CIVIL LIBERTIES
AND THE CONSTITUTION

SEVENTH EDITION

CIVIL LIBERTIES AND THE CONSTITUTION

Cases and Commentaries

LUCIUS J. BARKER

Stanford University

TWILEY W. BARKER, JR.

University of Illinois at Chicago

Prentice Hall
Englewood Cliffs, New Jersey 07632

Library of Congress Cataloging-in-Publication Data

Barker, Lucius Jefferson, (date)–
    Civil liberties and the Constitution: cases and commentaries /
  Lucius J. Barker, Twiley W. Barker, Jr.—7th ed.
      p.   cm.
    Includes bibliographical references.
    ISBN 0-13-137209-2
    1. Civil rights—United States—Cases. I. Barker, Twiley
Wendell, (date)– . II. Title.
KF4748.B2   1994
342.73'085—dc20
[347.30285]
                                 93-23785
                                    CIP

Acquisitions editor: Maria DiVencenzo
Editorial assistant: Nicole Signoretti
Editorial/production supervision and
   interior design: P. M. Gordon Associates
Copy editor: Sherry Babbitt
Cover design: John Thomas Judy
Production coordinator: Mary Ann Gloriande

© 1994, 1990, 1986, 1982, 1978, 1975, 1970 by Prentice-Hall, Inc.
A Paramount Communications Company
Englewood Cliffs, New Jersey 07632

Printed in the United States of America
10 9 8 7 6 5 4 3 2 1

ISBN 0-13-137209-2

Prentice-Hall International (UK) Limited, *London*
Prentice-Hall of Australia Pty. Limited, *Sydney*
Prentice-Hall Canada Inc., *Toronto*
Prentice-Hall Hispanoamericana, S.A., *Mexico*
Prentice-Hall of India Private Limited, *New Delhi*
Prentice-Hall of Japan, Inc., *Tokyo*
Simon & Schuster Asia Pte. Ltd., *Singapore*
Editora Prentice-Hall do Brasil, Ltda., *Rio de Janeiro*

To
Maud, Tracey, Heidi, Valerie, Sheri,
and the late Ruth Jamason Barker

Contents

4   THE RIGHTS OF THE ACCUSED   295

5   RACE, COLOR, AND THE CONSTITUTION   *431*

Featured Cases:

Preface

This seventh edition of *Civil Liberties and the Constitution* is marked by several new features. One of the most obvious (and we hope helpful) features is an expanded first chapter that introduces the volume. Here we attempt to paint a fuller picture of various factors and forums that constitute the overall contextual framework in which ongoing battles over our rights and liberties are fought. This includes a new section on the operation of the Supreme Court, with particular attention to the nature and dynamics of judicial selection and judicial decisionmaking.

Another new feature concerns the introductory essays and the arrangement of featured cases for the chapters involved. Rather than having one long continuous essay that introduces all cases for each given chapter, this new edition places featured cases immediately after text that illuminates the specific historical-legal context of which they are a part. For example, in Chapter 3 ("Freedom of Expression, Assembly, and Association") cases such as *Texas v. Johnson* and *R.A.V. v. St. Paul* follow immediately after that part of the introductory essay that focuses on "Symbolic Speech."

Aside from these new features, the major burden of the volume remains unchanged: to increase our understanding of civil liberty problems through a study of leading judicial decisions, primarily those of the United States Supreme Court. Though always challenging, the task is made considerably easier by the many comments and sug-gestions from instructors and students who have used the book. As a result, we approach new editions with added confidence that the experiences of our users have richly informed and influenced our own views as to what changes or directions each succeeding edition should take.

The new features referred to earlier have evolved mainly as a result of faculty and student comments and suggestions. For example, the need for an expanded Chapter 1 supports the view that our understanding of civil liberties is greatly enhanced and enriched by an assessment of the overall political-social context in which the formulation and implementation of civil liberties policies take place. Thus, Chapter 1 on political-social context remains a central feature of the volume. To be sure, viewing law and legal problems in broad political-social context is now commonplace among social scientists who study law and courts. Even so, however, comments we have received suggest that Chapter 1 provides users a necessary and convenient reference point and framework in which to more accurately evaluate and assess the role and function of courts, especially in relation to *other institutions and actors,* in the formulation and implementation of civil liberty policy.

Overall, we trust that the changes in this edition will strengthen and facilitate the two major features that characterize this volume: 1) in-depth introductory commentaries that introduce each chapter and the particular cases involved, and 2) a reasonable sample of such cases across a broad spectrum of our rights and liberties so as to enhance student analysis and discussion. We believe we have maintained and strengthened both features.

The introductory commentaries, for example, attempt to place case developments in historical perspective, especially for those cases that have been edited and reprinted here. The commentaries allow us to see more clearly changes and continuity in legal doctrines and, in particular, judicial policies. They allow us to continuously evaluate, for example, how the substance and tone of judicial policies of the Warren and Burger Courts are now being affected by actions of the Rehnquist Court. Consistent with the framework outlined in Chapter 1, the commentaries also allow us to take account of developments in other forums and institutions, such as the impact of the 1992 elections and the Clinton presidency on our rights and liberties.

Second, the number of cases for student analysis and discussion has been maintained and even increased. Where appropriate and profitable, however, old cases have been replaced by new ones so as to illustrate the continuous and changing nature of civil liberty problems. As before, cases are edited to promote a general rather than technically legal understanding of the issues involved. In doing so, an attempt is made to allow students to examine significant portions of court opinions, including major arguments from majority, concurring, and dissenting opinions. Overall, we have attempted to structure the volume so it is more adaptable to a variety of learning situations.

We remain grateful for the many persons who have played roles in the early development and continuation of this volume. Their names are far too numerous to mention, but they should know that their encouragement and assistance remain important to us. However, there are some acknowledgments that we feel compelled to make for this edition. We continue to be both amazed and delighted by the many comments and suggestions that come to us from professional colleagues who use the volume. Particularly, we appreciate—more than meets the eye—reactions in our own classes that keep us constantly alert to the interests and concerns of our primary users, the students.

We also appreciate the many valuable contributions of our research assistants and secretarial staff. Research assistance at Stanford was thoroughly and cheerfully provided by Tracey George, Roy Swan, and Tony West, all of whom are now graduates of Stanford Law School. The interactions of a political scientist with them during their second and third years of law school were always helpful, informative, and, hopefully, a mutually rewarding experience. The same is true and must be underscored with respect to Patrick DeSousa, a Yale Law School graduate ('86) who at the time (1992–93) was completing his Ph.D. work in political science at Stanford. For valuable clerical assistance we wish to thank Delia Gutierrez-James and Karen Shoen at the University of Illinois-Chicago, and Ora Hurd, Kim Shaver, and Daisy Sanchez at Stanford. Clearly, of course, any errors of commission or omission that inevitably persist are solely the responsibility of the authors.

Chapter 1

Civil Liberties in Political-Social Context

Abortion, the death penalty, school prayers, affirmative action, school desegregation, and lifestyle practices encapsulize issues that continue to evoke and engender sharp division and debate in our society and politics. This division and debate penetrates both private and public sectors and is clearly evident in our politics—in elections, in state and local governments, in congressional and presidential politics, in the Supreme Court, and in our courts generally. Thus, a continuing analysis of the overall political-social context remains an important consideration for students and others interested in a study of civil liberties.

This political-social context influences and is in turn influenced by actions and policies, including those relating to civil liberties, that emanate from elective political institutions (e.g., the president and Congress) and from nonelective governmental institutions (e.g., administrative agencies and federal courts). Actions and policies of the Reagan-Bush administrations, as well as of the Rehnquist Court, exemplify vividly how these institutions affect our civil liberties. They also demonstrate the important interaction of law and politics in the development and enforcement of civil liberty policies. The major point here is that, given the inextricable relationships of courts, law, and politics, this overall political-social context should be kept in mind as we discuss various issues in civil liberties.

In the main, this book represents a collation of leading decisions of the Supreme Court on civil liberties. This, of course, is a recognition of the important role of the U.S. Supreme Court in dealing with civil liberties and civil rights problems. Indeed, the Court exercises final authority with respect to legal interpretations of our national Constitution and federal laws. As such, its decisions are analyzed and studied with special care and attention. Although terribly important, decisions of the Court cannot be studied in a vacuum. This is especially true of positions of the Court on highly controversial questions, as civil liberties and civil rights issues tend to be. Under such circumstances, court decisions become only one consideration, albeit a very important one, in the determination of policy and practice in given issue areas. Consider, for example, the celebrated decisions of the Warren Court in the 1954 school segregation cases. Certainly, public policy involving school desegregation, much less actual practice, cannot be discussed by a mere reading of decisions of the Court. Many other factors must be considered to determine the policy and practice of school desegregation, such as the policy positions and attitudes of executive, legislative, and administrative officials including the president, governors, mayors, Congress and state legislatures, city councils, school boards, school superintendents, and chiefs of police. Of course, public opinion and community attitudes must also be considered.

The same or similar factors must be considered in discussing the policy and practice with respect to other salient civil liberty problems such as abortion, capital punishment, obscenity and pornography, privacy, state aid to parochial schools, affirmative action, and rights of the accused. The fact is that court decisions on matters of great controversy, just as decisions emanating from other decision-making institutions, are seldom if ever final. They continue to be subject to the pushes and pulls of interests that stand to gain or lose depending on particular outcomes. It is in this overall context that the purpose of this chapter becomes apparent. Certainly, we cannot fully explore in a single short chapter the many factors that may be and are involved in the definition and implementation of civil liberties and civil rights policies. In short, one volume cannot be all things to all people, not even to all students of civil liberties. Our hope is, however, that this chapter will serve as a constant reminder that leading cases of the Supreme Court, which constitute the bulk of this volume, must be placed in the overall political-social context of which they are a part. This context includes such considerations as the nature of constitutional and political values, the role and relation of the Court to the Congress and the president as policy-making institutions, and the role of interest groups.

LAW AND COURTS IN POLITICAL-SOCIAL CONTEXT

Americans are very much legally oriented. This legal orientation is symbolized by our almost reverent allegiance to doing things *according to law*. It is this attachment to law, based on very strong traditions, that allows courts and the legal profession to exercise an enormous amount of power and influence in the American political system. It is not surprising then that many people interested in bringing about changes in civil liberties have taken the judicial route in attempts to achieve their objectives. Consequently, in discussing policy development in general, especially civil liberties policy, close attention must be given to the role of courts.

The highest law in the American legal order is the Constitution. All other types of law—rules, regulations, practices, statutes, administrative orders, customs—must be in conformity with the Constitution. Herein lies the crucial role of courts, especially the Supreme Court. Long ago, in *Marbury* v. *Madison* (1 Cr. 137, 1803), Chief Justice John Marshall proclaimed that it is "emphatically" the province of the judiciary to determine whether particular laws, rules, regulations, etc., conform

with the Constitution. Thus, according to Marshall, the Constitution had authorized the courts, and no other institution of government, to make such a determination of the Constitution. This, in effect, is the power of judicial review that has long since become firmly entrenched in our constitutional and legal fabric.

Judicial review, as such, gives courts an important and crucial role in American politics and in the determination of public policies. Nowhere is this more true than in the articulation and development of civil rights and civil liberties policy. Consider the important values embodied in the Bill of Rights. The First Amendment, for example, declares that Congress may not pass laws "respecting an establishment of religion, or prohibiting the free exercise thereof; or abridging the freedom of speech, or of the press; or the right of the people peaceably to assemble, and to petition the Government for a redress of grievances." Or consider other provisions of the Bill of Rights, such as the prohibitions against unreasonable searches and seizures, and against self-incrimination, and other provisions safeguarding the rights of the accused. In addition, consider provisions of the Civil War amendments, the Thirteenth, Fourteenth, and Fifteenth Amendments. These amendments prohibit slavery and involuntary servitude; guarantee due process and equal protection; and prohibit denial of the right to vote on account of race, color, and previous condition of servitude. The Nineteenth Amendment prohibits abridging the right to vote on account of sex. The Twenty-fourth Amendment forbids denial of the right to vote in national elections for failure to pay any poll tax or other tax. (*Harper* v. *Virginia*, 1966, outlawed payment of poll taxes in state elections.) The Twenty-sixth Amendment says that "the right of citizens of the United States, who are eighteen years of age or older, to vote shall not be denied or abridged by the United States or by any State on account of age." Judicial review permits courts to determine whether these rights or guarantees have been violated in particular cases.

But courts do more than exercise the power of judicial review, that is, determining whether various acts are in accord with the Constitution. A major part of the workload of courts consists of cases dealing with statutory interpretation. Here, courts are called upon to interpret and apply statutes (laws and ordinances), such as those enacted by Congress. In many ways, then, how judges interpret statutes can prove crucial in determining who wins or loses as a result of specific legislative enactments. For example, Title IX of a 1972 federal law prohibits sex discrimination in "any education program or activity receiving federal financial assistance" and declares that failure to comply with the law could result in termination of such federal assistance. But in interpreting this provision of the law, the Supreme Court in its 1984 decision in *Grove City College* v. *Bell* ruled that although the college was such a "recipient," the force of the law's antisex discrimination provisions could be applied only to the specific program or unit receiving such financial assistance and not to the college as a whole. In short, failure to abide by antisex discrimination provisions in one such program or activity would not subject the college to institutional-wide coverage under Title IX. Undoubtedly, this Court interpretation of the statute severely limited its scope and effect as a tool for combating sex discrimination. As a result, *Grove City* created a storm of protests from civil rights groups and many others who saw the decision as a threat not only to federal laws banning sex discrimination, but to laws that ban other forms of discrimination as well, for example, race discrimination or discrimination against the handicapped. Thus, here, as in other instances, what a particular statute means is what the courts say it means. If Congress does not like how the Supreme Court interpreted a statute, however, it may change the law to overcome the Court's interpretation. And this is exactly what Congress did in 1988 when it passed the Civil Rights Restoration Act to overcome the effects of *Grove City*. Similarly, after protracted battles between President Bush and the Congress, including several leading Republicans, the Congress passed the Civil Rights Act of 1991 in an attempt to overcome a number of controversial Supreme Court decisions involving interpretations of affirmative action policies under several congressional statutes. In any event, the ambiguity of language found in many statutes, which might reflect compromises needed for their initial enactment, obviously means that "the opportunities for the exercise of judicial discretion in statutory interpretation are both frequent and wide."[1] When we combine this role of courts in statutory interpretation with that of constitutional interpretation (judicial review),[2] we begin to understand more clearly the enormous importance of courts and judges in the formulation of civil liberties policies and in the political process generally. And that importance, as the above mentioned Civil Rights Act of 1991 indicates, suggests that how courts interpret statutes passed by legislative bodies is likely to play an increasing role in the battle over civil rights and civil liberties.

In this volume, however, we are concerned mostly with cases involving judicial review, those in which courts are asked to determine the constitutionality of statutes and various other actions. The primary focus is on rights that are guaranteed in the Bill of Rights and the Fourteenth Amendment. These constitutional provisions, of course, were and are considered very important in safeguarding the rights of the excluded, the unpopular, or those who differ with the majority. As experience has shown, majorities do attempt to deny or abridge these freedoms and rights.

Consequently, since the very purpose of the Bill of Rights—and similar constitutional provisions— was to safeguard guarantees from majority abuse and tyranny, it may be said that courts bear a special duty under our constitutional system to protect and defend such rights. Courts, after all, are to make decisions according to *law*, not according to *majority rule*. And the fact that federal judges, unlike officials in the elective political branches, enjoy life tenure, gives them the sort of independence and detachment that might be needed to withstand majority pressures and to render what might be unpopular decisions. This by no means is to suggest that courts are aloof or are not influenced by the total political context in which they function. But it does suggest that courts and judges are accorded a special and unique role in the American political system that is not enjoyed by other political institutions and actors. This role, of course, is enhanced and perpetuated by the norms, procedures, and traditions that provide the *legal* context in which courts and judges operate. In any event, courts are looked upon as key protectors of civil liberties and civil rights in America. Many aspects of the judicial process lend an aura of fairness and justice to actions of the courts: the ornate courtrooms with robed judges who are stationed above all others; the semblance of equality accorded to interests before the courts through their representation by persons trained in the *law*; the studied and sometimes prolonged deliberations of judges before arriving at decisions; and the careful intoning of *legal* language of the judicial process. Characteristics such as these *symbolize* the belief that judicial decisions are determined in accord with *law* and not with popular or majority will or whim.

[1] See Walter Murphy and C. Herman Pritchett, *Courts, Judges and Politics*, 2nd ed. (New York: Random House, 1974), p. 408.

[2] Consider, for example, the role of courts in the interpretation of administrative regulations, hence their role in administrative law making. See Martin Shapiro, *The Supreme Court and Administrative Agencies* (New York: The Free Press, 1968).

But neither the *law* nor judicial decisions are neutral. They advantage certain interests and disadvantage others. For some time, for example, the *law* (Constitution, statutes, judicial decisions, customs, and practices) supported the interests of those who practiced racial segregation. As thus interpreted, the *law* disadvantaged black Americans. However, as we discuss in a later chapter, the strong positions taken by the Warren Court did much to change the *law* in this area. However, in more recent times, some analysts contend that the Burger Court and now the Rehnquist Court have acted to narrow, evade, and slow decisional trends of the Warren Court not only in areas relating to race but in other *civil liberty* areas as well. But it is just this sort of change, or perceived change, that vividly illustrates the dynamics of judicial decision making and its relation to the overall political-social context. Indeed, although law and judicial decisions help to shape that context, that context itself helps to shape the law and judicial decisions. In any event, the norms, procedures, and traditions of the judicial process contribute greatly to the importance and credibility accorded to decisions emanating from that process.

CONGRESS, THE PRESIDENT, AND ADMINISTRATIVE OFFICIALS

Although they alone are very important, judicial decisions must be considered in the total political-social context of which they are a part. Thus, a discussion of civil liberties and civil rights policies in the United States must perforce consider more than activities and decisions of courts. We must also consider the activity of other governmental institutions such as the Congress, the president, and administrative agencies and bureaus. Certainly, both the president and the Congress play important roles in the development of national civil rights and civil liberties policies. This is true if for no other reason than that our government is composed of three *interdependent* rather than three *independent* branches. In short, the *separation of powers* doctrine is more doctrine than practice; the "checks and balances" see to this. In some way, decisions of any one branch can be influenced (or checked) by the other branches. This is why students of civil liberties cannot focus solely on judicial decisions. Decisions of Congress, the president, and administrative officials can prove very important, even determinative, in certain situations. Consider, for example, the importance of such congressional legislation as the Civil Rights Act of 1964

and the Voting Rights Act of 1965. Certainly, the importance of *presidential leadership* loomed great in the passage of such legislation. To be sure, Supreme Court decisions gave judicial approval to these 1964 and 1965 actions of Congress and the president. But by the same token, one can scarcely fathom the vitality (or fate) of the Court's 1954 school desegregation decision had Congress and the president not passed the 1964 and 1965 legislation.

However, actions of Congress and the president may also impede or restrict civil liberties. Certainly, when Congress passed the Eagleton-Biden Amendment in 1977, it eliminated busing as one of the tools that the Department of Health, Education, and Welfare, or HEW (now the Education Department) could use to achieve public school desegregation under the 1964 Civil Rights Act. Congress may also impede civil liberties should it act to curb the jurisdiction of federal courts in certain areas. To be sure, such attempts have been made. But these attempts—covering such controversial issues as abortion and school prayer, have all met with failure.

Of course, congressional action to remove federal court jurisdiction in such highly controversial areas as civil liberties problems tend to be would perhaps bring us full circle, since federal courts would undoubtedly be asked to determine the constitutionality of such congressional action. In addition, adverse Court decisions may also be overcome through passing appropriate constitutional amendments, but this is a much more difficult route to negotiate.

Civil liberties are affected in still other ways. For example, the fact that Senator Joseph Biden and the Democratic majority, rather than Senator Orrin Hatch and the Republicans, control the Senate Judiciary Committee will obviously influence congressional action. What this suggests is that actions of the Congress can go far toward advancing (or retarding) civil rights and liberties. It becomes important then to study the Congress—its composition, powers, practices, and procedures—and how these factors can influence congressional policies generally and civil rights and liberties policies in particular.

Similarly, it is important to give attention to the president, his selection, his vast powers and authority, his leadership, and how these factors can shape and influence the course of civil liberties and civil rights policy. Consider, for example, the power of the president in the appointment of federal judges. How this appointment power might affect civil liberties–civil rights interests was illuminated vividly in the abortive attempt of President Reagan to appoint Judge Robert Bork to the Supreme Court. It has also been highlighted by the vast opportunities given President Carter under the Omnibus Judges Act of 1978 to appoint more than 152 judges to the federal courts. These appointments allowed Carter to appoint more blacks, Hispanics, and women to the federal bench than any other president.[3] The different life experiences and legal outlooks of these judges could have profound influence on the role and character of the federal judiciary.

But Ronald Reagan defeated President Carter in the 1980 election, and during his eight years in office Reagan had the opportunity to fashion further and different changes in appointments to the judiciary, including the appointment of three new justices to the Supreme Court (O'Connor, Scalia, and Kennedy) and the naming of a new Chief Justice (Rehnquist). Overall, President Reagan had the opportunity to appoint about 50 percent of the judges to our federal courts.

The matter of judicial appointments to our federal courts was also raised during the 1988 Bush-Dukakis presidential election. For example, at the time of the 1988 elections, there were three Supreme Court justices over age 75, making vacancies very likely to occur. That these three justices (Brennan, Marshall, and Blackmun) constituted the "liberal" bloc on the Court indicated that their possible replacements could bring about profound changes in our law. This fact, of course, did not go unnoticed during the presidential campaign, with both Republicans and Democrats listing the "parade of horribles" that would be visited upon the Court should either side win. In the end, the ensuing resignations of Justices William Brennan and Thurgood Marshall gave President Bush the opportunity to replace these two most liberal justices with justices more in tune with his own conservative positions. This was particularly salient in the appointment of Judge Clarence Thomas, who, although an African American like Justice Marshall, wore conservative credentials that were much more obvious than those of Justice David Souter, who replaced Brennan. While it is true that judges enjoy life tenure, the appointments of Thomas and Souter suggest that presidents clearly weigh carefully the type of persons they appoint. Indeed, judicial policies emanating from a Souter or Thomas are likely to be quite different from those

coming from a Brennan or Marshall, and this difference can prove crucial in fashioning public policy, including that relating to civil rights and civil liberties.

Indeed, who the judges are definitely affects what the judges do. This is vividly illuminated by Justice Marshall in his dissent in *Lloyd* v. *Tanner* (1972), where he protested the fact that the Court was, in his opinion, departing from an earlier ruling (*Amalgamated Food Employees* v. *Logan Valley*, 1968). Said Marshall: "The vote in *Logan Valley* (1968) was 6–3, and that decision is only four years old. But I am aware that the composition of this Court has radically changed in four years." And in a 1991 dissent (*Payne* v. *Tennessee*) suggesting how changes in judicial personnel were effecting changes in judicial policies, Marshall charged that "power, not reason, is the new currency of this Court's decision making." To Marshall, then, changes in Court personnel had brought with them changes in the Court's position. Overall, who the judges are can affect not only changes in civil liberty policy but policy change in general.

Still further, consider the fact that the president appoints other key administrative officials such as the attorney general, the directors of the CIA and the FBI, and secretaries of the various cabinet departments such as Housing and Urban Development (HUD), Education, and Health and Human Services. That these officials have important influences on civil liberties and civil rights was clearly illustrated by officials of the Reagan administration, whose policy stances were certainly quite different from policies supported during the Carter administration. Take, for example, the position of Attorney General William French Smith. During Reagan's first year in office, Smith made it clear that the administration would oppose mandatory busing and racial hiring quotas, since they not only "compromised the principle of color-blindness" but had also proven "counterproductive." Generally, this position was pursued during both terms of the Reagan administration.[4]

Similarly, the Reagan administration was aggressive in promoting actions: (1) that strengthened the interests of "society" as opposed to the rights of the accused (e.g., by facilitating convictions through working for exceptions and limitations of the "exclusionary rule"); (2) that attempted to put God "back into the public schools" through prayers, silent meditation, etc.; and (3) that allowed the president to put more of *his* people into sensitive

[3]See "Carter's Efforts to Diversify the Bench . . . Leave Reagan a Tough Act to Follow," *Congressional Quarterly* (Feb. 14, 1981), pp. 300–301.

[4]See "Departure from Busing Pledged in Rights Cases," *The New York Times*, May 23, 1981, p. 9."

positions (e.g., the Commission on Civil Rights). Actions and attitudes of the Reagan administration, although varying in degree and nature, suggest vividly how any president, his key officials, and many other appointments might influence the structure of policies and practices that determine our civil liberties and civil rights.

As reflected in this volume, this continued to prove true during the Bush administration and is likely to remain the case during the Clinton administration. This was evidenced by Clinton's quick overturning (only two days after taking office) of certain rules on abortion, such as the ban on abortion counseling in federally funded clinics, which in effect overcame a Republican-imposed rule that had been legitimated by the Supreme Court in *Rust* v. *Sullivan.*

INTEREST GROUPS AND THE DYNAMICS OF CIVIL LIBERTIES

When we combine the role of interest groups and public opinion with the role of the president, the courts, and other participants and factors in the political process, we begin to get the feel of the dynamics involved in the formulation of civil liberties policy. Interest groups have long played a role in shaping such policies. Pro-civil liberties groups such as the National Association for the Advancement of Colored People (NAACP) and the American Civil Liberties Union (ACLU) readily come to mind. But other groups, holding all sorts of views, also attempt to influence civil liberties policy. When stakes are high and deeply held values are involved, as often occurs in civil liberty conflicts, intense feelings and prolonged battles can be expected. And the battle is forged along many lines and in various arenas.

Groups such as the ACLU, NAACP, and the Jehovah's Witnesses have a long history of attempting to protect and vindicate their rights and liberties through the courts. Many of the judicial episodes in which these groups have been participants are well chronicled. They illustrate how those who are otherwise disadvantaged in the political process have resorted to the judiciary to achieve their objectives. Indeed, the resources needed to do battle in the courts are markedly different from resources needed to prevail in the elective political institutions. These groups have more access to courts than they do to elective forums. In short, they think their chances of achieving favorable policy outcomes are greater in the courts than in the elective political institutions.

Undoubtedly, it has been a recognition of this fact that has led groups such as the NAACP to hone skills and resources carefully to negotiate the judicial process. Numbers, popularity, and money are presumably less important in judicial combat than are skilled lawyers, reasoned arguments, and a good case. But even these limited resources, in comparison with those needed in the elective political arena, are more often than not beyond the capacity of those persons who need their rights vindicated.

Interest groups have played and continue to play an important role in the formulation of civil liberties policy. They provide the counsel, the money, and the psychological support that individual litigants often need to withstand the pressures and strains of fighting for unpopular causes. Without these kinds of support provided by the NAACP, for example, it is doubtful that advances made in our civil rights laws with respect to racial discrimination and segregation would have come about as readily or peacefully. Certainly, the resources needed for these cases were enormous: courageous litigants, skilled lawyers, expert witnesses, dedicated researchers, and an incalculable amount of fortitude and patience.

The two principal techniques used by interest groups to lobby the courts are the initiation and sponsorship of test cases and the filing of *amici curiae* briefs (friends of the court). Test cases provide opportunities for the judiciary to define and articulate particular policies with respect to the protection of civil liberties and civil rights. The *amicus* brief brings information that allows the courts to overcome the constraints of the adversary system and consider the broader political-social ramifications of the *legal* questions presented in particular cases. Of course, as exemplified vividly by Solicitor General Robert Fried, the *amicus* brief may also be used to promote through the courts policy objectives of a particular administration (e.g., the Reagan administration) that the administration had not been able to achieve in other forums. This suggests that conservative as well as liberal groups may and do resort to courts to achieve their policy goals.

Groups may also seek to achieve policy objectives through the legislature and may use a variety of lobbying techniques to press their respective causes. In short, major policy conflicts in civil liberties, just as in other policy areas, are fought out in many arenas and on many fronts—in elections, in Congress, and in administrative agencies as well as in the courts. Those who prevail in one arena (courts) might find their efforts frustrated in other arenas. Prevailing interests at a certain point or phase of the policy process must maintain a constant vigilance. For example, those who prevail at the policy *declaration* stage must be alert to the pitfalls that might be involved at the policy *implementation* stage.

MORE ON THE COURT: INSIDE THE MARBLE PALACE

The integral role and importance of the judiciary in American politics and policy-making impels us to take a closer look at the Supreme Court, at what happens inside the "Marble Palace."[5] Here we shall consider the justices—who they are, why they are important, and how they are appointed to the Court—as well as the basic workings of the Court as an institution—how it decides what cases to hear, and how it goes about the business of judicial decision-making.

Getting on the Court: A Note on Judicial Selection

As suggested above, who is on the Court greatly influences what comes out of the Court,[6] as the televised furor over the 1991 nomination (and eventual confirmation) of Clarence Thomas vividly reflects. Organized interest groups, Congress, and the president were all vying to determine who would fill the vacancy left by retiring Justice Thurgood Marshall. These actors believed that by influencing the selection of the new justice, they would also influence future Court decisions. Their reasoning is quite simple: as with other policy-making institutions, the Court's decisions are, in large part, a product of the views and predilections of its members.

Indeed, the debates over Supreme Court appointments are special, and they generate intense, bitter, and broad controversy. Contrast, for example, the raucous battle over Thomas with the confirmation hearings of Robert Gates, another presidential nominee who was under review by the Senate Intelligence Committee at roughly the same time as the Senate Judiciary Committee was considering the Thomas nomination. Like the Thomas situation, many questions surrounded Gates's nomination to head the CIA, and the posi-

tion involved was one of great national importance. But even though controversy erupted, the Senate panel conducting the Gates hearing was able to overcome their differences, resulting in strong bipartisan support for the president's nomination. One partial explanation for the difference is simply that many more people feel more personally affected by the Court than by the CIA. In addition, of course, is the fact that Supreme Court justices have life tenure, and are not subject to the tenure limits and constraints imposed by the electoral and political controls placed on legislators and political appointees.

When one of the nine Supreme Court justices retires or dies, the president has the opportunity to nominate a replacement.[7] After Marshall stepped down, Bush nominated Clarence Thomas. Thomas's nomination was the 146th to the high court, the 60th in this century. And after the retirement of Justice Byron White in 1993, President Clinton nominated Judge Ruth Bader Ginsburg of the U.S. Court of Appeals of Washington, D.C. She became only the second woman to be appointed to the Supreme Court. Of all the nominations, only 28 have failed to secure confirmation, indicating that the president's choice will likely become the next justice.

In making their nominations, presidents generally consult a number of persons,[8] including members of their own party in Congress, especially in the Senate, and their White House staff. In addition, other interested groups and persons who have the president's ear will try to influence selection. During the Reagan-Bush years, however, judicial selection at all levels came under increasing control of the White House.[9] Additionally, of course, presidents consider a number of other factors in deciding on their judicial appointments. And although the Constitution does not require the president to weigh any particular factors,[10] it is clear that *party affiliation* and *ideology* stand out as important considerations.

After the president has submitted a nomination

[5]Completed in 1932, the current Supreme Court building is made entirely of marble and is constructed in the Corinthian style.

[6]For a most extensive discussion of the selection process, see Lawrence Baum, *The Supreme Court,* 3rd ed. (Washington, D.C.: Congressional Quarterly Press, 1989), pp. 27–52.

[7]The president "shall nominate, and by and with the advice and consent of the Senate, shall appoint . . . judges of the Supreme Court." U.S. Constitution, Art. II, sec. 2.

[8]For a fascinating look at presidential nominations, see Henry J. Abraham, *Justices and Presidents,* 2nd ed. (New York: Oxford University Press, 1985).

[9]For an informative analysis in this regard, see Sheldon Goldman, "The Bush Imprint on the Judiciary: Carrying on a Tradition," 74 *Judicature* 294 (April–May 1991).

[10]In fact, the Constitution does not even require that a justice be an attorney, although all nominees in this century have attended accredited law schools.

to the Senate, the Senate Judiciary Committee takes over, holding hearings and then recommending Senate action in either support or opposition. Next, if the committee approves, the nomination is referred to the Senate floor, where it is debated and a confirmation vote is taken. On rare occasions, however, as in the case of the Bork and Thomas nominations, the Judiciary Committee may decide to send the matter to the entire Senate without the committee's approval. In general, the length of time spent at each of these two stages—in Senate Judiciary Committee hearings and in Senate open debate—depends on both the controversy surrounding the nomination and the relationship between the president and the Senate.

The number of factors and forces attending judicial nominations makes for a dynamic process, especially when controversial nominations are involved.[11] In the Thomas nomination, for example, the Senate considered a vast array of factors regarding Thomas, including his legal experience and credentials; his views on hotly contested issues such as affirmative action and abortion; his past actions as the head of the Equal Employment Opportunity Commission; and his alleged sexual harassment of a former employee. In addition, the Senate may consider issues, such as the current ideological balance of the Court and the views of the justice to be replaced, that are not unique to a particular nominee, as it did with respect to Bork and to some extent with Thomas.

The Senate, however, does not consider these myriad factors in isolation; rather, individuals and groups dutifully come before the Judiciary Committee stating reasons that support or oppose particular nominees. Again, during the Thomas hearings, those on both sides of the affirmative action and abortion issues expressed concerns and encouraged supporters to contact senators from their home states. In addition, a number of legal groups, such as the American Bar Association and the NAACP's Legal Defense Fund (LDF), stated their support or opposition to the nomination. Legal scholars also offered testimony as to the nominee's qualifications. Yet of all the outside forces, perhaps none placed as much pressure on the Senate as the media, particularly television.

In the end, as with most nominees, Thomas was confirmed, although by the lowest margin in this century, 52 to 48. But the general outcry following the raucous hearings led to repeated and open avowals (from in and outside the Senate) to do something about the "process." Predictably, however, such interest has since died down, and given the infrequency of Supreme Court appointments, the relative inertia of the political system, and the ever rapidly changing political agenda, it is unlikely that we will see any significant changes in the "process."

The Supreme Court in Operation

The Court,[12] not unlike other governmental institutions in Washington, has a fairly intricate system to handle the day-to-day activities (i.e., the many cases) for which it is responsible. Since 1917, the Court must by law begin its regular annual session on the first Monday in October. The regular session, now known as the October term, lasts approximately nine months. The Chief Justice is responsible for adjourning the Court and usually does so in late June or early July, depending on the caseload.

Yet, all through the year parties ask the Court to resolve their disputes. Those disputes that are in the Court's original jurisdiction may be heard by the Court in the first instance;[13] however, very few cases are filed under this jurisdiction. The bulk of the cases reaching the Court are those arising under its appellate jurisdiction—cases in which the Court would be reviewing the decisions of a lower court. Under the Judiciary Act of 1925, the Court has almost complete discretion in deciding whether to hear these cases. For such a case to be reviewed, one party must ask the Court to review the case (petitioning the Court for a writ of certiorari) and at least four justices must agree to do so (granting certiorari). The Court is asked to review between four thousand and five thousand such cases annually. Usually, the Court will agree to give full consideration to less than two hundred of these cases.

This suggests that "deciding to decide," as H. W. Perry aptly describes it, is a most crucial stage in judicial policy-making. The dynamics of agenda formation in policy institutions such as the Court is of central concern to scholars and many others. As Perry states:

[11]For an extensive consideration of the role of the Senate in Supreme Court nominations, see Joel B. Grossman and Stephen L. Wasby, "The Senate and Supreme Court Nominations: Some Reflections," *Duke Law Journal* 563 (1972).

[12]A more detailed explanation of the Court's operations can be found in Elder Witt, *Congressional Quarterly's Guide to the U.S. Supreme Court*, 2nd ed. (Washington, D.C.: CQ Press, 1990).

[13]U.S. Constitution, Art. III, sec. 2.

The need to examine the agenda-setting process is particularly relevant to the United States Supreme Court, an institution that has virtually complete discretion in setting its own agenda. When the Court hands down a decision, the impact often reaches far beyond the litigants and those similarly situated. A decision may set the agenda, or a large part of it, for political, social, and legal institutions for years to come. A seminal opinion often opens the floodgates for future litigation, legislation, and social reform. Even less than seminal decisions can be important and have widespread impact. But before the Court can render a decision, it must decide to decide. We know little about how the Court does this.[14]

Perry describes succinctly the basic procedure used by the Court in deciding what cases to hear: "The chief justice begins discussion of the first case on the discuss list. Each justice, in order of seniority, gives his [or her] comments on the case and usually announces his [or her] vote at that time. If a case receives four votes—the 'rule of four'—it is granted certiorari. Though formal votes are rare, if one is required, it, too, is taken in order of seniority."[15]

Given the heavy workload involved, particularly in "deciding what to decide," each justice is assisted by a number of law clerks, usually four. Individual justices use their own procedure for selecting their clerks. Traditionally, however, most clerks are recent honor graduates of the nation's prestigious law schools, such as Stanford, Harvard, and Yale. Although clerks usually serve one-year terms, their role and influence on "their justice" and judicial decision-making are subject to many and varied interpretations. Some, for example, compare the role of clerks to that of congressional staffs. Relevant here are Perry's comments, who in turn gives a very extended quote from a former law clerk:

Though the comparison is flawed, clerks are not completely unlike congressional staff. No staff member "controls" or "manipulates" a senator, but to deny the importance, or ignore the role staff members play in the legislative process, would be foolish. Likewise, the clerks. They cannot control their justice, and the process has checks and balances, but they play a crucial role. One clerk described the clerks' influence this way: "[On really important cases] what the clerks have to say is really less important. Justice——had his views. . . . I would tell him my constitutional views, but that is kind of preposter-

ous. I mean, if he has been doing his job and has been on the Court that long, he damn well better have his views about what the Constitution means. . . . Now the law clerks have more influence, I would say, on the areas of law that are less socially important. Given their law review experience and usually having worked on the Court of Appeals, they may be up on some [aspect] of this law and be able to have more of an impact. . . . Every clerk thought he was going to get there and would help his justice change America. . . . But we only had the opportunity to persuade him on an opinion here or there, because he had his own views on the major stuff".[16]

Overall, and regardless of their role and influence, it is clear that the justices rely a great deal on their clerks in deciding what cases to hear.

Once the Court grants certiorari, the clerk of the Court schedules the case for oral argument, usually two to three months later. Within the month prior to oral argument, the parties to the case and other interested parties (*amici curiae*) may seek and receive permission to file briefs with the Court. Such briefs broaden the base of information from which the justices may choose to make their decisions. In addition, the justices and their clerks will do further research on the issues involved. The amount of time and attention a justice gives to a certain case is a function of both her interest in the case and her approach to decision-making.

After oral argument in a given case, the Court will typically make its decision in conference. By tradition, conferences begin with the justices shaking hands with each other. Conferences are open to justices only and are held in strict secrecy. The exact procedures in the conference are not well known; however, we do know that each justice has an opportunity to speak without being interrupted and that at the end of the discussion a voice vote is taken, beginning with the senior justice and working down to the most junior justice.[17]

Once the justices have voted, one is assigned to write the majority opinion, or the "opinion of the court," for the case. The Chief Justice, or the senior justice in the majority, if he is in the majority, assigns this responsibility. In addition, any justice may write a separate opinion concurring in the

[14]H. W. Perry Jr., *Deciding to Decide: Agenda Setting in the U.S. Supreme Court* (Cambridge, MA: Harvard University Press, 1991), p. 6.

[15]Ibid., pp. 43–44 (footnotes omitted).

[16]Ibid., p. 70.

[17]Scholarly discussions of the voting procedure have been inconsistent, but conventional wisdom had always held that voting began with the most junior justice. Perry contends, however, based on his own interviews with justices and those of others, that this is simply not the case. For a discussion, refer to ibid., pp. 44–45.

judgment (agreeing with the outcome but not with the reasoning or some aspects of the majority opinion), or file a dissenting opinion.

Once the opinion drafts are written, they are circulated for review by all members, who then discuss them via their clerks, the telephone, and responding memos. It is possible that after the circulation of opinions, particular justices will change their votes, and a majority opinion will become a dissent. To prevent such mutinies, however, the majority opinion writer will attempt to make the changes needed to hold on to the majority. In contrast, justices writing concurrences or dissents are less concerned about winning the support of other justices.

Once all has been said and done, the final opinions are printed and publicly announced from the bench by their respective authors. Opinions are announced as they come down throughout the term, but typically a large number are announced in the final months of the term.

As the above procedures indicate, the justices are in constant contact and discussion. In fact, not only do they spend a great deal of time together, but they spend very little time with anyone else. Many justices have described their lives as cloistered—most of their time is spent in the Supreme Court building surrounded only by their clerks, administrative staffs, and the other justices. Not surprisingly, then, some scholarly research suggests that the dynamics of the Court—how the members interact and relate to one another—has a significant impact on Court decisions.

Consider, for example, the likely change in the Court's dynamics when the first woman, Sandra Day O'Connor, was named to the bench. Intuitively, we would expect that the Court's dynamics and discussion would change (at least to some extent) when one of its members represents a previously unrepresented group in society (such as it did after Thurgood Marshall was appointed by Lyndon Johnson). And, indeed, we have some reason to suspect that the Court's dynamics did change with the O'Connor appointment. For example, the success rate of women's rights advocates in the 1980s was even higher than it had been in the 1970s, despite a clear conservative shift in the ideology of the Court. While we can only hypothesize that the increased success rate was due in part to the presence of Justice O'Connor, it clearly is one possible explanation, especially given the frequency with which she wrote opinions.[18]

The Chief Justice

No discussion of the Court would be complete without a consideration of the role of the Chief Justice, who gains the position by virtue of presidential appointment. As with many aspects of the Court, the role and responsibilities of the Chief Justice are somewhat hazy. The only constitutional reference to the office is that "When the President of the United States is tried, the Chief Justice shall preside."[19] Indeed, originally, few expected that the Chief Justice position would become a significant one, and the first three Chief Justices are hardly remembered today. But this changed in 1801 when John Marshall was named to the Chief Justiceship. His command of the office would indelibly alter its image.

Interestingly, the tangible powers of Chief Justices are few. The Chief Justice develops the agenda of cases he considers worthy of discussion (the "discuss list"), and leads and presides over private sessions (conferences) of the Court. Hence, the Chief Justice might influence the flow of the proceedings as well as the decisional outcomes in particular cases. In addition, regardless of when appointed, the Chief Justice is considered the most senior member of the Court and thus may assign opinions for Court majorities of which the Chief Justice is a part. The Chief Justice also presides over the Court's public sessions and serves as chair of the Judicial Conference of the United States (a body made up of lower federal court judges that makes administrative decisions for the federal judicial system). In general, the Chief Justice is the most visible of the justices—administering the oath of office to the president and having the Court labeled by his name, for example, the Rehnquist Court.

Overall, however, the authority of a Chief Justice is largely a product of her person. As John P. Frank has explained, a Chief Justice

> must get his real eminence not from the office but from the qualities he brings to it. He must possess the mysterious quality of leadership. In this respect the outstanding Chief was John Marshall, who for 35 years presided over a Court largely populated by Justices of an opposing political party. . . . Nonetheless, Marshall dominated his Court as has no other Chief Justice.[20]

[18]See Tracey George and Lee Epstein, "Women's Rights Litigation in the 1980s: More of the Same?" 74 *Judicature* 314 (1991).

[19]U.S. Constitution, Art. I, sec. 3.

[20]John P. Frank, *Marble Palace: The Supreme Court in American Life* (New York: Alfred A. Knopf, 1958), pp. 78–79.

After this brief overview of life in the "Marble Palace," let us now turn our attention to several other contextual factors that shape the overall environment that influences both the Court and the nature and scope of our civil liberties.

THE "RULES OF THE GAME" AND AMERICAN POLITICAL VALUES

Civil liberty policy actors (such as the president, Congress, courts, administrators, and interest groups) must "play" the civil liberty policy "game" in keeping with certain rules and values. However, the "rules of the game" concerning civil liberties conflict suggest the difficulty in resolving or settling such matters. There is constant conflict over these "rules," that is, over very basic civil liberties guarantees such as those included in the Bill of Rights. The conflict occurs not only among interested publics but also within the judiciary itself, including the Supreme Court. Most of us agree with and extol the time-honored values that underlie these basic guarantees. For example, we believe in *individualism* and extol the importance and intrinsic worth of each and every person. Individuals have certain rights with which no state or government should interfere.

We also believe in the necessity and value of *freedom.* Individuals should have maximum freedom to determine their own interests as they see fit without external interference, especially from government. This also applies in the realm of business and economics. To be sure, individual liberty in the economic realm (i.e., economic rights) is believed to be important to democracy and to the maintenance of civil liberties.[21] Americans strongly believe in the sanctity of private property and more generally in the private enterprise market system. However, the result has been that a few individuals exercise important controls and influence over the operation, development, and management of important "public" functions[22] (e.g., employment, housing) that directly affect the quality of life or lack thereof for all segments of society. The intimate relation and importance of such functions to public needs allow these private business elites to wield great and disproportionate weight in our politics and government.[23] That we have been able to live with such obvious inequities between business elites and the masses may be said to result primarily from our strong attachment to the essentiality of *individualism* and *freedom* to democratic government.

Simultaneously, however, we are also strongly attached to the concept of equality, one of the very important "rules of the game" in democratic government. We believe that every person is equal under the law and that one person's vote should count the same as that of any other person. There should not be different treatment by government of individuals because of their station in life or the circumstances of their birth. All persons should be equal under the law. However, some people, the wealthy, for example, do exercise or are accorded more influence in our polity than others.[24] In addition, the theory of equality postulates that each person should enjoy an equal chance to succeed in life and to develop to his or her full potential. Herein lies the idea of "equality of opportunity," a concept that continues to be hotly debated in dealing with important civil rights issues, such as school desegregation and affirmative action in university and professional school admissions policies. One aspect of the debate focuses on the propriety, necessity, and extent of government regulations and involvement in certain private sector "public" functions, such as requiring affirmative action in employment, in order to make "equality" a more meaningful concept.

However, when and if government does become involved in such matters, do we not encroach upon other important values, such as *individualism* and *freedom*? On the other hand, does not ritualistic attachment to the notion of "equality of opportunity," without serious attempts to monitor its instrumental worth or to assess the relative well-

[21]Charles Lindblom, *The Policy Making Process* (Englewood Cliffs, NJ: Prentice-Hall, 1980), p. 71. In addition, for an interesting discussion of the relation between economic rights and civil liberties, see Robert G. McCloskey, "Economic Due Process and The Supreme Court: An Exhumation and Reburial," *The Supreme Court Review* 34 (1962).

[22]Lindblom, op. cit., pp. 72ff.

[23]Ibid. See generally ch. 9, "The Privileged Position of Business in Policy Making," p. 71, esp. pp. 72–78.

[24]Ibid., ch. 11, "Political Inequality," esp. pp. 100–102. In addition, the Supreme Court's decision in *Buckley* v. *Valco* (424 U.S. 1, 1976) was judicial support for the disproportionate influence of the wealthy in politics, or at least support for maintaining things as they are. In *Buckley*, the Court struck down as violative of freedom of political expressions and association protected by the First Amendment a congressional attempt through the Federal Campaign Election Act Amendments of 1974 to limit the undue influence of money in politics by placing ceilings on campaign expenditures, on independent expenditures by individuals and groups in support of a candidate, and on the amount that candidates could spend on their campaigns from their own funds. (For additional discussion of *Buckley*, see Chapter 3.)

being of all Americans, allow us to ignore or obscure certain inequities that might not be due to lack of individual initiative? Might this not seriously impair the basic idea of equality? To be sure, considerations such as these also bring to surface another thorny dimension of the contemporary debate over equality, that is, whether government has an affirmative obligation to provide more substantive benefits (e.g., welfare decent and sanitary housing) so as to assure a minimum level of economic subsistence for all persons. Put another way, is it necessary under the equal protection clause to redress certain economic inequities in order to make *equality* a more meaningful concept to those in poverty? Given the interests and stakes involved, problems such as these are not likely to disappear. However, despite the intensity of the debate, there remains a broad consensus, at least in theory, as to the importance of *equality* as well as *individualism* and *freedom* to the maintenance of civil liberties and democratic government. But *how* these values are put into practice is another matter. There remains

> intense controversy . . . over the definition, scope, and application of these values. For one thing, in particular circumstances these values may and do collide and conflict with each other. Individualism, for example, may conflict with what many might think is necessary to safeguard the "public interest" or to promote the "general welfare." Then again, suppose these values are denied by government itself (and others) to particular individuals. How and to what extent should government intervene to rectify the damage that has been done? And might such intervention itself be viewed as an encroachment upon these very values, e.g., individual freedom? These questions continue to pose a dilemma for American politics and politicians."[25]

That these questions do pose a dilemma is borne out by the perennial conflicts that occur in various arenas, such as the Supreme Court and the Congress. Data from public opinion polls and surveys also continue to illuminate differences that many of us hold between theory and practice.

Other values or concepts are also interwoven in the political-social context in which the formulation of civil liberties policy takes place. Consider, for example, our belief in *majority rule* and *minority rights,* two ideas that seem contradictory. There is a strong preference and necessity that decisions of the majority should prevail over those of any minority. The efficacy of majority rule as a way of making decisions depends as much on the acquiescence of the minority as it does on the sheer weight of numbers of the majority. While Americans believe in both majority rule and minority rights, we have not been able to resolve the built-in tension between the two values. We must be concerned not only with *how* decisions are made (the process) but with the content (the substance) of the decisions as well. The legitimacy of majority rule is very much related to its respect for minority rights. And by holding to minority rights, we do put some limits on majority rule.

As mentioned, we Americans also believe in doing things "according to law," and we consistently extol the view that "ours is a government of laws, not of men." We have a strong attachment to *legalism* and to the idea of written law. The chief symbol of this attachment is the written Constitution, the fundamental law. Indeed, the importance and necessity of legalism penetrate all our governmental institutions, taking the form of statutes, executive orders, and administrative rules and regulations. The idea of written legal forms extends even to our private life and organizations, where many social groups, for example, are not content unless they have written bylaws.

This preoccupation with law and legalism gives importance to those trained in the law. It allows lawyers to exercise a role in politics and government far beyond their sheer numbers. It also illuminates the role and importance of courts in the formulation of public policy, including civil liberties policy.

"*Conflict but compromise*" is another concept that shapes the character of our government and public policy. Americans have come to expect conflict, but they also have come to expect that conflicts can be resolved through restraint and reason. Basically, this means that contending interests must give a little and compromise their differences. Willingness to compromise ranks as one of the most important characteristics of American politics. This strong belief in managing conflict through compromise undoubtedly influences policy outcomes, including those resulting from civil liberties conflicts. It also leads to the related assumptions that: (1) all problems can be settled; and (2) the system provides ways for such settlements. Moreover, most Americans believe that such conflicts can be resolved peacefully and without violence. It matters not that violence has occurred or was even necessary in the past; the fact is that today violence and disruptive actions are no

[25]Lucius J. Barker and Jesse J. McCorry, *Black Americans and the Political System,* 2nd ed. (Englewood Cliffs, NJ: Prentice-Hall, 1980), p. 69.

longer considered necessary to resolve differences. There is a strong belief that such differences should be resolved peacefully. "Conflict but compromise" is still the order of the day.

Various structural features of the political system also foster both conflict and compromise, such as federalism, separation of powers, checks and balances, bicameralism, overlapping terms of office, and elections from various constituencies. These arrangements reflect the diversity of interests in American politics, and they also tend to institutionalize and preserve *prevailing* rather than *aspiring* interests. Hence, they promote *incrementalism* and *marginal* change rather than *decisive* and *fundamental* change. While these features have their virtues, they also have biases. The discussion of federalism that follows reflects how these structural features might affect the formulation of civil liberties policy.

CIVIL LIBERTIES IN THE CONTEXT OF FEDERALISM

Our civil liberties and civil rights are intimately connected with the nature and dynamics of the federal system. The impact of federalism on the scope and nature of civil liberties and rights is enormous. On the one hand, some states have shown the way in the protection and enforcement of civil liberties. Some state constitutions and laws obviously reflect a healthy respect and regard for civil liberties. For example, notwithstanding the Supreme Court decision in *Rodriguez* (*San Antonio Independent School District* v. *Rodriguez*, 1973), some state supreme courts now require "equal financing" of public schools based on provisions of their own state constitutions.[26]

It may also be the case, as Justice William Brennan suggested, that increasing restrictive policies of the Supreme Court (and of other federal institutions and agencies) might lead individuals and groups to look to state courts and agencies for relief.[27] Brennan cited an example from the California Supreme Court in which it held "that statements taken from suspects before first giving them *Miranda* warning are inadmissible in

California courts to impeach an accused who testifies in his own defense."[28] Brennan went on to quote the California Supreme Court as follows:

> We . . . declare[29] that [the decision to the contrary of the United States Supreme Court] is not persuasive authority in any state prosecution in California. . . . We pause . . . to reaffirm the independent nature of the California Constitution and our responsibility to separately define and protect the right of California citizens despite conflicting decisions of the United States Supreme Court interpreting the federal Constitution.[30]

Brennan cited other examples "where state courts have independently considered the merits of constitutional arguments and declined to follow opinions of the United States Supreme Court they find unconvincing, even where the state and federal constitutions are similarly or identically phrased."[31] "As the Supreme Court of Hawaii has observed," continued Brennan, "while this results in a divergence of meaning between words which are the same in both federal and state constitutions, the system of federalism envisaged by the United States Constitution tolerates such divergence where the result is greater protection of individual rights under state law than under federal law."[32]

On the other hand, however, some of the most dramatic confrontations between state and national authority have occurred in disputes over problems such as these. It is hard to imagine a more dramatic confrontation than that which occurred in early 1981 between a Louisiana state judge and a federal judge who issued conflicting orders as to which school three white girls would attend.[33] The state judge not only issued an order for the girls to attend an all-white private neighborhood school (Buckeye High), but he also personally escorted the girls there. However, the state judge's order was issued to counter an earlier parishwide (county) desegregation order of a federal judge that had assigned the three girls to the predominantly black school to bring about more racial balance in public schools. The confrontation

---

[26]*Serrano* v. *Priest II*, 557 P.2d 929 (1977). See "State Court Intervention in School Finance Reform," 28 Cleveland State Law Review 325.

[27]William J. Brennan, Jr., "State Constitutions and the Protection of Individual Rights," 90 *Harvard Law Review* 489 (1977).

[28]Ibid., pp. 498–499.

[29]Ibid., p. 498 (reference is to *Harris* v. *New York*, 401 U.S. 222, 1971).

[30]Ibid., p. 499 (reference is to *People* v. *Disrow*, 16 Cal.3d 101, 113, 114–115, 545 P.2d, 272, 280, 127 Cal. Reptr. 360, 368, 1970).

[31]Ibid., p. 500 (see note 76).

[32]Ibid., p. 500 (reference is to *State* v. *Kaluna*, 55 Hawaii 361, 369 n. 6, 320 P. 2d, 51, 58 n. 6, 1974).

[33]See, e.g., *Time,* Jan. 19, 1981, p. 49.

escalated when the federal judge, upon motion of the federal government, ordered the state judge not only to cease and desist but also to answer to the federal court as to why he should not be held in contempt. The students as well as the school officials were caught in the middle of the tug of war between federal and state courts. Although the federal court prevailed, the story nevertheless illustrates vividly the continuing conflict between federal and state authority.

A basic question underlying many of these disputes has been the extent to which states are obliged to follow the commands of the Constitution as interpreted by the U.S. Supreme Court not only in highly visible areas such as school desegregation but in other areas as well. In the more general controversy over the application of the Bill of Rights to the states, as we discuss later, there was the prior question of whether states were restricted *at all* by the terms of the Bill of Rights. Closely related to and interwoven with these issues has been the continuing controversy over the nature and scope of the restrictions imposed upon the states by the Civil War amendments, in particular the Fourteenth Amendment. May states, for example, notwithstanding the strictures of the First Amendment, give financial aid to parochial schools or allow prayers or other religious activities in public schools? How and to what extent and under what circumstances may states limit certain types of speech and expression, and remain consistent with the First Amendment? How, if at all, and in what ways may states draw distinctions among their inhabitants based upon such classifications as race, sex, age, wealth, and poverty in the formulation and enforcement of their policies and practices? To what extent are states obliged to follow procedural provisions of the Bill of Rights in dealing with persons accused of a crime? In one form or another, these questions illustrate some of the most salient civil liberties and civil rights problems that we face today. They go to the heart of the impact of federalism on our civil rights and liberties. This impact, of course, is determined by a number of institutions and officials, but since many of these questions relate to the *constitutional legal* boundaries of state and national authority, it is obvious that the judiciary—especially the U.S. Supreme Court—has had and continues to have a major role in determining how federalism affects our rights and liberties. We might gain a better understanding of this whole matter by surveying how the Supreme Court has dealt with such problems.

THE SUPREME COURT, THE BILL OF RIGHTS, AND THE FOURTEENTH AMENDMENT

The framers of the Bill of Rights considered federal power the major threat to individual liberties. The injunction of the First Amendment, "Congress shall make no law . . . ," is indicative of that concern. But there were others who viewed the Bill of Rights as restricting state power as well. This view was urged in *Barron* v. *Baltimore* (Pet. 243, 1833), but the Supreme Court rejected such a construction. Speaking for a unanimous Court, Chief Justice John Marshall said:

> The Constitution was ordained and established by the people of the United States for themselves, for their own government, and not for the government of the individual states. . . . The powers they conferred on this government were to be exercised by itself; and the limitations on power, if expressed in general terms are . . . necessarily applicable to the government created by the instrument. They are limitations of power granted in the instrument itself: not of distinct governments framed by different persons and for different purposes.

He concluded that if his propositions were correct, the Fifth Amendment (and hence the Bill of Rights) must be understood as restraining the power of the national government and not that of the states. Then came the Civil War and the enactment of the Civil War amendments. Ratified by Congress in 1866 and adopted by the states in 1868, the Fourteenth Amendment has had perhaps the most far-reaching impact of these amendments, indeed of any amendment outside the Bill of Rights, in the development of our rights and liberties. From the very beginning, the Fourteenth has prompted fierce debate over its meaning and sparked considerable litigation, particularly over the Court's evolving interpretation of its rights and protections.

What are its provisions? Although the Fourteenth Amendment defines citizenship, most relevant for our purposes are the three clauses that provide protection against the states: privileges and immunities, due process, and equal protection. Congress is also granted the power to enforce these protections through legislation. It is these constitutional clauses, particularly due process and equal protection, that have provided the basis for the modern expansion of civil rights and civil liberties. Let us consider this matter a bit further.

The Fourteenth Amendment forbids the states from abridging by law any privilege or immunity of U.S. citizens. But what are these "privileges and immunities"? Representative John A. Bingham, an Ohio Republican who authored the amendment, believed that "the privileges and immunities of citizens of the United States . . . are chiefly defined in the first eight amendments to the Constitution. . . . These eight articles . . . were never limitations upon the power of the States, until made so by the Fourteenth Amendment."[34]

But any semblance of this expansive interpretation of the privileges and immunities clause was clearly rejected by the Supreme Court in the well-known Slaughterhouse Cases (83 U.S. 36, 21 L.Ed. 394, 1873). By a 5 to 4 majority, the Court's narrow construction of the clause effectively gutted its protections. (The Court also construed the due process and equal protection clauses narrowly.) Here the Court drew a sharp distinction between state citizenship and national citizenship, holding that the mass of basic civil and economic rights—including the right to pursue one's business opportunities—accrue from the privileges and immunities of state citizenship, not national citizenship. The effect of the Court's decisions, as the four dissenters pointed out, meant that the privileges and immunities clause provided no more protection than that which existed prior to the adoption of the amendment.

Indeed, the Court's decision effectively rendered the clause meaningless, providing no independent rights or protections to individuals. Although a few attempts have been made to revive the provision, most notably by Justice Hugo Black, the Court's original interpretation, in the Slaughterhouse Cases, continues to prove an almost insurmountable barrier. Whether and how the privileges and immunities clause will become an important pillar in the protection of civil rights and civil liberties remains to be seen. But today, it is not.

Unlike privileges and immunities, the due process and equal protection clauses have been far from dormant. Their evolution and development have been dynamic, even if stormy and controversial, and remain so today. The due process clause prevents states from depriving any person of life, liberty, or property without "due process" of law. While this language is used in the Fifth Amendment, it has taken on a much more expansive meaning in the Fourteenth Amendment.

Ironically, however, it was primarily used at first not to protect individual rights but to protect businesses from economic regulation.

Under the guise of "substantive due process," the Court struck down Progressive Era legislation, such as minimum wage and maximum hour laws, on the grounds that it deprived individuals of their liberty to contract without due process of law. "Due process" was interpreted as not merely a *procedural* protection but as a requirement of substantive fairness. This doctrine dominated Court decisions in the early part of the Twentieth Century but began to disintegrate in the 1930s, until it all but disappeared in 1937, when the Court did an about face and began to uphold President Franklin D. Roosevelt's New Deal legislation (see *West Coast Hotel* v. *Parrish*, 1937).

The year 1937 was a significant turning point for the due process clause, not only because of decisions such as *West Coast Hotel*, but also because the Court now began to focus on the protection of civil rights and civil liberties as one of its major functions. Indeed, the Court began to accelerate its march toward applying certain provisions of the Bill of Rights to states through the use of the due process clause of the Fourteenth Amendment.

Let us backtrack and describe in somewhat more detail how this march toward incorporation came about. As discussed, from the very outset some, including its author, believed that the Fourteenth Amendment incorporated the first eight amendments of the Bill of Rights as limitations on powers of the states. But for some time the Court continued to hold to its earlier decision (*Barron* v. *Baltimore*, 1833), which held that the Bill of Rights did not protect against state action, only federal.

This principle was reaffirmed in a number of cases prior to the Civil War and continued to be a guide for the Court in decisions following the adoption of the Fourteenth Amendment in 1868. Indeed, the Court heard several cases in which counsel argued that the Fourteenth Amendment had as one of its objectives the incorporation of the Bill of Rights. But the Court steadfastly refused to interpret the Fourteenth Amendment in this way.

Then, in 1925, in a historic statement in *Gitlow* v. *New York* (268 U.S. 652, 1925), the Court said:

> For present purposes we may and do assume that freedom of speech and of the press which are protected by the First Amendment from abridgement by Congress are among the fundamental personal rights and liberties protected by the due process clause of

[34]Quoted in Irving Brant, *The Bill of Rights* (Indianapolis, IN: Bobbs-Merrill Co., 1965), p. 333.

the Fourteenth Amendment from impairment by the States.

As such, *Gitlow* may be viewed as a case of major, almost revolutionary significance, which pointed in favor of those who saw the provisions of the Bill of Rights as effective limitations on the states through the Fourteenth Amendment. Two years after *Gitlow,* for example, the Court reversed a conviction under a Kansas criminal syndicalism act, saying that the application of the act imposed "an arbitrary and unreasonable exercise of the police power of the State . . . in violation of the due process clause of the Fourteenth Amendment" (*Fiske* v. *Kansas,* 274 U.S. 380, 1927). Four years later, in *Near* v. *Minnesota* (283 U.S. 679, 1931), the Court struck down a Minnesota statute as an abridgment of freedom of the press. Chief Justice Charles Evans Hughes asserted in the opinion for the Court that "it is no longer open to doubt that the liberty of the press, and of speech, is within the liberty safeguarded by the due process clause of the Fourteenth Amendment from invasion by state action."

The Court continued to erode the effect of the *Barron* rule, at least as far as First Amendment freedoms were concerned, when, in *De Jonge* v. *Oregon* (299 U.S. 353, 1937), it held peaceable assembly a right cognate to those of free speech and free press, and hence protected against state impairment by the due process clause of the Fourteenth Amendment.

But any notion that this trend of decisions would lead to a reversal of *Barron* v. *Baltimore* and to the total incorporation of the first eight amendments into the Fourteenth Amendment was dispelled by Justice Benjamin Cardozo in a decision handed down just eleven months after *De Jonge.* In *Palko* v. *Connecticut* (302 U.S. 319, 1937), the Court refused to apply the double jeopardy provision of the Fifth Amendment to a state criminal prosecution. Justice Cardozo argued that only those guarantees of the first eight amendments that are "implicit in the concept of ordered liberty" are to be construed as valid restrictions on state power through the Fourteenth Amendment. In effect, he enunciated a doctrine of "selective incorporation" of specific Bill of Rights guarantees into the Fourteenth Amendment based on the test of their essentiality to his concept of "ordered liberty."

In 1940 the "selective incorporation" process resulted in the Court's holding in *Cantwell* v. *Connecticut* (310 U.S. 296, 1940) that the free exercise of religion clause of the First Amendment is applicable to the states. In this case the Court struck down a state statute that allowed officials unfettered discretion in regulating religious advocacy and solicitation. In his opinion for a unanimous Court, Justice Owen Roberts contended:

> The fundamental concept of liberty embodied in that [the Fourteenth] Amendment embraces the liberties guaranteed by the First Amendment . . . [which] declares that Congress shall make no law respecting an establishment of religion or prohibiting the free exercise thereof. The Fourteenth Amendment has rendered the legislatures of the states as incompetent as Congress to enact such laws.

This expansive interpretation of the scope of the Fourteenth Amendment was followed by an application of the establishment clause of the First Amendment to the states in *Everson* v. *Board of Education* (330 U.S. 1, 1947). In that case the Court considered the troublesome issue of public aid to parochial schools and held that the due process clause of the Fourteenth Amendment enjoins the states from rendering such aid, just as the First Amendment restrains Congress.

The most comprehensive arguments supporting the total incorporation theory were made in *Adamson* v. *California* (332 U.S. 46, 1947). Here the Court's five-man majority refused to upset a state conviction where the appellant argued that the state procedure infringed the Fifth Amendment guarantee against compulsory self-incrimination, which was made applicable to the states through the Fourteenth Amendment. The four dissenters—Justices Hugo Black, William O. Douglas, Frank Murphy, and Wiley B. Rutledge—contended that all the specific guarantees of the first eight amendments should be read into the due process clause of the Fourteenth Amendment and made applicable to the states. Justice Black's dissenting opinion is most often cited in support of this thesis. He maintained that the legislative history of the Fourteenth Amendment, as well as the debates in the state legislatures ratifying it, clearly revealed that the Fourteenth Amendment was designed to make the Bill of Rights applicable to the states. In effect, his position was that the framers of the Fourteenth Amendment intended the due process clause to be a shorthand restatement of the specific guarantees of the Bill of Rights, *but no more.*

In a concurring opinion, Justice Felix Frankfurter not only questioned Black's reading and interpretation of history but contended that incorporation of the specific guarantees of the Bill of Rights into the due process clause would impart to it a far more expansive meaning than intended in some cases and a more restricted meaning than intended in others. To him, such a construction would also do violence to the principle of federalism upon which the republic was founded. As he put it:

> A construction which gives to due process no independent function but turns it into a summary of the specific provisions of the Bill of Rights would . . . tear up the fabric of law in the several States, and would deprive the States of the opportunity for reforms in legal process designed for extending the area of freedom. It would assume that no other abuses would reveal themselves in the course of time than those which had become manifest in 1791.

On the other hand, two of Black's fellow dissenters did not share his view of the limited protection afforded by the due process clause. It was their view that restricting the scope of the clause only to the Bill of Rights guarantees and *no more* fails to include enough. As Murphy contended in a separate opinion in which Rutledge joined:

> Occasions may arise where a proceeding falls so far short of conforming to fundamental standards of procedure as to warrant constitutional condemnation in terms of lack of due process despite the absence of a specific provision in the Bill of Rights.

In subsequent cases, Justice Black reaffirmed his total incorporation position and continued to urge a narrow, or strict, interpretation of the specific guarantees of the Bill of Rights. In *Wolf* v. *Colorado* (338 U.S. 25, 1949), for example, he concurred in the Court's action of "selectively incorporating" the Fourth Amendment into the Fourteenth *without* the exclusionary rule. He contended that the rule, which holds that evidence obtained in violation of the Fourth Amendment is inadmissible in criminal prosecutions, "is not a command of the Fourth Amendment" but instead is a "judicially created" one. Justices Murphy and Rutledge were joined this time by Justice Douglas in taking issue with Black's narrow construction of the Fourth Amendment. In their view, not only does the Fourteenth Amendment incorporate the guarantees of the Fourth, but the exclusionary rule must be construed as embraced in the amendment if its command is to be an effective sanction against the evil to which it is directed. But in decisions interpreting *Mapp*, it seems as if the Burger Court was more disposed to follow a narrow construction and to reject the view that the exclusionary rule is a necessary corollary of the Fourth Amendment.

Although the "total incorporation" theory has never gained majority support, its proponents have virtually accomplished their goal. Note the forward thrust of incorporation since 1961: *Mapp* v. *Ohio*, where the exclusionary rule was made obligatory on the states, thereby making the Fourth Amendment an effective restraint on state action; *Malloy* v. *Hogan* and *Benton* v. *Maryland*, making the Fifth Amendment's self-incrimination and double jeopardy provisions applicable to the states; *Gideon* v. *Wainwright, Pointer* v. *Texas, Klopfer* v. *North Carolina*, and *Duncan* v. *Louisiana*, incorporating into the Fourteenth Amendment the Sixth Amendment guarantees of counsel, confrontation, a speedy trial, and trial by jury for serious criminal offenses; and *Robinson* v. *California*, tying to the Fourteenth Amendment the Eighth Amendment's protection against cruel and unusual punishment.

Only a few provisions of the Bill of Rights have not been incorporated into the Fourteenth Amendment. These include the Second and Third Amendments (which have no practical significance for the states), the grand jury indictment requirement of the Fifth Amendment, and the provision prohibiting excessive bail and the imposition of excessive fines of the Eighth Amendment. For all practical purposes, however, imposition of excessive bail and fines by a state would violate the due process clause of the Fourteenth Amendment. Consequently, and in general, the major controversy in this area is not whether specific guarantees of the Bill of Rights apply to the states, but whether judges narrowly or broadly interpret specific provisions of those guarantees as restrictions on the states.

A Note on Equal Protection

The final clause of the Fourteenth Amendment forbids states from denying any person "equal protection of the laws." This clause was intended, according to one of its fervent supporters, the Republican Senator Jacob M. Howard of Michigan, to give "to the humblest, the poorest, the most despised of the [human] race, the same rights and same protection before the law as it gives to the most powerful, the most wealthy, or the most haughty."[35] The amendment would not offer that protection to such persons until well into the middle of the twentieth century.

As interpreted by the Court, *equal protection* is a limitation on the exercise of government power that invalidates any government regulation that is "arbitrarily discriminatory." This is not to say that

---

[35]Ibid., p. 337.

laws may not treat individuals differently; indeed, all laws are to some extent inherently unequal, because part of the purpose of legislation is to distinguish among individuals. Rather, the clause prevents unreasonable classifications of individuals.

To aid decision-making in such cases, the Court has developed three major tests or standards of review: rational basis, strict scrutiny, and intermediate scrutiny. These tests or standards, as well as litigation under equal protection, are discussed in Chapter 5.

CONCLUSION

Overall, students of civil liberties must look to a number of legal sources in dealing with the problems and issues involved. At the national level, we must consider the Constitution, including the Bill of Rights and other relevant amendments. Legislation passed by the Congress, such as the Civil Rights Act of 1991, and rules and regulations issued by administrative agencies are also important to our study of civil liberties. So also are relevant decisions of federal courts and actions of the president and administrative agencies. Similarly, given the nature of the federal system, we must also consider various sources at the state (and local) level.

Indeed, the extent to which people more or less enjoy certain liberties or rights might depend upon the nature of *particular* state constitutions, state statutes, local ordinances, and administrative rules and regulations, and how these are interpreted and enforced by various officials. We must also consider pertinent decisions of state and local courts and actions of administrative officials.

Finally, students of civil liberties must remember that policies emanating from constitutions, court decisions, and statutes are not automatically put into practice, nor do they automatically change the behavior of those for whom they were intended. For example, whether a particular policy in court decisions will meet with compliance depends on a number of factors, including the decisiveness and clarity of the court's position; whether the policy is perceived as legitimate (within the court's authority); congruence of the policy with prevailing norms and mores of the community; the costs of noncompliance; and the attitudes of public officials and employees, especially those who must enforce or implement the court decision.[36]

It is hoped that the various factors and considerations summarized in this chapter will allow us to discern more clearly the nature and dimensions of the many civil liberty problems discussed in this volume.

SELECTED REFERENCES

Abraham, Henry J. *The Judiciary: The Supreme Court in the Governmental Process,* 8th ed. (Dubuque, IA: William C. Brown, 1991).

Barker, Lucius J., and McCorry, Jesse J. *Black Americans and the Political System,* 2nd ed. (Englewood Cliffs, NJ: Prentice-Hall, 1980).

Baum, Lawerence, *The Supreme Court,* 4th ed. (Washington, D.C.: Congressional Quarterly Press, 1992).

Caldeira, Gregory A., and Wright, John R. "Organized Interests and Agenda Setting in the U.S. Supreme Court," 82 *American Political Science Review* 1109 (1988).

Casper, Jonathan. "Supreme Court and National Policy-making," 70 *American Political Science Review* 50 (1979).

Choper, Jesse H. *Judicial Review and the National Political Process: A Functional Reconsideration of the Role of the Supreme Court* (Chicago: University of Chicago Press, 1980).

Ely, John Hart. *Democracy and Distrust: A Theory of Judicial Review* (Cambridge, MA: Harvard University Press, 1980).

Emerson, Thomas I. "First Amendment Doctrine and the Burger Court," 68 *California Law Review* 422 (1980).

Fino, Susan P. *The Role of State Supreme Courts in the New Judicial Federalism* (Westport, CT: Greenwood Press, 1987).

Horowitz, Donald L. *The Courts and Social Policy* (Washington, D.C.: The Brookings Institution, 1977).

Krislov, Samuel. "The Amicus Curiae Brief: From Friendship to Advocacy," 72 *Yale Law Journal* 694 (1963).

Lindblom, Charles E. *The Policy Making Process* (Englewood Cliffs, NJ: Prentice-Hall, 1980).

Marshall, Thomas. *Public Opinion and the Supreme Court* (Boston: Unwin/Hyman, 1989).

McCloskey, Robert G. *The American Supreme Court* (Chicago: University of Chicago Press, 1960).

McClosky, Herbert, and Brill, Alida. *Dimensions of Tolerance: What Americans Believe about Civil Liberties* (New York: Russell Sage Foundation, 1983).

Murphy, Walter F. *Elements of Judicial Strategy* (Chicago: University of Chicago Press, 1964).

O'Brien, David M. *Storm Center,* 2nd ed. (New York: W. W. Norton, 1990).

[36]Stephen Wasby, *The Supreme Court in the Federal Judicial System* (New York: Holt, Rinehart & Winston, 1988).

Perry, H. W., Jr. *Deciding to Decide: Agenda Setting in the U.S. Supreme Court* (Cambridge, MA: Harvard University Press, 1991)

Rehnquist, William H. *The Supreme Court: How It Was, How It Is* (New York: Morrow, 1987).

Rosenberg, Gerald. *The Hollow Hope* (Chicago: University of Chicago Press, 1991).

Schwartz, Herman. *Packing the Courts: The Conservative Campaign to Rewrite the Constitution* (New York: Charles Scribner's Sons, 1988).

Shapiro, Martin. *Freedom of Speech: The Supreme Court and Judicial Review* (Englewood Cliffs, NJ: Prentice-Hall, 1966), esp. ch. 1.

Sullivan, John; Pierson, James; and Marcus, George E. *Political Tolerance and American Democracy* (Chicago: University of Chicago Press, 1982).

Truman, David. *The Governmental Process: Political Interests and Public Opinion*, 2nd ed. (New York: Alfred A. Knopf, 1971).

Wasby, Stephen. *The Supreme Court in the Federal Judicial System* (New York: Holt, Rinehart & Winston, 1988).

Witt, Elder. *Congressional Quarterly's Guide to the U.S. Supreme Court*, 2nd ed. (Washington, D.C.: CQ Press, 1990).

Woodward, Bob, and Armstrong, Scott. *The Brethren* (New York: Simon and Schuster, 1979).

Religious Liberty

Introductory Commentary

The framers of the Bill of Rights guaranteed religious liberty in the United States by proclaiming in the First Amendment to the Constitution that "Congress shall make no law respecting an establishment of religion, or prohibiting the free exercise thereof. . . . " Despite the potential for litigation in this area, only a few controversies over religious liberty issues reached the Supreme Court in the century following the amendment's adoption.[1] And, for the most part, such litigation focused on the scope and meaning of the free exercise clause. But during the twentieth century, particularly since 1940, the Supreme Court has ruled on a large number of cases raising both establishment and free exercise issues. And, as we move closer toward the twenty-first century, some of the major policy issues that gave rise to the religious liberty cases from the 1940s through the 1980s—public financial support for sectarian schools, prayer and religious observances in public schools, and tax exemptions for religious activities—still produce lively debate in the political arena. To be sure, the elevation of Justice William Rehnquist to the Chief Justiceship in 1988 and the appointment of four new justices in the late 1980s and early 1990s by conservative Republican Presidents Ronald Reagan and George Bush spurred the move by the Court to reexamine and alter doctrines that had guided decision-making in religious liberty cases for decades. The commentary in this chapter, along with selected edited cases, examines several of the most celebrated policy questions on the religious liberty issue as we chronicle the development of constitutional law in this area.

[1]See, e.g., *Watson* v. *Jones*, 80 U.S. 679 (1871); *Reynolds* v. *United States*, 98 U.S. 145 (1879); *Church of the Holy Trinity* v. *United States*, 143 U.S. 457 (1892); and *Bradfield* v. *Roberts*, 175 U.S. 291 (1899).

The Everson *Case and the Emergence of Parochiaid Controversies: From Transportation to Textbooks*

FEATURED CASES

Everson v. *Board of Education*   *Board of Education* v. *Allen*

In 1941, New Jersey enacted legislation authorizing school districts to subsidize the transportation of pupils who attended church-related schools. Under this legislation the Ewing Township district decided to reimburse parents for money spent by their children to get to and from school on the regular transit system. A taxpayer objected to this reimbursement scheme and challenged the practice as a violation of the establishment clause. In the end, however, the Supreme Court upheld the reimbursement scheme in *Everson* v. *Board of Education* (330 U.S. 1, 1947). Justice Hugo Black, speaking for the five-to-four majority, emphasized the "child benefit," "secular legislative purpose," and "public welfare" aspects of the New Jersey legislation.

In dissent, Justice Wiley B. Rutledge, with whom Justices Felix Frankfurter, Robert H. Jackson, and Harold Burton agreed, warned of the efforts to use the taxing power to support parochial schools and to inject religious training and exercises into the public schools. Rutledge concluded that these two "great drives are constantly in motion to abridge, in the name of education, the complete division of religion and civil authority" that the First Amendment commands, and he concluded that neither should be supported by the Court.

Justice Rutledge's warning was reflected in the subsequent surge of legislative proposals for various forms of assistance to sectarian schools. The purchase of textbooks, for example, is a major expense for those attending nonpublic schools. As a result, over the years sectarian interest groups have made major efforts to influence legislative bodies to appropriate funds for textbooks. In addition to the *Everson* precedent, these advocates could point to the Court's decision in *Cochran* v. *Louisiana State Board of Education* (218 U.S. 370, 1930) for support. Here a Louisiana textbook aid statute was sustained against a due process challenge (the nonpublic purpose of the expenditure to provide secular books for pupils attending parochial schools); the establishment issue was not considered. Nevertheless, the child benefit nature of the expenditure emphasized by the *Cochran* case is now an essential ingredient of the

secular legislative purpose dimension of the three-pronged test the Court applies in establishment clause cases.

The leading establishment clause challenge to the state provision of secular textbooks for parochial school children came in *Board of Education* v. *Allen* (392 U.S. 236, 1968). At issue was a New York statute that required local school boards to provide the free loan of textbooks to students in grades 7–12, including those attending parochial and other private schools. In upholding the statute, the Court reaffirmed the general welfare and secular legislative purpose doctrine of *Everson*. In addition, Justice Byron White, who wrote the Court's opinion, thought the law met the test ("the purpose and primary effect of the enactment") enunciated in *School District of Abington Township* v. *Schempp* (discussed *infra*). He contended that the purpose of the legislation was to expand educational opportunity by making textbooks available free of charge. The financial benefit was to the student and the parent, and not to the school.

Both Justices Hugo Black and William O. Douglas, in their separate dissents, felt that the majority's reliance on *Everson* was grossly misplaced. Black charged that the law "is a flat, flagrant and open violation" of the establishment clause, and warned that it would take "no prophet to foresee" that similar arguments could be used to support and uphold legislation funding parochial school construction and teachers' salaries.

Justice Douglas was troubled with the ideological bias possible in the selection of textbooks. He noted that the initial selection was in the hands of those who could exercise an ideological (sectarian) bias, and that, whatever the subsequent action of the public school board, the church-state problem was aggravated. In distinguishing this case from *Everson*, Douglas stressed the possible ideological bias of a textbook as compared to a school bus, hot lunches, and scholarships. To him, the textbook "is the chief . . . instrumentality for propagating a particular religious creed or faith."

Despite such concerns, the Court's majority

continued to find state textbook aid statutes constitutionally acceptable in the decade following *Allen*. The Pennsylvania textbook arrangement was sustained in *Meek* v. *Pittinger* (421 U.S. 349) in 1975, and the Ohio textbook loan program was sustained in *Wolman* v. *Walter* (433 U.S. 229) in 1977. In the former, Justice Potter Stewart spoke for the Court and emphasized that the books were being loaned directly to the pupils and that there was no financial benefit to the sectarian schools they attended. Justice Harry Blackmun used similar reasoning in upholding the Ohio textbook provision in *Wolman*. Additionally, Blackmun underscored the state's "legitimate interest in providing a fertile educational environment" for all its pupils in both public and sectarian schools.

EVERSON v. BOARD OF EDUCATION
330 U.S. 1; 91 L. Ed. 711; 67 S. Ct. 504 (1947)

JUSTICE BLACK *delivered the opinion of the Court.*

A New Jersey statute authorizes its local school districts to make rules and contracts for the transportation of children to and from schools. The appellee, a township board of education, acting pursuant to this statute, authorized reimbursement to parents of money expended by them for the bus transportation of their children on regular busses operated by the public transportation system. Part of this money was for the payment of transportation of some school children in the community to Catholic parochial schools. These church schools give their students, in addition to secular education, regular religious instruction conforming to the religious tenets and modes of worship of the Catholic Faith. The superintendent of these schools is a Catholic priest.

The appellant, in his capacity as a district taxpayer, filed suit in a state court challenging the right of the Board to reimburse parents of parochial school students. He contended that the statute and the resolution passed pursuant to it violated both the State and Federal Constitutions. That court held that the legislature was without power to authorize such payments under the state constitution. . . . The New Jersey Court of Errors and Appeals reversed, holding that neither the statute nor the resolution passed pursuant to it was in conflict with the State Constitution or the provisions of the Federal Constitution in issue. . . . The Case is here on appeal under 28 U.S.C. sec. 344(a). . . .

The only contention here is that the state statute and the resolution, insofar as they authorize reimbursement to parents of children attending parochial schools, violate the Federal Constitution in these two aspects, which to some extent overlap. *First.* They authorize the State to take by taxation the private property of some and bestow it upon others, to be used for their own private purposes. This, it is alleged, violates the due process clause of the Fourteenth Amendment. *Second.* The statute and the resolution forced inhabitants to pay taxes to help support and maintain schools which are dedicated to, and which regularly teach, the Catholic Faith. This is alleged to be a use of state power to support church schools contrary to the prohibition of the First Amendment which the Fourteenth Amendment made applicable to the states.

First. The due process argument that the state law taxes some people to help others carry out their private purposes is framed in two phases. The first phase is that a state cannot tax A to reimburse B for the cost of transporting his children to church schools. This is said to violate the due process clause because the children are sent to these church schools to satisfy the personal desires of their parents, rather than the public's interest in the general education of all children. . . .

It is much too late to argue that legislation intended to facilitate the opportunity of children to get a secular education serves no public purpose. *Cochran* v. *Louisiana State Board of Education*, 281 U.S. 340: Holmes, J., in *Interstate Ry.* v. *Massachusetts*, 207 U.S. 79, 87. . . .

Second. The New Jersey statute is challenged as a "law respecting an establishment of religion." The First Amendment, as made applicable to the states by the Fourteenth, *Murdock* v. *Pennsylvania*, 319 U.S. 105, commands that a state "shall make no law respecting an establishment of religion, or prohibiting the free exercise thereof. . . ."

The "establishment of religion" clause of the First Amendment means at least this: Neither a state nor the Federal Government can set up a church. Neither can pass laws which aid one religion, aid all religions, or prefer one religion over another. Neither can force nor influence a person to go to or to remain away from church against his will or force him to profess a belief or disbelief in any religion. No person can be punished for entertaining or professing religious beliefs or disbeliefs, for church attendance or non-attendance. No tax in any amount, large or small, can be levied to support any religious activities or institutions, whatever they may be called or whatever form they may adopt to teach or practice religion. Neither a state nor the Federal Government can, openly or secretly, participate in the affairs of any religious organizations or groups and *vice versa.* In the words of Jefferson, the clause against establishment of religion by law was intended to erect "a wall of Separation between church and State. . . ."

We must consider the New Jersey statute in accordance with the foregoing limitations imposed by the First Amendment. But we must not strike that state statute down if it is within the State's constitutional power even though it approaches the verge of that power. . . . New Jersey cannot consistently with the "establishment of religion" clause of the First Amendment contribute tax-raised funds to the support of an institution which teaches the tenets and faith of any church. On the other hand, other language of the amendment commands that New Jersey cannot hamper its citizens in the free exercise of their own religion. Consequently, it cannot exclude individual Catholics, Lutherans, Mohammedans, Baptists, Jews, Methodists, Non-believers, Presbyterians, or the members of any other faith, because of their faith, or lack of it, from receiving the benefits of public welfare legislation. . . .

Measured by these standards, we cannot say that the First Amendment prohibits New Jersey from spending tax-raised funds to pay the bus fares of parochial school pupils as a part of a general program under which it pays the fares of pupils attending public and other schools. It is undoubtedly true that children are helped to get to church schools. There is even a possibility that some of the children might not be sent to the church schools if the parents were compelled to pay their children's bus fares out of their own pockets when transportation to a public school would have been paid for by the State. The same possibility exists where the state requires a local transit company to provide reduced fares to school children including those attending parochial schools, or where a municipally owned transportation system undertakes to carry all school children free of charge. Moreover, state-paid policemen, detailed to protect children going to and from church schools from the very real hazards of traffic, would serve much the same purpose and accomplish much the same result as state provisions intended to guarantee free transportation of a kind which the state deems to be best for the school children's welfare. And parents might refuse to risk their children to the serious danger of traffic accidents going to and from parochial schools, the approaches to which were not protected by the policemen. Similarly, parents might be reluctant to permit their children to attend schools which the state had cut off from such general government services as ordinary police and fire protection, connections for sewage disposal, public highways and sidewalks. Of course, cutting off church schools from these services, so separate and so indisputably marked off from the religious function, would make it far more difficult for the schools to operate. But such is obviously not the purpose of the First Amendment. That Amendment requires the state to be a neutral in its relations with groups of religious believers and non-believers: it does not require the state to be their adversary. . . .

. . . The State contributes no money to the schools. It does not support them. Its legislation, as applied, does no more than provide a general program to help parents get their children, regardless of their religion, safely and expeditiously to and from accredited schools.

The First Amendment has erected a wall between church and state. That wall must be kept high and impregnable. We could not approve the slightest breach. New Jersey has not breached it here.

Affirmed.

JUSTICE JACKSON, *dissenting.*

I find myself, contrary to first impressions, unable to join in this decision. I have a sympathy, though it is not ideological, with Catholic citizens who are compelled by law to pay taxes for public schools, and also feel constrained by conscience and discipline to support other schools for their own children. Such relief to them as this case involves is not in itself a serious burden to taxpayers and I had assumed it to be as little serious in principle. Study of this case convinces me otherwise. The Court's opinion marshals every argument in favor of state aid and puts the case in its most favorable light, but much of its reasoning confirms my conclusions that there are no good grounds upon which to support the present legislation. In fact, the undertones of the opinion, advocating complete and uncompromising separation of Church from State, seem utterly discordant with its conclusion yielding support to their commingling in educational matters. The case which irresistibly comes to mind as the most fitting precedent is that of Julia who, according to Byron's reports, "whispering 'I will ne'er consent.'—consented." . . .

The Township of Ewing is not furnishing transportation to the children in any form: it is not operating school busses itself or contracting for their operation; and it is not performing any public service of any kind with this taxpayer's money. All school children are left to ride as ordinary paying passengers on the regular busses operated by the public transportation system. What the Township does, and what the taxpayer complains of, is at stated intervals to reimburse parents for the fares paid, provided the children attend either public schools or Catholic Church schools. This expenditure of tax funds has no possible effect on the child's safety or expedition in transit. As passengers on the public busses they travel as fast and no faster, and are as safe and no safer, since their parents are reimbursed as before.

In addition to thus assuming a type of service that does not exist, the Court also insists that we must close our eyes to a discrimination which does exist. The resolution which authorizes disbursement of this taxpayer's money limits reimbursement to those who attend public schools and Catholic schools. That is the way the Act is applied to this taxpayer.

The New Jersey Act in question makes the character of the school, not the needs of the children, determine the eligibility of parents for reimbursement. The Act permits payment for transportation to parochial schools or public schools but prohibits it to private schools operated in whole or in part for profit. Children often are sent to private schools because their parents feel that they require more individual instruction than public schools can provide, or because they are backward or defective and need special attention. If all children of the state were objects of impartial solicitude, no reason is obvious for denying transportation reimbursement to students of this class, for these often are as needy and as worthy as those who go to public or parochial schools. Refusal to reimburse those who attend such schools is understandable only in the light of a purpose to aid the schools, because the state might well abstain from aiding a profit-making private enterprise. Thus, under the Act and resolution brought to us by this case, children are classified according to the schools they attend and are to be aided if they attend private secular schools or private religious schools of other faiths. . . .

It is no exaggeration to say that the whole historic conflict in temporal policy between the Catholic Church and non-Catholics comes to a focus in their respective school policies. The Roman Catholic Church, counseled by experience in many ages and many lands and with all sorts and conditions of men, takes what, from the viewpoint of its own progress and the success of its mission, is a wise estimate of the importance of education to religion. . . .

I should be surprised if any Catholic would deny that the parochial school is a vital, if not the most vital part of the Roman Catholic Church. If put to the choice, that venerable institution, I should expect, would forego its whole service for mature persons before it would give up education of the young, and it would be a wise choice. Its growth and cohesion, discipline and loyalty, spring from its schools. Catholic education is the rock on which the whole structure rests, and to render tax aid to its Church school is indistinguishable to me from rendering the same aid to the Church itself. . . .

[W]e cannot have it both ways. Religious teaching cannot be a private affair when the state seeks to impose regulations which infringe on it indirectly, and a public affair when it comes to taxing citizens of one faith to aid another, or those of no faith to aid all. If these principles seem harsh in prohibiting aid to Catholic education, it must not be forgotten that it is the same Constitution that alone assures Catholics the right to maintain these schools at all when predominant local sentiment would forbid them. *Pierce* v. *Society of Sisters*, 268 U.S. 510. Nor should I think that those who have done so well without this aid would want to see this separation between Church and State broken down. If the state may aid these religious schools, it may therefore regulate them. . . .

JUSTICE FRANKFURTER *joins in this opinion.*

JUSTICE RUTLEDGE, *with whom* JUSTICE FRANKFURTER, JUSTICE JACKSON, *and* JUSTICE BURTON *agree, dissenting.*

* * *

II

. . . [T]oday, apart from efforts to inject religious training or exercises and sectarian issues into the public schools, the only serious surviving threat to maintaining that complete and permanent separation of religion and civil power which the First

Amendment commands is through use of the taxing power to support religion, religious establishments, or establishments having a religious foundation whatever their form of special religious function.

Does New Jersey's action furnish support for religion by use of the taxing power? Certainly it does if the test remains undiluted as Jefferson and Madison made it, that money taken by taxation from one is not to be used or given to support another's religious training or belief, or indeed one's own. Today as then the furnishing of "contributions of money for the propagation of opinions which he disbelieves" is the forbidden exaction; and the prohibition is absolute for whatever measure brings that consequence and whatever amount may be sought or given to that end. . . .

New Jersey's action therefore exactly fits the type of exaction and the kind of evil at which Madison and Jefferson struck. Under the test they framed it cannot be said that the cost of transportation is no part of the cost of education or of the religious instruction given. That it is a substantial and a necessary element is shown most plainly by the continuing and increasing demand for the state to assume it. Nor is there pretense that it relates only to the secular instruction given in religious schools or that any attempt is or could be made toward allocating proportional shares as between the secular and the religious instruction. It is precisely because the instruction is religious and relates to a particular faith, whether one or another, that parents send their children to religious schools under the *Pierce* doctrine. And the very purpose of the state's contribution is to defray the cost of conveying the pupil to the place where he will receive not simply secular, but also and primarily religious, teaching and guidance. . . .

Finally, transportation, where it is needed, is as essential to education as any other element. Its cost is as much a part of the total expense, except at times in amount, as the of textbooks, of school lunches, or athletic equipment, of writing and other materials; indeed of all other items composing the total burden. . . . Without buildings, without equipment, without library, textbooks and other materials, and without transportation to bring teacher and pupil together in such an effective teaching environment, there can be not even the skeleton of what our times require. Hardly can it be maintained that transportation is the least essential of these items, or that it does not in fact aid, encourage, sustain and support, just as they do, the very process which is its purpose to accomplish. . . .

For me, therefore, the feat is impossible to select so indispensable an item from the composite of total costs, and characterize it as not aiding, contributing to, promoting or sustaining the propagation of beliefs which it is the very end of all to bring about. . . .

* * *

IV

No one conscious of religious value can be unsympathetic toward the burden which our constitutional separation puts on parents who desire religious instruction mixed with security for their children. They pay taxes for others' children's education, at the same time the added cost of instruction for their own. Nor can one happily see benefits denied to children which others receive, because in conscience they or their parents desire for them a different kind of training others do not demand.

But if those feelings should prevail, there would be an end to our historic constitutional policy and command. No more unjust or discriminatory in fact is it to deny attendance at religious schools the cost of their transportation than it is to deny them tuitions, sustenance for their teachers, or any other additional expense which others receive at public cost.

Two great drives are constantly in motion to abridge, in the name of education, the complete division of religion and civil authority which our forefathers made. One is to introduce religious education and observances into the public schools. The other, to obtain public funds for the aid and support of various private religious schools. See Johnson, *The Legal Status of Church-State Relationships in the United States* (1934); Thayer, *Religion in Public Education* (1947); Note (1941) 50 Yale L.J. 917. In my opinion both avenues were closed by the Constitution. Neither should be opened by this Court. The matter is not one of quantity, to be measured by the amount of money expended. Now as in Madison's day it is one of principle, to keep separate the separate spheres as the First Amendment drew them; to prevent the first experiment upon our liberties; and to keep the question from becoming entangled in corrosive precedents. We should not be less strict to keep strong and untarnished the one side of the shield of religious freedom than we have been of the other. The judgment should be reversed.

JUSTICE WHITE *delivered the opinion of the Court.*

A law of the State of New York requires local public school authorities to lend textbooks free of charge to all students in grades seven through 12: students attending private schools are included. This case presents the question whether this statute is a "law respecting the establishment of religion or prohibiting the free exercise thereof," and so in conflict with the First and Fourteenth Amendments to the Constitution, because it authorizes the loan of textbooks to students attending parochial schools. We hold that the law is not in violation of the Constitution.

. . . Beginning with the 1966–1967 school year, local school boards were required to purchase textbooks and lend them without charge "to all children residing in such district who are enrolled in grades seven to twelve of a public or private school which complies with the compulsory education law." The books now loaned are "text-books which are designated for use in any public, elementary or secondary schools of the state or are approved by any boards of education," and which—according to a 1966 amendment—"a pupil is required to use as a text for a semester or more in a particular class in the school he legally attends."

Appellants, [the members of the Board of Education of Central School District No. 1 in Rensselaer and Columbia Counties] . . . sought a declaration that Sec. 701 [of the state education law] was invalid, an order barring appellee Allen from removing appellants from office for failing to comply with it, and another order restraining him from apportioning state funds to school districts for the purchase of textbooks to be lent to parochial students. After answer, and upon cross-motions for summary judgment, the trial court held the law unconstitutional under the First and Fourteenth Amendments and entered judgment for appellants. . . . The Appellate Division reversed, ordering the complaint dismissed on the ground that appellant school boards had no standing to attack the validity of a state statute. . . . On appeal, the New York Court of Appeals concluded by a 4–3 vote that appellants did have standing but by a different 4–3 vote held that Sec. 701 was not in violation of either the State or the Federal Constitution. . . . The Court of Appeals said that

the law's purpose was to benefit all school children, regardless of the type of school they attended, and that only textbooks approved by public school authorities could be loaned. It therefore considered Sec. 701 "completely neutral with respect to religion, merely making available secular textbooks at the request of the individual student and asking no question about what school he attends." Section 701, the Court of Appeals concluded, is not a law which "established a religion or constitutes the use of public funds to aid religious schools." . . .

Everson v. *Board of Education*, is the case decided by this Court that is most nearly in point in today's problem. New Jersey reimbursed parents for expenses incurred in bussing their children to parochial schools. The Court stated that the Establishment Clause . . . does not prevent a State from extending the benefits of state laws to all citizens without regard for their religious affiliation and does not prohibit "New Jersey from spending tax-raised funds to pay the bus fares of parochial school pupils as part of a general program under which it pays the fares of pupils attending public and other schools." . . .

. . . Based on *Everson, Zorach, McGowan,* and other cases, *Abington School District* v. *Schempp*, fashioned a test ascribed to by eight Justices for distinguishing between forbidden involvements of the State with religion and those contacts which the Establishment Clause permits:

The test may be stated as follows: what are the purpose and the primary effect of the enactment? If either is the advancement or inhibition of religion then the enactment exceeds the scope of legislative power as circumscribed by the Constitution. That is to say that to withstand the strictures of the Establishment Clause there must be a secular legislative purpose and a primary effect that neither advances nor inhibits religion. . . .

This test is not easy to apply, but the citation of *Everson* by the *Schempp* Court to support its general standard made clear how the *Schempp* rule would be applied to the facts of *Everson*. The statute upheld in *Everson* would be considered a law having "a secular legislative purpose and a primary effect that neither advances nor inhibits religion." We reach the same result with respect to the New York law requiring school books to be loaned free of charge to all students in specified grades. The express purpose of Sec. 701 was stated by the New York Legislature to be furtherance of educational opportunities available to the young. Appellants have shown us nothing about the necessary effects of the statute that is contrary to its stated purpose. The law merely makes available to all children the benefits of a general program to lend school books free of charge. Books are furnished at the request of the pupil and ownership remains, at least technically, in the State. Thus no funds or books are furnished to parochial schools, and the financial benefit is to parents and children, not to schools. Perhaps free books make it more likely that some children choose to attend a sectarian school, but that was true of the state-paid bus fares in *Everson* and does not alone demonstrate an unconstitutional degree of support for a religious institution.

Of course books are different from buses. Most bus rides have no inherent religious significance, while religious books are common. However, the language of Sec. 701 does not authorize the loan of religious books and the State claims no right to distribute religious literature. Although the books loaned are those required by the parochial school for use in specific courses, each book loaned must be approved by the public school authorities; only secular books may receive approval. . . .

The major reason offered by appellants for distinguishing free textbooks from free bus fares is that books, but not buses, are critical to the teaching process, and in a sectarian school that process is employed to teach religion. However, this Court has long recognized that religious schools pursue two goals, religious instruction and secular education. In the leading case of *Pierce* v. *Society of Sisters*, the Court held that although it would not question Oregon's power to compel school attendance or require that the attendance be at an institution meeting State-imposed requirements as to quality and nature of curriculum, Oregon had not shown that its interest in secular education required that all children attend publicly operated schools. . . . Since *Pierce*, a substantial body of case law has confirmed the power of the States to insist that attendance at private schools, if it is to satisfy state compulsory-attendance laws, be at institutions which provide minimum hours of instruction, employ teachers of specified training, and cover prescribed subjects of instruction. Indeed, the State's interest in assuring that these standards are being met has been considered a sufficient reason for refusing to accept instruction at home as compliance with compulsory education statutes. These cases were a sensible corollary of *Pierce* v. *Society of Sisters*: if the State must satisfy its interest in secular education through the instrument of private schools, it has a proper interest in the manner in which those schools perform their secular educational function. Another corollary was *Cochran* v. *Louisiana State Board of Education*, where appellants said that a statute requiring school books to be furnished without charge to all students, whether they attended public or private schools, did not serve a "public purpose," and so offended the Fourteenth Amendment. Speaking through Chief Justice Hughes, the Court summarized as follows its conclusion that Louisiana's interest in the secular education being provided by private schools made provision of textbooks to students in those schools a properly public concern: "[The State's] interest is education, broadly; its method, comprehensive. Individual interests are sided only as the common interest is safeguarded." . . .

Underlying these cases, and underlying also the legislative judgments that have preceded the court decisions, has been a recognition that private education has played and is playing a significant and valuable role in raising national levels of knowledge, competence, and experience. Americans care about the quality of the secular education available to their children. They have considered high quality education to be an indispensable ingredient for achieving the kind of nation, and the kind of citizenry, that they have desired to create. Considering this attitude, the continued willingness to rely on private school systems, including parochial systems, strongly suggests that a wide segment of informed opinion, legislative and otherwise, has found that those schools do an acceptable job of providing secular education to their students. . . .

Against this background of judgment and experience, unchallenged in the meager record before us in this case, we cannot agree with appellants either that all teaching in a sectarian school is religious or that the processes of secular and religious training are so intertwined that secular textbooks furnished to students by the public are in fact instrumental in the teaching of religion. . . . Nothing in this record supports the proposition that all textbooks, whether they deal with mathematics, physics, foreign languages, history, or literature, are used by the parochial schools to teach religion. . . . We are unable to hold, based solely on judicial notice, that this statute results in unconstitutional involvement of the State with religious instruction or that Sec. 701, for this or the other reasons urged, is a law respecting the establishment of religion within the meaning of the First Amendment.

Appellants also contend that Sec. 701 offends the Free Exercise Clause of the First Amendment. However, "it is necessary in a free exercise case for one to show the coercive effect of the enactment as it operates against him in the practice of his religion," . . . and appellants have not contended that the New York law in any way coerces them as individuals in the practice of their religion.

The judgment is affirmed.

JUSTICE HARLAN'S *brief concurring opinion is not reprinted here.*

JUSTICE BLACK, *dissenting.*

. . . I believe the New York law held valid is a flat, flagrant, open violation of the First and Fourteenth Amendments which together forbid Congress or state legislatures to enact any law "respecting an establishment of religion." . . . This, I am confident, would be in keeping with the deliberate statement we made in *Everson* v. *Board of Education*, 330 U.S. 1, (1947) and repeated in *McCollum* v. *Board of Education*, 333 U.S. 203, (1948). . . .

The *Everson* and *McCollum* cases plainly interpret the First and Fourteenth Amendments as protecting the taxpayers of a State from being compelled to pay taxes to their government to support the agencies of private religious organizations the taxpayers oppose. To authorize a State to tax its residents for such church purposes is to put the State squarely in the religious activities of certain religious groups that happen to be strong enough politically to write their own religious preferences and prejudices into the laws. This links state and churches together in controlling the lives and destinies of our citizenship—a citizenship composed of people of myriad religious faiths, some of them bitterly hostile to and completely intolerant of the others. It was to escape laws precisely like this that a large part of the Nation's early immigrants fled to this country. It was also to escape such laws and such consequences that the First Amendment was written in language strong and clear barring passage of any law "respecting establishment of religion."

It is true, of course, that the New York law does not as yet formally adopt or establish a state religion. But it takes a great stride in that direction and coming events cast their shadows before them. The same powerful sectarian religious propagandists who have succeeded in securing passage of the present law to help religious schools carry on their sectarian religious purposes can and doubtless will continue their propaganda, looking toward complete domination and supremacy of their particular brand of religion. And it nearly always is by insidious approaches that the citadels of liberty are most successfully attacked.

I know of no prior opinion of this Court upon which the majority here can rightfully rely to support its holding this New York law constitutional. In saying this, I am not unmindful of the fact that the New York Court of Appeals purported to follow *Everson* v. *Board of Education.* . . .

. . . The First Amendment's bar to establishment of religion must preclude a State from using funds levied from all of its citizens to purchase books for use by sectarian schools which, although "secular," realistically will in some way inevitably tend to propagate the religious views of the favored sect. Books are the most essential tool of education since they contain the resources of knowledge which the educational process is designed to exploit. In this sense it is not difficult to distinguish books, which are the heart of any school, from bus fares, which provide a convenient and helpful general public transportation service. With respect to the former, state financial support actively and directly assists the teaching and propagation of sectarian religious viewpoints in clear conflict with the First Amendment's establishment bar; with respect to the latter, the State merely provides a general and nondiscriminatory transportation service in no way related to substantive religious views and beliefs.

* * *

I still subscribe to the belief that tax-raised funds cannot constitutionally be used to support religious schools, buy their school books, erect their buildings, pay their teachers, or pay any other of their maintenance expenses, even to the extent of one penny. The First Amendment's prohibition against governmental establishment of religion was written on the assumption that state aid to religion and religious schools generates discord, disharmony, hatred, and strife among our people, and that any government that supplies such aids is to that extent a tyranny. And I still believe that the only way to protect minority religious groups from majority groups in this country is to keep the wall of separation between church and state high and impregnable as the First and Fourteenth Amendments provide. The Court's affirmance here bodes nothing but evil to religious peace in this country.

JUSTICE DOUGLAS, *dissenting.*

*   *   *

Whatever may be said of *Everson*, there is nothing ideological about a bus. There is nothing ideological about a school lunch, nor a public nurse, nor a scholarship. The constitutionality of such public aid to students in parochial schools turns on considerations not present in this textbook case. The textbook goes to the very heart of education in a parochial school. It is the chief, although not solitary, instrumentality for propagating a particular religious creed or faith. How can we possibly approve such state aid to a religion? A parochial school textbook may contain many, many more seeds of creed and dogma than a prayer. Yet we struck down in *Engel* v. *Vitale*, [*infra*], an official New York prayer for its public schools, even though it was not plainly denominational. For we emphasized the violence done the Establishment Clause when the power was given religious-political groups "to write their own prayers into law." . . . That risk is compounded here by giving parochial schools the initiative in selecting the textbooks they desire to be furnished at public expense.

*   *   *

It will be often difficult, as Mr. Justice Jackson said, to say "where the secular ends and the sectarian begins in education." *McCollum* v. *Board of Education*, 333 U.S., at 237–238. But certain it is that once the so-called "secular" textbook is the prize to be won by that religious faith which selects the book, the battle will be on for those positions of control. . . . Others fear that one sectarian group, gaining control of the state agencies which approve the "secular" textbooks, will use their control to disseminate ideas most congenial to their faith. It must be remembered that the very existence of the religious school—whether Catholic or Mormon, Presbyterian or Episcopalian—is to provide an education oriented to the dogma of the particular faith.

*   *   *

The challenged New York law leaves to the Board of Regents, local boards of education, trustees, and other school authorities the supervision of the textbook program.

The Board of Regents (together with the Commissioner of Education) has powers of censorship over all textbooks that contain statements seditious in character, or evince disloyalty to the United States or are favorable to any nation with which we are at war. . . . Those powers can cut a wide swathe in many areas of education that involve the ideological element.

In general textbooks are approved for distribution by "boards of education, trustees or such body or officer as performs the function of such boards. . . ." N.Y. Educ. Law Sec. 701(1). These school boards are generally elected. Sections 2013, 2502(2), though in a few cities they are appointed. Sec. 2553. Where there are trustees, they are elected. Sections 1523, 1602, 1702. And superintendents who advise on textbook selection are appointed by the board of education or the trustees. Sections 1711, 2503(5), 2507.

The initiative to select and requisition "the books desired" is with the parochial school. Powerful religious political pressures will therefore be on the state agencies to provide the books that are desired.

These then are the battlegrounds where control of textbook distribution will be won or lost. Now that "secular" textbooks will pour into religious schools, we can rest assured that a contest will be on to provide those books for religious schools which the dominant religious group concludes best reflect the theocentric or other philosophy of the particular church.

The stakes are now extremely high . . . to obtain approval of what is "proper." For the "proper" books will radiate the "correct" religious view not only in the parochial school but in the public school as well.

*   *   *

What Madison wrote in his famous Memorial and Remonstrance against Religious Assessments is highly pertinent here:

Who does not see that the same authority which can establish Christianity, in exclusion of all other Religions, may establish with the same case any particular sect of Christians, in exclusion of all other Sects? That the same authority which can force a citizen to contribute three pence only of his property for the support of any one establishment, may force him to conform to any other establishment in all cases whatsoever?

[JUSTICE FORTAS's *brief dissenting opinion is not reprinted here.*]

Expanding Parochiaid: The Lemon Test Emerges

FEATURED CASES

Lemon v. *Kurtzman*　　*Committee for Public Education and Religious Liberty* v. *Nyquist*　　*Mueller* v. *Allen*

The Johnson administration's heightened effort to enhance the nation's educational programs during the 1960s spurred similar efforts at the state level. Some of the state efforts went beyond mere provision for "buses and books" (found constitutionally acceptable in *Everson* and *Allen*) to focus on a variety of educational needs, such as other instructional materials, teacher pay, and physical plant. Recognizing the secular educational activities of sectarian schools, the statutes typically directed aid to shore up the educational efforts of those schools also. Of course, attempts to give such extensive public support to church-related schools produced great tension on the line separating church and state, providing the Court with several cases through which it would clarify further establishment clause law.

Shortly after Chief Justice Warren Burger settled in, the Court indicated its unwillingness to accommodate the lawmakers of Pennsylvania and Rhode Island in their sectarian school aid packages that went beyond textbooks to other instructional materials and teacher salaries. Under the Pennsylvania statute of 1968, the State Superintendent of Public Instruction was authorized to purchase secular educational services from nonpublic schools and to reimburse them for teacher salaries, textbooks, and other instructional materials. The Rhode Island statute, enacted one year later, provided for a 15 percent salary supplement for teachers in nonpublic schools where the average per pupil expenditure on secular instruction was below the average in the public schools. Speaking for the seven-to-one majority in *Lemon* v. *Kurtzman* 403 U.S. 602 (1971) (the Pennsylvania case, consolidated with *Earley* v. *Dicenso* and *Robinson* v. *Dicenso* of Rhode Island), the Chief Justice reviewed the Court's establishment clause rulings over the years and articulated a three-pronged test gleaned from those several actions. To withstand an establishment clause challenge, he asserted, the statutory program at issue must have a *secular legislative purpose.* Next, its *principal or primary effect* must neither advance nor inhibit religion. And finally, the statutory arrangement must not foster *an excessive government entanglement with religion.* This formulation became popularized as the *Lemon* test and guided the Court's decision-

making in the church-state area for the next two decades. Applying the test to the Pennsylvania and Rhode Island programs at issue, the Chief Justice pointed to the "intimate and continuing relationship(s)" between church and state in order to accomplish the statutory objectives.

In a concurring opinion, Justice Douglas expressed concern about the surveillance that would be required to monitor the grants effectively. He further expressed great impatience with those who still have "the courage to announce that a state may . . . finance the secular part of a sectarian school's educational program." However, in a partial dissent, Justice Byron White found enough in prior holdings of the Court to sustain the statutes against the establishment clause challenge. For him, state support of a "separable secular function of overriding importance" was sufficient to sustain the program's constitutionality.

The disappointment for the supporters of this form of parochiaid was mitigated somewhat when the Court on the same day upheld the federal program for aid to higher educational facilities in *Tilton* v. *Richardson* (403 U.S. 672, 1971) (*infra*). The *Tilton* ruling, when coupled with the 1970 decision sustaining the exemption of church property used for religious purposes from taxation (see *Walz* v. *Tax Commission* [397 U.S. 664, 1970] *infra*), appeared to provide a small ray of hope for those advocating the use of public funds to shore up the steadily deteriorating financial position of parochial schools. This hope was further buttressed by what was deemed to be a more sympathetic Supreme Court, with the four Nixon appointees (Burger, Blackmun, Powell, and Rehnquist) aware of the president's promise to give financial relief for nonpublic schools through federal tax credits for parents of children attending those schools.

This hope was crushed, however, when the Supreme Court held in 1973 that the New York legislative program that provided for nonpublic school aid through maintenance and repair grants, tuition reimbursement, and tax credits, and a Pennsylvania statute that authorized tuition reimbursements, amounted to unconstitutional aid to religious establishments. In the New York case (*Committee for Public Education and Religious Liberty* v. *Nyquist*, 413 U.S. 756, 1973), Justice Lewis F. Powell, Jr., speaking for the six-to-three majority, noted that the purpose and primary effect of the program was to "advance activities of sectarian elementary and secondary schools." Furthermore, Justice Powell discounted the notion that parents could serve as conduits for such aid by employing tuition reimbursement and tax credits. Rejecting one of the most often cited justifications for public aid to parochial schools, Justice Powell concluded:

> However great our sympathy for the burdens of those who must pay public school taxes at the same time they support other schools because of the constraints of "conscience and discipline," and notwithstanding the "high social importance" of the state's purposes, neither may justify an eroding of the limitations of the Establishment Clause now firmly emplanted.

For similar reasons, the Pennsylvania tuition reimbursement program was struck down in *Sloan* v. *Lemon* (413 U.S. 825, 1973).

In dissent, Chief Justice Burger, supported by Justices White and Rehnquist, emphasized the secular purpose and general welfare nature of the benefits embraced by the legislative programs. He argued that the *Everson* and *Allen* precedents fully supported this attempt to equalize the costs incurred by parents who send their children to non-public schools. To him, the establishment clause limitations are attenuated "when the legislation moves away from direct aid to religious institutions and takes on the character of general aid to individual families."

Another attempt by Pennsylvania in 1972 to provide aid in the form of a variety of auxiliary services that included counseling, testing, psychological services, speech and hearing therapy, and remedial services for the educationally disadvantaged failed the Court's establishment clause test because the programs were held (1) to substantially aid in the advancement of religion; and (2) to foster excessive entanglement between state and church authorities, which would be required in implementation (*Meek* v. *Pittinger*, 421 U.S. 349, 1975).[2] The inclusion of a secular textbook loan provision held constitutional under the *Allen* precedent did not save the other provisions of the statute. In his plurality opinion, Justice Potter Stewart was not impressed with the provision limiting loans to secular resources. He thought it was simply unrealistic to attempt separation of the predominantly religious role of many church-related schools from their secular functions. Hence, this view suggests that the Court was taking the position that the impact of such aid on the total mission of the parochial school must be considered. At the time, this "aid-to-the-total-enterprise" position suggested possible greater scrutiny of the various forms of parochiaid that states were providing. But two years later, in *Wolman* v. *Walter* (433 U.S. 229, 1977), the Court moved away from the more restrictive position of the *Meek* decision and approved several components of Ohio's parochiaid program that provided for certain forms of therapeutic, counseling, and remedial services that were administered near parochial schools in mobile units. To be sure, the Court was making very fine distinctions here, as it found a counseling component that included a broadly gauged testing program acceptable, but found unacceptable a provision for instructional resources such as slide projectors, wall charts, and field trips.

Similarly, New York was successful in a statutory scheme providing for public funds to reimburse sectarian schools for performing state-mandated testing and reporting services in *Committee for Public Education and Religious Liberty* v. *Regan* (444 U.S. 646, 1980). Apparently, the Court felt that the defects of the earlier program invalidated in *Levitt* v. *Committee for Public Education* (discussed in footnote 2) were remedied by an auditing provision designed to ensure that costs incurred were only for secular services performed. The Court emphasized that *Meek* was not to be construed as barring any aid to the secular educational functions of a sectarian school.

During its 1983 term the Court continued its accommodationist stance when it approved

---

[2]Note also *Levitt* v. *Committee for Public Education*, 413 U.S. 472 (1973), where the Court struck down a state program for reimbursement of sectarian schools for performing such state-mandated services as administering, grading, and reporting the results of tests because there was no provision to ensure that such tests would be "free of religious instruction." In addition, the remedial and enrichment programs initiated under Title I of the Elementary and Secondary Education Act of 1965 delivered by public school teachers in parochial school facilities in New York City were held to violate the establishment clause in *Aguilar* v. *Felton*, 473 U.S. 402 (1985). Focusing on the excessive entanglement prong of the *Lemon* test, Justice William J. Brennan noted with disapproval that the system devised to monitor religious content to prevent courses from advancing religion "would require a permanent and pervasive state presence" in the church-related schools in which the programs would be offered. But note that the Court, with newly appointed Justice Anthony Kennedy delivering the key fifth vote, swung back to an accommodationist stance in *Bowen* v. *Kendrick* (108 S. Ct. 2562, 1988) in approving federal grants to church-related groups for counseling programs for teenage girls where chastity and avoidance of abortions were emphasized.

Minnesota's tax deduction program for tuition, textbook, and transportation costs in *Mueller* v. *Allen*, 463 U.S. 388, 1983. Unlike the various reimbursement arrangements of the past, this measure made the relief available to parents of pupils attending either public or nonpublic schools. But in practical terms, however, the primary beneficiaries were those whose children attended parochial schools. Justice William Rehnquist's opinion for the five-to-four majority emphasized the policy's conformity with the *Lemon* test. The secular purpose enhanced by the tax deduction for educational expenses would help improve education for all children. Additionally, he reasoned that the tax deduction was not primarily to advance religion, but it must be considered as just one of a number of tax deductions available to all those who send their children to either public or parochial schools. Hence, he found the Minnesota statute neutral on its face. But in reality, the tax deduction was of primary benefit to those who paid tuition and other fees for their children to attend parochial schools, as Justice Thurgood Marshall pointed out in dissent. Joined by Justices Brennan, Blackmun, and Stevens, he condemned the statute as a parochial school tuition subsidy "masquerading as a subsidy of general education expenses," since parents of public school children do not, as a rule, incur the expenses covered for which a deduction could be claimed.

Finally, the operation of the Minnesota statute did not present any excessive entanglement problems, since no official action was needed to insure that the money would be used only for secular purposes. On this point, Justice Rehnquist argued that where there is no surveillance, there can be no excessive entanglement.

Federal tax relief for parents who send their children to nonpublic schools was urged by President Reagan in the 1980 campaign. His supporters found a ray of optimism from *Mueller*, as they pushed a Reagan-sponsored tuition tax credit proposal in the first session of the 98th Congress. The measure, geared to low- and middle-income families, would have allowed a federal tax credit of up to $500 when fully operational, but after a number of amendments, the proposal was soundly defeated in the Republican-controlled Senate, and a similar measure was killed in the House Ways and Means Committee.

But the concept did not go away. It has continued to linger in the national debate over the use of educational "vouchers" as a mechanism for financing elementary and secondary education into the mid-1990s. Not only was the approach supported by President Bush in his national crusade to reverse the erosion of the quality of education in the nation, but a major corporate initiative to establish a system of "for-profit" elementary and secondary schools launched in the spring of 1992 enhanced interest in the "voucher" concept. Because the plan would allow students to use the publicly financed vouchers in any school of choice, significant First Amendment questions will be raised when students attempt to apply them to cover tuition and fees at church-related schools. Many voucher advocates, however, are optimistic that such challenges would eventually be brushed aside by the Rehnquist Court as it continues to dismantle the *Lemon* test.

LEMON v. KURTZMAN*
403 U.S. 602; 29 L. Ed. 2d 745; 91 S. Ct. 2105 (1971)

CHIEF JUSTICE BURGER *delivered the opinion of the Court.*

These two appeals raise questions as to Pennsylvania and Rhode Island statutes providing state aid to church-related elementary and secondary schools. Both statutes are challenged as violative of the Establishment and Free Exercise Clauses of the First Amendment and the Due Process Clause of the Fourteenth Amendment. . . .

*Decided with the companion cases of *Earley* v. *Dicenso* and *Robinson* v. *Dicenso*.

I

The Rhode Island Statute

The Rhode Island Salary Supplement Act was enacted in 1969. It rests on the legislative finding that the quality of education available in nonpublic elementary schools has been jeopardized by the rapidly rising salaries needed to attract competent and dedicated teachers. The Act authorizes state officials to supplement the salaries of teachers of secular subjects in nonpublic elementary schools by paying directly to a teacher an amount not in excess of 15% of his current annual salary. As supplemented, however, a nonpublic school teacher's salary cannot exceed the maximum paid to teachers in the State's public schools, and the recipient must be certified by the state board of education in substantially the same manner as public school teachers.

In order to be eligible for the Rhode Island salary supplement, the recipient must teach in a nonpublic school at which the average per-pupil expenditure on secular education is less than the average in the State's public schools during a specified period. Appellant state Commissioner of Education also requires eligible schools to submit financial data. If this information indicates a per-pupil expenditure in excess of the statutory limitation, the records of the school in question must be examined in order to assess how much of the expenditure is attributable to secular education and how much to religious activity.

The Act also requires that teachers eligible for salary supplement must teach only those subjects that are offered in the State's public schools. They must use "only teaching materials which are used in the public schools." Finally, any teacher applying for a salary supplement must first agree in writing "not to teach a course in religion for so long as or during such time as he or she receives any salary supplements" under the Act. . . .

A three-judge federal court was convened . . . [and] found that Rhode Island's nonpublic elementary schools accommodated approximately 25% of the State's pupils. About 95% of these pupils attended schools affiliated with the Roman Catholic church. To date some 250 teachers have applied for benefits under the Act. All of them are employed by Roman Catholic schools.

The court held a hearing at which extensive evidence was introduced concerning the nature of the secular instruction offered in the Roman Catholic schools whose teachers would be eligible for salary assistance under the Act. Although the court found that concern for religious values does not necessarily affect the content of secular subjects, it also found that the parochial school system was "an integral part of the religious mission of the Catholic Church."

The District Court concluded that the Act violated the Establishment Clause, holding that it fostered "excessive entanglement" between government and religion. . . .

The Pennsylvania Statute

. . . The Pennsylvania Nonpublic Elementary and Secondary Education Act was passed in 1968 in response to a crisis that the Pennsylvania legisla-

ture found existed in the State's nonpublic schools due to rapidly rising costs. . . .

The statute authorizes appellee state Superintendent of Public Instruction to "purchase" specified "secular educational services" from nonpublic schools. Under the "contracts" authorized by the statute, the State directly reimburses nonpublic schools solely for their actual expenditures for teachers' salaries, textbooks and instructional materials. A school seeking reimbursement must maintain prescribed accounting procedures that identify the "separate" cost of the "secular educational service. . . ."

There are several significant statutory restrictions on state aid. Reimbursement is limited to courses "presented in the curricula of the public schools." It is further limited "solely" to courses in the following "secular" subjects: mathematics, modern foreign languages, physical science, and physical education. Textbooks and instructional materials included in the program must be approved by the state Superintendent of Public Instruction. Finally, the statute prohibits reimbursement for any course that contains "any subject matter expressing religious teaching, or the morals or forms of worship of any sect."

. . . It appears that some $5 million has been expended annually under the Act. The State has now entered into contracts with some 1,181 nonpublic elementary and secondary schools with a student population of some 535,215 pupils—more than 20% of the total number of students in the State. More than 96% of these pupils attend church-related schools, and most of these schools are affiliated with the Roman Catholic church. . . .

The [District] court granted Pennsylvania's motion to dismiss the complaint for failure to state a claim for relief. . . . It held that the Act violated neither the Establishment nor the Free Exercise Clauses. CHIEF JUDGE HASTIE *dissenting. We reverse.*

II

In *Everson* v. *Board of Education* . . . this Court upheld a state statute which reimbursed the parents of parochial school children for bus transportation expenses. There Mr. Justice Black, writing for the majority, suggested that the decision carried to "the verge" of forbidden territory under the Religion Clauses. . . . Candor compels acknowledgment, moreover, that we can only dimly perceive the lines of demarcation in this extraordinarily sensitive area of constitutional law.

[1] The language of the Religion Clauses of the First Amendment is at best opaque, particularly when compared with other portions of the Amendment. . . . A law may be one "respecting" the forbidden objective while falling short of its total realization. A law "respecting" the proscribed result, that is, the establishment of religion, is not always easily identifiable as one violative of the Clause. A given law might not *establish* a state religion but nevertheless be one "respecting" that end in the sense of being a step that could lead to such establishment and hence offend the First Amendment.

In the absence of precisely stated constitutional prohibitions, we must draw lines with reference to the three main evils against which the Establishment Clause was intended to afford protection: "sponsorship, financial support, and active involvement of the sovereign in religious activity." *Walz* v. *Tax Commission*, 397 U.S. 664, 668. . . .

Every analysis in this area must begin with consideration of the cumulative criteria developed by the Court over many years. Three such tests may be gleaned from our cases. First, the statute must have a secular legislative purpose; second, its principal or primary effect must be one that neither advances nor inhibits religion . . .; finally, the statute must not foster "an excessive government entanglement with religion." *Walz, supra* [397 U.S.], at 674. . . .

Inquiry into the legislative purposes of the Pennsylvania and Rhode Island statutes affords no basis for a conclusion that the legislative intent was to advance religion. On the contrary, the statutes themselves clearly state that they are intended to enhance the quality of the secular education in all schools covered by the compulsory attendance laws. There is no reason to believe the legislatures meant anything else. . . .

The two legislatures . . . have . . . recognized that church-related elementary and secondary schools have a significant religious mission and that a substantial portion of their activities are religiously oriented. They have therefore sought to create statutory restrictions designed to guarantee the separation between secular and religious educational functions and to ensure that State financial aid supports only the former. . . . We need not decide whether these legislative precautions restrict the principal or primary effect of the programs to the point where they do not offend the Religion Clauses, for we conclude that the cumulative impact of the entire relationship arising under the statutes in each State involves excessive entanglement between government and religion.

III

Our prior holdings do not call for total separation between church and state; total separation is not possible in an absolute sense. Some relationship between government and religious organizations is inevitable. *Zorach* v. *Clauson*, 343 U.S. 306, 312, 72 S. Ct. 679, 683, 96 L. Ed. 954 (1952); *Sherbert* v. *Verner*, 374 U.S. 398, 422, 83 S. Ct. 1790, 1803, 10 L. Ed. 2d 965 (1963) (Harlan, J., dissenting). Fire inspections, building and zoning regulations, and state requirements under compulsory school attendance laws are examples of necessary and permissible contacts. Indeed, under the statutory exemption before us in *Walz*, the State had a continuing burden to ascertain that the exempt property was in fact being used for religious worship. Judicial caveats against entanglement must recognize that the line of separation, far from being a "wall," is a blurred, indistinct and variable barrier depending on all the circumstances of a particular relationship. . . .

In order to determine whether the government entanglement with religion is excessive, we must examine the character and purposes of the institutions which are benefited, the nature of the aid that the State provides, and the resulting relationship between the government and the religious authority. . . . Here we find that both statutes foster an impermissible degree of entanglement.

(a) Rhode Island Program

The District Court made extensive findings on the grave potential for excessive entanglement that inheres in the religious character and purpose of the Roman Catholic elementary schools of Rhode Island, to date the sole beneficiaries of the Rhode Island Salary Supplement Act.

The church schools involved in the program are located close to parish churches. This understandably permits convenient access for religious exercises since instruction in faith and morals is part of the total educational process. The school buildings contain identifying religious symbols such as crosses on the exterior and crucifixes, religious paintings and statues either in the classrooms or hallways. Although only approximately 30 minutes a day are devoted to direct religious instruction, there are religiously oriented extracurricular activities. Approximately two-thirds of the teachers in these schools are nuns of various religious orders. Their dedicated efforts provide an atmosphere in which religious instruction and religious vocations are natural and proper parts of life in such schools. . . .

On the basis of these findings the District Court concluded that the parochial schools constituted "an integral part of the religious mission of the Catholic Church." The various characteristics of the schools make them "a powerful vehicle for transmitting the Catholic faith to the next generation." This process of inculcating religious doctrine is, of course, enhanced by the impressionable age of the pupils, in primary schools particularly. . . .

The substantial religious character of these church-related schools gives rise to entangling church-state relationships of the kind the Religion Clauses sought to avoid. . . .

The dangers and corresponding entanglements are enhanced by the particular form of aid that the Rhode Island Act provides. Our decisions from *Everson* to *Allen* have permitted the States to provide church-related schools with secular, neutral, or non-ideological services, facilities, or materials. Bus transportation, school lunches, public health services, and secular textbooks supplied in common to all students were not thought to offend the Establishment Clause. We note that the dissenters in *Allen* seemed chiefly concerned with the pragmatic difficulties involved in ensuring the truly secular content of the textbooks provided at state expense. . . .

In our view the record shows these dangers are present to a substantial degree. The Rhode Island Roman Catholic elementary schools are under the general supervision of the Bishop of Providence and his appointed representative, the Diocesan Superintendent of Schools. . . . With only two exceptions, school principals are nuns appointed either by the Superintendent or the Mother Provincial of the order whose members staff the school. By 1969 lay teachers constituted more than a third of all teachers in the parochial elementary schools, and their number is growing. They are first interviewed by the superintendent's office and then by the school principal. The contracts are signed by the parish priest, and he retains some discretion in negotiating salary levels. Religious authority necessarily pervades the school system. . . .

Several teachers testified, however, that they did not inject religion into their secular classes. And the District Court found that religious values did not necessarily affect the content of the secular instruction. But what has been recounted suggests the potential if not actual hazards of this form of state aid. The teacher is employed by a religious organization, subject to the direction and discipline of religious authorities, and works in a system dedicated to rearing children in a particular faith. These controls are not lessened by the fact that most of the lay teachers are of the Catholic faith. Inevitably some of a teacher's responsibilities hover on the border between secular and religious orientation.

We need not and do not assume that teachers in parochial schools will be guilty of bad faith or any conscious design to evade the limitations imposed by the statute and the First Amendment. We simply recognize that a dedicated religious person, teaching in a school affiliated with his or her faith and operated to inculcate its tenets, will inevitably experience great difficulty in remaining religiously neutral. Doctrines and faith are not inculcated or advanced by neutrals. With the best of intentions such a teacher would find it hard to make a total separation between secular teaching and religious doctrine. What would appear to some to be essential to good citizenship might well for others border on or constitute instruction in religion. Further difficulties are inherent in the combination of religious discipline and the possibility of disagreement between teacher and religious authorities over the meaning of the statutory restrictions. . . .

. . . The Rhode Island Legislature has not, and could not, provide state aid on the basis of a mere assumption that secular teachers under religious discipline can avoid conflicts. The State must be certain, given the Religion Clauses, that subsidized teachers do not inculcate religion—indeed the State here has undertaken to do so. To ensure that no trespass occurs, the State has therefore carefully conditioned its aid with pervasive restrictions. . . .

[But] comprehensive, discriminating, and continuing state surveillance will inevitably be required to ensure that these restrictions are obeyed and the First Amendment otherwise respected. Unlike a book, a teacher cannot be inspected once so as to determine the extent and intent of his or her personal beliefs and subjective acceptance of the limitations imposed by the First Amendment. These prophylactic contacts will involve excessive and enduring entanglement between state and church.

There is another area of entanglement in the Rhode Island program that gives concern. The statute excludes teachers employed by nonpublic schools whose average per-pupil expenditures on secular education exceed the comparable figures for public schools. In the event that the total expenditures of an otherwise eligible school exceed this norm, the program requires the government to examine the school's record in order to determine how much of the total expenditures are attributable to secular education and how much to religious activity. This kind of state inspection and evaluation of the religious content of a religious organization is fraught with the sort of entanglement that the Constitution forbids. . . .

(b) Pennsylvania Program

The Pennsylvania statute also provides state aid to church-related schools for teachers' salaries. . . . As we noted earlier, the very restrictions and surveillance necessary to ensure that teachers play a strictly non-ideological role give rise to entanglements between church and state. The Pennsylvania statute, like that of Rhode Island, fosters this kind of relationship. Reimbursement is not only limited to courses offered in the public schools and materials approved by state officials, but the statute excludes "any subject matter expressing religious teaching, or the morals or forms of worship of any sect." In addition, schools seeking reimbursement must maintain accounting procedures that require the State to establish the cost of the secular as distinguished from the religious instruction.

The Pennsylvania statute, moreover, has the further defect of providing state financial aid directly to the church-related schools. This factor distinguishes both *Everson* and *Allen*, for in both those cases the Court was careful to point out that state aid was provided to the student and his parents— not to the church-related school. . . . The history of government grants of a continuing cash subsidy indicates that such programs have almost always been accompanied by varying measures of control and surveillance. The government cash grants before us now provide no basis for predicting that comprehensive measures of surveillance and controls will not follow. In particular the government's post-audit power to inspect and evaluate a church-related school's financial records and to determine which expenditures are religious and which are secular creates an intimate and continuing relationship between church and state.

IV

A broader base of entanglement of yet a different character is presented by the divisive political potential of these state programs. In a community where such a large number of pupils are served by church-related schools, it can be assumed that state assistance will entail considerable political activity. Partisans of parochial schools, understandably concerned with rising costs and sincerely dedicated to both the religious and secular educational missions of their schools, will inevitably champion this cause and promote political action to achieve their goals. Those who oppose state aid, whether for constitutional, religious, or fiscal reasons, will inevitably respond and employ all of the usual political campaign techniques to prevail. Candidates will be forced to declare and voters to choose. It would be unrealistic to ignore the fact that many people confronted with issues of this kind will find their votes aligned with their faith.

Ordinarily political debate and division, however vigorous or even partisan, are normal and healthy manifestations of our democratic system of government, but political division along religious lines was one of the principal evils against which the First Amendment was intended to protect. . . . To have States or communities divide on the issues presented by state aid to parochial schools would tend to confuse and obscure other issues of great urgency. We have an expanding array of vexing issues, local and national, domestic and international, to debate and divide on. It conflicts with our whole history and tradition to permit questions of the Religion Clauses to assume such importance in our legislatures and in our elections that they could divert attention from the myriad issues and problems which confront every level of government. The highways of church and state relationships are not likely to be one-way streets, and the Constitution's authors sought to protect religious worship from the pervasive power of government. The history of many countries attests to the hazards of religion intruding into the political arena or of political power intruding into the legitimate and free exercise of religious belief. . . .

The potential for political divisiveness related to religious belief and practice is aggravated in these two statutory programs by the need for continuing annual appropriations and the likelihood of larger and larger demands as costs and populations grow. The Rhode Island District Court found that the parochial school system's "monumental and deepening financial crisis" would "inescapably" require larger annual appropriations subsidizing greater percentages of the salaries of lay teachers. Although no facts have been developed in this respect in the Pennsylvania case, it appears that such pressures for expanding aid have already required the state legislature to include a portion of the state revenues from cigarette taxes in the program.

V

In *Walz* it was argued that a tax exemption for places of religious worship would prove to be the first step in an inevitable progression leading to the establishment of state churches and state religion. That claim could not stand up against more than 200 years of virtually universal practice imbedded in our colonial experience and continuing into the present.

The progression argument, however, is more persuasive here. We have no long history of state aid to church-related educational institutions comparable to 200 years of tax exemption for churches. Indeed, the state programs before us today represent something of an innovation. We have already noted that modern governmental programs have self-perpetuating and self-expanding propensities. These internal pressures are only enhanced when the schemes involve institutions whose legitimate needs are growing and whose interests have substantial political support. . . .

Finally, nothing we have said can be construed to disparage the role of church-related elementary and secondary schools in our national life. Their contribution has been and is enormous. Nor do we ignore their economic plight in a period of rising costs and expanding need. Taxpayers generally have been spared vast sums by the maintenance of these educational institutions by religious organizations, largely by the gifts of faithful adherents.

The merit and benefits of these schools, however, are not the issue before us in these cases. The sole question is whether state aid to these schools can be squared with the dictates of the Religion Clauses. Under our system the choice has been made that government is to be entirely excluded from the area of religious instruction and churches excluded from the affairs of government. The Constitution decrees that religion must be a private matter for the individual, the family, and the institutions of private choice, and that while some involvement and entanglement is inevitable, lines must be drawn.

The decision of the Rhode Island District Court . . . is affirmed. The decision of the Pennsylvania District Court . . . is reversed, and the case is remanded for further proceedings consistent with this opinion.

JUSTICE DOUGLAS, *whom* JUSTICE BLACK *joins, concurring.*

* * *

Under these laws there will be vast governmental suppression, surveillance, or meddling in church affairs. . . . [S]chool prayers, the daily routine of parochial schools, must go if our decision in *Engel* v. *Vitale* . . . is honored. If it is not honored, then the state has established a religious sect. Elimination of prayers is only part of the problem. The curriculum presents subtle and difficult problems. The constitutional mandate can in part be carried out by censoring the curricula. What is palpably a sectarian course can be marked for deletion. But the problem only starts there. Sectarian instruction, in which of course a State may not indulge, can take place in a course on Shakespeare or in one on mathematics. No matter what the curriculum offers, the question is, what is *taught*? We deal not with evil teachers but with zealous ones who may use any opportunity to indoctrinate a class.

It is well-known that everything taught in most parochial schools is taught with the ultimate goal of religious education in mind. Rev. Joseph H. Fichter, S.J., stated in Parochial Schools: A Sociological Study, 86 (1958):

> It is a commonplace observation that in the parochial school religion permeates the whole curriculum and is not confined to a single half hour period of the day. Even arithmetic can be used as an instrument of pious thought, as in the case of the teacher who gave this problem to her class: 'If it takes forty thousand priests and a hundred forty thousand sisters to care for forty million Catholics in the United States, how many more priests and sisters will be needed to convert and care for the hundred million non-Catholics in the United States?'

One can imagine what a religious zealot, as contrasted to a civil liberatarian, can do with the Reformation or with the Inquisition. Much history can be given the gloss of a particular religion. I would think that policing these grants to detect sectarian instruction would be insufferable to religious partisans and would breed division and dissension between church and state. . . .

We said in unequivocal words in *Everson* v. *Board of Education*. . . ."No tax in any amount, large or small, can be levied to support any religious activities or institutions, whatever they may be called, or whatever form they may adopt to teach or practice religion." We reiterated the same idea in *Zorach* v. *Clauson*. . . . We repeated the same idea in *McCollum* v. *Board of Education* . . . and added that a State's tax-supported public schools could not be used "for the dissemination of religious doctrines" nor could a State provide the church "pupils for their religious classes through use of the state's compulsory public school machinery. . . ."

Yet in spite of this long and consistent history there are those who have the courage to announce that a State may nonetheless finance the *secular* part of a sectarian school's educational program. That, however, makes a grave constitutional decision turn merely on cost accounting and bookkeeping entries. A history class, literature class, a science class in a parochial school is not a separate institute; it is part of the organic whole which the State subsidizes. The funds are used in these cases to pay or help pay the salaries of teachers in parochial schools; and the presence of teachers is critical to the essential purpose of the parochial school, *viz.* to advance the religious endeavors of the particular church. It matters not that the teacher receiving taxpayers' money only teaches religion a fraction of the time. Nor does it matter that he or she teaches no religion. The school is an organism living on one budget. What the taxpayers give for salaries of those who teach only the humanities or science without any trace of proseletyzing enables the school to use all of its own funds for religious training. As Judge Coffin said, 316 F. Supp. 112, we would be blind to realities if we let "sophisticated bookkeeping" sanction "almost total subsidy of a religious institution by assigning the bulk of the institution's expenses to 'secular' activities." And sophisticated attempts to avoid the Constitution are just as invalid as simpleminded ones. . . .

In my view the taxpayers' forced contribution to the parochial schools in the present cases violates the First Amendment. . . .

COMMITTEE FOR PUBLIC EDUCATION AND RELIGIOUS LIBERTY v. NYQUIST
413 U.S. 756; 37 L Ed. 2d 948; 93 S. Ct. 2955 (1973)

JUSTICE POWELL *delivered the opinion of the Court.*

[This case] raises a challenge under the Establishment Clause of the First Amendment to the constitutionality of a . . . New York law which provides financial assistance . . . to nonpublic elementary and secondary schools in that state. . . .

. . . The first five sections of these amendments [to the New York Education and Tax Laws] established three distinct financial aid programs for nonpublic elementary and secondary schools. . . . [A] complaint was filed in the United States District Court for the Southern District of New York challenging each of the three forms of aid as violative of the Establishment Clause. . . . By consent of the parties, a three-judge court was convened . . . and the case was decided without an evidentiary hearing. Because the questions before the District Court were resolved on the basis of the pleadings, that court's decision turned on the constitutionality of each provision on its face.

The first section of the challenged enactment, entitled "Health and Safety Grants for Nonpublic School Children," provides for direct money grants from the State to "qualifying" nonpublic schools to be used for the "maintenance and repair of . . . school facilities and equipment to ensure the health, welfare and safety of enrolled pupils." A "qualifying" school is any nonpublic, nonprofit elementary or secondary school which has been designated during the [immediately preceding] year as serving a high concentration of pupils from low income families for purposes of Title IV of the Federal Higher Education Act of 1965. . . . Such schools are entitled to receive a grant of $30 per pupil per year, or $40 per pupil per year if the facilities are more than 25 years old. Each school is required to submit to the Commissioner of Education an audited statement of its expenditures for maintenance and repair during the preceding year, and its grant may not exceed the total of such expenses. The Commissioner is also required to ascertain the average per-pupil cost for equivalent maintenance and repair services in the public schools, and in no event may the grant to nonpublic qualifying schools exceed 50% of that figure. . . .

. . . [The] section [on Maintenance and Repairs] is prefaced by a series of legislative findings which shed light on the State's purpose in enacting the law. These findings conclude that the State "has a primary responsibility to ensure the health, welfare and safety of children attending . . . nonpublic schools: that the fiscal crisis in nonpublic education . . . has caused a dimunition of proper maintenance and repair programs, threatening the health, welfare and safety of nonpublic school children" in low income urban areas; and that "a healthy and safe school environment" contributes "to the stability of urban neighborhoods." For these reasons, the statute declares that "the state has the right to make grants for maintenance and repair expenditures which are clearly secular, neutral and nonideological in nature."

The remainder of the challenged legislation—sections 2 through 5—is a single package captioned the "Elementary and Secondary Education Opportunity Program." It is composed essentially of two parts, a tuition grant program and a tax benefit program. Section 2 establishes a limited plan providing tuition reimbursements to parents of children attending elementary or secondary nonpublic schools. To qualify under this section the parent must have an annual taxable income of less than $5,000. The amount of reimbursement is limited to $50 for each grade school child and $100 for each high school child. Each parent is required, however, to submit to the Commissioner of Education a verified statement containing a receipted tuition bill, and the amount of state reimbursement may not exceed 50% of that figure. . . .

This section, like section 1, is prefaced by a series of legislative findings designed to explain the impetus for the State's action. Expressing a dedication to the "vitality of our pluralistic society," the findings state that a "healthy competitive and diverse alternative to public education is not only desirable but indeed vital to a state and nation that have continually reaffirmed the value of individual differences." The findings further emphasize that the right to select among alternative educational systems "is diminished or even denied to children of lower income families, whose parents, of all groups, have the least options in determining where their children are to be educated." . . . [T]he findings state [further] that any "precipitous decline in the number of nonpublic school pupils would cause a massive increase in public school enrollment and costs," an increase that would 'aggravate an already serious fiscal crisis in public education' and would 'seriously jeopardize the quality of education for all children.' " . . . Repeating the declaration contained in section 1, the findings conclude that "such assistance is clearly secular, neutral and non-ideological."

The remainder of the "Elementary and Secondary Education Opportunity Program" . . . is designed to provide a form of tax relief to those who fail to qualify for tuition reimbursement. Under these sections parents may subtract from their adjusted gross income for state income tax purposes a designated amount for each dependent for whom they have paid at least $50 in nonpublic school tuition. If the taxpayer's adjusted gross income is less than $9,000 he may subtract $1,000 for each of as many as three dependents. As the taxpayer's income rises, the amount he may subtract diminishes. Thus, if a taxpayer has adjusted gross income of $15,000, he may subtract only $400 per dependent, and if his income is $25,000 or more, no deduction is allowed. . . .

Although no record was developed in this case, a number of pertinent generalizations may be made about the nonpublic schools which would benefit from these enactments. The District Court . . . adopted [the following] profile, [noting that] [q]ualifying institutions . . . could be ones that:

(a) impose religious restrictions on admissions; (b) require attendance of pupils at religious activities; (c) require obedience by students to the doctrines and dogmas of a particular faith; (d) require pupils to attend instruction in the theology or doctrine of a particular faith; (e) are an integral part of the religious mission of the church sponsoring it; (f) have as a substantial purpose the inculcation of religious values; (g) impose religious restrictions on faculty appointments; and (h) impose religious restrictions on what or how the faculty may teach. 350 F. Supp., at 663.

. . . Some 700,000 to 800,000 students, constituting almost 20% of the State's entire elementary and secondary school population, attend over 2,000 nonpublic schools, approximately 85% of which are church affiliated. And while "all or practically all" of the 280 schools entitled to receive "maintenance and repair" grants "are related to the Roman Catholic Church and teach Catholic religious doctrine to some degree," institutions qualifying under the remainder of the statute include a substantial number of Jewish, Lutheran, Episcopal, Seventh Day Adventist, and other church-affiliated schools.

Plaintiffs argued below that because of the substantially religious character of the intended beneficiaries, each of the State's three enactments offended the Establishment Clause. The District Court . . . held unanimously that section 1 (maintenance and repair grants) and section 2 (tuition reimbursement grants) were invalid. As to the income tax provisions of sections 3, 4 and 5, however, a majority of the District Court . . . held that the Establishment Clause had not been violated. Finding the provisions of the law severable, it enjoined permanently any further implementation of sections 1 and 2 but declared the remainder of the law independently enforceable. . . . We affirm the District Court insofar as it struck down sections 1 and 2 and reverse its determination regarding sections 3, 4 and 5. . . .

. . . [Our past] decisions dictate that to pass muster under the Establishment Clause the law in question, first, must reflect a clearly secular legislative purpose, . . . second, must have a primary effect that neither advances nor inhibits religion, . . . and, third, must avoid excessive governmental entanglement with religion. . . .

In applying these criteria to the three distinct forms of aid involved in this case, we need touch only briefly on the requirement of a "secular legislative purpose." . . . [E]ach measure is adequately supported by legitimate, nonsectarian state interests. We do not question the propriety, and fully secular content, of New York's interest in preserving a healthy and safe educational environment for all of its school children. And we do not doubt—indeed, we fully recognize—the validity of the State's interests in promoting pluralism and diversity among its public and nonpublic schools. Nor do we hesitate to acknowledge the reality of its concern for an already overburdened public school system that might suffer in the event that a significant percentage of children presently attending nonpublic schools should abandon those schools in favor of the public schools.

But the propriety of a legislative purpose may not immunize from further scrutiny a law which either has a primary effect that advances religion, or which fosters excessive entanglements between Church and State. Accordingly, we must weigh . . . the three aid provisions challenged here against these criteria of effect and entanglement.

The "maintenance and repair" provisions. . . . authorize direct payments to nonpublic schools, virtually all of which are Roman Catholic schools in low income areas. . . . So long as expenditures do not exceed 50% of comparable expenses in the public school system, it is possible for a sectarian elementary or secondary school to finance its entire "maintenance and repair" from state tax-raised funds. No attempt is made to restrict payments to those expenditures related to the upkeep of facilities used exclusively for secular purposes, nor do we think it possible within the context of these religion-oriented institutions to impose such restrictions. Nothing in the statute . . . bars a qualifying school from paying out of state funds the salary of employees who maintain the school chapel, or the cost of renovating classrooms in which religion is taught, or the cost of heating and lighting those same facilities. Absent appropriate restrictions on expenditures for these and similar purposes, it simply cannot be denied that this section has a primary effect that advances religion. . . .

[Here, JUSTICE POWELL reviews the state's argument which relies on cases such as *Everson, Allen,* and *Tilton* to support such expenditures. In rejecting such arguments, he emphasizes the narrow channel for the infusion of aid to such nonpublic schools for their secular function only.]

What we have said demonstrates that New York's maintenance and repair provisions violate the Establishment Clause because their effect, inevitably, is to subsidize the religious mission of sectarian schools. We have no occasion, therefore, to consider the further question whether those provisions as presently written would also fail to survive scrutiny under the administrative entanglement aspect of the three-part test because assuring the secular use of all funds requires too intrusive and continuing a relationship between Church and State. . . .

New York's tuition reimbursement program also fails the "effect" test, for much the same reasons that govern its maintenance and repair grants. . . .

. . . The controlling question here…is whether the fact that the grants are delivered to parents rather than schools is of such significance as to compel a contrary result. The State and intervenor-appellees rely on *Everson* and *Allen* for their claim that grants to parents, unlike grants to institutions, respect the wall of separation required by the Constitution. . . . But those decisions make clear that, far from providing a *per se* immunity from examination of the substance of the State's program, the fact that aid is disbursed to parents rather than to the schools is only one among many factors to be considered. . . .

[I]n the tuition grants here . . . [t]here has been no endeavor "to guarantee the separation between secular and religious educational functions and to ensure that State financial aid supports only the former." . . . Indeed, it is precisely the function of New York's law to provide assistance to private schools, the great majority of which are sectarian. By reimbursing parents for a portion of their tuition bill, the State seeks to relieve their financial burdens sufficiently to assure that they continue to have the option to send their children to religion-oriented schools. And while the other purposes for that aid—to perpetuate a pluralistic educational environment and to protect the fiscal integrity of over-burdened public schools—are certainly unexceptionable, the effect of the aid is unmistakably to provide desired financial support for nonpublic, sectarian institutions. . . .

Although we think it clear . . . that New York's tuition grant program fares no better under the "effect" test than its maintenance and repair program, in view of the novelty of the question we will address briefly the subsidiary arguments made by the state officials. . . .

First, it has been suggested that it is of controlling significance that New York's program calls for *reimbursement* for tuition already paid rather than for direct contributions which are merely routed through the parents to the schools, in advance of or in lieu of payment by the parents. The parent is not a conduit, we are told, but is absolutely free to spend the money he receives in any manner he wishes. There is no element of coercion . . . , and no assurance that the money will end up in the hands of religious schools. The absence of any element of coercion, however, is irrelevant to questions arising under the Establishment Clause. . . . [But] while proof of coercion might provide a basis for a claim under the Free Exercise Clause, it [is] not a necessary element of any claim under the Establishment Clause. . . . [Such an] inquiry governs here: if the grants are offered as an incentive to parents to send their children to sectarian schools by making unrestricted cash payments to them, the Establishment Clause is violated whether or not the actual dollars given eventually find their way into the sectarian institutions. Whether the grant is labeled a reimbursement, a reward or a subsidy, its substantive impact is still the same. In sum, we agree with the conclusion of the District Court that "[w]hether he gets it during the current year, or as reimbursement for the past year, is of no constitutional importance." . . . [Two state officials argue] that it is significant here that the tuition reimbursement grants pay only a portion of the tuition bill, and an even smaller portion of the religious school's total expenses. . . . On the basis of [reimbursement limitations and the percentage of the cost of nonpublic education covered by tuition payments], appellee reasons that the "maximum tuition reimbursement by the State is thus only 15% of the educational costs in the nonpublic schools." And "since compulsory education laws of the State, by necessity require significantly more than 15% of school time to be devoted to teaching secular courses," the New York statute provides "a statistical guarantee of neutrality." . . . Obviously, if accepted, this argument would provide the foundation for massive, direct subsidization of sectarian elementary and secondary schools. Our cases, however, have long since foreclosed the notion that mere statistical assurances will suffice to sail between Scylla and Charybdis of "effect" and "entanglement."

Finally, the State argues that its program of tuition grants should survive scrutiny because it is designed to promote the free exercise of religion. The State notes that only "low-income parents" are aided by this law, and without state assistance their right to have their children educated in a religious environment "is diminished or even denied." It is true, of course, that this Court has long recognized and maintained the right to choose nonpublic over public education. It is also true that a state law interfering with a parent's right to have his child educated in a sectarian school would run afoul of the Free Exercise Clause. But this Court repeatedly has recognized that tension inevitably exists between the Free Exercise and the Establishment Clauses . . . and that it may often not be possible to promote the former without offending the latter. As a result of this tension, our cases require the State to maintain an attitude of "neutrality," neither "advancing" nor "inhibiting" religion. In its attempt to enhance the opportunities of the poor to choose between public and nonpublic education, the State has taken a step which can only be regarded as one "advancing" religion. However great our sympathy . . . for the burdens experienced by those who must pay public school taxes at the same time that they support other schools because of the constraints of "conscience and discipline," . . . and notwithstanding the "high social importance" of the State's purposes, . . . neither may justify an eroding of the limitations of the Establishment Clause now firmly emplanted.

Sections 3, 4, and 5 establish a system for providing income tax benefits to parents of children attending New York's nonpublic schools. In this Court, the parties have engaged in a considerable debate over what label best fits the New York law. . . . We see no reason to select one label over the other, as the constitutionality of this hybrid benefit does not turn in any event on the label we accord it. . . .

Appellees defend the tax portion of New York's legislative package on two grounds. First, they contend that it is of controlling significance that the . . . credits are directed to the parents rather than to the schools. Our treatment of this issue in Part II B, *supra,* is applicable here and requires rejection of this claim. Second, appellees place their strongest reliance on *Walz* v. *Tax Commission,* . . . in which New York's property tax exemption for religious organizations was upheld. We think that *Walz* provides no support for appellees' position. . . .

Because we have found that the challenged sections have the impermissible effect of advancing religion, we need not consider whether such aid would result in entanglement of the State with religion in the sense of "[a] comprehensive, discriminating, and continuing state surveillance." (*Lemon* v. *Kurtzman,* 403 U.S. at 619.) But the importance of the competing societal interests implicated in this case prompts us to make the further observation that, apart from any specific entanglement of the State in particular religious programs, assistance of the sort here involved carries grave potential for entanglement in the broader sense of continuing political strife over aid to education. . . .

Our examination of New York's aid provisions, in light of all relevant considerations, compels the judgment that each, as written, has a "primary effect that advances religion" and offends the constitutional prohibition against laws "respecting the establishment of religion." We therefore affirm the three-judge court's holding as to sections 1 and 2, and reverse as to sections 3, 4, and 5.

It is so ordered.

CHIEF JUSTICE BURGER, *joined in part by* JUSTICE WHITE, *and joined by* JUSTICE REHNQUIST, *concurring in part and dissenting in part.*

I join in that part of the Court's opinion . . . which holds the New York "maintenance and repair" provision unconstitutional . . . because it is a direct aid to religion. I disagree, however, with the Court's decisions in *Nyquist* and in *Sloan* v. *Lemon,* 413 U.S. 825, to strike down the New York and Pennsylvania tuition grant programs and the New York tax relief provisions. . . .

While there is no straight line running through our decisions interpreting the Establishment and Free Exercise Clauses of the First Amendment, our cases do, it seems to me, lay down one solid, basic principle: that the Establishment Clause does not forbid governments . . . from enacting a program of general welfare under which benefits are distributed to private individuals, even though many of those individuals may elect to use those benefits in ways that "aid" religious instruction or worship. . . .

This fundamental principle which . . . I believe governs the present cases, is premised more on experience and history than on logic. It is admittedly difficult to articulate the reasons why a State should be permitted to reimburse parents of private-school children—partially at least—to take into account the State's enormous savings in not having to provide schools for those children, when a State is not allowed to pay the same benefit directly to sectarian schools on a per-pupil basis. In either case, the private individual makes the ultimate decision that may indirectly benefit church sponsored schools; to that extent the state involvement with religion is substantially attenuated. The answer, I believe, lies in the experienced judgement of various members of this Court over the years that the balance between the policies of free exercise and establishment of religion tips in favor of the former when the legislation moves away from direct aid to religious institutions and takes on the character of general aid to individual families. This judgement reflects the caution with which we scrutinize any effort to give official support to religion and the tolerance with which we treat general welfare legislation. But, whatever its basis, that principle is established in our prior cases, . . . and ought to be followed here.

The tuition grant and tax relief programs now before us are, in my view, indistinguishable in principle, purpose and effect from the statutes in *Everson* and *Allen.* . . . The only discernible difference . . . is in the method of the distribution of benefits: here the particular benefits of the Pennsylvania and New York statutes are given only to parents of private school children, while in *Everson* and *Allen* the statutory benefits were made available to parents of both public and private school children. But to regard that difference as constitutionally meaningful is to exalt form over substance. It is beyond dispute that the parents of public school children in New York and Pennsylvania presently receive the "benefit" of having their children educated totally at state expense; the statutes enacted in those States and at issue here merely attempt to equalize that "benefit" by giving to parents of private school children, in the form of dollars or tax deductions, what the parents of public school children receive in kind. It is no more than simple equity to grant partial relief to parents who support the public schools they do not use. . . .

JUSTICE REHNQUIST *delivered the opinion of the Court.*

* * *

Minnesota . . . provides its citizens with free elementary schooling. . . . It seems to be agreed that about 820,000 students attended this school system in the most recent school year. During the same year, approximately 91,000 elementary and secondary students attended some 500 privately supported schools located in Minnesota, and about 95% of these students attended schools considering themselves to be sectarian.

Minnesota, by a law originally enacted in 1955 and revised in 1976 and again in 1978, permits state taxpayers to claim a deduction from gross income for certain expenses incurred in educating their children. The deduction is limited to actual expenses incurred for the "tuition, textbooks and transportation" of dependents attending elementary or secondary schools. A deduction may not exceed $500 per dependent in grades K through six and $700 per dependent in grades seven through twelve. . . .

Petitioners—certain Minnesota taxpayers—sued in the United States District Court for the District of Minnesota claiming that sec. 290.09(22) violated the Establishment Clause by providing financial assistance to sectarian institutions. . . . The district court granted respondent's motion for summary judgment, holding that the statute was "neutral on its face and in its application and does not have a primary effect of either advancing or inhibiting religion." . . . On appeal, the Court of Appeals affirmed, concluding that the Minnesota statute substantially benefited a "broad class of Minnesota citizens."

* * *

One fixed principle in this field is our consistent rejection of the argument that "any program which in some manner aids an institution with a religious affiliation" violates the Establishment Clause. . . . For example, it is now well-established that a state may reimburse parents for expenses incurred in transporting their children to school . . . and that it may loan secular textbooks to all schoolchildren within the state. . . .

Notwithstanding the repeated approval given programs such as those in *Allen* and *Everson*, our decisions also have struck down arrangements resembling, in many respects, these forms of assistance. See, e.g., *Lemon v. Kurtzman*, . . . *Levitt v. Committee for Public Education*, . . . *Meek v. Pittenger*. . . . In this case we are asked to decide whether Minnesota's tax deduction bears greater resemblance to those types of assistance to parochial schools we have approved, or to those we have struck down. Petitioners place particular reliance on our decision in *Committee for Public Education v. Nyquist*, . . . where we held invalid a New York statute providing public funds for the maintenance and repair of the physical facilities of private schools and granting thinly disguised "tax benefits," actually amounting to tuition grants, to the parents of children attending private schools. As explained below, we conclude that sec. 290.09(22) bears less resemblance to the arrangement struck down in *Nyquist* than it does to assistance programs upheld in our prior decisions and those discussed with approval in *Nyquist*.

The general nature of our inquiry in this area has been guided, since the decision in *Lemon v. Kurtzman* . . . by the "three-part" test laid down in that case:

> First, the statute must have a secular legislative purpose; second, its princip[al] or primary effect must be one that neither advances nor inhibits religion . . . ; finally, the statute must not foster 'an excessive government entanglement with religion.' . . .

* * *

Little time need be spent on the question of whether the Minnesota tax deduction has a secular purpose. Under our prior decisions, governmental assistance programs have consistently survived this inquiry even when they have run afoul of other aspects of the *Lemon* framework. . . . This reflects, at least in part, our reluctance to attribute unconstitutional motives to the states, particularly when a plausible secular purpose for the state's program may be discerned from the face of the statute.

A state's decision to defray the cost of educational expenses incurred by parents—regardless of the type of schools their children attend—evidences a purpose that is both secular and understandable. An educated populace is essential to the political and economic health of any community, and a state's efforts to assist parents in meeting the rising cost of educational expenses plainly serves this secular purpose of ensuring that the state's citizenry is well-educated. Similarly, Minnesota, like other states, could conclude that there is a strong public interest in assuring the continued financial health of private schools, both sectarian and non-sectarian. By educating a substantial number of students such schools relieve public schools of a correspondingly great burden—to the benefit of all taxpayers. In addition, private schools may serve as a benchmark for public schools, in a manner analogous to the "TVA yardstick" for private power companies. As JUSTICE POWELL has remarked:

> Parochial schools, quite apart from their sectarian purpose, have provided an educational alternative for millions of young Americans; they often afford wholesome competition with our public schools; and in some States they relieve substantially the tax burden incident to the operation of public schools. The State has, moreover, a legitimate interest in facilitating education of the highest quality for all children within its boundaries, whatever school their parents have chosen for them. *Wolman* v. *Walter*, 433 U.S. 229, 262, . . . (POWELL, J., concurring in part, concurring in judgment in part, and dissenting in part).

All these justifications are readily available to support sec. 290.09(22), and each is sufficient to satisfy the secular purpose inquiry of *Lemon*.

We turn therefore to the more difficult but related question whether the Minnesota statute has "the primary effect of advancing the sectarian aims of the non-public schools." . . . In concluding that it does not, we find several features of the Minnesota tax deduction particularly significant. First, an essential feature of Minnesota's arrangement is the fact that sec. 290.09(22) is only one among many deductions—such as those for medical expenses . . . and charitable contributions . . . available under the Minnesota tax laws. Our decisions consistently have recognized that traditionally "[l]egislatures have especially broad latitude in creating classifications and distinctions in tax statutes." . . . Under our prior decisions, the Minnesota legislature's judgment that a deduction for educational expenses fairly equalizes the tax burden of its citizens and encourages desirable expenditures for educational purposes is entitled to substantial deference.

Other characteristics of sec. 290.09(22) argue equally strongly for the provision's constitutionality. Most importantly, the deduction is available for educational expenses incurred by *all* parents, including those whose children attend public schools and those whose children attend non-sectarian private schools or sectarian private schools. Just as in *Widmar* v. *Vincent*, 454 U.S. 263 (1981), where we concluded that the state's provision of a forum neutrally "open to a broad class of non-religious as well as religious speakers" does not "confer any imprimatur of State approval," so here: "the provision of benefits to so broad a spectrum of groups is an important index of secular effect."

In this respect . . . this case is vitally different from the scheme struck down in *Nyquist*. There, public assistance amounting to tuition grants, was provided only to parents of children in *nonpublic* schools. . . . [W]e explicitly distinguished both *Allen* and *Everson* on the grounds that "In both cases the class of beneficiaries included *all* schoolchildren, those in public as well as those in private schools." . . . Moreover, we intimated that "public assistance (e.g., scholarships) made available generally without regard to the sectarian-nonsectarian or public-nonpublic nature of the institution benefited" . . . might not offend the Establishment Clause. We think the tax deduction adopted by Minnesota is more similar to this latter type of program than it is to the arrangement struck down in *Nyquist*. Unlike the assistance at issue in *Nyquist*, sec. 290.09(22) permits *all* parents—whether their children attend public school or private—to deduct their children's educational expenses. . . . [A] program, like [this], that neutrally provides state assistance to a broad spectrum of citizens is not readily subject to challenge under the Establishment Clause.

. . . [B]y channeling whatever assistance it may provide to parochial schools through individual parents, Minnesota has reduced the Establishment Clause objections to which its action is subject. It is true, of course, that financial assistance provided to parents ultimately has an economic effect comparable to that of aid given directly to the schools attended by their children. It is also true, however, that under Minnesota's arrangement public funds become available only as a result of numerous private choices of individual parents of school-age children. For these reasons, we recognized in *Nyquist* that the means by which state assistance flows to private schools is of some importance: we said that "the fact that aid is disbursed to parents rather than to . . . schools" is a material consideration in Establishment Clause analysis, albeit "only one among many to be considered." *Nyquist*, at 781. It is noteworthy that all but one of our recent cases invalidating state aid to parochial schools have involved the direct transmission of assistance from the state to the schools themselves. The exception, of course, was *Nyquist*. . . . Where, as here, aid to parochial schools is available only as a result of decisions of individual parents no "imprimatur of State approval," . . . can be deemed to have been conferred on any particular religion, or on religion generally. . . .

. . . The Establishment Clause of course extends beyond prohibition of a state church or payment of state funds to one or more churches. We do not think, however, that its prohibition extends to the type of tax deduction established by Minnesota. The historic purposes of the clause simply do not encompass the sort of attenuated financial benefit, ultimately controlled by the private choices of individual parents, that eventually flows to parochial schools from the neutrally available tax benefit at issue in this case.

Petitioners argue that, notwithstanding the facial neutrality of sec. 290.09(22), in application the statute primarily benefits religious institutions. Petitioners rely . . . on a statistical analysis of the type of persons claiming the tax deduction. They contend that most parents of public school children incur no tuition expenses . . . and that other expenses deductible under sec. 290.09(22) are negligible in value; moreover, they claim that 96 percent of the children in private schools in 1978–1979 attended religiously affiliated institutions. Because of all this, they reason, the bulk of deductions taken under sec. 290.09(22) will be claimed by parents of children in sectarian schools. Respondents reply that petitioners have failed to consider the impact of deductions for items such as transportation, summer school tuition, tuition paid by parents whose children attended schools outside the school districts in which they resided, rental or purchase costs for a variety of equipment, and tuition for certain types of instruction not ordinarily provided in public schools.

We need not consider these contentions in detail. We would be loath to adopt a rule grounding the constitutionality of a facially neutral law on annual reports reciting the extent to which various classes of private citizens claimed benefits under the law. Such an approach would scarcely provide the certainty that this field stands in need of, nor can we perceive principled standards by which such statistical evidence might be evaluated. Moreover, the fact that private persons fail in a particular year to claim the tax relief to which they are entitled— under a facially neutral statute—should be of little importance in determining the constitutionality of the statute permitting such relief.

Finally, private educational institutions, and parents paying for their children to attend these schools, make special contributions to the areas in which they operate. "Parochial schools, quite apart from their sectarian purpose, have provided an educational alternative for millions of young Americans: they often afford wholesome competition with our public schools; and in some States they relieve substantially the tax burden incident to the operation of public schools." *Wolman*, at 262, (POWELL, J., concurring and dissenting). If parents of children in private schools choose to take especial advantage of the relief provided by sec. 290.09(22), it is no doubt due to the fact that they bear a particularly great financial burden in educating their children. More fundamentally, whatever unequal effect may be attributed to the statutory classification can fairly be regarded as a rough return for the benefits . . . provided to the state and all taxpayers by parents sending their children to parochial schools. In the light of all this, we believe it wiser to decline to engage in the type of empirical inquiry into those persons benefited by state law which petitioners urge.

Thus, we hold that the Minnesota tax deduction for educational expenses satisfies the primary effect inquiry of our Establishment Clause cases.

Turning to the third part of the *Lemon* inquiry, we have no difficulty in concluding that the Minnesota statute does not "excessively entangle" the state in religion. The only plausible source of the "comprehensive, discriminating, and continuing state surveillance" . . . necessary to run afoul of this standard would lie in the fact that state officials must determine whether particular textbooks qualify for a deduction. . . . Making decisions such as this does not differ substantially from making the types of decisions approved in earlier opinions of this Court. In *Board of Education* v. *Allen*, . . . for example, the Court upheld the loan of secular textbooks to parents or children attending nonpublic schools; though state officials were required to determine whether particular books were or were not secular, the system was held not to violate the Establishment Clause. . . . The same result follows in this case. For the foregoing reasons, the judgment of the court of appeals is

Affirmed.

JUSTICE MARSHALL, *with whom* JUSTICE BRENNAN, JUSTICE BLACKMUN *and* JUSTICE STEVENS *join, dissenting.*

The Establishment Clause of the First Amendment prohibits a state from subsidizing religious education, whether it does so directly or indirectly. In my view, this principle of neutrality forbids. . . . any tax benefit, including the tax deduction at issue here, which subsidizes tuition payments to sectarian schools. I also believe that the Establishment Clause prohibits the tax deductions that Minnesota authorizes for the cost of books and other instructional materials used for sectarian purposes.

The majority today does not question the continuing vitality of this Court's decision in *Nyquist*. That decision established that a State may not support religious education either through direct grants to parochial schools or through financial aid to parents of parochial school students. . . . *Nyquist* also established that financial aid to parents of students attending parochial schools is no more permissible if it is provided in the form of a tax credit than if provided in the form of cash payments. . . . Notwithstanding these accepted principles, the Court today upholds a statute that provides a tax deduction for the tuition charged by religious schools. . . . The Minnesota tax statute violates the Establishment Clause for precisely the same reason as the statute struck down in *Nyquist*: it has a direct and immediate effect of advancing religion.

* * *

Indirect assistance in the form of financial aid to parents for tuition payments is . . . impermissible because it is not "subject to . . . restrictions" which " 'guarantee the separation between secular and religious educational functions and . . . ensure that State financial aid supports only the former.' " . . . By ensuring that parents will be reimbursed for tuition payments they make, the Minnesota statute requires that taxpayers in general pay for the cost of parochial education and extends a financial "incentive to parents to send their children to sectarian schools." *Nyquist, supra*, 413 U.S., at 786. . . .

* * *

That the Minnesota statute makes some small benefit available to all parents cannot alter the fact that the most substantial benefit provided by the statute is available only to those parents who send their children to schools that charge tuition. It is simply undeniable that the single largest expense that may be deducted under the Minnesota statute is tuition. The statute is little more than a subsidy of tuition masquerading as a subsidy of general educational expenses. The other deductible expenses are *de minimis* in comparison to tuition expenses.

Contrary to the majority's suggestion, . . . the bulk of the tax benefits afforded by the Minnesota scheme are enjoyed by parents of parochial school children not because parents of public school children fail to claim deductions to which they are entitled, but because the latter are simply *unable* to claim the largest tax deduction that Minnesota authorizes. Fewer than 100 of more than 900,000 school-age children in Minnesota attend public schools that charge a general tuition. Of the total number of taxpayers who are eligible for the tuition deduction, approximately 96 percent send their children to religious schools. Parents who send their children to free public schools are simply ineligible to obtain the full benefit of the deduction except in the unlikely event that they buy $700 worth of pencils, notebooks, and bus rides for their school-age children. Yet parents who pay at least $700 in tuition to nonpublic, sectarian schools can claim the full deduction even if they incur no other educational expenses.

* * *

There can be little doubt that the State of Minnesota intended to provide, and has provided, "[s]ubstantial aid to the educational function of [church-related] schools," and that the tax deduction for tuition and other educational expenses "necessarily results in aid to the sectarian school enterprise as a whole." *Meek* v. *Pittenger*, 421 U.S., at 366. . . . It is beside the point that the state may have legitimate secular reasons for providing such aid. In focusing upon the contributions made by church-related schools, the majority has lost sight of the issue before us in this case.

> The sole question is whether state aid to these schools can be squared with the dictates of the Religion Clauses. Under our system the choice has been made that government is to be entirely excluded from the area of religious instruction. . . . The Constitution decrees that religion must be a private matter for the individual, the family, and the institutions of private choice, and that while some involvement and entanglement are inevitable, lines must be drawn. *Lemon* v. *Kurtzman*, 403 U.S. 602, 625, (1971).

In my view, the lines drawn in *Nyquist* were drawn on a reasoned basis with appropriate regard for the principles of neutrality embodied by the Establishment Clause. I do not believe that the same can be said of the lines drawn by the majority today. For the first time, the Court has upheld financial support for religious schools without any reason at all to assume that the support will be restricted to the secular functions of those schools and will not be used to support religious instruction. This result is flatly at odds with the fundamental principle that a State may provide no financial support whatsoever to promote religion. As the Court stated in *Everson*, 330 U.S., at 16, and has often repeated . . .

> No tax in any amount, large or small, can be levied to support any religious activities or institutions, whatever they may be called, or whatever form they may adopt to teach or practice religion.

I dissent.

Parochiaid and Institutions of Higher Learning

While finding a number of schemes expending public funds to support certain dimensions of secular education in parochial elementary and secondary schools constitutionally defective, the Court appears not to have been as unyielding in weighing the constitutionality of public aid to church-related colleges and universities. For example, on the same day that it struck down the Pennsylvania and Rhode Island parochiaid programs for elementary and secondary schools in the *Lemon* and *Dicenso* cases, the Court sustained the expenditure of federal funds, some of which were targeted to support the construction of educational facilities at church-related colleges and universities. In *Tilton* v. *Richardson* (403 U.S. 672, 1971), funds to be funneled to such institutions through the Higher Educational Facilities Act of 1963 were deemed acceptable because the Court did not feel that the act's enforcement provisions would produce the kind of "excessive entanglement" between the government and church-related schools that the establishment clause forbids. Chief Justice Warren Burger, speaking for Justices John M. Harlan II, Potter Stewart, and Harry A. Blackmun, noted that the act provided for facilities that were "religiously neutral" and that the "one-shot" grants did not require the continuous surveillance condemned in *Kurtzman* and *Dicenso*. Furthermore, he contended that there was far less danger of religious matter permeating secular education and indoctrinating its recipients at this level than is possible at the elementary and secondary levels. However, the Court felt that the provision limiting federal interest in the facility to a period of twenty years did not provide adequate safeguards against impermissible aid to religious establishments. Consequently, their unrestricted use by religious bodies thereafter would constitute the

kind of aid the establishment clause proscribes. But in the end, Burger held that under the doctrine of separability, this defect was not fatal to the remainder of the statute.

In his dissent, Justice William O. Douglas, with whom Justices Hugo Black and Thurgood Marshall concurred, pointed to President Kennedy's statement in March 1961 in which the president flatly asserted that there was no doubt that "the Constitution clearly prohibits aid to . . . parochial schools [as] the correct constitutional principle for this case." Douglas had no doubt that the statute furthered education, but the aid accruing to parochial schools therefrom constituted a fatally defective constitutional flaw. To him, "excessive entanglements" of secular and sectarian officials and actions permeated the entire scheme.

The Court used the *Tilton* precedent to sustain two state programs providing for aid to church-related institutions of higher learning. The first involved a South Carolina plan for financing construction of secular facilities at church-related colleges by revenue bonds issued by state authority. In *Hunt* v. *McNair* (413 U.S. 734, 1973), the Court felt that since the college serviced and repaid the bonds (although at a lower rate stemming from the tax-free status for the interest payments), the aid resulting therefrom did not have the "primary effect" of advancing the religious mission of the college. Furthermore, the Court noted that the college was similar to those in *Tilton* and not "pervasively sectarian."

A more generous aid program for such institutions was authorized by a 1971 Maryland statute. Utilizing a noncategorical grant format, it authorized the payment of an annual subsidy to private institutions, including church-related ones, that met certain requirements. In recognition of First Amendment constraints, the act expressly excluded schools that award "only seminarian or theological degrees." An amendment to the statute in 1972 proscribes use of the funds for sectarian purposes.

In rejecting an establishment clause challenge that followed, a three-judge district court found: (1) that the act had a secular legislative purpose; (2) that the aid did not have a primary effect of advancing religion; (3) that the recipient institutions were not "pervasively sectarian"; (4) that the aid in fact was extended only to "the secular side" of the schools; and (5) that no "excessive entanglement" between church and state was fostered by the act. The Supreme Court affirmed this lower court holding in *Roemer* v. *Board of Public Works of Maryland* (426 U.S. 736, 1976).

FEATURED CASES

School District of Abington Township, Pennsylvania v. *Schempp*
Board of Education of Westside Community Schools v. *Mergens*
Wallace v. *Jaffree*   *Edwards* v. *Aguillard*   *Lee* v. *Weisman*

For many Americans, the principle of the separation of church and state need not be construed so rigidly as to prevent the nation's religious heritage and values from being imparted to pupils in public schools. Two of the most widely used mechanisms for the accomplishment of such purpose are the prayer and Bible-reading programs in schools' opening exercises and the released-time programs for religious instruction. What has made Supreme Court rulings in this area particularly controversial is the difficulty in reconciling the establishment and free exercise clauses of the First Amendment. Justice Potter Stewart phrased the issue succinctly when, in *Sherbert* v. *Verner* (*infra*), he noted that a "mechanistic" application of the establishment clause may result in a decision that compels government to violate the clause to guarantee the free exercise of religion and vice versa. He concluded that as long as that dilemma is unresolved, "consistent and perceptive" decisions in such cases will be "impeded and impaired."

The prayer exercise as a part of the daily opening ceremony of the public schools was first before the Supreme Court in *Engel* v. *Vitale* (370 U.S. 471) in 1962. At issue was the constitutionality of the use of a twenty-two-word prayer composed by the State Board of Regents of New York. School districts had an option in the matter, and the prayer was strictly voluntary for children if adopted in their district. However, if a school board opted for prayer in the opening ceremony, the Regents' prayer was to be used. Despite the "voluntarism" safeguards and the "nonsectarian" characterization claims of the prayer's sponsors, the Court declared its use an infringement of the establishment clause. Justice Hugo Black's opinion for the six-to-one majority stressed that it was not prayer but an "officially prescribed prayer" that was being condemned. He warned that in this country it is not the business of any government to compose official prayers for any group of people.

In dissent, Justice Stewart focused on the conflict between the two clauses, declaring that he could not "see how an 'official religion' is established by letting those who want to say a prayer say it." He contended that to deny use of the prayer to children who desire it "is to deny them the opportunity of sharing in the spiritual heritage of our Nation."

Although Justice Black stressed that it was not prayer but a governmentally prescribed prayer that the Court was condemning, critics warned that the Court should be checked before it struck down other types of activities that are considered a part of our heritage as a religious people.

The emotional outburst in response to the *Engel* decision had hardly subsided when, just one year later, the Court "dropped the other shoe" in this twofold controversy. In companion cases arising from school districts in Pennsylvania and Maryland (*School District of Abington Township, Pennsylvania* v. *Schempp* and *Murray* v. *Curlett*, 374 U.S. 203, 1963), public school opening exercises using the more traditional Lord's Prayer and Bible reading were held violative of the establishment clause. Speaking for the Court, Justice Tom Clark set forth the "purpose and primary effect" test as a measure of constitutional permissibility of such public-sponsored activity. Said Clark: "What are the purpose and primary effect of the enactment? If either is the advancement or inhibition of religion then the enactment exceeds the legislative power. . . ."

In his dissent, Justice Stewart advanced the view that the free exercise of religion is the central value embodied in the First Amendment. Consequently, he argued that the Court's action striking down the prayer exercises constituted a denial of a substantial free exercise claim of those desiring the exercises.

The immediate response to the *Engel* and *Schempp* rulings in the political arena brought forth scores of proposals to amend the Constitution to permit various forms of voluntary prayer in public schools. But the vigorous efforts mounted by Representatives Frank Becker (R., N.Y.) in the House of Representatives in 1963 and followed by those of Senator Everett M. Dirksen (R., Ill.) in 1966 came to naught, although the Dirksen proposal fell just nine votes short of the necessary two-thirds vote in the Senate. Vigorous efforts to get prayer exercises back into the public schools either through constitutional amendment or federal court-curbing legislation during the 1970s met a similar fate.[3]

Probably the most vigorous effort to restore voluntary prayer in the public schools was made by the Reagan administration in 1984 during the second session of the 98th Congress. Construing his election as a mandate to "put God back in the public school rooms" and supported by a wide variety of conservative and religious groups, the president opted for the constitutional certainty of the prayer exercise, offering the following proposal to amend the Constitution:

Nothing in this Constitution shall be construed to prohibit individual or group prayer in public schools or other public institutions. No person shall be required by the United States or by any state to participate in prayer.

In its consideration of the proposal the Senate Judiciary Committee added a provision to prohibit governments from composing a prayer, as was the case in *Engel* v. *Vitale.*

Senate debate on the proposal in March 1984 revealed that the arguments advanced on the issue had not changed significantly during the twenty-five years since *Engel* was decided. The following excerpts from the debate on the president's proposal in the Senate on March 5 and March 6, 1984, underscore this point:

Senator Strom Thurmond (R., S.C.)
. . . This amendment to the Constitution, as President Reagan has repeatedly emphasized, is of vital importance to the well-being of our nation. . . .

In writing the establishment clause . . . our Founding Fathers wanted to prevent . . . an official state religion. At the same time they sought, through the free exercise clause, to guarantee . . . the freedom to worship God without government interference or restraint. In their wisdom, they recognized that true religious liberty precludes the Government from both forcing and preventing worship.

The unfortunate constitutional interpretation which has banned voluntary prayer in our public schools runs contrary to this dual intent of the framers. They understood . . . that the general wel-

fare of our Republic depends to a large degree on the spiritual and moral fiber of the citizenry. That fiber is, in turn, dependent upon the guidance given our young people. A ban on school prayer is, therefore, contrary to the best interests of our Nation as a whole. . . .

[L]et there be no doubt about the constituency involved here. The movement to restore prayer to the public schools . . . is not an attempt by a small minority to impose their views upon an apathetic majority. Public opinion polls show strong support for a constitutional amendment. . . .

I believe the latest poll showed around 80 percent of our people favored prayers in the public schools. These are not religious zealots, but average Americans who want their children and grandchildren to enjoy the same simple privilege that they had as public school students. . . .

Senator Lowell Weicker (R., Conn.)
School children of America enjoy—at least if the Constitution is being enforced, and it may be that it is not being enforced in some jurisdictions—do enjoy voluntary prayer—truly voluntary. In no ways are they restricted from uttering their own prayer at any time of the day in school.

What is prohibited is the institutionalization of prayer in the school, and the minute you do that, it is no longer voluntary.

So let us understand clearly that those who are for voluntary prayer are for the law as it now stands.

What is attempted here . . . is to achieve an involuntary status for prayer in the United States. What is sought to be achieved is a state prayer. . . .

This is not some academic debate on the floor of the U.S. Senate. This [debate] relates to our freedom as Americans. This relates as to whether or not each of us will be able to find our own way to God, bound in our own way, to pray in our own way, or whether we go back to the history which we had denied and allow the state to do that for us. The one is the first step, the other the last, in the career of intolerance. . . .

Senator Jesse Helms (R., N.C.)
Mr. President, it is this Senator's strong conviction that we in the Senate today would do well to heed divine wisdom and the pleas of our children, and restore the right to pray in the schools once again. If we do, it is likely that not only will the children be closer to God but that we—including the Justices of the United States Supreme Court—will be drawn closer as well. . . .

It is no mere chance coincidence that the decline in American public education has roughly paralleled the banning of school prayer by the Supreme Court in the early 1960s. Sure, there have been other factors as well, but banning prayer removed a fundamental in the educational process. . . .

Mr. President, many Americans are baffled at how

[3]The most serious of these efforts was spearheaded by Senator Jesse Helms (R., N.C.) in 1979. His court-curbing proposal would have denied jurisdiction to the Supreme Court to review cases arising under state legislation relating to voluntary prayers in public schools and public buildings. The measure passed the Senate but was killed in the House.

we got to a point in our history where both Houses of Congress start every day with a prayer delivered by a tax-paid chaplain; where Presidential inaugurations always begin with an invocation; where the Supreme Court opens its sessions with the traditional "God Save the United States and this honorable Court"; where our money has "In God We Trust" printed on it; where all manner of state and local public and private meetings begin with a prayer, but their teachers in public schools may not lead their children in voluntary group prayer to start the day. . . .

Senator John Danforth (R., Mo.)

I do not stand here today to argue for one religious position or another. That is not my place. All I want to point out is that within America there are at least two positions on school prayer which are strongly held by very religious people. Some devout people, acting out their faith, ask us to amend the Constitution to permit prayer in public school. Other people, equally devout, ask us not to amend the Constitution. My only point today is to explain to the Senate some religious objections to the amendment, to state that many denominations ask us not to act, and to note that their position is deeply felt and can be advanced with a plenitude of Biblical references.

So . . . we have a choice to make. We can choose to do nothing, to keep the Constitution as it is, to allow personal prayer in public school, but not officially sanctioned group prayer. Or, we can choose to amend the Constitution, to weigh in on the side of those many religious people who favor the sanctioning of group prayer in public schools. . . .

My own view is that in this case the best course for the Senate to follow is to do nothing. To allow a child to pursue his own religious life without the structure of school sponsored observances is as close to neutrality as we can come. To take the affirmative step of amending the Constitution is to decide that now is the time to foster one religious position against another.

. . . [E]ven under the most narrow definition, establishment of religion includes an affirmative step, taken by Government to favor one religious position over another. That is what we are asked to do [by this amendment]. . . . We are asked to permit in public schools religious observances which are desirable to some and offensive to others. To vote for this amendment is to vote for the establishment of religion. That is a step we should not take.

Senator Howard Baker (R., Tenn.)

We are all agreed . . . that the issue is religious liberty. Those opposed to this amendment contend that it is not the place of the state, and should not be within the power of the State, to mandate religious activity or prescribe the form or substance of that activity. Those of us who support the amendment entirely agree.

But is mandating religious activity worse than pro-

hibiting it, or are these equal offenses before the law and the Constitution? That, I believe, is the crux of the issue before us. I believe the Government has no right either to force or forbid the voluntary exercise of religion in our schools or in any other place. But the Government, through the Courts, has assumed this right for 20 years, and the Government, through the Congress, has an opportunity . . . to remedy this constitutional and historical mistake. . . .

Although the strong pressure from the president and his religious and conservative constituencies produced 56 votes for the amendment, that was 11 votes shy of the two-thirds majority required in the constitutional amendment initiation stage. But as soon as the vote was taken on March 20, 1984, several proprayer senators indicated their intentions to push other efforts to get prayer exercises back into the public schools. As Senator Helms stated:

> [W]e have just begun to fight. Round 1 is over, but so long as I am in the U.S. Senate there will be many more rounds to come. . . . [T]here is more than one way to skin a cat. . . .

Condemning federal judges for imposing their personal policy views on the American public—views that he felt were hostile to both the Constitution and American traditions—Helms indicated a renewed effort to push jurisdiction-curbing legislation.

Meanwhile, in June 1984 proprayer supporters in the Senate were able to attach an "equal access" rider to an education appropriation measure that guaranteed any student group wishing to discuss religious issues (and possibly to pray) the use of school facilities on the same basis as any other student groups who are allowed use of school facilities for political discussion and consideration of a wide variety of secular issues. Although narrowly rejecting a similar measure prior to the Senate action, the House accepted the Senate measure in conference, and the president approved it on August 11, 1984. While not the straightforward school prayer amendment vigorously pushed earlier, many proponents accepted the Equal Access Act (20 U.S.C., Secs. 4071–4074) as a significant step in the direction of the eventual restoration of organized prayer in the public schools.

Not unexpectedly, this new act confronted a constitutional challenge within six months of its passage. A group of students in the Westside High School of Omaha, Nebraska, cited the act to support their request to establish a Christian club that would be accorded operational privileges and benefits available to all other recognized student clubs at the school. The students indicated that among the club's purposes was to provide a forum for them "to read and discuss the Bible, to have fellowship, and to pray together." School authorities denied this request on the ground that to permit such an activity, even with the support of the Equal Access Act, would violate the establishment clause. A federal district court sustained this interpretation, but the Court of Appeals for the Eighth Circuit reversed, and the Supreme Court agreed with the appeals tribunal.

Justice Sandra Day O'Connor's opinion for the Court in *Mergens* applied the *Lemon* three-prong test, and found that the Equal Access Act and the proposed Christian club met the threshold requirements of each. Additionally, the justice cited *Widmar* v. *Vincent* (454 U.S. 263, 1981) as authority supporting such student activity in the public secondary school context. In *Widmar*, which concerned student religious club activity within a university student body, the Court held that "an open-forum policy, including nondiscrimination against religious speech, would have a secular purpose." Consequently, O'Connor did not see how permitting these kinds of student-initiated activities could be construed as the school's endorsement of religious activity.

On a state front, the Alabama legislature attempted to put prayer back in its public schools in the late 1970s and early 1980s through the "period of silence for meditation and voluntary prayer" format. While a sympathetic federal district court upheld the several statutes involved (taking the novel position that although the statutes were religiously motivated, the state had the power to establish a state religion if it desired), the Court of Appeals reversed and the Supreme Court affirmed that reversal in *Wallace* v. *Jaffree* (472 U.S. 38, 1985). Citing *Lemon*, Justice John Paul Stevens emphasized the statutes' lack of a secular legislative purpose, noting that the legislature had made clear its promotion of religion with the 1981 voluntary prayer amendment. A review of the legislative history reveals that legislators made no attempt to camouflage their intent.

Could a meditation statute that did not contain a provision authorizing voluntary prayer get by the *Lemon* test? Many thought that the 1982 New Jersey statute that required public school administrators to permit students to observe a moment of silence prior to the commencement of each school day "for quiet and private contemplation or introspection" was the appropriate vehicle for a definitive answer by the Supreme Court. A federal district court had held the statute unconstitutional under all three prongs of the *Lemon* test, while the court of appeals' affirmance was based on the statute's lack of a secular purpose. When the case reached the Supreme Court in *Karcher* v. *May* (108 S. Ct. 388, 1988), review was limited to the question of the proper standing of the appellants, and a unanimous Court dismissed the appeal because the party-appellants no longer held the position that was required to pursue the appeal beyond the decision of the appeals court. Hence, the Supreme Court's stand on the moment of silence and meditation and reflection observances must await another case.

Another dimension of the school prayer controversy involves the common practice in many communities around the country of opening graduation exercises with an invocation in the form of prayers by a clergyman and closing the exercises with a benediction (another form of prayer by a clergyman). Whether such practices in the context of the public schools are permissible under the establishment clause was presented the Court in *Lee* v. *Weisman* (112 S. Ct. 2649, 1992) at the beginning of its 1991 term. That case presented the Court (then with a solid conservative majority) with yet another opportunity to determine what it wished to do with the *Lemon* test.

But in the end, three justices of the conservative bloc (O'Connor, Kennedy, and Souter) joined with the Court's fading liberal bloc (Blackmun and Stevens) to reject the school commencement invocation-benediction ceremony as an unconstitutional departure from establishment clause jurisprudence of the last quarter of a century. Justice Anthony Kennedy's opinion for the Court reemphasized the principle that government promotion of religious activity in the context of a public school ceremony is contrary to the strictures of the establishment clause, for in this case "persuasive coercion" of the nonconformist student was a distinct possibility. The majority agreed that, contrary to the expressions of several of the justices over the last decade, there was no need to reexamine and possibly reconfigure or discard the *Lemon* test.

And the Court did not do so while holding that public support for a parochial school deaf student's language interpreter was constitutionally permissible in *Zobrest* v. *Catalina School District* (113 S. Ct., 1993). Chief Justice William Rehnquist was able to marshall a 5-to-4 majority behind the general government benefit theory in the category of fire and police protection. Additionally, he cited *Witters* v. *Washington Department of Services for the Blind* (474 U. S. 481, 1986) (where the Court sustained a blind student's use of public vocational funds to pay for his seminary training) as similar to the language interpreter aid. Indeed, for him the benefit to the religious establishment was remote at best.

But the dissenters, led by Justices Harry Blackmun and David Souter, were not so generous in their characterization of this expenditure of public funds. They contended that the interpreter's role was critical as a significant participant in the delivery not only of secular matter, but in the propagation of religious doctrine as well.

The lineup of the justices in *Zobrest* suggests that the pendulum is likely to swing the other way in the future as Justice White as an accommodationist in the majority retires at the end of the 1992 term and will be succeeded by Judge Ruth Bader Ginsburg, who appears to be supportive of the separationist theory. *Lemon* could well get a new lease on life!

Organized prayer is not the only mechanism through which religious and other groups have sought to have their interests furthered through the public schools. But unlike the prayer issue, the so-called released-time programs in the public school context did not produce extended controversy, because the Supreme Court's last pronouncement on the subject in 1952 did not close the door to such programs. Just one year after Justice Wiley B. Rutledge had sounded his *Everson* warning about the drive to introduce religious instruction in the public schools, the Supreme Court was confronted with the issue in *McCollum* v. *Champaign Board of Education* (333 U.S. 203, 1948). The program was conducted in the Champaign, Illinois, public school system on a voluntary basis and provided religious instruction separately for Protestants, Catholics, and Jews. Instruction was the responsibility of the religious authorities and took place during regular school hours and in the school classrooms. Students not participating in the program were required to leave their regular classrooms and pursue their school activities elsewhere in the school building; on the other hand, students who volunteered to participate in the program were required to attend religious classes. The public school teachers assisted in several routine matters such as distributing permission slips and keeping attendance records.

This arrangement was rejected by the Court in an eight-to-one decision as a flat contravention of the establishment clause. Justice Black, whose opinion was supported by five other justices, maintained that the use of the public school classrooms to conduct religious instruction, the operation of the compulsory school attendance machinery to provide audiences for the propagation of the sectarian dogma, and the close cooperation between religious and school authorities in promoting the program constituted "beyond all question a utilization of the . . . tax-supported public school system to aid religious groups to spread their faith."

Only Justice Stanley Reed dissented, contending that the framers of the establishment clause did not intend to exclude religious education from the public schools. In his considered analysis, he concluded that they had instead meant for the clause to prohibit the establishment of a state church and/or a state religion, and nothing more.

The decision in *McCollum* met with widespread criticism, since in communities across the country such programs were commonly accepted. Apparently a majority of the justices were not oblivious to such reaction when they decided to limit the *McCollum* ruling four years later in *Zorach* v. *Clauson* (343 U.S. 306, 1952).

The only significant difference between the two programs was the place where the religious classes were conducted. In Champaign, Illinois, they were held inside the regular school classrooms. In New York, they were conducted off school property. For the six-person majority, however, this difference was sufficient to save New York's program from constitutional infirmity. Justice William O. Douglas, writing the majority opinion, rejected the view of rigid and absolute separation of church and state. He maintained that the First Amendment does not say that in all respects there must be a separation of church and state, for if that thesis were accepted, "the state and religion would be alien to each other—hostile, suspicious, and even unfriendly." But he argued that our religious heritage supports such accommodation between religion and secular authorities.

For the three dissenters—Justices Black, Frankfurter, and Jackson—there was no consequential difference between this program and the one struck down in *McCollum*. Operationally, they argued, public school authorities were still delivering aid to sectarian groups by securing audiences of schoolchildren for the propagation of religious dogma.

The Court appeared to move toward an accommodationist stance in *Zorach* without rejecting *McCollum*. Hence, those promoting such instructional arrangements would find the Court more tolerant if the classes were conducted off school premises.

Some groups have advocated a "shared-time" arrangement as a mechanism that would allow students to receive religious instruction while taking secular courses in the public schools. The basic plan calls for the dual enrollment of students in public and sectarian schools (the student attends the public school part of the day for secular subjects such as math, science, and physical education, and then moves to a sectarian school for the remainder of the school day to obtain religion courses in addition to some secular courses). Lower courts approved the implementation of such programs in a few states in the late 1960s and early 1970s,[4] but the Supreme Court did not review them directly. Instead, the Court examined a version of shared-time when it considered a challenge to the educational enrichment and remedial programs funded under Title I of the federal Elementary and Secondary Education Act (ESEA) in *Grand Rapids School District* v. *Ball* (473 U.S. 373, 1985). The challenge focused on that Michigan school district's program in which ESEA funds were used to pay public school employees to teach secular courses to sectarian pupils in their parochial school facilities during the normal school day. In striking down that "enrichment and remedial" program, Justice Brennan cited the second prong of the *Lemon* test, noting that, in reality, the program had the primary effect of advancing religion through a public subsidy. In a companion case (*Aguilar* v. *Felton*, 473 U.S. 402, 1985) involving New York City's use of Title I ESEA funds to meet special needs of educationally deprived children attending parochial schools, Brennan held that the totality of instructional and supervisory activities and interactions resulted in excessive entanglement between public and sectarian authorities.

While *Ball* and *Aguilar*, along with the general decline of public revenue for education, appear to have blunted this public-sectarian cooperative effort to enhance the educational experience of pupils in parochial schools, the Court's recent moves toward reformulating the *Lemon* test[5] may well make it possible for such educational initiatives to pass constitutional muster in the future.

The movement to include the so-called creation science courses in the public school curriculum represents yet another effort to get religious instruction in the public schools. Typical of such efforts was that of the state of Louisiana in 1981. That state's legislature mandated that instruction in the biblical account of the creation must accompany instruction in any secular theories of evolution. The statute's supporters emphasized that this "balanced treatment" of competing theories of evolution has the secular purpose of furthering academic inquiry. But this attempt to push sectarian instruction in secular packaging was rejected by the Supreme Court in *Edwards* v. *Aguillard* (107 S. Ct. 2573, 1987), as eight of the nine members agreed that the statute's clear religious purpose was in conflict with the *Lemon* test.

Finally, ingenuity knows no end in the efforts of some persons to "put God back into the public schools." For example, an interesting strategy to get sectarian matter into the public classroom was brought to the nation's attention in 1980 when the Court struck down a Kentucky statute requiring the posting of a copy of the Ten Commandments in each public classroom in the state. In *Stone* v. *Graham* (449 U.S. 39, 1980), the Court noted that the "avowed" secular purpose justification urged by the state was insufficient to avoid conflict with the establishment clause. The state's effort, the Court continued, had as its central purpose the advancement of religion. While some Kentucky school districts openly disregarded the ruling and continued to post the Commandments, some students evaded the decision by wearing T-shirts on which the Commandments were printed.

SCHOOL DISTRICT OF ABINGTON TOWNSHIP, PENNSYLVANIA v. SCHEMPP*
374 U.S. 203; 10 L. Ed. 2d 844; 83 S. Ct. 1560 (1963)

JUSTICE CLARK *delivered the opinion of the Court.*

Once again we are called upon to consider the scope of the provision of the First Amendment to

the United States Constitution which declares that "Congress shall make no law respecting an establishment of religion, or prohibiting the free exercise thereof. . . ." These companion cases present the issues in the context of state action requiring that schools begin each day with readings from the Bible. While raising the basic questions under slightly different factual situations, the cases permit of joint treatment. In light of the history of the

---

[4]See *Morton* v. *Board of Education of Chicago* (216 N.E. 2d 205, 1966) and *In re Proposal C* (185 N.W. 2d 9, 1971).

[5]See p. 178, *infra.*

*Decided with the companion case of Murray v. Curlett.

First Amendment and of our cases interpreting and applying its requirements, we hold that the practices at issue and the laws respecting them are unconstitutional under the Establishment Clause, as applied to the states through the Fourteenth Amendment. . . . [In] No. 142 [t]he Commonwealth of Pennsylvania by law, 24 Pa. Stat. Sec. 15-1516, as amended, . . . requires that "At least ten verses from the Holy Bible shall be read, without comment, at the opening of each public school on each school day. Any child shall be excused from such Bible reading, or attending such Bible reading, upon the written request of his parent or guardian." The Schempp family, husband and wife and two of their three children, brought suit to enjoin enforcement of the statute, contending that their rights under the Fourteenth Amendment to the Constitution of the United States are, have been, and will continue to be violated unless this statute be declared unconstitutional as violative of these provisions of the First Amendment. They sought to enjoin the appellant school district . . . from continuing to conduct such readings and recitation of the Lord's Prayer in the public schools of the district. . . . A three-judge statutory District Court for the Eastern District of Pennsylvania held that the statute is violative of the Establishment Clause of the First Amendment as applied to the States by the Due Process Clause of the Fourteenth Amendment and directed that appropriate injunctive relief issue. . . .

The appellees . . . are of the Unitarian faith . . . [and] they . . . regularly attend religious services. . . . The . . . children attend the Abington Senior High School, which is a public school operated by appellant district.

On each school day at the Abington Senior High School between 8:15 and 8:30 A.M., while the pupils are attending their home rooms or advisory sections, opening exercises are conducted pursuant to the statute. The exercises are broadcast into each room in the school building through an intercommunications system and are conducted under the supervision of a teacher by students attending the school's radio and television workshop. Selected students from this course gather each morning in the school's workshop studio for the exercises, which include readings by one of the students of 10 verses of the Holy Bible, broadcast to each room in the building. This is followed by the recitation of the Lord's Prayer, likewise over the intercommunications system, but also by the students in the various classrooms, who are asked to stand and join in repeating the prayer in unison. The exercises are closed with the flag salute and such pertinent announcements as are of interest to the students. Participation in the opening exercises, as directed by the statute, is voluntary. The student reading the verses from the Bible may select the passages and read from any version he chooses, although the only copies furnished by the school are the King James version, copies of which were circulated to each teacher by the school district. During the period in which the exercises have been conducted the King James, the Douay and the Revised Standard versions of the Bible have been used, as well as the Jewish Holy Scriptures. There are no prefatory statements, no questions asked or solicited, no comments or explanations made and no interpretations given at or during the exercises. The students and parents are advised that the student may absent himself from the classroom or, should he elect to remain, not participate in the exercises.

It appears from the record that in schools not having an intercommunications system the Bible reading and the recitation of the Lord's Prayer were conducted by the homeroom teacher, who chose the text of the verses and read them herself or had students read them in rotation or by volunteers. . . .

At the first trial Edward Schempp and the children testified as to specific religious doctrines purveyed by a literal reading of the Bible "which were contrary to the religious beliefs which they held and to their familial teaching." . . . Edward Schempp testified at the second trial that he had considered having . . . [his children] excused from attendance at the exercises but decided against it for several reasons, including his belief that the children's relationships with their teachers and classmates would be adversely affected.

* * *

The trial court, in striking down the practices and the statute requiring them, made specific findings of fact that the children's attendance at Abington Senior High School is compulsory and that the practice of reading 10 verses from the Bible is also compelled by law. It also found that:

The reading of the verses, even without comment, possesses a devotional and religious character and constitutes in effect a religious observance. The devotional and religious nature of the morning exercises is made all the more apparent by the fact that the Bible reading is followed immediately by a recital in unison by the pupils of the Lord's Prayer. . . . The exercises are held in the school buildings and perforce are conducted by and under the authority of the local school authorities and during school sessions. Since the statute requires the reading of the "Holy Bible," a Christian document, the practice . . . prefers the Christian religion. . . .

[The facts in] no. 119 [show that] [i]n 1905 the Board of School Commissioners of Baltimore City adopted a rule pursuant to . . . [state law which] . . . provided for the holding of opening exercises in the schools of the city, consisting primarily of the "reading, without comment, of a chapter in the Holy Bible and/or the use of the Lord's Prayer." The petitioners, Mrs. Madalyn Murray and her son, William J. Murray III, are both professed atheists. Following unsuccessful attempts to have the respondent school board rescind the rule, this suit was filed for mandamus to compel its rescission and cancellation. It was alleged that William was a student in a public school of the city and Mrs. Murray, his mother, was a taxpayer therein; . . . that at petitioners' insistence the rule was amended to permit children to be excused from the exercise on request of the parent and that William had been excused pursuant thereto. . . .

The respondents demurred and the trial court, recognizing that the demurrer admitted all facts well pleaded, sustained it without leave to amend. The Maryland Court of Appeals affirmed, the majority of four justices holding the exercise not in violation of the First and Fourteenth Amendments, with three justices dissenting. . . .

It is true that religion has been closely identified with our history and government. . . . The fact that the Founding Fathers believed devoutly that there was a God and that the unalienable rights of man were rooted in Him is clearly evidenced in their writings, from the Mayflower Compact to the Constitution itself. This background is evidenced today in our public life through the continuance in our oaths of office from the Presidency to the Alderman of the final supplication, "So help me God." Likewise each House of the Congress provides through the Chaplain an opening prayer, and the sessions of this Court are declared open by the crier in a short ceremony the final phrase of which invokes the grace of God. Again, there are such manifestations in our military forces, where those of our citizens who are under the restrictions of military service wish to engage in voluntary worship. Indeed, only last year an official survey of the country indicated that 64% of our people have church membership . . . while less than 3% profess no religion whatever. . . . It can be truly said, therefore, that today, as in the beginning, our national life reflects a religious people who, in the words of Madison are "earnestly praying, as . . . in duty bound, that the Supreme Lawgiver of the Universe . . . guide them into every measure which may be worthy of His [blessing . . .]"

Almost a hundred years ago in *Minor* v. *Board of Education of Cincinnati,* Judge Alphonzo Taft, father of the revered Chief Justice, in an unpublished opinion stated the ideal of our people as to religious freedom as one of:

> absolute equality before the law of all religious opinions and sects. . . . The government is neutral, and while protecting all, it prefers none, and it *disparages* none. . . .

The wholesome "neutrality" of which this Court's cases speak thus stems from a recognition of the teachings of history that powerful sects or groups might bring about a fusion or a concert or dependency of one upon the other to the end that official support of the State or Federal Government would be placed behind the tenets of one or of all orthodoxies. This the Establishment Clause prohibits. And a further reason for neutrality is found in the Free Exercise Clause, which recognizes the value of religious training, teaching and observance and, more particularly, the right of every person to freely choose his own course with reference thereto, free of any compulsion from the state. This the Free Exercise Clause guarantees. Thus, as we have seen, the two clauses may overlap. As we have indicated, the Establishment Clause has been directly considered by this Court eight times in the past score of years and, with only one Justice dissenting on the point, it has consistently held that the clause withdrew all legislative power respecting religious belief or the exercise thereof. The test may be stated as follows: what are the purpose and primary effect of the enactment? If either is the advancement or inhibition of religion then the enactment exceeds the scope of legislative power as circumscribed by the Constitution. That is to say that to withstand the strictures of the Establishment Clause there must be a secular legislative purpose and a primary effect that neither advances nor inhibits religion. . . . The Free Exercise Clause, likewise considered many times here, withdraws from legislative power, state and federal, the exertion of any restraint on the free exercise of religion. Its purpose is to secure religious liberty in the individual by prohibiting any invasions thereof by civil authority. Hence it is necessary in a free exercise case for one to show the coercive effect of the enactment as it operates against him in the practice of his religion. The distinction between the two clauses is apparent—a violation of the Free Exercise Clause is predicated on coercion while the Establishment Clause violation need not be so attended.

Applying the Establishment Clause principles to the cases at bar we find that the States are requiring the selection and reading at the opening of the school day of verses from the Holy Bible and the recitation of the Lord's Prayer by the students in unison. These exercises are prescribed as part of the curricular activities of students who are required by law to attend school. They are held in the school buildings under the supervision and with the participation of teachers employed in those schools. None of these factors, other than compulsory school attendance, was present in the program upheld in *Zorach* v. *Clauson*. The trial court in [*Schempp*] has found that such an opening exercise is a religious ceremony and was intended by the State to be so. We agree with the trial court's finding as to the religious character of the exercises. Given that finding the exercises and the law requiring them are in violation of the Establishment Clause.

There is no such specific finding as to the religious character of the exercises in [*Murray*], and the state contends (as does the state in [*Schempp*]) that the program is an effort to extend its benefits to all public school children without regard to their religious belief. Included within its secular purposes, it says, are the promotion of moral values, the contradiction to the materialistic trends of our times, the perpetuation of our institutions and the teaching of literature. The case came up on demurrer, of course, to a petition which alleged that the uniform practice under the rule had been to read from the King James version of the Bible and that the exercise was sectarian. The short answer, therefore, is that the religious character of the exercise was admitted by the State. But even if its purpose is not strictly religious, it sought to be accomplished through readings, without comment, from the Bible. Surely the place of the Bible as an instrument of religion cannot be gain-said, and the State's recognition of the pervading religious character of the ceremony is evident from the rule's specific permission of the alternative use of the Catholic Douay version as well as the recent amendment permitting nonattendance at the exercises. None of these factors is consistent with the contention that the Bible is here used either as an instrument for nonreligious moral consideration or as a reference for the teaching of secular subjects.

The conclusion follows that in both cases the laws require religious exercises and such exercises are being conducted in direct violation of the rights of the appellees and petitioners. Nor are these required exercises mitigated by the fact that individual students may absent themselves upon parental request, for that fact furnishes no defense to a claim of unconstitutionality under the Establishment Clause. . . . Further, it is no defense to urge that the religious practices here may be relatively minor encroachments on the First Amendment. The breach of neutrality that is today a trickling stream may all too soon become a raging torrent and, in the words of Madison, "it is proper to take alarm at the first experiment on our liberties." . . .

It is insisted that unless these religious exercises are permitted a "religion of secularism" is established in the schools. We agree of course that the State may not establish a "religion of secularism" in the sense of affirmatively opposing or showing hostility to religion, thus "preferring those who believe in no religion over those who do believe." . . . We do not agree, however, that this decision in any sense has that effect. In addition, it might well be said that one's education is not complete without a study of comparative religion or the history of religion and its relationship to the advancement of civilization. It certainly may be said that the Bible is worthy of study for its literary and historic qualities. Nothing we have said here indicates that such study of the Bible or of religion, when presented objectively as part of a secular program of education, may not be effected consistent with the First Amendment. But the exercises here do not fall into those categories. . . .

Finally, we cannot accept that the concept of neutrality, which does not permit a State to require a religious exercise even with the consent of the majority of those affected, collides with the majority's right to free exercise of religion. While the Free Exercise Clause clearly prohibits the use of state action to deny the rights of free exercise to *anyone*, it has never meant that a majority could use the machinery of the State to practice its beliefs. Such a contention was effectively answered by Mr. Justice Jackson for the Court in *West Virginia Board of Education* v. *Barnette*, 319 U.S. 624, 638, 63 S. Ct. 1178, 1185, 87 L. Ed. 1628, (1943):

The very purpose of a Bill of Rights was to withdraw certain subjects from the vicissitudes of political controversy, to place them beyond the reach of majorities and officials and to establish them as legal principles to be applied by the courts. One's right to . . . freedom of worship . . . and other fundamental rights may not be submitted to vote; they depend on the outcome of no elections.

The place of religion in our society is an exalted one, achieved through a long tradition of reliance on the home, the church and the inviolable citadel of the individual heart and mind. We have come to recognize through bitter experience that it is not within the power of government to invade that citadel, whether its purpose or effect be to aid or oppose, to advance or retard. In the relationship between man and religion, the State is firmly committed to a position of neutrality. . . .

It is so ordered.

Judgment in [*Schempp*] affirmed: judgment in [*Murray*] reversed and case remanded with directions.

[The concurring opinions of JUSTICE DOUGLAS and JUSTICE BRENNAN are not reprinted here.]

JUSTICE STEWART, *dissenting.*

I think the records in the two cases before us are so fundamentally deficient as to make impossible an informed or responsible determination of the constitutional issues presented. Specifically, I cannot agree that on these records we can say that the Establishment Clause has necessarily been violated. But I think there exist serious questions under both that provision and the Free Exercise Clause . . . which require the remand of these cases for the taking of additional evidence.

. . . It is, I think, a fallacious oversimplification to regard these two provisions as establishing a single constitutional standard of "separation of church and state," which can be mechanically applied in every case to delineate the required boundaries between government and religion. We err in the first place if we do not recognize, as a matter of history and as a matter of the imperatives of our free society, that religion and government must necessarily interact in countless ways. Secondly, the fact is that while in many contexts the Establishment Clause and the Free Exercise Clause fully complement each other, there are areas in which a doctrinaire reading of the Establishment Clause leads to irreconcilable conflict with the Free Exercise Clause.

A single obvious example should suffice to make the point. Spending federal funds to employ chaplains for the armed forces might be said to violate the Establishment Clause. Yet a lonely soldier stationed at some faraway outpost could surely complain that a government which did not provide him the opportunity for pastoral guidance was affirmatively prohibiting the free exercise of his religion. And such examples could readily be multiplied. The short of the matter is simply that the two relevant clauses of the First Amendment cannot accurately be reflected in a sterile metaphor which by its very nature may distort rather than illumine the problems involved in a particular case.

* * *

That the central value embodied in the First Amendment—and, more particularly, in the guarantee of "liberty" contained in the Fourteenth—is the safeguarding of an individual's right to free exercise of his religion has been consistently recognized. . . .

It is this concept of constitutional protection embodied in our decisions which makes the cases before us such difficult ones for me. For there is involved in these cases a substantial free exercise claim on the part of those who affirmatively desire to have their children's school day open with the reading of passages from the Bible.

* * *

It might also be argued that parents who want their children exposed to religious influences can adequately fulfill that wish off school property and outside school time. With all its surface persuasiveness, however, this argument seriously misconceives the basic constitutional justification for permitting the exercises at issue in these cases. For a compulsory state educational system so structures a child's life that if religious exercises are held to be an impermissible activity in schools, religion is placed at an artificial and state created disadvantage. Viewed in this light, permission of such exercises for those who want them is necessary if the schools are truly to be neutral in the matter of religion. And a refusal to permit religious exercises thus is seen, not as the realization of state neutrality, but rather as the establishment of a religion of secularism, or at the least, as government support of the beliefs of those who think that religious exercises should be conducted only in private.

What seems to me to be of paramount importance, then, is recognition of the fact that the claim advanced here in favor of Bible reading is sufficiently substantial to make simple reference to the constitutional phrase of "establishment of religion" as inadequate an analysis of the cases before us as the ritualistic invocation of the nonconstitutional phrase "separation of church and state." What these cases compel, rather, is an analysis of just what the "neutrality" is which is required by the interplay of the Establishment and Free Exercise Clauses of the First Amendment, as imbedded in the Fourteenth.

I have said that these provisions authorizing religious exercises are properly to be regarded as measures making possible the free exercise of religion. But it is important to stress that, strictly speaking, what is at issue here is a privilege rather than a right. In other words, the question presented is not whether exercises such as those at issue here are constitutionally compelled, but rather whether they are constitutionally invalid. And that issue, in my view, turns on the question of coercion.

It is clear that the dangers of coercion involved in the holding of religious exercises in a schoolroom differ qualitatively from those presented by the use of similar exercises or affirmations in ceremonies attended by adults. Even as to children, however, the duty laid upon government in connection with religious exercises in the public schools is that of refraining from so structuring the school environment as to put any kind of pressure on a child to participate in those exercises; it is not that of providing an atmosphere in which children are kept scrupulously insulated from any awareness that some of their fellows may want to open the school day with prayer, or of the fact that there exist in our pluralistic society differences of religious belief.

* * *

[I]t seems to me clear that certain types of exercises would present situations in which no possibility of coercion on the part of secular officials could be claimed to exist. Thus, if such exercises were held either before or after the official school day, or if the school schedule were such that participation were merely one among a number of desirable alternatives, it could hardly be contended that the exercises did anything more than to provide an opportunity for the voluntary expression of religious belief. On the other hand, a law which provided for religious exercises during the school day and which contained no excusal provision would obviously be unconstitutionally coercive upon those who did not wish to participate. And even under a law containing an excusal provision, if the exercises were held during the school day, and no equally desirable alternative were provided by the school authorities, the likelihood that children might be under at least some psychological compulsion to participate would be great. In a case such as the latter, however, I think we would err if we assumed such coercion in the absence of any evidence.

Viewed in this light, it seems to me clear that the records in both of the cases before us are wholly inadequate to support an informed or responsible decision. Both cases involve provisions which explicitly permit any student who wishes, to be excused from participation in the exercises. There is no evidence in either case as to whether there would exist any coercion of any kind upon a student who did not want to participate. . . .

. . . It is conceivable that these school boards, or even all school boards, might eventually find it impossible to administer a system of religious exercises during school hours in such a way to meet this constitutional standard—in such a way as completely to free from any kind of official coercion those who do not affirmatively want to participate. But I think we must not assume that school boards so lack the qualities of inventiveness and good will as to make impossible the achievement of the goal.

I would remand both cases for further hearings.

BOARD OF EDUCATION OF WESTSIDE COMMUNITY SCHOOLS v. MERGENS
496 U.S. 226; 110 L. Ed. 2d 191; 110 S. Ct. 2356 (1990)

JUSTICE O'CONNOR *delivered the opinion of the Court except as to Part III.*

The case requires us to decide whether the Equal Access Act prohibits Westside High School from denying a student religious group permission to meet on school premises during noninstructional time, and if so, whether the Act so construed, violates the Establishment Clause of the First Amendment.

I

Respondents are current and former students at Westside High School, a public secondary school in Omaha, Nebraska. At the time this suit was filed, the school enrolled about 1,450 students and included grades 10 to 12; in the 1987–1988 school year, ninth graders were added . . .

Students at Westside High School are permitted to join various student groups and clubs, all of which meet after school hours on school premises. . . .

School board policy 5610 recognizes these student clubs as a "vital part of the total education program as a means of developing citizenship, wholesome attitudes, good human relations, knowledge and skills." [That policy] also provides that each club shall have faculty sponsorship and that "clubs and organizations shall not be sponsored by any political or religious organization, or by any organization which denies membership on the basis of race, color, creed, sex or political belief." Board Policy 6180 on "Recognition of Religious Beliefs and Customs" requires that "[s]tudents adhering to a specific set of religious beliefs or holding to little or no belief shall be alike respected." In addition, Board Policy 5450 recognizes its students' "Freedom of Expression," consistent with the authority of the Board.

In January 1985, respondent Bridget Mergens met with Westside's principal Dr. Findley, and requested permission to form a Christian club at the school. The proposed club would have the same privileges and meet on the same terms and conditions as other Westside student groups, except that the proposed club would not have a faculty sponsor. According to the student's testimony at trial, the club's purpose would have been, among other things, to permit the students to read and discuss the Bible, to have fellowship, and to pray together. Membership would have been voluntary and open to all students regardless of religious affiliation.

Findley denied the request, as did associate superintendent Tangdell. . . . The school officials explained that school policy required all student clubs to have a faculty sponsor, which the proposed religious club would not or could not have, and that a religious club at the school would violate the Establishment Clause. In March 1985, Mergens appealed the denial of her request to the Board of Education, but the Board voted to uphold the denial.

Respondents, by and through their parents as next friends, then brought this suit in the United States District Court for the District of Nebraska seeking declaratory and injunctive relief. They alleged that petitioners' refusal to permit the proposed club to meet at Westside violated the Equal Access Act, which prohibits public secondary schools that receive federal financial assistance and that maintain a "limited open forum" from denying "equal access" to students who wish to meet within the forum on the basis of the content of the speech at such meetings. Respondents further alleged that petitioners' actions denied them their First and Fourteenth Amendment rights to freedom of speech, association, and the free exercise of religion. Petitioners responded that the Equal Access Act did not apply to Westside and that, if the Act did apply, it violated the Establishment Clause of the First Amendment and was therefore unconstitutional. The United States intervened in the action to defend the constitutionality of the Act.

The District Court entered judgment for petitioners. The court held that the Act did not apply in this case because Westside did not have a "limited open forum" as defined by the Act—all of Westside's student clubs, the court concluded, were curriculum-related and tied to the educational function of the school. The court rejected respondents' constitutional claims, reasoning that Westside did not have a limited public forum as set forth in *Widmar* v. *Vincent* and that Westside's denial of respondents' request was reasonably related to legitimate pedagogical concerns.

The United States Court of Appeals for the Eighth Circuit reversed. . . . The Court of Appeals noted that the "broad interpretation" advanced by the Westside school officials "would make the [Equal Access Act] meaningless" and would allow any school to "arbitrarily deny access to school facilities to any unfavored student club on the basis of its speech content," which was "exactly the result that Congress sought to prohibit by enacting the [Act]." The Court of Appeals instead found that "[m]any of the student clubs at WHS . . . are noncurriculum-related. Accordingly, because it found that Westside maintained a limited open forum under the Act, the Court of Appeals concluded that the Act applied to "forbi[d] discrimination against [respondents'] proposed club on the basis of its religious content." . . .

II

A

In *Widmar* v. *Vincent* we invalidated, on free speech grounds, a state university regulation that prohibited student use of school facilities " 'for purposes of religious worship or religious teaching.' " In doing so, we held that an "equal access" policy would not violate the Establishment Clause under our decision in *Lemon* v. *Kurtzman*. In particular, we held that such a policy would have a secular purpose, would not have the primary effect of advancing religion, and would not result in excessive entanglement between government and religion. We noted, however, that "[u]niversity students are, of course, young adults. They are less impressionable than younger students and should be able to appreciate that the University's policy is one of neutrality toward religion."

In 1984 Congress extended the reasoning of *Widmar* to public secondary schools. Under the Equal Access Act, a public secondary school with a "limited open forum" is prohibited from discriminating against students who wish to conduct a meeting within that forum on the basis of the "religious, political, philosophical, or other content of the speech at such meetings." . . .

B

The parties agree that Westside High School receives federal financial assistance and is a public secondary school within the meaning of the Act. The Act's obligation to grant equal access to student groups is therefore triggered if Westside maintains a "limited open forum"—i.e., if it permits one or more "noncurriculum related student groups" to meet on campus before or after classes. . . .

We think it significant that the Act . . . reflects at least some consensus on a broad legislative purpose. The committee reports indicate that the Act was intended to address perceived widespread discrimination against religious speech in public schools, and, as the language of the Act indicates, its sponsors contemplated that the Act would do more than merely validate the status quo. The committee reports also show that the Act was enacted in part in response to two federal appellate court decisions holding that student religious groups could not, consistent with the Establishment Clause, meet on school premises during noninstructional time. A broad reading of the Act would be consistent with the views of those who sought to end discrimination by allowing students to meet and discuss religion before and after classes.

In light of this legislative purpose, we think that the term "noncurriculum related student group" is best interpreted broadly to mean any student group that does not directly relate to the body of courses offered by the school. In our view, a student group directly relates to a school's curriculum if the subject matter of the group is actually taught, or will soon be taught, in a regularly offered course; if the subject matter of the group concerns the body of courses as a whole; if partici-

pation in the group is required for a particular course, or if participation in the group results in academic credit. We think this limited definition of groups that directly relate to the curriculum is a commonsense interpretation of the Act that is consistent with Congress' intent to provide a low threshold for triggering the Act's requirements.

For example, a French club would directly relate to the curriculum if a school taught French in a regularly offered course or planned to teach the subject in the near future. A school's student government would generally relate directly to the curriculum to the extent that it addresses concerns, solicits opinions, and formulates proposals pertaining to the body of courses offered by the school. If participation in a school's band or orchestra were required for the band or orchestra classes, or resulted in academic credit, then those groups would also directly relate to the curriculum. The existence of such groups at a school would not trigger the Act's obligations.

On the other hand, unless a school could show that groups such as a chess club, a stamp collecting club, or a community service club fell within our description of groups that directly relate to the curriculum, such groups would be "noncurriculum-related student groups" for purposes of the Act. The existence of such groups would create a "limited open forum" under the Act and would prohibit the school from denying equal access to any other student group on the basis of the content of that group's speech. Whether a specific student group is a "noncurriculum-related student group" will therefore depend on a particular school's curriculum, but such determinations would be subject to factual findings well within the competence of trial courts to make. . . .

C

The parties in this case focus on 10 of Westside's approximately 30 voluntary student clubs: Interact (a student club related to Rotary International); Chess; Subsurfers (a club for students interested in scuba diving); National Honor Society; Photography; Welcome to Westside (a club to introduce new students to the school); Future Business Leaders of America; Zonta (the female counterpart to Interact); Student Advisory Board (student government); and Student Forum (student government). Petitioners contend that all of these student activities are curriculum-related because they further the goals of particular aspects of the school's curriculum. . . .

To the extent that petitioners contend that "curriculum related" means anything remotely related to abstract educational goals, however, we reject that argument. To define "curriculum related" in a way that results in almost no schools having limited open fora, or in a way that permits schools to evade the Act by strategically describing existing student groups, would render the Act merely hortatory. . . .

. . . [W]e think it clear that Westside's existing student groups include one or more "noncurriculum related student groups." . . . The record therefore supports a finding that Westside has maintained a limited open forum under the Act.

Although our definition of "noncurriculum related student activities" looks to a school's actual practice rather than its stated policy, we note that our conclusion is also supported by the school's own description of its student activities. . . . The school states that Band "is included in our regular curriculum"; Choir "is a course offered as part of the curriculum"; International Club is "developed through our foreign language classes"; Latin Club is "designed for those students who are taking Latin as a foreign language"; Student Publications "includes classes offered in preparation of the yearbook (Shield) and the student newspaper (Lance)"; Dramatics "is an extension of a regular academic class"; and Orchestra "is an extension of our regular curriculum." These descriptions constitute persuasive evidence that these student clubs directly relate to the curriculum. By inference, however, the fact that the descriptions of student activities such as Subsurfers and chess do not include such references strongly suggests that those clubs do not, by the school's own admission, directly relate to the curriculum. We therefore conclude that Westside permits "one or more noncurriculum related student groups to meet on school premises during noninstructional time." Because Westside maintains a "limited open forum" under the Act, it is prohibited from discriminating, based on the content of the students' speech, against students who wish to meet on school premises during noninstructional time.

The remaining statutory question is whether petitioners' denial of respondents' request to form a religious group constitutes a denial of "equal access" to the school's limited open forum. Although the school apparently permits respondents to meet informally after school, respondents seek equal access in the form of official recognition by the school. Official recognition allows student clubs to be part of the student activities program and carries with it access to the school newspaper, bulletin boards, the public address system, and the annual Club Fair. Given that the Act explicitly prohibits denial of "equal access . . . to . . . any students who wish to conduct a meeting within [the school's] limited open forum" on the basis of the religious content of the speech at such meetings, we hold that Westside's denial of respondents' request to form a Christian club denies them "equal access" under the Act.

Because we rest our conclusion on statutory grounds, we need not decide—and therefore express no opinion on—whether the First Amendment requires the same result.

III

Petitioners contend that even if Westside has created a limited open forum within the meeting of the Act, its denial of official recognition to the proposed Christian club must nevertheless stand because the Act violates the Establishment Clause of the First Amendment, as applied to the States through the Fourteenth Amendment. Specifically, petitioners maintain that because the school's recognized student activities are an integral part of its educational mission, official recognition of respondents' proposed club would effectively incorporate religious activities into the school's official program, endorse participation in the religious club, and provide the club with an official platform to proselytize other students.

We disagree. In *Widmar*, we applied the three-part *Lemon* test to hold that an "equal access" policy, at the university level, does not violate the Establishment Clause. We concluded that "an open-forum policy, including nondiscrimination against religious speech, would have a secular purpose" and would in fact *avoid* entanglement with religion. . . . We also found that although incidental benefits accrued to religious groups who used university facilities, this result did not amount to an establishment of religion. First, we stated that a university's forum does not "confer any imprimatur of state approval on religious sects or practices." Indeed, the message is one of neutrality rather than endorsement; if a State refused to let religious groups use facilities open to others, then it would demonstrate not neutrality but hostility toward religion. "The Establishment Clause does not license government to treat religion and those who teach or practice it, simply by virtue of their status as such, as subversive of American ideals and therefore subject to unique disabilities." Second, we noted that "[t]he [University's] provision of benefits to [a] broad . . . spectrum of groups"— both nonreligious and religious speakers—was "an important index of secular effect."

We think the logic of *Widmar* applies with equal force to the Equal Access Act. As an initial matter, the Act's prohibition of discrimination on the basis of "political, philosophical, or other" speech as well as religious speech is a sufficient basis for meeting the secular purpose prong of the *Lemon* test. . . . Congress' avowed purpose—to prevent discrimination against religious and other types of speech—is undeniably secular. . . . Even if some legislators were motivated by a conviction that religious speech in particular was valuable and worthy of protection, that alone would not invalidate the Act, because what is relevant is the legislative *purpose* of the statute, not the possibly religious *motives* of the legislators who enacted the law. Because the Act on its face grants equal access to both secular and religious speech, we think it clear that the Act's purpose was not to " 'endorse or disapprove of religion.' " . . .

Petitioners' principal contention is that the Act has the primary effect of advancing religion. Specifically, petitioners urge that, because the student religious meetings are held under school aegis, and because the state's compulsory attendance laws bring the students together (and thereby provide a ready-made audience for student evangelists), an objective observer in the position of a secondary school student will perceive official school support for such religious meetings.

We disagree. First, although we have invalidated the use of public funds to pay for teaching state-required subjects at parochial schools, in part because of the risk of creating "a crucial symbolic link between government and religion, thereby enlisting—at least in the eyes of impressionable youngsters—the powers of government to the support of the religious denomination operating the school," there is a crucial difference between *government* speech endorsing religion, which the Establishment Clause forbids, and *private* speech endorsing religion, which the Free Speech and Free Exercise Clauses protect. We think that secondary school students are mature enough and are likely to understand that a school does not endorse or support student speech that it merely permits on a nondiscriminatory basis. . . . The proposition that schools do not endorse everything they fail to censor is not complicated. "[P]articularly in this age of massive media information . . . the few years difference in age between high school and college students [does not] justif[y] departing from *Widmar*." . . .

Second, we note that the Act expressly limits participation by school officials at meetings of student religious groups and that many such meet-ings must be held during "noninstructional time." The Act therefore avoids the problems of "the student's emulation of teachers as role models" and "mandatory attendance requirements." . . . To be sure, the possibility of *student* peer pressure remains, but there is little if any risk of official state endorsement or coercion where no formal classroom activities are involved and no school officials actively participate. Moreover, petitioners' fear of a mistaken inference of endorsement is largely self-imposed, because the school itself has control over any impressions it gives its students. To the extent a school makes clear that its recognition of respondents' proposed club is not an endorsement of the views of the club's participants, students will reasonably understand that the school's official recognition of the club evinces neutrality toward, rather than endorsement of, religious speech.

Third, the broad spectrum of officially recognized student clubs at Westside, and the fact that Westside students are free to initiate and organize additional student clubs . . . counteract any possible message of official endorsement of or preference for religion or a particular religious belief. . . . Under the Act, a school with a limited open forum may not lawfully deny access to a Jewish students' club, a Young Democrats club, or a philosophy club devoted to the study of Nietzsche. To the extent that a religious club is merely one of many different student-initiated voluntary clubs, students should perceive no message of government endorsement of religion. Thus, we conclude that the Act does not, at least on its face and as applied to Westside, have the primary effect of advancing religion.

Petitioners' final argument is that by complying with the Act's requirement, the school risks excessive entanglement between government and religion. The proposed club, petitioners urge, would be required to have a faculty sponsor who would be charged with actively directing the activities of the group, guiding its leaders, and ensuring balance in the presentation of controversial ideas. Petitioners claim that this influence over the club's religious program would entangle the government in day-to-day surveillance of religion of the type forbidden by the Establishment Clause. . . .

Under the Act, however, faculty monitors may not participate in any religious meetings, and nonschool persons may not direct, control, or regularly attend activities of student groups. Moreover, the Act prohibits school "sponsorship" of any religious meetings, which means that school officials may not promote, lead, or participate in any such meeting. Although the Act permits "[t]he assignment of a teacher, administrator, or other school employee to the meeting for custodial purposes," such custodial oversight of the student-initiated religious group merely to ensure order and good behavior, does not impermissibly entangle government in the day-to-day surveillance or administration of religious activities. Indeed, as the Court noted in *Widmar,* a denial of equal access to religious speech might well create greater entanglement problems in the form of invasive monitoring to prevent religious speech at meetings at which such speech might occur.

Accordingly, we hold that the Equal Access Act does not on its face contravene the Establishment Clause. Because we hold that petitioners have violated the Act, we do not decide respondents' claims under the Free Speech and Free Exercise Clauses. For the foregoing reasons, the judgment of the Court of Appeals is affirmed.

It is so ordered.

JUSTICE KENNEDY, *with whom* JUSTICE SCALIA *joins, concurring in part and concurring in the judgment.*

* * *

II

I agree with the plurality [in Part III] that a school complying with the statute by satisfying the criteria in §4071(c) does not violate the Establishment Clause. The accommodation of religion mandated by the Act is a neutral one, and in the context of this case it suffices to inquire whether the Act violates either one of two principles. The first is that the government cannot "give direct benefits to religion in such a degree that it in fact 'establishes a [state] religion or religious faith, or tends to do so.'" Any incidental benefits that accompany official recognition of a religious club under the criteria set forth in the [statute] do not lead to the establishment of religion under this standard. The second principle controlling the case now before us, in my view, is that the government cannot coerce any student to participate in a religious activity. The Act is consistent with this standard as well. Nothing on the face of the Act or in the facts of the case as here presented demonstrate that enforcement of the statute will result in the coercion of any student to participate in a religious activity. . . .

The plurality uses a different test, one which asks whether school officials, by complying with the Act, have endorsed religion. It is true that when government gives permissible assistance to a religion it can be said to have "endorsed" religion; but endorsement cannot be the test. The word *endorsement* has insufficient content to be dispositive. And its literal application may result in neutrality in name but hostility in fact when the question is the government's proper relation to those who express some religious preference.

I should think it inevitable that a public high school "endorses" a religious club, in a common-sense use of the term, if the club happens to be one of many activities that the school permits students to choose in order to further the development of their intellect and character in an extracurricular setting. But no constitutional violation occurs if the school's action is based upon a recognition of the fact that membership in a religious club is one of many permissible ways for a student to further his or her own personal enrichment. The inquiry with respect to coercion must be whether the government imposes pressure upon a student to participate in a religious activity. This inquiry, of course, must be undertaken with sensitivity to the special circumstances that exist in a secondary school where the line between voluntary and coerced participation may be difficult to draw. No such coercion, however, has been shown to exist as a necessary result of this statute, either on its face or as respondents seek to invoke it on the facts of this case.

For these reasons, I join Parts I and II of the Court's opinion, and concur in the judgment.

[The opinion of JUSTICE MARSHALL, with whom JUSTICE BRENNAN joins, concurring in the judgment is not reprinted here.]

JUSTICE STEVENS, *dissenting.*

The dictionary is a necessary, and sometimes sufficient aid to the judge confronted with the task of construing an opaque act of Congress. In a case like this, however, I believe we must probe more deeply to avoid a patently bizarre result. Can Congress really have intended to issue an order to every public high school in the nation stating, in substance, that if you sponsor a chess club, a scuba diving club, or a French club—without having formal classes in those subjects—you must also open your doors to every religious, political, or social organization, no matter how controversial or distasteful its views may be? I think not. A fair review of the legislative history of the Equal Access Act discloses that Congress intended to recognize a much narrower forum than the Court has legislated into existence today. . . .

My construction of the act makes it unnecessary to reach the Establishment Clause question that the Court decides. It is nevertheless appropriate to point out that the question is much more difficult than the Court assumes. The Court focuses upon whether the Act might run afoul of the Establishment Clause because of the danger that some students will mistakenly believe that the student-initiated religious clubs are sponsored by the school. I believe that the majority's construction of the statute obliges it to answer a further question: whether the Act violates the Establishment Clause by authorizing religious organizations to meet on high school grounds even when the high school's teachers and administrators deem it unwise to admit controversial or partisan organizations of any kind.

Under the Court's interpretation of the Act, Congress has imposed a difficult choice on public high schools receiving federal financial assistance. If such a school continues to allow students to participate in such familiar and innocuous activities as a school chess or scuba diving club, it must also allow religious groups to make use of school facilities. Indeed it is hard to see how a cheerleading squad or a pep club, among the most common student groups in American high schools, could avoid being "noncurriculum related" under the majority's test. The Act, as construed by the majority, comes perilously close to an outright command to allow organized prayer, and perhaps the kind of religious ceremonies involved in *Widmar* on school premises.

We have always treated with special sensitivity the Establishment Clause problems that result when religious observances are moved into the public schools. "The public school is at once the symbol of our democracy and the most pervasive means for promoting our common destiny. In no activity of the State is it more vital to keep out divisive forces than in its schools. . . ." As the majority recognizes, student initiated religious groups may exert a considerable degree of pressure even without official school sponsorship. "The law of imitation operates, and nonconformity is not an outstanding characteristic of children." Testimony in this case indicated that one purpose of the proposed Bible Club was to convert students to Christianity. The influence that could result is the product not only of the Equal Access Act and student-initiated speech, but also of the compulsory attendance laws, which we have long recognized to be of special constitutional importance in this context. . . .

I tend to agree with the Court that the Constitution does not forbid a local school district, or Congress, from bringing organized religion into the schools so long as all groups, religious or not, are welcomed equally if "they do not break either the laws or the furniture." That Congress has such authority, however, does not mean that the concerns underlying the Establishment Clause are irrelevant when, and if, that authority is exercised. Certainly we should not rush to embrace the conclusion that Congress swept aside these concerns by the hurried passage of clumsily drafted legislation.

There is an additional reason, also grounded in constitutional structure, why the Court's rendering of the Act is unsatisfying; so construed, the Act alters considerably the balance between state and federal authority over education, a balance long respected by both Congress and this Court. . . . The Court's construction of this Act . . . leads to a sweeping intrusion by the federal government into the operation of our public schools, and does so despite the absence of any indication that Congress intended to divest local school districts of their power to shape the educational environment. If a high school administration continues to believe that it is sound policy to exclude controversial groups, such as political clubs, the Ku Klux Klan, and perhaps gay rights advocacy groups, from its facilities, it now must also close its doors to traditional extracurricular activities that are noncontroversial but not directly related to any course being offered at the school. Congress made frequent reference to the primacy of local control in public education, and the legislative history of the Act is thus inconsistent with the Court's rigid definition of "noncurriculum related groups." Indeed, the very fact that Congress omitted any definition in the statute itself is persuasive evidence of an intent to allow local officials broad discretion in deciding whether or not to create limited public fora. I see no reason—and no evidence of congressional intent—to constrain that discretion any more narrowly than our holding in *Widmar* requires. . . .

I respectfully dissent.

[Initially, three statutes were involved in this litigation: (1) a 1978 statute authorized a one-minute period of silence in all public schools for meditation; (2) a 1981 statute authorized a period of silence for meditation or voluntary prayer; and (3) a 1982 statute which authorized teachers to lead "willing students" in a prescribed prayer to "Almighty God . . . the Creator and Supreme Judge of the world." The District Court found nothing wrong with the 1978 statute and, although finding that the sole purpose of the 1981 and 1982 statutes was to encourage religious activity, upheld their constitutionality because in its view of the Constitution the State of Alabama possessed the power to establish a state religion if it desired to do so. The Court of Appeals reversed and the state appealed to the Supreme Court.]

JUSTICE STEVENS *delivered the opinion of the Court.*

* * *

[T]he narrow question for decision is whether [Alabama's statute] which authorizes a period of silence for "meditation or voluntary prayer" is a law respecting the establishment of religion within the meaning of the First Amendment.

I

Appellee Ishmael Jaffree . . . filed a complaint on behalf of three of his minor children; two of them were second-grade students and the third was then in kindergarten, . . . [alleging] that . . . allowing the maintenance of regular religious prayer services or other forms of religious observances in the Mobile County Public Schools [is] in violation of the First Amendment as made applicable to states by the Fourteenth Amendment to the United States Constitution. The complaint further alleged that two of the children had been subjected to various acts of religious indoctrination "from the beginning of the school year in September, 1981"; that the defendant teachers had "on a daily basis" led their classes in saying certain prayers in unison: that the minor children were exposed to ostracism from their peer group class members if they did not participate; and that Ishmael Jaffree had repeatedly but unsuccessfully requested that the devotional services be stopped. . . .

[At the trial on the merits] the District Court . . . embarked on a fresh examination of the question whether the First Amendment imposes any barrier to the establishment of an official religion by the State of Alabama. After reviewing at length what it perceived to be newly discovered historical evidence, the District Court concluded that "the establishment clause of the first amendment to the United States Constitution does not prohibit the state from establishing a religion," . . . [and] dismissed appellees' challenge to the . . . Alabama statutes . . . [T]he Court of Appeals concluded that [Alabama's] statutes were "specifically the type which the Supreme Court addressed in *Engel v. Vitale* and reversed."

II

Our unanimous affirmance of the Court of Appeals' judgment concerning [the statute] makes it unnecessary to comment at length on the District Court's remarkable conclusion that the Federal Constitution imposes no obstacle to Alabama's establishment of a state religion. Before analyzing the precise issue that is presented to us, it is nevertheless appropriate to recall how firmly embedded in our constitutional jurisprudence is the proposition that the several States have no greater power to restrain the individual freedoms protected by the First Amendment than does the Congress of the United States.

As is plain from its text, the First Amendment was adopted to curtail the power of Congress to interfere with the individual's freedom to believe, to worship, and to express himself in accordance with the dictates of his own conscience. Until the Fourteenth Amendment was added to the Constitution, the First Amendment's restraints on the exercise of federal power simply did not apply to the States. But when the Constitution was amended to prohibit any State from depriving any person of liberty without due process of law, that Amendment imposed the same substantive limitations on the States' power to legislate that the First Amendment had always imposed on the Congress' power. This Court has confirmed and endorsed this elementary proposition of law time and time again. . . .

Just as the right to speak and the right to refrain from speaking are complementary components of a broader concept of individual freedom of mind, so also the individual's freedom to choose his own creed is the counterpart of his right to refrain from accepting the creed established by the majority. At one time it was thought that this right merely proscribed the preference of one Christian sect over another, but would not require equal respect for the conscience of the infidel, the atheist, or the adherent of a non-Christian faith such as Mohammedanism or Judaism. But when the underlying principle has been examined in the crucible of litigation, the Court has unambiguously concluded that the individual freedom of conscience protected by the First Amendment embraces the right to select any religious faith or none at all. This conclusion derives support not only from the interest in respecting the individual's freedom of conscience, but also from the conviction that religious beliefs worthy of respect are the product of free and voluntary choice by the faithful, and from recognition of the fact that the political interest in forestalling intolerance extends beyond intolerance among Christian sects— or even intolerance among "religions"—to encompass intolerance of the disbeliever and the uncertain. As Justice Jackson eloquently stated in *Board of Education* v. *Barnette*, 319 U.S. 624, 642 (1943):

> If there is any fixed star in our constitutional constellation, it is that no official, high or petty, can prescribe what shall be orthodox in politics, nationalism, religion, or other matters of opinion or force citizens to confess by word or act their faith therein.

The State of Alabama, no less than the Congress of the United States, must respect that basic truth.

III

When the Court has been called upon to construe the breadth of the Establishment Clause, it has examined the criteria developed over a period of many years. Thus, in *Lemon* v. *Kurtzman* [supra], 403 U.S. 602, 612–613 (1971), we wrote:

> Every analysis in this area must begin with consideration of the cumulative criteria developed by the Court over many years. Three such tests may be gleaned from our cases. First, the statute must have a secular legislative purpose; second, its principal or primary effect must be one that neither advances nor inhibits religion; . . . finally, the statute must not foster 'an excessive government entanglement with religion.' . . .

It is the first of these three criteria that is most plainly implicated by this case. As the District Court correctly recognized, no consideration of the second or third criteria is necessary if a statute does not have a clearly secular purpose. For even though a statute that is motivated in part by a religious purpose may satisfy the first criterion, . . . the First Amendment requires that a statute must be invalidated if it is entirely motivated by a purpose to advance religion.

In applying the purpose test, it is appropriate to ask "whether government's actual purpose is to endorse or disapprove of religion." In this case, the answer to that question is dispositive. For the record not only provides us with an unambiguous affirmative answer, but it also reveals that the enactment of [the statute] was not motivated by any clearly secular purpose—indeed, the statute had no secular purpose.

IV

The legislative intent to return prayer to the public schools is, of course, quite different from merely protecting every student's right to engage in voluntary prayer during an appropriate moment of silence during the school day. The 1978 statute already protected that right, containing nothing that prevented any student from engaging in voluntary prayer during a silent minute of meditation. Appellants have not identified any secular purpose that was not fully served by [the 1978 statute] before the enactment of [the 1981 statute]. Thus, only two conclusions are consistent with the text of [the latter]: (1) the statute was enacted to convey a message of State endorsement and promotion of prayer, or (2) the statute was enacted for no purpose. No one suggests that the statute was nothing but a meaningless or irrational act.

We must, therefore, conclude that the Alabama Legislature intended to change existing law and . . . for the sole purpose of expressing the State's endorsement of prayer activities for one minute at the beginning of each school day. The addition of "or voluntary prayer" indicates that the State intended to characterize prayer as a favored practice. Such an endorsement is not consistent with the established principle that the Government must pursue a course of complete neutrality toward religion.

The importance of that principle does not permit us to treat this as an inconsequential case involving nothing more than a few words of symbolic speech on behalf of the political majority. For whenever the State itself speaks on a religious subject, one of the questions that we must ask is "whether the Government intends to convey a message of endorsement or disapproval of religion." The well-supported concurrent findings of the District Court and the Court of Appeals—that [the statute] was intended to convey a message of State-approval of prayer activities in the public schools—make it unnecessary, and indeed inappropriate, to evaluate the practical significance of the addition of the words "or voluntary prayer" to the statute. Keeping in mind, as we must, "both the fundamental place held by the Establishment Clause in our constitutional scheme and the myriad, subtle ways in which Establishment Clause values can be eroded," we conclude that [the statute] violates the First Amendment.

The judgment of the Court of Appeals is affirmed.

It is so ordered.

[The concurring opinion of JUSTICE POWELL is not reprinted here.]

JUSTICE O'CONNOR *concurring in the judgment.*

. . . Despite its initial promise, the *Lemon* test has proven problematic. The required inquiry into "entanglement" has been modified and questioned, see *Mueller* v. *Allen* [*supra*], 463 U.S. 388, 403, n. 11 (1983), and in one case we have upheld state action against an Establishment Clause challenge without applying the *Lemon* test at all. *Marsh* v. *Chambers*, 463 U.S. 783 (1983). The author of *Lemon* himself apparently questions the test's general applicability. . . . JUSTICE REHNQUIST today suggests that we abandon *Lemon* entirely, and in the process limit the reach of the Establishment Clause to state discrimination between sects and governmental designation of a particular church as a "state" or "national" one.

Perhaps because I am new to the struggle, I am not ready to abandon all aspects of the *Lemon* test. I do believe, however, that the standards announced in *Lemon* should be reexamined and refined in order to make them more useful in achieving the underlying purpose of the First Amendment. We must strive to do more than erect a constitutional "signpost" . . . to be followed or ignored in a particular case as our predilections dictate. Instead, our goal should be "to frame a principle for constitutional adjudication that is not only grounded in the history and language of the First Amendment, but one that is also capable of consistent application to the relevant problems." Choper, "Religion in the Public Schools: A Proposed Constitutional Standard," 47 *Minn. L. Rev.* 329, 332–333 (1963). Last Term, I proposed a refinement of the *Lemon* test with this goal in mind. *Lynch* v. *Donnelly*. . . .

The *Lynch* concurrence suggested that the religious liberty protected by the Establishment Clause is infringed when the Government makes adherence to religion relevant to a person's standing in the political community. Direct governmental action endorsing religion or a particular religious practice is invalid under this approach because it "sends a message to nonadherents that they are outsiders, not full members of the political community, and an accompanying message to adherents that they are insiders, favored members of the political community." . . . Under this view, *Lemon*'s inquiry as to the purpose and effect of a statute requires courts to examine whether government's purpose is to endorse religion and whether the statute actually conveys a message of endorsement.

The endorsement test is useful because of the analytical content it gives to the *Lemon*-mandated inquiry into legislative purpose and effect. . . . A statute that ostensibly promotes a secular interest often has an incidental or even a primary effect of helping or hindering a sectarian belief. Chaos would ensue if every such statute were invalid under the Establishment Clause. . . . The task for the Court is to sort out those statutes and government practices whose purpose and effect go against the grain of religious liberty protected by the First Amendment.

The endorsement test does not preclude government from acknowledging religion or from taking religion into account in making law and policy. It does preclude government from conveying or attempting to convey a message that religion or a particular religious belief is favored or preferred. Such an endorsement infringes the religious liberty of the nonadherent, for "[w]hen the power, prestige, and financial support of government is placed behind a particular religious belief, the indirect coercive pressure upon religious minorities to conform to the prevailing officially approved religion is plain." *Engel* v. *Vitale*, 370 U.S., at 431. At issue today is whether state moment of silence statutes . . . embody an impermissible endorsement of prayer in public schools.

* * *

II

In his dissenting opinion, JUSTICE REHNQUIST reviews the text and history of the First Amendment religious clauses. His opinion suggests that a long line of this Court's decisions are inconsistent with the intent of the drafters of the Bill of Rights. He urges the Court to correct the historical inaccuracies in its past decisions by embracing a far more restricted interpretation of the Establishment Clause, an interpretation that presumably would permit vocal group prayer in public schools.

. . . In the Federal Government's view [set forth in its amicus brief], a state-sponsored moment of silence is merely an "accommodation" of the desire of some public school children to practice their religion by praying silently. Such an accommodation is contemplated by the First Amendment's guaranty that the Government will not prohibit free exercise of religion. Because the moment of silence implicates free exercise values, the United States suggests that the *Lemon*-mandated inquiry into purpose and effect should be modified. . . .

The element of truth in the United States' argument, I believe, lies in the suggestion that Establishment Clause analysis must comport with the mandate of the Free Exercise Clause that government make no law prohibiting the free exercise of religion. . . . The challenge posed by the United States argument is now to define the proper Establishment Clause limits on voluntary government efforts to facilitate the free exercise of religion. On the one hand, a rigid application of the *Lemon* test would invalidate legislation exempting religious observers from generally applicable government obligations. By definition such legislation has a religious purpose and effect in promoting the free exercise of religion. On the other hand, judicial deference to all legislation that purports to facilitate the free exercise of religion would completely vitiate the Establishment Clause. Any statute pertaining to religion can be viewed as an "accommodation" of free exercise rights. Indeed, the statute at issue in *Lemon* . . . can be viewed as an accommodation of the religious beliefs of parents who choose to send their children to religious schools.

It is obvious that either of the two Religion Clauses, "if expanded to a logical extreme, would tend to clash with the other." *Walz*, 397 U.S., at 668–669. The Court has long exacerbated the conflict by calling for government "neutrality" toward religion. It is difficult to square any notion of "complete neutrality" with the mandate of the Free Exercise Clause that government must sometimes exempt a religious observer from an otherwise generally applicable obligation. A government that confers a benefit on an explicitly religious basis is not neutral toward religion. . . .

The solution to the conflict between the Religion Clauses lies not in "neutrality," but rather in identifying workable limits to the Government's license to promote the free exercise of religion. The text of the Free Exercise Clause speaks of laws that prohibit the free exercise of religion. On its face, the Clause is directed at government interference with Free Exercise Clause values when it lifts a government-imposed burden on the free exercise of religion. If a statute falls within this category, then the standard Establishment Clause test should be modified accordingly. It is disingenuous to look for a purely secular purpose when the manifest objective of a statute is to facilitate the free exercise of religion by lifting a government-imposed burden. Instead, the Court should simply acknowledge that the religious purpose of such a statute is legitimated by the Free Exercise Clause. I would also go further. In assessing the effect of such a statute—that is, in determining whether the statute conveys the message of endorsement of religion or a particular religious belief—courts should assume that the "objective observer" is acquainted with the Free Exercise Clause and the values it promotes. Thus individual perceptions, or resentment that a religious observer is exempted from a particular government requirement, would be entitled to little weight if the Free Exercise Clause strongly supported the exemption. . . .

* * *

III

The Court does not hold that the Establishment Clause is so hostile to religion that it precludes the States from affording school children an opportunity for voluntary silent prayer. To the contrary, the moment of silence statutes of many States should satisfy the Establishment Clause standard we have here applied. The Court holds only that Alabama has intentionally crossed the line between creating a quiet moment during which those so inclined may pray, and affirmatively endorsing the particular religious practice of prayer. This line may be a fine one, but our precedents and the principles of religious liberty require that we draw it. . . .

JUSTICE REHNQUIST, *dissenting*.

[At the outset, JUSTICE REHNQUIST gives a lengthy review of the intention of the framers of the religious liberty clauses of the First Amendment along with the last thirty years of Establishment Clause jurisprudence as a predicate for condemnation of the "wall-of-separation" doctrine and the *Lemon* test.]

It would seem from this evidence that the Establishment Clause of the First Amendment had acquired a well-accepted meaning: it forbade establishment of a national religion, and forbade preference among religious sects or denominations. Indeed, the first American dictionary defined the word "establishment" as "the act of establishing, founding, ratifying or ordaining," such as in "[t]he episcopal form of religion, so called, in England." 1 N. Webster, *American Dictionary of the English Language* (1st ed., 1828). The Establishment Clause did not require government neutrality between religion and irreligion nor did it prohibit the Federal Government from providing nondiscriminatory aid to religion. There is simply no historical foundation for the proposition that the Framers intended to build the "wall of separation" that was constitutionalized in *Everson*.

Notwithstanding the absence of an historical basis for this theory of rigid separation, the wall idea might well have served as a useful albeit misguided analytical concept, had it led this Court to unified and principled results in Establishment Clause cases. The opposite, unfortunately, has been true; in the 38 years since *Everson* our Establishment Clause cases have been neither principled nor unified. Our recent opinions, many of them hopelessly divided pluralities, have with embarrassing candor conceded that the "wall of separation" is merely a "blurred, indistinct, and variable barrier," which "is not wholly accurate" and can only be "dimly perceived."

Whether due to its lack of historical support or its practical unworkability, the *Everson* "wall" has proven all but useless as a guide to sound constitutional adjudication. It illustrates only too well the wisdom of Benjamin Cardozo's observation that "[m]etaphors in law are to be narrowly watched, for starting as devices to liberate thought, they end often by enslaving it." *Berkey* v. *Third Avenue R. Co.*, 244 N.Y. 84, 94, 155 N.E. 58, 61 (1926).

But the greatest injury of the "wall" notion is its mischievous diversion of judges from the actual intentions of the drafters of the Bill of Rights. The "crucible of litigation" is well adapted to adjudicating factual disputes on the basis of testimony presented in court, but no amount of repetition of historical errors in judicial opinions can make the errors true. The "wall of separation between church and state" is a metaphor which has proved useless as a guide to judging. It should be frankly and explicitly abandoned.

The Court has more recently attempted to add some mortar to *Everson*'s wall through the three-part test of *Lemon* v. *Kurtzman*, which served at first to offer a more useful test for purposes of the Establishment Clause than did the "wall" metaphor. . . .

[Inconsistencies in the application of the Establishment Clause to cases continue] because the *Lemon* test has no more grounding in the history of the First Amendment than does the wall theory upon which it rests. The three-part test represents a determined effort to craft a workable rule from a historically faulty doctrine; but the rule can only be as sound as the doctrine it attempts to service. The three-part test has simply not provided adequate standards for deciding Establishment Clause cases, as this Court has slowly come to realize. Even worse, the *Lemon* test has caused this Court to fracture into unworkable plurality opinions, depending upon how each of the three factors applies to a certain state action. The results from our school service cases show the difficulty we have encountered in making the *Lemon* test yield principled results.

For example, a State may lend to parochial school children geography textbooks that contain maps of the United States, but the State may not lend maps of the United States for use in geography class. A State may lend textbooks on American colonial history, but it may not lend a film on George Washington, or a film projector to show it in history class. A State may lend classroom workbooks, but may not lend workbooks in which the parochial school children write, thus rendering them nonreusable. A State may pay for bus transportation to religious schools, but may not pay for bus transportation from the parochial school to the public zoo or natural history museum for a field trip. A State may pay for diagnostic services conducted in the parochial school, but therapeutic services must be given in a different building; speech and hearing "services" conducted by the State inside the sectarian school are forbidden, . . . but the State may conduct speech and hearing diagnostic testing inside the sectarian school. Exceptional parochial school students may receive counseling, but it must take place outside of the parochial school, such as in a trailer parked down the street. A State may give cash to a parochial school to pay for the administration of State-written tests and State-ordered reporting services, but it may not provide funds for teacher-prepared tests on secular subjects. Religious instruction may not be given in public school, but the public school may release students during the day for religion classes elsewhere, and may enforce attendance at those classes with its truancy laws.

These results violate the historically sound principle "that the Establishment Clause does not forbid governments . . . to [provide] general welfare under which benefits are distributed to private individuals, even though many of those individuals may elect to use those benefits in ways that 'aid' religious instruction or worship." . . . It is not surprising in the light of this record that our most recent opinions have expressed doubt on the usefulness of the *Lemon* test. . . .

If a constitutional theory has no basis in the history of the amendment it seeks to interpret, is difficult to apply, and yields unprincipled results, I see little use in it. The "crucible of litigation" has produced only consistent unpredictability, and today's effort is just a continuation of "the Sisyphean task of trying to patch together the 'blurred, indistinct and variable barrier' described in *Lemon* v. *Kurtzman*." . . . We have done much straining since 1947, but still we admit that we can only "dimly perceive" the *Everson* wall. Our perception has been clouded not by the Constitution but by the mists of an unnecessary metaphor.

The true meaning of the Establishment Clause can only be seen in its history. . . . As drafters of our Bill of Rights, the Framers inscribed the principles that control today. Any deviation from their intentions frustrates the permanence of that Charter and will only lead to the type of unprincipled decision making that has plagued our Establishment Clause cases since *Everson*.

The Framers intended the Establishment Clause to prohibit the designation of any church as a "national" one. The Clause was also designed to stop the Federal Government from asserting a preference for one religious denomination or sect over others. Given the "incorporation" of the Establishment Clause as against the States via the Fourteenth Amendment in *Everson*, States are prohibited as well from establishing a religion or discriminating between sects. As its history abundantly shows, however, nothing in the Establishment Clause requires government to be strictly neutral between religion and irreligion, nor does that Clause prohibit Congress or the States from pursuing legitimate secular ends through nondiscriminatory sectarian means.

The Court strikes down the Alabama statute in . . . *Wallace* v. *Jaffree*, because the State wished to "endorse prayer as a favored practice." It would come as much of a shock to those who drafted the Bill of Rights as it will to a large number of thoughtful Americans today to learn that the Constitution as construed by the majority, prohibits the Alabama Legislature from "endorsing" prayer. George Washington himself, at the request of the very Congress which passed the Bill of Rights, proclaimed a day of "public thanksgiving and prayer, to be observed by acknowledging with grateful hearts the many and signal favors of Almighty God." History must judge whether it was the father of his country in 1789, or a majority of the Court today, which has strayed from the meaning of the Establishment Clause. . . .

EDWARDS v. AGUILLARD
476 U.S. 1103; 96 L. Ed. 2d 510; 107 S. Ct. 2573 (1987)

JUSTICE BRENNAN *delivered the opinion of the Court.*

The question for decision is whether Louisiana's "Balanced Treatment for Creation-Science and Evolution-Science in Public School Instruction" Act (Creationism Act) is facially invalid as violative of the Establishment Clause of the First Amendment.

I

The Creationism Act forbids the teaching of the theory of evolution in public schools unless accompanied by instruction in "creation science." No school is required to teach evolution or creation science. If either is taught, however, the other must also be taught. The theories of evolution and creation science are statutorily defined as "the scientific evidences for [creation or evolution] and inferences from those scientific evidences."

Appellees, who include parents of children attending Louisiana public schools, Louisiana teachers, and religious leaders, challenged the constitutionality of the Act in District Court, seeking an injunction and declaratory relief. Appellants, Louisiana officials charged with implementing the Act, defended on the ground that the purpose of the Act is to protect a legitimate secular interest, namely, academic freedom. Appellees attacked the

Act as facially invalid because it violated the Establishment Clause and made a motion for summary judgment. The District Court granted the motion. The court held that there can be no valid secular reason for prohibiting the teaching of evolution, a theory historically opposed by some religious denominations. The court further concluded that "the teaching of 'creation-science' and 'creationism,' as contemplated by the statute, involves teaching 'tailored to the principles' of a particular religious sect or group of sects." The District Court therefore held that the Creationism Act violated the Establishment Clause either because it prohibited the teaching of evolution or because it required the teaching of creation science with the purpose of advancing a particular religious doctrine.

The Court of Appeals affirmed. The court observed that the statute's avowed purpose of protecting academic freedom was inconsistent with requiring, upon risk of sanction, the teaching of creation science whenever evolution is taught. The court found that the Louisiana Legislature's actual intent was "to discredit evolution by counterbalancing its teaching at every turn with the teaching of creationism, a religious belief." Because the Creationism Act was thus a law furthering a particular religious belief, the Court of Appeals held that the Act violated the Establishment Clause. . . .

* * *

II

In this case, the Court must determine whether the Establishment Clause was violated in the special context of the public elementary and secondary school system. States and local school boards are generally afforded considerable discretion in operating public schools. "At the same time . . . we have necessarily recognized that the discretion of the States and local school boards in matters of education must be exercised in a manner that comports with the transcendent imperatives of the First Amendment."

The Court has been particularly vigilant in monitoring compliance with the Establishment Clause in elementary and secondary schools. Families entrust public schools with the education of their children, but condition their trust on the understanding that the classroom will not purposely be used to advance religious views that may conflict with the private beliefs of the student and his or her family. Students in such institutions are impressionable, and their attendance is involuntary.

The State exerts great authority and coercive power through mandatory attendance requirements, and because of the students' emulation of teachers as role models and the children's susceptibility to peer pressure. Furthermore, "[t]he public school is at once the symbol of our democracy and the most pervasive means for promoting our common destiny. In no activity of the State is it more vital to keep out divisive forces than in its schools. . . ."

. . . [I]n employing the three-pronged *Lemon* test, we must do so mindful of the particular concerns that arise in the context of public elementary and secondary schools. We now turn to the evaluation of the Act under the *Lemon* test.

III

Lemon's first prong focuses on the purpose that animated adoption of the Act. "The purpose prong of the *Lemon* test asks whether government's actual purpose is to endorse or disapprove of religion." A governmental intention to promote religion is clear when the State enacts a law to serve a religious purpose. This intention may be evidenced by promotion of religion in general, . . . or by advancement of a particular religious belief. . . . If the law was enacted for the purpose of endorsing religion, "no consideration of the second or third criteria [of *Lemon*] is necessary." In this case, the petitioners have identified no clear secular purpose for the Louisiana Act.

True, the Act's stated purpose is to protect academic freedom. This phrase might, in common parlance, be understood as referring to enhancing the freedom of teachers to teach what they will. The Court of Appeals, however, correctly concluded that the Act was not designed to further that goal. We find no merit in the State's argument that the "legislature may not [have] use[d] the terms 'academic freedom' in the correct legal sense. They might have [had] in mind, instead, a basic concept of fairness; teaching all of the evidence." Even if "academic freedom" is read to mean "teaching all of the evidence" with respect to the origin of human beings, the Act does not further this purpose. The goal of providing a more comprehensive science curriculum is not furthered either by outlawing the teaching of evolution or by requiring the teaching of creation science.

A

While the Court is normally deferential to a State's articulation of a secular purpose, it is required that the statement of such purpose be sincere and not a sham. As JUSTICE O'CONNOR stated in *Wallace* [v. *Jaffree*]: "It is not a trivial matter, however, to require that the legislature manifest a secular purpose and omit all sectarian endorsements from its laws. That requirement is precisely tailored to the Establishment Clause's purpose of assuring that Government not intentionally endorse religion or a religious practice."

It is clear from the legislative history that the purpose of the legislative sponsor, Senator Bill Keith, was to narrow the science curriculum. During the legislative hearings, Senator Keith stated: "My preference would be that neither [creationism nor evolution] be taught." Such a ban on teaching does not promote—indeed, it undermines—the provision of a comprehensive scientific education.

It is equally clear that requiring schools to teach creation science with evolution does not advance academic freedom. The Act does not grant teachers a flexibility that they did not already possess to supplant the present science curriculum with the presentation of theories, besides evolution, about the origin of life. Indeed, the Court of Appeals found that no law prohibited Louisiana public schoolteachers from teaching any scientific theory.

. . . [T]he goal of basic "fairness" is hardly furthered by the Act's discriminatory preference for the teaching of creation science and against the teaching of evolution. While requiring that curriculum guides be developed for creation science, the Act says nothing of comparable guides for evolution. Similarly, research services are supplied for creation science but not for evolution. Only "creation scientists" can serve on the panel that supplies the resource services. The Act forbids school boards to discriminate against anyone who "chooses to be a creation-scientist" or to teach "creationism," but fails to protect those who choose to teach evolution or any other noncreation science theory, or who refuse to teach creation science.

If the Louisiana Legislature's purpose was solely to maximize the comprehensiveness and effectiveness of science instruction, it would have encouraged the teaching of all scientific theories about the origins of humankind. But under the Act's requirements, teachers who were once free to teach any and all facets of this subject are now unable to do so. Moreover, the Act fails even to ensure that creation science will be taught, but instead requires the teaching of this theory only when the theory of evolution is taught. Thus we agree with the Court of Appeals' conclusion that the Act does not serve to protect academic freedom, but has the distinctly different purpose of discrediting "evolution by counterbalancing its teaching at every turn with the teaching of creation science. . . ."

B

* * *

. . . The preeminent purpose of the Louisiana Legislature was clearly to advance the religious viewpoint that a supernatural being created humankind. The term "creation science" was defined as embracing this particular religious doctrine by those responsible for the passage of the Creationism Act. Senator Keith's leading expert on creation science, Edward Boudreaux, testified at the legislative hearings that the theory of creation science included belief in the existence of a supernatural creator. Senator Keith also cited testimony from other experts to support the creation-science view that "a creator [was] responsible for the universe and everything in it." The legislative history therefore reveals that the term "creation science," as contemplated by the legislature that adopted this Act, embodies the religious belief that a supernatural creator was responsible for the creation of humankind.

Furthermore, it is not happenstance that the legislature required the teaching of a theory that coincided with this religious view. The legislative history documents that the Act's primary purpose was to change the science curriculum of public schools in order to provide persuasive advantage to a particular religious doctrine that rejects the factual basis of evolution in its entirety. The sponsor of the Creationism Act . . . explained during the legislative hearings that his disdain for the theory of evolution resulted from the support that evolution supplied to views contrary to his own religious beliefs. According to [him], the theory of evolution was consonant with the "cardinal principle[s] of religious humanism, secular humanism, theological liberalism, aetheistism [*sic*]." The state senator repeatedly stated that scientific evidence supporting his religious views should be included in the public school curriculum to redress the fact that the theory of evolution incidentally coincided with what he characterized as religious beliefs antithetical to his own. The legislation therefore sought to alter the science curriculum to reflect endorsement of a religious view that is antagonistic to the theory of evolution.

In this case, the purpose of the Creationism Act was to restructure the science curriculum to conform with a particular religious viewpoint. Out of many possible science subjects taught in the public schools, the legislature chose to affect the teaching of the one scientific theory that historically has been opposed by certain religious sects. As in *Epperson*, the legislature passed the Act to give preference to those religious groups which have as one of their tenets the creation of humankind by a divine creator. The "overriding fact" that confronted the Court in *Epperson* was "that Arkansas' law selects from the body of knowledge a particular segment which it proscribes for the sole reason that it is deemed to conflict with . . . a particular interpretation of the Book of Genesis by a particular religious group." Similarly, the Creationism Act is designed *either* to promote the theory of creation science which embodies a particular religious tenet by requiring that creation science be taught whenever evolution is taught *or* to prohibit the teaching of a scientific theory disfavored by certain religious sects by forbidding the teaching of evolution when creation science is not also taught. The Establishment Clause, however, "forbids *alike* the preference of a religious doctrine *or* the prohibition of theory which is deemed antagonistic to a particular dogma" (emphasis added). Because the primary purpose of the Creationism Act is to advance a particular religious belief, the Act endorses religion in violation of the First Amendment. . . .

V

The Louisiana Creationism Act advances a religious doctrine by requiring either the banishment of the theory of evolution from public school classrooms or the presentation of a religious viewpoint that rejects evolution in its entirety. The Act violates the Establishment Clause of the First Amendment because it seeks to employ the symbolic and financial support of government to achieve a religious purpose. The judgment of the Court of Appeals therefore is

Affirmed.

[The concurring opinion of JUSTICE POWELL, with whom JUSTICE O'CONNOR joins, is not reprinted here.]

[The concurring opinion of JUSTICE WHITE is not reprinted here.]

JUSTICE SCALIA, *with whom* THE CHIEF JUSTICE *joins, dissenting.*

Even if I agreed with the questionable premise that legislation can be invalidated under the Establishment Clause on the basis of its motivation alone, without regard to its effects, I would still find no justification for today's decision. The Louisiana legislators who passed the "Balanced Treatment for Creation-Science and Evolution-Science Act," each of whom had sworn to support the Constitution, were well aware of the potential Establishment Clause problems and considered that aspect of the legislation with great care. After seven hearings and several months of study, resulting in substantial revision of the original proposal, they approved the Act overwhelmingly and specifically articulated the secular purpose they meant it to serve. Although the record contains abundant evidence of the sincerity of that purpose (the only issue pertinent to this case), the Court today holds, essentially on the basis of "its visceral knowledge regarding what *must* have motivated the legislators," that the members of the Louisiana Legislature knowingly violated their oaths and then lied about it. I dissent. Had requirements of the Balanced Treatment Act that are not apparent on its face been clarified by an interpretation of the Louisiana Supreme Court, or by the manner of its implementation, the Act might well be found unconstitutional; but the question of its constitutionality cannot rightly be disposed of on the gallop by impugning the motives of its supporters. . . .

* * *

I

This Court has said little about the first component of the *Lemon* test. Almost invariably, we have effortlessly discovered a secular purpose for measures challenged under the Establishment Clause, typically devoting no more than a sentence or two to the matter. . . .

Nevertheless, a few principles have emerged from our cases, principles which should, but to an unfortunately large extent do not, guide the Court's application of *Lemon* today. It is clear, first of all, that regardless of what "legislative purpose" may mean in other contexts, for the purpose of the *Lemon* test it means the "actual" motives of those responsible for the challenged action. . . . Thus, if those legislators who supported the Balanced Treatment Act *in fact* acted with a "sincere" secular purpose, the Act survives the first component of the *Lemon* test, regardless of whether that purpose is likely to be achieved by the provisions they enacted.

Our cases have also confirmed that when the *Lemon* Court referred to "a secular . . . purpose," it meant "a secular purpose." The author of *Lemon*, writing for the Court, has said that invalidation under the purpose prong is appropriate when "there [is] *no question* that the statute or activity was motivated *wholly* by religious considerations." In . . . cases in which we struck down laws under the Establishment Clause for lack of a secular purpose, we found that the legislature's sole motive was to promote religion. . . . Thus, the majority's invalidation of the Balanced Treatment Act is defensible only if the record indicates that the Louisiana Legislature had no secular purpose.

It is important to stress that the purpose forbidden by *Lemon* is the purpose to "advance religion." . . . Our cases in no way imply that the Establishment Clause forbids legislators merely to act upon their religious convictions. We surely would not strike down a law providing money to feed the hungry or shelter the homeless if it could be demonstrated that, but for the religious beliefs of the legislators, the funds would not have been approved. Also, political activism by the religiously motivated is part of our heritage. Notwithstanding the majority's implication to the contrary, we do not presume that the sole purpose of a law is to advance religion merely because it was supported strongly by organized religions or by adherents of particular faiths. To do so would deprive religious men and women of their right to participate in the political process. Today's religious activism may give us the Balanced Treatment Act, but yesterday's resulted in the abolition of slavery, and tomorrow's may bring relief for famine victims.

Similarly, we will not presume that a law's purpose is to advance religion merely because it " 'happens to coincide or harmonize with the tenets of some or all religions,' " or because it benefits religion, even substantially. We have, for example, turned back Establishment Clause challenges to restrictions on abortion funding, and to Sunday closing laws, despite the fact that both "agre[e] with the dictates of [some] Judaeo-Christian religions." "In many instances, the Congress or state legislatures conclude that the general welfare of society, wholly apart from any religious considerations, demands such regulation." On many past occasions we have had no difficulty finding a secular purpose for governmental action far more likely to advance religion than the Balanced Treatment Act. . . .

Finally, our cases indicate that even certain kinds of governmental actions undertaken with the specific intention of improving the position of religion do not "advance religion" as that term is used in *Lemon*. Rather, we have said that in at least two circumstances government *must* act to advance religion, and that in a third it *may* do so.

First, since we have consistently described the Establishment Clause as forbidding not only state action motivated by the desire to *advance* religion, but also that intended to "disapprove," "inhibit," or evince "hostility" toward religion, . . . and since we have said that governmental "neutrality" toward religion is the preeminent goal of the First Amendment, a State which discovers that its employees are inhibiting religion must take steps to prevent them from doing so, even though its purpose would clearly be to advance religion. Thus, if the Louisiana Legislature sincerely believed that the State's science teachers were being hostile to religion, our cases indicate that it could act to eliminate that hostility without running afoul of *Lemon's* purpose test.

Second, we have held that intentional governmental advancement of religion is sometimes required by the Free Exercise Clause. For example in *Hobbie* v. *Unemployment Appeals Comm'n of Fla.*, 480 U.S. 136 (1987) [and in] *Thomas* v. *Review Bd., Indiana Employment Security Div.*, 450 U.S. 707 (1981) . . . we held that in some circumstances States must accommodate the beliefs of religious citizens by exempting them from generally applicable regulations. We have not yet come close to reconciling *Lemon* and our Free Exercise cases, and typically we do not really try. . . . It is clear, however, that members of the Louisiana Legislature were not impermissibly motivated for purpose of the *Lemon* test if they believed that approval of the Balanced Treatment Act was *required* by the Free Exercise Clause.

We have also held that in some circumstances government may act to accommodate religion, even if that action is not required by the First Amendment. It is well established that "[t]he limits of permissible state accommodation to religion are by no means co-extensive with the noninterference mandated by the Free Exercise Clause." We have implied that voluntary governmental accommodation of religion is not only permissible, but desirable. Thus, few would contend that Title VII of the Civil Rights Act of 1964, which both forbids religious discrimination by private-sector employers, and requires them reasonably to accommodate the religious practices of their employees, violates the Establishment Clause, even though its "purpose" is, of course, to advance religion, and even though it is almost certainly not required by the Free Exercise Clause. While we have warned that at some point, accommodation may devolve into "an unlawful fostering of religion," we have not suggested precisely (or even roughly) where that point might be. It is possible, then, that even if the sole motive of those voting for the Balanced Treatment Act was to advance religion, and its passage was not actually required or even believed to be required by either the Free Exercise or Establishment Clauses, the Act would nonetheless survive scrutiny under *Lemon*'s purpose test.

One final observation about the application of that test: Although the Court's opinion gives no hint of it, in the past we have repeatedly affirmed "our reluctance to attribute unconstitutional motives to the States." We "presume that legislatures act in a constitutional manner." Whenever we are called upon to judge the constitutionality of an act of a state legislature, "we must have 'due regard to the fact that this Court is not exercising a primary judgment but is sitting in judgment upon those who also have taken the oath to observe the Constitution and who have the responsibility for carrying on government.' "

With the foregoing in mind, I now turn to the purposes underlying adoption of the Balanced Treatment Act.

II

A

We have relatively little information upon which to judge the motives of those who supported the Act. About the only direct evidence is the statute itself and transcripts of the seven committee hearings at which it was considered. Unfortunately, several of those hearings were sparsely attended, and the legislators who were present revealed little about their motives. We have no committee reports, no floor debates, no remarks inserted into the legislative history, no statement from the Governor, and no postenactment statements or testimony from the bill's sponsor or any other legislators. Nevertheless, there is ample evidence that the majority is wrong in holding that the Balanced Treatment Act is without secular purpose.

At the outset, it is important to note that the Balanced Treatment Act did not fly through the Louisiana Legislature on wings of fundamentalist religious fervor—which would be unlikely, in any event, since only a small minority of the State's citizens belong to fundamentalist religious denominations. . . . The Act had its genesis (so to speak) in legislation introduced by Senator Bill Keith in June 1980. After two hearings before the Senate Committee on Education, Senator Keith asked that his bill be referred to a study commission composed of members of both houses of the Louisiana Legislature. He expressed hope that the joint committee would give the bill careful consideration and determine whether his arguments were "legitimate." . . . [Here follows a brief discussion of the legislative history of the Act.]

B

Even with nothing more than this legislative history to go on, I think it would be extraordinary to invalidate the Balanced Treatment Act for lack of a valid secular purpose. Striking down a law approved by the democratically elected representatives of the people is no minor matter. "The cardinal principle of statutory construction is to save and not to destroy. We have repeatedly held that as between two possible interpretations of a statute, by one of which it would be unconstitutional and by the other valid, our plain duty is to adopt that which will save the act." . . . So, too, it seems to me, with discerning statutory purpose. Even if the legislative history were silent or ambiguous about the existence of a secular purpose—and here it is not—the statute should survive *Lemon*'s purpose test. But even more validation than mere legislative history is present here. The Louisiana Legislature explicitly set forth its secular purpose ("protecting academic freedom") in the very text of the Act. We have in the past repeatedly relied upon or deferred to such expressions. . . .

The Court seeks to evade the force of this expression of purpose by stubbornly misinterpreting it, and then finding that the provisions of the Act do not advance that misinterpreted purpose, thereby showing it to be a sham. The Court first surmises that "academic freedom" means "enhancing the freedom of teachers to teach what they will," even though "academic freedom" in that sense has little scope in the structured elementary and secondary curriculums with which the Act is concerned. Alternatively, the Court suggests that it might mean "maximiz[ing] the comprehensiveness and effectiveness of science instruction," though that is an exceeding strange interpretation of the words, and one that is refuted on the very face of the statute. Had the Court devoted to this central question of the meaning of the legislatively expressed purpose a small fraction of the research into legislative history that produced its quotations of religiously motivated statements by individual legislators, it would have discerned quite readily what "academic freedom" meant: *student's* freedom from *indoctrination*. The legislature wanted to ensure that students would be free to decide for themselves how life began, based upon a fair and balanced presentation of the scientific evidence—

that is, to protect "the right of each [student] voluntarily to determine what to believe (and what not to believe) free of any coercive pressures from the State." The legislature did not care *whether* the topic of origins was taught; it simply wished to ensure that *when* the topic was taught, students would receive " 'all of the evidence.' "

As originally introduced, the "purpose" section of the Balanced Treatment Act read: "This Chapter is enacted for the purposes of protecting academic freedom . . . *of students* . . . and assisting *students* in their search for truth." . . .

If one adopts the obviously intended meaning of the statutory terms "academic freedom," there is no basis whatever for concluding that the purpose they express is a "sham." To the contrary, the Act pursues that purpose plainly and consistently. It requires that, whenever the subject of origins is covered, evolution be "taught as a theory, rather than as proven scientific fact" and that scientific evidence inconsistent with the theory of evolution (viz., "creation science") be taught as well. Living up to its title of "Balanced Treatment for Creation-Science and Evolution-Science Act," it treats the teaching of creation the same way. It does *not* mandate instruction in creation science; [the Act] *forbids* teachers to present creation science "as proven scientific fact," . . . and bans the teaching of creation science unless the theory is (to use the Court's terminology) "discredit[ed] ' . . . at every turn' " with the teaching of evolution. It surpasses understanding how the Court can see in this a purpose "to restructure the science curriculum to conform with a particular religious viewpoint," "to provide a persuasive advantage to a particular religious doctrine," "to promote the theory of creation science which embodies a particular religious tenet," and "to endorse a particular religious doctrine."

The Act's reference to "creation" is not convincing evidence of religious purpose. . . . We have no basis on the record to conclude that creation science need be anything other than a collection of scientific data supporting the theory that life abruptly appeared on earth. Creation science, its proponents insist, no more must explain *whence* life came than evolution must explain whence came the inanimate materials from which it says life evolved. But even if that were not so, to posit a past creator is not to posit the eternal and personal God who is the object of religious veneration. Indeed, it is not even to posit the *"unmoved mover"* hypothesized by Aristotle and other notably nonfundamentalist philosophers. . . .

The legislative history gives ample evidence of

the sincerity of the Balanced Treatment Act's articulated purpose. Witness after witness urged the legislators to support the Act so that students would not be "indoctrinated" but would instead be free to decide for themselves, based upon a fair presentation of the scientific evidence, about the origin of life. . . .

Legislators other than Senator Keith made only a few statements providing insight into their motives, but those statements cast no doubt upon the sincerity of the Act's articulated purpose. The legislators were concerned primarily about the manner in which the subject of origins was presented in Louisiana schools—specifically, about whether scientifically valuable information was being censored and students misled about evolution. . . .

It is undoubtedly true that what prompted the legislature to direct its attention to the misrepresentation of evolution in the schools (rather than the inaccurate presentation of other topics) was its awareness of the tension between evolution and the religious beliefs of many children. But even appellees concede that a valid secular purpose is not rendered impermissible simply because its pursuit is prompted by concern for religious sensitivities. If a history teacher falsely told her students that the bones of Jesus Christ had been discovered, or a physics teacher that the Shroud of Turin had been conclusively established to be inexplicable on the bases of natural causes, I cannot believe (despite the majority's implication to the contrary) that legislators or school board members would be constitutionally prohibited from taking corrective action, simply because that action was prompted by concern for the religious beliefs of the misinstructed students.

In sum, even if one concedes, for the sake of argument, that a majority of the Louisiana Legislature voted for the Balanced Treatment Act partly in order to foster (rather than merely eliminate discrimination against) Christian fundamentalist beliefs, our cases establish that that alone would not suffice to invalidate the Act, so long as there was a genuine secular purpose as well. We have, moreover, no adequate basis for disbelieving the secular purpose set forth in the Act itself, or for concluding that it is a sham enacted to conceal the legislators' violation of their oaths of office. I am astonished by the Court's unprecedented readiness to reach such a conclusion, which I can only attribute to an intellectual predisposition created by the facts and the legend of *Scopes* v. *State*, 154 Tenn. 105, 289 S.W. 363 (1927)—an instinctive reaction that any governmentally imposed requirements bearing upon the teaching of evolution must be a manifestation of Christian fundamentalist repression. In this case, however, it seems to me the Court's position is the repressive one. The people of Louisiana, including those who are Christian fundamentalists, are quite entitled as a secular matter, to have whatever scientific evidence there may be against evolution presented in their schools, just as Mr. Scopes was entitled to present whatever scientific evidence there was for it. Perhaps what the Louisiana Legislature has done is unconstitutional because there *is* no such evidence, and the scheme they have established will amount to no more than a presentation of the Book of Genesis. But we cannot say that on the evidence before us in this summary judgment context, which includes ample uncontradicted testimony that "creation science" is a body of scientific knowledge rather than revealed belief. *Infinitely less* can we say (or should we say) that the scientific evidence for evolution is so conclusive that no one could be gullible enough to believe that there is any real scientific evidence to the contrary, so that the legislation's stated purpose must be a lie. Yet that liberal judgment, that *Scopes*-in-reverse, is ultimately the basis on which the Court's facile rejection of the Louisiana Legislature's purpose must rest. . . .

Because I believe that the Balanced Treatment Act had a secular purpose, which is all the first component of the *Lemon* test requires, I would reverse the judgment of the Court of Appeals and remand for further consideration.

III

I have to this point assumed the validity of the *Lemon* "purpose" test. In fact, however, I think the pessimistic evaluation that THE CHIEF JUSTICE made of the totality of *Lemon* is particularly applicable to the "purpose" prong: it is "a constitutional theory [that] has no basis in the history of the amendment it seeks to interpret, is difficult to apply and yields unprincipled results." *Wallace* v. *Jaffree*, 472 U.S., at 112, 105 S. Ct., at 2519 (REHNQUIST, J., dissenting).

Our cases interpreting and applying the purpose test have made such a maze of the Establishment Clause that even the most conscientious governmental officials can only guess what motives will be held unconstitutional. We have said essentially the following: Government may not act with the purpose of advancing religion, except when forced to do so by the Free Exercise Clause (which is now and then); or when eliminating existing governmental hostility to religion (which exists sometimes); or even when merely accommo-

dating governmentally uninhibited religious practices, except that at some point (it is unclear where) intentional accommodation results in the fostering of religion, which is of course unconstitutional.

But the difficulty of knowing what vitiating purpose one is looking for is as nothing compared with the difficulty of knowing how or where to find it. For while it is possible to discern the objective "purpose" of a statute (i.e., the public good at which its provisions appear to be directed), or even the formal motivation for a statute where that is explicitly set forth (as it was, to no avail, here), discerning the subjective motivation of those enacting the statute is, to be honest, almost always an impossible task. The number of possible motivations, to begin with, is not binary, or indeed even finite. In the present case, for example, a particular legislator need not have voted for the Act either because he wanted to foster religion or because he wanted to improve education. He may have thought the bill would provide jobs for his district, or may have wanted to make amends with a faction of his party he had alienated on another vote, or he may have been a close friend of the bill's sponsor, or he may have been repaying a favor he owed the Majority Leader, or he may have hoped the Governor would appreciate his vote and make a fund-raising appearance for him, or he may have been pressured to vote for a bill he disliked by a wealthy contributor or by a flood of constituent mail, or he may have been seeking favorable publicity, or he may have been reluctant to hurt the feelings of a loyal staff member who worked on the bill, or he may have been settling an old score with a legislator who opposed the bill, or he may have been mad at his wife who opposed the bill, or he may have been intoxicated and utterly *un*motivated when the vote was called, or he may have accidentally voted "yes" instead of "no," or, of course, he may have had (and very likely did have) a combination of some of the above and many other motivations. To look for *the sole purpose* of even a single legislator is probably to look for something that does not exist.

Putting that problem aside, however, where ought we to look for the individual legislator's purpose? We cannot of course assume that every member present (if, as is unlikely, we know who or even how many they were) agreed with the motivation expressed in a particular legislator's pre-enactment floor or committee statement. Quite obviously, "[w]hat motivates one legislator to make a speech about a statute is not necessarily what motivates scores of other to enact it." *United States* v.

O'Brien, 391 U.S. 367, 384; 10 L. Ed. 2d 672; 88 S. Ct. 1673, 1683 (1968). Can we assume, then, that they all agree with the motivation expressed in the staff-prepared committee reports they might have read—even though we are unwilling to assume that they agreed with the motivation expressed in the very statute that they voted for? Should we consider postenactment floor statements? Or postenactment testimony from legislators, obtained expressly for the lawsuit? Should we consider media reports on the realities of the legislative bargaining? All of these sources, of course, are eminently manipulable. Legislative histories can be contrived and sanitized, favorable media coverage orchestrated, and postenactment recollections conveniently distorted. Perhaps most valuable of all would be more objective indications—for example, evidence regarding the individual legislator's religious affiliations. And if that, why not evidence regarding the fervor or tepidity of their beliefs?

Having achieved, through these simple means, an assessment of what individual legislators intended, we must still confront the question (yet to be addressed in any of our cases) of how *many* of them must have the invalidating intent. If a state senate approves a bill by vote of 26 to 25, and only one of the 26 intended solely to advance religion, is the law unconstitutional? What if 13 of the 26 had that intent? What if 3 of the 26 had the impermissible intent, but 3 of the 25 voting against the bill were motivated by religious hostility or were simply attempting to "balance" the votes of their impermissibly motivated colleagues? Or is it possible that the intent of the bill's sponsor is alone enough to invalidate it—on a theory, perhaps, that even though everyone else's intent was pure, what they produced was the fruit of a forbidden tree?

Because there are no good answers to these questions, this Court has recognized from Chief Justice Marshall, that determining the subjective intent of legislators is a perilous enterprise. It is perilous, I might note, not just for the judges who will very likely reach the wrong result, but also for the legislators who find that they must assess the validity of proposed legislation—and risk the condemnation of having voted for an unconstitutional measure—not on the basis of what the legislation contains, nor even on the basis of what they themselves intend, but on the basis of what *others* have in mind.

Given the many hazards involved in assessing the subjective intent of governmental decision makers, the first prong of *Lemon* is defensible, I think, only if the text of the Establishment Clause demands it. That is surely not the case. The Clause states that "Congress shall make no law respecting an establishment of religion." One could argue, I suppose, that any time Congress acts with the *intent* of advancing religion, it has enacted a "law respecting an establishment of religion"; but far from being an unavoidable reading, it is quite an unnatural one. I doubt, for example, that the Clayton Act could reasonably be described as a "law respecting an establishment of religion" if bizarre new historical evidence revealed that it lacked a secular purpose, even though it has no discernible nonsecular effect. It is, in short, far from an inevitable reading of the Establishment Clause that it forbids all governmental action intended to advance religion; and if not inevitable, any reading with such untoward consequences must be wrong.

In the past we have attempted to justify our embarrassing Establishment Clause jurisprudence on the ground that it "sacrifices clarity and predictability for flexibility." One commentator has aptly characterized this as "a euphemism . . . for . . . the absence of any principled rationale." Choper, *supra*, n. 7, at 681. I think it time that we sacrifice some "flexibility" for "clarity and predictability." Abandoning *Lemon*'s purpose test—a test which exacerbates the tension between the Free Exercise and Establishment Clauses, has no basis in the language or history of the Amendment, and, as today's decision shows, has wonderfully flexible consequences—would be a good place to start.

LEE v. WEISMAN
___ U.S. ___; ___ L. Ed. 2d ___; 112 S. Ct. 2649 (1992)

JUSTICE KENNEDY, *delivered the opinion of the Court.*

School principals in the public school system of the city of Providence, Rhode Island, are permitted to invite members of the clergy to offer invocation and benediction prayers as part of the formal graduation ceremonies for middle schools and for high schools. The question before us is whether including clerical members who offer prayers as part of the official school graduation ceremony is consistent with the Religion Clauses of the First Amendment, provisions the Fourteenth Amendment makes applicable with full force to the States and their school districts.

I

A

Deborah Weisman graduated from Nathan Bishop Middle School, a public school in Providence, at a formal ceremony in June 1989. She was about 14 years old. For many years it has been the policy of the Providence School Committee and the Superintendent of Schools to permit principals to invite members of the clergy to give invocations and benedictions at middle school and high school graduations. Many, but not all, of the principals elected to include prayers as part of the graduation ceremonies. Acting for himself and his daughter, Deborah's father, Daniel Weisman, objected to any prayers at Deborah's middle school graduation, but to no avail. The school principal, petitioner Robert E. Lee, invited a rabbi to deliver prayers at the graduation exercises for Deborah's class. . . .

It has been the custom of Providence school officials to provide invited clergy with a pamphlet entitled "Guidelines for Civic Occasions," prepared by the National Conference of Christians and Jews. The Guidelines recommend that public prayers at nonsectarian civic ceremonies be composed with "inclusiveness and sensitivity," though they acknowledge that "[p]rayer of any kind may be inappropriate on some civic occasions." The principal gave Rabbi Gutterman the pamphlet before the graduation and advised him the invocation and benediction should be nonsectarian.

Rabbi Gutterman's prayers were as follows:

"INVOCATION

"God of the Free, Hope of the Brave:
"For the legacy of America where diversity is celebrated and the rights of minorities are protected, we thank You. May these young men and women grow up to enrich it.
"For the liberty of America, we thank You. May these new graduates grow up to guard it.
"For the political process of America in which all its citizens may participate, for its court system where all may seek justice we thank You. May those we honor this morning always turn to it in trust.
"For the destiny of America we thank You. May the

graduates of Nathan Bishop Middle School so live that they might help to share it.
"May our aspirations for our country and for these young people, who are our hope for the future, be richly fulfilled.
AMEN"

"BENEDICTION

"O God, we are grateful to You for having endowed us with the capacity for learning which we have celebrated on this joyous commencement.
"Happy families give thanks for seeing their children achieve an important milestone. Send Your blessings upon the teachers and administrators who helped prepare them.
"The graduates now need strength and guidance for the future, help them to understand that we are not complete with academic knowledge alone. We must strive to fulfill what You require of us all: To do justly, to love mercy, to walk humbly.
"We give thanks to You, Lord, for keeping us alive, sustaining us and allowing us to reach this special, happy occasion.
AMEN"

. . . [A]ttendance at graduation ceremonies is voluntary. The graduating students enter as a group in a processional, subject to the direction of teachers and school officials, and sit together, apart from their families. We assume the clergy's participation in any high school graduation exercise would be about what it was at Deborah's middle school ceremony. There the students stood for the Pledge of Allegiance and remained standing during the Rabbi's prayers. Even on the assumption that there was a respectful moment of silence both before and after the prayers, the Rabbi's two presentations must not have extended much beyond a minute each, if that. We do not know whether he remained on stage during the whole ceremony, or whether the students received individual diplomas on stage, or if he helped to congratulate them.

The school board (and the United States, which supports it as *amicus curiae*) argued that these short prayers and others like them at graduation exercises are of profound meaning to many students and parents throughout this country who consider that due respect and acknowledgement for divine guidance and for the the deepest spiritual aspirations of our people ought to be expressed at an event as important in life as a graduation. We assume this to be so in addressing the difficult case now before us, for the significance of the prayers lies also at the heart of Daniel and Deborah Weisman's case.

B

Deborah's graduation was held on the premises of Nathan Bishop Middle School on June 29, 1989. Four days before the ceremony, Daniel Weisman, in his individual capacity as a Providence taxpayer and as next friend of Deborah, sought a temporary restraining order in the United States District Court for the District of Rhode Island to prohibit school officials from including an invocation or benediction in the graduation ceremony. The court denied the motion for lack of adequate time to consider it. Deborah and her family attended the graduation, where the prayers were recited. In July 1989, Daniel Weisman filed an amended complaint seeking a permanent injunction barring petitioners, various public officials of the Providence public schools, from inviting the clergy to deliver invocations and benedictions at future graduations. . . .

. . . The District Court held that petitioners' practice of including invocations and benedictions in public school graduations violated the Establishment Clause of the First Amendment, and it enjoined petitioners from continuing the practice. The court applied the three-part Establishment Clause test set forth in *Lemon* v. *Kurtzman* . . . [and] held that petitioners' actions violated the second part of the test. . . . The court decided, based on its reading of our precedents, that the effects test of *Lemon* is violated whenever government action "creates an identification of the state with a religion, or with religion in general," or when "the effect of the governmental action is to endorse one religion over another, or to endorse religion in general." The court determined that the practice of including invocations and benedictions, even so-called nonsectarian ones, in public school graduations creates an identification of governmental power with religious practice, endorses religion, and violates the Establishment Clause. In so holding the court expressed the determination not to follow *Stein* v. *Plainwell Community Schools*, 822 F.2d 1406 (1987), in which the Court of Appeals for the Sixth Circuit, relying on our decision in *Marsh* v. *Chambers*, 463 U.S. 783 (1983), held that benedictions and invocations at public school graduations are not always unconstitutional. In *Marsh*, we upheld the constitutionality of the Nebraska State Legislature's practice of opening each of its sessions with a prayer offered by a chaplain paid out of public funds. The District Court in this case disagreed with the Sixth Circuit's reasoning because it believed that *Marsh* was a narrow decision, "limited to the unique situation of legislative prayer," and did not have any relevance to school prayer cases.

. . . *[The] Court of Appeals for the First Circuit affirmed. . . .*

II

These dominant facts mark and control the confines of our decision: State officials direct the performance of a formal religious exercise at promotional and graduation ceremonies for secondary schools. Even for those students who object to the religious exercise, their attendance and participation in the state-sponsored religious activity are in a fair and real sense obligatory, though the school district does not require attendance as a condition for receipt of the diploma.

This case does not require us to revisit the difficult questions dividing us in recent cases, questions of the definition and full scope of the principles governing the extent of permitted accommodation by the State for the religious beliefs and practices of many of its citizens. . . . For without reference to those principles in other contexts, the controlling precedents as they relate to prayer and religious exercise in primary and secondary public schools compel the holding here that the policy of the city of Providence is an unconstitutional one. We can decide the case without reconsidering the general constitutional framework by which public schools' efforts to accommodate religion are measured. Thus we do not accept the invitation of petitioners and *amicus* the United States to reconsider our decision in *Lemon* v. *Kurtzman*. The government involvement with religious activity in this case is pervasive, to the point of creating a state-sponsored and state-directed religious exercise in a public school. Conducting this formal religious observance conflicts with settled rules pertaining to prayer exercises for students, and that suffices to determine the question before us.

The principle that government may accommodate the free exercise of religion does not supersede the fundamental limitations imposed by the Establishment Clause. It is beyond dispute that, at a minimum, the Constitution guarantees that government may not coerce anyone to support or participate in religion or its exercise, or otherwise act in a way which "establishes a [state] religion or religious faith, or tends to do so." The State's involvement in the school prayers challenged today violates these central principles.

That involvement is as troubling as it is undenied. A school official, the principal, decided that an invocation and a benediction should be given, this is a choice attributable to the State, and from a constitutional perspective it is as if a state statute decreed that the prayers must occur. The principal chose the religious participant, here a rabbi, and that choice is also attributable to the State. The reason for the choice of a rabbi is not disclosed by the record, but the potential for divisiveness over the choice of a particular member of the clergy to conduct the ceremony is apparent. . . .

The State's role did not end with the decision to include a prayer and with the choice of clergyman. Principal Lee provided Rabbi Gutterman with a copy of the "Guidelines for Civic Occasions," and advised him that his prayers should be nonsectarian. Through these means the principal directed and controlled the content of the prayer. . . . It is a cornerstone principle of our Establishment Clause jurisprudence that "it is no part of the business of government to compose official prayers for any group of the American people to recite as a part of a religious program carried on by government," and that is what the school officials attempted to do. . . .

The First Amendment's Religious Clauses mean that religious beliefs and religious expression are too precious to be either proscribed or prescribed by the State. The design of the Constitution is that preservation and transmission of religious beliefs and worship is [sic] a responsibility and a choice committed to the private sphere, which itself is promised freedom to pursue that mission. It must not be forgotten then, that while concern must be given to define the protection granted to an objector or a dissenting nonbeliever, these same Clauses exist to protect religion from government interference. . . .

These concerns have particular application in the case of school officials, whose effort to monitor prayer will be perceived by the students as inducing a participation they might otherwise reject. Though the efforts of the school officials in this case to find common ground appear to have been a good-faith attempt to recognize the common aspects of religions and not the divisive ones, our precedents do not permit school officials to assist in composing prayers as an incident to a formal exercise for their students. And these same precedents caution us to measure the idea of a civic religion against the central meaning of the Religion Clauses of the First Amendment, which is that all creeds must be tolerated and none favored. The suggestion that government may establish an official or civic religion as a means of avoiding the establishment of a religion with more specific creeds strikes us as a contradiction that cannot be accepted.

The degree of school involvement here made it clear that the graduation prayers bore the imprint of the State and thus put school-age children who objected in an untenable position. We turn our attention now to consider the position of the students, both those who desired the prayer and she who did not. . . .

The First Amendment protects speech and religion by quite different mechanisms. Speech is protected by insuring its full expression even when the government participates, for the very object of some of our most important speech is to persuade the government to adopt an idea as its own. The method for protecting freedom of worship and freedom of conscience in religious matters is quite the reverse. In religious debate or expression the government is not a prime participant, for the Framers deemed religious establishment antithetical to the freedom of all. The Free Exercise Clause embraces a freedom of conscience and worship that has close parallels in the speech provisions of the First Amendment, but the Establishment Clause is a specific prohibition on forms of state intervention in religious affairs with no precise counterpart in the speech provisions. The explanation lies in the lesson of history that was and is the inspiration for the Establishment Clause, the lesson that in the hands of government what might begin as a tolerant expression of religious views may end in a policy to indoctrinate and coerce. A state-created orthodoxy puts at grave risk that freedom of belief and conscience which are [sic] the sole assurance that religious faith is real, not imposed.

The lessons of the First Amendment are as urgent in the modern world as in the 18th Century when it was written. One timeless lesson is that if citizens are subjected to state-sponsored religious exercises, the State disavows its own duty to guard and respect that sphere of inviolable conscience and belief which is the mark of a free people. To compromise that principle today would be to deny our own tradition and forfeit our standing to urge others to secure the protections of that tradition for themselves. . . .

As we have observed before, there are heightened concerns with protecting freedom of conscience from subtle coercive pressure in the elementary and secondary public schools. . . . The concern may not be limited to the context of schools, but it is most pronounced there. What to most believers may seem nothing more than a reasonable request that the nonbeliever respect their religious practices, in a school context may appear to the nonbeliever or dissenter to be an attempt to employ the machinery of the State to enforce a religious orthodoxy.

We need not look beyond the circumstances of this case to see the phenomenon at work. The undeniable fact is that the school district's supervision and control of a high school graduation ceremony places public pressure, as well as peer pressure, on attending students to stand as a group or, at least, maintain respectful silence during the Invocation and Benediction. This pressure, though subtle and indirect, can be as real as any overt compulsion. Of course, in our culture standing or remaining silent can signify adherence to a view or simple respect for the views of others. And no doubt some persons who have no desire to join a prayer have little objection to standing as a sign of respect for those who do. But for the dissenter of high school age, who has a reasonable perception that she is being forced by the State to pray in a manner her conscience will not allow, the injury is no less real. There can be no doubt that for many, if not most, of the students at the graduation, the act of standing or remaining silent was an expression of participation in the Rabbi's prayer. That was the very point of the religious exercise. It is of little comfort to a dissenter, then, to be told that for her the act of standing or remaining in silence signifies mere respect, rather than participation. What matters is that, given our social conventions, a reasonable dissenter in this milieu could believe that the group exercise signified her own participation or approval of it. . . .

The injury caused by the government's action, and the reason why Daniel and Deborah Weisman object to it, is that the State, in a school setting, in effect required participation in a religious exercise. It is, we concede, a brief exercise during which the individual can concentrate on joining its message, meditate on her own religion, or let her mind wander. But the embarrassment and the intrusion of the religious exercise cannot be refuted by arguing that these prayers, and similar ones to be said in the future, are of a *de minimis* character. To do so would be an affront to the Rabbi who offered them and to all those for whom the prayers were an essential and profound recognition of divine authority. And for the same reason, we think that the intrusion is greater than the two minutes or so of time consumed for prayers like these. Assuming, as we must, that the prayers were offensive to the student and the parent who now object, the intrusion was both real and, in the context of a secondary school, a violation of the objectors' rights. That the intrusion was in the course of pro-

mulgating religion that sought to be civic or nonsectarian rather than pertaining to one sect does not lessen the offense or isolation to the objectors. At best it narrows their number, at worst increases their sense of isolation and affront.

There was a stipulation in the District Court that attendance at graduation and promotional ceremonies is voluntary. Petitioners and the United States, as *amicus*, made this a center point of the case, arguing that the option of not attending the graduation excuses any inducement or coercion in the ceremony itself. The argument lacks all persuasion. Law reaches past formalism. And to say a teenage student has a real choice not to attend her high school graduation is formalistic in the extreme. True, Deborah could elect not to attend commencement without renouncing her diploma; but we shall not allow the case to turn on this point. Everyone knows that in our society and in our culture high school graduation is one of life's most significant occasions. A school rule which excuses attendance is beside the point. Attendance may not be required by official decree, yet it is apparent that a student is not free to absent herself from the graduation exercise in any real sense of the term "voluntary," for absence would require forfeiture of those intangible benefits which would have motivated the student through youth and all her high school years. Graduation is a time for family and those closest to the student to celebrate success and express mutual wishes of gratitude and respect, all to the end of impressing upon the young person the role that it is his or her right and duty to assume in the community and all of its diverse parts. . . .

The government's argument gives insufficient recognition to the real conflict of conscience faced by the young student. The essence of the Government's position is that with regard to a civic, social occasion of this importance it is the objector, not the majority, who must take unilateral and private action to avoid compromising religious scruples, here by electing to miss the graduation exercise. This turns conventional First Amendment analysis on its head. It is a tenet of the First Amendment that the State cannot require one of its citizens to forfeit his or her rights and benefits as the price of resisting conformance to state-sponsored religious practice. To say that a student must remain apart from the ceremony at the opening invocation and closing benediction is to risk compelling conformity in an environment analogous to the classroom setting, where we have said the risk of compulsion is especially high. . . .

We do not hold that every state action implicating religion is invalid if one or a few citizens find it offensive. People may take offense at all manner of religious as well as nonreligious messages, but offense alone does not in every case show a violation. We know too that sometimes to endure social isolation or even anger may be the price of conscience or nonconformity. But, by any reading of our cases, the conformity required of the student in this case was too high an exaction to withstand the test of the Establishment Clause. The prayer exercises in this case are especially improper because the State has in every practical sense compelled attendance and participation in an explicit religious exercise at an event of singular importance to every student, one the objecting student had no real alternative to avoid. . . .

Our society would be less than true to its heritage if it lacked abiding concern for the values of its young people, and we acknowledge the profound belief of adherents to many faiths that there must be a place in the student's life for precepts of a morality higher than even the law we today enforce. We express no hostility to those aspirations, nor would our oath permit us to do so. A relentless and all-pervasive attempt to exclude religion from every aspect of public life could itself become inconsistent with the Constitution. We recognize that, at graduation time and throughout the course of the educational process, there will be instances when religious persons will have some interaction with the public schools and their students. But these matters, often questions of accommodation of religion, are not before us. The sole question presented is whether a religious exercise may be conducted at a graduation ceremony in circumstances where, as we have found, young graduates who object are induced to conform. No holding by this Court suggests that a school can persuade or compel a student to participate in a religious exercise. That is being done here, and it is forbidden by the Establishment Clause of the First Amendment.

For the reasons we have stated, the judgment of the Court of Appeals is

Affirmed.

JUSTICE BLACKMUN, *with whom* JUSTICE STEVENS *and* JUSTICE O'CONNOR *join, concurring.*

Nearly half a century of review and refinement of Establishment Clause jurisprudence has distilled one clear understanding: Government may neither promote nor affiliate itself with any religious doctrine or organization, nor may it obtrude itself in the internal affairs of any religious institution. The application of these principles to the present case mandates the decision reached today by the Court. . . .

II

I join the Court's opinion today because I find nothing in it inconsistent with the essential precepts of the Establishment Clause developed in our precedents. . . . Although our precedents make clear that proof of government coercion is not necessary to prove an Establishment Clause violation, it is sufficient. Government pressure to participate in a religious activity is an obvious indication that the government is endorsing or promoting religion.

But it is not enough that the government restrain from compelling religious practices: it must not engage in them either. . . . The Establishment Clause proscribes public schools from "conveying or attempting to convey a message that religion or a particular religious belief is *favored* or *preferred*," *County of Allegheny* v. *ACLU* 492 U.S. 573, 593 (1989) (emphasis in original), even if the schools do not actually "impos(e) pressure upon a student to participate in a religious activity." *Westside Community Bd. of Ed.* v. *Mergens*, 496 U.S. 226, 261, (1990). . . .

. . . The Establishment Clause protects religious liberty on a grand scale; it is a social compact that guarantees for generations a democracy and a strong religious community—both essential to safeguarding religious liberty. "Our fathers seem to have been perfectly sincere in their belief that the members of the Church would be more patriotic, and the citizens of the State more religious, by keeping their respective functions entirely 'separate.' " Religious Liberty, in Essays and Speeches of Jeremiah S. Black 53 (C. Black ed. 1885) (Chief Justice of the Commonwealth of Pennsylvania).

The mixing of government and religion can be a threat to free government, even if no one is forced to participate. When the government puts its imprimatur on a particular religion, it conveys a message of exclusion to all those who do not adhere to the favored beliefs. A government cannot be premised on the belief that all persons are created equal when it asserts that God prefers some. Only "[a]nguish, hardship and bitter strife" result "when zealous religious groups struggl[e] with one another to obtain the Government's stamp of approval." *Engel*, 370 U.S., at 429. Such a struggle can "strain a political system to the breaking point." *Walz* v. *Tax Commission*, 397 U.S. 664, 694 (1970).

When the government arrogates to itself a role in religious affairs, it abandons its obligation as guarantor of democracy. Democracy requires the nourishment of dialogue and dissent, while religious faith puts its trust in an ultimate divine authority above all human deliberation. When the government appropriates religious truth, it "transforms rational debate into theological decree." Nuechterlein, Note, The Free Exercise Boundaries of Permissible Accommodation Under the Establishment Clause, 99 Yale L. J. 1127, 1131 (1990). Those who disagree no longer are questioning the policy judgment of the elected but the rules of a higher authority who is beyond reproach. . . .

. . . [W]e have recognized that "[r]eligion flourishes in greater purity, without than with the aid of Gov[ernment]." To "make room for as wide a variety of beliefs and creeds as the spiritual needs of man deem necessary," the government must not align itself with any one of them. When the government favors a particular religion or sect, the disadvantage to all others is obvious, but even the favored religion may fear being "taint[ed] . . . with a corrosive secularism." The favored religion may be compromised as political figures reshape the religion's beliefs for their own purposes; it may be reformed as government largesse brings government regulation. Keeping religion in the hands of private groups minimizes state intrusion on religious choice and best enables each religion to "flourish according to the zeal of its adherents and the appeal of its dogma."

It is these understandings and fears that underlie our Establishment Clause jurisprudence. We have believed that religious freedom cannot exist in the absence of a free democratic government, and that such a government cannot endure when there is fusion between religion and the political regime. We have believed that religious freedom cannot thrive in the absence of a vibrant religious community and that such a community cannot prosper when it is bound to the secular. And we have believed that these were the animating principles behind the adoption of the Establishment Clause. To that end, our cases have prohibited government endorsement of religion, its sponsorship, and active involvement in religion, whether or not citizens were coerced to conform. . . .

JUSTICE SOUTER, *with whom* JUSTICE STEVENS *and* JUSTICE O'CONNOR *join, concurring.*

I join the whole Court's opinion, and fully agree that prayers at public school graduation ceremonies indirectly coerce religious observance. I write separately nonetheless on two issues of Establishment Clause analysis that underlie my independent resolution of this case: whether the Clause applies to governmental practices that do not favor one religion or denomination over others, and whether state coercion of religious conformity, over and above state endorsement of religious exercise or belief, is a necessary element of an Establishment Clause violation.

I

Forty-five years ago, this Court announced a basic principle of constitutional law from which it has not strayed: the Establishment Clause forbids not only state practices that "aid one religion . . . or prefer one religion over another," but also those that "aid all religions." Today we reaffirm that principle, holding that the Establishment Clause forbids state-sponsored prayers in public school settings no matter how nondenominational the prayers may be. In barring the State from sponsoring generically Theistic prayers where it could not sponsor sectarian ones, we hold true to a line of precedent from which there is *no adequate historical case to depart.* (Emphasis added). . . .

A

Such is the settled law. Here, as elsewhere, we should stick to it absent some compelling reason to discard it. . . .

B

Some have challenged this precedent by reading the Establishment Clause to permit "nonpreferential" state promotion of religion. The challengers argue that, as originally understood by the Framers, "[t]he Establishment Clause did not require government neutrality between religion and irreligion nor did it prohibit the Federal Government from providing nondiscriminatory aid to religion." *Wallace* [v. *Jaffree*, 472 U.S. 38] at 106, (REHNQUIST, J., dissenting); see also R. Cord, Separation of Church and State: Historical Fact and Current Fiction (1988). While a case has been made for this position, it is not so convincing as to warrant reconsideration of our settled law; indeed, I find in the history of the Clause's textual development a more powerful argument supporting the Court's jurisprudence following *Everson.* . . .

. . . [O]n balance, history neither contradicts nor warrants reconsideration of the settled principle that the Establishment Clause forbids support for religion in general no less than support for one religion or some.

C

While these considerations are, for me, sufficient to reject the nonpreferentialist position, one further concern animates my judgment. In many contexts, including this one, nonpreferentialism requires some distinction between "sectarian" religious practices and those that would be, by some measure, ecumenical enough to pass Establishment Clause muster. Simply by requiring the inquiry, nonpreferentialists invite the courts to engage in comparative theology. I can hardly imagine a subject less amenable to the competence of the federal judiciary, or more deliberately to be avoided where possible.

This case is nicely in point. Since the nonpreferentialty of a prayer must be judged by its text, JUSTICE BLACKMUN pertinently observes, *ante*, at 2664, n. 5, that Rabbi Gutterman drew his exhortation "[t]o do justly, to love mercy, to walk humbly" straight from the King James version of Micah, ch. 6, v. 8. At some undefinable point, the similarities between a state-sponsored prayer and the sacred text of a specific religion would so closely identify the former with the latter that even a nonpreferentialist would have to concede a breach of the Establishment Clause. And even if Micah's thought is sufficiently generic for most believers, it still embodies a straightforwardly Theistic premise, and so does the Rabbi's prayer. Many Americans who consider themselves religious are not Theistic; some, like several of the Framers, are Deists who would question Rabbi Gutterman's plea for divine advancement of the country's political and moral good. Thus, a nonpreferentialist who would condemn subjecting public school graduates to, say, the Anglican liturgy would still need to explain why the government's preference for Theistic over non-Theistic religion is constitutional.

Nor does it solve the problem to say that the State should promote a "diversity" of religious views; that position would necessarily compel the government and, inevitably, the courts to make wholly inappropriate judgments about the number of religions the State should sponsor and the relative frequency with which it should sponsor each. In fact, the prospect would be even worse than that. As Madison observed in critizing religious presidential proclamations, the practice of sponsoring religious messages tends, over time, "to narrow the recommendation to the standard of the predominant sect." . . . We have not changed much since the days of Madison, and the judiciary should not willingly enter the political arena to battle the centripetal force leading from religious pluralism to official preference for the faith with the most votes.

II

Petitioners rest most of their argument on a theory that, whether or not the Establishment Clause permits extensive nonsectarian support for religion, it does not forbid the state to sponsor affirmations of religious beliefs that coerce neither support for religion nor participation in religious observance. I appreciate the force of some of the arguments supporting a "coercion" analysis of the Clause. . . . But we could not adopt that reading without abandoning our settled law, a course that, in my view, the text of the Clause would not readily permit. Nor does the extratextual evidence of original meaning stand so unequivocally at odds with the textual premise inherent in existing precedent that we should fundamentally reconsider our course.

A

Over the years, this Court has declared the invalidity of many noncoercive state laws and practices conveying a message of religious endorsement. . . .

Our precedents may not always have drawn perfectly straight lines. They simply cannot, however, support the position that a showing of coercion is necessary to a successful Establishment Clause claim.

B

Like the provisions about "due" process and "unreasonable" searches and seizures, the constitutional language forbidding laws "respecting an establishment of religion" is not pellucid. But virtually everyone acknowledges that the Clause bans more than formal establishments of religion in the traditional sense, that is, massive state support for religion through, among other means, comprehensive schemes of taxation. . . . This much follows from the Framers' explicit rejection of simpler provisions prohibiting either the establishment of a religion or laws "establishing religion" in favor of the broader ban on laws "respecting an establishment of religion." . . .

While petitioners insist that the prohibition extends only to the "coercive" features and incidents of establishment, they cannot easily square that claim with the constitutional text. The First

Amendment forbids not just laws "respecting an establishment of religion," but also those "prohibiting the free exercise thereof." Yet laws that coerce nonadherents to "support or participate in any religion or its exercise," would virtually by definition violate their right to religious free exercise. . . . Thus, a literal application of the coercion test would render the Establishment Clause a virtual nullity. . . .

III

While the Establishment Clause's concept of neutrality is not self-revealing, our recent cases have invested it with specific content: the state may not favor or endorse either religion generally over nonreligion or one religion over others. . . . This principle against favoritism and endorsement has become the foundation of Establishment Clause jurisprudence, ensuring that religious belief is irrelevant to every citizen's standing in the political community. . . . Now, as in the early Republic, "religion & Govt. will both exist in greater purity, the less they are mixed together." Letter from J. Madison to E. Livingston (10 July 1822), in 5 The Founders' Constitution, at 106. Our aspiration to religious liberty, embodied in the First Amendment, permits no other standard.

A

That government must remain neutral in matters of religion does not foreclose it from ever taking religion into account. The State may "accommodate" the free exercise of religion by relieving people from generally applicable rules that interfere with their religious callings. Contrary to the views of some, such accommodation does not necessarily signify an official endorsement of religious observance over disbelief.

In everyday life, we routinely accommodate religious beliefs that we do not share. A Christian inviting an Orthodox Jew to lunch might take pains to choose a kosher restaurant; an atheist in a hurry might yield the right of way to an Amish man steering a horse-drawn carriage. In so acting, we express respect for, but not endorsement of, the fundamental values of others. We act without expressing a position on the theological merit of those values or of religious belief in general, and no one perceives us to have taken such a position.

The government may act likewise. . . .

B

Whatever else may define the scope of accommodation permissible under the Establishment Clause, one requirement is clear: accommodation must lift a discernible burden on the free exercise of religion. . . . Concern for the position of religious individuals in the modern regulatory state cannot justify official solicitude for a religious practice unburdened by general rules; such gratuitous largesse would effectively favor religion over disbelief. By these lights one easily sees that, in sponsoring the graduation prayers at issue here, the State has crossed the line from permissible accommodation to unconstitutional establishment.

Religious students cannot complain that omitting prayers from their graduation ceremony would, in any realistic sense, "burden" their spiritual callings. To be sure, many of them invest this rite of passage with spiritual significance, but they may express their religious feelings about it before and after the ceremony. They may even organize a privately sponsored baccalaureate if they desire the company of like-minded students. Because they accordingly have no need for the machinery of the State to affirm their beliefs, the government's sponsorship of prayer at the graduation ceremony is most reasonably understood as an official endorsement of religion and, in this instance, of Theistic religion. One may fairly say, as one commentator has suggested, that the government brought prayer into the ceremony "precisely because some people want a symbolic affirmation that government approves and endorses their religion, and because many of the people who want this affirmation place little or no value on the costs to religious minorities." . . .

. . . When public school officials, armed with the State's authority, convey an endorsement of religion to their students, they strike at the core of the Establishment Clause. However "ceremonial" their messages may be, they are flatly unconstitutional.

JUSTICE SCALIA, *with whom* THE CHIEF JUSTICE, JUSTICE WHITE, *and* JUSTICE THOMAS *join, dissenting.*

Three Terms ago, I joined an opinion recognizing that the Establishment Clause must be construed in light of the "[g]overnment policies of accommodation, acknowledgment, and support for religion [that] are an accepted part of our political and cultural heritage." That opinion affirmed that "the meaning of the Clause is to be determined by reference to historical practices and understandings." It said that "[a] test for implementing the protections of the Establishment Clause that, if applied with consistency, would invalidate longstanding traditions cannot be a proper reading of the

Clause." *Allegheny County* v. *Greater Pittsburgh ACLU,* 492 U.S. 573, 657, 670 (1989).

These views of course prevent me from joining today's opinion, which is conspicuously bereft of any reference to history. In holding that the Establishment Clause prohibits invocations and benedictions at public-school graduation ceremonies, the Court—with nary a mention that it is doing so—lays waste a tradition that is as old as public-school graduation ceremonies themselves, and that is a component of an even more longstanding American tradition of nonsectarian prayer to God at public celebrations generally. As its instrument of destruction, the bulldozer of its social engineering, the Court invents a boundless, and boundlessly manipulable, test of psychological coercion, which promises to do for the Establishment Clause what the *Durham* rule did for the insanity defense. See *Durham* v. *United States,* 94 U.S. App. D.C. 228, 214 F.2d 862 (1954). Today's opinion shows more forcefully than volumes of argumentation why our Nation's protection, that fortress which is our Constitution, cannot possibly rest upon the changeable philosophical predilections of the Justices of this Court, but must have deep foundations in the historic practices of our people.

I

Justice Holmes' aphorism that "a page of history is worth a volume of logic," *New York Trust Co.* v. *Eisner,* 256 U.S. 345, 349 (1921), applies with particular force to our Establishment Clause jurisprudence. As we have recognized, our interpretation of the Establishment Clause should "compor[t] with what history reveals was the contemporaneous understanding of its guarantees." "[T]he line we must draw between the permissible and the impermissible is one which accords with history and faithfully reflects the understanding of the Founding Fathers." "[H]istorical evidence sheds light not only on what the draftsmen intended the Establishment Clause to mean, but also on how they thought that Clause applied" to contemporaneous practices. Thus, "[t]he existence from the beginning of the Nation's life of a practice, [while] not conclusive of its constitutionality . . . is a fact of considerable import in the interpretation" of the Establishment Clause. *Walz* v. *Tax Comm'n of New York City,* 397 U.S. 664, 681 (1970). . . .

In addition to [the] general tradition of prayer at public ceremonies, there exists a more specific tradition of invocations and benedictions at public-school graduation exercises. By one account, the first public-high-school graduation ceremony

took place in Connecticut in July 1868—the very month, as it happens, that the Fourteenth Amendment (the vehicle by which the Establishment Clause has been applied against the States) was ratified—when 15 seniors from the Norwich Free Academy marched in their best Sunday suits and dresses into a church hall and waited through majestic music and long prayers." . . . As the Court obliquely acknowledges in describing the "customary features" of high school graduations, and as respondents do not contest, the invocation and benediction have long been recognized to be "as traditional as any other parts of the [school] graduation program and are widely established." . . .

A

The Court declares that students' "attendance and participation in the [invocation and benediction] are in a fair and real sense obligatory." *Ibid.* But what exactly is this "fair and real sense"? According to the Court, students at graduation who want "to avoid the fact or appearance of participation" in the invocation and benediction are *psychologically* obligated by "public pressure, as well as peer pressure, . . . to stand as a group or, at least, maintain respectful silence" during those prayers. This assertion— *the very linchpin of the Court's opinion*—is almost as intriguing for what it does not say as for what it says. It does not say, for example, that students are psychologically coerced to bow their heads, place their hands in a Dürer-like prayer position, pay attention to the prayers, utter "Amen," or in fact pray. . . . It claims only that students are psychologically coerced "to stand . . . *or*, at least, maintain respectful silence" (emphasis added). . . . The Court's notion that a student who simply *sits* in "respectful silence" during the invocation and benediction (when all others are standing) has somehow joined—or would somehow be perceived as having joined—in the prayers is nothing short of ludicrous. We indeed live in a vulgar age. But surely "our social conventions" have not coarsened to the point that anyone who does not stand on his chair and shout obscenities can reasonably be deemed to have assented to everything said in his presence. Since the Court does not dispute that students exposed to prayer at graduation ceremonies retain (despite "subtle coercive pressures") the free will to sit, there is absolutely no basis for the Court's decision. It is fanciful enough to say that "a reasonable dissenter," standing head erect in a class of bowed heads, "could believe that the group exercise signified her own participation or approval of it." It is beyond the absurd to say that she could entertain such a belief while pointedly declining to rise. . . .

I also find it odd that the Court concludes that high school graduates may not be subjected to this supposed psychological coercion, yet refrains from addressing whether "mature adults" may. I had thought that the reason graduation from high school is regarded as so significant an event is that it is generally associated with transition from adolescence to young adulthood. Many graduating seniors, of course, are old enough to vote. Why, then, does the Court treat them as though they were first-graders? Will we soon have a jurisprudence that distinguishes between mature and immature adults? . . .

IV

Our religion-clause jurisprudence has become bedeviled (so to speak) by reliance on formulaic abstractions that are not derived from, but positively conflict with, our long-accepted constitutional traditions. Foremost among these has been the so-called *Lemon* test, which has received well-earned criticism from many members of this Court. . . . The Court today demonstrates the irrelevance of *Lemon* by essentially ignoring it, and the interment of that case may be the one happy by-product of the Court's otherwise lamentable decision. Unfortunately, however, the Court has replaced *Lemon* with its psycho-coercion test, which suffers the double disability of having no roots whatever in our people's historic practice, and being as infinitely expandable as the reasons for psychotherapy itself.

Another happy aspect of the case is that it is only a jurisprudential disaster and not a practical one. Given the odd basis for the Court's decision, invocations and benedictions will be able to be given at public-school graduations next June, as they have for the past century and a half, so long as school authorities make clear that anyone who abstains from screaming in protest does not necessarily participate in the prayers. All that is seemingly needed is an announcement, or perhaps a written insertion at the beginning of the graduation program, to the effect that, while all are asked to rise for the invocation and benediction, none is compelled to join in them, nor will be assumed, by

rising, to have done so. That obvious fact recited, the graduates and their parents may proceed to thank God, as Americans have always done, for the blessings He has generously bestowed on them and on their country. . . .

The narrow context of the present case involves a community's celebration of one of the milestones in its young citizens' lives, and it is a bold step for this Court to seek to banish from that occasion, and from thousands of similar celebrations throughout this land, the expression of gratitude to God that a majority of the community wishes to make. The issue before us today is not the abstract philosophical question whether the alternative of frustrating this desire of a religious majority is to be preferred over the alternative of imposing "psychological coercion," or a feeling of exclusion, upon nonbelievers. Rather, the question is *whether a mandatory choice in favor of the former has been imposed by the United States Constitution.* As the age-old practices of our people show, the answer to that question is not at all in doubt.

I must add one final observation: The founders of our Republic knew the fearsome potential of sectarian religious belief to generate civil dissension and civil strife. And they also knew that nothing, absolutely nothing, is so inclined to foster among religious believers of various faiths a toleration—no, an affection—for one another than voluntarily joining in prayer together, to the God whom they all worship and seek. Needless to say, no one should be compelled to do that, but it is a shame to deprive our public culture of the opportunity, and indeed the encouragement, for people to do it voluntarily. The Baptist or Catholic who heard and joined in the simple and inspiring prayers of Rabbi Gutterman on this official and patriotic occasion was inoculated from religious bigotry and prejudice in a manner that cannot be replicated. To deprive our society of that important unifying mechanism, in order to spare the nonbeliever what seems to me the minimal inconvenience of standing or even sitting in respectful nonparticipation, is as senseless in policy as it is unsupported in law.

For the foregoing reasons, I dissent.

FEATURED CASES

Lynch v. *Donnelly*   *County of Allegheny* v. *American Civil Liberties Union*

In 1984 a longstanding American tradition was considered by the Court in *Lynch* v. *Donnelly* (465 U.S. 668). At issue was a city-sponsored Christmas display that included a depiction of the birth of Christ. It was argued that the city of Pawtucket, Rhode Island, was conveying a sectarian message in aid of Christians. But the Court did not consider the nativity scene an infringement of the establishment clause. Chief Justice Warren Burger's opinion for the five-to-four majority considered the crèche within the context of the total display, which included a Christmas tree, reindeer, and other decorative ornaments. He called it merely "passive art" and concluded that the challenged display met the three-pronged *Lemon* test. But Justice William J. Brennan, in a sharp dissent supported by Justices Thurgood Marshall, Harry Blackmun, and John Paul Stevens, considered Pawtucket's involvement in the production of the display an unconstitutional governmental endorsement of the Christian faith; they warned that it was a small, although dangerous, step toward the establishment of majority sectarian preferences.

Five years later, in *County of Allegheny* v. *American Civil Liberties Union Greater Pittsburgh Chapter* (109 S. Ct. 3086, 1989), the Court appeared to reaffirm the *Lynch* "cultural context" approach when it held that a crèche and a banner reading "Glory to God in the Highest" could not withstand establishment clause strictures because of the "unmistakably clear" religious message. But Justice Blackmun, who spoke for the five-to-four majority, underscored the secular context requirement in a companion case, *City of Pittsburgh* v. *American Civil*

Liberties Union Greater Pittsburgh Chapter involving a challenge to the display of a Chanukah menorah in another public building. Because the menorah stood next to a Christmas tree and a sign saluting liberty, he called the display a "recognition of cultural diversity" that recognized the "secular status" of the holiday season. Justice Anthony Kennedy's dissent in the crèche decision not only criticized the majority for its view of the establishment clause that "reflects an unjustified hostility towards religion," but also called for a "substantial revision" of establishment clause law. Two tests would be the core of the doctrinal reformulation: (1) whether anyone was coerced into supporting religion or participating in a religious observance and (2) whether the government program gave direct benefits to religion in such a degree that it in fact established a state religion or religious faith.

To be sure, these several cases once again underscored the growing disagreement among the justices on establishment clause doctrine.[6] The accommodationists have often construed the *Lemon* test narrowly or called for its reformulation or complete abandonment in support of more governmental latitude and flexibility to allow accommodation of a wide range of religious activities. On the other hand, a declining bloc of strict separationist justices call for the continued application of *Lemon*'s three prongs as essential to enforce the command of the establishment clause. Inconsistent decisions in this area of church-state relations will continue to be spawned so long as the justices are all over the constitutional landscape on the meaning of the clause.

LYNCH v. DONNELLY
___ U.S. ___; ___ L. Ed. 2d ___; 104 S. Ct. 1355 (1984)

CHIEF JUSTICE BURGER *delivered the opinion of the Court.*

We granted certiorari to decide whether the Establishment Clause of the First Amendment prohibits a municipality from including a crèche, or

Nativity scene, in its annual Christmas display.

Each year, in cooperation with the downtown re-

[6]For further discussion of the *Lemon* doctrinal debate see Justice O'Connor's concurring opinion in *County of Allegheny* v. *American Civil Liberties Union*, pp. 201–206, *infra*, and the dissenting opinion of Justice Rehnquist in *Wallace* v. *Jaffree*, pp. 123–125, *supra*.

tail merchants' association, the City of Pawtucket, Rhode Island, erects a Christmas display as part of its observance of the Christmas holiday season. The display is situated in a park owned by a nonprofit organization and located in the heart of the shopping district. The display is essentially like those to be found in hundreds of towns or cities across the Nation—often on public grounds—during the Christmas season. The Pawtucket display comprises many of the figures and decorations traditionally associated with Christmas, including, among other things, a Santa Claus house, reindeer pulling Santa's sleigh, candy-striped poles, a Christmas tree, carolers, cutout figures representing such characters as a clown, an elephant, and a teddy bear, hundreds of colored lights, a large banner that reads "SEASONS GREETINGS," and the crèche at issue here. All components of this display are owned by the City.

The crèche, which has been included in the display for 40 or more years, consists of the traditional figures, including the Infant Jesus, Mary and Joseph, angels, shepherds, kings, and animals, all ranging in height from 5" to 5'. In 1973, when the present crèche was acquired, it cost the City $1365; it now is valued at $200. The erection and dismantling of the crèche costs the City about $20 per year; nominal expenses are incurred in lighting the crèche. No money has been expended on its maintenance for the past 10 years.

Respondents, Pawtucket residents and individual members of the Rhode Island affiliate of the American Civil Liberties Union, and the affiliate itself, brought this action in the United States District Court for Rhode Island, challenging the City's inclusion of the crèche in the annual display. The District Court held that the City's inclusion of the crèche in the display violates the Establishment Clause. . . . The . . . Court found that, by including the crèche in the Christmas display, the City has "tried to endorse and promulgate religious beliefs," 525 F. Supp., at 1173, and that "erection of the crèche has the real and substantial effect of affiliating the City with the Christian beliefs that the crèche represents." . . . [A]lthough the court acknowledged the absence of administrative entanglement, it found that excessive entanglement has been fostered as a result of the political divisiveness of including the crèche in the celebration. *Id.*, at 1179–1180. The City was permanently enjoined from including the crèche in the display.

A divided panel of the Court of Appeals for the First Circuit affirmed. . . .

[W]e reverse.

* * *

In every Establishment Clause case, we must reconcile the inescapable tension between the objective of preventing unnecessary intrusion of either the church or the state upon the other, and the reality that, as the Court has so often noted, total separation of the two is not possible. . . .

No significant segment of our society and no institution within it can exist in a vacuum or in total or absolute isolation from all the other parts, much less from government. "It has never been thought either possible or desirable to enforce a regime of total separation. . . ." *Committee for Public Education & Religious Liberty* v. *Nyquist*, 413 U.S. 756 (1973). Nor does the Constitution require complete separation of church and state; it affirmatively mandates accommodation, not merely tolerance, of all religions, and forbids hostility toward any. . . .

There is an unbroken history of official acknowledgment by all three branches of government of the role of religion in American life from at least 1789. Seldom in our opinions was this more affirmatively expressed than in Justice Douglas's opinion for the Court validating a program allowing release of public school students from classes to attend off-campus religious exercises. [in *Zorach* v. *Clauson*]. . . . [T]he Court asserted pointedly:

> We are a religious people whose institutions presuppose a Supreme Being. . . .

Our history is replete with official references to the value and invocation of divine guidance in deliberations and pronouncements of the Founding Fathers and contemporary leaders. . . . President Washington and his successors proclaimed Thanksgiving, with all its religious overtones, a day of national celebration and Congress made it a national holiday more than a century ago. . . . That holiday has not lost its theme of expressing thanks for divine aid any more than has Christmas lost its religious significance.

Executive Orders and other official announcements of Presidents and of the Congress have proclaimed both Christmas and Thanksgiving National Holidays in religious terms. And, by Acts of Congress, it has long been the practice that federal employees are released from duties on these National Holidays, while being paid from the same public revenues that provide the compensation of the Chaplains of the Senate and the House and the military services. . . . Thus, it is clear that

Government has long recognized—indeed it has subsidized—holidays with religious significance. . . .

* * *

. . . In our modern, complex society, whose traditions and constitutional underpinnings rest on and encourage diversity and pluralism in all areas, an absolutist approach in applying the Establishment Clause is simplistic and has been uniformly rejected by the Court.

Rather than mechanically invalidating all governmental conduct or statutes that confer benefits or give special recognition to religion in general or to one faith—as an absolutist approach would dictate—the Court has scrutinized challenged legislation or official conduct to determine whether, in reality, it establishes a religion or religious faith, or tends to do so. . . . Joseph Story wrote a century and a half ago:

> The real object of the [First] Amendment was . . . to prevent any national ecclesiastical establishment, which should give to an hierarchy the exclusive patronage of the national government. (3 Story, Commentaries on the Constitution of the United States 728, 1883. . . .)

In this case, the focus of our inquiry must be on the crèche in the context of the Christmas season. . . . In *Stone* v. *Graham* for example, we invalidated a state statute requiring the posting of a copy of the Ten Commandments on public classroom walls. But the Court carefully pointed out that the commandments were posted purely as a religious admonition, not "integrated into the school curriculum, where the Bible may constitutionally be used in an appropriate study of history, civilization, ethics, comparative religion, or the like." 449 U.S., at 42 (1980). Focus exclusively on the religious component of any activity would inevitably lead to its invalidation under the Establishment Clause.

The Court has invalidated legislation or governmental action on the ground that a secular purpose was lacking, but only when it has concluded there was no question that the statute or activity was motivated wholly by religious considerations. . . . Even where the benefits to religion were substantial. . . .

The District Court inferred from the religious nature of the crèche that the City has no secular purpose for the display. In so doing, it rejected the City's claim that its reasons for including the crèche are essentially the same as its reasons for sponsoring the display as a whole. The District Court plainly erred by focusing almost exclusively on the crèche. When viewed in the proper context of the Christmas Holiday season, it is apparent that, on this record, there is insufficient evidence to establish that the inclusion of the crèche is a purposeful or surreptitious effort to express some kind of subtle governmental advocacy of a particular religious message. In a pluralistic society a variety of motives and purposes are implicated. The City, like the Congress and Presidents, however, has principally taken note of a significant historical religious event long celebrated in the Western World. The crèche in the display depicts the historical origins of this traditional event long recognized as a National Holiday. . . .

The narrow question is whether there is a secular purpose for Pawtucket's display of the crèche. The display is sponsored by the City to celebrate the Holiday and to depict the origins of that Holiday. These are legitimate secular purposes. The District Court's inference, drawn from the religious nature of the crèche, that the City has no secular purpose was, on this record, clearly erroneous.

The District Court found that the primary effect of including the crèche is to confer a substantial and impermissible benefit on religion in general and on the Christian faith in particular. Comparisons of the relative benefits to religion of different forms of governmental support are elusive and difficult to make. But to conclude that the primary effect of including the crèche is to advance religion in violation of the Establishment Clause would require that we view it as more beneficial to and more an endorsement of religion, for example, than expenditure of large sums of public money for textbooks supplied throughout the country to students attending church-sponsored schools, . . . expenditure of public funds for transportation of students to church-sponsored schools, . . . federal grants for college buildings of church-sponsored institutions of higher education combining secular and religious education, [etc.]. . . . It would also require that we view it as more of an endorsement of religion than the Sunday Closing Laws upheld in *McGowan* v. *Maryland*, . . . the release-time program for religious training in *Zorach*, . . . and the legislative prayers upheld in *Marsh*. . . .

We are unable to discern a greater aid to religion deriving from inclusion of the crèche than from these benefits and endorsements previously held not violative of the Establishment Clause. What was said about the legislative prayers in *Marsh*, . . . and implied about the Sunday Closing

Laws in *McGowan* is true of the City's inclusion of the crèche: its "reason or effect merely happens to coincide or harmonize with the tenets of some . . . religions." See *McGowan*, 366 U.S., at 442. . . .

The dissent asserts some observers may perceive that the City has aligned itself with the Christian faith by including a Christian symbol in its display and that this serves to advance religion. We can assume *arguendo*, that the display advances religion in a sense; but our precedents plainly contemplate that on occasion some advancement of religion will result from governmental action. The Court has made it abundantly clear, however, that "not every law that confers an 'indirect,' 'remote,' or 'incidental' benefit upon [religion] is, for that reason alone, constitutionally invalid." . . . Here, whatever benefit to one faith or religion or to all religions, is indirect, remote and incidental; display of the crèche is no more an advancement or endorsement of religion than the Congressional and Executive recognition of the origins of the Holiday itself as "Christ's Mass," or the exhibition of literally hundreds of religious paintings in governmentally supported museums.

The District Court found that there had been no administrative entanglement between religion and state resulting from the City's ownership and use of the crèche. But it went on to hold that some political divisiveness was engendered by this litigation. Coupled with its finding of an impermissible sectarian purpose and effect, this persuaded the court that there was "excessive entanglement." The Court of Appeals expressly declined to accept the District Court's finding that inclusion of the crèche has caused political divisiveness along religious lines, [noting] that this Court has never held that political divisiveness alone was sufficient to invalidate government conduct.

Entanglement is a question of kind and degree. In this case, however, there is no reason to disturb the District Court's finding on the absence of administrative entanglement. There is no evidence of contact with church authorities concerning the content or design of the exhibit prior to or since Pawtucket's purchase of the crèche. No expenditures for maintenance of the crèche have been necessary; and since the City owns the crèche, now valued at $200, the tangible material it contributes is *de minimis*. In many respects the display requires far less ongoing, day-to-day interaction between church and state than religious paintings in public galleries. . . .

The Court of Appeals correctly observed that this Court has not held that political divisiveness alone can serve to invalidate otherwise permissible conduct. And we decline to so hold today. . . . [A]part from this litigation there is no evidence of political friction or divisiveness over the crèche in the 40-year history of Pawtucket's Christmas celebration. The District Court stated that the inclusion of the crèche for the 40 years has been "marked by no apparent dissension" and that the display has had a "calm history." 525 F. Supp., at 1179. Curiously, it went on to hold that the political divisiveness engendered by this lawsuit was evidence of excessive entanglement. A litigant cannot, by the very act of commencing a lawsuit, however, create the appearance of divisiveness and then exploit it as evidence of entanglement.

We are satisfied that the City has a secular purpose for including the crèche, that the City has not impermissibly advanced religion, and that including the crèche does not create excessive entanglement between religion and government. . . .

JUSTICE BRENNAN describes the crèche as a "re-creation of an event that lies at the heart of Christian faith," *post*, at 1377. The crèche, like a painting, is passive; admittedly it is a reminder of the origins of Christmas. Even the traditional, purely secular displays extant at Christmas, with or without a crèche, would inevitably recall the religious nature of the Holiday. The display engenders a friendly community spirit of good will in keeping with the season. The crèche may well have special meaning to those whose faith includes the celebration of religious masses, but none who sense the origins of the Christmas celebration would fail to be aware of its religious implications. That the display brings people into the central city, and serves commercial interests and benefits merchants and their employees, does not, as the dissent points out, determine the character of the display. That a prayer invoking divine guidance in Congress is preceded and followed by debate and partisan conflict over taxes, budgets, national defense, and myriad mundane subjects, for example, has never been thought to demean or taint the sacredness of the invocation.

Of course the crèche is identified with one religious faith but no more so than the examples we have set out from prior cases in which we found no conflict with the Establishment Clause. . . . It would be ironic, however, if the inclusion of a single symbol of a particular historic religious event, as part of a celebration acknowledged in the Western World for 20 centuries, and in this country by the people, by the Executive Branch, by the Congress, and the courts for two centuries, would so "taint" the City's exhibit as to render it violative of the Establishment Clause. To forbid the use of this one passive symbol—the crèche—at the very time people are taking note of the season with Christmas hymns and carols in public schools and other public places, and while the Congress and legislatures open sessions with prayers by paid chaplains would be a stilted over-reaction contrary to our history and to our holdings. If the presence of the crèche in this display violates the Establishment Clause, a host of other forms of taking official note of Christmas, and of our religious heritage, are equally offensive to the Constitution. . . .

We hold that, notwithstanding the religious significance of the crèche, the City of Pawtucket has not violated the Establishment Clause of the First Amendment. Accordingly, the judgment of the Court of Appeals is *reversed*.

It is so ordered.

[The concurring opinion of JUSTICE O'CONNOR is not reprinted here.]

JUSTICE BRENNAN, *with whom* JUSTICE MARSHALL, JUSTICE BLACKMUN *and* JUSTICE STEVENS *join, dissenting.*

. . . [T]he Court reaches an essentially narrow result which turns largely upon the particular holiday context in which the City of Pawtucket's nativity scene appeared. The Court's decision implicitly leaves open questions concerning the constitutionality of the public display on public property of a crèche standing alone, or the public display of other distinctively religious symbols such as a cross. Despite the narrow contours of the Court's opinion, our precedents in my view compel the holding that Pawtucket's inclusion of a life-sized display depicting the biblical description of the birth of Christ as part of its annual Christmas celebration is unconstitutional. Nothing in the history of such practices or the setting in which the City's crèche is presented obscures or diminishes the plain fact that Pawtucket's action amounts to an impermissible governmental endorsement of a particular faith.

Last Term, I expressed the hope that the Court's decision in *Marsh* v. *Chambers*, . . . would prove to be only a single, aberrant departure from our settled method of analyzing Establishment Clause cases. . . . That the Court today returns to the settled analysis of our prior cases gratifies that hope. At the same time, the Court's less than vigorous application of the *Lemon* test suggests that its commitment to those standards may only be super-

ficial. After reviewing the Court's opinion, I am convinced that this case appears hard not because the principles of decision are obscure, but because the Christmas holiday seems so familiar and agreeable. Although the Court's reluctance to disturb a community's chosen method of celebrating such an agreeable holiday is understandable, that cannot justify the Court's departure from controlling precedent. In my view, Pawtucket's maintenance and display at public expense of a symbol as distinctively sectarian as a crèche simply cannot be squared with our prior cases. And it is plainly contrary to the purposes and values of the Establishment Clause to pretend, as the Court does, that the otherwise secular setting of Pawtucket's nativity scene dilutes in some fashion the crèche's singular religiosity, or that the City's annual display reflects nothing more than an "acknowledgment" of our shared national heritage. Neither the character of the Christmas holiday itself, nor our heritage of religious expression supports this result. Indeed, our remarkable and precious religious diversity as a nation, . . . which the Establishment Clause seeks to protect, runs directly counter to today's decision. . . .

Applying the three-part [*Lemon*] test to Pawtucket's crèche, I am persuaded that the City' inclusion of the crèche in its Christmas display simply does not reflect a "clearly secular purpose." . . . Unlike the typical case in which the record reveals some contemporaneous expression of a clear purpose to advance religion . . . here we have no explicit statement of purpose by Pawtucket's municipal government accompanying its decision to purchase, display and maintain the crèche. Governmental purpose may nevertheless be inferred. . . . In the present case, the City claims that its purposes were exclusively secular. Pawtucket sought, according to this view, only to participate in the celebration of a national holiday and to attract people to the downtown area in order to promote pre-Christmas retail sales and to help engender the spirit of goodwill and neighborliness commonly associated with the Christmas season. . . .

. . . [A]ll of Pawtucket's valid secular objectives can be readily accomplished by other means. Plainly, the City's interest in celebrating the holiday and in promoting both retail sales and goodwill are fully served by the elaborate display of Santa Claus, reindeer, and wishing wells that are already a part of Pawtucket's annual Christmas display. More importantly, the nativity scene, unlike every other element of the . . . display, reflects a sectarian exclusivity that the avowed purposes of celebrating the holiday season and promoting retail commerce simply do not encompass. To be found constitutional, Pawtucket's seasonal celebration must at least be non-denominational and not serve to promote religion. The inclusion of a distinctively religious element like the crèche, however, demonstrates that a narrower sectarian purpose lay behind the decision to include a Nativity scene. That the crèche retained this religious character for the people and municipal government of Pawtucket is suggested by the Mayor's testimony at trial in which he stated that for him, as well as others in the City, the effort to eliminate the nativity scene from Pawtucket's Christmas celebration "is a step toward establishing another religion, non-religion that it may be." . . . Plainly the City and its leaders understood that the inclusion of the crèche in its display would serve the wholly religious purpose of "keep[ing] 'Christ in Christmas'." . . . From this record, therefore, it is impossible to say . . . that a wholly secular goal predominates.

The "primary effect" of including a nativity scene in the City's display is, as the District Court found, to place the government's imprimatur of approval on the particular religious beliefs exemplified by the crèche. Those who believe in the message of the nativity receive the unique and exclusive benefit of public recognition and approval of their views. For many, the City's decision to include the crèche as part of its extensive and costly efforts to celebrate Christmas can only mean that the prestige of the government has been conferred on the beliefs associated with the crèche, thereby providing "a significant symbolic benefit to religion. . . ." *Larkin* v. *Grendel's Den, Inc.* . . .

Finally, it is evident that Pawtucket's inclusion of a crèche as part of its annual Christmas display does pose a significant threat of fostering "excessive entanglement." . . . [T]he District Court found no administrative entanglement in this case, primarily because the City had been able to administer the annual display without extensive consultation with religious officials. . . . Of course, there is no reasons to disturb that finding, but it is worth noting that after today's decision, administrative entanglements may well develop. Jews and other non-Christian groups, prompted perhaps by the Mayor's remark that he will include a Menorah in future displays, can be expected to press government for inclusion of their symbols, and faced with such requests, government will have to become involved in accommodating the various demands. . . . More importantly, although no political divisiveness was apparent in Pawtucket prior to the filing of respondents' lawsuit, that act, . . . unleashed powerful emotional reactions which divided the City along religious lines. . . . Of course, the Court is correct to note that we have never held that the potential for divisiveness alone is sufficient to invalidate a challenged governmental practice; we have, nevertheless, repeatedly emphasized that "too close a proximity" between religious and civil authorities . . . may represent a "warning signal" that the values embodied in the Establishment Clause are at risk. . . . Furthermore, the Court should not blind itself to the fact that because communities differ in religious composition, the controversy over whether local governments may adopt religious symbols will continue to fester. In many communities, non-Christian groups can be expected to combat practices similar to Pawtucket's; this will be so especially in areas where there are substantial non-Christian minorities.

In sum, considering the District Court's careful findings of fact under the three-part analysis called for by our prior cases, I have no difficulty concluding that Pawtucket's display of the crèche is unconstitutional. . . .

Under our constitutional scheme, the role of safeguarding our "religious heritage" and of promoting religious beliefs is reserved as the exclusive prerogative of our nation's churches, religious institutions and spiritual leaders. Because the Framers of the Establishment Clause understood that "religion is too personal, too sacred, too holy to permit its 'unhallowed perversion' by civil [authorities]," *Engel* v. *Vitale* [*supra*], 370 U.S. at 432, 82 S. Ct., at 1267, the clause demands that government play no role in this effort. The Court today brushes aside these concerns by insisting that Pawtucket has done nothing more than include a "traditional" symbol of Christmas in its celebration of this national holiday, thereby muting the religious content of the crèche. *Ante*, at 1365. But the City's action should be recognized for what it is: a coercive, though perhaps small, step toward establishing the sectarian preferences of the majority at the expense of the minority, accomplished by placing public facilities and funds in support of the religious symbolism and theological tidings that the crèche conveys. As Justice Frankfurter, writing in *McGowan* v. *Maryland*, observed, the Establishment Clause "withdr[aws] from the sphere of legitimate legislative concern and competence a specific, but comprehensive area of human conduct: man's belief or disbelief in the verity of some transcendental idea and man's expression in action of that belief or disbelief." *Id.*, 366 U.S., at 465–466, 81 S. Ct., at 1156–1157 (separate opinion). That the Constitution sets this realm of thought and feeling apart from the pressures and antagonisms of government is one of its supreme achievements. Regrettably, the Court today tarnishes that achievement.

I dissent.

[The dissenting opinion of JUSTICE BLACKMUN, with whom JUSTICE STEVENS joins, is omitted.]

COUNTY OF ALLEGHENY v. AMERICAN CIVIL LIBERTIES UNION
___ U.S. ___; ___ L. Ed. 2d ___; 109 S. Ct. 3086 (1989)

JUSTICE BLACKMUN *announced the judgment of the Court and delivered the opinion of the Court with respect to Parts III-A, IV, and V, an opinion with respect to Parts I and II, in which* JUSTICE O'CONNOR *and* JUSTICE STEVENS *join, an opinion with respect to Part III-B, in which* JUSTICE STEVENS *joins, and an opinion with respect to Part VI.*

This litigation concerns the constitutionality of two recurring holiday displays located on public property in downtown Pittsburgh. The first is a crèche placed on the Grand Staircase of the Allegheny County Courthouse. The second is a Chanukah menorah placed just outside the City-County Building, next to a Christmas tree and a sign saluting liberty. The Court of Appeals for the Third Circuit ruled that each display violates the Establishment Clause of the First Amendment because each has the impermissible effect of endorsing religion. We agree that the crèche display has that unconstitutional effect but reverse the Court of Appeals' judgment regarding the menorah display.

I

* * *

Since 1981, the county has permitted the Holy Name Society, a Roman Catholic group, to display a crèche in the County Courthouse during the Christmas holiday season. Christmas is the holiday when Christians celebrate the birth of Jesus of Nazareth, whom they believe to be the Messiah. . . . As observed in this Nation, Christmas has a secular as well as a religious dimension.

The crèche in the County Courthouse . . . is a visual representation of the scene in the manger in Bethlehem shortly after the birth of Jesus. [It], . . . described in the Gospels of Luke and Matthew, includes figures of the infant Jesus, Mary, Joseph, farm animals, shepherds, and wise men, all places in or before a wooden representation of a manger, which has at its crest an angel bearing a banner that proclaims "Gloria in Excelsis Deo!"

During the 1986–1987 holiday season, the crèche was on display on the Grand Staircase. . . . It had a wooden fence on three sides and bore a plaque stating: "This Display Donated by the Holy Name Society." Sometime during the week of December 2, the county placed red and white poinsettia plants around the fence [and] . . . a small evergreen tree, decorated with a red bow, behind each of the two endposts of the fence. . . . Altogether, the crèche, the fence, the poinsettias, and the trees occupied a substantial amount of space on the Grand Staircase. No figures of Santa Claus or other decorations appeared on the Grand Staircase.

The county uses the crèche as the setting for its annual Christmas-carol program. During the 1986 season, the county invited high school choirs and other musical groups to perform during weekday lunch hours from December 3 through December 23. The county dedicated this program to world peace and to the families of prisoners-of-war and of persons missing-in-action in Southeast Asia.

Near the Grand Staircase is an area of the County Courthouse known as the "gallery forum" used for art and other cultural exhibits. The crèche, with its fence-and-floral frame, was distinct and not connected with any exhibit in the gallery forum. . . .

B

The City-County Building is separate and a block removed from the County Courthouse and . . . is jointly owned by the city of Pittsburgh and Allegheny County. The city's portion of the building houses the city's principal offices. . . . The city is responsible for the building's Grand Street entrance which has three rounded arches supported by columns.

For a number of years, the city has had a large

Christmas tree under the middle arch outside the Grand Street entrance. . . . [O]n November 17, 1986 [the city] erected a 45-foot tree under the middle arch and decorated it with lights and ornaments. . . . [P]laced at the foot of the tree [was] a sign bearing the Mayor's name and entitled "Salute to Liberty." Beneath the title, the sign stated:

> During this holiday season, the City of Pittsburgh salutes liberty. Let these festive lights remind us that we are the keepers of the flame of liberty and our legacy of freedom.

At least since 1982, the city has expanded its Grand Street holiday display to include a symbolic representation of Chanukah, an 8-day Jewish holiday [that] usually occurs in December. . . . In 1986, Chanukah began at sundown on December 26. . . .

Chanukah, like Christmas, is a cultural event as well as a religious holiday. . . . Also, Chanukah, like Christmas, is a winter holiday. . . . Just as some Americans celebrate Christmas without regard to its religious significance, some nonreligious American Jews celebrate Chanukah as an expression of ethnic identity, and "as a cultural or national event, rather than as a specifically religious event." . . .

The cultural significance of Chanukah varies with the setting in which the holiday is celebrated. . . . Indeed, some have suggested that the proximity of Christmas accounts for the social prominence of Chanukah in this country. Whatever the reason, Chanukah is observed by American Jews to an extent greater than its religious importance would indicate: in the hierarchy of Jewish holidays, Chanukah ranks fairly low in religious significance. This socially heightened status of Chanukah reflects its cultural or secular dimension.

On December 22 of the 1986 holiday season, the city placed at the Grand Street entrance to the City-County Building an 18-foot Chanukah menorah of an abstract tree-and-branch design. The menorah was placed next to the city's 45-foot Christmas tree, against one of the columns that supports the arch into which the tree was set. The menorah is owned by Chabad, a Jewish group, but is stored, erected, and removed each year by the city.

II

. . . [In] 1986 . . . the Greater Pittsburgh Chapter of the American Civil Liberties Union and seven local residents filed suit against the county and the city, seeking permanently to enjoin the county from dis-

playing the menorah in front of the City-County Building. Respondents claim that the displays of the crèche and the menorah each violate the Establishment Clause of the First Amendment. . . .

[T]he District Court denied respondent's request for a permanent injunction. Relying on *Lynch* v. *Donnelly,* the court stated that "the crèche was but part of the holiday decoration of the stairwell and a foreground for the high-school choirs which entertained each day at noon." Regarding the menorah, the court concluded that "it was but an insignificant part of another holiday display." The court also found that "the displays had a secular purpose" and "did not create an excessive entanglement of government with religion."

. . . [A] divided panel of the Court of Appeals reversed. Distinguishing *Lynch* v. *Donnelly,* the panel majority determined that the crèche and the menorah must be understood as endorsing Christianity and Judaism. The court observed: "Each display was located at or in a public building devoted to core functions of government." The court also stated: "Further, while the menorah was placed near a Christmas tree, neither the crèche nor the menorah can reasonably be deemed to have been subsumed by a larger display of non-religious items." Because the impermissible effect of endorsing religion was a sufficient basis for holding each display to be in violation of the Establishment Clause under *Lemon* v. *Kurtzman,* the Court of Appeals did not consider whether either one had an impermissible purpose or resulted in an unconstitutional entanglement between government and religion. . . .

III

A

* * *

In the course of adjudicating specific cases, this Court has come to understand the Establishment Clause to mean that government may not promote or affiliate itself with any religious doctrine or organization, may not discriminate among persons on the basis of their religious beliefs and practices, may not delegate a government power to a religious institution, and may not involve itself too deeply in such an institution's affairs. Although the myriad, subtle ways in which Establishment Clause values can be eroded . . . are not susceptible to a single verbal formulation, this Court has attempted to encapsulate the essential precepts of the Establishment Clause. . . .

In *Lemon* v. *Kurtzman,* . . . the Court [set forth] three "tests" for determining whether a government practice violates the Establishment Clause. Under the *Lemon* analysis, a statute or practice which touches upon religion, if it is to be permissible under the Establishment Clause, must have a secular purpose; it must neither advance nor inhibit religion in its principal or primary effect; and it must not foster an excessive entanglement with religion. This trilogy of tests has been applied regularly in the Court's later Establishment Clause cases.

Our subsequent decisions further have refined the definition of governmental action that unconstitutionally advances religion. In recent years, we have paid particularly close attention to whether the challenged governmental practice either has the purpose or effect of "endorsing" religion, a concern that has long had a place in our Establishment Clause jurisprudence. Thus, in *Wallace* v. *Jaffree*, the Court held unconstitutional Alabama's moment-of-silence statute because it was "enacted . . . for the sole purpose of expressing the State's endorsement of prayer activities." The Court similarly invalidated Louisiana's "Creationism Act" because it "endorses religion" in its purpose, *Edwards* v. *Aguillard*. And the educational program in *School District of Grand Rapids* v. *Ball* was held to violate the Establishment Clause because of its "endorsement" effect. . . .

Of course, the word "endorsement" is not self-defining. Rather, it derives its meaning from other words that this Court has found useful over the years in interpreting the Establishment Clause. Thus, it has been noted that the prohibition against governmental endorsement of religion "preclude[s] government from conveying or attempting to convey a message that religion or a particular religious belief is *favored or preferred*. . . ." Moreover, the term "endorsement" is closely linked to the term "promotion," and this Court long since has held that government "may not . . . promote one religion or religious theory against another or even against the militant opposite." . . .

Whether the key word is "endorsement," "favoritism," or "promotion," the essential principle remains the same. The Establishment Clause, at the very least, prohibits government from appearing to take a position on questions of religious belief or from "making adherence to a religion relevant in any way to a person's standing in the political community."

B

We have had occasion in the past to apply Establishment Clause principles to the government's display of objects with religious significance. In *Stone*

v. *Graham*, 449 U.S. 39, (1980), we held that the display of a copy of the Ten Commandments on the walls of public classrooms violates the Establishment Clause. Closer to the facts of this litigation is *Lynch* v. *Donnelly* [465 U.S. 691, 1984], in which we considered whether the city of Pawtucket, R.I., had violated the Establishment Clause by including a crèche in its annual Christmas display, located in a private park within the downtown shopping district. By a 5–4 decision in that difficult case, the Court upheld inclusion of the crèche in the Pawtucket display, holding, *inter alia*, that the inclusion of the crèche did not have the impermissible effect of advancing or promoting religion. . . .

Although JUSTICE O'CONNOR joined the majority opinion in *Lynch*, she wrote a concurrence that differs in significant respects from the majority opinion. The main difference is that the concurrence provides a sound analytical framework for evaluating governmental use of religious symbols.

First and foremost, the concurrence squarely rejects any notion that this Court will tolerate some government endorsement of religion. Rather, the concurrence recognizes any endorsement of religion as "invalid," because it "sends a message to nonadherents that they are outsiders, not full members of the political community, and an accompanying message to adherents that they are insiders, favored members of the political community."

Second, the concurrence articulates a method for determining whether the government's use of an object with religious meaning has the effect of endorsing religion. The effect of the display depends upon the message that the government's practice communicates: the question is "what viewers may fairly understand to be the purpose of the display." That inquiry, of necessity, turns upon the context in which the contested object appears: "a typical museum setting, though not neutralizing the religious content of a religious painting, negates any message of endorsement of that content." The concurrence thus emphasizes that the constitutionality of the crèche in that case depended upon its "particular physical setting," and further observes: "Every government practice must be judged in its unique circumstances to determine whether it [endorses] religion."

The concurrence applied this mode of analysis to the Pawtucket crèche, seen in the context of that city's holiday celebration as a whole. In addition to the crèche the city's display contained: a Santa Claus House with a live Santa distributing candy; reindeer pulling Santa's sleigh; a live 40-

foot Christmas tree strung with lights; statutes of carolers in old-fashioned dress; candy-striped poles; a "talking" wishing well; a large banner proclaiming "SEASONS GREETINGS"; a miniature "village" with several houses and a church; and various "cut-out" figures including those of a clown, a dancing elephant, a robot, and a teddy bear. The concurrence concluded that both because the crèche is a "traditional symbol" of Christmas, a holiday with strong secular elements, and because the crèche was "displayed along with purely secular symbols," the crèche's setting "changes what viewers may fairly understand to be the purpose of the display" and "negates any message of endorsement" of "the Christian beliefs represented by the crèche."

The four *Lynch* dissenters agreed with the concurrence that the controlling question was "whether Pawtucket ha[d] run afoul of the Establishment Clause by endorsing religion through its display of the crèche." The dissenters also agreed with the general proposition that the context in which the government uses a religious symbol is relevant for determining the answer to that question. They simply reached a different answer: the dissenters concluded that the other elements of the Pawtucket display did not negate the endorsement of Christian faith caused by the presence of the crèche. They viewed the inclusion of the crèche in the city's overall display as placing "the government's imprimatur of approval on the particular religious beliefs exemplified by the crèche." Thus, they stated: "The effect on minority religious groups, as well as on those who may reject all religion, is to convey the message that their views are not similarly worthy of public recognition nor entitled to public support."

Thus, despite divergence at the bottom line, the five Justices in concurrence and dissent in *Lynch* agreed upon the relevant constitutional principles: the government's use of religious symbolism is unconstitutional if it has the effect of endorsing religious beliefs, and the effect of the government's use of religious symbolism depends upon its context. These general principles are sound, and have been adopted by the Court in subsequent cases. Since *Lynch,* the Court has made clear that, when evaluating the effect of government conduct under the Establishment Clause, we must ascertain whether "the challenged governmental action is sufficiently likely to be perceived by adherents of the controlling denominations as an endorsement, and by the nonadherents as a disapproval, of their individual religious choices." Accordingly, our present task is to determine whether the display of the crèche and the menorah, in their respective "particular physical settings," has the effect of endorsing or disapproving religious beliefs.

IV

We turn first to the county's crèche display. There is no doubt, of course, that the crèche itself is capable of communicating a religious message. Indeed, the crèche in this lawsuit uses words, as well as the picture of the nativity scene, to make its religious meaning unmistakably clear. "Glory to God in the Highest!" says the angel in the crèche—Glory to God because of the birth of Jesus. This praise to God in Christian terms is indisputably religious—indeed sectarian—just as it is when said in the Gospel or in a church service.

Under the Court's holding in *Lynch* the effect of a crèche display turns on its setting. Here, unlike in *Lynch,* nothing in the context of the display detracts from the crèche's religious message. The *Lynch* display comprised a series of figures and objects, each group of which had its own focal point. Santa's house and his reindeer were objects of attention separate from the crèche, and had their specific visual story to tell. Similarly, whatever a "talking" wishing well may be, it obviously was a center of attention separate from the crèche. Here, in contrast, the crèche stands alone: it is the single element of the display on the Grand Staircase.

The floral decoration surrounding the crèche cannot be viewed as somehow equivalent to the secular symbols in the overall *Lynch* display. . . . The floral decoration surrounding the crèche contributes to, rather than detracts from, the endorsement of religion conveyed by the crèche. . . .

Nor does the fact that the crèche was the setting for the county's annual Christmas carol-program diminish its religious meaning. . . . The effect of the crèche on those who viewed it when the choirs were not singing—the vast majority of the time—cannot be negated by the presence of the choir program. Second, because some of the carols performed at the site of the crèche were religious in nature, those carols were more likely to augment the religious quality of the scene than to secularize it.

Furthermore, the crèche sits on the Grand Staircase, the "main" and "most beautiful part" of the building that is the seat of county government. No viewer could reasonably think that it occupies this location without the support and approval of the government. Thus, by permitting the "display of the crèche in this particular physical setting," the county sends an unmistakable message that it supports and promotes the Christian praise to God that is the crèche's religious message.

The fact that the crèche bears a sign disclosing its ownership by a Roman Catholic organization does not alter this conclusion. On the contrary, the sign simply demonstrates that the government is endorsing the religious message of that organization, rather than communicating a message of its own. But the Establishment Clause does not limit only the religious content of the government's own communications. It also prohibits the government's support and promotion of religious communications by religious organizations. . . . Thus, by prohibiting government endorsement of religion, the Establishment Clause prohibits precisely what occurred here: the government's lending its support to the communication of a religious organization's religious message . . . by suggesting that people praise God for the birth of Jesus.

. . . *Lynch* teaches that government may celebrate Christmas in some manner and form, but not in a way that endorses Christian doctrine. Here, Allegheny County has transgressed this line. It has chosen to celebrate Christmas in a way that has the effect of endorsing a patently Christian message: Glory to God for the birth of Jesus Christ. Under *Lynch,* and the rest of our cases, nothing more is required to demonstrate a violation of the Establishment Clause. The display of the crèche in this context, therefore, must be permanently enjoined. . . .

V

* * *

Of course, not all religious celebrations of Christmas located on government property violate the Establishment Clause. It obviously is not unconstitutional, for example, for a group of parishioners from a local church to go caroling through a city park on any Sunday in Advent or for a Christian club at a public university to sing carols during their Christmas meeting. The reason is that activities of this nature do not demonstrate the government's allegiance to, or endorsement of, the Christian faith.

Equally obvious, however, is the proposition that not all proclamations of Christian faith located on government property are permitted by the Establishment Clause just because they occur during the Christmas holiday season, as the example of a Mass in the courthouse surely illustrates. And once the judgment has been made that a par-

ticular proclamation of Christian belief, when disseminated from a particular location on government property, has the effect of demonstrating the government's endorsement of Christian faith, then it necessarily follows that the practice must be enjoined to protect the constitutional rights of those citizens who follow some creed other than Christianity. It is thus incontrovertible that the Court's decision today, premised on the determination that the crèche display on the Grand Staircase demonstrates the county's endorsement of Christianity does not represent a hostility or indifference to religion but, instead, the respect for religious diversity that the Constitution requires.

VI

The display of the Chanukah menorah in front of the City-County Building may well present a closer constitutional question. The menorah . . . is a religious symbol: it serves to commemorate the miracle of the oil as described in the Talmud. But the menorah's message is not exclusively religious. The menorah is the primary visual symbol for a holiday that, like Christmas, has both religious and secular dimensions.

Moreover, the menorah here stands next to a Christmas tree and a sign saluting liberty. While no challenge has been made here to the display of the tree and the sign their presence is obviously relevant in determining the effect of the menorah's display. The necessary result of placing a menorah next to a Christmas tree is to create an "overall holiday setting" that represents both Christmas and Chanukah—two holidays, not one.

. . . If the city celebrates both Christmas and Chanukah as religious holidays, then it violates the Establishment Clause. The simultaneous endorsement of Judaism and Christianity is no less constitutionally infirm than the endorsement of Christianity alone.

Conversely, if the city celebrates both Christmas and Chanukah as secular holidays, then its conduct is beyond reach of the Establishment Clause. Because government may celebrate Christmas as a secular holiday, it follows that government may also acknowledge Chanukah as a secular holiday. Simply put, it would be a form of discrimination against Jews to allow Pittsburgh to celebrate Christmas as a cultural tradition while simultaneously disallowing the city's acknowledgment of Chanukah as a contemporaneous cultural tradition.

Accordingly, the relevant question for Establishment Clause purposes is whether the combined display of the tree, the sign, and the menorah has the effect of endorsing both Christian and Jewish faiths, or rather simply recognizes that both Christmas and Chanukah are part of the same winter-holiday season, which has attained a secular status in our society. Of the two interpretations of this particular display, the latter seems far more plausible and is also in line with *Lynch*.

The Christmas tree, unlike the menorah, is not itself a religious symbol. Although Christmas trees once carried religious connotations, today they typify the secular celebration of Christmas. . . . The widely accepted view of the Christmas tree as the preeminent secular symbol of the Christmas holiday season serves to emphasize the secular component of the message communicated by other elements of an accompanying holiday display, including the Chanukah menorah.

The tree . . . is clearly the predominant element in the city's display. [It] . . . occupies the central position beneath the middle archway in front of the Grand Street entrance to the City-County Building: the 18-foot menorah is positioned to one side. Given this configuration, it is much more sensible to interpret the meaning of the menorah in light of the tree, rather than *vice versa*. In the shadow of the tree, the menorah is readily understood as simply a recognition that Christmas is not the only traditional way of observing the winter-holiday season. In these circumstances, then, the combination of the tree and the menorah communicates, not a simultaneous endorsement of both Christian and Jewish faith, but instead, a secular celebration of Christmas coupled with an acknowledgment of Chanukah as a contemporaneous alternative tradition.

Although the city has used a symbol with religious meaning as its representation of Chanukah, this is not a case in which the city has reasonable alternatives that are less religious in nature. It is difficult to imagine a predominantly secular symbol of Chanukah that the city could place next to its Christmas tree. An 18-foot dreidel would look out of place, and might be interpreted by some as mocking the celebration of Chanukah. The absence of a more secular alternative symbol is itself part of the context in which the city's actions must be judged in determining the likely effect of its use of the menorah. Where the government's secular message can be conveyed by two symbols, only one of which carries religious meaning, an observer reasonably might infer from the fact that the government has chosen to use the religious symbol that the government means to promote religious faith. But where, as here, no such choice has been made, this inference of endorsement is not present. . . .

Given all these considerations, it is not "sufficiently likely" that residents of Pittsburgh will perceive the combined display of the tree, the sign, and the menorah as an "endorsement" or "disapproval . . . of their individual religious choices." While an adjudication of the display's effect must take into account the perspective of one who is neither Christian nor Jewish, as well as of those who adhere to either of these religions, the constitutionality of its effect must also be judged according to the standard of a "reasonable observer." When measured against this standard, the menorah need not be excluded from this particular display. The Christmas tree alone in the Pittsburgh location does not endorse Christian belief; and, on the facts before us, the addition of the menorah "cannot fairly be understood to" result in the simultaneous endorsement of Christian and Jewish faiths. On the contrary, for purposes of the Establishment Clause, the city's overall display must be understood as conveying the city's secular recognition of different traditions for celebrating the winter-holiday season. . . .

VII

Lynch v. *Donnelly* confirms, and in no way repudiates, the longstanding constitutional principle that government may not engage in a practice that has the effect of promoting or endorsing religious beliefs. The display of the crèche in the County Courthouse has this unconstitutional effect. The display of the menorah in front of the City-County Building, however, does not have this effect, given its "particular physical setting."

The judgment of the Court of Appeals is affirmed in part and reversed in part, and the cases are remanded for further proceedings.

It is so ordered.

JUSTICE O'CONNOR, *with whom* JUSTICE BRENNAN *and* JUSTICE STEVENS *join as to Part II, concurring in part and concurring in the judgment.*

I

* * *

In my concurrence in *Lynch*, I suggested a clarification of our Establishment Clause doctrine to reinforce the concept that the Establishment Clause "prohibits government from making adherence to a religion relevant in any way to a person's standing in the political community." The government violates this prohibition if it endorses or disapproves of religion. "Endorsement sends a message to non-adherents that they are outsiders, not full members of the political community, and an accompanying message to adherents that they are insiders, favored members of the political community." Disapproval of religion conveys that opposite message. Thus, in my view, the central issue in *Lynch* was whether the city of Pawtucket had endorsed Christianity by displaying a crèche as part of a larger exhibit of traditional secular symbols of the Christmas holiday season.

In *Lynch*, I concluded that the city's display of a crèche in its larger holiday exhibit in a private park in the commercial district had neither the purpose nor the effect of conveying a message of government endorsement of Christianity or disapproval of other religions. The purpose of including the crèche in the larger display was to celebrate the public holiday through its traditional symbols, not to promote the religious content of the crèche. Nor, in my view, did Pawtucket's display of the crèche along with secular symbols of the Christmas holiday objectively convey a message of endorsement of Christianity.

For the reasons stated in Part IV of the Court's opinion in this case, I agree that the crèche displayed on the Grand Staircase of the Allegheny Courthouse, the seat of county government, conveys a message to nonadherents of Christianity that they are not full members of the political community, and a corresponding message to Christians that they are favored members of the political community. In contrast to the crèche in *Lynch*, which was displayed in a private park in the city's commercial district as part of a broader display of traditional secular symbols of the holiday season, this crèche stands alone in the County Courthouse. The display of religious symbols in public areas of core government buildings runs a special risk of "mak[ing] religion relevant, in reality or public perception, to status in the political community." . . . The Court correctly concludes that placement of the central religious symbol of the Christmas holiday season at the Allegheny County Courthouse has the unconstitutional effect of conveying a government endorsement of Christianity. . . .

II

* * *

I continue to believe that the endorsement test asks the right question about governmental practices challenged on Establishment Clause grounds, including challenged practices involving the display of religious symbols. Moreover, commentators in the scholarly literature have found merit in the approach. . . . I also remain convinced that the endorsement test is capable of consistent application. Indeed, it is notable that three Circuit courts which have considered challenges to the display of a crèche standing alone at city hall have each concluded, relying in part on endorsement analysis, that such a practice sends a message to nonadherents of Christianity that they are outsiders in the political community. To be sure, the endorsement test depends on a sensitivity to the unique circumstances and context of a particular challenged practice and, like any test that is sensitive to context, it may not always yield results with unanimous agreement at the margins. But that is true of many standards in constitutional law. . . .

Under the endorsement test, the "history and ubiquity" of a practice is relevant not because it creates an "artificial exception" from that test. On the contrary, the "history and ubiquity" of a practice is relevant because it provides part of the context in which a reasonable observer evaluates whether a challenged governmental practice conveys a message of endorsement of religion. It is the combination of the longstanding existence of practices such as opening legislative sessions with legislative prayers or opening Court sessions with "God save the United States and this honorable Court," as well as their nonsectarian nature, that lead me to the conclusion that those particular practices, despite their religious roots, do not convey a message of endorsement of particular religious belief. . . . The question under endorsement analysis, in short, is whether a reasonable observer would view such longstanding practices as a disapproval of their particular religious choices, in light of the fact that they serve a secular purpose rather than a sectarian one and have largely lost their religious significance over time. Although the endorsement test requires careful and often difficult line-drawing and is highly context-specific, no alternative test has been suggested that captures the essential mandate of the Establishment Clause as well as the endorsement test does, and it warrants continued application and refinement.

. . . [N]either the endorsement test nor its application in this case reflect "an unjustified hostility toward religion." Instead, the endorsement standard recognizes that the religious liberty so precious to the citizens who make up our diverse country is protected, not impeded, when government avoids endorsing religion or favoring particular beliefs over other. Clearly, the government can *acknowledge* the role of religion in our society in numerous ways that do not amount to an endorsement. Moreover, the government can *accommodate* religion by lifting government-imposed burdens on religion. Indeed, the Free Exercise Clause may mandate that it do so in particular cases. In cases involving the lifting of government burdens on the free exercise of religion, a reasonable observer would take into account the values underlying the Free Exercise Clause in assessing whether the challenged practice conveyed a message of endorsement. By "build[ing] on the concerns at the core of nonestablishment doctrine and recogniz[ing] the role of accommodations in furthering free exercise," the endorsement test "provides a standard capable of consistent application and avoids the criticism leveled against the *Lemon* test." The case before the Court today, however, does not involve lifting a governmental burden on the free exercise of religion. . . . Christians remain free to display their crèches at their homes and churches. Allegheny County has neither placed nor removed a governmental burden on the free exercise of religion but rather, for the reasons stated in Part IV of the Court's opinion, has conveyed a message of governmental endorsement of Christian beliefs. This the Establishment Clause does not permit.

III

For reasons which differ somewhat from those set forth in Part VI of JUSTICE BLACKMUN's opinion, I also conclude that the city of Pittsburgh's combined holiday display of a Chanukah menorah, a Christmas tree, and a sign saluting liberty does not have the effect of conveying an endorsement of religion. I agree with JUSTICE BLACKMUN that the Christmas tree, whatever its origins, is not regarded today as a religious symbol. . . . A Christmas tree displayed in front of city hall, in my view, cannot fairly be understood as conveying governmental endorsement of Christianity. . . .

[T]he question here is whether Pittsburgh's holiday display conveys a message of endorsement of Judaism, when the menorah is the only religious symbol in the combined display and when the opinion acknowledges that the tree cannot reasonably be understood to convey an endorsement of Christianity. One need not characterize Chanukah as a "secular holiday" or strain to argue that the menorah has a "secular dimension" in order to conclude that the city of Pittsburgh's combined display does not convey a message of endorsement of Judaism or of religion in general. . . .

My conclusion does not depend on whether or not the city had "a more secular alternative symbol" of Chanukah, just as the Court's decision in *Lynch* clearly did not turn on whether the city of Pawtucket could have conveyed its tribute to the Christmas holiday season by using a "less religious" alternative to the crèche symbol in its display of traditional holiday symbols. . . . In my view, JUSTICE BLACKMUN's new rule that an inference of endorsement arises every time government uses a symbol with religious meaning if a "more secular alternative" is available, is too blunt an instrument for Establishment Clause analysis, which depends on sensitivity to the context and circumstances presented by each case. Indeed, the opinion appears to recognize the importance of this contextual sensitivity by creating an exception to its new rule in the very case announcing it: the opinion acknowledges that "a purely secular symbol" of Chanukah is available, namely, a dreidel or four-sided top, but rejects the use of such a symbol because it "might be interpreted by some as mocking the celebration of Chanukah." This recognition that the more religious alternative may, depending on the circumstances, convey a message that is least likely to implicate Establishment Clause concerns is an excellent example of the need to focus on the specific practice in question in its particular physical setting and context in determining whether government has conveyed or attempted to convey a message that religion or a particular religious belief is favored or preferred. . . .

[The opinion of JUSTICE BRENNAN, with whom JUSTICE MARSHALL and JUSTICE STEVENS join, concurring in part and dissenting in part, is not reprinted here.]

[The opinion of JUSTICE STEVENS, with whom JUSTICE BRENNAN and JUSTICE MARSHALL join, concurring in part and dissenting in part, is not reprinted here.]

JUSTICE KENNEDY, *with whom the* CHIEF JUSTICE, JUSTICE WHITE, *and* JUSTICE SCALIA *join, concurring in the judgment in part and dissenting in part.*

The majority holds that the County of Allegheny violated the Establishment Clause by displaying a crèche in the County Courthouse, because the "principle or primary effect" of the display is to advance religion within the meaning of *Lemon* v.

Kurtzman. This view of the Establishment Clause reflects an unjustified hostility toward religion, a hostility inconsistent with our history and our precedents, and I dissent from this holding. The crèche display is constitutional, and, for the same reasons, the display of a menorah by the city of Pittsburgh is permissible as well. On this latter point, I concur in the result, but not the reasoning, of Part VI of JUSTICE BLACKMUN's opinion.

I

In keeping with the usual fashion of recent years, the majority applies the *Lemon* test to judge the constitutionality of the holiday displays here in question. I am content for present purposes to remain within the *Lemon* framework, but do not wish to be seen as advocating, let alone adopting, that test as our primary guide in this difficult area. Persuasive criticism of *Lemon* has emerged. . . . Our cases often question its utility in providing concrete answers to Establishment Clause questions, calling it but a " 'helpful signpos[t]' " or " 'guidelin[e]' ", to assist our deliberations rather than a comprehensive test. . . . Substantial revision of our Establishment Clause doctrine may be in order; but it is unnecessary to undertake that task today, for even the *Lemon* test, when applied with proper sensitivity to our traditions and our caselaw, supports the conclusion that both the crèche and the menorah are permissible displays in the context of the holiday season. . . .

. . . I would not commit this Court to the test applied by the majority today. The notion that cases arising under the Establishment Clause should be decided by an inquiry into whether a " 'reasonable observer' " may " 'fairly understand' " government action to " 'sen[d] a message to nonadherents that they are outsiders, not full members of the political community,' " is a recent, and in my view most unwelcome, addition to our tangled Establishment Clause jurisprudence. Although a scattering of our cases have used "endorsement" as another word for "preference" or "imprimatur," the endorsement test applied by the majority had its genesis in JUSTICE O'CONNOR's concurring opinion in *Lynch.* . . . Only one opinion for the Court has purported to apply it in full, see *School District of Grand Rapids* v. *Ball,* 473 U.S. 373, 389–392 (1985), but the majority's opinion in this case suggests that this novel theory is fast becoming a permanent accretion to the law. For the reasons expressed below, I submit that the endorsement test is flawed in its fundamentals and unworkable in practice. The uncritical adoption of this standard is every bit as troubling as the bizarre result it produces in the case before us.

A

I take it as settled law that, whatever standard the Court applies to Establishment Clause claims, it must at least suggest results consistent with our precedents and the historical practices that, by tradition, have informed our First Amendment jurisprudence. It is true that, for reasons quite unrelated to the First Amendment, displays commemorating religious holidays were not commonplace in 1791. But the relevance of history is not confined to the inquiry whether the challenged practice itself is a part of our accepted traditions dating back to the Founding.

Our decision in *Marsh* v. *Chambers* illustrates this proposition. The dissent in that case sought to characterize the decision as "carving out an exception to the Establishment Clause rather than reshaping Establishment Clause doctrine to accommodate legislative prayer," but the majority rejected the suggestion that "historical patterns ca[n] justify contemporary violations of constitutional guarantees." *Marsh* stands for the proposition, not that specific practices common in 1791 are an exception to the otherwise broad sweep of the Establishment Clause, but rather that the meaning of the Clause is to be determined by reference to historical practices and understandings. Whatever test we choose to apply must permit not only legitimate practices two centuries old but also any other practices with no greater potential for an establishment of religion. . . .

If the endorsement test, applied without artificial exceptions for historical practice, reached results consistent with history, my objections to it would have less force. But, as I understand that test, the touchstone of an Establishment Clause violation is whether nonadherents would be made to feel like "outsiders" by government recognition or accommodation of religion. Few of our traditional practices recognizing the part religion plays in our society can withstand scrutiny under a faithful application of this formula.

Some examples suffice to make plain my concerns. Since the Founding of our Republic, American Presidents have issued Thanksgiving Proclamations establishing a national day of celebration and prayer. The first such proclamation was issued by President Washington at the request of the First Congress. . . . Most of President Washington's successors have followed suit, and the forthrightly religious nature of these proclamations has not waned with the years. President

Franklin D. Roosevelt went so far as to "suggest a nationwide reading of the Holy Scriptures during the period from Thanksgiving Day to Christmas" so that "we may bear more earnest witness to our gratitude to Almighty God." It requires little imagination to conclude that these proclamations would cause nonadherents to feel excluded, yet they have been a part of our national heritage from the beginning.

The Executive has not been the only branch of our Government to recognize the central role of religion in our society. The fact that this Court opens its sessions with the request that "God save the United States and this honorable Court" has been noted elsewhere. The Legislature has gone much further, not only employing legislative chaplains, but also setting aside a special prayer room in the Capitol for use by Members of the House and Senate. The room is decorated with a large stained glass panel that depicts President Washington kneeling in prayer; around him is etched the first verse of the 16th Psalm: "Preserve me, O God, for in Thee do I put my trust." Beneath the panel is a rostrum on which a Bible is placed; next to the rostrum is an American Flag. Some endorsement is inherent in these reasonable accommodations, yet the Establishment Clause does not forbid them.

The United States Code itself contains religious references that would be suspect under the endorsement test. Congress has directed the President to "set aside and proclaim a suitable day each year . . . as a National Day of Prayer, on which the people of the United States may turn to God in prayer and meditation at churches, in groups, and as individuals." This statute does not require anyone to pray, of course, but it is a straightforward endorsement of the concept of "turn[ing] to God in prayer." Also by statute, the Pledge of Allegiance to the Flag describes the United States as "one Nation under God." To be sure, no one is obligated to recite this phrase, but it borders on sophistry to suggest that the " 'reasonable' " atheist would not feel less than a " 'full membe[r] of the political community' " every time his fellow Americans recited, as part of their expression of patriotism and love for country, a phrase he believed to be false. Likewise, our national motto, "In God we trust," which is prominently engraved in the wall above the Speaker's dais in the Chamber of the House of Representatives and is reproduced on every coin minted and every dollar printed by the Federal Government, must have the same effect.

If the intent of the Establishment Clause is to protect individuals from mere feelings of exclusion, then legislative prayer cannot escape invalidation. It has been argued that "[these] government acknowledgments of religion serve, in the only ways reasonably possible in our culture, the legitimate secular purposes of solemnizing public occasions, expressing confidence in the future, and encouraging the recognition of what is worthy of appreciation in society." I fail to see why prayer is the only way to convey these messages: appeals to patriotism, moments of silence, and any number of other approaches would be as effective, were the only purposes at issue the ones described by the *Lynch* concurrence. Nor is it clear to me why "encouraging the recognition of what is worthy of appreciation in society" can be characterized as a purely secular purpose, if it can be acheived only through religious prayer. No doubt prayer is "worthy of appreciation," but that is most assuredly not because it is secular. Even accepting the secular-solemnization explanation at face value, moreover, it seems incredible to suggest that the average observer of legislative prayer who either believes in no religion or whose faith rejects the concept of God would not receive the clear message that his faith is out of step with the political norm. Either the endorsement test must invalidate scores of traditional practices recognizing the place religion holds in our culture, or it must be twisted and stretched to avoid inconsistency with practices we know to have been permitted in the past, while condemning similar practices with no greater endorsement effect simply by reason of their lack of historical antecedent. Neither result is acceptable.

* * *

B

My description of the majority's test, though perhaps uncharitable, is intended to illustrate the inevitable difficulties with its application. This test could provide workable guidance to the lower courts, if ever, only after this Court has decided a long series of holiday display cases, using little more than intuition and a tape measure. Deciding cases on the basis of such an unguided examination of marginalia is irreconcilable with the imperative of applying neutral principles in constitutional adjudication. "It would be appalling to conduct litigation under the Establishment Clause as if it were a trademark case, with experts testifying about whether one display is really like another, and witnesses testifying they were offended—but would have been less so were the crèche five feet closer to the jumbo candy cane."

The result the Court reaches in this case is perhaps the clearest illustration of the unwisdom of the endorsement test. Although JUSTICE O'CONNOR disavows JUSTICE BLACKMUN's suggestion that the minority or majority status of a religion is relevant to the question whether government recognition constitutes a forbidden endorsement, the very nature of the endorsement test, with its emphasis on the feelings of the objective observer, easily lends itself to this type of inquiry. If there be such a person as the "reasonable observer," I am quite certain that he or she will take away a salient message from our holding in this case: the Supreme Court of the United States has concluded that the First Amendment creates classes of religions based on the relative numbers of their adherents. Those religions enjoying the largest following must be consigned to the status of least-favored faiths so as to avoid any possible risk of offending members of minority religions. I would be the first to admit that many questions arising under the Establishment Clause do not admit of easy answers, but whatever the Clause requires, it is not the result reached by the Court today.

IV

The approach adopted by the majority contradicts important values embodied in the Clause. Obsessive, implacable resistance to all but the most carefully scripted and secularized forms of accommodation requires this Court to act as a censor, issuing national decrees as to what is orthodox and what is not. What is orthodox, in this context, means what is secular, the only Christmas the State can acknowledge is one in which references to religion have been held to a minimum. The Court thus lends its assistance to an Orwellian rewriting of history as many understand it. I can conceive of no judicial function more antithetical to the First Amendment. The case before us is admittedly a troubling one. It must be conceded that however neutral the purpose of the city and county, the eager proselytizer may seek to use these symbols for his own ends. The urge to use them to teach or to taunt is always present. It is also true that some devout adherents of Judaism or Christianity may be as offended by the holiday display as are nonbelievers, if not more so. To place these religious symbols in a common hallway or sidewalk, where they may be ignored or even insulted, must be distasteful to many who cherish their meaning.

For these reasons, I might have voted against installation of these particular displays were I a local legislative official. But we have no jurisdiction over matters of taste within the realm of constitutionally permissible discretion. Our role is enforcement of a written Constitution. In my view, the principles of the Establishment Clause and our Nation's historic traditions of diversity and pluralism allow communities to make reasonable judgments respecting the accommodation or acknowledgment of holidays with both cultural and religious aspects. No constitutional violation occurs when they do so by displaying a symbol of the holiday's religious origins.

I dissent.

Taxes and Churches: A Continuing Controversy

FEATURED CASES

Walz v. *Tax Commission of City of New York*   *Jimmy Swaggart Ministries* v. *Board of Equalization of California*

In his landmark opinion in *Everson* v. *Board of Education,* Justice Black emphasized the constitutional ban on governmental taxing authority to support churches and religious activity when he asserted that:

> No tax in any amount, large or small, can be levied to support any religious activities or institutions, whatever they may be called, or whatever form they may adopt to teach or practice religion.

Such a principle is deeply rooted in American jurisprudence, as is also the principle that religious bodies and their widespread ministries should not be subjected to the taxes imposed on the general citizenry. In two cases almost 50 years ago (*Murdock* v. *Pennsylvania*, 319 U.S. 105, 1943; *Follett* v. *McCormick*, 321 U.S. 573, 1944), the Court rejected the imposition of license taxes on the evangelistic activities of Jehovah's Witnesses and a local preacher. Striking down a local ordinance in

Murdock that required those engaged in the sale of merchandise of any kind (including religious books and pamphlets) to register and pay an annual license tax, the Court took note of this "age-old form of missionary evangelism" and asserted that such "religious activity occupies the same high estate under the First Amendment as do worship in the churches and preaching in the pulpits." *Murdock* was extended the next term to strike down a similar ordinance in *Follett* as the Court reaffirmed the observation it has advanced in the former that "the power to tax the exercise of a privilege is the power to control or suppress its enjoyment."

Forty-seven years later, however, the Rehnquist Court was unwilling to extend the *Murdock-Follett* holdings to negate California's imposition of its sales and use taxes on a wide variety of religious materials sold by the nationally heralded ministry of the Reverend Jimmy Swaggart In *Jimmy Swaggart Ministries* v. *Board Equalization of California* (110 S. Ct. 688, 1990), Justice Sandra Day O'Connor emphasized the need to distinguish *Murdock* and *Follett* from *Swaggart*. She noted that the early holdings had been limited only to cases "where a flat license tax operates as a prior restraint on the free exercise of religious beliefs." The California tax imposed on the sales of *Swaggart*, however, was not of this character. Hence, she concluded that "[t]he Free Exercise Clause . . . does not *require* the State to grant [such ministries] . . . an exemption from its generally applicable sales and use taxes." Additionally, Justice O'Connor had little difficulty disposing of Swaggart's argument that the excessive entanglement prong of the *Lemon* test was infringed by the imposition of the taxes on his ministry by noting, among other factors, "that the evidence of administrative entanglement . . . is thin" and "does not rise to a constitutionally significant level."

In the final analysis, Swaggart, and others engaged in such merchandising as a part of their total ministries, sought a form of tax exemption so that what they believed to be an aspect of their free exercise of religion would not be adversely affected by demands of the tax collector.

The longstanding policy of exempting church property from public taxation has been considered by some to be an unconstitutional aid to religious establishments. But when the Supreme Court made a definitive pronouncement on the issue in *Walz* v. *Tax Commission of City of New York* (397 U.S. 664, 1970), it found such a policy to be in furtherance of the state's neutrality within the meaning of the establishment clause. Chief Justice Warren Burger made it clear that the tax exemption "is neither the advancement nor the inhibition of religion"; rather, he contended, it is an indirect economic benefit that should be distinguished from the direct subsidy that produces the "excessive governmental entanglement" that the establishment clause prohibits. He also expressed concern for the burden on the free exercise that a non–tax exemption policy would cause.

In dissent, Justice William O. Douglas focused on the discrimination issue raised in the tax exemption policy. He discussed the nature of governmental subsidies, and raised the question of whether religious bodies with their vast real estate holdings and their lucrative annual incomes should be allowed this government largess.

The New York law upheld in *Walz* did not embrace church property used for commercial purposes. However, shortly after *Walz* was announced, a federal district court in Florida used it as authority to sustain a Florida tax exemption for a church parking lot that was used commercially six days a week. Proceeds from it were used to support the church's religious activities and charitable projects.

An interesting controversy over tax exemption policy and the impact on the religious clauses was presented in *Bob Jones University* v. *United States* and *Goldsboro Christian Schools* v. *United States* (461 U.S. 574, 1983). There, the church-related educational institutions resisted an Internal Revenue Service (IRS) ruling denying them tax exempt status because of their racially discriminatory admissions policies. The schools argued that their policies were derived from their religious dogmas and that the tax exemption revocation amounted to a violation of both the free exercise and establishment clauses. But in rejecting those claims, the Court felt that the government's interest in eradicating racial discrimination far outweighs any burden on free exercise alleged to result from the denial of a tax exemption benefit. And the Court dismissed the establishment argument by simply noting that religion is not advanced merely because the IRS tax exemption regulation happens to coincide with the tenets of those religions that espouse racial intermixing. Hence the preference argument was without substance.

CHIEF JUSTICE BURGER *delivered the opinion of the Court.*

Appellant, owner of real estate in Richmond County, New York, sought an injunction in the New York courts to prevent the New York City Tax Commission from granting property tax exemptions to religious organizations for religious properties used solely for religious worship. The exemption from state taxes is authorized by . . . the New York Constitution. . . .

The essence of appellant's contention was that the New York State Tax Commission's grant of an exemption to church property indirectly requires the appellant to make a contribution to religious bodies and thereby violates provisions prohibiting establishment of religion under the First Amendment which under the Fourteenth Amendment is binding on the States.

Appellee's motion for summary judgment was granted and the Appellate Division, New York Supreme Court, and the New York Court of Appeals affirmed. We . . . affirm. . . .

Prior opinions of this Court have discussed the development and historical background of the First Amendment in detail. . . . It would therefore serve no useful purpose to review in detail the background of the Establishment and Free Exercise Clauses of the First Amendment or to restate what the Court's opinions have reflected over the years.

[At the outset, it] is sufficient to note that for the men who wrote the Religious Clauses of the First Amendment the "establishment" of a religion connoted sponsorship, financial support, and active involvement of the sovereign in religious activity. . . .

The Establishment and Free Exercise Clauses of the First Amendment are not the most precisely drawn portions of the Constitution. The sweep of the absolute prohibitions in the Religion Clauses may have been calculated; but the purpose was to state an objective not to write a statute. In attempting to articulate the scope of the two Religious Clauses, the Court's opinions reflect the limitations inherent in formulating general principles on a case-by-case basis. The considerable internal inconsistency in the opinions of the Court derives from what, in retrospect, may have been too sweeping utterances on aspects of these clauses that seemed clear in relation to the particular cases but have limited meaning as general principles.

The Court has struggled to find a neutral course between the two Religion Clauses, both of which are cast in absolute terms, and either of which, if expanded to a logical extreme, would tend to clash with the other. . . .

The course of constitutional neutrality in this area cannot be an absolutely straight line: rigidity could well defeat the basic purpose of these provisions, which is to insure that no religion be sponsored or favored, none commanded, and none inhibited. The general principle deducible from the First Amendment and all that has been said by the Court is this: that we will not tolerate either governmentally established religion or governmental interference with religion. Short of those expressly proscribed governmental acts there is room for play in the joints productive of a benevolent neutrality which will permit religious exercise to exist without sponsorship and without interference.

Each value judgment under the Religion Clauses must therefore turn on whether particular acts in question are intended to establish or interfere with religious beliefs and practices or have the effect of doing so. Adherence to the policy of neutrality that derives from an accommodation of the Establishment and Free Exercise Clauses has prevented the kind of involvement that would tip the balance toward government control of churches or governmental restraint on religious practice.

Adherents of particular faiths and individual churches frequently take strong positions on public issues including, as this case reveals in the several briefs *amici*, vigorous advocacy of legal or constitutional positions. Of course, churches as much as secular bodies and private citizens have that right. No perfect or absolute separation is really possible; the very existence of the Religion Clauses is an involvement of sorts—one which seeks to mark boundaries to avoid excessive entanglement. . . .

In *Everson* the Court declined to construe the religion clauses with a literalness that would undermine the ultimate constitutional objective as illuminated by history. Surely, bus transportation and police protection to pupils who receive religious instruction "aid" that particular religion to maintain schools that plainly tend to assure future adherents to a particular faith by having control of their total education at an early age. No religious body that maintains schools would deny this as an affirmative if not dominant policy of church schools. But if as in *Everson* buses can be provided to carry and policemen to protect church school pupils, we fail to see how a broader range of police and fire protection given equally to all churches along with nonprofit hospitals, art galleries, and libraries receiving the same tax exemption, is different for purposes of the religion clauses.

Similarly, making textbooks available to pupils in parochial schools in common with public schools was surely an "aid" to the sponsoring churches because it relieved those churches of an enormous aggregate cost for those books. Supplying of costly teaching materials was not seen either as manifesting a legislative purpose to aid or as having a primary effect of aid contravening the First Amendment. . . .

With all the risks inherent in programs that bring about administrative relationships between public education bodies and church-sponsored schools, we have been able to chart a course that preserved the autonomy and freedom of religious bodies while avoiding any semblance of established religion. This is a "tight rope" and one we have successfully traversed.

The legislative purpose of a property tax exemption is neither the advancement nor the inhibition of religion; it is neither sponsorship nor hostility. New York, in common with the other States, has determined that certain entities that exist in a harmonious relationship to the community at large, and that foster its "moral or mental improvement," should not be inhibited in their activities by property taxation or the hazard of loss of those properties for nonpayment of taxes. It has not singled out one particular church or religious group or even churches as such; rather, it has granted exemption to all houses of religious worship within a broad class of property owned by non-profit, quasi-public corporations which include hospitals, libraries, playgrounds, scientific, professional, historical and patriotic groups. The State has an affirmative policy that considers these groups as beneficial and stabilizing influences in community life and finds this classification useful, desirable, and in the public interest. Qualification for tax exemption is not perpetual or immutable; some tax exempt groups lose that status when their activities take them outside the classification and new entities can come into being and qualify for exemption.

Governments have not always been tolerant of religious activity, and hostility toward religion has taken many shapes and forms—economic, political, and sometimes harshly oppressive. Grants of exemption historically reflect the concern of authors of constitutions and statutes as to the latent dangers inherent in the imposition of property taxes; exemption constitutes a reasonable and balanced attempt to guard against those dangers. The limits of permissible state accommodation to religion are by no means co-extensive with the noninterference mandated by the Free Exercise Clause. To equate the two would be to deny a national heritage with roots in the Revolution itself. . . . We cannot read New York's statute as attempting to establish religion; it is simply sparing the exercise of religion from the burden of property taxation levied on private profit institutions.

We find it unnecessary to justify the tax exemption on the social welfare services or "good works" that some churches perform for parishioners and others—family counselling, aid to the elderly and the infirm, and to children. Churches vary substantially in the scope of such services; programs expand or contract according to resources and need. As public-sponsored programs enlarge, private aid from the church sector may diminish. The extent of social services may vary, depending on whether the church serves an urban or rural, a rich or poor constituency. To give emphasis to so variable an aspect of the work of religious bodies would introduce an element of governmental evaluation and standards as to the worth of particular social welfare programs, thus producing a kind of continuing day-to-day relationship which the policy of neutrality seeks to minimize. . . .

Determining that the legislative purpose of tax exemption is not aimed at establishing, sponsoring, or supporting religion does not end the inquiry, however. We must also be sure that the end result—the effect—is not an excessive government entanglement with religion. The test is inescapably one of degree. Either course, taxation of churches or exemption, occasions some degree of involvement with religion. Elimination of exemption would tend to expand the involvement of government by giving rise to tax valuation of church property, tax liens, tax foreclosures, and the direct confrontations and conflicts that follow in the train of those legal processes.

Granting tax exemptions to churches necessarily operates to afford an indirect economic benefit and also gives rise to some, but yet a lesser, involvement than taxing them. In analyzing either alternative the questions are whether the involvement is excessive, and whether it is a continuing one calling for official and continuing surveillance leading to an impermissible degree of entanglement. Obviously a direct money subsidy would be a relationship pregnant with involvement and, as with most governmental grant programs, could encompass sustained and detailed administrative relationships for enforcement of statutory or administrative standards, but that is not this case. . . .

The grant of a tax exemption is not sponsorship since the government does not transfer part of its revenue to churches but simply abstains from demanding that the church support the state. No one has ever suggested that tax exemption has converted libraries, art galleries, or hospitals into arms of the state or employees "on the public payroll." There is no genuine nexus between tax exemption and establishment of religion. . . . The exemption creates only a minimal and remote involvement between church and state and far less than taxation of churches. It restricts the fiscal relationship between church and state, and tends to complement and reinforce the desired separation insulating each from the other.

Separation in this context cannot mean absence of all contact: the complexities of modern life inevitably produce some contact and the fire and police protection received by houses of religious worship are no more than incidental benefits accorded all persons or institutions within a State's boundaries, along with many other exempt organizations. The appellant has not established even an arguable quantitative correlation between the payment of an ad valorem property tax and the receipt of these municipal benefits.

All of the 50 States provide for tax exemption of places of worship, most of them doing so by constitutional guarantees. For so long as federal income taxes have had any potential impact on churches—over 75 years—religious organizations have been expressly exempt from the tax. Such treatment is an "aid" to churches no more and no less in principle than the real estate tax exemption granted by States. Few concepts are more deeply embedded in the fabric of our national life, beginning with pre-Revolutionary colonial times, than for the government to exercise at the very least this kind of benevolent neutrality toward churches and religious exercise generally so long as none was favored over others and none suffered interference. . . .

Nothing in this national attitude toward religious tolerance and two centuries of uninterrupted freedom from taxation has given the remotest sign of leading to an established church or religion and on the contrary it has operated affirmatively to help guarantee the free exercise of all forms of religious beliefs. Thus, it is hardly useful to suggest that tax exemption is but the "foot in the door" or the "nose of the camel in the tent" leading to an established church. If tax exemption can be seen as this first step toward "establishment" of religion, as Mr. Justice Douglas fears, the second step has been long in coming. Any move which realistically "establishes" a church or tends to do so can be dealt with "while this Court sits." . . .

Affirmed.

[The concurring opinions of JUSTICE BRENNAN and JUSTICE HARLAN are not reprinted here.]

JUSTICE DOUGLAS, *dissenting.*

. . . The question in the case . . . is whether believers—organized in church groups—can be made exempt from real estate taxes, merely because they are believers, while nonbelievers, whether organized or not, must pay the real estate taxes.

My Brother Harlan says he "would suppose" that the tax exemption extends to "groups whose avowed tenets may be antitheological, atheistic and agnostic." . . . If it does, then the line between believers and nonbelievers has not been drawn. But, with all respect, there is not even a suggestion in the present record that the statute covers property used exclusively by organizations for "antitheological purposes," "atheistic purposes," or "agnostic purposes."

In *Torcaso* v. *Watkins,* 367 U.S. 488 (1961), . . . we held that a State could not bar an atheist from public office in light of the freedom of belief and religion guaranteed by the First and Fourteenth Amendments. Neither the State nor the Federal Government, we said, "can constitutionally pass laws or impose requirements which aid all religions as against non-believers, and neither can aid those religions based on a belief in the existence of God as against those religions founded on different beliefs." . . .

That principle should govern this case.

There is a line between what a State may do in encouraging "religious" activities . . . and what a State may not do by using its resources to promote "religious" activities . . . or bestowing benefits because of them. Yet that line may not always be clear. Closing public schools on Sunday is in the former category; subsidizing churches, in my view, is in the latter. Indeed I would suppose that in common understanding one of the best ways to "establish" one or more religions is to subsidize them, which a tax exemption does. . . .

In affirming this judgment the Court largely overlooks the revolution initiated by the adoption of the Fourteenth Amendment. That revolution involved the imposition of new and far-reaching constitutional restraints on the States. Nationalization of many civil liberties has been the consequence of the Fourteenth Amendment, reversing the historic position that the foundations of those liberties rested largely in state law. . . .

Hence the question in the present case makes irrelevant the "two centuries of uninterrupted freedom from taxation," referred to by the Court. . . . If history be our guide, then tax exemption of church property in this country is indeed highly suspect, as it arose in the early days when the church was an agency of the state. . . . The question here, though, concerns the meaning of the Establishment Clause and the Free Exercise Clause made applicable to the States for only a few decades at best.

With all due respect the governing principle is not controlled by *Everson* v. *Board of Education, supra.* . . .

This case . . . is quite different. Education is not involved. The financial support rendered here is to the church, the place of worship. A tax exemption is a subsidy. Is my Brother Brennan correct in saying that we would hold that state or federal grants to churches, say, to construct the edifice itself would be unconstitutional? What is the difference between that kind of subsidy and the present subsidy? . . .

State aid to places of worship, whether in the form of direct grants, or tax exemption, takes us back to the *Assessment Bill* and the *Remonstrance*. The church *qua* church would not be entitled to that support from believers and from nonbelievers alike. Yet the church *qua* nonprofit, charitable institution is one of many that receives a form of subsidy through tax exemption. To be sure, the New York statute does not single out the church for grant or favor. It includes churches in a long list of nonprofit organizations. . . . While the beneficiaries cover a wide range, "atheistic," "agnostic," or "anti-theological" groups do not seem to be included. . . .

If believers are entitled to public financial support, so are nonbelievers. A believer and nonbeliever under the present law are treated differently because of the articles of their faith. Believers are doubtless comforted that the cause of religion is being fostered by this legislation. Yet one of the mandates of the First Amendment is to promote a viable, pluralistic society and to keep government neutral, not only between sects but between believers and nonbelievers. The present involvement of government in religion may seem *de mimimis*. But it is, I fear, a long step down the Establishment path. Perhaps I have been misinformed. But as I have read the Constitution and its philosophy, I gathered that independence was the price of liberty.

I conclude that this tax exemption is unconstitutional.

JIMMY SWAGGART MINISTRIES v. BOARD OF EQUALIZATION OF CALIFORNIA
493 U.S. 378; 107 L. Ed. 2d 796; 110 S. Ct. 688 (1990)

JUSTICE O'CONNOR *delivered the opinion for a unanimous Court.*

This case presents the question whether the Religion Clauses of the First Amendment prohibit a State from imposing a generally applicable sales and use tax on the distribution of religious materials by a religious organization.

I

California's Sales and Use Tax Law requires retailers to pay a sales tax "[f]or the privilege of selling tangible personal property at retail." . . . A "sale" includes any transfer of title or possession of tangible personal property for consideration. . . .

The use tax, as a complement to the sales tax, reaches out-of-state purchases by residents of the State. It is "imposed on the storage, use, or other consumption in this state of tangible personal property purchased from any retailer" at the same rate as the sales tax (6 percent). Although the use tax is imposed on the purchaser, it is generally collected by the retailer at the time the sale is made. Neither the State Constitution nor the State Sales and Use Tax Law exempts religious organizations from the sales and use tax, apart from a limited exemption for the serving of meals by religious organizations.

During the tax period in question (1974 to 1981), appellant Jimmy Swaggart Ministries was a religious organization incorporated as a Louisiana nonprofit corporation and recognized as such by the Internal Revenue Service . . . and by the California State Controller. . . . Appellant's constitution and by-laws provide that it "is called for the purpose of establishing and maintaining an evangelistic outreach for the worship of Almighty God." This outreach is to be performed "by all available means, both at home and in foreign lands," and

> shall specifically include evangelistic crusades; missionary endeavors; radio broadcasting (as owner, broadcaster, and placement agency); television broadcasting (both as owner and broadcaster); and audio production and reproduction of music; audio production and reproduction of preaching; audio production and reproduction of teaching; writing, printing and publishing; and, any and all other individual or mass media methods that presently exist or may be devised in the future to proclaim the good news of Jesus Christ.

From 1974 to 1981, appellant conducted numerous "evangelistic crusades" in auditoriums and arenas across the country in cooperation with local churches. During this period, appellant held 23 crusades in California—each lasting one to three days, with one crusade lasting six days—for a total of 52 days. At the crusades, appellant conducted religious services that included preaching and singing. Some of these services were recorded for later sale or broadcast. Appellant also sold religious books, tapes, records, and other religious and nonreligious merchandise at the crusades.

Appellant also published a monthly magazine, "The Evangelist," which was sold nationwide by subscription. The magazine contained articles of a religious nature as well as advertisements for appellant's religious books, tapes, and records. . . . Appellant also offered its items for sale through radio, television, and cable television broadcasts, including broadcasts through local California stations.

In 1980, appellee Board of Equalization of the State of California (Board) informed appellant that religious materials were not exempt from the sales tax and requested appellant to register as a seller to facilitate reporting and payment of the tax. . . . Appellant responded that it was exempt from such taxes under the First Amendment. In 1981, the Board audited appellant and advised appellant that it should register as a seller and report and pay taxes on all sales made at its California crusades. The Board also opined that appellant had a sufficient nexus with the State of California

to require appellant to collect and report use tax on its mail-order sales to California purchasers.

Based on the Board's review of appellant's records, the parties stipulated "that appellant sold for use in California tangible personal property for the period April 1, 1974, through December 31, 1981, measured by payment to appellant of $1,702,942.00 for mail order sales from Baton Rouge, Louisiana and $240,560.00 for crusade merchandise sales in California." These figures represented the sales and use in California of merchandise with specific religious content—bibles, bible study manuals, printed sermons and collections of sermons, audiocassette tapes of sermons, religious books and pamphlets, and religious music in the form of songbooks, tapes, and records. Based on the sales figures for appellant's religious materials, the Board notified appellant that it owed sales and use taxes of $118,294.54, plus interest of $36,021.11, and a penalty of $11,829.45, for a total amount due of $166,145.10. Appellant did not contest the Board's assessment of tax liability for the sale and use of certain nonreligious merchandise, including such items as "T-shirts with JSM logo, mugs, bowls, plates, replicas of crown of thorns, ark of the covenant, Roman coin, candlesticks, Bible stand, pen and pencil sets, prints of religious scenes, bud vase, and communion cups."

Appellant filed a petition for redetermination with the Board, reiterating its view that the tax on religious materials violated the First Amendment. Following a hearing and an appeal to the Board, the Board deleted the penalty but otherwise redetermined the matter without adjustment in the amount of $118,294.54 in taxes owed plus $65,043.55 in interest. Pursuant to state procedural law, appellant paid the amount and filed a petition for redetermination and refund with the Board. The Board denied appellant's petition, and appellant brought suit in state court, seeking a refund of the tax paid.

The trial court entered judgment for the Board. The California Court of Appeal affirmed, and the California Supreme Court denied discretionary review. . . .

II

. . . Appellant challenges the sales and use tax law under both the Free Exercise and Establishment Clauses.

A

Our cases have established that "[t]he free exercise inquiry asks whether government has placed a substantial burden on the observation of a central religious belief or practice and, if so, whether a compelling governmental interest justifies the burden." *Hernandez* v. *Commissioner*, 490 U.S. 680 (1989).

Appellant relies almost exclusively on our decisions in *Murdock* v. *Pennsylvania*, 319 U.S. 105 (1944), and *Follett* v. *McCormick*, 321 U.S. 573, 576 (1944), for the proposition that a State may not impose a sales or use tax on the evangelical distribution of religious material by a religious organization. Appellant contends that the State's imposition of use and sales tax liability on it burdens its evangelical distribution of religious materials in a manner identical to the manner in which the evangelists in *Murdock* and *Follett* were burdened.

We reject appellant's expansive reading of *Murdock* and *Follett* as contrary to the decisions themselves. In *Murdock*, we considered the constitutionality of a city ordinance requiring all persons canvassing or soliciting within the city to procure a license by paying a flat fee. Reversing the convictions of Jevohah's Witnesses convicted under the ordinance of soliciting and distributing religious literature without a license, we explained:

> The hand distribution of religious tracts is an age-old form of missionary evangelism . . . [and] has been a potent force in various religious movements down through the years. This form of evangelism is utilized today on a large scale by various religious sects whose colporteurs carry the Gospel to thousands upon thousands of homes and seek through personal visitations to win adherents to their faith. It is more than preaching; it is more than distribution of religious literature. It is a combination of both. Its purpose is as evangelical as the revival meeting. This form of religious activity occupies the same high estate under the First Amendment as do worship in the churches and preaching in the pulpits. 319 U.S., at 108–109.

Accordingly, we held that "spreading one's religious beliefs or preaching the Gospel through distribution of religious literature and through personal visitations is an age-old type of evangelism with a claim to constitutional protection as the more orthodox types." . . .

We extended *Murdock* the following Term by invalidating, as applied to "one who earns his livelihood as an evangelist or preacher in his home town," an ordinance (similar to that involved in *Murdock*) that required all booksellers to pay a flat fee to procure a license to sell books. *Follett* v. *McCormick*, 321 U.S., at 576. . . .

Our decisions in these cases, however, resulted from the particular nature of the challenged taxes—flat license taxes that operated as a prior re-

straint on the exercise of religious liberty. . . ." We have here something quite different, for example, from a tax on the income of one who engages in religious activities or a tax on property used or employed in connection with those activities." . . . In *Follett*, we reiterated that a preacher is not "free from all financial burdens of government, including taxes on income or property" and, "like other citizens, may be subject to *general* taxation" (emphasis added).

Significantly, we noted in both cases that a primary vice of the ordinances at issue was that they operated as prior restraints of constitutionally protected conduct. . . . Thus, although *Murdock* and *Follett* establish that appellant's form of religious exercise has "as high a claim to constitutional protection as the more orthodox," those cases are of no further help to appellant. Our concern in *Murdock* and *Follett*—that a flat license tax would act as a *precondition* to the free exercise of religious beliefs—is simply not present where a tax applies to all sales and uses of tangible personal property in the State.

Our reading of *Murdock* and *Follett* is confirmed by our decision in *Minneapolis Star Tribune Co.* v. *Minnesota Commissioner of Revenue*, 460 U.S. 575 (1983), where we considered a newspaper's First Amendment challenge to a state use tax on ink and paper products used in the production of periodic publications. In the course of striking down the tax, we rejected the newspaper's suggestion, premised on *Murdock* and *Follett*, that a generally applicable sales tax could not be applied to publications. . . .

We also note that just last Term a plurality of the Court rejected the precise argument appellant now makes. In *Texas Monthly, Inc.* v. *Bullock*, 489 U.S. 1 (1989), JUSTICE BRENNAN, writing for three Justices, held that a state sales tax exemption for religious publications violated the Establishment Clause. In so concluding, the plurality further held that the Free Exercise Clause did not prevent the State from withdrawing its exemption, noting that "[t]o the extent our opinions in *Murdock* and *Follett* might be read . . . to suggest that the State and the Federal Government may never tax the sale of religious or other publications, we reject those dicta." JUSTICE WHITE, concurring in the judgment, concluded that the exemption violated the Free Press Clause because the content of a publication determined its tax exempt status. JUSTICE BLACKMUN, joined by JUSTICE O'CONNOR, concurred in the plurality's holding that the tax exemption at issue in that case contravened the Establishment Clause, but reserved the question whether "the Free Exercise Clause requires a tax exemption for the sale of religious literature by a religious organization; in other words, defining the ultimate scope of *Follett* and *Murdock* may be left for another day." In this case, of course, California has not chosen to create a tax exemption for religious materials, and we therefore have no need to revisit the Establishment Clause question presented in *Texas Monthly*.

We do, however, decide the Free Exercise question left open by JUSTICE BLACKMUN's concurrence in *Texas Monthly* by limiting *Murdock* and *Follett* to apply only where a flat license tax operates as a prior restraint on the free exercise of religious beliefs. As such, *Murdock* and *Follett* plainly do not support appellant's free exercise claim. California's generally applicable sales and use tax is not a flat tax, represents only a small fraction of any retail sale, and applies neutrally to all retail sales of tangible personal property made in California. California imposes its sales and use tax even if the seller or the purchaser is charitable, religious, nonprofit, or state local governmental in nature. . . . Thus, the sales and use tax is not a tax on the right to disseminate religious information, ideas, or beliefs *per se*; rather, it is a tax on the privilege of making retail sales of tangible personal property and on the storage, use or other consumption of tangible personal property in California. . . . There is no danger that appellant's religious activity is being singled out for special and burdensome treatment.

Moreover, our concern in *Murdock* and *Follett* that flat license taxes operate as a precondition to the exercise of evangelistic activity is not present in this case, because the registration requirement and the tax itself do not act as prior restraints—no fee is charged for registering, the tax is due regardless of preregistration, and the tax is not imposed as a precondition of disseminating the message. . . .

In addition to appellant's misplaced reliance on *Murdock* and *Follett*, appellant's free exercise claim is also in significant tension with the Court's decision last Term in *Hernandez* v. *Commissioner*, 490 U.S. 680 (1989), holding that the Government's disallowance of a tax deduction for religious "auditing" and "training" services did not violate the Free Exercise Clause. . . . There is no evidence in this case that collection and payment of the tax violates appellant's sincere religious beliefs. California's nondiscriminatory sales and use tax law requires only that appellant collect the tax from its California purchasers and remit the tax money to the State. The only burden on appellant is the claimed reduction in income resulting from the presumably lower demand for appellant's wares (caused by the marginally higher price) and from the costs associated with administering the tax. As the Court made clear in *Hernandez*, however, to the extent that imposition of a generally applicable tax merely decreases the amount of money appellant has to spend on its religious activities, any such burden is not constitutionally significant. . . .

Finally, because appellant's religious beliefs do not forbid payment of the sales and use tax, appellant's reliance on *Sherbert* v. *Verner*, 374 U.S. 398 (1963), and its progeny is misplaced, because in no sense has the State " 'condition[ed] receipt of an important benefit upon conduct proscribed by a religious faith, or . . . denie[d] such a benefit because of conduct mandated by religious belief, thereby putting substantial pressure on an adherent to modify his behavior and to violate his beliefs.' " . . . Appellant has never alleged that the mere act of paying the tax, by itself, violates its sincere religious beliefs.

We therefore conclude that the collection and payment of the generally applicable tax in this case imposes no constitutionally significant burden on appellant's religious practices or beliefs. The Free Exercise Clause accordingly does not *require* the State to grant appellant an exemption from its generally applicable sales and use tax. . . .

B

Appellant also contends that application of the sales and use tax to its sale of religious materials violates the Establishment Clause because it fosters " 'an excessive government entanglement with religion.' " . . . Appellant alleges, for example, that the present controversy has featured on-site inspections of appellant's evangelistic crusades, lengthy on-site audits, examinations of appellant's books and records, threats of criminal prosecution, and layers of administrative and judicial proceeding. . . .

The Establishment Clause prohibits "sponsorship, financial support, and active involvement of the sovereign in religious activity."

. . . The "excessive entanglement" prong of the tripartite purpose-effect-entanglement *Lemon* test, requires examination of "the character and purposes of the institutions that are benefited, the nature of the aid that the State provides, and the resulting relationship between the government and the religious authority." . . . The issue presented . . . is whether the imposition of sales and use tax liability in this case on appellant results in "excessive" involvement between appellant and the State and "continuing surveillance leading to an impermissible degree of entanglement." . . .

. . . [W]hatever the precise contours of the Establishment Clause . . . its undisputed core values are not even remotely called into question by the generally applicable tax in this case.

Even applying the "excessive entanglement" prong of the *Lemon* test, however, we hold that California's imposition of sales and use tax liability on appellant threatens no excessive entanglement between church and state First, we note that the evidence of administrative entanglement in this case is thin. Appellant alleges that collection and payment of the sales and use tax impose severe accounting burdens on it. The Court of Appeals however, expressly found that the record did not support appellant's factual assertions, noting that appellant "had a sophisticated accounting staff and had recently computerized its accounting and that [appellant] in its own books and for purposes of obtaining a federal income tax exemption segregated 'retail sales' and 'donations.' " . . .

Second, even assuming that the tax imposes substantial administrative burdens on appellant, such administrative and recordkeeping burdens do not rise to a constitutionally significant level. Collection and payment of the tax will of course require some contact between appellant and the State, but we have held that generally applicable administrative and recordkeeping regulations may be imposed on religious organization without running afoul of the Establishment Clause. . . .

Most significantly, the imposition of the sales and use tax without an exemption for appellant does not require the State to inquire into the religious content of the items sold or the religious motivation for selling or purchasing the items, because the materials are subject to the tax regardless of content or motive. From the State's point of view, the critical question is not whether the materials are religious, but whether there is a sale or use, a question which involves only a secular determination. . . . Although appellant asserts that donations often accompany payments made for the religious items and that items are sometimes given away without payment (or only nominal payment), it is plain that, in the first case, appellant's use of "order forms" and "price lists" renders illusory any difficulty in separating the two portions and that, in the second case, the question is only whether any particular transfer constitutes a "sale." Ironically, appellant's theory, under which government may not tax "religious core" activities but may tax "nonreligious" activities, would require government to do precisely what appellant asserts the Religion Clauses prohibit: "determine which expenditures are religious and which are secular."

Accordingly, because we find no excessive entanglement between government and religion in this case, we hold that the imposition of sales and use tax liability on appellant does not violate the Establishment Clause. . . .

The judgment of the California Court of Appeal is affirmed.

It is so ordered.

The State, Religious Beliefs and Practices, and the Free Exercise Clause

FEATURED CASES

Hobbie v. *Unemployment Appeals Commission of Florida*   *Wisconsin* v. *Yoder*
Employment Division, Department of Human Resources of Oregon v. *Smith*

During the 1960s, the 1970s, and the 1980s, the Supreme Court considered a number of cases in which it was asked to ascertain the permissible limits of legislative authority to enact regulations that have free exercise implications. In two of the four Sunday closing law cases decided by the Court in 1961—*Braunfeld* v. *Brown* (366 U.S. 617) and *Gallagher* v. *Crown Kasher Super Market* (366 U.S. 617)[7]—the Court deferred to the judgment of the

legislature of Pennsylvania and rejected the claim of several Orthodox Jewish merchants that the state law compelling them to close their businesses on Sundays effectively placed them at an economic disadvantage since their businesses were closed on Saturdays in observance of their Sabbath. Brushing

[7]The establishment issue was considered in *McGowan* v. *Maryland* and *Two Guys from Harrison-Allentown* v. *McGinley*.

aside the merchants' argument that this policy amounted to a penalty on them for adherence to their religious tenets, Chief Justice Earl Warren held that while the operational consequence of the statute was to make their religious beliefs and practices "more expensive," the alleged economic injury cannot be translated into a free exercise claim. When a statute regulates conduct, he argued, the imposition of an indirect burden on the exercise of religion does not necessarily render it unconstitutional. He set the constitutional limits of state regulatory power in this area this way:

> [I]f the State regulates conduct by enacting a general law within its power, the purpose and effect of which is to advance the State's secular goals, the statute is valid despite its indirect burden on religious observance unless the State may accomplish its purpose by means which do not impose such a burden. . . .

Justice William J. Brennan's dissent, supported by Justice Potter Stewart, complained about the law putting these merchants to what he considered to be an unconstitutional choice between their religion and economic survival. Suggesting the need for the Court to adopt a different standard for review of such governmental regulations, he argued that the Court should not limit its inquiry of challenged legislation in this area to substantiality and importance of interests, legitimacy of legislative purpose, and rationality. For him, the appropriate test should be that set forth in *Barnette*, where regulations infringing on the free exercise clause could be constitutionally sustained only to prevent "grave and immediate danger to interests the State may lawfully protect."

This more stringent test advanced in Brennan's dissent was accepted by a majority just two years later in *Sherbert* v. *Verner* (374 U.S. 398, 1963). The case resulted from a ruling of the South Carolina Unemployment Compensation Commission (sustained by the state supreme court) holding that a member of the Seventh-Day Adventist faith was ineligible for benefits because of her unwillingness to accept jobs requiring work on Saturdays (her day of worship). In a seven-to-two decision, the Court held that the state's action imposed an unconstitutional burden on the free exercise of religion. Justice Brennan reiterated his opposition to the kind of choice imposed on Mrs. Sherbert by the enforcement of the state statute. Logically following from his *Braunfeld* dissent, Brennan held that in order to sustain state regulation that places a burden on the free exercise of religion, there must be evidence of a "compelling state interest in

the regulation of a subject within the State's constitutional power to regulate." Furthermore, he argued, in addition to a showing of a "compelling state interest," the state must demonstrate "that no alternative forms of regulation would combat such abuses without infringing First Amendment rights."

In a concurring opinion, Justice Stewart was troubled by the Court's handling of what he termed the "double-barreled dilemma" presented by the case. First, he thought that the Court's action sustaining the free exercise claim forced South Carolina to violate the establishment clause. He believed that this case demonstrated the need for the Court to come to grips with "the dilemma posed by the conflict between 'the establishment and free exercise clauses.'" Additionally, he was troubled by the Court's inconsistency in this area, as he could not accept Brennan's reasoning in distinguishing this case from *Braunfeld*.

In dissent, Justice John Marshall Harlan was troubled by the apparent disregard of the *Braunfeld* precedent and the ruling's "implications for the future." To him, the burden imposed on Mrs. Sherbert's free exercise of religion by the state action was too "indirect, remote, and insubstantial" to warrant rejection of the state's regulatory action.

Almost two decades later, the Court reaffirmed its *Sherbert* position in *Thomas* v. *Review Board* (450 U.S. 707, 1981). There, as in *Sherbert*, unemployment benefits were at issue. When his employment situation was changed, requiring him to work in a job producing armaments, Thomas quit in deference to his religious beliefs as a Jehovah's Witness. His subsequent application for unemployment compensation was rejected by a state agency, and he sought judicial relief under the free exercise clause. Citing *Sherbert*, Chief Justice Burger argued that the alleged interests being promoted by Indiana in denying Thomas's claim were not "sufficiently compelling" to justify the resulting burden on the free exercise of religion by enforcing the policy. But in dissent, Justice William Rehnquist expressed his concern about the exacerbation of free exercise–establishment clause tension resulting from the decision and the continuing tendency of the majority to interpret the free exercise clause too broadly.

Sherbert was reaffirmed once again in 1987 in *Hobbie* v. *Unemployment Appeals Commission of Florida* (107 S. Ct. 1046) as the Court reiterated that the free exercise of religion is abridged when state policy forces a claimant to a choice of abandoning religious beliefs and practices in order to retain employment or of adhering to religious precepts and practices and forfeiting compensatory benefits. Of particular significance here, however, was the vigorous call of the lone dissenter, Chief Justice Rehnquist, for the reexamination of First Amendment religious liberty jurisprudence as essential to more consistent rulings in this area.

The rule emerging from *Sherbert*—that it is constitutionally permissible for government to remove impediments to Sabbath observances to ensure the guarantee of the free exercise of religion—undergirded a congressional amendment to Title VII of the 1964 Civil Rights Act in 1972 that provided statutory protection for the Sabbatarian worker that was not available to Mrs. Sherbert. Before amendment, the title made unlawful employee practices that discriminated in hiring, compensation, terms of employment, and so forth because of religion. Pursuant to that statutory proscription, the Equal Employment Opportunity Commission (EEOC) promulgated in 1967 a regulation obligating an employer to make *reasonable accommodations* to the religious needs of employees where such accommodations can be made without *undue hardship* on the conduct of the employer's business (emphasis added). Thereafter, Congress included similar language in the 1972 amendments to Title VII of the Act.

Most of the litigation emanating from the provision has focused on whether employers had met their obligations under the reasonable accommodations requirement. In a number of lower court cases, for example, employers were found to have offered arrangements to reasonably accommodate religious needs of employees (usually Sabbatarians seeking work schedule adjustment to free them from work on their Sabbath—Saturdays) despite demands of uncooperative employees.[8] On the other hand, other courts have found that the options offered by the employer did not constitute the required *reasonable accommodation* of employee religious needs. In *Cummins* v. *Parker Seal Co.* (516 F.2d 544, 1975), for example, the employer's attempt to use general employee discontent resulting from accommodation of a Sabbatarian employee's religious needs was rejected. Only a showing that such discontent would produce chaotic personnel problems will constitute "undue hardship."

The Supreme Court's leading statement on the issue came in its review of *Trans World Airlines, Inc.* v. *Hardison* (432 U.S. 63, 1977). There, it reversed a court of appeals ruling that had rejected the airline's offer of accommodation as inadequate. The Court noted that, to accommodate the claimant's religious needs, the airline would have to abrogate its neutral system of seniority and that Title VII does not contemplate such action to accommodate religious needs.

It has been suggested that the reasonable accommodations requirement is an unconstitutional aid to religion, and a few lower courts have so held.[9] On the other hand, other lower federal tribunals have rejected such a claim,[10] and the Supreme Court apparently agreed with that position when it affirmed, without opinion, the Sixth Circuit's *Cummins* ruling in 1976. But while TWA raised the establishment issue in its certiorari petition in the *Hardison* case, Justice Byron White saw no need to consider it, as he noted that the conflict could be resolved on nonconstitutional grounds.

A related clash of state and religious interests, although not involving Sabbatarians, was presented to the Court in *Wisconsin* v. *Yoder* (406 U.S. 205, 1972). Echoing the refrain of the popular song of another era, "Give Me the Simple Life," the Old Order Amish religious group resisted the state's compulsory school attendance policy as it applied to their children beyond the eighth grade. Not only was formal education unnecessary for the simple agrarian life to which they were committed, the Amish argued, but compelling their children to attend high school would expose them to cultural influences that threatened to undermine their religious beliefs and practices.

Recognizing some responsibility for the educational needs of their children, the Amish had sought unsuccessfully to meet the state requirements by setting up a program based on the Pennsylvania model of community-controlled vocational training. Under this plan, the children would be required to attend an Amish vocational school for three hours per week, where they would be given instruction by an Amish teacher in English, mathematics, health, and social studies. The remainder of the week would be devoted to performance of farm and household duties under parental supervision. A unanimous Court (Justice William O. Douglas dissenting only in part), with Justice Burger applying the "compelling state in-

---

[8]*Johnson* v. *United States Postal Service* (497 F.2d 128, 1974); *United States* v. *City of Albuquerque* (10 F.E.P. Cases 771, 1975); *Dewey* v. *Reynolds Metals Co.* (429 F.2d 324, 1970).

[9]*Reid* v. *Memphis Publishing Co.* (521 F.2d 512, 1975); *Dewey* v. *Reynolds Metal Co.*

[10]*Cummins* v. *Parker Seal Co., supra; Hardison* v. *Trans World Airlines* (375 F. Supp. 877, 1974).

terest—no alternative means" test, held that the enforcement of the law against the Amish abridged their free exercise of religion.[11]

But the attempt of the Amish to extend the free exercise shield to resist payment of the employer's share of the tax liability under FICA and FUTA was not accepted by the Court in *United States* v. *Lee* (455 U.S. 252, 1982). While acknowledging the sincerity of the religious beliefs asserted, the Court, nevertheless, concluded that the government's interest in imposing the tax was sufficient to override the free exercise claim. (Cf. *Bowen* v. *Roy*, 106 S. Ct. 2147, decided four years later, where the Court rejected the free exercise assertion of Native Americans in resisting the statutory requirement that Social Security numbers must be obtained for minors as a condition for participation in the federal food stamp program. In his opinion, Chief Justice Burger articulated a less rigorous test than that applied by the Court in *Sherbert* and *Thomas* when he asserted that "the Government meets its burden when it demonstrates that a challenged requirement for governmental benefits, neutral and uniform in its application, is a reasonable means of promoting a legitimate public interest.")

The *Yoder*, *Lee*, and *Roy* cases raised the free exercise claim in the civilian context, and the rulings in *Lee* and *Roy* accorded a greater deference to the legislative policy determination than that accepted by the Court in *Yoder* and in *Sherbert* and its progeny. Likewise, in *Goldman* v. *Weinberger* (106 S. Ct. 1310, 1986), the Court deferred to military interests served by a uniform dress code in rejecting the free exercise claim of a Jewish military officer that he should be allowed to wear the yarmulke while on duty in a military health facility. Justice Rehnquist's opinion for the Court noted that the Air Force regulation was reasonable and evenhanded in making a distinction between nonmilitary apparel that is visible and that which is not.

In terms of free exercise jurisprudence, Justice Sandra Day O'Connor's dissent is noteworthy. In it, she underscored the need for the Court to "articulate and apply an appropriate standard for [application to] a free exercise claim in the military context." Noting the Court's long-term ambiguity in articulating an appropriate standard to evaluate free exercise claims in a civilian context, she thought a standard of review appropriate for a military context requires a showing: (1) that the governmental interest at stake is of "unusual importance"; and (2) that "substantial harm" to such interest would result if the free exercise claim would prevail.

Two years later, in *Lyng* v. *Northwest Indian Cemetery Protective Association* (108 S. Ct. 1319, 1988), Justice O'Connor led the majority in refusing to construe the free exercise clause expansively to protect traditional religious practices conducted on public lands. Specifically, three Native American groups alleged that a U.S. Forest Service decision to allow timber harvesting and the construction of a new highway in a National Forest area that they had traditionally used to conduct religious rituals would have an adverse effect on their religious practices as protected by the free exercise clause. In rejecting this claim, Justice O'Connor advanced a noncoercive test that in effect held that the free exercise guarantee condemns only those governmental actions that would "coerce individuals into acting contrary to their religious beliefs," but does not disallow actions (like that taken by the Forest Service here) that merely have an "incidental effect on certain religious practices." Using such a test in the future (as appears likely from the division of the justices in *Lyng*) will not permit accommodation of religious claims such as those presented in *Sherbert*, *Yoder*, *Thomas*, and *Hobbie*.

The Rehnquist Court continued its restricted view of the free exercise guarantee when it considered a state's enforcement of its criminal laws against the sacramental use of the drug peyote in *Department of Human Resources of Oregon* v. *Smith*. There, two members of the Native American Church were dismissed from their jobs with a private drug rehabilitation agency because they had engaged in the use of peyote in a sacramental ceremony in their church. Their subsequent application for unemployment compensation was denied because the loss of employment was attributed to "misconduct." In explaining its action, the state commission responsible for ruling on the claims took the position that the claimants had forfeited their right to compensation by consuming peyote,

[11]Of course, religious groups have sought free exercise protection for a number of other practices. Included among them are the use of drugs in religious ceremonies (see *Employment Division, Department of Human Resources of Oregon* v. *Smith* 494 U.S. 872, 1990), the handling of poisonous snakes as a facet of the worship ritual, and the refusal of medical treatment such as blood transfusions and vaccination. For a good analysis of some of those issues, see Note, "Medical Care, Freedom of Religion, and Mitigation of Damages," 87 Yale Law Journal 1466 (June 1978); P. J. Riga, "Compulsory Medical Treatment of Adults," 22 Catholic Review 353 (Spring 1976); and Note, "Their Life Is the Blood: Jehovah's Witnesses, Blood Transfusions, and the Courts," 10 Northern Kentucky University Law Review 281 (1983).

which was criminal behavior under Oregon law. While the Oregon appellate courts disagreed on free exercise grounds (citing *Sherbert* and its progeny), the Supreme Court upheld the commission's view that the state's criminal law should override the free exercise claim in this context. In his opinion for the Court, Justice Antonin Scalia skirted the *Sherbert* core inquiry usually applied in such cases where government is required "to justify any substantial burden on religiously motivated conduct by a compelling state interest and by means narrowly tailored to achieve that interest." Instead, he argued that the Court should be guided by an inquiry that focuses on criminal law prohibitions. Thus, he concluded, "unless it purposely targets religious expression, a law that burdens a religious practice is fully consistent with the free exercise clause as long as a generally applicable criminal law prohibits that practice." In short, the Court's ruling allows regulations that merely have an incidental effect on the free exercise so long as the prohibitions imposed are generally applicable.

Justice Harry Blackmun's dissent, in which Justices William J. Brennan and Thurgood Marshall joined, lamented the Court's abandonment of what he thought was a "settled and inviolate principle of the Court's First Amendment jurisprudence." That principle stipulates that a regulatory statute that imposes burdens on the free exercise of religion can pass constitutional muster "only if the law in general, and the state's refusal to allow a religious exemption in particular, are justified by a compelling interest that cannot be served by less restrictive means."

Broad concern that state and local governments might construe the *Smith* ruling to impose a variety of burdens on religious practices led Congress to consider the Religious Freedom Restoration Act (H.R. 1308 and S.578) during the first session of the 103rd Congress. The measure would reinstate pre-*Smith* standards that require a showing of compelling state interest to be accomplished in the least burdensome manner to justify regulation in this area. The bill passed the House and was sent to the Senate on May 11, 1993.

In the meantime, the Court appeared to back away from *Smith* when it struck down Hialeah, Florida's ordinances banning animal sacrifices in *Church of Lukumi Babalu Aye, Inc.* v. *Hialeah, Florida* (113 S. Ct., 1993). Justice Anthony Kennedy, speaking for a unanimous Court, emphasized the requirement of carefully tailored regulations in this area that must avoid overbreadth and underinclusiveness. On their face, the Hialeah ordinances were not neutral, but were designed to suppress the central ritual practice of the religious group. In the end, he concluded that the city's asserted interests (prevention of cruelty to animals and protection of the public health) could be accomplished by less drastic means.

HOBBIE v. UNEMPLOYMENT APPEALS COMMISSION OF FLORIDA
480 U.S. 136; 94 L. Ed. 2d 190; 107 S. Ct. 1046 (1987)

JUSTICE BRENNAN *delivered the opinion of the Court.*

Appellant's employer discharged her when she refused to work certain scheduled hours because of sincerely held religious convictions adopted after beginning employment. The question to be decided is whether Florida's denial of unemployment compensation benefits to appellant violates the Free Exercise Clause of the First Amendment of the Constitution, as applied to the States through the Fourteenth Amendment.

I

Lawton and Company (Lawton), a Florida jeweler, hired appellant Paula Hobbie in October 1981. She was employed by Lawton for 2½ years, first as trainee and then as assistant manager of a retail jewelry store. In April 1984, Hobbie informed her immediate supervisor that she was to be baptized into the Seventh-Day Adventist Church and that, for religious reasons, she would no longer be able to work on her Sabbath, from sundown on Friday to sundown Saturday. The supervisor devised an arrangement with Hobbie: she agreed to work evenings and Sundays, and he agreed to substitute for her whenever she was scheduled to work on a Friday evening or a Saturday.

This arrangement continued until the general manager of Lawton learned of it in June 1984. At that time, after a meeting with Hobbie and her minister, the general manager informed appellant that she could either work her scheduled shifts or submit her resignation to the company. When Hobbie refused to do either, Lawton discharged her.

On June 4, 1984, appellant filed a claim for unemployment compensation with the Florida Department of Labor and Employment Security. Under Florida law, unemployment compensation benefits are available to persons who become "unemployed through no fault of their own." Fla. Stat. §443.021 (1985). Lawton contested the payment of benefits on the ground that Hobbie was "disqualified for benefits" because she had been discharged for "misconduct connected with [her] work." §443.101(1)(a).*

A claims examiner for the Bureau of Unemployment Compensation denied Hobbie's claim for benefits, and she appealed that determination. Following a hearing before a referee, the Unemployment Appeals Commission (Appeals Commission) affirmed the denial of benefits, agreeing that Hobbie's refusal to work scheduled shifts constituted "misconduct connected with [her] work."

Hobbie challenged the Appeals Commission's order in the Florida Fifth District Court of Appeal [and] . . . that court summarily affirmed the Appeals Commission. . . . [W]e now reverse.

II

Under our precedents, the Appeals Commission's disqualification of appellant from receipt of benefits violates the Free Exercise Clause of the First Amendment, applicable to the States through the Fourteenth Amendment. *Sherbert* v. *Verner*, 374 U.S. 398 (1963); *Thomas* v. *Review Board of the Indiana Employment Security Div.*, 450 U.S. 707 (1981). In *Sherbert* we considered South Carolina's denial of unemployment compensation benefits to a Sabbatarian who, like Hobbie, refused to work on Saturdays. The Court held that the State's disqualification of Sherbert

> force[d] her to choose between following the precepts of her religion and forfeiting benefits, on the one hand, and abandoning one of the precepts of her religion in order to accept work, on the other hand.

*The Florida statute defines "misconduct" as follows:
"Misconduct" includes, but is not limited to, the following, which shall not be construed in pari materia with each other:
"(a) Conduct evincing such willful or wanton disregard of an employer's interests as is found in deliberate violation or disregard of standards of behavior which the employer has the right to expect of his employee; or
"(b) Carelessness or negligence of such a degree or recurrence as to manifest culpability, wrongful intent, or evil design or to show an intentional and substantial disregard of the employer's interests or of the employee's duties and obligations to his employer." Fla. Stat. §443.036(24)-(1985).

Governmental imposition of such a choice puts the same kind of burden upon the free exercise of religion as would a fine imposed against [her] for her Saturday worship. 374 U.S., at 404.

We concluded that the State had imposed a burden upon Sherbert's free exercise rights that had not been justified by a compelling state interest.

In *Thomas*, too, the Court held that a State's denial of unemployment benefits unlawfully burdened an employee's right to free exercise of religion. Thomas, a Jehovah's Witness, held religious beliefs that forbade his participation in the production of armaments. He was forced to leave his job when the employer closed his department and transferred him to a division that fabricated turrets for tanks. Indiana then denied Thomas unemployment compensation benefits. The Court found that the employee had been "put to a choice between fidelity to religious belief or cessation of work" and that the coercive impact of the forfeiture of benefits in this situation was undeniable. . .

We see no meaningful distinction among the situations of Sherbert, Thomas, and Hobbie. We again affirm, as stated in *Thomas*:

> Where the State conditions receipt of an important benefit upon conduct proscribed by a religious faith, or *where it denies such a benefit because of conduct mandated by religious belief, thereby putting substantial pressure on an adherent to modify his behavior and to violate his beliefs*, a burden upon religion exists. While the compulsion may be indirect, the infringement upon free exercise is nonetheless substantial. *Id.*, 450 U.S., at 717–718 (emphasis added).

Both *Sherbert* and *Thomas* held that such infringements must be subjected to strict scrutiny and could be justified only by proof by the State of a compelling interest. The Appeals Commission does not seriously contend that its denial of benefits can withstand strict scrutiny; rather it urges that we hold that its justification should be determined under the less rigorous standard articulated in Chief Justice Burger's opinion in *Bowen* v. *Roy*: "the Government meets its burden when it demonstrates that a challenged requirement for governmental benefits, neutral and uniform in its application, is a reasonable means of promoting a legitimate public interest." 476 U.S. 693, 708 (1986). Five Justices expressly rejected this argument in *Roy*. . . . We reject the argument again today. As JUSTICE O'CONNOR pointed out in *Roy*, "[s]uch a test has no basis in precedent and relegates a serious First Amendment value to the barest level of minimal scrutiny that the Equal Protection Clause already provides." . . . ("[O]nly those interests of the highest order and those not otherwise served can overbalance legitimate claims to the free exercise of religion.")

The Appeals Commission also suggests two grounds upon which we might distinguish *Sherbert* and *Thomas* from the present case. First, the Appeals Commission points out that in *Sherbert* the employee was deemed completely ineligible for benefits under South Carolina's unemployment insurance scheme because she would not accept work that conflicted with her Sabbath. The Appeals Commission contends that, under Florida law, Hobbie faces only a limited disqualification from receipt of benefits, and that once this fixed term has been served, she will again "be on an equal footing with all other workers, provided she avoids employment that conflicts with her religious beliefs." . . . The Appeals Commission argues that such a disqualification provision is less coercive than the ineligibility determination in *Sherbert*, and that the burden it imposes on free exercise is therefore permissible.

This distinction is without substance. The immediate effects of ineligibility and disqualification are identical, and the disqualification penalty is substantial. Moreover, *Sherbert* was given controlling weight in *Thomas*, which involved a disqualification provision similar in all relevant respects to the statutory section implicated here. . . .

The Appeals Commission also attempts to distinguish this case by arguing that, unlike the employees in *Sherbert* and *Thomas*, Hobbie was the "agent of change" and is therefore responsible for the consequences of the conflict between her job and her religious beliefs. In *Sherbert* and *Thomas*, the employees held their respective religious beliefs at the time of hire; subsequent changes in the conditions of employment made *by the employer* caused the conflict between work and belief. In this case, Hobbie's beliefs changed during the course of her employment, creating a conflict between job and faith that had not previously existed. The Appeals Commission contends that "it is . . . unfair for an employee to adopt religious beliefs that conflict with existing employment and expect to continue the employment without compromising those beliefs" and that this "intentional

disregard of the employer's interests . . . constitutes misconduct." . . .

In effect, the Appeals Commission asks us to single out the religious convert for different, less-favorable treatment than that given an individual whose adherence to his or her faith precedes employment. We decline to do so. The First Amendment protects the free exercise rights of employees who adopt religious beliefs or convert from one faith to another after they are hired. The timing of Hobbie's conversion is immaterial to our determination that her free exercise rights have been burdened; the salient inquiry under the Free Exercise Clause is the burden involved. In *Sherbert, Thomas,* and the present case, the employee was forced to choose between fidelity to religious belief and continued employment; the forfeiture of unemployment benefits for choosing the former over the latter brings unlawful coercion to bear on the employee's choice.

Finally, we reject the Appeals Commission's argument that the awarding of benefits to Hobbie would violate the Establishment Clause. This Court has long recognized that the Government may (and sometimes must) accommodate religious practices and that it may do so without violating the Establishment Clause. . . . As in *Sherbert*, the accommodation at issue here does not entangle the State in an unlawful fostering of religion. . . .

III

We conclude that Florida's refusal to award unemployment compensation benefits to appellant violated the Free Exercise Clause of the First Amendment. . . . The judgment of the Florida Fifth District Court of Appeal is therefore

Reversed.

CHIEF JUSTICE REHNQUIST, *dissenting.*

I adhere to the views I stated in dissent in *Thomas* v. *Review Board of the Indiana Employment Security Div.* . . . Accordingly, I would affirm.

[The brief concurring opinions of JUSTICE POWELL and JUSTICE STEVENS are not reprinted here.]

CHIEF JUSTICE BURGER *delivered the opinion of the Court.*

. . . [W]e granted the writ in this case to review a decision of the Wisconsin Supreme Court holding that respondents' convictions for violating the State's compulsory school attendance law were invalid under the Free Exercise Clause of the First Amendment to the United States Constitution made applicable to the States by the Fourteenth Amendment . . . [and] we affirm the judgment of the Supreme Court of Wisconsin.

Respondents Jonas Yoder and Adin Yutzy are members of the Old Order Amish Religion, and respondent Wallace Miller is a member of the Conservative Amish Mennonite Church. They and their families are residents of Green County, Wisconsin. Wisconsin's compulsory school attendance law required them to cause their children to attend public or private school until reaching age 16 but the respondents declined to send their children, ages 14 and 15, to public school after completing the eighth grade. The children were not enrolled in any private school, or within any recognized exception to the compulsory attendance law, and they are conceded to be subject to the Wisconsin statute.

. . . [R]espondents were charged, tried and convicted of violating the compulsory attendance law in Green County Court and were fined the sum of $5 each. . . . The trial testimoney showed that respondents believed, in accordance with the tenets of Old Order Amish communities generally, that their children's attendance at high school, public or private, was contrary to the Amish religion and way of life. They believed that by sending their children to high school, they would not only expose themselves to the danger of the censure of the church community, but, as found by the county court, endanger their own salvation and that of their children. . . .

Amish . . . object to the high school and higher education generally because the values it teaches are in marked variance with Amish values and the Amish way of life; they view secondary school education as an impermissible exposure of their children to a "worldly" influence in conflict with their beliefs. The high school tends to emphasize intellectual and scientific accomplishments, self-distinction, competitiveness, worldly success, and social life with other students. Amish society emphasizes informal learning-through-doing, a life of "goodness," rather than a life of intellect, wisdom, rather than technical knowledge, community welfare rather than competition, and separation rather than integration with contemporary worldly society.

Formal high school education beyond the eighth grade is contrary to Amish beliefs . . . because it takes [the children] away from their community, physically and emotionally, during the crucial and formative adolescent period of life. During this period, the children must acquire Amish attitudes favoring manual work and self-reliance and the specific skills needed to perform the adult role of an Amish farmer or housewife. They must learn to enjoy physical labor. . . .

The Amish do not object to elementary education through the first eight grades as a general proposition because they agree that their children must have basic skills in the "three R's" in order to read the Bible, to be good farmers and citizens and to be able to deal with non-Amish people when necessary in the course of daily affairs. . . .

. . . The Wisconsin Circuit Court affirmed the convictions. The Wisconsin Supreme Court, however, sustained respondents' claim under the Free Exercise Clause of the First Amendment and reversed the convictions. . . .

. . . [As] *Pierce* v. *Society of Sisters,* 268 U.S. 510, 534 (1925) . . . suggests, the values of parental direction of the religious upbringing and education of their children in their early and formative years have a high place in our society. . . . Thus, a State's interest in universal education, however highly we rank it, is not totally free from a balancing process when it impinges on other fundamental rights and interests, such as those specifically protected by the Free Exercise Clause of the First Amendment and the traditional interest of parents with respect to the religious upbringing of their children. . . .

It follows that in order for Wisconsin to compel school attendance beyond the eighth grade against a claim that such attendance interferes with the practice of a legitimate religious belief, it must appear either that the State does not deny the free exercise of religious belief by its requirement, or that there is a state interest of sufficient magnitude to override the interest claiming protection under the Free Exercise Clause. . . .

The essence of all that has been said and written on the subject is that only those interests of the highest order and those not otherwise served can overbalance legitimate claims to the free exercise of religion. We can accept it as settled, therefore, that however strong the State's interest in universal compulsory education, it is by no means absolute to the exclusion or subordination of all other interests. . . .

We come then to the quality of the claims of the respondents concerning the alleged encroachment of Wisconsin's compulsory school attendance statute on their rights and the rights of their children to the free exercise of the religious beliefs they and their forebears have adhered to for almost three centuries. In evaluating those claims we must be careful to determine whether the Amish religious faith and their mode of life are . . . inseparable and interdependent. A way of life, however virtuous and admirable, may not be interposed as a barrier to reasonable state regulation of education if it is based on purely secular considerations; to have the protection of the Religion Clauses, the claims must be rooted in religious belief. . . .

Giving no weight to such secular considerations, however, we see that the record in this case abundantly supports the claim that the traditional way of life of the Amish is not merely a matter of personal preference, but one of deep religious conviction, shared by an organized group, and intimately related to daily living. That the Old Order Amish daily life and religious practice stems from their faith is shown by the fact that it is in response to their literal interpretation of the Biblical injunction from the Epistle of Paul to the Romans, "Be not conformed to this world. . . ." This command is fundamental to the Amish faith. Moreover, for the Old Order Amish, religion is not simply a matter of theocratic belief. As the expert witnesses explained, the Old Order Amish religion pervades and determines virtually their entire way of life. . . .

The record shows that the respondents' religious beliefs and attitude toward life, family, and home have remained constant—perhaps some would say static—in a period of unparalleled progress in human knowledge generally and great changes in education. The respondents freely concede, and indeed assert as an article of faith, that their religious beliefs and what we would today call "life style" has not altered in fundamentals for centuries. Their way of life in a church-oriented community, separated from the outside world and "worldly" influences, their attachment to nature and the soil, is a way inherently simple and uncomplicated, albeit difficult to preserve against the pressure to conform. Their rejection of tele-

phones, automobiles, radios, and television, their mode of dress, of speech, their habits of manual work do indeed set them apart from much of contemporary society. . . .

. . . The Amish mode of life has . . . come into conflict increasingly with requirements of contemporary society exerting a hydraulic insistence on conformity to majoritarian standards. So long as compulsory education laws were confined to eight grades of elementary basic education imparted in a nearby rural schoolhouse, with a large proportion of students of the Amish faith, the Old Order Amish had little basis to fear that school attendance would expose their children to the wordly influence they reject. But modern compulsory secondary education in rural areas is now largely carried on in a consolidated school, often remote from the student's home and alien to his daily home life. As the record so strongly shows, the values and programs of the modern secondary school are in sharp conflict with the fundamental mode of life mandated by the Amish religion. . . . The conclusion is inescapable that secondary schooling, by exposing Amish children to worldly influences in terms of attitudes, goals and values contrary to beliefs, and by substantially interfering with the religious development of the Amish child and his integration into the way of life of the Amish faith community at the crucial adolescent state of development, contravenes the basic religious tenets and practices of the Amish faith, both as to the parent and the child.

The impact of the compulsory attendance law on respondents' practice of the Amish religion is not only severe, but inescapable, for the Wisconsin law affirmatively compels them, under threat of criminal sanction, to perform acts undeniably at odds with fundamental tenets of their religious beliefs. . . . Nor is the impact of the compulsory attendance law confined to grave interference with important Amish religious tenets from a subjective point of view. It carries with it precisely the kind of objective danger to the free exercise of religion which the First Amendment was designed to prevent. As the record shows, compulsory school attendance to age 16 for Amish children carries with it a very real threat of undermining the Amish community and religious practice as it exists today; they must either abandon belief and be assimilated into society at large, or be forced to migrate to some other and more tolerant region. . . .

* * *

Wisconsin concedes that under the Religion Clauses religious beliefs are absolutely free from the State's control, but it argues that "actions," even though religiously grounded, are outside the protection of the First Amendment. But our decisions have rejected the idea that religiously grounded conduct is always outside the protection of the Free Exercise Clause. It is true that activities of individuals, even when religiously based, are often subject to regulation by the States in the exercise of their undoubted power to promote the health, safety, and general welfare, or the Federal Government in the exercise of its delegated powers. . . . But to agree that religiously grounded conduct must often be subject to the broad police power of the State is not to deny that there are areas of conduct protected by the Free Exercise Clause of the First Amendment and thus beyond the power of the State to control. . . .

We turn, then to the State's . . . contention that its interest in its system of compulsory education is so compelling that even the established religious practices of the Amish must give way. . . .

The State advances two primary arguments in support of its system of compulsory education. It notes, as Thomas Jefferson pointed out early in our history, that some degree of education is necessary to prepare citizens to participate effectively and intelligently in our open political system if we are to preserve freedom and independence. Further, education prepared individuals to be self-reliant and self-sufficient participants in society. We accept these propositions.

However, the evidence adduced by the Amish in this case is persuasively to the effect that an additional one or two years of formal high school for Amish children in place of their long established program of informal vocational education would do little to serve those interests. Respondents' experts testified at trial, without challenge, that the value of all education must be assessed in terms of its capacity to prepare the child for life. It is one thing to say that compulsory education for a year or two beyond the eighth grade may be necessary when its goal is the preparation of the child for life in modern society as the majority live, but it is quite another if the goal of education be viewed as the preparation of the child for life in the separated agrarian community that is the keystone of the Amish faith. . . .

The State attacks respondents' position as one fostering "ignorance" from which the child must be protected by the State. No one can question the State's duty to protect children from ignorance but this argument does not square with the facts disclosed in the record. Whatever their idiosyncrasies as seen by the majority, this record strongly shows that the Amish community has been a highly successful social unit within our society even if apart from the conventional "mainstream." Its members are productive and very law-abiding members of society; they reject public welfare in any of its usual modern forms. . . .

It is neither fair nor correct to suggest that the Amish are opposed to education beyond the eighth grade level. What this record shows is that they are opposed to conventional formal education of the type provided by a certified high school because it comes at the child's crucial adolescent period of religious development. . . .

We must not forget that in the Middle Ages important values of the civilization of the western world were preserved by members of religious orders who isolated themselves from all worldly influences against great obstacles. There can be no assumption that today's majority is "right" and the Amish and others like them are "wrong." A way of life that is odd or even erratic but interferes with no rights or interests of others is not to be condemned because it is different.

The State, however, supports its interest in providing an additional one or two years of compulsory high school education to Amish children because of the possibility that some such children will choose to leave the Amish community, and that if this occurs they will be ill-equipped for life. The State argues that if Amish children leave their church they should not be in the position of making their way in the world without the education available in the one or two additional years the State requires. However, on this record, that argument is highly speculative. There is no specific evidence of the loss of Amish adherents by attrition, nor is there any showing that upon leaving the Amish community Amish children, with their practical agricultural training and habits of industry and self-reliance, would become burdens on society because of educational shortcomings. Indeed, this argument of the State appears to rest primarily on the State's mistaken assumption, already noted, that the Amish do not provide any education for their children beyond the eighth grade, but allow them to grow in "ignorance." To the contrary, not only do the Amish accept the necessity for formal schooling through the eighth grade level, but continue to provide what has been characterized by the undisputed testimony of expert educators as an "ideal" vocational education for their children in the adolescent years. . . .

Insofar as the State's claim rests on the view that a brief additional period of formal education is imperative to enable the Amish to participate effectively and intelligently in our democratic process, it must fail. The Amish alternative to formal secondary school education has enabled them to function effectively in their day-to-day life under self-imposed limitations on relations with the world, and to survive and prosper in contemporary society as a separate, sharply identifiable and highly self-sufficient community for more than 200 years in this country. In itself this is strong evidence that they are capable of fulfilling the social and political responsibilities of citizenship without compelled attendance beyond the eighth grade at the price of jeopardizing their free exercise of religious belief. . . .

. . . The independence and successful social functioning of the Amish community for a period approaching almost three centuries and more than 200 years in this country is strong evidence that there is at best a speculative gain, in terms of meeting the duties of citizenship, from an additional one or two years of compulsory formal education. Against this background it would require a more particularized showing from the State on this point to justify the severe interference with religious freedom such additional compulsory attendance would entail.

We should also note that compulsory education and child labor laws find their historical origin in common humanitarian instincts, and that the age limits of both laws have been coordinated to achieve their related objectives. In the context of this case, such considerations, if anything, support rather than detract from respondents' position. . . .

The requirement of compulsory schooling to age 16 must therefore be viewed as aimed not merely at providing educational opportunities for children, but as an alternative to the equally undesirable consequence of unhealthful child labor displacing adult workers, or, on the other hand, forced idleness. The two kinds of statutes—compulsory school attendance and child labor laws—tend to keep children of certain ages off the labor market and in school; this in turn provides opportunity to prepare for a livelihood of a higher order than that children could perform without education and protects their health in adolescence.

In these terms, Wisconsin's interest in compelling the school attendance of Amish children to age 16 emerges as somewhat less substantial than requiring such attendance for children generally. For, while agricultural employment is not totally outside the legitimate concerns of the child labor laws, employment of children under parental guidance and on the family farm from age 14 to 16 is

an ancient tradition which lies at the periphery of the objectives of such laws. There is no intimation that the Amish employment of their children on family farms is in any way deleterious to their health or that Amish parents exploit children at tender years. Any such inference would be contrary to the record before us. Moreover, employment of Amish children on the family farm does not present the undesirable economic aspects of eliminating jobs which might otherwise be held by adults.

Finally, the State, on authority of *Prince* v. *Massachusetts*, argues that a decision exempting Amish children from the State's requirement fails to recognize the substantive right of the Amish child to a secondary education, and fails to give due regard to the power of the state as *parens patrias* to extend the benefit of secondary education to children regardless of the wishes of their parents. Taken at its broadest sweep, the Court's language in *Prince* might be read to give support to the State's position. However, the Court was not confronted in *Prince* with a situation comparable to that of the Amish as revealed in this record. . . .

This case, of course, is not one in which any harm to the physical or mental health of the child or to the public safety, peace, order, or welfare has been demonstrated or may be properly inferred. The record is to the contrary, and any reliance on that theory would find no support in the evidence.

Contrary to the suggestion of the dissenting opinion of JUSTICE DOUGLAS, our holding today in no degree depends on the assertion of the religious interest of the child as contrasted with that of the parents. It is the parents who are subject to prosecution here for failing to cause their children to attend school, and it is their right of free exercise, not that of their children, that must determine Wisconsin's power to impose criminal penalties on the parent. The dissent argues that a child who expresses a desire to attend public high school in conflict with the wishes of his parents should not be prevented from doing so. There is no reason for the Court to consider that point since it is not an issue in the case. The children are not parties to this litigation. The State has at no point tried this case on the theory that respondents were preventing their children from attending school against their expressed desires, and indeed the record is to the contrary. The State's position from the outset has been that it is empowered to apply its compulsory attendance law to Amish parents in the same manner as to other parents—that is, without regard to the wishes of the child. That is the claim we reject today.

Our holding in no way determines the proper resolution of possible competing interests of parents, children, and the State in an appropriate state court proceeding in which the power of the State is asserted on the theory that Amish parents are preventing their minor children from attending high school despite their expressed desires to the contrary. Recognition of the claim of the State in such a proceeding would, of course, call into question traditional concepts of parental control over the religious upbringing and education of their minor children recognized in this Court's past decisions. It is clear that such an intrusion by a State into family decisions in the area of religious training would give rise to grave questions of religious freedom comparable to those raised here and those presented in *Pierce* v. *Society of Sisters*. On this record we neither reach nor decide those issues.

The State's argument proceeds without reliance on any actual conflict between the wishes of parents and children. It appears to rest on the potential that exemption of Amish parents from the requirements of the compulsory education law might allow some parents to act contrary to the best interests of their children by foreclosing their opportunity to make an intelligent choice between the Amish way of life and that of the outside world. The same argument could, of course, be made with respect to all church schools short of college. There is nothing in the record or in the ordinary course of human experience to suggest that non-Amish parents generally consult with children up to ages 14–16 if they are placed in a church school of the parents' faith.

Indeed it seems clear that if the State is empowered, as *parens patriae*, to "save" a child from himself or his Amish parents by requiring an additional two years of compulsory formal high school education, the State will in large measure influence, if not determine, the religious future of the child. Even more markedly than in *Prince*, therefore, this case involves the fundamental interest of parents, as contrasted with that of the State, to guide the religious future and education of their children. The history and culture of western civilization reflect a strong tradition of parental concern for the nurture and upbringing of their children. This primary role of the parents in the upbringing of their children is now established beyond debate as an enduring American tradition. . . .

For the reasons stated we hold, with the Supreme Court of Wisconsin, that the First and Fourteenth Amendments prevent the State from compelling respondents to cause their children to attend formal high school to age 16. . . .

Nothing we hold is intended to undermine the general applicability of the State's compulsory school attendance statutes or to limit the power of the State to promulgate reasonable standards that, while not impairing the free exercise of religion, provide for continuing agricultural vocational education under parental and church guidance by the Old Order Amish or others similarly situated. The States have had a long history of amicable and effective relationships with church-sponsored schools, and there is no basis for assuming that, in this related context, reasonable standards cannot be established concerning the content of the continuing vocational education of Amish children under parental guidance, provided always that state regulations are not inconsistent with what we have said in this opinion.

Affirmed.

[The concurring opinion of JUSTICE WHITE, with whom JUSTICES BRENNAN and STEWART joined, is not reprinted here.]

JUSTICE DOUGLAS, *dissenting in part.*

I agree with the Court that the religious scruples of the Amish are opposed to the education of their children beyond the grade schools, yet I disagree with the Court's conclusion that the matter is within the dispensation of parents alone. The Court's analysis assumes that the only interests at stake in the case are those of the Amish parents on the one hand, and those of the State on the other. The difficulty with this approach is that, despite the Court's claim, the parents are seeking to vindicate not only their own free exercise claims, but also those of their high-school age children.

It is argued that the right of the Amish children to religious freedom is not presented by the facts of the case, as the issue before the Court involves only the Amish parents' religious freedom to defy a state criminal statute imposing upon them an affirmative duty to cause their children to attend high school.

First, respondents' motion to dismiss in the trial court expressly asserts, not only the religious liberty of the adults, but also that of the children, as a defense to the prosecutions. It is, of course, beyond question that the parents have standing as defendants in a criminal prosecution to assert the religious interests of their children as a defense. Although the lower courts and the majority in this Court assume an identity of interest between parent and child, it is clear that they have treated the religious interest of the child as a factor in the analysis.

Second, it is essential to reach the question to decide the case not only because the question was squarely raised in the motion to dismiss, but also because no analysis of religious liberty claims can take place in a vacuum. If the parents in this case are allowed a religious exemption, the inevitable effect is to impose the parents' notions of religious duty upon their children. Where the child is mature enough to express potentially conflicting desires, it would be an invasion of the child's rights to permit such an imposition without canvassing his views. As in *Prince*, it is an imposition resulting from this very litigation. As the child has no other effective forum, it is in this litigation that his rights should be considered. And, if an Amish child desires to attend high school, and is mature enough to have that desire respected, the State may well be able to override the parents' religiously motivated objections.

Religion is an individual experience. It is not necessary, not even appropriate, for every Amish child to express his views on the subject in a prosecution of a single adult. Crucial, however, are the views of the child whose parent is the subject of the suit. Freida Yoder has in fact testified that her own religious views are opposed to high school education. I therefore join the judgment of the Court as to respondent Jonas Yoder. But Freida Yoder's views may not be those of Vernon Yutzy or Barbara Miller. I must dissent, therefore, as to respondents Adin Yutzy and Wallace Miller as their motion to dismiss also raised the question of their children's religious liberty. . . .

On this important and vital matter of education, I think the children should be entitled to be heard. While the parents, absent dissent, normally speak for the entire family, the education of the child is a matter on which the child will often have decided views. He may want to be a pianist or an astronaut or an oceanographer. To do so he will have to break from the Amish tradition.

It is the future of the student, not the future of the parents, that is imperiled in today's decision. If a parent keeps his child out of school beyond the grade school, then the child will be forever barred from entry into the new and amazing world of diversity that we have today. The child may decide that that is the preferred course, or he may rebel. It is the student's judgment, not his parent's, that is essential if we are to give full meaning to what we have said about the Bill of Rights and of the right of students to be masters of their own destiny. If he is harnessed to the Amish way of life by those in authority over him and if his education is truncated, his entire life may be stunted and deformed. The child, therefore, should be given an opportunity to be heard before the State gives the exemption which we honor today. . . .

EMPLOYMENT DIVISION, DEPARTMENT OF HUMAN RESOURCES OF OREGON v. ALFRED L. SMITH
494 U.S. 872; 108 L. Ed. 2d 876; 110 S. Ct. 1595 (1990)

JUSTICE SCALIA *delivered the opinion of the Court.*

This case requires us to decide whether the Free Exercise Clause of the First Amendment permits the State of Oregon to include religiously inspired peyote use within the reach of its general criminal prohibition on use of that drug, and thus permits the State to deny unemployment benefits to persons dismissed from their jobs because of such religiously inspired use.

I

Oregon law prohibits the knowing or intentional possession of a "controlled substance" unless the substance has been prescribed by a medical practitioner. . . .

Respondents Alfred Smith and Galen Black were fired from their jobs with a private drug reha-bilitation organization because they ingested peyote for sacramental purposes at a ceremony of the Native American Church, of which both are members. When respondents applied to petitioner Employment Division for unemployment compensation, they were determined to be ineligible for benefits because they had been discharged for "misconduct." The Oregon Court of Appeals reversed that determination, holding that the denial of benefits violated respondents' free exercise rights under the First Amendment.

On appeal to the Oregon Supreme Court, petitioner argued that the denial of benefits was permissible because respondents' consumption of peyote was a crime under Oregon law. The Oregon Supreme Court reasoned, however, that the criminality of respondents' peyote use was irrelevant to resolution of their constitutional claim. . . .

Citing our decisions in *Sherbert* v. *Verner*, and

Thomas v. *Review Board, Indiana Employment Security Div.*, the court concluded that respondents were entitled to payment of unemployment benefits. We granted certiorari.

Before this Court in 1987, petitioner continued to maintain that the illegality of respondents' peyote consumption was relevant to their constitutional claim. We agreed, concluding that "if a State has prohibited through its criminal laws certain kinds of religiously motivated conduct without violating the First Amendment, it certainly follows that it may impose the lesser burden of denying unemployment compensation benefits to persons who engage in that conduct." We noted, however, that the Oregon Supreme Court had not decided whether respondents' sacramental use of peyote was in fact proscribed by Oregon's controlled substance law, and that this issue was a matter of dispute between the parties. Being "uncertain about the legality of the religious use of peyote in Oregon, we determined that it would not be appropriate for us to decide whether the practice is protected by the Federal Constitution." Accordingly, we vacated the judgment of Oregon Supreme Court and remanded for further proceedings.

On remand, the Oregon Supreme Court held that respondents' religiously inspired use of peyote fell within the prohibition of the Oregon statute, which "makes no exception for the sacramental use" of the drug. It then considered whether that prohibition was valid under the Free Exercise Clause, and concluded that it was not [and] reaffirmed its previous ruling that the State could not deny unemployment benefits to respondents. . . . We again granted certiorari.

II

Respondents' claim for relief rests on our decision in *Sherbert* v. *Verner, Thomas* v. *Review Board, Indiana Employment Security Div.*, and *Hobbie* v. *Unemployment Appeals Comm'n of Florida*, in which we held that a State could not condition the availability of unemployment insurance on an individual's willingness to forgo conduct required by his religion. As we observed in *Smith I*, however, the conduct at issue in those cases was not prohibited by law. We held that distinction to be critical, for "if Oregon does prohibit the religious use of peyote, and if that prohibition is consistent with the Federal Constitution, there is no federal right to engage in that conduct in Oregon." . . . Now that the Oregon Supreme Court has confirmed that Oregon does prohibit the religious use of peyote, we proceed to consider whether that prohibition is permissible under the Free Exercise Clause.

A

The Free Exercise Clause of the First Amendment . . . often involves not only belief and profession but the performance of or abstention from physical acts: assembling with others for a worship service, participating in sacramental use of bread and wine, proselytizing, abstaining from certain foods or certain modes of transportation. It would be true, we think, though no case of ours has involved the point, that a state would be "prohibiting the free exercise [of religion] if it sought to ban such acts or abstentions only when they are engaged in for religious belief that they display. It would doubtless be unconstitutional, for example, to ban the casting of "statues that are to be used for worship purposes," or to prohibit bowing down before a golden calf.

Respondents in the present case, however, seek to carry the meaning of "prohibiting the free exercise [of religion] one large step further. They contend that their religious motivation for using peyote places them beyond the reach of a criminal law that is not specifically directed at their religious practice, and that is concededly constitutional as applied to those who use the drug for other reasons. They assert, in other words, that "prohibiting the free exercise [of religion]" includes requiring any individual to observe a generally applicable law that requires or forbids the performance of an act that his religious belief forbids or requires. As a textual matter, we do not think the words must be given that meaning. . . .

. . . We have never held that an individual's beliefs excuse him from compliance with an otherwise valid law prohibiting conduct that the State is free to regulate. On the contrary, the record of more than a century of our free exercise jurisprudence contradicts that proposition. As described succinctly by Justice Frankfurter in *Minersville School Dist. Bd. of Educ.* v. *Gobitis* [in 1940]: "Conscientious scruples have not, in the course of the long struggle for religious toleration, relieved the individual from obedience to a general law not aimed at the promotion or restriction of religious beliefs. The mere possession of religious convictions which contradict the relevant concerns of a political society does not relieve the citizen from the discharge of political responsibilities." . . .

The only decisions in which we have held that the First Amendment bars application of a neutral, generally applicable law to religiously motivated action have involved not the Free Exercise Clause alone, but the Free Exercise Clause in conjunction with other constitutional protections, such as freedom of speech and of the press, see *Cantwell* v. *Connecticut*, (invalidating a licensing system for religious and charitable solicitations under which the administrator had discretion to deny a license to any cause he deemed nonreligious); *Murdock* v. *Pennsylvania*, 319 U.S. 105, (1943) (invalidating a flat tax on solicitation as applied to the dissemination of religious ideas); . . . or the right of parents, acknowledged in *Pierce* v. *Society of Sisters*, 268 U.S. 510, (1925), to direct the education of their children, see [also] *Wisconsin* v. *Yoder*, 406 U.S. 205, (1972) (invalidating compulsory school-attendance laws as applied to Amish parents who refused on religious grounds to send their children to school). Some of our cases prohibiting compelled expression, decided exclusively upon free speech grounds, have also involved freedom of religion, cf *Wooley* v. *Maynard*, 430 U.S. 705, (1977) (invalidating compelled display of a license plate slogan that offended individual religious beliefs); *West Virginia Board of Education* v. *Barnette*, 319 U.S. 624, (1943) (invalidating compulsory flag salute challenged by religious objectors). And it is easy to envision a case in which a challenge on freedom of association grounds would likewise be reinforced by Free Exercise Clause concerns. . . .

The present case does not present such a hybrid situation, but a free exercise claim unconnected with any communicative activity or parental right. Respondents urge us to hold, quite simply, that when otherwise prohibitable conduct is accompanied by religious convictions, not only the convictions but the conduct itself must be free from governmental regulation. We have never held that, and decline to do so now. There being no contention that Oregon's drug law represents an attempt to regulate religious beliefs, the communication of religious beliefs, or the raising of one's children in those beliefs, the rule to which we have adhered ever since *Reynolds* plainly controls. . . .

B

Respondents argue that even though exemption from generally applicable criminal laws need not automatically be extended to religiously motivated actors, at least the claim for a religious exemption must be evaluated under the balancing test set forth in *Sherbert* v. *Verner*. Under the *Sherbert* test, governmental actions that substantially burden a religious practice must be justified by a compelling governmental interest. . . . We have never invalidated any governmental action on the basis of the *Sherbert* test except the denial of unemployment compensation. Although we have sometimes purported to apply the *Sherbert* test in contexts other than that, we have always found the test satisfied. In recent years we have abstained from applying the *Sherbert* test (outside the unemployment compensation field) at all.

Even if we were inclined to breathe into *Sherbert* some life beyond the unemployment compensation field, we would not apply it to require exemptions from a generally applicable criminal law. The *Sherbert* test, it must be recalled, was developed in a context that lent itself to individualized governmental assessment of the reasons for the relevant conduct. As a plurality of the Court noted in *Bowen* v. *Roy*, 476 U.S. 693, (1986) a distinctive feature of unemployment compensation programs is that their eligibility criteria invite consideration of the particular circumstances behind an applicant's unemployment: "The statutory conditions [in *Sherbert* and *Thomas*] provided that a person was not eligible for unemployment compensation benefits if, 'without good cause,' he had quit work or refused available work. The 'good cause' standard created a mechanism for individualized exemptions". . . .

Whether or not the decisions are that limited, they at least have nothing to do with an across-the-board criminal prohibition or a particular form of conduct. Although . . . we have sometimes used the *Sherbert* test to analyze free exercise challenges to such law, we have never applied the test to invalidate one. We conclude today that the sounder approach, and the approach in accord with the vast majority of our precedent, is to hold the test inapplicable to such challenges. The government's ability to enforce generally applicable prohibitions of socially harmful conduct, like its ability to carry out other aspects of public policy, "cannot depend on measuring the effects of a governmental action on a religious objector's spiritual development." To make an individual's obligation to obey such a law contingent upon the law's coincidence with his religious beliefs, except where the State's interest is "compelling"—permitting him, by virtue of his beliefs, "to become a law unto himself," contradicts both constitutional tradition and common sense. . . .

Nor is it possible to limit the impact of respondents' proposal by requiring a "compelling state interest" only when the conduct prohibited is "central" to the individual's religion. It is no more appropriate for judges to determine the "centrality" of religious beliefs before applying a "compelling interest" test in the free exercise field, than it would be for them to determine the "importance" of ideas before applying the "compelling interest" test in the free speech field. What principle of law or logic can be brought to bear to contradict a believer's assertion that a particular act is "central" to his personal faith? Judging the centrality of different religious practices is akin to the unacceptable "business of evaluating the relative merits of differing religious claims." As we reaffirmed only last Term, "[i]t is not within the judicial ken to question the centrality of particular beliefs or practices to a faith, or the validity of particular litigants' interpretation of those creeds." *Hernandez* v. *Commissioner*. Repeatedly and in many different contexts, we have warned that courts must not presume to determine the place of a particular belief in a religion or the plausibility of a religious claim. If the "compelling interest" test is to be applied at all, then, it must be applied across the board, to all actions thought to be religiously commanded. . . . Precisely because "we are a cosmopolitan nation made up of people of almost every conceivable religious preference," and precisely because we value and protect that religious divergence, we cannot afford the luxury of deeming presumptively invalid as applied to the religious objector, every regulation of conduct that does not protect an interest of the highest order. The rule respondents favor would open the prospect of constitutionally required religious exemptions from civic obligations of almost every conceivable kind. . . .

The First Amendment's protection of religious liberty does not require this. Values that are protected against government interference through enshrinement in the Bill of Rights are not thereby banished from the political process. Just as a society that believes in the negative protection accorded to the press by the First Amendment is likely to enact laws that affirmatively foster the dissemination of the printed word, so also a society that believes in the negative protection accorded to religious belief can be expected to be solicitous of that value in its legislation as well. It is therefore not surprising that a number of States have made an exception to their drug laws for sacramental peyote use. But to say that a nondiscriminatory religious-practice exemption is permitted, or even that it is desirable, is not to say that it is constitutionally required, and that the appropriate occasions for its creation can be discerned by the courts. It may fairly be said that leaving accommodation to the political process will place at a relative disadvantage those religious practices that are not widely engaged in; but that unavoidable consequence of democratic government must be preferred to a system in which each conscience is a

law unto itself or in which judges weigh the social importance of all laws against the centrality of all religious beliefs.

Because respondents' ingestion of peyote was prohibited under Oregon law, and because that prohibition is constitutional, Oregon may, consistent with the Free Exercise Clause, deny respondents unemployment compensation when their dismissal results from the use of the drug. The decision of the Oregon Supreme Court is accordingly reversed.

It is so ordered.

JUSTICE O'CONNOR *with whom* JUSTICE BRENNAN, JUSTICE MARSHALL, *and* JUSTICE BLACKMUN *join as to Parts I and II, concurring in the judgment.*

[Although JUSTICE BRENNAN, JUSTICE MARSHALL, and JUSTICE BLACKMUN join as to Parts I and II of this opinion, they do not concur in the judgment.]

Although I agree with the result the Court reaches in this case, I cannot join its opinion. In my view, today's holding dramatically departs from well-settled First Amendment jurisprudence, appears unnecessary to resolve the question presented, and is incompatible with our Nation's fundamental commitment to individual religious liberty . . . .

II

The Court today extracts from our long history of free exercise precedents the single categorical rule that "if prohibiting the exercise of religion . . . is . . . merely the incidental effect of a generally applicable and otherwise valid provision, the First Amendment has not been offended." Indeed, the Court holds that where the law is a generally applicable criminal prohibition, our usual free exercise jurisprudence does not even apply. To reach this sweeping result, however, the Court must not only give a strained reading of the First Amendment but must also disregard our consistent application of free exercise doctrine to cases involving generally applicable regulations that burden religious conduct.

A

. . . As the Court recognizes, however, the "free exercise" of religion often, if not invariably, requires the performance of (or abstention from) certain acts. . . . Because the First Amendment does not distinguish between religious belief and religious conduct, conduct motivated by sincere religious belief, like the belief itself, must therefore be at least presumptively protected by the Free Exercise Clause.

The Court today, however, interprets the Clause to permit the government to prohibit, without justification, conduct mandated by an individual's religious beliefs, so long as that prohibition is generally applicable. But a law that prohibits certain conduct—conduct that happens to be an act of worship for someone—manifestly does prohibit that person's free exercise of his religion. A person who is barred from engaging in religiously motivated conduct is barred from freely exercising his religion. Moreover, that person is barred from freely exercising his religion regardless of whether the law prohibits the conduct only when engaged in for religious reason, only by members of that religion, or by all persons. It is difficult to deny that a law that prohibits religiously motivated conduct, even if the law is generally applicable, does not at least implicate First Amendment concerns.

The Court responds that generally applicable laws are "one large step" removed from laws aimed at specific religious practices. The First Amendment, however, does not distinguish between laws that are generally applicable and laws that target particular religious practices. Indeed, few States would be so naive as to enact a law directly prohibiting or burdening a religious practice as such. Our free exercise cases have all concerned generally applicable laws that had the effect of significantly burdening a religious practice. If the First Amendment is to have any vitality, it ought not be construed to cover only the extreme and hypothetical situation in which a State directly targets a religious practice. As we have noted in a slightly different context, " '[s]uch a test has no basis in precedent and relegates a serious First Amendment value to the barest level of minimum scrutiny that the Equal Protection Clause already provides.' " . . .

In my view . . . the essence of a free exercise claim is relief from a burden imposed by government on religious practices or beliefs, whether the burden is imposed directly through laws that prohibit or compel specific religious practices, or indirectly through laws that, in effect, make abandonment of one's own religion or conformity to the religious beliefs of others the price of an equal place in the civil community. . . . A State that makes criminal an individual's religiously motivated conduct burdens that individual's free exercise of religion in the severest manner possible, for it "results in the choice to the individual of either

abandoning his religious principle or facing criminal prosecution." . . . I would reaffirm that principle today: a neutral criminal law prohibiting conduct that a State may legitimately regulate is, if anything, more burdensome than a neutral civil statute placing legitimate conditions on the award of a state benefit. . . .

The Court today gives no convincing reason to depart from settled First Amendment jurisprudence. There is nothing talismanic about neutral laws of general applicability or general criminal prohibitions, for laws neutral toward religion can coerce a person to violate his religious conscience or intrude upon his religious duties just as effectively as laws aimed at religion. Although the Court suggests that the compelling interest test, as applied to generally applicable laws, would result in a "constitutional anomaly," the First Amendment unequivocally makes freedom of religion, like freedom from race discrimination and freedom of speech, a "constitutional nor[m]," not an "anomaly." . . .

Finally the Court today suggests that the disfavoring of minority religions is an "unavoidable consequence" under our system of government and that accommodation of such religions must be left to the political process. In my view, however, the First Amendment was enacted precisely to protect the right of those whose religious practices are not shared by the majority and may be viewed with hostility. The history of our free exercise doctrine amply demonstrates the harsh impact majoritarian rule has had on unpopular or emerging religious groups such as the Jehovah's Witnesses and the Amish. Indeed, the words of Justice Jackson, in *West Virginia Board of Education* v. *Barnette* (overruling *Minersville School District* v. *Gobitis*) are apt:

> The very purpose of a Bill of Rights was to withdraw certain subjects from the vicissitudes of political controversy, to place them beyond the reach of majorities and officials and to establish them as legal principles to be applied by the courts. One's right to life, liberty, and property, to free speech, a free press, freedom of worship and assembly, and other fundamental rights may not be submitted to vote; they depend on the outcome of no elections. . . .

III

The Court's holding today not only misreads settled First Amendment precedent; it appears to be unnecessary to this case. I would reach the same result applying our established free exercise jurisprudence.

A

There is no dispute that Oregon's criminal prohibition of peyote places a severe burden on the ability of respondents to freely exercise their religion. Peyote is a sacrament of the Native American Church and is regarded as vital to respondents' ability to practice their religion. . . . Under Oregon law, as construed by that State's highest court, members of the Native American Church must choose between carrying out the ritual embodying their religious beliefs and avoidance of criminal prosecution. That choice is, in my view, more than sufficient to trigger First Amendment scrutiny.

There is also no dispute that Oregon has a significant interest in enforcing laws that control the possession and use of controlled substances by its citizens. . . .

B

Thus, the critical question in this case is whether exempting respondents from the State's general criminal prohibition "will unduly interfere with fulfillment of the governmental interest." . . . Although the question is close, I would conclude that uniform application of Oregon's criminal prohibition is "essential to accomplish," its overriding interest in preventing the physical harm caused by the use of a . . . controlled substance. Oregon's criminal prohibition represents that State's judgment that the possession and use of controlled substances, even by only one person, is inherently harmful and dangerous. Because the health effects caused by the use of controlled substances exist regardless of the motivation of the user, the use of such substances, even for religious purposes, violates the very purpose of the laws that prohibit them. . . .

For these reasons, I believe that granting a selective exemption in this case would seriously impair Oregon's compelling interest in prohibiting possession of peyote by its citizens. Under such circumstances, the Free Exercise Clause does not require the State to accommodate respondents' religiously motivated conduct. . . . I would therefore adhere to our established free exercise jurisprudence and hold that the State in this case has a compelling interest in regulating peyote use by its citizens and that accommodating respondents' religiously motivated conduct "will unduly interfere with fulfillment of the governmental interest." *Accordingly, I concur in the judgment of the Court.*

JUSTICE BLACKMUN, *with whom* JUSTICE BRENNAN *and* JUSTICE MARSHALL *join, dissenting.*

This Court over the years painstakingly has developed a consistent and exacting standard to test the constitutionality of a state statute that burdens the free exercise of religion. Such a statute may stand only if the law in general, and the State's refusal to allow a religious exemption in particular, are justified by a compelling interest that cannot be served by less restrictive means.

Until today, I thought this was a settled and inviolate principle of this Court's First Amendment jurisprudence. The majority, however, perfunctorily dismisses it as a "constitutional anomaly." . . . The Court discards leading free exercise cases such as *Cantwell* v. *Connecticut* (1940), and *Wisconsin* v. *Yoder* (1972), as "hybrid." The Court views traditional free exercise analysis as somehow inapplicable to criminal prohibitions (as opposed to conditions on the receipt of benefits), and to state laws of general applicability (as opposed, presumably, to laws that expressly single out religious practices). . . . In short, it effectuates a wholesale overturning of settled law concerning the Religion Clauses of our Constitution. One hopes that the Court is aware of the consequences, and that its result is not a product of overreaction to the serious problems the country's drug crisis has generated. . . . The State's interest in enforcing its prohibition, in order to be sufficiently compelling to outweigh a free exercise claim, cannot be merely abstract or symbolic. The State cannot plausibly assert that unbending application of a criminal prohibition is essential to fulfill any compelling interest, if it does not, in fact, attempt to enforce that prohibition. In this case, the State actually has not evinced any concrete interest in enforcing its drug laws against religious users of peyote. Oregon has never sought to prosecute respondents, and does not claim that it has made significant enforcement efforts against other religious users of peyote. The State's asserted interest thus amounts only to the symbolic preservation of an unenforced prohibition. But a government interest in "symbolism, even symbolism for so worthy a cause as the abolition of unlawful drugs," cannot suffice to abrogate the constitutional rights of individuals.

Similarly, this Court's prior decisions have not allowed a government to rely on mere speculation about potential harms, but have demanded evidentiary support for a refusal to allow a religious exception. . . . In this case, the State's justification for refusing to recognize an exception to its criminal laws for religious peyote use is entirely speculative.

The State proclaims an interest in protecting the health and safety of its citizens from the dangers of unlawful drugs. It offers, however, no evidence that the religious use of peyote has ever harmed anyone. The factual findings of other courts cast doubt on the State's assumption that religious use of peyote is harmful. . . .

The fact that peyote is classified as a Schedule I controlled substance does not, by itself, show that any and all uses of peyote, in any circumstance, are inherently harmful and dangerous. The Federal Government, which created the classification of unlawful drugs from which Oregon's drug laws are derived, apparently does not find peyote so dangerous as to preclude an exemption for religious use. . . .

The carefully circumscribed ritual context in which respondents used peyote is far removed from the irresponsible and unrestricted recreational use of unlawful drugs. The Native American Church's internal restrictions on, and supervision of, its members' use of peyote substantially obviate the State's health safety concerns. . . .

III

Finally, although I agree with JUSTICE O'CONNOR that courts should refrain from delving into questions of whether, as a matter of religious doctrine, a particular practice is "central" to the religion, I do not think this means that the courts must turn a blind eye to the severe impact of a State's restrictions on the adherents of a minority religion. . . .

Respondents believe, and their sincerity has never been at issue, that the peyote plant embodies their deity, and eating it is an act of worship and communion. Without peyote, they could not enact the essential ritual of their religion. . . .

If Oregon can constitutionally prosecute them for this act of worship, they, like the Amish, may be "forced to migrate to some other and more tolerant region." This potentially devastating impact must be viewed in light of the federal policy—reached in reaction to many years of religious persecution and intolerance—of protecting the religious freedom of Native Americans. . . . Congress recognized that certain substances, such as peyote, "have religious significance because they are sacred, they have power, they heal, they are necessary to the cultural integrity of the tribe, and therefore, religious survival."

The American Indian Religious Freedom Act, in itself, may not create rights enforceable against government action restricting religious freedom, but this Court must scrupulously apply its free exercise analysis to the religious claims of Native Americans, however unorthodox they may be. Otherwise, both the First Amendment and the stated policy of Congress will offer to Native Americans merely an unfulfilled and hollow promise. . . .

Commentary

Religious Liberty, the Military Draft, and Patriotic Ceremony

Since World War I, persons opposed to participating in wars have questioned whether the conscientious objection provision of selective service legislation was consistent with the religious liberty clauses of the First Amendment. The Supreme Court, however, has steadfastly side-stepped the establishment and free exercise claims pressed and has disposed of the cases on other grounds. Beginning with the Selective Draft Law Cases of 1918 (245 U.S. 366), Chief Justice Edward Douglas White said of the claims, "we pass without anything but statement the proposition that an establishment of a religion or an interference with the free exercise thereof . . . resulted from the exemption clause . . . because we think its unsoundness is too apparent to require us to do more."

Opposition to U.S. participation in the Vietnam War in the 1960s once again brought to the Court the religious liberty–compulsory military service question, in which both free exercise and establishment issues were raised. As draft-eligible college students lost their student deferment classification (II-S), a number of them sought the conscientious objector classification (I-O). Denials of their petitions and subsequent refusals to submit to induction precipitated prosecutorial actions that resulted in several constitutional challenges to the conscientious objector provision, Section 6(j), of the Universal Military Training and Service Act on its face and as applied.

In *United States* v. *Seeger* (380 U.S. 163, 1965) and two companion cases (*United States* v. *Jakobson* and *Peter* v. *United States*), for example, the constitutionality of the clause that defines the term "religious training and belief" was at issue. While the appeals pressed both establishment and free exercise challenges, the Court chose to side-step them. Instead, it construed the statute in its most favorable light and held that Congress had not intended to give preference to believers in a conventional God when it employed in section 6(j) the term "religious training and belief . . . in relation to a Supreme Being. . . ." Justice Tom Clark, in writing the Court's opinion, noted that with the "vast panoply of beliefs" that abound in our society, construing the phrase to embrace all religions was consistent with the long-established congressional policy "of not picking and choosing among religious beliefs." Justice Clark provided draft boards and lower courts with some guidance for the future by proposing a test to determine whether a belief was within the statutory definition of Section 6(j): "A sincere and meaningful belief which occupies in the life of its possessor a place parallel to that filled by the God of those admittedly qualifying for the exemption." What the Court said in effect was that adherence to formal religious principles was no longer the sole ground for granting conscientious objector status.

Congressional response to the decision was in the form of a 1967 amendment to the Selective Service Law, eliminating the clause that defines "religious training and belief" in terms of an individual's belief in relation to a Supreme Being. However, the lawmakers retained the provision that "religious training and belief" does not include political, sociological, or philosophical views and personal moral codes.

Three years later, in *Welsh* v. *United States* (308 U.S. 333, 1970), the Court rendered this provision meaningless. In reversing Welsh's conviction for refusing to submit to induction after his request for conscientious objector status had been denied, Justice Hugo Black spoke for the Court and held that "essentially political, sociological, or philosophical views or a merely personal moral code" should not be read to exclude persons with strong beliefs about the nation's domestic and foreign affairs. Furthermore, Black contended that Section 6(j) does *not* require exclusion of those whose conscientious objection is grounded to a great degree "on considerations of public policy."

Justice John M. Harlan II concurred in the result, but expressed serious concern about the length to which the majority had gone in statutory construction to avoid facing the constitutional issues presented. To him, the Court, in the face of compelling legislative history, had interpreted the statute to produce a policy outcome that Congress did not intend. He felt that the majority had performed this "lobotomy" to save the statute since it was clear to him that section 6(j)'s theistic bias abridged the establishment clause.

Justice Byron White's dissent, in which Chief Justice Warren Burger and Justice Potter Stewart joined, supported Harlan's attack on the Court's "rewriting" of the statute. Since the First Amendment does not forbid the congressional policy in this area, he argued, certainly the Court should not "frustrate the legislative will."

In 1971, the Court examined further the meaning of Section 6(j) in the companion cases of *Gillette* v. *United States* and *Negre* v. *Larsen* (401 U.S. 437, 1971) and rejected the concept of "selective conscientious objection." Petitioners argued that the statutory requirement that one must be opposed to participation in all wars rather than to a particular war to be eligible for a I-O status results in discrimination among religions in violation of the establishment clause. Hence, even those who are acting in accordance with "religious training and belief" (such as Negre, a devout Catholic) and who are opposed to participating in "unjust wars" only (like Vietnam) cannot qualify for exemption.

But Justice Thurgood Marshall insisted for the Court that no religious preference was reflected in the statute; its underlying purposes were neutral and secular. As an example, Marshall noted "the hopelessness of converting a sincere conscientious objector into an effective fighting man." Certainly, he concluded, such a pragmatic consideration has nothing to do with aiding or fostering any religious sect.

Can a person who is exempted from the military service as a conscientious objector, but meets his obligation through "alternative civilian service," be denied educational benefits under the Veterans Readjustment Act of 1966? In *Johnson* v. *Robinson* (415 U.S. 361, 1974), an eight-to-one majority said yes. Justice William J. Brennan's opinion for the Court emphasized that the distinction that Congress made between the veteran of military service and the conscientious objector performing "alternative service" for purposes of receiving educational benefits was based on a rational classification scheme and did not deny the latter the equal protection of the laws. In rejecting Robinson's free exercise claim, Brennan had serious doubts that the statutory exclusion of benefits from his class imposed a burden on free exercise of religion and, at most, if such a burden did result, it was only an incidental one.

In dissent, Justice William O. Douglas urged that *Sherbert* v. *Verner* should be controlling. To him this was a simple case of the government penalizing people "for asserting their religious scruples."

The Jehovah's Witnesses had created a patriotism controversy just prior to World War II when their children, as an expression of religious belief, refused to participate in the flag salute ceremony while attending public schools. Essentially, this ceremony required all " . . . public school children, as a part of the daily opening exercises, to salute the United States Flag and repeat the Pledge of Allegiance." Two children of a member of the Jehovah's Witnesses were expelled from school for refusing to participate in the ceremony. A federal district court agreed with the contention of the Witnesses that compulsory participation in the ceremony infringed upon their free exercise of religion and enjoined the school district from its continued use. Upon appeal, the Supreme Court reversed (*Minersville School District* v. *Gobitis*, 310 U.S. 586, 1940). Justice Felix Frankfurter, speaking for the eight-man majority, rejected the religious liberty claims and, instead, stressed the relationship between such symbolism and national unity. He maintained that "we live by symbols" and that "the flag is a symbol of our national unity, transcending all internal differences, however large, within the framework of the Constitution." In addition, Frankfurter urged judicial restraint in such matters of "educational policy." Justice Harlan F. Stone, the lone dissenter, stressed the need to protect the right of the individual to hold and to express opinions. He contended that the liberty protected by the Constitution from state infringement includes "the freedom of the individual from compulsion as to what he shall say, at least where the compulsion is to bear false witness to his religion."

Three years later, the Court did a complete about-face on the flag salute issue in *West Virginia State Board of Education* v. *Barnette* (319 U.S. 624, 1943). Factors usually cited in explaining this turnabout include: (1) the addition of two new associate justices—Justice Robert H. Jackson filled the vacancy created by the retirement of Chief Justice Charles Evans Hughes in 1941 (Justice Harlan Fiske Stone was elevated to the Chief Justiceship),

and Justice Wiley B. Rutledge replaced Justice James C. McReynolds in 1943; and (2) while dissenting in *Jones* v. *Opelika* (316 U.S. 584) a year earlier, the unusual admission of three justices of the *Gobitis* majority that they believed *Gobitis* was wrongly decided.

Justice Jackson's opinion for the six-man majority was not based on the Witnesses' assertions of religious liberty. Rather, it stressed freedom of speech and conscience and the implied right to remain silent. Noting that "the compulsory flag salute and pledge requires affirmation of a belief and an attitude of mind," Jackson argued:

> To sustain the compulsory flag salute we are required to say that a Bill of Rights which guards the individual's right to speak his own mind left it open to public authorities to compel him to utter what is not in his mind.

In an oft-quoted passage in defense of freedom of expression and conscience, Jackson concluded:

> If there is any fixed star in our constitutional constellation, it is that no official, high or petty, can prescribe what shall be orthodox in politics, nationalism, religion, or other matters of opinion or force citizens to confess by word or act their faith therein. . . .

Several later policies designed to evade *Barnette* have continuously met judicial rebuffs. Typical of such policies was that enforced under authority of a New Jersey statute in *Lipp* v. *Norris* (579 F.2d 834, 1977), which required students not participating in the flag salute ceremony merely to stand at "respectful attention." Both the district court and the Court of Appeals for the Third Circuit struck down the statute with a simple adherence to *Barnette*. Undoubtedly, the proscription laid down by Justice Jackson in that case, in which he said that the students there could not be compelled by word or act to affirm their loyalty, had controlling significance for these lower court jurists. See also *Goetz* v. *Ansell* (477 F.2d 63, 1973) and *Banks* v. *Board of Public Instruction of Dade County, Florida* (314 F. Supp. 285, 1970).

SELECTED REFERENCES

Brisbin, Richard A. "The Rehnquist Court and the Free Exercise of Religion," 34 *Journal of Church and State* 577 (Winter, 1992)

Choper, Jesse H. "Separation of Church and State: 'New' Directions by the 'New' Supreme Court," 34 *Journal of Church and State* 363 (Spring, 1992)

Dolbeare, Kenneth and Hammond, Phillip. "The School Prayer Decisions: From Court Policy to Local Practice," (Chicago: Univ. of Chicago Press, 1977)

Ellsworth, J. E. "Religion in Secondary Schools: An Apparent Conflict of Rights—Free Exercise, the Establishment Clause, and Equal Access," 26 *Gonzaga Law Review* 505 (1990-/91)

Hamre, James. "The Creationist—Evolutionist Debate

and the Public Schools," 33 *Journal of Church and State* 765 (Autumn, 1991)

Hosteller, John A. "The Amish and the Law: A Religious Minority and its Legal Encounters," 41 *Washington and Lee Law Review* 33 (Winter, 1984)

Howard, J. Woodford, Jr. "The Robe and the Cloth: The Supreme Court and Religion in the United States," 7 *Journal of Law and Politics* 481 (Spring, 1991)

Iron, Diane G. "Religious Discrimination in Employment: Title VII and the Constitution," 29 *Journal of Church and State* 253 (Spring, 1987)

Preville, Joseph R. "Catholic Colleges and the Supreme Court: The Case of *Tilton* v. *Richardson*," 30 *Journal of Church and State* 291 (Spring, 1988)

Wood, James Z. "Abridging the Free Exercise Clause," 32 *Journal of Church and State* 741 (Autumn, 1983).

Chapter 3

Freedom of Expression, Assembly, and Association

Dennis v. *United States*   *Connick* v. *Myers*
Village of Schaumburg v. *Citizens for a Better Environment et al.*   *Adderly* v. *Florida*
Ward v. *Rock against Racism*
Consolidated Edison Company of New York Inc. v. *Public Service Commission of New York*   *Frisby* v. *Schultz*
PruneYard Shopping Center v. *Robins*   *Texas* v. *Johnson*   *United States* v. *Eichman*
R.A.V. v. *St. Paul*   *Wisconsin* v. *Mitchell*   *Bethel School District* v. *Fraser*
Hazelwood School District v. *Kuhlmeier*   *Nebraska Press Association* v. *Stuart*
New York Times Company v. *Sullivan*   *Miller* v. *California*   *Barnes* v. *Glen Theatre*

Introductory Commentary

First Amendment freedoms of expression, assembly, and association go to the heart of what a democracy is all about. But what really is the theory of free speech and expression embodied in the First Amendment? What functions are served by First Amendment freedoms, and how are they put into practice? How do these relate to what a democracy is "all about"? What do we do when the right of free speech and free expression collides with other rights that we hold dear? One of the most celebrated theories of freedom of expression is that put forth by Justice Oliver Wendell Holmes:

> Persecution for the expression of opinions seems to be perfectly logical. If you have no doubt of your premises or your power and want a certain result with all your heart you naturally express your wishes in law and sweep away all opposition. To allow opposition by speech seems to indicate that you think the speech impotent, as when a man says that he has squared the circle, or that you do not care whole-heartedly for the result, or that you doubt either your power or your premises. But when men have realized that time has upset many fighting faiths, they may come to believe even more than they believe the very foundations of their own conduct that the ultimate good desired is better achieved by free trade in ideas—that the best test of truth is the power of thought to get itself accepted in the competition of the market, and that truth is the only ground upon which their wishes safely can be carried out. That at any rate is the theory of our Constitution. It is an experiment. Every year if not every day we have to wager our salvation

upon some prophecy based upon imperfect knowledge. While that experiment is part of our system I think that we should be eternally vigilant against attempts to check the expression of opinions that we loathe and believe to be fraught with death, unless they so imminently threaten immediate interference with the lawful and pressing purpose of the law that an immediate check is required to save the country.

While rhetorically flourishing and of obvious instrumental value, Holmes's theory is not without problems. Fortunately for students of civil liberties, some of these problems have been faced very directly by Laurence Tribe in his forceful and convincing analysis of free speech theory. For example, as to Holmes's "marketplace of ideas" thesis, Tribe cuts through the rhetoric with enviable precision:

> How do we know that the analogy of the market is an apt one? Especially when the wealthy have more access to the most potent media of communication than the poor, how sure can we be that "free trade in ideas" is likely to generate truth? And what of falsity: Is not the right to differ about what is "the truth" subtly endangered by a theory that perceives communication as no more than a system of transactions for vanquishing what is false? What, finally, of speech as an expression of self? As a cry of impulse no less than as a dispassionate contribution to intellectual dialogue?[1]

---

[1]*American Constitution Law* (Mineola, NY: Foundation Press, 1978), pp. 576–79.

Similarly, Tribe criticizes Alexander Meiklejohn's theory that posits that free speech is protected by the First Amendment as "essential to intelligent self-government in a democratic system." In fact, he finds Meiklejohn's view "even narrower in its reach and more preclusive in its implications" than Holmes's. As to both Holmes and Meiklejohn, Tribe concludes that both were "far too focused on intellect and rationality to accommodate the emotive role of free expression—its place in the evolution, definition, and proclamation of individual and group identity."

Tribe develops his own more expansive view of free speech with perceptive force and clarity. And in doing so he quotes with approval from *Cohen* v. *California* 403 U.S. 15 (1971), where Justice John Marshall Harlan, speaking for the Court majority, recognized "that expression 'conveys not only ideas capable of precise, detached explication, but otherwise inexpressible emotions as well.' " This indicates, observes Tribe, that Harlan's opinion "implicitly rejected the hoary dichotomy between reason and desire that so often constricts the reach of the First Amendment." Similarly, Tribe cites with approval the "broader vision" of the First Amendment as stated by Justice Louis Brandeis while concurring in *Whitney* v. *California* (1927):

> Those who won our independence believed that the final end of the State was to make men free to develop their faculties. . . They valued liberty both as an end and as a means. They believed liberty to be the secret of happiness and courage to be the secret of liberty. . . .

In short, Tribe alerts us to both the very human intrinsic functions served by free expression (self-realization of individual and group identity) as well as the more extrinsic instrumental political functions served by free expression in democratic government. Both are of vital central importance to our theory of First Amendment freedoms.

Yet what happens if speech is harmful to one's self-realization, as in the circumstance of "hate speech"? Do we allow "political" statements made by Nazis or the Ku Klux Klan, or do we protect the right of Jews and African Americans not to hear (or see?) speech that evokes emotions harmful to one's self-realization? Consider the 1992 case *R.A.V.* v. *City of St. Paul* (505 U.S.), where a Supreme Court majority found facially invalid a St. Paul city ordinance banning the display of symbols, such as a burning cross, that would arouse anger in others on the basis of race, color, creed, religion, or gender. Here, speaking for the majority, Justice Scalia put forth a view of the First Amendment that argued that the city's desire to limit "group hatred" of bias-motivated speech did not justify selectively silencing speech on the basis of its content. To what extent does Scalia's view suggest that the Court majority in *St. Paul*—in terms of free speech jurisprudence—did not think that such justification can be made and that government cannot prohibit "hate speech" directed toward such groups, even if it hurts such persons in their ability to realize or achieve their own self-worth and potential? (Compare *R.A.V.* with the 1993 unanimous Court decision in *Wisconsin* v. *Mitchell*, in which the Court made a sharp distinction between voiding a city ordinance making criminal certain *expressions* of racial hatred [*R.A.V.*], and upholding a state law aimed at imposing stiffer penalties on persons convicted of bias-motivated criminal conduct [*Mitchell*].)

In general, as we shall see, Americans hold ambivalent views about their freedoms. A number of surveys have found that large majorities of the American public believe strongly in "free speech," "free association," "free press," and related First Amendment rights as *abstract concepts*. But these large majorities dwindle when these particular concepts are applied in *concrete* situations. Take, for example, the attempt of a New York school board to remove from its school library books that the board characterized as "anti-American, anti-Christian, anti-Semitic, and just plain filthy." By a five-to-four decision in *Board of Education* v. *Pico* (457 U.S. 853, 1982), the Supreme Court struck down the board's attempt to remove such books. And in a plurality opinion, Justice William J. Brennan reiterated the strong position the Court has given in a "variety of contexts" to the principle that " 'the Constitution protects the right to receive information and ideas.' " Said Brennan: "We hold that local school boards may not remove books from school library shelves simply because they dislike the ideas contained in those books and seek by their removal to 'prescribe what shall be orthodox in politics, nationalism, religion, or other matters of opinion.' " "Such purposes," concluded Brennan, "stand inescapably condemned by our precedents."

Overall, protection of First Amendment freedoms has never been automatic. Its boundaries have changed through the years, reflecting changes in public opinion, scientific and technological advances, changes in interpersonal relationships, changes in the political realities of the country (and at times of the world), and of course, changes in Supreme Court personnel. To be sure,

First Amendment rights—speech, press, assembly, petition—are not exercised in a vacuum. They frequently run afoul of restrictive legislation, governmental regulation, and community mores. When these constitutional rights hang in the balance, sooner or later the courts—and ultimately the U.S. Supreme Court—become the arenas for resolving (or accommodating) the disputes. Judicial decisions thus become guidelines in determining which forms of expression are to be granted constitutional protection. Consequently, let us take a closer look at what the federal judiciary, especially the U.S. Supreme Court, has done in these areas.

Some Judicial Guidelines

FEATURED CASE
Dennis v. *United States*

Although the First Amendment guarantees are couched as absolutes, the Supreme Court has never interpreted them without limitations. The Court has repeatedly attempted to distinguish between speech that is protected by the Constitution and speech that is not. In doing so, the Court has developed several tests or doctrines to serve as guidelines. Although judges rather than tests or doctrines decide cases that come before them, a brief look at these tests or doctrines might help explain how the Court has gone about the difficult task of safeguarding First Amendment freedoms in the face of substantial societal interests, such as the preservation of peace and order.

Perhaps the first test to be adopted by the Court was the "clear-and-present-danger" test. "The question in every case," said Justice Holmes for a unanimous Court in *Schenck* v. *United States* (249 U.S. 47, 1919), "is whether the words used are used in such circumstances and are of such a nature as to create a clear and present danger that they will bring about the substantive evils that Congress has a right to prevent." Although destined to become a sort of "libertarian" test (see *Bridges* v. *California*, 314 U.S. 252, 1941), its early effect was to restrict rather than broaden the scope of First Amendment freedoms.[2] Since it was formulated, however, the test has traveled a rather rocky road. (Cf. *Landmark Communication, Inc.* v. *Virginia*, 435 U.S. 829, 1978.) This, of course, illustrates the fact that judges rather than doctrines decide cases.

"Legislative reasonableness" or "bad tendency" has been another guideline used by the Court in some free speech cases, most notably in *Gitlow* v. *New York* (268 U.S. 652, 1925), *supra.* Here, in effect, was the "reasonable-man (-person)" theory, so widely applied in the economic field, now being applied to First Amendment freedoms. This doctrine or test gives great deference to the *legislative* determination that certain kinds of speech have a tendency to lead to substantive evils and therefore do not enjoy constitutional protection. In upholding a New York statute prohibiting certain kinds of utterances, the Court said:

> By enacting the present statute the State has determined, through its legislative body, that utterances advocating the overthrow of organized government by force, violence and unlawful means, are so inimical to the general welfare and involve such danger of substantive evil that they may be penalized in the exercise of its police power. That determination must be given great weight. . . . We cannot hold that the present statute is an arbitrary or unreasonable exercise of the police power of the State unwarrantably infringing the freedom of speech or press; and we must and do sustain its constitutionality.

The effect of *Gitlow* was the revival of an earlier standard of judicial review, the reasonable-man (-person) test, which brought it into conflict with the emerging "clear-and-present-danger" test. The latter gives the judiciary great latitude in determining whether the circumstances warrant restrictions on First Amendment freedoms, while the former limits the judiciary to deciding whether a reasonable man (person) could have reached the legislative conclusion that the statute was necessary to prevent substantive evils. In the late 1930s, clear and present danger became the more acceptable doctrine for determining the constitutionality of restrictions on free expression.

---

[2]For the development and early application of clear and present danger, see pp. 141–142, *infra.*

Another judicial guideline used in dealing with free expression cases is the "preferred-position" doctrine. The doctrine was spurred by Justice Harlan Stone's famous footnote 4 in *U.S. v. Carolene Products Co.* (304 U.S. 144, 1938). Here Stone stated that the First Amendment freedoms are so important to the democratic process that they occupy—or should occupy—a preferred position in our constitutional hierarchy. Hence, legislation restricting First Amendment freedoms is presumed to be unconstitutional, and courts bear a heavy responsibility to scrutinize such legislation with care. While having roots in several cases in the late 1930s and early 1940s, perhaps the first clear statement of the preferred-position doctrine that commanded support of the Court majority occurred in *Thomas* v. *Collins* (323 U.S. 516, 1945), in which Justice Wiley Rutledge, speaking for the majority, stated:

> The case confronts us again with the duty our system places on this Court to say where the individual's freedom ends and the State's power begins. Choice on that border, now as always delicate, is perhaps more so where the usual presumption supporting legislation is balanced by the preferred place given in our scheme to the great, the indispensable democratic freedoms secured by the First Amendment. . . . That priority gives these liberties a sanctity and a sanction not permitting dubious intrusions. And it is the character of the right, not of the limitation, which determines what standard governs the choice. . . .

The preferred-position doctrine, thus stated, could be considered as an extension of the clear-and-present-danger doctrine to its outermost limits. In fact, of all the doctrines used by the court, it comes closest to an absolutist position with regard to First Amendment freedoms.

In general, the Court has steadfastly held to the view that the First Amendment forbids *prior restraint* on the exercise of those freedoms. Government cannot prevent a speech or publication *before* the act takes place but can take such action as might be appropriate *after* the act. For example, in *Near* v. *Minnesota* (283 U.S. 697, 1931) the Court declared unconstitutional a state statute that allowed a newspaper to be enjoined from future publication on the ground that it constituted a "public nuisance" by engaging "in the business of regularly and customarily producing . . . a malicious, scandalous and defamatory newspaper, magazine or other periodical. . . ." The paper enjoined was a Minneapolis weekly, *The Saturday Press*, which had directed charges against law enforcement officers, including the chief of police, county attorney,

and mayor. In effect, the paper charged that these officials were allowing a "Jewish gangster" to control illegal operations—gambling, bootlegging, racketeering—and were not "energetically performing their duties." Some, principally the chief of police, were charged with "gross neglect of duty, illicit relations with gangsters, and with participation in graft." But by a five-to-four decision, the Court stated that the statute authorizing an injunction was an unconstitutional prior restraint on freedom of the press as protected by the First and Fourteenth Amendments. Chief Justice Charles Evans Hughes, speaking for the Court, found that the statute was directed not against the publication of scandalous and defamatory statements about private citizens but at the continued publication of such matters against public officials. Moreover, the statute operated not only to suppress the offending publication but to put the publisher under effective censorship as well. The Court found this to be the essence of censorship, which is inconsistent with the constitutional guarantee of liberty of the press. The extent of that constitutional guarantee has been generally, if not universally, considered, said Hughes, to "prevent previous restraints upon publication." He quoted Blackstone with approval: "The liberty of the press is indeed essential to the nature of a free state; but this consists in laying no *previous* [italics Blackstone's] restraints upon publications." Hughes said that "for whatever wrong the appellant has committed or may commit, by his publications, the state appropriately affords both public and private redress by its libel laws." However, the Chief Justice said that the protection against previous restraint is not "absolutely unlimited." "But," he contended, "the limitation has been recognized only in exceptional cases."

In its decision in the widely publicized "Pentagon Papers" case (*New York Times* v. *United States*, 403 U.S. 713, 1971), the Supreme Court held firm to its earlier decisions that the First Amendment generally forbids prior restraints on the exercise of those freedoms. The Court held to this view even though the government alleged that continued publication by the *New York Times* (and others) of secret papers on the "History of United States Decision-Making on Vietnam Policy" could seriously endanger national security interests. Of course, such publication undoubtedly added fuel to an increasingly popular Vietnam War protest movement. Nonetheless, in a six-to-three per curiam decision, the Court held that the government had not met its "heavy burden of showing justification for the imposition of such a [prior] restraint on publication of the 'Pentagon Papers.' " And in

Nebraska Press Association v. *Stuart* (1976), the Court continued to look askance at attempts to impose prior restraints on First Amendment freedoms. (For further discussion of *Stuart*, see p. 249, *infra*.)

Judges also use other tests, or "rules of thumb," in arriving at decisions in First Amendment cases, especially in those dealing with free expression. Laws are unconstitutionally vague, for example, when "men of common intelligence must necessarily guess at [their] meaning and differ as to [their] application" (*Lanzetta* v. *New Jersey*, 306 U.S. 451, 1939). Indeed, this "void-for-vagueness" test, as it is called, applies with special force and with "stricter standards of permissible statutory vagueness" in laws that deal with speech "because the free dissemination of ideas may be the loser" (*Smith* v. *California*, 361 U.S. 147, 1959). The void-for-vagueness test was used by the Court in a 1976 New Jersey case (*Hynes* v. *Oradell*, 425 U.S. 510, 1976). Here an ordinance of the Borough of Oradell required persons, including representatives of "Borough Civic Groups and Organizations," who wished to engage in door-to-door solicitation for a "recognized charitable cause" to notify the police department in writing. Such notification, according to the ordinance, was for "identification" purposes only. But a majority of members of the Supreme Court found the ordinance unconstitutionally vague. The Court not only found the coverage of the ordinance unclear (for example, what was a "recognized charity"?) but it also thought that the ordinance did not sufficiently specify what actions were necessary for compliance (what must be included in the notice of what the police would consider sufficient "identification"?). Moreover, the ordinance did not provide explicit standards for those who were to apply it.

Two other tests—"overbreadth" and "least means"—are clearly related to the vagueness test. Statutes may not be so overly broad as to bring within their prohibition protected activities as well as those that are not protected. In order to avoid such overbreadth, such legislation must be drawn with "narrow specificity." (See *NAACP* v. *Button*, 571 U.S. 415, 1963. Also see *Schad* v. *Borough of Mt. Ephraim*, 452 U.S. 61, 1981.) Moreover, "even though the governmental purpose be legitimate and substantial, that purpose cannot be pursued by means that broadly stifle fundamental personal liberties when the end can be more narrowly achieved" (*Shelton* v. *Tucker*, 364 U.S. 479, 1960). Here is the least-means test, which states in essence that "the breadth of the legislative abridgement must be viewed in the light of the least drastic means for achieving the same basic purpose"

(*Shelton* v. *Tucker*). While these two tests were not specifically relied upon by the Court in voiding the New Jersey ordinance discussed above, it is clear that both tests are very much interwoven in the decision of the Court in that case.

In general, the Court will allow states to enforce narrowly drawn rules or regulations that impose reasonable "time, place, and manner" restrictions on free expression activities (e.g., speechmaking, solicitations, and demonstrations) in order to protect compelling governmental interests. The Court, for example, upheld a Minnesota state fair regulation that restricted the distribution or sale of material to certain fixed locations on state fairgrounds. The Court found the state interest sufficient to justify the restriction. (*Heffron* v. *International Society for Krishna Consciousness*, 452 U.S. 640, 1982). But the Court looks askance at licensing statutes that give governmental officials unbridled discretion to permit or forbid expressive activity. In *Lovell* v. *City of Griffin* (Georgia) (1938), the Court held that such statutes may be challenged on their face. And in *City of Lakewood* v. *Plain Dealer Pub. Co.* (1988), the Court shored up and perhaps expanded this "facial challenge" approach to speech-related activities.

Overall, it is apparent that judges weigh a variety of factors in making their decisions. However, when some judges, such as Justices Felix Frankfurter and Harlan, began to articulate the weighing of interests in particular cases, the "balancing doctrine" began to take on a more special meaning. Those who espouse the balancing doctrine reject the notion that the First Amendment should be read in absolute terms—that those freedoms should stand on a higher plane or be preferred more than other constitutional freedoms. They view a judge's responsibility regarding the protection of First Amendment freedoms as no more or no less than that in any other area. Justice Frankfurter's concurring opinion in *Dennis* v. *United States* provides a good example of the balancing doctrine in operation.

In contrast, Justices Hugo Black and William O. Douglas were highly critical of "balancing" away First Amendment freedoms. As Black said in his dissent in *Barenblatt* v. *United States* (360 U.S. 109, 1959), applying the balancing test is like reading the First Amendment to say, "Congress shall pass no law abridging freedom of speech, press, assembly, and petition unless Congress and the Supreme Court reach the joint conclusion that on balance the interests of the Government in stifling these freedoms is greater than the interest of the people in having them exercised." Instead, when it comes to expression, these justices urged an absolutist-literal view. Justice Black explained the doctrine in *Smith* v. *California, supra,* when he said:

> I read "no law abridging" to mean no law abridging. The First Amendment, which is the supreme law of the land, has thus fixed its own value on freedom of speech and press by putting those freedoms wholly "beyond the reach of federal power to abridge." No other provision of the Constitution purports to dilute the scope of these unequivocal commands of the First Amendment. Consequently, I do not believe that any federal agencies, including Congress and this Court, have power or authority to subordinate speech and press to what they think are "more important interests."

In a much broader sense judges seem to use a general balancing approach regardless of the test or doctrine used. Balancing in this context simply means, as stated earlier, that judges invariably weigh a number of factors in making their decisions. The priority judges give to these factors or interests on their particular scale of values determines whether the balance is struck in favor of or against First Amendment guarantees.

It is also important to remember, as noted at the beginning of this section, that doctrines and tests arise in part against the backdrop of changing social circumstances and political realities. Several of the tests discussed above, which articulate the nature and scope of free expression guarantees, did indeed come about during times of crises with respect to international or national security. Seen in this light, one may well be concerned with the value of a constitutional "guarantee" if it is permitted to vary based on changing times. Consider, for example, the case of *Schenck* v. *United States* (249 U.S. 47, 1919), where the validity of the Espionage Act of 1917 was at issue. Schenck was convicted for printing and circulating leaflets allegedly calculated to obstruct recruiting and to cause insubordination in the military forces during World War I. One side of the leaflet in question proclaimed that the Conscription Act violated the Thirteenth Amendment in that "a conscript is little more than a convict." It also intimated that the war was a monstrous wrong against humanity perpetrated by Wall Street interests. On the other side of the leaflet, in an article entitled "Assert Your Rights," reference was made to arguments in support of the draft as coming from "cunning politicians" and "a mercenary capitalist press." It further encouraged people to speak out in opposition to the draft, for "silent consent [helps] to support an infamous conspiracy."

In appealing the conviction, Schenck argued that the statute infringed his freedom of speech and press guarantees of the First Amendment. However, Justice Holmes, speaking for a unanimous Court, rejected this contention. It was here that Holmes put forth the now familiar clear-and-present-danger test. Said Holmes: "The question in every case is whether the words used are used in such circumstances and are of such a nature as to create a clear and present danger that they will bring about the substantive evils that Congress has a right to prevent." Applying this test, Holmes rejected the notion that freedom of speech and freedom of the press were absolutes; rather, he contended, judges must consider the circumstances in which such expressions are made. "The most stringent protection of free speech," said Holmes, "would not protect a man in falsely shouting fire in a theater and causing a panic." He concluded by noting that "[w]hen a nation is at war, many things that might be said in time of peace are such a hindrance to its effort that their utterance will not be endured so long as men fight, and no Court could regard them as protected by any constitutional right."

Consider, moreover, the case of *Dennis* v. *United States,* where the Court engaged in sharp debate over the meaning and application of the clear-and-present-danger test, and where a number of other tests were also discussed. In *Dennis,* the validity of certain provisions of the 1940 Alien Registration Act, now popularly known as the Smith Act, was at stake. The *Dennis* litigation involved the advocacy, conspiracy, and membership clauses of Section 2 of the Act. Specifically, these provisions made it illegal for any person to:

1. knowingly or willfully advocate. . .or teach the overthrow or destruction of any government in the United States by force and violence;
2. print, publish, and disseminate written matter advocating such overthrow;
3. participate in the organization of any group dedicated to such purposes; and
4. acquire and hold membership in such a group with knowledge of its purposes.

In the years immediately following World War II, relations between the United States and the Soviet Union deteriorated to the point of a "cold war" impasse. Suspicion mounted that an international Communist conspiracy was being actively supported by native Communists. These suspicions were stirred into a kind of widespread public hysteria as some Republican politicians charged that Communists were occupying positions in government and had infiltrated the military-industrial complex. Stung by Republican charges of official insensitivity to and toleration of Communists in such vital places, the Democratic Party realized that being tagged with a "soft on Communism" label could be very damaging in the forthcoming general elections. Hence, in 1948 the Justice Department moved to enforce the Smith Act against the American Communist Party, when 11 of its leaders were indicted on charges of willfully and knowingly: (1) conspiring to organize the Communist Party, a group of persons who teach and advocate the overthrow of the government by force and violence; and (2) advocating and teaching the duty and necessity of overthrowing the government by force and violence.

After a marathon trial lasting nine months, the Communist leaders were found guilty as charged. Subsequently, their convictions were affirmed by both the Court of Appeals for the Second Circuit and the Supreme Court in *Dennis* v. *United States.* Both courts found that the act, on its face and as applied, did not cut too deeply into constitutional guarantees. In fact, Chief Justice Fred Vinson, writing the leading opinion for the Supreme Court, adopted as correct and appropriate the test applied in the Court of Appeals by Judge Learned Hand. To Judge Hand, the crucial question was "whether the gravity of the evil, discounted by its improbability, justifies such invasion of free speech as is necessary to avoid the danger." The Chief Justice reasoned that since the government's very existence was at stake, the clear-and-present-danger test did not mean that the government could not act until the *putsch* was about to be executed. Knowledge of the existence of a group aiming to overthrow the government "as speedily as circumstances would permit" was

deemed sufficient to justify restrictive governmental action.

The dissenters sharply disagreed with Chief Justice Vinson and criticized, among other things, what they considered his tortured construction of the clear-and-present-danger test. Even those who concurred with the Court's decision questioned the wisdom of using "clear and present danger" in a case like *Dennis*, and suggested instead what they considered more appropriate standards by which to uphold the conviction of the Communist leaders.

As the *Dennis* case so vividly illustrates, and regardless of the free speech area involved, it becomes quite clear that no matter what test or doctrine is used, or even if one is used at all—individual judges invariably weigh or balance a number of factors and interests in reaching their decisions. Thus, when viewed in overall perspective, judicial guidelines (either doctrines or tests) are not able to answer definitively the questions with which we opened this section. What is the theory of free speech and expression embodied in the First Amendment? What functions are served by First Amendment freedoms, and how are these functions put into practice? How do these functions relate to the fundamentals of democracy? It may well be that social circumstances and prevailing political forces set the terms of First Amendment jurisprudence. Thus, rather than law shaping free expression values to promote a fuller realization of democracy, perhaps law is merely an expression of how much democracy is possible given current circumstances and social preferences. Or does how much democracy is possible depend upon an interaction of both of these factors? Reconsider *R.A.V.* v. *St. Paul* and *Wisconsin* v. *Mitchell* in this context.

DENNIS v. UNITED STATES
341 U.S. 494; 95 L. Ed. 1137; 71 S. Ct. 857 (1951)

CHIEF JUSTICE VINSON *announced the judgment of the Court and an opinion in which* JUSTICE REED, JUSTICE BURTON, *and* JUSTICE MINTON *join.*

Petitioners were indicted in July 1948, for violation of the conspiracy provisions of the Smith Act, 54 Stat. 670, 671, ch. 439, 18 U.S.C. (1946 ed.) section 11, during the period of April, 1945, to July, 1948. . . . [T]he case was set for trial on January 17, 1949 [and a] verdict of guilty as to all the petitioners was returned by the jury on October 14, 1949.

The Court of Appeals affirmed the convictions. . . . We granted certiorari . . . limited to the following two questions: (1) Whether either section 2 or section 3 of the Smith Act, inherently or as construed and applied in the instant case, violates the First Amendment and other provisions of the Bill of Rights; (2) whether either section 2 or section 3 of the Act, inherently or as construed and applied in the instant case, violates the First and Fifth Amendments because of indefiniteness.

Sections 2 and 3 of the Smith Act, 54 Stat. 670,

671, ch. 439, 18 U.S.C. (1946 ed.) sections 10, 11 (see present 18 U.S.C. Section 2385), provide as follows:

> Sec. 2.
>
> (a) It shall be unlawful for any person
>
> (1) to knowingly or willfully advocate, abet, advise, or teach the duty, necessity, desirability, or propriety of overthrowing or destroying any government in the United States by force or violence, or by the assassination of any officer of such government;
>
> (2) with the intent to cause the overthrow or destruction of any government in the United States, to print, publish, edit, issue, circulate, sell, distribute, or publicly display any written or printed matter advocating, advising, or teaching the duty, necessity, desirability, or propriety of overthrowing or destroying any government in the United States by force or violence;
>
> (3) to organize or help to organize any society, group, or assembly of persons who teach, advocate, or encourage the overthrow or destruction of any government in the United States by force or violence; or to be or become a member of, or affiliate with, any such society, group, or assembly of persons knowing the purposes thereof.
>
> (b) for the purposes of this section, the term "government in the United States" means the Government of the United States, the government of any State, Territory, or possession of the United States, the government of the District of Columbia, or the government of any political subdivision of any of them.
>
> Sec. 3. It shall be unlawful for any person to attempt to commit, or to conspire to commit, any of the acts prohibited by the provision of . . . this title.

The indictment charged the petitioners with willfully and knowingly conspiring (1) to organize as the Communist Party of the United States of America a society, group and assembly of persons who teach and advocate the overthrow and destruction of the Government of the United States by force and violence, and (2) knowingly and willfully to advocate and teach the duty and necessity of overthrowing and destroying the Government of the United States by force and violence. The indictment further alleged that section 2 of the Smith Act proscribes these acts and that any conspiracy to take such actions is a violation of section 3 of the Act.

. . . Our limited grant of the writ of certiorari has removed from our consideration any question as to the sufficiency of the evidence to support the jury's determination that petitioners are guilty of the offense charged. Whether on this record petitioners did in fact advocate the overthrow of the Government by force and violence is not before us, and we must base any discussion of this point upon the conclusions stated in the opinion of the Court of Appeals, which treated the issue in great detail. That court held that the record in this case amply supports the necessary finding of the jury that petitioners, the leaders of the Communist Party in this country, were unwilling to work within our framework of democracy, but intended to initiate a violent revolution whenever the propitious occasion appeared.

* * *

It will be helpful in clarifying the issues to treat next the contention that the trial judge improperly interpreted the statute by charging that the statute required an unlawful intent before the jury could convict. More specifically, he charged that the jury could not find the petitioners guilty under the indictment unless they found that petitioners had the intent "to overthrow the government by force and violence as speedily as circumstances permit."

. . . The structure and purpose of the statute demanded the inclusion of intent as an element of the crime. Congress was concerned with those who advocate and organize for the overthrow of the Government. Certainly those who recruit and combine for the purpose of advocating overthrow intend to bring about that overthrow. We hold that the statute requires as an essential element of the crime proof of the intent of those who are charged with its violation to overthrow the Government by force and violence.

* * *

The obvious purpose of the statute is to protect existing Government, not from change by peaceable, lawful and constitutional means, but from change by violence, revolution and terrorism. That it is within the *power* of the Congress to protect the Government of the United States from armed rebellion is a proposition which requires little discussion. Whatever theoretical merit there may be to the argument that there is a "right" to rebellion against dictatorial governments is without force where the existing structure of the government provides for peaceful and orderly change. We reject any principle of governmental helplessness in the face of preparation for revolution, which principle, carried to its logical conclusion, must lead to anarchy. No one could conceive that it is not within the power of Congress to prohibit acts intended to overthrow the Government by force and violence. The question with which we are concerned here is not whether Congress has such *power*, but whether the *means* which it has employed conflict with the First and Fifth Amendments to the Constitution.

One of the bases for the contention that the means which Congress has employed are invalid takes the form of an attack on the face of the statute on the grounds that by its terms it prohibits academic discussion of the merits of Marxism-Leninism, that it stifles ideas and is contrary to all concepts of a free speech and a free press. Although we do not agree that the language itself has that significance, we must bear in mind that it is the duty of the federal courts to interpret federal legislation in a manner not inconsistent with the demands of the Constitution. . . .

The very language of the Smith Act negates the interpretation which petitioners would have us impose on that Act. It is directed at advocacy, not discussion. Thus, the trial judge properly charged the jury that they could not convict if they found that petitioners did "no more than pursue peaceful studies and discussions or teaching and advocacy in the realm of ideas." He further charged that it was not unlawful "to conduct in an American college and university a course explaining the philosophical theories set forth in the books which have been placed in evidence." Such a charge is in strict accord with the statutory language, and illustrates the meaning to be placed on those words. Congress did not intend to eradicate the free discussion of political theories, to destroy the traditional rights of Americans to discuss and evaluate ideas without fear of governmental sanction. Rather Congress was concerned with the very kind of activity in which the evidence showed these petitioners engaged. . . .

* * *

[Here JUSTICE VINSON examines the application of clear and present danger between *Schenck* and *Gitlow*.]

* * *

The rule we deduce from these cases is that where an offense is specified by a statute in nonspeech or nonpress terms, a conviction relying upon speech or press as evidence of violation may be sustained only when the speech or publication created a "clear and present danger" of attempting or accomplishing the prohibited crime, e.g., interference with enlistment. The dissents, we repeat, in emphasizing the value of speech, were addressed to the argument of the sufficiency of the evidence. . . .

In this case we are squarely presented with the application of the "clear and present danger" test, and must decide what that phrase imports. We first note that many of the cases in which this Court has reversed convictions by use of this or similar tests have been based on the fact that the interest which the State was attempting to protect was itself too insubstantial to warrant restriction to speech. . . . Overthrow of the Government by force and violence is certainly a substantial enough interest for the Government to limit speech. Indeed, this is the ultimate value of any society, for if a society cannot protect its very structure from armed internal attack, it must follow that no subordinate value can be protected. If, then, this interest may be protected, the literal problem which is presented is what has been meant by the use of the phrase "clear and present danger" of the utterances bringing about the evil within the power of Congress to punish.

Obviously, the words cannot mean that before the Government may act, it must wait until the *putsch* is about to be executed, the plans have been laid and the signal is awaited. If Government is aware that a group aiming at its overthrow is attempting to indoctrinate its members and to commit them to a course whereby they will strike when the leaders feel the circumstances permit, action by the Government is required. The argument that there is no need for Government to concern itself, for Government is strong, it possesses ample powers to put down a rebellion, it may defeat the revolution with ease needs no answer. For that is not the question. Certainly an attempt to overthrow the Government by force even though doomed from the outset because of inadequate numbers or power of the revolutionists, is a sufficient evil for Congress to prevent. The damage which such attempts create both physically and politically to a nation makes it impossible to measure the validity in terms of the probability of success, or the immediacy of a successful attempt. In the instant case the trial judge charged the jury that they could not convict unless they found that petitioners intended to overthrow the Government "as speedily as circumstances would permit." This does not mean, and could not properly mean, that they would not strike until there was certainty of success. What was meant was that the revolutionists would strike when they thought the time was ripe. We must therefore reject the contention that success or probability of success is the criterion.

The situation with which Justices Holmes and Brandeis were concerned in *Gitlow* was a comparatively isolated event, bearing little relation in their minds to any substantial threat to the safety of the community. . . . They were not confronted with any situation comparable to the instant one—the development of an apparatus designed and dedicated to the overthrow of the Government, in the context of world crisis after crisis.

Chief Judge Learned Hand, writing for the majority below, interpreted the phrase as follows: "In each case [courts] must ask whether the gravity of the 'evil,' discounted by its improbability, justifies such invasion of free speech as is necessary to avoid the danger." 183 F.2d at 212. We adopt this statement of the rule. . . . [I]t is as succinct and inclusive as any other we might devise at this time. It takes into consideration those factors which we deem relevant, and relates their significances. More we cannot expect from words.

Likewise, we are in accord with the court below, which affirmed the trial court's finding that the requisite danger existed. The mere fact that from the period 1945 to 1948 petitioners' activities did not result in an attempt to overthrow the Government by force and violence is of course no answer to the fact that there was a group that was ready to make the attempt. The formation by petitioners of such a highly organized conspiracy, with rigidly disciplined members subject to call when the leaders, these petitioners, felt that the time had come for action, coupled with the inflammable nature of world conditions, similar uprisings in other countries, and the touch-and-go nature of our relations with countries with whom petitioners were in the very least ideologically attuned, convince us that their convictions were justified on this score. And this analysis disposes of the contention that a conspiracy to advocate as distinguished from the advocacy itself, cannot be constitutionally restrained, because it comprises only the preparation. It is the existence of the conspiracy which creates the danger. . . . If the ingredients of the reaction are present, we cannot bind the Government to wait until the catalyst is added.

Although we have concluded that the finding that there was a sufficient danger to warrant the application of the statute was justified on the merits, there remains the problem of whether the trial judge's treatment of the issue was correct. He charged the jury, in relevant part, as follows:

In further construction and interpretation of the statute I charge you that it is not the abstract doctrine of overthrowing or destroying organized government by unlawful means which is denounced by this law, but the teaching and advocacy of action for the accomplishment of that purpose, by language reason-ably and ordinarily calculated to incite persons to such action. Accordingly, you cannot find the defendants or any of them guilty of the crime charged unless you are satisfied beyond a reasonable doubt that they conspired to organize a society, group and assembly of persons who teach and advocate the overthrow or destruction of the Government of the United States by force and violence and to advocate and teach the duty and necessity of overthrowing or destroying the Government of the United States by force and violence, with the intent that such teaching and advocacy be of a rule or principle of action and by language reasonably and ordinarily calculated to incite persons to such action, all with the intent to cause the overthrow or destruction of the Government of the United States by force and violence as speedily as circumstances would permit.

* * *

If you are satisfied that the evidence establishes beyond a reasonable doubt that the defendants, or any of them, are guilty of a violation of the statute, as I have interpreted it to you, I find as a matter of law that there is sufficient danger of a substantive evil that the Congress has a right to prevent to justify the application of the statute under the First Amendment of the Constitution. . . .

It is thus clear that he reserved the question of the existence of the danger for his own determination, and the question becomes whether the issue is of such a nature that it should have been submitted to the jury.

. . . The argument that the action of the trial court is erroneous, in declaring as a matter of law that such violation shows sufficient danger to justify the punishment despite the First Amendment, rests on the theory that a jury must decide a question of the application of the First Amendment. We do not agree.

When facts are found that establish the violation of a statute, the protection against conviction afforded by the First Amendment is a matter of law. The doctrine that there must be a clear and present danger of a substantive evil that Congress has a right to prevent is a judicial rule to be applied as a matter of law by the courts. The guilt is established by proof of facts. Whether the First Amendment protects the activity which constitutes the violation of the statute must depend upon a judicial determination of the scope of the First Amendment applied to the circumstances of the case. . . .

The question in this case is whether the statute which the legislature has enacted may be constitutionally applied. In other words, the Court must examine judicially the application of the statute to the particular situation to ascertain if the Constitution prohibits the conviction. We hold that the statute may be applied where there is a "clear and present danger" of the substantive evil which the legislature had the right to prevent. Bearing, as it does, the marks of a "question of law," the issue is properly one for the judge to decide.

There remains to be discussed the question of vagueness whether the statute as we have interpreted it is too vague, not sufficiently advising those who would speak of the limitations upon their activity. It is urged that such vagueness contravenes the First and Fifth Amendments. This argument is particularly nonpersuasive when presented by petitioners, who, the jury found, intended to overthrow the Government as speedily as circumstances would permit. . . .

We agree that the standard as defined is not a neat, mathematical formulary. Like all verbalizations it is subject to criticism on the score of indefiniteness. But petitioners themselves contend that the verbalization, "clear and present danger," is the proper standard. We see no difference from the standpoint of vagueness, whether the standard of "clear and present danger" is one contained in *haec verba* within the statute, or whether it is the judicial measure of constitutional applicability. We have shown the indeterminate standard the phrase necessarily connotes. We do not think we have rendered that standard any more indefinite by our attempt to sum up the factors which are included within its scope. . . . Where there is doubt as to the intent of the defendants, the nature of their activities, or their power to bring about the evil, this Court will review the convictions with the scrupulous care demanded by our Constitution. But we are not convinced that because there may be borderline cases at some time in the future, these convictions should be reversed because of the argument that these petitioners could not know that their activities were constitutionally proscribed by the statute.

We hold that sections 2(a)(1), (2)(a)(3) and 3 of the Smith Act, do not inherently, or as construed or applied in the instant case, violate the First Amendment and other provisions of the Bill of Rights, or the First and Fifth Amendments because of indefiniteness. Petitioners intended to overthrow the Government of the United States as speedily as the circumstances would permit. Their conspiracy to organize the Communist Party and to teach and advocate the overthrow of the Government of the United States by force and violence created a "clear and present danger" of an attempt to overthrow the Government by force and violence. They were properly and constitutionally convicted for violation of the Smith Act. The judgments of conviction are

Affirmed.

[JUSTICE CLARK took no part in the consideration of this case.]

JUSTICE FRANKFURTER, *concurring in affirmance of the judgment.*

* * *

The demands of free speech in a democratic society as well as the interest in national security are better served by candid and informed weighing of the competing interests, within the confines of the judicial process, than by announcing dogmas too inflexible for the non-Euclidian problems to be solved.

But how are competing interests to be assessed? Since they are not subject to quantitative ascertainment, the issue necessarily resolves itself into asking, who is to make the adjustment, who is to balance the relevant factors and ascertain which interest is in the circumstances to prevail? Full responsibility for the choice cannot be given to the courts. Courts are not representative bodies. They are not designed to be a good reflex of a democratic society. Their judgment is best informed, and therefore most dependable, within narrow limits. Their essential quality is detachment, founded on independence. History teaches that the independence of the judiciary is jeopardized when courts become embroiled in the passions of the day and assume primary responsibility in choosing between competing political, economic, and social pressures.

Primary responsibility for adjusting the interests which compete in the situation before us of necessity belongs to the Congress. The nature of the power to be exercised by this Court has been delineated in decisions not charged with the emotional appeal of situations such as that now before us. We are to set aside the judgment of those whose duty is to legislate only if there is no reasonable basis for it. . . . [W]e must scrupulously observe the narrow limits of judicial authority even though self-restraint is alone set over us. Above all we must remember that this Court's power of judicial review is not "an exercise of the powers of a super-legislature."

* * *

It is not for us to decide how we would adjust the clash of interests which this case presents were the primary responsibility for reconciling it ours. Congress has determined that the danger created by advocacy of overthrow justifies the ensuing restriction on freedom of speech. The determination was made after due deliberation, and the seriousness of the congressional purpose is attested by the volume of legislation passed to effectuate the same ends.

Can we then say that the judgment Congress exercised was denied it by the Constitution? Can we establish a constitutional doctrine which forbids the elected representatives of the people to make this choice? Can we hold that the First Amendment deprives Congress of what it deemed necessary for the Government's protection?

To make validity of legislation depend on judicial reading of events still in the womb of time a forecast, that is, of the outcome of forces at best appreciated only with knowledge of the topmost secrets of nations—is to charge the judiciary with duties beyond its equipment. . . .

Our duty to abstain from confounding policy with constitutionality demands perceptive humility as well as self-restraint in not declaring unconstitutional what in a judge's private judgment is deemed unwise and even dangerous.

Even when moving strictly within the limits of constitutional adjudication, judges are concerned with issues that may be said to involve vital finalities. The too easy transition from disapproval from what is undesirable to condemnation as unconstitutional, has led some of the wisest judges to question the wisdom of our scheme in lodging such authority in courts. But it is relevant to remind that in sustaining the power of Congress in a case like this nothing irrevocable is done. The democratic process at all events is not impaired or restricted. Power and responsibility remain with the people and immediately with their presentation. All the Court says is that Congress was not forbidden by the Constitution to pass this enactment and that a prosecution under it may be brought against a conspiracy such as the one before us. . . .

* * *

JUSTICE JACKSON, *concurring.*

The Communist Party . . . does not seek its strength primarily in numbers. Its aim is a relatively small party whose strength is in selected, dedicated, indoctrinated, and rigidly disciplined members. From established policy it tolerates no deviation and no debate. It seeks members that are, or may be, secreted in strategic posts in transportation, communications, industry, government, and especially in labor unions where it can compel employers to accept and retain its members. It also seeks to infiltrate and control organizations of professional and other groups. Through these placements in positions of power it seeks a leverage over society that will make up in power of coercion what it lacks in power of persuasion.

The Communists have no scruples against sabotage, terrorism, assassination, or mob disorder, but violence is not with them, as with the anarchists, an end in itself. The Communist Party advocates force only when prudent and profitable. Their strategy of stealth precludes premature or uncoordinated outbursts of violence, except, of course, when the blame will be placed on shoulders other than their own. They resort to violence as to truth, not as a principle but as an expedient. Force or violence, as they would resort to it, may never be necessary, because infiltration and deception may be enough.

Force would be utilized by the Communist Party not to destroy Government but for its capture.

* * *

The foregoing is enough to indicate that, either by accident or design, the Communist stratagem outwits the antianarchist pattern of statute aimed against "overthrow by force and violence" if qualified by the doctrine that only "clear and present danger" of accomplishing that result will sustain the prosecution.

The "clear-and-present-danger" test was an innovation by Justice Holmes in the Schenck Case, reiterated and refined by him and Justice Brandeis in later cases, all arising before the era of World War II revealed the subtlety and efficacy of modernized revolutionary techniques used by totalitarian parties. In those cases, they were faced with convictions under so-called criminal syndicalism statutes aimed at anarchists but which, loosely construed, had been applied to punish socialism, pacifism, and left-wing ideologies, the charges often resting on far-fetched inferences which, if true, would establish only technical or trivial violations. They proposed "clear and present danger" as a test for the sufficiency of evidence in particular cases.

I would save it, unmodified, for application as a "rule of reason" in the kind of case for which it was devised. When the issue is criminality of a hot-headed speech on a street corner, or circulation of a few incendiary pamphlets, or parading by some zealots behind a red flag, or refusal of a handful of school children to salute our flag, it is not beyond the capacity of the judicial process to gather, comprehend, and weigh the necessary materials for decision whether it is a clear and present danger of substantive evil or a harmless letting off of steam. It is not a prophecy, for the danger in such cases has matured by the time of trial or it was never present. The test applies and has meaning where a conviction is sought to be based on a speech or writing which does not directly or explicitly advocate a crime but to which such tendency is sought to be attributed by construction or by implication from external circumstances. The formula in such cases favors freedoms that are vital to our society, and, even if sometimes applied too generously, the consequences cannot be grave. But its recent expansion has extended, in particular to Communists, unprecedented immunities. Unless we are to hold our Government captive in a judge-made verbal trap, we must approach the problem of a well-organized nation-wide conspiracy, such as I have described, as realistically as our predecessors faced the trivialities that were being prosecuted until they were checked with a rule of reason.

I think reason is lacking for applying that test to this case.

If we must decide that this Act and its application are constitutional only if we are convinced that petitioners' conduct creates a "clear and present danger" of violent overthrow, we must appraise imponderables, including international and national phenomena which baffle the best informed foreign offices and our most experienced politicians. We would have to foresee and predict the effectiveness of Communist propaganda, opportunities for infiltration, whether, and when, a time will come that they consider propitious for action, and whether and how fast our existing government will deteriorate. And we would have to speculate as to whether an approaching Communist coup would not be anticipated by a nationalistic fascist movement. No doctrine can be sound whose application requires us to make a prophecy of that sort in the guise of a legal decision. The judicial process simply is not adequate to a trial of such far-flung issues. The answers given would reflect our own political predilections and nothing more.

The authors of the clear-and-present-danger test never applied it to a case like this, nor would I. If applied as it is proposed here, it means that the Communist plotting is protected during its period of incubation; its preliminary stages of organization and preparation are immune from the law; the Government can move only after imminent action is manifest, when it would, of course, be too late.

* * *

What really is under review here is a conviction of conspiracy, after a trial for conspiracy, on an indictment charging conspiracy, brought under a statute outlawing conspiracy. With due respect to my colleagues, they seem to me to discuss anything under the sun except the law of conspiracy. One of the dissenting opinions even appears to chide me for "invoking the law of conspiracy." As that is the case before us, it may be more amazing that its reversal can be proposed without even considering the law of conspiracy.

* * *

I do not suggest that Congress could punish conspiracy to advocate something, the doing of which it may not punish. Advocacy or exposition of the doctrine of communal property ownership, or any political philosophy unassociated with advocacy of its imposition by force or seizure of government by unlawful means would not be reached through conspiracy prosecution. But it is not forbidden to punish its teaching of advocacy, and the end being punishable, there is no doubt of the power to punish conspiracy for the purpose. . . .

JUSTICE DOUGLAS, *dissenting*.

If there were a case where those who claimed protection under the First Amendment were teaching the techniques of sabotage, the assassination of the president, the filching of documents from public files, the planting of bombs, the art of street warfare, and the like, I would have no doubt. The freedom to speak is not absolute; the teaching of methods of terror and other seditious conduct should be beyond the pale along with obscenity and immorality. This case was argued as if those were the facts. The argument imported much seditious conduct into the record. That is easy and it has popular appeal, for the activities of Communists in plotting and scheming against the free world are common knowledge. But the fact is that no such evidence was introduced at the trial. There is a statute which makes a seditious conspiracy unlawful. Petitioners, however, were not charged with a "conspiracy to overthrow" the Government. They were charged with a conspiracy to form a party and groups and assemblies of people who teach and advocate the overthrow of our Government by force or violence and with a conspiracy to advocate and teach its overthrow by force and violence. It may well be that indoctrination in the techniques of terror to destroy the Government would be indictable under either statute. But the teaching which is condemned here is of a different character.

So far as the present record is concerned, what petitioners did was to organize people to teach and themselves teach the Marxist-Leninist doctrine contained chiefly in four books: *Foundations of Leninism* by Stalin (1924), *The Communist Manifesto* by Marx and Engels (1848), *State and Revolution* by Lenin (1917), *History of the Communist Party of the Soviet Union* (1939).

Those books are to Soviet Communism what *Mein Kampf* was to Nazism. If they are understood, the ugliness of Communism is revealed, its deceit and cunning are exposed, the nature of its activities becomes apparent, and the chances of its success less likely. That is not, of course, the reason why petitioners chose these books for their classrooms. They are fervent Communists to whom these volumes are gospel. They preached the creed with the hope that some day it would be acted upon.

The opinion of the Court does not outlaw these texts nor condemn them to the fire, as the Communists do literature offensive to their creed. But if the books themselves are not outlawed, if they can lawfully remain on library shelves, by what reasoning does their use in a classroom become a crime? It would not be a crime under the Act to introduce these books to a class, though that would be teaching what the creed of violent overthrow of Government is. The Act, as construed, requires the element of intent—that those who teach the creed believe in it. The crime then depends not on what is taught but on who the teacher is. That is to make freedom of speech turn not on *what is said*, but on the intent from which it is said. Once we start down that road we enter territory dangerous to the liberties of every citizen. . . .

Full and free discussion has indeed been the first article of our faith. We have founded our political system on it. It has been the safeguard of every religious, political, philosophical, economic, and racial group amongst us. We have counted on it to keep us from embracing what is cheap and false; we have trusted the common sense of our people to choose the doctrine true to our genius and to reject the rest. This has been the one single outstanding tenet that has made our institutions the symbol of freedom and equality. We have deemed it more costly to liberty to suppress a despised minority than to let them vent their spleen. We have above all else feared the political censor. We have wanted a land where our people can be exposed to all the diverse creeds and cultures of the world.

There comes a time when even speech loses its constitutional immunity. Speech innocuous one year may at another time be halted in the interests of the safety of the Republic. That is the meaning of the clear-and-present-danger test. When conditions are so critical that there will be no time to avoid the evil that the speech threatens, it is time to call a halt. Otherwise, free speech which is the strength of the Nation, will be the cause of its destruction.

Yet free speech is the rule, not the exception. The restraint to be constitutional must be based on more than fear, on more than passionate opposition against the speech, on more than a revolted dislike for its contents. There must be some immediate injury to society that is likely if speech is allowed.

* * *

The nature of Communism as a force on the world scene would, of course, be relevant to the issue of clear and present danger of petitioners' advocacy within the United States. But the primary consideration is the strength and tactical position of petitioners and their converts in this country. On that there is no evidence in the record. If we are to take judicial notice of the threat of Communists within the nation, it should not be difficult to conclude that as a *political party* they are of little consequence. Communists in this country have never made a respectable or serious showing in any election. I would doubt that there is a village, let alone a city or county or state, which the Communists could carry. Communism in the world scene is no bogey-man; but Communists as a political faction or party in this country plainly is. Communism has been so thoroughly exposed in this country that it has been crippled as a political force. Free speech has destroyed it as an effective political party. It is inconceivable that those who went up and down this country preaching the doctrine of revolution which petitioners espouse would have any success. In days of trouble and confusion when bread lines were long, when the unemployed walked the streets, when people were starving, the advocates of a short-cut by revolution might have a chance to gain adherents. But today there are no such conditions. The country is not in despair; the people know Soviet Communism; the doctrine of Soviet revolution is exposed in all of its ugliness and the American people want none of it.

How it can be said that there is a clear and present danger that this advocacy will succeed is, therefore, a mystery. Some nations less resilient than the United States, where illiteracy is high and where democratic traditions are only budding, might have to take drastic steps and jail these men for merely speaking their creed. But in America they are miserable merchants of unwanted ideas; their wares remain unsold. The fact that their ideas are abhorrent does not make them powerful.

The political impotence of the Communists in this country does not, of course, dispose of the problem. Their numbers; their positions in industry and government; the extent to which they have in fact infiltrated the police, the armed services, transportation, stevedoring, power plants, munitions works, and other critical places—these facts all bear on the likelihood that their advocacy of the Soviet theory of revolution will endanger the Republic. But the record is silent on these facts. If we are to proceed on the basis of judicial notice, it is impossible for me to say that the Communists in this country are so potent or so strategically deployed that they must be suppressed for their speech. I could not so hold unless I were willing to conclude that the activities in recent years of committees of Congress, of the Attorney General, of labor unions, of state legislatures, and of Loyalty Boards were so futile as to leave the country on the edge of grave peril. To believe that petitioners and their following are placed in such positions as to endanger the Nation is to believe the incredible. It is safe to say that the followers of the creed of Soviet Communism are known to the F.B.I.; that in case of war with Russia they will be picked up overnight as were all prospective saboteurs at the commencement of World War II; that the invisible army of petitioners is the best known, the most beset, and the least thriving of any fifth column in history. Only those held by fear and panic could think otherwise.

Rights of Public Employees: Free Speech Issues

FEATURED CASE

Connick v. *Myers*

The anti-Communism and proloyalty fervor of the 1950s illuminated quite vividly the whole question of the constitutional rights of public employees, especially as related to First Amendment freedoms. The 1967 case of *Keyishian* v. *Board of Regents* (385 U.S. 589), for example, raised the general issue of the extent to which government may condition public employment on the surrender of constitutional rights. Specifically, the Court declared invalid a New York law making membership in the Communist Party prima facie evidence for the disqualification of public school teachers. In short, it held that government cannot condition employment on the surrender of First Amendment rights. But one year later, in *Pickering* v. *Board of Education* (391 U.S. 563, 1968), the Court narrowed the sweep of *Keyishian*. In so doing, the Court constructed a balancing test whereby the Court would weigh the free speech interests against the government's ability to provide functions and services. In *Pickering*, for example, the Court did not believe that a teacher's dismissal would be justified on the basis of a letter written to a newspaper, absent proof of knowingly and recklessly making false statements, unless it was shown that such exercise of free expression (i.e., the letter) interfered with the teacher's performance of classroom duties or with operation of the school. (Cf. *Smith* v. *Arkansas Highway Employees*, 441 U.S. 463, 1979; and *Abood* v. *Detroit Board of Education*, 431 U.S. 209, 1977).

However, in the 1983 New Orleans case of *Connick* v. *Myers*, the Court brought to the fore once again the whole question of the rights of governmental employees, that is, the extent to which the constitutional rights of public employees may be restricted by virtue of public employment. In *Connick*, the Court upheld the dismissal of Sheila Myers, an assistant district attorney in New Orleans, whose complaints about her working conditions her employer felt undermined his authority and disrupted the operation of his office. In so doing, the Court refined its *Pickering* balancing test by attempting to balance between the interests of the employees as citizens in commenting upon matters of public concern and the interest of the state, as an employer, in promoting the efficiency of the public services it performs through its employees. It is this "balancing" that portends to inhibit First

Amendment rights of public employees, making it possible to construe governmental employment as a "benefit" or a "privilege." (Cf. *Rankin* v. *McPherson*, 107 S. Ct. 2891, 1987, where the Court upheld the free speech rights of a public employee.)

The Court did qualify *Connick* four years later in *Rankin* v. *McPherson* (107 S. Ct. 2891, 1987). By a six-to-three margin, the Court upheld an appellate court's reinstatement of a clerical worker who had been dismissed by her employer, a county constable, for commenting on the attempted assassination of President Reagan, "If they go for him again, I hope they get him." Writing for the Court, Justice Marshall applied the balancing test from *Pickering* and held that while McPherson's comments clearly dealt with a matter of public concern, they did not adversely affect the constable's office's performance or any other state interest that might outweigh McPherson's free speech rights. Although the state has an interest in preserving an agency's mission, the ability of the state to limit an employee's speech must take into account the role played by that employee within the agency: "Where . . . an employee serves no confidential, policymaking, or public contact role, the danger to the agency's successful functioning from that employee's private speech is minimal." Thus, McPherson's free speech rights outweighed her employer's right to dismiss her.

CONNICK v. MYERS
461 U.S. 138; 75 L. Ed. 2d 708; 103 S. Ct. 1684 (1983)

JUSTICE WHITE *delivered the opinion of the Court.*

In *Pickering* v. *Board of Education*, . . . (1968), we stated that a public employee does not relinquish First Amendment rights to comment on matters of public interest by virtue of government employment. We also recognized that the State's interests as an employer in regulating the speech of its employees "differ significantly from those it possesses in connection with regulation of the speech of the citizenry in general." . . . The problem, we thought, was arriving "at a balance between the interests of the [employee], as a citizen, in commenting upon matters of public concern and the interest of the State, as an employer, in promoting the efficiency of the public services it performs through its employees." . . . We return to this problem today and consider whether the First and Fourteenth Amendments prevent the discharge of a state employee for circulating a questionnaire concerning internal office affairs.

The respondent, Sheila Myers, was employed as an Assistant District Attorney in New Orleans for five and a half years. She served at the pleasure of petitioner Harry Connick, the District Attorney for Orleans Parish. During this period Myers competently performed her responsibilities of trying criminal cases.

In the early part of October 1980, Myers was informed that she would be transferred to prosecute cases in a different section of the criminal court. Myers was strongly opposed to the proposed transfer and expressed her view to several of her supervisors, including Connick. Despite her objections, on October 6 Myers was notified that she was being transferred. Myers again spoke with Dennis Waldron, one of the first assistant district attorneys, expressing her reluctance to accept the transfer. A number of other office matters were discussed, and Myers later testified that, in response to Waldron's suggestion that her concerns were not shared by others in the office, she informed him that she would do some research on the matter.

That night Myers prepared a questionnaire soliciting the views of her fellow staff members concerning office transfer policy, office morale, the need for a grievance committee, the level of confidence in supervisors, and whether employees felt pressured to work in political campaigns. Early the following morning, Myers typed and copied the questionnaire. She also met with Connick, who urged her to accept the transfer. She said she would "consider" it. Connick then left the office. Myers then distributed the questionnaire to fifteen assistant district attorneys. Shortly after noon, Dennis Waldron learned that Myers was distributing the survey. He immediately phoned Connick and informed him that Myers was creating a "mini-insurrection" within the office. Connick returned to the office and told Myers that she was being terminated because of her refusal to accept the transfer. She was also told that her distribution of the questionnaire was considered an act of insubordination. Connick particularly objected to the question which inquired whether employees "had confidence in and would rely on the word" of various supervisors in the office, and to a question concerning pressure to work in political campaigns, which he felt would be damaging if discovered by the press.

Myers filed suit . . . contending that her employment was wrongfully terminated because she had exercised her constitutionally protected right of free speech. The District Court agreed, ordered Myers reinstated, and awarded back pay, damages, and attorney's fees. . . . The District Court found that although Connick informed Myers that she was being fired because of her refusal to accept a transfer, the facts showed that the questionnaire was the real reason for her termination. The court then proceeded to hold that Myers's questionnaire involved matters of public concern and that the State had not "clearly demonstrated" that the survey "substantially interfered" with the operations of the District Attorney's office.

Connick appealed to the United States Court of Appeals for the Fifth Circuit, which affirmed on the basis of the District Court's opinion. . . . Connick then sought review in this Court by way of certiorari, which we granted. . . .

[1] For at least fifteen years, it has been settled that a state cannot condition public employment on a basis that infringes the employee's constitutionally protected interest in freedom of expression. . . . Our task, as we defined it in *Pickering*, is to seek "a balance between the interests of the [employee], as a citizen, in commenting upon matters of public concern and the interest of the State, as an employer, in promoting the efficiency of the public services it performs through its employees." . . .The District Court, and thus the Court of Appeals as well, misapplied our decision in *Pickering* and consequently, in our view, erred in striking the balance for respondent. . . .

The repeated emphasis in *Pickering* on the right of a public employee "as a citizen, in commenting upon matters of public concern," was not accidental. This language, reiterated in all of *Pickering*'s progeny, reflects both the historical evolvement of the rights of public employees, and the common-sense realization that government offices could not function if every employment decision became a constitutional matter.

For most of this century, the unchallenged dogma was that a public employee had no right to object to conditions placed upon the terms of employment—including those which restricted the exercise of constitutional rights. The classic formulation of this position was Justice Holmes's, who, when sitting on the Supreme Judicial Court of Massachusetts, observed: "A policeman may have a

constitutional right to talk politics, but he has no constitutional right to be a policeman." . . .

The Court cast new light on the matter in a series of cases arising from the widespread efforts in the 1950s and early 1960s to require public employees, particularly teachers, to swear oaths of loyalty to the State and reveal the groups with which they associated. . . . By the time *Sherbert* v. *Verner* (1963) was decided, it was already "too late in the day to doubt that the liberties of religion and expression may be infringed by the denial of or placing of conditions upon a benefit or privilege." . . . It was therefore no surprise when in *Keyishian* v. *Board of Regents* (1967), the Court invalidated New York statutes barring employment on the basis of membership in "subversive" organizations, observing that the theory that public employment which may be denied altogether may be subjected to any conditions, regardless of how unreasonable, had been uniformly rejected. . . .

In all of these cases, the precedents in which *Pickering* is rooted, the invalidated statutes and actions sought to suppress the rights of public employees to participate in public affairs. The issue was whether government employees could be prevented or "chilled" by the fear of discharge from joining political parties and other associations that certain public officials might find "subversive." The explanation for the Constitution's special concern with threats to the right of citizens to participate in political affairs is no mystery. The First Amendment "was fashioned to assure unfettered interchange of ideas for the bringing about of political and social changes desired by the people." . . . "[S]peech concerning public affairs is more than self-expression; it is the essence of self-government," *Garrison* v. *Louisiana*, . . . (1964). Accordingly, the court has frequently reaffirmed that speech on public issues occupies the "highest rung of the hierarchy of First Amendment values" and is entitled to special protection. *NAACP* v. *Claiborne Hardware Co.*, . . . (1980).

Pickering v. *Board of Education, supra,* followed from this understanding of the First Amendment. In *Pickering,* the Court held impermissible under the First Amendment the dismissal of a high school teacher for openly criticizing the Board of Education on its allocation of school funds between athletics and education and its methods of informing taxpayers about the need for additional revenue. Pickering's subject was "a matter of legitimate public concern" upon which "free and open debate is vital to informed decision-making by the electorate." . . .

Pickering, its antecedents and progeny, lead us

to conclude that if Myers's questionnaire cannot be fairly characterized as constituting speech on a matter of public concern, it is unnecessary for us to scrutinize the reasons for her discharge. When employee expression cannot be fairly considered as relating to any matter of political, social, or other concern to the community, government officials should enjoy wide latitude in managing their offices, without intrusive oversight by the judiciary in the name of the First Amendment. Perhaps the government employer's dismissal of the worker may not be fair, but ordinary dismissals from government service which violate no fixed tenure or applicable statute of regulation are not subject to judicial review even if the reasons for the dismissal are alleged to be mistaken or unreasonable. *Board of Regents* v. *Roth*, . . . (1976).

We do not suggest, however, that Myers's speech, even if not touching upon a matter of public concern, is totally beyond the protection of the First Amendment. "The First Amendment does not protect speech and assembly only to the extent that it can be characterized as political. 'Great secular causes, with smaller ones, are guarded.' " . . . We in no sense suggest that speech on private matters falls into one of the narrow and well-defined classes of expression which carries so little social value, such as obscenity, that the state can prohibit and punish such expression by all persons in its jurisdiction. . . . For example, an employee's false criticism of his employer on grounds not of public concern may be cause for his discharge but would be entitled to the same protection in a libel action accorded an identical statement made by a man on the street. We hold only that when a public employee speaks not as a citizen upon matters of public concern, but instead as an employee upon matters only of personal interest, absent the most unusual circumstances, a federal court is not the appropriate forum in which to review the wisdom of a personnel decision taken by a public agency allegedly in reaction to the employee's behavior. . . . Our responsibility is to ensure that citizens are not deprived of fundamental rights by virtue of working for the Government; this does not require a grant of immunity for employee grievances not afforded by the First Amendment to those who do not work for the State.

Whether an employee's speech addresses a matter of public concern must be determined by the content, form, and context of a given statement, as revealed by the whole record. In this case, with but one exception, the questions posed by Myers to her coworkers do not fall under the rubric of matters of "public concern." We view the questions pertaining to the confidence and trust that Myers's coworkers possess in various supervisors, the level of office morale, and the need for a grievance committee as mere extensions of Myers's dispute over her transfer to another section of the criminal court. Unlike the dissent, . . . we do not believe these questions are of public import in evaluating the performance of the District Attorney as an elected official. Myers did not seek to inform the public that the District Attorney's office was not discharging its governmental responsibilities in the investigation and prosecution of criminal cases. Nor did Myers seek to bring to light actual or potential wrongdoing or breach of public trust on the part of Connick and others. Indeed, the questionnaire, if released to the public, would convey no information at all other than the fact that a single employee is upset with the status quo. While discipline and morale in the workplace are related to an agency's efficient performance of its duties, the focus of Myers's questions is not to evaluate the performance of the office but rather to gather ammunition for another round of controversy with her superiors. These questions reflect one employee's dissatisfaction with a transfer and an attempt to turn that displeasure into a cause célèbre.

To presume that all matters which transpire within a government office are of public concern would mean that virtually every remark—and certainly every criticism directed at a public official—would plant the seed of a constitutional case. While as a matter of good judgment, public officials should be receptive to constructive criticism offered by their employees, the First Amendment does not require a public office to be run as a roundtable for employee complaints over internal office affairs.

One question in Myers's questionnaire, however, does touch upon a matter of public concern. Question 11 inquires if assistant district attorneys "ever feel pressured to work in political campaigns on behalf of office-supported candidates." We have recently noted that official pressure upon employees to work for political candidates not of the worker's own choice constitutes a coercion of belief in violation of fundamental constitutional rights. . . . In addition, there is a demonstrated interest in this country that government service should depend upon meritorious performance rather than political service. . . . Given this history, we believe it apparent that the issue of whether assistant district attorneys are pressured to work in political campaigns is a matter of interest to the community upon which it is essential that public employees be able to speak out freely without fear of retaliatory dismissal.

Because one of the questions in Myers's survey touched upon a matter of public concern and contributed to her discharge, we must determine whether Connick was justified in discharging Myers. Here the District Court again erred in imposing an unduly onerous burden on the State to justify Myers's discharge. The District Court viewed the issue of whether Myers's speech was upon a matter of "public concern" as a threshold inquiry, after which it became the government's burden to "clearly demonstrate" that the speech involved "substantially interfered" with official responsibilities. Yet *Pickering* unmistakably states, and respondent agrees, that the State's burden in justifying a particular discharge varies depending upon the nature of the employee's expression. Although such particularized balancing is difficult, the courts must reach the most appropriate possible balance of the competing interests.

The *Pickering* balance requires full consideration of the Government's interest in the effective and efficient fulfillment of its responsibilities to the public. . . .

Connick's judgment, and apparently also that of his first assistant, Dennis Waldron, who characterized Myers's actions as causing a "mini-insurrection," was that Myers's questionnaire was an act of insubordination which interfered with working relationships. When close working relationships are essential to fulfilling public responsibilities, a wide degree of deference to the employer's judgment is appropriate. Furthermore, we do not see the necessity for an employer to allow events to unfold to the extent that the disruption of the office and the destruction of working relationships are manifest before taking action. We caution that a stronger showing may be necessary if the employee's speech more substantially involved matters of public concern.

The District Court rejected Connick's position because "Unlike a statement of fact which might be deemed critical of one's superiors, [Myers's] questionnaire was not a statement of fact, but the presentation and solicitation of ideas and opinions," which are entitled to greater constitutional protection because "under the First Amendment there is no such thing as a false idea.". . . This approach, while perhaps relevant in weighing the value of Myers's speech, bears no logical relationship to the issue of whether the questionnaire undermined office relationships. Questions, no less than forcefully stated opinions and facts, carry messages, and it requires no unusual insight to conclude that the purpose, if not the likely result,

of the questionnaire is to seek to precipitate a vote of no confidence in Connick and his supervisors. Thus, Question 10, which asked whether or not the assistants had confidence in and relied on the word of five named supervisors, is a statement that carries the clear potential for undermining office relations.

Also relevant is the manner, time, and place in which the questionnaire was distributed. . . . ". . .When a government employee personally confronts his immediate superior, the employing agency's institutional efficiency may be threatened not only by the content of the employee's message but also by the manner, time, and place in which it is delivered." Here the questionnaire was prepared and distributed at the office; the manner of distribution required not only Myers to leave her work but for others to do the same in order that the questionnaire be completed. Although some latitude in when official work is performed is to be allowed when professional employees are involved, and Myers did not violate announced office policy, the fact that Myers, unlike Pickering, exercised her rights to speech at the office supports Connick's fears that the functioning of his office was endangered.

Finally, the context in which the dispute arose is also significant. This is not a case where an employee, out of purely academic interest, circulated a questionnaire so as to obtain useful research. Myers acknowledges that it is no coincidence that the questionnaire followed upon the heels of the transfer notice. When employee speech concerning office policy arises from an employment dispute concerning the very application of that policy to the speaker, additional weight must be given to the supervisor's view that the employee has threatened the authority of the employer to run the office. Although we accept the District Court's factual finding that Myers's reluctance to accede to the transfer order was not a sufficient cause in itself for her dismissal, . . . this does not render irrelevant the fact that the questionnaire emerged after a persistent dispute between Myers and Connick and his deputies over office transfer policy.

Myers's questionnaire touched upon matters of public concern in only a most limited sense; her survey, in our view, is most accurately characterized as an employee grievance concerning internal office policy. The limited First Amendment interest involved here does not require that Connick tolerate action which he reasonably believed would disrupt the office, undermine his authority, and destroy close working relationships. Myers's discharge therefore did not offend the First Amendment. We reiterate, however, the caveat we expressed in *Pickering* . . . : "Because of the enormous variety of fact situations in which critical statements by . . . public employees may be thought by their superiors . . . to furnish grounds for dismissal, we do not deem it either appropriate or feasible to lay down a general standard against which all such statements may be judged."

Our holding today is grounded in our long-standing recognition that the First Amendment's primary aim is the full protection of speech upon issues of public concern, as well as the practical realities involved in the administration of a government office. Although today the balance is struck for the government, this is no defeat for the First Amendment. For it would indeed be a Pyrrhic victory for the great principles of free expression if the Amendment's safeguarding of a public employee's right, as a citizen, to participate in discussions concerning public affairs were confused with the attempt to constitutionalize the employee grievance that we see presented here. The judgment of the Court of Appeals is

Reversed.

* * *

JUSTICE BRENNAN, *with whom* JUSTICE MARSHALL, JUSTICE BLACKMUN, *and* JUSTICE STEVENS *join, dissenting.*

* * *

The Court's decision today is flawed in three respects. First, the Court distorts the balancing analysis required under *Pickering* by suggesting that one factor, the context in which a statement is made, is to be weighed *twice*—first in determining whether an employee's speech addresses a matter of public concern and then in deciding whether the statement adversely affected the Government's interest as an employer. . . . Second, in concluding that the effect of respondent's personnel policies on employee morale and the work performance of the District Attorney's office is not a matter of public concern, the Court impermissibly narrows the class of subjects on which public employees may speak out without fear of retaliatory dismissal. . . . Third, the Court misapplies the *Pickering* balancing test in holding that Myers could constitutionally be dismissed for circulating a questionnaire addressed to at least one subject that *was* "a matter of interest to the community," . . . in the absence of evidence that her conduct disrupted the efficient functioning of the District Attorney's office. . . .

The standard announced by the Court suggests that the manner and context in which a statement is made must be weighed on *both* sides of the *Pickering* balance. It is beyond dispute that how and where a public employee expresses his views are relevant in the second half of the *Pickering* inquiry—determining whether the employee's speech adversely affects the Government's interests as an employer. The Court explicitly acknowledged this in *Givhan* v. *Western Line Consolidated School District*, . . . (1979), where we stated that when a public employee speaks privately to a supervisor, "the employing agency's institutional efficiency may be threatened not only by the content of the . . . message but also by the manner, time, and place in which it is delivered." . . . But the fact that a public employee has chosen to express his views in private has nothing whatsoever to do with the first half of the *Pickering* calculus—whether those views relate to the matter of public concern. This conclusion is implicit in *Givhan*'s holding that the freedom of speech guaranteed by the First Amendment is not "lost to the public employee who arranges to communicate privately with his employer rather than to spread his views before the public.". . .

The Court seeks to distinguish *Givhan* on the ground that speech protesting racial discrimination is "inherently of public concern." . . . In so doing, it suggests that there are two classes of speech of public concern: statements "of public import" because of their content, form and context, and statements that, by virtue of their subject matter, are "inherently of public concern." In my view, however, whether a particular statement by a public employee is addressed to a subject of public concern does not depend on where it was said or why. The First Amendment affords special protection to speech that may inform public debate about how our society is to be governed—regardless of whether it actually becomes the subject of a public controversy. . . .

Unconstrained discussion concerning the manner in which the Government performs its duties is an essential element of the public discourse necessary to informed self-government. . . .

The constitutionally protected right to speak out on governmental affairs would be meaningless if it did not extend to statements expressing criticism of governmental officials. In *New York Times Co.* v. *Sullivan* . . . we held that the Constitution prohibits an award of damages in a libel action brought by a public official for criticism of his official conduct absent a showing that the false statements at issue were made with "actual malice." . . .

We stated there that the First Amendment expresses "a profound national commitment to the principle that debate on public issues should be uninhibited, robust, and wide-open, and that it may well include vehement, caustic, and sometimes unpleasantly sharp attacks on government and public officials." . . .

In *Pickering* we held that the First Amendment affords similar protection to critical statements by a public school teacher directed at the Board of Education for whom he worked. . . . In so doing, we recognized that "free and open debate" about the operation of public schools "is vital to informed decision-making by the electorate." . . .

Applying these principles, I would hold that Myers's questionnaire addressed matters of public concern because it discussed subjects that could reasonably be expected to be of interest to persons seeking to develop informed opinions about the manner in which the Orleans Parish District Attorney, an elected official charged with managing a vital governmental agency, discharges his responsibilities. The questionnaire sought primarily to obtain information about the impact of the recent transfers on morale in the District Attorney's

office. It is beyond doubt that personnel decisions that adversely affect discipline and morale may ultimately impair an agency's efficient performance of its duties. . . . Because I believe the First Amendment protects the right of public employees to discuss such matters so that the public may be better informed about how their elected officials fulfill their responsibilities, I would affirm the District Court's conclusion that the questionnaire related to matters of public importance and concern. . . .

* * *

The Court's decision today inevitably will deter public employees from making critical statements about the manner in which government agencies are operated for fear that doing so will provoke their dismissal. As a result, the public will be deprived of valuable information with which to evaluate the performance of elected officials. Because protecting the dissemination of such information is an essential function of the First Amendment,

I dissent.

Speech-making, Solicitations, and Demonstrations

FEATURED CASES

Village of Schaumburg v. Citizens for a Better Environment et al.   Adderly v. Florida
Ward v. Rock against Racism
Consolidated Edison Company of New York, Inc. v. Public Service Commission of New York   Frisby v. Schultz

---

The street-corner speaker, the demonstrator, the distributor of handbills, the labor organizer who solicits members, and the person who uses the sound amplifier—all are exercising what they consider their First Amendment freedoms. But sometimes these activities run counter to some state law or local ordinance designed to preserve peace and order or some other societal value. The crucial question then becomes how and under what conditions may a state control speech-making, solicitations, or demonstrations in public places such as streets and parks.

STRUCTURING THE TERMS AND CONDITIONS

Permit systems have been one way that state and local governments have attempted to cope with this

problem. For example, the Court, in *Lovell* v. *Griffin*, invalidated a city ordinance that gave too much discretion to officials to decide whether to permit or forbid distribution of leaflets. And the next year, in *Hague* v. *CIO* (307 U.S. 496, 1939), the Court declared unconstitutional a Jersey City ordinance that prohibited public parades or public assemblies "in or upon the public streets, highways, public parks, or public buildings" without first securing a permit from the director of public safety. Here Jersey City, under Mayor Hague, was preventing members of the Congress of Industrial Organizations (CIO) from distributing materials and holding a meeting to discuss the National Labor Relations Act. The ordinance enabled the director of safety "to refuse a permit on his mere opinion that such refusal will prevent riots, disturbances, or disorderly assemblage." By investing such uncontrolled authority in the director of public safety, said Justice Owen Roberts, the ordinance can "be made the instrument of arbitrary suppression of free expression of views on national affairs, for the prohibition of all speaking will undoubtedly prevent such eventualities."

It was in *Hague* that Justice Roberts made what has now become a classic comment on the use of public streets and parks for speech making, soliciting, and assembly:

> Wherever the title of streets and parks may rest, they have immemorially been held in trust for the use of the public and, time out of mind, have been used for purposes of assembly, communicating thoughts between citizens, and discussing public questions. Such use of the streets and public places has, from ancient times, been a part of the privileges, immunities, rights, and liberties of citizens. The privilege of a citizen of the United States to use the streets and parks for communication of views on national questions may be regulated in the interest of all; it is not absolute, but relative, and must be exercised in subordination to the general comfort and convenience, and in consonance with peace and good order; but it must not, in the guise of regulation, be abridged or denied.

Although there was no majority opinion in *Hague* (some of the majority justices acted on the due process clause, others on privileges and immunities), it was generally assumed in later decisions that the public had a basic constitutional right to use the streets and parks and other public places in the exercise of First Amendment freedoms subject to reasonable state regulations, such as protecting public safety. In *Cox* v. *New Hampshire* (312 U.S. 529, 1941), the Court unanimously upheld convictions of Jehovah's Witnesses who marched along downtown streets of Manchester without first securing a special permit (license) as required by state statutes for "parades or processions" on public streets. Here the Court found that the statute, as construed by the state supreme court, provided for reasonable and nondiscriminatory regulations with respect to the use of streets. Chief Justice Charles Evans Hughes, who delivered the opinion of the Court, said that "[c]ivil liberties, as guaranteed by the Constitution, imply the existence of an organized society maintaining public order without which liberty itself would be lost in the excesses of unrestrained abuses."

During the 1950s the Court continued its close scrutiny of permit and licensing systems. And in such cases as *Niemotko* v. *Maryland* (340 U.S. 268, 1959), *Staub* v. *Baxley* (355 U.S. 313, 1958), *Kunz* v. *New York* (340 U.S. 395, 1953), and *Cantwell* v.

Connecticut, infra, it condemned licensing and permit systems that vested unfettered discretion in administrative officials as working a prior restraint on the First Amendment freedoms involved. And more recently in its 1988 decision in *City of Lakewood* v. *Plain Dealer Pub. Co.* (486 U.S. 750), the Court continued to look askance at speech-related control systems that vest unbridled discretion in administrative officials, i.e., the city mayor.

By contrast, the Court, in *Poulos* v. *New Hampshire* (345 U.S. 395, 1953), upheld a city ordinance providing a permit system for "open air public meetings" on the ground that "by its construction of the ordinance the state left in the licensing officials no discretion as to granting permits, no power to discriminate, no control over speech." But in *Hynes* v. *Oradell* (425 U.S. 510, 1976), the Court continued to look askance at regulatory systems that could substantially impede the exercise of First Amendment freedoms if they are "unacceptably vague." An ordinance in the Village of Schaumburg, Illinois, met a similar fate. Here the Court found unconstitutionally overbroad and in violation of the First and Fourteenth Amendments a village ordinance that prohibited door-to-door or on-street solicitation of contributions by charitable organizations not using at least 75 percent of their receipts for "charitable purposes." The Court said that the ordinance could not be justified on the basis that such limitation was "intimately related to substantial governmental interest in the preventing of fraud and protecting public safety and residential privacy." (*Schaumburg* v. *Citizens for a Better Environment*). In 1984 in *Maryland* v. *Munson* (104 S. Ct. 2839, 1984) the Court followed *Schaumburg* and struck down a Maryland law which required similar restrictions on charitable contributions.

Demonstrations may also be limited by court injunctions. Indeed, when Nobel Peace Prize winner Martin Luther King, Jr., and his followers deliberately violated a state court injunction forbidding them to participate in or encourage "mass street parades or mass processions" without a permit, as required by a Birmingham city ordinance, the Supreme Court affirmed their convictions for criminal contempt (*Walker* v. *Birmingham*, 388 U.S. 307, 1967). Although Justice Stewart, who spoke for the five-to-four Court majority, admitted that both the injunction and the city ordinance raised "substantial" constitutional questions, he nevertheless maintained that the petitioners should have followed the orderly procedures of the law rather than ignoring them altogether and carrying "their battle to the streets." "One may sympathize with the petitioners' impatient commitment to their cause," said Stewart, "but respect for judicial process is a small price to pay for the civilizing hand of law, which alone can give abiding meaning to constitutional freedom." However, Justice Brennan, in a dissent joined by Chief Justice Warren and Justices Douglas and Fortas, bitterly assailed the majority for letting "loose a devastatingly destructive weapon [the injunction] for infringement of freedom. . . ." "Convictions for contempt of court orders which invalidly abridge First Amendment freedoms," said Brennan, "must be condemned equally with convictions for violation of statutes which do the same thing."

An interesting contrast to *Walker* is afforded by *Carroll* v. *President and Commissioners of Princess Anne* (393 U.S. 175, 1968). There a white supremacist organization called the National States Rights Party was enjoined from resuming a rally that had been held the night before and that was characterized by Justice Abe Fortas as militantly racist and aimed primarily at blacks and Jews. It was against the resumption of the rally the second night that law enforcement officials in Princess Anne and Somerset counties, Maryland, sought and obtained a restraining order in ex parte proceedings from the county circuit court. The order, originally issued for 10 days and later extended for 10 months, sought to restrain petitioners from holding rallies "which . . . tend to disturb and endanger the citizens of the County." No notice was given to the petitioners, and apparently, as Justice Fortas observed, no effort was made to otherwise communicate with them as was "expressly contemplated under Maryland law." In any case, the petitioners obeyed the injunction and took their battle to the courts.

The Maryland Court of Appeals subsequently upheld the 10-day injunction but reversed the 10-month order on the ground that "the period of time was unreasonable and that it was arbitrary to assume that a clear and present danger of civil disturbance and riot would persist for ten months." However, on certiorari, Justice Fortas, speaking for the U.S. Supreme Court, brushed aside the 10-day order "because of a basic infirmity in the procedure by which it was obtained."

The Court remains apprehensive of injunctions that restrain the exercise of First Amendment freedoms in public places. For example, in *Organization for a Better Austin* v. *Keefe* (402 U.S. 415, 1971), the Court set aside an Illinois state court injunction that barred a community organization from distributing leaflets. The leaflets alleged that respondent (a real estate broker) was engaged in "blockbusting" and "panic peddling"

activities in the Austin area of Chicago. Chief Justice Burger, who spoke for a unanimous Court, observed that the Illinois court "was apparently of the view that petitioners' purpose in distributing their literature was not to inform the public but to force respondent to sign a non-solicitation agreement." "But even if this coercive impact was intended," Burger continued, "it does not remove the petitioner's expressions [leaflets] from the reach of the First Amendment."

In *National Socialist Party of America* v. *Skokie* (432 U.S. 43, 1977), a narrow five-to-four majority reversed and remanded an Illinois Supreme Court decision that had denied a stay of trial court injunction prohibiting Nazi party members from parading or marching in uniform in Skokie, a predominantly Jewish suburb of Chicago. The order also prohibited Nazi party members from "distributing pamphlets or displaying any materials which incite or promote hatred against persons of Jewish faith or ancestry or hatred against persons of any faith or ancestry, race or religion." The Court majority, in effect, held that by its refusal either to stay the lower court order or to grant an expedited appeal, the Illinois Supreme Court had rendered a final determination as to the merits of petitioners' claim that the injunction denied them their First Amendment rights. "If a State seeks to impose a restraint of this kind," said the Court, "it must provide strict procedural safeguards, . . . including immediate appellate review."

PRESERVING THE PEACE AND THE RELEVANT FORUM

Government also seeks to preserve public peace and order through laws relating to unlawful assembly, breach of the peace, disorderly conduct, and incitement to riot. But the enforcement of these laws may, and sometimes does, collide with the exercise of constitutional guarantees. Governmental restrictions on unpopular speakers, street-corner preachers, picketers, protesters, and demonstrators have produced an almost endless stream of Supreme Court cases.

Two of the early cases in this area involved Jehovah's Witnesses. In *Cantwell* v. *Connecticut*, a Jehovah's Witness approached two men in the street, asked and received permission to play, and played a phonograph record entitled "Enemies," which contained a vitriolic attack on organized religion and the Catholic Church. Coincidentally, both men were Catholics and were incensed by the contents of the record. They testified that they were tempted to strike Cantwell, but on being told to be on his way, he left. There was no evidence that Cantwell was personally offensive or entered into any argument with the persons he stopped. Cantwell was charged with and convicted of inciting a breach of the peace. The Supreme Court reversed the conviction, as Justice Roberts, who wrote the majority opinion, declared "that a State may not unduly suppress free communication of views, religious or other, under the guise of conserving desirable conditions." "Here we have a situation," said Justice Roberts, "analogous to a conviction under a statute sweeping in a great variety of conduct under a general and indefinite characterization, and leaving to the executive and judicial branches too wide a discretion in its application. . . ."

In *Chaplinsky* v. *New Hampshire* (315 U.S. 568, 1942), another Jehovah's Witness was convicted under a state law for calling a city marshal a "God damned racketeer" and a "damned Fascist." The state law made it a crime for any person to address "any offensive, derisive or annoying word" to another person or call him or her by "any offensive or derisive name. . . ." In an opinion by Justice Murphy, the Supreme Court affirmed the conviction stating that "it is well understood that the right of free speech is not absolute at all times and under all circumstances." Said Justice Murphy:

> There are certain well-defined and narrowly limited classes of speech, the prevention and punishment of which have never been thought to raise any Constitutional problem. These include the lewd and obscene, the profane, the libelous, and the insulting or "fighting" words those which by their very utterance inflict injury or tend to incite an immediate breach of the peace. It has been well observed that such utterances are no essential part of any exposition of ideas and are of such slight social value as a step to truth that any benefit that may be derived from them is clearly outweighed by the social interest in order and morality. . . .

Another case that could have extended or clarified the "fighting words" doctrine of *Chaplinsky* was *Terminiello* v. *Chicago* (337 U.S. 1, 1947). However, the Court decided the case on another basis. Terminiello, a defrocked Catholic priest, was well known for his vicious attacks on Jews, blacks, Communists, and others. The instant case arose when he spoke in a Chicago auditorium to a crowd of about eight hundred. An even larger crowd gathered outside, picketing the auditorium, throwing ice picks, stones, and bottles, and attempting to storm the doors. In his speech Terminiello con-

demned the conduct of the crowd outside and bitterly criticized various political, racial, and religious groups whose activities he denounced as "inimical to the welfare of the nation." Terminiello was arrested and convicted under a breach of the peace ordinance. The Supreme Court, however, reversed the conviction on an issue that neither party brought to the Court—the trial judge's charge to the jury. The trial judge charged the jury that "breach of the peace" includes "misbehavior" (or speech) that "stirs the public to anger, invites dispute, brings about a condition of unrest, or creates a disturbance, or if it molests the inhabitants in the enjoyment of peace and quiet by arousing alarm." Justice Douglas, who spoke for the majority, read this construction of the breach of the peace ordinance as "part of the ordinance" itself and binding upon the Court. Consequently, Douglas and the majority of his colleagues ignored completely the facts or circumstances of the situation and rested their decision on the fact that the ordinance, as construed by the trial judge in his charge to the jury, was too broad and might encompass speech that is constitutionally protected. Said Justice Douglas:

> . . .[A] function of free speech under our system of government is to invite dispute. It may indeed best serve its high purpose when it induces a condition of unrest, creates dissatisfaction with conditions as they are, or even stirs people to anger. Speech is often provocative and challenging. It may strike at prejudices and preconceptions and have profound *unsettling* effects as it presses for acceptance of an idea. . . . The ordinance as construed by the trial court seriously invaded this province. It permitted conviction of petitioner if his speech stirred people to anger, invited public dispute, or brought about a condition of unrest. A conviction resting on any of those grounds may not stand.

Justice Jackson, in a dissent joined by Justices Frankfurter and Burton, sharply criticized the majority for ignoring the facts of the highly explosive situation that existed in *Terminiello* and for not giving sufficient weight to the importance of order in the enjoyment of liberty. Said Jackson: "The choice is not between order and liberty. It is between liberty with order and anarchy without either. There is danger that, if the Court does not temper its doctrinaire logic with a little practical wisdom, it will convert the constitutional Bill of Rights into a suicide pact."

Although in *Terminiello* the Court avoided the problem of free speech when a threat to public peace and order is imminent, the problem was before the Court again a short time later in *Feiner* v. *New York* (310 U.S. 315, 1951). Given the nature of his speech and the circumstances in which it was given, Feiner was arrested and convicted under a breach of the peace statute. Eventually, his conviction was upheld by the Supreme Court, where Chief Justice Fred Vinson said that Feiner had gone beyond the "bounds of argument and persuasion" and had undertaken "incitement to riot." Justices Black, Douglas, and Minton dissented. Black issued a particularly sharp dissent, saying that he was convinced that Feiner was convicted for his unpopular views, nothing more.

The *Feiner* case was only a prelude to a number of cases the Court faced in the 1960s, when civil rights demonstrators and protesters took to the streets and other public places to press their causes. In *Edwards* v. *South Carolina* (372 U.S. 229, 1963), the Supreme Court reversed breach of peace convictions of 187 black student demonstrators who had marched in small groups to the South Carolina State House grounds to protest segregation practices. A crowd of some two hundred onlookers gathered, but there was no disturbance or obstruction of any kind. Accordingly, the Court found insufficient evidence to support breach of peace convictions. "The Fourteenth Amendment," said Justice Stewart, speaking for the majority, "does not permit a state to make criminal the peaceful expression of unpopular views." While Stewart attempted to distinguish *Edwards* from *Feiner*, Justice Tom Clark, in dissent, did not see any distinction. Said Clark: "We upheld a breach of the peace in a situation [in *Feiner*] no more dangerous than found here." Nevertheless, the Court continued to support its *Edwards* position in several subsequent cases. (Cf. *Fields* v. *South Carolina*, 375 U.S. 44, 1963; *Henry* v. *Rock Hill*, 376 U.S. 776, 1964; and *Gregory* v. *City of Chicago*, 394 U.S. 111, 1969.)

Far more difficult questions reached the Court in 1965 in two cases (*Cox* v. *Louisiana*, No. 24; and *Cox* v. *Louisiana*, No. 49, 379 U.S. 536, 1965) arising out of the same set of facts. In 1961 over two thousand students from Southern University, a predominantly black institution, converged on downtown Baton Rouge and conducted a protest rally near the Old State Capitol Building in the vicinity of the courthouse. They were protesting segregation practices generally as well as the arrest the day before of 23 of their fellow students who had been picketing downtown stores that maintained segregated lunch counters. The leader of the group, an ordained Congregational minister, the Reverend Mr. B. Elton Cox, was arrested and

convicted on three charges: (1) disturbing the peace under Louisiana's breach of the peace statute; (2) obstructing public passages; and (3) picketing before a courthouse. The Supreme Court reversed convictions on all three charges. The first *two* charges were heard in *Cox* No. 24, the third in *Cox* No. 49.

The Court voted unanimously to reverse the breach of the peace conviction, saying that it infringed on Cox's rights of free speech and free assembly. The Court relied on grounds similar to those in *Edwards*, and as in *Edwards*, found the situation a "far cry from *Feiner*." The Court held that not only was there insufficient evidence to support the breach of the peace charge but also that the statute as interpreted by the Louisiana Supreme Court was unconstitutionally broad in scope.

The Court next considered Cox's conviction on the "obstructing public passages" charge and voted seven-to-two for reversal. Speaking for five members of the Court, Justice Goldberg said that "although the statute . . . on its face precludes all street assemblies and parades, it has not been so applied and enforced by the Baton Rouge authorities." Goldberg said that "city officials who testified for the state clearly indicated that certain meetings and parades are permitted in Baton Rouge, even though they have the effect of obstructing traffic, provided prior approval is obtained." Goldberg also found that "[t]he statute itself provides no standards for the determination of local officials as to which assemblies to permit or which to prohibit. . . ." Consequently, he concluded that the practice of allowing such "unfettered discretion" in local officials in regulating the use of the streets for peaceful parades and meetings "[was] an unwarranted abridgement of the appellant's freedom of speech and assembly. . . ."

In *Cox* No. 49, the Court, by a five-to-four majority, also reversed the appellant's conviction on the third charge of picketing before a courthouse. The relevant state law prohibited picketing or parading "in or near" a building housing a state court "with the intent of interfering with, obstructing, or impeding the administration of justice or with the intent of influencing any judge, juror, witness, or court officer in the discharge of his duty. . . ." Justice Goldberg again spoke for the majority. He found that the state statute was precise and well drawn, and that its purpose of protecting the state's judicial system was wholly within the legitimate interest of the state. In general, Goldberg's opinion supported the proposition that the state had a right to forbid what the demonstrators had done. "There can be no question," said Goldberg, "that a state has a legitimate interest in protecting its judicial system from pressures which picketing near a courthouse might create." Despite the principled rhetoric, however, Goldberg and a majority of his colleagues reversed Cox's conviction on the ground that:

> [T]he highest police officials of the city, in the presence of the Sheriff and Mayor, in effect told the demonstrators that they could meet where they did, 101 feet from the courthouse steps, but could not meet closer to the courthouse. In effect, appellant was advised that a demonstration at the place it was held would not be one "near" the courthouse within the terms of the statute.

Justice Black, along with Justices Clark, White, and Harlan, dissented. In his dissent, Black said that he could not "understand how the Court can justify the reversal of these convictions [in No. 49] because of a permission which testimony in the record denies was given, which could not have been authoritatively given anyway, and which even if given was soon afterward revoked."

What of mass demonstrations and protests that take place on public properties other than streets? The Court considered this question in two cases decided in 1966. In *Brown* v. *Louisiana* (383 U.S. 131, 1966), the demonstrations did not take place on the streets but in a public library. When the five black demonstrators refused to leave, they were arrested and convicted for violating Louisiana's "breach of the peace" statute, the same statute involved in *Cox*. By a five-to-four decision, the Supreme Court reversed the convictions on the ground that there was, in fact, no violation of the statute. As Justice Abe Fortas said for the majority, there was no disorder, no intent to provoke a breach of the peace, and no circumstances indicating a breach might be occasioned by petitioners' actions. They were merely exercising their constitutional right to protest unconstitutional segregation. However, Justice Black, joined by Justices Clark, Harlan, and Stewart, issued a strong dissent. Black said that he did not believe that the First Amendment guarantees to any person "the right to use someone else's property, even that owned by government and dedicated to other purposes, as a stage to express dissident ideas," especially in a library, where tranquillity is of the highest priority.

Black did not have to wait long for his views to gain majority support. In *Adderly* v. *Florida* (385 U.S. 39, 1966), the Court upheld the convictions of student demonstrators under a state trespass statute. The demonstrators, students at Florida

A & M University, had marched to the jailhouse to protest segregation, including segregation in the jail. But Justice Black, now speaking for the majority, emphasized the significant difference between this case and *Edwards*. In *Edwards*, the demonstrators went to the state capitol grounds, whereas in this case they went to the jail. Traditionally, state capitol grounds are open to the public, said Black, but jails, built for security purposes, are not. The Constitution does not prevent Florida, Black continued, from "even-handed enforcement of its general trespass statute . . . to preserve the property under its control for the use to which it is lawfully dedicated." People who wish to propagandize protests or views do not have a constitutional right to do so "whenever and however and wherever they please."

Essentially, this was the reasoning followed by the Court in upholding a federal statute prohibiting groups and individuals from depositing unstamped letters or notices in mailboxes used by the United States Postal Service for mail delivery. (*U.S. Postal Service* v. *Greenburgh Civic Assns.*, 453 U.S. 114, 1981).

A number of cases reaching the Court in the 1970s and 1980s continued to focus on the scope of constitutional protections afforded speech-making and demonstrations. In the main, these cases were the outgrowth of state and local governmental actions designed to maintain peace and order. While some of these actions survived constitutional challenges, others ran afoul of constitutional limitation. In *Coates* v. *Cincinnati* (402 U.S. 611, 1971), for example, a city ordinance made it a criminal offense for "three or more persons to assemble . . . on any of the sidewalks . . . and there conduct themselves in a manner annoying to persons passing by." However, Justice Stewart, who spoke for the Court, found the ordinance unconstitutional on its face without reaching the merits of the case. Stewart said that "the vice of the ordinance lies not alone in its violation of the due process standard of vagueness," but that it "also violates the constitutional rights of free assembly and association."

Similarly, in *Police Department of the City of Chicago* v. *Mosley* (408 U.S. 92, 1972), the Court held unconstitutional a Chicago ordinance that banned all picketing within 150 feet of a school building while school was in session, except "the peaceful picketing of any school involved in a labor dispute." Justice Thurgood Marshall, who spoke for the Court, said that the ordinance made an "impermissible distinction between labor picketing and other peaceful picketing." For him, the fatal defect of the ordinance was its description of impermissible picketing in terms of subject matter.

In 1983 the Court declared unconstitutional a federal law prohibiting the "display of any flags, banner, or device designed or adapted to bring into public notice any party organization, or movement" in the Supreme Court building or its grounds, including public sidewalks that constitute the outer boundaries of such grounds. Specifically, in *United States* v. *Grace* (461 U.S. 171) the Court held that the federal law as applied to public sidewalks surrounding the Court building was unconstitutional, since " 'public places,' such as streets, sidewalks, and parks, historically associated with the free exercise of expressive activities, are considered . . . to be 'public forums.' " And in such places, said the Court, the government may enforce "time, place and manner" restrictions but cannot ban such activities altogether except through narrowly drawn statutes and regulations designed to achieve compelling governmental interests.

In *Perry Education Assn.* v. *Perry Local Educators Assn.* (460 U.S. 337, 1983), the Court upheld a labor contract, against First and Fourteenth Amendment challenges, wherein a public school district agreed to give exclusive use of the school's internal mail system to the teachers' union that won the right through a representational election (over a rival union) to be the official bargaining agent for the district teachers. In response to the losing union's claims that its constitutional rights were being violated, the Court majority (per Justice White) held that the school mail system was not a "public forum," and hence the school district was under "no constitutional obligation *per se* to let any organization use the school's mail boxes." Justice White divided speech forums into three categories: traditional public forums (e.g., streets, public parks); limited public forums (designated free speech areas); and nonpublic forums. The first two forums embrace greatest free speech protections, although the Court indicated that the State "may enforce regulations of the time, place, and manner of expression which are content neutral, are narrowly tailored to serve a significant governmental interest, and leave open ample alternative channels of communication."

The Court made use of *Perry* in its 1985 decision in *Cornelius* v. *NAACP Legal Defense and Educational Fund*. Here Justice O'Connor, speaking for the Court, held under *Perry* that a federal government–sponsored charitable contributions program was a "nonpublic forum," and as such the government could exclude legal defense organizations such as the NAACP from using the program.

Justice O'Connor examined the government's justifications for excluding legal defense organizations and concluded that the exclusion did indeed meet *Perry's* "touchstone" requirement that limits on speech in "nonpublic" forums be "reasonable in light of the purpose which the forum at issue serves." (Cf. *Lamb's Chapel v. Steigerwald*, where the U.S. Supreme Court held violative of free speech guarantees of the First and Fourteenth Amendments a New York local district school board regulation that allowed after-hours use of school property by groups for certain specified purposes, but prohibiting use by any group for religious purposes.)

Similarly, the Court, in 1988 decision (*Frisby* v. *Schultz*, 108 S. Ct. 2495), also used *Perry* to uphold a Brookfield, Wisconsin, ordinance banning picketing in residential neighborhoods. Justice O'Connor, who once again spoke for the Court, interpreted the "public forum" doctrine of *Perry* so as to completely prohibit picketing that focused on and took place in front of a particular house, in that such activity is by its very nature destructive of residential privacy. Indeed, Justice O'Connor noted that *Perry* allows a state to enforce content-neutral time, place, and manner regulations of expression in public forums, if such regulations "are narrowly tailored to serve a significant government interest and leave open ample alternative channels for communication."

Recently, the Supreme Court made a variety of distinctions in developing the public forum doctrine. In a series of three separately paginated opinions arising out of the case of *International Society for Krishna Consciousness, Inc.* [*ISKCON*] v. *Lee* (*ISKCON* I, 112 S. Ct. 2701, 1992; *ISKCON* II, 112 S. Ct. 2709, 1992; *ISKCON* III, 112 S. Ct. 2711, 1992), the Court set forth typologies, tests, and standards that offer no coherent method by which to analyze speech regulation in government–run airport terminals.

With respect to solicitation, the Supreme Court held that a Port Authority of New York and New Jersey ban on soliciting money within airport terminals was reasonable and therefore valid. Chief Justice Rehnquist divided governmental property into the categories of traditional public forums, designated public forums, and nonpublic forums. It was only traditional forums, as defined by the property's history, that required legislation to be drawn narrowly to serve a compelling state interest. Under this scheme, Chief Justice Rehnquist considered an airport to be a nonpublic forum requiring only that regulation be reasonable.

With respect to the ban on the distribution of

literature that arose out of the same regulation, the Court affirmed that although an airport was a nonpublic forum, such conduct was protected by the First Amendment. However, the splintering of concepts, tests, and standards was apparent. Justice O'Connor applied a different standard of reasonableness in evaluating a nonpublic forum for the conduct of distribution. Justice Kennedy, meanwhile, proposed an alternative "unified" test balancing the nature of the property with the objective manifestation of its permitted uses.

The scattered reasoning evident in the Court's analysis of the public forum doctrine with respect to government property indicates that there exists as much confusion in this area as in the circumstances in which the Court must balance the rights of private property owners against the protections of the First Amendment. (See *PruneYard, infra*; see also *Lechmere, infra*.)

Whether because of "permissiveness" or "telling it like it is," the Court has been faced with several so-called offensive-word cases. (See *Chaplinsky v. New Hampshire, supra*.) The charge in such cases is that certain words in and of themselves may be so "offensive" to the community or to individuals that the words alone disturb the peace or provoke others to do so. These are so-called fighting words, which might stir those to whom they are addressed to breach the peace or to react predictably and angrily. However, in *Cohen v. California* (1971), the Court reversed a conviction based on a general state disturbing-the-peace statute that prohibits "maliciously and willfully disturbing the peace or quiet of any neighborhood or person by offensive conduct." Cohen had worn a jacket that plainly bore the words "Fuck the Draft" in a Los Angeles courthouse corridor where women and children were present. Cohen testified that he wore the jacket to demonstrate to the public the intensity of his feelings against the Vietnam War and the military draft. Cohen did not engage in any act of violence, nor did anyone who saw him in the courthouse corridor. There was no evidence that he had "uttered any sound prior to his arrest." Accordingly, said Justice John Marshall Harlan, who spoke for the Court, "the conviction quite clearly rests upon the asserted offensiveness of the *words* Cohen used to convey his message to the public. The only 'conduct' which the state sought to punish is the fact of communication." For the conviction to stand, Harlan said, the state needed to show that the statute sought to preserve "an appropriately decorous atmosphere in the courthouse where Cohen was arrested" or that it falls within the gambit of prior decisions establishing the "power of government to deal more comprehensively with certain forms of individual expression simply upon a showing that such a form was employed." But to Harlan, neither of these showings was made. The decorous courthouse atmosphere failed, he noted, because the statute did not put Cohen "on notice that certain kinds of otherwise permissible speech or conduct would nevertheless, under California law, not be tolerated in certain places." Nor did he feel that the "fighting words" doctrine applied. Cf. *Gooding* v. *Wilson* (405 U.S. 518, 1972) and *Rosenfeld* v. *New Jersey* (408 U.S. 901, 1972).

In a 1974 Vietnam War–related case, *Parker* v. *Levy* (417 U.S. 733), the Court upheld the validity of Articles 133 and 134 of the Uniform Code of Military Justice against claims of vagueness. The two articles punish, respectively, "conduct unbecoming an officer and a gentleman" and "all disorders and neglect to the prejudice of good order and discipline in the armed forces." After publicly declaring his opposition to the war and openly encouraging black enlisted men to refuse orders to serve in Vietnam, Captain Howard B. Levy was convicted by court-martial for violation of the Uniform Code of Military Justice. On a petition for federal habeas corpus, the U.S. Court of Appeals for the Third Circuit unanimously reversed Levy's conviction, finding Articles 133 and 134 unconstitutionally vague. Reinstating the conviction, the Supreme Court, through Justice Rehnquist, emphasized the special nature of the military context, which requires greater restrictions on expression than are permitted in the civilian sector. Hence, whatever vagueness existed in the wording of the two articles was insufficient to warrant overturning Levy's conviction.

The Court reiterated the "military-civilian difference" argument in *Greer* v. *Spock* (424 U.S. 828, 1976) and rejected the view that there is "a generalized constitutional right to make political speeches or distribute leaflets" at a military base, in this instance at Fort Dix, New Jersey. Indeed, by a six-to-two majority, the Court upheld the right of a military base commander to prohibit all political speeches and demonstrations on the base. "[T]he business of a military installation like Fort Dix," said Justice Stewart in his opinion for majority, "is to train soldiers, not to provide a public forum."

What about political or religious speech-making in public places with the use of sound amplifiers? This is an attempt by the speech-maker to reach a wider audience, but what about unwilling listeners, those who do not wish to be disturbed? In *Saia* v. *New York* (334 U.S. 558, 1948), the Court was faced with a city ordinance that forbade use of sound amplification devices except "public dissemination through radio loudspeakers of items of news and matters of public concern . . . provided that the same be done under permission obtained from the Chief of Police." Here the appellant, a Jehovah's Witness, was refused a new permit since complaints had been received concerning his speeches and sermons delivered under an earlier permit. Nevertheless, the lack of a permit did not keep the appellant from delivering speeches over a loudspeaker in a small public park used primarily for recreational purposes. He was subsequently tried and convicted for violating the ordinance. By a five-to-four majority, the Supreme Court held the ordinance unconstitutional on its face as a prior restraint on freedom of speech.

In a subsequent case (*Kovacs* v. *Cooper*, 336 U.S. 77, 1949), however, the Court retreated and upheld a Trenton, New Jersey, loudspeaker ordinance that prohibited use of sound trucks and similar amplifying devices that emit "loud and raucous noises." Justice Reed announced the judgment of the five-to-four majority and, in an opinion joined by Chief Justice Vinson and Justice Burton, accepted the state supreme court's construction of the ordinance to apply only to vehicles with sound amplifiers emitting "loud and raucous noises." An interesting sequel to these cases occurred in 1989, when in, *Ward* v. *Rock against Racism* (109 S. Ct. 2746), the Court, by a six-to-three decision, found constitutional a New York City regulation restricting sound equipment in Central Park to that provided by the City and operated by an independent technician. The Court upheld the regulation as a reasonable regulation of the "time, place, and manner" of protected speech.

BLURRED DISTINCTIONS AND CONFLICTING INTERESTS

Saia and *Kovacs* portend the potential conflict between explicit constitutional rights such as free speech and the merging constitutional right to privacy, or "the right to be let alone." These cases and the right to privacy generally are discussed in a later chapter. However, one way in which the Court attempted to deal with certain aspects of the problem of privacy in free speech cases was to focus on the *nature* of the speech involved. In *Martin* v. *Struthers* (319 U.S. 141, 1943), for example, the Court struck down an ordinance as a denial of speech and press that made it unlawful for Jehovah's Witnesses to engage in door-to-door canvass-

ing to advertise a religious meeting. But in *Breard* v. *Alexandria* (341 U.S. 622, 1951), the Court, despite free speech claims, upheld a city ordinance against door-to-door canvassing as applied against persons soliciting magazine subscriptions. The difference in the two cases seemed to indicate that the Court was disposed to give more protection to "noncommercial" as opposed to "commercial" speech.

However, this noncommercial/commercial distinction seems to have now been substantially eroded. Commercial speech, or "purely commercial advertising," since the 1942 case, *Valentine* v. *Chrestensen* (316 U.S. 52, 1942), was generally considered to warrant either *no* First Amendment protection or *less* protection than other speech in the face of government regulation. The 1951 *Breard* v. *Alexandria* case is illustrative of this view. But in the 1975 case of *Bigelow* v. *Virginia* (421 U.S. 809), this view was substantially limited. In *Bigelow*, a seven-to-two Court majority held that speech cannot be denied constitutional protection solely because of its commercial form or because it relates to commercial activity. The question arose when Jeffrey Bigelow, managing editor of a Virginia newspaper, published an advertisement for a New York abortion referral service, stating: "Abortions are now legal in New York. . . . There is no residency requirement. . . ." Bigelow was charged and ultimately convicted under a Virginia statute that prohibited all advertising or other dissemination of information having the effect of encouraging an abortion. On review, the Supreme Court of Virginia ruled that because the speech was commercial in nature it was not protected by rights covering noncommercial speech. Moreover, the state court noted that Virginia had a particularly strong interest in regulating speech that might affect the health of its citizens.

Proposing the criteria of the "public interest" content of the advertisement and the legality of the underlying commercial activity to determine the weightiness of the commercial speech, Justice Blackmun concluded for the majority that Bigelow possessed a strong claim for protection. Moreover, the defendant's status as a member of the press "augmented" the strength of the speech interest. On the other hand, the Court recognized the state's particular interest in the health care of its citizenry but concluded that Virginia could not "bar a citizen of another State from disseminating information about an activity that is legal in that State."

In the following term the Court decided *Virginia State Board of Pharmacy* v. *Virginia Citizens Consumer Council, Inc.* (425 U.S. 748, 1976). Here the Court ruled that pharmacists cannot be constitutionally restricted from advertising prices of prescription drugs except to restrict the "time, place, and manner" of the advertisements, or to prohibit "false or misleading" or "deceptive" advertisements. The Court held that "commercial speech, like other varieties, is protected" by the First Amendment. (Cf. *Linmark Associates* v. *Township of Willingboro*, 431 U.S. 85, 1977, where the Court continued the thrust of its *Bigelow* and *Virginia Pharmacy* decisions by holding that an ordinance forbidding "For Sale" signs outside one's home constitutionally impaired "the free flow of truthful and legitimate commercial information" about real estate properties. Also see *Carey* v. *Population Int'l*, 431 U.S. 678, 1977. Additionally, see *Metromedia, Inc.* v. *San Diego*, 453 U.S. 490, 1981, where the Court declared invalid an ordinance that imposed substantial prohibitions on the erection of outdoor advertising billboards within the city. While *Metromedia* dealt with the problem of signs on private property, such restrictions fared no better, since the Court also upheld similar restrictions when applied to public property in *Los Angeles* v. *Taxpayers for Vincent*, 466 U.S. 789, 1984.)

An interesting aspect of *Virginia Pharmacy* is that specific mention was made that the case did not apply to the legal profession or the medical profession. Subsequently, however, in *Bates and O'Steen* v. *Arizona State Bar* (433 U.S. 350, 1977), the Court, citing *Virginia Pharmacy*, held that the First Amendment protects lawyers in advertising fees for routine legal services. (Cf. *Ohralik* v. *Ohio State Bar Assn.*, 436 U.S. 447, 1978; and *Zauderer* v. *Ofc. of Disciplinary Counsel*, 105 S. Ct. 2265, 1985.) In *Friedman* v. *Rogers* (440 U.S. 1, 1979) the Court upheld the Texas Optometry Act, which prohibited the practice of optometry under a trade name. The Court concluded that the state's interest in protecting the public from "deceptive and misleading use of optometrical trade names is substantial and well demonstrated in this case, and the prohibition against the use of trade names is a constitutionally permissible regulation in furtherance of this interest." (Cf. *Edenfield* v. *Fane*, where the U.S. Supreme Court held that a Florida Board of Accountancy rule that prohibited CPAs from engaging in "direct, in-person, uninvited solicitation" to obtain new clients was inconsistent with the free speech guarantees of the First and Fourteenth amendments.)

A decision of the Supreme Court in 1980 (*Central Hudson Gas and Electric Corporation* v. *Public Service Commission*, 447 U.S. 557) held invalid a regulation of the Public Service Commission (PSC) that, in order to conserve power, prohibited promotional advertising by Central except for encouraging shifts of consumption from peak demand times. Justice Powell, who spoke for the Court in *Central Hudson*, stated that although the Constitution accords lesser protection to commercial speech than to other constitutionally guaranteed forms of expression, the First Amendment nevertheless does protect commercial speech from unwarranted governmental regulation. For commercial speech to come within the First Amendment, it at least must concern lawful activity and not be misleading, and it must be determined whether the asserted governmental interest to be served by the restriction on commercial speech is substantial. If there are positive answers on these criteria, it must be decided whether the regulation directly advances the governmental interest asserted, and whether it is not more extensive than is necessary to serve the particular interest involved. The Court, in *Bolger* v. *Youngs Drugs Products Corp.* (456 U.S. 970, 1983), reinforced this line of reasoning when it declared unconstitutional a federal statute that prohibited the unsolicited mailing of contraceptive advertisements. Essentially, *Central Hudson* represents the Court's attempt to accord a level of First Amendment protection to commercial speech that would be consistent with both (1) the "free marketplace of ideas" concept; and (2) the legitimate interests of the state in protecting consumers from harmful, misleading, and deceptive commercial speech. In a 1986 ruling (*Posadas de Puerto Rico Associates* v. *Tourism Company of Puerto Rico*), the Court upheld a Puerto Rican law that forbids advertisements that invite Puerto Rican citizens to gamble legally in casinos. Although *Posadas* purported to follow *Central Hudson*, it seems clear that the Court accorded more weight to the "consumer protection" interest than to the "free marketplace of ideas" interest.

In *Consolidated Edison Company of New York, Inc.* v. *Public Service Commission of New York* (447 U.S. 530, 1980), the Court found invalid a New York Public Service Commission order that prohibited public utility companies from including in monthly bills inserts discussing "controversial issues" of public policy. Justice Powell, who spoke for the Court majority, found the PSC prohibition order a direct infringement on freedom of speech protected by the First and Fourteenth Amendments. Powell warned of the First Amendment's hostility to such content-based regulations, which in effect allow government the choice of selecting permissible subjects for public debate. Nor did he find that the prohibition order met any of the requirements in which government regulation of speech is constitutionally permissible.

Essentially, *Consolidated Edison* protects corporate free speech rights, as was done earlier by the Court in *First National Bank of Boston* v. *Bellotti* by negating restrictions on corporate spending in election referenda.

In *Pacific Gas and Electric Co.* v. *Public Utilities Commission of California* (106 S. Ct. 903, 1986), the Court also protected corporate free speech rights, but in this instance the Court held that corporate interests (e.g., Pacific Gas) have a right *not* to associate with speech with which they disagree. For some time *Pacific Gas*, not unlike Consolidated Edison of New York, had included a newsletter in its monthly billing envelopes. A public interest consumer group asked the Public Utilities Commission to forbid Pacific Gas from using its billing envelopes to distribute the newsletter, which contained political editorials. The Public Utilities Commission responded by ordering Pacific Gas to allow the consumer group access to "extra space" so as to include in the billing envelopes a greater variety of views. It was this order that the Court overturned.

In a plurality opinion for four members of the Court, Justice Powell indicated that, like individuals, the First Amendment protects not only the right to speak but also the right *not* to associate with speech with which they disagree. To be sure, the Court followed this concept of "negative free speech" in striking down New Hampshire's law requiring car owners to include the state's motto ("Live Free or Die") on their license plates (*Wooley* v. *Maynard*); and similarly, the Court found unconstitutional a Florida "right to reply" statute that required newspapers to accord candidates a right to respond to editorials that attacked the character and records of candidates.

Justice Marshall, in a concurring opinion in *Pacific Gas*, compared the instant case to *Prune-Yard*, (*infra*) and agreed that Pacific Gas's free speech rights had been unconstitutionally restricted, since, unlike *PruneYard*, giving access would allow the consumer public interest group to intrude on property that was never opened to the public. Marshall, however, did not agree with the plurality opinion that corporate free speech rights are the same as those for individuals.

Overall, *Pacific Gas* represents somewhat of a retreat by the Court from its 1969 holding in *Red Lion Broadcasting Co.* v. *Federal Communications Commission (FCC)*, where the Court upheld the FCC's fairness doctrine granting access rights to those holding views different from those put forth by the broadcast media.

VILLAGE OF SCHAUMBURG v. CITIZENS FOR A BETTER ENVIRONMENT ET AL.
444 U.S. 620; 63 L. Ed. 2d 73; 100 S. Ct. 826 (1980)

JUSTICE WHITE *delivered the opinion of the Court.*

The issue in this case is the validity under the First and Fourteenth Amendments of a municipal ordinance prohibiting the solicitation of contributions by charitable organizations that do not use at least 75 percent of their receipts for "charitable purposes," those purposes being defined to exclude solicitation expenses, salaries, overhead and other administrative expenses. The Court of Appeals held the ordinance unconstitutional. We affirm that judgment.

The Village of Schaumburg (Village) is a suburban community located 25 miles northwest of Chicago, Ill. On March 12, 1974, the Village adopted "An Ordinance Regulating Soliciting by Charitable Organizations," codified as Art. III of chapter 22 of the Schaumburg Village Code (Code), which regulates the activities of "peddlers and solicitors,"...(1974). Article III provides that

"[e]very charitable organization, which solicits or intends to solicit contributions from persons in the village by door-to-door solicitation or the use of public streets and public ways, shall prior to such solicitation apply for a permit. ... Solicitation of contributions for charitable organizations without a permit is prohibited and is punishable by a fine of up to $500 for each offense...."

Section 22-20(g), which is the focus of the constitutional challenge involved in this case, requires that permit applications, among other things, contain "[s]atisfactory proof that at least seventy-five percent of the proceeds of such solicitations will be used directly for the charitable purpose of the organization." In determining whether an organization satisfies the 75-percent requirement, the ordinance provides that:

the following items shall not be deemed to be used

for the charitable purposes of the organization, to wit:

(1) Salaries or commissions paid to solicitors;

(2) Administrative expenses of the organization, including, but not limited to, salaries, attorneys' fees, rents, telephone, advertising expenses, contributions to other organizations and persons, except as charitable contribution and related expenses incurred as administrative or overhead items. Schaumburg Village Code 22-20(g).

Respondent Citizens for a Better Environment (CBE) is an Illinois not-for-profit corporation organized for the purpose of promoting "the protection of the environment." CBE is registered with the Illinois Attorney General's Charitable Trust Division pursuant to Illinois law, and has been afforded tax-exempt status by the United States Internal Revenue Service, and gifts to it are deductible for federal income tax purposes. CBE requested permission to solicit contributions in the Village of Schaumburg, but the Village denied CBE a permit because CBE could not demonstrate that 75 percent of its receipts would be used for "charitable purposes" as required by . . . the Village code. CBE then sued the Village in the United States District Court for the Northern District of Illinois, charging that the 75-percent requirement . . . violated the First and Fourteenth Amendments. Declaratory and injunctive relief were sought.

In its amended complaint, CBE alleged that "[i]t was organized for the purpose, among others, of protecting, maintaining, and enhancing the quality of the Illinois environment." The complaint also alleged:

[t]hat incident to its purpose, CBE employs "canvassers" who are engaged in door-to-door activity in the Chicago metropolitan area, endeavoring to distribute literature on environmental topics and answer questions of an environmental nature when posed; solicit contributions to financially support the organization and its program; receive grievances and complaints of an environmental nature regarding which CBE may afford assistance in the evaluation and redress of these grievances and complaints.

The Village's answer to the complaint averred that the foregoing allegations, even if true, would not be material to the issues of the case, acknowledged that CBE employed "canvassers" to solicit funds, but alleged that "CBE is primarily raising funds for the benefit and salary of its employees and that its charitable purposes are negligible as compared with the primary objective of raising

funds." The Village also alleged "that more than 60% of the funds collected [by CBE] have been spent for benefits of employees and not for any charitable purposes."

CBE moved for summary judgment and filed affidavits describing its purposes and the activities of its "canvassers" as outlined in the complaint. The affidavit also alleged that "the door-to-door canvass is the single most important source of funds" for CBE. A second affidavit offered by CBE stated that in 1975 the organization spent 23.3% of its income on fundraising and 21.5% of its income on administration, and that in 1976 these figures were 23.3% and 16.5%, respectively. The Village opposed the motion but filed no counter affidavits taking issue with the factual representations in CBE's affidavits.

The District Court awarded summary judgment to CBE. The court recognized that although "the government may regulate solicitation in order to protect the community from fraud, . . . [a]ny action impinging upon the freedom of expression and discussion. . .must be minimal, and intimately related to an articulated, substantial government interest." The court concluded that the 75-percent requirement of . . . the Village Code on its face was "a form of censorship" prohibited by the First and Fourteenth Amendments. Section 22-20(g) was declared void on its face, its enforcement was enjoined, and the Village was ordered to issue a charitable solicitation permit to CBE.

The Court of Appeals for the Seventh Circuit affirmed. The court rejected the Village's argument that summary judgment was inappropriate because material issues of fact were disputed. Because CBE challenged the facial validity of the Village ordinance on First Amendment grounds, the court held that "any issue of fact as to the nature of CBE's particular activities is not material . . . and is therefore not an obstacle to the granting of summary judgment." . . . Like the District Court, the Court of Appeals recognized that the Village had a legitimate interest in regulating solicitation to protect its residents from fraud and the disruption of privacy, but that such regulation "must be done 'with narrow specificity' " when First Amendment interests are affected.

We granted certiorari, . . . to review the Court of Appeals' determination that the Village ordinance violates the First and Fourteenth Amendments.

It is urged that the ordinance should be sustained because it deals only with solicitation and because any charity is free to propagate its views from door to door in the Village without a permit as long as it refrains from soliciting money. But this represents a far too limited view of our prior cases relevant to canvassing and soliciting by religious and charitable organizations.

In *Schneider* v. *State (Town of Irvington)* . . . (1939), a canvasser for a religious society, who passed out booklets from door to door and asked for contributions, was arrested and convicted under an ordinance which prohibited canvassing, soliciting or distribution of circulars from house to house without a permit, the issuance of which rested much in the discretion of public officials. The state courts construed the ordinance as aimed mainly at house-to-house canvassing and solicitation. This distinguished the case from *Lovell* v. *Griffin* . . . (1938), which had invalidated on its face and on First Amendment grounds an ordinance criminalizing the distribution of any handbill at any time or place without a permit. Because the canvasser's conduct "amounted to the solicitation and acceptance of money contributions without a permit" and because the ordinance was thought to be valid as a protection against fraudulent solicitations, the conviction was sustained. This Court disagreed, noting that the ordinance not only applied to religious canvassers but also to "one who wishes to present his views on political, social, or economic questions," . . . and holding that the city could not, in the name of preventing fraudulent appeals, subject door-to-door advocacy and the communication of views to the discretionary permit requirement. The Court pointed out that the ordinance was not limited to those "who canvass for profit," . . . and reserved the question whether "commercial soliciting and canvassing" could be validly subjected to such controls. . . .

Cantwell v. *Connecticut* . . . (1940) involved a state statute forbidding the solicitation of contributions of anything of value by religious, charitable or philanthropic causes without obtaining official approval. Three members of a religious group were convicted under the statute for selling books, distributing pamphlets and soliciting contributions or donations. Their convictions were affirmed in the state courts on the ground that they were soliciting funds and that the statute was valid as an attempt to protect the public from fraud. This Court set aside the convictions, holding that although "[a] general regulation, in the public interest, of solicitation, which does not involve any religious test and does not unreasonably obstruct or delay the collection of funds, is not open to any constitutional objection," . . . to "condition the solicitation of aid for the perpetuation of religious views or systems upon a license, the grant of which rests in the exercise of a determination by state authority as to

what is a religious cause," . . . was considered to be an invalid prior restraint on the free exercise of religion. Although *Cantwell* turned on the free exercise clause, the Court has subsequently understood *Cantwell* to have implied that soliciting funds involves interests protected by the First Amendment's guarantee of freedom of speech. *Virginia Pharmacy Board* v. *Virginia Consumer Council* . . . (1976); *Bates* v. *State Bar of Arizona* . . . (1977).

In *Valentine* v. *Chrestensen* . . . (1942), an arrest was made for distributing on the public streets a commercial advertisement in violation of an ordinance forbidding this distribution. Addressing the question left open in *Schneider*, the Court recognized that while municipalities may not unduly restrict the right of communicating information in the public streets, the "Constitution imposes no such restraint on government as respects purely commercial advertising." . . . The Court reasoned that unlike speech "communicating information and disseminating opinion" commercial advertising implicated only the solicitor's interest in pursuing "a gainful occupation.". . .

The following Term in *Jamison* v. *Texas* . . . (1942), the Court, without dissent, and with the agreement of the author of the *Chrestensen* opinion, held that although purely commercial leaflets could be banned from the streets, a State could not "prohibit the distribution of handbills in the pursuit of a clearly religious activity merely because the handbills invite the purchase of books for the improved understanding of the religion or because the handbills seek in a lawful fashion to promote the raising of funds for religious purposes." . . . The Court reaffirmed what it deemed to be an identical holding in *Schneider*, as well as the ruling in *Cantwell* that "a State might not prevent the collection of funds for a religious purpose by unreasonably obstructing or delaying their collection." . . .

In the course of striking down a tax on the sale of religious literature, the majority opinion in *Murdock* v. *Pennsylvania* . . . (1943) reiterated the holding in *Jamison* that the distribution of handbills was not transformed into an unprotected commercial activity by the solicitation of funds. Recognizing that drawing the line between purely commercial ventures and protected distributions of written material was a difficult task, the Court went on to hold that the sale of religious literature by itinerant evangelists in the course of spreading their doctrine was not a commercial enterprise beyond the protection of the First Amendment.

On the same day, the Court invalidated a municipal ordinance that forbade the door-to-door distribution of handbills, circulars or other advertisements. None of the justifications for the general prohibition was deemed sufficient; the right of the individual resident to warn off such solicitors was deemed sufficient protection for the privacy of the citizen. *Martin* v. *Struthers* . . . (1943). On its facts, the case did not involve the solicitation of funds or the sale of literature.

Thomas v. *Collins* . . . (1945) held that the First Amendment barred enforcement of a state statute requiring a permit before soliciting membership in any labor organization. Solicitation and speech were deemed to be so intertwined that a prior permit could not be required. The Court also recognized that "espousal of the cause of labor is entitled to no higher constitutional protection than the espousal of any other lawful cause." . . . The Court rejected the notion that First Amendment claims could be dismissed merely by urging "that an organization for which the rights of free speech and free assembly are claimed is one 'engaged in business activities' or that the individual who leads it in exercising these rights receives compensation for doing so." . . . Concededly, the "collection of funds" might be subject to reasonable regulation, but the Court ruled that such regulation "must be done, and the restriction applied, in such a manner as not to intrude upon the rights of free speech and free assembly." . . .

In 1951, *Breard* v. *Alexandria* . . . was decided. That case involved an ordinance making it criminal to enter premises without an invitation to sell goods, wares and merchandise. The ordinance was sustained as applied to door-to-door solicitation of magazine subscriptions. The Court held that the sale of literature introduced "a commercial feature," . . . and that the householder's interest in privacy outweighed any rights of the publisher to distribute magazines by uninvited entry on private property. The Court's opinion, however, did not indicate that the solicitation of gifts or contributions by religious or charitable organizations should be deemed commercial activities, nor did the facts of *Breard* involve the sale of religious literature or similar materials. *Martin* v. *Struthers* . . . was distinguished but not overruled.

Hynes v. *Mayor of Oradell* . . . (1976) dealt with a city ordinance requiring an identification permit for canvassing or soliciting from house to house for charitable or political purposes. Based on its review of prior cases, the Court held that soliciting and canvassing from door to door were subject to reasonable regulation so as to protect the citizen against crime and undue annoyance, but that the First Amendment required such controls to be drawn with "narrow specificity." . . . The ordinance was invalidated as unacceptably vague.

Prior authorities, therefore, clearly establish that charitable appeals for funds, on the street or door to door, involve a variety of speech interests—communication of information, the dissemination and propagation of views and ideas, and the advocacy of causes—that are within the protection of the First Amendment. Soliciting financial support is undoubtedly subject to reasonable regulation, but the latter must be undertaken with due regard for the reality that solicitation is characteristically intertwined with informative and perhaps persuasive speech seeking support for particular causes or for particular views on economic, political or social issues, and for the reality that without solicitation the flow of such information and advocacy would likely cease. Canvassers in such contexts are necessarily more than solicitors for money. Furthermore, because charitable solicitation does more than inform private economic decisions and is not primarily concerned with providing information about the characteristics and costs of goods and services, it has not been dealt with in our cases as a variety of purely commercial speech.

The issue before us, then, is not whether charitable solicitations in residential neighborhoods are within the protections of the First Amendment. It is clear that they are. [O]ur cases long have protected speech even though it is in the form of . . . a solicitation to pay or contribute money.

The issue is whether the Village has exercised its power to regulate solicitation in such a manner as not unduly to intrude upon the rights of free speech.

Although indicating that the 75-percent limitation might be enforceable against "the more traditional charitable organizations" or "where solicitors represent themselves as mere conduits for contributions," . . . the Court of Appeals identified a class of charitable organizations as to which the 75-percent rule could not constitutionally be applied. These were the organizations whose primary purpose is not to provide money or services for the poor, the needy, or other worthy objects of charity, but to gather and disseminate information about and advocate positions on matters of public concern. These organizations characteristically use paid solicitors who "necessarily combine" the solicitation of financial support with the "functions of information dissemination, discussion, and advocacy of public issues." . . . These organizations also pay other employees to obtain and process the necessary information and to arrive at and announce in suitable form the organizations' preferred positions on the issues of interest to them. Organizations of this kind, although they might pay only reasonable salaries, would necessarily spend more than 25 percent of their budgets on salaries and administrative expenses and would be completely barred from solicitation in the Village. The Court of Appeals concluded that such a prohibition was an unjustified infringement of the First and Fourteenth Amendments.

We agree with the Court of Appeals that the 75-percent limitation is a direct and substantial limitation on protected activity that cannot be sustained unless it serves a sufficiently strong, subordinating interest that the Village is entitled to protect. We also agree that the Village's proferred justifications are inadequate and that the ordinance cannot survive scrutiny under the First Amendment.

The Village urges that the 75-percent requirement is intimately related to substantial governmental interests "in protecting the public from fraud, crime and undue annoyance." These interests are indeed substantial, but they are only peripherally promoted by the 75-percent requirement and could be sufficiently served by measures less destructive of First Amendment interests.

Prevention of fraud is the Village's principal justification for prohibiting solicitation by charities that spend more than one-quarter of their receipts on salaries and administrative expenses. The submission is that any organization using more than 25 percent of its receipts on fundraising, salaries and overhead is not a charitable, but a commercial, for profit enterprise and that to permit it to represent itself as a charity is fraudulent. But, as the Court of Appeals recognized, this cannot be true of those organizations that are primarily engaged in research, advocacy or public education and that use their own paid staff to carry out these functions as well as to solicit financial support. The Village, consistent with the First Amendment, may not label such groups "fraudulent" and bar them from canvassing on the streets and house to house. Nor may the Village lump such organizations with those that in fact are using the charitable label as a cloak for profitmaking and refuse to employ more precise measures to separate one kind from the other. The Village may serve its legitimate interests, but it must do so by narrowly drawn regulations designed to serve those interests without unnecessarily interfering with First Amendment freedoms. . . .

The Village's legitimate interest in preventing fraud can be better served by measures less intrusive than a direct prohibition on solicitation. Fraudulent misrepresentations can be prohibited and the penal laws used to punish such conduct directly. Efforts to promote disclosure of the finances of charitable organizations also may assist in preventing fraud by informing the public of the ways in which their contributions will be employed. Such measures may help make contribution decisions more informed, while leaving to individual choice the decision whether to contribute to organizations that spend large amounts on salaries and administrative expenses.

We also fail to perceive any substantial relationship between the 75-percent requirement and the protection of public safety or of residential privacy. There is no indication that organizations devoting more than one-quarter of their funds to salaries and administrative expenses are any more likely to employ solicitors who would be a threat to public safety than are other charitable organizations. Other provisions in the ordinance that are not challenged here, such as the provision making it unlawful for charitable organizations to use convicted felons as solicitors, . . . may bear some relation to public safety; the 75-percent requirement does not.

The 75-percent requirement in the Village ordinance plainly is insufficiently related to the governmental interests asserted in its support to justify its interference with protected speech.

We find no reason to disagree with the Court of Appeals' conclusion that 22-20(g) is unconstitutionally overbroad. Its judgment is therefore affirmed.

It is so ordered.

JUSTICE REHNQUIST, *dissenting.*

The Court holds that Art. III of the Schaumburg Village Code is unconstitutional as applied to prohibit respondent Citizens for a Better Environment (CBE) from soliciting contributions door to door. If read in isolation, today's decision might be defensible. When combined with this Court's earlier pronouncements on the subject, however, today's decision relegates any local government interest in regulating door-to-door activities to the role of Sisyphus.

The Court's opinion first recites the litany of language from 40 years of decisions in which this Court has considered various restrictions on the right to distribute information or solicit door to door, concluding from these decisions that "charitable appeals for funds, on the street or door to door, involve a variety of speech interests . . . that are within the protection of the First Amendment." . . . I would have thought this proposition self-evident now that this Court has swept even the most banal commercial speech within the ambit of the First Amendment. See *Virginia Board of Pharmacy* v. *Virginia Consumer Council* ... (1976). But, having arrived at this conclusion on the basis of earlier cases, the Court effectively departs from the reasoning of those cases in discussing the limits on Schaumburg's authority to place limitations on so-called "charitable" solicitors who go from house to house in the village.

The Court's neglect of its prior precedents in this regard is entirely understandable since the earlier decisions striking down various regulations covering door-to-door activities turned upon factors not present in the instant case. A plurality of these decisions turned primarily, if not exclusively, upon the amount of discretion vested in municipal authorities to grant or deny permits on the basis of vague or even nonexistent criteria. See *Schneider* v. *State (Town of Irvington)* ... (1939). In *Schneider,* for example, the Court invalidated such an ordinance as applied to Jehovah's Witnesses because "[i]n the end, [the applicant's] liberty to communicate with the residents of the town at their homes depends upon the exercise of the officer's discretion." ... These cases clearly do not control the validity of Schaumburg's ordinance, which leaves virtually no discretion in the hands of the licensing authority.

Another line of earlier cases involved the distribution of information, as opposed to requests for contributions. *Martin* v. *Struthers* ... (1943), for example, dealt with Jehovah's Witnesses who had gone door to door with invitations to a religious meeting despite a local ordinance prohibiting distributions of any "handbills, circulars, or other advertisements" door to door. The Court noted that such an ordinance "limits the dissemination of knowledge," and that it could "serve no purpose but that forbidden by the Constitution, the naked restriction of the dissemination of ideas." ...

Here, however, the challenged ordinance deals not with the dissemination of ideas, but rather with the solicitation of money. That the *Martin* Court would have found this distinction important is apparent not only from *Martin*'s emphasis on the dissemination of knowledge, but also from various other decisions of the same period. In *Breard* v. *Alexandria* ... (1951), for example, the Court upheld an ordinance prohibiting "solicitors, peddlers, hawkers, itinerant merchants or transient vendors of merchandise" from entering private property without permission. The petitioner in *Breard* had been going door to door soliciting subscriptions for magazines. Despite petitioner's invocation of both freedom of speech and freedom of the press, the Court distinguished the "commercial

feature" of the transactions from their informational overtone. ... Because *Martin* "was narrowly limited to the precise fact of the free distribution of an invitation to religious services," the Court found that it was "not necessarily inconsistent with the conclusion reached in this case.". ...

Shunning the guidance of these cases, the Court sets out to define a new category of solicitors who may not be subjected to regulation. According to the Court, Schaumburg cannot prohibit door-to-door solicitation for contributions by "organizations whose primary purpose is ... to gather and disseminate information about the advocate positions on matters of public concern." ... In another portion of its opinion, the majority redefines this immunity as extending to all organizations "primarily engaged in research, advocacy, or public education and that use their own paid staff to carry out these functions as well as to solicit financial support." ... This result—or perhaps, more accurately, these results—seem unwarranted by the First and Fourteenth Amendments for three reasons.

First, from a legal standpoint, the Court invites municipalities to draw a line it has already erased. Today's opinion strongly, and I believe correctly, implies that the result here would be otherwise if CBE's primary objective were to provide "information about the characteristics and costs of goods and services," ... rather than to "advocate positions on matters of public concern." ... Four years ago, however, the Court relied upon the supposed bankruptcy of this very distinction in overturning a prohibition on advertising by pharmacists. See *Virginia Pharmacy Board* v. *Virginia Consumer Council* ... (1976). According to *Virginia Pharmacy,* while "not all commercial messages contain the same or even a very great public interest element[,] [t]here are few to which such an element ... could not be added." ... This and other considerations led the Court in that case to conclude that "no line between publicly 'interesting' or 'important' commercial advertising and the [other] kind could ever be drawn." ... To the extent that the Court found such a line elusive in *Virginia Pharmacy,* I venture to suggest that the Court, as well as local legislators, will find the line equally elusive in the context of door-to-door solicitation.

Second, from a practical standpoint, the Court gives absolutely no guidance as to how a municipality might identify those organizations "whose primary purpose is ... to gather and disseminate information about and advocate positions on matters of public concern," and which are therefore exempt from Art. III. Earlier cases do provide one guideline: the municipality must rely on objective criteria, since reliance upon official discretion in any significant degree would clearly run afoul of *Schneider, Cantwell, Largent* v. *Texas,* and *Hynes.* In requiring municipal authorities to use "more precise measures to separate" constitutionally preferred counterparts, . . . the Court would do well to remember that these local bodies are poorly equipped to investigate and audit the various persons and organizations that will apply to them for preferred status. Stripped of discretion, they must be able to resort to a line-drawing test capable of easy and reliable application without the necessity for an exhaustive case-by-case investigation of each applicant.

Finally, I believe that the Court overestimates the value, in a constitutional sense, of door-to-door solicitation for financial contributions and simultaneously underestimates the reasons why a village board might conclude that regulation of such activity was necessary. In *Hynes* v. *Mayor of Oradell,* . . . this Court referred with approval to Professor Zechariah Chafee's observation that "[o]f all the methods of spreading unpopular ideas, [house-to-house canvassing] seems the least entitled to extensive protection." . . . Quoting Z. Chafee, *Free Speech in the United States,* 406 (1954). While such activity may be worthy of heightened protection when limited to the dissemination of information, see, e.g., *Martin* v. *Struthers,* . . . or when designed to propagate reli-

gious beliefs, see, e.g., *Cantwell* v. *Connecticut,* . . . I believe that a simple request for money lies far from the core protections of the First Amendment as heretofore interpreted. In the case of such solicitation, the community's interest in ensuring that the collecting organization meet some objective financial criteria is indisputably valid. Regardless whether one labels noncharitable solicitation "fraudulent," nothing in the United States Constitution should prevent residents of a community from making the collective judgment that certain worthy charities may solicit door to door while at the same time insulating themselves against panhandlers, profiteers, and peddlers.

The central weakness of the Court's decision, I believe, is its failure to recognize, let alone confront, the two most important issues in this case: how does one define a "charitable" organization, and to which authority in our federal system is application of that definition confided? I would uphold Schaumburg's ordinance as applied to CBE because that ordinance, while perhaps too strict to suit some tastes, affects only door-to-door solicitation for financial contributions, leaves little or no discretion in the hands of municipal authorities to "censor" unpopular speech, and is rationally related to the community's collective desire to bestow its largess upon organizations that are truly "charitable."

I therefore dissent.

ADDERLY v. FLORIDA
385 U.S. 39; 17 L. Ed. 2d 149; 87 S. Ct. 242 (1966)

JUSTICE BLACK *delivered the opinion of the Court.*

Petitioners, Harriett Louise Adderly and 31 other persons, were convicted by a jury in a joint trial. . .on a charge of "trespass with a malicious and mischievous intent" upon the premises of the county jail contrary to section 821.18 of the Florida statutes set out below.* Petitioners, apparently all students of the Florida A. & M. University in Tallahassee, had gone from the school to the jail

about a mile away, along with many other students, to "demonstrate" at the jail their protests because of arrests of other protesting students the day before, and perhaps to protest more generally against state and local policies and practices of racial segregation, including segregation of the jail. The county sheriff, legal custodian of the jail and jail grounds, tried to persuade the students to leave the jail grounds. When this did not work, he notified them that they must leave or he would arrest them for trespassing, and notified them further that if they resisted arrest he would arrest them for resisting arrest as well. Some of the students left, but others, including petitioners, remained and they were arrested. On appeal the convictions were affirmed by the Florida [appellate courts]. . . . [P]etitioners applied to us for certio-

---

*"Every trespass upon property of another, committed with a malicious and mischievous intent, the punishment of which is not specially provided for, shall be punished by imprisonment not exceeding three months, or by fine not exceeding one hundred dollars." Fla. Stat. section 821.18 (1965).

rari contending that, in view of petitioners' purpose to protest against jail and other segregation policies, their conviction denied them "rights of free speech, assembly, petition, due process of law and equal protection of the laws as guaranteed by the Fourteenth Amendment to the Constitution of the United States." On this "Question Presented" we granted certiorari. . . .

Petitioners have insisted from the beginning of these cases that they are controlled and must be reversed because of our prior cases of *Edwards* v. *South Carolina,* 372 U. S. 229 (1963), . . . and *Cox* v. *Louisiana,* 379 U. S. 536 (1965). . . . We cannot agree.

The *Edwards* case, like this one, did come up when a number of persons demonstrated on public property against their State's segregation policies. They also sang hymns and danced, as did the demonstrators in this case. But here the analogies to this case end. In *Edwards*, the demonstrators went to the South Carolina State Capitol grounds to protest. In this case they went to the jail. Traditionally, state capitol grounds are open to the public. Jails, built for security purposes, are not. The demonstrators at the South Carolina Capitol went in through a public driveway, and as they entered they were told by state officials there that they had a right as citizens to go through the State House grounds as long as they were peaceful. Here the demonstrators entered the jail grounds through a driveway used only for jail purposes and without warning to or permission from the sheriff. More importantly, South Carolina sought to prosecute its State Capitol demonstrators by charging them with the common-law crime of breach of the peace. This Court in *Edwards* took pains to point out at length the indefinite, loose, and broad nature of this charge. . . . The South Carolina breach-of-the-peace statute was thus struck down as being so broad and all-embracing as to jeopardize speech, press, assembly and petition. . . . And it was on this same ground of vagueness that in *Cox* v. *Louisiana* . . . the Louisiana breach-of-the-peace law used to prosecute Cox was invalidated.

The Florida trespass statute under which these petitioners were charged cannot be challenged on this ground. It is aimed at conduct of one limited kind, that is for one person or persons to trespass upon the property of another with a malicious and mischievous intent. There is no lack of notice in this law, nothing to entrap or fool the unwary.

Petitioners seem to argue that the Florida trespass law is void for vagueness because it requires a trespass to be "with a malicious and mischievous intent. . . ." But these words do not broaden the scope of trespass so as to make it cover a multitude of types of conduct as does the common-law breach-of-the-peace charge. On the contrary, these words narrow the scope of the offense. The trial court charged the jury as to their meaning, and petitioners have not argued that this definition, set out below,** is not a reasonable and clear definition of the terms. The use of these terms in the statute, instead of contributing to uncertainty and misunderstanding, actually makes its meaning more understandable and clear.

Petitioners in this Court invoke the doctrine of abatement announced by this Court in *Hamm* v. *City of Rock Hill,* 379 U.S. 306. . . . But that holding was that the Civil Rights Act of 1964 . . . which made it unlawful for places of public accommodation to deny service to any person because of race, effected an abatement of prosecutions of persons for seeking service in establishments covered by the Act. It involves only an alleged trespass on jails grounds—a trespass which can be prosecuted regardless of the fact that it is the means of protesting segregation of establishments covered by the Act.

Petitioners next argue that "petty criminal statutes may not be used to violate minorities' constitutional rights." This of course is true, but this abstract proposition gets us nowhere in deciding the case.

Petitioners . . . contend that "[their] convictions are based on a total lack of relevant evidence." If true, this would be a denial of due process under *Garner* v. *Louisiana,* 368 U.S. 157 . . ., and *Thompson* v. *City of Louisville,* 362 U.S. 199. . . . Both in the petition for certiorari and in the brief on the merits petitioners state that their summary of the evidence "does not conflict with the facts contained in the Circuit Court's opinion" which was in effect affirmed by the District Court of Appeals. . . .

In summary both these statements show testimony ample to prove this: Disturbed and upset by the arrest of their schoolmates the day before, a

---

**"Malicious", means wrongful; you remember back in the original charge, the State has to prove beyond a reasonable doubt there was a malicious and mischievous intent. The word "malicious" means that the wrongful act shall be done voluntarily, unlawfully, and without excuse or justification. The word "malicious" that is used in these affidavits does not necessarily allege nor require the State to prove that the defendant had actual malice in his mind at the time of the alleged trespass. Another way of stating the definition of 'malicious' is by 'malicious' is meant the act was done knowingly and willfully and without any legal justification.

"Mischievous," which is also required, means that the alleged trespass shall be inclined to cause petty and trivial trouble, annoyance and vexation to others in order for you to find that the alleged trespass was committed with mischievous intent. R74.

large number of Florida A. & M. students assembled on the school grounds and decided to march down to the county jail. Some apparently wanted to get themselves put in jail too, along with the students already there. A group of around 200 marched from the school and arrived at the jail singing and clapping. They went directly to the jail door entrance where they were met by a deputy sheriff, evidently surprised by their arrival. He asked them to move back, claiming they were blocking the entrance to the jail and fearing that they might attempt to enter the jail. They moved back part of the way, where they stood or sat, singing, clapping and dancing, on the jail driveway and on an adjacent grassy area upon the jail premises. This particular jail entrance and driveway were not normally used by the public, but the sheriff's department for transporting prisoners to and from the courts several blocks away and by commercial concerns for servicing the jail. Even after their partial retreat, the demonstrators continued to block vehicular passage over this driveway up to the entrance of the jail. Someone called the sheriff who was at the moment apparently conferring with one of the state court judges about incidents connected with prior arrests for demonstrations. When the sheriff returned to the jail, he immediately inquired if all was safe inside the jail and was told it was. He then engaged in a conversation with two of the leaders. He told them that they were trespassing upon jail property and that he would give them 10 minutes to leave or he would arrest them. Neither of the leaders did anything to disperse the crowd, and one of them told the sheriff that they wanted to get arrested. A local minister talked with some of the demonstrators and told them not to enter the jail, because they could not arrest themselves, but just to remain where they were. After about 10 minutes, the sheriff, in a voice loud enough to be heard by all, told the demonstrators that he was the legal custodian of the jail and its premises, that they were trespassing on county property in violation of the law, that they should all leave forthwith or he would arrest them, and that if they attempted to resist arrest, he would charge them with that as a separate offense. Some of the group left. Others, including all petitioners, did not leave. Some of them sat down. In a few minutes, realizing that the remaining demonstrators had no intention of leaving, the sheriff ordered his deputies to surround those remaining on jail premises and placed them, 107 demonstrators, under arrest. The sheriff unequivocally testified that he did not arrest any person other than those who were on the jail premises. Of the three petitioners testifying, two insisted that they were arrested before they had a chance to leave, had they wanted to, and one testified that she did not intend to leave. The sheriff again explicitly testified that he did not arrest any person who was attempting to leave.

Under the foregoing testimony the jury was authorized to find that the State had proven every essential element of the crime, as it was defined by the state court. That interpretation is, of course, binding on us, leaving only the question of whether conviction of the state offense, thus defined, unconstitutionally deprives petitioners of their rights to freedom of speech, press, assembly, or petition. We hold it does not. The sheriff, as jail custodian, had power as the state courts have here held, to direct that this large crowd of people get off the grounds. There is not a shred of evidence in this record that this power was exercised, or that its exercise was sanctioned by the lower courts, because the sheriff objected to what was being sung or said by the demonstrators or because he disagreed with the objectives of their protest. The record reveals that he objected only to their presence on that part of the jail grounds reserved for jail uses. There is no evidence at all that on any other occasion had similarly large groups of the public been permitted to gather on this portion of the jail grounds for any purpose. Nothing in the Constitution of the United States prevents Florida from even-handed enforcement of its general trespass statute against those refusing to obey the sheriff's order to remove themselves from what amounted to the curtailage of the jailhouse. The State, no less than a private owner of property, has power to preserve the property under its control for the use to which it is lawfully dedicated. For this reason there is no merit to the petitioners' argument that they had a constitutional right to stay on the property, over the jail custodian's objections, because this "area chosen for the peaceful civil rights demonstration was not only 'reasonable' but also particularly appropriate. . . ." Such an argument has as its major unarticulated premise the assumption that people who want to propagandize protests or views have a constitutional right to do so whenever and however and wherever they please. . . . We reject [that concept] . . . . [T]he United States Constitution does not forbid a State to control the use of its own property for its own lawful nondiscriminatory purpose.

These judgments are affirmed.

JUSTICE DOUGLAS, *with whom the* CHIEF

JUSTICE, JUSTICE BRENNAN, *and* JUSTICE FORTAS *concur, dissenting.*

...With all respect, the Court errs in treating the case as if it were an ordinary trespass case or an ordinary picketing case.

The jailhouse, like an executive mansion, a legislative chamber, a courthouse, or the statehouse itself . . . is one of the seats of government, whether it be the Tower of London, the Bastille, or a small county jail. And when it houses political prisoners or those whom many think are unjustly held, it is an obvious center for protest. The right to petition for the redress of grievances has an ancient history and is not limited to writing a letter or sending a telegram to a congressman; it is not confined to appearing before the local city council, or writing letters to the President or Governor or Mayor. . . . Conventional methods of petitioning may be, and often have been, shut off to large groups of our citizens. Legislators may turn deaf ears; formal complaints may be routed endlessly through a bureaucratic maze; courts may let the wheels of justice grind very slowly. Those who do not control television and radio, those who cannot afford to advertise in newspapers or circulate elaborate pamphlets may have only a more limited type of access to public officials. Their methods should not be condemned as tactics of obstruction and harassment as long as the assembly and petition are peaceable, as these were.

There is no question that petitioners had as their purpose a protest against the arrest of Florida A. & M. students for trying to integrate public theatres. The sheriff's testimony indicates that he well understood the purpose of the rally. The petitioners who testified unequivocally stated that the group was protesting the arrests, and state and local policies of segregation, including segregation of the jail. This testimony was not contradicted or even questioned. The fact that no one gave a formal speech, that no elaborate handbills were distributed, and that the group was not laden with signs would seem immaterial. Such methods are not the sine qua non of petitioning for the redress of grievances. The group did sing "freedom" songs. And history shows that a song can be a powerful tool of protest. . . . There was no violence; no threats of violence; no attempted jail break; no storming of a prison; no plan or plot to do anything but protest. The evidence is uncontradicted that the prisoners' conduct did not upset the jailhouse routine; things went on as they normally would. None of the group entered the jail. Indeed, they moved back from the entrance as they were

instructed. There was no shoving, no pushing, no disorder or threat of riot. It is said that some of the group blocked part of the driveway leading to the jail entrance. The chief jailer to be sure testified that vehicles would not have been able to use the driveway. Never did the students locate themselves so as to cause interference with persons or vehicles going to or coming from the jail. Indeed, it is undisputed that the sheriff and deputy sheriff, in separate cars, were able to drive up this driveway to the parking places near the entrance and that no one obstructed their path. Further, it is undisputed that the entrance to the jail was not blocked. And wherever the students were requested to move they did so. If there was congestion, the solution was a further request to move to lawns or parking areas, not complete ejection and arrest. The claim is made that a tradesman waited inside the jail because some of the protestants were sitting around and leaning on his truck. The only evidence supporting such a conclusion is the testimony of a deputy sheriff that the tradesman "came to the door and then did not leave." His remaining is just as consistent with a desire to satisfy his curiosity as it is with a restraint. Finally, the fact that some of the protestants may have felt their cause so just that they were willing to be arrested for making their protest outside the jail seems wholly irrelevant. A petition is nonetheless a petition, though its futility may make martyrdom attractive.

We do violence to the First Amendment when we permit this "petition for redress of grievances" to be turned into a trespass action. It does not help to analogize this problem to the problem of picketing. Picketing is a form of protest usually directed against private interests. I do not see how rules governing picketing in general are relevant to this express constitutional right to assemble and to petition for redress of grievances, in the first place the jailhouse grounds were not marked with "NO TRESPASSING!" signs, nor does respondent claim that the public was generally excluded from the grounds. Only the sheriff's fiat transformed lawful conduct into an unlawful trespass. To say that a private owner could have done the same if the rally had taken place on private property is to speak of a different case, as an assembly and a petition for redress of grievances run to government not to private proprietors.

* * *

. . . When we allow Florida to construe her "malicious trespass" statute to bar a person from going on property knowing it is not his own and to apply that prohibition to public property, we discard *Cox* and *Edwards*. Would the case be any different if, as is common, the demonstration took place outside a building which housed both the jail and the legislative body? I think not.

There may be some public places which are so clearly committed to other purposes that their use for the airing of grievances is anomalous. There may be some instances in which assemblies and petitions for redress of grievances are not consistent with other necessary purposes of public property. A noisy meeting may be out of keeping with the serenity of the statehouse or the quiet of the courthouse. No one, for example, would suggest that the Senate gallery is the proper place for a vociferous protest rally. And, in other cases it may be necessary to adjust the right to petition for redress of grievances to the other interests inherent in the uses to which the public property is normally put. . . . But this is quite different than saying that all public places are off-limits to people with grievances. . . . And it is farther yet from saying that the "custodian" of the public property in his discretion can decide when public places shall be used for the communication of ideas, especially the constitutional right to assemble and petition for redress of grievances. . . . For to place such discretion in any public official, be he the "custodian" of the public property or the local police commissioner, . . . is to place those who assert their First Amendment rights at his mercy. It gives him the awesome power to decide whose ideas may be expressed and who shall be denied a place to air their claims and petition their government. Such power is out of step with all our decisions prior to today where we have insisted that before a First Amendment right may be curtailed under the guise of a criminal law, any evil that may be collateral to the exercise of that right must be isolated and defined in a "narrowly drawn" statute . . . lest the power to control excesses of conduct be used to suppress the constitutional right itself. . . .

That tragic consequence happens today when a trespass law is used to bludgeon those who peacefully exercise a First Amendment right to protest to government against one of the most grievous of all modern oppressions which some of our states are inflicting on our citizens.

* * *

Today a trespass law is used to penalize people for exercising a constitutional right. Tomorrow a disorderly conduct statute, a breach of the peace statute, a vagrancy statute will be put to the same end. It is said that the sheriff did not make the arrests because of the views which petitioners espoused. That excuse is usually given, as we know from the cases involving arrests of minority groups for breaches of the peace, unlawful assemblies, and parading without a permit. The charge against William Penn, who preached a nonconformist doctrine in a street in London, was that he caused "a great concourse and tumult of people" in contempt of the King and "to the great disturbance of the peace." That was in 1670. In modern times also such arrests are usually sought to be justified by some legitimate function of government. Yet by allowing these orderly and civilized protests against injustice to be suppressed, we only increase the forces of frustration which the conditions of second-class citizenship are generating amongst us.

WARD, ET AL., v. ROCK AGAINST RACISM
491 U.S. 781; 109 S. Ct. 2746; 105 L. Ed. 661 (1989)

KENNEDY, J., *delivered the opinion of the Court, in which* REHNQUIST, C. J., *and* WHITE, O'CONNOR, *and* SCALIA, JJ., *joined.* BLACKMUN, J., *filed a dissenting opinion, in which* BRENNAN *and* STEVENS, JJ., *joined.*

JUSTICE KENNEDY *delivered the opinion of the Court.*

In the southeast portion of New York City's Central Park, about 10 blocks upward from the park's beginning point at 59th Street, there is an amphitheater and stage structure known as the Naumberg Acoustic Bandshell. The Bandshell faces west across the remaining width of the park. In close proximity to the Bandshell, and lying within the directional path of its sound, is a grassy open area called the Sheep Meadow. The city has designated the Sheep Meadow as a quiet area for passive recreations like reclining, walking, and reading. Just beyond the park, and also within the potential sound range of the Bandshell, are the apartments and residences of Central Park West.

This case arises from the city's attempt to regulate the volume of amplified music at the bandshell so the performances are satisfactory to the audience without intruding upon those who use the Sheep Meadow or live on Central Park West and in its vicinity.

The city's regulation requires Bandshell performers to use sound-amplification equipment and a sound technician provided by the city. The challenge to this volume control technique comes from the sponsor of a rock concert. The trial court sustained the noise control measures, but the Court of Appeals for the Second Circuit reversed. We granted certiorari to resolve the important First Amendment issues presented by the case.

Rock against Racism [RAR], respondent in this case, is an unincorporated association which, in its own words, is "dedicated to the espousal and promotion of antiracist views." Each year from 1979 through 1986, RAR has sponsored a program of speeches and rock music at the Bandshell. RAR has furnished the sound equipment and sound technician used by the various performing groups at these annual events.

Over the years, the city received numerous complaints about excessive sound amplification at respondent's concerts from park users and residents of areas adjacent to the park. On some occasions RAR was less than cooperative when city officials asked that the volume be reduced; at one concert, police felt compelled to cut off the power to the sound system, an action that caused the audience to become unruly and hostile.

Before the 1984 concert, city officials met with RAR representatives to discuss the problem of excessive noise. It was decided that the city would monitor sound levels at the edge of the concert ground, and would revoke respondent's event permit if specific volume limits were exceeded. Sound levels did exceed acceptable levels for sustained periods of time, despite repeated warnings and requests that the volume be lowered. Two citations for excessive volume were issued to respondent during the concert. When the power was eventually shut off, the audience became abusive and disruptive.

The following year, when respondent sought permission to hold its upcoming concert at the Bandshell, the city declined to grant an event permit, citing its problems with noise and crowd control at RAR's previous concerts. The city suggested some other city-owned facilities as alternative sites for the concert. RAR declined the invitation and filed suit in United States District Court against the city, its mayor, and various police and parks department officials, seeking an injunction directing issuance of an event permit. After respondent agreed to abide by all applicable regulations, the parties reached agreement and a permit was issued.

The city then undertook to develop comprehensive Use Guidelines for the Bandshell. A principal problem to be addressed by the guidelines was controlling the volume of amplified sound at Bandshell events. A major concern was that at some Bandshell performances the event sponsors had been unable to "provide the amplification levels required and 'crowds unhappy with the sound became disappointed or unruly.' " The city found that this problem had several causes, including inadequate sound equipment, sound technicians who were either unskilled at mixing sound outdoors or unfamiliar with the acoustics of the Bandshell and its surrounding, and the like. Because some performers compensated for the poor sound mix by raising volume, these factors tended to exacerbate the problem of excess noise.

The city considered various solutions to the sound amplification problem. The idea of a fixed decibel limit for all performers using the Bandshell was rejected because the impact on listeners of a single decibel level is not constant, but varies in response to changes in air temperature, foliage, audience size, and like factors. The city also rejected the possibility of employing a sound technician to operate the equipment provided by the various sponsors of Bandshell events, because the city's technician might have had difficulty satisfying the needs of sponsors while operating unfamiliar, and perhaps inadequate, sound equipment. Instead, the city concluded that the most effective way to achieve adequate but not excessive sound amplification would be for the city to furnish high quality sound equipment and retain an independent, experienced sound technician for all performances at the Bandshell. After extensive search the city hired a private sound company capable of meeting the needs of all the varied users of the Bandshell.

The Use Guidelines were promulgated on March 21, 1986. After learning that it would be expected to comply with the guidelines at its upcoming annual concert in May 1986, respondent returned to the District Court and filed a motion for an injunction against the enforcement of certain aspects of the guidelines. The District Court preliminarily enjoined enforcement of the sound-amplification rule on May 1, 1986. Under the protection of the injunction, and alone among users of the Bandshell in the 1986 season, RAR was permitted to use its own sound equipment and technician, just as it had done it prior years. RAR's 1986 concert again generated complaints about excessive noise from the park users and nearby residents.

After the concert, respondent amended its complaint to seek damages and a declaratory judgment striking down the guidelines as facially invalid. After hearing five days of testimony about various aspects of the guidelines, the District Court issued its decision upholding the sound-amplification guidelines. The court found that the city had been "motivated by a desire to obtain top-flight sound equipment and experienced operators" in selecting an independent contractor to provide the equipment and technician for Bandshell events, and that the performers who did use the city's sound system in the 1986 season, in performances "which ran the full cultural gamut from grand opera to salsa to reggae," were uniformly pleased with the quality of the sound provided.

Although the city's sound technician controlled both sound volume and sound mix by virtue of his position at the mixing board, the court found that the city's practice for events at the Bandshell is to give the sponsor autonomy with respect to the sound mix: balancing treble with bass, highlighting a particular instrument or voice, and the like, and that the city's sound technician "does all he can to accommodate the sponsor's desires in those regards." Even with respect to volume control, the city's practice was to confer with the sponsor before making any decision to turn the volume down. In some instances, as with a New York Grand Opera performance, the sound technician accommodated the performers' unique needs by integrating special microphones with the city's equipment. The court specifically found "[t]he City's implementation of the Bandshell guidelines provides for a sound amplification system capable of meeting RAR's technical needs and leaves control of the sound 'mix' in the hands of RAR." Applying this Court's three-part test for judging the constitutionality of government regulation of the time, place, or manner of protected speech, the court found the city's regulations valid.

The Court of Appeals reversed. After recognizing that the "[c]ontent neutral time, place and manner regulations are permissible so long as they are narrowly tailored to serve a substantial government interest and do not unreasonably limit alternative avenues of expression," the court added the proviso that "the method and extent of such regulation must be reasonable, that is, it must be the least intrusive upon the freedom of expression as is reasonably necessary to achieve a legitimate purpose of the regulation." (citing *United States* v.

O'Brien, [1968]). Applying this test the court determined that the city's guideline was valid only to the extent necessary to achieve the city's legitimate interest in controlling excessive volume, but found there were various alternative means of controlling volume without also intruding on respondent's ability to control the sound mix.

For example, the city could have directed respondent's sound technician to keep the volume below specified levels. Alternatively, a volume-limiting device could have been installed; and as a "last resort," the court suggested, "the plug can be pulled on the sound to enforce the volume limit." In view of the potential availability of these seemingly less-restrictive alternatives, the Court of Appeals concluded that the sound-amplification guideline was invalid because the city had failed to prove that its regulation "was the least intrusive means of regulating the volume."

We granted certiorari, (1988), to clarify the legal standard applicable to governmental regulation of the time, place, or manner of protected speech. Because the Court of Appeals erred in requiring the city to prove that its regulation was the least intrusive means of furthering its legitimate governmental interest, and because the ordinance is valid on its face, we now reverse.

Music is one of the oldest forms of human expression. From Plato's discourse in the Republic to the totalitarian state in our own times, rulers had known its capacity to appeal to the intellect and to the emotions, and had censored musical compositions to serve the needs of the state. . . . The Constitution prohibits any like attempts in our own legal order. Music, as a form of expression and communication, is protected under the First Amendment. In the case before us the performances apparently consisted of remarks by speakers, as well as rock music, but the case has been presented as one in which the constitutional challenge is to the city's regulation of the musical aspects of the concert; and based on the principle we have stated, the city's guidelines must meet the demands of the First Amendment. The parties do not appear to dispute that proposition.

We need not here discuss whether a municipality which owns a band stand or stage facility may exercise, in some circumstances, a proprietary right to select performances and control their quality. . . . Here the Bandshell was open, apparently, to all performers; and we decide the case as one in which the Bandshell is a public forum for performances in which the government's right to regulate expression is subject to the protections of the First Amendment. *United States* v. *Grace*, (1983);

see *Frisby* v. *Schultz*, (1988); *Perry Education Assn.* v. *Perry Local Educators' Assn.*, (1983). Our cases make clear, however, that even in a public forum the government may impose reasonable restrictions on the time, place, or manner of protected speech, provided the restrictions "are justified without reference to the content of the regulated speech, that they are narrowly tailored to serve a significant governmental interest, and that they leave open ample alternative channels for communication of the information." We consider these requirements in turn.

The principle inquiry in determining content neutrality, in speech cases generally and in time, place, or manner cases in particular, is whether the government has adopted a regulation of speech because of disagreement with the message it conveys. The government's purpose is the controlling consideration. A regulation that serves purposes unrelated to the content of expression is deemed neutral, even if it has an incidental effect on some speakers or messages but not others. Government regulation of expressive activity is content-neutral so long as it is "justified without reference to the content of the regulated speech." . . .

The principal justification for the sound-amplification guideline is the city's desire to control noise levels at Bandshell events, in order to retain the character of the Sheep Meadow and its more sedate activities, and to avoid undue intrusion into residential areas and other areas of the park. This justification for the guideline "ha[s] nothing to do with the content," and it satisfies the requirement that time, place, or manner regulations be neutral.

The only other justification offered below was the city's interest in "ensur[ing] the quality of sound at Bandshell events." Respondent urges that this justification is not content-neutral because it is based upon the quality, and thus the content, of the speech being regulated. In respondent's view, the city is seeking to assert artistic control over performers at the Bandshell by enforcing a bureaucratically determined, value-laden conception of good sound. That all performers who have used the city's sound equipment have been completely satisfied is of no moment, respondent argues, because "[t]he First Amendment does not permit and cannot tolerate state control of artistic expression merely because the State claims that [its] efforts will lead to 'top-quality' results."

While respondent's arguments that the government may not interfere with artistic judgment may have much force in other contexts, they are inapplicable to the facts of this case. The city has disclaimed in express terms any interest in imposing its own view of appropriate sound mix on performers. To the contrary, as the District Court found, the city requires its sound technician to defer to the wishes of event sponsors concerning sound mix. On this record, the city's concern with sound quality extends only to the clearly content-neutral goals of ensuring adequate sound amplification and avoiding the volume problems associated with inadequate sound mix. Any governmental attempt to serve purely aesthetic goals by imposing subjective standards of acceptable sound mix on performers would raise serious First Amendment concerns, but this case provides us with no opportunity to address those questions. As related above, the District Court found that the city's equipment and its sound technician could meet all the standards requested by the performers.

Respondent argues further that the guideline, even if not content-based in explicit terms, is nonetheless invalid on its face because it places unbridled discretion in the hands of city officials charged with enforcing it. . . .

As a threshold matter, it is far from clear that respondent should be permitted to bring a facial challenge to this aspect of the regulation. Our cases permitting facial challenges to regulations that allegedly grant officials unconstrained authority to regulate speech have generally involved licensing schemes that "ves[t] unbridled discretion in a government official over whether to permit or deny expressive activity." The grant of discretion that respondent seeks to challenge here is of an entirely different, and lesser, order of magnitude, because respondent does not suggest that city officials enjoy unfettered discretion to deny Bandshell permits altogether. Rather, respondent contends only that the city, by exercising what is concededly its right to regulate amplified sound, could choose to provide inadequate sound for performers based on the content of the speech. Since respondent does not claim that city officials enjoy unguided discretion to deny the right to speak altogether, it is open to question whether respondent's claim falls within the narrow class of permissible facial challenges to allegedly unconstrained grants of regulatory authority. . . .

We need to decide, however, whether the "extraordinary doctrine" that permits facial challenges to some regulations of expression, should be extended to the circumstances of this case, for respondent's facial challenge fails on its merits. The city's guideline states that its goals are to "provide the best sound for all events" and to "insure appropriate sound quality balanced with respect for nearby residential neighbors and mayorally decreed quiet zone of [the] Sheep Meadow." While these standards are undoubtedly flexible, and the officials implementing them will exercise considerable discretion, perfect clarity and precise guidance have never been required even of regulations that restrict expressive activity. . . . By its own terms the city's sound-amplification guideline must be interpreted to forbid city officials purposely to select inadequate sound systems or to vary the sound quality or volume based on the message being delivered by performers. The guideline is not vulnerable to respondent's facial challenge.

Even if the language of the guideline were not sufficient on its face to withstand challenge, our ultimate conclusion would be the same, for the city has interpreted the guideline in such a manner as to provide additional guidance to the officials charged with its enforcement. . . .

Any inadequacy on the face of the guideline would have been more than remedied by the city's narrowing construction.

The city's regulation is also "narrowly tailored to serve a significant governmental interest." . . . This interest is perhaps at its greatest when government seeks to protect "'the well-being, tranquility and privacy of the home,'" *Frisby* v. *Schultz*, but it is by no means limited to that context, for the government may act to protect even such traditional public forums as city streets and parks from excessive noise. *Kovacs* v. *Cooper*. . . .

We think it also apparent that the city's interest in ensuring the sufficiency of sound amplification at Bandshell events is a substantial one. The record indicates that the inadequate sound amplification has had an adverse affect on the ability of some audiences to hear and enjoy performances at the Bandshell. The city enjoys a substantial interest in ensuring the ability of its citizens to enjoy whatever benefits the city parks have to offer, from amplified music to silent meditation.

The Court of Appeals recognized the city's substantial interest in limiting the sound emanating from the Bandshell. The court concluded, however, that the city's sound-amplification guideline was not narrowly tailored to further this interest, because "it has not [been] shown . . . that the requirement of the use of the city's sound system and technician was the least intrusive means of regulating the volume." In the court's judgment, there were several alternative methods of achieving the desired end that would have been less restrictive of respondent's First Amendment rights.

The Court of Appeals erred in sifting through all the available or imagined alternative means of regulating sound volume in order to determine whether the city's solution was "the least intrusive means" of achieving the desired end. This "less-restrictive-alternative analysis . . . has never been a part of the inquiry into the validity of a time, place, and manner regulation." Instead, our cases quite clearly hold that restrictions on the time, place, or manner of protected speech are not invalid "simply because there is some imaginable alternative that might be less burdensome on speech."

The Court of Appeals apparently drew its least-intrusive-means requirement from *United States* v. *O'Brien*, (1968), the case in which we established the standard for judging the validity of restrictions of expressive conduct. The court's reliance was misplaced, however, for we have held that the O'Brien test "in the last analysis is little, if any, different from the standard applied to time, place, or manner restrictions.". . .

Lest any confusion on the point remain, we reaffirm today that a regulation of the time, place, or manner of protected speech must be narrowly tailored to serve the government's legitimate content-neutral interests but that it need not be the least-restrictive or least-intrusive means of doing so. Rather, the requirement of narrow tailoring is satisfied "so long as the . . . regulation promotes a substantial government interest that would be achieved less effectively absent the regulation." To be sure, this standard does not mean that a time, place, or manner regulation may burden substantially more speech than is necessary to further the government's legitimate interests. Government may not regulate expression in such a manner that a substantial portion of the burden on speech does not serve to advance its goals. . . . So long as the means chosen are not substantially broader than necessary to achieve the government's interest, however, the regulation will not be invalid simply because a court concludes that the government's interest could be adequately served by some less-speech-restrictive alternative. "The validity of [time, place, or manner] regulations does not turn on a judge's agreement with the responsible decisionmaker concerning the most appropriate method for promoting significant government interests" or the degree to which those interests should be promoted.

It is undeniable that the city's substantial interest in limiting sound volume is served in a direct and effective way by the requirement that the city's sound technician control the mixing board during performances. Absent this requirement, the city's interest would have been served less well, as is evidenced by the complaints about excessive volume generated by respondent's past concerts. The alternative regulatory methods hypothesized by the Court of Appeals reflect nothing more than a disagreement with the city over how much control of volume is appropriate or how that level of control is to be achieved. The Court of Appeals erred in failing to defer to the city's reasonable determination that its interest in controlling volume would be best served by requiring Bandshell performers to utilize the city's sound technician.

The city's second content-neutral justification for the guideline, that of ensuring "that the sound amplification [is] sufficient to reach all listeners within the defined concertground," also supports the city's choice of regulatory methods. By providing competent sound technicians and adequate amplification equipment, the city eliminated the problems of inexperienced technicians and insufficient sound volume that had plagued some Bandshell performers in the past. No doubt this concern is not applicable to respondent's concerts, which apparently were characterized by more-than-adequate sound amplification. But that fact is beside the point, for the validity of the regulation depends on the relation it bears to the overall problem the government seeks to correct, not on the extent to which it furthers the government's interests in an individual case. Here, the regulation's effectiveness must be judged by considering all the varied groups that use the Bandshell, and it is valid so long as the city could reasonably have determined that its interest overall would be served less effectively without the sound-amplification guideline than with it. Considering these proffered justifications together, therefore, it is apparent that the guideline directly furthers the city's legitimate governmental interests and that those interests would have been less well served in the absence of the sound-amplification guideline.

Respondent nonetheless argues that the sound-amplification guideline is not narrowly tailored because, by placing control of sound mix in the hands of the city's technician, the guideline sweeps far more broadly than is necessary to further the city's legitimate concern with sound volume. According to respondent, the guideline "targets . . . more than the exact source of the 'evil' it seeks to remedy."

If the city's regulatory scheme has a substantial deleterious effect on the ability of Bandshell performers to achieve the quality of sound they desired, respondent's concerns would have considerable force. The District Court found, however, that pursuant to city policy, the city's sound technician "give[s] the sponsor autonomy with respect to the sound mix . . . [and] does all that he can to accom-

modate the sponsor's desires in those regards." The court squarely rejected respondent's claim that the city's "technician is not able properly to implement a sponsor's instructions as to sound quality or mix," finding that "[n]o evidence to that effect was offered at trial; as noted, the evidence is to the contrary." In view of these findings, which were not disturbed by the Court of Appeals, we must conclude that the city's guideline has no material impact on any performer's ability to exercise complete artistic control over sound quality. Since the guideline allows the city to control volume without interfering with the performer's desired sound mix, it is not "substantially broader than necessary" to achieve the city's legitimate ends, and thus it satisfies the requirement of narrow tailoring.

The final requirement, that the guideline leave open ample alternative channels of communication, is easily met. Indeed, in this respect the guideline is far less restrictive than regulations we have upheld in other cases, for it does not attempt to ban any particular manner or type of expression at a given place or time. Rather, the guideline continues to permit expressive activity in the Bandshell, and has no effect on the quantity or content of that expression beyond regulating the extent of amplification. . . .

The city's sound-amplification guideline is narrowly tailored to serve the substantial and content-neutral governmental interests of avoiding excessive sound volume and providing sufficient amplification within the Bandshell concertground, and the guideline leaves open ample channels of communication. Accordingly, it is valid under the First Amendment as a reasonable regulation of the place and manner of expression. The judgment of the Court of Appeals is

Reversed.

JUSTICE BLACKMUN *concurs in the result.*

JUSTICE MARSHALL, *with whom* JUSTICE BRENNAN *and* JUSTICE STEVENS *join, dissenting.*

No one can doubt that government has substantial interest in regulating the barrage of excessive sound that can plague urban life. Unfortunately, the majority plays to our shared impatience with loud noise to obscure the damage that it does to our First Amendment rights. Until today, a key safeguard of free speech has been government's obligation to adopt the least intrusive restriction necessary to achieve its goals. By abandoning the requirement that time, place, and manner regulations must be narrowly tailored, the majority's willingness to give government officials a free hand in achieving their policy ends extends so far as to permit, in this case, government control of speech in advance of its dissemination. Because New York City's Sound Amplification Guidelines (Guidelines) are not narrowly tailored to serve its interest in regulating loud noise, and because they constitute an impermissible prior restraint, I dissent.

The majority sets forth the appropriate standard for assessing the constitutionality of the Guidelines. A time, place, and manner regulation of expression must be content-neutral, serve a significant government interest, and leave open ample alternative channels of communication. The Guidelines indisputably are content-neutral as they apply to all Bandshell users irrespective of the message of their music. They also serve government's significant interests in limiting loud noise in public places, by giving the city exclusive control of all sound equipment.

My complaint is with the majority's serious distortion of the narrow tailoring requirement. Our cases have not, as the majority asserts, "clearly" rejected a less restrictive alternative test. On the contrary, just last Term, we held that a statute is narrowly tailored only "if it targets and eliminates no more than the exact source of the 'evil' it seeks to remedy." *Frisby* v. *Schultz*. While there is language in a few opinions which, taken out of context, supports the majority's position, in practice, the Court has interpreted the narrow tailoring requirement to mandate an examination of alternative methods of serving the asserted governmental interest and a determination whether the greater efficacy of the challenged regulation outweighs the increased burden it places on protected speech. . . . In *Schneider,* for example, the Court invalidated a ban on handbill distribution on public streets, notwithstanding that it was the most effective means of serving government's legitimate interest in minimizing litter, noise, and traffic congestion, and in preventing fraud. The Court concluded that punishing those who actually litter or perpetrate frauds was a much less intrusive, albeit not quite as effective, means to serve those significant interests. . . .

The Court's past concern for the extent to which a regulation burdens speech more than would a satisfactory alternative is noticeably absent from today's decision. The majority requires only that government show that its interest cannot be served as effectively without the challenged restriction. It will be enough, therefore, that the challenged regulation advances the government's in-

terest only in the slightest, for any differential burden on speech that results does not enter the calculus. Despite its protestations to the contrary, the majority thus has abandoned the requirement that restrictions on speech be narrowly tailored in any ordinary use of the phrase. Indeed, after today's decision, a city could claim that bans on handbill distribution or on door-to-door solicitation are the most effective means of avoiding littering and fraud, or that a ban on loud-speakers and radios in a public park is the most effective means of avoiding loud noise. Logically extended, the majority's analysis would permit such far-reaching restrictions on speech.

True, the majority states that "[g]overnment may not regulate expression in such a manner that a substantial portion of the burden on speech does not serve to advance its goals." But this means that only those regulations that "engage in the gratuitous inhibition of expression" will be invalidated. Moreover, the majority has robbed courts of the necessary analytic tools to make even this limited inquiry. The Court of Appeals examined "how much control of volume is appropriate [and] how that level of control is to be achieved," but the majority admonishes that court for doing so, stating that it should have "defer[red] to the city's reasonable determination." The majority thus instructs courts to refrain from examining how much speech may be restricted to serve an asserted interest and how that level of restriction is to be achieved. If a court cannot engage in such inquiries, I am at a loss to understand how a court can ascertain whether the government has adopted a regulation that burdens substantially more speech than is necessary.

Had the majority not abandoned the narrow tailoring requirement, the Guidelines could not possibly survive constitutional scrutiny. Government's interest in avoiding loud sounds cannot justify giving government total controls over sound equipment, any more than its interest in avoiding litter could justify a ban on handbill distribution. In both cases, government's legitimate goals can be effectively served by directly punishing the evil— the persons responsible for excessive sounds and the persons who litter. Indeed, the city confessed that it has an ordinance generally limiting noise but has chosen not to enforce it.

By holding that the Guidelines are valid time, place, and manner restrictions, notwithstanding the availability of less intrusive means of controlling volume, the majority deprives the narrow tailoring requirement of all meaning. Today, the majority enshrines efficacy but sacrifices free speech.

The majority's conclusion that the city's exclusive control of sound equipment is constitutional is deeply troubling for another reason. It places the Court's imprimatur on a quintessential prior restraint, incompatible with fundamental First Amendment values. See *Near* v. *Minnesota,* (1931). Indeed, just as "[m]usic is one of the oldest forms of human expression," the city's regulation is one of the oldest forms of speech repression. In 16th and 17th century England, government controlled speech through its monopoly of printing presses. See L. Levy, *Emergence of a Free Press 6* (1985). Here, the city controls the volume and mix of sound through its monopoly on sound equipment. In both situations, government's exclusive control of the means of communication enables public officials to censor speech in advance of its expression. Under more familiar prior restraints, government officials censor speech "by a simple stroke of the pen. . . ." Here, it is done by a single turn of a knob.

The majority's implication that government control of sound equipment is not a prior restraint because city officials do not "enjoy unguided discretion to deny the right to speak altogether" is startling. In the majority's view, this case involves a question of "different and lesser" magnitude—the discretion to provide inadequate sound for performers. But whether the city denies a performer a Bandshell permit or grants the permit and then silences or distorts the performer's music, the result is the same—the city censors speech. . . .

As a system of prior restraint, the Guidelines are presumptively invalid. They may be constitutional only if accompanied by the procedural safeguards necessary "to avoid the dangers of a censorship system." The city must establish neutral criteria embodied in "narrowly drawn, reasonable and definite standards," in order to ensure that discretion is not exercised based on the content of speech. *Niemotko* v. *Maryland,* (1951). . . . Moreover, there must be "an almost immediate judicial determination" that the restricted material was unprotected by the First Amendment. *Bantam Books (Inc.* v. *Sullivan,* [1963]).

The Guidelines contain neither of these procedural safeguards. First, there are no "narrowly drawn, reasonable and definite standards" guiding the hands of the city's sound technician as he mixes the sound.

The Guidelines state that the goals are "to provide the best sound for all events" and to "insure appropriate sound quality balanced with respect for nearby residential neighbors and the mayorally decreed quiet zone." But the city never defines

"best sound" or "appropriate sound quality." The Bandshell program director-manager testified that quality of sound refers to tone and to sound mix. Yet questions of tone and mix cannot be separated from musical expression as a whole. . . . Because judgments that sounds are too loud, noise-like, or discordant can mask disapproval of the music itself, government control of the sound mixing equipment necessitates detailed and neutral standards.

The majority concedes that the standards in the Guidelines are "undoubtedly flexible" and that "the officials implementing them will exercise considerable discretion." Nevertheless, it concludes that "[b]y its own terms the city's sound-amplification guideline must be interpreted to forbid city officials purposefully to select the inadequate sound systems or to vary the sound quality or volume based on the message being delivered by performers." Although the majority wishes it were so, the language of the Guidelines simply does not support such a limitation on the city's discretion. Alternatively, the majority finds a limitation in the city's practice of deferring to the sponsor with respect to sound mix, and of conferring "with the sponsor if any questions of excessive sound arise, before taking any corrective action." A promise to consult, however, does not provide the detailed "neutral criteria" necessary to prevent future abuses of discretion any more than did the city's promise in *Lakewood* to deny permit applications only for reasons related to the health, safety, or welfare of Lakewood citizens. Indeed, a presumption that city officials will act in good faith and adhere to standards absent from a regulation's face is "the very presumption that the doctrine forbidding unbridled discretion disallows."

Second, even if there were narrowly drawn guidelines limiting the city's discretion, the Guidelines would be fundamentally flawed. For the requirement that there be detailed standards is of value only so far as there is a judicial mechanism to enforce them. Here, that necessary safeguard is absent. The city's sound technician consults with the performers for several minutes before the performance and then decides how to present each song or piece of music. During the performance itself, the technician makes hundreds of decisions affecting the mix of volume of sound. The music is played immediately after each decision. There is, of course, no time for appeal in the middle of a song. As a result, no court ever determines that a particular restraint on speech is necessary. The city's admission that it does not impose sanctions on violations of its general sound ordinance because the necessary litigation is too costly and time consuming only underscores its contempt for the need for judicial review of restrictions on speech. With neither prompt judicial review nor detailed and neutral standards fettering the city's discretion to restrict protected speech, the Guidelines constitute a quintessential, and unconstitutional, prior restraint.

Today's decision has significance far beyond the world of rock music. Government no longer need balance the effectiveness of regulation with the burdens on free speech. After today, government need only assert that it is most effective to control speech in advance of its expression. Because such a result eviscerates the First Amendment,

I dissent.

**CONSOLIDATED EDISON COMPANY OF NEW YORK, INC. v.
PUBLIC SERVICE COMMISSION OF NEW YORK
447 U.S. 530; 65 L. Ed. 2d 319; 100 S. Ct. 2326 (1980)**

JUSTICE POWELL *delivered the opinion of the Court.*

The question in this case is whether the First Amendment, as incorporated by the Fourteenth Amendment, is violated by an order of the Public Service Commission of the State of New York that prohibits the inclusion in monthly electric bills of inserts discussing controversial issues of public policy.

The Consolidated Edison Company of New York, appellant in this case, placed written material entitled "Independence Is Still a Goal, and Nuclear Power Is Needed to Win the Battle" in its January 1976 billing envelope. The bill insert stated Consolidated Edison's views on "the benefits of nuclear power," saying that they "far outweigh any potential risk" and that nuclear power plants are safe, economical, and clean. . . . The utility also contended that increased use of nuclear energy would further this country's independence from foreign energy sources.

In March 1976, the Natural Resources Defense Council, Inc. (NRDC) requested Consolidated Edison to enclose a rebuttal prepared by NRDC in its next billing envelope. . . . When Consolidated Edison refused, NRDC asked the Public Service Commission of the State of New York to open Consolidated Edison's billing envelopes to contrasting views on controversial issues of public importance. . . .

On February 17, 1977, the Commission, appellee here, denied NRDC's request, but prohibited "utilities from using bill inserts to discuss political matters, including the desirability of future development of nuclear power." . . . The Commission explained its decision in a Statement of Policy on Advertising and Promotion Practices of Public Utilities issued on February 25, 1977. The

Commission concluded that Consolidated Edison customers who receive bills containing inserts are a captive audience of diverse views who should not be subjected to the utility's beliefs. Accordingly, the Commission barred utility companies from including bill inserts that express "their opinions or viewpoints on controversial issues of public policy." . . . The Commission did not, however, bar utilities from sending bill inserts discussing topics that are not "controversial issues of public policy." The Commissioner later denied petitions for rehearing filed by Consolidated Edison and other utilities. . . .

Consolidated Edison sought review of the Commission's order in the New York state courts. The State Supreme Court, Special Term, held the order unconstitutional . . . but the State Supreme Court, Appellate Division, reversed . . . (1978), . . . and the New York Court of Appeals affirmed that judgment . . . (1979). The Court of Appeals held that the order did not violate the Constitution because it was a valid time, place, and manner regulation designed to protect the privacy of Consolidated Edison's customers. . . . We noted probable jurisdiction. . .(1979). We reverse. . . .

The restriction on bill inserts cannot be upheld on the ground that Consolidated Edison is not entitled to freedom of speech. In *First National Bank of Boston* v. *Bellotti,* . . . (1978), we rejected the contention that a State may confine corporate speech to specified issues. That decision recognized that "[t]he inherent worth of the speech in terms of its capacity for informing the public does not depend upon the identity of its source, whether corporation, association, union, or individual." . . . Because the state action limited protected speech, we concluded that the regulation could not stand absent a showing of a compelling state interest. . . .

The First and Fourteenth Amendments guarantee that no State shall "abridg[e] the freedom of speech." See *Joseph Burstyn, Inc.* v. *Wilson* . . . (1952). Freedom of speech is "indispensable to the discovery and spread of political truth." *Whitney* v. *California*. . .(1927)(Brandeis, J., concurring), and "the best test of truth is the power of the thought to get itself accepted in the competition of the market . . ." *Abrams* v. *United States* . . . (1919)(Holmes, J., dissenting). The First and Fourteenth Amendments remove "governmental restraints from the arena of public discussion, putting the decision as to what views shall be voiced largely into the hands of each of us, in the hope that use of such freedom will ultimately produce a more capable citizenry and more perfect polity . . ." *Cohen* v. *California* . . . (1971).

The Court has emphasized that the First Amendment "embraces at the least the liberty to discuss publicly and truthfully all matters of public concern . . ." *Thornhill* v. *Alabama* . . . (1940). . . . In the mailing that triggered the regulation at issue, Consolidated Edison advocated the use of nuclear power. The Commission has limited the means by which Consolidated Edison may participate in the public debate on this question and other controversial issues of national interest and importance. Thus, the Commission's prohibition of discussion of controversial issues strikes at the heart of the freedom to speak. . . .

The Commission's ban on bill inserts is not, of course, invalid merely because it imposes a limitation upon speech. . . . We must consider whether the State can demonstrate that its regulation is constitutionally permissible. The Commission's arguments require us to consider three theories that might justify the state action. We must determine whether the prohibition is (i) a reasonable time, place or manner restriction, (ii) a permissible subject-matter regulation, or (iii) a narrowly tailored means of serving a compelling state interest.

This Court has recognized the validity of reasonable time, place, or manner regulations that serve a significant governmental interest and leave ample alternative channels for communication. . . . In *Cox* v. *New Hampshire* . . . (1941) this Court upheld a licensing requirement for parades through city streets. The Court recognized that the regulation, which was based on time, place or manner criteria, served the municipality's legitimate interests in regulating traffic, securing public order, and ensuring that simultaneous parades did not prevent all speakers from being heard. . . . Similarly, in *Grayned* v. *Rockford* . . . (1972), we upheld an antinoise regulation prohibiting demonstrations that would disturb the good order of an educational facility. The narrowly drawn restriction constitutionally advanced the city's interest "in having an undisrupted school session conducive to students' learning. . . ." . . . Thus, the essence of time, place, or manner regulation lies in the recognition that various methods of speech, regardless of their content, may frustrate legitimate governmental goals. No matter what its message, a roving sound truck that blares at 2 A.M. disturbs neighborhood tranquility.

A restriction that regulates only the time, place or manner of speech may be imposed so long as it's reasonable. But when regulation is based on the content of speech, governmental action must be scrutinized more carefully to ensure that communication has not been prohibited "merely because public officials disapprove the speaker's views." *Niemotko* v. *Maryland* . . . (1951)(Frankfurter, J., concurring in the result). As a consequence, we have emphasized that time, place, and manner regulations must be "applicable to all speech irrespective of content." *Erznoznick* v. *City of Jacksonville* . . . (1975). . . . Governmental action that regulates speech on the basis of its subject matter "slip[s] from the neutrality of time, place, and circumstance into a concern about content." . . . Therefore, a constitutionally permissible time, place, or manner restriction may not be based upon either the content or subject matter of speech.

The Commission does not pretend that its action is unrelated to the content or subject matter of bill inserts. Indeed, it has undertaken to suppress certain bill inserts precisely because they address controversial issues of public policy. The Commission allows inserts that present information to consumers on certain subjects, such as energy conservation measures, but it forbids the use of inserts that discuss public controversies. The Commission, with commendable candor, justifies its ban on the ground that consumers will benefit from receiving "useful" information, but not from the prohibited information. . . . The Commission's own rationale demonstrates that its action cannot be upheld as a content-neutral time, place, or manner regulation.

The Commission next argues that its order is acceptable because it applies to all discussion of nuclear power, whether pro or con, in bill inserts. The prohibition, the Commission contends, is related to subject matter rather than to the views of a particular speaker. Because the regulation does not favor either side of a political controversy, the Commission asserts that it does not unconstitutionally suppress freedom of speech.

The First Amendment's hostility to content-based regulation extends not only to restrictions on particular viewpoints, but also to prohibition of public discussion of an entire topic. As a general matter "the First Amendment means that the government has no power to restrict expression because of its message, its ideas, its subject matter, or its content." *Police Department* v. *Mosley* . . . (1972). . . . In *Mosley*, we held that a municipality could not exempt labor picketing from a general prohibition on picketing at a school even though the ban would have reached both pro- and anti-union demonstrations. If the marketplace of ideas is to remain free and open, governments must not be allowed to choose "which issues are worth discussing or debating. . . ." . . . To allow a government the choice of permissible subjects for public debate would be to allow that government control over the search for political truth.

Nevertheless, governmental regulation based on subject matter has been approved in narrow circumstances. The court below relied upon two cases in which this Court has recognized that the government may bar from its facilities certain speech that would disrupt the legitimate governmental purpose for which the property has been dedicated. . . . In *Greer* v. *Spock* . . . (1976), we held that the Federal Government could prohibit partisan political speech on a military base even though civilian speakers had been allowed to lecture on other subjects. . . . In *Lehman* v. *Shaker Heights* . . . (1974) (opinion of Blackmun, J.), a plurality of the Court similarly concluded that a city transit system that rented space in its vehicles for commercial advertising did not have to accept partisan political advertising. The municipality's refusal to accept political advertising was based upon fears that partisan advertisements might jeopardize long-term commercial revenue, that commuters would be subjected to political propaganda, and that acceptance of particular political advertisements might lead to charges of favoritism. . . .

Greer and *Lehman* properly are viewed as narrow exceptions of the general prohibition against subject-matter distinctions. In both cases, the Court was asked to decide whether a public facility was open to all speakers. The plurality in *Lehman* and the Court in *Greer* concluded that partisan political speech would disrupt the operation of governmental facilities even though other forms of speech posed no such danger.

The analysis of *Greer* and *Lehman* is not applicable to the Commission's regulation of bill inserts. In both cases, a private party asserted a right of access to public facilities. Consolidated Edison has not asked to use the offices of the Commission as a forum from which to promulgate its views. Rather, it seeks merely to utilize its own billing envelopes to promulgate its views on controversial issues of public policy. The Commission asserts that the billing envelope, as a necessary adjunct to the operations of a public utility, is subject to the State's plenary control. To be sure, the State has a legitimate regulatory interest in controlling Consolidated Edison's activities, just as local governments always have been able to use their police powers in the public interest to regulate private behavior. . . . But the Commission's attempt to restrict the free expression of a private party cannot be upheld by reliance upon precedent that rests on the special interests of a government in overseeing the use of its property.

Where a government restricts the speech of a private person, the state action may be sustained only if the government can show that the regulation is a precisely drawn means of serving a compelling state interest. . . . The Commission argues finally that its prohibition is necessary (i) to avoid forcing Consolidated Edison's views on a captive audience, (ii) to allocate limited resources to the public interest, and (iii) to ensure that ratepayers do not subsidize the cost of the bill inserts.

The State Court of Appeals largely based its approval of the prohibition upon its conclusion that the bill inserts intruded upon individual privacy. The court stated that the Commission could act to protect the privacy of the utility's customers because they have no choice whether to receive the insert and the views expressed in the insert may inflame their sensibilities. . . . But the Court of Appeals erred in its assessment of the seriousness of the intrusion.

Even if a short exposure to Consolidated Edison's views may offend the sensibilities of some consumers, the ability of government "to shut off discourse solely to protect others from hearing it [is] dependent upon a showing that substantial privacy interests are being invaded in an essentially intolerable manner.". . . A less stringent analysis would permit a government to slight the First Amendment's role "in affording the public access to discussion, debate and the dissemination of information and ideas.". . . Where a single speaker communicates to many listeners, the First Amendment does not permit the government to prohibit speech as intrusive unless the "captive" audience cannot avoid objectional speech.

Passengers on public transportation, . . . or residents of a neighborhood disturbed by the raucous broadcasts from a passing sound-truck . . . may well be unable to escape an unwanted message. But customers who encounter an objectionable billing insert may "effectively avoid further bombardment of their sensibilities simply by averting their eyes." ... The customers of Consolidated Edison may escape exposure to objectionable material simply by transferring the bill insert from envelope to wastebasket.

The Commission contends that because a billing envelope can accommodate only a limited amount of information, political messages should not be allowed to take the place of inserts that promote energy conservation or safety, or that remind consumers of their legal rights. The Commission relies upon *Red Lion Broadcasting* v. *Federal Communications Commission* ... (1969), in which the Court held that the regulation of radio and television broadcast frequencies permit the Federal Government to exercise unusual authority over speech. But billing envelopes differ from broadcast frequencies in two ways. First, a broadcaster communicates through use of a scarce, publicly owned resource. No person can broadcast without a license, whereas all persons are free to send correspondence to private homes through the mails. Thus, it cannot be said that billing envelopes are a limited resource comparable to the broadcast spectrum. Second, the Commission has not shown on the record before us that the presence of the bill inserts at issue would preclude the inclusion of other inserts that Consolidated Edison might be ordered lawfully to include in the billing envelope. Unlike radio or television stations broadcasting on a single frequency, multiple bill inserts will not result in a "cacophony of competing voices." ...

Finally, the Commission urges that its prohibition would prevent ratepayers from subsidizing the costs of policy-oriented bill inserts. But the Commission did not base its order on an inability to allocate costs between the shareholders of Consolidated Edison and the ratepayers. Rather the Commission stated "that using bill inserts to proclaim a utility's viewpoint on controversial issues (*even when the stockholder pays for it in full*) is tantamount to taking advantage of a captive audience ..." (emphasis added). ... Accordingly, there is no basis on this record to assume that the Commission could not exclude the cost of these bill inserts from the utility's rate base. Mere speculation of harm does not constitute a compelling state interest. ... The Commission's suppression of bill inserts that discuss controversial issues of public policy directly infringes the freedom of speech-protected by the First and Fourteenth Amendments. The state action is neither a valid time, place, or manner restriction, nor a permissible subject-matter regulation, nor a narrowly drawn prohibition justified by a compelling state interest. Accordingly, the regulation is invalid. ...

The decision of the New York Court of Appeals is
Reversed.

JUSTICE MARSHALL, *concurring.*

I join the Court's opinion. I write separately to emphasize that our decision today in no way addresses the question whether the Commission may exclude the costs of bill inserts from the rate base, nor does it intimate any view on the appropriateness of any allocation of such costs the Commission might choose to make. ... The Commission did not rely on the argument that the use of bill inserts required ratepayers to subsidize the dissemination of management's view in issuing its order, and we therefore are precluded from sustaining the order on that ground. ... ("[A]n administrative order cannot be upheld unless the grounds upon which the agency acted in exercising its powers were those upon which its action can be sustained.") ...

JUSTICE STEVENS, *concurring in the judgment.*

Any student of history who has been reprimanded for talking about the World Series during a class discussion of the First Amendment knows that it is incorrect to state that a "time, place, or manner restriction may not be based upon either the content or subject matter of speech." ... And every lawyer who has read our Rules, or our cases upholding various restrictions on speech with specific reference to subject matter must recognize the hyperbole in the dictum, "But, above all else, the First Amendment means that Government has no power to restrict expression because of its message, its ideas, its subject matter or its content." ... Indeed, if that were the law, there would be no need for the Court's detailed rejection of the justifications put forward by the State for the restriction involved in this case. ...

There are, in fact, many situations in which the subject matter, or indeed, even the point of view of the speaker, may provide a justification for a time, place and manner regulation. Perhaps the most obvious example is the regulation of oral argument in this Court; the appellant's lawyer precedes his adversary solely because he seeks reversal of a judgment. As is true of many other aspects of liberty, some forms of orderly regulation actually promote freedom more than would a state of total anarchy.

Instead of trying to justify our conclusion by reasoning from honey-combed premises, I prefer to identify the basis of decision in more simple terms. . . . A regulation of speech that is motivated by nothing more than a desire to curtail expression of a particular point of view on controversial issues of general interest is the purest example of a "law abridging the freedom of speech, or of the press." A regulation that denies one group of persons the right to address a selected audience on "controversial issues of public policy" is plainly such a regulation.

The only justification for the regulation relied on by the New York Court of Appeals is that the utilities' bill inserts may be "offensive" to some of their customers. But a communication may be offensive in two different ways. Independently of the message the speaker intends to convey, the form of his communication may be offensive—perhaps because it is too loud or too ugly in a particular setting. Other speeches, even though elegantly phrased in dulcet tones, are offensive simply because the listener disagrees with the speaker's message. The fact that the offensive form of some communication may subject it to appropriate regulation surely does not support the conclusion that the offensive character of an idea can justify an attempt to censor its expression. Since the Public Service Commission has candidly put forward this impermissible justification for its censorial regulation, it plainly violates the First Amendment.

Accordingly, I concur in the judgment of the Court.

JUSTICE BLACKMUN, *with whom* JUSTICE REHNQUIST *as to Parts I and II joins, dissenting.*

My dissent in this case in no way indicates any disapprobation on my part of the previous rights of free speech (so carefully catalogued by the Court in its opinion) that are protected by the First and Fourteenth Amendments against repression by the State. My prior writings for the Court in the speech area prove conclusively my sensitivity about these rights and my concern for them. . . .

But I cannot agree with the Court that the New York Public Service Commission's ban on the utility bill insert somehow deprives the utility of its First and Fourteenth Amendment rights. Because of Consolidated Edison's monopoly status and its rate structure, the use of the insert amounts to an exaction from the utility's customers by way of forced aid for the utility's speech. And, contrary to the Court's suggestion, an allocation of the insert's cost between the utility's shareholders and the ratepayers would not eliminate this coerced subsidy. . . .

Although monopolies generally are against the public policies of the United States and of the State of New York, Consolidated Edison and other utilities are permitted to operate as monopolies because of a determination by the State that the public interest is better served by protecting them from competition. . . .

This exceptional grant of power to private enterprises justifies extensive oversight on the part of the State to protect the ratepayers from exploitation of the monopoly power through excessive rates and other forms of overreaching. For this reason, the State regulates the rates that utilities may charge. . . . In addition, New York law gives its Public Service Commission plenary supervisory powers over all property, real and personal, "used or to be used for or in connection with or to facilitate the . . . sale or furnishing of electricity for light, heat or power." . . . State law explicitly gives the Commission control over the format of the utility bill and any material included in the envelope with the bill. . . .

The rates authorized by the Public Service Commission may reflect only the costs of providing necessary services to customers plus a reasonable rate of return to the utility's shareholders. . . . The entire bill payment system—meters, meter-reading, bill mailings, and bill inserts—are paid for by the customers under Commission rules permitting recovery of necessary operating expenses. . . . Under the laws of New York and other states, however, a public utility cannot include in the rate base the costs of political advertising and lobbying. . . . These costs cannot be passed on to consumers because ratepayers derive no service-related benefits from political advertisements. The purpose of such advertising and lobbying is to benefit the utility's shareholders, and its cost must be deducted from profits otherwise available for the shareholders. The Federal Energy Regulatory Commission, formerly the Federal Power Commission, has adopted this rule as well.

The Commission concluded, properly in my view, that use of the billing envelope to distribute management's pamphlets amounts to a forced subsidy of the utility's speech by the ratepayers. Consolidated Edison would counter this argument by pointing out that it is willing to allocate to shareholders the *additional* costs attributable to the inserts. It maintains: "The fact that the utilities may incidentally save money by the use of bill inserts, at no expense to the ratepayers, is not detrimental to the ratepayers or the public.". . .

I do not accept appellant's argument that preventing a "free ride" for the utility's message, is not a substantial, legitimate state concern. Even though the free ride may cost the ratepayers nothing additional by way of specific dollars, it still qualifies as forced support of the utility's speech. . . . If the State compelled an individual to help defray the utility's speech expenses, that compulsion surely would violate that person's First and Fourteenth Amendment rights. . . . The fact that providing such aid costs the individual nothing extra does not make the compulsion any less offensive. See *Wooley* v. *Maynard* . . . (1977). . . .

Of course, a private business does not deprive an individual of his constitutional rights unless state action is involved. Although the State has given utilities their monopoly power and thus contributed to a situation in which coerced support of the utility's speech is possible, the state action requirement of the Fourteenth Amendment may not be met in this situation. . . .

I do find it necessary, however, to decide whether state action in the Fourteenth Amendment sense has occurred here. It is not necessary to decide whether the ratepayers' First and Fourteenth Amendment rights have been infringed in order to determine whether the State

has the power to prevent the utility from exacting aid from the ratepayers in dissemination of a message with which they do not all agree. Even if the State is not so entwined in the activities of Consolidated Edison to meet the state action requirement, the State has made a monopoly possible by preventing others from competing with the utility. Thus the State is legitimately concerned with preventing the utility from taking advantage of this monopoly power to force consumers to subsidize dissemination of its viewpoint on political issues. . . .

The Commission's ban on bill inserts does not restrict the utility from using the shareholders' resources to finance communication of its viewpoints on any topic. Consolidated Edison is completely free to use the mails and any other medium of communication on the same basis as any other speaker. The order merely prevents the utility from relying on a forced subsidy from the ratepayers. This leads me to conclude that the State's attempt here to protect the ratepayers from unwillingly financing the utility's speech and to preserve the billing envelope for the sole benefit of the customers who pay for it does not infringe upon the First and Fourteenth Amendment rights of the utility.

FRISBY v. SCHULTZ
487 U.S. 474; 108 S. Ct.; 101 L. Ed. 420 (1988)

O'CONNOR, J., *delivered the opinion of the Court, in which* REHNQUIST, C. J., *and* BLACKMUN, SCALIA, *and* KENNEDY, JJ., *joined.* WHITE, J., *filed an opinion concurring in the judgment,* BRENNAN, J., *filed a dissenting opinion, in which* MARSHALL, J., *joined.* STEVENS, J., *filed a dissenting opinion.*

JUSTICE O'CONNOR *delivered the opinion of the Court.*

Brookfield, Wisconsin, has adopted an ordinance that completely bans picketing "before or about" any residence. This case presents a facial First Amendment challenge to that ordinance.

I

Brookfield, Wisconsin, is a residential suburb of Milwaukee with a population of approximately 4,300. The appellees, Sandra C. Schultz and Robert C. Braun, are individuals strongly opposed to abor-

tion and wish to express their views on the subject by picketing on a public street outside the Brookfield residence of a doctor who apparently performs abortions at two clinics in neighboring towns. Appellees and others engaged in precisely that activity, assembling outside the doctor's home on at least six occasions between April 20, 1985, and May 20, 1985, for periods ranging from one to one and a half hours. The size of the group varied from 11 to more than 40. The picketing was generally orderly and peaceful; the town never had occasion to invoke any of its various ordinances prohibiting obstruction of the streets, loud and unnecessary noises, or disorderly conduct. Nonetheless, the picketing generated substantial controversy and numerous complaints.

The Town Board therefore resolved to enact an ordinance to restrict the picketing. On May 7, 1985, the town passed an ordinance that prohibited all picketing in residential neighborhoods except for labor picketing. But after reviewing this

Court's decision in *Carey* v. *Brown* (1980), which invalidated a similar ordinance as a violation of the Equal Protection Clause, the town attorney instructed the police not to enforce the new ordinance and advised the Town Board that the ordinance's labor picketing exception likely rendered it unconstitutional. This ordinance was repealed on May 15, 1985, and replaced with the following flat ban on all residential picketing:

> It is unlawful for any person to engage in picketing before or about the residence or dwelling of any individual in the Town of Brookfield.

The ordinance itself recites the primary purpose of this ban: "the protection and preservation of the home" through assurance "that members of the community enjoy in their homes and dwellings a feeling of well-being, tranquility, and privacy." The Town Board believed that a ban was necessary because it determined that "the practice of picketing before or about residences and dwellings causes emotional disturbance and distress to the occupants . . ." [and] "has as its object the harassing of such occupants." The ordinance also evinces a concern for public safety, noting that picketing obstructs and interferes with "the free use of public sidewalks and public ways of travel."

On May 18, 1985, appellees were informed by the town attorney that enforcement of the new, revised ordinance would begin on May 21, 1985. Faced with this threat of arrest and prosecution, appellees ceased picketing in Brookfield and filed this lawsuit in the United States District Court for the Eastern District of Wisconsin. The complaint sought declaratory as well as preliminary and permanent injunctive relief on the grounds that the ordinance violated the First Amendment. . . .

The District Court granted appellees' motion for a preliminary injunction. The court concluded that the ordinance was not narrowly tailored enough to restrict protected speech in a public forum. . . .

A divided panel of the United States Court of Appeals for the Seventh Circuit affirmed. (1986). The Court of Appeals subsequently vacated this decision, however, and ordered a rehearing en banc. (1987). After rehearing, the Court of Appeals affirmed the judgment of the District Court by an equally divided vote. . . .

II

The antipicketing ordinance operates at the core of the First Amendment by prohibiting appellees from engaging in picketing on an issue of public concern. Because of the importance of "uninhibited, robust, and wide-open" debate on public issues, *New York Times Co.* v. *Sullivan,* (1964), we have traditionally subjected restrictions on public issue picketing to careful scrutiny. Of course, "[e]ven protected speech is not equally permissible in all places and at all times." *Cornelius* v. *NAACP Legal Defense & Educational Fund, Inc.,* (1985).

To ascertain what limits, if any, may be placed on protected speech, we have often focused on the "place" of that speech, considering the nature of the forum the speaker seeks to employ. Our cases have recognized that the standards by which limitations on speech must be evaluated "differ depending on the character of the property at issue." *Perry Education Assn.* v. *Perry Local Educators' Assn.,* (1983). Specifically, we have identified three types of fora: "the traditional public forum, the public forum created by government designation, and the nonpublic forum."

The relevant forum here may be easily identified: appellees wish to picket on the public streets of Brookfield. Ordinarily, a determination of the nature of the forum would follow automatically from this identification; we have repeatedly referred to public streets as the archetype of a traditional public forum. "[T]ime out of mind" public streets and sidewalks have been used for public assembly and debate, the hallmarks of a traditional public forum. Appellants, however, urge us to disregard these "clichés." They argue that the streets of Brookfield should be considered a nonpublic forum. Pointing to the physical narrowness of Brookfield's streets as well as to their residential character, appellants contend that such streets have not by tradition or designation been held open for public communication.

We reject this suggestion. Our prior holdings make clear that a public street does not lose its status as a traditional public forum simply because it runs through a residential neighborhood. In *Carey* v. *Brown*—which considered a statute similar to the one at issue here, ultimately striking it down as a violation of the Equal Protection Clause because it included an exception for labor picketing—we expressly recognized that "public streets and sidewalks in residential neighborhoods," were "public for[a]." This rather ready identification virtually forecloses appellants' argument.

In short, our decisions identifying public streets and sidewalks as traditional public fora are not accidental invocations of a "cliché," but recognition that "[w]herever the title of streets and parks may rest, they have immemorially been held in trust for the use of the public." No particularized inquiry into the precise nature of a specific street is necessary; all public streets are held in the public trust and are properly considered traditional public fora. Accordingly, the streets of Brookfield are traditional public fora. The residential character of those streets may well inform the application of the relevant test, but it does not lead to a different test; the antipicketing ordinance must be judged against the stringent standards we have established for restrictions on speech in traditional public fora:

> In these quintessential public for[a], the government may not prohibit all communicative activity. For the State to enforce a content-based exclusion it must show that its regulation is necessary to serve a compelling state interest and that it is narrowly drawn to achieve that end. . . . The State may also enforce regulations of the time, place, and manner of expression which are content-neutral, are narrowly tailored to serve a significant government interest, and leave open ample alternative channels of communication. *Perry.*

As *Perry* makes clear, the appropriate level of scrutiny is initially tied to whether the statute distinguishes between prohibited and permitted speech on the basis of content. Appellees argue that despite its facial content-neutrality, the Brookfield ordinance must be read as containing an implied exception for labor picketing. The basis for appellees' argument is their belief that an express protection of peaceful labor picketing in state law must take precedence over Brookfield's contrary efforts. The District Court, however, rejected this suggested interpretation of state law, and the Court of Appeals affirmed, albeit ultimately by an equally divided court. Following our normal practice, "we defer to the construction of a state statute given it by the lower federal courts . . . to reflect our belief that district courts and courts of appeals are better schooled in and more able to interpret the laws of their respective States." . . . Thus, we accept the lower courts' conclusion that the Brookfield ordinance is content-neutral. Accordingly, we turn to consider whether the ordinance is "narrowly tailored to serve a significant government interest" and whether it "leave[s] open ample alternative channels of communication."

Because the last question is so easily answered, we address it first. Of course, before we are able to assess the available alternatives, we must consider more carefully the reach of the ordinance. The precise scope of the ban is not further described within the text of the ordinance, but in our view the ordinance is readily subject to a narrowing construction that avoids constitutional difficulties. Specifically, the use of the singular form of the words "residence" and "dwelling" suggests that the ordinance is intended to prohibit only picketing focused on, and taking place in front of, a particular residence.

. . . Accordingly, we construe the ban to be a limited one; only focused picketing taking place solely in front of a particular residence is prohibited.

So narrowed, the ordinance permits the more general dissemination of a message. As appellants explain, the limited nature of the prohibition makes it virtually self-evident that ample alternatives remain:

> Protestors have not been barred from the residential neighborhoods, alone or in groups, even marching. . . . They may go door-to-door to proselytize their views. They may distribute literature in this manner . . . or through the mails. They may contact residents by telephone, short of harassment.

We readily agree that the ordinance preserves ample alternative channel of communication and thus move on to inquire whether the ordinance serves a significant government interest. We find that such an interest is identified within the text of the ordinance itself: the protection of residential privacy.

"The State's interest in protecting the well-being, tranquility, and privacy of the home is certainly of the highest order in a free and civilized society." *Carey* v. *Brown.* Our prior decisions have often remarked on the unique nature of the home, "the last citadel of the tired, the weary, and the sick," and have recognized that "[p]reserving the sanctity of the home, the one retreat to which men and women can repair to escape from the tribulations of their daily pursuits, is surely an important value."

One important aspect of residential privacy is protection of the unwilling listener. Although in many locations, we expect individuals simply to avoid speech they do not want to hear, the home is different. "That we are often 'captives' outside the sanctuary of the home and subject to objectionable speech . . . does not mean we must be captive everywhere." Instead, a special benefit of the privacy all citizens enjoy within their own walls, which the State may legislate to protect, is an ability to avoid intrusions. Thus, we have repeatedly held that individuals are not required to welcome unwanted speech into their own homes and that the government may protect this freedom.

This principle is reflected even in prior decisions in which we have invalidated complete bans on expressive activity, including bans operating in residential areas. . . . There simply is no right to force speech into the home of an unwilling listener.

It remains to be considered, however, whether the Brookfield ordinance is narrowly tailored to protect only unwilling recipients of the communications. A statute is narrowly tailored if it targets and eliminates no more than the exact source of the "evil" it seeks to remedy. A complete ban can be narrowly tailored, but only if each activity within the proscription's scope is an appropriately targeted evil. . . .

The type of focused picketing prohibited by the Brookfield ordinance is fundamentally different from more generally directed means of communication that may not be completely banned in residential areas. . . . Here, in contrast, the picketing is narrowly directed at the household, not the public. The type of picketers banned by the Brookfield ordinance generally do not seek to disseminate a message to the general public, but to intrude upon the targeted resident, and to do so in an especially offensive way. Moreover, even if some such picketers have a broader communicative purpose, their activity nonetheless inherently and offensively intrudes on residential privacy. . . .

In this case, for example, appellees subjected the doctor and his family to the presence of a relatively large group of protesters on their doorstep in an attempt to force the doctor to cease performing abortions. But the actual size of the group is irrelevant; even a solitary picket can invade residential privacy. . . .

The First Amendment permits the government to prohibit offensive speech as intrusive when the "captive" audience cannot avoid the objectionable speech. The target of the focused picketing banned by the Brookfield ordinance is just such a "captive." The resident is figuratively and perhaps literally trapped within the home, and because of the unique and subtle impact of such picketing is left with no ready means of avoiding the unwanted speech. Thus, the "evil" of targeted residential picketing, "the very presence of an unwelcome visitor at the home," is "created by the medium of expression itself." Accordingly, the Brookfield ordinance's complete ban of that particular medium of expression is narrowly tailored.

Of course, this case presents only a facial challenge to the ordinance. Particular hypothetical applications of the ordinance—to, for example, a particular resident's use of his or her home as a place of business or public meeting, or to picketers present at a particular home by invitation of the resident—may present somewhat different questions. Initially, the ordinance by its own terms may not apply in such circumstances, since the ordinance's goal is the protection of residential privacy, and since it speaks only of a "residence or dwelling," not a place of business. Moreover, since our First Amendment analysis is grounded in protection of the unwilling residential listener, the constitutionality of applying the ordinance to such hypotheticals remains open to question. These are, however, questions we need not address today in order to dispose of appellees' facial challenge.

Because picketing prohibited by the Brookfield ordinance is speech directed primarily at those who are presumptively unwilling to receive it, the State has a substantial and justifiable interest in banning it. The nature and scope of this interest make the ban narrowly tailored. The ordinance also leaves open ample alternative channels of communication and is content-neutral. Thus, largely because of its narrow scope, the facial challenge to the ordinance must fail. The contrary judgment of the Court of Appeals is

Reversed.

[The concurring opinion of JUSTICE WHITE is omitted.]

JUSTICE BRENNAN, *with whom* JUSTICE MARSHALL *joins, dissenting.*

The Court today sets out the appropriate legal tests and standards governing the question presented, and proceeds to apply most of them correctly. Regrettably, though, the Court errs in the final step of its analysis, and approves an ordinance banning significantly more speech than is necessary to achieve the government's substantial and legitimate goal. Accordingly, I must dissent.

The ordinance before us absolutely prohibits picketing "before or about" any residence in the town of Brookfield, thereby restricting a manner of speech in a traditional public forum. Consequently, as the Court correctly states, the ordinance is subject to the well-settled time, place, and manner test: the restriction must be content and viewpoint neutral, leave open ample alternative channels of communication, and be narrowly tailored to further a substantial governmental interest.

Assuming one construes an ordinance as the Court does, I agree that the regulation reserves ample alternative channels of communication. I also agree with the Court that the town has a substantial interest in protecting its residents' right to be left alone in their homes. It is, however, critical to specify the precise scope of this interest. The mere fact that speech takes place in a residential neighborhood does not automatically implicate a residential privacy interest. It is the intrusion of speech into the home or the unduly coercive nature of a particular manner of speech around the home that is subject to more exacting regulation. . . . Similarly, the government may prohibit unduly coercive conduct around the home, even though it involves expressive elements. A crowd of protesters need not be permitted virtually to imprison a person in his or her own house merely because they shout slogans or carry signs. But so long as the speech remains outside the home and does not unduly coerce the occupant, the government's heightened interest in protecting residential privacy is not implicated.

The foregoing distinction is crucial here because it directly affects the last prong of the time, place, and manner test: whether the ordinance is narrowly tailored to achieve the governmental interest. . . .

Without question there are many aspects of residential picketing that, if unregulated, might easily become intrusive or unduly coercive. Indeed, some of these aspects are illustrated by this very case. As the District Court found, before the ordinance took effect up to 40 sign-carrying, slogan-shouting protesters regularly converged on Dr. Victoria's home and, in addition to protesting, warned young children not to go near the house because Dr. Victoria was a "baby killer." Further, the throng repeatedly trespassed onto the Victoria property and at least once blocked the exits to their home. Surely it is within the government's power to enact regulations as necessary to prevent such intrusive and coercive abuses. Thus, for example, the government could constitutionally regulate the number of residential picketers, the hours during which a residential picket may take place, or the noise level of such a picket. In short, substantial regulation is permitted to neutralize the intrusive or unduly coercive aspects of picketing around the home. But to say picketing may be substantially regulated is not to say that it may be prohibited in its entirety. Once size, time, volume, and the like have been controlled to ensure that the picket is no longer intrusive or coercive, only the speech itself remains, conveyed perhaps by a lone, silent individual, walking back and forth with a sign. Such speech, which no longer implicates the heightened governmental interest in residential privacy, is nevertheless banned by the Brook-field law. Therefore, the ordinance is not narrowly tailored. . . .

A valid time, place, or manner law neutrally regulates speech only to the extent necessary to achieve a substantial governmental interest, and no further. Because the Court is unwilling to examine the Brookfield ordinance in light of the precise governmental interest at issue, it condones a law that suppresses substantially more speech than is necessary. I dissent.

JUSTICE STEVENS, *dissenting.*

"GET WELL CHARLIE—OUR TEAM NEEDS YOU."

In Brookfield, Wisconsin, it is unlawful for a fifth grader to carry such a sign in front of a residence for the period of time necessary to convey its friendly message to its intended audience.

The Court's analysis of the question whether Brookfield's ban on picketing is constitutional begins with an acknowledgment that the ordinance "operates at the core of the First Amendment," and that the streets of Brookfield are a "traditional public forum." It concludes, however, that the total ban on residential picketing is "narrowly tailored" to protect "only unwilling recipients of the communications." The plain language of the ordinance, however, applies to communications to willing and indifferent recipients as well as to the unwilling. . . .

Two characteristics of picketing—and of speech more generally—make this a difficult case. First, it is so important to recognize that, "[l]ike so many other kinds of expression, picketing is a mixture of conduct and communication." If we put the speech element to one side, I should think it perfectly clear that the town could prohibit pedestrians from loitering in front of a residence. On the other hand, it seems equally clear that a sign carrier has a right to march past a residence—and presumably pause long enough to read his or her message—regardless of whether the reader agrees, disagrees, or is simply indifferent to the point of view being expressed.

Second, it bears emphasis that:

[A] communication may be offensive in two different ways. Independently of the message the speaker intends to convey, the form of his communication may be offensive—perhaps because it is too loud or too ugly in a particular setting. Other speeches, even though elegantly phrased in dulcet tones, are offensive simply because the listener disagrees with the speaker's message. *Consolidated Edison Co.* v. *Public Service Comm'n of New York.*

Picketing is a form of speech that, by virtue of its repetition of message and often hostile repetition of message and often hostile presentation, may be disruptive of an environment irrespective of the substantial message conveyed.

The picketing that gave rise to the ordinance enacted in this case was obviously intended to do more than convey a message of opposition to the character of the doctor's practice; it was intended to cause him and his family substantial psychological distress. As the record reveals, the picketer's message was repeatedly redelivered by a relatively large group—in essence, increasing the volume and intrusiveness of the same message with each repeated assertion. As is often the function of picketing, during the periods of protest the doctor's home was held under a virtual siege. I do not believe that picketing for the sole purpose of imposing psychological harm on a family in the shelter of their home is constitutionally protected. I do believe, however, that the picketers have a right to communicate their opposition to abortion to the doctor, but after they have had a fair opportunity to communicate that message, I see little justification for allowing them to remain in front of his home and repeat it over and over again simply to harm the doctor and his family. Thus, I agree that the ordinance may be constitutionally applied to the kind of picketing that gave rise to its enactment.

On the other hand, the ordinance is unquestionably "overbroad" in that it prohibits some communication that is protected by the First Amendment. The question, then, is whether to apply the overbreadth doctrine's "strong medicine," or to put that approach aside "and await further developments.". . .

In this case the overbreadth is unquestionably "real." Whether or not it is "substantial" in relation to the "plainly legitimate sweep" of the ordinance is a more difficult question. My hunch is that the town will probably not enforce its ban against friendly, innocuous, or even brief unfriendly picketing, and that the Court may be right in concluding that its legitimate sweep makes its overbreadth insubstantial. But there are two countervailing considerations that are persuasive to me. The scope of the ordinance gives the town officials far too much discretion in making enforcement decisions; while we sit by and await further developments, potential picketers must act at their peril. Second, it is a simple matter for the town to amend its ordinance and to limit the ban to conduct that unreasonably interferes with the privacy of the home and does not serve a reasonable communicative purpose.

Accordingly, I respectfully dissent.

Picketing and Handbilling: From Public Places to Private Property

---

FEATURED CASE

PruneYard Shopping Center v. *Robins*

When Alabama banned all peaceful picketing regardless of purpose, the Supreme Court declared the law unconstitutional as an invasion of freedom of speech. The statute swept too broadly. Speaking for the Court in *Thornhill* v. *Alabama* (310 U.S. 88, 1940), Justice Frank Murphy contended:

The freedom of speech and of the press guaranteed by the Constitution embraces at the least the liberty to discuss publicly and truthfully all matters of public concern without previous restraint or fear of subsequent punishment. . . . Freedom of discussion, if it would fulfill its historic function in this nation, must embrace all issues about which information is needed or appropriate to enable the members of society to cope with the exigencies of their period.

In the circumstances of our times the dissemination of information concerning the facts of a labor dispute must be regarded as within that area of free discussion that is guaranteed by the Constitution. . . .

Thornhill recognizes that the Constitution may protect more than "pure speech"; in some instances it may protect "speech plus," e.g., peaceful picketing and demonstrations—which might be used as ways of expression or petition to more effectively and dramatically express and communicate an idea or point of view. This glowing language of *Thornhill*, however, has since been narrowed in subsequent Court decisions. Thus, even peaceful picketing can be constitutionally enjoined if it prevents the effectuation of valid state policies. (See, e.g., *Hughes* v. *Superior Court of California*, 339 U.S. 460, 1950; and *International Brotherhood of Teamsters* v. *Vogt*, 354 U.S. 284, 1957.) Indeed, picketing, the traditional method used by workers to convey their views to the public, involves more than speech; it involves elements of both speech and conduct. And the Court indicated in *Hughes* and *Vogt* that, due to the intermingling of protected and unprotected elements, picketing can be controlled in ways that pure speech cannot. But in *Amalgamated Food Employees Local 590* v. *Logan Valley Plaza, Inc.* (391 U.S. 308, 1968), Justice Thurgood Marshall rejected the notion that "the nonspeech aspects of peaceful picketing are so great as to render the provisions of the First Amendment inapplicable to it altogether." Here, the Court held that the First Amendment protects peaceful picketing within a privately owned shopping center "because the shopping center serves as the community business block and is freely accessible and open to the people in the area and those passing through."

However, the Burger Court was not as scrupulous in protecting those who distribute handbills on private property. In *Lloyd Corporation* v. *Tanner* (407 U.S. 551, 1972) Justice Byron White, for a closely divided five-to-four Court, upheld the right of a privately owned shopping center, open to the public, to prohibit the distribution of handbills on its property when the handbilling is unrelated to the shopping center's operations. The handbills advertised a meeting to protest the draft and the Vietnam War. The Court distinguished this case from *Logan Valley* by focusing on the "shopping center's operations" language and not on the "community business block" phrase. In a strong defense of private property rights, Justice White reemphasized the basic principle that "the First and Fourteenth Amendments safeguard the rights of free speech and assembly by limitations on state action, not on action by the owner of private property used nondiscriminatorily for private purposes only."

Dissenting, Justice Thurgood Marshall, also speaking for Justices Brennan, Douglas, and Stewart, thought that the majority had strayed from time-honored precedents such as *Marsh* v. *Alabama* (326 U.S. 501, 1946) and *Logan Valley*. In a sharply worded observation, Marshall said:

[O]ne may suspect from reading the opinion of the Court that it is *Logan Valley* itself that the Court finds bothersome. The vote in *Logan Valley* was 6–3, and that decision is only four years old. But I am aware that the composition of the Court has radically changed in four years. The fact remains that *Logan Valley* is binding unless it is overruled. There is no valid distinction between that case and this one. . . .

Noting the increasing reliance of governments on private enterprise, Marshall warned that "only the wealthy may find effective communication possible unless we adhere to *Marsh* v. *Alabama* and continue to hold that '[t]he more an owner, for his advantage, opens up his property for use by the public in general the more do his rights become circumscribed by the statutory and constitutional rights of those who use it.' "

By 1976, however, Justice Stewart apparently had changed from his position in *Tanner*. In *Hudgens* v. *National Labor Relations Board* (424 U.S. 507, 1976), Stewart was joined by the four Nixon appointees and spoke for the majority in upholding the private property rights of a shopping center owner against the First Amendment claims of workers who were picketing one of the resident stores of the shopping mall. "[W]e make clear now," Justice Stewart asserted, "if it was not clear before, that the rationale of *Logan Valley* did not survive the Court's decision in the *Lloyd* case. . . . Not only did the *Lloyd* opinion incorporate lengthy excerpts from two of the dissenting opinions in *Logan Valley* . . . ," said Stewart, "the ultimate holding in *Lloyd* amounted to a total rejection of the holding in *Logan Valley*." Justice White, who dissented from the *Logan Valley* decision, concurred in the result but refused to accept the majority's reasoning that that precedent had been overruled.

In a lengthy dissent, Justice Marshall, joined by Justice Brennan, argued that the case should have been decided as a "statutory question without reference to the First Amendment." The U.S. Court of Appeals for the Fifth Circuit had based its decision in favor of the picketers on Section 7 of the National Labor Relations Act. "By bypassing that question," Justice Marshall charged, "and reaching out to overrule a constitutionally based decision, the Court surely departs from traditional modes of adjudication." "I cannot escape the feeling," he continued, "that *Logan Valley* has been laid to rest without ever having been accorded a proper burial."

In *PruneYard Shopping Center* v. *Robins* (447 U.S. 74, 1980), however, the Supreme Court upheld the authority of a state, under its own constitution, to grant individuals the right to solicit signatures for a petition in the central courtyard of a private shopping center even though owners of the center objected. Here the California Supreme Court construed its own constitution in such a way as to extend individual rights beyond those found in the

U.S. Constitution. And the Supreme Court, not-withstanding its earlier rulings (*Lloyd, Hudgens*), supported the position of the California court.

In effect, the Supreme Court was creating a new vision for federalism by setting a floor for constitutional rights beyond which it was up to states to decide what protections for free expression would be supplied. From a different angle, one might consider the Supreme Court's decision to be signaling a new day in which the Court was the follower, not the leader, in constitutional jurisprudence.

It is important to note that recently the Supreme Court clarified its interpretation of Section 7 of the National Labor Relations Act in a decision that was both ironic and troublesome in terms of its broader First Amendment implications. In *Lechmere, Inc.* v. *NLRB* (112 S. Ct. 841, 1992), the Supreme Court, in reversing the decision of the National Labor Relations Board (NLRB), held six-to-three that a privately owned shopping plaza could exclude nonemployee union organizers from distributing organizing leaflets in the parking lot. The holding was that by its plain terms, the National Labor Relations Act gave rights only to employees, not unions or their nonemployee organizers. The decision was ironic in that it was the first authored by Justice Marshall's successor, Justice Clarence Thomas. In light of both Justice Marshall's and Justice White's dissents in *Hudgens,* Justice Thomas's dicta is startling:

> *Central Hardware Co.* v. *NLRB*, 407 U.S. 539 (1972), and *Hudgens* v. *NLRB*, 424 U.S. 507 (1976), involved activity by union supporters on employee-owned property. The principle issue in both cases was whether, based upon *Food Employees* v. *Logan Valley Plaza, Inc.*, 391 U.S. 308 (1968), the First Amendment protected such activities. In both cases, we *rejected* the First Amendment claims, and in *Hudgens* we made it clear that *Logan Valley was overruled.* (emphasis added)

Against the backdrop of *PruneYard*, one might ask whether the Supreme Court is preparing the way to restrict access to forums, such as shopping centers, based on distinctions in the content of speech, such as political solicitations (*PruneYard*), as opposed to labor organizing (*Hudgens, Lechmere*).

PRUNEYARD SHOPPING CENTER v. ROBINS
447 U.S. 74; 64 L. Ed. 2d 741; 100 S. Ct. 2035 (1980)

JUSTICE REHNQUIST *delivered the opinion of the Court.*

We postponed jurisdiction of this appeal from the Supreme Court of California to decide the important federal constitutional questions it presented. Those are whether state constitutional provisions, which permit individuals to exercise free speech and petition rights on the property of a privately owned shopping center to which the public is invited, violate the shopping center owner's property rights under the Fifth and Fourteenth Amendments or his free speech rights under the First and Fourteenth Amendments.

Appellant PruneYard is a privately owned shopping center in the city of Campbell, Cal. It covers approximately 21 acres—five devoted to parking and 16 occupied by walkways, plazas, sidewalks, and buildings that contain more than 65 specialty shops, 10 restaurants, and a movie theater. The PruneYard is open to the public for the purpose of encouraging the patronizing of its commercial establishments. It has a policy not to permit any visitor or tenant to engage in any publicly expressive activity, including the circulation of petitions, that is not directly related to its commercial purposes. This policy has been strictly enforced in a non-discriminatory fashion. The PruneYard is owned by appellant Fred Sahadi.

Appellees are high school students who sought to solicit support for their opposition to a United Nations resolution against "Zionism." On a Saturday afternoon they set up a card table in a corner of PruneYard's central courtyard. They distributed pamphlets and asked passersby to sign petitions, which were to be sent to the President and Members of Congress. Their activity was peaceful and orderly and so far as the record indicates was not objected to by PruneYard's patrons.

Soon after appellees had begun soliciting signatures, a security guard informed them that they would have to leave because their activity violated PruneYard regulations. The guard suggested that they move to the public sidewalk at the PruneYard perimeter. Appellees immediately left the premises and later filed this lawsuit in the California Superior Court of Santa Clara County. They sought to enjoin appellants from denying them access to the PruneYard for the purpose of circulating their petitions.

The Superior Court held that appellees were not entitled under either the Federal or California Constitution to exercise their asserted rights on the shopping center property. . . . The California Court of Appeals affirmed.

The California Supreme Court reversed, holding that the California Constitution protects "speech and petitioning, reasonably exercised, in shopping centers even when the centers are privately owned." . . . It concluded that appellees are entitled to conduct their activity on PruneYard property. In rejecting appellants' contention that such a result infringed property rights protected by the Federal Constitution, the California Supreme Court observed:

> It bears repeated emphasis that we do not have under consideration the property or privacy rights of an individual homeowner or the proprietor of a modest retail establishment. As a result of advertising and the lure of a congenial environment, 25,000 persons are induced to congregate daily to take advantage of the numerous amenities offered by the [shopping center there]. A handful of additional orderly persons soliciting signatures and distributing handbills in connection therewith, under reasonable regulations adopted by defendant to assure that these activities do not interfere with normal business operations . . . would not markedly dilute defendant's property rights.

The California Supreme Court thus expressly overruled its earlier decision in *Diamond II*, which had reached an opposite conclusion. . . . Before this Court, appellants contend that their "constitutionally established rights under the Fourteenth Amendment to exclude appellees from adverse use of appellants' private property cannot be denied by invocation of a state constitutional provision or by judicial reconstruction of a state's laws of private property." . . . We postponed consideration of the question of jurisdiction until the hearing of the case on the merits. We now affirm.

We initially conclude that this case is properly before us as an appeal under 28 U.S.C. §1257(2). It has long been established that a state constitutional provision is a "statute" within the meaning of §1257(2). . . . Here the California Supreme Court decided that Art. 1, §§2 and 3 of the California Constitution gave appellees the right to solicit signatures on appellants' property in exercising their state rights of free expression and petition. In so doing, the California Supreme Court rejected appellants' claim that recognition of such a right violated appellants' "right to exclude others,"

which is a fundamental component of their federally protected property rights. Appeal is thus the proper method of review.

Appellants first contend that *Lloyd* v. *Tanner* . . . prevents the State from requiring a private shopping center owner to provide access to persons exercising their state constitutional rights of free speech and petition when adequate alternative avenues of communication are available. *Lloyd* dealt with the question whether under the Federal Constitution a privately owned shopping center may prohibit the distribution of handbills on its property when the handbilling is unrelated to the shopping center's operations. . . . The shopping center had adopted a strict policy against thee distribution of handbills within the building complex and its malls, and it made no exceptions to this rule. . . . Respondents in *Lloyd* argued that because the shopping center was open to the public, the First Amendment prevents the private owner from enforcing the handbilling restriction on shopping center premises. . . . In rejecting this claim we substantially repudiated the rationale of *Logan Valley*, which was later overruled in *Hudgens* v. *NLRB*. . . . We stated that property does not "lose its private character merely because the public is generally invited to use it for designated purposes," and that "[t]he essentially private character of a store and its privately owned abutting property does not change by virtue of being large or clustered with other stores in a modern shopping center.". . .

Our reasoning in *Lloyd*, however, does not ex proprio vigore limit the authority of the State to exercise its policy power or its sovereign right to adopt in its own Constitution individual liberties more expansive than those conferred by the Federal Constitution. . . . In *Lloyd*, there was no state constitutional or statutory provision that had been construed to create rights to the use of private property by strangers, comparable to those found to exist by the California Supreme Court here. It is, of course, well-established that a State in the exercise of its police power may adopt reasonable restrictions on private property so long as the restrictions do not amount to a taking without just compensation or contravene any other federal constitutional provision. . . . *Lloyd* held that when a shopping center owner opens his private property to the public for the purpose of shopping, the First Amendment to the United States Constitution does not thereby create individual rights in expression beyond those already existing under applicable law. . . .

Appellants next contend that a right to exclude others underlies the Fifth Amendment guarantee against the taking of property without just compensation and the Fourteenth Amendment guarantee against the deprivation of property without due process of law.

It is true that one of the essential sticks in the bundle of property rights is the right to exclude others. . . . And here there has literally been a "taking" of that right to the extent that the California Supreme Court has interpreted the state constitution to entitle its citizens to exercise free expression and petition rights on shopping center property. But it is well-established that "not every destruction or injury to property by governmental action has been held to be a 'taking' in the constitutional sense.". . . Rather, the determination whether a state law unlawfully infringes a landowner's property in violation of the Taking Clause requires an examination of whether the restriction on private property "force[s] some people alone to bear public burdens which, in all fairness and justice, should be borne by the public as a whole.". . . This examination entails inquiry into such factors as the character of the governmental action, its economic impact, and its interference with reasonable investment backed expectations. . . . When "regulation goes too far it will be recognized as a taking."

Here the requirement that appellants permit appellees to exercise state-protected rights of free expression and petition on shopping center property clearly does not amount to an unconstitutional infringement of appellants' property rights under the Taking Clause. There is nothing to suggest that preventing appellants from prohibiting this sort of activity will unreasonably impair the value or use of their property as a shopping center. The PruneYard is a large commercial complex that covers several city blocks, contains numerous separate business establishments, and is open to the public at large. The decision of the California Supreme Court makes it clear that the PruneYard may restrict expressive activity by adopting time, place and manner regulations that will minimize any interference with its commercial functions. Appellees were orderly, and they limited their activity to the common areas of the shopping center. In these circumstances, the fact that they may have "physically invaded" appellants' property cannot be viewed as determinative. . . .

There is also little merit to appellants' argument that they have been denied their property without due process of law. In *Nebbia* v. *New York* . . . (1934), this Court stated that

> [Neither] property rights nor contract rights are absolute. . . . Equally fundamental with the private right is that of the public to regulate it in the common interest. . . . [T]he guaranty of due process, as has often been held, demands only that the law shall not be unreasonable, arbitrary or capricious, and that the means selected shall have a real and substantial relation to the objective sought to be [obtained]. . . .

Appellants have failed to provide sufficient justification for concluding that this test is not satisfied by the State's asserted interest in promoting more expansive rights of free speech and petition than conferred by the Federal Constitution.

Appellants finally contend that a private property owner has a First Amendment right not to be forced by the State to use his property as a forum for the speech of others. They state that in *Wooley* v. *Maynard* . . . (1977), this Court concluded that a State may not constitutionally require an individual to participate in the dissemination of an ideological message by displaying it on his private property in a manner and for the express purpose that it be observed and read by the public. This rationale applies here, they argue, because the message of *Wooley* is that the State may not force an individual to display any message at all.

Wooley, however, was a case in which the government itself prescribed the message, required it to be displayed openly on appellee's personal property that was used "as part of his daily life," and refused to permit him to take any measures to cover up the motto even though the Court found the display of the motto served no important state interest. Here, by contrast, there are a number of distinguishing factors. Most important, the shopping center by choice of its owner is not limited to the personal use of appellants. It is instead a business establishment that is open to the public to come and go as they please. The views expressed by members of the public in passing out pamphlets or seeking signatures for a petition thus will not likely be identified with those of the owner. Second, no specific message is dictated by the State to be displayed on appellants' property. There consequently is no danger of governmental discrimination for or against a particular message. Finally, as far as appears here appellants can expressly disavow any connection with the message by simply posting signs in the area where the speakers or handbillers stand. Such signs, for example, could disclaim any sponsorship of the message and could explain that the persons are communicating their own messages by virtue of state law.

Appellants also argue that their First Amendment rights have been infringed in light of *West Virginia State Board of Education* v. *Barnette* . . .

(1943) and *Miami Herald Publishing Co.* v. *Tornillo* . . . (1974). *Barnette* is inapposite because it involved the compelled recitation of a message containing an affirmation of belief. This Court held such compulsion unconstitutional because it "require[d] the individual to communicate by word and sign his acceptance" of government-dictated political ideas, whether or not he subscribed to them. . . . Appellants are not similarly being compelled to affirm their belief in any governmentally prescribed position or view, and they are free to publicly dissociate themselves from the views of the speakers or handbillers.

Tornillo struck down a Florida statute requiring a newspaper to publish a political candidate's reply to criticism previously published in that newspaper. It rests on the principle that the State cannot tell a newspaper what it must print. The Florida statute contravened this principle in that it "exact[ed] a penalty on the basis of the content of a newspaper.". . . There also was a danger in *Tornillo* that the statute would "dampen the vigor and limit the variety of public debate" by deterring editors from publishing controversial political statements that might trigger the application of the statute. . . . Thus the statute was found to be an "intrusion into the function of editors." . . . These concerns obviously are not present here.

We conclude that neither appellant's federally recognized property rights nor their First Amendment rights have been infringed by the California Supreme Court's decision recognizing a right of appellees to exercise protected rights of expression and petition on the appellants' property. The judgment of the Supreme Court of California is therefore

Affirmed.

JUSTICE MARSHALL, *concurring.*

I join the opinion of the Court, but write separately to make a few additional points.

In *Food Employees* v. *Logan Valley Plaza* . . . (1968), this Court held that the First and Fourteenth Amendments prevented a state court from relying on its law of trespass to enjoin the peaceful picketing of a business enterprise located within a shopping center. The Court concluded that because the shopping center "serves as the community business block" and is open to the general public, "the State may not delegate the power, through the use of its trespass laws, wholly to exclude those members of the public wishing to exercise their First Amendment rights on the premises." . . . The Court rejected the suggestion that such an abroga-

tion of the state law of trespass would intrude on the constitutionally protected property rights of shopping center owners. And it emphasized that the shopping center was open to the public and that reasonable restrictions on the exercise of communicative activity would be permitted. "[N]o meaningful claim to protection of a right of privacy can be advanced by respondents here. Nor on the facts of the case can any significant claim to protection of the normal business operation of the property be raised. Naked title is essentially all that is at issue.". . .

The Court in *Logan Valley* emphasized that if the property rights of shopping center owners were permitted to overcome the First Amendment rights of prospective petitioners, a significant intrusion on communicative activity would result. Because "[t]he large-scale movement of this country's population from the cities to the suburbs has been accompanied by the advent of the suburban shopping center," a contrary decision would have "substantial consequences for workers seeking to challenge substandard working conditions, consumers protesting shoddy or over-priced merchandise, and minority groups seeking nondiscriminatory hiring policies." . . . In light of these realities, we concluded that the First and Fourteenth Amendments prohibited the State from using its trespass laws to prevent the exercise of expressive activities on privately owned shopping centers, at least when those activities were related to the operations of the store at which they were directed.

In *Lloyd Corp.* v. *Tanner* . . . (1972), the Court confined *Logan Valley* to its facts, holding that the First and Fourteenth Amendments were not violated when a State prohibited petitioning that was not designed to convey information with respect to the operation of the store that was being picketed. The Court indicated that a contrary result would constitute "an unwarranted infringement of property rights." . . . And in *Hudgens* v. *National Labor Relations Board* . . . (1976), the Court concluded that *Lloyd* had in fact overruled *Logan Valley.*

I continue to believe that *Logan Valley* was rightly decided, and that both *Lloyd* and *Hudgens* were incorrect interpretations of the First and Fourteenth Amendments. State action was present in all three cases. In all of them the shopping center owners had opened their centers to the public at large, effectively replacing the State with respect to such traditional First Amendment forums as streets, sidewalks, and parks. The State had in turn made its laws of trespass available to shopping center owners, enabling them to exclude those who wished to engage in expressive activity on their premises. Rights of free expression become illusory when a State has operated in such a way as to shut off effective channels of communication. I continue to believe, then, that "the Court's rejection of any role for the First Amendment in the privately owned shopping center complex stems . . . from an overly formalistic view of the relationship between the institution of private ownership of property and the First Amendment's guarantee of freedom of speech." *Hudgens* v. *NLRB* . . . (dissenting opinion).

In the litigation now before the Court, the Supreme Court of California construed the California Constitution to protect precisely those rights of communication and expression that were at stake in *Logan Valley, Lloyd,* and *Hudgens.* The California court concluded that its state "constitution broadly proclaims speech and petition rights. Shopping centers to which the public is invited can provide an essential and invaluable forum for exercising those rights." . . . Like the Court in *Logan Valley,* the California court found that access to shopping centers was crucial to the exercise of rights of free expression. And like the Court in *Logan Valley,* the California court rejected the suggestion that the Fourteenth Amendment barred the intrusion on the property rights of the shopping center owners. I applaud the court's decision, which is a part of a very healthy trend of affording state constitutional provisions a more expansive interpretation than this Court has given to the Federal Constitution. See Brennan, State Constitutions and the Protection of Individual Rights, 90 Harv. L. Rev. 489 (1977).

From Symbolic Speech to Bias-Motivated Crimes

FEATURED CASES

Texas v. *Johnson*   *United States* v. *Eichman*   *R.A.V.* v. *St. Paul*   *Wisconsin* v. *Mitchell*

Is the communication of an idea by conduct protected by the First Amendment? The answer to this question is not easy. This is especially true in certain activities (e.g., door-to-door solicitation, various "cause" demonstrations, posting of outdoor signs) where the conduct (activity) is intertwined with speech or petition, obvious concerns of the First Amendment. But does the First Amendment offer protection to activities where the *conduct* rather than "pure speech" itself becomes the focal point of the communication? In other words, what about symbolic speech? The issue was raised when four persons stood on the steps of the South Boston Courthouse on March 13, 1966, and burned their draft cards as a way of expressing opposition to the Vietnam War. They were tried and convicted under a 1965 congressional law that made it a crime to knowingly destroy or mutilate draft cards. But burning draft cards, they argued, was "symbolic speech" or "communication of ideas by conduct," which is protected by the First Amendment. The Supreme Court disagreed. In *United States* v. *O'Brien* (391 U.S. 367, 1968), the Court by a seven-to-one vote said it could not accept the position that an "apparently limitless variety of conduct can be labelled 'speech' whenever the person engaging in the conduct intends there-by to express an idea." Moreover, continued Chief Justice Warren, who spoke for the majority, when "speech" and "non-speech" elements are "combined in the same course of conduct, a sufficiently important governmental interest in regulating the non-speech element can justify incidental limitations on First Amendment freedoms." The Court found that the governmental regulation as imposed by the 1965 law was sufficiently justified. Justice Douglas, the lone dissenter, thought that the basic question in the case was "whether conscription is permissible in the absence of a declaration of war." He argued that the Court should make a ruling on it. (Cf. *Schacht* v. *United States*, 398 U.S. 58, 1970.)

In *Street* v. *New York* (394 U.S. 577, 1969), a case similar to *O'Brien*, the Court skirted the question of whether a person could be punished for burning or defacing an American flag. After learning that James Meredith[3] had been shot from ambush in Mississippi in 1966, Street, a Brooklyn black, in apparent disgust, burned the American flag that he

---

[3]After a protracted legal and political battle, and amidst campus turmoil, Meredith became the first black student admitted to the University of Mississippi in 1962.

had always displayed on national holidays. When encountered by a police officer, Street remarked: "We don't need no damn flag." He was convicted under a New York law that makes it a crime to "publicly mutilate, deface, defile or defy, trample upon or cast contempt upon either by word or act" the state or national flag. By a five-to-four majority the Court voted to set aside Street's conviction. Justice John Marshall Harlan delivered the Court's opinion and emphasized the overbreadth of the statute under which Street was convicted. Harlan noted that the judge (Street was tried before a judge without a jury) did not make a distinction between the actual act of burning and the contemptuous remarks about the flag. Consequently, he held that the statute "was unconstitutionally applied [to Street] because it permitted him to be punished merely for [his] defiant or contemptuous words about the flag"—words which, Harlan contended, were constitutionally protected. Even assuming that the conviction could have been based solely on the act of burning the flag, Harlan argued that the conviction should be reversed because a guilty verdict ensued from the indictment, which charged the commission of a crime by use of words and the act of flag burning without elucidation, and it is possible that the trial judge could have considered the two acts as "intertwined, . . . [resting] the conviction on both together." Harlan concluded that while "disrespect for our flag is to be deplored no less in these vexed times than in calmer periods of our history," a conviction that may have been based on a form of expression that the Constitution protects cannot be sustained. For, he continued, "the right to differ as to things that touch the heart of the existing order' encompass[es] the freedom to express publicly one's opinions about our flag, including those opinions which are defiant or contemptuous."

The dissenters took sharp exception to the majority's avoidance of the crucial constitutional issue presented in the case. To them, this case was not one in which constitutionally protected expression had been sacrificed to protect the flag; rather, at issue was whether the deliberate act of burning the American flag is symbolic expression protected by the Constitution. In his dissent, Chief Justice Warren noted that the record indicated clearly that all parties focused on the "flag burning as symbolic expression" issue and so did the state appellate court. Warren argued that where a constitutional issue is presented to the Court, as this one had been, the Court has the "responsibility to confront [it] squarely and resolve it." He warned that facing the flag burning and desecration issue was

particularly pressing because the "flag has increasingly become an integral part of public protests." (Cf. *Spence* v. *Washington*, 418 U.S. 405, 1974, where the unorthodox use of the American flag by a college student for symbolic expression is held to be protected expression. See also *Wooley* v. *Maynard*, in which the Court held that New Hampshire could not force citizens to display the state motto, "Live Free or Die," on their license plates. 430 U.S. 705, 1977.)

In 1989 a sharply divided five-to-four Court in *Texas* v. *Johnson* (109 S. Ct. 2533) held that laws prohibiting peaceful political protesters from burning the American Flag were unconstitutional under the First Amendment. Justice Brennan, speaking for a court majority that cut across ideological lines, said, "If there is a bedrock principle underlying the First Amendment, it is that the Government may not prohibit the expression of an idea simply because society finds the idea itself offensive or disagreeable."

Congress, in an attempt to placate the majority of Americans upset at the *Johnson* decision, passed legislation protecting the American flag in a "content-neutral" manner in the belief that the new statute would survive the *Johnson* test. Congress did not have long to wait, however, before the Supreme Court reacted by holding that this congressional attempt to protect the American flag did not survive a "content-neutral" standard. (See *United States* v. *Eichman*, 110 S. Ct. 2404, 1990).

In this light, consider *R.A.V.* v. *St. Paul.* We had originally raised the case to explore the difficulty of achieving Tribe's view that the First Amendment serves two functions: "instrumental political functions" and the "self-realization of individual and group identity". While *Texas* v. *Johnson* involved the former, *R.A.V.* presents tough choices to be made about the latter. In *R.A.V.*, the Supreme Court overturned a local ordinance that forbade symbols that aroused "anger, alarm, or resentment in others on the basis of race, color, creed, [or] religion." The ordinance then enumerated certain symbols, such as a burning cross or a Nazi swastika. In the case, teenagers had burned a crudely made cross in the yard of a black family. The Supreme Court held that the ordinance was unconstitutional in that it restricted speech on the basis of content. It forbade certain categories of speech, such as that relating to race, and did not forbid others, such as that relating to patriotism.

Despite *R.A.V.*, however, it is clear that, unlike symbolic speech or certain expressions indicative of hatred or bias directed toward certain groups, the Court nonetheless is willing to uphold harsher sentences for bias-motivated crimes. The raging controversy over how best to deal with a seeming proliferation of "hate crimes" came to fore in *Wisconsin* v. *Mitchell*. Here, a unanimous Court upheld enhanced penalties for crimes motivated by hatred based in race, religion or other similar characteristics.

Mitchell tested the constitutionality of a Wisconsin hate-crimes statute that increased the maximum sentences for crimes in which the defendant "[i]ntentionally selects the person against whom the crime . . . is committed . . . because of the race, religion, color, disability, sexual orientation, national origin or ancestry of that person." Writing for the Court, Chief Justice Rehnquist rejected Mitchell's First Amendment claim for two reasons.

First, Rehnquist noted that sentencing judges consider various factors other than evidence concerning guilt when passing sentence. While a judge may not consider a defendant's "abstract beliefs, however obnoxious to most people," that judge may consider evidence of bias if such evidence is relevant to determining motive, a factor whose use in determining violations of federal and state anti-discrimination laws has been upheld by the courts. Second, in distinguishing *Mitchell* from *R.A.V.*, Rehnquist argued that the Wisconsin law regulates conduct unprotected by the First Amendment and likely to cause significant and individual societal harm, while the St. Paul statute in *R.A.V.* was specifically directed at speech protected by the First Amendment.

TEXAS v. JOHNSON
491 U.S. 397; 105 L. Ed. 2d 342; 109 S. Ct. 2533 (1989)

JUSTICE BRENNAN *delivered the opinion of the Court.*

After publicly burning an American flag as a means of political protest, Gregory Lee Johnson was convicted of desecrating a flag in violation of Texas law. This case presents the question whether his conviction is consistent with the First Amendment. We hold that it is not.

I

While the Republican National Convention was taking place in Dallas in 1984, respondent Johnson participated in a political demonstration dubbed the "Republican War Chest Tour."

. . . [T]he purpose of this event was to protest the policies of the Reagan administration and of certain Dallas-based corporations. The demonstrators marched through the Dallas streets, chanting political slogans and stopping at several corporate locations to stage "die-ins" intended to dramatize the consequences of nuclear war. On several occasions they spray painted the walls of buildings and overturned potted plants, but Johnson himself took no part in such activities. He did, however, accept an American flag handed to him by a fellow protestor who had taken it from a flagpole outside one of the targeted buildings.

The demonstration ended in front of Dallas City Hall, where Johnson unfurled the American flag, doused it with kerosene, and set it on fire.

While the flag burned, the protestors chanted, "America, the red, white and blue, we spit on you." After the demonstrators dispersed, a witness to the flag-burning collected the flag's remains and buried them in his backyard. No one was physically injured or threatened with injury, though several witnesses testified that they had been seriously offended by the flagburning. . . .

. . . Johnson alone was charged with a crime. . . . After a trial, he was convicted, sentenced to one year in prison, and fined $2,000. The Court of Appeals for the Fifth District of Texas at Dallas affirmed, . . . but the Texas Court of Criminal Appeals reversed, holding that the State could not, consistent with the First Amendment, punish Johnson for burning the flag in these circumstances . . . [for his] conduct was symbolic speech protected by the First Amendment. . . .

Because it reversed Johnson's conviction on the ground that [the statute] was unconstitutional as applied to him, the state court did not address Johnson's argument that the statute was, on its face, unconstitutionally vague and overbroad. We granted certiorari . . . and now affirm.

II

Johnson was convicted of flag desecration for burning the flag rather than uttering insulting words. This fact somewhat complicates our consideration of his conviction under the First Amendment. We must first determine whether Johnson's burning of the flag constituted expressive conduct, permitting him to invoke the First Amendment in challenging his conviction. . . . If his conduct was expressive, we next decide whether the State's regulation is related to the suppression of free expression. . . . If the State's regulation is not related to expression, then the less stringent standard we announced in *United States* v. *O'Brien* for regulations of noncommunicative conduct controls. . . . If it is, then we are outside of *O'Brien*'s test, and we must ask whether this interest justifies Johnson's conviction under a more demanding standard. . . . A third possibility is that the State's asserted interest is simply not implicated on these facts, and in that event the interest drops out of the picture. . . .

The First Amendment literally forbids the abridgement only of "speech," but we have long recognized that its protection does not end at the spoken or written word. While we have rejected "the view that an apparently limitless variety of conduct can be labeled 'speech' whenever the person engaging in the conduct intends thereby to express an idea," . . . we have acknowledged that conduct may be "sufficiently imbued with elements of communication to fall within the scope of the First and Fourteenth Amendments." . . .

In deciding whether particular conduct possesses sufficient communicative elements to bring the First Amendment into play, we have asked whether "[a]n intent to convey a particularized message was present, and [whether] the likelihood was great that the message would be understood by those who viewed it." . . . Hence, we have recognized the expressive nature of students' wearing of black armbands to protest American military involvement in Vietnam; . . . of a sit-in by blacks in a "whites only" area to protest segregation; . . . of the wearing of American military uniforms in a dramatic presentation criticizing American involvement in Vietnam; . . . and of picketing about a wide variety of causes. . . .

Especially pertinent to this case are our decisions recognizing the communicative nature of conduct relating to flags. . . . That we have had little difficulty identifying an expressive element in conduct relating to flags should not be surprising. The very purpose of a national flag is to serve as a symbol of our country; it is, one might say, "the one visible manifestation of two hundred years of nationhood." . . . Pregnant with expressive content, the flag as readily signifies this Nation as does the combination of letters found in "America."

We have not automatically concluded, however, that any action taken with respect to our flag is expressive. Instead, in characterizing such action for First Amendment purposes, we have considered the context in which it occurred. . . .

The State of Texas conceded for purposes of its oral argument in this case that Johnson's conduct was expressive conduct, . . . and this concession seems to us . . . prudent. . . . Johnson burned an American flag as part—indeed, as the culmination—of a political demonstration that coincided with the convening of the Republican Party and its renomination of Ronald Reagan for President. The expressive, overtly political nature of this conduct was both intentional and overwhelmingly apparent. At his trial, Johnson explained his reasons for burning the flag as follows: "The American Flag was burned as Ronald Reagan was being renominated as President. And a more powerful statement of symbolic speech, whether you agree with it or not, couldn't have been made at that time. It's quite a just position [juxtaposition]. We had new patriotism and no patriotism." In these circumstances, Johnson's burning of the flag was conduct "sufficiently imbued with elements of communication," . . . to implicate the First Amendment.

III

The Government generally has a freer hand in restricting expressive conduct than it has in restricting the written or spoken word. . . . It may not, however, proscribe particular conduct *because* it has expressive elements. "[W]hat might be termed the more generalized guarantee of freedom of expression makes the communicative nature of conduct an inadequate *basis* for singling out that conduct for proscription. A law *directed at* the communicative nature of conduct must, like a law directed at speech itself, be justified by the substantial showing of need that the First Amendment requires.". . . It is, in short, not simply the verbal or nonverbal nature of the expression, but the governmental interest at stake, that helps to determine whether a restriction on that expression is valid.

Thus, although we have recognized that where " 'speech' and 'nonspeech' elements are combined in the same course of conduct, a sufficiently important governmental interest in regulating the nonspeech element can justify incidental limitations on First Amendment freedoms,". . . we have limited the applicability of *O'Brien*'s relatively lenient standard to those cases in which "the governmental interest is unrelated to the suppression of free expression." In stating, moreover, that *O'Brien*'s test "in the last analysis is little, if any, different from the standard applied to time, place, or manner restrictions," . . . we have highlighted the requirement that the governmental interest in question be unconnected to expression in order to come under *O'Brien*'s less demanding rule.

In order to decide whether *O'Brien*'s test applies here, . . . we must decide whether Texas has asserted an interest in support of Johnson's conviction that is unrelated to the suppression of expression. If we find that an interest asserted by the State is simply not implicated on the facts before us, we need not ask whether *O'Brien*'s test applies. . . . The State offers two separate interests to justify this conviction: preventing breaches of the peace, and preserving the flag as a symbol of nationhood and national unity. We hold that the first interest is not implicated on this record and that the second is related to the suppression of expression.

A

Texas claims that its interest in preventing breaches of the peace justifies Johnson's conviction for flag desecration. However, no disturbance of the peace actually occurred or threatened to occur because of Johnson's burning of the flag. . . . The State's emphasis on the protestors' disorderly actions prior to arriving at City Hall is not only somewhat surprising given that no charges were brought on the basis of this conduct, but it also fails to show that a disturbance of the peace was a likely reaction to Johnson's conduct. . . .

The State's position, therefore, amounts to a claim that an audience that takes serious offense at particular expression is necessarily likely to disturb the peace and that the expression may be prohibited on this basis. Our precedents do not countenance such a presumption. . . .

Nor does Johnson's expressive conduct fall within that small class of "fighting words" that are "likely to provoke the average person to retaliation, and thereby cause a breach of the peace.". . . No reasonable onlooker would have regarded Johnson's generalized expression of dissatisfaction with the policies of the Federal Government as a direct personal insult or an invitation to exchange fisticuffs. . . .

We thus conclude that the State's interest in maintaining order is not implicated on these facts. . . .

B

The State also asserts an interest in preserving the flag as a symbol of nationhood and national unity. . . . We are . . . persuaded that this interest is related to expression in the case of Johnson's burning of the flag. The State, apparently, is concerned that such conduct will lead people to believe either that the flag does not stand for nationhood and national unity, but instead reflects other, less positive concepts, or that the concepts reflected in the flag do not in fact exist, that is, we do not enjoy unity as a Nation. These concerns blossom only when a person's treatment of the flag communicates some message, and thus are related "to the suppression of free expression" within the meaning of *O'Brien*. We are thus outside of *O'Brien*'s test altogether.

IV

It remains to consider whether the State's interest in preserving the flag as a symbol of nationhood and national unity justifies Johnson's conviction. . . .

According to the principles announced in *Boos* [v. *Barry*, 485 U. S. 312 (1988)], Johnson's political expression was restricted because of the content of the message he conveyed. We must therefore subject the State's asserted interest in preserving the special symbolic character of the flag to "the most exacting scrutiny.". . .

If there is a bedrock principle underlying the First Amendment, it is that the Government may not prohibit the expression of an idea simply because society finds the idea itself offensive or disagreeable. . . .

. . . [N]othing in our precedents suggests that a State may foster its own view of the flag by prohibiting expressive conduct relating to it. To bring its argument outside our precedents, Texas attempts to convince us that even if its interest in preserving the flag's symbolic role does not allow it to prohibit words or some expressive conduct critical of the flag, it does permit it to forbid the outright destruction of the flag. The State's argument cannot depend here on the distinction between written or spoken words and nonverbal conduct. That distinction . . . is of no moment where the nonverbal conduct is expressive, as it is here, and where the regulation of that conduct is related to expression, as it is here. . . .

Texas' focus on the precise nature of Johnson's expression . . . misses the point of our prior decisions: their enduring lesson, that the Government may not prohibit expression simply because it disagrees with its message, is not dependent on the particular mode in which one chooses to express an idea. If we were to hold that a State may forbid flag-burning wherever it is likely to endanger the flag's symbolic role, but allow it wherever burning a flag promotes that role—as where, for example, a person ceremoniously burns a dirty flag—we would be saying that when it comes to impairing the flag's physical integrity, the flag itself may be used as a symbol—as a substitute for the written or spoken word or a "short cut from mind to mind"—only in one direction. We would be permitting a State to "prescribe what shall be orthodox" by saying that one may burn the flag to convey one's attitude toward it and its referents only if one does not endanger the flag's representation of nationhood and national unity.

We never before have held that the Government may ensure that a symbol be used to express only one view of that symbol or its referents. . . . To conclude that the Government may permit designated symbols to be used to communicate only a limited set of messages would be to enter territory having no discernible or defensible boundaries. Could the Government, on this theory, prohibit the burning of state flags? Of copies of the Presidential seal? Of the Constitution? In evaluating these choices under the First Amendment, how would we decide which symbols were sufficiently special to warrant this unique status? To do so, we would be forced to consult our own political preferences, and impose them on the citizenry, in the very way that the First Amendment forbids us to do. . . .

There is, moreover, no indication—either in the text of the Constitution or in our cases interpreting it—that a separate juridical category exists for the American flag alone. Indeed, we would not be surprised to learn that the persons who framed our Constitution and wrote the Amendment that we now construe were not known for their reverence for the Union Jack. The First Amendment does not guarantee that other concepts virtually sacred to our Nation as a whole—such as the principle that discrimination on the basis of race is odious and destructive—will go unquestioned in the marketplace of ideas. . . . We decline, therefore, to create for the flag an exception to the joust of principles protected by the First Amendment. . . .

We are fortified in today's conclusion by our conviction that forbidding criminal punishment for conduct such as Johnson's will not endanger the special role played by our flag or the feelings it inspires. To paraphrase Justice Holmes, we submit that nobody can suppose that this one gesture of an unknown man will change our Nation's attitude towards its flag. . . .

We are tempted to say, in fact, that the flag's deservedly cherished place in our community will be strengthened, not weakened, by our holding today. Our decision is a reaffirmation of the principles of freedom and inclusiveness that the flag best reflects, and of the conviction that our toleration of criticism such as Johnson's is a sign and source of our strength. . . . It is the Nation's resilence, not its rigidity that Texas sees reflected in the flag—and it is that resilience that we reassert today.

The way to preserve the flag's special role is not to punish those who feel differently about these matters. It is to persuade them that they are wrong.

> To courageous, self-reliant men, with confidence in the power of free and fearless reasoning applied through the processes of popular government, no danger flowing from speech can be deemed clear and present, unless the incidence of the evil apprehended is so imminent that it may befall before there is opportunity for full discussion. If there be time to expose through discussion the falsehood and fallacies, to avert the evil by the processes of education, the remedy to be applied is more speech, not enforced silence. . . . *Whitney* v. *California* (1927).

And, precisely because it is our flag that is involved, one's response to the flag-burner may exploit the uniquely persuasive power of the flag itself. We can imagine no more appropriate response to burning a flag than waving one's own, no better way to counter a flag-burner's message than by saluting the flag that burns, no surer means of preserving the dignity even of the flag that burned than by—as one witness here did—according its remains a respectful burial. We do not consecrate the flag by punishing its desecration, for in doing so we dilute the freedom that this cherished emblem represents. . . .

. . . The judgment of the Texas Court of Criminal Appeals is therefore

Affirmed.

JUSTICE KENNEDY, *concurring.*

. . . I join JUSTICE BRENNAN's opinion without reservation, but with a keen sense that this case, like others before us from time to time, exacts its personal toll. This prompts me to add to our pages these few remarks.

The case before us illustrates better than most that the judicial power is often difficult in its exercise. We cannot here ask another branch to share responsibility, as when the argument is made that a statute is flawed or incomplete. For we are presented with a clear and simple statute to be judged against a pure command of the Constitution. The outcome can be laid at no door but ours.

The hard fact is that sometimes we must make decisions we do not like. We make them because they are right, right in the sense that the law and the Constitution, as we see them, compel the result. And so great is our commitment to the process that, except in the rare case, we do not pause to express distaste for the result, perhaps for fear of undermining a valued principle that dictates the decision. This is one of those rare cases.

Our colleagues in dissent advance powerful arguments why respondent may be convicted for his expression, reminding us that among those who will be dismayed by our holding will be some who have had the singular honor of carrying the flag in battle. . . .

With all respect to those views, I do not believe the Constitution gives us the right to rule as the dissenting members of the Court urge, however painful this judgment is to announce. Though symbols often are what we ourselves make of them, the flag is constant in expressing beliefs Americans share, beliefs in law and peace and that freedom which sustains the human spirit. The case here today forces recognition of the costs to which those beliefs commit us. It is poignant but fundamental that the flag protects those who hold it in contempt.

For all the record shows, this respondent was not a philosopher and perhaps did not even possess the ability to comprehend how repellent his statements must be to the Republic itself. But whether or not he could appreciate the enormity of the offense he gave, the fact remains that his acts were speech, in both the technical and the fundamental meaning of the Constitution. So I agree with the Court that he must go free.

CHIEF JUSTICE REHNQUIST, *with whom* JUSTICE WHITE *and* JUSTICE O'CONNOR *join, dissenting.*

In holding this Texas statute unconstitutional, the Court ignores Justice Holmes' familiar aphorism that "a page of history is worth a volume of logic." *New York Trust Co.* v. *Eisner,* 256 U. S. 345, 349 (1921). For more than 200 years, the American flag has occupied a unique position as the symbol of our Nation, a uniqueness that justifies a governmental prohibition against flag burning in the way respondent Johnson did here. . . .

[Here follows a lengthy review of the role of the flag in our national history.]

The American flag . . . throughout more than 200 years of history, has come to be the visible symbol of our Nation. It does not represent the views of any particular political party, and it does not represent any particular political party, and it does not represent any particular political philosophy. The flag is not simply another "idea" or "point of view" competing for recognition in the marketplace of ideas. Millions and millions of Americans regard it with an almost mystical reverence regardless of what sort of social, political, or philosophical beliefs they may have. I cannot agree that the First Amendment invalidates the Act of Congress, and the laws of 48 of the 50 States, which make criminal the public burning of the flag. . . .

Here it may . . . well be said that the public burning of the American flag by Johnson was no essential part of any exposition of ideas, and at the same time it had a tendency to incite a breach of the peace. Johnson was free to make any verbal denunciation of the flag that he wished; indeed, he was free to burn the flag in private. He could publicly burn other symbols of the Government or effigies of political leaders. He did lead a march through the streets of Dallas, and conducted a rally in front of the Dallas City Hall. He engaged in a "die-in" to protest nuclear weapons. He shouted out various slogans during the march, including: "Reagan, Mondale which will it be? Either one means World War III"; "Ronald Reagan, killer of the hour, Perfect example of U. S. power"; and "Red, white and blue, we spit on you, you stand for plunder, you will go under." . . . For none of these acts was he arrested or prosecuted; it was only when he proceeded to burn publicly an American flag stolen from its rightful owner that he violated the Texas statute. . . .

. . . Johnson's public burning of the flag in this case . . . obviously did convey Johnson's bitter dislike of his country. But his act . . . conveyed nothing that could not have been conveyed and was not conveyed just as forcefully in a dozen different ways. As with "fighting words," so with flag burning, for purposes of the First Amendment: It is "no essential part of any exposition of ideas, and [is] of such slight social value as a step to truth that any benefit that may be derived from [it] is clearly outweighed" by the public interest in avoiding a probable breach of the peace. The highest courts of several States have upheld state statutes prohibiting the public burning of the flag on the grounds that it is so inherently inflammatory that it may cause a breach of public order. . . .

The result of the Texas statute is obviously to deny one in Johnson's frame of mind of many means of "symbolic speech." Far from being a case of "one picture being worth a thousand words," flag burning is the equivalent of an inarticulate grunt or roar that, it seems fair to say, is most likely to be indulged in not to express any particular idea, but to antagonize others. . . . The Texas statute deprived Johnson of only one rather inarticulate symbolic form of protest—a form of protest that was profoundly offensive to many—and left him with a full panoply of other symbols and every conceivable form of verbal expression to express his deep disapproval of national policy. Thus, in no way can it be said that Texas is punishing him because his hearers—or any other group of people—were profoundly opposed to the message that he sought to convey. Such opposition is no proper basis for restricting speech or expression under the First Amendment. It was Johnson's use of this particular symbol, and not the idea that he sought to convey by it or by his many other expressions, for which he was punished. . . .

But the Court today will have none of this. The uniquely deep awe and respect for our flag felt by virtually all of us are bundled off under the rubric of "designated symbols" . . . that the First Amendment prohibits the government from "establishing." But the government has not "established" this feeling; 200 years of history have done that. The government is simply recognizing as fact the profound regard for the American flag created by that history when it enacts statutes prohibiting the disrespectful public burning of the flag.

The Court concludes its opinion with a regrettably patronizing civics lecture, presumably addressed to the Members of both Houses of Congress, the members of the 50 state legislatures that enacted prohibitions against flag burning, and the troops fighting under that flag in Vietnam who objected to its being burned: "The way to preserve the flag's special role is not to punish those who feel differently about these matters. It is to persuade them that they are wrong." The Court's role

as the final expositor of the Constitution is well established, but its role as a platonic guardian admonishing those responsible to public opinion as if they were truant school children has no similar place in our system of government. The cry of "no taxation without representation" animated those who revolted against the English Crown to found our Nation—the idea that those who submitted to government should have some say as to what kind of laws would be passed. Surely one of the high purposes of a democratic society is to legislate against conduct that is regarded as evil and profoundly offensive to the majority of people—whether it be murder, embezzlement, pollution, or flag burning.

Our Constitution wisely places limits on powers of legislative majorities to act, but the declaration of such limits by this Court "is, at all times, a question of much delicacy, which ought seldom, if ever, to be decided in the affirmative, in a doubtful case." . . . Uncritical extension of constitutional protection to the burning of the flag risks the frustration of the very purpose for which organized governments are instituted. The Court decides that the American flag is just another symbol, about which not only must opinions pro and con be tolerated, but for which the most minimal public respect may not be enjoined. The government may conscript men into the Armed Forces where they must fight and perhaps die for the flag, but the government may not prohibit the public burning of the banner under which they fight. I would uphold the Texas statute as applied in this case.

[The dissenting opinion of JUSTICE STEVENS is not reprinted here.]

UNITED STATES v. EICHMAN
496 U.S. 310; 110 L. Ed. 287; 110 S. Ct. 2404 (1990)

BRENNAN, J., *delivered the opinion of the Court, in which* MARSHALL, BLACKMUN, SCALIA, *and* KENNEDY, JJ., *joined.* STEVENS, J., *filed a dissenting opinion, in which* REHNQUIST, C. J., *and* WHITE *and* O'CONNOR, JJ., *joined.*

JUSTICE BRENNAN *delivered the opinion of the Court.*

In these consolidated appeals, we considered whether appellees' prosecution of burning a

United States flag in violation of the Flag Protection Act of 1989 is consistent with the First Amendment. Applying our recent decision in *Texas* v. *Johnson*, (1989), the District Courts held that the Act cannot constitutionally be applied to appellees. We affirm.

I

In No. 89-1433, the United States prosecuted certain appellees for violating the Flag Protection

Act of 1989, by knowingly setting fire to several United States flags on the steps of the United States Capitol while protesting various aspects of the Government's domestic and foreign policy. In No. 89-1434, the United States prosecuted other appellees for violating the Act by knowingly setting fire to a United States flag while protesting the Act's passage. In each case, the respective appellees moved to dismiss the flag-burning charge on the ground that the Act, both on its face and as applied, violates the First Amendment. Both the United States District Court for the Western District of Washington, and the United States District Court for the District of Columbia, following *Johnson, supra,* held the Act unconstitutional as applied to appellees and dismissed the charges. The United States appealed both decisions directly to this Court. . . . We noted probable jurisdiction and consolidated the two cases.

II

Last term in *Johnson*, we held that a Texas statute criminalizing the desecration of venerated objects, including the United States flag, was unconstitutional as applied to an individual who had set such a flag on fire during a political demonstration. The Texas statute provided that "[a] person commits an offense if he intentionally or knowingly desecrates . . . [a] national flag," where "desecrate" meant to "deface, damage, or otherwise physically mistreat in a way that the actor knows will seriously offend one or more persons likely to observe or discover his action." We first held that Johnson's flag-burning was "conduct 'sufficiently imbued with elements of communication' to implicate the First Amendment." We next considered and rejected the State's contention that, under *United States* v. *O'Brien*, (1968), we ought to apply the deferential standard with which we have reviewed Government regulations of conduct containing both speech and non-speech elements where "the governmental interest is unrelated to the suppression of free expression." We reasoned that the State's asserted interest "in preserving the flag as a symbol of nationhood and national unity," was an interest "related 'to the suppression of free expression' within the meaning of *O'Brien*" because the State's concern with protecting the flag's symbolic meaning is implicated "only when a person's treatment of the flag communicates some message." We therefore subjected the statute to " 'the most exacting scrutiny,' " and we concluded that the State's asserted interests could not justify the infringement on the demonstrator's First Amendment rights.

After our decision in *Johnson*, Congress passed the Flag Protection Act of 1989. The Act provides in relevant part:

> (a)(1) Whoever knowingly mutilates, defaces, physically defiles, burns, maintains on the floor or ground, or tramples upon any flag of the United States shall be fined under this title or imprisoned for not more than one year, or both.
> (2) This subsection does not prohibit any conduct consisting of the disposal of a flag when it has become worn or soiled.
> (b) As used in this section, the term "flag of the United States" means any flag of the United States, or any part thereof, made of any substance, of any size, in a form that is commonly displayed.

The Government concedes in this case, as it must, that appellees' flag-burning constituted expressive conduct, but invites us to reconsider our rejection in *Johnson* of the claim that flag-burning as a mode of expression, like obscenity or "fighting words," does not enjoy full protection of the First Amendment. This we decline to do. The only remaining question is whether the Flag Protection Act is sufficiently distinct from the Texas statute that it may constitutionally be applied to proscribe appellees' expressive conduct.

The Government contends that the Flag Protection Act is constitutional because, unlike the statute addressed in *Johnson*, the Act does not target expressive conduct on the basis of the content of its message. The Government asserts an interest in "protect[ing] the physical integrity of the flag under all circumstances" in order to safeguard the flag's identity " 'as the unique and unalloyed symbol of the Nation.' " The Act proscribes conduct (other than disposal) that damages or mistreats a flag, without regard to the actor's motive, his intended message, or the likely effects of his conduct on onlookers. By contrast, the Texas statute expressly prohibited only those acts of physical flag desecration "that the actor knows will seriously offend" onlookers, and the former federal statute prohibited only those acts of desecration that "cas[t] contempt upon" the flag.

Although the Flag Protection Act contains no explicit content-based limitation on the scope of prohibited conduct, it is nevertheless clear that the Government's asserted *interest* is "related 'to the suppression of free expression,' " and concerned with the content of such expression. The Government's interest in protecting the "physical integrity" of a privately owned flag rests upon a perceived need to preserve the flag's status as a symbol of our Nation and certain national ideals.

But the mere destruction or disfigurement of a particular physical manifestation of the symbol, without more, does not diminish or otherwise affect the symbol itself in any way. For example, the secret destruction of a flag in one's own basement would not threaten the flag's recognized meaning. Rather, the Government's desire to preserve the flag as a symbol for certain national ideals is implicated "only when a person's treatment of the flag communicates [a] message" to others that is inconsistent with those ideals.

Moreover, the precise language of the Act's prohibitions confirms Congress' interest in the communicative impact of flag destruction. The Act criminalizes the conduct of anyone who "knowingly mutilates, defaces, physically defiles, burns, maintains on the floor or ground, or tramples upon any flag." Each of the specified terms—with the possible exception of "burns"—unmistakably connotes disrespectful treatment of the flag and suggests a focus on those acts likely to damage the flag's symbolic value. And the explicit exemption for disposal of "worn or soiled" flags protects certain acts traditionally associated with patriotic respect for the flag. . . .

Although Congress cast the Flag Protection Act in somewhat broader terms than the Texas statute at issue in *Johnson*, the Act still suffers from the same fundamental flaw: it suppresses expression out of concern for its likely communicative impact. Despite the Act's wider scope, its restriction on expression cannot be " 'justified without reference to the content of the regulated speech.' "

. . . The Act therefore must be subjected to "the most exacting scrutiny," and for the reasons stated in *Johnson*, the Government's interest cannot justify its infringement on First Amendment rights. We decline the Government's invitation to reassess this conclusion in light of Congress' recent recognition of a purported "national consensus" favoring a prohibition on flag-burning. Even assuming such a consensus exists, any suggestion that the Government's interest in suppressing speech becomes more weighty as popular opposition to that speech grows is foreign to the First Amendment.

III

. . . Government may create national symbols, promote them, and encourage their respectful treatment. But the Flag Protection Act goes well beyond this by criminally proscribing expressive conduct because of its likely communicative impact.

We are aware that desecration of the flag is deeply offensive to many. But the same might be said, for example, of virulent ethnic and religious epithets, see *Terminiello* v. *Chicago*, (1949); vulgar repudiations of the draft, see *Cohen* v. *California*, (1971); and scurrilous caricatures, see *Hustler Magazine, Inc.* v. *Falwell*, (1988). "If there is a bedrock principle underlying the First Amendment, it is that the Government may not prohibit the expression of an idea simply because society finds the idea itself offensive or disagreeable." *Johnson.* Punishing desecration of the flag dilutes the very freedom that makes this emblem so revered, and worth revering. The judgments are

Affirmed.

JUSTICE STEVENS, *with whom* THE CHIEF JUSTICE, JUSTICE WHITE, *and* JUSTICE O'CONNOR *join, dissenting.*

The Court's opinion ends where proper analysis of the issue should begin. Of course "the Government may not prohibit the expression of an idea simply because society finds the idea itself offensive or disagreeable." None of us disagrees with that proposition. But it is equally well settled that certain methods of expression may be prohibited if (a) the prohibition is supported by a legitimate societal interest that is unrelated to suppression of the ideas the speaker desires to express; (b) the prohibition does not entail any interference with the speaker's freedom to express those ideas by other means; and (c) the interest in allowing the speaker complete freedom of choice among alternative methods of expression is less important than the societal interest supporting the prohibition.

Contrary to the position taken by counsel for the flag burners in *Texas* v. *Johnson*, it is now conceded that the Federal Government has a legitimate interest in protecting the symbolic value of the American flag. Obviously that value cannot be measured, or even described, with any precision. It has at least these two components: in times of national crisis, it inspires and motivates the average citizen to make personal sacrifices in order to achieve societal goals of overriding importance; at all times, it serves as a reminder of the paramount importance of pursuing the ideals that characterize our society.

The first question the Court should consider is whether the interest in preserving the value of that symbol is unrelated to suppression of the ideas that flag burners are trying to express. In my judgment the answer depends, at least in part, on what those ideas are. A flag burner might intend various messages. The flag burner may wish simply to convey hatred, contempt, or sheer opposition directed at the United States. This might be the case if the flag were burned by an enemy during time of war. A flag burner may also, or instead, seek to convey the depth of his personal conviction about some issue, by willingly provoking the use of force against himself. In so doing, he says that "my disagreement with certain policies is so strong that I am prepared to risk physical harm (and perhaps imprisonment) in order to call attention to my views." This second possibility apparently describes the expressive conduct of the flag burners in these cases. Like the protesters who dramatized their opposition to our engagement in Vietnam by publicly burning their draft cards—and who were punished for doing so—their expressive conduct is consistent with affection for this country and respect for the ideals that the flag symbolizes. There is at least one further possibility: a flag burner may intend to make an accusation against the integrity of the American people who disagree with him. By burning the embodiment of America's collective commitment to freedom and equality, the flag burner charges that the majority has forsaken that commitment—that continued respect for the flag is nothing more than hypocrisy. Such a charge may be made even if the flag burner loves the country and zealously pursues the ideals that the country claims to honor.

The idea expressed by a particular act of flag burning is necessarily dependent on the temporal and political context in which it occurs. In the 1960's it may have expressed opposition to the country's Vietnam policies, or at least to the compulsory draft. In *Texas* v. *Johnson*, it apparently expressed opposition to the platform of the Republican Party. In these cases, the respondents have explained that it expressed their opposition to racial discrimination, to the failure to care for the homeless, and of course to statutory prohibitions of flag burning. In any of these examples, the protestors may wish both to say that their own position is the only one faithful to liberty and equality, and to accuse their fellow citizens of hypocritical indifference to—or even of a selfish departure from—the ideals which the flag is supposed to symbolize. The ideas expressed by flag burners are thus various and often ambiguous.

The Government's legitimate interest in preserving the symbolic value of the flag is, however, essentially the same regardless of which of many different ideas may have motivated a particular act of flag burning. . . .

Thus, the Government may—indeed, it should—protect the symbolic value of the flag without regard to the specific content of the flag burners' speech. The prosecution in this case does not depend upon the object of the defendant's protest. It is, moreover, equally clear that the prohibition does not entail any interference with the speaker's freedom to express his or her ideas by other means. It may well be true that other means of expression may be less effective in drawing attention to those ideas, but that is not itself a sufficient reason for immunizing flag burning. Presumably a gigantic fireworks display or a parade of nude models in a public park might draw even more attention to a controversial message, but such methods of expression are nevertheless subject to regulation.

This case therefore comes down to a question of: Does the admittedly important interest in allowing every speaker to choose the method of expressing his or her ideas that he or she deems most effective and appropriate outweigh the societal interest in preserving the symbolic value of the flag? This question, in turn, involves three different interests: (1) The importance of the individual interest in selecting the preferred means of communication; (2) the importance of the national symbol; and (3) the question whether tolerance of flag burning will enhance or tarnish that value. The opinions in *Texas* v. *Johnson* demonstrate that reasonable judges may differ with respect to each of these interests.

The individual interest is unquestionably a matter of great importance. Indeed, it is one of the critical components of the ideas of liberty that the flag itself is intended to symbolize. Moreover, it is buttressed by the societal interest in being alerted to the need for thoughtful response to voices that might otherwise go unheard. The freedom of expression protected by the First Amendment embraces not only the freedom to communicate particular ideas, but also the right to communicate them effectively. That right, however, is not absolute—the communicative value of a well-placed bomb in the Capitol does not entitle it to the protection of the First Amendment.

Burning a flag is not, of course, equivalent to burning a public building. Assuming that the protester is burning his own flag, it causes no physical harm to other persons or to their property. The impact is purely symbolic, and it is apparent that some thoughtful persons believe that impact, far from depreciating the value of the symbol, will actually enhance its meaning. I most respectfully disagree. Indeed, what makes this case particularly difficult for me is what I regard as the damage to the symbol that has already occurred as a result of this Court's decision to place its stamp of approval on the act of flag burning. A formerly dramatic expression of protest is now rather commonplace. In today's marketplace of ideas, the public burning of a Vietnam draft card is probably less provocative than lighting a cigarette. Tomorrow flag burning may produce a similar reaction. There is surely a direct relationship between the communicative value of the act of flag burning and the symbolic value of the object being burned.

The symbolic value of the American flag is not the same today as it was yesterday. Events during the last three decades have altered the country's image in the eyes of numerous Americans, and some now have difficulty understanding the message that the flag conveyed to their parents and grandparents—whether born abroad and naturalized or native born. Moreover, the integrity of the symbol has been compromised by those leaders who seem to advocate compulsory worship of the flag even by individuals whom it offends, or who seem to manipulate the symbol of national purpose into a pretext for partisan disputes about meaner ends. And, as I have suggested, the residual value of the symbol after this Court's decision in *Texas* v. *Johnson* is surely not the same as it was a year ago.

Given all these consideration, plus the fact that the Court today is really doing nothing more than reconfirming what it has already decided, it might be appropriate to defer to the judgment of the majority and merely apply the doctrine of *stare decisis* to the case at hand. That action, however, would not honestly reflect my considered concerning the relative importance of the conflicting interests that are at stake. I remain persuaded that the considerations identified in my opinion in *Texas* v. *Johnson* are of controlling importance in this case as well.

Accordingly, I respectfully dissent.

R.A.V., PETITIONER v. CITY OF ST. PAUL, MINNESOTA
505 U.S. ___; 120 L. Ed. 305; 112 S. Ct. 2538 (1992)

JUSTICE SCALIA *delivered the opinion of the Court.*

In the predawn hours of June 21, 1990, petitioner and several other teenagers allegedly assembled a crudely-made cross by taping together broken chair legs. They then allegedly burned the cross inside the fenced yard of a black family that lived across the street from the house where petitioner was staying. Although this conduct could have been punished under any of a number of laws, one of the two provisions under which respondent city of St. Paul chose to charge petitioner (then a juvenile) was the St. Paul Bias-Motivated Crime Ordinance, St. Paul, Minn. Legis. Case 292.02 (1990), which provides:

> Whoever places on public or private property a symbol, object, appellation, characterization or graffiti, including, but not limited to, a burning cross or Nazi swastika, which one knows or has reasonable grounds to know arouses anger, alarm or resentment in others on the basis of race, color, creed, religion or gender commits disorderly conduct and shall be guilty of a misdemeanor.

Petitioner moved to dismiss this count on the ground that the St. Paul ordinance was substantially overbroad and impermissibly content-based and therefore facially invalid under the First Amendment. The trial court granted this motion, but the Minnesota Supreme Court reversed. That court rejected petitioner's overbreadth claim because, as construed in prior Minnesota cases, the modifying phrase "arouses anger, alarm or resentment in others" limits the reach of the ordinance to "conduct that itself inflicts injury or tends to incite immediate violence . . . ," and therefore the ordinance reached only expression "that the first amendment does not protect." The court also concluded that the ordinance was not impermissibly content-based because, in its view, "the ordinance is a narrowly tailored means toward accomplishing the compelling governmental interest in protecting the community against bias-motivated threats to public safety and order." We granted certiorari.

I

In construing the St. Paul ordinance, we are bound by the construction given to it by the Minnesota court. Accordingly, we accept the Minnesota Supreme Court's authoritative statement that the ordinance reaches only those expressions that constitute "fighting words" within the meaning of *Chaplinsky* v. *New Hampshire* (1942). Petitioner and his *amici* urge us to modify the scope of the *Chaplinsky* formulation, thereby invalidating the ordinance as "substantially overbroad." We find it unnecessary to consider this issue. Assuming, *arguendo*, that all of the expression reached by the ordinance is proscribable under the "fighting words" doctrine, we nonetheless conclude that the ordinance is facially unconstitutional in that it prohibits otherwise permitted speech solely on the basis of the subjects the speech addresses.

The First Amendment generally prevents government from proscribing speech, see, e.g., *Cantwell* v. *Connecticut*, (1940), or even expressive conduct, see, e.g., *Texas* v. *Johnson*, (1989), because of disapproval of the ideas expressed. Content-based regulations are presumptively invalid. From 1791 to the present, however, our society, like other free but civilized societies, has permitted restrictions upon the content of speech in a few limited areas, which are "of such slight social value as a step to truth that any benefit that may be derived from them is clearly outweighed by the social interest in order and morality." *Chaplinsky* [v. *New Hampshire*, 1942.] We have recognized that "the freedom of speech" referred to by the First Amendment does not include a freedom to disregard these traditional limitations. Our decisions since the 1960's have narrowed the scope of the traditional categorical exceptions for defamation, and for obscenity, but a limited categorical approach has remained an important part of our First Amendment jurisprudence.

We have sometimes said that these categories of expression are "not within the area of constitutionally protected speech," or that the "protection of the First Amendment does not extend" to them. Such statements must be taken in context, however, and are no more literally true than is the occasionally repeated shorthand characterizing obscenity "as not being speech at all." What they mean is that these areas of speech can, consistently with the First Amendment, be regulated *because of their constitutionally proscribable content* (obscenity, defamation, etc.)—not that they are categories of speech entirely invisible to the Constitution, so that they may be made the vehicles for content discrimination unrelated to their distinctively proscribable content. Thus, the government may proscribe libel; but it may not make the further content discrimination of proscribing *only* libel critical of the government. We recently acknowledged this distinction in *Ferber*, where, in upholding New York's child pornography law, we expressly recognized that there was no "question here of censoring a particular literary theme . . . ."

Our cases surely do not establish the proposition that the First Amendment imposes no obstacle whatsoever to regulation of particular instances of such proscribable expression, so that the government "may regulate [them] freely." That would mean that the city council could enact an ordinance prohibiting only those legally obscene works that contain criticism of the city government or, indeed, that do not include endorsement of the city government. Such a simplistic, all-or-nothing-at-all approach to the First Amendment protection is at odds with common sense and with our jurisprudence as well. It is not true that "fighting words" have at most a "*de minimis*" expressive content, or that their content is in *all respects* "worthless and undeserving of constitutional protection." Sometimes they are quite expressive indeed. We have not said that they constitute "no part of the expression of ideas," but only that they constitute "no *essential* part of any exposition of ideas."

The proposition that a particular instance of speech can be proscribable on the basis of one feature (e.g., obscenity) but not on the basis of another (e.g., opposition to the city government) is commonplace, and has found application in many contexts. We have long held, for example, that nonverbal expressive activity can be banned because of the action it entails, but not because of the ideas it expresses—so that burning a flag in violation of an ordinance against outdoor fires could be punishable, whereas burning a flag in violation of an ordinance against dishonoring the flag is not. Similarly, we have upheld reasonable "time, place, or manner" restrictions, but only if they are "justified without reference to the content of the regulated speech." *Ward* v. *Rock against Racism*, (1989). And just as the power to proscribe particular speech on the basis of a noncontent element (e.g., noise) does not entail the power to proscribe the same speech on the basis of a content element; so also, the power to proscribe it on the basis of *one* content element (e.g., obscenity) does not entail the power to proscribe it on the basis of *other* content elements.

In other words, the exclusion of "fighting words" from the scope the First Amendment simply means that, for purposes of that Amendment, the unprotected features of the words are, despite their verbal character, essentially a "nonspeech" element of communication. Fighting words are thus analogous to a noisy sound truck: Each is, as Justice Frankfurter recognized, a "mode of speech." *Niemotko* v. *Maryland*, (1951). Both convey an idea; but neither has, in and of itself, a claim upon the First Amendment. As with the sound truck, however, so also with fighting words: The government may not regulate use based on hostility—or favoritism—towards the underlying message expressed. Compare *Frisby* v. *Schultz*, (1988) (upholding, against facial challenge, a content-neutral ban on targeted residential picketing) with *Carey* v. *Brown* 447 U.S. 455 (1980) (invalidating a ban on residential picketing that exempted labor picketing).

The concurrences describe us as setting forth a new First Amendment principle that prohibition of constitutionally proscribable speech cannot be "underinclusiv[e],"—a First Amendment "absolutism" whereby "within a particular 'proscribable' category of expression, . . . a government must either proscribe *all* speech or no speech at all." That easy target is of the concurrences' own invention. In our view, the First Amendment imposes not an "underinclusiveness" limitation but a "content discrimination" limitation upon a State's prohibition of proscribable speech. There is no problem whatever, for example, with a State's prohibiting obscenity (and other forms of proscribable expression) only in certain media or markets, for although that prohibition would be "underinclusive," it would not discriminate on the basis of content. See, e.g., *Sable Communications*, 492 U.S., at 124–126 (upholding [legislation]) which prohibits obscene *telephone* communications).

Even the prohibition against content discrimination that we assert the First Amendment requires is not absolute. It applies differently in the context of proscribable speech than in the area of fully protected speech. The rationale of the general prohibition, after all, is that the content discrimination "rais[es] the specter that the Government may effectively drive certain ideas or viewpoints from the marketplace." But content discrimination among various instances of a class of proscribable speech often does not pose this threat.

When the basis for the content discrimination consists entirely of the very reason the entire class of speech at issue is proscribable, no significant danger of idea or viewpoint discrimination exists. Such a reason, having been adjudged neutral enough to support exclusion of the entire class of speech from First Amendment protection, is also neutral enough to form the basis of distinction within the class. To illustrate: A State might choose to prohibit only that obscenity which is the most patently offensive *in its prurience*—i.e., that which involves the most lascivious displays of sexual activity. But it may not prohibit, for example, only that obscenity which includes offensive *political* messages. And the Federal Government can criminalize only those threats of violence that are directed against the President,—since the reasons why threats of violence are outside the First Amendment (protecting individuals from the fear of violence, from the disruption that fear engenders, and from the possibility that the threatened violence will occur) have special force when applied to the person of the President. See *Watts* v. *United States*, (1969) (upholding the facial validity of [18 U.S.C. Sec.] 871 because of the "overwhelmin[g] interest in protecting the safety of [the] Chief Executive and in allowing him to perform his duties without interference from threats of physical violence"). But the Federal Government may not criminalize only those threats against the President that mention his policy on aid to inner cities. And to take a final example, a State may choose to regulate price advertising in one industry but not in others, because the risk of fraud (one of the characteristics of commercial speech that justifies depriving it of full First Amendment protection, see *Virginia Pharmacy Bd.* v. *Virginia Citizens Consumer Council, Inc.*, [1976]) is in its view greater there.

Another valid basis for according differential treatment to even a content-defined subclass of proscribable speech is that the subclass happens to be associated with particular "secondary effects" of the speech, so that the regulation is "*justified* without reference to the content of the . . . speech [. . . .]" A State could, for example, permit all obscene live performances except those involving minors. Moreover, since words can in some circumstances violate laws directed not against speech but against conduct (a law against treason, for example, is violated by telling the enemy the nation's defense secrets), a particular content-based subcategory of a proscribable class of speech can be swept up incidentally within the reach of a statute directed at conduct rather than speech. Thus, for example, sexually derogatory "fighting words," among other words, may produce a violation of Title VII's general prohibition against sexual discrimination in employment practices. Where the government does not target conduct on the basis of its expressive content, acts are not shielded from regulation merely because they express a discriminatory idea or philosophy. . . .

II

Applying these principles to the St. Paul ordinance, we conclude that, even as narrowly construed by the Minnesota Supreme Court, the ordinance is facially unconstitutional. Although the phrase in the ordinance, "arouses anger, alarm or resentment in others," has been limited by the Minnesota

Supreme Court's construction to reach only those symbols or displays that amount to "fighting words," the remaining unmodified terms make clear that the ordinance applies only to "fighting words" that insult, or provoke violence, "on the basis of race, color, creed, religion or gender." Displays containing abusive invective, no matter how vicious or severe, are permissible unless they are addressed to one of the specified disfavored topics. Those who wish to use "fighting words" in connection with other ideas—to express hostility, for example, on the basis of political affiliation, union membership, or homosexuality—are not covered. The First Amendment does not permit St. Paul to impose special prohibitions on those speakers who express views on disfavored subjects.

In its practical operation, moreover, the ordinance goes even beyond mere content discrimination, to actual viewpoint discrimination. Displays containing some words—odious racial epithets, for example—would be prohibited to proponents of all views. But "fighting words" that do not themselves invoke race, color, creed, religion, or gender—aspersions upon a person's mother, for example—would seemingly be usable *ad libitum* in the placards of those arguing *in favor* of racial, color, etc. tolerance and equality, but could not be used by that speaker's opponents. One could hold up a sign saying, for example, that all "anti-Catholic bigots" are misbegotten; but not that all "papists" are, for that would insult and provoke violence "on the basis of religion." St. Paul has no such authority to license one side of a debate to fight freestyle, while requiring the other to follow Marquis of Queensbury Rules.

What we have here, it must be emphasized, is not a prohibition of fighting words that are directed at certain persons or groups (which would be *facially* valid if it met the requirements of the Equal Protection Clause); but rather, a prohibition of fighting words that contain (as the Minnesota Supreme Court repeatedly emphasized) messages of "bias-motivated" hatred and in particular, as applied to this case, messages "based on virulent notions of racial supremacy." One must wholeheartedly agree with the Minnesota Supreme Court that "[i]t is the responsibility, even the obligation of diverse communities to confront such notions in whatever form they appear," *ibid.*, but the manner of that confrontation cannot consist of selective limitations upon speech. St. Paul's brief asserts that a general "fighting words" law would not meet the city's needs because only a content-specific measure can communicate to minority groups that the "group hatred" aspect of such speech "is not condoned by the majority." The point of the First Amendment is that majority preferences must be expressed in some fashion other than silencing speech on the basis of its content.

Despite the fact that the Minnesota Supreme Court and St. Paul acknowledge that the ordinance is directed at expression of group hatred, JUSTICE STEVENS suggests that this "fundamentally misreads" the ordinance. It is directed, he claims, not to speech of a particular content, but to particular "injur[ies]" that are "qualitatively different" from other injuries. This is word-play. What makes the anger, fear, sense of dishonor, etc. produced by violation of this ordinance distinct from the anger, fear, sense of dishonor, etc. produced by other fighting words is nothing other than the fact that it is caused by a distinctive idea, conveyed by a distinctive message. The First Amendment cannot be evaded that easily. It is obvious that the symbols which will arouse "anger, alarm or resentment in others on the basis of race, color, creed, religion or gender" are those symbols that communicate a message of hostility based on one of these characteristics. St. Paul concedes in its brief that the ordinance applies only to "racial, religious, or gender-specific symbols" such as "a burning cross, Nazi swastika or other instrumentality of like import." Indeed, St. Paul argued in the Juvenile Court that "[t]he burning of a cross does express a message and it is, in fact, the content of that message which the St. Paul Ordinance attempts to legislate."

The content-based discrimination reflected in the St. Paul ordinance comes within neither any of the specific exceptions to the First Amendment prohibition we discussed earlier, nor within a more general exception for content discrimination based on the very reasons why the particular class of speech at issue (here, fighting words) is proscribable. As explained earlier, the reason why fighting words are categorically excluded from the protection of the First Amendment is not that their content communicates any particular idea, but that their content embodies a particularly intolerable (and socially unnecessary) *mode* of expressing *whatever* idea the speaker wishes to convey. St. Paul has not singled out an especially offensive mode of expression—it has not, for example, selected for prohibition only those fighting words that communicate ideas in a threatening (as opposed to a merely obnoxious) manner. Rather, it has proscribed fighting words of whatever manner that communicate messages of racial, gender, or religious intolerance. Selectivity of this sort creates the possibility that the city is seeking to handicap the expression of particular ideas. That possibility would alone be enough to render the ordinance presumptively invalid, but St. Paul's comments and concessions in this case elevate the possibility to a certainty. . . .

Finally, St. Paul and its *amici* defend the conclusion of the Minnesota Supreme Court that, even if the ordinance regulates expression based on hostility towards its protected ideological content, this discrimination is nonetheless justified because it is narrowly tailored to serve compelling state interests. Specifically, they assert that the ordinance helps to ensure the basic human rights of members to live in peace where they wish. We do not doubt that these interests are compelling, and that the ordinance can be said to promote them. But the "danger of censorship" presented by a facially content-based statute requires that that weapon be employed only where it is "necessary to serve the asserted [compelling] interest." The dispositive question in this case, therefore, is whether content discrimination is reasonably necessary to achieve St. Paul's compelling interests; it plainly is not. An ordinance not limited to the favored topics, for example, would have precisely the same beneficial effect. In fact the only interest distinctively served by the content limitation is that of displaying the city council's special hostility towards the particular biases thus singled out. That is precisely what the First Amendment forbids. The politicians of St. Paul are entitled to express that hostility—but not through the means of imposing unique limitations upon speakers who (however benightedly) disagree.

* * *

Let there be no mistake about our belief that burning a cross in someone's front yard is reprehensible. But St. Paul has sufficient means at its disposal to prevent such behavior without adding the First Amendment to the fire.

The judgment of the Minnesota Supreme Court is reversed, and the case is remanded for proceedings not inconsistent with this opinion.

It is so ordered.

JUSTICE WHITE, *with whom* JUSTICE BLACKMUN *and* JUSTICE O'CONNOR *join, and with whom* JUSTICE STEVENS *joins except as to Part I(A), concurring in the judgment.*

I agree with the majority that the judgment of the Minnesota Supreme Court should be reversed. However, our agreement ends there.

This case could easily be decided within the contours of established First Amendment law by holding, as petitioner argues, that the St. Paul ordinance is fatally overbroad because it criminalizes not only unprotected expression but expression protected by the First Amendment. . . .

But in the present case, the majority casts aside long established First Amendment doctrine without the benefit of briefing and adopts an untried theory. This is hardly a judicious way of proceeding, and the Court's reasoning in reaching its result is transparently wrong.

I

A

This Court's decisions have plainly stated that expression falling within certain limited categories so lacks the values the First Amendment was designed to protect that the Constitution affords no protection to that expression. *Chaplinsky* v. *New Hampshire* (1942), made the point in the clearest possible terms:

> There are certain well-defined and narrowly limited classes of speech, the prevention and punishment of which have never been thought to raise any Constitutional problem. . . . It has been well observed that such utterances are no essential part of any exposition of ideas, and are of such slight social value as a step to truth that any benefit that may be derived from them is clearly outweighed by the social interest in order and morality.

Thus, as the majority concedes, this Court has long held certain discrete categories of expression to be proscribable on the basis of their content. For instance, the Court has held that the individual who falsely shouts "fire" in a crowded theatre may not claim the protection of the First Amendment. *Schenck* v. *United States*, (1919). The Court has concluded that neither child pornography, nor obscenity, is protected by the First Amendment. *New York* v. *Ferber*, (1973); *Roth* v. *United States*, (1957).

All of these categories are content based. But the Court has held that First Amendment does not apply to them because their expressive content is worthless or of *de minimis* value to society. We have not departed from this principle, emphasizing repeatedly that, "within the confines of [these] given classification[s], the evil to be restricted so overwhelmingly outweighs the expressive interests, if any, at stake that no process of case-by-case adjudication is required." This categorical approach has provided a principled and narrowly focused means for distinguishing between expression that the government may regulate freely and that which it may regulate on the basis of content only upon a showing of compelling need.

Today, however, the Court announces that earlier Courts did not mean their repeated statements that certain categories of expression are "not within the area of constitution protected speech." The present Court submits that such clear statements "must be taken in context" and are not "literally true."

To the contrary, those statements meant precisely what they said: The categorical approach is a firmly entrenched part of our First Amendment jurisprudence. Indeed, the Court in *Roth* reviewed the guarantees of freedom of expression in effect at the time of the ratification of the Constitution and concluded, "[i]n light of this history, it is apparent that the unconditional phrasing of the First Amendment was not intended to protect every utterance."

In its decision today, the Court points to "[n]othing . . . in this Court's precedents warrant[ing] disregard of this longstanding tradition." Nevertheless, the majority holds that the First Amendment protects those narrow categories of expression long held to be undeserving of First Amendment protection—at least to the extent that the lawmakers may not regulate some fighting words more strictly than others because of their content. The Court announces that such content-based distinctions violate the First Amendment because "the government may not regulate use based on hostility—or favoritism—towards the underlying message expressed." Should the government want to criminalize certain fighting words, the Court now requires it to criminalize all fighting words.

To borrow a phrase, "Such a simplistic, all-or-nothing-at-all approach to the First Amendment protection is at odds with common sense and with our jurisprudence as well." It is inconsistent to hold that the government may proscribe an entire category of speech because the content of that speech is evil, *Ferber*, but that the government may not treat a subset of that category differently without violating the First Amendment; the content of the subset is by definition worthless and undeserving protection.

The majority's observation that fighting words are "quite expressive indeed," is no answer. Fighting words are not a means of exchanging views, rallying supporters, or registering a protest; they are directed against individuals to provoke violence or to inflict injury. Therefore, a ban on all fighting words or on a subset of the fighting words category would restrict only the social evil of hate speech, without creating the danger of driving viewpoints from the marketplace.

Therefore, the Court's insistence on inventing its brand of First Amendment underinclusiveness puzzles me. The overbreadth doctrine has the redeeming virtue of attempting to avoid the chilling of protected expression, but the Court's new "underbreadth" creation serves no desirable function. Instead, it permits, indeed invites, the continuation of expressive conduct that in this case is evil and worthless in First Amendment terms, until the city of St. Paul cures the underbreadth by adding to its ordinance a catch-all phrase such as "and all other fighting words that may constitutionally be subject to this ordinance."

Any contribution of this holding to First Amendment jurisprudence is surely a negative one, since it necessarily signals that expressions of violence, such as the message of intimidation and racial hatred conveyed by burning a cross on someone's lawn, are of sufficient value to outweigh the social interest in order and morality that has traditionally placed such fighting words outside the First Amendment. Indeed, by characterizing fighting words as a form of "debate," the majority legitimates hate speech as a form of public discussion.

Furthermore, the Court obscures the line between speech that could be regulated freely on the basis of content (i.e., the narrow categories of expression falling outside the First Amendment) and that which could be regulated on the basis of content only upon a showing of a compelling state interest (i.e., all remaining expression). By placing fighting words, which the Court has long held to be valueless, on at least equal constitutional footing with political discourse and other forms of speech that we have deemed to have the greatest social value, the majority devalues the latter category.

B

In a second break with precedent, the Court refuses to sustain the ordinance even though it would survive under the strict scrutiny applicable to other protected expression. Assuming, *arguendo*, that the St. Paul ordinance is a content-based regulation of protected expression, it nevertheless would pass First Amendment review under settled law upon a showing that the regulation " 'is necessary to serve a compelling state interest and is narrowly drawn to achieve that end.' " *Simon & Schuster, Inc.* v. *New York Crime Victims Board*, (1991). St. Paul has urged that its ordinance, in the words of the majority, "helps to ensure the basic human rights of members of groups that have historically been subjected to discrimination. . . . " The Court expressly concedes that this interest is compelling and is promoted by the ordinance. Nevertheless, the Court treats strict scrutiny analysis as irrelevant to the constitutionality of the legislation:

> The dispositive question . . . is whether content discrimination is reasonably necessary in order to achieve St. Paul's compelling interests; it plainly is not. An ordinance not limited to the favored topics would have precisely the same beneficial effect.

Under the majority's view, a narrowly drawn, content-based ordinance could never pass constitutional muster if the object of that legislation could be accomplished by banning a wider category of speech. This appears to be a fundamental tool of First Amendment analysis.

. . . As with its rejection of the Court's categorical analysis, the majority offers no reasoned basis for discarding our firmly established strict scrutiny analysis at this time. The majority appears to believe that its doctrinal revisionism is necessary to prevent our elected lawmakers from prohibiting libel against members of one political party but not another and from enacting similarly preposterous laws. The majority is misguided.

Although the First Amendment does not apply to categories of unprotected speech, such as fighting words, the Equal Protection Clause requires that the regulation of unprotected speech be rationally related to a legitimate government interest. A defamation statute that drew distinctions on the basis of political affiliation or "an ordinance prohibiting only those legally obscene works that contain criticism of the city government," would unquestionably fail rational basis review.

Turning to the St. Paul ordinance and assuming *arguendo*, as the majority does, that the ordinance is not constitutionally overbroad, there is no question that it would pass equal protection review. The ordinance proscribes a subset of "fighting words," those that injure "on the basis of race, color, creed, religion or gender." This selective regulation reflects the City's judgment that harms based on race, color, creed, religion, or gender are more pressing public concerns than the harms caused by other fighting words. In light of our Nation's long and painful experience with discrimination, this determination is plainly reasonable. Indeed, as the majority concedes, the interest is compelling. . . .

C

As I see it, the Court's theory does not work and will do nothing more than confuse the law. Its selection of this case to rewrite First Amendment law is particularly inexplicable, because the whole problem could have been avoided by deciding this case under settled First Amendment principles.

II

Although I disagree with the Court's analysis, I do agree with its conclusion. The St. Paul ordinance is unconstitutional. However, I would decide the case on overbreadth grounds.

. . . I agree with petitioner that the ordinance is invalid on its face. Although the ordinance as construed reaches categories of speech that are constitutionally unprotected, it also criminalizes a substantial amount of expression that—however repugnant—is shielded by the First Amendment.

. . . In the First Amendment context, "[c]riminal statutes must be scrutinized with particular care; those that make unlawful a substantial amount of constitutionally protected conduct may be held facially invalid even if they also have legitimate application." The St. Paul antibias ordinance is such a law. Although the ordinance reaches conduct that is unprotected, it also makes criminal expressive conduct that causes only hurt feelings, offense, or resentment, and is protected by the First Amendment. The ordinance is therefore fatally overbroad and invalid on its face.

III

Today, the Court has disregarded two established principles of First Amendment law without providing a coherent replacement theory. Its decision is an arid, doctrinaire interpretation, driven by the frequently irresistible impulse of judges to tinker with the First Amendment. The decision is mischievous at best and will surely confuse the lower courts. I join the judgment, but not the folly of the opinion.

JUSTICE BLACKMUN, *concurring in the judgment.*

I regret what the Court has done in this case. The majority opinion signals one of two possibilities; it will serve as precedent for future cases, or it will not. Either result is disheartening.

In the first instance, by deciding that a State cannot regulate speech that causes great harm unless it also regulates speech that does not (setting law and logic on their heads), the Court seems to abandon the categorical approach, and inevitably to relax the level of scrutiny applicable to content-based laws. As JUSTICE WHITE points out, this weakens the traditional protections of speech. If all expressive activity must be accorded the same protection, that protection will be scant. The simple reality is that the Court will never provide child pornography or cigarette advertising the level of protection customarily granted political speech. If we are forbidden from categorizing, as the Court has done here, we shall reduce protection across the board. It is sad that in its effort to reach a satisfying result in this case, the Court is willing to weaken First Amendment protections.

In the second instance is the possibility that this case will not significantly alter First Amendment jurisprudence, but, instead, will be regarded as an aberration—a case where the Court manipulated doctrine to strike down an ordinance whose premise it opposed, namely, that racial threats and verbal assaults are of greater harm than other fighting words. I fear that the Court has been distracted from its proper mission by the temptation to decide the issue over "politically correct speech" and "cultural diversity," neither of which is presented here. If this is the meaning of today's opinion, it is perhaps even more regrettable.

I see no First Amendment values that are compromised by a law that prohibits hoodlums from driving minorities out of their homes by burning crosses on their lawns, but I see great harm in preventing the people of St. Paul from specifically punishing the race-based fighting words that so prejudice their community.

I concur in the judgment, however, because I agree with JUSTICE WHITE that this particular ordinance reaches beyond fighting words to speech protected by the First Amendment.

JUSTICE STEVENS, *with whom* JUSTICE WHITE *and* JUSTICE BLACKMUN *join as to Part I, concurring in the judgment.*

Conduct that creates special risks or causes special harms may be prohibited by special rules. Lighting a fire near an ammunition dump or a gasoline storage tank is especially dangerous; such behavior may be punished more severely than burning trash in a vacant lot. Threatening someone because of her race or religious beliefs may cause particularly severe trauma or touch off a riot, and threatening a high public official may cause substantial social disruption; such threats may be punished more severely than threats against someone based on, say, his support of a particular athletics team. There are legitimate, reasonable, and neutral justifications for such special rules.

This case involves the constitutionality of one such ordinance. Because the regulated conduct has some communicative content—a message of racial, religious, or gender hostility—the ordinance raises two quite different First Amendment questions. Is the ordinance "overbroad" because it prohibits too much speech? If not, is it "underbroad" because it does not prohibit enough speech?

In answering these questions, my colleagues today wrestle with two broad principles: first, that certain "categories of expression [including 'fighting words'] are 'not within the area of constitutionally protected speech,'" *ante*, and second, that "[c]ontent-based regulations [of expression] are presumptively invalid." Although in past opinions the Court has repeated both of these maxims, it has—quite rightly—adhered to neither with the absolutism suggested by my colleagues. Thus, while I agree that the St. Paul ordinance is unconstitutionally overbroad for the reasons stated in Part II of JUSTICE WHITE's opinion, I write separately to suggest how the allure of absolute principles has skewed the analysis of both the majority and concurring opinions.

I

Fifty years ago, the Court articulated a categorical approach to First Amendment jurisprudence. . . .

We have, as JUSTICE WHITE observes, often described such categories of expression as "not within the area of constitutionally protected speech." *Roth* v. *United States*, (1957).

The Court today revises this categorical approach. It is not, the Court rules, that certain "categories" of expression are "unprotected," but rather that certain "elements" of expression are wholly "proscribable." To the Court, an expressive act, like a chemical compound, consists of more than one element. Although the act may be regulated because it contains a proscribable element, it may not be regulated on the basis of another (nonproscribable) element it also contains. Thus, obscene antigovernment speech may be regulated because it is obscene, but not because it is antigovernment. It is this revision of the categorical approach that allows the Court to assume that the St.

Paul ordinance proscribes *only* fighting words, while at the same time concluding that the ordinance is invalid because it imposes a content-based regulation on expressive activity.

As an initial matter, the Court's revision of the categorical approach seems to me something of an adventure in a doctrinal wonderland, for the concept of "obscene antigovernment" speech is fantastical. The category of the obscene is very narrow; to be obscene, expression must be found by the trier of fact to "appea[l] to the prurient interest, . . . depic[t] or describ[e], in a patently offensive way, sexual conduct, [and] taken as a whole, *lac[k] serious literary, artistic, political or scientific value." Miller* v. *California,* (1973) (emphasis added). "Obscene antigovernment" speech, then, is a contradiction in terms: If expression is antigovernment, it does not "lac[k] serious . . . political . . . value" and cannot be obscene.

The Court attempts to bolster its argument by likening its novel analysis to that applied to restrictions on the time, place, or manner of expression or on expressive conduct. It is true that loud speech in favor of the Republican Party can be regulated because it is loud, but not because it is pro-Republican; and it is true that the public burning of the American flag can be regulated because it involves public burning and not because it involves the flag. But these analogies are inapposite. In each of these examples, the two elements (e.g., loudness and pro-Republican orientation) can coexist; in the case of "obscene antigovernment" speech, however, the presence of one element ("obscenity") by definition means the absence of the other. To my mind, it is unwise and unsound to craft a new doctrine based on such highly speculative hypotheticals.

I am, however, even more troubled by the second step of the Court's analysis—namely, its conclusion that the St. Paul ordinance is an unconstitutional content-based regulation of speech. Drawing on broadly worded *dicta,* the Court establishes a near-absolute ban on content-based regulations of fighting words by subject matter. Thus, while the Court rejects the "all-or-nothing-at-all" nature of the categorical approach, it promptly embraces an absolutism of its own: within a particular "proscribable" category of expression, the Court holds, a government must either proscribe *all* speech or no speech at all. This aspect of the Court's ruling fundamentally misunderstands the role and constitutional status of content-based regulations on speech, conflicts with the very nature of First Amendment jurisprudence, and disrupts well-settled principles of First Amendment law.

Although the Court has, on occasion, declared that content-based regulations of speech are "never permitted," *Police Dept. of Chicago* v. *Mosley,* (1972), such claims are overstated. Indeed, in *Mosley* itself, the Court indicated that Chicago's selective proscription of nonlabor picketing was not *per se* unconstitutional, but rather could be upheld if the City demonstrated that nonlabor picketing was "clearly more disruptive than [labor] picketing." Contrary to the broad *dicta* in *Mosley* and elsewhere, our decisions demonstrate that content-based distinctions, far from being presumptively invalid, are an inevitable and indispensable aspect of a coherent understanding of the First Amendment.

This is true at every level of the First Amendment law. In broadest terms, our entire First Amendment jurisprudence creates a regime based on the content of speech. The scope of the First Amendment is determined by the content of expressive activity: Although the First Amendment broadly protects "speech," it does not protect the right to "fix prices, breach contracts, make false warranties, place bets with bookies, threaten, [or] extort." Similarly, "the line between permissible advocacy and impermissible incitation to crime or violence depends, not merely on the setting which the speech occurs, but also on exactly what the speaker had to say." *Young* v. *American Mini Theaters, Inc.,* (1976).

Likewise, whether speech falls within one of the categories of "unprotected" or "proscribable" expression is determined, in part, by its content. Whether a magazine is obscene, a gesture a fighting word, or a photograph child pornography is determined, in part, by its content. Even within categories of protected expression, the First Amendment status of speech is fixed by its content. *New York Times Co.* v. *Sullivan,* (1964), and *Dun & Bradstreet, Inc.* v. *Greenmoss Builders, Inc.,* (1985), establish that the level of protection given to speech depends upon its subject matter: speech about public officials or matters of public concern receives greater protection than speech about other topics. It can, therefore, scarcely be said that the regulation of expressive activity cannot be predicated on its content: much of our First Amendment jurisprudence is premised on the assumption that content makes a difference.

. . . All of these cases involved the selective regulation of speech based on content—precisely the sort of regulation the Court invalidates today. Such selective regulations are unavoidably content based, but they are not, in my opinion, "presumptively invalid." As these many decisions and examples demonstrate, the prohibition on content based regulations is not nearly as total as the *Mosley* dictum suggests.

Disregarding this vast body of case law, the Court today goes beyond even the overstatement in *Mosley* and applies the prohibition on content-based regulation to speech that the Court had until today considered wholly "unprotected" by the First Amendment—namely, fighting words. This new absolutism in the prohibition of content-based regulations severely contorts the fabric of settled First Amendment law.

Our First Amendment decisions have created a rough hierarchy in the constitutional protection of speech. Core political speech occupies the highest, most protected position; commercial speech and nonobscene, sexually explicit speech are regarded as a sort of second-class expression; obscenity and fighting words receive the least protection of all. Assuming that the Court is correct that this last class of speech is not wholly "unprotected," it certainly does not follow that fighting words and obscenity receive the *same* sort of protection afforded core political speech. Yet in ruling that proscribable speech cannot be regulated based on subject matter, the Court does just that. Perversely, this gives fighting words *greater* protection than is afforded commercial speech. If Congress can prohibit false advertising directed at airline passengers without also prohibiting false advertising directed at bus passengers and if a city can prohibit political advertisements in its busses while allowing other advertisements, it is ironic to hold that a city cannot regulate fighting words based on "race, color, creed, religion or gender" while leaving unregulated fighting words based on "union membership or homosexuality." The Court today turns First Amendment law on its head: Communication that was once entirely unprotected (and that still can be wholly proscribed) is now entitled to greater protection than commercial speech—and possibly greater protection than core political speech.

Perhaps because the Court recognizes these perversities, it quickly offers some ad hoc limitations on its newly extended prohibition on content-based regulations. First, the Court states that a content-based regulation is valid "[w]hen the content discrimination is based upon the very reason the entire class of speech . . . is proscribable." In a pivotal passage, the Court writes

the Federal Government can criminalize only those physical threats that are directed against the President,—since the reasons why threats of violence are outside the First Amendment (protecting individuals from the fear of violence, from the disruption that fear engenders, and from the possibility that the threatened violence will occur) have special force when applied to the . . . President.

As I understand this opaque passage, Congress may choose from the set of unprotected speech (all threats) to proscribe only a subset (threats against the President) because those threats are particularly likely to cause "fear of violence," "disruption," and actual "violence."

Precisely this same reasoning, however, compels the conclusion that St. Paul's ordinance is constitutional. Just as Congress may determine that threats against the President entail more severe consequences than other threats, so St. Paul's City Council may determine that threats based on the target's race, religion, or gender cause more severe harm to both the target and to society than other threats. This latter judgment—that harms caused by racial, religious, and gender-based invective are qualitatively different from that caused by other fighting words—seems to me eminently reasonable and realistic.

In sum, the central premise of the Court's ruling—that "[c]ontent-based regulations are presumptively invalid"—has simplistic appeal, but lacks support in our First Amendment jurisprudence. To make matters worse, the Court today extends this overstated claim to reach categories of hitherto unprotected speech and, in doing so, wreaks havoc in an area of settled law. Finally, although the Court recognizes exceptions to its new principle, those exceptions undermine its very conclusion that the St. Paul ordinance is unconstitutional. Stated directly, the majority's position cannot withstand scrutiny.

II

Although I agree with much of JUSTICE WHITE's analysis, I do not join Part I-A of his opinion because I have reservations about the "categorical approach" to the First Amendment.

. . . Admittedly, the categorical approach to the First Amendment has some appeal: either expression is protected or it is not—the categories create safe harbors for governments and speakers alike. But this approach sacrifices subtlety for clarity and is, I am convinced, ultimately unsound. As an initial matter, the concept of "categories" fits poorly with the complex reality of expression. Few dividing lines in First Amendment law are straight and unwavering, and efforts at categorization inevitably give rise only to fuzzy boundaries. Our definitions of "obscenity," and "public forum," illustrate this all too well. The quest for doctrinal certainty through the definition of categories and subcategories is, in my opinion, destined to fail.

Moreover, the categorical approach does not take seriously the importance of *context*. The meaning of any expression and legitimacy of its regulation can only be determined in context. Whether, for example, a picture or a sentence is obscene cannot be judged in the abstract, but rather only in the context of its setting, its use, and its audience.

. . . In short, the history of the categorical approach is largely the history of narrowing the categories of unprotected speech.

This evolution, I believe, indicates that the categorical approach is unworkable and the quest for absolute categories of "protected" and "unprotected" speech ultimately futile. My analysis of the faults and limits of this approach persuades me that the categorical approach presented in Part I-A of JUSTICE WHITE's opinion is not an adequate response to the novel "underbreadth" analysis the Court sets forth today.

III

As the foregoing suggests, I disagree with both the Court's and part of JUSTICE WHITE's analysis of the constitutionality [of the] St. Paul ordinance. Unlike the Court, I do not believe that all content-based regulations are equally infirm and presumptively invalid; unlike JUSTICE WHITE, I do not believe that fighting words are wholly unprotected by the First Amendment. To the contrary, I believe our decisions establish a more complex and subtle analysis, one that considers the content and context of the regulated speech, and the nature and scope of the restriction on speech. Applying this analysis and assuming *arguendo* (as the Court does) that the St. Paul ordinance is *not* overbroad, I conclude that such a selective, subject-matter regulation on proscribable speech is constitutional.

Not all content-based regulations are alike; our decisions clearly recognize that some content-based restrictions raise more constitutional questions than others. Although the Court's analysis of content-based regulations cannot be reduced to a simple formula, we have considered a number of factors in determining the validity of such regulations.

First, as suggested above, the scope of protection provided expressive activity depends in part upon its content and character.

. . . The protection afforded expression turns as well on the context of the regulated speech.

. . . The nature of a contested restriction of speech also informs our evaluation of its constitutionality. Thus, for example, "[a]ny system of prior restraints of expression comes to this Court bearing a heavy presumption against its constitutional validity."

. . . Finally, in considering the validity of content-based regulations we have also looked more broadly at the scope of the restrictions. For example, in *Young* v. *American Mini Theaters*, we found significant the fact that "what [was] ultimately at stake [was] nothing more than a limitation on the place where adult films may be exhibited."

. . . All of these factors play some role in our evaluation of content-based regulations on expression. Such a multifaceted analysis cannot be conflated into two dimensions. Whatever the allure of absolute doctrines, it is just too simple to declare expression "protected" or "unprotected" or to proclaim a regulation "content-based" or "content-neutral."

In applying this analysis to the St. Paul ordinance, I assume *arguendo*—as the Court does—that the ordinance regulates *only* fighting words and therefore is *not* overbroad. Looking to the content and character of the regulated activity, two things are clear. First, by hypothesis the ordinance bars only low-value speech, namely, fighting words. By definition such expression constitutes "no essential part of any exposition of ideas, and [is] of such slight social value as a step to truth that any benefit that may be derived from [it] is clearly outweighed by the social interest in order and morality." Second, the ordinance regulates "expressive conduct [rather] than . . . the written or spoken word." *Texas* v. *Johnson*.

Looking at the context of the regulated activity, it is again significant that the statute (by hypothesis) regulates *only* fighting words. Whether words are fighting words is determined in part by their context. Fighting words are not words that merely cause offense; fighting words must be directed at individuals so as to "by their very utterance inflict injury." By hypothesis, then, the St. Paul ordinance restricts speech in confrontational and potentially violent situations. The case at hand is illustrative. The cross-burning in this case—directed as it was to a single African-American family trapped in their home—was nothing more that a crude form of physical intimidation. That this cross-burning sends a message of racial hostility does not automatically endow it with complete constitutional protection.

Significantly, the St. Paul ordinance regulates speech not on the basis of its subject matter or the viewpoint expressed, but rather on the basis of the *harm* the speech causes. In this regard, the Court fundamentally misreads the St. Paul ordinance . . . , Contrary to the Court's suggestions, the ordinance regulates only a subcategory of expression that causes *injuries* based on "race, color, creed, religion or gender," not a subcategory that involves *discussions* that concern those characteristics. The ordinance, as construed by the Court, criminalizes expression that "one knows . . . [by its very utterance inflicts injury on] others on the basis of race, color, creed, religion or gender." In this regard, the ordinance resembles the child pornography law at issue in *Ferber*, which in effect singled out child pornography because those publications caused far greater harms than pornography involving adults.

. . . The St. Paul ordinance is evenhanded. In a battle between advocates of tolerance and advocates of intolerance, the ordinance does not prevent either side from hurling fighting words at the other on the basis of their conflicting ideas, but it does bar *both* sides from hurling such words on the basis of the text's "race, color, creed, religion or gender." To extend the Court's pugilistic metaphor, the St. Paul ordinance simply bans punches "below the belt"—*by either party*. It does not, therefore, favor one side of any debate.

Finally, it is noteworthy that the St. Paul ordinance is, as construed by the Court today, quite narrow. The St. Paul ordinance does not ban all "hate speech," nor does it ban, say, all cross-burnings or all swastika displays. Rather it only bans a subcategory of the already narrow category of fighting words. Such a limited expression leaves open and protected a vast range of expression on the subjects of racial, religious, and gender equality. As construed by the Court today, the ordinance certainly does not " 'raise the specter that the Government may effectively drive certain ideas or viewpoints from the marketplace.' " Petitioner is free to burn a cross to announce a rally or to express views about racial supremacy; he may do so on private property or public land, at day or at night, so long as the burning is not so threatening and so directed at an individual as to "by its very [execution] inflict injury." Such a limited proscription scarcely offends the First Amendment.

In sum, the St. Paul ordinance, (as construed by the Court) regulates expressive activity that is wholly proscribable and does so not on the basis of viewpoint, but rather in recognition of the different harms caused by such activity. Taken together, these several considerations persuade me that the St. Paul ordinance is not an unconstitutional content-based regulation of speech. Thus, were the ordinance not overbroad, I would vote to uphold it.

WISCONSIN v. MITCHELL
___ U. S. ___; ___ L. Ed. ___; ___ S. Ct. ___ (1993)

CHIEF JUSTICE REHNQUIST *delivered the opinion for a unanimous Court.*

Respondent Todd Mitchell's sentence for aggravated battery was enhanced because he *intentionally selected his victim on account of the victim's race.* The question presented in this case is whether this penalty enhancement is prohibited by the First and Fourteenth Amendments. We hold that it *is not.*

On the evening of October 7, 1989, a group of young black men and boys, including Mitchell, gathered at an apartment complex in Kenosha, Wisconsin. Several members of the group discussed a scene from the motion picture "Mississippi Burning," in which a white man beat a young black boy who was praying. The group moved outside and Mitchell asked them: " 'Do you all feel hyped up to move on some white people?' "

Shortly thereafter, a young white boy approached the group on the opposite side of the street where they were standing. As the boy walked by, Mitchell said: " 'You all want to fuck somebody up? There goes a white boy; go get him.' " Mitchell counted to three and pointed in the boy's direction. The group ran towards the boy, beat him severely, and stole his tennis shoes. The boy was rendered unconscious and remained in a coma for four days.

After a jury trial in the Circuit Court for Kenosha County, Mitchell was convicted of aggravated battery. That offense ordinarily carries a maximum sentence of two years' imprisonment. But because the jury found that Mitchell had intentionally selected his victim because of the boy's race, the maximum sentence for Mitchell's offense was increased to seven years under [a provision that] enhances the maximum penalty for an offense whenever the defendant "[i]ntentionally selects the person against whom the crime . . . is committed. . . because of the race, religion, color, disability, sexual orientation, national origin or ancestry of that person. . . ." The Circuit Court sentenced Mitchell to four years' imprisonment for the aggravated battery.

Mitchell unsuccessfully sought postconviction relief in the Circuit Court. Then he appealed his conviction and sentence, challenging the constitutionality of Wisconsin's penalty-enhancement provision on First Amendment grounds. The Wisconsin Court of Appeals rejected Mitchell's challenge (1991), but the Wisconsin Supreme Court reversed. The Supreme Court held that the statute "violates the First Amendment directly by punishing what the legislature has deemed to be offensive thought." (1992) It rejected the State's contention "that the statute punishes only the 'conduct' of intentional selection of a victim." According to the court, "[t]he statute punishes the 'because of' aspect of the defendant's selection, the reason the defendant selected the victim, the motive behind the selection." And under *R. A. V. v. St. Paul*, 505 U. S. ___ (1992), "the Wisconsin legislature cannot criminalize bigoted thought with which it disagrees."

The Supreme Court also held that the penalty-enhancement statute was unconstitutionally overbroad. It reasoned that, in order to prove that a defendant intentionally selected his victim because of the victim's protected status, the State would often have to introduce evidence of the defendant's prior speech, such as racial epithets he may have uttered before the commission of the offense. This evidentiary use of protected speech, the court thought, would have a "chilling effect" on those who feared the possibility of prosecution for offenses subject to penalty enhancement. Finally, the court distinguished antidiscrimination laws, which have long been held constitutional, on the ground that the Wisconsin statute punishes the "subjective mental process" of selecting a victim because of his protected status, whereas antidiscrimination laws prohibit "objective acts of discrimination."

We granted *certiorari* because of the importance of the question presented and the existence of a conflict of authority among state high courts on the constitutionality of statutes similar to Wisconsin's penalty-enhancement provision. We reverse.

Mitchell argues that we are bound by the Wisconsin Supreme Court's conclusion that the statute punishes bigoted thought and not conduct. There is no doubt that we are bound by a state court's construction of a state statute. *R. A. V.*,

supra, at ___ (slip op. at 2–3); *New York* v. *Ferber*, 458 U. S. 747, 769, n. 24 (1982); *Terminello* v. *Chicago*, 337 U. S. 1, 4 (1949). In *Terminello*, for example, the Illinois courts had defined the term " 'breach of the peace,' " in a city ordinance prohibiting disorderly conduct, to include " 'stirs the public to anger . . . or creates a disturbance.' " We held this construction to be binding on us. But here the Wisconsin Supreme Court did not, strictly speaking, construe the Wisconsin statute in the sense of defining the meaning of a particular statutory word or phrase. Rather, it merely characterized the "practical effect" of the statute for First Amendment purposes. ("Merely because the statute refers in a literal sense to the intentional 'conduct' of selecting, does not mean the court must turn a blind eye to the intent and practical effect of the law—punishment of motive or thought"). This assessment does not bind us. Once any ambiguities as to the meaning of the statute are resolved, we may form our own judgment as to its operative effect.

The State argues that the statute does not punish bigoted thought, as the Supreme Court of Wisconsin said, but instead punishes only conduct. While this argument is literally correct, it does not dispose of Mitchell's First Amendment challenge. To be sure, our cases reject the "view that an apparently limitless variety of conduct can be labeled 'speech' whenever the person engaging in the conduct intends thereby to express an idea." . . . Thus, a physical assault is not by any stretch of the imagination expressive conduct protected by the First Amendment. ("[V]iolence or other types of potentially expressive activities that produce special harms distinct from their communicative impact . . . are entitled to no constitutional protection"); *NAACP* v. *Claiborne Hardware Co.*, 458 U. S. 886, 916 (1982) ("The First Amendment does not protect violence").

But the fact remains that under the Wisconsin statute the same criminal conduct may be more heavily punished if the victim is selected because of his race or other protected status than if no such motive obtained. Thus, although the statute punishes criminal conduct, it enhances the maximum penalty for conduct motivated by a discriminatory point of view more severely than the same conduct engaged in for some other reason or for no reason at all. Because the only reason for the enhancement is the defendant's discriminatory motive for selecting his victim, Mitchell argues (and the Wisconsin Supreme Court held) that the statute violates the First Amendment by punishing offenders' bigoted beliefs.

Traditionally, sentencing judges have considered a wide variety of factors in addition to evidence bearing on guilt in determining what sentence to impose on a convicted defendant. See *Payne* v. *Tennessee*, 501 U. S. ___ (1991). The defendant's motive for committing the offense is one important factor. See I. W. LeFave & A. Scott, Substantive Criminal Law §3.6(b), p. 324 (1986). "Motives are most relevant when the trial judge sets the defendant's sentence, and it is not uncommon for a defendant to receive a minimum sentence because he was acting with good motives, or a rather high sentence because of his bad motives."

But it is equally true that a defendant's abstract beliefs, however obnoxious to most people, may not be taken into consideration by a sentencing judge. *Dawson* v. *Delaware*, 503 U. S. ___ (1992). In *Dawson*, the State introduced evidence at a capital-sentencing hearing that the defendant was a member of a white supremacist prison gang. Because "the evidence proved nothing more than [the defendant's] abstract beliefs," we held that its admission violated the defendant's First Amendment rights. In so holding, however, we emphasized that "the Constitution does not erect a *per se* barrier to the admission of evidence concerning one's beliefs and associations at sentencing simply because those beliefs and associations are protected by the First Amendment." Thus, in *Barclay* v. *Florida*, 463 U. S. 939 (1983) (plurality opinion), we allowed the sentencing judge to take into account the defendant's racial animus towards his victim. The evidence in that case showed that the defendant's membership in the Black Liberation Army and desire to provoke a "race war" were related to the murder of a white man for which he was convicted. Because "the elements of racial hatred in [the] murder" were relevant to several aggravating factors, we held that the trial judge permissibly took this evidence into account in sentencing the defendant to death.

Mitchell suggests that *Dawson* and *Barclay* are inapposite because they did not involve application of a penalty-enhancement provision. But in *Barclay* we held that it was permissible for the sentencing court to consider the defendant's racial animus in determining whether he should be sentenced to death, surely the most severe "enhancement" of all. And the fact that the Wisconsin Legislature has decided, as a general matter, that bias-motivated offenses warrant greater maximum penalties across the board does not alter the result here. For the primary responsibility for fixing criminal penalties lies with the legislature. . . .

Mitchell argues that the Wisconsin penalty-enhancement statute is invalid because it punishes the defendant's discriminatory motive, or reason, for acting. But motive plays the same role under the Wisconsin statute as it does under federal and state antidiscriminatory laws, which we have previously upheld against constitutional challenge. See *Roberts* v. *Jaycees*, 468 U. S., at 628; *Hishon* v. *King & Spalding*, 467 U. S. 69, 78 (1984); *Runyon* v. *McCrary*, 427 U. S. 160, 176 (1976). Title VII, for example, makes it unlawful for an employer to discriminate against an employee "*because of* such individual's race, color, religion, sex, or national origin." In *Hishon*, we rejected the argument that Title VII infringed employers' First Amendment rights. And more recently, in *R. A. V.* v. *St. Paul*, 505 U. S., at ___, we cited Title VII (as well as 18 U. S. C. §242 and 42 U. S. C. §§1981 and 1982) as an example of a permissible content-neutral regulation of conduct.

Nothing in our decision last term in *R. A. V.* compels a different result here. That case involved a First Amendment challenge to a municipal ordinance prohibiting the use of " 'fighting words' that insult or provoke violence, 'on the basis of race, color, creed, religion or gender.' " 505 U. S., at (quoting St. Paul Bias-Motivated Crime Ordinance, St. Paul, Minn., Legis. Code §292.02 [1990]). Because the ordinance only proscribed a class of "fighting words" deemed particularly offensive by the city—i.e., those "that contain. . .messages of bias-motivated' hatred" we held that it violated the rule against content-based discrimination. But whereas the ordinance struck down in *R. A. V.* was explicitly directed at expression (i.e., "speech" or "messages"), the statute in this case is aimed at conduct unprotected by the First Amendment.

Moreover, the Wisconsin statute singles out for enhancement bias-inspired conduct because this conduct is thought to inflict greater individual and societal harm. For example, according to the State and its *amici*, bias-motivated crimes are more likely to provoke retaliatory crimes, inflict distinct emotional harms on their victims, and incite community unrest . . . . The State's desire to redress these perceived harms provides an adequate explanation for its penalty-enhancement provision over and above mere disagreement with offenders' beliefs or biases. As Blackstone said long ago, "it is but reasonable that among crimes of different natures those should be most severely punished, which are the most destructive of the public safety and happiness." 4 W. Blackstone, Commentaries.

Finally, there remains to be considered Mitchell's argument that the Wisconsin statute is unconstitutionally overbroad because of its "chilling effect" on free speech. Mitchell argues (and the Wisconsin Supreme Court agreed) that the statute is "overbroad" because evidence of the defendant's prior speech or associations may be used to prove that the defendant intentionally selected his victim on account of the victim's protected status. Consequently, the argument goes, the statute impermissibly chills free expression with regard to such matters by those concerned about the possibility of enhanced sentences if they should in the future commit a criminal offense covered by the statute. We find no merit in this contention.

The sort of chill envisioned here is far more attenuated and unlikely than that contemplated in traditional "overbreadth" cases. We must conjure up a vision of a Wisconsin citizen suppressing his unpopular bigoted opinions for fear that if he later commits an offense covered by the statute, these opinions will be offered at trial to establish that he selected his victim on account of the victim's protected status, thus qualifying him for penalty-enhancement. To stay within the realm of rationality, we must surely put to one side minor misdemeanor offenses covered by the statute, such as negligent operation of a motor vehicle, for it is difficult, if not impossible, to conceive of a situation where such offenses would be racially motivated. We are left, then, with the prospect of a citizen suppressing his bigoted beliefs for fear that evidence of such beliefs will be introduced against him at trial if he commits a more serious offense against person or property. This is simply too speculative a hypothesis to support Mitchell's overbreadth claim.

The First Amendment, moreover, does not prohibit the evidentiary use of speech to establish the elements of a crime or to prove motive or intent. Evidence of a defendant's previous declarations or statements is commonly admitted in criminal trials subject to evidentiary rules dealing with relevancy, reliability and the like. Nearly half a century ago, in *Haupt* v. *United States*, 330 U. S. 631 (1947), we rejected a contention similar to that advanced by Mitchell here. Haupt was tried for the offense of treason, which, as defined by the Constitution (Art. III, §3), may depend very much on proof of motive. To prove that the acts in question were committed out of "adherence to the enemy" rather than "parental solicitude," the Government introduced evidence of conversations that had taken place long prior to the indictment, some of which consisted of statements showing Haupt's sympathy with Germany and Hitler and hostility towards the United States. We rejected Haupt's argument that this evidence was improperly admitted. While "[s]uch testimony is to be scrutinized with care to be certain the statements are not expressions of mere lawful and permissible difference of opinion with our own government or quite proper appreciation of the land of birth," we held that "these statements . . . clearly were admissible on the question of intent and adherence to the enemy." . . .

For the foregoing reasons, we hold that Mitchell's First Amendment rights were not violated by the application of the Wisconsin penalty-enhancement provision in sentencing him. The judgment of the Supreme Court of Wisconsin is therefore reversed, and the case is remanded for further proceedings not inconsistent with this opinion.

It is so ordered.

Student Rights and Free Expression

FEATURED CASES

Bethel School District v. *Fraser*   *Hazelwood School District* v. *Kuhlmeier*

Free expression rights of the First Amendment are the focus of increasing debate and division among students and educators. The debate focuses on the authority and responsibilities of public schools to carry out the schools' educational mission against charges that such authority unconstitutionally intrudes upon self-expression rights of students. This debate was dramatically brought before the Court in *Tinker* v. *Des Moines.* Here public school officials, under the claim of maintaining orderly processes and decorum, suspended students who persisted in wearing black armbands to express opposition to United States involvement in Vietnam. Justice Fortas, speaking for the Court, viewed the black armbands as peaceful expression of political opinion and thus protected by the First Amendment. The students' behavior did not cause disorder or disruption of school activities, observed Fortas, and "undifferentiated fear or apprehension of disturbance is not enough to overcome the right to freedom of expression." In any event, since school officials had permitted students in Des Moines to wear other symbols, such as political campaign buttons, Fortas saw the prohibition against armbands as a method to suppress opposition to the Vietnam War. "In our system," said Fortas, "students may not be regarded as closed-circuit recipients of only that which the state chooses to communicate." Thus, the Court ruled that public school students are entitled to free speech guarantees of the First Amendment. However, Fortas was careful to point out that the Court's decision pertained only to "symbolic speech" or speech itself and did not extend to protest demonstrations.

Nonetheless, Justice Hugo Black issued a sharp dissent. He complained that the Court's decision ushers in "a new revolutionary era of permissiveness in this country in which the power of school officials to control pupils is substantially weakened." Black took judicial notice of the timing of the decision and noted that "groups of students all over the land . . . [were] running loose, conducting break-ins, sit-ins, lie-ins, and smash-ins." Decisions like *Tinker*, warned Black, "subject all the public schools in the country to the whims and caprices of their loudest-mouthed, but maybe not their brightest students." He was certain that students were not wise enough to run the public school system.

Two more recent cases also illuminate vividly the increasing tension between the authority of educators in public schools to protect and promote the state's educational interests and the rights of students to exercise their First Amendment rights of free expression. In *Bethel School District No.403* v. *Fraser* (478 U.S. 675, 1986), the Court upheld disciplinary actions taken by school officials against a student (Fraser) who, in a nominating speech before a high school student assembly, "referred to his candidate in terms of an elaborate, graphic, and explicit sexual metaphor." Prior to the speech, Fraser discussed the speech with two teachers who advised him that the speech was inappropriate and that he probably should not deliver it since the "delivery of the speech might have 'severe consequences.' "

Subsequently, Fraser was disciplined pursuant to a school "disruptive-conduct" rule prohibiting "conduct which materially and substantially interferes with the educational process . . . , including the use of obscene, profane language or gestures."

In upholding the school's disciplinary action, Chief Justice Burger stated that the inculcation of "fundamental values is necessary to the maintenance of a democratic political system . . . is truly the 'work of the schools' " and that "nothing in the Constitution prohibits the states from insisting that certain modes of expression are inappropriate and subject to sanctions." As a result the Court somewhat modified *Tinker* by suggesting that interference with the inculcation of "fundamental values" could itself be viewed as a material disruption of the school's educational mission.

The Court also seemed to have moved a bit more from *Tinker* in its 1988 decision in *Hazelwood School District* v. *Kuhlmeier* (484 U.S. 260). Here the Court upheld the authority of a high school principal to stop publication of two articles in the student newspaper (the *Spectrum*): one relating stories of three pregnant Hazelwood students and the other describing reactions of students to their parents' divorces. The newspaper was written by students in a regular journalism class of the school wherein the teacher was required to submit page proofs to the principal for his approval prior to publication.

In the instant case, the principal objected to the pregnancy article since he viewed it as "inappropriate" for some of the younger students in the school; he objected to the divorce story since a student who complained of her father's conduct was identified by name. Student editors brought suit alleging that the principal's censorship violated their First Amendment rights. By a five-to-three vote, however, a Supreme Court majority disagreed with the students and indicated that the paper was a "nonpublic forum"; it was school-sponsored and under the circumstances could be subject to standards "reasonably related to legitimate pedagogical concerns." By so doing, the Court departed from *Tinker's* "material disruption" standard and found that the principal's conduct met the "reasonableness" standard mentioned above.

In recent years, much of the intense controversy over the free expression rights of students has shifted from public schools to colleges and universities. A number of these institutions have passed "antihate" speech codes that are designed to prohibit derogatory and demeaning remarks directed at certain individuals or groups who are targeted because of their race or sexual orientation. These codes have sparked controversy on university and college campuses as well as in the courts. Do you agree with such restrictions? Might restrictions of this type be more appropriate at the secondary school level rather than in higher education?

CHIEF JUSTICE BURGER *delivered the opinion of the Court.*

We granted certiorari to decide whether the First Amendment prevents a school district from disciplining a high school student for giving a lewd speech at a school assembly.

I

On April 26, 1983, respondent Matthew N. Fraser, a student at Bethel High School in Bethel, Washington, delivered a speech nominating a fellow student for student elective office. Approximately 600 high school students, many of whom were 14-year-olds, attended the assembly. Students were required to attend the assembly or to report to the study hall. The assembly was part of a school-sponsored educational program in self-government. Students who elected not to attend the assembly were required to report to study hall. During the entire speech, Fraser referred to his candidate in terms of an elaborate, graphic, and explicit sexual metaphor.

Two of Fraser's teachers, with whom he discussed the content of his speech in advance, informed him that the speech was "inappropriate and that he probably should not deliver it" and that his delivery of the speech might have "severe consequences."

During Fraser's delivery of the speech, a school counselor observed the reaction of students to the speech. Some students hooted and yelled; some by gestures graphically simulated the sexual activities pointedly alluded to in respondent's speech. Other students appeared to be bewildered and embarrassed by the speech. One teacher reported that on the day following the speech, she found it necessary to forgo a portion of the scheduled class lesson in order to discuss the speech with the class.

A Bethel High School disciplinary rule prohibiting the use of obscene language in the school provides:

> Conduct which materially and substantially interferes with the educational process is prohibited, including the use of obscene, profane language or gestures.

The morning after the assembly, the Assistant Principal called Fraser into her office and notified him that the school considered his speech to have been a violation of this rule. Fraser was presented with copies of four letters submitted by teachers, describing his conduct in the assembly; he was given a chance to explain his conduct. He admitted to having given the speech described and that he deliberately used sexual innuendo in the speech. Fraser was then informed that he would be suspended for three days, and that his name would be removed from the list of candidates for graduation speaker at the school's commencement exercises.

Fraser sought review of this disciplinary action through the School District's grievance procedures. The hearing officer determined that the speech given by respondent was "indecent, lewd, and offensive to students and faculty in attendance at the assembly." The examiner determined that the speech fell within the ordinary meaning of "obscene," as used in the disruptive-conduct rule, and affirmed the discipline in its entirety. Fraser served two days of his suspension and was allowed to return to school on the third day.

Respondent, by his father as guardian, then brought this action in the United States District Court for the Western District of Washington. Respondent alleged a violation of his First Amendment right to freedom of speech and sought both injunctive relief and monetary damages under 42 U.S.C., 1983. The District Court held that the school's sanctions violated respondent's right to freedom of speech under the First Amendment to the United States Constitution, that the school's disruptive-conduct rule is unconstitutionally vague and overbroad, and that the removal of respondent's name from the graduation speaker's list violated the Due Process Clause of the Fourteenth Amendment because the disciplinary rule makes no mention of such removal as a possible sanction. The District Court awarded respondent $278 in damages, $12,750 in litigation costs and attorney's fees, and enjoined the School District from preventing respondent from speaking at the commencement ceremonies. Respondent, who had been elected graduation speaker by a write-in vote of his classmates, delivered a speech at the commencement ceremonies on June 8, 1983.

The Court of Appeals for the Ninth Circuit affirmed the judgment of the District Court (1985), holding that respondent's speech was indistinguishable from the protest armband in *Tinker* v. *Des Moines Independent Community School* (1969). The court explicitly rejected the School District's argument that the speech, unlike the passive conduct of wearing a black armband, had a disruptive effect on the educational process. The Court of Appeals also rejected the School District's argument that it had an interest in protecting an essentially captive audience of minors from lewd and indecent language in a setting sponsored by the school, reasoning that the school board's "unbridled discretion" to determine what discourse is "decent" would "increase the risk of cementing white, middle-class standards for determining what is acceptable and proper speech and behavior in our public schools." Finally, the Court of Appeals rejected the School District's argument that, incident to its responsibility for the school curriculum, it had the power to control the language used to express ideas during a school-sponsored activity.

We granted certiorari (1985).

We reverse.

II

This Court acknowledged in *Tinker* that students do not "shed their constitutional rights to freedom of speech or expression at the schoolhouse gate." The Court of Appeals read that case as precluding any discipline of Fraser for indecent speech and lewd conduct in the school assembly. That court appears to have proceeded on the theory that the use of lewd and obscene speech in order to make what the speaker considered to be a point in a nominating speech for a fellow student was essentially the same as the wearing of an armband in *Tinker* as a form of protest or the expression of a political position.

The marked distinction between the political "message" of the armbands in *Tinker* and the sexual content of the respondent's speech in this case seems to have been given little weight by the Court of Appeals. In upholding the students' right to engage in a nondisruptive, passive expression of a political viewpoint in *Tinker*, this Court was careful to note that the case did "not concern speech or action that intrudes upon the work of the schools or the rights of other students."

It is against this background that we turn to consider the level of First Amendment protection accorded to Fraser's utterances and actions before an official high school assembly attended by 600 students.

III

The role and purpose of the American public school system was well described by two historians, saying "public education must prepare pupils for citizenship in the Republic. . . . It must inculcate the habits and manners of civility as values in themselves conducive to happiness and as indispensable to the practice of self-government in the community and the nation." See C. Beard and M. Beard, *New Basic History of the United States* 228 (1968). In *Ambach* v. *Norwick*, 441 U.S. 68 (1979), we echoed the essence of this statement of the objectives of public education as the "inculcat[ion of] fundamental values necessary to the maintenance of a democratic political system."

These fundamental values of "habits and manners of civility" essential to a democratic society must, of course, include tolerance of divergent political and religious views, even when the views expressed may be unpopular. But these "fundamental values" must also take into account consideration of the sensibilities of others and, in the case of a school, the sensibilities of fellow students. The undoubted freedom to advocate unpopular and controversial views in schools and classrooms must be balanced against the society's countervailing interest in teaching students the boundaries of socially appropriate behavior. Even the most heated political discourse in a democratic society requires consideration for the personal sensibilities of the other participants and audiences.

In our Nation's legislative halls, where some of the most vigorous political debates in our society are carried on, there are rules prohibiting the use of expressions offensive to other participants in the debate. Can it be that what is proscribed in the halls of Congress is beyond the reach of school officials to regulate?

The First Amendment guarantees wide freedom in matters of adult public discourse. A sharply divided Court upheld the right to express an antidraft viewpoint in a public place, albeit in terms highly offensive to most citizens. See *Cohen* v. *California* (1971). It does not follow, however, that simply because the use of an offensive form of expression may not be prohibited to adults making what the speaker considers a political point, that the same latitude must be permitted to children in a public school. In *New Jersey* v. *T.L.O.* (1985), we reaffirmed that the constitutional rights of students in public school are not automatically coextensive with the rights of adults in other settings. As cogently expressed by Judge Newman, "the First Amendment gives a high school student the classroom right to wear Tinker's armband, but not Cohen's jacket." *Thomas* v. *Board of Education, Grenville Central School Dist.*, 607 F.2d 1043, 1057 (CA2 1979) (opinion, concurring in result).

Surely it is a highly appropriate function of public school education to prohibit the use of vulgar and offensive terms in public discourse. Indeed, the "fundamental values necessary to the maintenance of a democratic political system" disfavor the use of terms of debate highly offensive or highly threatening to others. Nothing in the Constitution prohibits the States from insisting that certain modes of expression are inappropriate and subject to sanctions. The inculcation of these values is truly the "work of the schools." The determination of what manner of speech in the classroom or in school assembly is inappropriate properly rests with the school board.

The process of educating our youth for citizenship in public schools is not confined to books, the curriculum, and the civics class; schools must teach by example the shared values of a civilized social order. Consciously or otherwise, teachers—and indeed the older students—demonstrate the appropriate form of civil discourse and political expression by their conduct and deportment in and out of class. Inescapably, like parents, they are role models. The schools, as instruments of the State, may determine that the essential lessons of civil, mature conduct cannot be conveyed in a school that tolerates lewd, indecent, or offensive speech and conduct such as that indulged in by this confused boy.

The pervasive sexual innuendo in Fraser's speech was plainly offensive to both teachers and students—indeed to any mature person. By glorifying male sexuality, and in its verbal content, the speech was acutely insulting to teenage girl students. The speech could well be seriously damaging to its less mature audience, many of whom were only fourteen years old and on the threshold of awareness of human sexuality. Some students were reported as bewildered by the speech and the reaction of mimicry it provoked.

This Court's First Amendment jurisprudence has acknowledged limitations on the otherwise absolute interest of the speaker in reaching an unlimited audience where the speech is sexually explicit and the audience may include children. In *Ginsberg* v. *New York* (1968), this Court upheld a New York statute banning the sale of sexually oriented material to minors, even though the material in question was entitled to First Amendment protection with respect to adults. And in addressing the question whether the First Amendment

places any limit on the authority of public schools to remove books from a public school library, all Members of the Court, otherwise sharply divided, acknowledged that the school board has the authority to remove books that are vulgar. *Board of Education* v. *Pico* (1982). These cases recognize the obvious concern on the part of parents and school authorities acting in *in loco parentis* to protect children—especially in a captive audience—from exposure to sexually explicit, indecent, or lewd speech. . . .

We hold that petitioner School District acted entirely within its permissible authority in imposing sanctions upon Fraser in response to his offensively lewd and indecent speech. Unlike the sanctions imposed on the students wearing armbands in *Tinker*, the penalties imposed in this case were unrelated to any political view-point. The First Amendment does not prevent the school officials from determining that to permit a vulgar and lewd speech such as respondent's would undermine the school's basic educational mission. A high school assembly or classroom is no place for a sexually explicit monologue directed towards an unsuspecting audience of teenage students. Accordingly, it was perfectly appropriate for the school to disassociate itself to make the point to the pupils that vulgar speech and lewd conduct are wholly inconsistent with the "fundamental values" of public school education. Justice Black, dissenting in *Tinker*, made a point that is especially relevant in this case:

> I wish therefore . . . to disclaim any purpose . . . to hold that the federal Constitution compels the teachers, parents and elected school officials to surrender control of the American public school system to public school students.

IV

Respondent contends that the circumstances of his suspension violated due process because he had no way of knowing that the delivery of the speech in question would subject him to disciplinary sanctions. This argument is wholly without merit. We have recognized that "maintaining security and order in the schools requires a certain degree of flexibility in school disciplinary procedures, and we have respected the value of preserving the informality of the student-teacher relationship." Given the school's need to be able to impose disciplinary sanctions for a wide range of unanticipated conduct disruptive of the educational process, the school disciplinary rules need not be as detailed as a criminal code which imposes criminal sanctions. Two days' suspension from school does not rise to the level of a penal sanction calling for the full panoply of procedural due process protections applicable to a criminal prosecution. The school disciplinary rule proscribing "obscene" language and the prespeech admonitions of teachers gave adequate warning to Fraser that his lewd speech could subject him to sanctions.*

The judgment of the Court of Appeals for the Ninth Circuit is

Reversed.

JUSTICE BLACKMUN *concurs in the result.*

JUSTICE BRENNAN, *concurring in the judgment.*

Respondent gave the following speech at a high school assembly in support of a candidate for student government office:

> I know a man who is firm—he's firm in his pants, he's firm in his shirt, his character is firm—but most . . . of all, his belief in you, the students of Bethel, is firm.
>
> Jeff Kuhlman is a man who takes his point and pounds it in. If necessary, he'll take an issue and nail it to the wall. He doesn't attack things in spurts—he drives hard, pushing and pushing until finally—he succeeds.
>
> Jeff is a man who will go to the very end—even the climax, for each and every one of you.
>
> So vote for Jeff for A.S.R. vice-president—he'll never come between you and the best our high school can be.

The Court, referring to these remarks as "obscene," "vulgar," "lewd," and "offensively lewd" concludes that school officials properly punished respondent for uttering the speech. Having read the full text of respondent's remarks, I find it difficult to believe that it is the same speech the Court describes. To my mind, the most that can be said about respondent's speech—and all that need be said—is that in light of the discretion school officials have to teach high school students how to conduct civil and effective public discourse and to prevent disruption

of school educational activities, it was not unconstitutional for school officials to conclude, under the circumstances of this case, that respondent's remarks exceeded permissible limits. Thus, while I concur in the Court's judgment, I write separately to express my understanding of the breadth of the Court's holding.

The Court today reaffirms the unimpeachable proposition that students do not " 'shed their constitutional rights to freedom of speech or expression at the schoolhouse gate.' " If respondent had given the same speech outside of the school environment, he could not have been penalized simply because government officials considered his language to be inappropriate; the Court's opinion does not suggest otherwise. Moreover, despite the Court's characterizations, the language respondent used is far removed from the very narrow class of "obscene" speech which the Court has held is not protected by the First Amendment. It is true, however, that the state has interests in teaching high school students how to conduct civil and effective public discourse and in avoiding disruption of educational school activities. Thus, the Court holds that under certain circumstances, high school students may properly be reprimanded for giving a speech at a high school assembly which school officials conclude disrupted the school's educational mission. Respondent's speech may well have been protected had he given it in school but under different circumstances, where the school's legitimate interests in teaching and maintaining civil public discourse were less weighty.

In the present case, school officials sought only to ensure that high school assembly proceed in an orderly manner. There is no suggestion that school officials attempted to regulate respondent's speech because they disagreed with the views he sought to express. (Cf. *Tinker, supra.*) Nor does this case involve an attempt by school officials to ban written materials they consider "inappropriate" for high school students, cf. *Board of Education* v. *Pico* (1982), or to limit what students should hear, read, or learn about. Thus, the Court's holding concerns only the authority that school officials have to restrict a high school student's use of disruptive language in a speech given to a high school assembly.

The authority school officials have to regulate such speech by high school students is not limitless. ("[S]chool officials . . . do [not] have limitless discretion to apply their own notions of indecency. Courts have a First Amendment responsibility to insure that robust rhetoric . . . is not suppressed by prudish failures to distinguish the vigorous from

---

*Petitioners also challenge the ruling of the District Court that the removal of Fraser's name from the ballot for graduation speaker violated his due process rights because that sanction was not indicated as a potential punishment in the school's disciplinary rules. We agree with the Court of Appeals that this issue has become moot, since the graduation ceremony has long since passed and Fraser was permitted to speak in accordance with the District Court's injunction. No part of the damage award was based upon the removal of Fraser's name from the list, since damages were based upon the loss of two day's schooling.

the vulgar.") Under the circumstances of this case, however, I believe that school officials did not violate the First Amendment in determining that respondent should be disciplined for the disruptive language he used while addressing a high school assembly. Thus, I concur in the judgment reversing the decision of the Court of Appeals.

JUSTICE MARSHALL, *dissenting*.

I agree with the principles that JUSTICE BRENNAN sets out in his opinion concurring in the judgment. I dissent from the Court's decision, however, because in my view the School District failed to demonstrate that respondent's remarks were indeed disruptive. The District Court and Court of Appeals conscientiously applied *Tinker* v. *Des Moines School District* (1968) and concluded that the board had not demonstrated any disruption of the educational process. I recognize that the school administration must be given wide latitude to determine what forms of conduct are inconsistent with the school's educational mission; nevertheless, where speech is involved, we may not unquestioningly accept a teacher's or administrator's assertion that certain pure speech interfered with education. Here the board, despite a clear opportunity to do so, failed to bring in evidence sufficient to convince either of the two lower courts that education at Bethel School was disrupted by respondent's speech. I therefore see no reason to disturb the Court of Appeals' judgment.

JUSTICE STEVENS, *dissenting*.

"Frankly, my dear, I don't give a damn."
When I was a high school student, the use of those words in a public forum shocked the Nation. Today Clark Gable's four-letter expletive is less offensive than it was then. Nevertheless, I assume that high school administrators may prohibit the use of that word in classroom discussion and even in extracurricular activities that are sponsored by the school and held on school premises. For I believe a school faculty must regulate the content as well as the style of student speech in carrying out its educational mission. It does seem to me, however, that if a student is to be punished for using offensive speech, he is entitled to fair notice of the scope of the prohibition and the consequences of its violation. The interest in free speech protected by the First Amendment and the interest in fair procedure protected by the Due Process Clause of the Fourteenth Amendment combine to require this conclusion.

* * *

One might conclude that respondent should have known that he would be punished for giving this speech on three quite different theories: (1) it violated the "Disruptive Conduct" rule published in the student handbook; (2) he was specifically warned by his teachers; or (3) the impropriety is so obvious that no specific notice was required. I discuss each theory in turn.

The Disciplinary Rule

At the time discipline was imposed, as well as in its defense of this lawsuit, the school took the position that respondent violated the following published rule:

> In addition to the criminal acts defined above, the commission of, or participation in certain noncriminal activities or acts may lead to disciplinary action. Generally, these are acts which disrupt and interfere with the educational process.

* * *

> *Disruptive conduct.* Conduct which materially and substantially interferes with the educational process is prohibited, including the use of obscene, profane language or gestures.

Based on the findings of fact made by the District Court, the Court of Appeals concluded that the evidence did not show "that the speech had a materially disruptive effect on the educational process." The Court of Appeals explained the basis for this conclusion:

> [T]he record now before us yields no evidence that Fraser's use of a sexual innuendo in his speech materially interfered with activities at Bethel High School. While the students' reaction to Fraser's speech may fairly be characterized as boisterous, it was hardly disruptive of the educational process. In the words of Mr. McCutcheon, the school counselor whose testimony the District relies upon, the reaction of the student body 'was not atypical to a high school auditorium assembly.' In our view, a noisy response to a speech and sexually suggestive movements by three students in a crowd of 600 fail to rise to the level of a material interference with the educational process that justifies impinging upon Fraser's First Amendment right to express himself freely.

We find it significant that although four teachers delivered written statements to an assistant principal commenting on Fraser's speech, none of them suggested that the speech disrupted the assembly or otherwise interfered with school activities. Nor can a finding of material disruption be based upon the evidence that the speech proved to be a lively topic of conversation among students the following day.

Thus, the evidence in the record, as interpreted by the District Court and the Court of Appeals, makes it perfectly clear that respondent's speech was not "conduct" prohibited by the disciplinary rule. Indeed, even if the language of the rule could be stretched to encompass the nondisruptive use of obscene or profane language, there is no such language in respondent's speech. What the speech does contain is a sexual metaphor that may unquestionably be offensive to some listeners in some settings. But if an impartial judge puts his or her own views about the metaphor to one side, I simply cannot understand how he or she could conclude that it is embraced by the above quoted rule. At best, the rule is sufficiently ambiguous that without a further explanation or construction it could not advise the reader of the student handbook that the speech would be forbidden.

The Specific Warning by the Teachers

Respondent read his speech to three different teachers before he gave it. Mrs. Irene Hicks told him that she thought the speech "was inappropriate and that he probably should not deliver it." Steven DeHart told respondent "that this would indeed cause problems in that it would raise eyebrows." The third teacher, Shawn Madden, did not testify. None of the three suggested that the speech might violate a school rule.

The fact that respondent reviewed the text of his speech with three different teachers before he gave it does indicate that he must have been aware of the possibility that it would provoke an adverse reaction, but the teachers' responses certainly did not give him any better notice of the likelihood of discipline than did the student handbook itself. In my opinion, therefore, the most difficult question is whether the speech was so obviously offensive that an intelligent high school student must be presumed to have realized that he would be punished for giving it.

Obvious Impropriety

Justice Sutherland taught us that a "nuisance may be merely a right thing in the wrong place—like a pig in the parlor instead of the barnyard." *Euclid* v. *Ambler Realty Co.* (1926). Vulgar language, like vulgar animals, may be acceptable in some contexts and intolerable in others. Indeed, even ordinary, inoffensive speech may be wholly unacceptable in some settings.

It seems fairly obvious that respondent's speech would be inappropriate in certain classroom and formal social settings. On the other hand, in a locker room or perhaps in a school corridor the metaphor in the speech might be regarded as rather routine comment. If this be true, and if respondent's audience consisted almost entirely of young people with whom he conversed on a daily basis, can we—at this distance—confidently assert that he must have known that the school administration would punish him for delivering it?

For three reasons, I think not. First, it seems highly unlikely that he would have decided to deliver the speech if he had known that it would result in his suspension and disqualification from delivering the school commencement address. Second, I believe a strong presumption in favor of free expression should apply whenever an issue of this kind is arguable. Third, because the Court has adopted the policy of applying contemporary community standards in evaluating expression with sexual connotations, the Court should defer to the views of the district and circuit judges who are in a much better position to evaluate this speech than we are.

I would affirm the judgment of the Court of Appeals.

HAZELWOOD SCHOOL DISTRICT (ST. LOUIS) v. CATHY KUHLMEIER ET AL.
484 U.S. 260; 98 L. Ed. 2d 592; 108 S. Ct. 562 (1988)

JUSTICE WHITE *delivered the opinion of the Court.*

This case concerns the extent to which educators may exercise editorial control over the contents of a high school newspaper produced as part of the school's journalism curriculum.

I

Petitioners are the Hazelwood School District in St. Louis County, Missouri; various school officials; Robert Eugene Reynolds, the principal of Hazelwood East High School; and Howard Emerson, a teacher in the school district. Respondents are three former Hazelwood East students who were staff members of Spectrum, the school newspaper. They contend that school officials violated their First Amendment rights by deleting two pages of articles from the May 13, 1983, issue of Spectrum.

Spectrum was written and edited by the Journalism II class at Hazelwood East. The newspaper was published every three weeks or so during the 1982–1983 school year. More than 4,500 copies of the newspaper were distributed during that year to students, school personnel, and members of the community.

The Board of Education allocated funds from its annual budget for the printing of Spectrum. These funds were supplemented by proceeds from sales of the newspaper. The printing expenses during the 1982–1983 school year totaled $4,668.50; revenue from sales was $1,166.84. The other costs associated with the newspaper—such as supplies, textbooks, and a portion of the journalism teacher's salary—were borne entirely by the Board.

The Journalism II course was taught by Robert Stergos for most of the 1982–1983 academic year. Stergos left Hazelwood East to take a job in private industry on April 29, 1983, when the May 13 edition of Spectrum was nearing completion, and petitioner Emerson took his place as newspaper adviser for the remaining weeks of the term.

The practice at Hazelwood East during the spring of 1983 semester was for the journalism teacher to submit page proofs of each Spectrum issue to Principal Reynolds for his review prior to publication. On May 10, Emerson delivered the proofs of the May 13 edition to Reynolds, who objected to two of the articles scheduled to appear in that edition. One of the stories described three Hazelwood East students' experiences with pregnancy; the other discussed the impact of divorce on students at the school.

Reynolds was concerned that, although the pregnancy story used false names "to keep the identity of these girls a secret," the pregnant students still might be identifiable from the text. He also believed that the article's references to sexual activity and birth control were inappropriate for some of the younger students at the school. In addition, Reynolds was concerned that a student identified by name in the divorce story had complained that her father "wasn't spending enough time with my mom, my sister and I" prior to the divorce, "was always out of town on business or out late playing cards with the guys," and "always argued about everything" with her mother. Reynolds believed that the student's parents should have

been given an opportunity to respond to these remarks or to consent to their publication. He was unaware that Emerson had deleted the student's name from the final version of the article.

Reynolds believed that there was no time to make the necessary changes in the stories before the scheduled press run and that the newspaper would not appear before the end of the school year if printing were delayed to any significant extent. He concluded that his only options under the circumstances were to publish a four-page newspaper instead of the planned six-page newspaper, eliminating the two pages on which the offending stories appeared, or to publish no newspaper at all. Accordingly, he directed Emerson to withhold from publication the two pages containing the stories on pregnancy and divorce.* He informed his superiors of the decision, and they concurred.

Respondents subsequently commenced this action in the United States District Court for the Eastern District of Missouri seeking a declaration that their First Amendment rights had been violated, injunctive relief, and monetary damages. After a bench trial, the District Court denied an injunction, holding that no First Amendment violation had occurred.

The District Court concluded that school officials may impose restraints on students' speech in activities that are " 'an integral part of the school's educational function' "—including the publication of a school-sponsored newspaper by a journalism class—so long as their decision has " 'a substantial and reasonable basis.' " The court found that Principal Reynolds' concern that the pregnant students' anonymity would be lost and their privacy invaded was "legitimate and reasonable," given "the small number of pregnant students at Hazelwood East and several identifying characteristics that were disclosed in the article." The court held that Reynolds' action was also justified "to avoid the impression that [the school] endorses the sexual norms of the subjects" and to shield younger students from exposure to unsuitable material. The deletion of the article on divorce was seen by the court as a reasonable response to the invasion of privacy concerns raised by the named student's remarks. Because the article did not indicate that the student's parents had been offered

*The two pages deleted from the newspaper also contained articles on teenage marriage, runaways, and juvenile delinquents, as well as a general article on teenage pregnancy. Reynolds testified that he had no objection to these articles and that they were deleted only because they appeared on the same pages as the two objectionable articles.

an opportunity to respond to her allegations, said the court, there was cause for "serious doubt that the article complied with the rules of fairness which are standard in the field of journalism and which were covered in the textbook used in the Journalism II class." Furthermore, the court concluded that Reynolds was justified in deleting two full pages of the newspaper, instead of deleting only the pregnancy and divorce stories or requiring that those stories be modified to address his concerns, based on his "reasonable belief that he had to make an immediate decision and that there was no time to make modifications to the articles in question."

The Court of Appeals for the Eighth Circuit reversed. The court held at outset that Spectrum was not only "a part of the school adopted curriculum" but also a public forum, because the newspaper was "intended to be and operated as a conduit for student viewpoint." The court then concluded that Spectrum's status as a public forum precluded school officials from censoring its contents except when " 'necessary to avoid material and substantial interference with school work or discipline . . . or the rights of others' " (quoting *Tinker* v. *Des Moines Independent Community School Dist.*, 393 U.S. 503, 511 [1969]).

The Court of Appeals found "no evidence in the record that the principal could have reasonably forecast that the censored articles or any materials in the censored articles would have materially disrupted classwork or given rise to substantial disorder in the school." School officials were entitled to censor the articles on the ground that they invaded the rights of others, according to the court, only if publication of the articles could have resulted in tort liability to the school. The court concluded that no tort action for libel or invasion of privacy could have been maintained against the school by the subjects of the two articles or by their families. Accordingly, the court held that school officials had violated respondents' First Amendment rights by deleting the two pages of the newspaper.

We granted certiorari, and we now reverse.

II

Students in the public schools do not "shed their constitutional rights to freedom of speech or expression at the schoolhouse gate." *Tinker, supra.* They cannot be punished merely for expressing their personal views on the school premises— whether "in the cafeteria, or on the playing field, or on the campus during the authorized hours"— unless school authorities have reason to believe that such expression will "substantially interfere with the work of the school or impinge upon the rights of other students."

We have nonetheless recognized that the First Amendment rights of students in the public schools "are not automatically coextensive with the rights of adults in other settings," *Bethel School District No. 403* v. *Fraser* (1968), and must be "applied in light of the special characteristics of the school environment." *Tinker, supra.* A school need not tolerate student speech that is inconsistent with its "basic educational mission," *Fraser, supra,* even though the Government could not censor similar speech outside the school. Accordingly, we held in *Fraser* that a student could be disciplined for having delivered a speech that was "sexually explicit" but not legally obscene at an official school assembly, because the school was entitled to "disassociate itself" from the speech in a manner that would demonstrate to others that such vulgarity is "wholly inconsistent with the 'fundamental values' of public school education." *Ibid.* We thus recognized that "[t]he determination of what manner of speech in the classroom or in school assembly is inappropriate properly rests with the school board," rather than with the federal courts. It is in this context that respondents' First Amendment claims must be considered.

We deal first with the question whether Spectrum may appropriately be characterized as a forum for public expression. The public schools do not possess all of the attributes of streets, parks, and other traditional public forums that "time out of mind, have been used for purposes of assembly, communicating thoughts between citizens, and discussing public questions." *Hague* v. *CIO* (1939). Hence, school facilities may be deemed to be public forums only if school authorities have "by policy or by practice" opened those facilities "for indiscriminate use by the general public," *Perry Education Assn.* v. *Perry Local Educators' Assn.* (1983), or by some segment of the public, such as student organizations. If the facilities have instead been reserved for other intended purposes, "communicative or otherwise," then no public forum has been created, and school officials may impose reasonable restrictions on the speech of students, teachers, and other members of the school community. *Ibid.* "The government does not create a public forum by inaction or by permitting limited discourse, but only by intentionally opening a nontraditional forum for public discourse."

The policy of school officials toward Spectrum was reflected in Hazelwood School Board Policy

348.51 and the Hazelwood East Curriculum Guide. Board Policy 348.51 provided that "[s]chool sponsored publications are developed within the adopted curriculum and its educational implications in regular classroom activities." The Hazelwood East Curriculum Guide described the Journalism II course as a "laboratory situation in which the students publish the school newspaper applying skills they have learned in Journalism I." The lessons that were to be learned from the Journalism II course, according to the Curriculum Guide, included development of journalistic skills under deadline pressure, "the legal, moral, and ethical restrictions imposed upon journalists within the school community," and "responsibility and acceptance of criticism for articles of opinion." *Ibid.* Journalism II was taught by a faculty member during regular class hours. Students received grades and academic credit for their performance in the course.

School officials did not deviate in practice from their policy that production of Spectrum was to be part of the educational curriculum and a "regular classroom activit[y]." The District Court found that Robert Stergos, the journalism teacher during most of the 1982–1983 school year, "both had the authority to exercise and in fact exercised a great deal of control over Spectrum." For example, Stergos selected the editors of the newspaper, scheduled publication dates, decided the number of pages for each issue, assigned story ideas to class members, advised students on the development of their stories, reviewed the use of quotations, edited stories, selected and edited the letters to the editor, and dealt with the printing company. Many of these decisions were made without consultation with the Journalism II students. The District Court thus found it "clear that Mr. Stergos was the final authority with respect to almost every aspect of the production and publication of Spectrum, including its content." Moreover, after each Spectrum issue had been finally approved by Stergos or his successor, the issue still had to be reviewed by Principal Reynolds prior to publication. Respondents' assertion that they had believed that they could publish "practically anything" in Spectrum was therefore dismissed by the District Court as simply "not credible." These factual findings are amply supported by the record and were not rejected as clearly erroneous by the Court of Appeals.

The evidence relied upon by the Court of Appeals in finding Spectrum to be a public forum is equivocal at best. For example, Board Policy 348.51, which stated in part that "[s]chool sponsored student publications will not restrict free expression or diverse viewpoints within the rules of responsible journalism," also stated that such publications were "developed within the adopted curriculum and its educational implications." One might reasonably infer from the full text of Policy 348.51 that school officials retained ultimate control over what constituted "responsible journalism" in a school-sponsored newspaper. Although the Statement of Policy published in the September 14, 1982, issue of Spectrum declared that "Spectrum, as a student-press publication, accepts all rights implied by the First Amendment," this statement, understood in the context of the paper's role in the school's curriculum, suggests at most that the administration will not interfere with the students' exercise of those First Amendment rights that attend the publication of a school-sponsored newspaper. It does not reflect an intent to expand those rights by converting a curricular newspaper into a public forum. Finally, that students were permitted to exercise some authority over the contents of Spectrum was fully consistent with the Curriculum Guide objective of teaching the Journalism II students "leadership responsibilities as issue and page editors." A decision to teach leadership skills in the context of a classroom activity hardly implies a decision to relinquish school control over that activity. In sum, the evidence relied upon by the Court of Appeals fails to demonstrate the "clear intent to create a public forum" that existed in cases in which we found public forums to have been created. School officials did not evince either "by policy or by practice" any intent to open the pages of Spectrum to "indiscriminate use" by its student reporters and editors or by the student body generally. Instead, they "reserve[d] the forum for its intended purpos[e]," as a supervised learning experience for journalism students. Accordingly, school officials were entitled to regulate the contents of Spectrum in any reasonable manner. It is this standard, rather than our decision in *Tinker*, that governs this case.

The question whether the First Amendment requires a school to tolerate particular student speech—the question that we addressed in *Tinker*—is different from the question whether the First Amendment requires a school affirmatively to promote particular student speech. The former question addresses educators' ability to silence a student's personal expression that happens to occur on the school premises. The latter question concerns educators' authority over school-sponsored publications, theatrical productions, and other expressive activities that students, parents, and members of the public might reasonably perceive to bear the imprimatur of the school. These activities may fairly be characterized as part of the school curriculum, whether or not they occur in a traditional classroom setting, so long as they are supervised by faculty members and designed to impart particular knowledge or skills to student participants and audiences.

Educators are entitled to exercise greater control over this second form of student expression to assure that participants learn whatever lessons the activity is designed to teach, that readers or listeners are not exposed to material that may be inappropriate for their level of maturity, and that the views of the individual speaker are not erroneously attributed to the school. Hence, a school may in its capacity as publisher of a school newspaper or producer of a school play "disassociate itself," not only from speech that would "substantially interfere with [its] work . . . or impinge upon the rights of other students," but also from speech that is, for example, ungrammatical, poorly written, inadequately researched, biased or prejudiced, vulgar or profane, or unsuitable for immature audiences. A school must be able to set high standards for the student speech that is disseminated under its auspices—standards that may be higher than those demanded by some newspaper publishers or theatrical producers in the "real" world—and may refuse to disseminate student speech that does not meet those standards. In addition, a school must be able to take into account the emotional maturity of the intended audience in determining whether to disseminate student speech on potentially sensitive topics, which might range from the existence of Santa Claus in an elementary school setting to the particulars of teenage sexual activity in a high school setting. A school must also retain the authority to refuse to sponsor student speech that might reasonably be perceived to advocate drug or alcohol use, irresponsible sex, or conduct otherwise inconsistent with "the shared values of a civilized social order," or to associate the school with any position other than neutrality on matters of political controversy. Otherwise, the schools would be unduly constrained from fulfilling their role as "a principal instrument in awakening the child to cultural values, in preparing him for later professional training, and in helping him to adjust normally to his environment."

Accordingly, we conclude that the standard articulated in *Tinker* for determining when a school may punish student expression need not also be the standard for determining when a school may refuse to lend its name and resources to the dissemination of student expression. Instead we hold that educators do not offend the First Amendment by exercising editorial control over the style and content of student speech in school-sponsored expressive activities so long as their actions are reasonably related to legitimate pedagogical concerns.

This standard is consistent with our oft-expressed view that the education of the Nation's youth is primarily the responsibility of parents, teachers, and state and local school officials, and not of federal judges. It is only when the decision to censor a school-sponsored publication, theatrical production, or other vehicle of student expression has no valid educational purpose that the First Amendment is so "directly and sharply implicate[d]" as to require judicial intervention to protect students' constitutional rights.

III

We also conclude that Principal Reynolds acted reasonably in requiring the deletion from the May 13 issue of Spectrum of the pregnancy article, the divorce article, and the remaining articles that were to appear on the same pages of the newspaper.

The initial paragraph of the pregnancy article declared that "[a]ll names have been changed to keep the identity of these girls a secret." The principal concluded that the students' anonymity was not adequately protected, however, given the other identifying information in the article and the small number of pregnant students at the school. Indeed, a teacher at the school credibly testified that she could positively identify at least one of the girls and possibly all three. It is likely that many students at Hazelwood East would have been at least as successful in identifying the girls. Reynolds therefore could reasonably have feared that the article violated whatever pledge of anonymity had been given to the pregnant students. In addition, he could reasonably have been concerned that the article was not sufficiently sensitive to the privacy interests of the students' boyfriends and parents, who were discussed in the article but who were given no opportunity to consent to its publication or to offer a response. The article did not contain graphic accounts of sexual activity. The girls did comment in the article, however, concerning their sexual histories and their use or nonuse of birth control. It was not unreasonable for the principal to have concluded that such frank talk was inappropriate in a school-sponsored publication distributed to 14-year-old freshmen and presumably taken home to be read by students' even younger brothers and sisters.

The student who was quoted by name in the version of the divorce article seen by Principal Reynolds made comments sharply critical of her father. The principal could reasonably have concluded that an individual publicly identified as an inattentive parent—indeed, as one who chose "playing cards with guys" over home and family—was entitled to an opportunity to defend himself as a matter of journalistic fairness. These concerns were shared by both of Spectrum's faculty advisers for the 1982–1983 school year, who testified that they would not have allowed the article to be printed without deletion of the student's name.

Principal Reynolds testified credibly at trial that, at the time that he reviewed the proofs of the May 13 issue during an extended telephone conversation with Emerson, he believed that there was no time to make any changes in the articles and that the newspaper had to be printed immediately or not at all. It is true that Reynolds did not verify whether the necessary modifications could still have been made in the articles, and that Emerson did not volunteer the information that printing could be delayed until the changes were made. We nonetheless agree with the District Court that the decision to excise the two pages containing the problematic articles was reasonable given the particular circumstances of this case. These circumstances included the very recent replacement of Stergos by Emerson, who may not have been entirely familiar with Spectrum editorial and production procedures, and the pressure felt by Reynolds to make an immediate decision so that students would not be deprived of the newspaper altogether.

In sum, we cannot reject as unreasonable Principal Reynolds' conclusion that neither the pregnancy article nor the divorce article was suitable for publication in Spectrum. Reynolds could reasonably have concluded that the students who had written and edited these articles had not sufficiently mastered those portions of the Journalism II curriculum that pertained to the treatment of controversial issues and personal attacks, the need to protect the privacy of individuals whose most intimate concerns are to be revealed in the newspaper, and "the legal, moral, and ethical restrictions imposed upon journalists within [a] school community" that includes adolescent subjects and readers. Finally, we conclude that the principal's decision to delete two pages of Spectrum, rather than to delete only the offending articles or to require that they be modified, was reasonable under the circumstances as he understood them.

Accordingly, no violation of First Amendment rights occurred.

The judgment of the Court of Appeals for the Eighth Circuit is therefore

Reversed.

JUSTICE BRENNAN, *with whom* JUSTICE MARSHALL *and* JUSTICE BLACKMUN *join, dissenting.*

When the young men and women of Hazelwood East High School registered for Journalism II, they expected a civics lesson. Spectrum, the newspaper they were to publish, "was not just a class exercise in which students learned to prepare papers and hone writing skills, it was a . . . forum established to give students an opportunity to express their views while gaining an appreciation of their rights and responsibilities under the First Amendment to the United States Constitution. . . ." "[A]t the beginning of each school year," the student journalists published a Statement of Policy—tacitly approved each year by school authorities—announcing their expectation that "Spectrum, as a student-press publication, accepts all rights implied by the First Amendment. . . . Only speech that 'materially and substantially interferes with the requirements of appropriate discipline' can be found unacceptable and therefore prohibited" (quoting *Tinker*). The school board itself affirmatively guaranteed the students of Journalism II an atmosphere conducive to fostering such an appreciation and exercising the full panoply of rights associated with a free student press. "School sponsored student publications," it vowed, "will not restrict free expression or diverse viewpoints within the rules of responsible journalism" (Board Policy Section 348.51).

This case arose when the Hazelwood East administration breached its own promise, dashing its students' expectations. The school principal, without prior consultation or explanation, excised six articles—comprising two full pages—of the May 13, 1983, issue of Spectrum. He did so not because any of the articles would "materially and substantially interfere with the requirements of appropriate discipline," but simply because he considered two of the six "inappropriate, personal, sensitive, and unsuitable" for student consumption.

In my view the principal broke more than just a promise. He violated the First Amendment's prohibitions against censorship of any student expression that neither disrupts classwork nor invades the rights of others, and against any censorship that is not narrowly tailored to serve its purpose.

I

While the "constitutional rights of students in public school are not automatically coextensive with the rights of adults in other settings," *Fraser*, students in the public schools do not "shed their constitutional rights to freedom of speech or expression at the schoolhouse gate." *Tinker*. Just as the public on the street corner must, in the interest of fostering "enlightened opinion," tolerate speech that "tempt[s] [the listener] to throw [the speaker] off the street," public educators must accommodate some student expression even if it offends them or offers views or values that contradict those the school wishes to inculcate.

In *Tinker*, this Court struck the balance. We held that official censorship of student expression—there the suspension of several students until they removed their armbands protesting the Vietnam War—is unconstitutional unless the speech "materially disrupts classwork or involves substantial disorder or invasion of the rights of others. . . ." School officials may not suppress "silent, passive expression of opinion, unaccompanied by any disorder or disturbance on the part of" the speaker. The "mere desire to avoid the discomfort and unpleasantness that always accompany an unpopular viewpoint" does not justify official suppression of student speech in the high school.

This Court applied the *Tinker* test just a term ago in *Fraser, supra*, upholding an official decision to discipline a student for delivering a lewd speech in support of a student government candidate. The Court today casts no doubt on *Tinker's* vitality. Instead it erects a taxonomy of school censorship, concluding that *Tinker* applies to one category and not another. On the one hand is censorship "to silence a student's personal expression that happens to occur on the school premises." On the other hand is censorship of expression that arises in the context of "school-sponsored . . . expressive activities that students, parents, and members of the public might reasonably perceive to bear the imprimatur of the school."

The Court does not, for it cannot, purport to discern from our precedents the distinction it creates. One could, I suppose, readily characterize the Tinkers' symbolic speech as "personal expression that happens to [have] occur[red] on school premises," although *Tinker* did not even hint that the personal nature of the speech was of any (much less dispositive) relevance. But that same description could not by any stretch of the imagination fit Fraser's speech. He did not just "happen" to deliver his lewd speech to an ad hoc gathering on the playground. As the second paragraph of *Fraser* evinces, if ever a forum for student expression was "school-sponsored," Fraser's was:

> Fraser . . . delivered a speech nominating a fellow student for student elective office. Approximately 600 high school students . . . attended the assembly. Students were required to attend the assembly or to report to study hall. The assembly was part of a *school-sponsored* educational program in self-government (emphasis added).

Yet, from the first sentence of its analysis, *Fraser* faithfully applied *Tinker*.

Nor has this Court ever intimated a distinction between personal and school-sponsored speech in any other context. Particularly telling is this Court's heavy reliance on *Tinker* in two cases of First Amendment infringement on state college campuses, See *Papish* v. *University of Missouri Board of Curators*, 410 U.S. 667 (1973); *Healy* v. *James*, 408 U. S. 169 (1972). One involved the expulsion of a student for lewd expression in a newspaper that she sold on campus pursuant to university authorization, see *Papish, supra*; and the other involved the denial of university recognition and concomitant benefits to a political student organization, see *Healy, supra*. Tracking *Tinker's* analysis, the Court found each act of suppression unconstitutional. In neither case did this Court suggest the distinction, which the Court today finds dispositive, between school-sponsored and incidental student expression.

II

Even if we were writing on a clean slate, I would reject the Court's rationale for abandoning *Tinker* in this case. The Court offers no more than an obscure tangle of three excuses to afford educators "greater control" over school-sponsored speech than the *Tinker* test would permit: the public educator's prerogative to control curriculum; the pedagogical interest in shielding the high school audience from objectionable viewpoints and sensitive topics; and the school's need to dissociate itself from student expression. None of the excuses, once disentangled, supports the distinction that the Court draws. *Tinker* fully addresses the first concern; the second is illegitimate; and the third is readily achievable through less oppressive means.

The Court is certainly correct that the First Amendment permits educators "to assure that participants learn whatever lessons the activity is designed to teach. . . ." That is, however, the essence of the *Tinker* test, not an excuse to abandon it. Under *Tinker*, school officials may censor only such student speech as would "materially disrup[t]" a legitimate curricular function. Manifestly, student speech is more likely to disrupt a curricular function when it arises in the context of a curricular activity—one that "is designed to teach" something—than when it arises in the context of a noncurricular activity. Thus, under *Tinker*, the school may constitutionally punish the budding political orator if he disrupts calculus class but not if he holds his tongue for the cafeteria. That is not because some more stringent standard applies in the curricular context. (After all, the Court applied the same standard whether the Tinkers wore their armbands to the "classroom" or the "cafeteria.") It is because student speech in the noncurricular context is less likely to disrupt materially any legitimate pedagogical purpose.

I fully agree with the Court that the First Amendment should afford an educator the prerogative not to sponsor the publication of a newspaper article that is "ungrammatical, poorly written, inadequately researched, biased or prejudiced," or that falls short of the "high standards . . . student speech that is disseminated under [the school's] auspices. . . ." But we need not abandon *Tinker* to reach that conclusion; we need only apply it. The enumerated criteria reflect the skills that the curricular newspaper "is designed to teach." The educator may, under *Tinker* constitutionally "censor" poor grammar, writing, or research because to reward such expression would "materially disrup[t]" the newspaper's curricular purpose.

The same cannot be said of official censorship designed to shield the audience or dissociate the sponsor from the expression. Censorship so motivated might well serve (although, as I demonstrate *infra*, cannot legitimately serve) some other school purpose. But it in no way furthers the curricular purposes of a student newspaper, unless one believes that the purpose of the school newspaper is to teach students that the press ought never report bad news, express unpopular views, or print a thought that might upset its sponsors. Unsurprisingly, Hazelwood East claims no such pedagogical purpose.

The Court relies on bits of testimony to portray the principal's conduct as a pedagogical lesson to Journalism II students who "had not sufficiently mastered those portions of the . . . curriculum that pertained to the treatment of controversial issues and personal attacks, the need to protect the privacy of individuals . . . , and 'the legal, moral, and ethical restrictions imposed upon journalists. . . .' "

But the principal never consulted the students before censoring their work. "[T]hey learned of the deletions when the paper was released." Further, he explained the deletions only in the broadest of generalities. In one meeting called at the behest of seven protesting Spectrum staff members (presumably a fraction of the full class), he characterized the articles as "'too sensitive' for 'our immature audience of readers,' " and in a later meeting he deemed them simply "inappropriate, personal, sensitive and unsuitable for the newspaper." The Court's supposition that the principal intended (or the protesters understood) those generalities as a lesson on the nuances of journalistic responsibility is utterly incredible. If he did, a fact that neither the District Court nor the Court of Appeals found, the lesson was lost on all but the psychic Spectrum staffer.

The Court's second excuse for deviating from precedent is the school's interest in shielding an impressionable high school audience from material whose substance is "unsuitable for immature audiences." Specifically, the majority decrees that we must afford educators authority to shield high school students from exposure to "potentially sensitive topics" (like "the particulars of teenage sexual activity") or unacceptable social viewpoints (like the advocacy of "irresponsible se[x] or conduct otherwise inconsistent with 'the shared values of a civilized social order' ") through school-sponsored student activities. . . .

The mere fact of school sponsorship does not, as the Court suggests, license such thought control in the high school, whether through school suppression of disfavored viewpoints or through official assessment of topic sensitivity. The former would constitute unabashed and unconstitutional viewpoint discrimination, as well as an impermissible infringement of the students' " 'right to receive information and ideas.' " Just as a school board may not purge its state-funded library of all books that " 'offen[d] [its] social, political and moral tastes,' " school officials may not, out of like motivation, discriminatorily excise objectionable ideas from a student publication. The State's prerogative to dissolve the student newspaper entirely (or to limit its subject matter) no more entitles it to dictate which viewpoints students may express on its pages, than the State's prerogative to close down the schoolhouse entitles it to prohibit the nondisruptive expression of antiwar sentiment within its gates.

Official censorship of student speech on the ground that it addresses "potentially sensitive topics" is, for related reasons, equally impermissible. I would not begrudge an educator the authority to limit the substantive scope of a school-sponsored publication to a certain, objectively definable topic, such as literary criticism, school sports, or an overview of the school year. Unlike those determinate limitations, "potential topic sensitivity" is a vaporous nonstandard—like " 'public welfare, peace, safety, health, decency, good order, morals or convenience,' " *Shuttlesworth* v. *Birmingham* (1969), or " 'general welfare of citizens,' " *Staub* v. *Baxley* (1958)—that invites manipulation to achieve ends that cannot permissibly be achieved through blatant viewpoint discrimination and chills student speech to which school officials might not object. In part because of those dangers, this Court has consistently condemned any scheme allowing a state official boundless discretion in licensing speech from a particular forum.

The case before us aptly illustrates how readily school officials (and courts) can camouflage viewpoint discrimination as the "mere" protection of students from sensitive topics. Among the grounds that the Court advances to uphold the principal's censorship of one of the articles was the potential sensitivity of "teenage sexual activity." Yet the District Court specifically found that the principal "did not, as a matter of principle, oppose discussion of said topi[c] in Spectrum." That much is also clear from the same principal's approval of the "squeal law" article on the same page, dealing forthrightly with "teenage sexuality," "the use of contraceptives by teenagers," and "teenage pregnancy." If topic sensitivity were the true basis of the principal's decision, the two articles should have been equally objectionable. It is much more likely that the objectionable article was objectionable because of the viewpoint it expressed: It might have been read (as the majority apparently does) to advocate "irresponsible sex."

The sole concomitant of school sponsorship that might conceivably justify the distinction that the Court draws between sponsored and nonsponsored student expression is the risk "that the views of the individual speaker [might be] erroneously attributed to the school." Of course, the risk of erroneous attribution inheres in any student expression, including "personal expression" that, like the Tinkers' armbands, "happens to occur on the school premises." Nevertheless, the majority is certainly correct that indicia of school sponsorship increase the likelihood of such attribution, and that state educators may therefore have a legitimate interest in dissociating themselves from student speech.

But " '[e]ven though the governmental purpose be legitimate and substantial, that purpose cannot be pursued by means that broadly stifle fundamental personal liberties when the end can be more narrowly achieved.' " Dissociative means short of censorship are available to the school. It could, for example, require the student activity to publish a disclaimer, such as the "Statement of Policy" that Spectrum published each school year announcing that "[a]ll . . . editorials appearing in this newspaper reflect the opinions of the Spectrum staff, which are not necessarily shared by the administrators or faculty of Hazelwood East"; or it could simply issue its own response clarifying the official position on the matter and explaining why the student position is wrong. Yet, without so much as acknowledging the less oppressive alternatives, the Court approves of brutal censorship.

III

Since the censorship served no legitimate pedagogical purpose, it cannot by any stretch of the imagination have been designed to prevent "materia[l] disrup[tion of] classwork." Nor did the censorship fall within the category that *Tinker* described as necessary to prevent student expression from "inva[ding] the rights of others." If that term is to have any content, it must be limited to rights that are protected by law. "Any yardstick less exacting than [that] could result in school officials curtailing speech at the slightest fear of disturbance," a prospect that would be completely at odds with this Court's pronouncement that the "undifferentiated fear or apprehension of disturbance is not enough [even in the public-school context] to overcome the right to freedom of expression" (*Tinker*). And, as the Court of Appeals correctly reasoned, whatever journalistic impropriety these articles may have contained, they could not conceivably be tortious, much less criminal.

Finally, even if the majority were correct that the principal could constitutionally have censored the objectionable material, I would emphatically object to the brutal manner in which he did so. Where "[t]he separation of legitimate from illegitimate speech calls for more sensitive tools" the principal used a paper shredder. He objected to some material in two articles but excised six entire articles. He did not so much as inquire into obvious alternatives, such as precise deletions or additions (one of which had already been made), rearranging the layout, or delaying publication. Such unthinking contempt for individual rights is intolerable from any state official. It is particularly insidious from one to whom the public entrusts the task of inculcating in its youth an appreciation for the cherished democratic liberties that our Constitution guarantees.

IV

The Court opens its analysis in this case by purporting to reaffirm *Tinker's* time-tested proposition that public school students "do not 'shed their constitutional rights to freedom of speech or expression at the schoolhouse gate.'" That is an ironic introduction to an opinion that denudes high school students of much of the First Amendment protection that *Tinker* itself prescribed. Instead of "teach[ing] children to respect the diversity of ideas that is fundamental to the American system" and "that our Constitution is a living reality, not parchment preserved under glass," the Court today "teach[es] youth to discount important principles of our government as mere platitudes." The young men and women of Hazelwood East expected a civics lesson, but not the one the Court teaches them today.

I dissent.

The Free Press in a Modern Context

FEATURED CASES

Nebraska Press Association v. *Stuart*   *New York Times* v. *Sullivan*   *Cohen* v. *Cowles Media Co.*

The protection of freedom of the press is a long-standing tradition in the United States. But like other freedoms, freedom of the press is not absolute. We still face such problems as how, to what extent, and under what circumstances this freedom is to be protected (or restricted). And these problems have become more complicated with advances in media technology. Newsprint today has to compete with more instant and dramatic communication media such as radio and television. This, of course, maximizes the people's right to know and to gain information.

But the pursuit of this goal, even armed with "free press protection," can sometimes collide with other rights and interests. It is certainly understandable for the media to insist on "full coverage" and "full disclosure." But it is also understandable when others contend that such activity encroaches on their rights and interests. Consider, for example, the defendant who feels that widespread pretrial publicity prejudiced his right to a "fair" trial, or the defendant who alleges a denial of due process if a judge allows television coverage of her trial. Or consider the attempt by law enforcement officials to compel reporters to divulge their news sources when such information could be important in the prevention or prosecution of criminal activity. Consider, moreover, the attempts of certain governmental officials to withhold information from the press or to prevent its publication on the grounds that such divulgence might endanger "national security." These are the types of "free press" problems that now reach our courts. In this section, we review briefly how the Supreme Court has dealt with them.

Another dimension of maintaining a free press in modern society has to do with the general problem of access to mass communications media, such as newspapers, radio, and television. This problem is reflected in a number of situations and cases, including *Lloyd Corporation* v. *Tanner, supra.* To be sure, the access problem was involved in the decision of the Court in *Miami Herald Publishing Co.* v. *Tornillo* (418 U. S. 241, 1974). There a Florida "right-to-reply" statute was struck down as offending freedom of the press because of its "intrusion into the functions of editors in choosing what materials they wish to print" and on what issues and public officials they wish to comment. Such governmental regulation of editorial control and judgment, Chief Justice Burger concluded, is inconsistent with the First Amendment guarantee of a free press. The implication from this case is that under the First Amendment, compulsory access should be treated much the same as prior restraint—that is, presumed to be invalid. And the practical effect of the decision was to deny to political candidates free space to reply to editorial comment that criticized them.

But due to its unique nature, the Court tends to treat the broadcast media differently. For example, in *CBS* v. *Federal Communications Commission* (453 U.S. 367, 1981), the Court upheld a federal law imposing on broadcasters the obligation to provide an affirmative right of access to broadcast facilities for individual candidates seeking federal office. However, in 1984, the Court struck down a law banning editorials on public broadcasting stations (*FCC* v. *League of Women Voters of California*, 104 S. Ct. 3106). Additionally, the Court renewed its longstanding skepticism of tax schemes that seem to impact especially hard on the press, and in 1983 once again declared such schemes unconstitutional (*Minneapolis Star* v. *Commissioner of Revenue*, 460 U.S. 575).

In a 1991 decision, *Simon & Schuster, Inc.* v. *Members of New York Crime Victims Board* (112 S. Ct. 501), the Court struck down the "Son of Sam" law designed to prevent criminals from profiting from notoriety resulting from their crimes or from the sale of such stories. The law required publishers to deposit with the Victims Board all earnings and royalties accruing from contracts with accused or convicted criminals. Such monies were to be held by the Board for five years, during which time victims could bring litigation to seek financial restitution. The law also extended to persons not charged, tried, or convicted but who later admitted the commission of such crimes in books or other commercial forms. In the instant case, the Victims Board notified Simon & Schuster of violating the law by not turning over monies owed to a Henry Hill, who recounted his involvement in organized crime in the book *Wiseguy*.

Against charges that the New York law violated First Amendment free speech and press guarantees, Justice O'Connor held that the law was "presumptively inconsistent with the First Amendment" by exacting "a financial burden on speakers because of the content of their speech." O'Connor reasoned that as such the law could drive certain viewpoints from the marketplace. O'Connor did, however, think the law served a compelling state interest that could not be met through less restrictive means such as restitution-type statutes. At bottom, she viewed the law "as significantly overinclusive" and said that:

> the statute's broad definition of "person convicted of a crime" enables the Board to escrow the income of any author who admits in his work to having committed a crime, whether or not the author was ever actually accused or convicted. These two provisions combine to encompass a potentially very large number of works. Had the Son of Sam law been in effect at the time and place of publication, it would have escrowed payment for such works as *The Autobiography of Malcolm X*, which describes crimes committed by the civil rights leader before he became a public figure; *Civil Disobedience*, in which Thoreau acknowl-

edges his refusal to pay taxes and recalls his experience in jail; and even the *Confessions of Saint Augustine*, in which the author laments "my past foulness and the carnal corruptions of my soul," one instance of which involved the theft of pears from a neighboring vineyard.

Freedom of the Press and the Judicial Process

1. *Free Press v. Fair Trial: Access to News Sources.* One of the most controversial issues to reach the Court during the 1960s involved the conflicting constitutional claims of the accused to a fair trial free from prejudicial publicity and of a "free press" to gather and report news about a criminal case. Put another way, how free is a "free press" in having access to gather and to report on certain public matters where—as in the criminal process—conflicting interests may be at stake. In balancing these interests, for example, the Court in one case emphasized that the maintenance of an atmosphere free from inflamed public opinion is essential to the selection of an unbiased jury. Thus in *Irwin* v. *Dowd* (366 U.S. 717, 1961) the Court, for the first time, reversed a state conviction solely on the ground of prejudicial pretrial publicity. Justice Tom Clark's opinion for the Court cited the "pattern of deep and bitter prejudice" permeating the community, which was reflected in the "*voir dire* examination of the majority of the jurors finally" selected to hear the case. He further noted that eight of the twelve jurors had expressed the belief that the petitioner was guilty. Consequently, he concluded that the sincere assurances of fairness and impartiality proclaimed by jurors could be given little weight in meeting the constitutional requirement of impartiality, particularly where a life was at stake.

Five years later, in *Sheppard* v. *Maxwell* (384 U. S. 333, 1966), the Court reversed a state murder conviction because of prejudicial publicity both before and during the trial. Referring to the "Roman holiday" atmosphere created by "circulation conscious editors catering to the insatiable interest of the American public in the bizarre," Justice Tom Clark contended that the public had been so inflamed and prejudiced as to make impossible a fair trial before an impartial jury. He condemned the trial court for permitting the trial to take place in a "carnival atmosphere" and for its failure to take necessary precautions for insulation of the jury.*

---

*In 1968, the American Bar Association made significant modifications in its Canons of Professional Ethics. Recommended by a committee headed by Massachusetts Supreme Court Judge

The use of television has presented the Court with another dimension of the free press—fair trial issue. In *Rideau* v. *Louisiana* (373 U. S. 723, 1963), the Court reversed a murder conviction where the defendant's confession was presented on "live" television and then rerun by videotape on two other occasions. Noting that the station's viewing range covered the entire area from which jurors were drawn, the Court held that refusal of the defendant's request for a change of venue was a denial of due process.

Televising of the actual trial was at issue in *Estes* v. *Texas* (381 U. S. 532, 1965). The case presented an appeal of the conviction of Texas financier Billie Sol Estes for swindling. Under Texas law, the question of televising court proceedings was left to the discretion of the trial judge. A motion to prohibit televising the trial was rejected (the hearing on the motion was itself televised) and it proceeded under limited video coverage. In a five-to-four decision, the Court reversed the conviction and emphasized the right of the accused to have his day in court free from the distractions inherent in telecasting. Justice Clark, again speaking for the majority, said that "the chief function of our judicial machinery is to ascertain the truth" and that the use of television injects a factor irrelevant toward that end. Furthermore, he noted that television has an infectious impact on the participants in a trial. The jury, "nerve center of the factfinding process," is subjected to considerable distraction. The testimony of witnesses will often be impaired. If the trial is being conducted before an elective

Paul C. Reardon, the major thrust of the rules is directed at the conduct and responsibilities of prosecutors, defense attorneys, judges, court employees, and law enforcement officials in the discharge of their duties in criminal proceedings. Attorneys, for example, are forbidden to release or authorize the release of information in connection with pending or imminent criminal litigation with which they are associated if there is a reasonable likelihood that such dissemination will interfere with a fair trial. This restriction applies to such matters as comment on prior criminal record, the existence or contents of a confession or statement of the accused, the results of any tests or the refusal to submit to tests, the identity of prospective witnesses, and the possible nature of the plea. The restrictions recommended to govern the conduct of court employees and law enforcement officers are similar in nature, and the new rules simply recommend that "judges should refrain from any conduct or the making of any statements that may tend to interfere with the right of the people or of the defendant to a fair trial." The 1968 modifications were incorporated in the ABA Code of Professional Responsibility, which replaced the Canons in 1970. Canon 7 of the Code—specifically EC 7-33 and DR 7-107—provide both minimum standards relating to trial publicity and sanctions upon attorneys who breach the disciplinary rules. Judicial and law enforcement officials are urged to adopt similar standards.

judge, the political capital to be gained from such exposure may impair his or her effectiveness. And finally, the defendant may suffer from "a form of mental harassment resembling a police lineup or the third degree."

In the major dissent, Justice Potter Stewart thought the introduction of television into the courtroom an unwise policy but that on the specific record of the "limited use of the medium," the defendant's constitutional rights were not impaired. Stewart expressed great concern about the "intimation" in the majority and concurring opinions that "there are limits upon the public's right to know what goes on in the courts" and the implicit limitations on First Amendment guarantees.

In *Nebraska Press Association* v. *Stuart* (427 U. S. 539, 1976), the Court once again confronted the longstanding conflict between the First Amendment's guarantee of a free press and the Sixth Amendment's right to a fair trial. The defendant, Erwin Charles Simants, was charged with the 1975 mass murder of six people in a small Nebraska town. To protect the defendant from prejudicial publicity, Judge Stuart of the Lincoln County District Court entered an order restraining the publication or broadcast of accounts of "confessions or admissions made by the accused or facts 'strongly implicative' of the accused" in the widely reported murder. The order applied to all pretrial events, including a public preliminary hearing, until a jury could be impaneled. The Nebraska Press Association challenged the gag order and carried the issue to the state supreme court. The Nebraska Supreme Court upheld the order in the interest of the defendant but modified the "absolutist position" of the district court. The modified order prohibited the reporting of "the existence and nature of any confessions or admissions" made to law enforcement officials or any third party except members of the press, and other information "strongly implicative of the accused." However, a unanimous Supreme Court found the order to be unconstitutionally vague and an unacceptable prior restraint on speech.

As suggested earlier, a general question raised by *Stuart* (and other cases) has to do with journalists' right of access to public records and public facilities. That question continues to be raised in various contexts. For example, in an invasion of privacy suit the Court set aside an award for damages against a television station that aired the name of a rape victim (*Cox Broadcasting Co.* v. *Conn*, 420 U. S. 469, 1975). Here the Court reasoned that since the name of the victim was already a part of public trial records, the media could not be prevented from reporting it to the public. However, two 1978 Court decisions blunted efforts of the press to gather and report information. In *Houchins* v. *KQED*, by a four-to-three majority, the Court reversed a lower court decision that preliminary enjoined Sheriff Houchins from denying KQED news personnel reasonable access to the county jail, including a portion of the jail where a prisoner's suicide had reportedly occurred. While there was no majority opinion to support the Court's position, the opinion of Chief Justice Burger commanded support of three members of the four-man majority. In that opinion, Burger, joined by Justices White and Rehnquist, concluded that neither the First nor Fourteenth Amendments provides a right of access to government information or sources of information within government's control. Burger said that the "news media have no constitutional right of access to the county jail, over and above that of other persons, to interview inmates and make sound recordings, films, and photographs, for publication and broadcasting by newspapers, radio, and television."

Similarly, in *Nixon* v. *Warner Communications, Inc.* (435 U. S. 589, 1978), television networks and others appealed from a district court order that networks could not make copies of tapes introduced at the Watergate criminal trial of the defendants, at least until appeals from convictions obtained in the criminal trial were decided. But in a five-to-four ruling, the Court said that release of the tapes is not required by First Amendment guarantees of freedom of press nor by the Sixth Amendment guarantee of public trial. Rather, the Court majority held that through the Presidential Recordings Act Congress had created an administrative procedure for the processing and releasing of materials to the public, including the tapes at issue. The Court stated that "the guarantee of a public trial confers no special benefit on the press nor does it require that the trial . . . be broadcast live or on tape to the public, but such guarantee is satisfied by the opportunity of the public and the press to attend the trial to report what they have observed."

And in a 1979 decision in *Gannett* v. *DePasquale* (443 U. S. 368), the Court once again failed to expand access rights of the press. Here a newspaper brought suit to vacate and prohibit enforcement of trial court orders that excluded the public and press from a pretrial suppression hearing in a murder prosecution. The New York Court of Appeals upheld the exclusion orders, and the Supreme Court affirmed. The Court, in an opinion by Justice Stewart, said that "members of the public have no constitutional right under the Sixth and Fourteenth Amendments to attend criminal trials," and that the exclusion orders, designed to ensure defendant's right to a fair trial, did not violate any First and Fourteenth Amendment right of the press to attend criminal trials.

By 1980, however, the Court seems to have modified its stance in *Gannett*. In *Richmond Newspapers, Inc.* v. *Virginia*, by a seven-to-one vote, the Court reversed a trial court order barring press and public from a murder trial. Although there was no majority opinion, several opinions filed by the justices seem to reflect the view that the right of the press and public to attend criminal trials is constitutionally based in the guarantees and protections of the First Amendment.

The Court followed its *Richmond* principles in *Chandler* v. *Florida* (449 U. S. 560, 1981), where it permitted television coverage of court trials. Similarly, in *Globe Newspaper Co.* v. *Superior Ct.* (457 U.S. 596, 1982), it found violative of the First Amendment a Massachusetts law that required the exclusion of the press and the public from the courtroom during testimony of a minor who allegedly has been the victim of a sex offense. The Court also followed *Richmond* in its 1984 decision in *Press-Enterprise Co.* v. *Superior Ct.* (104 S. Ct. 819). The Court, in an opinion by Chief Justice Burger, said that the press could not be excluded from the *voir dire* examination of prospective jurors in a criminal trial, in the instant case involving charges of rape and murder of a teenage girl.

In *CNN* v. *Noriega* (111 S. Ct. 451, 1990), and despite "prior restraint" charges based on strong precedents (e.g., *Near* v. *Minnesota*), the Court, without oral argument, refused to lift a restraining order that barred Cable News Network (CNN) from disclosing information secured from tape recordings of conversations between Manuel Noriega and his attorney. Justices Marshall and O'Connor dissented in *Noriega*, charging that the decision "could not be reconciled with the teachings" of leading cases such as *Near, Nebraska Press Association* v. *Stuart*, and *New York Times* v. *Sullivan*.

2. *Confidentiality of News Sources v. Law Enforcement and Laws of General Applicability.* Rights protected under the freedom of the press have also come in conflict with other interests. At times, for example, the right to protect the confidentiality of news sources and thus to maintain a continued supply of information has collided with the needs and interests of law enforcement. And as discussed later, interesting questions are also raised when the value of confidentiality to nonmedia persons comes in conflict with freedom of the press itself.

Beginning in the 1960s, a number of dissident, militant groups not only *vocally expressed* their opposition to policies of the government and to the political system generally, but *demonstrated* their opposition through illegal, obstructive actions. Under such circumstances, these organizations aroused the concern both of the government, for surveillance and security purposes, and of enterprising newspeople, for news-gathering and reporting purposes. And whereas these groups attempted to erect an iron curtain between themselves and the government, they did on occasion grant reporters access to their meetings, provided confidentiality was assured.

But when a news story in the morning paper gives law enforcement officials reason to believe that internal security (e.g., the prevention of civil disorders) or criminal activity (e.g., the use of drugs) may be involved, can reporters be compelled to reveal their sources pursuant to certain governmental investigations or grand jury inquiries.? This was the question presented to the Court in *Branzburg* v. *Hayes, In re Pappas*, and *United States* v. *Caldwell* (408 U.S. 665), decided together in 1972. In all three cases, reporters had attempted to avoid testifying before grand juries. In *Branzburg*, a Kentucky reporter who had written several major articles on the drug traffic sought to avoid being required to name the persons he saw possessing marijuana and hashish. In *Pappas*, a Massachusetts television reporter sought to have quashed a grand jury summons requiring him to report on activities that he observed while in a Black Panther Party headquarters. And in *Caldwell*, the government appealed a Court of Appeals decision that held that a *New York Times* reporter was not to be held in contempt for refusing to appear before a federal grand jury to discuss certain interviews he had had with Black Panther Party members. In another five-to-four decision, in which the four Nixon appointees were joined by Justice White, the Supreme Court held that reporters, like other citizens, had no privilege to refuse to appear before a grand jury and to answer questions as to their information or sources. In his majority opinion, Justice White rejected the claims made by the reporters that there must be demonstrated a compelling need for the information in their possession because of its relevance to a crime and because it is unavailable from other sources to override their First Amendment guarantees to protect their sources and information from compelled disclosure. "The heart of the claim," said White, "is that the burden on news gathering resulting from compelling reporters to disclose confidential information outweighs any public interest in obtaining the information." White proceeded to discuss generally testimonial privilege for reporters, saying that none existed at common law and that none exists by federal statute. He declined to establish such a privilege in these cases. "On the records now before us," said White, "we perceive no basis for holding that the public interest in law enforcement in ensuring effective grand jury proceedings is insufficient to override the consequential, but uncertain, burden on news gathering which is said to result from insisting that reporters, like other citizens, respond to relevant questions put to them in the course of a valid grand jury investigation or criminal trial." Justice Stewart, joined by Justices Brennan and Marshall, issued a strong dissent. Stewart charged that the "Court's crabbed view of the First Amendment reflects a disturbing insensitivity to the critical role of an independent press in our society. . . ."*

Similarly, some viewed a 1978 Court decision as subordinating the First Amendment rights of the press to the needs of law enforcement. Indeed, in *Zurcher* v. *Stanford Daily* (436 U.S. 547, 1978) law enforcement officials obtained a search warrant issued upon a judge's finding of probable cause that the editors of the *Stanford Daily* (student newspaper) had notes and photo negatives in their possession that could identify demonstrators who had assaulted the police. The newspaper brought action claiming a deprivation of constitutional rights under the Fourth and First Amendments. But a Supreme Court majority, led by Justice White, could find no constitutional violation. As to the Fourth Amendment, the Court said that "the critical element in a reasonable search is not that the property owner is suspected of crime but that there is reasonable cause to believe that the things to be searched for and seized are located on the property to which entry is sought." Moreover, the Court held that, properly administered, the preconditions for a search warrant (probable cause, specificity with respect to the place to be searched and the things to be seized, and overall reasonableness), "which must be applied with particular exactitude when First Amendment interests would be endangered by the search, are adequate safeguards against the interference with the press's ability to gather, analyze, and disseminate news that respondents claim would ensue from use of warrants for third-party searches of newspaper offices."

*For state legislative developments and reactions relative to *Branzburg*, see Kathryn J. Humphrey, "Shield Statutes: A Changing Problem in Light of Branzburg," 25 *Wayne Law Review* 1381 (1979).

But what happens when the value of confidentiality to nonmedia persons collides with the rights of freedom of the press in news reporting? In the 1991 case (*Cohen* v. *Cowles Media Co.*, 111 S. Ct. 2513), the Supreme Court held that the First Amendment did not bar a suit for damages based on the breach of a promise of confidentiality made by a reporter to his news source. Here a supporter of an Independent-Republican candidate for the governorship of Minnesota gave false information about the Democratic rival to some newspapers based on a promise of confidentiality. Two newspapers ran editorials exposing such "dirty tricks" despite the promise of confidentiality made to the news source involved. The source, who was subsequently fired from his employment, sued and received compensatory and punitive damages arising out of the breach of promise of confidentiality. The Supreme Court held that the First Amendment's protection of freedom of the press did not exempt the press from laws of "general applicability," such as state contract law, that only incidentally affect First Amendment values.

The Press and Damage to Reputation

In his opinion in *Near* v. *Minnesota*, Chief Justice Charles Evans Hughes emphasized the need for "a vigilant and courageous press" to focus attention on malfeasance and corruption of unfaithful public officials.* But when does comment on official conduct lose its character as constitutionally protected expression and become subject to the sanctions of state libel laws? The Supreme Court supplied the answer in 1964 in *New York Times Co.* v. *Sullivan* in reversing a $500,000 judgment against the New York Times Publishing Company, which had been awarded to a local public official by an Alabama court. Paradoxically, the allegedly defamatory publication did not deal with the traditional subjects on which there has been criticism of official conduct, such as alliances with criminal elements and malfeasance in office. Instead, the publication was an editorial advertisement on the civil rights movement in the South.

In setting aside the judgment, the Supreme Court applied the brakes to southern public officials who tried to stifle comment critical of their conduct in actions involving race relations. Thus, Sullivan's allegation that the advertisement contained a number of inaccuracies and was injurious

*Probably the most significant rulings on freedom of the press since *Near* were the Pentagon Papers cases decided by the Court in 1972 in *New York Times* v. *United States* (403 U.S. 713).

to his reputation as a public official was rejected. Justice William J. Brennan, who wrote the opinion of the Court, noted that the case must be considered "against the background of a profound national commitment to the principle that debate on public issues should be uninhibited, robust, and wide open, and that it may well include vehement, caustic, and sometimes unpleasant sharp attacks . . . on public officials." With this principle in mind, Brennan held that the crucial question is whether the advertisement forfeited its status as constitutionally protected expression because it contained some false statements and allegedly defamed the respondent. Advancing the proposition that "erroneous statement is inevitable in free debate and . . . must be protected if the freedoms of expression are to have the 'breathing space' that they 'need . . . to survive,' " he concluded that "neither factual error nor defamatory content" nor "the combination of the two elements" can justify removal of "the constitutional shield from criticism of official conduct" unless there is proof of "actual malice."

Justice Hugo Black's concurring opinion, supported by Justice William O. Douglas, set forth the absolutist position that the *Times* and the sponsors of the ad had an "unconditional constitutional right to publish . . . their criticisms of the Montgomery agencies and officials."

Later that year, the Court extended its *New York Times* rule to limit state power to impose criminal sanctions for criticism of the official conduct of public officials. In *Garrison* v. *Louisiana* (379 U.S. 64, 1964), a unanimous Court reversed the conviction of District Attorney Jim Garrison of Orleans Parish (County), Louisiana, on a charge of criminal defamation based on his criticism of the official conduct of judges of the parish's Criminal District Court. In an opinion supported by five members of the Court, Justice Brennan rejected the contention that because "criminal libel laws serve distinct interests from those secured by civil libel laws" they should not be subject to the limitations laid down in the *New York Times* case. Said Brennan, "[t]he *New York Times* rule is not rendered inapplicable merely because an official's private reputation, as well as his public reputation, is harmed. . . . [A]nything which might touch an official's fitness for office is relevant." He concluded that "even where the utterance is false, the great principles of the Constitution . . . preclude attaching adverse consequences to any except the knowing or reckless falsehood."

As in *New York Times*, the concurring opinions of Justices Black and Douglas once again emphasized that the absolutist position is the only rule that makes sense.

The Court examined further the scope of the term "public official" and the meaning of "malice" in *Rosenblatt* v. *Baer* (383 U.S. 75, 1966). Here the Court reversed a state libel judgment against a newspaper columnist for using defamatory falsehoods in commentary about the performance of a supervisor of a county recreation area. Justice William J. Brennan held that since the position of "supervisor of the Belknap County Recreation Area" was embraced within the term "public official" as construed in *New York Times*, the instructions to the jury (which permitted the jury to find that negligent misstatement of fact would abrogate the commentary's privileged status) were defective.

Regarding "malice," Brennan contended that the state court definition, which includes "ill will, evil motive [and] intention to injure," was "constitutionally insufficient where discussion of public affairs is concerned." It did not square with the definition set forth in *New York Times*, which requires a showing that the statement was made with knowledge of its falsity or "reckless disregard of whether it was false or not."

In another dimension of the defamation issue, the Court, in *Time, Inc.* v. *Hill* (385 U.S. 374, 1967) applied the *New York Times* rule in holding that a New York "right of privacy" statute was unconstitutionally applied to redress false reports of matters of public interest in the absence of proof of actual malice. The case involved a *Life* magazine article in which the fictionalized play "The Desperate Hours" was portrayed as a reenactment of the ordeal of a family held captive by three escaped convicts. Taking cognizance of the "exposure of one's self to others [as] a concomitant of life in a civilized community," Justice William J. Brennan contended that such a risk "is an essential incident of life in a society which places a primary value on freedom of speech and of press."

In the companion cases of *Curtis Publishing Co.* v. *Butts* and *Associated Press* v. *Walker* (388 U.S. 130, 1967) the Court considered whether its ruling in *New York Times* extended to libel actions brought by "public figures" who are "involved in issues in which the public has a justified and important interest." The *Butts* case involved a federal district court libel judgment of $460,000 against the Curtis Publishing Company for publication of an article in *The Saturday Evening Post* in which Wally Butts, longtime football coach and athletic director of the University of Georgia, was accused of plotting to fix a football game between his school and the University of Alabama. The *Walker* case was an appeal from a state court libel judgment of $500,000 against the Associated Press for publication of news stories describing the role of retired Major General Edwin A. Walker in the campus disorders accompanying the enrollment of James Meredith at the University of Mississippi.

In examining the constitutional issues presented by these cases, Justice Harlan, who wrote the plurality opinion, counseled against "blind application" of the *New York Times* rule. He stressed that "none of the particular considerations involved in *New York Times*" were present in *Butts* and *Walker*. Hence, it was necessary to formulate a new rule of libel, which he stated as follows:

> [A] "public figure" who is not a public official may . . . recover damages for a defamatory falsehood whose substance makes substantial danger to reputation apparent, on a showing of highly unreasonable conduct constituting an extreme departure from standards of investigation and reporting ordinarily adhered to by responsible publishers.

Applying this new rule to the cases, Harlan concluded that there was enough evidence to support the judgment in *Butts* but that the evidence was insufficient to prove "a severe departure from accepted publishing standards" in *Walker*.

The *New York Times* doctrine was further expanded in a 1971 decision—*Rosenbloom* v. *Metromedia, Inc.* (403 U.S. 29)—that involved a libel suit brought by a private individual against a radio broadcasting corporation. Rosenbloom, a distributor of nudist magazines, was arrested for possession of obscene literature. One of Metromedia's radio stations, in reports concerning Rosenbloom's subsequent suit alleging that the magazines he distributed were not obscene, described Rosenbloom and the publisher of the magazines involved as "girlie-book peddlers" and as part of the "smut literature racket." Rosenbloom initiated the libel suit against Metromedia after being acquitted of criminal obscenity charges. The Court held that the *New York Times* standard applied to libel suits brought by private individuals as well as to suits brought by "public officials" or "public figures" so long as the subject of the suit was a matter of "public or general concern." Justice Brennan's opinion, in which Chief Justice Burger and Justice Blackmun joined, explained that

> [d]rawing a distinction between "public" and "private" figures makes no sense in terms of the First Amendment guarantees. The *New York Times* standard was applied to libel of a public official or public

figure to give effect to the Amendment's function to encourage ventilation of public issues, not because the public official has any less interest in protecting his reputation than an individual in private life.

The Court's decision in the case indicated that there was no evidence to support the contention that Metromedia's descriptions of Rosenbloom, even if defamatory, were made with knowledge of their falsity or with a reckless disregard therefor.

Dissenting, Justice Harlan, who had defined the "public figure" libel rule only four years earlier, contended that "those special considerations" compelling a different test when public officials or public figures are the plaintiffs "do not obtain where the litigant is a purely private individual." Justice Marshall's dissent was critical of Brennan's "public or general concern" test, arguing that it "threatens society's interest in protecting private individuals from being thrust into the public eye by the distorting light of defamation" since "all human events are arguably within the area of public or general concern."

In *Gertz* v. *Robert Welch, Inc.* (418 U.S. 323, 1974) three years later, the Court eliminated some of the confusion fostered by the five separate opinions in *Rosenbloom* when it held the *New York Times Co.* v. *Sullivan* rule was not applicable in determining media liability for alleged defamation of private persons. Specifically, the Court held that private individuals, in contrast to public figures, did not have to prove "actual malice" to recover damages in libel actions. In his opinion for the Court, Justice Lewis Powell took notice of the greater access of public officials and public figures to the media for counteracting false statements. Contrariwise, he felt that the private individual is much "more vulnerable to injury and [hence] the state's interest in protecting him is correspondingly greater." Consequently, states should be accorded "substantial latitude" in fashioning legal remedies for such relief.

In dissent, Chief Justice Burger complained about the Court's departure from the orderly development of the law of defamation since the decision in *New York Times Co.* v. *Sullivan.* He indicated his preference for the development of law as it had existed up to then with respect to private persons, rather than embarking "on a new doctrinal theory which has no jurisprudential ancestry." And Justice Douglas's dissent echoed his familiar theme that the First Amendment prohibits such laws absolutely.

Early in 1976 the Court applied the new *Gertz* rule in *Time* v. *Firestone* (424 U.S. 448). *Time* magazine had erred in a published account of the divorce of Russell A. Firestone, Jr., the tire fortune heir. Although Mr. Firestone had charged his wife with "extreme cruelty and adultery," the presiding judge did not specify these charges as the grounds upon which he granted the divorce. The *Time* article did specify these charges as the grounds accepted by the trial court, and, when the magazine refused Mrs. Firestone's request to retract the statement, she filed a libel suit. Upon losing a $100,000 damage judgment, *Time* appealed, arguing that because she was a public figure, Mrs. Firestone would have to prove malicious intent on the part of the magazine under the *New York Times* rule.

Speaking for the five-to-three majority, Justice Rehnquist opined that Mrs. Firestone "did not assume any role of especial prominence in the affairs of society . . . and she did not thrust herself to the forefront of any public controversy in order to influence the resolution of the issues involved in it." In short, she was deemed not to be a public figure, and according to the *Gertz* decision, she need only prove negligence in order to recover damages from the publication. Because no fault was proven in state court, the case was remanded.

Similarly, in a 1979 decision (*Wolston* v. *Reader's Digest Association, Inc.*, 443 U.S. 157), an eight-to-one Court majority stated that Wolston was not a public figure within the meaning of its defamation cases and therefore "was not required by the First Amendment to meet the 'actual malice' standard of *New York Times Co.* v. *Sullivan.*"

However, a "public figure" or "public official" must continue to meet the "actual malice" standard. But another 1979 decision appears to give such plaintiffs additional grounds in which to probe for evidence. In *Herbert* v. *Lando* (441 U.S. 153, 1979), the Court held that the "First Amendment does not bar plaintiff from inquiring into editorial process and state of mind of those responsible for publication." Such inquiries may indeed hold far-reaching implication for defamation litigation.

In *Dun & Broadstreet* v. *Greenmoss Builders* (105 S. Ct. 2939, 1985), the Court held that not even the lesser standards of *Gertz* had to be applied to libel defendants if their speech was unrelated to matters of public concern. Here a credit reporting agency (Dun & Broadstreet) passed on to five subscribers an unsubstantiated and inaccurate report to the effect that Greenmoss Builders had filed for bankruptcy. Although Dun & Broadstreet attempted to overcome the error through a corrective notice, Greenmoss nonetheless filed a defamation suit and was awarded damages.

Justice Powell spoke for a five-to-four Court majority and held that in addition to the public/private figure distinction, *Gertz* should also be viewed as drawing a distinction between matters of public and private concern, the latter commanding lesser First Amendment protection and thus according more consideration to state libel laws. Indeed, the Court held that even absent a showing of actual malice, the First Amendment does not prevent a private person from receiving awards for presumed and punitive damages if the defamatory statements do not focus on matters of public concern. Cf. *Masson* v. *New Yorker Magazine, Inc.* (111 S. Ct. 2419, 1991).

NEBRASKA PRESS ASSOCIATION v. STUART
427 U.S. 539; 49 L. Ed. 2d 683; 96 S. Ct. 2791 (1976)

CHIEF JUSTICE BURGER *delivered the opinion of the Court.*

The respondent State District Judge entered an order restraining the petitioners from publishing or broadcasting accounts of confessions or admissions made by the accused or facts "strongly implicative" of the accused in a widely reported murder of six persons. We granted certiorari to decide whether the entry of such an order on the showing made before the state court violated the constitutional guarantee of freedom of the press.

I

On the evening of October 18, 1975, local police found the six members of the Henry Kellie family murdered in their home in Sutherland, Neb., a town of about 850 people. Police released the description of a suspect, Erwin Charles Simants, to the reporters who had hastened to the scene of the crime. Simants was arrested and arraigned in Lincoln County Court that following morning. . . .

The crime immediately attracted widespread news coverage, by local, regional, and national newspapers, radio and television stations. Three days after the crime, the County Attorney and Simants' attorney joined in asking the County Court to enter a restrictive order relating to "matters that may or may not be publicly reported or disclosed to the public," because of the "mass coverage by news media" and the "reasonable likelihood of prejudicial news which would make difficult, if not impossible, the impaneling of an impartial jury and tend to prevent a fair trial." The County Court heard oral argument but took no evidence; no attorney for members of the press appeared at this stage. The County Court granted the prosecutor's motion for a restrictive order and entered it the next day, October 22. The order prohibited everyone in attendance from "releas[ing] or authoriz[ing] for public dissemination in any form or manner whatsoever any testimony given or evidence adduced"; the order also required members of the press to observe the Nebraska Bar-Press Guidelines.*

Simants' preliminary hearing was held the same day, open to the public but subject to the order. The County Court bound over the defendant for trial to the State District Court. The charges, as amended to reflect the autopsy findings, were that Simants had committed the murders in the course of a sexual assault.

Petitioners—several press and broadcast associations, publishers, and individual reporters—moved on October 23 for leave to intervene in the District Court, asking that the restrictive order imposed by the County Court be vacated. The District Court conducted a hearing, at which the County Judge testified and newspaper articles about the Simants case were admitted in evidence. The District Judge granted petitioners' motion to intervene and, on October 27, entered his own restrictive order. The judge found "because of the nature of the crimes charged in the complaint that there is a clear and present danger that pretrial publicity could impinge upon the defendant's right to a fair trial." The order applied only until the jury was impaneled, and specifically prohibited petitioners from

*The Nebraska Guidelines are voluntary standards adopted by members of the state bar and news media to deal with the reporting of crimes and criminal trials. They outline the matters of fact that may appropriately be reported, and also list what items are not generally appropriate for reporting, including: confessions, opinions on guilt or innocence, statements that would influence the outcome of a trial, the results of tests or examinations, comments on the credibility of witnesses, and evidence presented in the jury's absence. The publication of an accused's criminal record should, under the Guidelines, be "considered very carefully." The Guidelines also act out standards for taking and publishing photographs, and set up a joint bar-press committee to foster cooperation in resolving particular problems that emerge.

reporting five subjects: (1) the existence or contents of a confession Simants had made to law enforcement officers, which had been introduced in open court at arraignment; (2) the fact or nature of statements Simants had made to other persons; (3) the contents of a note he had written the night of the crime; (4) certain aspects of the medical testimony at the preliminary hearing; (5) the identity of the victims of the alleged sexual assault and the nature of the assault. It also prohibited reporting the exact nature of the restrictive order itself. Like the County Court's order, this order incorporated the Nebraska Bar-Press Guidelines. Finally, the order set out a plan for attendance, seating and courthouse traffic control during the trial.

The problems presented by this case are almost as old as the Republic. Neither in the Constitution nor in contemporaneous writing do we find that the conflict between these two important rights was anticipated, yet it is inconceivable that the authors of the Constitution were unaware of the potential conflicts between the right to an unbiased jury and the guarantee of freedom of the press. . . . [T]heir chief concern was the need for freedom of expression in the political arena and the dialogue in ideas. But they recognized that there were risks to private rights from an unfettered press. . . .

The speed of communication and the pervasiveness of the modern news media have exacerbated these problems, however, as numerous appeals demonstrate. The trial of Bruno Hauptmann in a small New Jersey community for the abduction and murder of Charles Lindbergh's infant child probably was the most widely covered trial up to that time, and the nature of the coverage produced widespread public reaction. Criticism was directed at the "carnival" atmosphere that pervaded the community and the courtroom itself. Responsible leaders of press and the legal profession—including other judges—pointed out that much of this sorry performance could have been controlled by a vigilant trial judge and by other public officers subject to the control of the court. . . .

The excesses of press and radio and lack of responsibility of those in authority in the Hauptmann case and others of that era led to efforts to develop voluntary guidelines for courts, lawyers, press and broadcasters. . . .

In practice, of course, even the most ideal guidelines are subjected to powerful strains when a case such as Simants arises, with reporters from many parts of the country on the scene. Reporters from distant places are unlikely to consider themselves bound by local standards. They report to editors outside the area covered by the guidelines, and their editors are likely to be guided only by their own standards. To contemplate how a state court can control acts of a newspaper or broadcaster outside its jurisdiction, even though the newspapers and broadcasts reach the very community from which jurors are to be selected, suggests something of the practical difficulties of managing such guidelines.

The problems presented in this case have a substantial history outside the reported decisions of the courts, in the efforts of many responsible people to accommodate the competing interests. We cannot resolve all of them, for it is not the function of this Court to write a code. . . .

IV

The Sixth Amendment in terms guarantees "trial by an impartial jury" in federal criminal prosecutions. Because "trial by jury in criminal cases is fundamental to the American scheme of justice," the Due Process Clause of the Fourteenth Amendment guarantees the same right in state criminal prosecutions. . . .

Taken together, . . . cases [decided by this Court] demonstrate that pretrial publicity—even pervasive, adverse publicity—does not inevitably lead to an unfair trial. The capacity of the jury eventually impaneled to decide the case fairly is influenced by the tone and extent of the publicity, which is in part, and often in large part, shaped by what attorneys, police, and other officials do to precipitate news coverage. The trial judge has a major responsibility. What the judge says about the case, in or out of the courtroom, is likely to appear in newspapers and broadcasts. More important, the measures a judge takes or fails to take to mitigate the effects of pretrial publicity . . . may well determine whether the defendant receives a trial consistent with the requirements of due process. . . .

The costs of failure to afford a fair trial are high. In the most extreme cases . . . the risk of injustice was avoided when the convictions were reversed. But a reversal means that justice has been delayed for both the defendant and the State; in some cases, because of lapse of time retrial is impossible or further prosecution is gravely handicapped. Moreover, in borderline cases in which the conviction is not reversed, there is some possibility of an injustice unredressed. . . .

The state trial judge in the case before us acted responsibly, out of a legitimate concern, in an effort to protect the defendant's right to a fair trial. What we must decide is not simply whether the

Nebraska courts erred in seeing the possibility of real danger to the defendant's rights, but whether in the circumstances of this case the means employed were foreclosed by another provision of the Constitution.

V

* * *

. . . [P]rior restraints on speech and publication are the most serious and the least tolerable infringement on First Amendment rights. A criminal penalty or a judgment in a defamation case is subject to the whole panoply of protections afforded by deferring the impact of the judgment until all avenues of appellate review have been exhausted. Only after judgment has become final, correct or otherwise, does the law's sanction become fully operative.

A prior restraint, by contrast and by definition, has an immediate and irreversible sanction. If it can be said that threat of criminal or civil sanctions after publication "chills" speech, prior restraint "freezes" it at least for the time.

The damage can be particularly great when the prior restraint falls upon the communication of news and commentary on current events. Truthful reports of public judicial proceedings have been afforded special protection against subsequent punishment. . . . For the same reasons the protection against prior restraint should have particular force as applied to reporting of criminal proceedings, whether the crime in question is a single isolated act or a pattern of criminal conduct . . . . The extraordinary protections afforded by the First Amendment carry with them something in the nature of a fiduciary duty to exercise the protected rights responsibly—a duty widely acknowledged but not always observed by editors and publishers. It is not asking too much to suggest that those who exercise First Amendment rights in newspapers or broadcasting enterprises direct some effort to protect the rights of an accused to a fair trial by unbiased jurors. . . .

VI

We now turn to the record in this case to determine whether, as Learned Hand put it, "the gravity of the 'evil,' discounted by its improbability, justifies such invasion of free speech as is necessary to avoid the danger." *United States* v. *Dennis*, 183 F.2d 201, 212 (1950), aff'd, 341 U.S. 494. . . .

A

In assessing the probable extent of publicity, the trial judge had before him newspapers demonstrating that the crime had already drawn intensive news coverage, and the testimony of the County Judge, who had entered the initial restraining order based on the local and national attention the case had attracted. The District Judge was required to assess the probable publicity that would be given these shocking crimes prior to the time a jury was selected and sequestered. He then had to examine the probable nature of the publicity and determine how it would affect prospective jurors.

Our review of the pretrial record persuades us that the trial judge was justified in concluding that there would be intense and pervasive pretrial publicity concerning the case. He could also reasonably conclude, based on common human experience, that publicity might impair the defendant's right to a fair trial. He did not purport to say more, for he found only a clear and present danger that pretrial publicity *could* impinge upon the defendant's right to a fair trial. His conclusion as to the impact of such publicity on prospective jurors was of necessity speculative, dealing as he was with factors unknown and unknowable.

B

We find little in the record that goes to another aspect of our task, determining whether measures short of an order restraining all publication would have ensured the defendant a fair trial. Although the entry of the order might be read as a judicial determination that other measures would not suffice, the trial court made no express findings to that effect; the Nebraska Supreme Court referred to the issue only by implication. . . .

We have . . . examined this record to determine the probable efficacy of the measures short of prior restraint on the press and speech. There is no finding that alternative measures would not have protected Simants' rights, and the Nebraska Supreme Court did no more than imply that such measures might not be adequate. Moreover, the record is lacking in evidence to support such a finding.

C

We must also assess the probable efficacy of prior restraint on publication as a workable method of protecting Simants' right to a fair trial, and we cannot ignore the reality of the problems of managing and enforcing pretrial restraining orders. The territorial jurisdiction of the issuing court is limited by concepts of sovereignty. . . . The need for *in person-*

am jurisdiction also presents an obstacle to a restraining order that applies to publication at large as distinguished from restraining publication within a given jurisdiction.

The Nebraska Supreme Court narrowed the scope of the restrictive order, and its opinion reflects awareness of the tensions between the need to protect the accused as fully as possible and the need to restrict publication as little as possible. The dilemma posed underscores how difficult it is for trial judges to predict what information will in fact undermine the impartiality of jurors, and the difficulty of drafting an order that will effectively keep prejudicial information from prospective jurors. When a restrictive order is sought, a court can anticipate only part of what will develop that may injure the accused. But information not so obviously prejudicial may emerge, and what may properly be published in these "gray zone" circumstances may not violate the restrictive order and yet be prejudicial.

Finally, we note that the events disclosed by the record took place in a community of 850 people. It is reasonable to assume that, without any news accounts being printed or broadcast, rumors would travel swiftly by word of mouth. One can only speculate on the accuracy of such reports, given the generative propensities of rumors; they could well be more damaging than reasonably accurate news accounts. But plainly a whole community cannot be restrained from discussing a subject intimately affecting life within it.

Given these practical problems, it is far from clear that prior restraint on publication would have protected Simants' rights.

D

Finally, another feature of this case leads us to conclude that the restrictive order entered here is not supportable. At the outset the County Court entered a very broad restrictive order, the terms of which are not before us; it then held a preliminary hearing open to the public and the press. There was testimony concerning at least two incriminating statements made by Simants to private persons; the statement—evidently a confession—that he gave to law enforcement officials was also introduced. . . .

To the extent that this order prohibited the reporting of evidence adduced at the open preliminary hearing, it plainly violated settled principles: "there is nothing that proscribes the press from reporting events that transpire in the courtroom.". . . The County Court could not know that closure of the preliminary hearing was an alternative open to it until the Nebraska Supreme Court so construed state law; but once a public hearing had been held, what transpired there could not be subject to prior restraint.

E

The record demonstrates . . . that there was indeed a risk that pretrial news accounts, true or false, would have some adverse impact on the attitudes of those who might be called as jurors. But on the record now before us it is not clear that further publicity, unchecked, would so distort the views of potential jurors that twelve could not be found who would, under proper instructions, fulfill their sworn duty to render a just verdict exclusively on the evidence presented in open court. We cannot say on this record that alternatives to a prior restraint on petitioners would not have sufficiently mitigated the adverse effects of pretrial publicity so as to make prior restraint unnecessary. Nor can we conclude that the restraining order actually entered would serve its intended purpose. Reasonable minds can have few doubts about the gravity of the evil pretrial publicity can work, but the probability that it would do so here was not demonstrated with the degree of certainty our cases on prior restraint require.

Of necessity our holding is confined to the record before us. But our conclusion is not simply a result of assessing the adequacy of the showing made in this case; it results in part from the problems inherent in meeting the heavy burden of demonstrating, in advance of trial, that without prior restraint a fair trial will be denied. The practical problems of managing and enforcing restrictive orders will always be present. In this sense, the record now before us is illustrative rather than exceptional. It is significant that when this Court has reversed a state conviction, because of prejudicial publicity, it has carefully noted that some course of action short of prior restraint would have made a critical difference. . . .

Our analysis ends as it began, with a confrontation between prior restraint imposed to protect one vital constitutional guarantee and the explicit command of another that the freedom to speak and publish shall not be abridged. We reaffirm that the guarantees of freedom of expression are not an absolute prohibition under all circumstances, but the barriers to prior restraint remain high and the presumption against its use continues intact. We hold that, with respect to the order entered in this case prohibiting reporting or commentary on judicial proceedings held in public, the barriers have not been overcome; to the extent that this order restrained publication of such material, it is clearly invalid. To the extent that it prohibited publication based on information gained from other sources, we conclude that the heavy burden imposed as a condition to securing a prior restraint was not met and the judgment of the Nebraska Supreme Court is therefore

Reversed.

NEW YORK TIMES COMPANY v. SULLIVAN
376 U.S. 254; 11 L. Ed. 2d 686; 84 S. Ct. 710 (1964)

JUSTICE BRENNAN *delivered the opinion of the Court.*

We are required for the first time in this case to determine the extent to which the constitutional protections for speech and press limit a state's power to award damages in a libel action brought by a public official against critics of his official conduct.

Respondent L. B. Sullivan is one of the three elected Commissioners of the City of Montgomery, Alabama. He testified that he was "Commissioner of Public Affairs and the duties are supervision of the Police Department, Fire Department, Department of Cemetery and Department of Scales." He brought this civil libel action against the four individual petitioners, who are Negroes and Alabama clergymen, and against petitioner, the New York Times Company . . . which publishes *The New York Times*. . . . A jury in the Circuit Court of Montgomery County awarded him damages of $500,000, the full amount claimed, against all the petitioners, and the Supreme Court of Alabama affirmed.

Respondent's complaint alleged that he had been libeled by statements in a full-page advertisement that was carried in *The New York Times* on March 29, 1960. Entitled "Heed Their Rising Voices," the advertisement began by stating that "As the whole world knows by now, thousands of Southern Negro students are engaged in widespread nonviolent demonstrations in positive affirmation of the right to live in human dignity as guaranteed by the U.S. Constitution and the Bill of Rights." It went on to charge that "in their efforts to uphold these guarantees, they are being met by an unprecedented wave of terror by those who would deny and negate that document which the whole world looks upon as setting the pattern for modern freedom. . . ." Succeeding paragraphs purported to illustrate the "wave of terror" by describing certain alleged events. The text concluded with an appeal for funds for three purposes: support of the student movement, "the struggle for the right-to-vote," and the legal defense of Dr. Martin Luther King, Jr., leader of the movement, against a perjury indictment then pending in Montgomery.

The text appeared over the names of 64 persons, many widely known for their activities in public affairs, religion, trade unions, and the performing arts. Below these names, and under a line reading "We in the South who are struggling daily for dignity and freedom warmly endorse this appeal," appeared the names of the four individual petitioners and of 16 other persons, all but two of whom were identified as clergymen in various Southern cities. The advertisement was signed at the bottom of the page by the "Committee to Defend Martin Luther King and Struggle for Freedom in the South," and the officers of the Committee were listed.

Of the 10 paragraphs of text in the advertisement, the third and a portion of the sixth were the basis of respondent's claim of libel. They read as follows:

Third paragraph:

> In Montgomery, Alabama, after students sang "My Country, 'Tis of Thee" on the State Capitol steps, their leaders were expelled from school, and truckloads of police armed with shotguns and teargas ringed the Alabama State College Campus. When the entire student body protested to state authorities by refusing to reregister, their dining hall was padlocked in an attempt to starve them into submission.

Sixth paragraph:

> Again and again the Southern violators have answered Dr. King's peaceful protests with intimidation and violence. They have bombed his home almost killing his wife and child. They have assaulted his person. They have arrested him seven times for "speeding," "loitering" and similar "offenses." And now they have charged him with "perjury"—*a felony* under which they would imprison him for *ten years*. . . .

Although neither of these statements mentions respondent by name, he contended that the word "police" in the third paragraph referred to him as the Montgomery Commissioner who supervised the Police Department, so that he was being accused of "ringing" the campus with police. He further claimed that the paragraph would be read as imputing to the police, and hence to him, the padlocking of the dining hall in order to starve the students into submission. As to the sixth paragraph, he contended that since arrests are ordinarily made by the police, the statement "They have arrested [Dr. King] seven times" would be read as referring to him; he further contended that the "They" who did the arresting would be equated with the "They" who committed the other described acts and with the "Southern violators." Thus, he argued, the paragraph would be read as accusing the Montgomery police, and hence him, of answering Dr. King's protests with "intimidation and violence," bombing his home, assaulting his person, and charging him with perjury. Respondent and six other Montgomery residents testified that they read some or all of the statements as referring to him in his capacity as Commissioner.

It is uncontroverted that some of the statements contained in the two paragraphs were not accurate descriptions of events which occurred in Montgomery. Although Negro students staged a demonstration on the State Capitol steps, they sang the National Anthem and not "My Country, 'Tis of Thee." Although nine students were expelled by the State Board of Education, this was not for leading the demonstration at the Capitol, but for demanding service at a lunch counter in the Montgomery County Courthouse on another day. Not the entire student body, but most of it, had protested the expulsion, not by refusing to register, but by boycotting classes on a single day; virtually all the students did register for the ensuing semester. The campus dining hall was not padlocked on any occasion, and the only students who may have been barred from eating there were the few who had neither signed a preregistration application nor requested temporary meal tickets. Although the police were deployed near the campus in large numbers on three occasions, they did not at any time "ring" the campus, and they were not called to the campus in connection with the demonstration on the State Capitol steps, as the third paragraph implied. Dr. King had not been arrested seven times, but only four; and although he claimed to have been assaulted some years earlier in connection with his arrest for loitering outside a courtroom, one of the officers who made the arrest denied that there was such an assault.

On the premise that the charges in the sixth paragraph could be read as referring to him, respondent was allowed to prove that he had not participated in the events described. Although Dr. King's home had in fact been bombed twice when his wife and child were there, both of these occasions antedated respondent's tenure as Commissioner, and the police were not only not implicated in the bombings, but had made every effort to apprehend those who were. Three of Dr. King's four arrests took place before respondent became Commissioner. Although Dr. King had in fact been indicted (he was subsequently acquitted) on two counts of perjury, each of which carried a possible five-year sentence, respondent had nothing to do with procuring the indictment.

Respondent made no effort to prove that he suffered actual pecuniary loss as a result of the alleged libel.* One of his witnesses, a former employer, testified that if he had believed the statements, he doubted whether he "would want to be associated with anybody who would be a party to such things as are stated in that ad," and that he would not re-employ respondent if he believed "that he allowed the Police Department to do the things that the paper said he did." But neither this witness nor any of the others testified that he had actually believed the statements in their supported reference to respondent.

The cost of the advertisement was approximately $4800, and it was published by the *Times* upon an order from a New York advertising agency acting for the signatory Committee. The agency submitted the advertisement with a letter from A. Philip Randolph, Chairman of the Committee, certifying that the persons whose names appeared on the advertisement had given their permission. Mr. Randolph was known to the Times' Advertising Acceptability Department as a responsible person, and in accepting the letter as sufficient proof of authorization it followed its established practice. There was testimony that the copy of the advertisement which accompanied the letter listed only the sixty-four names appearing under the text, and that the statement "We in the South . . . warmly endorse this appeal" and the list of names thereunder, which included those of the individual petitioners, were subsequently added when the first

---

*Approximately 394 copies of the edition of the *Times* containing the advertisement were circulated in Alabama. Of these about 35 copies were distributed in Montgomery County. The total circulation of the *Times* for that day was approximately 650,000 copies.

proof of the advertisement was received. Each of the individual petitioners testified that he had not authorized the use of his name, and that he had been unaware of its use until receipt of respondent's demand for a retraction. The manager of the Advertising Acceptability Department testified that he had approved the advertisement for publication because he knew nothing to cause him to believe that anything in it was false, and because it bore the endorsement of "a number of people who are well known and whose reputation" he "had no reason to question." Neither he nor anyone else at the Times made an effort to confirm the accuracy of the advertisement, either by checking it against recent Times news stories relating to some of the described events or by some other means.

Alabama law denies a public officer recovery of punitive damages in a libel action brought on account of a publication concerning his official conduct unless he first makes a written demand for a public retraction and the defendant fails or refuses to comply. Respondent served such a demand upon each of the petitioners. None of the individual petitioners responded to the demand, primarily because each took the position that he had not authorized the use of his name on the advertisement and therefore had not published the statements that respondent alleged to have libeled him. The Times did not publish a retraction in response to the demand, but wrote respondent a letter stating, among other things, that "we . . . are somewhat puzzled as to how you think the statements in any way reflect on you," and "you might, if you desire, let us know in what respect you claim that the statements in the advertisement reflect on you." Respondent filed this suit a few days later without answering the letter. The Times did, however, subsequently publish a retraction of the advertisement upon the demand of Governor John Patterson of Alabama, who asserted that the publication charged him with "grave misconduct and . . . improper actions and omissions as Governor of Alabama and Ex-Officio Chairman of the State Board of Education in Alabama." When asked to explain why there had been a retraction for the Governor but not for respondent, the Secretary of the Times testified: "We did that because we didn't want anything that was published by the Times to be a reflection on the State of Alabama and the Governor was, as far as we could see, the embodiment of the State of Alabama and the proper representative of the State and, furthermore, we had by that time learned more of the actual facts which the ad purported to recite and, finally, the ad did

refer to the action of the State authorities and the Board of Education presumably of which the Governor is ex-officio, chairman. . . ." On the other hand, he testified that he did not think that "any of the language in there referred to Mr. Sullivan."

The trial judge submitted the case to the jury under instructions that the statements in the advertisement were "libelous per se" and were not privileged, so that petitioners might be held liable if the jury found that they had published the advertisement and that the statements were made "of and concerning" respondent. The jury was instructed that, because the statements were libelous per se, "the law . . . implies legal injury from the bare fact of publication itself," "falsity and malice are presumed," "general damages need not be alleged or proved but are presumed," and "punitive damages may be awarded by the jury even though the amount of actual damages is neither found nor shown." An award of punitive damages as distinguished from "general" damages, which are compensatory in nature—apparently requires proof of actual malice under Alabama law, and the judge charged that "mere negligence or carelessness is not evidence of actual malice or malice in fact, and does not justify an award of exemplary or punitive damages." He refused to charge, however, that the jury must be "convinced" of malice, in the sense of "actual intent" to harm or "gross negligence and recklessness," to make such an award, and he also refused to require that a verdict for respondent differentiate between compensatory and punitive damages. The judge rejected petitioners' contention that his rulings abridged the freedoms of speech and of the press that are guaranteed by the First and Fourteenth Amendments.

In affirming the judgment, the Supreme Court of Alabama sustained the trial judge's rulings and instructions in all respects. . . .

. . . We reverse the judgment. We hold that the rule of law applied by the Alabama courts is constitutionally deficient for failure to provide the safeguards for freedom of speech and of the press that are required by the First and Fourteenth Amendments in a libel action brought by a public official against critics of his official conduct. We further hold that under the proper safeguards the evidence presented in this case is constitutionally insufficient to support the judgment for respondent.

We may dispose at the outset of two grounds asserted to insulate the judgment of the Alabama courts from constitutional scrutiny. The first is the proposition relied on by the State Supreme

Court—that "The Fourteenth Amendment is directed against State action and not private action." That proposition has no application to this case. Although this is a civil lawsuit between private parties, the Alabama courts have applied a state rule of law which petitioners claim to impose invalid restrictions on their constitutional freedoms of speech and press. It matters not that the law has been applied in a civil action and that it is common law only, though supplemented by statute. . . .

The second contention is that the constitutional guarantees of freedom of speech and of the press are inapplicable here, at least so far as the Times is concerned, because the allegedly libelous statements were published as part of a paid, "commercial" advertisement. The argument relies on *Valentine* v. *Chrestensen*, 316 U.S. 52, where the Court held that a city ordinance forbidding street distribution of commercial and business advertising matter did not abridge the First Amendment freedoms, even as applied to a handbill having a commercial message on one side but a protest against certain official action on the other. The reliance is wholly misplaced. . . .

The publication here was not a "commercial" advertisement in the sense in which the word was used in *Chrestensen*. It communicated information, expressed opinion, recited grievances, protested claimed abuses, and sought financial support on behalf of a movement whose existence and objectives are matters of the highest public interest and concern. That the Times was paid for publishing the advertisement is as immaterial in this connection as is the fact that newspapers and books are sold. Any other conclusion would discourage newspapers from carrying "editorial advertisements" of this type, and so might shut off an important outlet for the promulgation of information and ideas by persons who do not themselves have access to publishing facilities.

Under Alabama law as applied in this case, a publication is "libelous per se" if the words "tend to injure a person . . . in his reputation" or to "bring [him] into public contempt"; the trial court stated that the standard was met if the words are such as to injure him in his public office, or impute misconduct to him in his office, or want of official integrity, or want of fidelity to a public trust. . . ." The jury must find that the words were published "of and concerning" the plaintiff, but where the plaintiff is a public official his place in the governmental hierarchy is sufficient evidence to support a finding that his reputation has been af-

fected by statements that reflect upon the agency of which he is in charge. Once "libel per se" has been established, the defendant has no defense as to stated facts unless he can persuade the jury that they were true in all their particulars. His privilege of "fair comment" for expressions of opinion depends on the truth of the facts upon which the comment is based. Unless he can discharge the burden of proving truth, general damages are presumed, and may be awarded without proof of pecuniary injury. A showing of actual malice is apparently a prerequisite to recovery of punitive damages, and the defendant may in any event forestall these by a retraction meeting the statutory requirements. Good motives and belief in truth do not negate an inference of malice, but are relevant only in mitigation of punitive damages if the jury chooses to accord them weight.

The question before us is whether this rule of liability, as applied to an action brought by a public official against critics of his official conduct, abridges the freedom of speech and of the press that is guaranteed by the First and Fourteenth Amendments. . . .

. . . [W]e consider this case against the background of a profound national commitment to the principle that debate on public issues should be uninhibited, robust, and wide open, and that it may well include vehement, caustic, and sometimes unpleasantly sharp attacks on government and public officials. The present advertisement, as an expression of grievance and protest on one of the major public issues of our time, would seem clearly to qualify for the constitutional protection. The question is whether it forfeits that protection by the falsity of some of its factual statements and by its alleged defamation of respondent. . . .

Authoritative interpretations of the First Amendment guarantees have consistently refused to recognize an exception for any test of truth, whether administered by judges, juries, or administrative officials and especially not one that puts the burden of proving truth on the speaker. The constitutional protection does not turn upon "the truth, popularity, or social utility of the ideas and beliefs which are offered." *N.A.A.C.P.* v. *Button*, 371 U.S. 415, 445. . . .

. . . [E]rroneous statement is inevitable in free debate, and . . . it must be protected if the freedoms of expression are to have the "breathing space" that they "need . . . to survive," *N.A.A.C.P.* v. *Button*. . . .

. . . Criticism of their official conduct does not

lose its constitutional protection merely because it is effective criticism and hence diminishes their official reputations.

If neither factual error nor defamatory content suffices to remove the constitutional shield from criticism of official conduct, the combination of the two elements is no less inadequate. This is the lesson to be drawn from the great controversy over the Sedition Act of 1798, 1 Stat. 596, which first crystallized a national awareness of the central meaning of the First Amendment. . . .

What a State may not constitutionally bring about by means of a criminal statute is likewise beyond the reach of its civil law of libel. The fear of damage awards under a rule such as that invoked by the Alabama courts here may be markedly more inhibiting than the fear of prosecution under a criminal statute. Alabama, for example, has a criminal libel law which subjects to prosecution "any person who speaks, writes, or prints of and concerning another any accusation falsely and maliciously importing the commission by such person of a felony, or any other indictable offense involving moral turpitude," and which allows as punishment upon conviction a fine not exceeding $500 and a prison sentence of six months. Alabama Code, Tit. 14, §350. Presumably a person charged with violation of this statute enjoys ordinary criminal-law safeguards such as the requirement of an indictment and of proof beyond a reasonable doubt. These safeguards are not available to the defendant in a civil action. The judgment awarded in this case without the need for any proof of actual pecuniary loss—was one thousand times greater than the maximum fine provided by the Alabama criminal statute, and one hundred times greater than that provided by the Sedition Act. And since there is no double-jeopardy limitation applicable to civil lawsuits, this is not the only judgment that may be awarded against petitioners for the same publication. Whether or not a newspaper can survive a succession of such judgments, the pall of fear and timidity imposed upon those who would give voice to public criticism is an atmosphere in which the First Amendment freedoms cannot survive. Plainly the Alabama law of civil libel is "a form of regulation that creates hazards to protected freedoms markedly greater than those that attend reliance upon the criminal law."

The state rule of law is not saved by its allowance of the defense of truth. A defense for erroneous statements honestly made is no less essential here than was the requirement of proof of guilty knowledge which, in *Smith* v. *California*, 361 U.S. 147, we held indispensable to a valid conviction of a bookseller for possessing obscene writings for sale. . . . A rule compelling the critic of official conduct to guarantee the truth of all his factual assertions and to do so on pain of libel judgments virtually unlimited in amount leads to a comparable "self-censorship." Allowance of the defense of truth, with the burden of proving it on the defendant, does not mean that only false speech will be deferred. Even courts accepting this defense as an adequate safeguard have recognized the difficulties of adducing legal proofs that the alleged libel was true in all its factual particulars. Under such a rule, would-be critics of official conduct may be deterred from voicing their criticism, even though it is believed to be true and even though it is in fact true, because of doubt whether it can be proved in court or fear of the expense of having to do so. They tend to make only statements which "steer far wider of the unlawful zone." The rule thus dampens the vigor and limits the variety of public debate. It is inconsistent with the First and Fourteenth Amendments.

The constitutional guarantees require, we think, a federal rule that prohibits a public official from recovering damages for a defamatory falsehood relating to his official conduct unless he proves that the statement was made with "actual malice"—that is, with knowledge that it was false or with reckless disregard of whether it was false or not. . . .

We hold today that the Constitution delimits a State's power to award damages for libel in actions brought by public officials against critics of their official conduct. Since this is such an action, the rule requiring proof of actual malice is applicable. While Alabama law apparently requires proof of actual malice for an award of punitive damages, where general damages are concerned malice is "presumed." Such a presumption is inconsistent with the federal rule. . . . Since the trial judge did not instruct the jury to differentiate between general and punitive damages, it may be that the verdict was wholly an award of one or the other. But it is impossible to know, in view of the general verdict returned. Because of this uncertainty, the judgment must be reversed and the case remanded. . . .

Applying these standards, we consider that the proof presented to show actual malice lacks the convincing clarity which the constitutional standard demands, and hence that it would not constitutionally sustain the judgment for respondent under the proper rule of law. The case of the individual petitioners requires little discussion. Even assuming that they could constitutionally be found to have authorized the use of their names on the advertisement, there was no evidence whatever that they were aware of any erroneous statements or were in any way reckless in that regard. The judgment against them is thus without constitutional support.

As to the Times, we similarly conclude that the facts do not support a finding of actual malice. The statement by the Times' Secretary that, apart from the padlocking allegation, he thought the advertisement was "substantially correct," affords no constitutional warrant for the Alabama Supreme Court's conclusion that it was a "cavalier ignoring of the falsity of the advertisement [from which], the jury could not have but been impressed with the bad faith of The Times, and its maliciousness inferable therefrom." The statement does not indicate malice at the time of the publication; even if the advertisement was not "substantially correct although respondent's own proofs tend to show that it was—that opinion was at least a reasonable one, and there was no evidence to impeach the witness's good faith in holding it. The Times' failure to retract upon respondent's demand, although it later retracted upon the demand of Governor Patterson, is likewise not adequate evidence of malice for constitutional purposes. Whether or not a failure to retract may ever constitute such evidence, there are two reasons why it does not here. *First,* the letter written by the Times reflected a reasonable doubt on its part as to whether the advertisement could reasonably be taken to refer to respondent at all. *Second,* it was not a final refusal, since it asked for an explanation on this point—a request that respondent chose to ignore. Nor does the retraction upon the demand of the Governor supply the necessary proof. It may be doubted that a failure to retract which is not itself evidence of malice can retroactively become such by virtue of a retraction subsequently made to another party. But in any event, that did not happen here, since the explanation given by the Times' Secretary for the distinction drawn between respondent and the Governor was a reasonable one, the good faith of which was not impeached.

Finally, there is evidence that the Times published the advertisement without checking its accuracy against the news stories in the Times' own files. The mere presence of the stories in the files does not, of course, establish that the Times "knew" the advertisement was false, since the state of mind required for actual malice would have to be brought home to the persons in the Times' organization having responsibility for the publication of the advertisement. With respect to the failure of those persons to make the check, the record shows that they relied upon their knowledge of the good reputation of many of those whose names were listed as sponsors of the advertisement, and upon the letter from A. Philip Randolph, known to them as a responsible individual, certifying that the use of the names was authorized. There was testimony that the persons handling the advertisement saw nothing in it that would render it unacceptable under the Times' policy of rejecting advertisements containing "attacks of a personal character"; their failure to reject it on this ground was not unreasonable. We think the evidence against the Times supports at most a finding of negligence in failing to discover the misstatements, and is constitutionally insufficient to show the recklessness that is required for a finding of actual malice. . . . There is no legal alchemy by which a State may thus create the cause of action that would otherwise be denied for a publication which, as respondent himself said of the advertisement, "reflects not only on me but on the other Commissioners of the community." Raising as it does the possibility that a good-faith critic of government will be penalized for his criticism, the proposition relied on by the Alabama courts strikes at the very center of the constitutionally protected area of free expression. We hold that such a proposition may not constitutionally be utilized to establish that an otherwise impersonal attack on governmental operations was a libel of an official responsible for those operations. . . .

The judgment of the Supreme Court of Alabama is reversed and the case is remanded to that court for further proceedings not inconsistent with this opinion.

Reversed and remanded.

JUSTICE BLACK *with whom* JUSTICE DOUGLAS *joins, concurring.*

. . . I base my vote to reverse on the belief that the First and Fourteenth Amendments not merely "delimit" a State's power to award damages to "a public official against critics of his official conduct" but completely prohibit a State from exercising such a power. . . . Unlike the Court . . . I vote to reverse exclusively on the ground that the Times and the individual defendants had an absolute, unconditional constitutional right to publish in the Times advertisement their criticisms of the Montgomery agencies and officials. I do not base my vote to reverse on any failure to prove that these individual defendants signed the advertisement or that their criticism of the Police Department was aimed at the respondent Sullivan, who was then the Montgomery City Commissioner having supervision of the city's police; for present purposes I assume these things were proved. Nor is my reason for reversal the size of the half-million-dollar judgment.

The half-million-dollar verdict does give dramatic proof, however, that state libel laws threaten the very existence of an American press virile enough to publish unpopular views on public affairs and bold enough to criticize the conduct of public officials. The factual background of this case emphasizes the imminence and enormity of that threat. One of the acute and highly emotional issues in this country arises out of efforts of many people, even including some public officials, to continue state-commanded segregation of races in the public schools and other public places, despite our several holdings, that such a state practice is forbidden by the Fourteenth Amendment. Montgomery is one of the localities in which widespread hostility to desegregation has been manifested. This hostility has sometimes extended itself to persons who favor desegregation, particularly to so-called "outside agitators," a term which can be made to fit papers like the Times. . . . The scarcity of testimony to show that Commissioner Sullivan suffered any actual damages at all suggests that these feelings of hostility had at least as much to do with rendition of this half-million-dollar verdict as did an appraisal of damages. Viewed realistically, this record lends support to an inference that instead of being damaged Commissioner Sullivan's political, social, and financial prestige has likely been enhanced by the Times' publication. Moreover, a second half-million-dollar libel verdict against the Times based on the same advertisement has already been awarded to another Commissioner. There a jury again gave the full amount claimed. There is no reason to believe that there are not more such huge verdicts lurking just around the corner for the Times or any other newspaper or broadcaster which might dare to criticize public officials. In fact, briefs before us show that in Alabama there are now pending eleven libel suits by local and state officials against the Times seeking $5,600,000, and five such suits against the Columbia Broadcasting System seeking $1,700,000. Moreover, this technique for harassing and punishing a free press now that it has been shown to be possible is by no means limited to cases with racial overtones: it can be used in other fields where public feelings may make local as well as out-of-state newspapers easy prey for libel verdict seekers.

In my opinion the Federal Constitution has dealt with this deadly danger to the press in the only way possible without leaving the free press open to destruction by granting the press an absolute immunity for criticism of the way public officials do their public duty. Stopgap measures like those the Court adopts are in my judgment not enough. This record certainly does not indicate that any different verdict would have been rendered here whatever the Court had charged the jury about "malice," "truth," "good motives," "justifiable ends," or any other legal formulas which in theory would protect the press. Nor does the record indicate that any of these legalistic words would have caused the courts below to set aside or to reduce the half-million-dollar verdict in any amount. . . .

We would . . . more faithfully interpret the First Amendment by holding that at the very least it leaves the people and the press free to criticize officials and discuss public affairs with impunity. This Nation of ours elects many of its important officials; so do the States, the municipalities, the counties, and even many precincts. These officials are responsible to the people for the way they perform their duties. . . . [F]reedom to discuss public affairs and public officials is unquestionably . . . the kind of speech the First Amendment was primarily designed to keep within the area of free discussion. To punish the exercise of this right to discuss public affairs or to penalize it through libel judgments is to abridge or shut off discussion of the very kind most needed. This Nation, I suspect, can live in peace without libel suits based on public discussions of public affairs and public officials. But I doubt that a country can live in freedom where its people can be made to suffer physically or financially for criticizing their government, its actions, or its officials. . . .

JUSTICE WHITE *delivered the opinion of the court.*

The question before us is whether the First Amendment prohibits a plaintiff from recovering damages, under state promissory estoppel law, for a newspaper's breach of a promise of confidentiality given to the plaintiff in exchange for information. We hold that it does not.

During the closing days of 1982 Minnesota gubernatorial race, Dan Cohen, an active Republican associated with Wheelock Whitney's Independent-Republican gubernatorial campaign, approached reports from the St. Paul Pioneer Press Dispatch (Pioneer Press) and the Minneapolis Star and Tribune (Star Tribune) and offered to provide documents relating to a candidate in the upcoming election. Cohen made clear to the reporters that he would provide the information only if he was given a promise of confidentiality. Reporters from both papers promised to keep Cohen's identity anonymous and Cohen turned over copies of two public court records concerning Marlene Johnson, the Democratic Farmer-Labor candidate for Lieutenant Governor. The first record indicated that Johnson had been charged in 1969 with three counts of unlawful assembly, and the second that she had been convicted in 1970 of petit theft. Both newspapers interviewed Johnson for her explanation and one reporter tracked down the person who had found the records for Cohen. As it turned out, the unlawful assembly charges arose out of Johnson's participation in a protest of an alleged failure to hire minority workers on municipal construction projects and the charges were eventually dismissed. The petit theft conviction was for leaving a store without paying for $6.00 worth of sewing materials. The incident apparently occurred at a time during which Johnson was emotionally distraught, and the conviction was later vacated.

After consultation and debate, the editorial staffs of the two newspapers independently decided to publish Cohen's name as part of their stories, both papers identified Cohen as the source of the court records, indicated his connection to the Whitney campaign, and included denials by Whitney campaign officials of any role in the matter. The same day the stories appeared, Cohen was fired by his employer.

Cohen sued respondents, the publishers of the Pioneer Press and Star Tribune, in Minnesota state court, alleging fraudulent misrepresentation and breach of contract. The trial court rejected respondents' argument that the First Amendment barred Cohen's lawsuit. A jury returned a verdict in Cohen's favor, awarding him $200,000 in compensatory damages and $500,000 in punitive damages.

The Minnesota Court of Appeals, in a split decision, reversed the award of punitive damages after concluding that Cohen had failed to establish a fraud claim, the only claim that would support such an award. However, the court upheld the finding of liability for breach of contract and the $200,000 compensatory damage award.

A divided Minnesota Supreme Court reversed the compensatory damages award. After affirming the Court of Appeals' determination that Cohen had not established a claim for fraudulent misrepresentation, the court considered his breach of contract claim and concluded that "a contract cause of action is inappropriate for these particular circumstances." The court then went on to address the question whether Cohen could establish a cause of action under Minnesota law on a promissory estoppel theory. Apparently, a promissory estoppel theory was never tried to the jury, nor briefed nor argued by the parties; it first arose during oral argument in the Minnesota Supreme Court when one of the justices asked a question about equitable estoppel.

In addressing the promissory estoppel question, the court decided that the most problematic element in establishing such a cause of action here was whether injustice could be avoided only by enforcing the promise of confidentiality made to Cohen. The court stated that "[u]nder a promissory estoppel analysis there can be no neutrality towards the First Amendment. In deciding whether it would be unjust not to enforce the promise, the court must necessarily weigh the same considerations that are weighed for whether the First Amendment has been violated. The court must balance the constitutional rights of a free press against the common law interest in protecting a promise of anonymity." After a brief discussion, the court concluded that "in this case enforcement of the promise of confidentiality under a promissory estoppel theory would violate defendants' First Amendment rights."

We granted *certiorari* to consider the First Amendment implications of this case.

Respondents initially contend that the Court should dismiss this case without reaching the merits because the promissory estoppel theory was not argued or presented in the courts below and because the Minnesota Supreme Court's decision rests entirely on the interpretation of state law. These contentions do not merit extended discussion. It is irrelevant to this Court's jurisdiction whether a party raised below and argued a federal-law issue that the state supreme court actually considered and decided. Moreover, that the Minnesota Supreme Court rested its holding on federal law could not be made more clear than by its conclusion that "in this case enforcement of the promise of confidentiality under a promissory estoppel theory would violate defendants' First Amendment rights." It can hardly be said that there is no First Amendment issue present in the case when respondents have defended against this suit all along by arguing that the First Amendment barred the enforcement of the reporters' promises to Cohen. We proceed to consider whether that Amendment bars a promissory estoppel cause of action against respondents.

The initial question we face is whether a private cause of action for promissory estoppel involves "state action" within the meaning of the Fourteenth Amendment such that the protections of the First Amendment are triggered. For if it does not, then the First Amendment has no bearing on this case. The rationale of our decision in *New York Times Co.* v. *Sullivan,* (1964), and subsequent cases compels the conclusion that there is state action here. Our cases teach that the application of state rules of law in the state courts in a manner alleged to restrict First Amendment freedoms constitutes "state action" under the Fourteenth Amendment. . . .

In this case, the Minnesota Supreme Court held that if Cohen could recover at all it would be on the theory of promissory estoppel, a state-law doctrine which, in the absence of a contract, creates obligations never explicitly assumed by the parties. These legal obligations would be enforced through the official power of the Minnesota courts. Under our cases, that is enough to constitute "state action" for purposes of the Fourteenth Amendment.

Respondents rely on the proposition that "if a newspaper lawfully obtains truthful information about a matter of public significance then state officials may not constitutionally punish publication of the information, absent a need to further a state interest of the highest order." That proposition is unexceptionable, and it has been applied in various cases that have found insufficient the asserted state interests in preventing publication of truthful, lawfully obtained information.

This case however, is not controlled by this line of cases but rather by the equally well-established line of decisions holding that generally applicable laws do not offend the First Amendment simply because their enforcement against the press has incidental effects on its ability to gather and report the news. As the cases relied on by respondents recognize, the truthful information sought to be published must have been lawfully acquired. The press may not with impunity break and enter an office or dwelling to gather news. Neither does the First Amendment relieve a newspaper reporter of the obligation shared by all citizens to respond to a grand jury subpoena and answer questions relevant to a criminal investigation, even though the reporter might be required to reveal a confidential source. *Branzburg* v. *Hayes,* (1972). The press, like others interested in publishing, may not publish copyrighted material without obeying the copyright laws. . . . Similarly, the media must obey the National Labor Relations Act, and the Fair Labor Standards Act . . . may not restrain trade in violation of the antitrust laws; and must pay non-discriminatory taxes. It is therefore beyond dispute that "[t]he publisher of a newspaper has no special immunity from the application of general laws. He has no special privilege to invade the rights and liberties of others." 301 U.S., at 132–133. Accordingly, enforcement of such general laws against the press is not subject to stricter scrutiny than would be applied to enforcement against other persons or organizations.

There can be little doubt that the Minnesota doctrine of promissory estoppel is a law of general applicability. It does not target or single out the press. Rather, in so far as we are advised, the doctrine is generally applicable to the daily transactions of all the citizens of Minnesota. The First Amendment does not forbid its application to the press.

JUSTICE BLACKMUN suggests that applying Minnesota promissory estoppel doctrine in this case will "punish" Respondents for publishing truthful information that was lawfully obtained. *Post,* at____. This is not strictly accurate because compensatory damages are not a form of punishment, as were the criminal sanctions at issue in *Smith*. If the contract between the parties in this case had contained a liquidated damages provision, it would be perfectly clear that the payment to petitioner would represent a cost of acquiring newsworthy material to be published at a profit, rather than a punishment imposed by the State. The payment of compensatory damages in this case is constitutionally indistinguishable from a generous bonus paid to a confidential news source. In any event, as indicated above, the characterization of the payment makes no difference for First Amendment purposes when the law being applied is a general law and does not single out the press. Moreover, JUSTICE BLACKMUN'S reliance on cases like *The Florida Star and Smith* v. *Daily Mail* is misplaced. In those cases, the State itself defined the content of publications that would trigger liability. Here, by contrast, Minnesota law simply requires those making promises to keep them. The parties themselves, as in this case, determine the scope of their legal obligations and any restrictions which may be placed on the publication of truthful information are self imposed.

Also, it is not at all clear that Respondents obtained Cohen's name "lawfully" in this case, at least for purposes of publishing it. Unlike the situation in *The Florida Star*, where the rape victim's name was obtained through lawful access to a police report, respondents obtained Cohen's name only by making a promise which they did not honor. The dissenting opinions suggest that the press should not be subject to any law, including copyright law for example, which in any fashion or to any degree limits or restricts the press' right to report truthful information. The First Amendment does not grant the press such limitless protection.

Nor is Cohen attempting to use a promissory estoppel cause of action to avoid the strict requirements for establishing a libel or defamation claim. As the Minnesota Supreme Court observed here, "Cohen could not sue for defamation because the information disclosed [his name] was true." Cohen is not seeking damages for injury to his reputation or his state of mind. He sought damages in excess of $50,000 for a breach of a promise that caused him to lose his job and lowered his earning capacity . . . respondents and *amici* argue that permitting Cohen to maintain a cause of action for promissory estoppel will inhibit truthful reporting because news organizations will have legal incentives not to disclose a confidential source's identity [and] is itself newsworthy. JUSTICE SOUTER makes a similar argument. But if this is the case, it is no more than the incidental, and constitution-

ally insignificant, consequence of applying to the press a generally applicable law that requires those who make certain kinds of promises to keep them. Although we conclude that the First Amendment does not confer on the press a constitutional right to disregard promises that would otherwise be enforced under state law, we reject Cohen's request that in reversing the Minnesota Supreme Court's judgment we reinstate the jury verdict awarding him $200,000 in compensatory damages. The Minnesota Supreme Court's incorrect conclusion that the First Amendment barred Cohen's claim may well have truncated its consideration of whether a promissory estoppel claim had otherwise been established under Minnesota law and whether Cohen's jury verdict could be upheld on a promissory estoppel basis. Or perhaps the State Constitution may be construed to shield the press from a promissory estoppel cause of action such as this one. These are matters for the Minnesota Supreme Court to address and resolve in the first instance on remand. Accordingly, the judgment of the Minnesota Supreme Court is reversed, and the case is remanded for further proceedings not inconsistent with this opinion.

So ordered.

JUSTICE BLACKMUN, *with whom* JUSTICE MARSHALL *and* JUSTICE SOUTER *join, dissenting.*

I agree with the Court that the decision of the Supreme Court of Minnesota rested on federal grounds and that the judicial enforcement of petitioner's promissory estoppel claim constitutes state action under the Fourteenth Amendment. I do not agree, however, that the use of that claim to penalize the reporting of truthful information regarding a political campaign does not violate the First Amendment. Accordingly,

I dissent.

The majority concludes that this case is not controlled by the decision in *Smith* v. *Daily Mail Publishing Co.*, to the effect that a State may not punish the publication of lawfully obtained, truthful information "absent a need to further a state interest of the highest order." Instead, we are told, the controlling precedent is "the equally well-established line of decisions holding that generally applicable laws do not offend the First Amendment simply because their enforcement against the press "has incidental effects on its ability to gather and report the news. . . . I disagree.

I do not read the decision of the Supreme Court of Minnesota to create any exception to or immunity from the laws of that State for members of the press. In my view, the court's decision is premised, not on the identity of the speaker, but on the speech itself. Thus, the court found it to be of "critical significance," that "the promise of anonymity arises in the classic First Amendment context of the quintessential public debate in our democratic society, namely, a political source involved in a political campaign." The majority's admonition that " '[t]he publisher of a newspaper has no special community from the application of general laws,' " and its reliance on the cases that support that principle, are therefore misplaced.

Contrary to the majority, I regard our decision in *Hustler Magazine, Inc.* v. *Falwell*, to be precisely on point. There, we found that the use of a claim of intentional infliction of emotional distress to impose liability for the publication of a satirical critique violated the First Amendment. There was no doubt that Virginia's tort of intentional infliction of emotional distress was "a law of general applicability" unrelated to the suppression of speech. Nonetheless, a unanimous Court found that, when used to penalize the expression of opinion, the law was subject to the strictures of the First Amendment. In a applying that principal, we concluded, *id.*, at 56, 108 S. Ct., at 882, that "public figures and public officials may not recover for the tort of intentional infliction of emotional distress by reason of publications such as the one here at issue without showing in addition that the publication contains a false statement of fact which was made with 'actual malice,'" as defined by *New York Times Co.* v. *Sullivan*, 376 U.S. 254, 84 S.Ct. 710, 11 L.Ed.2d 686 (1964). In so doing, we rejected the argument that Virginia's interest in protecting its citizens from emotional distress was sufficient to remove from First Amendment protection a "patently offensive" expression of opinion. 485 U.S., at 50, 108 S.Ct., at 879.

As in *Hustler*, the operation of Minnesota's doctrine of promissory estoppel in this case cannot be said to have a merely "incidental" burden on speech; the publication of important political speech *is* the claimed violation. Thus, as in *Hustler*, the law may not be enforced to punish the expression of truthful information or opinion. In the instant case, it is undisputed that the publication at issue was true.

To the extent that truthful speech may ever be sanctioned consistent with the First Amendment, it must be in furtherance of a state interest "of the highest order." (*Smith*). Because the Minnesota

Supreme Court's opinion makes clear that the State's interest in enforcing its promissory estoppel doctrine in this case was far from compelling, I would affirm that court's decision.

I respectfully dissent.

JUSTICE SOUTER, *with whom* JUSTICE MARSHALL, JUSTICE BLACKMUN *and* JUSTICE O'CONNOR *join, dissenting.*

I agree with JUSTICE BLACKMUN that this case does not fall within the line of authority holding the press to laws of general applicability where commercial activities and relationships, not the content of publication, are at issue. Even such general laws as to entail effects on the content of speech, like the one in question, may of course be found constitutional. . . . Thus, "[t]here is nothing talismanic about neutral laws of general applicability," *Employment Division, Dept. of Human Resources of Oregon* v. *Smith*, 1612, 108 L.Ed.2d 876 (1990). Because I do not believe the fact of general applicability to be dispositive, I find it necessary to articulate, measure, and compare the competing interests involved in any given case to determine the legitimacy of burdening constitutional interests, and such has been the Court's recent practice in publication cases. . . .

Nor can I accept the majority's position that we may dispense with balancing because the burden on publication is in a sense "self-imposed" by the newspaper's voluntary promise of confidentiality. This suggests both possibility of waiver, the requirements for which have been met here . . . as well as a conception of First Amendment rights as those of the speaker alone, with a value that may be measured without reference to the importance of the information to public discourse. But freedom of the press is ultimately founded and thus more prudently self-governed. "[T]he First Amendment goes beyond protection of the press and the self-expression of individuals to prohibit government from limiting the stock of information from which members of the public may draw." *First National Bank of Boston* v. *Bellotti*, (1978). In this context, " '[i]t is the right of the [public], not the right of the [media], which is paramount.' "

The importance of this public interest is integral to the balance that should be struck in this case. There can be no doubt that the fact of Cohen's identity expanded the universe of information relevant to the choice faced by Minnesota voters in that State's 1982 gubernatorial election, the publication of which was thus of the sort quintessentially subject to strict First Amendment protection. The propriety of his leak to respondents could be taken to reflect on his character, which in turn could be taken to reflect on the character of the candidate who had retained him as an adviser. An election could turn on just such a factor; if it should, I am ready to assume that it would be to the greater public good, at least over the long run.

This is not to say that the breach of such a promise of confidentiality could never give rise to liability. One can conceive of situations in which the injured party is a private individual, whose identity is of less public concern than that of the petitioner; liability there might not be constitutionally prohibited. Nor do I mean to imply that the circumstances of acquisition are irrelevant to the balance, although they may go only to what balances against, and not to diminish, the First Amendment value of any particular piece of information.

Because I believe the State's interest in enforcing a newspaper's promise of confidentiality insufficient to outweigh the interest in unfettered publication of the information revealed in this case,

I respectfully dissent.

Assembly and Association

FEATURED CASES

National Association for the Advancement of Colored People v. *State of Alabama*
New York State Club Association v. *City of New York*

In *Dejonge* v. *Oregon* (299 U.S. 353, 1937) the Supreme Court made it clear that the "right of peaceable assembly is a right cognate to those of free speech and free press and equally fundamental." DeJonge was indicted for violating the state criminal syndicalism law. He was convicted of assisting in the conduct of a meeting called under the auspices of the Communist Party. The fact that nothing unlawful took place at the meeting was immaterial, since the indictment was not concerned with specific conduct at the meeting in question but rather with the fact that DeJonge assisted in the conduct of a public meeting held under the auspices of the Communist Party. The Supreme Court reversed the conviction saying that "peaceable assembly for lawful discussion cannot be made a crime." Chief Justice Hughes, in his strongly worded opinion for the Court, hit hard at the "broad reach" of the statute and said that "the question, if the rights of free speech and peaceable assembly are to be preserved, is not as to the auspices under which the meeting is held but as to its purposes; not as to the relations of the speakers, but whether their utterances transcend the bounds of the freedom of speech which the Constitution protects."

The right of assembly of *DeJonge* was greatly bolstered in 1958 when the Court in *National Association for the Advancement of Colored People* v. *State of Alabama* clearly recognized that the First Amendment protected freedom of association.

Here the Court overturned Alabama's attempt to compel the NAACP to disclose its membership list. Speaking for a unanimous Court, Justice Harlan said that the NAACP had conclusively shown that, in the past, revealing the identity of rank-and-file members had resulted in "economic reprisals, loss of employment, threat of physical coercion, and other manifestations of public hostility." Under such circumstances, the Court thought, compelled disclosure of membership would be likely to affect adversely the petitioner's freedom of association.

Similarly, in 1982, the Court struck down Mississippi's attempt to impose civil liability on the NAACP as a deprivation of free association rights of the group to promote its objectives through a boycott of local businesses (*NAACP* v. *Claiborne*, 458 U.S. 886, 1982).

Following *NAACP* v. *Alabama*, in *Shelton* v. *Tucker* (364 U.S. 479, 1960) the Court declared unconstitutional an Arkansas statute on the ground that it violated the "associational freedom" of the First Amendment. The statute required every teacher, "as a condition of employment in a state supported school or college, to file annually an affidavit listing without limitation every organization to which he has belonged or regularly contributed within the preceding five years." Unlike the *NAACP* case, the Court acknowledged that Arkansas had a legitimate interest to inquire into the fitness and competence of its teachers. Nevertheless, the Court thought the statute went "far beyond what might be justified in the exercise of the state's legitimate inquiry" and thus greatly interfered with associational freedom.

But the Court did not hold that assocational rights had been unconstitutionally impaired by statutes designed to eliminate discrimination against certain groups such as women. For example, in *Roberts* v. *U.S. Jaycees* (104 S.Ct. 3244) the Court upheld Minnesota's Human Rights statute that was interpreted to forbid Jaycees from denying women full membership in that organization. The Court majority, among other things, held that the statute did not transgress "constitutional freedom of association asserted by members of a private organization." Subsequently, the Court relied heavily on *Roberts* and *Board of Directors of Rotary International* v. *Rotary Club* (107 S.Ct. 1940, 1987) in upholding a New York law prohibiting discrimination in certain private clubs based on race, sex, or similar grounds. (*New York State Club Association* v. *City of New York*, 487 U.S. 101, 1988). The Court stated that on its face, the New York law "does not affect 'in any significant' way the ability of individuals to form associations that will advocate public or private viewpoints."

Associational freedom for college students was also the crucial issue in *Healy* v. *James* (408 U.S. 169, 1972). Here the Court held that a college's "denial of recognition without justification" to a chapter of the Students for a Democratic Society (SDS) interfered improperly with the students' associational rights under the First and Fourteenth Amendments. The denial of recognition precluded the students' use of campus facilities ranging from bulletin boards to meeting rooms.

The Court has also addressed associational rights in the context of partisan and electoral politics. For example, in the Chicago case of *Elved* v. *Burns* (427 U.S. 347, 1976) the Court placed "free association" roadblocks against the firing of employees on the basis of traditional party patronage politics, indicating that such "patronage dismissals severely restrict political belief and association." The Court suggested that less "restrictive means" could be found to promote the "vital need for government efficiency and effectiveness."

Similarly, the Court has struck down particular laws that imposed certain requirements and limitations on minor or third parties. In *Brown* v. *Socialist Workers* (459 U.S. 87, 1982), the Court held that the disclosure provisions of an Ohio Campaign Expense Reporting Law "could not constitutionally be applied to the Socialist Workers Party since the First Amendment prohibits a state from compelling disclosure by minor political parties that would subject those persons identified to a reasonable probability of threats, harassment, or reprisals." And in *Anderson* v. *Calabrezze* (456 U.S. 960, 1983) the Court held that an Ohio statute requiring independent candidates for president to file a statement of candidacy and nomination petition in March in order to appear on the general election ballot in November was violative of the voting and associational rights of supporters of independent candidates.

NATIONAL ASSOCIATION FOR THE ADVANCEMENT OF COLORED PEOPLE v. STATE OF ALABAMA
357 U.S. 449; 2 L. Ed. 2d 1488; 78 S. Ct. 1163 (1958)

JUSTICE HARLAN *delivered the opinion of the Court.*

We review from the standpoint of its validity under the Federal Constitution a judgment of civil contempt entered against petitioner, the National Association for the Advancement of Colored People, in the courts of Alabama. The question presented is whether Alabama, consistently with the Due Process Clause of the Fourteenth Amendment, can compel petitioner to reveal to the State's Attorney General the names and addresses of all its Alabama members and agents, with regard to their positions or functions in the Association. The judgment of contempt was based upon petitioner's refusal to comply fully with a court order requiring in part the production of membership lists. Petitioner's claim is that the order, in the circumstances shown by this record, violated rights assured to petitioner and its members under the Constitution.

Alabama has a statute similar to those of many other States which requires a foreign corporation, except as exempted, to qualify before doing business by filing its corporate charter with the Secretary of State. . . . The statute imposes a fine on a corporation transacting intrastate business before qualifying and provides for criminal prosecution of officers of such a corporation. . . . The

National Association for the Advancement of Colored People is a non-profit membership corporation organized under the laws of New York. Its purposes, fostered on a nationwide basis, are those indicated by its name, and it operates through chartered affiliates which are independent unincorporated associations, with membership therein equivalent to membership in petitioner. The first Alabama affiliates were chartered in 1918. Since that time the aims of the Association have been advanced through activities of its affiliates, and in 1951 the Association itself opened a regional office in Alabama, at which it employed two supervisory persons and one clerical worker. The Association has never complied with the qualification statute, from which it considered itself exempt.

In 1956 the Attorney General of Alabama brought an equity suit in the State Circuit Court, Montgomery County, to enjoin the Association from conducting further activities within, and to oust it from, the State. Among other things the bill in equity alleged that the Association had opened a regional office and had organized various affiliates in Alabama; had recruited members and solicited contributions within the State; had given financial support and furnished legal assistance to Negro students seeking admission to the state university; and had supported a Negro boycott of the bus lines in Montgomery to compel the seating of passengers without regard to race. The bill recited that the Association, by continuing to do business in Alabama without complying with the qualification statute, was ". . . causing irreparable injury to the property and civil rights of the residents and citizens of the State of Alabama for which criminal prosecution and civil actions of law afford no adequate relief. . . ." On the day the complaint was filed, the Circuit Court issued ex parte an order restraining the Association, *pendrate lite,* from engaging in further activities within the State and forbidding it to take any steps to qualify itself to do business therein.

Petitioner demurred to the allegations of the bill and moved to dissolve the restraining order. It contended that its activities did not subject it to the qualification requirements of the statute and that in any event what the State sought to accomplish by its suit would violate rights to freedom of speech and assembly guaranteed under the Fourteenth Amendment to the Constitution of the United States. Before the date set for a hearing on this motion, the State moved for the production of a large number of the Association's records and papers, including bank statements, leases, deeds, and records containing the names and addresses of all Alabama "members" and "agents" of the Association. It alleged that all such documents were necessary for adequate preparation for the hearing, in view of petitioner's denial of the conduct of intrastate business within the meaning of the qualification statute. Over petitioner's objections, the court ordered the production of a substantial part of the requested records, including the membership lists, and postponed the hearing on the restraining order to a date later than the time ordered for production.

Thereafter petitioner filed its answer to the bill in equity. It admitted its Alabama activities substantially as alleged in the complaint and that it had not qualified to do business in the State. Although still disclaiming the statute's application to it, petitioner offered to qualify if the bar from qualification made part of the restraining order were lifted, and it submitted with the answer an executed set of the forms required by the statute. However petitioner did not comply with the production order, and for this failure was adjudged in civil contempt and fined $10,000. The contempt judgment provided that the fine would be subject to reduction or remission if compliance were forthcoming within five days but otherwise would be increased to $100,000.

At the end of the five-day period petitioner produced substantially all the data called for by the production order except its membership lists, as to which it contended that Alabama could not constitutionally compel disclosure, and moved to modify or vacate the contempt judgment, or stay its execution pending appellate review. This motion was denied. While a similar stay application, which was later denied, was pending before the Supreme Court of Alabama, the Circuit Court made a further order adjudging petitioner in continuing contempt and increasing the fine already imposed to $100,000. Under Alabama law . . . the effect of the contempt adjudication was to foreclose petitioner from obtaining a hearing on the merits of the underlying ouster action, or from taking any steps to dissolve the temporary restraining order which had been issued ex parte, until it purged itself of contempt. . . .

The State Supreme Court thereafter twice dismissed petitions for certiorari to review this final contempt judgment.

* * *

The Association both urges that it is constitutionally entitled to resist official inquiry into its membership lists, and that it may assert, on behalf of its members, a right personal to them to be protected from compelled disclosure by the State of their affiliation with the Association as revealed by the membership lists. We think that petitioner argues more appropriately the rights of its members, and that its nexus with them is sufficient to permit that it act as their representative before this Court. In so concluding, we reject respondent's argument that the Association lacks standing to assert here constitutional rights pertaining to the members, who are not of course parties to the litigation.

To limit the breadth of issues which must be dealt with in particular litigation, this Court has generally insisted that parties rely only on constitutional rights which are personal to themselves. . . . This rule is related to the broader doctrine that constitutional adjudication should where possible be avoided. . . . The principle is not disrespected where constitutional rights of persons who are not immediately before the Court could not be effectively vindicated except through an appropriate representative before the Court. . . .

If petitioner's rank-and-file members are constitutionally entitled to withhold their connection with the Association despite the production order, it is manifest that this right is properly assertable by the Association. To require that it be claimed by the members themselves would result in nullification of the right at the very moment of its assertion. Petitioner is the appropriate party to assert these rights, because it and its members are in every practical sense identical. The Association, which provides in its constitution that "[a]ny person who is in accordance with [its] principles and policies . . ." may become a member, is but the medium through which its individual members seek to make more effective the expression of their own views. The reasonable likelihood that the Association itself through diminished financial support and membership may be adversely affected if production is compelled is a further factor pointing towards our holding that petitioner has standing to complain of the production order on behalf of its members. . . .

We thus reach petitioner's claim that the production order in the state litigation trespasses upon fundamental freedoms protected by the Due Process Clause of the Fourteenth Amendment. Petitioner argues that in view of the facts and circumstances shown in the record, the effect of compelled disclosure of the membership lists will be to abridge the rights of its rank-and-file members to engage in lawful association in support of their common beliefs. It contends that governmental action, which although not directly suppressing association, nevertheless carries this consequence, can

be justified only upon some overriding valid interest of the State.

Effective advocacy of both public and private points of view, particularly controversial ones, is undeniably enhanced by group association, as this Court has more than once recognized by remarking upon the close nexus between the freedoms of speech and assembly. . . . It is beyond debate that freedom to engage in association for the advancement of beliefs and ideas is an inseparable aspect of the "liberty" assured by the Due Process Clause of the Fourteenth Amendment, which embraces freedom of speech. . . . Of course, it is immaterial whether the beliefs sought to be advanced by association pertain to political, economic, religious or cultural matters, and state action which may have the effect of curtailing the freedom is subject to the closest scrutiny.

* * *

It is hardly a novel perception that compelled disclosure of affiliation with groups engaged in advocacy may constitute as effective a restraint on freedom of association as the forms of governmental action in the cases above were thought likely to produce upon the particular constitutional rights there involved. This Court has recognized the vital relationship between freedom to associate and privacy in one's associations. When referring to the varied forms of governmental action which might interfere with freedom of assembly, it said in *American Communications Assn.* v. *Douds* (339 U.S. 402): "A requirement that adherents of particular religious faiths or political parties wear identifying armbands, for example, is obviously of this nature." Compelled disclosure of membership in an organization engaged in advocacy of particular beliefs is of the same order. Inviolability of privacy in group association may in many circumstances be indispensable to preservation of freedom of association, particularly where a group espouses dissident beliefs. . . .

We think that the production order, in the respects here drawn in question, must be regarded as entailing the likelihood of a substantial restraint upon the exercise by petitioner's members of their right to freedom of association. Petitioner has made an uncontroverted showing that on past occasions revelation of the identity of its rank-and-file members has exposed these members to economic reprisal, loss of employment, threat of physical coercion, and other manifestations of public hostility. Under these circumstances, we think it apparent that compelled disclosure of petitioner's Alabama membership is likely to affect adversely the ability of petitioner and its members to pursue their collective effort to foster beliefs which they admittedly have the right to advocate, in that it may induce members to withdraw from the Association and dissuade others from joining it because of fear of exposure of their beliefs shown through their associations and of the consequences of this exposure.

It is not sufficient to answer, as the State does here, that whatever repressive effect compulsory disclosure of names of petitioner's members may have upon participation by Alabama citizens in petitioner's activities follows not from *state* action but from *private* community pressures. The crucial factor is the interplay of governmental and private action, for it is only after the initial exertion of state power represented by the production order that private action takes hold.

We turn to the final question whether Alabama has demonstrated an interest in obtaining the disclosures it seeks from petitioner which is sufficient to justify the deterrent effect which we have concluded these disclosures may well have on the free exercise by petitioner's members of their constitutionally protected right of association. . . .

It is important to bear in mind that petitioner asserts no right to absolute immunity from state investigation, and no right to disregard Alabama's laws. As shown by its substantial compliance with the production order, petitioner does not deny Alabama's right to obtain from it such information as the State desires concerning the purposes of the Association and its activities within the State. Petitioner has not objected to divulging the identity of its members who are employed by or hold official positions with it. It has urged the rights solely of its ordinary rank-and-file members. This is therefore not analogous to a case involving the interest of a State in protecting its citizens in their dealings with paid solicitors or agents of foreign corporations by requiring identification.

* * *

. . . [W]e think it apparent that *New York* ex. rel. *Bryant* v. *Zimmerman*, 278 U.S. 63 . . . cannot be relied on in support of the State's position, for that case involved markedly different considerations in terms of the interest of the State in obtaining disclosure. There, this Court upheld as applied to a member of a local chapter Ku Klux Klan, a New York statute requiring any unincorporated association which demanded an oath as a condition of membership to file with state officials copies of its ". . . constitution, by-laws, rules, regulations, and oath of membership, together with a roster of its membership and a list of its officers for the current year." NY Laws 1923, ch. 664, sections 53, 56. In its opinion, the Court took care to emphasize the nature of the organization which New York sought to regulate. The decision was based on the particular character of the Klan's activities, involving acts of unlawful intimidation and violence, which the Court assumed was before the state legislature when it enacted the statute, and of which the Court itself took judicial notice. Furthermore the situation before us is significantly different from that in *Bryant*, because the organization there had made no effort to comply with any of the requirements of New York's statute but rather had refused to furnish the State with any information as to its local activities.

We hold that the immunity from state scrutiny of membership lists which the Association claims on behalf of its members is here so related to the right of the members to pursue their lawful private interests privately and to associate freely with others in so doing as to come within the protection of the Fourteenth Amendment. And we conclude that Alabama has fallen short of showing a controlling justification for the deterrent effect on the free enjoyment of the right to associate which disclosure of membership lists is likely to have. Accordingly, the judgment of civil contempt and the $100,000 fine which resulted from petitioner's refusal to comply with the production order in this respect must fall.

* * *

Reversed.

JUSTICE WHITE *delivered the opinion of the Court.*

New York City has adopted a local law that forbids discrimination by certain private clubs. The New York Court of Appeals rejected a facial challenge to this law based on the First and Fourteenth Amendments. We sit in review of that judgment.

In 1965, New York City adopted a Human Rights Law that prohibits discrimination by any "place of public accommodation, resort or amusement."[*] This term is defined broadly in the Law to cover such various places as hotels, restaurants, retail stores, hospitals, laundries, theaters, parks, public conveyances, and public halls, in addition to numerous other places that are specifically listed. Yet the Law also exempted from its coverage various public educational facilities and "any institution, club or place of accommodation which proves that it is in its nature distinctly private." The city adopted this Law soon after the Federal Government adopted civil rights legislation to bar discrimination in places of public accommodation, *Civil Rights Act of 1964.*

In 1984, New York City amended its Human Rights Law. The basic purpose of the amendment is to prohibit discrimination in certain private clubs that are determined to be sufficiently "public" in nature that they do not fit properly within the exemption for "any institution, club or place of accommodation which is in its nature distinctly private." As the City Council stated at greater length:

[*]The Human Rights Law (Local Law No. 97 of 1965) makes it "an unlawful discriminatory practice for any person, being the owner, lessee, proprietor, manager, superintendent, agent or employee of any place of public accommodation, resort or amusement, because of the race, creed, color, national origin or sex of any person directly or indirectly, to refuse, withhold from or deny to such person any of the accommodations, advantages, facilities or privileges thereof, or, directly or indirectly, to publish, circulate, issue, display, post or mail any written or printed communication, notice or advertisement, to the effect that any of the accommodations, advantages, facilities and privileges of any such place shall be refused, withheld from or denied to any person on account of race, creed, color, national origin or sex or that the patronage or custom thereon of any person belonging to or purporting to be of any particular race, creed, color, national origin, or sex is unwelcome, objectionable or not acceptable, desired or solicited." N.Y.C. Admin. Code 8-107(2) (1986) (1986). The city has also extended the Law's coverage to discrimination against "an otherwise qualified person who is physically or mentally handicapped," §8-106, and to discrimination against "individuals because of their actual or perceived sexual orientation," §8-1.108.

It is hereby found and declared that the city of New York has a compelling interest in providing its citizens an environment where all persons, regardless of race, creed, color, national origin or sex, have a fair and equal opportunity to participate in the business and professional life of the city, and may be unfettered in availing themselves of employment opportunities. Although city, state and federal laws have been enacted to eliminate discrimination in employment, women and minority group members have not attained equal opportunity in business and the professions. One barrier to the advancement of women and minorities in the business and professional life of the city is the discriminatory practices of certain membership organizations where business deals are often made and personal contacts valuable for business purposes, employment and professional advancements are formed. While such organizations may avowedly be organized for social, cultural, civil or educational purposes, and while many perform valuable services to the community, the commercial nature of some of the activities occurring therein and the prejudicial impact of these activities on business, professional and employment opportunities of minorities and women cannot be ignored. *Local Law No. 63 of 1984.*

For these reasons, the City Council found that "the public interest in equal opportunity" outweighs "the interest in private association asserted by club members." It cautioned, however, that it did not purpose "to interfere in club activities or subject club operations to scrutiny beyond what is necessary in good faith to enforce the human rights law," and the amendments were not intended as an attempt "to dictate the manner in which certain private clubs conduct their activities or select their members, except insofar as is necessary to ensure that clubs do not automatically exclude persons from consideration for membership or enjoyment of club accommodations and facilities and the advantages and privileges of membership, on account of invidious discrimination."

The specific change wrought by the amendment is to extend the antidiscrimination provisions of the Human Rights Law to any "institution, club or place of accommodation [that] has more than four hundred members, provides regular meal service and regularly receives payment for dues, fees, use of space, facilities, services, meals or beverages directly or indirectly from or on behalf of nonmembers for the furtherance of trade or business." Any such club "shall not be considered in its nature distinctly private." Nonetheless, the city also stated that any such club "shall be deemed to be in its nature distinctly private" if it is "a corporation incorporated under the benevolent orders law or described in the benevolent orders law but formed under any other law of this state, or a religious corporation incorporated under the education law or the religious corporations law." The City Council explained that it drafted the amendment in this way so as to meet the specific problem confronting women and minorities in the city's business and professional world: "Because small clubs, benevolent orders and religious corporations have not been identified in testimony before the Council as places where business activity is prevalent, the Council has determined not to apply the requirements of this local law to such organizations."

Immediately after the 1984 Law became effective, the New York State Club Association filed suit against the city and some of its officers in state court, seeking a declaration that the Law is invalid on various state grounds and is unconstitutional on its face under the First and Fourteenth Amendments and requesting that defendants be enjoined from enforcing it. [T]he trial court upheld the Law against all challenges, including the federal constitutional challenges. The intermediate state appellate court affirmed this judgment on appeal. . . . The State Club Association appealed this decision to the New York Court of Appeals, which affirmed in a unanimous opinion. The court rejected the First Amendment challenge to Local Law 63, relying heavily on the decisions in *Roberts* v. *United States Jaycees* (1984) and *Board of Directors of Rotary Int'l* v. *Rotary Club* (1987). It ruled that any infringement on associational rights is amply justified by the city's compelling interest in eliminating discrimination against women and minorities. In addition, the Law employs the least restrictive means to achieve its ends because it interferes with the policies and activities of private clubs only "to the extent necessary to ensure that they do not automatically exclude persons from membership or use of the facilities on account of invidious discrimination." The court denied relief on the equal protection claim without discussing it.

The State Club Association appealed to this Court. We noted probable jurisdiction, and we now affirm the judgment below, upholding Local Law 63 against appellant's facial attack on its constitutionality.

The initial question in this case is whether appellant has standing to challenge the constitution-

ality of Local Law 63 in this Court. We hold that it does.

Appellant is a nonprofit corporation, which essentially consists of a consortium of 125 other private clubs and associations in the State of New York, many of which are located in New York City. In *Hunt* v. *Washington Apple Advertising Comm'n*, we held that an association has standing to sue on behalf of its members "when (a) its members would otherwise have standing to sue in their own right; (b) the interests it seeks to protect are germane to the organization's purpose; and (c) neither the claim asserted nor the relief requested requires the participation of individual members in the lawsuit.". . .

[T]he appellant consortium has standing to sue on behalf of its member associations as long as those associations would have standing to bring the same challenge to Local Law 63. In this regard, it is sufficient to note that appellant's member associations would have standing to bring this same suit on behalf of their own individual members, since those individuals "are suffering immediate or threatened injury" to their associational rights as a result of the Law's enactment. *Werth* v. *Seldin* (1975). Thus the case is properly before us.

New York City's Human Rights Law authorizes the city's Human Rights Commission or any aggrieved individual to initiate a complaint against any "place of public accommodation, resort or amusement" that is alleged to have discriminated in violation of the Law. The Commission investigates the complaint and determines whether probable cause exists to find a violation. When probable cause is found, the Commission may settle the matter by conciliatory measures, if possible; if the matter is not settled, the Commission schedules a hearing in which the defending party may present evidence and answer the charges against it. After the hearing is concluded, the Commission states its findings of fact and either dismisses the complaint or issues a cease-and-desist order. Any person aggrieved by an order of the Commission is entitled to seek judicial review of the order, and the Commission may seek enforcement of its orders in judicial proceedings.

None of these procedures has come into play in this case, however, for appellant brought this suit challenging the constitutionality of the statute on its face before any enforcement proceedings were initiated against any of its member associations. Although such facial challenges are sometimes permissible and often have been entertained, especially when speech protected by the First Amendment is at stake, to prevail on a facial attack the plaintiff must demonstrate that the challenged law either "could never be applied in a valid manner" or that even though it may be validly applied to the plaintiff and others, it nevertheless is so broad that it "may inhibit the constitutionally protected speech of third parties." *City Council* v. *Taxpayers for Vincent* (1964). Properly understood, the latter kind of facial challenge is an exception to ordinary standing requirements, and is justified only by the recognition that free expression may be inhibited almost as easily by the potential or threatened use of power as by the actual exercise of that power. Both exceptions, however, are narrow ones: the first kind of facial challenge will not succeed unless that court finds that "every application of the statute created an impermissible risk of suppression of ideas," and the second kind of facial challenge will not succeed unless the statute is "substantially" overbroad, which requires the court to find "a realistic danger that the statute itself will significantly compromise recognized First Amendment protections of parties not before the Court."

We are unpersuaded that appellant is entitled to make either one of these two distinct facial challenges. Appellant conceded at oral argument, understandably we think, that the antidiscrimination provisions of the Law certainly could be constitutionally applied at least to some of the large clubs, under this Court's decisions in *Rotary* and *Roberts*. The clubs that are covered under the Law contain at least 400 members. They thus are comparable in size to the local chapters of the Jaycees that we found not to be protected private associations in *Roberts*, and they are considerably larger than many of the local clubs that were found to be unprotected in *Rotary*, some which included as few as 20 members. The clubs covered by Local Law 63 also provide "regular meal service" and receive regular payments "directly or indirectly from or on behalf of nonmembers for the furtherance of trade or business." The city found these two characteristics to be significant in pinpointing organizations which are "commercial" in nature, "where business deals are often made and personal contacts valuable for business purposes, employment and professional advancement are formed."

These characteristics are at least as significant in defining the nonprivate nature of these associations because of the kind of role that strangers play in their ordinary existence, as is the regular participation of strangers at meetings, which we emphasized in *Roberts* and *Rotary*. It may well be that a considerable amount of private or intimate association occurs in such a setting, as is also true

in many restaurants and other places of public accommodation, but that fact alone does not afford the entity as a whole any constitutional immunity to practice discrimination when the Government has barred it from doing so. *Hishon* v. *King & Spalding* (1984). Although there may be clubs that would be entitled to constitutional protection despite the presence of these characteristics, surely it cannot be said that Local Law 63 is invalid on its face because it infringes the private associational rights of each and every club covered by it.

The same may be said about the contention that the Law infringes upon every club member's right of expressive association. The ability and the opportunity to combine with others to advance one's views is a powerful practical means of ensuring the perpetuation of the freedoms the First Amendment has guaranteed to individuals as against the Government. "Effective advocacy of both public and private points of view, particularly controversial ones, is undeniably enhanced by group association, as this Court has more than once recognized by remarking upon the close nexus between the freedoms of speech and assembly." *NAACP* v. *Alabama ex rel. Patterson* (1958). This is not to say, however, that in every setting in which individuals exercise some discrimination in choosing associates, their selective process of inclusion and exclusion is protected by the Constitution.

On its face, Local Law 63 does not affect "in any significant way" the ability of individuals to form associations that will advocate public or private viewpoints. *Rotary*. It does not require the clubs "to abandon or alter" any activities that are protected by the First Amendment. If a club seeks to exclude individuals who do not share the views that the club's members wish to promote, the Law erects no obstacle to this end. Instead, the Law merely prevents an association from using race, sex, and the other specified characteristics as shorthand measures in place of what the city considers to be more legitimate criteria for determining membership. It is conceivable, of course, that an association might be able to show that it is organized for specific expressive purposes and that it will not be able to advocate its desired viewpoints nearly as effectively if it cannot confine its membership to those who share the same sex, for example, or the same religion. In the case before us, however, it seems sensible enough to believe that many of the large clubs covered by the Law are not of this kind. We could hardly bold otherwise on the record before us, which contains no specific evidence on the characteristics of any club covered by the Law.

The facial attack based on the claim that Local

Law 63 is invalid in all of its applications must therefore fail. Appellant insists, however, that there are some clubs within the reach of the Law that are "distinctively private" and that the Law is therefore overbroad and invalid on its face. But as we have indicated, this kind of facial challenge also falls short.

The overbreadth doctrine is "strong medicine" that is used "sparingly and only as a last resort." *Broadrick* v. *Oklahoma* (1973). A law is constitutional unless it is "substantially overbroad." To succeed in its challenge, appellant must demonstrate from the text of the Law and from actual fact that a substantial number of instances exist in which the Law cannot be applied constitutionally. Yet appellant has not identified those clubs for whom the antidiscrimination provisions will impair their ability to associate together or to advocate public or private viewpoints. No record was made in this respect; we are not informed of the characteristics of any particular clubs, and hence we cannot conclude that the Law threatens to undermine the associational or expressive purposes of any club, let alone a substantial number of them. We therefore cannot conclude that the Law is substantially overbroad and must assume that "whatever overbreadth may exist should be cured through case-by-case analysis of the fact situations to which its sanctions, assertedly, may not be applied." . . . [O]pportunities for individual associations to contest the constitutionality of the Law as it may be applied against them are adequate to assure that any overbreadth under the Law will be curable through case-by-case analysis of specific facts.

Appellant also contends that the exemption in Local Law 63 for benevolent and religious corporations, which deems them to be "distinctly private" in nature, violates the Equal Protection Clause. . . .

As written, the legislative classification on its face is not manifestly without reasoned support. The City Council explained that it limited the Law's coverage to large clubs and excluded smaller clubs, benevolent orders, and religious corporations because the latter associations "have not been identified in testimony before the Council as places where business activity is prevalent." . . . It is plausible that these associations differ in their practices and purposes from other private clubs that are now covered under the Law. As the Appellate Division in this case pointed out, the benevolent orders are organized under the relevant law " 'solely for the benefit of [their] membership and their beneficiaries,' " and thus are not "public" organizations. Similarly, religious organizations are " 'created for religious purposes' " and are "patently not engaged in commercial activity for the benefit of non-members."

Appellant contends, however, that the benevolent and religious corporations exempted in the Law are in fact no different in nature from the other clubs and associations that are now made subject to the city's antidiscrimination restrictions. Because the Equal Protection Clause "is essentially a direction that all persons similarly situated should be treated alike," appellant contends that the exemption violates the Clause.

In support of its argument, appellant observes that appellees offered no evidence to support the city's position that benevolent and religious groups are actually different from other private associations. Legislative classifications, however, are presumed to be constitutional, and the burden of showing a statute to be unconstitutional is on the challenging party, not on the party defending the statute: "those challenging the legislative judgment must convince the court that the legislative facts on which the classification is apparently based could not reasonably be conceived to be true by the governmental decisionmaker." In a case such as this, the plaintiff can carry this burden by submitting evidence to show that the asserted grounds for the legislative classification lack any reasonable support in fact, but this burden is nonetheless a considerable one.

The City Council's explanation for exempting benevolent orders and religious corporations from the Law's coverage reflects a view that these associations are different in kind, at least in the crucial respect of whether business activity is prevalent among them, from the associations on whose behalf appellant has brought suit. Appellant has the burden of showing that this view is erroneous and that the issue is not truly debatable, a burden that appellant has failed to carry. There is no evidence in record to indicate that a detailed examination of the practices, purposes, and structures of benevolent orders and religious corporations would show them to be identical in this and other critical respects to the private clubs that are covered under the city's antidiscrimination provisions. Without any such showing, appellant's facial attack on the Law under the Equal Protection Clause must founder.

We therefore affirm the judgment below.

In response to scandals revealed during the Watergate hearings, including public disclosures of illegal campaign contributions in the 1972 presidential election, Congress passed the Campaign Finance Law of 1974.* The legislation placed limits on campaign contributions and expenditures, called for public disclosure of the names of contributors to political campaigns, provided for matching federal grants to finance presidential primary campaigns, and the public financing of national party conventions and presidential elections. It also set up a Federal Election Commission with authority to implement the new statute. Soon after its passage, Senator James Buckley (R., N.Y.) and former Senator Eugene McCarthy (D., Minn.), a third-party candidate in the 1976 elections, charged that the law gave favored status to the two major political parties to the detriment of candidates from third or minor parties. Subsequently they challenged the constitutionality of the statute, which eventuated in the Supreme Court decision in *Buckley* v. *Valeo* (424 U.S. 1, 1976).

The Court upheld some provisions of the law and voided others. For example, the Court upheld provisions of the law that placed limits on campaign contributions against arguments that such provisions violated free speech guarantees of the First Amendment. The Court reasoned that "the contribution provisions, along with those covering disclosure, are appropriate legislative weapons against the reality or appearance of improper influence stemming from the dependence of candidates on large campaign contributions, and the ceilings imposed accordingly, serve the basic governmental interest in safeguarding the integrity of the electoral process without directly impinging upon the rights of individual citizens and candidates to engage in political debate and discussion."

But the Court found that ceilings on campaign expenditures, on independent expenditures by individuals and groups, and on the amount that candidates themselves could spend on their campaigns from their own personal funds, were clear violations of the First Amendment. These provisions, said the Court, "place substantial and direct restrictions on the ability of candidates, citizens, and associations to engage in protected political expression, restrictions that the First Amendment

cannot tolerate." The Court distinguished the First Amendment implications of campaign spending and contributions by arguing that "expenditure ceilings impose significantly more severe restrictions on protected freedom of political expression and association than do its limitations on financial contributions." In effect, "a restriction on the amount of money a person or group can spend on political communication during a campaign necessarily reduces the quantity of expression by restricting the number of issues discussed, the depth of their exploration, and the size of the audience reached." "This," says the Court, "is because virtually every means of communicating in today's mass society requires the expenditure of money." At the same time the court found that "a limitation upon the amount that any one person or group may contribute to a candidate or political committee entails only a marginal restriction upon the contributor's ability to engage in free communication. . . . [The limits do not] infringe upon the contributor's freedom to discuss candidates and issues."

Perhaps most important, however, the Court did not find persuasive the asserted interest of "equalizing the relative ability of individuals and groups to influence the outcome of elections." "[T]he concept that the government," said the Court, "may restrict the speech of some elements of our society in order to enhance the relative voice of others is wholly foreign to the First Amendment, which was designed "to secure the widest possible dissemination of information from diverse and antagonistic sources," and " 'to assure unfettered interchange of ideas for the bringing about of political and social changes desired by the people.' "

In a related decision in 1985 (*Federal Election Commission* v. *National Conservative Political Action Committee*, 470 U.S. 480) the Court in a seven-to-two ruling declared unconstitutional provisions of the Presidential Campaign Funds Act which placed a $1,000 limit on the amount "political committees" could spend in behalf of a candidate. Just as in *Buckley*, the Court found crucial the determination that the expenditures in the instant case "were 'independent' in that they were not made at the request of or in coordination with the official Reagan election campaign committee or any of its agents." Thus, Justice Rehnquist, who spoke for the Court, said that "there can be no doubt that the expenditures at issue . . . produce speech at

*Passed as amendments to the Federal Election Campaign Act of 1971.

the core of the First Amendment." To allow the "protection of views" while forbidding the expenditures of more than $1,000 to present them, he reasoned, "is much like allowing a speaker in a public hall to express his views while denying him the use of an amplifying system."

The matter of corporate spending and influence in elections has come up in other litigation contexts. In *First National Bank of Boston* v. *Bellotti* (435 U.S. 765, 1978), a Massachusetts law that prohibited corporate spending to influence voting in state referenda elections was found violative of the First Amendment. In its opinion, the Court noted that the First Amendment makes no distinction among speakers in the context of referendum campaigns, and consequently, government could not restrict corporate speech in such contexts. But the Court did suggest that since corporate spending in candidate elections could pose greater threats of corruption, it might as a result be appropriate to allow greater regulation of corporate speech. This suggestion was given support in a 1986 case (*Federal Election Commission* v.

Massachusetts Citizens for Life, Inc., 107 S. Ct. 616), when for the first time a court majority indicated that it might uphold limits on corporate speech in elections even if the threat of corruption was not clearly present. Here, the Court found a provision of the Federal Election Campaign Act requiring corporations to establish a segregated fund for political spending was applied unconstitutionally to nonprofit, nonstock corporations (MCFL). The exemption of such nonprofit corporations indicated the Court's new inclination to scrutinize content-neutral regulations that disproportionately hurt poorer corporate speakers. Even the Court acknowledged and indicated that it might uphold legislative regulations designed to overcome the disproportionate and distorting influence of corporate speech in the marketplace of ideas, that might be caused by aggregated wealth of business corporations. In the past, the Court has apparently disregarded the adverse impact that content-neutral regulations might have on poorly funded speakers. (See *Los Angeles* v. *Taxpayers for Vincent*, 466 U.S. 789, 1984.)

Obscenity

FEATURED CASES

Miller v. *California*   *Barnes* v. *Glen Theatre*

Justice William J. Brennan noted in his opinion in *Roth v. United States* that "sex . . . has indisputably been a subject of absorbing interest through the ages. . . ." The portrayal of sex in books, magazines, motion pictures, the legitimate theater, and television is now commonplace. Sex and obscenity are not synonymous, but the various media have the potential for portraying sex in an obscene manner. hence, governments have instituted various types of regulatory actions to protect the public morals. Statutes have been enacted to prohibit the publication, ptoduction, sale, and exhibition of obscene books, magazines, motion pictures, and other matter. Administrative agencies have been established to review and license motion pictures prior to their exhibition. Postal and customs authorities have exercised regulatory powers in prohibiting the dissemination of obscene materials through their channels.

In addition, statutes have also been passed to

regulate other forms of expressive conduct such as nude dancing. Some statutes have been upheld while others have been invalidated. Compare *Schad* v. *Borough of Mount Ephraim* (452 U.S. 61, 1981, overturning local ordinance banning all live entertainment, including nude dancing) with *Barnes* v. *Glen Theater, Inc.* (111 S. Ct. 2456, 1991, upholding ordinance, discussed *infra* p. 285).

It is interesting to consider how regulations vary depending on the form of the subject matter—books, movies, live entertainment. Enforcement of such regulations has raised many troublesome questions involving the federal constitutional guarantees of freedom of speech and freedom of the press—questions that have inevitably ended up in the Supreme Court for resolution.

The Court first considered the difficult problem of defining obscenity in 1957. In companion cases arising under the federal obscenity statute (*Roth* v. *United States,* 354 U.S. 476) and the California obscenity code *(Alberts v. California),* the Court sustained convictions (in *Roth)* for use of the mails to disseminate obscene matter and (in *Alberts)* for possession of obscene matter for sale by mail order. In his opinion for the Court, Justice William J. Brennan emphasized that ideas with the "slightest redeeming social importance" must be accorded the full protection of the First Amendment. But since obscene matter is "utterly without redeeming social importance," it is not protected expression. The test, said Brennan, is "whether to the average person, applying contemporary community standards, the dominant theme of the material taken as a whole appeals to prurient interest." While this test was considered an improvement over the earlier *Hicklis* test, which allowed material to be judged "by the effect of an isolated [passage] upon particularly susceptible persons," in practice it opened up a Pandora's box of questions for law enforcement officials and the lower courts. What does the term "prurient interest" mean? Who is "the average person"? What is "redeeming social importance"? Who determines "contemporary community standards," and what is the "relevant community"?

In subsequent decisions, the Court provided some answers to these questions. In *Manual Enterprises* v. *Day* (370 U.S. 478, 1962), the Court narrowed the sweep of its "prurient interest" test by holding that to be adjudged obscene, material must not only have "prurient interest" appeal but its "patent offensiveness" must also be demonstrated. Furthermore, Justice Harlan held that the two elements "must conjoin" to support a finding of obscenity. Applying this test to reverse an obscenity finding of postal authorities, Harlan contended that the magazines in question (containing photographs of nude males), while "dismally unpleasant, uncouth, and tawdry," were not "under any permissible constitutional standard . . . beyond the pale of contemporary notions of rudimentary decency."

Jacobellis v. *Ohio* (378 U.S. 184, 1964) was used by Justice Brennan to expand upon the "redeeming social importance" concept. In that case, a state court obscenity conviction for exhibiting the movie *Les Amants* was reversed by the Court, with Justice Brennan stressing that obscene material is that which is "utterly without redeeming social importance." Conversely, he argued, if material "has literary or scientific or any other form of social importance [it] may not be branded as obscenity. . . ." Brennan also focused attention on the "contemporary community standards" concept.

The "relevant community," he held, must be construed in the broad sense of "society at large."

The significance of the "redeeming social importance" test is well illustrated in *A Book Named John Cleland's Memoirs of a Woman of Pleasure* v. *Attorney General of Massachusetts* (383 U.S. 413, 1966). The controversial novel *Fanny Hill,* in which a prostitute reviews her life's experiences, was adjudged obscene by Massachusetts courts. The Supreme Court reversed that holding, and, in the opinion for the Court, Justice Brennan emphasized that although a book may have "prurient interest" appeal and is "patently offensive," it may not be held obscene unless it is "utterly without redeeming social value." To him, each of these criteria is to be applied independently, but material must have all three qualities to be proscribed as obscene. Hence, because the trial court found that *Fanny Hill* contained at least "a modicum of social value," its obscenity finding was erroneous.

A further criterion for determining obscenity was set forth in *Ginzburg* v. *United States* (383 U.S. 463, 1966). Apparently frowning on the "sordid business" of commercializing sex engaged in by some publishers under the guise of freedom of expression, the Court affirmed a federal obscenity conviction on the basis of the publisher's motives as revealed by his advertising and promotion methods. Conceding that the materials under "a different setting" might not be obscene, Justice Brennan, speaking for the majority, made it clear that "where the purveyor's sole emphasis is on the sexually provocative aspects of his publications, that fact may be decisive in the determination of obscenity." Furthermore, he assumed that the prosecution could not have succeeded otherwise.

The obvious difficulty with Brennan's opinion is that it provides for the evaluation of the substantive content of a work partly on the basis of the use to which it is put. Actually, Brennan was focusing on "pandering," and in doing so, as Justice Harlan pointed out, the conviction was affirmed upon something quite different from that on which Ginzburg was charged and tried. Harlan contended that if there is any validity in adding the "pandering" dimension to the existing obscenity tests, then the least the Court could do would be to remand the case so Ginzburg could "have his day in court" on the "amended" charges. (Cf. *Splawn* v. *California,* 431 U.S. 595, 1977.)

The Court continued to recognize the need for more legislative flexibility in dealing with obscenity when it held in *Ginsberg* v. *New York* (390 U.S. 629, 1968) that what may be obscene for minors may not be for adults. Speaking for the Court, Justice Brennan accepted the state's "variable obscenity" standard and held that government can impose stricter standards on materials sold to juveniles than on those sold to adults. "The state has an independent interest in the well-being of its youth," said Brennan, and can constitutionally accord them "a more restricted right than that assured to adults."

The Court firmed up this "independent interest" in *New York* v. *Ferber* (458 U.S. 787, 1982), where it classified "child pornography as a category of material outside the protection of the First Amendment." But even the "variable obscenity" doctrine does not give states unfettered discretion in this area. In *Interstate Circuit, Inc.* v. *Dallas* (390 U.S. 676, 1968), for example, the Court held void for vagueness a city ordinance that empowered a board to ban from exhibition for persons under sixteen years of age motion pictures in which the portrayal of brutality and sex would tend to incite crime and encourage sexual promiscuity among youth. Justice Thurgood Marshall, who wrote the Court's opinion, pointed out that the inclusion of such undefined terms as "sacrilegious" and "sexual promiscuity" rendered the ordinance fatally defective. Such loose language, said Marshall, left the censors free to apply their own mores in regulating the film fare of others.

The indefiniteness resulting from these several "tests" had the result of providing publishers, moviemakers, and others wide latitude in the treatment of sexual matters in their works. Consequently, there was a major boom in so-called smut and pornography in the late 1960s and the early 1970s. As never before, motion pictures with "X" ratings for "Adults Only" depicted graphically a wide variety of sexual activities. In addition, "Adults Only" bookstores openly promoted as having "a modicum of redeeming social value" books and magazines that many considered to be hard-core pornography. Alarmed at this trend, many Americans pointed an accusing finger at the Supreme Court as a major causal agent of this crisis in morals. President Nixon had echoed a similar view in 1970 in rejecting the recommendation of the Commission on Obscenity and Pornography that advocated unrestricted access to sexual materials by consenting adults.

When this latest dimension of the obscenity debate reached the Court in 1973, the four Nixon appointees (Burger, Blackmun, Powell, and Rehnquist) were joined by Warren Court holdover Byron White in a major overhaul of obscenity law that had developed since the 1957 *Roth-Alberts* decision. In *Miller* v. *California* (413 U.S. 15) and four companion cases, the Court emphasized the need for more definitive standards than those employed in the past. Chief Justice Burger, speaking for the Court, set forth the following test:

> (a) [W]hether "the average person, applying contemporary community standards" would find that the work, taken as a whole, appeals to the prurient interest;
> (b) whether the work depicts or describes, in a patently offensive way, sexual conduct specifically defined by the applicable state law; and
> (c) whether the work, taken as a whole, lacks serious literary, artistic, political or scientific value.

Careful examination of this test reveals a major modification of the "contemporary community" concept and the "redeeming social value" standard. Rejecting the "national standards" concept implicit in Justice Brennan's "society-at-large" language in the 1964 *Jacobellis* case, the Chief Justice emphasized the need for standards to reflect local views. Notwithstanding the national implications of the First Amendment, he held that it was "neither realistic nor constitutionally sound" to demand "that the people of Maine or Mississippi accept public depiction of conduct found tolerable in Las Vegas or New York City."

Under the new test, the publishers of controversial works like *Fanny Hill* will no longer be able to protect their works by arguing their "redeeming social value." Instead, the more demanding modification allows authorities to inquire if the work, "taken as a whole, lacks serious literary, artistic, political or scientific value." The trier of facts makes this determination.

That *Miller* marked a more restrictive posture of the Court with regard to the First Amendment and obscenity was underscored by the sharp dissents of Justices Douglas, Brennan, Stewart, and Marshall, all holdovers from the Warren Court. For example, Justice Douglas, after reviewing the Court's major prior decisions on obscenity, asserted:

> Today the Court retreats from the earlier formulations of the constitutional test and undertakes to make new definitions. This effort, like the earlier ones, is earnest and well-intentioned. The difficulty is that we do not deal with constitutional terms, since "obscenity" is not mentioned in the Constitution or Bill of Rights. . . . So there are no constitutional guidelines for deciding what is and what is not "obscene." The Court is at large because we deal with tastes and standards of literature. What shocks me may be sustenance for my neighbor. . . . We deal here

with problems of censorship which, if adopted, should be done by constitutional amendment after full debate by the people.

Such an amendment, said Douglas, would give courts "some guidelines." "Now," he concluded, "we have none except our predilections."

In its first application of the *Miller* standards, the Court reversed the obscenity conviction of a theater owner for exhibiting the motion picture *Carnal Knowledge* in *Jenkins* v. *Georgia* (418 U.S. 153, 1974), and in doing so appeared to be continuing a case-by-case adjudication, which it had hoped to avoid with its *Miller* decision. Such was suggested by Justice William Rehnquist, who spoke for a unanimous court, when he said that "*our own view* of the film satisfies us" that it is not obscene under the *Miller* standard, which requires a finding that sexual conduct is depicted in a "patently offensive way."

Various methods used by state and local government to control the dissemination of obscene matter have resulted in considerable litigation producing a number of significant Supreme Court decisions. With regard to books and other printed matter, the Court has: (1) approved a New York statute authorizing limited injunctive proceedings against the sale of obscene books (*Kingsley Books* v. *Brown*, 354 U.S. 436, 1957), reaffirmed in *A Quantity of Copies of Books* v. *Kansas* (378 U.S. 205, 1964); (2) declared a Michigan statute unconstitutional that made it a crime to sell to the general public materials that tended to "incite minors to violent or depraved or immoral acts, manifestly tending to the corruption of the morals of youth" (*Butler* v. *Michigan*, 352 U.S. 380, 1957); (3) invalidated a city ordinance because it did not contain "scienter"—a provision that the bookseller knowingly offered an obscene book for sale (*Smith* v. *California*, 361 U.S. 147, 1959); (4) declared the "informal practices" of a Rhode Island statutory Commission to Encourage Morality in Youth unconstitutional as a form of prior restraint abridging freedom of the press (*Bantam Books* v. *Sullivan*, 372 U.S. 58, 1963); and (5) invalidated the search and seizure procedures of a Kansas law because the procedures lacked sufficient safeguards for the protection of nonobscene materials and allowed law enforcement officials too much discretion to determine which publication should be seized (*Marcus* v. *Search Warrant*, 376 U.S. 717, 1961).

The Court has also held that mere possession of obscene matter in the home for personal use is not a crime. In *Stanley* v. *Georgia* (394 U.S. 557, 1969), a unanimous Court overturned a Georgia conviction for possession of obscene matter where law en-

forcement officers had raided Stanley's home searching for gambling paraphernalia and in the process discovered and seized three reels of "stag movies" from a desk drawer in the bedroom. These movies were used as evidence to support the obscenity conviction. In overturning the conviction, Justice Thurgood Marshall emphasized the constitutional right of an individual "to satisfy his intellectual and emotional needs in the privacy of his own home." "If the First Amendment means anything," said Marshall, "it means that a state has no business telling a man sitting alone in his own house, what books he may read or what films he may watch."

Four subsequent rulings, however, severely limit this decision. In two 1971 cases—*United States* v. *Reidel* (402 U.S. 351) and *United States* v. *Thirty-Seven Photographs* (402 U.S. 363)—the Supreme Court indicated that although the *Stanley* holding remained viable, its extension was unlikely. Justice White's opinion for the Court in *Reidel*, for example, stated:

> To extrapolate from Stanley's right to have and peruse obscene material in the privacy of his own home, a First Amendment right in *Reidel* to sell it to him would effectively scuttle *Roth*, the precise result that the *Stanley* opinion abjured. Whatever the scope of the "right to receive" referred to in *Stanley*, it is not so broad as to immunize the dealings in obscenity in which Reidel engaged here—dealings which *Roth* held unprotected by the First Amendment.

Reidel upheld the right of Congress to prevent the mail distribution of pornography, while *Thirty-Seven Photographs* sustained its right to prohibit importation of obscene materials. Moreover, the trend indicated in *Reidel* and *Thirty-Seven Photographs* was continued in two 1973 decisions, *United States* v. *Orito* (413 U.S. 139) and *United States* v. *12,200-Ft. Reels* (413 U.S. 123). In *Orito*, the Court held that the *Stanley* rationale did not go so far as to permit interstate transportation of obscene material by a passenger on a common carrier even if such material was for purely personal use. And in *12,200-Ft. Reels*, the Court clarified the *Thirty-Seven Photographs* decision by holding that Congress could prohibit importation of obscene material intended solely for personal use.

In the 1989 "dial-a-porn" case (*Sable Communications* v. *Federal Communications Commission*, 109 S. Ct. 2829), the Court unanimously held that a federal law banning commercial telephone messages that are "indecent" but not "obscene" is unconstitutional under the free speech guarantee of the First Amendment. Simultaneously, the Court by a six-to-three vote upheld that portion of the law banning "obscene" telephone messages. Just as in the federal law, however, the Court did nothing to define the difference between "indecency" and "obscenity."

Motion pictures, unlike books and other printed matter, were long considered entertainment and not a medium for the communication of ideas protected by the First Amendment. Justice Joseph McKenna stated the principle in *Mutual Film Corporation* v. *Industrial Commission of Ohio* (236 U.S. 230, 1915), when he said that the production and exhibition of motion pictures is "a business, pure and simple," and is not "to be regarded. . .as part of the press of the country, or as organs of public opinion." As such, and recognizing the medium's "capacity for evil," the Court approved state censorship of motion pictures. By 1948, however, a change in the judicial attitude on the subject was indicated in the antitrust case of *United States* v. *Paramount Pictures, Inc.* (331 U.S. 131, 1948), when Justice Douglas remarked: "We have no doubt that moving pictures like newspapers and radio, are included in the press whose freedom is guaranteed by the First Amendment." Four years later, in *Burstyn* v. *Wilson* (343 U.S. 495, 1952), the controversy over New York's banning of the Italian film *The Miracle* put the constitutional issue squarely before the Court. The Court struck down the New York ban and in so doing overruled the *Mutual* precedent. There can be no longer any doubt, said the Court, "that motion pictures are a significant medium for the communication of ideas." However, because the New York statute contained vague and meaningless standards, the Court found it unnecessary to rule on whether censorship would be valid under a narrowly drawn statute directed at obscene films.

The Court reemphasized the need for definitive standards in clearly drawn statutes in *Kingsley International Pictures* v. *Regents of State University of New York* (360 U.S. 684, 1959). In his opinion for the Court, Justice Potter Stewart said that the manner in which the state court construed the movie licensing statute "struck at the very heart of constitutionally protected liberty." The state court had sustained a ban on the movie *Lady Chatterly's Lover* because it advocated the unorthodox idea that adultery may be proper behavior under certain circumstances. While Justice Stewart was careful to indicate that this case was not an occasion to consider the scope of state power to censor movies, two concurring justices—Black and Douglas—did. They expressed the view that prior censorship of motion pictures was just as offensive to the First and Fourteenth Amendments as is prior censorship of newspapers and books.

A full examination of the extent of state movie censorship authority came two years later in *Times Film Corporation* v. *City of Chicago* (365 U.S. 43, 1961). In question was the constitutionality of the Chicago movie censorship ordinance, which required the submission of motion pictures to a censorship agency before exhibition. No issue of standards was raised. The distributor applied for a permit and paid the license fee, but refused to submit the film *Don Juan* for screening by the censors. He urged on the Court an absolute privilege against prior restraint, thereby challenging the basic authority of the censor. A closely divided Court (five to four) rejected that claim and held that motion picture censorship per se was not necessarily unconstitutional. Justice Tom Clark's majority opinion recognized the motion picture medium's "capacity for evil" as a relevant factor "in determining the permissible scope of community control." Consequently, he argued, since the Court had held in *Burstyn* that motion pictures were not "necessarily subject to the precise rules governing any other particular method of expression," states should not be limited in the selection of the remedy they considered most effective to deal with the problem. In exercising such authority, however, Justice Clark warned against regulations that allowed censors unfettered discretion.

Chief Justice Earl Warren, writing the major dissent (in which Justices Black, Douglas, and Brennan joined), contended that the majority's action amounted to approval of unlimited motion picture censorship by an administrative agency and could also subject other media—newspapers, books, television, radio—to the same type of unlimited censorship.

Four years later, in *Freedman* v. *Maryland* (380 U.S. 51, 1965), the Court restricted its *Times Film* ruling, and outlined certain specific and permissible constitutional standards that must be included in laws calling for prior submission of all films to a review board. They provide that: (1) the burden of proving that the film is unprotected expression must rest on the censor; (2) only a procedure requiring a judicial determination suffices to impose a valid final restraint; and (3) any restraint imposed in advance of a final judicial determination on the merits of the case must be limited to the preservation of the status quo for the shortest fixed period compatible with sound judicial resolution. These standards were reaffirmed in *Teitel Film Corporation* v. *Cusak* (390 U.S. 139, 1968), where the Court invalidated the Chicago motion picture censorship ordinance because of the lengthy administration licensing process (50 to 75 days) required before initiation of judicial proceedings.

In a 1975 case, *Erzoznick* v. *City of Jacksonville* (422 U.S. 219, 1975), the Court reaffirmed the vitality of the *Miller* standard concerning adult obscenity but avoided the necessity of defining obscenity as to minors by declaring a local ordinance void on its face. Justifying its actions on the basis of a community's police power to ameliorate traffic problems and to protect children, the Jacksonville, Florida, city government enacted an ordinance prohibiting the exhibition of motion pictures visible from "any public street or public place" in which "the human male or female bare buttocks, human female bare breasts, or human bare pubic areas are shown." After showing a nonobscene picture that did contain nudity, the manager of a local drive-in theater was prosecuted and convicted for violating the ordinance.

Justice Powell, writing for the six-to-three majority, declared the ordinance an overbroad restraint of both minors' and film exhibitors' First Amendment rights and void on its face. Without explicitly defining obscenity as to minors, Justice Powell did observe that all nudity is not obscene, but that under the Jacksonville ordinance a film "containing a picture of baby's buttocks," for instance, could provoke a prosecution.

Restrictive zoning ordinances were at issue in *Young* v. *American Mini Theatres, Inc.* (427 U.S. 50, 1976). Here Detroit attempted to restrict, or "zone out," commercial establishments in certain neighborhoods, in this instance, an "adult" movie house. Justice Stevens, for the five-to-four majority, stated that the city's interests in planning and regulating the use of commercial property to avoid deterioration of neighborhoods were sufficient to outweigh the theatre operator's claims that the restrictions acted as a prior restraint upon expression protected by the First Amendment. (But cf. *Schad et al.* v. *Borough of Mount Ephraim*, 452 U.S. 61, 1981.)

In the 1986 case of *City of Renton* v. *Playtime Theatres* (495 U.S. 41), the Court reinforced *American Mini Theatres* and upheld a city ordinance prohibiting any "adult motion picture theater" from locating "within 1,000 feet of any residential zone, single- or multiple-family dwelling, church, park, or within one mile of any school." Although the ordinance facially discriminated against adult theatres, Justice Rehnquist, who spoke for the seven-to-two Court majority, found that the ordinance was a "content-neutral" regulation in that it could be "justified without reference to the content of the regulated speech." The major concern of the city, as Rehnquist saw it, was not an attempt to suppress messages of particular films shown in such theaters, but rather to prevent the "secondary effects" of adult theaters such as a decrease in retail trade, decline in property values, increase in crime, and overall urban decay. The use of this "secondary effects" approach to find the ordinance content-neutral represented a departure from *American Mini Theatres* and was strongly criticized by the dissenters (Justices Brennan and Marshall), who saw such "secondary effects" as a pretext for banning films based on content.

Although the Supreme Court has made distinctions between written materials and films, the parameters of other modes of expression, such as nude dancing, have been only vaguely outlined. Recently, the Supreme Court tried to clarify some of its jurisprudence by making a variety of distinctions with respect to nude dancing. Because of the nature of the plurality opinion in *Barnes* v. *Glen Theatre, Inc.* of 1991, the Court may have only clouded the picture. While affirming that nude dancing was protected expression under the First Amendment, the Court nevertheless upheld Indiana's public indecency statute, which prohibited totally nude dancing. The statute required that the dancers wear pasties and a G-string to make the message less graphic. Chief Justice Rehnquist, writing for a three-person plurality, argued that totally nude dancing was expressive conduct but fell "within the outer perimeters of the First Amendment." Rehnquist borrowed the *O'Brien* test from the jurisprudence on symbolic speech (*supra*) to analyze whether an "important or substantial" governmental interest existed. The Chief Justice held that Indiana had such an important and substantial interest in promoting public morality and that the statute was narrowly tailored to further that governmental interest.

In contrast, Justice Scalia wrote a concurring opinion arguing that the statute should not be subjected to First Amendment scrutiny at all. He argued that the statute was not directed at expressive conduct in that it regulated public nudity, not dancing. In this respect, there was no reason for the Court to get involved in the business of assessing governmental interests. In dissent, Justice White rejected the argument that expressive conduct was not being regulated and concluded that the statute should be subject to the highest level of First Amendment scutiny.

In understanding the distinctions made with respect to nude dancing, one might ask whether it is possible to separate laws regulating conduct that implicates morals from those regulating conduct that is expressive. In this respect, it is interesting to consider closely Justice Souter's concurrence, which rejected the characterization of the governmental interest as the protection of morality. Justice Souter focused on the governmental interest in fighting the side effects of such as prostitution and sexual assaults. In reorienting the discussion toward obscenity's social effects on women, one might be seeing the "secularization" of such regulated conduct.

MILLER v. CALIFORNIA
413 U.S. 5; 36 L. Ed. 2d 419; 93 S. Ct. 2607 (1973)

CHIEF JUSTICE BURGER *delivered the opinion of the Court.*

This is one of a group of "obscenity-pornography" cases being reviewed by the Court in a re-examination of standards enunciated in earlier cases involving what Justice Harlan called "the intractable obscenity problem." *Interstate Circuit, Inc.* v. *Dallas*, 390 U. S. 676, 704 (concurring and dissenting opinion) (1968).

Appellant conducted a mass mailing campaign to advertise the sale of illustrated books euphemistically called "adult" material. After a jury trial, he was convicted of violating California Penal Code . . . by knowledgeably distributing obscene matter, and the Appellate Department, Superior Court of California, County of Orange, summarily affirmed the judgment without opinion. Appellant's conviction was specifically based on his conduct in causing five unsolicited advertising brochures to be sent through the mail in an envelope addressed to a restaurant in Newport Beach, California. The envelope was opened by the manager of the restaurant and his mother. They had not requested the brochures; they complained to the police.

The brochures advertise four books entitled "Intercourse," "Man-Woman," "Sex Orgies Illustrated," and "An Illustrated History of Pornography," and a film entitled "Marital Intercourse." While the brochures contain some descriptive printed material, primarily they consist of pictures and drawings very explicitly depicting men and women in groups of two or more engaging in a variety of sexual activities, with genitals often prominently displayed.

This case involves the application of a State's criminal obscenity statute to a situation in which sexually explicit materials have been thrust by aggressive sales action upon unwilling recipients who had in no way indicated any desire to receive such materials. . . .

The dissent of Justice Brennan reviews the background of the obscenity problem, but since the Court now undertakes to formulate standards more concrete than those in the past, it is useful for us to focus on two of the landmark cases in the somewhat tortured history of the Court's obscenity decisions. In *Roth* v. *United States*, 354 U. S. 476 (1957), the Court sustained a conviction under a federal statute punishing the mailing of "obscene, lewd, lascivious or filthy . . ." materials. The key to that holding was the Court's rejection of the claim that obscene materials were protected by the First Amendment. Five justices joined in the opinion stating:

> All ideas having even the slightest redeeming social importance—unorthodox ideas, controversial ideas, even ideas hateful to the prevailing climate of opinion—have full protection of the First Amendment guarantees, unless excludable because they encroach upon the limited area of more important interests. But implicit in the history of the First Amendment is the rejection of obscenity as utterly without redeeming social importance.

Nine years later in *Memoirs* v. *Massachusetts*, 383 U.S. 413 (1966), the Court veered sharply away from the *Roth* concept and, with only three justices in the plurality opinion, articulated a new test of obscenity. The plurality held that under the *Roth* definition:

> . . . as elaborated in subsequent cases, three elements must coalesce: it must be established that (a) the dominant theme of the material taken as a whole appeals to a prurient interest in sex; (b) the material is patently offensive because it affronts contemporary community standards relating to the description or representation of sexual matters; and (c) the material is utterly without redeeming social value. . . .

The sharpness of the break with *Roth*, represented by the third element of the *Memoirs* test . . . was further underscored when the *Memoirs* plurality went on to state:

The Supreme Judicial Court erred in holding that a book need not be "unqualifiedly worthless before it can be deemed obscene." A book cannot be proscribed unless it is found to be *utterly* without redeeming social value. (Emphasis in original.) 383 U. S., at 419.

While *Roth* presumed "obscenity" to be "utterly without redeeming social value," *Memoirs* required that to prove obscenity it must be affirmatively established that the material is "utterly without redeeming social value." Thus, even as they repeated the words of *Roth*, the *Memoirs* plurality produced a drastically altered test that called on the prosecution to prove a negative, i.e., that the material was "*utterly* without redeeming social value"—a burden virtually impossible to discharge under our criminal standards of proof. Such considerations caused Justice Harlan to wonder if the "*utterly* without redeeming social value" test had any meaning at all. . . .

Apart from the initial formulation in the *Roth* case, no majority of the Court has at any given time been able to agree on a standard to determine what constitutes obscene, pornographic material subject to regulation under the States' police power. . . . We have seen "a variety of views among the members of the Court unmatched in any other course of constitutional adjudication. . . ."

The case we now review was tried on the theory that the California Penal Code . . . approximately incorporates the three-stage *Memoirs* test. . . . But now the *Memoirs* test has been abandoned as unworkable by its author [Justice Brennan] and no member of the Court today supports the *Memoirs* formulation.

. . . We acknowledge . . . the inherent dangers of undertaking to regulate any form of expression. State statutes designed to regulate obscene materials must be carefully limited. . . . As a result, we now confine the permissible scope of such regulation to works which depict or describe sexual conduct. That conduct must be specifically defined by the applicable state law, as written or authoritatively construed. A state offense must also be limited to works which, taken as a whole, appeal to the prurient interest in sex, which portray sexual conduct in a patently offensive way, and which, taken as a whole, do not have serious literary, artistic, political, or scientific value.

The basic guidelines for the trier of fact must be: (a) whether "the average person, applying contemporary community standards" would find that the work, taken as a whole, appeals to the prurient interest, . . .(b) whether the work depicts or describes, in a patently offensive way, sexual conduct specifically defined by the applicable state law, and (c) whether the work, taken as a whole, lacks serious literary, artistic, political, or scientific value. We do not adopt as a constitutional standard the "*utterly* without redeeming social value" test of *Memoirs* v. *Massachusetts*; that concept has never commanded the adherence of more than three Justices at one time. If a state law that regulates obscene materials is thus limited, as written or construed, the First Amendment values applicable to the States through the Fourteenth Amendment are adequately protected by the ultimate power of appellate courts to conduct an independent review of constitutional claims when necessary. . . .

We emphasize that it is not our function to propose regulatory schemes for the States. That must await their concrete legislative efforts. It is possible, however, to give a few plain examples of what a state statute could define for regulation under the second part (b), of the standard announced in this opinion, *supra*:

(a) Patently offensive representations or descriptions of ultimate sexual acts, normal or perverted, actual or simulated.

(b) Patently offensive representations or descriptions of masturbation, excretory functions, and lewd exhibition of the genitals.

Sex and nudity may not be exploited without limit by films or pictures exhibited or sold in places of public accommodation any more than live sex and nudity can be exhibited or sold without limit in such public places. At a minimum, prurient, patently offensive depiction or description of sexual conduct must have serious literary, artistic, political, or scientific value to merit First Amendment protection. . . . For example, medical books for the education of physicians and related personnel necessarily use graphic illustrations and descriptions of human anatomy. . . .

Justice Brennan, author of the opinions of the Court, or the plurality opinions, in *Roth* v. *United States, Jacobellis* v. *Ohio, Ginzburg* v. *United States, Mishkin* v. *New York*, and *Memoirs* v. *Massachusetts* has abandoned his former positions and now maintains that no formulation of this Court, the Congress, or the States can adequately distinguish obscene material unprotected by the First Amendment from protected expression. . . . Paradoxically, Justice Brennan indicates that suppression of unprotected obscene material is permissible to avoid exposure to unconsenting adults, as in this case, and to juveniles, although he gives no indication of how the division between protected and nonprotected materials may be drawn with greater precision for these purposes than for regulation of commercial exposure to consenting adults only. Nor does he indicate where in the Constitution he finds the authority to distinguish between a willing "adult" one month past the state law age of majority and a willing "juvenile" one month younger.

Under the holdings announced today, no one will be subject to prosecution for the sale or exposure of obscene materials unless these materials depict or describe patently offensive "hard core" sexual conduct specifically defined by the regulating state law, as written or construed. We are satisfied that these specific prerequisites will provide fair notice to a dealer in such materials that his public and commercial activities may bring prosecution. . . . If the inability to define regulated materials with ultimate, god-like precision altogether removes the power of the States or the Congress to regulate, then "hard core" pornography may be exposed without limit to the juvenile, the passerby, and the consenting adult alike, as, indeed Justice Douglas contends. . . . In this belief, however, Justice Douglas now stands alone. . . .

It is certainly true that the absence, since *Roth*, of a single majority view of this Court as to proper standards for testing obscenity has placed a strain on both state and federal courts. But today, for the first time since *Roth* was decided in 1957, a majority of this Court has agreed on concrete guidelines to isolate "hard core" pornography from expression protected by the First Amendment. . . .

This may not be an easy road, free from difficulty. But no amount of "fatigue" should lead us to adopt a convenient "institutional" rationale—an absolutist, "anything goes" view of the First Amendment—because it will lighten our burdens. "Such an abnegation of judicial supervision in this field would be inconsistent with our duty to uphold constitutional guarantees. . . ."

Under a national Constitution, fundamental First Amendment limitations on the powers of the States do not vary from community to community, but this does not mean that there are, or should be, fixed, uniform national standards of precisely what appeals to the "prurient interest" or is "patently offensive." These are essentially questions of fact, and our Nation is simply too big and diverse for this Court to reasonably expect that such standards could be articulated for all 50 States in a single formulation, even assuming the prerequisite consensus exists. When triers of fact are asked to decide whether "the average person, applying contemporary community standards" would consider certain materials "prurient," it would be unrealistic to re-

quire that the answer be based on some abstract formulation. The adversary system, with lay jurors as the usual ultimate fact-finders in criminal prosecutions, has historically permitted triers-of-fact to draw on the standards of their community, guided always by limiting instructions on the law. To require a State to structure obscenity proceedings around evidence of a *national* "community standard" would be an exercise in futility. . . .

We conclude that neither the State's alleged failure to offer evidence of "national standards," nor the trial court's charge that the jury consider state community standards, were constitutional errors. Nothing in the First Amendment requires that a jury must consider hypothetical and unascertainable "national standards" when attempting to determine whether certain materials are obscene as a matter of fact. . . .

It is neither realistic nor constitutionally sound to read the First Amendment as requiring that the people of Maine or Mississippi accept public depiction of conduct found tolerable in Las Vegas, or New York City. . . . People in different States vary in their tastes and attitudes, and this diversity is not to be strangled by the absolutism of imposed uniformity. . . .

In sum we (a) affirm the *Roth* holding that obscene material is not protected by the First Amendment, (b) hold that such material can be regulated by the States, subject to the specific safeguards enunciated above, without a showing that the material is "*utterly* without redeeming social value," and (c) hold that obscenity is to be determined by applying "contemporary community standards," . . . not "national standards." The judgment of the Appellate Department of the Superior Court, Orange County, California, is vacated and the case remanded to that court for further proceedings not inconsistent with the First Amendment standards established by this opinion. . . .

Vacated and remanded for further proceedings.

JUSTICE BRENNAN's *views in dissent are set forth in* Paris Adult Theater v. Slaton, *413 U.S. 49, decided the same day.*

* * *

The view that, until today, enjoyed the most, but not majority, support was an interpretation of *Roth* (and not, as the Court suggests, a veering "sharply away from the *Roth* concept" and the articulation of "a new test of obscenity," *ante*, at 6) adopted by Chief Justice Warren. Justice Fortas, and the author of this opinion in *Memoirs* v. *Massachusetts, 383 U.S.*

413 (1966). We expressed the view that Federal or State Governments could control the distribution of material where "three elements . . . coalesce: it must be established that (a) the dominant theme of the material taken as a whole appeals to a prurient interest in sex; (b) the material is patently offensive because it affronts contemporary community standards relating to the description or representation of sexual matters; and (c) the material is utterly without redeeming social value." Even this formulation, however, concealed differences of opinion. . . . Nor, finally, did it ever command a majority of the Court. Aside from the other views described above, Justice Clark believed that "social importance" could only "be considered together with evidence that the material in question appeals to prurient interest and is patently offensive. . . ." Similarly, Justice White regarded "a publication to be obscene if its predominant theme appeals to the prurient interest in a manner exceeding customary limits of candor,". . .and regarded " 'social importance'. . .not [as] an independent test of obscenity, but [as] relevant only to determining the predominant prurient interest of the material. . . ."

In the face of this divergence of opinion the Court began the practice in 1967 in *Redrup* v. *New York*, 386 U.S. 767, of *per curiam* reversals of convictions for the dissemination of materials that at least five members of the Court, applying their separate tests, deemed not to be obscene.

Our experience with the *Roth* approach has certainly taught us that the outright suppression of obscenity cannot be reconciled with the fundamental principles of the First and Fourteenth Amendments. For we have failed to formulate a standard that sharply distinguishes protected from unprotected speech, and out of necessity, we have resorted to the *Redrup* approach, which resolves cases as between the parties, but offers only the most obscure guidance to legislation, adjudication by other courts, and primary conduct. By disposing of cases through summary reversal or denial of certiorari we have deliberately and effectively obscured the rationale underlying the decision. It comes as no surprise that judicial attempts to follow our lead conscientiously have often ended in hopeless confusion. . . .

I need hardly point out that the factors which must be taken into account are judgmental and can only be applied on "a case-by-case, sight-by-sight" basis. These considerations suggest that no one definition, no matter how precisely or narrowly drawn, can possibly suffice for all situations, or carve out fully suppressible expression from all media without also creating a substantial risk of encroachment upon the guarantees of the Due Process Clause and the First Amendment. . . .

The approach requiring the smallest deviation from our present course would be to draw a new line between protected and unprotected speech, still permitting the States to suppress all material on the unprotected side of the line. In my view, clarity cannot be obtained pursuant to this approach except by drawing a line that resolves all doubts in favor of state power and against the guarantees of the First Amendment. We could hold, for example, that any depiction or description of human sexual organs, irrespective of the manner or purpose of the portrayal, is outside the protection of the First Amendment and therefore open to suppression by the States. That formula would, no doubt, offer much fairer notice of the reach of any state statute drawn at the boundary of the State's constitutional power. And it would also, in all likelihood, give rise to a substantial probability of regularity in most judicial determinations under the standard. But such a standard would be appallingly overbroad, permitting the suppression of a vast range of literary, scientific, and artistic masterpieces. Neither the First Amendment nor any free community could possibly tolerate such a standard. Yet short of that extreme it is hard to see how any choice of words could reduce the vagueness problem to tolerable proportions, so long as we remain committed to the view that some class of materials is subject to outright suppression by the State. . . .

Of course, the Court's restated *Roth* test does limit the definition of obscenity to depictions of physical conduct and explicit sexual acts. And that limitation may seem, at first glance, a welcome and clarifying addition to the *Roth-Memoirs* formula. But just as the agreement in *Roth* on an abstract definition of obscenity gave little hint of the extreme difficulty that was to follow in attempting to apply that definition to specific material, the mere formulation of a "physical conduct" test is no assurance that it can be applied with any greater facility. The Court does not indicate how it would apply its test to the materials involved in *California* v. *Miller*, and we can only speculate as to its application. But even a confirmed optimist could find little realistic comfort in the adoption of such a test. Indeed, the valiant attempt of one lower federal court to draw the constitutional line at depictions of explicit sexual conduct seems to belie any suggestion that this approach marks the road to clarity. The Court surely demonstrates little sensitivity to our own institutional problems, much less the other vagueness-related difficulties, in establishing a system that requires us to consider whether a description of human genitals is sufficiently "lewd" to deprive it of constitutional protection; whether a sexual act is "ultimate"; whether the conduct depicted in materials before us fits within one of the categories of conduct whose depiction the state or federal governments have attempted to suppress; and a host of equally pointless inquiries. In addition, adoption of such a test does not, presumably, obviate the need for consideration of the nuances of presentation of sexually oriented material, yet it hardly clarifies the application of those opaque but important factors.

If the application of the "physical conduct" test to pictorial material is taught with difficulty, its application to textual material carries the potential for extraordinary abuse. Surely we have passed the point where the mere written description of sexual conduct is deprived of First Amendment protection. Yet the test offers no guidance to us, or anyone else, in determining which written descriptions of sexual conduct are protected, and which are not.

Ultimately, the reformulation must fail because it still leaves in this Court the responsibility of determining in each case whether the materials are protected by the First Amendment. The Court concedes that even under its restated formulation, the First Amendment interests at stake require "appellate courts to conduct an independent review of constitutional claims when necessary. . . ." Thus, the Court's new formulation will not relieve us of "the awesome task of making case by case at once the criminal and the constitutional law." And the careful efforts of state and lower federal courts to apply the standard will remain an essentially pointless exercise, in view of the need for an ultimate decision by this Court. . . .

Finally, I have considered the view, urged so forcefully since 1957 by our Brothers Black and Douglas, that the First Amendment bars the suppression of any sexually oriented expression. That position would effect a sharp reduction, although perhaps not a total elimination, of the uncertainty that surrounds our current approach. Nevertheless, I am convinced that it would achieve that desirable goal only by stripping the States of power to an extent that cannot be justified by the commands of the Constitution, at least as long as there is available an alternative approach that strikes a better balance between the guarantee of free expression and the States' legitimate interests.

Our experience since *Roth* requires us not only to abandon the effort to pick our obscene materials on a case-by-case basis, but also to reconsider a fun-

damental postulate of *Roth*: that there exists a definable class of sexually oriented expression that may be totally suppressed by the Federal and State Governments. Assuming that such a class of expression does in fact exist, I am forced to conclude that the concept of "obscenity" cannot be defined with sufficient specificity and clarity to provide fair notice to persons who create and distribute sexually oriented materials, to prevent substantial erosion of protected speech as a by-product of the attempt to suppress unprotected speech, and to avoid very costly institutional harms. Given these inevitable side-effects of state efforts to suppress what is assumed to be *unprotected* speech, we must scrutinize with care the state interest that is asserted to justify the suppression. For in the absence of some very substantial interest in suppressing such speech, we can hardly condone the ill-effects that seem to flow inevitably from the effort. . . .

If, as the Court today assumes, "a state legislature may . . . act on the . . . assumption that . . . commerce in obscene books, or public exhibitions focused on obscene conduct, have a tendency to exert a corrupting debasing impact leading to antisocial behavior,". . . then it is hard to see how state-ordered regimentation of our minds can ever be forestalled. For if a State may, in an effort to maintain or create a particular moral tone, prescribe what its citizens cannot read or cannot see, then it would seem to follow that in pursuit of that same objective a State could decree that its citizens must read certain books or must view certain films. . . . However laudable its goal—and that is obviously a question on which reasonable minds may differ— the State cannot proceed by means that violate the Constitution. . . .

Recognizing these principles, we have held that so-called thematic obscenity—obscenity which might persuade the viewer or reader to engage in "obscene" conduct—is not outside the protection of the First Amendment. . . . Even a legitimate, sharply focused state concern for the morality of the community cannot, in other words, justify an assault on the protections of the First Amendment. . . . Where the state interest in regulation of morality is vague and ill-defined, interference with the guarantees of the First Amendment is even more difficult to justify.

In short, while I cannot say that the interests of the State—apart from the question of juveniles and unconsenting adults—are trivial or nonexistent, I am compelled to conclude that these interests cannot justify the substantial damage to constitutional rights and to this Nation's judicial machinery that inevitably results from state efforts to bar the distribution even of unprotected material to consenting adults. . . . I would hold, therefore, that at least in the absence of distribution to juveniles or obtrusive exposure to unconsenting adults, the First and Fourteenth Amendments prohibit the State and Federal Governments from attempting wholly to suppress sexually oriented material on the bases of their allegedly "obscene" contents. Nothing in this approach precludes those governments from taking action to serve what may be strong and legitimate interests through regulation of the manner of distribution of sexually oriented material. . . .

BARNES v. GLEN THEATRE
501 U.S. ___; 115 L. Ed. 2d 504; 111 S. Ct. 2456 (1991)

CHIEF JUSTICE REHNQUIST *announced the judgment of the Court and delivered an opinion in which* O'CONNOR *and* KENNEDY, JJ., *joined.*

Respondents are two establishments in South Bend, Indiana, that wish to provide totally nude dancing as entertainment, and individual dancers who are employed at these establishments. They claim that the First Amendment's guarantee of freedom of expression prevents the State of Indiana from enforcing its public indecency law to prevent this form of dancing. We reject their claim.

* * *

Respondent Glen Theatre, Inc., is an Indiana corporation with a place of business in South Bend. Its primary business is supplying so-called adult entertainment through written and printed materials, movie showings, and live entertainment at an enclosed "bookstore." The live entertainment at the "bookstore" consists of nude and seminude performances and showings of the female body through glass panels. Customers sit in a booth and insert coins into a timing mechanism that permits them to observe the live nude and seminude dancers for a period of time. One of Glen Theatre's dancers, Gayle Ann Marie Sutro, has danced, modeled, and acted professionally for more than 15 years, and in addition to her performances at the Glen Theatre, can be seen in a pornographic movie at a nearby theater.

Respondents sued in the United States District Court for the Northern District of Indiana to enjoin the enforcement of the Indiana public indecency statute, (1988), asserting that its prohibition against complete nudity in public places violated the First Amendment. The District Court originally granted respondents' prayer for an injunction, finding that the statute was facially overbroad. The Court of Appeals for the Seventh Circuit reversed, deciding that previous litigation with respect to the statute in the Supreme Court of Indiana and this Court precluded the possibility of such a challenge, and remanded to the District Court in order for the plaintiffs to pursue their claim that the statute violated the First Amendment as applied to their dancing. On remand, the District Court concluded that "the type of dancing these plaintiffs wish to perform is not expressive activity protected by the Constitution of the United States," and rendered judgment in favor of the defendants. The case was again appealed to the Seventh Circuit, and a panel of that court reversed the District Court, holding that the nude dancing involved here was expressive conduct protected by the First Amendment. The Court of Appeals then heard the case *en banc*, and the court rendered a series of comprehensive and thoughtful opinions. The majority concluded that nonobscene nude dancing performed for entertainment is expression protected by the First Amendment, and that the public indecency statute was an improper infringement of that expressive activity because its purpose was to prevent the message of eroticism and sexuality conveyed by the dancers. We granted certiorari, and now hold that the Indiana statutory requirement that the dancers in the establishments involved in this case must wear pasties and a G-string does not violate the First Amendment.

Several of our cases contain language suggesting that nude dancing of the kind involved here is expressive conduct protected by the First Amendment. In *Doran* v. *Salem Inn, Inc.*, (1975), we said: "[A]lthough the customary 'barroom' type of nude dancing may involve only the barest minimum of protected expression, we recognized in *California* v. *LaRue*, (1972) that this form of entertainment might be entitled to First and Fourteenth Amendment protection under some circumstances." In *Schad* v. *Borough of Mount Ephraim*, we said that "[f]urthermore, as the state courts in this case recognized, nude dancing is not without its First Amendment protections from official regulation." These statements support the conclusion of the Court of Appeals that nude dancing of the kind sought to be performed here is expressive conduct within the outer perimeters of the First Amendment, though we view it as only marginally so. This, of course, does not end our inquiry. We must determine the level of protection to be afforded to the expressive conduct at issue, and must determine whether the Indiana statute is an impermissible infringement of that protected activity.

Indiana, of course, has not banned nude dancing as such, but has proscribed public nudity across the board. The Supreme Court of Indiana has construed the Indiana statute to preclude nudity in what are essentially places of public accommodation such as the Glen Theatre and the Kitty Kat Lounge. In such places, respondents point out, minors are excluded and there are no non-consenting viewers. Respondents contend that while the state may license establishment such as the ones involved here, and limit the geographical area in which they do business, it may not in any way limit the performance of the dances within them without violating the First Amendment. The petitioner contends, on the other hand, that Indiana's restriction on nude dancing is a valid "time, place or manner" restriction under cases such as *Clark* v. *Community for Creative Non-Violence*, (1984).

The "time, place, or manner" test was developed for evaluating restrictions on expression taking place on public property which had been dedicated as a "public forum," *Ward* v. *Rock against Racism*, (1989), although we have on at least one occasion applied it to conduct occurring on private property. See *Renton* v. *Playtime Theatres, Inc.*, (1986). In *Clark* we observed that this test has been interpreted to embody much the same standards as those set forth in *United States* v. *O'Brien*, (1968), and we turn, therefore, to the rule enunciated in *O'Brien*.

O'Brien burned his draft card on the steps of the South Boston courthouse in the presence of a sizable crowd, and was convicted of violating a statute that prohibited the knowing destruction or mutilation of such a card. He claimed that his conviction was contrary to the First Amendment because his act was a "symbolic speech"—expressive conduct. The court rejected his contention that symbolic speech is entitled to full First Amendment protection, saying:

[E]ven on the assumption that the alleged communicative element in O'Brien's conduct is sufficient to bring into play the First Amendment, it does not necessarily follow that the destruction of a registration certificate is constitutionally protected activity. This Court has held that when "speech" and "nonspeech" elements are combined in the same course of conduct, a sufficiently important governmental interest in regulating the nonspeech element can justify incidental limitations on First Amendment freedoms. To characterize the quality of the governmental interest which must appear, the Court has employed a variety of descriptive terms: compelling; substantial; subordinating; paramount; cogent; strong. Whatever imprecision inheres in these terms, we think it clear that a government regulation is sufficiently justified if it is within the constitutional power of the Government; if it furthers an important or substantial governmental interest; if the governmental interest is unrelated to the suppression of free expression; and if the incidental restriction on alleged First Amendment freedoms is no greater than is essential to the furtherance of that interest.

Applying the four-part *O'Brien* test enunciated above, we find that Indiana's public indecency statute is justified despite its incidental limitations on some expressive activity. The public indecency statute is clearly within the constitutional power of the State and furthers substantial governmental interests. It is impossible to discern, other than from the text of the statute, exactly what governmental interest the Indiana legislators had in mind when they enacted this statute, for Indiana does not record legislative history, and the state's highest court has not shed additional light on the statute's purpose. Nonetheless, the statute's purpose of protecting societal order and morality is clear from its text and history. Public indecency statutes of this sort are of ancient origin, and presently exist in at least 47 States. . . . Public indecency statutes such as the one before us reflect moral disapproval of people appearing in the nude among strangers in public places.

This public indecency statute follows a long line of earlier Indiana statutes banning all public nudity. The history of Indiana's public indecency statute shows that it predates barroom nude dancing and was enacted as a general prohibition.

* * *

This and other public indecency statutes were designed to protect morals and public order. The traditional police power of the States is defined as the authority to provide for the public health, safety, and morals, and we have upheld such a basis for legislation. In *Paris Adult Theatre I* v. *Slaton*, (1973), we said:

> In deciding *Roth* [v. *United States*, (1957)], this Court implicitly accepted that a legislature could legitimately act on such a conclusion to protect "the social interest in order and morality." [*Id.*], at 485. (Emphasis omitted.)

And in *Bowers* v. *Hardwick*, (1986), we said:

> The law, however, is constantly based on notions of morality, and if all laws representing essentially moral choices are to be invalidated under the Due Process Clause, the courts will be very busy indeed.

Thus, the public indecency statute furthers a substantial government interest in protecting order and morality.

This interest is unrelated to the suppression of free expression. Some may view restricting nudity on moral grounds as necessarily related to expression. We disagree. It can be argued, of course, that almost limitless types of conduct—including appearing in the nude in public—are "expressive," and in one sense of the word this is true. People who go about in the nude in public may be expressing something about themselves by so doing. But the court rejected this expansive notion of "expressive conduct" in *O'Brien* saying:

> We cannot accept the view that an apparently limitless variety of conduct can be labelled "speech" whenever the person engaging in the conduct intends thereby to express an idea. 391 U.S. at 376.

And in *Dallas* v. *Stanglin*, we further observed:

> It is possible to find some kernel of expression in almost every activity a person undertakes—for example, walking down the street or meeting one's friends at a shopping mall—but such a kernel is not sufficient to bring the activity within the protection of the First Amendment. We think the activity of these dance-hall patrons coming together to engage in recreational dancing—is not protected by the First Amendment.

Respondents contend that even though prohibiting nudity in public generally may not be related to suppressing expression, prohibiting the performance of nude dancing is related to expression because the state seeks to prevent its erotic message. Therefore, they reason that the application of the Indiana statute to the nude dancing in this case violates the First Amendment, because it fails the third part of the *O'Brien* test, viz.: the gov-ernmental interest must be unrelated to the suppression of free expression.

But we do not think that when Indiana applies its statute to the nude dancing in these nightclubs it is proscribing nudity because of the erotic message conveyed by the dancers. Presumably numerous other erotic performances are presented at these establishments and similar clubs without any interference from the state, so long as the performers wear a scant amount of clothing. Likewise, the requirement that the dancers don pasties and a G-string does not deprive the dance of whatever erotic message it conveys; it simply makes the message slightly less graphic. The perceived evil that Indiana seeks to address is not erotic dancing, but public nudity. The appearance of people of all shapes, sizes and ages in the nude at a beach, for example, would convey little if any erotic message, yet the state still seeks to prevent it. Public nudity is the evil the state seeks to prevent, whether or not it is combined with expressive activity.

This conclusion is buttressed by a reference to the facts of *O'Brien*. An act of Congress provided that anyone who knowingly destroyed a selective service registration certificate committed an offense. O'Brien burned his certificate on the steps of the South Boston Courthouse to influence others to adopt his anti-war beliefs. This Court upheld his conviction, reasoning that the continued availability of issued certificates served a legitimate and substantial purpose in the administration of the selective service system. O'Brien's deliberate destruction of his certificate frustrated this purpose and "for this non-communicative aspect of his conduct, and for nothing else, he was convicted." It was assumed that O'Brien's act in burning the certificate had a communicative element in it sufficient to bring into play the First Amendment, but it was for the non-communicative element that he was prosecuted. So here with the Indiana statute; while the dancing to which it was applied had a communicative element, it was not the dancing that was prohibited, but simply its being done in the nude.

The fourth part of the *O'Brien* test requires that the incidental restriction on First Amendment freedom be no greater than is essential to the furtherance of the governmental interest. As indicated in the discussion above, the governmental interest served by the text of the prohibition is societal disapproval of nudity in public places and among strangers. The statutory prohibition is not a means to some greater end, but an end in itself. It is without cavil that the pubic indecency statute is "narrowly tailored"; Indiana's requirement that the dancers wear at least pasties and a G-string is modest, and the bare minimum necessary to achieve the state's purpose.

The judgment of the Court of Appeals accordingly is

Reversed.

* * *

JUSTICE SCALIA, *concurring in the judgment.*

I agree that the judgment of the Court of Appeals must be reversed. In my view, however, the challenged regulation must be upheld, not because it survives some lower level of First Amendment scrutiny, but because, as a general law regulating conduct and not specifically directed at expression, it is not subject to First-Amendment scrutiny at all.

I

Indiana's public indecency statute provides:

(a) A person who knowingly or intentionally, in a public place:
   (1) engages in sexual intercourse;
   (2) engages in deviate sexual conduct;
   (3) appears in a state of nudity; or
   (4) fondles the genitals of himself or another person; commits public indecency, a Class A misdemeanor.
(b) "Nudity" means the showing of the human male or female genitals, pubic area, or buttocks with less than a fully opaque covering, the showing of the female breast with less than a fully opaque covering of any part of the nipple, or the showing of covered male genitals in a discernibly turgid state. Ind. Code Sec. 35-45-4-1 (1988).

On its face, this law is not directed at expression in particular. As Judge Easterbrook put it in his dissent: "Indiana does not regulate dancing. It regulates public nudity. . . . Almost the entire domain of Indiana's statute is unrelated to expression, unless we view nude beaches and topless hot dog vendors as speech." (Easterbrook, J., dissenting). The intent to convey a "message of eroticism" (or any other message) is not a necessary element of the statutory offense of public indecency; nor does one commit that statutory offense by conveying the most explicit "message of eroticism," so long as he does not commit any of the four specified acts in the process.

Indiana's statute is in the line of a long tradition of laws against public nudity, which have never been thought to run afoul of traditional understanding of "the freedom of speech." Public indecency—including public nudity—has long been an offense at common law. Indiana's first public nudity statute, (1831), predated by many years the appearance of nude barroom dancing. It was general in scope, directed at all public nudity, and not just at public nude expression; and all succeeding statutes, down to the present one, have been the same.

* * *

The dissent confidently asserts . . . that the purpose of restricting nudity in public places in general is to protect nonconsenting parties from offense; and argues that since only consenting, admission-paying patrons see respondents dance, that purpose cannot apply and the only remaining purpose must relate to the communicative elements of the performance. Perhaps the dissenters believe that "offense to others" *ought* to be the only reason for restricting nudity in public places generally, but there is no basis for thinking that our society has ever shared that Thoreauvian "you-may-do-what-you-like-so-long-as-it-does-not-injure-someone-else" beau ideal—much less for thinking that it was written into the Constitution. The purpose of Indiana's nudity law would be violated, I think, if 60,000 fully consenting adults crowded into the Hoosierdome to display their genitals to one another, even if there were not an offended innocent in the crowd. Our society prohibits, and all human societies have prohibited, certain activities not because they harm others but because they are considered, in the traditional phrase, "*contra bonos mores,*" i.e., immoral. In American society, such prohibitions have included, for example, sadomasochism, cockfighting, bestiality, suicide, drug use, prostitution, and sodomy. While there may be great diversity of view on whether various of these prohibitions should exist (though I have found few ready to abandon, in principle, all of them) there is no doubt that, absent specific constitutional protection for the conduct involved, the Constitution does not prohibit them simply because they regulate "morality." See *Bowers* v. *Hardwick,* 478 U.S. 186, 196 (1986) (upholding prohibition of private homosexual sodomy enacted solely on "the presumed belief of a majority of the electorate in [the jurisdiction] that homosexual sodomy is immoral and unacceptable"). . . . The purpose of the Indiana statute, as both its text and the manner of its enforcement demonstrate, is to enforce the traditional moral belief that people should not expose their private parts indiscriminately, regardless of whether those who see them are disedified. Since that is so, the dissent has no basis for positing that, where only thoroughly edified adults are present, the purpose must be repression of communication.

* * *

II

Since the Indiana regulation is a general law not specifically targeted at expressive conduct, its application to such conduct does not in my view implicate the First Amendment.

* * *

This is not to say that the First Amendment affords no protection to expressive conduct. Where the government prohibits conduct precisely because of its communicative attributes, we hold the regulation unconstitutional. See, e.g., *United States* v. *Eichman,* 496 U.S. 310 (1990) (burning flag); *Texas* v. *Johnson,* 491 U.S. 397 (1989) (same); *Spence* v. *Washington,* 418 U.S. 405 (1974) (defacing flag); *Tinker* v. *Des Moines Independent Community School District,* 393 U.S. 503 (1969) (wearing black arm bands); *Brown* v. *Louisiana,* 383 U.S. 131 (1966) (participating in silent sit-in); *Stromberg* v. *California,* 283 U.S. 359 (1931) (flying a red flag). In each of the foregoing cases, we explicitly found that suppressing communication was the object of the regulation of conduct. Where that has not been the case, however—where suppression of communicative use of the conduct was merely the incidental effect of forbidding the conduct for other reasons—we have allowed the regulation to stand. *O'Brien,* 391 U.S., at 377 (law banning destruction of draft card upheld in application against cardburning to protest war); *FTC* v. *Superior Court Trial Lawyers Assn.,* 493 U.S. 411 (1990) (Sherman Act upheld in application against restraint of trade to protest low pay); cf. *United States* v. *Albertini,* 472 U.S. 675, 678–688 (1985) (rule barring petitioner from military base upheld in application against entrance on base to protest war); *Clark* v. *Community for Creative Non-Violence,* 468 U.S. 288 (1984) (rule barring sleeping in parks upheld in application against persons engaging in such conduct to dramatize plight of homeless).

* * *

III

While I do not think the plurality's conclusions differ greatly from my own, I cannot entirely endorse its reasoning. The plurality purports to apply to this general law, insofar as it regulates this allegedly expressive conduct, an intermediate level of First Amendment scrutiny: the government interest in the regulation must be " 'important or substantial.' " As I have indicated, I do not believe such a heightened standard exists. I think we should avoid wherever possible, moreover, a method of analysis that requires judicial assessment of the "importance" of government interest—and especially of government interests in various aspects of morality.

Neither of the cases that the plurality cites to support the "importance" of the State's interest here is in point. *Paris Adult Theatre I* v. *Slaton* and *Bowers* v. *Hardwick* did uphold laws prohibiting private conduct based on concerns of decency and morality; but neither opinion held that those concerns were particularly "important" or "substantial," or amounted to anything more than a *rational basis* for regulation. *Slaton* involved an exhibition which, since it was obscene and at least to some extent public, was unprotected by the First Amendment; the State's prohibition could therefore be invalidated only if it had no rational basis. We found that the State's "right . . . to maintain a decent society" provided a "legitimate" basis for regulation—even as to obscene material viewed by consenting adults. In *Bowers,* we held that since homosexual behavior is not a fundamental right, a Georgia law prohibiting private homosexual intercourse needed only a rational basis in order to comply with the Due Process Clause. Moral opposition to homosexuality, we said, provided that rational basis. I would uphold the Indiana statute on precisely the same ground: moral opposition to nudity supplies a rational basis for its prohibition, and since the First Amendment has no application to this case no more than that is needed.

* * *

Indiana may constitutionally enforce its prohibition of public nudity even against those who choose to use public nudity as a means of communication. The State is regulating conduct, not expression, and those who choose to employ conduct as a means of expression must make sure that the conduct they select is not generally forbidden. For these reasons, I agree that the judgment should be reversed.

JUSTICE SOUTER, *concurring in the judgment.*

Not all dancing is entitled to First Amendment protection as expressive activity.

* * *

Although such performance dancing is inherently expressive, nudity per se is not. It is a condition, not an activity, and the voluntary assumption of that condition, without more, apparently expresses nothing beyond the view that the condition is somehow appropriate to the circumstances. But every voluntary act implies some such idea, and the implication is thus so common and minimal that calling all voluntary activity expressive would reduce the concept of expression to the point of the meaningless. A search for some expression beyond the minimal in the choice to go nude will often yield nothing: a person may choose nudity, for example, for maximum sunbathing. But when nudity is combined with expressive activity, its stimulative and attractive value certainly can enhance the force of expression, and a dancer's acts in going from clothed to nude, as in a strip-tease, are integrated into the dance and its expressive function. Thus I agree with the plurality and the dissent that an interest in freely engaging in the nude dancing at issue here is subject to a degree of First Amendment protection.

I also agree with the plurality that the appropriate analysis to determine the actual protection required by the First Amendment is the four-part enquiry described in *United States* v. *O'Brien*, for judging the limits of appropriate state action burdening expressive acts as distinct from pure speech or representation. I nonetheless write separately to rest my concurrence in the judgment, not on the possible sufficiency of society's moral views to justify the limitations at issue, but on the State's substantial interest in combating the secondary effects of adult entertainment establishments of the sort typified by respondents' establishments.

It is, of course, true that this justification has not been articulated by Indiana's legislature or by its courts. As the plurality observes, "Indiana does not record legislative history, and the state's highest court has not shed additional light on the statute's purpose." While it is certainly sound in such circumstances to infer general purposes "of protecting societal order and morality . . . from [the statute's] text and history," I think that we need not so limit ourselves in identifying the justification for the legislation at issue here, and may legitimately consider petitioners' assertion that the statute is applied to nude dancing because such dancing "encourag[es] prostitution, increas[es] sexual assaults, and attract[s] other criminal activity." Brief for Petitioners 37.

This asserted justification for the statute may not be ignored merely because it is unclear to what extent this purpose motivated the Indiana Legislature in enacting the statute. Our appropriate focus is not an empirical enquiry into the actual intent of the enacting legislature, but rather the existence or not of a current governmental interest in the service of which the challenged application of the statute may be constitutional. Cf. *McGowan* v. *Maryland*, 366 U.S. 420 (1961). At least as to the regulation of expressive conduct, "[w]e decline to void [a statute] essentially on the ground that it is unwise legislation which [the legislature] had the undoubted power to enact and which could be reenacted in its exact form if the same or another legislator made a 'wiser' speech about it." *O'Brien*. In my view, the interest asserted by petitioners in preventing prostitution, sexual assault, and other criminal activity, although presumably not a justification for all applications of the statute, is sufficient under *O'Brien* to justify the State's enforcement of the statute against the type of adult entertainment at issue here.

* * *

JUSTICE WHITE, *with whom* JUSTICE MARSHALL, JUSTICE BLACKMUN, *and* JUSTICE STEVENS *join, dissenting.*

The first question presented to us in this case is whether nonobscene nude dancing performed as entertainment is expressive conduct protected by the First Amendment. The Court of Appeals held that it is, observing that our prior decisions permit no other conclusion. Not surprisingly, then, the Court now concedes that "nude dancing of the kind sought to be performed here is expressive conduct within the outer perimeters of the First Amendment. . . ." This is no more than recognizing, as the Seventh Circuit observed, that dancing is an ancient art form and "inherently embodies the expression and communication of ideas and emotions."

Having arrived at the conclusion that nude dancing performed as entertainment enjoys First Amendment protection, the Court states that it must "determine the level of protection to be afforded to the expressive conduct at issue, and must determine whether the Indiana statute is an impermissible infringement of that protected activity." For guidance, the Court turns to *United States* v. *O'Brien*, (1968), which held that expressive conduct could be narrowly regulated or forbidden in pursuit of an important or substantial governmental interest that is unrelated to the content of the expression. The Court finds that the Indiana statute satisfies the *O'Brien* test in all respects.

The Court acknowledges that it is impossible to discern the exact state interests which the Indiana legislature had in mind when it enacted the Indiana statute, but the Court nonetheless concludes that it is clear from the statute's text and history that the law's purpose is to protect "societal order and morality." The Court goes on to conclude that Indiana's statute "was enacted as a *general prohibition*," (emphasis added), on people appearing in the nude among strangers in public places. The Court then points to cases in which we upheld legislation based on the State's police power, and ultimately concludes that the Indiana statute "furthers a substantial government interest in protecting order and morality." The Court also holds that the basis for banning nude dancing is unrelated to free expression and that it is narrowly drawn to serve the State's interest.

The Court's analysis is erroneous in several respects. Both the Court and JUSTICE SCALIA in his concurring opinion overlook a fundamental and critical aspect of our cases upholding the States' exercise of their police powers. None of the cases they rely upon, including *O'Brien* and *Bowers* v. *Hardwick*, (1986), involved anything less than truly general proscriptions on individual conduct. In *O'Brien*, for example, individuals were prohibited from destroying their draft cards at any time and in any place, even in completely private places such as the home. Likewise, in *Bowers*, the State prohibited sodomy, regardless of where the conduct might occur, including the home, as was true in that case. The same is true of cases like *Employment Division, Oregon Dept. of Human Resources* v. *Smith*, (1990), which, though not applicable here because it did not involve any claim that the peyote users were engaged in expressive activity, recognized that the State's interests in preventing the use of illegal drugs extends even into the home. By contrast, in this case Indiana does not suggest that its statute applies to, or could be applied to, nudity wherever it occurs, including the home. We do not understand the Court or JUSTICE SCALIA to be suggesting that Indiana could constitutionally enact such an intrusive prohibition, nor do we think such a suggestion would be tenable in light of our decision in *Stanley* v. *Georgia*, (1969), in which we held that States could not punish the mere possession of obscenity in the privacy of one's own home.

We are told by the Attorney General of Indiana that, in *State* v. *Baysinger*, (1979), the Indiana Supreme Court held that the statute at issue here cannot and does not prohibit nudity as a part of some larger form of expression meriting protection when the communication of ideas is involved. Petitioners also state that the evils sought to be avoided by applying the statute in this case would not obtain in the case of theatrical productions, such as *Salome* or *Hair*. Neither is there any evidence that the State has attempted to apply the statute to nudity in performances such as plays, ballets or operas. "No arrests have ever been made for nudity as part of a play or ballet."

Thus, the Indiana statute is not a general prohibition of the type we have upheld in the prior cases. As a result, the Court's and JUSTICE SCALIA's simple references to the State's general interest in promoting societal order and morality is not sufficient justification for a statute which concededly reaches a significant amount of protected expressive activity. Instead, in applying the *O'Brien* test, we are obligated to carefully examine the reasons the State has chosen to regulate this expressive conduct in a less than general statute. In other words, when the State enacts a law which draws a line between expressive conduct which is regulated and nonexpressive conduct of the same type which is not regulated, *O'Brien* places the burden on the State to justify the distinctions it has made. Closer inquiry as to the purpose of the statute is surely appropriate.

Legislators do not just randomly select certain conduct for proscription; they have reasons for doing so and those reasons illuminate the purpose of the law that is passed. Indeed, a law may have multiple purposes. The purpose of forbidding people from appearing nude in parks, beaches, hot dog stands, and like public places is to protect others from offense. But that could not possibly be the purpose of preventing nude dancing in theaters and barrooms since the viewers are exclusively consenting adults who pay money to see these dances. The purpose of the proscription in these contexts is to protect the viewers from what the State believes is the harmful message that nude dancing communicates. This is why *Clark* v. *Community for Creative Non-Violence*, (1984), is of no help to the State: "In *Clark* . . . the damage to the parks was the same whether the sleepers were camping out for fun, were in fact homeless, or wished by sleeping in the park to make a symbolic statement on behalf of the homeless." (Posner, J., concurring). That cannot be said in this case: the perceived damage to the public interest caused by appearing nude on the streets or in the parks, as I have said, is not what the State seeks to avoid in preventing nude dancing in theaters and taverns.

There the perceived harm is the communicative aspect of the erotic dance. As the State now tells us, and as JUSTICE SOUTER agrees, the State's goal in applying what it describes as its "content-neutral" statute to the nude dancing in this case is "deterrence of prostitution, sexual assaults, criminal activity, degradation of women, and other activities which break down family structure." The attainment of these goals, however, depends on preventing an expressive activity.

The Court nevertheless holds that the third requirement of the *O'Brien* test, that the governmental interest be unrelated to the suppression of free expression, is satisfied because in applying the statute to nude dancing, the State is not "proscribing nudity because of the erotic message conveyed by the dancers." The Court suggests that this is so because the State does not ban dancing that sends an erotic message; it is only nude erotic dancing that is forbidden. The perceived evil is not erotic dancing but public nudity, which may be prohibited despite any incidental impact on expressive activity. This analysis is transparently erroneous.

In arriving at its conclusion, the Court concedes that nude dancing conveys an erotic message and concedes that the message would be muted if the dancers wore pasties and G-strings. Indeed, the emotional or erotic impact of the dance is intensified by the nudity of the performers. As Judge Posner argues in his thoughtful concurring opinion in the Court of Appeals, the nudity of the dancer is an integral part of the emotions and thought that a nude dancing performance evokes. The sight of a fully clothed, or even a partially clothed, dancer generally will have a far different impact on a spectator than that of a nude dancer, even if the same dance is performed. The nudity is itself an expressive component of the dance, not merely incidental "conduct." We have previously pointed out that " '[n]udity alone' does not place otherwise protected material outside the mantle of the First Amendment." *Schad* v. *Mt. Ephraim*, (1981).

This being the case, it cannot be that the statutory prohibition is unrelated to expressive conduct. Since the State permits the dancers to perform if they wear pasties and G-strings but forbids nude dancing, it is precisely because of the distinctive, expressive content of the nude dancing performances at issue in this case that the State seeks to apply the statutory prohibition. It is only because nude dancing performances may generate emotions and feelings of eroticism and sensuality among the spectators that the State seeks to regulate such expressive activity, apparently on the assumption that creating or emphasizing such thoughts and ideas in the minds of the spectators may lead to increased prostitution and the degradation of women. But generating thoughts, ideas, and emotions is the essence of communication. The nudity element of nude dancing performances cannot be neatly pigeonholed as mere "conduct" independent of any expressive component of the dance.

That fact dictates the level of First Amendment protection to be accorded the performances at issue here. In *Texas* v. *Johnson*, (1989), the Court observed: "Whether Johnson's treatment of the flag violated Texas law thus depended on the likely communicative impact of his expressive conduct. . . . We must therefore subject the State's asserted interest in preserving the special symbolic character of the flag to 'the most exacting scrutiny.' *Boos* v. *Barry*, [(1980)]." Content-based restriction "will be upheld only if narrowly drawn to accomplish a compelling governmental interest." *United States* v. *Grace*, (1983); *Sable Communications of California, Inc.* v. *FCC*, (1989). Nothing could be clearer from our cases.

That the performances in the Kitty Kat Lounge may not be high art, to say the least, and may not appeal to the Court, is hardly an excuse for distorting and ignoring settled doctrine. The Court's assessment of the artistic merits of nude dancing performances should not be the determining factor in deciding this case. In the words of Justice Harlan, "it is largely because governmental officials cannot make principled decisions in this area that the Constitution leaves matters of taste and style so largely to the individual." *Cohen* v. *California*, (1971). "[W]hile the entertainment afforded by a nude ballet at Lincoln Center to those who can pay the price may differ vastly in content (as viewed by judges) or in quality (as viewed by critics), it may not differ in substance from the dance viewed by the person who. . .wants some 'entertainment' with his beer or shot of rye."

The Court and JUSTICE SOUTER do not go beyond saying that the state interests asserted here are important and substantial. But even if there were compelling interests, the Indiana statute is not narrowly drawn. If the State is genuinely concerned with prostitution and associated evils, as JUSTICE SOUTER seems to think, or the type of conduct that was occurring in *California* v. *LaRue*, (1972), it can adopt restrictions that do not interfere with the expressiveness of nonobscene nude dancing performances. For instance, the State could perhaps require that, while performing, nude performers remain at all times a certain minimum distance from spectators, that nude entertainment be limited to certain hours, or even that establishments providing such entertainment be dispersed throughout the city. Cf. *Renton* v. *Playtime Theatres, Inc.*, (1986). Likewise, the State clearly has the authority to criminalize prostitution and obscene behavior. Banning an entire category of expressive activity, however, generally does not satisfy the narrow tailoring requirement of strict First Amendment scrutiny. See *Frisby* v. *Schultz*, (1988). Furthermore, if nude dancing in barrooms, as compared with other establishments, is the most worrisome problem, the State could invoke its Twenty-first Amendment powers and impose appropriate regulation.

As I see it, our cases require us to affirm absent a compelling state interest supporting the statute. Neither the Court nor the State suggest that the statute could withstand scrutiny under that standard.

JUSTICE SCALIA's views are similar to those of the Court and suffer from the same defects. The Justice asserts that a general law barring specified conduct does not implicate the First Amendment unless the purpose of the law is to suppress the expressive quality of the forbidden conduct, and that, absent such purpose, First Amendment protections are not triggered simply because the incidental effect of the law is to proscribe conduct that is unquestionably expressive. The application of the Justice's proposition to this case is simple to state: The statute at issue is a general law banning nude appearances in public places, including barrooms and theaters. There is no showing that the purpose of this general law was to regulate expressive conduct; hence, the First Amendment is irrelevant and nude dancing in theaters and barrooms may be forbidden, irrespective of the expressiveness of the dancing.

As I have pointed out, however, the premise for the Justice's position—that the statute is a general law of the type our cases contemplate—is nonexistent in this case. Reference to JUSTICE SCALIA's own hypothetical makes this clear. We agree with JUSTICE SCALIA that the Indiana statute would not permit 60,000 consenting Hoosiers to expose themselves to each other in the Hoosierdome. No one can doubt, however, that those same 60,000 Hoosiers would be perfectly free to drive to their respective homes all across Indiana and, once there, to parade around, cavort, and revel in the nude for hours in front of relatives and friends. It is difficult to see why the State's interest in morality is any less in that situation, especially if, as JUSTICE SCALIA seems to suggest, nudity is inherently evil, but clearly the statute does not reach such activity. As we pointed out earlier, the State's failure to enact a truly general proscription requires closer scrutiny of the reasons for the distinctions the State has drawn.

As explained previously, the purpose of applying the law to the nude dancing performances in respondents' establishments is to prevent their customers from being exposed to the distinctive communicative aspects of nude dancing. That being the case, JUSTICE SCALIA's observation is fully applicable here: "Where a government prohibits conduct *precisely because of its communicative attributes*, we hold the regulation unconstitutional."

The *O'Brien* decision does not help JUSTICE SCALIA. Indeed, his position, like the Court's, would eviscerate the *O'Brien* test. *Employment Division, Oregon Dept. of Human Resources* v. *Smith*, (1990), is likewise not on point. The Indiana law, as applied to nude dancing, targets the expressive activity itself; in Indiana nudity in a dancing performance is a crime because of the message such dancing communicates. In *Smith*, the use of drugs was not criminal because the use was part of or occurred within the course of an otherwise protected religious ceremony, but because a general law made it so and was supported by the same interests in the religious context as in others.

Accordingly, I would affirm the judgment of the Court of Appeals, and dissent from this Court's judgment.

SELECTED REFERENCES

Arnone, James L. "Constitutional Law: Political Parties and Freedom of Association," *Harvard Journal of Law and Public Policy* (Summer 1988).

Baum, Lawrence. *The Supreme Court*. (Washington, D.C.: Congressional Quarterly Press), 1989.

Carter, T. Barton. *The First Amendment and the Fifth Estate: Regulation of Electronic Mass Media* (Westbury, NY: Foundation Press, 1989).

Chafee, Zechariah. *Free Speech in the United States*. (Cambridge, Mass.: Harvard University Press, 1948).

Curry, Richard O., ed. *Freedom at Risk: Secrecy, Censorship, and Repression in the 1980s* (Philadelphia: Temple University Press, 1988).

DeGrazia, Edward. *Girls Lean Back Everywhere: The Law on Obscenity and the Assault on Genius* (New York: Random House, 1992).

Emerson, Thomas I. *The System of Free Expression* (New York: Random House, 1970).

Fernandez, Joseph M. "Bringing Hate Crime Into Focus—The Hate Crimes Statistics Act of 1990," 26 *Harvard Civil Rights and Civil Liberties Law Review* 261 (1991).

Gellman, Susan. "Sticks and Stones Can Put You in Jail. . ." 39 *U.C.L.A. Law Review* 333 (1991).

Gey, Steven G. "The Apologetics of Suppression: The Regulation of Pornography as Act and Idea," 86 *Michigan Law Review* (June 1988).

Gomez, Jose. "The Public Expression of Lesbian/Gay Personhood as Protected Speech," 1 *Law and Inequality* 121-153, No. 1 (1983).

Hunter, James Davison, and Guinness, Os, eds. *Articles of Faith, Articles of Peace: The Religious Liberty Clauses and the American Public Philosophy* (Washington, D.C.: Brookings Institution, 1990).

Karst, Kenneth L. "The Freedom of Intimate Association," 89 *Yale Law Journal* 624 (1980).

Kobylka, Joseph Fiske. *The Politics of Obscenity: Group Litigation in a Time of Legal Change* (New York: Random House, 1992).

Lawrence, Charles R. "If He Hollers Let Him Go: Regulating Racist Speech on Campus," 1990 *Duke Law Review* 431 (1990).

Lewis, Anthony. *Make No Law* (New York: Random House, 1991).

Lynn, Barry W. *Polluting the Censorship Debate: A Summary and Critique of the Final Report of the Attorney General's Commission on Pornography* (Washington, D.C.: American Civil Liberties Union, 1986).

McClosky, Herbert, and Brill, Alida. *Dimensions of Tolerance: What Americans Believe About Civil Liberties* (New York: Russell Sage Foundation, 1983), chs. 2 and 3.

Office of Technology Assessment. *Science, Technology, and the First Amendment: A Special Report.* (Washington, D.C., 1988).

Smith, Norman B. "Constitutional Rights of Students, Their Families, and Teachers in the Public Schools," 10 *Campbell Law Review* 353 (Summer 1988).

Smith, Steven D. "Skepticism, Tolerance, and Truth in the Theory of Free Expression," 60 *Southern California Law Review* (March 1987).

Smolla, Rodney A. *Free Speech in an Open Society* (New York: Knopf, 1992).

Chapter 4

The Rights of the Accused

Mapp v. Ohio   United States v. Leon   California v. Greenwood   Florida v. Bostick
Miranda v. Arizona   New York v. Quarles   Illinois v. Perkins   Gideon v. Wainwright
Strickland v. Washington   Gregg v. Georgia   McCleskey v. Kemp   Stanford v. Kentucky
Payne v. Tennessee   Wilson v. Seiter   Hudson v. McMillian   Hernandez v. New York
Georgia v. McCollum   United States v. Salerno   Coy v. Iowa

Introductory Commentary

One of the most challenging problems facing government at all levels continues to be how best to protect persons and property from criminals and criminal activity. The crime rates in the United States are the highest in the Western world and show no signs of abating. Not only does such a phenomenon have major implications for policy-makers, but it tests the will of the nation to maintain its commitment to a Bill of Rights that guarantees certain rights to those accused of crime. In short, can we deal with crime and criminals expeditiously and effectively while at the same time holding to the values and concepts of the Bill of Rights and the Constitution? This is not an easy question. To be sure, "law and order" advocates and their sympathizers continue to denounce "overly permissive" courts for "coddling" criminals. Many charge that the Supreme Court, in its attempts to require strict adherence to the Bill of Rights,[1] has frustrated and randomly overruled longstanding law enforcement practices and procedures. They especially criticize the Supreme Court under Chief Justice Earl Warren for favoring what they consider the "criminal forces" over the "peace forces," thereby endangering important societal needs and interests. Certainly, the Warren Court did bring about revolutionary changes in criminal law during the 1960s, which did indeed, as the Court interpreted the Bill of

Rights, strengthen the protective shield of those accused of crime. However, as we shall see, the Burger Court, particularly since the mid-1970s, slowed the forward thrusts of the Warren Court, and narrowed and limited several important decisions of that era. The results of the Rehnquist Court, beginning in 1986, indicate a continuation of that trend into the 1990s.

Criminal law is probably the area that best illuminates how change in Supreme Court personnel has brought changes in our constitutional law. During the 1968 presidential campaign, criminal law decisions of the Supreme Court were frequently criticized by Republican candidate Richard Nixon. Nixon charged that such decisions were contributing to the increase of crime in our streets and in our communities. Reflecting the sentiments of many law enforcement officials (and others), Nixon saw the need for Supreme Court decisions that would support the "peace forces" and that would remove the "barbed wire of legalism" erected by the Warren Court to protect the "criminal forces."

As a result of the 1968 election, Candidate Nixon became President Nixon, and several factors combined to present the new president with the opportunity to do something about the decisional trends of the Warren Court. First, Chief Justice Warren's desire to retire in 1968 was thwarted when Associate Justice Abe Fortas (who was nominated by President Johnson to become Chief Jus-

---

[1]See Chapter 1 for a discussion of the application of the Bill of Rights to the states.

tice) was himself forced to resign from the Court. Fortas was accused of being involved in certain financial arrangements that many thought to be improper. Faced with the Fortas resignation and with his own "lame duck" status, President Johnson made no further attempt to name a Chief Justice to replace Warren, nor did he move to fill the seat vacated by Justice Fortas. As a result, the new president (Nixon) was presented with the rare opportunity to make two nominations to the Court shortly after taking office. In Nixon's appointment of a new Chief Justice (Warren E. Burger) and a replacement for Fortas (Harry A. Blackmun), the president, in his opinion, had two people who reflected the kind of "strict constructionism" needed to curb decisional trends in the criminal law area.

Following these two appointments, the president also had a chance in his first term (in 1971) to fill two other vacancies on the Court: one to replace Justice Hugo Black, who died in office; and another to take the seat vacated by Justice John Marshall Harlan II, who retired because of poor health. These two vacancies were filled by Lewis F. Powell of Virginia and William Rehnquist of Arizona. In Powell and Rehnquist, Nixon noted that the two appointees carried with them strong credentials consistent with his own "strict constructionist" views. In addition, had President Nixon not been forced to resign because of the Watergate scandal, he would also have had the opportunity to appoint a fifth justice, occasioned when Justice Douglas's failing health precipitated his retirement in 1975. (Douglas's successor, Justice John Paul Stevens, was appointed to the Court by President Ford.) When Justice Potter Stewart retired at the end of the 1980 term, President Reagan appointed Arizona State Court Judge Sandra Day O'Connor, who became the first woman to serve on the Court and one with an "acceptable" decisional stance on criminal law issues. The retirement of Chief Justice Burger in 1986 presented President Reagan with the opportunity to further the criminal law interests of his conservative constituency by elevating the Court's most consistent conservative member, Associate Justice William H. Rehnquist, to the chief justiceship. At the same time, the president nominated conservative Appeals Court Judge Antonin Scalia to the seat vacated by Rehnquist. The opportunity to solidify a conservative majority in the Court was presented to Reagan when centrist Justice Lewis Powell retired at the end of the Court's 1986 term. But the president's initial attempt to fill that vacancy with the high-profile conservative Appeals Court Judge Robert Bork was rebuffed by the Democratic-controlled Senate. And when disclosure of a personal behavior flaw derailed the nomination of his second choice, Appeals Court Judge Douglas Ginsburg, the president had to settle for his third choice, Appeals Court Judge Anthony Kennedy, whose stance on criminal law issues was not as clear and certain as that of Bork and Ginsburg. But in the few cases in which Kennedy participated toward the end of the Court's 1987 term, he provided the crucial fifth vote in support of the conservative position on criminal law issues. (This bloc consists of Chief Justice Rehnquist and Associate Justices White, O'Connor, Scalia, and Kennedy.) Both the election of George Bush in 1988 and the subsequent retirement of two of the Court's staunchest liberals (Brennan and Marshall) in 1990 and 1991, respectively, have enhanced the conservative position of the Court on criminal law issues for some time to come. Even with the election of President Clinton in 1992, his initial Supreme Court appointments do not portend any significant change in the Court's overall stance on criminal law issues.[2]

The commentary that follows examines the revolutionary expansion of the rights of the accused by the Warren Court (1953–69), the contraction and/or elimination of some of these rights by the Burger Court (1969–86), and the even more conservative trends emerging in the Rehnquist Court (since 1986).

[2]The speculation, as the Court began its 1992 term, was that the Court's two liberal members (Blackmun and Stevens) could be among the first to retire during the Clinton administration.

FEATURED CASES

Mapp v. *Ohio*   *United States* v. *Leon*

Despite the noble profession of justice expressed in the Fourth Amendment that "the right of the people to be secure in their persons, houses, papers, and effects, against unreasonable searches and seizures, shall not be violated," most people whose liberty was in conflict with state governmental authority were not initially the beneficiaries of this guarantee. The states, as primary enforcers of criminal law under our federal system were not bound by the Fourth Amendment. State actions were governed by similar provisions in state bills of rights, but the enforcement of those guarantees was at best wavering, uncertain, and uneven. By contrast, for those whose liberty was in conflict with federal authority, the Fourth Amendment had real meaning. As far back as 1886, in *Boyd* v. *United States* (116 U.S. 616), the Court, in effect, tied the Fourth Amendment to the Fifth Amendment's self-incrimination provision, indicating that the two "run almost into each other." An unreasonable search and seizure, the Court felt, is in reality a "compulsory extortion" of evidence that could result in compulsory self-incrimination. Subsequently, the Court ruled, in *Weeks* v. *United States* (232 U.S. 383, 1914), that evidence obtained in violation of the Fourth Amendment is inadmissible in federal criminal prosecutions.

Some states voluntarily adopted the *Weeks* rule, but most did not, and when, in *Wolf* v. *Colorado* (338 U.S. 25, 1949), the Court was urged to make the rule obligatory on the states, it refused to do so. Although the Court agreed that the Fourth Amendment guarantee against unreasonable searches and seizures was enforceable against the states through the Fourteenth Amendment, it nevertheless concluded that the exclusionary rule announced in *Weeks* was not an essential ingredient of that guarantee. The Court emphasized that the exclusionary rule was merely a rule of evidence imposed on federal courts, and state courts were free to admit or exclude illegally seized evidence as their laws might require.

Two cases decided during the next decade portended the demise of the *Wolf* rule. First, Chief Justice Earl Warren's sharp dissent in *Breithaupt* v. *Abram* (353 U.S. 43, 1957) indicated that at least four justices were ready to overrule *Wolf.* The Court

majority in that case upheld a conviction based on evidence obtained by taking a blood sample from the accused (while he was unconscious in a hospital) to prove intoxication. In the second action, in 1960, the Court struck down the "silver platter" doctrine in *Elkins* v. *United States* (364 U.S. 206). That doctrine had permitted evidence illegally obtained by state officers to be admitted in federal prosecutions as long as there was no complicity.

In 1961, the *Wolf* rule was finally laid to rest in *Mapp* v. *Ohio* (367 U.S. 643), which began a period of revolutionary holdings in criminal procedure by the Warren Court. Here the Court reversed a conviction for possession of obscene literature in which the evidence against the accused was obtained by forcible police entry without a search warrant. In his opinion for the five-man majority, Justice Tom Clark stressed the need to observe the command of the Fourth Amendment, and since *Wolf* had made it enforceable against the states, it should no longer be permitted "to remain an empty promise."

In its first application of the *Mapp* rule, the Court appeared to make a mild retreat. In *Ker* v. *California* (374 U.S. 23, 1963), the Court affirmed a conviction where the evidence was obtained without a search warrant and entry was gained by using the building manager's passkey. Justice Clark's opinion for the majority distinguished between state's evidence and evidence held inadmissible because it violated a federal statute. Noting that the evidence would have been inadmissible in a federal prosecution because a federal statute would bar it, he emphasized that such a prohibition had no application to a state prosecution "where admissibility is governed by constitutional standards." He thought that our federal system required recognition of state power to develop arrest and search and seizure rules (consistent with the Constitution) "to meet the practical demands of effective criminal investigation and law enforcement."

But if *Ker* implied any "soft" application of *Mapp*, it was quickly dispelled one year later in *Aguillar* v. *Texas* (378 U.S. 108, 1964). Here the Court reversed a narcotics conviction and in doing so made it clear that the *Mapp* rule must be obeyed and that no shabby subterfuges would be tolerated. In speaking for the Court, Justice Arthur Goldberg said that an inquiry as to the constitutionality of a search warrant should begin with the rule that "the informed and deliberate determinations of magistrates empowered to issue warrants . . . are to be preferred over the hurried action of officers . . . who may happen to make the arrests."

The Court explicated further these principles in *Spinelli* v. *United States* (393 U.S. 410, 1969), when it reversed a federal criminal conviction for interstate travel in aid of bookmaking. Justice Harlan's opinion for the Court reemphasized the Court's established propositions regarding issuance of warrants, which hold that:

1. Only the probability, and not a prima facie showing of criminal activity, is the standard of probable cause;
2. Affidavits of probable cause are tested by much less rigorous standards than those governing admissibility of evidence at trial;
3. In determining probable cause, issuing magistrates are not proscribed from the use of their common sense; and
4. Reviewing courts should accord great deference to determinations of probable cause by issuing magistrates.

The immediate response to *Mapp* in the law enforcement community was very negative. Generally, police officials saw the *Mapp* rule as judicial meddling with police procedures that made obtaining evidence of crimes much more difficult, if not impossible. For example, the head of the Minneapolis detective bureau was quoted as proclaiming during a burglary wave in that city in 1962: "I'd have 20 guys in jail right now if we didn't have to operate under present search and seizure laws."[3] Likewise, Chicago Superintendent of Police Orlando W. Wilson indicated his misgivings about the *Mapp* rule. Speaking to a conference of law enforcement officials, Wilson surmised that the police can probably live with the exclusionary rule since there appeared to be no alternative, but he wondered if the public could tolerate it. "If we followed some of our court decisions literally," said Wilson, "the public would be demanding my removal as Superintendent of Police . . . with justification."[4]

Additionally, some scholar-observers of police behavior have found that the primary purpose of the exclusionary rule—observance of Fourth Amendment requirements by law enforcement officials (police deterrence)—was not being realized.[5] Certainly such findings and the growing public concern over the steady increase in crime served to intensify the debate over the efficacy of the exclusionary rule in the early 1970s, leading some to call for its modification or abandonment.

Moving to the vanguard of the rule's critics in the 1970s was Chief Justice Warren E. Burger. In *Bivens* v. *Six Unknown Agents* (403 U.S. 388, 1971), decided near the end of the Court's 1970 term, the Chief Justice's sharp dissent portended an uncertain future for *Mapp*, particularly with the gradual depletion of the Warren Court "activist bloc." Here, the majority reaffirmed the suppression doctrine and construed the Fourth Amendment to permit actions for damages upon proof of injury resulting from the actions of federal officers operating in violation of the Fourth Amendment. But Burger objected to this act of "judicial legislation" and was greatly troubled by the "high price" that the exclusionary rule "extracts from society."

Three years later, in *United States* v. *Calandra* (414 U.S. 338, 1974), the contraction of the exclusionary rule forecasted in the Burger dissent in *Bivens* reached fruition. The case involved the use of illegally seized records from which questions were put to a witness in a federal grand jury investigation. A federal district court granted the motion to suppress the records, and the Court of Appeals for the Sixth Circuit, citing *Weeks*, affirmed. Chief Justice Burger and three other Nixon appointees (Blackmun, Powell, and Rehnquist) were joined by Warren Court holdovers Justices Stewart and White in reversal. Distinguishing the grand jury process from a criminal trial, Justice Powell, in his majority opinion, did not want the grand jury process to be hampered by "technical procedural and evidentiary rules" that apply to criminal trials. Powell tightened the reins on the exclusionary rule when he asserted that it was not "a personal constitutional right," but a "judicially created remedy" to deter illegal searches by law enforcement officials.

But such justifications did not satisfy Justices

---

[3]From a *Minneapolis Star* news item cited in Yale Kamisar, "On the Tactics of Police-Prosecutor Oriented Critics of the Courts," 49 *Cornell Law Quarterly* 436 (September 1964).

[4]Orlando W. Wilson. "Police Authority in a Free Society," 54 *Journal of Criminal Law, Crime, and Police Science*, 173 (March 1963). For a good review of much of the criticism of the *Mapp* rule, see Bradley Canon, "The Exclusionary Rule in Failing Health? Some New Data and a Plea Against a Precipitous Conclusion," 62 *Kentucky Law Journal* 681 (1974).

[5]See, for example, Dallin Oaks, "Studying the Exclusionary Rule in Search and Seizure." 37 *University of Chicago Law Review* 655 (1970). For an interesting perspective on the exclusionary rule controversy, see Lane V. Sunderland, "Liberals, Conservatives, and the Exclusionary Rule," 71 *Journal of Criminal Law and Criminology* 343 (1980).

Brennan, Douglas, and Marshall. In focusing on the "deterrent" purpose, Brennan contended that the majority had submerged the central purpose of the exclusionary rule. It was designed, he argued, to assure the people "that the government would not profit from its [own] lawless behavior."

The Burger Court continued to express its displeasure with the exclusionary rule when it refused to apply it to a federal tax proceeding in *United States* v. *Janis* (428 U.S. 433, 1976). Justice Harry A. Blackmun, who spoke for the five-to-three majority (Justice Stevens did not participate), questioned the rule's deterrence benefit. He argued that excluding the evidence, which had been seized by Los Angeles police, from the federal civil proceeding because it had been illegally seized by them, "[had] not been shown to have a sufficient likelihood of deterring the conduct of the police so that it outweighs the societal costs imposed by the exclusion." He made it clear that the judiciary should not confuse its role with that of the executive and legislative branches, which have the responsibility for supervising law enforcement.

Three holdovers from the Warren Court (Brennan, Marshall, and Stewart) disagreed. Justice Brennan, in whose dissent Justice Marshall concurred, characterized the majority holding as the continuing "slow strangulation of the exclusionary rule" and reiterated his view set forth in *Calandra*, that "the exclusionary rule is a necessary and inherent constitutional ingredient of the protections of the Fourth Amendment."

Justice Lewis Powell struck another blow at the exclusionary rule on the same day when the Court decided *Stone* v. *Powell* (428 U.S. 465, 1976). In rejecting federal habeas corpus relief to prisoners whose motions to suppress illegally obtained evidence were fully heard and denied by state courts, Powell questioned the exclusionary rule's value as a conservator of the integrity of the judicial process, particularly when balanced against the exclusion of "highly probative evidence." He warned that the "[a]pplication of the rule . . . deflects the truth finding process, affording a windfall to the guilty which often results in the inability to convict him."

The Burger Court continued its apparent disdain for the exclusionary rule in several decisions toward the end of the 1970s. Its holdings tended to reflect a balancing of the police misconduct deterrence rationale against societal costs in reduced prosecutions rather than acceptance of the rule as having a constitutional base. In two 1978 cases, for example—*United States* v. *Ceccolini* (435 U.S. 268) and *Rakas* v. *Illinois* (439 U.S. 128)—Justice Rehn-

quist led the Court first in refusing to affirm lower court suppression of "live" testimony and second in affirming a state court refusal to exclude evidence seized in an automobile in which the defendants had been passengers without property or possessory interest in the vehicle. Rehnquist was convinced that in the context of cases like *Ceccolini* and *Rakas*, application of the exclusionary rule exacted too high a societal cost for the minimal deterrence that exclusion of the evidence might have.

In addition to *Ceccolini* and *Rakas*, two 1980 rulings appeared to further the "slow strangulation" of the exclusionary rule. First, in *United States* v. *Salvucci* (448 U.S. 83), the "automatic standing" rule announced in *Jones* v. *United States* (362 U.S. 257, 1960),[6] under which those charged with crimes of possession could challenge the legality of a search that produced the evidence against them, was overturned in a seven-to-two decision. Accepting the defendants' claim of the constitutional inadequacy of the warrant authorizing the search, the district court granted a motion to suppress the evidence, and the court of appeals affirmed. But in overruling these lower court actions, Justice Rehnquist cited holdings that had eroded *Jones* and argued that now, standing to challenge the legality of the search that produced the evidence against an accused must be supported by a showing that his or her own Fourth Amendment rights were violated. This, he concluded, is essential to claim the benefits of the exclusionary rule. Underscoring his "law and order" commitment, Rehnquist noted that the "automatic standing" doctrine merely served to "afford a windfall to defendants whose Fourth Amendment rights have not been violated." The exclusion of probative evidence under such a rule was for him intolerable.

In the other 1980 ruling—*Rawlings* v. *Kentucky* (448 U.S. 48)—the Court, speaking through Justice Rehnquist, rejected an attempt to invoke the exclusionary rule in a drug conviction where the

[6]Here the Court recognized the dilemma facing accused persons when they are required to show that they have a property interest in the place searched, where evidence against them was seized in establishing their standing to challenge the constitutionality of the search. If they establish ownership or a possessory interest, such fact may be sufficient to convict them on a possession charge. The other horn of the dilemma is possible perjury as they attempt to establish standing. Justice Felix Frankfurter rejected such options afforded the accused, as the Court recognized that anyone legitimately on the premises where a search is conducted has "automatic standing" to challenge its legality in a suppression motion when the "fruits" of the search are proposed to be used against him or her (448 U.S. at 262–263, 1960).

petitioner pushed the "legitimate expectation of privacy" argument to establish his standing to assert a Fourth Amendment challenge to the search of his female companion's purse where his drugs were discovered. In such cases, Rehnquist asserted, trial courts may examine the "totality of the circumstances" to determine if a defendant had "made" a sufficient showing that his legitimate expectations of privacy were violated in the search. He concluded that the inquiry after *Rakas* focuses on the simple query: "whether governmental officials violated any legitimate expectation of privacy held by [a] petitioner."[7]

The Reagan administration's persistent attacks on the exclusionary rule in the early 1980s helped to produce three major decisions that narrowed significantly the Fourth Amendment's protective shield for the accused. First, in *Illinois* v. *Gates* (462 U.S. 213, 1983), the Court abandoned the two-pronged test emanating from *Aguillar* and *Spinelli* for assessing an informant's tip in establishing probable cause for issuance of a search warrant and supplanted it with a "totality of circumstances" approach. The issuing magistrate's "practical common-sense" judgment is emphasized, although he must have "a substantial basis for concluding that probable cause existed." The flexibility of such an approach, the Court felt, will produce a much better accommodation of the competing public and private interests at issue in the search.[8] While requesting additional argument on the question of whether there should be a "good faith" exception of the exclusionary rule, the Court declined ruling on it since the issue had not been presented to the state courts in the earlier stages of the proceeding.

But when it was appropriately presented to the Court one year later, the exception was permitted (*United States* v. *Leon*, 468 U.S. 897, and *Massachusetts* v. *Sheppard*, 468 U.S. 981). Justice Byron White's opinion for the six-to-three majority stressed that the purpose of the rule is to deter police misconduct. White stated that where police officers act in "objectively reasonable reliance" (good faith) on a warrant that is presumed to be valid but is subsequently found to be defective, the extreme sanction of exclusion is not required. For him, application of the exclusionary rule, in the context of *Leon*, would suppress "trustworthy" evidence at substantial costs to society. He reiterated

the rule's purpose—to deter police misconduct—not to punish the errors of issuing magistrates and judges.

While some analysts did not consider the "good faith" exception a mortal blow to the exclusionary rule, Justice William J. Brennan did. In dissent, he made a painstaking review of the Court's action on the rule during the last decade, characterizing that action as a "gradual but determined strangulation" of it. To him the majority had ignored the "fundamental importance" of the Fourth Amendment when it forged a cost/benefit analysis, where the "costs" of excluding evidence are "exaggerated" and the benefits are made to disappear with relative ease. But most troubling for him was the exception's impact on future police and judicial behavior. He feared that there will be less care in reviewing warrant applications and that police will not be as painstaking in providing information to support their applications for warrants.

Another significant modification of the exclusionary rule was announced by the Court in *Nix* v. *Williams* (467 U.S. 431, 1984), just three weeks before the "good-faith exception" ruling. Here, a seven-to-two majority fashioned the "inevitable discovery" exception that allows admission of "tainted evidence" if the prosecution can establish that such evidence would have inevitably been discovered by lawful means.[9] Chief Justice Burger emphasized that such an "inevitable discovery" exception is consistent with the rationale of the longstanding "independent source" doctrine, where deterrence of police misconduct interests and the interests of the law enforcement community in the admission of all probative evidence of crimes are "properly balanced" by leaving police officials in essentially the same investigation position they would have been in had there been no misconduct. But in dissent, Justice William J. Brennan pointed to the key distinction between the two exceptions—evidence sought to be admitted under the "inevitable discovery" exception could have the taint of police misconduct since it is not actually the product of an

[7]See also *United States* v. *Payner* (447 U.S. 727, 1980), where the Court held that the deterrent interest is not sufficient to justify exclusion of tainted evidence of third parties.

[8]The "totality of circumstances" approach was explicated further in *Massachusetts* v. *Upton* (466 U.S. 727, 1984).

[9]This case resulted from Williams's second conviction for murder. His first conviction was overturned in 1977 (*Brewer* v. *Williams*, 430 U.S. 387) because incriminating statements admitted as evidence at the trial, from which other evidence was derived, were obtained by police officers contrary to the constitutional guarantee of the right to assistance of counsel. The Court upheld the trial court's admission of evidence in the second trial that had been discovered as a result of the statements that had been held to be inadmissible in *Brewer*, accepting the state's argument that the evidence would have been "inevitably discovered" through independent means of law enforcement agencies.

independent source. Consequently, he argued that this distinction demanded "a heightened burden of proof" before admission of such evidence.

During President Reagan's second term (1985–89), Attorney General Edwin Meese was unsuccessful in his campaign to get the Court to abandon the rule altogether. Even with the elevation of staunch conservative Justice Rehnquist to Chief Justice in 1986 and the addition of conservatives Scalia (in 1986); Kennedy (in 1988); Souter (in 1990); and Thomas (in 1991), the Court had given no indication that it was ready to take that final action. Rather, in one of its last rulings on the issue during the 1987 term—*Murray* v. *United States* (108 S. Ct. 2529, 1988)—a narrow four-to-three majority was content to construe the "independent source" doctrine expansively in rejection of an attempt to suppress evidence that could well have been excluded in earlier years. In a drug-related prosecution, the evidence was initially discovered upon illegal entry and was later seized on authority of a valid warrant that was issued by a magistrate, where the fact of illegal entry was not disclosed by officers in their application for the warrant. In what appears to be a bow to added discretion of law enforcement officials, Justice Scalia contended for the Court that the "independent source" doctrine permits the introduction of evidence (even where there was an illegal initial entry) "obtained independently from lawful activities untainted by the initial illegality." Crucial for them is whether the information presented to support issuance of the warrant was of "a genuinely independent source." In short, would the warrant have been sought without the plain view of drugs during the illegal entry? While Scalia took judicial notice of the fact that knowledge of the existence of drugs was acquired at the illegal entry, he also noted that such knowledge was also acquired from entry pursuant to the warrant. Hence, if the latter acquisition did not flow from the former, then the "independent source" doctrine preserves admission of the evidence. But the Court remanded the case to the district court to determine if the warrant-authorized search was grounded on an independent source.

The dissenters, led by Justice Thurgood Marshall, were concerned that this latest construction of the "independent source" doctrine was bound to undermine the deterrence value that has been the mainstay of the exclusionary rule. Noting that the majority had certainly strained the "independent source" doctrine in applying it to the facts of this case, Marshall bluntly asserted that the majority "loses sight of the practical moorings of the independent source exception and creates an affirmative incentive for unconstitutional searches." Because the same team of investigators was involved in the illegal entry and the subsequent warrant-based search, he was very skeptical of the claim of "independent source." Hence, he urged that to ensure that a search is not tainted by a "prior illegal search," analysis should "focus . . . on 'demonstrated historical facts capable of ready verification or impeachment.' "

In the final analysis, the Court's position in *Murray* could well point the way for continued finessing of the exclusionary rule. To be sure, the rule will continue to be available for the accused, but in a successful application of it, the burden will be heightened. Certainly the Court's action in several warrantless search cases since 1987 (discussed below), when viewed with *Murray*, portends a less restrictive policy on the admissibility of evidence against the accused.

MAPP v. OHIO
367 U.S. 643; 6 L. Ed. 2d 1081; 81 S. Ct. 1684 (1961)

JUSTICE CLARK *delivered the opinion of the court.*

Appellant stands convicted of knowingly having had in her possession and under her control certain lewd and lascivious books, pictures, and photographs in violation of . . . Ohio's Revised Code. . . .

On May 23, 1957, three Cleveland police officers arrived at appellant's residence in that city pursuant to information that "a person [was] hiding out in the home, who was wanted for questioning in connection with a recent bombing, and that there was a large amount of policy paraphernalia being hidden in the home." Miss Mapp and her daughter by a former marriage lived on the top floor of the two-family dwelling. Upon their arrival at that house, the officers knocked on the door and demanded entrance, but appellant, after telephoning her attorney, refused to admit them without a search warrant. They advised their headquarters of the situation and undertook a surveillance of the house.

The officers again sought entrance some three hours later when four or more additional officers arrived on the scene. When Miss Mapp did not come to the door immediately, at least one of the several doors to the house was forcibly opened and the policemen gained admittance. Meanwhile Miss Mapp's attorney arrived, but the officers, having secured their own entry, and continuing in their defiance of the law, would permit him neither to see Miss Mapp nor to enter the house. It appears that Miss Mapp was halfway down the stairs from the upper floor to the front door when the officers, in this high-handed manner, broke into the hall. A paper, claimed to be a warrant, was held up by one of the officers. She grabbed the "warrant" and placed it in her bosom. A struggle ensued in which the officers recovered a piece of paper and as a result of which they handcuffed appellant because she had been "belligerent" in resisting their official rescue of the "warrant" from her person. Running roughshod over appellant, a policeman "grabbed her, "twisted [her] hand," and she "yelled [and pleaded with him" because "it was hurting." Appellant, in handcuffs, was then forcibly taken upstairs to her bedroom where the officers searched a dresser, a chest of drawers, closet and some suitcases. They also looked into a photo album and through personal papers belonging to the appellant. The search spread into the rest of the second floor including the child's bedroom, the living room, the kitchen and a dinette. The basement of the building and a trunk found therein were also searched. The obscene materials for possession of which she was ultimately convicted were discovered in the course of that widespread search.

At the trial no search warrant was produced by the prosecution, nor was the failure to produce one explained or accounted for. At best, [said the State Supreme Court,] "there is, in the record, considerable doubt as to whether there ever was any warrant for the search of defendant's home." . . . The Ohio Supreme Court believed a "reasonable argument" could be made that the conviction should be reversed "because the 'methods' employed to obtain the [evidence] . . . were such as to 'offend "a sense of justice," ' " but the court found determinative the fact that the evidence had not been taken "from defendant's person by the use of brutal or offensive physical force against defendant." . . . [Hence, it found that the conviction was valid.]

The State says that even if the search were made without authority, or otherwise unreasonably, it is not prevented from using the unconstitutionally seized evidence at trial, citing *Wolf* v. *Colorado* . . . in which this Court did indeed hold "that in a prosecution in a State court for a State crime the Fourteenth Amendment does not forbid the admission of evidence obtained by an unreasonable search and seizure." . . .

Seventy-five years ago in *Boyd* v. *United States*, 116 U.S. 616 (1886) . . . , considering the Fourth and Fifth Amendments as running "almost into each other" on the facts before it, this Court held that the doctrines of those Amendments "apply to all invasions on the part of the government and its employees of the sanctity of a man's home and the privacies of life. It is not the breaking of his doors, and the rummaging of his drawers, that constitutes the essence of the offense; but it is the invasion of his indefeasible right of personal security, personal liberty and private liberty. . . . Breaking into a house and opening boxes and drawers are circumstances of aggravation; but any forcible and compulsory extortion of a man's own testimony or of his private papers to be used as evidence to convict him of crime or to forfeit his goods, is within the condemnation . . . [of those Amendments]."

. . . The Court in the *Weeks* case clearly stated that use of the seized evidence involved "a denial of the constitutional rights of the accused." . . . Thus, in the year 1914, in the *Weeks* case, this Court "for the first time" held that "in a federal prosecution the Fourth Amendment barred the use of evidence secured through an illegal search and seizure." (*Wolf* v. *Colorado*. . . .) This Court has ever since required of federal law officers a strict adherence to that command which this Court has held so be a clear, specific, and constitutionally required—even if judicially implied—deterrent safeguard without insistence upon which the Fourth Amendment would have been reduced to "a form of words." . . . It meant, quite simply, that conviction by means of unlawful seizures and enforced confessions . . . should find no sanction in the judgments of the courts. . . ."

There are in the cases of this Court some passing references to the *Weeks* rule as being one of evidence. But the plain and unequivocal language of *Weeks*—and its later phrase in *Wolf*—to the effect that the *Weeks* rule is of constitutional origin, remains entirely undisturbed. . . .

In 1949, thirty-five years after *Weeks* was announced, this Court, in *Wolf* v. *Colorado*, . . . again for the first time, discussed the effect of the Fourth Amendment upon the States through the operation of the Due Process Clause of the Fourteenth Amendment. It said:

[W]e have no hesitation in saying that were a State affirmatively to sanction such police incursion into privacy it would run counter to the guaranty of the Fourteenth Amendment.

Nevertheless, after declaring that the "security of one's privacy against arbitrary intrusion by the police" is "implicit in the 'concept of ordered liberty' and as such enforceable against the States through the Due Process Clause," cf. *Palko* v. *Connecticut*, 302 U.S. 319 (1937) . . . , and announcing that it "stoutly adhere[d]" to the *Weeks* decision, the Court decided that the *Weeks* exclusionary rule would not then be imposed upon the States as "an essential ingredient of the right." . . . The Court's reasons for not considering essential to the right of privacy, as a curb imposed upon the States by the Due Process Clause, that which decades before had been posited as part and parcel of the Fourth Amendment's limitation upon federal encroachment of individual privacy, were bottomed on factual considerations.

While they are not basically relevant to a decision that the exclusionary rule is an essential ingredient of the Fourth Amendment as the right it embodies is vouchsafed against the States by the Due Process Clause, we will consider the current validity of the factual grounds upon which *Wolf* was based.

The Court in *Wolf* first stated that "[t]he contrariety of views of the States" on the adoption of the exclusionary rule of *Weeks* was "particularly impressive" . . . ; and, in this connection, that it could not "brush aside the experience of States which deem the incidence of such conduct by the police too slight to call for a deterrent remedy . . . by overriding the [States'] relevant rules of evidence." . . . While in 1949, prior to the *Wolf* case, almost two-thirds of the States were opposed to the use of the exclusionary rule, now, despite the *Wolf* case, more than half of those since passing upon it, by their own legislative or judicial decision, have wholly or partly adopted or adhered to the *Weeks* rule. See *Elkins* v. *United States*, 364 U.S. 206 (1960). . . . Significantly, among those now following the rule is California which, according to its highest court, was "compelled to reach that conclusion because other remedies have completely failed to secure compliance with the constitutional provisions. . . ." The experience of California that such other remedies have been worthless and futile is buttressed by the experience of other States. The obvious futility of relegating the Fourth Amendment to the protection of other remedies has, moreover, been recognized by this Court since *Wolf*. . . .

Likewise, time has set its face against what *Wolf* called the "weighty testimony" of *People* v. *Defore*, 242 N.Y. 13, 150 N.E. 585 (1962). There Justice (then Judge) Cardozo, rejecting adoption of the *Weeks* exclusionary rule in New York, had said that "the Federal rule as it stands is either too strict or too lax." . . . However, the force of that reasoning has been largely vitiated by later decisions of this Court. These include the recent discarding of the "silver platter" doctrine which allowed federal judicial use of evidence seized in violation of the Constitution by state agents, *Elkins* v. *United States*, 364 U.S. 206, 111; the relaxation to the formerly strict requirements as to standing to challenge the use of evidence thus seized, so that now the procedure of exclusion, "ultimately referable to constitutional safeguards," is available to anyone even "legitimately on [the] premises" unlawfully searched, *Jones* v. *United States*, 362 U.S. 257, 111 (1960); and, finally, the formulation of a method to prevent state use of evidence unconstitutionally seized by federal agents, *Rea* v. *United States*, 350 U.S. 214, 111 (1956). Because there can be no fixed formula, we are admittedly met with "recurring questions of the reasonableness of searches." But less is not to be expected when dealing with a Constitution, and, at any rate, "reasonableness is in the first instance for the [trial court] . . . to determine." *United States* v. *Rabinowitz*, 339 U.S. 56, . . . (1950).

It, therefore, plainly appears that the factual considerations supporting the failure of the *Wolf* Court to include the *Weeks* exclusionary rule when it recognized the enforceability of the right to privacy against the States in 1949, while not basically relevant to the constitutional consideration, could not, in any analysis, now be deemed controlling.

Since the Fourth Amendment's right of privacy has been declared enforceable against the States through the Due Process Clause of the Fourteenth, it is enforceable against them by the same sanction of exclusion as is used against the Federal Government. . . .

Moreover, our holding that the exclusionary rule is an essential part of both the Fourth and Fourteenth Amendments is not only the logical dictate of prior cases, but it also makes very good sense. There is no war between the Constitution and common sense. Presently, a federal prosecutor may make no use of evidence illegally seized, but a State's attorney across the street may, although he supposedly is operating under the enforceable prohibitions of the same Amendment. Thus the State, by admitting evidence unlawfully seized, serves to encourage disobedience to the Federal Constitution which it is bound to uphold. . . .

There are those who say, as did Justice (then Judge) Cardozo, that under our constitutional exclusionary doctrine "the criminal is to go free because the constable has blundered." *People* v. *Defore,* 242 N.Y. at 21. . . . In some cases this will undoubtedly be the result. But, as was said in *Elkins,* "there is another consideration—the imperative of judicial integrity." . . . The criminal goes free, if he must, but it is the law that sets him free. Nothing can destroy a government more quickly than its failure to observe its laws, or worse, its disregard of the charter of its own existence. . . .

The ignoble shortcut to conviction left open to the State tends to destroy the entire system of constitutional restraints on which the liberties of the people rest. Having once recognized that the right to privacy embodied in the Fourth Amendment is enforceable against the States, and that the right to be secure against rude invasions of privacy by state officers is, therefore, constitutional in origin, we can no longer permit that right to remain an empty promise. Because it is enforceable in the same manner and to like effect as other basic rights secured by the Due Process Clause, we can no longer permit it to be revocable at the whim of any police officer who, in the name of law enforcement itself, chooses to suspend its enjoyment. . . .

The judgment of the Supreme Court of Ohio is reversed and the cause remanded for further proceedings not inconsistent with this opinion.

Reversed and remanded.

JUSTICE BLACK, *concurring.*

I am still not persuaded that the Fourth Amendment, standing alone, would be enough to bar the introduction into evidence against an accused of papers and effects seized from him in violation of its commands. For the Fourth Amendment does not itself contain any provision expressly precluding the use of such evidence, and I am extremely doubtful that such a provision could properly be inferred from nothing more than the basic command against unreasonable searches and seizures. Reflection on the problem, however, in the light of cases coming before the Court since *Wolf,* has led me to conclude that when the Fourth Amendment's ban against unreasonable searches and seizures is considered together with the Fifth Amendment's ban against compelled self-incrimination, a constitutional basis emerges which not only justifies but actually requires the exclusionary rule. . . .

. . . As I understand the Court's opinion in this case, we again reject the confusing "shock the conscience" standard of the *Wolf* and *Rochin* cases and,

instead, set aside this state conviction in reliance upon the precise, intelligible and more predictable constitutional doctrine enunciated in the *Boyd* case. I fully agree with Justice Bradley's opinion that the two Amendments upon which the *Boyd* doctrine rests are of vital importance in our constitutional scheme of liberty and that both are entitled to a liberal rather than a niggardly interpretation. The courts of the country are entitled to know with as much certainty as possible what scope they cover. The Court's opinion, in my judgment, dissipates the doubt and uncertainty in this field of constitutional law, and I am persuaded, for this and other reasons stated, to depart from my prior views, to accept the *Boyd* doctrine as controlling in this state case, and to join the Court's judgment and opinion which are in accordance with that constitutional doctrine.

JUSTICE HARLAN, *whom* JUSTICE FRANKFURTER *and* JUSTICE WHITAKER *join, dissenting.*

In overruling the *Wolf* case the Court, in my opinion, has forgotten the sense of judicial restraint which, with due regard for *stare decisis,* is one element that should enter into deciding whether a past decision of this Court should be overruled. Apart from that I also believe that the *Wolf* rule represents sounder constitutional doctrine than the new rule which now replaces it. . . .

I would not impose upon the States this federal exclusionary remedy. The reasons given by the majority for now suddenly turning its back on *Wolf* seem to be notably unconvincing.

First, it is said that "the factual grounds upon which *Wolf* was based" have since changed, in that more States now follow the *Weeks* exclusionary rule than was so at the time *Wolf* was decided. While that is true, a recent survey indicated that at present one half of the States still adhere to the common-law nonexclusionary rule, and one, Maryland, retains the rule as to felonies. . . . But in any case surely all this is beside the point, as the majority itself indeed seems to recognize. Our concern here, as it was in *Wolf,* is not with the desirability of that rule but only with the question whether the States are constitutionally free to follow it or not as they may themselves determine, and the relevance of the disparity of views among the States on this point lies simply in the fact that the judgment involved is a debatable one. Moreover, the very fact on which the majority relies, instead of lending support to what is now being done, points away from the need of replacing voluntary state action with federal compulsion.

The preservation of a proper balance between state and federal responsibility in the administration of criminal justice demands patience on the part of those who might like to see things move faster among the States in this respect. Problems of criminal law enforcement vary widely from State to State. One State, in considering the totality of its legal picture, may conclude that the need for embracing the *Weeks* rule is pressing because other remedies are unavailable or inadequate to secure compliance with the substantive constitutional principle involved. Another, though equally solicitous of constitutional rights, may choose to pursue one purpose at a time, allowing all evidence relevant to guilt to be brought into a criminal trial, and dealing with constitutional infractions by other means. Still another may consider the exclusionary rule too rough and ready a remedy, in that it reaches only unconstitutional intrusions which eventuate in criminal prosecution of the victims. Further, a State after experimenting with the *Weeks* rule for a time may, because of unsatisfactory experience with it, decide to revert to a nonexclusionary rule. And so on. . . . For us the question remains, as it has always been, one of state power, not one of passing judgment on the wisdom of one state course or another. In my view this Court should continue to forbear from fettering the States with an adamant rule which may embarrass them in coping with their own peculiar problems in criminal law enforcement.

Further, we are told that imposition of the *Weeks* rule on the States makes "very good sense," in that it will promote recognition by state and federal officials of their "mutual obligation to respect the same fundamental criteria" in their approach to law enforcement, and will avoid "needless conflict between state and federal courts." Indeed the majority now finds an incongruity in *Wolf*'s discriminating perception between the demands of "ordered liberty" as respects the basic right of "privacy" and the means of securing it among the States. That perception, resting both on a sensitive regard for our federal system and a sound recognition of this Court's remoteness from particular state problems, is for me the strength of that decision.

An approach which regards the issue as one of achieving procedural symmetry or of serving administrative convenience surely disfigures the boundaries of this Court's functions in relation to the state and federal courts. Our role in promulgating the *Weeks* rule and its extensions . . . was quite a different one than it is here. There, in implementing the Fourth Amendment, we occupied the position of a tribunal having the ultimate responsibility for developing the standards and procedures of judicial administration within the judicial system over which it presides. Here we review state procedures whose measure is to be taken not against the specific substantive commands of the Fourth Amendment but under the flexible contours of the Due Process Clause. I do not believe that the Fourteenth Amendment empowers this Court to mould state remedies effectuating the right to freedom from "arbitrary intrusion by the police" to suit its own notions of how things should be done. . . .

In conclusion, it should be noted that the majority opinion in this is in fact an opinion only for the *judgment* overruling *Wolf*, and not for the basic rationale by which four members of the majority have reached that result. For my Brother Black is unwilling to subscribe to their view that the *Weeks* exclusionary rule derives from the Fourth Amendment itself . . . but joins the majority opinion on the premise that its end result can be achieved by bringing the Fifth Amendment to the aid of the Fourth. . . . On that score I need only say that whatever the validity of the "Fourth-Fifth Amendment" correlation which the *Boyd* case . . . found, . . . we have only very recently again reiterated the long-established doctrine of this Court that the Fifth Amendment privilege against self-incrimination is not applicable to the States. . . .

I regret that I find so unwise in principle and so inexpedient in policy a decision motivated by the high purpose of increasing respect for constitutional rights. But in the last analysis I think this Court can increase respect for the Constitution only if it rigidly respects the limitations which the Constitution places upon it. . . .

Memorandum of JUSTICE STEWART.

I express no view as to the merits of the constitutional issue which the Court today decides. I would, however, reverse the judgment in this case because I am persuaded that the provision of the statute upon which the petitioner's conviction was based is, in the words of JUSTICE HARLAN, not "consistent with the rights of free thought and expression. . . ."

JUSTICE WHITE *delivered the opinion of the Court.*

This case presents the question whether the Fourth Amendment exclusionary rule should be modified so as not to bar the use in the prosecution's case-in-chief of evidence obtained by officers acting in reasonable reliance on a search warrant issued by a detached and neutral magistrate but ultimately found to be unsupported by probable cause. To resolve this question, we must consider once again the tension between the sometimes competing goals of, on the one hand, deterring official misconduct and removing inducements to unreasonable invasions of privacy and, on the other, establishing procedures under which criminal defendants are "acquitted or convicted on the basis of all the evidence which exposes the truth." . . .

In August 1981, a confidential informant of unproven reliability informed an officer of the Burbank Police Department that two persons known to him as "Armando" and "Patsy" were selling large quantities of cocaine and methaqualone from their residence at 620 Price Drive in Burbank, California. The informant also indicated that he had witnessed a sale of methaqualone by "Patsy" at the residence approximately five months earlier and had observed at that time a shoebox containing a large amount of cash belonging to "Patsy." He further declared that "Armando" and "Patsy" generally kept only small quantities of drugs at their residence and stored the remainder at another location in Burbank.

On the basis of this information, the Burbank police initiated an extensive investigation. . . . During the course of the investigation, officers observed an automobile belonging to respondent Ricardo Del Castillo, who had previously been arrested for possession of 50 pounds of marijuana, arrive at the Price Drive residence. The driver of that car entered the house, exited shortly thereafter carrying a small paper sack, and drove away. A check of Del Castillo's probation records led the officers to respondent Alberto Leon, whose telephone number Del Castillo had listed as his employer's. Leon had been arrested in 1980 on drug charges, and a companion had informed the police at that time that Leon was heavily involved in the importation of drugs into this country. Before the current investigation began, the Burbank offi-

cers had learned that an informant had told a Glendale police officer that Leon stored a large quantity of methaqualone at his residence in Glendale. During the course of this investigation, the Burbank officers learned that Leon was living at 716 South Sunset Canyon in Burbank.

Subsequently, the officers observed several persons, at least one of whom had prior drug involvement, arriving at the Price Drive residence and leaving with small packages; observed a variety of other material activity at the two residences as well as at a condominium at 7902 Via Magdalena; and witnessed a variety of relevant activity involving respondents' automobiles. The officers also observed respondents Sanchez and Stewart board separate flights for Miami. The pair later returned to Los Angeles together, consented to a search of their luggage that revealed only a small amount of marijuana, and left the airport. Based on these and other observations . . . Officer Cyril Rombach of the Burbank Police Department, an experienced and well-trained narcotics investigator, prepared an application for a warrant to search 620 Price Drive, 716 South Sunset Canyon, 7902 Via Magdalena, and automobiles registered to each of the respondents for an extensive list of items believed to be related to respondents' drug-trafficking activities. Officer Rombach's extensive application was reviewed by several Deputy District Attorneys.

A facially valid search warrant was issued on September 1981 by a state superior court judge. The ensuing searches produced large quantities of drugs at the Via Magdalena and Sunset Canyon addresses and a small quantity at the Price Drive residence. Other evidence was discovered at each of the residences and in Stewart's and Del Castillo's automobiles. Respondents were indicted by a grand jury in the District Court for the Central District of California and charged with conspiracy to possess and distribute cocaine and a variety of substantive counts.

The respondents then filed motions to suppress the evidence seized pursuant to warrant. The District Court held an evidentiary hearing and . . . granted the motions to suppress in part. It concluded that the affidavit was insufficient to establish probable cause, but did not suppress all of the evidence as to all of the respondents because none of the respondents had standing to challenge all of the searches. In response to a request from the

Government, the court made clear that Officer Rombach had acted in good faith, but it rejected the Government's suggestion that the Fourth Amendment exclusionary rule should not apply where evidence is seized in reasonable, good-faith reliance on a search warrant.

The District Court denied the Government's motion for reconsideration, . . . and a divided panel of the Court of Appeals for the Ninth Circuit affirmed. The Court of Appeals first concluded that Officer Rombach's affidavit could not establish probable cause to search the Price Drive residence. To the extent that the affidavit set forth facts demonstrating the basis of the informant's knowledge of criminal activity, the information included was fatally stale. The affidavit, moreover, failed to establish the informant's credibility. Accordingly, the Court of Appeals concluded that the information was inadequate under both prongs of the two-part test established in *Aguilar* v. *Texas* . . . and *Spinelli* v. *United States.* . . . The Court of Appeals refused the Government's invitation to recognize a good-faith exception to the Fourth Amendment exclusionary rule. . . .

The Government's petition for certiorari presented only the question "[w]hether the Fourth Amendment exclusionary rule should be modified so as not to bar the admission of evidence seized in reasonable, good-faith reliance on a search warrant that is subsequently held to be defective." We granted certiorari to consider the propriety of such a modification. . . .

We have concluded that, in the Fourth Amendment context, the exclusionary rule can be modified somewhat without jeopardizing its ability to perform its intended functions. Accordingly, we reverse the judgment of the Court of Appeals. . . .

The Fourth Amendment contains no provision expressly precluding the use of evidence obtained in violation of its commands, and an examination of its origin and purposes makes clear that the use of fruits of a past unlawful search or seizure "work[s] no new Fourth Amendment wrong." *United States* v. *Calandra*, 414 U.S. 388, 354 . . . (1974). The wrong condemned by the Amendment is "fully accomplished" by the unlawful search or seizure itself, *ibid.*, and the exclusionary rule is neither intended nor able to "cure the invasion of the defendant's rights which he has already suffered." *Stone* v. *Powell*, 428 U.S., at 540. . . . (WHITE, J., *dissenting*). . . .

The substantial social costs exacted by the exclusionary rule for the vindication of Fourth Amendment rights have long been a source of concern. "Our cases have consistently recognized that unbending application of the exclusionary sanction to enforce ideals of governmental rectitude would impede unacceptably the truth-finding functions of judge and jury." *United States* v. *Payner*, 447 U.S. 727, 734 (1980). An objectionable collateral consequence of this interference with the criminal justice system's truth-finding function is that some guilty defendants may go free or receive reduced sentences as a result of favorable plea bargains. Particularly when law enforcement officers have acted in objective good faith or their transgressions have been minor, the magnitude of the benefit conferred on such guilty defendants offends basic concepts of the criminal justice system. . . . Indiscriminate application of the exclusionary rule, therefore, may well "generat[e] disrespect for the law and administration of justice." . . . Accordingly, "[a]s with any remedial device, the application of the rule has been restricted to those areas where its remedial objectives are thought most efficaciously served." *United States* v. *Calandra, supra*, 414 U.S., at 348. . . .

Close attention to those remedial objectives has characterized our recent decisions concerning the scope of the Fourth Amendment exclusionary rule. The Court has . . . not seriously questioned, "in the absence of a more efficacious sanction, the continued application of the rule to suppress evidence from the [prosecution's] case where a Fourth Amendment violation has been substantial and deliberate. . . ." *Franks* v. *Delaware*, 438 U.S. 154. . . . Nevertheless, the balancing approach, that has evolved in various contexts—including criminal trials—"forcefully suggest[s] that the exclusionary rule be more generally modified to permit the introduction of evidence obtained in the reasonable good-faith belief that a search or seizure was in accord with the Fourth Amendment." . . .

When considering the use of evidence obtained in violation of the Fourth Amendment in the prosecution's case-in-chief . . . we have declined to adopt a *per se* or but for rule that would render inadmissible any evidence that came to light through a chain of causation that began with an illegal arrest. . . . We also have held that a witness's testimony may be admitted even when his identity was discovered in an unconstitutional search. . . . The perception underlying these decisions—that the connection between police misconduct and evidence of crime may be sufficiently attenuated to permit the use of that evidence at trial—is a product of considerations relating to the exclusionary rule and the constitutional principles it is designed to protect. . . . In short, the "dissipation of the taint" concept that the Court has applied in deciding whether exclusion is appropriate in a particular case "attempts to mark the point at which the detrimental consequences of illegal police action become so attenuated that the deterrent effect of the exclusionary rule no longer justifies its cost." . . .

As yet, we have not recognized any form of good-faith exception of the Fourth Amendment exclusionary rule. But the balancing approach that has evolved during the years of experience with the rule provides strong support for the modification currently urged upon us. As we discuss below, our evaluation of the costs and benefits of suppressing reliable physical evidence seized by officers reasonably relying on a warrant issued by a detached and neutral magistrate leads to the conclusion that such evidence should be admissible in the prosecution's case-in-chief.

Because a search warrant "provides the detached scrutiny of a neutral magistrate, which is a more reliable safeguard against improper searches than the hurried judgment of a law enforcement officer 'engaged in the often competitive enterprise of ferreting out crime,' " . . . we have expressed a strong preference for warrants and declared that "in a doubtful or marginal case a search under a warrant may be sustainable where without one it would fail." . . . [W]e have thus concluded that the preference for warrants is most appropriately effectuated by according "great deference" to a magistrate's determination. . . .

Deference to the magistrate, however, is not boundless. It is clear, first, that the deference accorded to a magistrate's finding of probable cause does not preclude inquiry into the knowing or reckless falsity of the affidavit on which that determination was based. . . . Second, the courts must also insist that the magistrate purport to "perform his 'neutral and detached' function and not serve merely as a rubber stamp for the police." . . . A magistrate failing to "manifest that neutrality and detachment demanded of a judicial officer when presented with a warrant application" and who acts instead as "an adjunct law enforcement officer" cannot provide valid authorization for an otherwise unconstitutional search. . . .

Third, reviewing courts will not defer to a warrant based on an affidavit that does not "provide the magistrate with a substantial basis for determining the existence of probable cause." . . . "Sufficient information must be presented to the magistrate to allow that official to determine probable cause; his action cannot be a mere ratification of the bare conclusions of others." . . .

Only in the first of these three situations, however, has the Court set forth a rationale for suppressing evidence obtained pursuant to a search warrant; in the other areas, it has simply excluded such evidence without considering whether Fourth Amendment interests will be advanced. To the extent that proponents of exclusion rely on its behavioral effects on judges and magistrates in these areas, their reliance is misplaced. . . .

. . . [W]e discern no basis, and are offered none, for believing that exclusion of evidence seized pursuant to a warrant will have a significant deterrent effect on the issuing judge or magistrate. Many of the factors that indicate that the exclusionary rule cannot provide an effective "special" or "general" deterrent for individual offending law enforcement officers apply as well to judges or magistrates. And, to the extent that the rule is thought to operate as a "systemic" deterrent on a wider audience, it clearly can have no such effect on individuals empowered to issue search warrants. Judges and magistrates are not adjuncts to the law enforcement team; as neutral judicial officers, they have no stake in the outcome of particular criminal prosecutions. The threat of exclusion thus cannot be expected significantly to deter them. . . .

If exclusion of evidence obtained pursuant to a subsequently invalidated warrant is to have any deterrent effect, therefore, it must alter the behavior of individual law enforcement officers or the policies of their departments. One could argue that applying the exclusionary rule in cases where the police failed to demonstrate probable cause in the warrant application deters future inadequate presentations or "magistrate shopping" and thus promotes the ends of the Fourth Amendment. Suppressing evidence obtained pursuant to a technically defective warrant supported by probable cause also might encourage officers to scrutinize more closely the form of the warrant and to point out suspected judicial errors. We find such arguments speculative and conclude that suppression of evidence obtained pursuant to a warrant should be ordered only on a case-by-case basis and only in those unusual cases in which exclusion will further the purposes of the exclusionary rule. . . .

We have frequently questioned whether the exclusionary rule can have any deterrent effect when the offending officers acted in the objectively reasonable belief that their conduct did not violate the Fourth Amendment. "No empirical researcher, proponent or opponent of the rule, has yet been able to establish with any assurance whether the rule has a deterrent effect. . . ." But even assuming that the rule effectively deters some police misconduct and provides incentives for the law enforcement profession as a whole to conduct itself in accord with the Fourth Amendment, it cannot be expected, and should not be applied, to deter objectively reasonable law enforcement activity. . . .

. . . It is the magistrate's responsibility to determine whether the officer's allegations establish probable cause and, if so, to issue a warrant comporting in form with the requirements of the Fourth Amendment. In the ordinary case, an officer cannot be expected to question the magistrate's probable-cause determination or his judgment that the form of the warrant is technically sufficient. "[O]nce the warrant issues, there is literally nothing more the policeman can do in seeking to comply with the law." . . . Penalizing the officer for the magistrate's error, rather than his own, cannot logically contribute to the deterrence of Fourth Amendment violations.

We conclude that the marginal or nonexistent benefits produced by suppressing evidence obtained in objectively reasonable reliance on a subsequently invalidated search warrant cannot justify the substantial costs of exclusion. We do not suggest, however, that exclusion is always inappropriate in cases where an officer has obtained a warrant and abided by its terms. "[S]earches pursuant to a warrant will rarely require any deep inquiry into reasonableness," . . . for "a warrant issued by a magistrate normally suffices to establish" that a law enforcement officer has "acted in good faith in conducting the search." . . . Nevertheless, the officer's reliance on the magistrate's probable-cause determination and on the technical sufficiency of the warrant he issues must be objectively reasonable, . . . and it is clear that in some circumstances the officer will have no reasonable grounds for believing that the warrant was properly issued. . . .

In . . . limiting the suppression remedy, we leave untouched the probable-cause standard and the various requirements for a valid warrant. Other objections to the modification of the Fourth Amendment exclusionary rule we consider to be insubstantial. The good-faith exception for searches conducted pursuant to warrants is not intended to signal our unwillingness strictly to enforce the requirements of the Fourth Amendment, and we do not believe that it will have this effect. As we have already suggested, the good-faith exception, turning as it does on objective reasonableness, should not be difficult to apply in practice. When officers have acted pursuant to a warrant, the prosecution should ordinarily be able to establish objective good faith without a substantial expenditure of judicial time.

Nor are we persuaded that application of a good-faith exception to searches conducted pursuant to warrants will preclude review of the constitutionality of the search or seizure, deny needed guidance from the courts, or freeze Fourth Amendment law in its present state. There is no need for courts to adopt the inflexible practice of always deciding whether the officers' conduct manifested objective good faith before turning to the question whether the Fourth Amendment has been violated. Defendants seeking suppression of the fruits of allegedly unconstitutional searches or seizures undoubtedly raise live controversies which Article III empowers federal courts to adjudicate. As cases addressing questions of good-faith immunity under 42 U.S.C. § 1983 . . . and cases involving the harmless-error doctrine . . . make clear, courts have considerable discretion in conforming their decision-making processes to the exigencies of particular cases. . . .

When the principles we have enunciated today are applied to the facts of this case, it is apparent that the judgment of the Court of Appeals cannot stand. . . . [T]he officers' reliance on the magistrate's determination of probable cause was objectively reasonable, and application of the extreme sanction of exclusion is inappropriate.

Accordingly, the judgment of the Court of Appeals is

Reversed.

[The concurring opinion of JUSTICE BLACKMUN is not reprinted here.]

JUSTICE BRENNAN, *with whom* JUSTICE MARSHALL *joins, dissenting.*

Ten years ago in *United States* v. *Calandra,* 414 U.S. 338 . . . (1974), I expressed the fear that the Court's decision "may signal that a majority of my colleagues have positioned themselves to reopen the door [to evidence secured by official lawlessness] still further, and abandon altogether the exclusionary rule in search-and-seizure cases." . . . Since then, in case after case, I have witnessed the Court's gradual but determined strangulation of the rule. It now appears that the Court's victory over the Fourth Amendment is complete. That today's decision represents the *pièce de résistance* of the Court's past efforts cannot be doubted, for today the Court sanctions the use in the prosecution's case-in-chief of illegally obtained evidence against the individual whose rights have been violated—a result that had previously been thought to be foreclosed.

The Court seeks to justify on the ground that the "costs" of adhering to the exclusionary rule in cases like those before us exceed the "benefits." But the language of deterrence and of cost/benefit analysis, if used indiscriminately, can have a narcotic effect. It creates an illusion of technical precision and ineluctability. It suggests that not only constitutional principle but also empirical data supports the majority's result. When the Court's analysis is examined carefully, however, it is clear that we have not been treated to an honest assessment of the merits of the exclusionary rule, but have instead been drawn into a curious world where the "costs" of excluding illegally obtained evidence loom to exaggerated heights and where the "benefits" of such exclusion are made to disappear with a mere wave of the hand. The majority ignores the fundamental constitutional importance of what is at stake here. While the machinery of law enforcement and indeed the nature of crime itself have changed dramatically since the Fourth Amendment became part of the nation's fundamental law in 1791, what the Framers understood then remains true today—that the task of combating crime and convicting the guilty will in every era seem of such critical and pressing concern that we may be lured by the temptations of expediency into forsaking our commitment to protecting individual liberty and privacy. It was for that very reason that the Framers of the Bill of Rights insisted that law enforcement efforts be permanently and unambiguously restricted in order to preserve personal freedoms. In the constitutional scheme they ordained, the sometimes unpopular task of ensuring that the Government's enforcement efforts remain within the strict boundaries fixed by the Fourth Amendment was entrusted to the courts. . . . If those independent tribunals lose their resolve, however, as the Court has done today, and give way to the seductive call of expediency, the vital guarantees of the Fourth Amendment are reduced to nothing more than a "form of words." . . .

A proper understanding of the broad purposes sought to be served by the Fourth Amendment demonstrates that the principles embodied in the exclusionary rule rest upon a far firmer constitutional foundation than the shifting sands of the Court's deterrence rationale. But even if I were to accept the Court's chosen method of analyzing the question posed by these cases, I would still conclude that the Court's decision cannot be justified.

The Court holds that physical evidence seized by police officers reasonably relying upon a warrant issued by a detached and neutral magistrate is admissible in the prosecution's case-in-chief, even though a reviewing court has subsequently determined either that the warrant was defective . . . or that these officers failed to demonstrate when applying for the warrant that there was probable cause to conduct the search. I have no doubt that these decisions will prove in time to have been a grave mistake. But, as troubling and important as today's new doctrine may be for the administration of criminal justice in this country, the mode of analysis used to generate that doctrine also requires critical examination, for it may prove in the long run to pose the greater threat to our civil liberties.

At bottom, the Court's decision turns on the proposition that the exclusionary rule is merely a " 'judicially created remedy designed to safeguard Fourth Amendment rights generally through its deterrent effect, rather than a personal constitutional right.' " . . . [A]lthough I had thought that such a narrow conception of the rule had been forever put to rest by our decision in *Mapp* v. *Ohio*, . . . it has been revived by the present Court and reaches full flower with today's decision. The essence of this view . . . is that the sole "purpose of the Fourth Amendment is to prevent unreasonable government intrusions into the privacy of one's person, house, papers, or effects. The wrong condemned is the unjustified governmental invasion of these areas of an individual's life. That wrong . . . is *fully accomplished* by the original search without probable cause." . . . This reading of the Amendment implies that its proscriptions are directed solely at those government agents who may actually invade an individual's constitutionally protected privacy. The courts are not subject to any direct constitutional duty to exclude illegally obtained evidence, because the question of the admissibility of such evidence is not addressed by the Amendment. This view of the scope of the Amendment relegates the judiciary to the periphery. Because the only constitutionally cognizable injury has already been "fully accomplished" by the police by the time a case comes before the courts, the Constitution is not itself violated if the judge decides to admit the tainted evidence. Indeed, the most the judge *can* do is wring his hands and hope that perhaps by excluding such evidence he can deter future transgressions by the police.

Such a reading appears plausible because, as critics of the exclusionary rule never tire of repeating, the Fourth Amendment makes no express provision for the exclusion of evidence secured in violation of its commands. A short answer to this claim, of course, is that many of the Constitution's most vital imperatives are stated in general terms, and the task of giving meaning to these precepts is therefore left to subsequent judicial decision making in the context of concrete cases. . . .

A more direct answer may be supplied by recognizing that the Amendment, like other provisions of the Bill of Rights, restrains the power of the Government as a whole; it does not specify only a particular agency and exempt all others. The Judiciary is responsible, no less than the Executive, for ensuring that constitutional rights are respected.

When that fact is kept in mind, the role of the courts and their possible involvement in the concerns of the Fourth Amendment comes into sharper focus. Because seizures are executed principally to secure evidence, and because such evidence generally has utility in our legal system only in the context of a trial supervised by a judge, it is apparent that the admission of illegally obtained evidence implicates the same constitutional concerns as the initial seizure of that evidence. Indeed, by admitting unlawfully seized evidence, the Judiciary becomes a part of what is in fact a single governmental action prohibited by the terms of the Amendment. Once that connection between the evidence-gathering role of the police and the evidence-admitting function of the courts is acknowledged, the plausibility of the Court's interpretation becomes more suspect. Certainly nothing in the language or history of the Fourth Amendment suggests that a recognition of this evidentiary link between the police and the courts was meant to be foreclosed. . . . The Amendment . . . must be read to condemn not only the initial unconstitutional invasion of privacy—which is done, after all, for the purpose of securing evidence—but also the subsequent use of any evidence so obtained.

The Court evades this principle by drawing an artificial line between the constitutional rights and responsibilities that are engaged by actions of the police and those that are engaged when a defendant appears before the courts. . . .

I submit that such a crabbed reading of the Fourth Amendment casts aside the teaching of those justices who first formulated the exclusionary rule, and rests ultimately on an impoverished understanding of judicial responsibility in our constitutional scheme. For my part, "[t]he right of the people to be secure in their persons, houses, papers and effects, against unreasonable searches and seizures" comprises a personal right to exclude all evidence secured by means of unreasonable searches and seizures. The right to be free from the initial invasion of privacy and the right of exclusion are coordinate components of the central embracing right to be free from the unreasonable searches and seizures. . . .

[T]he Amendment plainly operates to disable the Government from gathering information and securing evidence in certain ways. In practical terms, of course, this restriction of official power means that some incriminating evidence inevitably will go undetected if the Government obeys these constitutional restraints. It is the loss of that evidence that is the "price" our society pays for enjoying the freedom and privacy safeguarded by the Fourth Amendment. Thus some criminals will go free *not* in Justice (then Judge) Cardozo's misleading epigram, "because the constable has blundered," *People* v. *Defore*, 242 N.Y. 13, 21, 150 N.E. 585, 587 (1926), but rather because official compliance with Fourth Amendment requirements makes it more difficult to catch criminals. Understood in this way, the amendment directly contemplates that some reliable and incriminating evidence will be lost to the Government; therefore, it is not the exclusionary rule, but the Amendment itself that has imposed this cost.

In addition, the Court's decisions over the past decade have made plain that the entire enterprise of attempting to assess the benefits and costs of the exclusionary rule in various contexts is a virtually impossible task for the judiciary to perform honestly or accurately. Although the Court's language in those cases suggests that some specific empirical basis may support its analyses, the reality is that the Court's opinions represent inherently unstable compounds of intuition, hunches, and occasional pieces of partial and often inconclusive data. . . . To the extent empirical data is available regarding the general costs and benefits of the exclusionary rule, it has shown, on the one hand, as the Court acknowledges today, that the costs are not as substantial as critics have asserted in the past . . . and, on the other hand, that while the exclusionary rule may well have certain deterrent effects, it is extremely difficult to determine with any degree of precision whether the incidence of unlawful conduct by police is now lower than it was prior to *Mapp*. . . . The Court has sought to turn this uncertainty to its advantage by casting the burden of proof upon proponents of the rule. . . . "Obviously," however, "the assignment of the burden of proof on an issue where evidence does not exist and cannot be obtained is outcome determinative.

[The] assignment of the burden is merely a way of announcing a predetermined conclusion."

By remaining within its redoubt of empiricism and by basing the rule solely on the deterrence rationale, the Court has robbed the rule of legitimacy. A doctrine that is explained as if it were an empirical proposition but for which there is only limited empirical support is both inherently unstable and an easy mark for critics. The extent of this Court's fidelity to Fourth Amendment requirements, however, should not turn on such statistical uncertainties. . . .

If the overall educational effect of the exclusionary rule is considered, application of the rule to even those situations in which individual police officers have acted on the basis of a reasonable but mistaken belief that their conduct was authorized can still be expected to have a considerable long-term deterrent effect. If evidence is consistently excluded in these circumstances, police departments will surely be prompted to instruct their officers to devote greater care and attention to providing sufficient information to establish probable cause when applying for a warrant, and to review with some attention the form of the warrant that they have been issued, rather than automatically assuming that whatever document the magistrate has signed will necessarily comport with Fourth Amendment requirements.

After today's decision, however, that institutional incentive will be lost. Indeed, the Court's "reasonable mistake" exception to the exclusionary rule will tend to put a premium on police ignorance of the law. Armed with the assurance provided by today's decision that evidence will always be admissible whenever an officer has "reasonably" relied upon a warrant, police departments will be encouraged to train officers that if a warrant has simply been signed, it is reasonable, without more, to rely on it. Since in close cases there will no longer be any incentive to err on the side of constitutional behavior, police would have every reason to adopt a "let's wait until it's decided" approach in situations in which there is a question about a warrant's validity or the basis for its issuance. . . .

A chief consequence of today's decision will be to convey a clear and unambiguous message to magistrates that their decisions to issue warrants are now insulated from subsequent judicial review. Creation of this new exception for good faith reliance upon a warrant implicitly tells magistrates that they need not take much care in reviewing warrant applications, since their mistakes will from now on have virtually no consequence: If their decision to issue a warrant was correct, the evidence will be admitted; if their decision was incorrect but the police relied in good faith on the warrant, the evidence will also be admitted. . . .

[T]he good faith exception will encourage police to provide only the bare minimum of information in future warrant applications. The police will now know that if they can secure a warrant, so long as the circumstances of its issuance are not "entirely unreasonable," . . . all police conduct pursuant to that warrant will be protected from further judicial review. The clear incentive that operated in the past to establish probable cause adequately because reviewing courts would examine the magistrate's judgment carefully . . . has now been so completely vitiated that the police need only show that it was not "entirely unreasonable" under the circumstances of a particular case for them to believe that the warrant they were issued was valid. . . . The long-run effect unquestionably will be to undermine the integrity of the warrant process.

Finally, even if one were to believe, as the Court apparently does, that police are hobbled by inflexible and hypertechnical warrant procedures, today's decision cannot be justified. This is because, given the relaxed standard for assessing probable cause, established just last Term in *Illinois* v. *Gates,* . . . the Court's newly fashioned good faith exception, when applied in the warrant context, will rarely, if ever, offer any greater flexibility for police than the *Gates* standard already supplies. In *Gates,* the Court held that "the task of an issuing magistrate is simply to make a practical, common-sense decision whether, given all the circumstances set forth in the affidavit before him, . . . there is a fair probability that contraband or evidence of a crime will be found in a particular place." . . . Given such a relaxed standard, it is virtually inconceivable that a reviewing court, when faced with a defendant's motion to suppress, could first find that a warrant was invalid under the new *Gates* standard, but then, at the same time, find that a police officer's reliance on such an invalid warrant was nevertheless "objectively reasonable" under the test announced today. Because the two standards overlap so completely, it is unlikely that a warrant could be found invalid under *Gates* and yet the police reliance upon it could be seen as objectively reasonable; otherwise, we would have to entertain the mind-boggling concept of objectively reasonable reliance upon an objectively unreasonable warrant. . . .

[A]lthough the Court's decisions are clearly limited to the situation in which police officers reasonably rely upon an apparently valid warrant in conducting a search, I am not at all confident that the exception unleashed today will remain so confined. Indeed, the full impact of the Court's regrettable decision will not be felt until the Court attempts to extend this rule to situations in which the police have conducted a warrantless search solely on the basis of their own judgment about the existence of probable cause and exigent circumstances. When that question is finally posed, I for one will not be surprised if my colleagues decide once again that we simply cannot afford to protect Fourth Amendment rights.

When the public, as it quite properly has done in the past as well as in the present, demands that those in Government increase their efforts to combat crime, it is all too easy for those government officials to seek expedient solutions. In contrast to such costly and difficult measures as building more prisons, improving law enforcement methods, or hiring more prosecutors and judges to relieve the overburdened court systems in the country's metropolitan areas, the relaxation of Fourth Amendment standards seems a tempting, costless means of meeting the public's demand for better law enforcement. In the long run, however, we as a society pay a heavy price for such expediency. . . . Once lost, such rights are difficult to recover. There is hope, however, that in time this or some later Court will restore these precious freedoms to their rightful place as a primary protection for our citizens against over reaching officialdom.

I dissent.

[The opinion of JUSTICE STEVENS concurring in *Sheppard* and dissenting in *Leon* is not reprinted here.]

Fourth Amendment Problems: Warrantless Searches

FEATURED CASES

California v. *Greenwood*   *Florida* v. *Bostick*

In the course of day-to-day law enforcement work, it is often not possible or feasible to obtain a warrant for searches and seizures in gathering evidence for the prosecution of criminal activity. For the most part, however, the Supreme Court has followed the basic constitutional doctrine that searches without prior approval of a "neutral and detached magistrate" are per se unreasonable under the Fourth Amendment and that any exceptions to this rule must be supported by a showing of special exigencies that make the warrantless search imperative.

One such exigency that the Supreme Court has recognized over the years is the "search incident to a lawful arrest." Beginning with its holding in *Carroll* v. *United States* (267 U.S. 132, 1925) that "[w]hen a man is legally arrested for an offense, whatever is found upon his person or in his control which it is unlawful for him to have and which may be used to prove the offense may be seized and held as evidence in the prosecution," the Court has accepted cases periodically that were vehicles for further explication of the doctrine. At times it adopted an expanded view of the doctrine and approved fairly extensive warrantless searches incident to arrests. This is well illustrated by such decisions as *Harris* v. *United States* (331 U.S. 145, 1947), where the Court validated an extensive search of a four-room apartment supported only by the arrest warrant, and *United States* v. *Rabinowitz* (399 U.S. 56, 1950), where a one and one-half hour search of an office, including desks, safes, and file cabinets, was approved as incident to the arrest. In the context of these and similar cases, the Court applied a "plain view" doctrine to validate the seizure of evidence clearly visible in the "immediate area" of the arrest.

On the other hand, the Supreme Court has at other times adopted a more limited view of the doctrine. In the 1931 and 1932 cases of *Go-Bart Importing Co.* v. *United States* (282 U.S. 344) and *United States* v. *Lefkowitz* (285 U.S. 452), for example, the Court held defective the less extensive searches of offices in which the arrest warrants were executed and the arresting officers "had an abundance of information and time to swear out a valid [search] warrant [and] failed to do so." Likewise, in *Trupiano* v. *United States* (334 U.S. 699, 1948), the Court, in reaffirming this position, asserted that "[i]t is a cardinal rule that in seizing goods and articles, law enforcement agents must secure and use search warrants wherever reasonably practicable" for "[a] search or seizure without a warrant as an incident to a lawful arrest has always been considered to be a strictly limited right."

The Court reiterated these principles in *Chimel* v. *California* (395 U.S. 752, 1969) and took the occasion to lay to rest the principles of *Harris* and *Rabinowitz*. In his opinion for the Court, Justice Potter Stewart stressed that such searches, to be consistent with the Fourth Amendment, must be limited to the arrestee's "person and the area from within which he might have obtained either a weapon" or something that could have been used as evidence against him.

The Court continued to stress the limited use of warrantless searches in *Vale* v. *Louisiana* (399 U.S. 30, 1976), where an extensive search of an arrestee's house was held invalid because it was not limited to the "immediate vicinity" of his arrest on the front steps. The Court took a similar position in *Coolidge* v. *New Hampshire* (403 U.S. 443, 1971), where the search of an accused's automobile was rejected because it was conducted two days after his arrest, although it was accessible in his driveway when he was arrested.

Apparently, concern for the sanctity of the home has continued to guide the Court in this area, particularly where residences were entered to effect arrests and/or conduct searches without valid warrants. For example, in *Payton* v. *New York* (445 U.S. 573, 1980), the Court struck down as violative of the Fourth Amendment a state statute that authorized police officers without warrants to make forceful entries of residences for routine felony arrests. Restricting police discretion in this area even further, the Court, in *Steagold* v. *United States* (451 U.S. 204, 1981), decided one year later, refused to allow an arrest warrant to justify the entry and search of a house belonging to someone other than the person to whom the arrest warrant was directed. Similarly, in *Welsh* v. *Wisconsin* (466 U.S. 740, 1984), the Court rejected warrantless entry of residences in order to arrest persons for civil, nonjailable traffic offenses.

A dimension of the warrantless search doctrine that has produced considerable controversy during the last two decades is the "stop-and-frisk" practice. Whether acting on the basis of statutory authorization or custom, many law enforcement agencies consider the procedure a valuable tool in their day-to-day battle to control criminal behavior. Although it is alleged that these practices do not conform to the "probable cause" requirement of the Fourth Amendment, the Supreme Court validated them in *Terry* v. *Ohio* (392 U.S. 1, 1968). Speaking for the eight-to-one majority, Chief Justice Earl Warren made it clear that the Court was not retreating from the warrant requirement of the Fourth Amendment but was merely applying a more practical standard in the limited search for weapons to prevent assault of the officer and others nearby. But to Justice Douglas, the lone dissenter, it was illogical to let police search without probable cause when they acted without a warrant, while they had to show probable cause if they applied to a magistrate for a warrant. He was troubled by the majority's concession of authority to the police to cope with the crisis in crime. If the strictures of the Fourth Amendment needed loosening, he felt, a constitutional amendment was necessary. But by invalidating a "frisk" in *Sibron* v. *New York* (392 U.S. 40), a case decided the same day as *Terry*, the Chief Justice appeared to allay such fears. Warren insisted that "before a police officer places a hand on . . . a citizen in search of anything," his actions must be supported by "constitutionally adequate reasonable grounds." Furthermore, he emphasized, the officer must be able to point to specific facts from which he could reasonably infer that the person stopped was armed and presented an immediate danger to him and others nearby to justify a warrantless "frisk."

In the succeeding years, however, the Burger Court rulings appeared to be considerably more flexible in applying constitutional standards to the procedure. In *Adams* v. *Williams* (407 U.S. 143, 1972), for example, a "stop-and-frisk" was held to meet constitutional requirements even if probable cause to effect an arrest was not evident. As Justice William Rehnquist, who wrote the Court's opinion, put it, "[t]he Fourth Amendment does not require a policeman who lacks the precise level of information necessary for probable cause to arrest to simply shrug his shoulders and allow a crime to occur or a criminal to escape." Furthermore, Rehnquist continued, an informant's tip, if supported by sufficient *indicia of reliability*, justifies the stop and subsequent frisk.

The three dissenters—Douglas, Brennan, and Marshall—decried this expansive interpretation of *Terry* and reiterated their understanding of the constitutional requirement that the procedure could only be invoked where direct observation of the police and other "well-authenticated information show 'that criminal activity may be afoot.'" They warned that by loosening constitutional requirements for this practice many innocent people would be subjected to police harassment with at most "the slightest suspicion of improper conduct."

In several cases following *Adams*, the Burger Court majority did not consider the "protective search" limitation of *Terry* applicable and held valid "stop-and-frisk" type searches as "incidental to lawful custodial arrests." (See *United States* v. *Robinson*, 414 U.S. 218, 1973; *Gustafson* v. *Florida*, 414 U.S. 260, 1973; and *Michigan* v. *DeFillippo*, 443 U.S. 31, 1979.) But in a 1980 "drug courier profile" case—*Reid* v. *Georgia* (448 U.S. 438)—the Court held that to justify a stop and subsequent search of a person under the Fourth Amendment more is required than an officer's conclusion that the person possesses the "characteristics . . . typical of persons unlawfully carrying narcotics." (Cf. *United States* v. *Mendenhall*, 466 U.S. 544, 1980.)

The Burger Court continued to construe *Terry* expansively well into the 1980s. In *Michigan* v. *Long* (463 U.S. 1032, 1983), for example, a roadside stop-and-frisk was approved because "roadside encounters between the police and suspects are especially hazardous," and the suspect could obtain a weapon if allowed to reenter the vehicle before it was searched. (Cf. *Kolender* v. *Lawson*, 461 U.S. 352, 1983, Justice Brennan concurring.) In another case decided two years later—*United States* v. *Hensley* (469 U.S. 221, 1985)—a wanted flyer was the justification for an investigatory stop-and-detention. Citing the "strong government interest" in controlling criminal activity and apprehending offenders. Justice O'Connor argued that reliance on a wanted flyer to stop and detain a suspect while attempting to obtain additional information can be justified under *Terry*. She noted that "restraining police action until after probable cause is obtained would not only hinder the investigation but might also enable the suspect to flee and remain at large."

Another controversial aspect of the warrantless search involves the searching of automobiles. The Supreme Court concluded more than a half-century ago in *Carroll* v. *United States*, *supra*, that it may not always be practical to obtain a warrant authorizing a search of a vehicle because it may be quickly moved out of the jurisdiction in which the warrant is sought. In his opinion for the Court, Chief Justice Taft noted that the laws of the United States recognize a difference between the searching of structures such as houses and offices and vehicular instruments such as automobiles and boats because of the different uses to which they may be put in criminal activity. The Chief Justice cautioned, however, that police do not possess the authority to indiscriminately stop people using the public highways and "subject them to the inconvenience and indignities of a search of their automobiles." Probable cause for believing that such vehicle is being used or has been used as an instrument of criminal activity must be shown.

One of the more troublesome problems for the Court in considering automobile searches has been the locus of the search. In some instances automobiles are stopped and the occupants are arrested, but the warrantless search of the impounded vehicle takes place later at the station house or in a garage. While the Court conceded that Fourth Amendment requirements are less stringent for the search of automobiles, it held, in *Preston* v. *United States* (376 U.S. 364, 1964), that such postarrest searches could not be justified as incident to arrest.

Subsequently, however, the Court construed *Preston* narrowly to uphold warrantless searches of automobiles conducted some time after arrest and impoundment upon a showing of probable cause. In *Cooper* v. *California* (386 U.S. 68, 1967), for example, the Court held valid a warrantless search of an automobile that was impounded at the time of arrest and was searched a week later in a garage. Justice Hugo Black, speaking for the five-to-four majority, emphasized that the search was "closely related" to the criminal activity for which Cooper was arrested. (See also *Chambers* v. *Maroney*, 399 U.S. 42, 1970.)

The automobile search exception to the warrant requirement was expanded significantly under the Burger Court in the 1970s and 1980s as a majority of the justices reflected an increasing sensitivity to the "realities" of current law enforcement. In *Cady* v. *Dombrowski* (413 U.S. 433, 1973), for example, the Court held that the police had followed "sound police procedure" when they had a car (disabled in a one-car accident) towed away and stored in a garage where a subsequent warrantless search uncovered evidence used to support a murder conviction. (The search was undertaken to find a gun that was thought to have been in possession of the driver, a Chicago policeman. Concern for public safety was accepted by the Court as sufficient justification.)

Likewise, in *Cardwell* v. *Lewis* (417 U.S. 583, 1974), the four Nixon appointees were joined by Justice Byron White to uphold a warrantless examination of the exterior of an automobile. The plurality opinion of Justice Blackmun emphasized that "the search of an automobile is far less intrusive on [Fourth Amendment rights] than the search of one's person or of a building." Hence, there is less expectation of privacy, and certainly, Blackmun contended, no privacy was infringed by taking scrapings of paint and an impression of a tire of an automobile while impounded by the police.

Controversial warrantless searches of automobiles by border patrol authorities enforcing immigration laws got the attention of the Burger Court in the mid-1970s. In *Almeida Sanchez* v. *United States* (413 U.S. 917, 1973), the Court recognized unconsented warrantless searches of vehicles by roving border patrols as constitutionally permissible. However, the Court cautioned that because such procedures "impinged so significantly on Fourth Amendment privacy interest," there must be probable cause to believe that the occupants of the vehicle are illegal aliens. But two years later, the Court relaxed Fourth Amendment requirements in *United States* v. *Brignoni Ponce* (422 U.S. 873, 1975). There, the majority felt that the practice of stopping motorists in the general vicinity of the Mexican border and inquiring as to their residence status was only a "modest" infringement on Fourth Amendment guarantees when balanced against governmental law enforcement interests. Consequently, the Court concluded that the stop need not be justified by probable cause; the "stopping officer's" suspicion that the vehicle contained illegal aliens would suffice.

In companion 1976 cases—*United States* v. *Martin-Fuerte* and *Sifuentes* v. *United States* (428 U.S. 543)—the probable cause requirements to support border patrol automobile searches were relaxed further. While reaffirming the *Brignoni Ponce* holding, the Court held that motorists routinely stopped at permanent checkpoints could be selectively sent to secondary screening areas for more extensive questioning about their immigration status. Furthermore, the Court saw no constitutional bar to referrals, even if Mexican ancestry of the motorist was the prime consideration.

During the same term, the Court approved a warrantless "caretaking inventory search" of an impounded automobile (*South Dakota* v. *Opperman*, 428 U.S. 364, 1976). Here the Court rejected a claim that the marijuana discovered during the search should have been suppressed at trial as "fruits of an illegal search" and emphasized the reduced expectation of privacy in one's automobile when compared to the home or office.

But three years later, the Court appeared to backtrack somewhat when it considered the routine "spot check" practice in *Delaware* v. *Prouse* (440 U.S. 686, 1979). Justice Byron White emphasized the probable cause requirement and asserted that the state's interest in promoting highway safety by employing the "spot check" practice does not outweigh the privacy interest of those randomly stopped. But a decade later, in *Michigan Department of State Police* v. *Sitz* (110 S. Ct. 2481, 1990), Chief Justice Rehnquist led the Court in a six-to-three decision in approving of Michigan's highway sobri-

ety checkpoint program that had been challenged as infringing the seizure protection of the Fourth Amendment. While recognizing that the checkpoint stop procedure constitutes a seizure within the meaning of the Fourth Amendment, Rehnquist emphasized that the state's "grave and legitimate interest in curbing drunken driving" along with the minimal intrusion resulting from the police practices and procedures leads to the conclusion that the program is a reasonable means of advancing that interest.

Justice Brennan's dissent, in which Justice Marshall joined, focused on the probable cause requirement of the Fourth Amendment for the seizure to be reasonable. To him, the essence of the majority's holding was that "no level of suspicion is necessary before" stopping a car in the enforcement of a drunk driving program. In the end, he warned that the relaxation of Fourth Amendment imperatives "for the purpose of preventing drunken driving" could have the potential of subjecting the public to police harassment.

While expanding the use of warrantless searches of automobiles, several decisions of the Court in the late 1970s and into the early 1980s evince some uncertainty in extending that exception to "containers" (such as luggage) and/or other articles that are found in the automobile being searched. For example, in *United States* v. *Chadwick* (433 U.S. 1, 1977), the Court would not allow either expansion of the automobile exception or a search incidental to a lawful arrest to justify the warrantless search of a closed footlocker that had been seized from the trunk of the suspect's automobile. Emphasizing the "expectation of privacy" principle, Chief Justice Warren Burger took judicial notice of the absence of "exigencies" that required an immediate search "without the safeguards a judicial warrant provides." The general principle was reaffirmed, and *Chadwick* was clarified in *Arkansas* v. *Sanders* (442 U.S. 753, 1979). Stressing the expectation of privacy principle and the fact that the luggage found in the vehicle was under police control with no danger of its contents being removed before obtaining a proper search warrant, the Court concluded that "there is no greater need for warrantless searches of luggage taken from automobiles than of luggage taken from other places."

Two years later, in *Robbins* v. *California* (453 U.S. 420, 1981), the Court (although only a plurality), refused to make a distinction between containers like luggage and "flimsier" items such as "plastic bags" and "cardboard boxes" discovered during the course of warrantless automobile searches. But the Court did suggest that "transparency" and "distinctive configuration" that make contents apparent could bring a warrantless search of such containers within the "plain view" exception.

In a decision on the same day, however, a different configuration of justices appeared to retreat from the *Chadwick-Sanders-Robbins* position. There, in *New York* v. *Belton* (453 U.S. 454, 1981), a warrantless search of an unzipped pocket of a jacket uncovered in the search of an automobile was held valid as a search incident to a lawful arrest. With such justification, the Court concluded, the search of a container may be conducted whether it is open or closed.

Finally, in *United States* v. *Ross* (456 U.S. 798, 1982), the Court rejected its *Robbins* decision and abandoned some of the reasoning supporting *Sanders* in expanding police discretion in container searches. The "nice distinctions" between opened and closed containers could be brushed aside when officers, having probable cause to stop and subsequently search an automobile, believe that containers found therein conceal contraband. As Justice John Paul Stevens pointed out, "the scope of [a] warrantless search of [an] automobile is not defined by [the] nature of [the] container in which the contraband is secreted but rather is defined by the object of the search and places in which there is probable cause to believe that it may be found."

Following this line of reasoning and buttressed by the "plain view" doctrine, the Court in *Texas* v. *Brown* (460 U.S. 730, 1983) did not consider unreasonable the warrantless seizure of balloons containing drugs from the opened glove compartment of an automobile that they observed during a routine license check. The fact that the officer spotted the contraband after shifting his position and shining his flashlight in the car was considered irrelevant "to Fourth Amendment analysis." And in 1985 in *United States* v. *Johns* (105 S. Ct. 881), the Court construed *Ross* expansively as authority for a warrantless search of several packages suspected of containing marijuana that had been seized from an automobile and held in a warehouse for three days before the search. The Court rejected the court of appeals' view that there had been ample time to obtain a search warrant.

The warrantless search was extended to the sensitive setting of the public school in *New Jersey* v. *T.L.O.* (469 U.S. 325) in 1985 to allow broadened discretion of school officials in their effort to combat the drug problem. While recognizing the Fourth Amendment rights of students, the six-to-three majority gave considerable weight to the school's "substantial interest" in maintaining discipline in the face of mounting drug and other criminal activity in the schools. Hence, it concluded that searches by school authorities should not be subjected to the more stringent probable cause requirement demanded of other public officials. Rather, a test of "reasonableness under all circumstances" was deemed sufficient.

However, the same Court did not think it was necessary to narrow Fourth Amendment rights in a different context—the apprehension of a fleeing unarmed felony suspect. Thus, in *Tennessee* v. *Garner* (471 U.S. 1, 1985), the Court agreed with the Court of Appeals for the Sixth Circuit that a Tennessee law that permitted police to "use all necessary means" to apprehend a fleeing felony suspect was unconstitutional because it made no distinction between an armed suspect and an unarmed one in the use of deadly force. Apprehending suspects by the use of deadly force is a seizure, Justice Byron White contended, and necessarily triggers the reasonableness requirement of the Fourth Amendment. For him, such cases present competing interests, and the government's interest in promoting effective law enforcement is insufficient to outweigh a fleeing suspect's "fundamental interest in his own life." Absent a threat to the officer and others, deadly force cannot be justified in apprehending a suspect. "A police officer," he concluded, "may not seize an unarmed, nondangerous suspect by shooting him."

But *Garner* does not represent a retreat from warrantless search doctrine. This was made clear in the first term of the Rehnquist Court when the Court, in *Colorado* v. *Bertine* (107 S. Ct. 738, 1987), reaffirmed warrantless "caretaking" searches of automobiles and, in *New York* v. *Burger* (107 S. Ct. 1492, 1987), approved a state statutory procedure for the warrantless inspection of certain commercial establishments. What was probably the strongest reaffirmation of the warrantless search doctrine of the initial Rehnquist Court was made by Justice Sandra Day O'Connor in *O'Connor* v. *Ortega* (107 S. Ct. 1492, 1987). In approving supervisory searches in work-related contexts, the justice held that only a standard of "reasonableness" is required of supervisors when they make warrantless searches of employees' desks, file cabinets, and so forth. The "operational realities of the workplace" justified, for her, this supervisory method of investigating employee work-related conduct and outweighed their privacy claims.[10] Certainly, *Ortega* has

[10]The conflict between privacy interests and administrative searches has been considered by the Court in a number of cases over the last several decades. See, for example, *Frank* v. *Maryland* (359 U.S. 360, 1959); *Camara* v. *Municipal Court of San*

implications for the issue of mandatory employee drug testing, but O'Connor indicated that the issue would not be addressed in the *Ortega* context. But this and other issues such as an employee's right to control the content of electronic mail (E-Mail) and computer discs, containing his/her creative input, will undoubtedly produce a variety of Fourth Amendment issues that will find their way to the Supreme Court during the remainder of the 1990s and into the 21st century.

One year later, approval of warrantless searches in the workplace was followed by approval of such searches in residential garbage containers. In *California* v. *Greenwood* (108 S. Ct. 1625, 1988), the justices gave the police a boost in their effort to track down drug pushers. Rejecting claims of expectation of privacy in garbage bags left at the curbside for the garbage truck, Justice White made it clear that when a garbage bag is left along the curb of a public street for the trash collector, it becomes readily accessible to the public passersby and that it is reasonable for the police to request those bags from the garbage collector. He concluded that in this context, Greenwood's expectation of privacy claim must be rejected because society at large does not accept such claims "as objectively reasonable."[11]

Greenwood illustrates well the continuing debate about the amount of latitude the Constitution allows law enforcement agencies in criminal investigations. Justice Brennan points to the dangers of approval of such police behavior for society at large in his dissent. Noting the potential that such a practice has for the invasion of intimate aspects of an individual's life, Brennan thought that police rummaging through one's garbage without a proper search warrant is "contrary to commonly accepted notions of civilized behavior." Brennan concluded with this view of liberty in our society:

> The American society with which I am familiar "chooses to dwell in reasonable security and freedom from surveillance," . . . and is more dedicated to individual liberty and more sensitive to intrusions on the sanctity of the home than the Court is willing to acknowledge.

On the other hand, however, given society's almost hysterical concern for control of criminal activity, the majority of the justices may well feel that the more restricted construction of the Fourth Amendment set forth in *Greenwood* comes closer to society's current notions on privacy and that they can more readily accept warrantless searches that are conducted in a variety of law enforcement contexts as we move toward the twenty-first century.

Francisco (387 U.S. 523, 1967); *United States* v. *Biswell* (406 U.S. 311, 1972); *Marshall* v. *Barlow* (436 U.S. 307, 1978); *Michigan* v. *Tyler* (436 U.S. 499, 1978); and *Donovan* v. *Dewey* (452 U.S. 594, 1981).

[11]Cf. *United States* v. *Knotts* (460 U.S. 276, 1983), where the Court did not consider police action to hide an electronic beeper monitoring device in materials purchased by a person for use in the production of illicit drugs in order to track him to his production facility an invasion of any lawful expectation of privacy. Recognizing as constitutionally permissible police use of "scientific and technological development" to augment their sensory faculties, Justice Rehnquist made it clear that the beeper is used to track movement on public streets and highways and that a person traveling in an automobile on such thoroughfares certainly "has no reasonable expectation of privacy." The attempt to taint the evidence obtained under a subsequent search warrant issued after intermittent surveillance of the "drug factory" because of the warrantless use of the "beeper" in locating the facility was rejected because use of the "beeper" to track the movement of a chemical in an automobile was "neither search nor seizure" within contemplation of the Fourth Amendment.

Note also the Court's rejection of the expectation of privacy claim in *California* v. *Ciraolo* (106 U.S. 1809, 1986), where the warrantless aerial observation of an enclosed backyard within the curtilage of a home identified growing marijuana was not considered to abridge Fourth Amendment rights. The justices reasoned that aircrafts flying over private property at an altitude of 1,000 feet (as in *Ciraolo*) are commonplace and that there cannot be a reasonable expectancy of privacy where such property is clearly visible to the "unaided eye."

The Court extended *Ciraolo* to cover low-flying helicopter observances over private property three years later in *Florida* v. *Riley* (109 S. Ct. 693, 1989), where evidence used to support a conviction for growing marijuana was developed from a helicopter flying 400 feet over a greenhouse. Justice Byron White's plurality opinion stressed the helicopter operator's conformity with regulations governing the use of airspace.

JUSTICE WHITE *delivered the opinion of the Court.*

The issue here is whether the Fourth Amendment prohibits the warrantless search and seizure of garbage left for collection outside the curtilage of a home. We conclude . . . that it does not.

I

In early 1984, Investigator Jenny Stracner of the Laguna Beach Police Department received information indicating that respondent Greenwood might be engaged in narcotics trafficking. Stracner learned that a criminal suspect had informed a federal drug-enforcement agent in February 1984 that a truck filled with illegal drugs was en route to the Laguna Beach address at which Greenwood resided. In addition, a neighbor complained of heavy vehicular traffic late at night in front of Greenwood's single-family home which . . . remained [there] . . . for only a few minutes.

Stracner sought to investigate this information by conducting a surveillance of Greenwood's home. . . .

On April 6, 1984, Stracner asked the neighborhood's regular trash collector to pick up the plastic garbage bags that Greenwood had left on the curb in front of his house and to turn the bags over to her without mixing their contents with garbage from other houses. The trash collector cleaned his truck bin of other refuse, collected the garbage bags from the street in front of Greenwood's house, and turned the bags over to Stracner. The officer searched through the rubbish and found items indicative of narcotics use. She recited the information that she had gleaned from the trash search in an affidavit in support of a warrant to search Greenwood's home.

Police officers encountered both respondents at the house later that day when they arrived to execute the warrant. The police discovered quantities of cocaine and hashish during their search of the house. Respondents were arrested on felony narcotics charges. . . .

The police continued to receive reports of many late-night visitors to the Greenwood house. On May 4, Investigator Robert Rahaeuser obtained Greenwood's garbage from the regular trash collector in the same manner as had Stracner. The garbage again contained evidence of narcotics use.

. . . [Another warrant was obtained on basis of the second trash search, and Greenwood was arrested for a second time.]

The Superior Court dismissed the charges against respondents . . . [holding] that warrantless trash searches violate the Fourth Amendment and the California Constitution. The court found that the police would not have had probable cause to search the Greenwood home without the evidence obtained from the trash searches.

The Court of Appeal affirmed . . . [and] [t]he California Supreme Court denied the State's petition for review of the Court of Appeals' decision. We granted certiorari . . . and now reverse.

II

The warrantless search and seizure of the garbage bags left at the curb outside the Greenwood house would violate the Fourth Amendment only if respondents manifested a subjective expectation of privacy in their garbage that society accepts as objectively reasonable. . . . Respondents do not disagree with this standard.

They assert, however, that they had, and exhibited, an expectation of privacy with respect to the trash that was searched by the police. The trash, which was placed on the street for collection at a fixed time, was contained in opaque plastic bags, which the garbage collector was expected to pick up, mingle with the trash of others, and deposit at the garbage dump. The trash was only temporarily on the street, and there was little likelihood that it would be inspected by anyone.

It may well be that respondents did not expect that the contents of their garbage bags would become known to the police or other members of the public. An expectation of privacy does not give rise to Fourth Amendment protection, however, unless society is prepared to accept that expectation as objectively reasonable.

Here, we conclude that respondents exposed their garbage to the public sufficiently to defeat their claim to Fourth Amendment protection. It is common knowledge that plastic garbage bags left on or at the side of a public street are readily accessible to animals, children, scavengers, snoops, and other members of the public. Moreover, respondents placed their refuse at the curb for the express purpose of conveying it to a third party, the trash collector, who might himself have sorted through respondents' trash or permitted others, such as the police, to do so. Accordingly, having deposited their garbage "in an area particularly suited for public inspection and, in a manner of speaking, public consumption, for the express purpose of having strangers take it," . . . respondents could have had no reasonable expectation of privacy in the inculpatory items that they discarded.

Furthermore, as we have held, the police cannot reasonably be expected to avert their eyes from evidence of criminal activity that could have been observed by any member of the public. Hence, "[w]hat a person knowingly exposes to the public, even in his own home or office, is not a subject of Fourth Amendment protection." . . .

Our conclusion that society would not accept as reasonable respondents' claim to an expectation of privacy in trash left for collection in an area accessible to the public is reinforced by the unanimous rejection of similar claims by the Federal Courts of Appeals. . . . In *United States* v. *Thornton*, 241 U.S. App.D.C. 46, 56, and n. 11, 746 F.2d 39, 49 and n. 11 (1984), the court observed that "the overwhelming weight of authority rejects the proposition that a reasonable expectation of privacy exists with respect to trash discarded outside the home and the curtilage [*sic*] thereof." In addition, of those state appellate courts that have considered the issue the vast majority have held that the police may conduct warrantless searches and seizures of garbage discarded in public areas. . . .

III

We reject respondent Greenwood's alternative argument for affirmance: that his expectation of privacy in his garbage should be deemed reasonable as a matter of federal constitutional law because the warrantless search and seizure of his garbage was impermissible as a matter of California law. He urges that the state-law right of Californians to privacy in their garbage, announced by the California Supreme Court in *People* v. *Krivda*, 486 P.2d 1262, survived the subsequent state constitutional amendment eliminating the suppression remedy as a means of enforcing that right. . . . Hence, he argues that the Fourth Amendment should itself vindicate that right.

Individual States may surely construe their own constitutions as imposing more stringent constraints on police conduct than does the Federal Constitution. We have never intimated, however, that whether or not a search is reasonable within

the meaning of the Fourth Amendment depends on the law of the particular State in which the search occurs. We have emphasized instead that the Fourth Amendment analysis must turn on such factors as "our *societal* understanding that certain areas deserve the most scrupulous protection from government invasion." . . . We have already concluded that society as a whole possesses no such understanding with regard to garbage left for collection at the side of a public street. Respondent's argument is no less than a suggestion that concepts of privacy under the laws of each State are to determine the reach of the Fourth Amendment. We do not accept this submission. . . .

The judgment of the California Court of Appeal is . . . reversed and this case is remanded for further proceedings not inconsistent with this opinion.

It is so ordered.

[JUSTICE KENNEDY took no part in the consideration or decision of this case.]

JUSTICE BRENNAN, *with whom* JUSTICE MARSHALL *joins, dissenting.*

Every week for two months, and at least once more a month later, the Laguna Beach police clawed through the trash that respondent Greenwood left in opaque, sealed bags on the curb outside his home. Complete strangers minutely scrutinized their bounty, undoubtedly dredging up intimate details of Greenwood's private life and habits. The intrusions proceeded without a warrant, and no court before or since has concluded that the police acted on probable cause to believe Greenwood was engaged in any criminal activity.

Scrutiny of another's trash is contrary to commonly accepted notions of civilized behavior. I suspect, therefore, that members of our society will be shocked to learn that the Court, the ultimate guarantor of liberty, deems unreasonable our expectation that the aspects of our private lives that are concealed safely in a trash bag will not become public.

I

"A container which can support a reasonable expectation of privacy may not be searched even on probable cause, without a warrant" *United States* v. *Jacobsen*, 466 U.S. 109, 120, n. 17 (1984). Thus, as the Court observes, if Greenwood had a reasonable expectation that the contents of the bags that he placed on the curb would remain private, the warrantless search of those bags violated the Fourth Amendment.

The Framers of the Fourth Amendment understood that "unreasonable searches" of "paper[s] and effects"—no less than "unreasonable searches" of "person[s] and houses"—infringe privacy. . . .

Our precedent . . . leaves no room to doubt that had respondents been carrying their personal effects in opaque, sealed plastic bags—identical to the ones they placed on the curb—their privacy would have been protected from warrantless police intrusion. So far as Fourth Amendment protection is concerned, opaque plastic bags are every bit as worthy as "packages wrapped in green opaque plastic" and "double-locked footlocker[s]." . . .

II

Respondents deserve no less protection just because Greenwood used the bags to discard rather than to transport his personal effects. Their contents are not inherently any less private, and Greenwood's decision to discard them, at least in the manner in which he did, does not diminish his expectation of privacy.

A trash bag, like any of the above-mentioned containers, "is a common repository for one's personal effects" and, even more than many of them, is "therefore . . . inevitably associated with the expectation of privacy." . . . A single bag of trash testifies eloquently to the eating, reading, and recreational habits of the person who produced it. A search of trash, like a search of the bedroom, can relate intimate details about sexual practices, health, and personal hygiene. Like rifling through desk drawers or intercepting phone calls, rummaging through trash can divulge the target's financial and professional status, political affiliations and inclinations, private thoughts, personal relationships, and romantic interests. It cannot be doubted that a sealed trash bag harbors telling evidence of the "intimate activity associated with the 'sanctity of a man's home and the privacies of life,'" which the Fourth Amendment is designed to protect. . . .

The Court properly rejects the State's attempt to distinguish trash searches from other searches on the theory that trash is abandoned and therefore not entitled to an expectation of privacy. As the author of the Court's opinion observed last Term, a defendant's "property interest [in trash] does not settle the matter for Fourth Amendment purposes, for the reach of the Fourth Amendment is not determined by state property law." . . .

Beyond a generalized expectation of privacy, many municipalities, whether for reasons of privacy, sanitation, or both, reinforce confidence in the integrity of sealed trash containers by "prohibit[ing] anyone, except authorized employees of the Town. . . . to rummage into, pick up, collect, move or otherwise interfere with articles or materials placed on . . . any public street for collection." *United States* v. *Dzialak*, 441 F.2d 212, 215 (CA2 1971) (paraphrasing ordinance for town of Cheektowaga, New York). . . .

That is not to deny that isolated intrusions into opaque, sealed trash containers occur. When, acting on their own, "animals, children, scavengers, snoops, [or] other members of the general public" . . . *actually* rummage through a bag of trash and expose its contents to plain view, "police cannot reasonably be expected to avert their eyes from evidence of criminal activity that could have been observed by any member of the public." . . .

Had Greenwood flaunted his intimate activity by strewing his trash all over the curb for all to see, or had some nongovernmental intruder invaded his privacy and done the same, I could accept the Court's conclusion that an expectation of privacy would have been unreasonable. Similarly, had police searching the city dump run across incriminating evidence that, despite commingling with the trash of others, still retained its identity as Greenwood's, we would have a different case. But all that Greenwood "exposed . . . to the public" were the exteriors of several opaque, sealed containers. Until the bags were opened by police, they hid their contents from the public's view. . . . Faithful application of the warrant requirement does not require police to "avert their eyes from evidence of criminal activity that could have been observed by any member of the public." Rather, it only requires them to adhere to norms of privacy that members of the public plainly acknowledge.

The mere *possibility* that unwelcome meddlers *might* open and rummage through the containers does not negate the expectation of privacy in its contents any more than the possibility of a burglary negates an expectation of privacy in the home; or the possibility of a private intrusion negates an expectation of privacy in an unopened package; or the possibility that an operator will listen in on a telephone conversation negates an expectation of privacy in the words spoken on the telephone. "What a person . . . seeks to preserve as private, *even in an area accessible to the public,* may be constitutionally protected." *Katz*, 389 U.S., at 351–352 (1967). . . .

III

In holding that the warrantless search of Greenwood's trash was consistent with the Fourth Amendment, the Court paints a grim picture of our society. It depicts a society in which local authorities may command their citizens to dispose of their personal effects in the manner least protective of the "sanctity of [the] home and the privacies of life," *Boyd* v. *United States*, 116 U.S., at 630 (1886), and then monitor them arbitrarily and without judicial oversight—a society that is not prepared to recognize as reasonable an individual's expectation of privacy in the most private of personal effects sealed in an opaque container and disposed of in a manner designed to commingle it imminently and inextricably with the trash of others. The American society with which I am familiar "chooses to dwell in reasonable security and freedom from surveillance," *Johnson* v. *United States*, 333 U.S. 10, 14 (1948), and is more dedicated to individual liberty and more sensitive to intrusions on the sanctity of the home than the Court is willing to acknowledge.

I dissent.

FLORIDA v. BOSTICK
___ U.S. ___; ___ L. Ed. 2d ___; 111 S. Ct. 2382 (1991)

JUSTICE O'CONNOR *delivered the opinion of the Court.*

I

Drug interdiction efforts have led to the use of police surveillance at airports, train stations, and bus depots. Law enforcement officers stationed at such locations routinely approach individuals, either randomly or because they suspect in some vague way that the individuals may be engaged in criminal activity, and ask them potentially incriminating questions. Broward County has adopted such a program. County Sheriff's Department officers routinely board buses at scheduled stops and ask passengers for permission to search their luggage.

In this case, two officers discovered cocaine when they searched a suitcase belonging to Terrance Bostick. The underlying facts of the search are in dispute, but the Florida Supreme Court, whose decision we review here, stated explicitly the factual premise for its decision:

> "Two officers, complete with badges, insignia and one of them holding a recognizable zipper pouch, containing a pistol, boarded a bus bound from Miami to Atlanta during a stopover in Fort Lauderdale. Eyeing the passengers, the officers admittedly without articulable suspicion, picked out the defendant passenger and asked to inspect his ticket and identification. The ticket, from Miami to Atlanta, matched the defendant's identification and both were immediately returned to him as unremarkable. However, the two police officers persisted and explained their presence as narcotics agents on the lookout for illegal drugs. In pursuit of that aim, they then requested the defendant's consent to search his luggage. Needless to say, there is a conflict in the evidence about whether the defendant consented to the search of the second bag in which the contraband was found and as to whether he was informed of his right to refuse consent. However, any conflict must be resolved in favor of the state, it being a question of fact decided by the trial judge." . . .

Two facts are particularly worth noting. First, the police specifically advised Bostick that he had the right to refuse consent. Bostick appears to have disputed the point, but, as the Florida Supreme Court noted explicitly, the trial court resolved this evidentiary conflict in the State's favor. Second, at no time did the officers threaten Bostick with a gun. The Florida Supreme Court indicated that one officer carried a zipper pouch containing a pistol—the equivalent of carrying a gun in a holster—but the court did not suggest that the gun was ever removed from its pouch, pointed at Bostick, or otherwise used in a threatening manner. The dissent's characterization of the officers [as] "gun-wielding inquisitor[s]" is colorful, but lacks any basis in fact.

Bostick was arrested and charged with trafficking in cocaine. He moved to suppress the cocaine on the grounds that it had been seized in violation of his Fourth Amendment rights. The trial court denied the motion but made no factual findings. Bostick subsequently entered a plea of guilty, but reserved the right to appeal the denial of motion to suppress.

The Florida District Court of Appeal affirmed, but considered the issue sufficiently important that it certified a question to the Florida Supreme Court. The Supreme Court reasoned that Bostick had been seized because a reasonable passenger in his situation would have felt free to leave the bus to avoid questioning by the police. It rephrased and answered the certified question so as to make the bus setting dispositive in every case. It ruled categorically that " 'an impermissible seizure result[s] when police mount a drug search on buses during scheduled stops and question boarded passengers without articulable reasons for doing so, thereby obtaining consent to search the passengers' luggage.' " The Florida Supreme Court thus adopted a *per se* rule that the Broward County Sheriff's practice of "working the buses" is unconstitutional. The result of this decision is that police in Florida, as elsewhere, may approach persons at random in most public places, ask them questions and seek consent to a search, but they may not engage in the same behavior on a bus. . . .

II

The sole issue presented for our review is whether a police encounter on a bus of the type described above necessarily constitutes a "seizure" within the meaning of the Fourth Amendment. The State concedes, and we accept for purposes of this decision, that the officers lacked the reasonable suspicion required to justify a seizure and that, if a seizure took place, the drugs found in Bostick's suitcase must be suppressed as tainted fruit.

Our cases make it clear that a seizure does not occur simply because a police officer approaches an individual and asks a few questions. So long as a reasonable person would feel free "to disregard the police and go about his business," the encounter is consensual and no reasonable suspicion is required. The encounter will not trigger Fourth Amendment scrutiny unless it loses its consensual nature. . . .

Since [*Terry* v. *Ohio*, 392 U.S. 1, 1968], we have held repeatedly that mere police questioning does not constitute seizure. In *Florida* v. *Royer*, 460 U.S. 491 (1983) (plurality opinion), for example, we explained that "law enforcement officers do not violate the Fourth Amendment by merely approaching an individual on the street or in another public place, by asking him if he is willing to answer some questions, by putting questions to him if the person is willing to listen, or by offering in evidence in a criminal prosecution his voluntary answers to such questions."

There is no doubt that if this same encounter had taken place before Bostick boarded the bus or in the lobby of the bus terminal, it would not rise to the level of a seizure. The Court has dealt with similar encounters in airports and has found them to be "the sort of consensual encounter[s] that implicat[e] no Fourth Amendment interest." *Florida* v. *Rodriguez*, 469 U.S. 1, 5–6, (1984). We have stated that even when officers have no basis for suspecting a particular individual, they may generally ask questions of that individual, ask to examine the individual's identification . . . and request consent to search his or her luggage, as long as the police do not convey a message that compliance with their requests is required.

Bostick insists that this case is different because it took place in the cramped confines of a bus. A police encounter is much more intimidating in this setting, he argues, because police tower over a seated passenger and there is little room to move around. . . . Bostick maintains that a reasonable bus passenger would not have felt free to leave under the circumstances of this case because there is nowhere to go on a bus. Also, the bus was about to depart. Had Bostick disembarked, he would have risked being stranded and losing whatever baggage he had locked away in the luggage compartment.

The Florida Supreme Court found this argument persuasive, so much so that it adopted a *per se* rule prohibiting the police from randomly boarding buses as a means of drug interdiction. The state court erred, however, in focusing on whether Bostick was "free to leave" rather than on the principle that those words were intended to capture. When police attempt to question a person who is walking down the street or through an airport lobby, it makes sense to inquire whether a reasonable person would feel free to continue walking. But when the person is seated on a bus and has no desire to leave, the degree to which a reasonable person would feel that he or she could leave is not an accurate measure of the coercive effect of the encounter.

Here, for example, the mere fact that Bostick did not feel free to leave the bus does not mean that the police seized him. Bostick was a passenger on a bus that was scheduled to depart. He would not have felt free to leave the bus even if the police had not been present. Bostick's movements were "confined" in a sense, but this was the natural result of his decision to take the bus; it says nothing about whether or not the police conduct at issue was coercive.

. . . [His] freedom of movement was restricted by a factor independent of police conduct—*i.e.*, by his being a passenger on a bus. Accordingly, the "free to leave" analysis on which Bostick relies is inapplicable. In such a situation, the appropriate inquiry is whether a reasonable person would feel free to decline the officers' request or otherwise terminate the encounter. This formulation follows logically from prior cases and breaks no new ground. We have said before that the crucial test is whether, taking into account all of the circumstances surrounding the encounter, the police conduct would "have communicated to a reasonable person that he was not at liberty to ignore the police presence and go about his business." . . . We have consistently held that a refusal to cooperate . . . does not furnish the minimal level of objective justification needed for a detention or seizure.

The facts of this case . . . leave some doubt whether a seizure occurred. . . . [N]o seizure occurs when police ask questions of an individual, ask to examine the individual's identification, and request consent to search his or her luggage—so long as the officers do not convey a message that compliance with their requests is not required. Here, the facts . . . indicate that the officers did not point guns at Bostick or otherwise threaten him and that they specifically advised Bostick that he could refuse consent.

Nevertheless, we refrain from deciding whether or not a seizure occurred in this case. The trial court made no express findings of fact, and the Florida Supreme Court rested its decision on a single fact—that the encounter took place on a bus—rather than on the totality of the circumstances. We remand so that the Florida courts may evaluate the seizure question under the correct legal standard. We do reject, however, Bostick's argument that he must have been seized because no reasonable person would freely consent to a search of luggage that he or she knows contains drugs. This argument cannot prevail because the "reasonable person" test presupposes an *innocent* person. . . .

. . . Clearly, a bus passenger's decision to cooperate with the law enforcement officers authorizes the police to conduct a search without first obtaining a warrant *only* if the cooperation is voluntary. "Consent" that is the product of official intimidation or harassment is not consent at all. Citizens do not forfeit their constitutional rights when they are coerced to comply with a request that they would prefer to refuse. The question to be decided by the Florida courts on remand is whether Bostick chose to permit the search of his luggage.

. . . Our Fourth Amendment inquiry in this case—whether a reasonable person would have felt free to decline the officers' requests or otherwise terminate the encounter—applies equally to police encounters that take place on trains, planes, and city streets. It is the dissent that would single out this particular mode of travel for differential treatment by adopting a *per se* rule that random bus searches are unconstitutional.

The dissent reserves its strongest criticism for the proposition that police officers can approach individuals as to whom they have no reasonable suspicion and ask them potentially incriminating questions. But this proposition is by no means novel; it has been endorsed by the Court any number of times. *Terry*, *Royer*, *Rodriguez*, and *Delgado* are just a few examples. As we have explained, today's decision follows logically from those decisions and breaks no new ground. Unless the dissent advocates overruling a long, unbroken line of decisions dating back more than 20 years, its criticism is not well taken. This Court . . . is not empowered to suspend constitutional guarantees so that the Government may more effectively wage a "war on drugs." If that war is to be fought, those who fight it must respect the rights of individuals, whether or not those individuals are suspected of having committed a crime. By the same token, this Court is not empowered to forbid law enforcement practices simply because it considers them distasteful. The Fourth Amendment proscribes unreasonable searches and seizures; it does not proscribe voluntary cooperation. The cramped confines of a bus are one relevant factor that should be considered in evaluating whether a passenger's consent is voluntary. We cannot agree, however, with the Florida Supreme Court that this single factor will be dispositive in every case.

We adhere to the rule that, in order to determine whether a particular encounter constitutes a seizure, a court must consider all the circumstances surrounding the encounter to determine whether the police conduct would have communicated to a reasonable person that the person was not free to decline the officers' requests or otherwise terminate the encounter. That rule applies to encounters that take place on a city street or in an airport lobby, and it applies equally on a bus. The Florida Supreme Court is reversed, and the case remanded for further proceedings not inconsistent with this opinion.

It is so ordered.

JUSTICE MARSHALL, *with whom* JUSTICE BLACKMUN *and* JUSTICE STEVENS *join, dissenting.*

* * *

I

At issue in this case is a "new and increasingly common tactic in the war on drugs": the suspicionless police sweep of buses in interstate or intrastate travel. . . . Typically under this technique, a group of state or federal officers will board a bus while it is stopped at an intermediate point on its route. Often displaying badges, weapons or other indications of authority, the officers identify themselves and announce their purpose to intercept drug traffickers. They proceed to approach individual passengers, requesting them to show identification, produce their tickets, and explain the purpose of their travels. Never do the officers advise the passengers that they are free not to speak with the officers. An "interview" of this type ordinarily culminates in a request for consent to search the passenger's luggage.

The sweeps are conducted in "dragnet" style. The police admittedly act without an "articulable suspicion" in deciding which buses to board and which passengers to approach for interviewing. By proceeding systematically in this fashion, the police are able to engage in a tremendously high volume of searches. . . .

To put it mildly, these sweeps "are inconvenient, intrusive, and intimidating." *United States* v. *Chandler*, 744 F. Supp., at 335. They occur within cramped confines, with officers typically placing themselves in between the passenger selected for an interview and the exit of the bus. Because the bus is only temporarily stationed at a point short of its destination, the passengers are in no position to leave as a means of evading the officers' questioning. Undoubtedly, such a sweep holds up the progress of the bus. . . . Thus, this "new and increasingly common tactic," burdens the experience of traveling by bus with a degree of governmental interference to which, until now, our society has been proudly unaccustomed. . . .

This aspect of the suspicionless sweep has not been lost on many of the lower courts called upon to review the constitutionality of this practice. Remarkably, the courts located at the heart of the "drug war" have been the most adamant in condemning this technique. As one Florida court put it:

"[T]he evidence in this cause has evoked images of other days, under other flags, when no man traveled his nation's roads or railways without fear of unwarranted interruption, by individuals who held temporary power in the Government. The spectre of American citizens being asked, by badge-wielding police, for identification, travel papers . . . is foreign to *any* fair reading of the Constitution, and its guarantee of human liberties. This is not Hitler's Berlin, nor Stalin's Moscow, nor is it white supremacist South Africa.

Yet in Broward County, Florida, these police officers approach every person on board buses and trains ('that time permits') and check identification [and] tickets, [and] ask to search luggage—all in the name of 'voluntary cooperation' with law enforcement. . . ."

The District Court for the District of Columbia spoke in equally pointed words:

It seems rather incongruous at this point in the world's history that we find totalitarian states becoming more like our free society while we in this nation are taking on their former trappings of suppressed liberties and freedoms.

* * *

"The random indiscriminate stopping and questioning of individuals on interstate buses seems to have gone too far. If this Court approves such 'bus stops' and allows prosecutions to be based on evidence seized as a result of such 'stops,' then we will have stripped our citizens of basic Constitutional protections. Such action would be inconsistent with what this nation has stood for during its 200 years of existence. If passengers on a bus passing through the Capital of this great nation cannot be free from police interference where there is absolutely no basis for the police officers to stop and question them, then the police will be free to accost people on our streets without any reason or cause. In this 'anything goes' war on drugs, random knocks on the doors of our citizens' homes seeking 'consent' to search for drugs cannot be far away. This is not America." *United States* v. *Lewis*, 728 F. Supp. 784, 788–789, rev'd, 287 U.S. App. D.C. 306, 921 F. 2d 1294 (1990). . . .

II

I have no objection to the manner in which the majority frames the test for determining whether a suspicionless bus sweep amounts to a Fourth Amendment "seizure." I agree that the appropriate question is whether a passenger who is approached during such a sweep "would feel free to decline the officers' requests or otherwise terminate the encounter." What I cannot understand is how the majority can possible suggest an affirmative answer to this question.

The majority reverses what it characterizes as the Florida Supreme Court's "*per se* rule" against suspicionless encounters between the police and bus passengers. . . . [T]he notion that the Florida Supreme Court decided this case on the basis of any "*per se* rule" *independent* of the facts of this case is wholly a product of the majority's imagination. As the majority acknowledges, the Florida

Supreme Court "stated explicitly the factual premise for its decision." This factual premise contained *all* of the details of the encounter between respondent and the police. The lower court's analysis of whether respondent was seized drew heavily on these facts, and the court repeatedly emphasized that its conclusion was based on "*all the circumstances*" of this case.

The majority's conclusion that the Florida Supreme Court, contrary to all appearances, *ignored* these facts is based solely on the failure of the lower court to expressly incorporate all of the facts into its reformulation of the certified question on which respondent took his appeal. The majority never explains the basis of its implausible assumption that the Florida Supreme Court intended its phrasing of the certified question to trump its opinion's careful treatment of the facts in this case. Certainly, when *this* Court issues an opinion, it does not intend lower courts and parties to treat as irrelevant the analysis of facts that the parties neglected to cram into the question presented in the petition for certiorari. But in any case, because the issue whether a seizure has occurred in any given factual setting is a question of law, nothing prevents this Court from deciding on its own whether a seizure occurred based on *all* of the facts of this case as they appear in the opinion of the Florida Supreme Court. . . .

As far as is revealed by facts on which the Florida Supreme Court premised its decision, the officers did not advise respondent that he was free to break off this "interview." Inexplicably, the majority repeatedly stresses the trial court's implicit finding that the police officers advised respondent that he was free to refuse permission to search his travel bag. This aspect of the exchange between respondent and the police is completely irrelevant to the issue before us. For as the State concedes, and as the majority purports to "accept," *if* respondent was unlawfully seized when the officers approached him and initiated questioning, the resulting search was likewise unlawful no matter how well advised respondent was of his right to refuse it. Consequently, the issue is not whether a passenger in respondent's position would have felt free to deny consent to the search of his bag, but whether such a passenger—without being apprised of his rights—would have felt free to terminate the antecedent encounter with the police.

Unlike the majority, I have no doubt that the answer to this question is no. Apart from trying to accommodate the officers, respondent had only two options. First, he could have remained seated while obstinately refusing to respond to the officers' questioning. But in light of the intimidating show of authority that the officers made upon boarding the bus, respondent reasonably could have believed that such behavior would only arouse the officers' suspicions and intensify their interrogation. Indeed, officers who carry out bus sweeps like the one at issue here frequently admit that this is the effect of a passenger's refusal to cooperate. The majority's observation that a mere refusal to answer questions, "without more," does not give rise to a reasonable basis for seizing a passenger . . . is utterly beside the point, because a passenger unadvised of his rights and otherwise unversed in constitutional law *has no reason to know* that the police cannot hold his refusal to cooperate against him. Second, respondent could have tried to escape the officers' presence by leaving the bus altogether. But because doing so would have required respondent to squeeze past the gun-wielding inquisitor who was blocking the aisle of the bus, this hardly seems like a course that respondent reasonably would have viewed as available to him. The majority lamely protests that nothing in the stipulated facts shows that the questioning officer "*point[ed]* [his] gu[n] at [respondent] or otherwise *threatened* him" with the weapon. Our decisions recognize the obvious point, however, that the choice of the police to "display" their weapons during an encounter exerts significant coercive pressure on the confronted citizen. We have never suggested that the police must go so far as to put a citizen in immediate apprehension of *being shot* before a court can take account of the intimidating effect of being questioned by an officer with weapon in hand.

Even if respondent had perceived that the officers would *let* him leave the bus, moreover, he could not reasonably have been expected to resort to this means of evading their intrusive questioning. For so far as respondent knew, the bus's departure from the terminal was imminent. Unlike a person approached by the police on the street, or at a bus or airport terminal after reaching his destination, a passenger approached by the police at an intermediate point in a long bus journey cannot simply leave the scene and repair to a safe haven to avoid unwanted probing by law-enforcement officials. The vulnerability that an intrastate or interstate traveler experiences when confronted by the police outside of his "own familiar territory" surely aggravates the coercive quality of such an encounter. . . .

Rather than requiring the police to justify the coercive tactics employed here, the majority blames respondent for his own sensation of constraint. The majority concedes that respondent "did not feel free to leave the bus" as a means of breaking off the interrogation by the Broward County officers. But this experience of confinement, the majority explains, "was the natural result of *his* decision to take the bus." Thus, in the majority's view, because respondent's "freedom of movement was restricted by a factor independent of police conduct," . . . respondent was not seized for purposes of the Fourth Amendment.

This reasoning borders on sophism and trivializes the values that underlie the Fourth Amendment. Obviously, a person's "voluntary decision" to place himself in a room with only one exit does not authorize the police to force an encounter upon him by placing themselves in front of the exit. It is no more acceptable for the police to force an encounter on a person by exploiting his "voluntary decision" to expose himself to perfectly legitimate personal or social constraints. By consciously deciding to single out persons who have undertaken interstate or intrastate travel, officers who conduct suspicionless, dragnet-style sweeps put passengers to the choice of cooperating or of exiting their buses and possibly being stranded in unfamiliar locations. It is exactly because this "choice" is no "choice" at all that police engage this technique.

In my view, the Fourth Amendment clearly condemns the suspicionless, dragnet-style sweep of intrastate or interstate buses. Withdrawing this particular weapon from the government's drug-war arsenal would hardly leave the police without any means of combatting the use of buses as instrumentalities of the drug trade. The police would remain free, for example, to approach passengers whom they have a reasonable, articulable basis to suspect of criminal wrongdoing. Alternatively, they could continue to confront passengers without suspicion so long as they took simple steps, like advising the passengers confronted of their right to decline to be questioned, to dispel the aura of coercion and intimidation that pervades such encounters. There is no reason to expect that such requirements would render the Nation's buses law-enforcement-free zones.

III

The majority attempts to gloss over the violence that today's decision does to the Fourth Amendment with empty admonitions. "If th[e] [war on drugs] is to be fought," the majority intones, "those who fight it must respect the rights of individuals, whether or not those individuals are suspected of having committed a crime." The majority's actions, however, speak louder than its words.

I dissent.

Protection Against Self-Incrimination, Right to Counsel, and Police Interrogation

FEATURED CASES

Miranda v. *Arizona*   *New York* v. *Quarles*   *Illinois* v. *Perkins*

Probably no case dealing with criminal procedure decided by the Warren Court provoked as much controversy as did its decision in *Miranda* v. *Arizona* (384 U.S. 436, 1966). Applying the guarantees of protection against compulsory self-incrimination and the assistance of counsel, state pretrial custodial procedures were subjected to searching scrutiny. In earlier years, the Court had outlawed "third degree" methods employed in a number of police departments to coerce confessions from defendants. In such cases as *Brown* v. *Mississippi* (297 U.S. 278, 1936) and *Chambers* v. *Florida* (309 U.S. 277, 1940), the Court made it clear that confessions obtained by physical coercion were inadmissible as evidence to support criminal convictions. Likewise, the Court held inadmissible confessions elicited by mental pressures and psychological ploys and trickery. (See *Spano* v. *New York*, 360 U.S. 315, 1959.)

With both physical and psychological coercion barred in eliciting confessions, the debate shifted to the appropriate test for "voluntariness." The totality of circumstances became the standard, making it considerably more difficult to make a confession stand up. In *Haynes* v. *Washington* (373 U.S. 503, 1963), for example, the Court held that a confession was involuntarily extracted because the accused was subjected to lengthy incommunicado questioning and was not allowed to call his family until after he had made a confession. The Court condemned what it characterized as a general "atmosphere of substantial coercion and inducement created by statements and actions of state authorities" in which the confession was obtained.

The long line of coerced confession cases and the more stringent requirements applied to determine voluntariness of confessions were logical developments leading to the imposition of the self-incrimination provision of the Fifth Amendment on the states in *Malloy* v. *Hogan* (378 U.S. 1, 1964). Justice William J. Brennan took note of the shift to the federal standard in many post-*Twining* and *Adamson* state cases and concluded that such a "shift reflects recognition that the American system of criminal prosecution is accusatory, not inquisitorial, and that the Fifth Amendment privilege is its essential mainstay."

Subsequent actions immediately following *Malloy* underscored the significance of the self-incrimination guarantee when applied to a number of then current criminal and administrative procedures. On the same day that it announced its *Malloy* ruling, the Court decided the related issue of whether one jurisdiction in our federal system (a state) may compel a witness to answer questions after a grant of immunity from prosecution under its laws, while simultaneously leaving him or her open to prosecution in another jurisdiction (the federal government) on the basis of testimony thus disclosed. In *Murphy* v. *Waterfront Commission of New York Harbor* (378 U.S. 52, 1964), the Court foreclosed this possibility and declared that "in light of the history, policies and purposes of the privilege against self-incrimination . . . [the privilege] protects a state witness against incrimination under federal as well as state law and a federal witness against incrimination under state law as well as federal law." And in *Griffin* v. *California* (380 U.S. 609, 1965), the Court cited *Malloy* as authority to strike down the "comment" rule (on the failure of the defendant to testify at his trial) that had been approved almost sixty years earlier in *Twining* and reaffirmed in *Adamson*.

But the Court was not so generous when asked to discard another precedent on the authority of *Malloy* and its earlier decision in *Mapp* v. *Ohio*. In *Schmerber* v. *California* (384 U.S. 755, 1966), the Court was asked to reverse a conviction where evidence of intoxication was obtained from a blood sample taken from the injured petitioner (at the direction of the police and over his objection) while in the emergency room of a hospital. In rejecting the petitioner's claim that the action abridged the privilege against self-incrimination, Justice William J. Brennan's opinion for the majority stressed the testimonial and communicative na-

ture of evidence to which the privilege extended. He concluded that the withdrawal of blood under the circumstances did not involve the type of compulsion condemned by the Constitution. This holding was extended 17 years later when, in *South Dakota* v. *Neville* (459 U.S. 553, 1983) the Court upheld a state statute that, while allowing a person suspected of drunk driving to refuse to submit to a blood-alcohol test, permits such refusal to be admitted as evidence against the suspect at trial. Justice Sandra Day O'Connor made it clear that a refusal to submit to the test after an officer has requested it and submission of that fact to the court is not a coercive act that infringes the guarantee against compulsory self-incrimination.[12]

Three years after deciding *Gideon* and two years after *Malloy*, the Court combined these "double-barrelled" guarantees to those accused of crime to place very strict restrictions on custodial interrogation practices of state law enforcement officers in the landmark case of *Miranda* v. *Arizona*. Over two decades earlier the Court had curbed federal officials when, in *McNabb* v. *United States* (318 U.S. 332, 1943), it construed federal rules of criminal procedure to require that persons arrested for federal crimes be taken before a U.S. Commissioner "without unnecessary delay" for a hearing in which the arresting officer would have to show that probable cause existed for the arrest and the accused would be informed of his or her rights. This sanction was enforced by excluding evidence obtained "in default of the statutory obligation." The Court reaffirmed this rule in *Mallory* v. *United States* (354 U.S. 449, 1957); this, together with stricter standards governing the determination of "voluntariness" of confessions and the *Gideon* and *Malloy* decisions obligating the states to abide by the Sixth Amendment requirement of counsel and the Fifth Amendment strictures on compulsory self-incrimination, respectively, inevitably led the Court to its

[12]Cf. *Winston* v. *Lee* (105 S. Ct. 1611, 1985), where the Court unanimously affirmed a ruling of the Court of Appeals for the Fourth Circuit that had rejected prosecutorial efforts to forceably extract a bullet from the chest of a robbery suspect for evidentiary use. Unlike the "minor intrusion" occasioned by the compulsory blood test in the drunk driving allegation in the *Schmerber* case, Justice Brennan contended that the compulsory surgical procedure sought here constituted a "major intrusion" (and a dangerous one) into an individual's body that had serious privacy and security implications. Because of this, and the state's failure to demonstrate a compelling need for the bullet as evidence, Brennan concluded that the individual's interest outweighed that of the state. He indicated his preference in such cases was a proper weighing of the competing interests of the individual and the state rather than the application of a specific rule.

holding in *Miranda*. In that five-to-four ruling, the Court, speaking through Chief Justice Earl Warren, made it clear that the prosecution may not use a statement against the accused elicited during custodial interrogation "unless it demonstrates the use of effective safeguards to secure" his or her constitutional rights, and they must be made known to the accused. Interrogation could proceed if the accused "voluntarily, knowingly, and intelligently" makes a waiver of the rights to which he or she is entitled.

In an extensive dissenting opinion, Justice John Marshall Harlan II noted that "the thrust of the new rules" was to eliminate "pressures" applied to the suspect and as such would most likely discourage any confessions. He doubted if such a "utopian" aim could be realized and renewed his call for judicial restraint on such issues of "pure policy."

Undoubtedly, the Court was not oblivious to the sweeping impact such rulings could have on the administration of state criminal law. Consequently, it held in *Johnson* v. *New Jersey* (384 U.S. 719, 1966), decided one week later, that both *Escobedo* and *Miranda* would be limited to a prospective application. In fact, the Court ruled that the new standards announced in *Escobedo* and *Miranda* would apply only to cases begun *after* the announcement of these two cases. Thus, the Court was even more restrictive here than in its earlier prospective application of *Mapp* and *Griffin*, where the new standards applied to cases *still pending* on direct appeal.

REFINING *MIRANDA*

Almost immediately, extensive and sharp criticism was directed at the Court for its *Miranda* ruling. Law enforcement officials complained of having their hands tied and of the needless interference with their primary concern for apprehending criminal suspects and solving crimes. Legislators and "law and order" proponents condemned the Court for "strait-jacketing" the police and "coddling" criminals with the *Miranda* requirements. To them, this was particularly appalling during an era of alarming increases in major crimes. Dissenting justices continued to criticize the rule, and in cases decided shortly after *Miranda*, voiced strong objections to what they viewed as extending the rules. In *Mathis* v. *United States* (391 U.S. 1, 1968), for example, the Court held that *Miranda* warnings were required in a case where the defendant, while incarcerated in a state jail on another charge, was "routinely" questioned by Internal Revenue Service

agents, and statements were elicited that were used to support a conviction for filing false tax claims. Justice Byron White, however, complained of this subtle extension of *Miranda* and issued a call for its abandonment. He continued to complain against the ruling as a "constitutional strait-jacket on law enforcement" when the Court, in *Orozco* v. *Texas* (394 U.S. 324, 1969), ruled one year later that the required warnings were not to be restricted to in-custody interrogation but were required even though questioning took place in the defendant's bedroom at 4:00 A.M. He noted that extending the rule to cover this kind of noncoercive interrogation actually "draws the strait-jacket even tighter."

Congressional action provided the first formal retreat from the requirements of the controversial ruling in a provision on the Omnibus Crime Control and Safe Streets Act in 1968. Title II of that act provided that any statements and/or confessions made within six hours after arrest while a suspect was in custody and had not been informed of his or her rights were admissible in federal prosecutions. The thrust of the provision was to restrict the requirements advanced in *McNabb*, *Mallory*, and *Miranda* in federal prosecutions.

When Chief Justice Warren Burger replaced Chief Justice Earl Warren in 1969 and Justice Harry Blackmun replaced Justice Abe Fortas in 1970, they immediately joined Justices Byron White, John Marshall Harlan II, and Potter Stewart in opposition to the expansion of the *Miranda* rule. These five justices constituted the majority in *Harris* v. *New York* (401 U.S. 222, 1971), indicating the beginning of a contracting trend for *Miranda*. Led by Chief Justice Burger, the Court held that the prosecution is not precluded from the use of statements that admittedly do not meet the *Miranda* test as an impeachment tool in attacking the credibility of an accused's trial testimony. The Chief Justice construed *Miranda* as proscribing use of the "warningless" statements only in the prosecution's "case in chief."

Miranda's erosion continued in several rulings of the Court's 1973, 1974, and 1975 terms. First, in *Michigan* v. *Tucker* (417 U.S. 433, 1974), the Court held that failure to inform a suspect of his right to appointed counsel before being interrogated (which incidentally took place a few months before *Miranda* was announced) was only a harmless error in the total circumstances of the case.[13] Then one year later, in *Oregon* v. *Haas* (420 U.S. 714,

---

[13]The Court has considered the issue of waiver of counsel under *Miranda* in a number of cases. See, for example, *Edwards* v. *Arizona* (451 U.S. 477, 1981).

1975), the Court reaffirmed *Harris* v. *New York*, (401 U.S. 22 *supra*), and allowed the use of a suspect's statements for impeachment purposes, although they had been made before arrival of counsel that he had requested prior to making any statements. And the next year, in *Michigan* v. *Mosley* (423 U.S. 96, 1976), the Court did not construe *Miranda* as invoking "a *per se* proscription of indefinite duration on any further questionings . . . on any subject." This ruling approved an interrogation process where a suspect had initially used the shield of *Miranda* to remain silent, but several hours later in a different room was administered the Miranda rights again and proceeded to respond to questions about a different crime. The Court continued to contract the ruling by refusing to extend it to grand jury proceedings in *United States* v. *Mandujano* (425 U.S. 564), also decided in 1976. In the context of that case, not even Justices Brennan and Marshall objected as Chief Justice Burger emphasized the difference between such proceedings and the criminal trial.[14]

The Burger Court also construed the in-custody dimension of the *Miranda* warnings to enhance interrogation efforts of law enforcement officials. In *Beckwith* v. *United States* (425 U.S. 319, 1976), for example, the Court held that a noncustodial interview of a person in his home by Internal Revenue Service agents, during which statements were made and were subsequently used against him in a tax fraud prosecution, was not the equivalent of the in-custody interrogation that triggers *Miranda* warnings. Chief Justice Burger noted that, while the investigation was focused on the defendant in the sense that his tax liability was under scrutiny, there was no need for *Miranda* warnings at this stage, since the agents did not take him into custody or deprive him of his freedom in "any significant way." In *Oregon* v. *Mathiason* (425 U.S. 492, 1977), a defendant "voluntarily" appeared at a police station after having been requested to do so in a telephone conversation. In his discussion of a crime with the police, he made a verbal confession although he was not under arrest, nor had he been advised of his *Miranda* rights. The Oregon Supreme Court's reversal of a subsequent conviction because of the failure to provide *Miranda* warnings prior to the police station "interview" was

overturned by the U.S. Supreme Court because the defendant was not in custody at the time of his verbal confession, nor had he been "deprived of his freedom of action in any significant way." The Court noted that even after the oral confession and a subsequent taping of it, the defendant was allowed to leave the police station without hindrance. In a similar vein, the Court held that a suspect's written statement is not essential in establishing proof of explicit waiver of counsel under *Miranda* (*North Carolina* v. *Butler*, 441 U.S. 369, 1979).

By 1980 Chief Justice Warren Burger expressed the view in *Rhode Island* v. *Innis* (446 U.S. 291) that the meaning of *Miranda* had become "reasonably clear" and that law enforcement officials had adjusted their practices to its strictures without major hindrance to their work. Consequently he saw no need to "overrule," "disparage," or "extend" it. The Court adhered to this approach when refusing to extend *Miranda* to cover interviews with probation officers (see footnote 14). Thus, it was somewhat surprising that just four years after *Innis*, the Court in *New York* v. *Quarles* (467 U.S. 649, 1984), adopted a "public-safety exception" to *Miranda*. Speaking for the five-man majority, Justice William Rehnquist indicated that "prophylactic rules" outlined in *Miranda* may be bypassed where overriding considerations of public safety require it. Applying a cost-benefit analysis, Rehnquist asserted that giving *Miranda* warnings within the context of the case could prove too costly by delaying immediate recovery of a dangerous weapon—a gun discarded by the suspect.

But in a rare dissent from her colleagues, Justice Sandra Day O'Connor expressed concern that the exception would "unnecessarily blur the edges" of *Miranda* and lessen the clarity that had been developed since it was first decided. Characterizing the "prophylactic rules" set forth in *Miranda* as one of the strengths of the decision, she warned of the possible evisceration of the "core virtue of *Miranda*" (clear guidance to police and courts in conducting custodial investigations), since law enforcement officers could freely ignore the rules under the guise of a "public safety exception." But in limiting her opposition to admission of the suspect's statements, O'Connor agreed with the majority's admission of the gun as evidence since it was her view that the source of *Miranda*—the self-incrimination provision of the Fifth Amendment—does not prohibit compelling surrender of nontestimonial evidence.

Notwithstanding her concern for exceptions that would "unnecessarily blur the edges" of *Mi-*

---

[14]See also *Fare* v. *Michael C.* (482 U.S. 707, 1979), where the Court refused to equate a request to talk with a probation officer with a *Miranda* request to see a lawyer; and *Minnesota* v. *Murphy* (104 S. Ct. 1136, 1984), where the Court refused to extend the *Miranda* requirement to interviews with probation officers.

randa, Justice O'Connor wrote the Court's opinion one year later in *Oregon* v. *Elstad* (105 S. Ct. 1285, 1985), which permits greater police discretion in the initial application of *Miranda* warnings. The case involved a suspect's inculpatory response to a police inquiry in the initial stage of a burglary investigation before *Miranda* warnings were given and a subsequent confession that was given at the stationhouse after *Miranda* warnings had been given and waived. Overturning an Oregon appeals court ruling that threw out both the initial statement (as a flat violation of *Miranda*) and the confession (as "fruit of the poisonous tree"), O'Connor emphasized the voluntariness of the initial statement and that it, although technically in violation of *Miranda*, does not preclude the suspect's subsequent confession after having received and waived the *Miranda* warnings.

Justice O'Connor wrote another opinion for the Court the next term in *Moran* v. *Burbine* (106 S. Ct. 1135, 1986), where police behavior in obtaining a waiver of *Miranda* rights from a suspect was at issue. Here, the police failed to inform the suspect of the attempt of counsel to contact him before he agreed to talk to them. O'Connor did not believe that knowledge of that fact was essential to the suspect's ability to "knowingly and intelligently" waive *Miranda* rights. Counseling against extending the reach of *Miranda* to situations where police are less than forthright in their dealings with suspects, she concluded that:

> [W]hile a rule requiring that the police inform a suspect of an attorney's efforts to reach him might add marginally to *Miranda*'s goal of dispelling the compulsion inherent in custodial interrogation, overriding practical considerations—particularly the case and clarity of *Miranda*'s application—counsel against adoption of the rule. Moreover, such a rule would work a substantial and inappropriate shift in the subtle balance struck in *Miranda* between society's legitimate law enforcement interests and the protection of the accused's Fifth Amendment rights.

The "overriding practical consideration" appeared to be crucial in the Court's refusal to strike down alleged police deception in *Colorado* v. *Spring* (107 S. Ct. 851, 1987) the next year. Speaking for the seven-to-two majority, Justice Lewis Powell reiterated the position of Justice O'Connor in the *Burbine* case that failure of the police to make certain information in their possession available to the suspect is not essential to his decision-making in the waiver of *Miranda* rights. (In *Spring*, the police did not inform the suspect of all the crimes about which he might be questioned.) In addition, the

majority in the same term refused to construe *Miranda* expansively to allow a limited invocation of the *Miranda* counsel guarantee with respect to written statements to proscribe verbal statements of the accused who had voluntarily participated in the oral dimension of the interrogation. In *Connecticut* v. *Barrett* (107 S. Ct. 828, 1987), the suspect had proclaimed that he would not sign anything, but then agreed to talk with the police about the criminal activity being investigated. Chief Justice Rehnquist considered Barrett's decision to talk with the police a valid waiver of his right to remain silent, noting that *Miranda* only guarantees a suspect the choice between "speech and silence."

That the Rehnquist Court will continue to limit the *Miranda* shield in criminal prosecutions is reflected in two cases decided by the Court in 1990 and 1991. First, in *Illinois* v. *Perkins* (110 S. Ct. 2394, 1990), the Court, in an eight-to-one ruling, refused to suppress the testimony of an undercover law enforcement agent who had obtained incriminating information while sharing a cell with the accused. Justice Anthony Kennedy, whose opinion was joined by six of the justices (even Justice Brennan concurred in the judgment with a separate opinion, leaving Justice Marshall as the lone dissenter), rejected the argument of the respondent that the "cellmate undercover agent" was constitutionally required to give the *Miranda* warnings before eliciting statements from him because he was working as a law enforcement officer. The critical factor for the justices was the noncoercive context in which the respondent's statements were made. Kennedy took judicial notice of the fact that the suspect was speaking "freely to someone that he believed to be a fellow inmate." Underscoring this point, he asserted that "*Miranda* forbids coercion, not mere strategic deception by taking advantage of a suspect's misplaced trust in one he supposes to be a fellow prisoner."

In dissent, Justice Thurgood Marshall was concerned that this "cellmate" exception "allows police officers intentionally to take advantage of suspects unaware of their constitutional rights." For him, the inmate's conversations with the "undercover cellmate" had all of the trappings of the in-custody interrogation that *Miranda* addresses, and he was concerned about the proliferation of policies that evade *Miranda* as the result of the Court's decision.

A year later, in *Arizona* v. *Fulminante* (111 S. Ct. 1246, 1991), a complex case in which the justices split significantly on the several key issues presented, the justices seemed to indicate their uncertainty about how far to cut back on *Miranda* in the future. A majority (Rehnquist, O'Connor, Scalia, Kennedy, and Souter) found the harmless error analysis appropriate for cases like *Fulminante,* where such analysis could allow the admission of a coerced confession if there is sufficient evidence (independently obtained) to support a conviction. But a different majority (White, Marshall, Blackmun, Stevens, and Scalia) threw out the confession as coerced and "not harmless beyond a reasonable doubt." (See also *McNeil* v. *Wisconsin,* 11 S. Ct. 2204, 1991, where the Rehnquist Court continued a restricted construction of *Miranda* and refused to allow the assignment of the Sixth Amendment counsel guarantee as the invocation of *Miranda* rights applicable to subsequent criminal proceedings of a suspect.)

As the Republican era drew to a close in 1993, criminal procedure conservatives constitute a dominant bloc in the Court. Hence, we will most likely witness the crafting of additional exceptions to *Miranda* but not its complete rejection.

MIRANDA v. ARIZONA
384 U.S. 436; 16 L. Ed. 2d 694; 86 S. Ct. 1602 (1966)*

CHIEF JUSTICE WARREN *delivered the opinion of the Court.*

The cases before us raise questions which go to the roots of our concepts of American criminal jurisprudence: the restraints society must observe consistent with the Federal Constitution in prosecuting individuals for crime. More specifically, we deal with the admissibility of statements obtained from an individual who is subjected to custodial police interrogation and the necessity for procedures which assure that the individual is accorded his privilege under the Fifth Amendment to the Constitution not to be compelled to incriminate himself.

We dealt with certain phases of this problem recently in *Escobedo* v. *State of Illinois.* . . .

. . . We granted certiorari in these cases . . . in order further to explore some facets of the problems, thus exposed, of applying the privilege against self-incrimination to in-custody interrogation, and to give concrete constitutional guidelines for law enforcement agencies and courts to follow.

We start here, as we did in *Escobedo,* with the premise that our holding is not an innovation in our jurisprudence, but is an application of principles long recognized and applied in other settings. We have undertaken a thorough re-examination of the *Escobedo* decision and the principles it announced, and we re-affirm it.

* * *

Our holding will be spelled out with some specificity in the pages which follow, but briefly stated it is this: the prosecution may not use statements, whether exculpatory or inculpatory, stemming from custodial interrogation of the defendant unless it demonstrates the use of procedural safeguards effective to secure the privilege against self-incrimination. By custodial interrogation we mean questioning initiated by law enforcement officers after a person has been taken into custody or otherwise deprived of his freedom of action in any significant way. As for the procedural safeguards to be employed, unless other fully effective means are devised to inform accused persons of their right of silence and to assure a continuous opportunity to exercise it, the following measures are required. Prior to any questioning, the person must be warned that he has a right to remain silent, that any statement he does make may be used as evidence against him, and that he has a right to the presence of any attorney, either retained or appointed. The defendant may waive effectuation of these rights, provided the waiver is made voluntarily, knowingly and intelligently. If, however, he indicates in any manner and at any stage of the process that he wishes to consult with an attorney before speaking there can be no questioning. Likewise, if the individual is alone and indicates in any manner that he does not wish to be interrogated, the police may not question him. The mere fact that he may have answered some questions or volunteered some statements on his own does not deprive him of the right to refrain from answering any further inquiries until he has consulted with an attorney and thereafter consents to be questioned.

The constitutional issue we decided in each of these cases is the admissibility of statements obtained from a defendant questioned while in cus-

---

*This opinion applies to the companion cases of *Vignera* v. *New York,* *Westover* v. *United States,* and *California* v. *Stewart.*

tody and deprived of his freedom of action. In each, the defendant was questioned by police officers, detectives, or a prosecuting attorney in a room in which he was cut off from the outside world. In none of these cases was the defendant given a full and effective warning of his rights at the outset of the interrogation process. In all the cases, the questioning elicited oral admissions, and in three of them, signed statements as well which were admitted at their trials. They all thus share salient features—incommunicado interrogation of individuals in a police-dominated atmosphere, resulting in self-incriminating statements without full warning of constitutional rights.

An understanding of the nature and setting of this in-custody interrogation is essential to our decisions today. The difficulty in depicting what transpires at such interrogations stems from the fact that in this country they have largely taken place incommunicado. From extensive factual studies undertaken in the early 1930s, including the famous Wickersham Report to Congress by a Presidential Commission, it is clear that police violence and the "third degree" flourished at that time. In a series of cases decided by this Court long after these studies, the police resorted to physical brutality—beating, hanging, whipping—and to sustained and protracted questioning incommunicado in order to extort confessions. The 1961 Commission on Civil Rights found much evidence to indicate that "some policemen still resort to physical force to obtain confessions." . . . The use of physical brutality and violence is not, unfortunately, relegated to the past or to any part of the country. . . .

The examples given above are undoubtedly the exception now, but they are sufficiently widespread to be the object of concern. Unless a proper limitation upon custodial interrogation is achieved—there can be no assurance that practices of this nature will be eradicated in the foreseeable future. . . .

[Here THE CHIEF JUSTICE reviewed some of the current literature which sets forth modern techniques of in-custody interrogation.]

The question in these cases is whether the privilege is fully applicable during a period of custodial interrogation. . . . We are satisfied that all the principles embodied in the privilege apply to informal compulsion exerted by law-enforcement officers during in-custody questioning. An individual swept from familiar surroundings into police custody, surrounded by antagonistic forces, and subjected to the techniques of persuasion described above cannot be otherwise than under compulsion to speak. As a practical matter, the compulsion to speak in the isolated setting of the police station may well be greater than in courts or other official investigations, where there are often impartial observers to guard against intimidation or trickery. . . .

Today, then, there can be no doubt that the Fifth Amendment privilege is available outside of criminal court proceedings and serves to protect persons in all settings in which their freedom of action is curtailed from being compelled to incriminate themselves. . . . In order to combat [inherently compelling] pressures and to permit a full opportunity to exercise the privilege against self-incrimination, the accused must be adequately and effectively apprised of his rights, and the exercise of those rights must be fully honored. . . .

At the outset, if a person in custody is to be subjected to interrogation he must first be informed in clear and unequivocal terms that he has the right to remain silent. For those unaware of the privilege the warning is needed simply to make them aware of it—the threshold requirement for an intelligent decision as to its exercise. More important, such a warning is an absolute prerequisite in overcoming the inherent pressures of the interrogation atmosphere. It is not just the subnormal or woefully ignorant who succumb to an interrogator's imprecations, whether implied or expressly stated, that the interrogation will continue until a confession is obtained or that silence in the face of accusation is itself damning and will bode ill when presented to a jury. Further, the warning will show the individual that his interrogators are prepared to recognize his privilege should he choose to exercise it. . . .

The warning of the right to remain silent must be accompanied by the explanation that anything said can and will be used against the individual in court. This warning is needed in order to make him aware not only of the privilege, but also of the consequences of forgoing it. It is only through an awareness of these consequences that there can be any assurance of real understanding and intelligent exercise of the privilege. Moreover, this warning may serve to make the individual more acutely aware that he is faced with a phase of the adversary system—that he is not in the presence of persons acting solely in his interest.

The circumstances surrounding in-custody interrogation can operate very quickly to overbear the will of one merely made aware of his privilege by his interrogators. Therefore, the right to have counsel present at the interrogation is indispensable to the protection of the Fifth Amendment privilege under the system we delineate today. Our aim is to assure that the individual's right to choose between silence and speech remains unfettered throughout the interrogation process. A once-stated warning, delivered by those who will conduct the interrogation cannot itself suffice to that end among those who most require knowledge of their rights. A mere warning given by the interrogators is not alone sufficient to accomplish that end. Prosecutors themselves claim that the admonishment of the right to remain silent without more "will benefit only the recidivist and the professional." Brief for the National District Attorneys Association as *amicus curiae*, p. 14. Even preliminary advice given to the accused by his own attorney can be swiftly overcome by the secret interrogation process. . . . Thus, the need for counsel to protect Fifth Amendment privilege comprehends not merely a right to consult prior to questioning, but also to have counsel present during any questioning if the defendant so desires.

The presence of counsel at the interrogation may serve several significant subsidiary functions as well. If the accused decides to talk to his interrogators, the assistance of counsel can mitigate the dangers of untrustworthiness. With a lawyer present, the likelihood that the police will practice coercion is reduced, and if coercion is nevertheless exercised the lawyer can testify to it in court. The presence of a lawyer can also help to guarantee that the accused gives a fully accurate statement to the police and that the statement is rightly reported by the prosecution at trial. . . .

An individual need not make a preinterrogation request for a lawyer. While such request affirmatively secures his right to have one, his failure to ask for a lawyer does not constitute a waiver. No effective waiver of the right to counsel during interrogation can be recognized unless specifically made after the warnings we here delineate have been given. The accused who does not know his rights and therefore does not make a request may be the person who most needs counsel. . . .

Accordingly, we hold that an individual held for interrogation must be clearly informed that he has the right to consult with a lawyer and to have the lawyer with him during interrogation under the system for protecting the privilege we delineate today. As with the warnings of the right to remain silent and that anything stated can be used in evidence against him, this warning is an absolute prerequisite to interrogation. . . .

If an individual indicates that he wishes the assistance of counsel before any interrogation oc-

curs, the authorities cannot rationally ignore or deny his request on the basis that the individual does not have or cannot afford a retained attorney. The financial ability of the individual has no relationship to the scope of the rights involved here. The privilege against self-incrimination secured by the Constitution applies to all individuals. The need for counsel in order to protect the privilege exists for the indigent as well as the affluent. In fact, were we to limit these constitutional rights to those who can retain an attorney, our decision today would be of little significance. . . . While authorities are not required to relieve the accused of his poverty, they have the obligation not to take advantage of indigence in the administration of justice. . . .

In order fully to apprise a person interrogated of the extent of his rights under this system then, it is necessary to warn him not only that he has the right to consult with an attorney, but also that if he is indigent a lawyer will be appointed to represent him. . . .

Once warnings have been given, the subsequent procedure is clear. If the individual indicates in any manner, at any time prior to or during questioning, that he wishes to remain silent, the interrogation must cease. At this point he has shown that he intends to exercise his Fifth Amendment privileges; any statement taken after the person invokes his privilege cannot be other than the product of compulsion, subtle or otherwise. Without the right to cut off questioning, the setting of in-custody interrogation operates on the individual to overcome free choice in producing a statement after the privilege has been once invoked. If the individual states that he wants an attorney, the interrogation must cease until an attorney is present. At that time, the individual must have an opportunity to confer with the attorney and to have him present during any subsequent questioning. If the individual cannot obtain an attorney and he indicates that he wants one before speaking to police, they must respect his decision to remain silent.

This does not mean, as some have suggested, that each police station must have a "station house lawyer" present at all times to advise prisoners. It does mean, however, that if police propose to interrogate a person they must make known to him that he is entitled to a lawyer and that if he cannot afford one, a lawyer will be provided for him prior to any interrogation. . . .

If the interrogation continues without the presence of an attorney and a statement is taken, a heavy burden rests on the Government to demonstrate that the defendant knowingly and intelligently waived his privilege against self-incrimination and his right to retained or appointed counsel. . . .

In dealing with statements obtained through interrogation, we do not purport to find all confessions inadmissible. Confessions remain a proper element in law enforcement. Any statement given freely and voluntarily without any compelling influences is, of course, admissible in evidence. The fundamental import of the privilege while an individual is in custody is not whether he is allowed to talk to the police without the benefit of warning and counsel, but whether he can be interrogated. There is no requirement that police stop a person who enters a police station and states that he wishes to confess to a crime, or a person who calls the police to offer a confession or any other statement he desires to make. Volunteered statements of any kind are not barred by the Fifth Amendment, and their admissibility is not affected by our holding today.

To summarize, we hold that when an individual is taken into custody or otherwise deprived of his freedom by the authorities and is subjected to questioning, the privilege against self-incrimination is jeopardized. Procedural safeguards must be employed to protect the privilege, and unless other fully effective means are adopted to notify the person of his right of silence and to assure that the exercise of the right will be scrupulously honored, the following measures are required. He must be warned prior to any questioning that he has the right to remain silent, that anything he says can be used against him in a court of law, that he has the right to the presence of an attorney, and that if he cannot afford an attorney one will be appointed for him prior to any questioning if he so desires. Opportunity to exercise these rights must be afforded to him throughout the interrogation. After such warnings have been given and such opportunity afforded him, the individual may knowingly and intelligently waive these rights and agree to answer questions or make a statement. But unless and until such warnings and waiver are demonstrated by the prosecution at trial, no evidence obtained as a result of interrogation can be used against him.

[Here CHIEF JUSTICE WARREN examines the argument that society's need for interrogation outweighs the privileges.]

* * *

Because of the nature of the problem and because of its recurrent significance in numerous cases, we have to this point discussed the relationship of the Fifth Amendment privilege to police interrogation without specific concentration on the facts of the cases before us. We turn now to these facts to consider the application to these cases of the constitutional principles discussed above. In each instance, we have concluded that statements were obtained from the defendant under circumstances that did not meet constitutional standards for protection of the privilege.

NO. 759
MIRANDA v. *ARIZONA*

On March 13, 1963, petitioner, Ernesto Miranda, was arrested at his home and taken in custody to a Phoenix police station. He was there identified by the complaining witness. The police then took him to Interrogation Room No. 2 of the detective bureau. There he was questioned by two police officers. The officers admitted at trial that Miranda was not advised that he had a right to have an attorney present. Two hours later, the officers emerged from the interrogation room with a written confession signed by Miranda. . . .

At his trial before a jury, the written confession was admitted into evidence over the objection of defense counsel. . . . Miranda was found guilty of kidnapping and rape. . . . On appeal, the Supreme Court of Arizona . . . affirmed the conviction. . . .

We reverse. From the testimony of the officers and by the admission of respondent, it is clear that Miranda was not in any way apprised of his right to consult with an attorney and to have one present during the interrogation, nor was his right not to be compelled to incriminate himself effectively protected in any other manner. Without these warnings the statements were inadmissible. The mere fact that he signed a statement which contained a typed-in clause stating that he had full knowledge of his legal rights does not approach the knowing and intelligent waiver required to relinquish constitutional rights. . . .

NO. 760
VIGNERA v. *NEW YORK*

Petitioner, Michael Vignera, was picked up by New York police on October 14, 1960, in connection with the robbery three days earlier of a Brooklyn dress shop. . . . [A] detective questioned Vignera with respect to the robbery. Vignera orally admitted the robbery to the detective. The detective was asked on cross-examination at trial by defense counsel whether Vignera was warned of his right to counsel before being interrogated. The prosecution objected to the question, and the trial judge sustained the objection. Thus, the defense was precluded from making any showing that warnings had not been given. . . . At Vignera's trial on a charge of first degree robbery, [a] detective testified as to the oral confession. . . . At the conclusion of the testimony, the trial judge charged the jury in part as follows:

> The law doesn't say that the confession is void or invalidated because the police officer didn't advise the defendant as to his rights. Did you hear what I said? I am telling you what the law of the State of New York is.

Vignera was found guilty of first degree robbery. . . . The conviction was affirmed without opinion by the Appellate Division, Second Department . . . and by the Court of Appeals, also without opinion. . . .

We reverse. . . . Vignera . . . was not effectively apprised of his Fifth Amendment privilege or of his right to have counsel present, and his statements are inadmissible.

NO. 761
WESTOVER v. UNITED STATES

At approximately 9:45 P.M. on March 20, 1963, petitioner . . . was arrested by local police in Kansas City as a suspect in two Kansas City robberies. A report was also received from the FBI that he was wanted on a felony charge in California. The local authorities took him to a police station and placed him in a line-up on the local charges, and at about 11:45 P.M. he was booked. Kansas City police interrogated Westover on the night of his arrest. He denied any knowledge of criminal activities. The next day local officers interrogated him again throughout the morning. Shortly before noon they informed the FBI that they were through interrogating Westover and that the FBI could proceed to interrogate him. There is nothing in the record to indicate that Westover was ever given any warning as to his rights by local police. . . .

After two or two and one-half hours, Westover signed separate confessions to each of these two robberies which had been prepared by one of the agents during this interrogation. . . .

Westover was tried by a jury in federal court and convicted of the California robberies. His statements were introduced at trial. . . . On appeal, the conviction was affirmed by the Court of Appeals for the Ninth Circuit. . . .

We reverse. On the facts of this case we cannot find that Westover knowingly and intelligently waived his right to remain silent and his right to consult with proper counsel prior to the time he made the statement. . . .

NO. 584
CALIFORNIA v. STEWART

. . . At the time of Stewart's arrest, police also arrested Stewart's wife and three other persons who were visiting him. These four were jailed along with Stewart and were interrogated. Stewart was taken to the University Station of the Los Angeles Police Department where he was placed in a cell. During the next five days, police interrogated Stewart on nine different occasions. Except during the first interrogation session, when he was confronted with an accusing witness, Stewart was isolated with his interrogators.

During the ninth interrogation session, Stewart admitted that he had robbed the deceased and stated that he had not meant to hurt her. Police then brought Stewart before a magistrate for the first time. Since there was no evidence to connect them with any crime, the police then released the other four persons arrested with him.

Nothing in the record specifically indicates whether Stewart was or was not advised of his right to remain silent or his right to counsel. . . .

. . . At his trial, transcripts of the first interrogation and the confession at the last interrogation were introduced in evidence. The jury found Stewart guilty of robbery and first degree murder and fixed the penalty as death. On appeal, the Supreme Court of California reversed. . . . It held that under this Court's decision in *Escobedo*, Stewart should have been advised of his right to remain silent and of his right to counsel and that it would not presume in the face of a silent record that the police advised Stewart of his rights.

We affirm. In dealing with custodial interrogation, we will not presume that a defendant has been effectively apprised of his rights and that his privilege against self-incrimination has been adequately safeguarded on a record that does not show that any warnings have been given or that any effective alternative has been employed. . . .

Therefore, in accordance with the foregoing, the judgments [below] . . . are reversed. It is so ordered.

[JUSTICE CLARK's opinion dissenting in Nos. 759, 760, and 761, and concurring in the result in No. 584 is not reprinted here.]

JUSTICE HARLAN, *whom* JUSTICE STEWART *and* JUSTICE WHITE *join, dissenting.*

I believe the decision of the Court represents poor constitutional law and entails harmful consequences for the country at large. How serious these consequences may prove to be only time can tell. But the basic flaws in the Court's justification seem to me readily apparent now once all sides of the problem are considered.

* * *

While the fine points of this scheme [the majority's requirement of warnings in interrogation] are far less clear than the Court admits, the tenor is quite apparent. The new rules are not designed to guard against police brutality or other unmistakably banned forms of coercion. Those who use third-degree tactics and deny them in court are equally able and destined to lie as skillfully about warnings and waivers. Rather, the thrust of the new rules is to negate all pressures, to reinforce the nervous or ignorant suspect, and ultimately to discourage any confession at all. The aim in short is toward "voluntariness" in a utopian sense, or to view it from a different angle, voluntariness with a vengeance.

To incorporate this notion into the Constitution requires a strained reading of history and precedent and a disregard of the very pragmatic concerns that alone may on occasion justify such strains. I believe that reasoned examination will show that the Due Process Clauses provide an adequate tool for coping with confessions and that, even if the Fifth Amendment privilege against self-incrimination be invoked, its precedents taken as a whole do not sustain the present rules. Viewed as a choice based on pure policy, these new rules prove to be a highly debatable if not one-sided appraisal of the competing interests imposed over widespread objection, at the very time when judicial restraint is most called for by the circumstances. . . .

The Court's new rules aim to offset . . . minor pressures and disadvantages intrinsic to any kind of police interrogation. . . . The rules work for reliability in confessions almost only in the Pickwickian sense that they can prevent some from being given at all. . . .

What the Court largely ignores is that its rules impair, if they will not eventually serve wholly to frustrate, an instrument of law enforcement that has long and quite reasonably been thought worth the price paid for it. There can be little doubt that the Court's new code would markedly decrease the number of confessions. To warn the suspect that he may remain silent and remind him that his confession may be used in court are minor obstructions. To require also an express waiver by the suspect and an end to questioning whenever he demurs must heavily handicap questioning. And to suggest or provide counsel for the suspect simply invites the end of the interrogation. . . .

How much harm this decision will inflict on law enforcement cannot fairly be predicted with accuracy. Evidence on the role of confessions is notoriously incomplete. . . . We do know that some crimes cannot be solved without confessions, that ample expert testimony attests to their importance in crime control, and that the Court is taking a real risk with society's welfare in imposing its new regime on the country. The social costs of crime are too great to call the new rules anything but a hazardous experimentation.

While passing over the costs and risks of its experiment, the Court portrayed the evils of normal police questioning in terms which I think are exaggerated. Albeit stringently confined by the due process standards, interrogation is no doubt often inconvenient and unpleasant for the suspect. However, it is not less so for a man to be arrested and jailed, to have his house searched, or to stand trial in court, yet all this may properly happen to the most innocent given probable cause, a warrant, or an indictment. Society has always paid a stiff price for law and order, and peaceful interrogation is not one of the dark moments of the law.

* * *

In closing this necessarily truncated discussion of policy considerations attending the new confession rules, some reference must be made to their ironic untimeliness. There is now in progress in this country a massive reexamination of criminal law enforcement procedures on a scale never before witnessed. . . .

It is no secret that concern has been expressed lest long-range and lasting reforms be frustrated by this Court's too rapid departure from existing constitutional standards. Despite the Court's disclaimer, the practical effect of the decision made today must inevitably be to handicap seriously sound efforts at reform. . . .

. . . I would adhere to the due process test and reject the new requirements inaugurated by the Court. On this premise my disposition of each of these cases can be stated briefly.

In two of the three cases coming from state courts, *Miranda* v. *Arizona* (No. 759) and *Vignera* v. *New York* (No. 760), the confessions were held admissible and no other errors worth comment are alleged by petitioners. I would affirm in these two cases. The other state case is *California* v. *Stewart*

(No. 584), where the state supreme court held the confession inadmissible and reversed the conviction. In that case I would dismiss the writ of certiorari on the ground that no final judgment is before us. . . . If the merits of the decision in *Stewart* be reached, then I believe it should be reversed and the case remanded so the state supreme court may pass on the other claims available to respondent.

In the federal case, *Westover* v. *United States* (No. 761) . . . [i]t is urged that the confession was . . . inadmissible because [it was] not voluntary even measured by due process standards and because federal-state cooperation brought the *McNabb-Mallory* rule into play under *Anderson* v. *United States*, 318 U.S. 350, 1943. . . . However, the facts alleged fall well short of coercion in my view, and I believe the involvement of federal agents in petitioner's arrest and detention by the State too slight to invoke *Anderson*. . . . I would therefore affirm Westover's conviction.

In conclusion: Nothing in the letter or the spirit of the Constitution or in the precedents squares with the heavy-handed and one-sided action that is so precipitously taken by the Court in the name of fulfilling its constitutional responsibilities. The foray which the Court takes today brings to mind the wise and farsighted words of Justice Jackson in *Douglas* v. *City of Jeanette*, 319 U.S. 157, 1943. . . . (separate opinion): "This Court is forever adding new stories to the temples of constitutional law, and the temples have a way of collapsing when one story too many is added." . . .

[The dissenting opinion of JUSTICE WHITE, with whom JUSTICE HARLAN and JUSTICE STEWART joined, is not reprinted here.]

NEW YORK v. QUARLES
467 U.S. 649; 81 L. Ed. 2d 550; 104 S. Ct. 2626 (1984)

JUSTICE REHNQUIST *delivered the opinion of the Court.*

Respondent Benjamin Quarles was charged . . . with criminal possession of a weapon. The trial court suppressed the gun in question, and a statement made by respondent, because the statement was obtained by police before they read respondent his *Miranda* rights. That ruling was affirmed on appeal through the New York Court of Appeals. We granted certiorari . . . , and we now reverse. We conclude that under the circumstances involved in this case, overriding considerations of public safety justify the officer's failure to provide *Miranda* warnings before he asked questions devoted to locating the abandoned weapon.

On September 11, 1980, at approximately 12:30 A.M., Officer Frank Kraft and Officer Sal Scarring were on road patrol in Queens, New York, when a young woman approached their car. She told them that she had just been raped by a black male, approximately six feet tall, who was wearing a black jacket with the name "Big Ben" printed in yellow letters on the back . . . [and] that the man had just entered an A & P supermarket located nearby and that the man was carrying a gun.

The officers drove the woman to the supermarket, and Officer Kraft entered the store while Officer Scarring radioed for assistance. Officer Kraft quickly spotted respondent, who matched the description given by the woman, approaching a check-out counter. Apparently upon seeing the officer, respondent turned and ran toward the rear of the store, and Officer Kraft pursued him with a drawn gun. When respondent turned the corner at the end of an aisle, Officer Kraft lost sight of him for several seconds, and upon regaining sight of respondent, ordered him to stop and put his hands over his head.

Although more than three other officers had arrived on the scene by that time, Officer Kraft was the first to reach respondent. He frisked him and discovered that he was wearing a shoulder holster which was then empty. After handcuffing him, Officer Kraft asked him where the gun was. Respondent nodded in the direction of some empty cartons and responded, "The gun is over there." Officer Kraft thereafter retrieved a loaded .38 caliber revolver from one of the cartons, formally placed respondent under arrest, and read him his *Miranda* rights from a printed card. Respondent indicated that he would be willing to answer questions without an attorney present. Officer Kraft then asked respondent if he owned the gun and where he had purchased it. Respondent answered that he did own it and that he had purchased it in Miami, Florida.

In subsequent prosecution of respondent for

criminal possession of a weapon, the judge excluded the statement "The gun is over there" and the gun because the officer had not given respondent the warnings required by our decision in *Miranda* v. *Arizona* . . . before asking him where the gun was located. The judge excluded the other statements about respondent's ownership of the gun and the place of purchase, as evidence tainted by the prior *Miranda* violation. The Appellate Division of the Supreme Court of New York affirmed without opinion. . . .

The Court of Appeals . . . concluded that respondent was in "custody" within the meaning of *Miranda* during all questioning and rejected the State's argument that the exigencies of the situation justified Officer Kraft's failure to read respondent his *Miranda* rights until after he had located the gun. The court declined to recognize an exigency exception to the usual requirements of *Miranda* because it found no indication from Officer Kraft's testimony at the suppression hearing that his subjective motivation in asking the question was to protect his own safety or the safety of the public. . . . For the reasons which follow, we believe that this case presents a situation where concern for public safety must be paramount to adherence to the literal language of the prophylactic rules enunciated in *Miranda*. . . .

In this case . . . [there is] no claim that respondent's statements were actually compelled by police conduct which overcame his will to resist. See *Beckwith* v. *United States*, 425 U.S. 341, 347–348 (1976). . . . Thus the only issue before us is whether Officer Kraft was justified in failing to make available to respondent the procedural safeguards associated with the privilege against compulsory self-incrimination since *Miranda*.

The New York Court of Appeals was undoubtedly correct in deciding that the facts of this case come within the ambit of the *Miranda* decision as we have subsequently interpreted it. We agree that respondent was in police custody because we have noted that "the ultimate inquiry is simply whether there is a 'formal arrest or restraint on freedom of movement' of the degree associated with a formal arrest." . . . Here Quarles was surrounded by at least four police officers and was handcuffed when the questioning at issue took place. As the New York Court of Appeals observed, there was nothing to suggest that any of the officers were any longer concerned for their own physical safety. . . . The New York Court of Appeals majority declined to express an opinion as to whether there might be an exception to the *Miranda* rule if the police had been acting to protect the public, because the

lower courts in New York had made no factual determination that the police had acted with that motive. . . .

We hold that on these facts there is a "public safety" exception to the requirement that *Miranda* warnings be given before a suspect's answers may be admitted into evidence, and that the availability of that exception does not depend upon the motivation of the individual officers involved. In a kaleidoscopic situation such as the one confronting these officers, where spontaneity rather than adherence to a police manual is necessarily the order of the day, the application of the exception which we recognize today should not be made to depend on *post hoc* findings at a suppression hearing concerning the subjective motivation of the arresting officer. Undoubtedly most police officers, if placed in Officer Kraft's position, would act out of a host of different, instinctive, and largely unverifiable motives—their own safety, the safety of others, and perhaps as well the desire to obtain incriminating evidence from the suspect.

Whatever the motivation of individual officers in such a situation, we do not believe that the doctrinal underpinnings of *Miranda* require that it be applied in all its rigor to a situation in which police officers ask questions reasonably prompted by a concern for the public safety. . . .

The police in this case, in the very act of apprehending a suspect, were confronted with the immediate necessity of ascertaining the whereabouts of a gun which they had every reason to believe the suspect had just removed from his empty holster and discarded in the supermarket. So long as the gun was concealed somewhere in the supermarket, with its actual whereabouts unknown, it obviously posed more than one danger to the public safety: an accomplice might make use of it, a customer or employee might later come upon it.

In such a situation, if the police are required to recite the familiar *Miranda* warnings before asking the whereabouts of the gun, suspects in Quarles' position might well be deterred from responding. Procedural safeguards which deter a suspect from responding were deemed acceptable in *Miranda* in order to protect the Fifth Amendment privilege; when the primary social cost of those added protections is the possibility of fewer convictions, the *Miranda* majority was willing to bear that cost. Here, had *Miranda* warnings deterred Quarles from responding to Officer Kraft's question about the whereabouts of the gun, the cost would have been something more than merely the failure to obtain evidence useful in convicting Quarles. Officer Kraft needed an answer to his question not simply to make his case against Quarles but to insure that further danger to the public did not result from the concealment of the gun in a public area.

We conclude that the need for answers to questions in a situation posing a threat to the public safety outweighs the need for the prophylactic rule protecting the Fifth Amendment's privilege against self-incrimination. We decline to place officers such as Officer Kraft in the untenable position of having to consider, often in a matter of seconds, whether it best serves society for them to ask the necessary questions without the *Miranda* warnings and render whatever probative evidence they uncover inadmissible, or for them to give the warnings in order to preserve the admissibility of evidence they might uncover but possibly damage or destroy their ability to obtain that evidence and neutralize the volatile situation confronting them.

In recognizing a narrow exception to the *Miranda* rule in this case, we acknowledge that to some degree we lessen the desirable clarity of that rule. At least in part in order to preserve its clarity, we have over the years refused to sanction attempts to expand our *Miranda* holding. . . . As we have in other contexts, we recognize here the importance of a workable rule "to guide police officers, who have only limited time and expertise to reflect on and balance the social and individual interests involved in the specific circumstances they confront." . . . But as we have pointed out, we believe that the exception which we recognize today lessens the necessity of that on-the-scene balancing process. The exception will not be difficult for police officers to apply because in each case it will be circumscribed by the exigency which justifies it. We think police officers can and will distinguish almost instinctively between questions necessary to secure their own safety or the safety of the public and questions designed solely to elicit testimonial evidence from a suspect.

The facts of this case clearly demonstrate that distinction and an officer's ability to recognize it. Officer Kraft asked only the question necessary to locate the missing gun before advising respondent of his rights. It was only after securing the loaded revolver and giving the warnings that he continued with investigatory questions about the ownership and place of purchase of the gun. The exception which we recognize today, far from complicating the thought processes and the on-the-scene judgments of police officers, will simply free them to follow their legitimate instincts when confronting situations presenting a danger to the public safety.

We hold that the Court of Appeals in this case

erred in excluding the statement "the gun is over there" and the gun because of the officer's failure to read respondent his *Miranda* rights before attempting to locate the weapon. Accordingly, we hold that it also erred in excluding the subsequent statements as illegal fruits of a *Miranda* violation. We therefore reverse and remand for further proceedings not inconsistent with this opinion.

It is so ordered.

JUSTICE O'CONNOR, *concurring in part in the judgment and dissenting in part.*

* * *

In my view, a "public safety" exception unnecessarily blurs the edges of the clear line heretofore established and makes *Miranda*'s requirements more difficult to understand. In some cases, police will benefit because a reviewing court will find that an exigency excused their failure to administer the required warnings. But in other cases, police will suffer because, though they thought an exigency excused their noncompliance, a reviewing court will view the "objective" circumstances differently and require exclusion of admissions thereby obtained. The end result will be a fine-spun new doctrine on public safety exigencies incident to custodial interrogation, complete with the hair-splitting distinctions that currently plague our Fourth Amendment jurisprudence. "While the rigidity of the prophylactic rules was a principal weakness in the view of dissenters and critics outside the Court, . . . that rigidity [has also been called a] strength of the decision. It [has] afforded police and courts clear guidance on the manner in which to conduct a custodial investigation: if it was rigid, it was also precise. . . . [T]his core virtue of *Miranda* would be eviscerated if the prophylactic rules were freely [ignored] by . . . courts under the guise of [reinterpreting] *Miranda* . . . " *Fare* v. *Michael C.*, 439 U.S. 1310, 1314 (1978). . . .

The justification the Court provides for upsetting the equilibrium that has finally been achieved—that police cannot and should not balance considerations of public safety against the individual's interest in avoiding compulsory testimonial self-incrimination—really misses the critical question to be decided. . . . *Miranda* has never been read to prohibit the police from asking questions to secure the public safety. Rather, the critical question *Miranda* addresses is, Who shall bear the cost of securing the public safety when such questions are asked and answered: the defendant or the State? *Miranda*, for better or worse, found the resolution of that question implicit in the prohibition against compulsory self-incrimination and placed the burden on the State. When police ask custodial questions without administering the required warnings, *Miranda* quite clearly requires that the answers received be presumed compelled and that they be excluded from evidence at trial. . . .

The Court concedes, as it must, both that respondent was in "custody" and subject to "interrogation" and that his statement "the gun is over there" was compelled within the meaning of our precedent. . . . In my view, since there is nothing about an exigency that makes custodial interrogation any less compelling, a principled application of *Miranda* requires that respondent's statement be suppressed. . . .

The gun respondent was compelled to supply is clearly evidence of the "real or physical" sort. What makes the question of its admissibility difficult is the fact that, in asking respondent to produce the gun, the police also "compelled" him, in the *Miranda* sense, to create an incriminating testimonial response. In other words, the case is problematic because police compelled respondent, not only to provide the gun but also to admit that he knew where it was and that it was his. . . .

[A]dmission of nontestimonial evidence secured through informal custodial interrogation will reduce the incentives to enforce the *Miranda* code. But that fact simply begs the question of *how much* enforcement is appropriate. There are some situations, as the Court's struggle to accommodate a "public safety" exception demonstrates, in which the societal cost of administering the *Miranda* warnings is very high indeed. The *Miranda* decision quite practically does not express any societal interest in having those warnings administered for their own sake. Rather, the warnings and waiver are only required to ensure that "testimony" used against the accused at trial is voluntarily given. Therefore, if the testimonial aspects of the accused's custodial communications are suppressed, the failure to administer the *Miranda* warnings should cease to be of concern. . . . The harm caused by failure to administer *Miranda* warnings relates only to admission of testimonial self-incriminations, and the suppression of such incriminations should by itself produce the optimal enforcement of the *Miranda* rule. . . .

In *Miranda*, the Court looked to the experience of countries like England, India, Scotland, and Ceylon in developing its code to regulate custodial interrogations. . . . Those countries had also adopted procedural rules to regulate the manner in which police secured confessions to be used

against accused persons at trial. . . . Confessions induced by trickery or physical abuse were never admissible at trial, and any confession secured without the required procedural safeguards could, in the courts' discretion, be excluded on grounds of fairness or prejudice. . . . But nontestimonial evidence derived from all confessions "not blatantly coerced" was and still is admitted. . . . Admission of nontestimonial evidence of this type is based on the very sensible view that procedural errors should not cause entire investigations and prosecutions to be lost. . . .

The learning of these countries was important to development of the initial *Miranda* rule. It therefore should be of equal importance in establishing the scope of the *Miranda* exclusionary rule today. I would apply that learning in this case and adhere to our precedents requiring that statements elicited in the absence of *Miranda* warnings be suppressed. But because nontestimonial evidence such as the gun should not be suppressed, I join in that part of the Court's judgment that reverses and remands for further proceedings with the gun admissible as evidence against the accused.

JUSTICE MARSHALL, *with whom* JUSTICE BRENNAN *and* JUSTICE STEVENS *join, dissenting.*

* * *

Before today's opinion, the procedures established in *Miranda* v. *Arizona* had "the virtue of informing police and prosecutors with specificity as to what they may do in conducting custodial interrogation, and of informing courts under what circumstances statements obtained during such interrogations are not admissible." . . . In a chimerical quest for public safety, the majority has abandoned the rule that brought eighteen years of doctrinal tranquility to the field of custodial interrogations. As the majority candidly concedes, . . . a public-safety exception destroys forever the clarity of *Miranda* for both law enforcement officers and members of the judiciary. The Court's candor cannot mask what a serious loss the administration of justice has incurred.

This case is illustrative of the chaos the "public-safety" exception will unleash. The circumstances of Quarles' arrest have never been in dispute. After the benefit of briefing and oral argument, the New York Court of Appeals concluded that there was "no evidence in the record before us that there were exigent circumstances posing a risk to the public safety." 58 N.Y. 2d, at 666. Upon reviewing the same facts and hearing the same arguments, a majority of this Court has come to precisely the opposite conclusion: "So long as the gun was concealed somewhere in the supermarket, with its actual whereabout unknown, it obviously posed more than one danger to the public safety. . . ."

If after plenary review two appellate courts so fundamentally differ over the threat to public safety presented by the simple and uncontested facts of this case, one must seriously question how law enforcement officers will respond to the majority's new rule in the confusion and haste of the real world. As the Chief Justice wrote in a similar context, "Few, if any, police officers are competent to make the kind of evaluation seemingly contemplated; . . . " *Rhode Island* v. *Innis*, 446 U.S. at 304 (1980), (concurring in the judgment). Not only will police officers have to decide whether the objective facts of an arrest justify an unconsented custodial interrogation; they will also have to remember to interrupt the interrogation and read the suspect his *Miranda* warnings once the focus of the inquiry shifts from protecting the public's safety to ascertaining the suspect's guilt. Disagreements of the scope of the "public-safety" exception and mistakes in its application are inevitable.

The end result, as JUSTICE O'CONNOR predicts, will be "a finespun new doctrine of public safety exigencies incident to custodial interrogation, complete with the hair-splitting distinctions that currently plague our Fourth Amendment jurisprudence." In the meantime, the courts will have to dedicate themselves to spinning this new web of doctrines, and the country's law enforcement agencies will have to suffer patiently through the frustrations of another period of constitutional uncertainty.

Though unfortunate, the difficulty of administering the "public-safety" exception is not the most profound flaw in the majority's decision. The majority has lost sight of the fact that *Miranda* v. *Arizona* and our earlier custodial-interrogation cases all implemented a constitutional privilege against self-incrimination. The rules established in these cases were designed to protect criminal defendants against prosecutions based on coerced self-incriminating statements. The majority today turns its back on these constitutional considerations and invites the government to prosecute through the use of what necessarily are coerced statements. . . .

In fashioning its "public-safety" exception to *Miranda*, the majority makes no attempt to deal with the constitutional presumption established by that case. The majority does not argue that police questioning about issues of public safety is any less coercive than custodial interrogations into other matters. The majority's only contention is that police officers could more easily protect the public if *Miranda* did not apply to custodial interrogations concerning the public's safety. But *Miranda* was not a decision about public safety; it was a decision about coerced confessions. Without establishing that interrogations concerning the public's safety are less likely to be coercive than other interrogations, the majority cannot endorse the "public-safety" exception and remain faithful to the logic of *Miranda* v. *Arizona.*

The majority's avoidance of the issue of coercion may not have been inadvertent. It would strain credulity to contend that Officer Kraft's questioning of respondent Quarles was not coercive. In the middle of the night and in the back of an empty supermarket, Quarles was surrounded by four armed police officers. His hands were handcuffed behind his back. The first words out of the mouth of the arresting officer were: "Where is the gun?" In the majority's phrase, the situation was "kaleidoscopic." Police and suspect were acting on instinct. Officer Kraft's abrupt and pointed question pressured Quarles in precisely the way that the *Miranda* Court feared the custodial interrogations would coerce self-incriminating testimony.

That the application of the "public-safety" exception in this case entailed coercion is no happenstance. The majority's *ratio decidendi* is that interrogating suspects about matters of public safety *will* be coercive. In its cost-benefit analysis, the Court's strongest argument in favor of a public-safety exception to *Miranda* is that the police would be better able to protect the public's safety if they were not always required to give suspects their *Miranda* warnings. The crux of this argument is that, by deliberately withholding *Miranda* warnings, the police can get information out of suspects who would refuse to respond to police questioning were they advised of their constitutional rights. The "public-safety" exception is efficacious precisely because it permits police officers to coerce criminal defendants into making involuntary statements.

Indeed, in the efficacy of the "public-safety" exception lies a fundamental and constitutional defect. Until today, this Court could truthfully state that the Fifth Amendment is given "broad scope" "where there has been genuine compulsion of testimony." . . . Coerced confessions were simply inadmissible in criminal prosecutions. The "public-safety" exception departs from this principle by expressly inviting police officers to coerce defendants into making incriminating statements, and then permitting prosecutors to introduce those statements at trial. . . .

The irony of the majority's decision is that the public's safety can be perfectly well protected without abridging the Fifth Amendment. If a bomb is about to explode or the public is otherwise imminently imperiled, the police are free to interrogate suspects without advising them of their constitutional rights. Such unconsented questioning may take place not only when police officers act on instinct but also when higher faculties lead them to believe that advising a suspect of his constitutional rights might decrease the likelihood that the suspect would reveal life-saving information. If trickery is necessary to protect the public, then the police may trick a suspect into confessing. While the Fourteenth Amendment sets limits on such behavior, nothing in the Fifth Amendment or our decision in *Miranda* v. *Arizona* proscribes this sort of emergency questioning. All the Fifth Amendment forbids is the introduction of coerced statements at trial. . . .

To a limited degree, the majority is correct that there is a cost associated with the Fifth Amendment's ban on introducing coerced self-incriminating statements at trial. Without a "public-safety" exception, there would be occasions when a defendant incriminated himself by revealing a threat to the public, and the State was unable to prosecute because the defendant retracted his statement after consulting with counsel and the police cannot find independent proof of guilt. Such occasions would not, however, be common. The prosecution does not always lose the use of incriminating information revealed in these situations. After consulting with counsel, a suspect may well volunteer to repeat his statement in hopes of gaining a favorable plea bargain or more lenient sentence. The majority thus overstates its case when it suggests that a police officer must necessarily choose between public safety and admissibility. . . .

The policies underlying the Fifth Amendment's privilege against self-incrimination are not diminished simply because testimony is compelled to protect the public's safety. The majority should not be permitted to elude the Amendment's absolute prohibition simply by calculating special costs that arise when the public's safety is at issue. Indeed, were constitutional adjudication always conducted in such an *ad hoc* manner, the Bill of Rights would be a most unreliable protector of individual liberties. . . .

ILLINOIS v. PERKINS
496 U.S. 292; ___ L. Ed. 2d ___; 110 S. Ct. 2394 (1990)

JUSTICE KENNEDY *delivered the opinion of the Court.*

An undercover government agent was placed in a cell of respondent Perkins, who was incarcerated on charges unrelated to the subject of the agent's investigation. Respondent made statements that implicated him in the crime that the agent sought to solve. Respondent claims that the statements should be inadmissible because he had not been given *Miranda* warnings by the agent. We hold that the statements are admissible. *Miranda* warnings are not required when the suspect is unaware that he is speaking to a law enforcement officer and gives a voluntary statement.

I

In November 1984, Richard Stephenson was murdered in a suburb of East St. Louis, Illinois. The murder remained unsolved until March 1986, when one Donald Charlton told police that he had learned about a homicide from a fellow inmate at the Graham Correctional Facility, where Charlton had been serving a sentence for burglary. The fellow inmate was Lloyd Perkins, who is the respondent here. Charlton told police that, while at Graham, he had befriended respondent, who told him in detail about a murder that respondent had committed in East St. Louis. On hearing Charlton's account, the police recognized details of the Stephenson murder that were not well known, and so they treated Charlton's story as a credible one.

By the time the police heard Charlton's account, respondent had been released from Graham, but police traced him to a jail in Montgomery County, Illinois, where he was being held pending trial on a charge of aggravated battery, unrelated to the Stephenson murder. The police wanted to investigate further respondent's connection to the Stephenson murder, but feared the use of an eavesdropping device would prove impractical and unsafe. They decided instead to place an undercover agent in the cellblock with respondent and Charlton. The plan was for Charlton and undercover agent John Parisi to pose as escapees from a work release program who had been arrested in the course of a burglary. Parisi and Charlton were instructed to engage respondent in casual conversation and report anything he said about the Stephenson murder.

Parisi, using the alias "Vito Bianco," and Charlton, both clothed in jail garb, were placed in the cellblock with respondent at the Montgomery County jail. . . . Respondent greeted Charlton, who, after a brief conversation with respondent, introduced Parisi by his alias. Parisi told respondent that he "wasn't going to do any more time," and suggested that the three of them escape. Respondent replied that the Montgomery County jail was "rinky-dink" and that they could "break out." The trio met in respondent's cell later that evening, after the other inmates were asleep, to refine their plan. Respondent said that his girlfriend could smuggle in a pistol. Charlton said, "Hey, I'm not a murderer, I'm a burglar. That's your guy's profession." After telling Charlton that he would be responsible for any murder that occurred, Parisi asked respondent if he had ever "done" anybody. Respondent said that he had, and proceeded to describe at length the events of the Stephenson murder. Parisi and respondent then engaged in some casual conversation before respondent went to sleep. Parisi did not give respondent *Miranda* warnings before the conversations.

Respondent was charged with the Stephenson murder. Before trial, he moved to suppress the statements made to Parisi in the jail. The trial court granted the motion to suppress, and the State appealed. The Appellate Court of Illinois affirmed, holding that *Miranda* v. *Arizona* prohibits all undercover contacts with incarcerated suspects which are reasonably likely to elicit an incriminating response. . . .

II

* * *

Conversations between suspects and undercover agents do not implicate the concerns underlying *Miranda*. The essential ingredients of a "police-dominated atmosphere" and compulsion are not present when an incarcerated person speaks freely to someone that he believes to be a fellow inmate. Coercion is determined from the prospective of

the suspect.When a suspect considers himself in the company of cellmates and not officers, the coercive atmosphere is lacking. . . . There is no empirical basis for the assumption that a suspect speaking to those whom he assumes are not officers will feel compelled to speak by the fear of reprisal for remaining silent or in the hope of more lenient treatment should he confess.

It is the premise of *Miranda* that the danger of coercion results from the interaction of custody and official interrogation. We reject the argument that *Miranda* warnings are required whenever a suspect is in custody in a technical sense and converses with someone who happens to be a government agent. Questioning by captors, who appear to control the suspect's fate, may create mutually reinforcing pressures that the Court has assumed will weaken the suspect's will, but where a suspect does not know that he is conversing with a government agent, these pressures do not exist. The State Court here mistakenly assumed that because the suspect was in custody, no undercover questioning could take place. When the suspect has no reason to think that the listeners have official power over him, it should not be assumed that his words are motivated by the reaction he expects from his listeners. "[W]hen the agent carries neither badge nor gun and wears not 'police blue,' but the same prison gray" as the suspect, there is no "interplay between police interrogation and police custody.". . .

Miranda forbids coercion, not mere strategic deception by taking advantage of a suspect's misplaced trust in one he supposes to be a fellow prisoner. As we recognized in *Miranda*, "[c]onfessions remain a proper element in law enforcement. Any statement given freely and voluntarily without any compelling influence is, of course, admissible as evidence." Ploys to mislead a suspect or lull him into a false sense of security that do not rise to the level of compulsion or coercion to speak are not within *Miranda*'s concerns. . . . *Miranda* was not meant to protect suspects from boasting about their criminal activities in front of persons whom they believe to be their cellmates. This case is illustrative. Respondent had no reason to feel that undercover agent Parisi had any legal authority to force him to answer questions or that Parisi could affect respondent's future treatment. Respondent viewed the cellmate-agent as an equal and showed no hint of being intimidated by the atmosphere of the jail. In recounting the details of the Stephenson murder, respondent was motivated solely by the desire to impress his fellow inmates. He spoke at his own peril.

The tacit employed here to elicit a voluntary confession from a suspect does not violate the Self-Incrimination Clause. We held in *Hoffa* v. *United States*, 385 U.S. 293 (1966), that placing an undercover agent near a suspect in order to gather incriminating information was permissible under the Fifth Amendment. . . . The only difference between this case and *Hoffa* is that the suspect here was incarcerated, but detention, whether or not for the crime in question, does not warrant a presumption that the use of an undercover agent to speak with an incarcerated suspect makes any confession thus obtained involuntary.

Our decision in *Mathis* v. *United States*, 391 U.S. 1 (1968), is distinguishable. In *Mathis*, an inmate in a state prison was interviewed by an Internal Revenue Service agent about possible tax violations. No *Miranda* warning was given before questioning. The Court held that the suspect's incriminating statements were not admissible at his subsequent trial on tax fraud charges. The suspect in *Mathis* was aware that the agent was a government official, investigating the possibility of noncompliance with the tax laws. The case before us now is different. Where the suspect does not know that he is speaking to a government agent there is no reason to assume the possibility that the suspect might feel coerced. . . .

This Court's Sixth Amendment decisions in *Massiah* v. *United States*, 377 U.S. 21 (1964), *United States* v. *Henry*, 447 U.S. 264 (1980), and *Maine* v. *Moulton*, 474 U.S. 159 (1985), also do not avail respondent. We held in those cases that the government may not use an undercover agent to circumvent the Sixth Amendment right to counsel once a suspect has been charged with the crime. After charges have been filed, the Sixth Amendment prevents the government from interfering with the accused's right to counsel. In the instant case no charges have been filed on the subject of the interrogation, and our Sixth Amendment precedents are not applicable.

Respondent can seek no help from his argument that a bright-line rule for the application of *Miranda* is desirable. Law enforcement officers will have little difficulty putting into practice our holding that undercover agents need not give *Miranda* warnings to incarcerated suspects. The use of undercover agents is a recognized law enforcement technique, often employed in the prison context to detect violence against correctional officials on inmates, as well as for the purpose served here. The interests protected by *Miranda* are not implicated in these cases, and the warnings are not required to safeguard the constitutional rights of inmates who make voluntary statements to undercover agents.

We hold that an undercover law enforcement officer posing as a fellow inmate need not give *Miranda* warnings to an incarcerated suspect before asking the questions that may elicit an incriminating response. The statements at issue in this case were voluntary, and there is no federal obstacle to their admissibility at trial. We now reverse and remand for proceedings not inconsistent with our opinion.

It is so ordered.

[The concurring opinion of JUSTICE BRENNAN is not reprinted here.]

JUSTICE MARSHALL, *dissenting.*

. . . The conditions that require the police to apprise a defendant of his constitutional rights—custodial interrogation conducted by an agent of the police—were present in this case. Because Lloyd Perkins received no *Miranda* warnings before he was subjected to custodial interrogation, his confession was not admissible.

The Court reaches the contrary conclusion by fashioning an exception to the *Miranda* rule that applies whenever "an undercover law enforcement officer posing as a fellow inmate . . . ask[s] questions that may elicit an incriminating response" from an incarcerated suspect. This exception is inconsistent with the rationale supporting *Miranda* and allows police officers intentionally to take advantage of suspects unaware of their constitutional rights. I therefore dissent.

The Court does not dispute the police officer here conducted a custodial interrogation of a criminal suspect. Perkins was incarcerated in county jail during the questioning at issue here; under these circumstances, he was in custody as that term is defined in *Miranda*. . . . The Solicitor General argues that Perkins was not in custody for purpose of *Miranda* because he was familiar with the custodial environment as a result of being in jail for two days and previously spending time in prison. Perkins' familiarity with confinement, however, does not transform his incarceration into some sort of noncustodial arrangement. . . .

. . . Although the Court does not dispute that Perkins was interrogated, it downplays the nature of the 35-minute questioning by disingenuously referring to it as a "conversatio[n]." The officer's narration of the "conversation" at Perkins' trial, however, reveals that it clearly was an interrogation.

"[*Agent:*] You ever do anyone?

"[*Perkins:*] Yeah, once in East St. Louis, in a rich white neighborhood.

"[*Informant:*] I didn't know they had any rich white neighborhoods in East St. Louis.

"[*Perkins:*] It wasn't in East St. Louis, it was by a race track in Fairview Heights. . . .

"[*Agent:*] You did a guy in Fairview Heights?

"[*Perkins:*] Yeah in a rich white section where most of the houses look the same.

"[*Informant:*] If all the houses look the same, how did you know you had the right house?

"[*Perkins:*] Me and two guys cased the house for about a week. I knew exactly which house, the second house on the left from the corner.

"[*Agent:*] How long ago did this happen?

"[*Perkins:*] Approximately about two years ago. I got paid $5,000 for that job.

"[*Agent:*] How did it go down?

"[*Perkins:*] I walked up to . . . this guy's house with a sawed-off shotgun under my trench coat.

"[*Agent:*] What type gun[?]

"[*Perkins:*] A .12 gauge Remmington [*sic*] Automatic Model 1100 sawed-off."

The police officer continued the inquiry, asking a series of questions designed to elicit specific information about the victim, the crime scene, the weapon, Perkins' motive, and his actions during and after the shooting. This interaction was not a "conversation;" Perkins, the officer, and the informant were not equal in a free-ranging discussion, with each man offering his views on different topics. Rather, it was an interrogation: Perkins was subjected to express questioning likely to evoke an incriminating response.

Because Perkins was interrogated by the police while he was in custody, *Miranda* required that the officer inform him of his rights. In rejecting that conclusion, the Court finds that "conversations" between undercover agents and suspects are devoid of the coercion inherent in stationhouse interrogations conducted by law enforcement officials who openly represent the State. *Miranda* was not, however, concerned soley with police *coercion*. It dealt with any police tactics that may operate to compel a suspect in custody to make incriminating statements without full awareness of his constitutional rights. . . . Thus, when a law enforcement agent structures a custodial interrogation so that a suspect feels compelled to reveal incriminating information, he must inform the suspect of his constitutional rights and give him an opportunity to decide whether or not to talk.

The compulsion proscribed by *Miranda* includes deception by the police. . . . Although the Court did not find trickery by itself sufficient to constitute compulsion in *Hoffa* v. *United States*, the defendant in that case was not in custody. Perkins, however, was interrogated while incarcerated. As the Court has acknowledged in the Sixth Amendment context: "[T]he mere fact of custody imposes pressures on the accused; confinement may bring into play subtle influences that will make him particularly susceptible to the ploys of undercover Government agents." *United States* v. *Henry*, 447 U.S. 264, 274 (1980). . . .

Custody works to the State's advantage in obtaining incriminating information. The psychological pressures inherent in confinement increase in the suspect's anxiety, making him likely to seek relief by talking to others. . . . The inmate is thus more susceptible to efforts by undercover agents to elicit information from him. Similarly, where the suspect is incarcerated, the constant threat of physical danger peculiar to the prison environment may make him demonstrate his toughness to other inmates by recounting or inventing past violent acts. "Because the suspect's ability to select people with whom he can confide is completely within their control, the police have a unique opportunity to exploit the suspect's vulnerability. In short, the police can insure that if the pressures of confinement lead the suspect to confide in anyone, it will be a police agent." . . . In this case, the police deceptively took advantage of Perkins' psychological vulnerability by including him in a sham escape plot, a situation in which he would feel compelled to demonstrate his willingness to shoot a prison guard by revealing his past involvement in a murder. . . .

Thus, the pressures unique to custody allow the police to use deceptive interrogation tactics to compel a suspect to make an incriminating statement. The compulsion is not eliminated by the suspect's ignorance of his interrogator's true identity. The Court therefore need not inquire past the bare facts of custody and interrogation to determine whether *Miranda* warnings are required.

The Court's adoption of an exception to the *Miranda* doctrine is incompatible with the principle, consistently applied by this Court, that the doctrine should remain simple and clear. We explained the benefits of a brightline rule in *Fare* v. *Michael C.*, 442 U.S. 707 (1979): "*Miranda's* holding has the virtue of informing police and prosecutors with specificity as to what they may do in conducting custodial interrogation, and of informing the courts under what circumstances statements obtained during such interrogation are not admissible."

The Court's holding today complicates a previously clear and straightforward doctrine. The Court opines that "[l]aw enforcement officers will have little difficulty putting into practice our holding that undercover agents need not give *Miranda* warnings to incarcerated suspects." Perhaps this prediction is true with respect to fact patterns virtually identical to the one before the Court today. But the outer boundaries of the exception created by the Court are by no means clear. Would *Miranda* be violated, for instance, if an undercover police officer beat a confession out of a suspect, but the suspect thought the officer was another prisoner who wanted the information for his own purposes?

Even if *Miranda*, as interpreted by the Court, would not permit such obviously compelled confessions, the ramifications of today's opinion are still disturbing. The exception carved out of *Miranda* doctrine today may well result in proliferation of departmental policies to encourage police officers to conduct interrogations of confined suspects through undercover agents, thereby circumventing the need to administer *Miranda* warnings. Indeed, if *Miranda* now requires a police officer to issue warnings only in those situations in which the suspect might feel compelled "to speak by the fear of reprisal for remaining silent or in the hope of more lenient treatment should he confess," presumably it allows custodial interrogation by an undercover officer posing as a member of the clergy or a suspect's defense attorney. Although such abhorrent tricks would cause the suspect's need to confide in a trusted advisor, neither would cause the suspect to "think that the listeners have official power over him." The Court's adoption of the "undercover agent" exception to the *Miranda* rule thus is necessary also the adoption of a substantial loophole in our jurisprudence protecting suspects' Fifth Amendment rights.

I dissent.

Right to Counsel

FEATURED CASES

Gideon v. *Wainwright*   *Strickland* v. *Washington*

A basic tenet of American jurisprudence is that a person charged with a criminal offense should have his or her day in court. Hence, the framers of the Bill of Rights included in the Sixth Amendment a provision that guarantees to the accused "in all criminal prosecutions" the right to assistance of counsel for his or her defense. Pursuant to that provision, congressional action and judicial decisions secured the right in federal prosecutions. (See *Johnson* v. *Zerbst*, 304 U.S. 458, 1938.) But as a result of the doctrine enunciated in *Barron* v. *Baltimore, supra*, the states were left free to determine their own rules on counsel.

Almost a century after *Barron* was decided, the due process clause of the Fourteenth Amendment began to be invoked as a limitation on the states with respect to the counsel guarantee. In 1932, the Court decided *Powell* v. *Alabama* (287 U.S. 45), the first of the celebrated *Scottsboro* cases, and held that in the circumstances of the case the manner in which counsel was provided offended the due process of the Fourteenth Amendment.[15] Noting the casual and callous manner in which the assignment of counsel was handled, Justice George Sutherland made it clear that the assistance of counsel was a fundamental ingredient of a fair trial. In reaching its decision, the Court took judicial notice of the youth of the defendants, their illiteracy, the public hostility, the incommunicado imprisonment while awaiting trial, and above all, the capital nature of the crime with which they were charged. Subsequently, Justice Sutherland's opinion was construed to require the assistance of counsel in capital cases to fulfill the due process guarantee of the Fourteenth Amendment.

The *Betts* v. *Brady* decision (310 U.S. 495, 1942), which followed ten years later, established the "special circumstances" rule to guide trial courts in their determination of the essentiality of assistance of counsel to a fair trial. Rejecting the "incorporation" argument, the Court did recognize that in some circumstances refusal to observe the counsel guarantee could result in a deprivation of due process.

After some two decades of uncertainties in the case-by-case approach, adopted in *Betts*, the Court abandoned it in *Gideon* v. *Wainwright* (372 U.S.

---

[15]The trial judge appointed all members of the local bar to serve as counsel for "the purpose of arraignment," but when the trial began six days later, no member of the local bar appeared to represent the defendants. Finally, responsibility for defense was reluctantly undertaken by one member of the local bar.

335, 1963). Justice Hugo Black's opinion for the Court made it clear that in its current view of the due process clause of the Fourteenth Amendment the counsel guarantee of the Sixth Amendment is obligatory on the states. Black indicated that the Court, in reality, was merely returning to the principles enunciated in *Powell* v. *Alabama.*

A major question left unanswered in *Gideon* was considered the following year in the well-publicized case of *Escobedo* v. *Illinois* (378 U.S. 478, 1964). At issue was the stage in the criminal process at which the suspect is entitled to the counsel guarantee. There, Escobedo's repeated requests to consult his lawyer were denied while the police interrogated him. Statements made during this interrogation were used to support a murder conviction. But, focusing on the denials of the requests to consult counsel, the Court overturned the conviction. Justice Arthur Goldberg's opinion for the majority stressed the need for counsel when the police action shifts from the investigatory to the accusatory stage, that is, when the focus is directed on the accused and the purpose of interrogation is to elicit a confession.

In subsequent cases, the Court extended the counsel guarantee to the traditional line-up procedure employed in identification of suspects. In *United States* v. *Wade* (338 U.S. 218, 1967), the Court ruled that not only is counsel required at this "critical stage" of a criminal proceeding, but the prosecution is required to notify counsel of the impending line-up. On the same day, the Court held this requirement applicable to state criminal proceedings in *Gilbert* v. *California* (388 U.S. 263). This guarantee in federal cases was negated, however, when Congress included in the Omnibus Crime Control Act of 1968 a provision permitting the admission of testimony in criminal prosecutions of those identifying a suspect even if the suspect had no counsel when identification took place in a police line-up.

Four years later, in *Kirby* v. *Illinois* (406 U.S. 682, 1972), the four Nixon appointees were joined by Justice Potter Stewart to narrow greatly line-up procedures employed in state criminal prosecutions. For them, the "critical stage" had not yet been reached at a police station line-up held prior to indictment or formal charge. Speaking for all the majority except Justice Powell, Justice Stewart argued that long-standing judicial precedents clearly established that the "right to counsel attaches only at or after the time that adversary judicial proceedings have been initiated against an accused." He concluded that only when "a defendant finds himself faced with the prosecutorial forces of organized society, and is immersed in the intricacies of substantive and procedural criminal law," is the "critical stage" reached where the command of the Sixth Amendment must be observed.

A subsequent attempt to expand the "critical stage" concept to photographic identification sessions was rejected by the Court in *United States* v. *Ash* (413 U.S. 300, 1973). The commencement of formal adversarial criminal proceedings, Justice Harry Blackmun emphasized, is essential to a determination of the "critical stage."

Initially, lower courts charted divergent courses in determining whether *Gideon* extended to nonfelonious criminal prosecutions (Cf. *In Application of Stevenson*, 458 P.2d 414, 1969; *Blake* v. *Municipal Court*, 41 Cal. Rptr. 771, 1966; and *James* v. *Headley*, 5th Cir. 410 F.2d 325, 1969). The Supreme Court considered the issue fully in *Argersinger* v. *Hamlin* (407 U.S. 25, 1972). In reversing a concealed weapons conviction of an indigent defendant (who was not provided counsel) where a ninety-day jail sentence was imposed, the Court emphasized that the Constitution proscribes imprisonment for any offense—petty, misdemeanor, or felony—unless the defendant is represented by counsel at his or her trial. Speaking for the Court, Justice William O. Douglas contended that in many instances the legal and constitutional issues and questions in a petty or misdemeanor case are just as complex as they are in a more serious felony. But Douglas tempered the requirement somewhat by indicating that this counsel rule applied only to cases where imprisonment may be imposed and would not apply to the general "run of misdemeanors."

Subsequently, however, the Burger Court refused to expand this actual imprisonment standard because it was feared that an extension would lead to unnecessary confusion with substantial costs to the states. In *Scott* v. *Illinois* (440 U.S. 367, 1979), for example, the Court refused to overturn a conviction where an indigent defendant, without counsel, was convicted on a $50 shoplifting charge. In affirming the state's denial of counsel, Justice Rehnquist emphasized for the Court that *Argersinger* does not require counsel where imprisonment is merely authorized. Rather, he held, the constitutional standard only prohibits imprisonment of a defendant when assistance of counsel is not provided. Hence, a statute (like the one under which Scott was convicted) that authorized imprisonment and/or fine does not automatically trigger a guarantee of counsel.

Gideon has also been construed to require the provision of counsel at various stages of the appellate process. Earlier, in *Griffin* v. *Illinois* (351 U.S.

12, 1956), the Court had ruled that states are obligated to provide indigents the necessary trial transcripts to appeal a noncapital conviction. The Court found no distinction between this kind of disability inflicted on the poor and the right to defense at trial. This line of reasoning was apparent when, on the same day that it decided *Gideon*, the Court held in *Douglas* v. *California* (372 U.S. 353, 1963) that the right to counsel extends to the first appeal from a criminal conviction where appeal is granted as a matter of right under state law.

The Burger Court, however, rejected attempts to extend *Douglas* beyond the first appeal where it is a matter of right. In *Ross* v. *Moffit* (417 U.S. 356, 1974), discretionary appeals and applications for Supreme Court review were held to be beyond the requirements of due process.

What is the extent of the duty of court-appointed counsel to pursue a first appeal from a conviction? The Court considered the issue in *Anders* v. *California* (386 U.S. 738, 1967) four years after it decided *Douglas*. There, court-appointed counsel for an appeal of a felony conviction reviewed the trial court record, consulted with the petitioner, and concluded that the appeal was without merit. Counsel advised the court by letter of his findings and indicated that the petitioner desired to file a brief in his own behalf. At the same time, the petitioner's request for appointment of another lawyer to handle his appeal was denied. He then proceeded to file his own brief *pro se*, but the state court of appeals affirmed his conviction. His attempts to have his case reopened via a writ of habeas corpus were rejected by both the state district court of appeals and the state supreme court. The United States Supreme Court, however, reversed, as Justice Tom Clark condemned the rather cavalier manner in which appointed counsel was permitted to dismiss his client's interest. He pointed to the *pro se* brief of the petitioner as evidence of the disadvantage suffered by a petitioner under the procedure permitted by California. Here, petitioner had failed to list as a possible error the comment of both judge and prosecutor on his failure to testify at his trial. Such comment procedures had been outlawed in *Griffin* v. *California* (380 U.S. 609, 1965). Clark concluded that "[t]he constitutional requirement of . . . fair process can only be attained where counsel acts in the role of an active advocate in behalf of his client" and certainly the "no merit letter" and the subsequent actions it triggered did "not reach that dignity." Counsel, Clark emphasized, is required to "support his client's appeal to the best of his ability." (Cf. *Evitts* v. *Lucey*, 105 S. Ct. 830, 1985, where

the Court held that the promise of *Douglas* of a criminal defendant's entitlement to counsel on the first appeal as of right would be a "futile gesture unless it comprehended the right to effective assistance of counsel.") But the Court indicated that this does not preclude counsel withdrawal from "wholly frivolous" cases. In pursuing such a course, counsel must submit to the court, with his request to withdraw, a brief that points out any issues that could "arguably support appeal." Merit of the appeal is then determined by the court after its examination of those issues. Sixteen years later, in further explication of *Anders*, the Court made it clear in *Jones* v. *Barnes* (103 S. Ct. 3308, 1983) that the indigent defendant does not have a constitutional right to compel his appointed counsel to pursue issues that counsel considers, based on his professional judgment, unworthy.

In the decade following *Gideon*, an extensive volume of case law in which the effectiveness of counsel was at issue developed in state and lower federal courts.[16] Where lack of knowledge of the relevant law or inadequate preparation produced glaring errors in defense of the accused, courts set aside convictions. (See *People* v. *Ibarra*, 386 P.2d 487, 1968, where the California Supreme Court cited ineffective counsel as a major contributor to making the trial a "farce or a sham.") Generally, however, the Supreme Court left the resolution of this problem to the lower courts and denied certiorari. But in 1970, in *McMann* v. *Richardson* (397 U.S. 759), the Supreme Court recognized the effectiveness of counsel as essential to the Sixth Amendment guarantee. The principle was underscored in subsequent cases where it held that government procedural actions had impaired "the ability of counsel to make independent decisions about how to conduct the defense." (See, for example, *Brooks* v. *Tennessee*, 406 U.S. 605, 1972; *Herring* v. *New York*, 422 U.S. 853, 1975; and *Geders* v. *United States*, 425 U.S. 80, 1976.) The Court's most significant holding on the issue came in 1984 in the case of *Strickland* v. *Washington* (446 U.S. 668), where the proper standards to be applied in making a determination of the ineffectiveness of counsel were set forth. Speaking for the Court, Justice O'Connor emphasized an "objective standard of reasonableness" and that "the benchmark for judging any claim of ineffectiveness must be whether counsel's conduct so un-

---

[16]For an excellent review of this problem, see Joel J. Finer, "Ineffective Assistance of Counsel," 58 *Cornell Law Review* 1077 (July 1973); and Robert A. Harper, Jr., "Effective Assistance of Counsel—Evolution of the Standard," 58 *Florida Bar Journal* 58 (January 1984).

dermined the proper functioning of the adversarial process that the trial cannot be relied on as having produced a just result." In short, the standards require of the claimant the heavy burden of showing that the outcome would have been different but for the ineffectiveness of his counsel. (Cf. *United States v. Cronic*, 466 U.S. 648, 1984, where Justice Stevens held that a claim of ineffective counsel must be supported by reference to specific errors committed by defense counsel.)

On a related issue, the Court has refused to di-

lute the counsel guarantee with the use of joint representation by a single counsel. In his opinion for the Court in *Holloway* v. *Arkansas* (435 U.S. 475, 1978), Chief Justice Burger made it clear that where counsel is compelled to undertake concurrent representation of defendants with conflicting interests over timely objections, making effective assistance for each problematic, the Sixth Amendment guarantee is abridged. See *Cuyler* v. *Sullivan* (446 U.S. 335, 1980), where the Court delineated further the standards for multiple representation.

GIDEON v. WAINWRIGHT
U.S. 335; 9 L. Ed. 2d 799; 83 S. Ct. 792 (1963)

JUSTICE BLACK *delivered the opinion of the Court.*

Petitioner was charged in a Florida state court with having broken and entered a pool room with intent to commit a misdemeanor. This offense is a felony under Florida law. Appearing in court without funds and without a lawyer, petitioner asked the court to appoint counsel for him, whereupon the following colloquy took place:

The Court: Mr. Gideon, I am sorry, but I cannot appoint Counsel to represent you in this case. Under the laws of the State of Florida, the only time the Court can appoint Counsel to represent a Defendant is when that person is charged with a capital offense. I am sorry, but I will have to deny your request to appoint Counsel to defend you in this case.

The Defendant: The United States Supreme Court says I am entitled to be represented by Counsel.

Put to trial before a jury, Gideon conducted his defense about as well as could be expected from a layman. He made an opening statement to the jury, cross-examined the State's witnesses, presented witnesses in his own defense, declined to testify himself, and made a short argument "emphasizing his innocence to the charge contained in the Information filed in this case." The jury returned a verdict of guilty, and petitioner was sentenced to serve five years in the state prison. Later, petitioner filed in the Florida Supreme Court this *habeas corpus* petition attacking his conviction and sentence on the ground that the trial court's refusal to appoint counsel for him denied him rights "guaranteed by the Constitution and the Bill of Rights by the United States Government." . . . [T]he State Supreme Court, "upon consideration thereof" but without

an opinion, denied all relief. . . . [W]e granted certiorari . . . and requested both sides to discuss in their briefs and oral arguments the following: "Should this Court's holding in *Betts* v. *Brady* (316 U.S. 455, 1942) be reconsidered?"

The facts upon which Betts claimed that he had been unconstitutionally denied the right to have counsel appointed to assist him are strikingly like the facts upon which Gideon here bases his federal constitutional claim. Betts was indicted for robbery in a Maryland state court. In arraignment, he told the trial judge of his lack of funds to hire a lawyer and asked the court to appoint one for him. Betts was advised that it was not the practice in that county to appoint counsel for indigent defendants except in murder and rape cases. He then pleaded not guilty, had witnesses summoned, cross-examined the State's witnesses, examined his own, and chose not to testify himself. He was found guilty by the judge, sitting without a jury, and sentenced to eight years in prison. Like Gideon, Betts sought release by *habeas corpus*, alleging that he had been denied the right to assistance of counsel in violation of the Fourteenth Amendment. Betts was denied any relief, and on review this Court affirmed. It was held that a refusal to appoint counsel for an indigent defendant charged with a felony did not necessarily violate the Due Process Clause of the Fourteenth Amendment, which for reasons given the Court deemed to be the only applicable federal constitutional provision. The Court said:

Asserting denial [of due process] is to be tested by an appraisal of the totality of facts in a given case. That which may, in one setting, constitute a denial of fundamental fairness, shocking to the universal sense of justice, may, in other circumstances, and in the light of other considerations, fall short of such denial. (316 U.S., at 462).

Treating due process as "a concept less rigid and more fluid than those envisaged in other specific and particular provisions of the Bill of Rights," the Court held that refusal to appoint counsel under the particular facts and circumstances in the *Betts* case was not so "offensive to the common and fundamental ideas of fairness" as to amount to a denial of due process. Since the facts and circumstances of the two cases are so nearly indistinguishable, we think the *Betts* v. *Brady* holding if left standing would require us to reject Gideon's claim that the Constitution guarantees him the assistance of counsel. Upon full reconsideration we conclude that *Betts* v. *Brady* should be overruled.

The Sixth Amendment provides, "In all criminal prosecutions, the accused shall enjoy the right . . . to have the Assistance of Counsel for his defense." We have construed this to mean that in federal courts counsel must be provided for defendants unable to employ counsel unless the right is competently and intelligently waived. (*Johnson* v. *Zerbst*, 304 U.S. 458, 1958.) Betts argued that this right is extended to indigent defendants in state courts by the Fourteenth Amendment. In response the Court stated that, while the Sixth Amendment laid down "no rule for the conduct of the states, the question recurs whether the constraint laid by the amendment upon the national courts expresses a rule so fundamental and essential to a fair trial, and so, to due process of law, that it is made obligatory upon the states by the Fourteenth Amendment." (316 U.S., at 463.) In order to decide whether the Sixth Amendment's guarantee of counsel is of this fundamental nature, the Court in *Betts* set out and considered "relevant data on the subject . . . afforded by constitutional and statutory provisions subsisting in the colonies and the states prior to the inclusion of the Bill of Rights in the national Constitution, and in the constitutional, legislative, and judicial history of the states to the present." (316 U.S., 471.) It was for this reason the *Betts* Court refused to accept the contention that the Sixth Amendment's guarantee of counsel for indigent federal defendants was extended to, or, in the words of that court, "made obligatory upon the states by the Fourteenth Amendment." Plainly, had the Court concluded that appointment of counsel for an indigent criminal defendant was "a fundamental right, essential to a fair trial," it would have held that the Fourteenth Amendment requires appointment of counsel in a state court, just as the Sixth Amendment requires in a federal court.

We think the Court in *Betts* had ample precedent for acknowledging that those guarantees of the Bill of Rights which are fundamental safeguards of liberty immune from federal abridgement are equally protected against state invasion by the Due Process Clause of the Fourteenth Amendment. This same principle was recognized, explained, and applied in *Powell* v. *Alabama*, 287 U.S. 45 (1932), a case upholding the right of counsel, where the Court held that despite sweeping language to the contrary in *Hurtado* v. *California*, 110 U.S. 516 (1884), the Fourteenth Amendment "embraced" those "fundamental principles of liberty and justice which lie at the base of all our civil and political institutions," even though they had been "specifically dealt with in another part of the federal Constitution" (287 U.S., at 67). In many cases other than *Powell* and *Betts*, this Court has looked to the fundamental nature of the original Bill of Rights guarantees to decide whether the Fourteenth Amendment makes them obligatory on the states. Explicitly recognized to be of this "fundamental nature" and therefore made immune from state invasion by the Fourteenth, or some part of it, are the First Amendment's freedoms of speech, press, religion, assembly, association, and petition for redress of grievances. For the same reason, though not always in precisely the same terminology, the Court has made obligatory on the States the Fifth Amendment's command that private property shall not be taken for public use without just compensation, the Fourth Amendment's prohibition of unreasonable searches and seizures, and the Eighth's ban on cruel and unusual punishment. On the other hand, this Court in *Palko* v. *Connecticut*, 302 U.S. 319 (1937), refused to hold that the Fourteenth Amendment made the double jeopardy provision of the Fifth Amendment obligatory on the States. Insofar as refusing, however, the Court, speaking through Justice Cardozo, was careful to emphasize that "immunities that are valid against the federal government by force of the specific pledges of particular amendments have been found to be implicit in the concept of ordered liberty, and thus, through the Fourteenth Amendment, become valid as against the states" and that guarantees "in their origin . . . effective against the federal government alone" had by prior cases "been taken over from the earlier articles of the Federal Bill of Rights and brought within the Fourteenth Amendment by a process of absorption." (302 U.S. at 324–325, 326.)

We accept *Betts* v. *Brady*'s assumption, based as it

was on our prior cases, that a provision of the Bill of Rights which is "fundamental and essential to a fair trial" is made obligatory upon the states by the Fourteenth Amendment. We think the Court in *Betts* was wrong, however, in concluding that the Sixth Amendment's guarantee of counsel is not one of these fundamental rights. Ten years before *Betts* v. *Brady*, this Court, after full consideration of all historical data examined in *Betts*, had unequivocally declared that "the right to the aid of counsel is of this fundamental character." *Powell* v. *Alabama*, 287 U.S. 45, 68 (1932). While the Court at the close of its *Powell* opinion did by its language, as it frequently does, limit its holding to the particular facts and circumstances of that case, its conclusions about the fundamental nature of the right to counsel are unmistakable. Several years later, in 1936, the Court reemphasized what it has said about the fundamental nature of the right to counsel in this language:

> We concluded that certain fundamental rights, safeguarded by the first eight amendments against federal action, were also safeguarded against state action by the due process clause of the Fourteenth Amendment, and among them the fundamental right of the accused to the aid of counsel in a criminal prosecution. *Grossjean* v. *American Press Co.*, 297 U.S. 233, 243–244 (1936).

And again in 1938 this Court said:

> [The assistance of counsel] is one of the safeguards of the Sixth Amendment deemed necessary to insure fundamental human rights of life and liberty. . . . The Sixth Amendment stands as a constant admonition that if the constitutional safeguards it provides be lost, justice will "still be done," *Johnson* v. *Zerbst*, 304 U.S. 458, 462 (1938). . . .

In the light of these and many other prior decisions of this Court, it is not surprising that the *Betts* Court, when faced with the contention that "one charged with crime, who is unable to obtain counsel, must be furnished counsel by the state," conceded that "expressions in the opinions of this court lend color to the argument . . . " 316 U.S., at 462–463. The fact is that in deciding as it did—that "appointment of counsel is not a fundamental right, essential to a fair trial"—the Court in *Betts* v. *Brady* made an abrupt break with its own well-considered precedents. In returning to these old precedents, sounder we believe than the new, we but restore constitutional principles established to achieve a fair system of justice. Not only these precedents but also reason and reflection require

us to recognize that in our adversary system of criminal justice, any person haled into court, who is too poor to hire a lawyer, cannot be assured a fair trial unless counsel is provided for him. This seems to us to be an obvious truth. Governments, both state and federal, quite properly spend vast sums of money to establish machinery to try defendants accused of crime. Lawyers to prosecute are everywhere deemed essential to protect the public's interest in an orderly society. Similarly, there are few defendants charged with crime, few, indeed, who fail to hire the best lawyers they can get to prepare and present their defenses. That government hires lawyers to prosecute and defendants who have the money hire lawyers to defend are the strongest indications of a widespread belief that lawyers in criminal courts are necessities, not luxuries. The right of one charged with crime to counsel may not be deemed fundamental and essential to fair trials in some countries, but it is in ours. From the very beginning, our state and national constitutions and laws have laid great emphasis on procedural and substantive safeguards designed to assure fair trials before impartial tribunals in which every defendant stands equal before the law. This noble ideal cannot be realized if the poor man charged with crime has to face his accusers without a lawyer to assist him. A defendant's need for a lawyer is nowhere better stated than in the moving words of Justice Sutherland in *Powell* v. *Alabama*:

> The right to be heard would be, in many cases, of little avail if it did not comprehend the right to be heard by counsel. Even the intelligent and educated layman has small and sometimes no skill in the science of law. If charged with crime, he is incapable, generally, of determining for himself whether the indictment is good or bad. He is unfamiliar with the rules of evidence. Left without the aid of counsel he may be put on trial without a proper charge, and convicted upon incompetent evidence, or evidence irrelevant to the issue or otherwise inadmissible. He lacks both the skill and knowledge adequately to prepare his defense, even though he has a perfect one. He requires the guiding hand of counsel at every step in the proceedings against him. Without it, though he be not guilty, he faces the danger of conviction because he does not know how to establish his innocence, 287 U.S., at 68–69.

The Court in *Betts* v. *Brady* departed from the sound wisdom upon which the Court's holding in *Powell* v. *Alabama* rested. Florida, supported by two other States, asked that *Betts* v. *Brady* be left intact. Twenty-two States, as friends of the Court, argue that *Betts* was "an anachronism when handed down" and that it should now be overruled. We agree.

> *The Judgment is reversed and the cause is remanded to the Supreme Court of Florida for further action not inconsistent with this opinion.*

JUSTICE CLARK, *concurring.*

I must conclude . . . that the Constitution makes no distinction between capital and noncapital cases. The Fourteenth Amendment requires due process of law for the deprival of "liberty" just as for deprival of "life," and there cannot constitutionally be a difference in the sanction involved. How can the Fourteenth Amendment tolerate a procedure which it condemns in capital cases on the ground that deprival of liberty may be less onerous than deprival of life—a value judgment not universally accepted—or that only the latter deprival is irrevocable? I can find no acceptable rationalization for such a result, and I therefore concur in the judgment of the Court.

JUSTICE HARLAN, *concurring.*

I agree that *Betts* v. *Brady* should be overruled, but consider it entitled to a more respectful burial than has been accorded, at least on the part of those of us who were not on the Court when that case was decided.

I cannot subscribe to the view that *Betts* v. *Brady* represented "an abrupt break with its own well-considered precedents." . . . The principles declared in *Powell* and *Betts* . . . had a troubled journey throughout the years that have followed first the one case and then the other. Even by the time of the *Betts* decision, dictum in at least one of the Court's opinions had indicated that there was an absolute right to the services of counsel in the trial of state capital cases. "Such dicta continued to appear in subsequent decisions," and any lingering doubts were finally eliminated by the holding of *Hamilton* v. *Alabama*, 368 U.S. 52, 1961.

In noncapital cases, the "special circumstances" rule has continued to exist in form while its substance has been substantially and steadily eroded.

. . . The Court has come to recognize, in other words, that the mere existence of a serious criminal charge constituted in itself special circumstances requiring the services of counsel at trial. In truth the *Betts* v. *Brady* rule is no longer a reality.

This evolution, however, appears not to have been fully recognized by many state courts, in this instance charged with the front-line responsibility for the enforcement of constitutional rights. . . . To continue a rule which is honored by this Court only with lip service is not a healthy thing and in the long run will do disservice to the federal system.

The special circumstances rule has been formally abandoned in capital cases, and the time has now come when it should be abandoned in noncapital cases, at least as to offenses which, as the one involved here, carry the possibility of a substantial prison sentence. (Whether the rule should extend to all criminal cases need not be decided.) This indeed does no more than to make explicit something that has long since been foreshadowed in our decisions.

In agreeing with the Court that the right to counsel in a case such as this should now be expressly recognized as a fundamental right embraced in the Fourteenth Amendment. I wish to make a further observation. When we hold a right or immunity, valid against the Federal Government, to be "implicit in the concept of ordered liberty" and thus valid against the States, I do not read our past decisions to suggest that by so holding, we automatically carry over an entire body of federal law and apply it in full sweep to the States. Any such concept would disregard the frequently wide disparity between the legitimate interests of the States and of the Federal Government, the divergent problems that they face, and the significantly different consequences of their actions. . . . In what is done today I do not understand the Court to depart from the principles laid down in *Palko* v. *Connecticut* . . . or to embrace the concept that the Fourteenth Amendment "incorporates" the Sixth Amendment as such.

On these premises I join in the judgment of the Court.

JUSTICE O'CONNOR *delivered the opinion of the Court.*

This case requires us to consider the proper standards for judging a criminal defendant's contention that the Constitution requires a conviction or death sentence to be set aside because counsel's assistance at the trial or sentencing was ineffective.

I

A

During a 10-day period in September 1976, respondent planned and committed three groups of crimes, which included three brutal stabbing murders, torture, kidnapping, severe assaults, attempted murders, attempted extortion, and theft. After his two accomplices were arrested, respondent surrendered to police and voluntarily gave a lengthy statement confessing to the third of the criminal episodes. The State of Florida indicted respondent for kidnapping and murder and appointed an experienced criminal lawyer to represent him.

Counsel actively pursued pretrial motions and discovery. He cut his efforts short, however, and he experienced a sense of hopelessness about the case when he learned that, against his specific advice, respondent had also confessed to the first two murders. By the date set for trial, respondent was subject to indictment for three counts of first-degree murder and multiple counts of robbery, kidnapping for ransom, breaking and entering and assault, attempted murder, and conspiracy to commit robbery. Respondent waived his right to a jury trial, again acting against counsel's advice, and pleaded guilty to all charges, including the three capital murder charges.

In the plea colloquy, respondent told the trial judge that, although he had committed string of burglaries, he had no significant prior criminal record and that at the time of his criminal spree he was under extreme stress caused by his inability to support his family. He also stated, however, that he accepted responsibility for the crimes. The trial judge told respondent that he had "a great deal of respect for people who are willing to step forward and admit their responsibility" but that he was making no statement at all about his likely sentencing decision.

Counsel advised respondent to invoke his right under Florida law to an advisory jury at his capital sentencing hearing. Respondent rejected the advice and waived the right. He chose instead to be sentenced by the trial judge without a jury recommendation.

In preparing for the sentencing hearing, counsel spoke with respondent about his background. He also spoke on the telephone with respondent's wife and mother, though he did not follow up on the one unsuccessful effort to meet with them. He did not otherwise seek out character witnesses for respondent. Nor did he request a psychiatric examination, since his conversations with his client gave no indication that respondent had psychological problems.

Counsel decided not to present and hence not to look further for evidence concerning respondent's character and emotional state. That decision reflected trial counsel's sense of hopelessness about overcoming the evidentiary effect of respondent's confessions to the gruesome crimes, it also reflected the judgment that it was advisable to rely on the plea colloquy for evidence about respondent's background and about his claim of emotional stress. The plea colloquy communicated sufficient information about these subjects, and by forgoing the opportunity to present new evidence on these subjects, counsel prevented the State from cross-examining respondent on his claim and from putting on psychiatric evidence of its own.

Counsel also excluded from the sentencing hearing other evidence he thought was potentially damaging. He successfully moved to exclude respondent's "rap sheet." Because he judged that a presentence report might prove more detrimental than helpful, as it would have included respondent's criminal history and thereby would have undermined the claim of no significant history of criminal activity, he did not request that one be prepared.

At the sentencing hearing, counsel's strategy was based primarily on the trial judge's remarks at the plea colloquy as well as on his reputation as a sentencing judge who thought it important for a convicted defendant to own up to his crime. Counsel argued that respondent's remorse and acceptance of responsibility justified sparing him from the death penalty. Counsel also argued that respondent had no history of criminal activity and that respondent committed the crimes under extreme mental or emotional disturbance, thus coming within the statutory list of mitigating circumstances. He further argued that respondent should be spared death because he had surrendered, confessed, and offered to testify against a codefendant, and because respondent was fundamentally a good person who had briefly gone badly wrong in extremely stressful circumstances. The State put on evidence and witnesses largely for the purpose of describing the details of the crimes. Counsel did not cross-examine the medical experts who testified about the manner of death of respondent's victims.

The trial judge found several aggravating circumstances with respect to each of the three murders. He found that all three murders were especially heinous, atrocious, and cruel, all involving repeated stabbings. All three murders were committed in the course of at least one other dangerous and violent felony, and since all involved robbery, the murders were for pecuniary gain. All three murders were committed to avoid arrest for the accompanying crimes and to hinder law enforcement. In the course of one of the murders, respondent knowingly subjected numerous persons to a grave risk of death by deliberately stabbing and shooting the murder victim's sisters-in-law, who sustained severe—in one case, ultimately fatal—injuries.

With respect to mitigating circumstances, the trial judge made the same findings for all three capital murders. First, although there was no admitted evidence of prior convictions, respondent had stated that he had engaged in a course of stealing. In any case, even if respondent had no significant history of criminal activity, the aggravating circumstances "would still clearly far outweigh" that mitigating factor. Second, the judge found that, during all three crimes, respondent was not suffering from extreme mental or emotional disturbance and could appreciate the criminality of his acts. Third, none of the victims was a participant in, or consented to, respondent's conduct. Fourth, respondent's participation in the crimes was neither minor nor the result of duress or domination by an accomplice. Finally, respondent's age (26) could not be considered a factor in mitigation, especially when viewed in light of respondent's planning of the crimes and disposition of the proceeds of the various accompanying thefts.

In short, the trial judge found numerous aggravating circumstances and no (or a single comparatively insignificant) mitigating circumstance. . . . He therefore sentenced respondent to death on each of the three counts of murder and to prison

terms for the other crimes. The Florida Supreme Court upheld the convictions and sentences on direct appeal.

B

Respondent subsequently sought collateral relief in state court on numerous grounds, among them that counsel had rendered ineffective assistance at the sentencing proceeding. Respondent challenged counsel's assistance in six respects. He asserted that counsel was ineffective because he failed to move for a continuance to prepare for sentencing, to request a psychiatric report, to investigate and present character witnesses, to seek a presentence investigation report, to present meaningful arguments to the sentencing judge, and to investigate the medical examiner's reports or cross-examine the medical experts. In support of the claim, respondent submitted 14 affidavits from friends, neighbors, and relatives stating that they would have testified if asked to do so. He also submitted one psychiatric report and one psychological report stating that respondent, though not under the influence of extreme mental or emotional disturbance, was "chronically frustrated and depressed because of his economic dilemma" at the time of his crimes.

The trial court denied relief without an evidentiary hearing, finding that the record evidence conclusively showed that the ineffectiveness claim was meritless. . . .

Applying the standard for ineffectiveness claims articulated by the Florida Supreme Court in *Knight* v. *State*, 394 So. 2d 997 (1981), the trial court concluded that respondent had not shown that counsel's assistance reflected any substantial and serious deficiency measurably below that of competent counsel that was likely to have affected the outcome of the sentencing proceeding. The court specifically found: "[A]s a matter of law, the record affirmatively demonstrates beyond any doubt that even if [counsel] had done each of the . . . things [that respondent alleged counsel had failed to do] at the time of sentencing, there is not even the remotest chance that the outcome would have been any different. The plain fact is that the aggravating circumstances proved in this case were completely *overwhelming*. . . ."

The Florida Supreme Court affirmed the denial of relief. . . .

C

Respondent next filed a petition for a writ of *habeas corpus* in the United States District Court for the Southern District of Florida. He advanced numerous grounds for relief, among them ineffective assistance of counsel based on the same errors, except for the failure to move for a continuance, as those he had identified in state court. The District Court held an evidentiary hearing to inquire into trial counsel's efforts to investigate and to present mitigating circumstances. Respondent offered the affidavits and reports he had submitted in the state collateral proceedings; he also called his trial counsel to testify. The State of Florida, over respondent's objection, called the trial judge to testify.

The District Court disputed none of the state court factual findings concerning trial counsel's assistance and made findings of its own that are consistent with the state court findings. The account of trial counsel's actions and decisions given above reflects the combined findings. On the legal issue of ineffectiveness, the District Court concluded that, although trial counsel made errors in judgment in failing to investigate nonstatutory mitigating evidence further than he did, no prejudice to respondent's sentence resulted from any such error in judgment. Relying in part on the trial judge's testimony but also on the same factors that led the state courts to find no prejudice, the District Court concluded that "there does not appear to be likelihood, or even a significant possibility" that any errors of trial counsel had affected the outcome of the sentencing proceeding and . . . accordingly denied the petition for a writ of *habeas corpus.*

On appeal, a panel of the United States Court of Appeals for the Fifth Circuit affirmed in part, vacated in part, and remanded with instructions to apply to the particular facts the framework for analyzing ineffectiveness claim that it developed in its opinion. The panel decision was itself vacated when Unit B of the former Fifth Circuit, now the Eleventh Circuit decided to rehear the case *en banc.* The full Court of Appeals developed its own framework for analyzing ineffective assistance claims and reversed the judgment of the District Court and remanded the case for new fact-finding under the newly announced standards. . . .

. . . The Court of Appeals stated that the Sixth Amendment right to assistance of counsel accorded criminal defendants a right to "counsel reasonably likely to render and rendering reasonably effective assistance given the totality of the circumstances." The court remarked in passing that no special standard applies in capital cases such as the one before it: the punishment that a defendant faces is merely one of the circumstances to be considered in determining whether counsel was reasonably effective. The court then addressed respondent's contention that his trial counsel's assistance was not reasonably effective because counsel breached his duty to investigate nonstatutory mitigating circumstances.

The court agreed that the Sixth Amendment imposes on counsel a duty to investigate, because reasonably effective assistance must be based on professional decisions and informed legal choices can be made only after investigation of options. The court observed that counsel's investigatory decisions must be assessed in light of the information known at the time of the decisions, not in hindsight, and that "[t]he amount of pretrial investigation that is reasonable defies precise measurement." Nevertheless, putting guilty-plea cases to one side, the court attempted to classify cases presenting issues concerning the scope of the duty to investigate before proceeding to trial.

If there is only one plausible line of defense, the court concluded, counsel must conduct a "reasonably substantial investigation" into that line of defense, since there can be no strategic choice that renders such an investigation unnecessary. . . .

If there is more than one plausible line of defense, the court held, counsel should ideally investigate each line substantially before making a strategic choice about which lines to rely on at trial. If counsel conducts such substantial investigations, the strategic choices made as a result "will seldom if ever" be found wanting. . . .

If counsel does not conduct a substantial investigation into each of several plausible lines of defense, assistance may nonetheless be effective. Counsel may not exclude certain lines of defense for other than strategic reasons. Limitations of time and money, however, may force early strategic choices, often based solely on conversations with the defendant and a review of the prosecutions' evidence. Those strategic choices about which lines of defense to pursue are owed deference commensurate with the reasonableness of the professional judgments on which they are based. Thus, "when counsel's assumptions are reasonable given the totality of the circumstances and when counsel's strategy represents a reasonable choice based upon those assumptions, counsel need not investigate lines of defense that he has chosen not to employ at trial." Among the factors relevant to deciding whether particular strategic choices are reasonable are the experience of the attorney, the inconsistency of unpursued lines of defense, and the potential for prejudice from taking an unpursued line of defense.

. . . [T]he Court of Appeals [next] turned its attention to the question of the prejudice to the defense that must be shown before counsel's errors justify reversal of the judgment. The court observed that only in cases of outright denial of counsel, of affirmative government interference in the representation process, or of inherently prejudicial conflicts of interest had this Court said that no special showing of prejudice need be made. For cases of deficient performance by counsel, where the Government is not directly responsible for the deficiencies and where evidence of deficiency may be more accessible to the defendant than to the prosecution, the defendant must show that counsel's errors "resulted in actual and substantial disadvantage to the course of his defense." This standard, the Court of Appeals reasoned, is compatible with the "cause and prejudice" standard for overcoming procedural defaults in federal collateral proceedings and discourages insubstantial claims by requiring more than a showing, which could virtually always be made, of some conceivable adverse effect on the defense from counsel's errors. The specified showing of prejudice would result in reversal of the judgment, the court concluded, unless the prosecution showed that the constitutionally deficient performance was, in light of all the evidence, harmless beyond a reasonable doubt. . . .

The Court of Appeals thus laid down the tests to be applied in the Eleventh Circuit in challenges to convictions on the ground of ineffectiveness of counsel. . . .

. . . [W]e granted certiorari to consider the standards by which to judge a contention that the Constitution requires that a criminal judgment be overturned because of the actual ineffective assistance of counsel. . . .

II

* * *

The Sixth Amendment recognizes the right to the assistance of counsel because it envisions counsel's playing a role that is critical to the ability of the adversarial system to produce just results. An accused is entitled to be assisted by an attorney, whether retained or appointed, who plays the role necessary to ensure that the trial is fair.

For that reason, the Court has recognized that "the right to counsel is the right to the effective assistance of counsel." *McMann* v. *Richardson*, 397 U.S. 759, 711, n. 14 (1970). Government violates the right to effective assistance when it interferes in certain ways with the ability of counsel to make decisions about how to conduct the defense. . . . Counsel, however, can also deprive a defendant of the right to effective assistance simply by failing to render "adequate legal assistance." *Cuyler* v. *Sullivan*, 446 U.S., at 344.

The Court has not elaborated on the meaning of the constitutional requirement of effective assistance. . . . In giving meaning to the requirement, however, we must take its purpose—to ensure a fair trial—as the guide. The benchmark for judging any claim of ineffectiveness must be whether counsel's conduct so undermined the proper functioning of the adversarial process that the trial cannot be relied on as having produced a just result. . . .

III

A convicted defendant's claim that counsel's assistance was so defective as to require reversal of a conviction or death sentence has two components. First, the defendant must show that counsel's performance was deficient. This requires showing that counsel made errors so serious that counsel was not functioning as the "counsel" guaranteed the defendant by the Sixth Amendment. Second, the defendant must show that the deficient performance prejudiced the defense. This requires showing that counsel errors were so serious as to deprive the defendant of a fair trial, a trial whose result is reliable. Unless a defendant makes both showings, it cannot be said that the conviction or death sentence resulted from a breakdown in the adversary process that renders the result unreliable.

A

As all the Federal Courts of Appeals have now held, the proper standard for attorney performance is that of reasonably effective assistance. The Court indirectly recognized as much when it stated in *McMann* v. *Richardson*, 397 U.S., at 770, 771, that a guilty plea cannot be attacked as based on inadequate legal advice unless counsel was not "a reasonably competent attorney" and the advice was not "within the range of competence demanded of attorneys in criminal cases." See also *Cuyler* v. *Sullivan, supra,* 446 U.S., at 344, 100 S. Ct., at 1716. When a convicted defendant complains of the ineffectiveness of counsel's assistance, the defendant must show that counsel's representation fell below an objective standard of reasonableness.

More specific guidelines are not appropriate. The Sixth Amendment refers simply to "counsel," not specifying particular requirements of effective assistance. It relies instead on the legal profession's maintenance of standards sufficient to justify the law's presumption that counsel will fulfill the role in the adversary process that the Amendment envisions. The proper measure of attorney performance remains simply reasonableness under prevailing professional norms. . . .

Prevailing norms of practice as reflected in American Bar Association standards and the like . . . are guides to determining what is reasonable, but they are only guides. No particular set of detailed rules for counsel's conduct can satisfactorily take account of the variety of circumstances faced by defense counsel or the range of legitimate decisions regarding how best to represent a criminal defendant. Any such set of rules would interfere with the constitutionally protected independence of counsel and restrict the wide latitude counsel must have in making tactical decisions. . . . [T]he purpose of the effective assistance guarantee of the Sixth Amendment is not to improve the quality of legal representation, although that is a goal of considerable importance to the legal system. The purpose is simply to ensure that criminal defendants receive a fair trial.

Judicial scrutiny of counsel's performance must be highly deferential. It is all too tempting for a defendant to second-guess counsel's assistance after conviction or adverse sentence, and it is all too easy for a court, examining counsel's defense after it has proved unsuccessful, to conclude that a particular act or omission of counsel was unreasonable. A fair assessment of attorney performance requires that every effort be made to eliminate the distorting effects of hindsight, to reconstruct the circumstances of counsel's challenged conduct, and to evaluate the conduct from counsel's perspective at the time. Because of the difficulties inherent in making the evaluation, a court must indulge a strong presumption that counsel's conduct falls within the wide range of reasonable professional assistance; that is, the defendant must overcome the presumption that, under the circumstances, the challenged action "might be considered sound trial strategy." . . .

The availability of intrusive post-trial inquiry into attorney performance or of detailed guidelines for its evaluation would encourage the proliferation of ineffectiveness challenges. Criminal trials resolved unfavorably to the defendant would increasingly come to be followed by a second trial, this one of counsel's unsuccessful defense. Counsel's performance and even willingness to serve could be adversely affected. Intensive scrutiny of counsel and rigid requirements for acceptable assistance could dampen the ardor and impair the independence of defense counsel, discourage the acceptance of assigned cases, and undermine the trust between attorney and client. . . .

IV

. . . Most important, in adjudicating a claim of actual ineffectiveness of counsel, a court should keep in mind that the principles we have stated do not establish mechanical rules. Although those principles should guide the process of decision, the ultimate focus of inquiry must be on the fundamental fairness of the proceeding whose result is being challenged. In every case the court should be concerned with whether, despite the strong presumption of reliability, the result of the particular proceeding is unreliable because of a breakdown in the adversarial process that our system counts on to produce just results.

To the extent that this has already been the guiding inquiry in the lower courts, the standards articulated today do not require reconsideration of ineffectiveness claims rejected under different standards. . . . In particular, the minor differences in the lower courts' precise formulations of the performance standard are insignificant: the different formulations are mere variations of the overarching reasonableness standard. . . .

V

* * *

Application of the governing principles is not difficult in this case. The facts . . . make clear that the conduct of respondent's counsel at and before respondent's sentencing proceeding cannot be found unreasonable. They also make clear that, even assuming the challenged conduct of counsel was unreasonable, respondent suffered insufficient prejudice to warrant setting aside his death sentence.

With respect to the performance component, the record shows that respondent's counsel made a strategic choice to argue for the extreme emotional distress mitigating circumstance and to rely as fully as possible on respondent's acceptance of responsibility for his crimes. Although counsel understandably felt hopeless about respondent's prospects, nothing in the record indicates . . . that counsel's sense of hopelessness distorted his professional judgment. Counsel's strategy choice was well within the range of professionally reasonable judgments, and the decision not to seek more character or psychological evidence than was already in hand was likewise reasonable. . . .

Failure to make the required showing of either deficient performance or sufficient prejudice defeats the ineffectiveness claim. Here there is a double failure. More generally, respondent has made no showing that the justice of his sentence was rendered unreliable by a breakdown in the adversary process caused by deficiencies in counsel's assistance. Respondent's sentencing proceeding was not fundamentally unfair.

We conclude, therefore, that the District Court properly declined to issue a writ of *habeas corpus.*

The judgment of the Court of Appeals is accordingly

Reversed.

[The opinion of JUSTICE BRENNAN, concurring in part and dissenting in part, is not reprinted here.]

The Death Penalty Controversy

FEATURED CASES

Gregg v. *Georgia*   *McCleskey* v. *Kemp*   *Stanford* v. *Kentucky*   *Payne* v. *Tennessee*

Since its 1972 decision in *Furman* v. *Georgia* (408 U.S. 238), the Court has remained embroiled in the continuing controversy over the death penalty. In *Furman,* the Court found violative of the Eighth and Fourteenth Amendments particular state statutes[17] that allowed juries unfettered discretion to impose the death penalty and that allowed for the arbitrary and discriminatory implementation of these laws.[18] Beyond this statement of principle, however, there was little agreement among the majority, and each wrote a concurring opinion without support from any of his associates. Three of the majority justices (Douglas, Stewart, and White) found the statutes defective because they failed to mandatorily impose the death penalty for specific crimes, allowing juries to exercise undirected discretion in each case. This led them to express concern about the discriminatory application of the penalty possible under such statutory schemes. Statistics were cited that revealed the substantial differential treatment between whites and nonwhites and between "the poor who lack 'political clout' " and the more socially prominent. Justice Potter Stewart set forth the argument that the death penalty in these cases is "cruel" because the juries in their discretion go "excessively . . . beyond, not in degree but in kind, the punishments that the state legislatures [had] determined to be necessary." It is "unusual," he continued, because of its infrequent imposition as punishment for murder and rape.

Because of this infrequent imposition, Justice Byron White could not see any effective contribution of the death penalty as a deterrent to crime. He characterized it as a "pointless and needless extinction of life with only marginal contributions to any discernible social or public purposes." And Justices Brennan and Marshall expressed the view that the death penalty was unconstitutional *per se.* Brennan argued that imposition of the death penalty as punishment for crimes is "cruel and unusual punishment" because "it does not comport with human dignity," and Justice Thurgood Marshall felt that such a mode of punishment was "no longer consistent with our 'self-respect.' "

Each of the dissenters wrote opinions, and, unlike the majority justices, they joined in each other's opinion. Essentially, theirs was a plea for judicial restraint and deference to legislatures in prescribing penalties deemed necessary as punishments for crime. And Chief Justice Burger emphasized that a thorough analysis of the intent of the framers of the Eighth Amendment does not support the conclusion that the death penalty was one of the cruel and unusual punishments banned by the Amendment.

The dissenters emphasized that only two members of the majority had held that the death penalty *per se* is cruel and unusual punishment. Hence, the ruling did not prevent legislatures from prescribing capital punishment for specified crimes. Undoubtedly, the state legislatures got this same message, and thirty-five of them moved at varying degrees of speed to bring their statutes into conformity with the standards enunciated in *Furman.* Some of the revamped statutes called for bifurcated proceedings—a trial segment followed

---

[17]The Georgia statute was at issue in *Furman* and *Jackson* v. *Georgia,* and the Texas law was at issue in *Branch* v. *Texas.*

[18]This holding was somewhat surprising, since the Court had approved broad jury discretion in capital cases one year earlier in *McGautha* v. *California* (402 U.S. 183, 1971).

by a separate sentencing proceeding. Missouri's unique bifurcated procedure, for example, where the sentencing phase resembles the trial on the issue of guilt or innocence gave rise to an interesting double jeopardy argument in *Bullington* v. *Missouri* (451 U.S. 430, 1981). Because of this and the statute's explicit requirement that the jury in the sentencing phase determine whether the prosecution has proved its case, the Court held that the protection afforded by the double jeopardy clause applied to the sentencing phase. Here, the death sentence was imposed after the second trial was based on the same aggravating circumstances that produced a life sentence in the first trial. Justice Harry Blackmun, who spoke for the Court, noted that when the jury imposed a life sentence after the first trial, it had found the aggravating factors that were again presented by the prosecution at the second trial inadequate to support imposition of the death penalty. Cf. *Arizona* v. *Rumsey* (104 S. Ct. 2405, 1984). In general, most of the several statutes mandate consideration of specified aggravating and mitigating circumstances, although some eliminated the sentencing discretion by specifying the crimes for which the death penalty could be imposed. However, they all mandate some type of appellate review.

Certain of these so-called revised death penalty statutes were once again before the Court in five cases arising in Florida, Georgia, Texas, North Carolina, and Louisiana during the 1975 term.[19] Seven justices were satisfied that the standards enunciated in *Furman* had been followed in Georgia, Florida, and Texas, but not in North Carolina and Louisiana. In the leading opinion of Justices Stewart, Powell, and Stevens, it was noted that the statutes of the three aforementioned states contained standards that would ensure that the death penalty could not be imposed "arbitrarily and capriciously." Furthermore, pointing to its long use in the United States and the reflection of "contemporary standards of decency" by the legislative bodies recently enacting capital punishment statutes, and the continued disposition of juries to impose the penalty, the three justices rejected the cruel and unusual punishment attack. The concurring justices echoed similar themes.

Employing reasoning similar to that in *Gregg* v. *Georgia*, the Court sustained the Florida and Texas statutes but set aside the Louisiana and North Carolina statutes for insufficient standards to control

court and jury discretion. In a subsequent review of the Louisiana statute one year later in *Harry Roberts* v. *Louisiana* (431 U.S. 633), the Court emphasized the need to allow the sentencing authority to consider mitigating circumstances to be consistent with *Gregg*. In striking down the mandatory death penalties prescribed by the statute, the Court reasserted its holding in *Woodson*, the North Carolina case of the previous year, that:

> the fundamental respect for humanity underlying the Eighth Amendment requires consideration of the character and record of the individual offender and the circumstances of the particular offense as a constitutionally indispensable part of the process of inflicting the penalty of death.

A steady stream of cases since *Gregg* has allowed the Court to explicate further the constitutional standards for imposition of the death penalty. Imposition of the penalty for rape was considered "excessive punishment" for the crime contrary to the cruel and unusual punishment prohibition of the Eighth Amendment in *Coker* v. *Georgia* (433 U.S. 584, 1977). Justice Byron White's plurality opinion emphasized that while "rape is without doubt deserving of serious punishment . . . in terms of moral depravity and . . . injury to the person and to the public, it does not compare with murder. . . ." In an action the next year—*Lockett* v. *Ohio* (438 U.S. 586, 1978), the Court made it clear that *Gregg* requires the "individualized consideration of mitigating circumstances" and that even where a statutory enumeration of such factors is made, such a listing should not be construed to preclude consideration of others by the sentencing authority (Cf. *Eddings* v. *Oklahoma*, 455 104, 1982). This was reemphasized two years later in *Beck* v. *Alabama* (447 U.S. 625, 1980), when the Court overturned a death sentence imposed for a "robbery-intentional killing" conviction where the jury was statutorily proscribed from considering a "lesser included offense"—felony, murder. Justice John Paul Stevens maintained that in withholding the "lesser included offense" option from the jury, the risk of an unwarranted conviction may well be enhanced. He concluded that "such a risk" was intolerable when a person's life is at stake. However, the Court, in *Spaziano* v. *Florida* (104 S. Ct. 3154, 1984), did not consider a trial court's refusal to instruct the jury on lesser included offenses, where the statute of limitations had run on such offenses, inconsistent with *Beck*.

On another key issue in *Spaziano*, the Court upheld the Florida capital sentencing scheme that al-

---

[19]*Profit* v. *Florida*, 428 U.S. 242; *Gregg* v. *Georgia*, 428 U.S. 153; *Jurek* v. *Texas*, 428 U.S. 262; *Woodson* v. *North Carolina*, 428 U.S. 280; and *Stanislaus Roberts* v. *Louisiana*, 428 U.S. 325.

lows a trial judge to disregard the jury's sentence recommendation. Here, the jury, after considering both aggravating and mitigating circumstances, recommended life imprisonment. But the trial judge disregarded their advice and imposed a death sentence because he concluded that the aggravating circumstances far outweighed the mitigating ones. To Justice Harry Blackmun, who authored the Court's opinion, the discretion permitted to the trial judge under the statute was not inconsistent with "contemporary standards of fairness and decency." It was sufficient, he concluded, that the statute required the judge to assess both aggravating and mitigating circumstances in making his determination whether death is an appropriate penalty for the crime. Further, in several post-*Gregg* cases, the Court has also considered the statutory "aggravating circumstance" issue. In *Godfrey* v. *Georgia* (446 U.S. 420, 1980), for example, the Court overturned a murder conviction because of the vague construction given to the aggravating circumstances provision of the statute by the court.[20] But in *Zant* v. *Stephens* (103 S. Ct. 2733, 1983), the Court referred to the jury's finding of a statutory aggravating circumstance as a "limited function" and refused to overturn a death sentence where one of three aggravating circumstances found was later held void for vagueness. The two remaining valid aggravating circumstances were considered sufficient to achieve their "narrowing function."

Likewise, the Court refused to overturn a death sentence in *Barclay* v. *Florida* (103 S. Ct. 3418, 1983), although the sentencing judge improperly went beyond the statute's enumeration of aggravating circumstances to find and include the defendant's criminal record as an aggravating circumstance. Indicating the trend of Court actions to allow states more latitude in implementing their sentencing procedure, Justice Rehnquist asserted that:

> The Constitution does not require that the sentencing process be transformed into a rigid and mechanical parsing of statutory aggravating factors. It is entirely fitting for the moral, factual and legal judgment of judges and juries to play a meaningful role in sentencing.

The Court scrutinized what some consider to be

[20] Under the statute, a person convicted of murder may be sentenced to death if it is found that the offense "was outrageously or wantonly vile, horrible or inhuman in that it involved torture, depravity of mind, or an aggravated battery to the victim."

an inordinately and unnecessarily drawn-out process of appellate review of applications for stays of execution in *Barefoot* v. *Estelle* (103 S. Ct. 3383, 1983). There, the Court held valid a court of appeals procedure in a habeas corpus action, where the merits of the appeal were decided in the course of denying a stay. Noting that it would have been better for the appeals court to expressly affirm the lower court's habeas corpus ruling and then proceed with the application for the stay, the Court, nevertheless, did not find the "merged" consideration of the appeal and the application for stay at variance with precedents so long as the petitioner was given "ample opportunity to address the merits." While such a procedure was considered "tolerable" in the context of *Barefoot*, the Court cautioned that it was not "preferred procedure." Consequently, it set forth several general guidelines for the courts of appeals to consider in formulating procedures for expediting the appellate stage of the federal habeas corpus process and the continuing flood of applications for stays of execution.

The Court's decision in *Pulley* v. *Harris* (104 S. Ct. 871) in 1984 appears to underscore its desire to lessen federal constitutional constraints on the states in the death penalty appellate process. Pursuant to *Furman*, some 35 states revised their death penalty statutes, and several of them provided for "comparative proportionality review"—an inquiry comparing a death penalty imposed in one case with that of others for similar crimes. However, the Court in *Pulley* indicated that this type of proportionality review is not necessary to meet constitutional standards set forth in *Gregg*. The constitution, said Justice White for the Court majority, only requires "traditional proportionality" to ensure that the penalty imposed is not "inherently disproportionate" to the offense committed. Thus, the fact that some states require a kind of "comparative proportionality review" before affirming a death sentence (and the statutes providing for that review have been declared constitutional by the Supreme Court) does not fasten it as a federal constitutional requirement on other states.

Over the years, the Court has been presented questions alleging racial discrimination in the administration of various aspects of the criminal justice system in several states, and one of the most troublesome of such allegations was presented in the context of the death penalty in *McCleskey* v. *Kemp* (107 S. Ct. 1756) in 1987. The conventional wisdom shared by many blacks over the years was that the death penalty was imposed on blacks who were convicted of capital crimes in much greater frequency than on whites who were convicted of similar crimes. One of the most oft-cited examples was that involving interracial crime. Simply put, "when the person convicted of the capital offense was black and the victim was white, the frequency of imposition of the death penalty was high. But when the capital offender was white, the death penalty was rarely imposed." In a last-ditch effort to save his life, McCleskey presented to the Court this argument in the context of a systematic scientific study using data gleaned from some 2,000 murder cases in Georgia during the 1970s. (McCleskey was convicted and sentenced to death in Georgia.) The Baldus study, as it was labeled by the Court, used the data to show that there is a disparity in the imposition of the death penalty in Georgia and that such disparity correlates with the race of both the defendant and the victim. Hence, McCleskey argued that because in Georgia black defendants who killed white victims have a far greater likelihood of being executed than do white defendants who killed white or black victims, the sentencing process is administered in a racially discriminatory manner that violates the equal protection clause of the Fourteenth Amendment.

But this did not impress the majority of the justices. Speaking for the five-person majority (Rehnquist, White, Powell, O'Connor, and Scalia), Justice Lewis Powell contended that the statistical analysis did not prove that race was the critical factor in the sentencing decision but merely showed only a likelihood that racial prejudices may have some influence. Furthermore, he thought that accepting the argument presented by McCleskey would negate the traditional discretion accorded juries so they would be in a position to consider leniency arguments of defendants as they weigh their "particularized characteristics." In the end, he cautioned that if the racial-disparity argument is taken to its logical conclusion, other claims of bias could very well be made that focus on "unexplained discrepancies that correlate to membership in other minority groups and even to gender."

Justices Brennan and Marshall, who have consistently opposed the imposition of the death penalty in all circumstances, were joined in dissent by Justices Blackmun and Stevens. They accepted the study's findings as valid and underscored the continued arbitrariness in the imposition of the death penalty in some jurisdictions. Brennan emphasized that the study was particularly important when viewed in the context of Georgia's past racial history and its legacy of a race-conscious criminal justice system. In a separate opinion, Justice Blackmun indicated that the statistical evidence made the case of prosecutorial racial bias, and consequently that the state should have been required to shoulder the burden of proof that it administered a capital sentencing process free of racial considerations.

Another dimension of death penalty jurisprudence that has commanded the Court's attention during the 1980s considers the penalty's appropriateness for accomplices to capital crimes. Initially, the Court confronted this question directly in 1982 in *Enmund* v. *Florida* (458 U.S. 782), and held that the Eighth Amendment prohibits the imposition of the death penalty on the nontriggerman accomplice whose participation in the activities that led to murder was *minimal* (emphasis ours). Contending that the death penalty is in fact excessive punishment for one who does not actually take human life, Justice Byron White reviewed the statutes of the 36 states that permit the use of the death penalty and noted that in only nine of them are there felony-murder provisions that allow under some circumstances imposition of the ultimate sanction on the accomplice who does not actually take the lethal action. (In the instant case, the defendant was not present at the actual scene of the murder but was waiting in the getaway car in front of the victims' house.) Florida was one of the nine, but Justice White concluded that the application of its statute to Enmund's level of involvement was at odds with the general societal view as expressed by most legislative bodies and juries and does not warrant the imposition of the death penalty.

In the succeeding years, courts differed as to the sweep of *Enmund*. Some construed it expansively as barring the imposition of the death penalty on all nontriggermen accomplices. Others held accomplices culpable depending on intent and the level of participation. The opportunity for the Court to eliminate some of the confusion about its *Enmund* ruling came when it decided *Tison* v. *Arizona* (107 S. Ct. 1676) in 1987. In what may be considered a contraction of the Eighth Amendment guarantee, the Court majority (Rehnquist, White, Powell, O'Connor, and Scalia) focused on the mental state of the accomplice and the degree of participation in the criminal activity that culminated in murder. Examining the facts in *Tison*, Justice Sandra Day O'Connor contended for the majority that the Eighth Amendment does not prohibit the imposition of the death penalty on a nontriggerman accomplice who "had the culpable mental state of reckless indifference to human life" and whose participation in the several activities that eventually resulted in murder was "major."

Justice Brennan wrote a sharp dissent, which

was joined by Justice Marshall and supported in part by Justices Blackmun and Stevens, in which he complained that the majority's approval of state felony-murder statutes represented a return to a legal era where those convicted for all kinds of felonies were subjected to capital punishment. Indeed, he noted, such a policy is at odds with doctrines adhered to in most of our states and in practically all of the Western world. Consequently, he would continue to adhere to the doctrine established in *Enmund*, which requires proof of "intent to kill" before the death penalty could be imposed on a nontriggerman accomplice.

Considerations in the penalty segment of the bifurcated death penalty trial have presented other controversial questions to the Court. In *California* v. *Brown* (107 S. Ct. 837, 1987), for example, the Court appeared to allow trial judges considerable discretion in guiding juries when listening to the presentation of evidence of mitigating circumstances. There, a bare majority of the justices did not consider a trial judge's caution to the sentencing jury that it should not be "swayed by sentiment, sympathy, public opinion, or passion, etc." an unconstitutional interference with the defendant in the presentation of evidence on mitigating circumstances. But in another ruling related to the introduction of evidence at the penalty phase, the Court disallowed the presentation of victim-impact statements. In *Booth* v. *Maryland* (107 S. Ct. 2529, 1987), a bare majority of the Court (Brennan, Marshall, Blackmun, Powell, and Stevens) held that statements describing the emotional impact of the crime on surviving family members is irrelevant to the sentence decision-making process.

A critical death penalty question was presented to the Court in *Ford* v. *Wainwright* (106 S. Ct. 2595, 1986), where the Court had to determine for the first time if the Eighth Amendment bars a state from executing an insane prisoner. Citing the common-law jurisprudence that has developed over the centuries and the constitutional law and practices of the several states, a majority of the Court concluded that it did. Both Justice Marshall in his plurality opinion and Justice Powell in his partial concurrence underscored the cruelty and inhumanity of a policy that permits the execution of a person who has lost his sanity. Both justices also concluded that Florida's procedures for determining the condemned prisoner's sanity were constitutionally inadequate. For Justice Powell the proper test is "whether the prisoner is aware of his impending execution and the reason for it."

The death penalty controversy spawned another difficult question for consideration by the Court in 1988—whether the Constitution allows the several states to execute minors. But the Court did not provide the definitive answer in *Thompson* v. *Oklahoma* (108 S. Ct. 2687), as only four justices agreed that the Eighth Amendment prohibits the execution of a person who was under 16 years of age at the time the offense was committed. Justice Stevens, in whose opinion Justices Brennan, Marshall, and Blackmun joined, argued that the appropriate Eighth Amendment standard "must be guided by the 'evolving standards of decency that mark the progress of a maturing society,' " and that the imposition of the death penalty on juveniles below 16 years old "is now generally abhorrent to the conscience of the community." Justice O'Connor agreed that Thompson's conviction should be vacated and remanded because of defects in the Oklahoma statute. However, she was not ready to accept the view that the Constitution prohibits states from executing juvenile offenders below the age of 16 until the Court is presented better evidence that there is societal consensus supporting the prohibition. Hence, whether and when a proscription on juvenile executions would become a dimension of our Eighth Amendment's jurisprudence had to await another such case in another term of the Court.

One year later, Justice O'Connor switched sides and joined the four *Thompson* dissenters to rule that there was no "national consensus" that the Eighth Amendment bars states from imposing the death penalty on juveniles less than 18 years of age. In the companion cases of *Stanford* v. *Kentucky* and *Wilkins* v. *Missouri* (109 S. Ct. 2969, 1989), the Court upheld the imposition of the death penalty on 16- and 17-year-old murderers. In his opinion for the Court, Justice Antonin Scalia reviewed the extant federal and state laws on the issue (which he considered "[t]he primary and most reliable evidence of national consensus") and concluded that the evidence of a national consensus opposing the death penalty for juveniles was insufficient to characterize the imposition of the death penalty in these contexts as cruel and unusual. Nor did he believe that these state policies were "contrary to the 'evolving standards of decency that mark the progress of a maturing society.' " As would be expected, the dissenters (Justices Brennan, Marshall, Blackmun, and Stevens) reviewed the same evidence and came to the opposite conclusion.

Continuing to show deference to legislative discretion on the capital punishment issue, the Court, on the same decision day, refused to place constitutional constraints on state power to impose the death penalty on mentally retarded murderers.

In *Penry* v. *Lynaugh* (109 S. Ct. 2934, 1989), Justice O'Connor played a pivotal role in crafting an opinion to dispose the two critical issues raised in the appeal. First, she joined the liberal bloc (Brennan, Marshall, Blackmun, and Stevens) to set aside Penry's death sentence because the trial judge's construction of relevant Texas law did not permit the sentencing jury to consider adequately his mental deficiency. On the central constitutional question, however, O'Connor joined her conservative colleagues (Rehnquist, White, Scalia, and Kennedy) to hold that the "evidence of a national consensus against the imposition of the death penalty on murderers with mental deficiencies was insufficient to conclude that the Eighth Amendment bars it absolutely."

The Rehnquist Court underscored its deepening impatience with lengthy appellate review procedures that have enabled some death row inmates to delay their execution for years when it decided *McCleskey* v. *Zant* (111 S. Ct. 1454) in 1991. There the Court heightened the burden on inmate use of habeas corpus petitions to raise constitutional claims challenging their sentences. Some death row inmates had engaged in the practice of raising different claims in successive separate actions, which had the practical effect of staying their execution date pending disposition of their petitions. (As soon as a claim in one petition would be denied, another petition raising a different claim would be filed.) In his opinion for the Court, Justice Anthony Kennedy focused on inmate abuse of the habeas corpus writ to set out standards, which would be applied to the consideration of petitions after the initial one, that would allow dismissal for abusive use unless the inmate shows that: (1) there was cause for not having raised the claim earlier; and (2) he or she had suffered "actual prejudice" from the constitutional error claimed in the trial and/or sentencing process. Undoubtedly, this redefined "abuse of writ" standard should make it easier for prosecutors to challenge the flow of habeas corpus petitions that Justice Kennedy thought had raised a threat to the integrity of the habeas corpus process.

On another front in the death penalty controversy, the Rehnquist Court underscored its sensitivity to prosecutorial forces seeking the death penalty in capital cases when it decided *Payne* v. *Tennessee* (111 S. Ct. 2597) in 1991. At issue in *Payne* was the admission of victim-impact statements in the sentencing phase of a capital case. In two earlier cases—*Booth* v. *Maryland* (482 U.S. 496) and *Gathers* v. *South Carolina* (490 U.S. 805), decided in 1987 and 1989, respectively—the Court had rejected the admission of such evidence as contrary to the Eighth Amendment. But in a six-to-three decision, the Chief Justice brushed aside those recent precedents in support of state procedures that provide sentencing authorities another method of informing themselves. For him, victim-impact evidence serves entirely legitimate purposes, and because in both *Booth* and *Gathers* the Court had wrongly characterized such evidence as leading "to the arbitrary imposition of the death penalty," the Court should not feel bound by these decisions as precedent. As Rehnquist stated bluntly, "when governing decisions are unworkable or are badly reasoned, 'this Court has never felt constrained to follow precedent.' "

In a particularly sharp dissent, Justice Thurgood Marshall hurled a parting shot at his conservative brethren. (This was to be his last opinion before retirement.) Apparently greatly disturbed by the majority's cavalier treatment of the stare decisis doctrine, he thundered that "power, not reason, is the new currency of this Court's decision making." Noting that "neither the law nor the facts supporting *Booth* and *Gathers*" had undergone change since they were decided, he warned that the majority's action in *Payne* "suggests that an even more extensive upheaval of . . . precedents may be in store."

GREGG v. GEORGIA
428 U.S. 153; 49 L. Ed. 2d 857; 96 S. Ct. 2906 (1976)

JUSTICE STEWART, JUSTICE POWELL, *and* JUSTICE STEVENS *announced the judgment of the Court and filed an opinion delivered by* JUSTICE STEWART.

The issue in this case is whether the imposition of the sentence of death for the crime of murder under the law of Georgia violates the Eighth and Fourteenth Amendments.

I

The petitioner, Troy Gregg, was charged with committing armed robbery and murder. In accordance with Georgia procedure in capital cases, the trial was in two stages, a guilt stage and a sentencing stage. The evidence at the guilt trial established that on November 21, 1973, the petitioner and a traveling companion, Floyd Allen, while hitchhiking north in Florida, were picked up by Fred Simmons and Bob Moore. Their car broke down, but they continued north after Simmons purchased another vehicle with some of the cash he was carrying. While still in Florida, they picked up another hitchhiker. Dennis Weaver, who rode with them to Atlanta, where he was let out about 11 P.M. A short time later the four men interrupted their journey for a rest stop along the highway. The next morning the bodies of Simmons and Moore were discovered in a ditch nearby.

On November 23, after reading about the shootings in an Atlanta newspaper, Weaver communicated with the Gwinnett County police and related information concerning the journey with the victims, including a description of the car. The next afternoon, the petitioner and Allen, while in Simmons's car, were arrested in Ashville, N.C. . . . After receiving the warnings required by *Miranda,* and signing a written waiver of his rights, the petitioner signed a statement in which he admitted shooting, then robbing, Simmons and Moore. He justified the slayings on grounds of self-defense. . . . [The next day Allen gave police his version of the events at the scene of the slayings. At the subsequent trial] the jury found the petitioner guilty of two counts of armed robbery and two counts of murder.

At the penalty stage, which took place before the same jury, . . . the judge instructed the jury that it "would not be authorized to consider [imposing] the sentence of death" unless it first found beyond a reasonable doubt one of these aggravating circumstances:

> One—That the offense of murder was committed while the offender was engaged in the commission o[f] two other capit[a]l felonies, to-wit the armed ro[b]bery of [Simmons and Moore].
> Two—That the offender committed the offense of murder for the purpose of receiving money and the automobile described in the indictment.
> Three—The offense of murder was outrageously and wantonly vile, horrible and inhuman, in that they [*sic*] involved the depravity of the mind of the defendant.

Finding the first and second of these circumstances, the jury returned verdicts of death on each count.

The Supreme Court of Georgia affirmed the convictions and the imposition of the death sentences for murder. . . . The death sentences imposed for armed robbery, however, were vacated on the grounds that the death penalty had rarely been imposed in Georgia for that offense. . . .

We granted the petitioner's application for a writ of certiorari challenging the imposition of the death sentence in this case as "cruel and unusual" punishment in violation of the Eighth and the Fourteenth Amendments. . . .

II

Before considering the issues presented it is necessary to understand the Georgia statutory scheme for the imposition of the death penalty. The Georgia statute, as amended after our decision in *Furman* . . . retains the death penalty for six categories of crime: murder, kidnapping for ransom or where the victim is harmed, armed robbery, rape, treason, and aircraft hijacking. . . . The capital defendant's guilt or innocence is determined in the traditional manner, either by a trial judge or a jury, in the first stage of a bifurcated trial.

If trial is by jury, the trial judge is required to charge lesser included offenses when they are supported by any view of the evidence. . . . After a verdict, finding or plea of guilty to a capital crime, a presentence hearing is conducted before whoever made the determination of guilt. The sentencing procedures are essentially the same in both bench and jury trials. At the hearing,

> the judge (or jury) shall hear additional evidence in extenuation, mitigation, and aggravation of punishment, including the record of any prior criminal convictions and pleas of guilty or pleas of nolo contendere of the defendant, or the absence of any prior conviction and pleas: Provided however, that only such evidence in aggravation as the State has made known to the defendant prior to his trial shall be admissible.

In the assessment of the appropriate sentence to be imposed the judge is also required to consider or to include in his instructions to the jury "any mitigating circumstances or aggravating circumstances otherwise authorized by law and any of (10) statutory aggravating circumstances which may be supported by the evidence. . . ." The scope of the nonstatutory aggravating or mitigating circumstances is not delineated in the statute. Before a convicted defendant may be sentenced to death, however, except in cases of treason or aircraft hijacking, the jury, or the trial judge in cases tried without a jury, must find beyond a reasonable doubt one of the 10 aggravating circumstances specified in the statute. . . . If the verdict is death the jury or judge must specify the aggravating circumstance(s) found. . . . In jury cases, the trial judge is bound by the jury's recommended sentence. . . .

In addition to the conventional appellate process available in all criminal cases, provision is made for special expedited direct review by the Supreme Court of Georgia of the appropriateness of imposing the sentence of death in the particular case. The court is directed to consider "the punishment as well as any errors enumerated by way of appeal," and to determine:

1. Whether the sentence of death was imposed under the influence of passion, prejudice, or any other arbitrary factor, and
2. Whether, in cases other than treason or aircraft hijacking, the evidence supports the jury's or judge's finding of a statutory aggravating circumstance as enumerated in section 27.2534.1(b), and
3. Whether the sentence of death is excessive or disproportionate to the penalty, imposed in similar cases considering both the crime and the defendant.

If the court affirms a death sentence, it is required to include in its decision reference to similar cases that it has taken into consideration. . . .

III

We address initially the basic contention that the punishment of death for the crime of murder is, under all circumstances, "cruel and unusual" in violation of the Eighth and Fourteenth Amendments of the Constitution. In Part IV of this opinion, we will consider the sentence of death imposed under the Georgia statutes at issue in this case.

The Court on a number of occasions has both assumed and asserted the constitutionality of capital punishment. In several cases that assumption provided a necessary foundation for the decision, as the Court was asked to decide whether a particular method of carrying out a capital sentence would be allowed to stand under the Eighth Amendment. But until *Furman* v. *Georgia*, (1972) the Court never confronted squarely the fundamental claim that the punishment of death always, regardless of the enormity of the offense or the procedure followed in imposing the sentence, is cruel and unusual punishment in violation of the Constitution. Although this issue was presented and addressed in *Furman*, it was not resolved by the Court. Four justices would have reached the oppo-

site conclusion; and three justices, while agreeing that the statutes then before the Court were invalid as applied, left open the question whether such punishment may ever be imposed. We now hold that the punishment of death does not invariably violate the Constitution.

The history of the prohibition of "cruel and unusual" punishment already has been reviewed by this Court at length. . . .

In the earliest cases raising Eighth Amendment claims, the Court focused on particular methods of execution to determine whether they were too cruel to pass constitutional muster. The constitutionality of the sentence of death itself was not at issue, and the criterion used to evaluate the mode of execution was its similarity to "torture" and other "barbarous" methods. . . .

But the Court has not confined the prohibition embodied in the Eighth Amendment to "barbarous" methods that were generally outlawed in the 18th century. Instead, the Amendment has been interpreted in a flexible and dynamic manner. The Court early recognized that "a principle to be vital must be capable of wider application than the mischief which gave it birth." *Weems* v. *United States*, 217 U.S. 349, 373 (1910). Thus the clause forbidding "cruel and unusual" punishments "is not fastened to the obsolete but may acquire meaning as public opinion becomes enlightened by a humane justice." *Id.*, at 378. . . .

It is clear that the Eighth Amendment has not been regarded as a static concept. As Chief Justice Warren said, in an oft-quoted phrase, "[t]he Amendment must draw its meaning from the evolving standards of decency that mark the progress of a maturing society." *Trop* v. *Dulles*, 356 U.S. at 101. . . . Thus, an assessment of contemporary values concerning the infliction of a challenged sanction is relevant to the application of the Eighth Amendment. . . . It requires, rather, that we look to objective indicia that reflect the public attitude toward a given sanction.

But our cases also make clear that public perceptions of standards of decency with respect to criminal sanctions are not conclusive. A penalty also must accord with "the dignity of man," which is the "basic concept underlying the Eighth Amendment." . . . This means, at least, that the punishment not be "excessive." When a form of punishment in the abstract . . . is under consideration, the inquiry into "excessiveness" has two aspects. First, the punishment must not involve the unnecessary and wanton infliction of pain. . . . Second, the punishment must not be grossly out of proportion to the severity of the crime. . . .

We now consider specifically whether the sentence of death for the crime of murder is a *per se* violation of the Eighth and Fourteenth Amendments to the Constitution. We note first that history and precedent strongly support a negative answer to this question.

The imposition of the death penalty for the crime of murder has a long history of acceptance both in the United States and in England. The common-law rule imposed a mandatory death sentence on all convicted murderers. . . . And the penalty continued to be used into the 20th century by most American States, although the breadth of the common-law rule was diminished, initially by narrowing the class of murders to be punished by death and subsequently by widespread adoption of laws expressly granting juries the discretion to recommend mercy. . . .

It is apparent from the test of the Constitution itself that the existence of capital punishment was accepted by the Framers. At the time the Eighth Amendment was ratified, capital punishment was a common sanction in every State. Indeed, the First Congress of the United States enacted legislation providing death as the penalty for specified crimes. . . . The Fifth Amendment, adopted at the same time as the Eighth, contemplated the continued existence of the capital sanction by imposing certain limits on the prosecution of capital cases. . . . And the Fourteenth Amendment, adopted over three-quarters of a century later, similarly contemplates the existence of the capital sanction in providing that no State shall deprive any person of "life, liberty, or property" without due process of law.

For nearly two centuries, this Court, repeatedly and often expressly, has recognized that capital punishment is not invalid per se. . . .

Four years ago, the petitioners in *Furman* and its companion cases predicated their argument primarily upon the asserted proposition that standards of decency had evolved to the point where capital punishment no longer could be tolerated. . . . This view was accepted by two justices. Three other justices were unwilling to go so far. . . .

The petitioners . . . before the Court today renew the "standards of decency" argument, but developments during the four years since *Furman* have undercut substantially the assumptions upon which their argument rested. Despite the continuing debate, dating back to the 19th century, over the morality and utility of capital punishment, it is now evident that a large proportion of American society continues to regard it as an appropriate and necessary criminal sanction.

The most marked indication of society's endorsement of the death penalty for murder is the legislative response to *Furman*. The legislatures of at least 35 States have enacted new statutes that provide for the death penalty for at least some crimes that result in the death of another person. And the Congress of the United States, in 1974, enacted a statute providing the death penalty for aircraft piracy that results in death. These recently adopted statutes have attempted to address the concerns expressed by the Court in *Furman*. . . . But all of the post-*Furman* statutes make clear that capital punishment itself has not been rejected by the elected representatives of the people. In the only state-wide referendum occurring since *Furman* brought to our attention, the people of California adopted a constitutional amendment that authorized capital punishment. . . .

The jury also is a significant and reliable objective index of contemporary values because it is so directly involved. . . . Indeed, the actions of juries in many States since *Furman* is [sic] fully compatible with the legislative judgments, reflected in the new statutes, as to the continued utility and necessity of capital punishment in appropriate cases. At the close of 1974 at least 254 persons had been sentenced to death since *Furman,* and by the end of March 1976, more than 460 persons were subject to death sentences. . . .

The death penalty is said to serve two principal social purposes: retribution and deterrence of capital crimes by prospective offenders.

In part, capital punishment is an expression of society's moral outrage at particularly offensive conduct. This function may be unappealing to many, but it is essential in an ordered society that asks its citizens to rely on legal processes rather than self-help to vindicate their wrongs. . . . "Retribution is no longer the dominant objective of the criminal law," *Williams* v. *New York,* 337 U.S. 241, 248 (1949), but neither is it a forbidden objective nor one inconsistent with our respect for the dignity of men. . . . Indeed, the decision that capital punishment may be the appropriate sanction in extreme cases is an expression of the community's belief that certain crimes are themselves so grievous an affront to humanity that the only adequate response may be the penalty of death.

Statistical attempts to evaluate the worth of the death penalty as a deterrent to crimes by potential offenders have occasioned a great deal of debate. The results simply have been inconclusive. . . .

Although some of the studies suggest that the death penalty may not function as a significantly greater deterrent than lesser penalties, there is no convincing empirical evidence either supporting or refuting this view. We may nevertheless assume safely that there are murderers, such as those who act in passion, for whom the threat of death has little or no deterrent effect. But for many others, the death penalty undoubtedly is a significant deterrent. . . .

The value of capital punishment as a deterrent of crime is a complex factual issue the resolution of which properly rests with the legislatures, which can evaluate the results of statistical studies in terms of their own local conditions and with a flexibility of approach that is not available to the courts. . . .

In sum, we cannot say that the judgment of the Georgia legislature that capital punishment may be necessary in some cases is clearly wrong. Considerations of federalism, as well as respect for the ability of a legislature to evaluate, in terms of its particular State the moral consensus concerning the death penalty and its social utility as a sanction, require us to conclude, in the absence of more convincing evidence, that the infliction of death as a punishment for murder is not without justification and thus is not unconstitutionally severe.

Finally, we must consider whether the punishment of death is disproportionate in relation to the crime for which it is imposed. There is no question that death as a punishment is unique in its severity and irrevocability. . . . When a defendant's life is at stake, the Court has been particularly sensitive to insure that every safeguard is observed. . . . But we are concerned here only with the imposition of capital punishment for the crime of murder, and when a life has been taken deliberately by the offender, we cannot say that the punishment is invariably disproportionate to the crimes. . . .

IV

[Here the Court reviews the mandate of *Furman* on sentencing discretion.]

B

We now turn to consideration of the constitutionality of Georgia's capital-sentencing procedures. In the wake of *Furman*, Georgia amended its capital punishment statute, but chose not to narrow the scope of its murder provisions. . . .

These procedures require the jury to consider the circumstances of the crime and the criminal before it recommends sentence. No longer can a Georgia jury do as *Furman*'s jury did: reach a finding of the defendant's guilt and then, without guidance or direction, decide whether he should live or die. . . .

Georgia's new sentencing procedures require as a prerequisite to the imposition of the death penalty, specific jury findings as to the circumstances of the crime or the character of the defendant. Moreover, to guard further against a situation comparable to that presented in *Furman*, the Supreme Court of Georgia compares each death sentence with the sentences imposed on similarly situated defendants to ensure that the sentence of death in a particular case is not disproportionate. On their face these procedures seem to satisfy the concerns of *Furman*. . . .

[The concurring opinion of JUSTICE WHITE, with whom THE CHIEF JUSTICE and JUSTICE REHNQUIST joined, is not reprinted here.]

JUSTICE BRENNAN, *dissenting*.

In *Furman* v. *Georgia*, . . . I read "evolving standards of decency" as requiring focus upon the essence of the death penalty itself and not primarily or solely upon the procedures under which the determination to inflict the penalty upon a particular person was made. I there said:

> At bottom, the battle has been waged on moral grounds. The country has debated whether a society for which the dignity of the individual is the supreme value can, without a fundamental inconsistency, follow the practice of deliberately putting some of its members to death. In the United States, as in other nations of the western world, the struggle about this punishment has been one between ancient and deeply rooted beliefs in retribution, atonement or vengeance on the one hand, and, on the other, beliefs in the personal value and dignity of the common man that were born of the democratic movement of the eighteenth century, as well as beliefs in the scientific approach to an understanding of the motive forces of human conduct, which are the result of the growth of the sciences of behavior during the nineteenth and twentieth centuries. It is this essentially moral conflict that forms the backdrop for the past changes in and the present operation of our system of imposing death as a punishment for crime.

That continues to be my view. For the Clause forbidding cruel and unusual punishments under our constitutional system of government embodies in unique degree moral principles restraining the punishments that our civilized society may impose on those persons who transgress its laws. . . .

This Court inescapably has the duty, as the ultimate arbiter of the meaning of our Constitution, to say whether, when individuals condemned to death stand before our Bar, "moral concepts" require us to hold that the law has progressed to the point where we should declare that the punishment of death, like punishments on the rack, the screw and the wheel, is no longer morally tolerable in our civilized society. . . . I emphasize only that foremost among the "moral concepts" recognized in our cases and inherent in the Clause is the primary moral principle that the State, even as it punishes, must treat its citizens in a manner consistent with their intrinsic worth as human beings—a punishment must not be so severe as to be degrading to human dignity. A judicial determination whether the punishment of death comports with human dignity is therefore not only permitted but compelled by the Clause. . . .

I do not understand that the Court disagrees that "[i]n comparison to all other punishments today . . . the deliberate extinguishment of human life by the State is uniquely degrading to human dignity." . . . For three of my Brethren hold today that mandatory infliction of the death penalty constitutes the penalty cruel and unusual punishment. I perceive no principled basis for this limitation. Death for whatever crime and under all circumstances "is truly an awesome punishment. The calculated killing of a human being by the State involves, by its very nature, a denial of the executed person's humanity. . . ."

* * *

The fatal constitutional infirmity in the punishment of death is that it treats "members of the human race as nonhumans, as objects to be toyed with and discarded. [It] is thus inconsistent with the fundamental premise of the Clause that even the vilest criminal remains a human being possessed of common human dignity." . . . As such it is a penalty that "subjects the individual to a fate forbidden by the principle of civilized treatment guaranteed by the [Clause]." . . .

McCLESKEY v. KEMP
481 279; 95 L. Ed. 2d 262; 107 S. Ct. 1756 (1987)

JUSTICE POWELL *delivered the opinion of the Court.*

This case presents the question whether a complex statistical study that indicates a risk that racial considerations enter into capital sentencing determinations proves that petitioner McCleskey's capital sentence is unconstitutional under the Eighth or Fourteenth Amendment.

I

McCleskey, a black man, was convicted of two counts of armed robbery and one count of murder in the Superior Court of Fulton County, Georgia, on October 12, 1978. McCleskey's convictions arose out of the robbery of a furniture store and the killing of a white police officer during the course of the robbery. The evidence at trial indicated that McCleskey and three accomplices planned and carried out the robbery. All four were armed. . . . During the course of the robbery, a police officer, answering a silent alarm, entered the store through the front door. As he was walking down the center aisle of the store, two shots were fired. Both struck the officer. One hit him in the face and killed him.

Several weeks later, McCleskey was arrested in connection with an unrelated offense. He confessed that he had participated in the furniture store robbery but denied that he had shot the police officer. At trial, the State introduced evidence that at least one of the bullets that struck the officer was fired from a .38 caliber Rossi revolver. This description matched the description of the gun that McCleskey had carried during the robbery. The State also introduced the testimony of two witnesses who had heard McCleskey admit to the shooting.

The jury convicted McCleskey of murder. At the penalty hearing, the jury heard arguments as to the appropriate sentence. Under Georgia law, the jury could not consider imposing the death penalty unless it found beyond a reasonable doubt that the murder was accompanied by one of the statutory aggravating circumstances. [I]t . . . found two aggravating circumstances to exist beyond a reasonable doubt: the murder was committed during the course of an armed robbery, . . . and the murder was committed upon a peace officer engaged in the performance of his duties. . . . In making its decision whether to impose the death sentence, the jury considered the mitigating and aggravating circumstances of McCleskey's conduct. . . . McCleskey offered no mitigating evidence. The jury recommended that he be sentenced to death on the murder charge and to consecutive life sentences on the armed robbery charges. The court followed the jury's recommendation and sentenced McCleskey to death.

On appeal, the Supreme Court of Georgia affirmed the convictions and the sentences. This Court denied a petition for a writ of certiorari. The Superior Court of Fulton County denied McCleskey's extraordinary motion for a new trial. McCleskey then filed a petition for a writ of *habeas corpus* in the Superior Court of Butts County. After holding an evidentiary hearing, the Superior Court denied relief. The Supreme Court of Georgia denied McCleskey's application for a certificate of probable cause to appeal the Superior Court's denial of his petition, and this Court again denied certiorari. . . .

McCleskey next filed a petition for a writ of *habeas corpus* in the federal District Court for the Northern District of Georgia. His petition raised 18 claims, one of which was that the Georgia capital sentencing process is administered in a racially discriminatory manner in violation of the Eighth and Fourteenth Amendments to the United States Constitution. In support of his claim, McCleskey proffered a statistical study performed by Professors David C. Baldus, George Woodworth, and Charles Pulanski (the Baldus study) that purports to show a disparity in the imposition of the death sentence in Georgia based on the race of the murder victim and, to a lesser extent, the race of the defendant. The Baldus study is actually two sophisticated statistical studies that examine over 2,000 murder cases that occurred in Georgia during the 1970s. The raw numbers collected by Professor Baldus indicate that defendants charged with killing white persons received the death penalty in 11% of the cases, but defendants charged with killing blacks received the death penalty in only 1% of the cases. The raw numbers also indicate a reverse racial disparity according to the race of the defendant: 4% of the black defendants received the death penalty, as opposed to 7% of the white defendants.

Baldus also divided the cases according to the combination of the race of the defendant and the race of the victim. He found that the death penalty was assessed in 22% of the cases involving black defendants and white victims; 8% of the cases involving white defendants and white victims; 1% of the cases involving black defendants and black victims;

and 3% of the cases involving white defendants and black victims. Similarly, Baldus found that prosecutors sought the death penalty in 70% of the cases involving black defendants and white victims; 32% of the cases involving white defendants and white victims; 15% of the cases involving black defendants and black victims; and 19% of the cases involving white defendants and black victims.

Baldus subjected his data to an extensive analysis, taking account of 230 variables that could have explained the disparities on nonracial grounds. One of his models concludes that, even after taking account of 39 nonracial variables, defendants charged with killing white victims were 4.3 times as likely to receive a death sentence as defendants charged with killing blacks. According to this model, black defendants were 1.1 times as likely to receive a death sentence as other defendants. Thus, the Baldus study indicates that black defendants, such as McCleskey, who kill white victims have the greatest likelihood of receiving the death penalty.*

The District Court held an extensive evidentiary hearing on McCleskey's petition [and] . . . considered the Baldus study with care. It concluded that McCleskey's "statistics do not demonstrate a prima facie case in support of the contention that the death penalty was imposed upon him because of his race, because of the race of the victim, or because of any Eighth Amendment concern." *McCleskey* v. *Zant*, 580 F. Supp. 338, 379 (ND Ga. 1984). As to McCleskey's Fourteenth Amendment claim, the court found that the methodology of the Baldus study was flawed in several respects.**

---

*Baldus's 230-variable model divided cases into eight different ranges, according to the estimated aggravation level of the offense. Baldus argued in his testimony to the District Court that the effects of racial bias were most striking in the mid-range cases. "[W]hen the cases become tremendously aggravated so that everybody would agree that if we're going to have a death sentence, these are the cases that should get it, the race effects go away. It's only in the mid-range of cases where the decision makers have a real choice as to what to do. If there's room for the exercise of discretion, then the [racial] factors begin to play a role." App. 36. Under this model, Baldus found that 14.4% of the black-victim mid-range cases received the death penalty, and 34.4% of the white-victim cases received the death penalty. See Exhibit DB 90, reprinted in Supplemental Exhibits 54. According to Baldus, the facts of McCleskey's case placed it within the mid-range. App. 45–46.

**Baldus, among other experts, testified at the evidentiary hearing. The District Court "was impressed with the learning of all of the experts." 580 F. Supp., at 353 (emphasis omitted). Nevertheless, the District Court noted that in many respects the data were incomplete. In its view, the questionnaires used to obtain the data failed to capture the full degree of the aggravating or mitigating circumstances. The court criticized the re-

Because of these defects, the court held that the Baldus study "fail[ed] to contribute anything of value" to McCleskey's claim, [and] ... dismissed the petition. . . .

The Court of Appeals affirmed the dismissal by the District Court ... with three judges dissenting as to McCleskey's claims based on the Baldus study. We granted certiorari and now affirm.

II

McCleskey's first claim is that the Georgia capital punishment statute violates the Equal Protection Clause of the Fourteenth Amendment. He argues that race has infected the administration of Georgia's statute in two ways: persons who murder whites are more likely to be sentenced to death than persons who murder blacks, and black murderers are more likely to be sentenced to death than white murderers. As a black defendant who killed a white victim, McCleskey claims that the Baldus study demonstrates that he was discriminated against because of his race and because of the race of his victim. . . .

A

Our analysis begins with the basic principle that a defendant who alleges an equal protection violation has the burden of proving "the existence of purposeful discrimination." A corollary to this principle is that a criminal defendant must prove that

searcher's decisions regarding unknown variables. The researchers could not discover whether penalty trials were held in many of the cases, thus undercutting the value of the study's statistics as to prosecutorial decisions. In certain cases, the study lacked information on the race of the victim in cases involving multiple victims, on whether or not the prosecutor offered a plea bargain, and on credibility problems with witnesses. The court concluded that McCleskey had failed to establish by a preponderance of the evidence that the data was trustworthy. "It is a major premise of a statistical case that the data base numerically mirrors reality. If it does not in substantial degree mirror reality, any inferences empirically arrived at are untrustworthy."

The District Court noted other problems with Baldus's methodology. First, the researchers assumed that all of the information available from the questionnaires was available to the juries and prosecutors when the case was tried. The court found this assumption "questionable." Second, the court noted the instability of the various models. Even with the 230-variable model, consideration of 20 further variables caused a significant drop in the statistical significance of race. In the court's view, this undermined the persuasiveness of the model that showed the greatest racial disparity, the 39-variable model. Third, the court found that the high correlation between race and many of the nonracial variables diminished the weight to which the study was entitled.

Finally, the District Court noted the inability of any of the models to predict the outcome of actual cases. . . .

the purposeful discrimination "had a discriminatory effect" on him. Thus, to prevail under the Equal Protection Clause, McCleskey must prove that the decision makers in his case acted with discriminatory purpose. He offers no evidence specific to his own case that would support an inference that racial considerations played a part in his sentence. Instead, he relies solely on the Baldus study. McCleskey argues that the Baldus study compels an inference that his sentence rests on purposeful discrimination. McCleskey's claim that these statistics are sufficient proof of discrimination, without regard to the facts of a particular case, would extend to all capital cases in Georgia, at least where the victim was white and the defendant black.

The Court has accepted statistics as proof of intent to discriminate in certain limited contexts. First, this Court has accepted statistical disparities as proof of an equal protection violation in the selection of the jury venire in a particular district. Although statistical proof normally must present a "stark" pattern to be accepted as the sole proof of discriminatory intent under the Constitution, "[b]ecause of the nature of the jury-selection task ... we have permitted a finding of constitutional violation even when the statistical pattern does not approach [such] extremes." Second, this Court has accepted statistics in the form of multiple regression analysis to prove statutory violations under Title VII [of the 1964 Civil Rights Act].

But the nature of the capital-sentencing decision, and the relationship of the statistics to that decision, are fundamentally different from the corresponding elements in the venire-selection or Title VII cases. Most importantly, each particular decision to impose the death penalty is made by a petit jury selected from a properly constituted venire. Each jury is unique in its composition, and the Constitution requires that its decision rest on consideration of innumerable factors that vary according to the characteristics of the individual defendant and the facts of the particular capital offense. Thus, the application of an inference drawn from the general statistics to a specific decision in a trial and sentencing simply is not comparable to the application of an inference drawn from general statistics to a specific venire-selection or Title VII case. In those cases, the statistics relate to fewer entities, and fewer variables are relevant to the challenged decision.

Another important difference between the cases in which we have accepted statistics as proof of discriminatory intent and this case is that, in the venire-selection and Title VII contexts, the decision maker has an opportunity to explain the statistical disparity. Here, the State has no practical opportunity to rebut the Baldus study. "[C]ontrolling considerations of . . . public policy" dictate that jurors "cannot be called . . . to testify to the motives and influences that led to their verdict." Similarly, the policy considerations behind a prosecutor's traditionally "wide discretion" suggest the impropriety of our requiring prosecutors to defend their decisions to seek death penalties "often years after they were made." Moreover, absent far stronger proof, it is unnecessary to seek such a rebuttal, because a legitimate and unchallenged explanation for the decision is apparent from the record: McCleskey committed an act for which the United States Constitution and Georgia laws permit imposition of the death penalty.

Finally, McCleskey's statistical proffer must be viewed in the context of his challenge. McCleskey challenges decisions at the heart of the State's criminal justice system. "[O]ne of society's most basic tasks is that of protecting the lives of its citizens, and one of the most basic ways in which it achieves the task is through criminal laws against murder." Implementation of these laws necessarily requires discretionary judgments. Because discretion is essential to the criminal justice process, we would demand exceptionally clear proof before we would infer that the discretion has been abused. The unique nature of the decisions at issue in this case also counsels against adopting such an inference from the disparities indicated by the Baldus study. Accordingly, we hold that the Baldus study is clearly insufficient to support an inference that any of the decision makers in McCleskey's case acted with discriminatory purpose.

B

McCleskey also suggests that the Baldus study proves that the State as a whole has acted with a discriminatory purpose. He appears to argue that the State has violated the Equal Protection Clause by adopting the capital punishment statute and allowing it to remain in force despite its allegedly discriminatory application. But " '[d]iscriminatory purpose' . . . implies more than intent as volition or intent as awareness of consequences. It implies that the decision maker, in this case a state legislature, selected or reaffirmed a particular course of action at least in part 'because of,' not merely 'in spite of,' its adverse effects upon an identifiable group." For this claim to prevail, McCleskey would have to prove that the Georgia Legislature enacted or maintained the death penalty statute because of an anticipated racially discriminatory effect. In *Gregg* v. *Georgia*, this Court found that the Georgia capital

sentencing system could operate in a fair and neutral manner. There was no evidence then, and there is none now, that the Georgia Legislature enacted the capital punishment statute to further a racially discriminatory purpose.

Nor has McCleskey demonstrated that the legislature maintains the capital punishment statute because of the racially disproportionate impact suggested by the Baldus study. As legislatures necessarily have wide discretion in the choice of criminal laws and penalties, and as there were legitimate reasons for the Georgia Legislature to adopt and maintain capital punishment, we will not infer a discriminatory purpose on the part of the State of Georgia. Accordingly, we reject McCleskey's equal protection claims.

III

McCleskey also argues that the Baldus study demonstrates that the Georgia capital sentencing system violates the Eighth Amendment. . . . [Here Justice Powell's analysis focuses on *Furman, Gregg,* and post-*Gregg* rulings to elucidate the requirements of the capital sentencing process.]

D

In sum, our decisions since *Furman* have identified a constitutionally permissible range of discretion in imposing the death penalty. First, there is a required threshold below which the death penalty cannot be imposed. In this context, the State must establish rational criteria that narrow the decision maker's judgment as to whether the circumstances of a particular defendant's case meet the threshold. Moreover, a societal consensus that the death penalty is disproportionate to a particular offense prevents a State from imposing the death penalty for that offense. Second, States cannot limit the sentencer's consideration of any relevant circumstance that could cause it to decline to impose the penalty. In this respect, the State cannot channel the sentencer's discretion, but must allow it to consider any relevant information offered by the defendant.

IV

A

In light of our precedents under the Eighth Amendment, McCleskey cannot argue successfully that his sentence is "disproportionate to the crime in the traditional sense." He does not deny that he committed a murder in the course of a planned robbery, a crime for which this Court has determined that the death penalty constitutionally may be imposed. His disproportionality claim "is of a different sort." McCleskey argues that the sentence in his case is disproportionate to the sentences in other murder cases.

On the one hand, he cannot base a constitutional claim on an argument that his case differs from other cases in which defendants did receive the death penalty. On automatic appeal, the Georgia Supreme Court found that McCleskey's death sentence was not disproportionate to other death sentences imposed in the State. The court supported this conclusion with an appendix containing citations to 13 cases involving generally similar murders. Moreover, where the statutory procedures adequately channel the sentencer's discretion, such proportionality review is not constitutionally required.

On the other hand, absent a showing that the Georgia capital punishment system operates in an arbitrary and capricious manner, McCleskey cannot prove a constitutional violation by demonstrating that other defendants who may be similarly situated did not receive the death penalty. . . .

Because McCleskey's sentence was imposed under Georgia sentencing procedures that focus discretion "on the particularized nature of the crime and the particularized characteristics of the individual defendant," we lawfully may presume that McCleskey's death sentence was not "wantonly and freakishly" imposed, and thus that the sentence is not disproportionate within any recognized meaning under the Eighth Amendment.

B

. . . McCleskey . . . further contends that the Georgia capital punishment system is arbitrary and capricious in application, and therefore his sentence is excessive, because racial considerations may influence capital sentencing decisions in Georgia. We now address this claim.

To evaluate McCleskey's challenge, we must examine exactly what the Baldus study may show. Even Professor Baldus does not contend that his statistics prove that race enters into any capital sentencing decisions, or that race was a factor in McCleskey's particular case. Statistics at most may show only a likelihood that a particular factor entered into some decisions. There is, of course, some risk of racial prejudice influencing a jury's decision in a criminal case. There are similar risks that other kinds of prejudice will influence other criminal trials. The question "is at what point that risk becomes constitutionally unacceptable." McCleskey asks us to accept the likelihood allegedly shown by the Baldus study as the constitutional

measure of an unacceptable risk of racial prejudice influencing capital sentencing decision. This we decline to do.

Because of the risk that the factor of race may enter the criminal justice process, we have engaged in "unceasing efforts" to eradicate racial prejudice from our criminal justice system. Our efforts have been guided by our recognition that "the inestimable privilege of trial by jury . . . is a vital principle, underlying the whole administration of criminal justice." Thus, it is the jury that is a criminal defendant's fundamental "protection of life and liberty against race or color prejudice." Specifically, a capital sentencing jury representative of a criminal defendant's community assures a " 'Diffused impartiality,' " in the jury's task of "express[ing] the conscience of the community on the ultimate question of life or death." . . .

McCleskey's argument that the Constitution condemns the discretion allowed decision makers in the Georgia capital sentencing system is antithetical to the fundamental role of discretion in our criminal justice system. Discretion in the criminal justice system offers substantial benefits to the criminal defendant. Not only can a jury decline to impose the death sentence, it can decline to convict or choose to convict of a lesser offense. Whereas decisions against a defendant's interest may be reversed by the trial judge or on appeal, these discretionary exercises of leniency are final and unreviewable. Similarly, the capacity of prosecutorial discretion to provide individualized justice is "firmly entrenched in American law." 2 W. LaFave & D. Israel, Criminal Procedure Section 13.2(a), p. 160 (1984). . . .

C

At most, the Baldus study indicates a discrepancy that appears to correlate with race. Apparent disparities in sentencing are an inevitable part of our criminal justice system. The discrepancy indicated by the Baldus study is "a far cry from the major systemic defects identified in *Furman*." As this Court has recognized, any mode for determining guilt or punishment "has its weaknesses and the potential for misuse." Specifically, "there can be 'no perfect procedure for deciding in which cases governmental authority should be used to impose death.' " Despite these imperfections, our consistent rule has been that constitutional guarantees are met when "the mode [for determining guilt or punishment] itself has been surrounded with safeguards to make it as fair as possible." Where the discretion that is fundamental to our criminal process is involved, we decline to assume that what is unexplained is invidious. In light of the safeguards designed to minimize racial bias in the process, the fundamental value of a jury trial in our criminal justice system, and the benefits that discretion provides to criminal defendants, we hold that the Baldus study does not demonstrate a constitutionally significant risk of racial bias affecting the Georgia capital sentencing process.

V

Two additional concerns inform our decision in this case. First, McCleskey's claim, taken to its logical conclusion, throws into serious question the principles that underlie our entire criminal justice system. The Eighth Amendment is not limited in application to capital punishment, but applies to all penalties. Thus, if we accepted McCleskey's claim that racial bias has impermissibly tainted the capital sentencing decision, we could soon be faced with similar claims as to other types of penalty. Moreover, the claim that his sentence rests on the irrelevant factor of race easily could be extended to apply to claims based on unexplained discrepancies that correlate to membership in other minority groups, and even to gender. Similarly, since McCleskey's claim relates to the race of his victim, other claims could apply with equally logical force to statistical disparities that correlate with the race or sex of other actors in the criminal justice system, such as defense attorneys or judges. Also, there is no logical reason that such a claim need be limited to racial or sexual bias. If arbitrary and capricious punishment is the touchstone under the Eighth Amendment, such a claim could—at least in theory—be based upon any arbitrary variable, such as the defendant's facial characteristics, or the physical attractiveness of the defendant or the victim, that some statistical study indicates may be influential in jury decision making. As these examples illustrate, there is no limiting principle to the type of challenge brought by McCleskey.

The Constitution does not require that a State eliminate any demonstrable disparity that correlates with a potentially irrelevant factor in order to operate a criminal justice system that includes capital punishment. As we have stated specifically in the context of capital punishment, the Constitution does not "plac[e] totally unrealistic conditions on its use."

Second, McCleskey's arguments are best presented to the legislative bodies. It is not the responsibility or indeed even the right of this Court to determine the appropriate punishment for particular crimes. It is the legislatures, the elected representatives of the people, that are "constituted to respond to the will and consequently the moral values of the people." Legislatures also are better qualified to weigh and "evaluate the results of statistical studies in terms of their own local conditions and with a flexibility of approach that is not available to the courts." Capital punishment is now the law in more than two-thirds of our States. It is the ultimate duty of courts to determine on a case-by-case basis whether these laws are applied consistently with the Constitution. Despite McCleskey's wide-ranging arguments that basically challenge the validity of capital punishment in our multiracial society, the only question before us is whether in his case the law of Georgia was properly applied. We agree with the District Court and the Court of Appeals for the Eleventh Circuit that this was carefully and correctly done in this case.

VI

Accordingly, we affirm the judgment of the Court of Appeals for the Eleventh Circuit.

It is so ordered.

JUSTICE BRENNAN, *with whom* JUSTICE MARSHALL *joins, and with whom* JUSTICE BLACKMUN *and* JUSTICE STEVENS *join in all but Part I, dissenting.*

I

. . . [M]urder defendants in Georgia with white victims are more than four times as likely to receive the death sentence as are defendants with black victims. Nothing could convey more powerfully the intractable reality of the death penalty: "that the effort to eliminate arbitrariness in the infliction of that ultimate sanction is so plainly doomed to failure that is—and the death penalty—must be abandoned altogether." . . .

II

At some point in this case, Warren McCleskey doubtless asked his lawyer whether a jury was likely to sentence him to die. A candid reply to this question would have been disturbing. First, counsel would have to tell McCleskey that few of the details of the crime or of McCleskey's past criminal conduct were more important than the fact that his victim was white. Furthermore, counsel would feel bound to tell McCleskey that defendants charged with killing white victims in Georgia are 4.3 times as likely to be sentenced to death as defendants charged with killing blacks. In addition, frankness would compel the disclosure that it was more likely than not that the race of McCleskey's victim would determine whether he received a death sentence: 6 of every 11 defendants convicted of killing a white person would not have received the death penalty if their victims had been black; while, among defendants with aggravating and mitigating factors comparable to McCleskey, 20 of every 34 would not have been sentenced to die if their victims had been black. Finally, the assessment would not be complete without the information that cases involving black defendants and white victims are more likely to result in a death sentence than cases featuring any other racial combination of defendant and victim. The story could be told in a variety of ways, but McCleskey could not fail to grasp its essential narrative line: there was a significant chance that race would play a prominent role in determining if he lived or died.

The Court today holds that Warren McCleskey's sentence was constitutionally imposed. It finds no fault in a system in which lawyers must tell their clients that race casts a large shadow on the capital sentencing process. The Court arrives at this conclusion by stating that the Baldus study cannot "prove that race enters into any capital sentencing decisions or that race was a factor in McCleskey's particular case." Since, according to Professor Baldus, we cannot say "to a moral certainty" that race influenced a decision, we can identify only "a likelihood that a particular factor entered into some decisions" and "a discrepancy that appears to correlate with race." This "likelihood" and "discrepancy," holds the Court, is [sic] insufficient to establish a constitutional violation. The Court reaches this conclusion by placing four factors on the scales opposite McCleskey's evidence: the desire to encourage sentencing discretion, the existence of "statutory safeguards" in the Georgia scheme, the fear of encouraging widespread challenges to other sentencing decisions, and the limits of the judicial role. The Court's evaluation of the significance of petitioner's evidence is fundamentally at odds with our consistent concern for rationality in capital sentencing, and the considerations that the majority invokes to discount that evidence cannot justify ignoring its force.

III

A

* * *

Defendants challenging their death sentences . . .

never have had to prove that impermissible considerations have actually infected sentencing decisions. We have required instead that they establish that the system under which they were sentenced posed a significant risk of such an occurrence. McCleskey's claim does differ, however, in one respect from these earlier cases: it is the first to base a challenge not on speculation about how a system might operate, but on empirical documentation of how it does operate.

The Court assumes the statistical validity of the Baldus study and acknowledges that McCleskey has demonstrated a risk that racial prejudice plays a role in capital sentencing in Georgia. Nonetheless, it finds the probability of prejudice insufficient to create constitutional concern. Close analysis of the Baldus study, however, in light of both statistical principles and human experience, reveals that the risk that race influenced McCleskey's sentence is intolerable by any imaginable standard.

B

The Baldus study indicates that, after taking into account some 230 nonracial factors that might legitimately influence a sentencer, the jury more likely than not would have spared McCleskey's life had his victim been black. The study distinguishes between (1) those cases in which the jury exercises virtually no discretion because the strength or weakness of aggravating factors usually suggests that only one outcome is appropriate, and (2) cases reflecting an "intermediate" level of aggravation, in which the jury has considerable discretion in choosing a sentence. McCleskey's case falls into the intermediate range. In such cases, death is imposed in 34% of the white-victim crimes and 14% of black-victim crimes, a difference of 139% in the rate of imposition of the death penalty. In other words, just under 59%—almost 6 in 10—defendants comparable to McCleskey would not have received the death penalty if their victims had been black.

Furthermore, even examination of the sentencing system as a whole, factoring in those cases in which the jury exercises little discretion, indicates the influence of race on capital sentencing. For the Georgia system as a whole, race accounts for a six-percentage-point difference in the rate at which capital punishment is imposed. Since death is imposed in 11% of all white-victim cases, the rate in comparably aggravated black-victim cases is 5%. The rate of capital sentencing in a white-victim case is thus 120% greater than the rate in a black-victim case. Put another way, over half—55%—of defendants in white-victim crimes in Georgia would not have been sentenced to die if their victims had been black. Of the more than 200 variables potentially relevant to a sentencing decision, race of the victim is a powerful explanation for variation in death sentence rates—as powerful as nonracial aggravating factors such as a prior murder conviction or acting as the principal planner of the homicide.

These adjusted figures are only the most conservative indication of the risk that race will influence the death sentences of defendants in Georgia. Data unadjusted for the mitigating or aggravating effect of other factors show an even more pronounced disparity by race. The capital sentencing rate for all white-victim cases was almost 11 times greater than the rate for black-victim cases. Furthermore, blacks who kill whites are sentenced to death at nearly 22 times the rate of blacks who kill blacks, and more than 7 times the rate of whites who kill blacks. In addition, prosecutors seek the death penalty for 70% of black defendants with white victims, but for only 15% of black defendants with black victims, and only 19% of white defendants with black victims. Since our decision upholding the Georgia capital sentencing system in *Gregg*, the State has executed 7 persons. All of the 7 were convicted of killing whites, and 6 of the 7 executed were black. Such execution figures are especially striking in light of the fact that, during the period encompassed by the Baldus study, only 9.2% of Georgia homicides involved black defendants and white victims, while 60.7% involved black victims.

McCleskey's statistics have particular force because most of them are the product of sophisticated multiple-regression analysis. Such analysis is designed precisely to identify patterns in the aggregate, even though we may not be able to reconstitute with certainty any individual decision that goes to make up that pattern. Multiple-regression analysis is particularly well suited to identify the influence of impermissible considerations in sentencing, since it is able to control for permissible factors that may explain an apparent arbitrary pattern. While the decision-making process of a body such as a jury may be complex, the Baldus study provides a massive compilation of the details that are most relevant to that decision. . . .

The statistical evidence in this case thus relentlessly documents the risk that McCleskey's sentence was influenced by racial considerations. This evidence shows that there is a better than even chance in Georgia that race will influence the decision to impose the death penalty: a majority of defendants in white-victim crimes would not have

been sentenced to die if their victims had been black. In determining whether this risk is acceptable, our judgment must be shaped by the awareness that "[t]he risk of racial prejudice infecting a capital sentencing proceeding is especially serious in light of the complete finality of the death sentence." . . . In light of the gravity of the interest at stake, petitioner's statistics on their face are a powerful demonstration of the type of risk that our Eighth Amendment jurisprudence has consistently condemned.

C

Evaluation of McCleskey's evidence cannot rest solely on the numbers themselves. We must also ask whether the conclusion suggested by those numbers is consonant with our understanding of history and human experience. Georgia's legacy of a race-conscious criminal justice system, as well as this Court's own recognition of the persistent danger that racial attitudes may affect criminal proceedings, indicate that McCleskey's claim is not a fanciful product of mere statistical artifice.

For many years, Georgia operated openly and formally precisely the type of dual system the evidence shows is still effectively in place. The criminal law expressly differentiated between crimes committed by and against blacks and whites, distinctions whose lineage traced back to the time of slavery. . . .

This historical review of Georgia criminal law is not intended as a bill of indictment calling the State to account for past transgressions. Citation of past practices does not justify the automatic condemnation of current ones. But it would be unrealistic to ignore the influence of history in assessing the plausible implications of McCleskey's evidence. . . .

History and its continuing legacy thus buttress the probative force of McCleskey's statistics. Formal dual criminal laws may no longer be in effect, and intentional discrimination may no longer be prominent. Nonetheless . . . "subtle, less consciously held racial attitudes" continue to be of concern, and the Georgia system gives such attitudes considerable room to operate. The conclusions drawn from McCleskey's statistical evidence are therefore consistent with the lessons of social experience.

The majority thus misreads our Eighth Amendment jurisprudence in concluding that McCleskey has not demonstrated a degree of risk sufficient to raise constitutional concern. The determination of the significance of his evidence is at its core an exercise in human moral judgment, not a mechanical statistical analysis. It must first and foremost be informed by awareness of the fact that death is irrevocable, and that as a result "the qualitative difference of death from all other punishments requires a greater degree of scrutiny of the capital sentencing determination." For this reason, we have demanded a uniquely high degree of rationality in imposing the death penalty. A capital sentencing system in which race more likely than not plays a role does not meet this standard. It is true that every nuance of decision cannot be statistically captured, nor can any individual judgment be plumbed with absolute certainty. Yet the fact that we must always act without the illumination of complete knowledge cannot induce paralysis when we confront what is literally an issue of life and death. Sentencing data, history, and experience all counsel that Georgia has provided insufficient assurance of the heightened rationality we have required in order to take a human life. . . .

IV

* * *

Considering the race of a defendant or victim in deciding if the death penalty should be imposed is completely at odds with this concern that an individual be evaluated as a unique human being. Decisions influenced by race rest in part on a categorical assessment of the worth of human beings according to color, insensitive to whatever qualities the individuals in question may possess. Enhanced willingness to impose the death sentence on black defendants, or diminished willingness to render such a sentence when blacks are victims, reflects a devaluation of the lives of black persons. When confronted with evidence that race more likely than not plays such a role in a capital sentencing system, it is plainly insufficient to say that the importance of discretion demands that the risk be higher before we will act—for in such a case the very end that discretion is designed to serve is being undermined. . . .

At the time our Constitution was framed 200 years ago this year, blacks "had for more than a century before been regarded as beings of an inferior order, and altogether unfit to associate with the white race, either in social or political relations; and so far inferior, that they had no rights which the white man was bound to respect." *Dred Scott* v. *Sandford*, 19 How. 393, 404 (1857). Only

130 years ago, this Court relied on these observations to deny American citizenship to blacks. *Ibid.* A mere three generations ago, this Court sanctioned racial segregation, stating that "[i]f one race be inferior to the other socially, the Constitution of the United States cannot put them upon the same plane." *Plessy* v. *Ferguson*, 163 U.S. 537, 552 (1896).

In more recent times, we have sought to free ourselves from the burden of this history. Yet it has been scarcely a generation since this Court's first decision striking down racial segregation, and barely two decades since the legislative prohibition of racial discrimination in major domains of national life. These have been honorable steps, but we cannot pretend that in three decades we have completely escaped the grip of a historical legacy spanning centuries. Warren McCleskey's evidence confronts us with the subtle and persistent influence of the past. His message is a disturbing one to a society that has formally repudiated racism, and a frustrating one to a Nation accustomed to regarding its destiny as the product of its own will. Nonetheless, we ignore him at our peril, for we remain imprisoned by the past as long as we deny its influence in the present.

It is tempting to pretend that minorities on death row share a fate in no way connected to our own, that our treatment of them sounds no echoes beyond the chambers in which they die. Such an illusion is ultimately corrosive, for the reverberations of injustice are not so easily confined. "The destinies of the two races in this country are indissolubly linked together." *id.*, at 560, (Harlan, J., dissenting), and the way in which we choose those who will die reveals the depth of moral commitment among the living.

The Court's decision today will not change what attorneys in Georgia tell other Warren McCleskeys about their chances of execution. Nothing will soften the harsh message they must convey nor alter the prospect that race undoubtedly will continue to be a topic of discussion. McCleskey's evidence will not have obtained judicial acceptance, but that will not affect what is said on death row. However many criticisms of today's decision may be rendered, these painful conversations will serve as the most eloquent dissents of all.

[The dissenting opinions of JUSTICE BLACKMUN and JUSTICE STEVENS are not reprinted here.]

STANFORD v. KENTUCKY
WILKINS v. MISSOURI
492 U.S. 361; 106 L. Ed. 2d. 306; 109 S. Ct. 2969 (1989)

JUSTICE SCALIA *announced the judgment of the Court and delivered the opinion of the Court with respect to Parts I, II, III, and IV-A, and an opinion with respect to Parts IV-B and V, in which* THE CHIEF JUSTICE, JUSTICE WHITE, *and* JUSTICE KENNEDY *joined.*

These two consolidated cases require us to decide whether the imposition of capital punishment on an individual for a crime committed at 16 or 17 years of age constitutes cruel and unusual punishment under the Eighth Amendment.

I

The first case . . . involves the shooting death of 20-year-old Baerbel Poore in Jefferson County, Kentucky. Petitioner Kevin Stanford committed the murder on January 7, 1981, when he was approximately 17 years and 4 months of age. Stanford and his accomplice repeatedly raped and sodomized Poore during and after their commission of a robbery at a gas station where she worked as an attendant. They then drove her to a secluded area near the station, where Stanford shot her point-blank in the face and then in the back of the head. The proceeds from the robbery were roughly 300 cartons of cigarettes, two gallons of fuel and a small amount of cash. A corrections officer testified that petitioner explained the murder as follows: " '[H]e said, I had to shoot her, [she] lived next door to me and she would recognize me. . . . I guess we could have tied her up or something or beat [her up] . . . and tell her if she tells, we would kill her. . . . Then after he said that he started laughing.' " . . .

After Stanford's arrest, a Kentucky juvenile court conducted hearings to determine whether he should be transferred for trial as an adult. . . . Stressing the seriousness of petitioner's offenses and the unsuccessful attempts of the juvenile system to treat him for numerous instances of past delinquency, the juvenile court found certification for trial as an adult to be in the best interest of petitioner and the community.

Stanford was convicted of murder, first-degree sodomy, first-degree robbery, and receiving stolen property, and was sentenced to death and 45 years in prison. The Kentucky Supreme Court affirmed the death sentence, rejecting Stanford's "deman[d] that he has a constitutional right to treatment." . . . Finding that the record clearly demonstrated that "there was no program or treatment appropriate for the appellent in the juvenile justice system," the court held that the juvenile court did not err in certifying petitioner for trial as an adult. . . .

The second case . . . involves the stabbing death of Nancy Allen, a 26-year-old mother of two who was working behind the sales counter of the convenience store she and David Allen owned and operated in Avondale, Missouri. Petitioner Heath Wilkins committed the murder on July 27, 1985, when he was approximately 16 years and 6 months of age. The record reflects that Wilkins' plan was to rob the store and murder "whoever was behind the counter" because "a dead person can't talk." While Wilkins' accomplice, Patrick Stevens, held Allen, Wilkins stabbed her, causing her to fall to the floor. When Stevens had trouble operating the cash register, Allen spoke up to assist him, leading Wilkins to stab her three more times in her chest. Two of these wounds penetrated the victim's heart. When Allen began to beg for her life, Wilkins stabbed her four more times in the neck, opening her carotid artery. After helping themselves to liquor, cigarettes, rolling papers, and approximately $450 in cash and checks, Wilkins and Stevens left Allen to die on the floor.

Because he was roughly six months short of the age of majority for purposes of criminal prosecution . . . Wilkins could not automatically be tried as an adult under Missouri law. Before that could happen, the juvenile court was required to terminate juvenile-court jurisdiction and certify Wilkins for trial as an adult [under Missouri law], which permits individuals between 14 and 17 years of age who have committed felonies to be tried as adults. Relying on the "viciousness, force, and violence" of the alleged crime, petitioner's maturity, and the failure of the juvenile justice system to rehabilitate him after previous delinquent acts, the juvenile court made the necessary certification.

Wilkins was charged with first-degree murder, armed criminal action, and carrying a concealed weapon. After the court found him competent, petitioner entered guilty pleas to all charges. A punishment hearing was held, at which both the State and petitioner himself urged imposition of the death sentence. Evidence at the hearing revealed that petitioner had been in and out of juvenile facilities since the age of eight for various acts of burglary, theft, and arson, had attempted to kill his mother by putting insecticide into Tylenol capsules, and had killed several animals in his neighborhood. Although psychiatric testimony indicated that Wilkins had "personality disorders," the witnesses agreed that Wilkins was aware of his actions and could distinguish right from wrong.

The trial court then determined that the death penalty was appropriate . . . and the Supreme Court of Missouri affirmed.

We granted certiorari in these cases . . . to decide whether the Eighth Amendment precludes the death penalty for individuals who commit crimes at 16 or 17 years of age.

II

The thrust of both Wilkins' and Stanford's arguments is that imposition of the death penalty on those who were juveniles when they committed their crimes falls within the Eighth Amendment's prohibition against "cruel and unusual punishments." Wilkins would have us define juveniles as individuals 16 years of age and under, Stanford would draw the line at 17.

Neither petitioner asserts that his sentence constitutes one of "those modes or acts of punishment that had been considered cruel and unusual at the time that the Bill of Rights was adopted." . . . Nor could they support such a contention. At that time, the common law set the rebuttable presumption of incapacity to commit any felony at the age of 14, and theoretically permitted capital punishment to be imposed on anyone over the age of 7. . . . In accordance with the standards of this common-law tradition, at least 281 offenders under the age of 18 have been executed in this country, and at least 126 under the age of 17. . . .

Thus, petitioners are left to argue that their punishment is contrary to the "evolving standards of decency that mark the progress of a maturing society." . . . They are correct in asserting that this Court has "not confined the prohibition embodied in the Eighth Amendment to 'barbarous' methods that were generally outlawed in the 18th century," but instead has interpreted the Amendment "in a flexible and dynamic manner." . . . In determining what standards have "evolved," however, we have looked not to our own conceptions of decency, but to those of modern American society as a whole. As we have said, "Eighth Amendment judgments should not be, or appear to be, merely the subjective views of individual Justices; judgment should

be informed by objective factors to the maximum possible extent." . . . This approach is dictated both by the language of the Amendment . . . and by the "deference we owe to the decisions of the state legislatures under our federal system." . . .

III

"[F]irst" among the " 'objective indicia that reflect the public attitude toward a given sanction' " are statutes passed by society's elected representatives. . . . Of the 37 States whose laws permit capital punishment, 15 decline to impose it upon 16-year-old offenders and 12 decline to impose it on 17-year-old offenders. This does not establish the degree of national consensus this Court has previously thought sufficient to label a particular punishment cruel and unusual. . . .

Since a majority of the States that permit capital punishment authorize it for crimes committed at age 16 or above, petitioners' cases are analogous to *Tison* v. *Arizona*, 481 U.S. 137, (1987). . . . In *Tison*, which upheld Arizona's imposition of the death penalty for major participation in a felony with reckless indifference to human life, we noted that only 11 of those jurisdictions imposing capital punishment rejected its use in such circumstances. As we noted earlier, here the number is 15 for offenders under 17, and 12 for offenders under 18. We think the same conclusion as in *Tison* is required in this case.

Petitioners make much of the recently enacted federal statute providing capital punishment for certain drug-related offenses, but limiting that punishment to offenders 18 and over. . . . That reliance is entirely misplaced. To begin with, the statute in question does not embody a judgment by the Federal Legislature that *no* murder is heinous enough to warrant the execution of such a youthful offender, but merely that the narrow class of offense it defines is not. The congressional judgment on the broader question, if apparent at all, is to be found in the law that permits 16- and 17-year-olds (after appropriate findings) to be tried and punished as adults for *all* federal offenses, including those bearing a capital penalty that is not limited to 18-year-olds. . . . Moreover, even if it were true that no federal statute permitted the execution of persons under 18, that would not remotely establish—in the face of a substantial number of state statutes to the contrary—a national consensus that such punishment is inhumane. . . . To be sure, the absence of a federal death penalty for 16- or 17-year-olds (if it existed) might be evidence that there is no national consensus *in favor* of such punishment. It is not the burden of Kentucky and Missouri, however, to establish a national consensus approving what their citizens have voted to do; rather, it is the "heavy burden" of petitioners . . . to establish a national consensus *against* it. As far as the primary and most reliable indication of consensus is concerned—the pattern of enacted laws—petitioners have failed to carry that burden.

IV

A

Wilkins and Stanford argue . . . that even if the laws themselves do not establish a settled consensus, the application of the laws does. That contemporary society views capital punishment of 16- and 17-year-old offenders as inappropriate is demonstrated, they say, by the reluctance of juries to impose, and prosecutors to seek, such sentences. Petitioners are quite correct that a far smaller number of offenders under 18 than over 18 have been sentenced to death in this country. From 1982 through 1988, for example, out of 2,106 total death sentences, only 15 were imposed on individuals who were 16 or under when they committed their crimes, and only 30 on individuals who were 17 at the time of their crime. . . . And it appears that actual executions for crimes committed under age 18 accounted for only about two percent of the total number of executions that occurred between 1642 and 1986. . . . These statistics, however, carry little significance. Given the undisputed fact that a far smaller percentage of capital crimes is committed by persons under 18 than over 18, the discrepancy in treatment is much less than might seem. Granted, however, that a substantial discrepancy exists, that does not establish the requisite proposition that the death sentence for offenders under 18 is categorically unacceptable to prosecutors and juries. To the contrary, it is not only possible but overwhelmingly probable that the very considerations which induce petitioners and their supporters to believe that death should *never* be imposed on offenders under 18 cause prosecutors and juries to believe that it should *rarely* be imposed.

V

Having failed to establish a consensus against capital punishment for 16- and 17-year-old offenders through state and federal statutes and the behavior of prosecutors and juries, petitioners seek to demonstrate it through other indicia, including public opinion polls, the views of interest groups and the positions adopted by various professional associations. We decline the invitation to rest constitutional law upon such uncertain foundations. A revised national consensus so broad, so clear and so enduring as to justify a permanent prohibition upon all units of democratic government must appear in the operative acts (laws and the application of laws) that the people have approved.

We also reject petitioners' argument that we should invalidate capital punishment of 16- and 17-year-old offenders on the ground that it fails to serve the legitimate goals of penology. According to petitioners, it fails to deter because juveniles, possessing less developed cognitive skills than adults, are less likely to fear death; and it fails to exact just retribution because juveniles, being less mature and responsible, are also less morally blameworthy. In support of these claims, petitioners and their supporting *amici* marshall an array of socioscientific evidence concerning the psychological and emotional development of 16- and 17-year-olds.

If such evidence could conclusively establish the entire lack of deterrent effect and moral responsibility, resort to the Cruel and Unusual Punishments Clause would be unnecessary; the Equal Protection Clause of the Fourteenth Amendment would invalidate these laws for lack of rational basis. . . . But as the adjective "socioscientific" suggests (and insofar as evaluation of moral responsibility is concerned perhaps the adjective "ethicoscientific" would be more apt), it is not demonstrable that no 16-year-old is "adequately responsible" or significantly deterred. It is rational, even if mistaken, to think the contrary. The battle must be fought, then, on the field of the Eighth Amendment; and in that struggle socioscientific, ethicoscientific, or even purely scientific evidence is not an available weapon. The punishment is either "cruel *and* unusual" or it is not. The audience for these arguments, in other words, is not this Court but the citizenry of the United States. It is they, not we, who must be persuaded. . . . [O]ur job is to *identify* the "evolving standards of decency;" to determine, not what they *should* be, but what they *are*. We have no power under the Eighth Amendment to substitute our belief in the scientific evidence for the society's apparent skepticism. In short, we emphatically reject petitioner's suggestion that the issues in this case permit us to apply our "own informed judgment" . . . regarding the desirability of permitting the death penalty for crimes by 16- and 17-year-olds.

We reject the dissent's contention that our approach, by "largely return[ing] the task of defining the contours of Eighth Amendment protection to political majorities," leaves " '[c]onstitutional doctrine [to] be formulated by the acts of those institutions which the Constitution is supposed to limit.' " . . . When this Court cast loose from the historical moorings consisting of the original application of the Eighth Amendment, it did not embark rudderless upon a wide-open sea. Rather, it limited the Amendment's extension to those practices contrary to the "evolving *standards* of decency that mark the progress of a maturing *society.*" . . .

We discern neither a historical nor a modern societal consensus forbidding the imposition of capital punishment on any person who murders at 16 or 17 years of age. Accordingly, we conclude that such punishment does not offend the Eighth Amendment's prohibition against cruel and unusual punishment.

The judgments of the Supreme Court of Kentucky and the Supreme Court of Missouri are therefore

Affirmed.

[JUSTICE O'CONNOR's concurring opinion is not reprinted here.]

JUSTICE BRENNAN, *with whom* JUSTICE MARSHALL, JUSTICE BLACKMUN, *and* JUSTICE STEVENS *join, dissenting.*

I

Our judgment about the constitutionality of a punishment under the Eighth Amendment is informed, though not determined, . . . by an examination of contemporary attitudes toward the punishment, as evidenced in the actions of legislatures and of juries. . . . The views of organizations with expertise in relevant fields and the choices of governments elsewhere in the world also merit our attention as indicators whether a punishment is acceptable in a civilized society.

A

The Court's discussion of state laws concerning capital sentencing gives a distorted view of the evidence of contemporary standards that these legislative determinations provide. Currently, 12 of the States whose statutes permit capital punishment specifically mandate that offenders under age 18 not be sentenced to death. When one adds to these 12 States the 15 (including the District of Columbia) in which capital punishment is not authorized at all, it appears that the governments in fully 27 of the States have concluded that no one under 18 should face the death penalty. A further 3 States explicitly refuse to authorize sentences of death for

those who committed their offenses when under 17, making a total of 30 States that would not tolerate the execution of petitioner Wilkins. Congress's most recent enactment of a death penalty statute also excludes those under 18. . . .

In 18 States that have a death penalty, no minimum age for capital sentences is set in the death penalty statute. . . . The notion that these States have consciously authorized the execution of juveniles derives from the congruence in those jurisdictions of laws permitting state courts to hand down death sentences, on the one hand, and, on the other, statutes permitting the transfer of offenders under 18 from the juvenile to state court systems for trial in certain circumstances. . . . I would not assume, however, in considering how the States stand on the moral issue that underlies the constitutional question with which we are presented, that a legislature that has never specifically considered the issue has made a conscious moral choice to permit the execution of juveniles. . . . On a matter of such moment that most States have expressed an explicit and contrary judgment, the decisions of legislatures that are only implicit, and that lack the "earmarks of careful consideration that we have required for other kinds of decisions leading to the death penalty," must count for little. I do not suggest, of course, that laws of these States cut *against* the constitutionality of the juvenile death penalty—only that accuracy demands that the baseline for our deliberations should be that 27 States refuse to authorize a sentence of death in the circumstances of petitioner Stanford's case, and 30 would not permit Wilkins' execution; that 18 States have not squarely faced the question; and that only the few remaining jurisdictions have explicitly set an age below 18 at which a person may be sentenced to death.

B

The application of these laws is another indicator the Court agrees to be relevant. The fact that juries have on occasion sentenced a minor to death shows, the Court says, that the death penalty for adolescents is not categorically unacceptable to juries. This, of course, is true; but it is not a conclusion that takes Eighth Amendment analysis very far. Just as we have never insisted that a punishment have been rejected unanimously by the States before we may judge it cruel and unusual, so we have never adopted the extraordinary view that a punishment is beyond Eighth Amendment challenge if it is sometimes handed down by a jury. . . .

Both in absolute and in relative terms, imposition of the death penalty on adolescents is distinctly unusual. Adolescent offenders make up only a small proportion of the current death row population. . . .

The Court speculates that this very small number of capital sentences imposed on adolescents indicates that juries have considered the youth of the offender when determining sentence, and have reserved the punishment for rare cases in which it is nevertheless appropriate. . . . It is certainly true that in the vast majority of cases, juries have not sentenced juveniles to death, and it seems to me perfectly proper to conclude that a sentence so rarely imposed is "unusual."

C

Further indicators of contemporary standards of decency that should inform our consideration of the Eighth Amendment question are the opinions of respected organizations. . . . Where organizations with expertise in a relevant area have given careful consideration to the question of a punishment's appropriateness, there is no reason why that judgment should not be entitled to attention as an indicator of contemporary standards. There is no dearth of opinion from such groups that the state-sanctioned killing of minors is unjustified. . . . The American Bar Association has adopted a resolution opposing the imposition of capital punishment upon any person for an offense committed while under age 18, as has the National Council of Juvenile and Family Court Judges. The American Law Institute's Model Penal Code similarly includes a lower age of 18 for the death sentence. And the National Commission on Reform of the Federal Criminal Laws also recommended that 18 be the minimum age.

Our cases recognize that objective indicators of contemporary standards of decency in the form of legislation in other countries is also of relevance to Eighth Amendment analysis. . . . Many countries, of course—over 50, including nearly all in Western Europe—have formally abolished the death penalty, or have limited its use to exceptional crimes such as treason. . . . Twenty-seven others do not in practice impose the penalty. Of the nations that retain capital punishment, a majority—65— prohibit the execution of juveniles. . . . Since 1979, Amnesty International has recorded only eight executions of offenders under 18 throughout the world, three of these in the United States. . . . In addition to national laws, three leading human rights treaties ratified or signed by the United States explicitly prohibit juvenile death penalties. Within the world community, the imposition of the death penalty for juvenile crimes appears to be overwhelmingly disapproved.

D

Together, the rejection of the death penalty for juveniles by a majority of the States, the rarity of the sentence for juveniles, both as an absolute and a comparative matter, the decisions of respected organizations in relevant fields that this punishment is unacceptable, and its rejection generally throughout the world, provide to my mind a strong grounding for the view that it is not constitutionally tolerable that certain States persist in authorizing the execution of adolescent offenders. It is unnecessary, however, to rest a view that the Eighth Amendment prohibits the execution of minors solely upon a judgment as to the meaning to be attached to the evidence of contemporary values outlined above, for the execution of juveniles fails to satisfy two well-established and independent Eighth Amendment requirements—that a punishment not be disproportionate, and that it make a contribution to acceptable goals of punishment. . . .

II

* * *

The Court has explicitly stated that "the attitude of state legislatures and sentencing juries do *not* wholly determine" a controversy arising under the Eighth Amendment. *Coker* v. *Georgia*, 433 U.S., at 597, 1977 (plurality opinion) (emphasis added), because "the Constitution contemplates that in the end our own judgment will be brought to bear on the question of the [constitutional] acceptability of" a punishment. . . .

Thus, in addition to asking whether legislative or jury rejection of a penalty shows that "society has set its face against it," . . . the Court asks whether "a punishment is 'excessive' and unconstitutional" because there is disproportion "between the punishment imposed and the defendant's blameworthiness" or because it "makes no measurable contribution to acceptable goals of punishment and hence is nothing more than the purposeless and needless imposition of pain and suffering." . . .

III

* * *

A

Legislative determinations distinguishing juveniles from adults abound. These age-based classifications reveal much about how our society regards juveniles as a class, and about societal beliefs regarding adolescent levels of responsibility. . . .

. . . In a host of . . . ways, minors are treated differently from adults in our laws, which reflects the simple truth derived from communal experience, that juveniles as a class have not the level of maturation and responsibility that we presume in adults and consider desirable for full participation in the rights and duties of modern life.

"The reasons why juveniles are not trusted with the privileges and responsibilities of an adult also explain why their irresponsible conduct is not as morally reprehensible as that of an adult." . . . Adolescents "are more vulnerable, more impulsive, and less self-disciplined than adults," and are without the same "capacity to control their conduct and to think in long-range terms." . . . Moreover, the very paternalism that our society shows towards youths and the dependency it forces upon them mean that society bears a responsibility for the actions of juveniles that it does not for the actions of adults who are at least theoretically free to make their own choices: youth crime . . . is not exclusively the offender's fault; offenses by the young represent a failure of family, school, and the social system, which share responsibility for the development of America's youth." . . .

To be sure, the development of cognitive and reasoning abilities and of empathy, the acquisition of experience upon which these abilities operate and upon which the capacity to make sound value judgments depends, and in general the process of maturation into a self-directed individual fully responsible for his or her actions, occurs by degrees. . . . But the factors discussed above indicate that 18 is the dividing line that society has generally drawn, the point at which it is thought reasonable to assume that persons have an ability to make and a duty to bear responsibility for their judgments. Insofar as age 18 is a necessarily arbitrary social choice as a point at which to acknowledge a person's maturity and responsibility, given the different developmental rates of individuals, it is in fact "a conservative estimate of the dividing line between adolescence and adulthood. . . ."

B

There may be exceptional individuals who mature more quickly than their peers, and who might be considered fully responsible for their actions prior to the age of 18, despite their lack of the experience upon which judgment depends. In my view, however, it is not sufficient to accommodate the facts about juveniles that an individual youth's cul-

pability may be taken into account in the decision to transfer him or her from the juvenile to adult court systems for trial, or that a capital sentencing jury is instructed to consider youth and other mitigating factors. I believe that the Eighth Amendment requires that a person who lacks that full degree of responsibility for his or her actions associated with adulthood not be sentenced to death. Hence it is constitutionally inadequate that a juvenile offender's level of responsibility be taken into account only along with a host of other factors that the court or jury may decide outweigh that want of responsibility. . . .

. . . Adolescents on death row appear typically to have a battery of psychological, emotional, and other problems going to their likely capacity for judgment and level of blameworthiness. . . .

The cases under consideration today certainly do not suggest that individualized consideration at transfer and sentencing ensure that only exceptionally mature juveniles, as blameworthy for their crimes as an adult, are sentenced to death. Transferring jurisdiction over Kevin Stanford to Circuit Court, the Juvenile Division of the Jefferson, Kentucky, District Court nevertheless found that Stanford, who was 17 at the time of his crime,

> has a low internalization of the values and morals of society and lacks social skills. That he does possess an institutionalized personality and has, in effect, because of his chaotic family life and lack of treatment, become socialized in delinquent behavior. That he is emotionally immature and could be amenable to treatment if properly done on a long term basis of psychotherap[eu]tic intervention and reality based therapy for socialization and drug therapy in a residential facility. . . .

At the penalty phase of Stanford's trial, witnesses testified that Stanford, who lived with various relatives, had used drugs from the age of about 13, and that his drug use had caused changes in his personality and behavior. . . . Stanford had been placed at times in juvenile treatment facilities, and a witness who had assessed him upon his admission to an employment skills project found that he lacked age-appropriate social interaction skills; had a history of drug abuse; and wanted for family support or supervision. . . .

Heath Wilkins was 16 when he committed the crime for which Missouri intends to kill him. The juvenile court, in ordering him transferred for trial to adult court, focused upon the viciousness of Wilkins' crime, the juvenile system's inability to rehabilitate him in the 17 months of juvenile confinement available, and the need to protect the public, though it also mentioned that Wilkins was, in its view, "an experienced person, and mature in his appearance and habits." . . . The Circuit Court found Wilkins competent to stand trial. . . . Wilkins then waived counsel, with the avowed intention of pleading guilty and seeking the death penalty and the Circuit Court accepted the waiver and later Wilkins' guilty plea. Wilkins was not represented by counsel at sentencing. Presenting no mitigating evidence, he told the court he would prefer the death penalty to life in prison "[o]ne I fear, the other one I don't," and after hearing evidence from the State, the Court sentenced Wilkins to die. Wilkins took no steps to appeal and objected to an *amicus*' efforts on his behalf. The Missouri Supreme Court, however, ordered an evaluation to determine whether Wilkins was competent to waive his right to appellate counsel. Concluding that Wilkins was incompetent to waive his rights, the state-appointed forensic psychiatrist found that Wilkins "suffers from a mental disorder" that affects his "reasoning and impairs his behavior." . . . It would be incredible to suppose, given this psychiatrist's conclusion and his summary of Wilkins' past . . . that Missouri's transfer and sentencing schemes had operated to identify in Wilkins a 16-year-old mature and culpable beyond his years.

C

Juveniles very generally lack that degree of blameworthiness that is, in my view, a constitutional prerequisite for the imposition of capital punishment under our precedents concerning the Eighth Amendment proportionality principle. The individualized consideration of an offender's youth and culpability at the transfer stage and at sentencing has not operated to ensure that the only offenders under 18 singled out for the ultimate penalty are exceptional individuals whose level of responsibility is more developed than that of their peers. In that circumstance, I believe that the same categorical assumption that juveniles as a class are insufficiently mature to be regarded as fully responsible that we make in so many areas is appropriately made in determining whether minors may be subjected to the death penalty. . . . [I]t would be ironic if the assumptions we so readily make about minors as a class were suddenly unavailable in conducting proportionality analysis. I would hold that the Eighth Amendment prohibits the execution of any person for a crime committed below the age of 18. . . .

I dissent.

PAYNE v. TENNESSEE
___ U.S. ___; ___ L. Ed. 2d ___; 111 S. Ct. 2597 (1991)

CHIEF JUSTICE REHNQUIST *delivered the opinion of the Court.*

In this case we reconsider our holdings in *Booth* v. *Maryland*, 482 U.S. 496, (1987), and *South Carolina* v. *Gathers*, 490 U.S. 805, (1989), that the Eighth Amendment bars the admission of victim impact evidence during the penalty phase of a capital trial.

The petitioner, Pervis Tyrone Payne, was convicted by a jury on two counts of first-degree murder and one count of assault with intent to commit murder in the first degree. He was sentenced to death for each of the murders, and to 30 years in prison for the assault.

The victims of Payne's offenses were 28-year-old Charisse Christopher, her 2-year-old daughter Lacie, and her 3-year-old son Nicholas. The three lived together in an apartment in Millington, Tennessee, across the hall from Payne's girlfriend, Bobbie Thomas. On Saturday, June 27, 1987, Payne visited Thomas' apartment several times in expectation of her return from her mother's house in Arkansas, but found no one at home. On one visit, he left his overnight bag, containing clothes and other items for his weekend stay, in the hallway outside Thomas' apartment. With the bag were three cans of malt liquor.

Payne passed the morning and early afternoon injecting cocaine and drinking beer. Later, he drove around the town with a friend in the friend's car, each of them taking turns reading a pornographic magazine. Sometime around 3 p.m., Payne returned to the apartment complex, and began making sexual advances toward Charisse. Charisse resisted and Payne became violent. A neighbor heard Charisse screaming, " 'Get out, get out,' as if she were telling the children to leave." The noise briefly subsided and then began, " 'horribly loud.' " The neighbor called the police after she heard a "blood-curdling scream" from the Christopher apartment.

When the first police officer arrived at the

scene, he immediately encountered Payne, who was leaving the apartment building, so covered with blood that he appeared to be " 'sweating blood.' " The officer confronted Payne, who responded, " 'I'm the complainant.' " When the officer asked, " 'What's going on up there?' " Payne struck the officer with the overnight bag, dropped his tennis shoes, and fled.

Inside the apartment, the police encountered a horrifying scene. Blood covered the walls and floor throughout the unit. Charisse and her children were lying on the floor in the kitchen. Nicholas, despite several wounds inflicted by a butcher knife that completely penetrated through his body from front to back, was still breathing. Miraculously, he survived, but not until after undergoing seven hours of surgery and a transfusion of 1700 cc's of blood—400 to 500 cc's more than his estimated blood volume. Charisse and Lacie were dead.

Charisse's body was found on the kitchen floor on her back, her legs fully extended. She had sustained 42 direct knife wounds and 42 defensive wounds on her arms and hands. The wounds were caused by 41 separate thrusts of a butcher knife. None of the 84 wounds inflicted by Payne were individually fatal; rather, the cause of death was most likely bleeding from all the wounds.

Lacie's body was on the kitchen floor near her mother. She had suffered stab wounds to the chest, abdomen, back, and head. The murder weapon, a butcher knife, was found at her feet. Payne's baseball cap was snapped on her arm near her elbow. Three cans of malt liquor bearing Payne's fingerprints were found on a table near her body, and a fourth empty one was on the landing outside the apartment door.

Payne was apprehended later that day hiding in the attic of the home of a former girlfriend. As he descended the stairs of the attic, he stated to the arresting officers, "Man, I aint killed no woman." According to one of the officers, Payne had "a wild look about him. His pupils were contracted. He was foaming at the mouth, saliva. He appeared to be very nervous. He was breathing real rapid." He had blood on his body and clothes and several scratches across his chest. It was later determined that the blood stains matched the victims' blood types. A search of his pockets revealed a packet containing cocaine residue, a hypodermic syringe wrapper, and a cap from a hypodermic syringe. His overnight bag, containing a bloody white shirt, was found in a nearby dumpster.

At trial, Payne took the stand and, despite the overwhelming and relatively uncontroverted evidence against him, testified that he had not harmed any of the Christophers. Rather, he asserted that another man had raced by him as he was walking up the stairs to the floor where the Christophers lived. He stated that he had gotten blood on himself when, after hearing moans from the Christophers' apartment, he had tried to help the victims. According to his testimony, he panicked and fled when he heard police sirens and noticed the blood on his clothes. The jury returned guilty verdicts against Payne on all counts.

During the sentencing phase of the trial, Payne presented the testimony of four witnesses: his mother and father, Bobbie Thomas, and Dr. John T. Huston, a clinical psychologist specializing in criminal court evaluation work. Bobbie Thomas testified that she met Payne at church, during a time when she was being abused by her husband. She stated that Payne was a very caring person, and that he devoted much time and attention to her three children, who were being affected by her marital difficulties. She said that the children had come to love him very much and would miss him, and that he "behaved just like a father that loved his kids." She asserted that he did not drink, nor did he use drugs, and that it was generally inconsistent with Payne's character to have committed these crimes.

Dr. Huston testified that based on Payne's low score on an IQ test, Payne was "mentally handicapped." Huston also said that Payne was neither psychotic nor schizophrenic, and that Payne was the most polite prisoner he had ever met. Payne's parents testified that their son had no prior criminal record and had never been arrested. They also stated that Payne had no history of alcohol or drug abuse, [that] he worked with his father as a painter, he was good with children, and that he was a good son.

The State presented the testimony of Charisse's mother, Mary Zvolanek. When asked how Nicholas had been affected by the murders of his mother and sister, she responded:

> He cries for his mom. He doesn't seem to understand why she doesn't come home. And he cries for his sister Lacie. He comes to me many times during the week and asks me, Grandmama, do you miss my Lacie. And I tell him yes. He says, I'm worried about my Lacie.

In arguing for the death penalty during closing argument, the prosecutor commented on the continuing effects of Nicholas' experience, stating:

> But we do know that Nicholas was alive. And Nicholas

was still conscious. His eyes were open. He responded to the paramedics. He was able to follow their directions. He was able to hold his intestines in as he was carried to the ambulance. So he knew what happened to his mother and baby sister.

There is nothing you can do to ease the pain of any of the families involved in this case. There is nothing you can do to ease the pain of Bernice or Carl Payne, and that's a tragedy. There is nothing you can do basically to ease the pain of Mr. and Mrs. Zvolanek, and that's a tragedy. They will have to live with it the rest of their lives. There is obviously nothing you can do for Charisse and Lacie Jo. But there is something you can do for Nicholas.

Somewhere down the road Nicholas is going to grow up, hopefully. He's going to want to know what happened. And he is going to know what happened to his baby sister and his mother. He is going to want to know what type of justice was done. He is going to want to know what happened. With your verdict, you will provide the answer.

In the rebuttal to Payne's closing argument, the prosecutor stated:

You saw the videotape this morning. You saw what Nicholas Christopher will carry in his mind forever. When you talk about cruel, when you talk about atrocious, and when you talk about heinous, that picture will always come into your mind, probably throughout the rest of your lives.

＊ ＊ ＊

. . . No one will ever know about Lacie Jo because she never had the chance to grow up. Her life was taken from her at the age of two years old. So, no, there won't be a high school principal to talk about Lacie Jo Christopher, and there won't be anybody to take her to her high school prom. And there won't be anybody there—there won't be her mother there or Nicholas' mother there to kiss him at night. His mother will never kiss him good night or pat him as he goes off to bed, or hold him and sing him a lullaby.

＊ ＊ ＊

[Petitioner's attorney] wants you to think about a good reputation, people who love the defendant and things about him. He doesn't want you to think about the people who love Charisse Christopher, her mother and daddy who loved her. The people who loved little Lacie Jo, the grandparents who are still here. The brother who mourns for her every single day and wants to know where his best little playmate is. He doesn't have anybody to watch cartoons with him, a little one.

These are the things that go into why it is especially cruel, heinous, and atrocious, the burden that that child will carry forever.

The jury sentenced Payne to death on each of the murder counts.

The Supreme Court of Tennessee affirmed the conviction and sentence. The court rejected Payne's contention that the admission of the grandmother's testimony and the State's closing argument constituted prejudicial violations of his rights under the Eighth Amendment as applied in *Booth* v. *Maryland,* and *South Carolina* v. *Gathers.* . . . The court concluded that any violation of Payne's rights under *Booth* and *Gathers* "was harmless beyond a reasonable doubt."

In *Booth,* the defendant robbed and murdered an elderly couple. As required by a state statute, a victim impact statement was prepared based on interviews with the victims' son, daughter, son-in-law, and granddaughter. The statement, which described the personal characteristics of the victims, the emotional impact of the crimes on the family, and set forth the family members' opinions and characterizations of the crimes and the defendant, was submitted to the jury at sentencing. The jury imposed the death penalty. The conviction and sentence were affirmed on appeal by the State's highest court.

This Court held by a 5-to-4 vote that the Eighth Amendment prohibits a jury from considering a victim impact statement at the sentencing phase of a capital trial. The Court made clear that the admissibility of victim impact evidence was not to be determined on a case-by-case basis, but that such evidence was *per se* inadmissible in the sentencing phase of a capital case except to the extent that it "relate[d] directly to the circumstances of the crime." In *Gathers,* decided two years later, the Court extended the rule announced in *Booth* to statements made by a prosecutor to the sentencing jury regarding the personal qualities of the victim.

The *Booth* Court began its analysis with the observation that the capital defendant must be treated as a " 'uniquely individual human bein[g],' " and therefore the Constitution requires the jury to make an individualized determination as to whether the defendant should be executed based on the " 'character of the individual and the circumstances of the crime.' " . . . The Court concluded that, except to the extent that victim impact evidence relates "directly to the circumstances of the crime," the prosecution may not introduce such evidence at a capital sentencing hearing because "it creates an impermissible risk that the capital sentencing decision will be made in an arbitrary manner."

Booth and *Gathers* were based on two premises: that evidence relating to a particular victim or to the harm that a capital defendant causes a victim's family do not in general reflect on the defendant's "blameworthiness," and that only evidence relating to "blameworthiness" is relevant to the capital sentencing decision. However, the assessment of harm caused by the defendant as a result of the crime charged has understandably been an important concern of the criminal law, both in determining the elements of the offense and in determining the appropriate punishment. Thus, two equally blameworthy criminal defendants may be guilty of different offenses solely because their acts cause differing amounts of harm. . . .

Wherever judges in recent years have had discretion to impose sentence, the consideration of the harm caused by the crime has been an important factor in the exercise of that discretion. . . .

Whatever the prevailing sentencing philosophy, the sentencing authority has always been free to consider a wide range of relevant material. In the federal system, we observed that "a judge may appropriately conduct an inquiry broad in scope, largely unlimited as to the kind of information he may consider, or the source from which it may come." Even in the context of capital sentencing, prior to *Booth* the joint opinion of Justices Stewart, Powell, and Stevens in *Gregg* v. *Georgia*, had rejected petitioner's attack on the Georgia statute because of the "wide scope of evidence and argument allowed at presentence hearings." The joint opinion stated:

> We think that the Georgia court wisely has chosen not to impose unnecessary restrictions on the evidence that can be offered at such a hearing and to approve open and far-ranging argument. . . . So long as the evidence introduced and the arguments made at the presentence hearing do not prejudice a defendant, it is preferable not to impose restrictions. We think it desirable for the jury to have as much information before it as possible when it makes the sentencing decision.

The Maryland statute involved in *Booth* required that the presentence report in all felony cases include a "victim impact statement" which would describe the effect of the crime on the victim and his family. Congress and most of the States have, in recent years, enacted similar legislation to enable the sentencing authority to consider information about the harm caused by the crime committed by the defendant. The evidence involved in the present case was not admitted pursuant to any such enactment, but its purpose and effect was much the same as if it had been. While the admission of

this particular kind of evidence—designed to portray for the sentencing authority the actual harm caused by a particular crime—is of recent origin, this fact hardly renders it unconstitutional. . . .

"We have held that a State cannot preclude the sentencer from considering 'any relevant mitigating evidence' that the defendant proffers in support of a sentence less than death." *Eddings* v. *Oklahoma*, 455 U.S. 14, 114, (1982). Thus we have, as the Court observed in *Booth*, required that the capital defendant be treated as a " 'uniquely individual human bein[g].' " But it was never held or even suggested in any of our cases preceding *Booth* that the defendant, entitled as he was to individualized consideration, was to receive that consideration wholly apart from the crime which he had committed. . . .

Booth reasoned that victim impact evidence must be excluded because it would be difficult, if not impossible, for the defendant to rebut such evidence without shifting the focus of the sentencing hearing away from the defendant, thus creating a " 'mini-trial' on the victim's character." In many cases the evidence relating to the victim is already before the jury at least in part because of its relevance at the guilt phase of the trial. But even as to additional evidence admitted at the sentencing phase, the mere fact that for tactical reasons it might not be prudent for the defense to rebut victim impact evidence makes the case no different than others in which a party is faced with this sort of dilemma. As we explained in rejecting the contention that expert testimony on future dangerousness should be excluded from capital trials, "the rules of evidence generally extant at the federal and state levels anticipate that relevant, unprivileged evidence should be admitted and its weight left to the factfinder, who would have the benefit of cross examination and contrary evidence by the opposing party."

Payne echoes the concern voiced in *Booth*'s case that the admission of victim impact evidence permits a jury to find that defendants whose victims were assets to their community are more deserving of punishment than those whose victims are perceived to be less worthy. As a general matter, however, victim impact evidence is not offered to encourage comparative judgments of this kind—for instance, that the killer of a hardworking, devoted parent deserves the death penalty, but that the murderer of a reprobate does not. It is designed to show instead each victim's "uniqueness as an individual human being," whatever the jury might think the loss to the community resulting from his death might be. . .

Under our constitutional system, the primary responsibility for defining crimes against state law, fixing punishments for the commission of these crimes, and establishing procedures for criminal trials rests with the States. . . . Where the State imposes the death penalty for a particular crime, we have held that the Eighth Amendment imposes special limitations upon that process.

First, there is a required threshold below which the death penalty cannot be imposed. In this context, the State must establish rational criteria that narrow the decisionmaker's judgment as to whether the circumstances of a particular defendant's case meet the threshold. Moreover, a societal consensus that the death penalty is disproportionate to a particular offense prevents a State from imposing the death penalty for that offense. Second, States cannot limit the sentencer's consideration of any relevant circumstance that could cause it to decline to impose the penalty. In this respect, the State cannot challenge the sentencer's discretion, but must allow it to consider any relevant information offered by the defendant. . . .

But, as we noted in *California* v. *Ramos,* 463 U.S. 992, 1983, "[b]eyond these limitations . . . the Court has deferred to the State's choice of substantive factors relevant to the penalty determination."

. . . The States remain free, in capital cases, as well as others, to devise new procedures and new remedies to meet felt needs. Victim impact evidence is simply another form or method of informing the sentencing authority about the specific harm caused by the crime in question, evidence of a general type long considered by sentencing authorities. We think the *Booth* Court was wrong in stating that this kind of evidence leads to the arbitrary imposition of the death penalty. In the majority of cases, and in this case, victim impact evidence serves entirely legitimate purposes. In the event that evidence is introduced that is so unduly prejudicial that it renders the trial fundamentally unfair, the Due Process Clause of the Fourteenth Amendment provides a mechanism for relief. . . .

We are now of the view that a State may properly conclude that for the jury to assess meaningfully the defendant's moral culpability and blameworthiness, it should have before it at the sentencing phase evidence of the specific harm caused by the defendant. "[T]he State has a legitimate interest in countering the mitigating evidence which the defendant is entitled to put in, by reminding the sentencer that just as the murderer should be considered as an individual, so too the victim is an individual whose death represents a unique loss to society and in particular to his family." . . . *Booth* deprives the State of the full moral force of its evidence and may prevent the jury from having before it all the information necessary to determine the proper punishment for a first-degree murder. . . .

. . . Under the aegis of the Eighth Amendment, we have given the broadest latitude to the defendant to introduce relevant mitigating evidence reflecting on his individual personality, and the defendant's attorney may argue that evidence to the jury. Petitioner's attorney in this case did just that. . . .

[W]e now reject the view that a State may not permit the prosecutor to similarly argue to the jury the human cost of the crime of which the defendant stands convicted. We reaffirm the view expressed by Justice Cardozo in *Snyder* v. *Massachusetts,* 291 U.S. 97, 122, (1934): "justice, though due to the accused, is due to the accuser also. The concept of fairness must not be strained till it is narrowed to a filament. We are to keep the balance true."

We thus hold that if the State chooses to permit the admission of victim impact evidence and prosecutorial argument on that subject, the Eighth Amendment erects no *per se* bar. A State may legitimately conclude that evidence about the victim and about the impact of the murder on the victim's family is relevant to the jury's decision as to whether or not the death penalty should be imposed. There is no reason to treat such evidence differently than other relevant evidence is treated.

Payne and his *amicus* argue that despite these numerous infirmities in the rule created by *Booth* and *Gathers,* we should adhere to the doctrine of *stare decisis* and stop short of overruling those cases. *Stare decisis* is the preferred course because it promotes the evenhanded, predictable, and consistent development of legal principles, fosters reliance on judicial decisions, and contributes to the actual and perceived integrity of the judicial process. Adhering to precedent "is usually the wise policy, because in most matters it is more important that the applicable rule of law be settled than it be settled right." Nevertheless, when governing decisions are unworkable or are badly reasoned, "this Court has never felt constrained to follow precedent." *Stare decisis* is not an inexorable command; rather, it "is a principle of policy and not a mechanical formula of adherence to the latest decision." This is particularly true in constitutional cases, because in such cases "correction through legislative action is practically impossible." Considerations in favor of *stare decisis* are at their acme in cases involving property and contract rights, where reliance interests are involved; . . . the opposite is true in cases such as the present one involving procedural and evidentiary rules.

Applying these general principles, the Court has during the past two terms overruled in whole or in part 33 of its previous constitutional decisions. *Booth* and *Gathers* were decided by the narrowest of margins over spirited dissents challenging the basic underpinnings of those decisions. They have been questioned by members of the Court in later decisions, and have defied consistent application by the lower courts. . . . Reconsidering these decisions now, we conclude for the reasons heretofore stated, that they were wrongly decided and should be, and now are, overruled. We accordingly affirm the judgment of the Supreme Court of Tennessee.

Affirmed.

[The concurring opinions of JUSTICE O'CONNOR, JUSTICE SCALIA, and JUSTICE SOUTER are not reprinted here.]

JUSTICE MARSHALL, *with whom* JUSTICE BLACKMUN *joins, dissenting.*

Power, not reason, is the new currency of this Court's decisionmaking. Four terms ago, a five-Justice majority of this Court held that "victim impact" evidence of the type at issue in this case could not constitutionally be introduced during the penalty phase of a capital trial. By another 5–4 vote, a majority of this Court rebuffed an attack upon this ruling just two terms ago. Nevertheless, having expressly invited respondent to renew the attack, today's majority overrules *Booth* and *Gathers* and credits the dissenting views expressed in those cases. Neither the law nor the facts supporting *Booth* and *Gathers* underwent any change in the last four years. Only the personnel of this Court did.

In dispatching *Booth* and *Gathers* to their graves, today's majority ominously suggest that an even more extensive upheaval of this Court's precedents may be in store. Renouncing this Court's historical commitment, to a conception of "the judiciary as a source of impersonal and reasoned judgments," the majority declares itself free to discard any principle of constitutional liberty which was recognized or reaffirmed over the dissenting votes of four Justices and with which five or more Justices *now* disagree. The implications of this radical new exception to the doctrine of *stare decisis* are

staggering. The majority of established constitutional liberties are now ripe for reconsideration, thereby inviting the very type of open defiance of our precedents that the majority rewards in this case. Because I believe that this Court owes more to its constitutional precedents in general and to *Booth* and *Gathers* in particular, I dissent.

I

Speaking for the Court as then constituted, Justice Powell and Justice Brennan set out the rationale for excluding victim-impact evidence from the sentencing proceedings in a capital case. As the majorities in *Booth* and *Gathers* recognized, the core principle of this Court's capital jurisprudence is that the sentence of death must reflect an " '*individualized* determination' " of the defendant's " 'personal responsibility and moral guilt' " and must be based upon factors that channel the jury's discretion " 'so as to minimize the risk of wholly arbitrary and capricious action.' " . . .

There is nothing new in the majority's discussion of the supposed deficiencies in *Booth* and *Gathers*. Every one of the arguments made by the majority can be found in the dissenting opinions filed in those two cases, and . . . each argument was convincingly answered by Justice Powell and Justice Brennan.

But contrary to the impression that one might receive from reading the majority's lengthy rehearsing of the issues addressed in *Booth* and *Gathers*, the outcome of this case does not turn simply on who—the *Booth* and *Gathers* dissenters—had the better of the argument. Justice Powell and Justice Brennan's position carried the day in those cases and became the law of the land. The real question, then, is whether today's majority has come forward with the type of extraordinary showing that this Court has historically demanded before overruling one of its precedents. In my view, the majority clearly has not made any such showing. Indeed, the striking feature of the majority's opinion is its radical assertion that it need not even try.

II

The overruling of one of this Court's precedents ought to be a matter of great moment and consequence. Although the doctrine of *stare decisis* is not an "inexorable command," this Court has repeatedly stressed that fidelity to precedent is fundamental to "a society governed by the rule of law." . . .

Consequently, this Court has never departed from precedent without "special justification."

Such justifications include the advent of "subsequent changes or development in the law" that undermine a decision's rationale, the need "to bring [a decision] into agreement with experience and with facts newly ascertained," and a showing that a particular precedent has become a "detriment to coherence and consistency in the law."

The majority cannot seriously claim that *any* of these traditional bases for overruling a precedent applies to *Booth* or *Gathers*. The majority does not suggest that the legal rationale of these decisions has been undercut by changes or developments in doctrine during the last two years. Nor does the majority claim that experience over that period of time has discredited the principle that "any decision to impose the death sentence be, and appear to be, based on reason rather than caprice or emotion," the larger postulate of political morality on which *Booth* and *Gathers* rest.

The majority does assert that *Booth* and *Gathers* "have defied consistent application by the lower courts," but the evidence that the majority proffers is so feeble that the majority cannot sincerely expect anyone to believe this claim. To support its contention, the majority points to JUSTICE O'CONNOR's dissent in *Gathers*, which noted a division among lower courts over whether *Booth* prohibited prosecutorial arguments relating to the victim's personal characteristics. That, of course, was the issue expressly considered and resolved in *Gathers*. The majority also cites THE CHIEF JUSTICE's dissent in *Mills* v. *Maryland*, 486 U.S. 367 (1988). That opinion does not contain a *single word* about any supposed "[in]consistent application" of *Booth* in the lower courts. Finally, the majority refers to a divided Ohio Supreme Court decision disposing of an issue concerning victim-impact evidence. Obviously, if a division among the members of a single lower court in a single case were sufficient to demonstrate that a particular precedent was a "detriment to coherence and consistency in the law," there would hardly be a decision in United States Reports that we would not be obliged to reconsider.

It takes little real detective work to discern just what has changed since this Court decided *Booth* and *Gathers*: this Court's own personnel. Indeed, the majority candidly explains why this particular contingency, which until now has been almost universally understood not to be sufficient to warrant overruling a precedent . . . is sufficient to justify overruling *Booth* and *Gathers*. "Considerations in favor of *stare decisis* are at their acme," the majority explains, "in cases involving property and contract rights, where reliance interests are involved[;] the opposite is true in cases such as the present one involving procedural and evidentiary rules." In addition, the majority points out, "*Booth* and *Gathers* were decided by the narrowest of margins, over spirited dissents," and thereafter were "questioned by members of the Court." Taken together, these considerations make it legitimate, in the majority's view, to elevate the position of the *Booth* and *Gathers* dissenters into the law of the land.

This truncation of the Court's duty to stand by its own precedents is astonishing. By limiting full protection of the doctrine of *stare decisis* to "cases involving property and contract rights," the majority sends a clear signal that essentially all decisions implementing the personal liberties protected by the Bill of Rights and the Fourteenth Amendment are open to reexamination. Taking into account the majority's additional criterion for overruling—that a case either was decided or reaffirmed by a 5–4 margin "over spirited dissen[t]," the continued vitality of literally scores of decisions must be understood to depend on nothing more than the proclivities of the individuals who now comprise a majority of this Court. . . .

In my view, this impoverished conception of *stare decisis* cannot possibly be reconciled with the values that inform the proper judicial function. Contrary to what the majority suggests, *stare decisis* is important not merely because individuals rely on precedent to structure their commercial activity but because fidelity to precedent is part and parcel of a conception of "the judiciary as a source of impersonal and reasoned judgments." Indeed, this function of *stare decisis* is in many respects even more critical in adjudication involving constitutional liberties than in adjudication involving commercial entitlements. Because enforcement of the Bill of Rights and the Fourteenth Amendment frequently requires this Court to rein in the forces of democratic politics, this Court can legitimately lay claim to compliance with its directives only if the public understands the Court to be implementing "principles . . . founded in the law rather than in the proclivities of individuals." Thus, as JUSTICE STEVENS has explained, the "stron[g] presumption of validity" to which "recently decided cases" are entitled "is an essential thread in the mantle of protection that the law affords the individual. . . . It is the unpopular or beleaguered individual—not the man in power—who has the greatest stake in the integrity of the law." . . .

Carried to its logical conclusion, the majority's debilitated conception of *stare decisis* would destroy the Court's very capacity to resolve authoritatively the abiding conflicts between those with power and those without. If this Court shows so little respect for its own precedents, it can hardly expect them to be treated more respectfully by the state actors whom these decisions are supposed to bind. By signaling its willingness to give fresh consideration to any constitutional liberty recognized by a 5–4 vote "over spirited dissen[t]," the majority invites state actors to renew the very policies deemed unconstitutional in the hope that this Court may now reverse course, even if it has only recently reaffirmed the constitutional liberty in question.

Indeed, the majority's disposition of this case nicely illustrates the rewards of such a strategy of defiance. The Tennessee Supreme Court did nothing in this case to disguise its contempt for this Court's decisions in *Booth* and *Gathers* . . .

Offering no explanation for how this case could possibly be distinguished from *Booth* and *Gathers*— for obviously, there is none to offer—the court perfunctorily declared that the victim-impact evidence and the prosecutor's argument based on this evidence "did not violate either [of those decisions]." It cannot be clearer that the court simply declined to be bound by this Court's precedents.

Far from condemning this blatant disregard for the rule of law, the majority applauds it. In the Tennessee Supreme Court's denigration of *Booth* and *Gathers* as "an affront to the civilized members of the human race," the majority finds only confirmation of "the unfairness of the rule pronounced by" the majorities in those cases. It is hard to imagine a more complete abdication of this Court's historic commitment to defending the supremacy of its own pronouncements on issues of constitutional liberty. . . . In light of the cost that such abdication exacts on the authoritativeness of all of this Court's pronouncements, it is also hard to imagine a more short-sighted strategy for effecting change in our constitutional order.

III

Today's decision charts an unmistakable course. If the majority's radical reconstruction of the rules for overturning this Court's decisions is to be taken at face value—and the majority offers us no reason why it should not—then the overruling of *Booth* and *Gathers* is but preview of an even broader and more far-reaching assault upon this Court's precedents. Cast aside today are those condemned to face society's ultimate penalty. Tomorrow's victims may be minorities, women, or the indigent. Inevitably, this campaign to resurrect yesterday's "spirited dissents" will squander the authority and the legitimacy of this Court as a protector of the powerless.

I dissent.

[The dissenting opinion of JUSTICE STEVENS, with whom JUSTICE BLACKMUN joins, is not reprinted here.]

Prisoners' Rights

FEATURED CASES

Wilson v. *Seiter*   *Hudson* v. *McMillian*

While many scholars and organizations have devoted years of extensive study to the conditions under which prisoners are forced to live during their incarceration, it was an apparent spin-off of the "rights revolution" of 1960s that focused the Court's attention on the constitutional rights of prisoners. More specifically, the Court has been asked to determine whether the guarantees of the Constitution apply to those incarcerated for crimes and, if so, to what extent the special status of criminals requires some modification of those guarantees when applied to them. Since the late 1960s, the Supreme Court has considered some of these questions, and several are examined briefly here.

In a number of cases, the Court has focused on prisoners' accessibility to courts for the adjudication of their claims. Although Congress had provided for the writ of habeas corpus in certain circumstances, persons incarcerated have occasionally encountered stiff resistance to their attempts to invoke it. Initially, the Court steadfastly held that such an access route is fundamental and struck down roadblocks thereto. In *Ex parte Hull* (312 U.S. 546, 1941), for example, a subtle state attempt to apply limited censorship by requiring initially that all habeas corpus petitions be submitted to prison authorities to determine whether they were "properly drawn" was struck down as an impairment of a prisoner's right to petition a federal court for the writ. In addition, the Court held in *Smith* v. *Bennett* (365 U.S. 708, 1961) that states are obligated to provide prisoners with a free transcript of their previous habeas corpus hearings. (See *Long* v. *District Court*, 385 U.S. 192, 1966; cf. *Younger* v. *Gilmore*, 404 U.S. 15, 1971.)

Undoubtedly as a logical extension of its concern for the right to counsel enunciated in *Gideon, supra*, the Court has required some form of legal assistance for prisoners attempting to assert their claims. Its sensitivity to such assistance was indicated in *Johnson* v. *Avery* (393 U.S. 483, 1969), when it nullified a prison regulation prohibiting inmates from assisting fellow prisoners in the preparation of legal papers seeking postconviction relief.[21] The Court reiterated its concern for prisoner access to the judicial process for the presentation of their constitutional claims when it held in *Haines* v. *Kerner* (404 U.S. 519, 1972) that a federal district court was in error for dismissing a prisoner's *pro se* pleading without allowing the presentation of evidence in support of the claim. Such pleadings, the Court conceded, should be considered with "less stringent standards [than those applied to] formal pleadings drafted by lawyers."

Recognizing the steady increase in the number of cases in which questions of prison regulatory authority and the scope of constitutional liberty of prisoners were at issue, the Court took the occasion of a challenge to California's mail censorship regulations in *Procunier* v. *Martinez* (416 U.S. 396, 1974) to set forth important principles that should govern judicial analysis of the constitutional claims of prisoners. These include: (1) judicial cognizance of a prisoner's "valid constitutional claims"; (2) inmate access to the judicial process; and (3) judicial deference to prison administrative authorities in the operation of such facilities, but without abdication of judicial responsibility to assure that prison regulations and practices do not offend fundamental constitutional guarantees. Then, without resolving the "broad question of prisoner rights," the Court struck down the content-based mail censorship regulations as an infringement of the First Amendment guaranty to prisoners and their communicants.

Following *Procunier*, a number of challenges to a wide variety of prison administrative practices were presented to the Burger Court. A leading case considering such issues as disciplinary proceedings, an inmate legal assistance program, and mail inspection regulations is *Wolff* v. *McDonnell* (418 U.S. 539, 1974). In that case, the Court, while recognizing that prison disciplinary proceedings are not subject to the procedural guarantees governing criminal trials, made it clear that where statutory rights (such as a reduction of time served for good behavior) are provided, a prisoner's interest is "sufficiently embraced within Fourteenth Amendment liberty" so that procedural due process protects him or her against arbitrary abrogation of the statutory right. In short, the Court emphasized the requirement of "some kind of hearing" before withdrawing a prisoner's statutory rights.

The Court considered further the extent of the constitutional rights of inmates in prison disciplinary proceedings in the consolidated cases of *Baxter* v. *Palmigiano* and *Enomoto* v. *Clutchette* (425 U.S. 308, 1976). At issue were procedures of the Rhode Island Adult Correctional Institutions (in *Palmigiano*) and California's San Quentin Prison (in *Clutchette*). Prisoners in both cases alleged that the procedures employed in their disciplinary proceedings for behavior constituting violations of prison regulations, and which could possibly be punished under state statutes as well, abridged their Fourteenth Amendment due process and equal protection guarantees.

The district court denied relief in *Palmigiano*, but it was granted in *Clutchette*. Thereupon, the Court of Appeals for the First Circuit reversed the district court in *Palmigiano*, while the Appeals Court in the Ninth Circuit affirmed in *Clutchette*, generally stressing the same kinds of guarantees that must be made available to an inmate confronted with the prison disciplinary process. The court in the Ninth Circuit, for example, held that inmates in such proceeding are entitled to:

1. notice of the charges against them;
2. a hearing in which they could present witnesses;
3. the right to confrontation and cross examination;
4. a neutral and detached hearing panel;
5. provision of counsel or a "counsel substitute" when the seriousness of the consequences of the disciplinary action warrant such; and

---

[21]A number of lower courts have dealt extensively with assistance provided by "jailhouse lawyers." See, for example, *Bears* v. *Alabama Board of Corrections* (413 F.2d 455, 5th Cir., 1969); *Novak* v. *Beto* (453 F.2d 661, 5th Cir., 1971); and *Lepiscopo* v. *United States* (469 F.2d 650, 5th Cir., 1972). Other cases have focused on the inmates' accessibility of law books and inmate law libraries. See *Hooks* v. *Wainwright* (352 F. Supp. 163, M.D. Fla., 1972).

6. a decision limited to the evidence presented at the hearing.

Relying heavily on its *Wolff* decision, the Supreme Court reversed the rulings of both appeals courts. Justice White's opinion for the Court took notice of the difference between a prison disciplinary proceeding and a criminal trial, and held that inmates are not constitutionally entitled to assistance of counsel. Nor are they entitled to the application of the *Griffin* rule (announced in *Griffin* v. *California*, 380 U.S. 609, 1965), which proscribes drawing adverse inferences from one's decision to remain silent in the face of probative evidence against him or her, and to unrestricted confrontation and cross-examination privileges. Regarding the extension of the minimum due process requirements (such as notice and opportunity to respond to charges) to "less serious" disciplinary actions, the Court held that the appeals court for the Ninth Circuit had acted prematurely in reaching that issue, since all of the inmates involved were charged with "serious misconduct."

The Burger Court continued to reject the assertion of prisoner rights in *Meachum* v. *Fano* (427 U.S. 215, 1976). Justice White's opinion for the Court made it clear that the decision of prison authorities to transfer an inmate from a "medium to maximum security" institution without a hearing does not abridge liberty protected by the due process clause of the Fourteenth Amendment. He concluded that as long as prison officials' discretion in transfers is not limited by state law, it is a matter of prison administration into which the judiciary should not inquire. (Cf. *Vitek* v. *Jones*, 445 U.S. 480, 1980, where the Court held that transfer of an inmate from a prison to a mental facility does not "implicate a liberty interest," and *Olim* v. *Wakinekona*, 461 U.S. 238, 1983, where the same reasoning was used to approve the interstate transfer of inmates.)

The Court has reviewed several cases in which the conditions under which inmates live and receive care were at issue. In *Hutto* v. *Finney* (437 U.S. 678, 1978), aspects of the relief ordered by a lower court to correct conditions and practices of the well-publicized Arkansas prison facilities were reviewed by the Court. In particular, the Court sustained a lower court holding that the conditions under which inmates were kept in isolated (solitary) confinement abridged the prohibition against cruel and unusual punishment of the Eighth Amendment. Justice John Paul Stevens made it clear that the length of isolated confinement standing alone would not in itself constitute a violation, but when it is considered together with the conditions to which an inmate is subjected while in an isolated cell (such as filth and inadequate diet), it is possible to conclude that a constitutional violation exists.

Two years earlier, the Court reached the same conclusion regarding medical care for inmates of a correctional facility. In *Estelle* v. *Gamble* (429 U.S. 97, 1976), the Court, while partially absolving prison officials, made it clear that the "deliberate indifference" of prison authorities to the "serious medical needs of prisoners" constitutes cruel and unusual punishment, thereby providing a cause of action under 42 U.S.C. 1983.

The Court indicated further its sensitivity to the health concerns of prisoners when it held in *Helling* v. *McKinney* (113 S. Ct. 2475, 1993) that an inmate has an Eighth Amendment cause of action to protect himself from the hazard of secondhand smoke to which he was subjected by the chain smoking of his cellmate. In his opinion for the Court, Justice Byron White asserted that the Eighth Amendment "requires that inmates be furnished with the basic human needs, one of which is reasonable safety." The Justice agreed with the lower court (Court of Appeals for the Ninth Circuit) that the inmate (McKinney) had stated a proper cause of action by alleging that prison authorities, "with deliberate indifference" had exposed him to levels of secondhand smoke that placed his future health at risk.

In addition to examining the conditions in prisons, the Court has also been presented with questions about the constitutionality of certain conditions under which those charged and awaiting trial are detained. In *Bell* v. *Wolfish* (441 U.S. 520, 1979), for example, the Court scrutinized several conditions, practices, and policies of a federal detention center—double bunking, the limiting of reading matter that can be received through the mail to that from publishers, body cavity and room searches—to determine whether they abridged the Fifth Amendment due process guarantees of the detainees. Emphasizing the marked difference between the innovative features and modern architectural design of the facilities in which the petitioners were detained and traditional jails, Justice William Rehnquist, speaking for the Court, considered the crucial issue to be whether the conditions and practices challenged amounted to the punishment of detainees. The loss of freedom of choice and the diminished privacy inherent in such detention facilities, he opined, cannot be equated with punishment. And "absent a showing of an expressed intent to punish" and balancing the governmental interests protected by the practices against the constitutional claims of the detainees, the challenges were dismissed with the statement that courts ought to refrain from becoming "enmeshed in the minutiae of prison operations."

The Court reaffirmed its position in *Wolfish* on diminished privacy rights for inmates when it considered the cell "shakedown search" practices in *Hudson* v. *Palmer* (104 S. Ct. 3194, 1984). Reversing a court of appeals ruling that acknowledged an inmate's "limited privacy rights" in his or her cell, where searches are conducted "solely to harass or to humiliate," Chief Justice Burger held for the Court that the Fourth Amendment does not extend to a prisoner any reasonable expectation of privacy in his or her cell. To recognize such a right would be inconsistent with the prison objective preventing the smuggling of weapons, drugs, and other contraband into cells and among the prison population. Burger concluded that the "shakedown search" was an effective weapon in prison administrators' efforts against the proliferation of weapons in cells that should not be blunted by an expansive interpretation of the Fourth Amendment. (See also *Block* v. *Rutherford*, 104 S. Ct. 3227, 1984, where the Court upheld the "shakedown" practice in county jails for pretrial detainees. Also at issue here was the blanket prohibition of contact visits between detainees and their spouses, children, relatives, and friends, a policy that the Court found constitutionally valid as "reasonably related to a legitimate governmental objective.")

Near the end of its 1980 term, the Court examined the serious problem of housing the spiraling increase in the prison population. Many states have been unwilling to tax further their dwindling financial resources in order to provide additional facilities to meet such housing demands. Consequently, officials in some institutions have had to resort to the practice of "double celling," or routinely assigning two inmates to a cell designed for one. Some inmates and their advocates contend that forcing such living arrangements on the incarcerated constitutes cruel and unusual punishment in violation of the Eighth Amendment. But the Court, apparently recognizing the serious consequences of accepting that position, ruled otherwise in *Rhodes* v. *Chapman* (452 U.S. 337, 1981). Justice Lewis Powell emphasized that the Constitution requires the maintenance of humane conditions, but not "comfort." Consequently, where prison conditions such as food, medical care, sanitation, and personal security are satisfactory, "double celling" is not constitutionally impermissible.

During its first term, the Rehnquist Court

(1986–87), in considering the constitutionality of Missouri's correspondence and marriage regulations, reexamined the level of judicial scrutiny that should be appropriate for determining if prison regulations and practices abridge the constitutional rights of inmates. In *Turner* v. *Safley* (107 S. Ct. 2254, 1987), Justice O'Connor's opinion for the Court contended that lower courts had misconstrued *Procunier* and its progeny as requiring a strict scrutiny level of review of such controversies. Instead, she argued that a lesser standard of review—"whether a prison regulation that impinges on inmates' constitutional rights is 'reasonably related' to legitimate penological interests"—was indicated in those cases and should be adhered to here. After reviewing several factors that are to be examined in determining if prison regulations and practices are "reasonably related to penological interests," she concluded that the inmate-correspondence regulation was in pursuance of "legitimate" prison security interests,[22] while the marriage restriction was not.[23]

The issue of the quality of living conditions for prison inmates was presented the Rehnquist Court for the first time in a challenge to the living conditions in Ohio prisons in *Wilson* v. *Seiter* (111 S. Ct. 2321) in 1991. Alleging that the facility in which he was incarcerated was overcrowded, had inadequate heating and lighting, was improperly ventilated, and had unsanitary food preparation and dining facilities, the inmate argued that such conditions of confinement constituted the cruel and unusual punishment proscribed by the Eighth Amendment. But the Court, following its position of deference to prison administrative authority, rejected the claim. In his opinion for the Court, Justice Scalia fastened a heavy burden on inmates raising such Eighth Amendment claims by requiring them to show that not only did the conditions exist but that the prison officials responsible for them had "a culpable state of mind." He also stressed that the "deliberate indifference" standard enunciated in *Estelle* v. *Gamble* in 1976 must be met in inmate challenges to their conditions of con-

---

[22]The regulation prescribed conditions for correspondence between inmates at different institutions. It permits correspondence with "immediate family members" and with inmates imprisoned at other institutions concerning legal matters. All other interinmate, interprison correspondence is permitted only if appropriate authorities determine it to be "in the best interest of the parties involved."

[23]The challenged regulation permitted inmate marriage only with the permission of the prison superintendent, whose consent was to be given only "when there are compelling reasons to do so."

finement. Scalia's assertion that the "indifference" standard could be applied to the conditions and deprivations suffered by inmates that *were not a part of the formal sentence* was challenged by Justice White in a concurring opinion, supported by Justices Marshall, Blackmun, and Stevens. He contended that "[t]he linchpin of the majority's analysis . . . is its assertion that '[i]f the pain inflicted is not formally meted out as punishment . . . [by the sentencer] some mental element must be attributed to the inflicting officer before it can qualify' " for Eighth Amendment scrutiny. This, he argued, was a serious disregard of the Court's prior decisions on conditions of confinement, where it had been made "clear that the conditions are themselves part of the punishment."

In a second cruel and unusual punishment case involving prison disciplinary action, the Rehnquist Court drew back from its earlier deference to prison authorities as it decided *Hudson* v. *McMillian* (112 S. Ct. 995) in 1992. There, a Louisiana prison inmate, after sustaining injuries (minor bruises, facial swelling, loosened teeth, and a cracked denture) from a beating by prison guards, convinced a seven-to-two majority of the Court that they should sustain his Eighth Amendment claim. In her opinion for the Court, Justice O'Connor noted that in cases like this, the "core of judicial inquiry is whether force is applied in a good-faith effort to maintain or restore discipline, or maliciously and sadistically to cause harm." Hence, she concluded that although the inmate did not suffer serious injuries, the use of excessive physical force is at odds with the Eighth Amendment's cruel and unusual punishments clause.

In a dissenting opinion in which Justice Scalia joined, Justice Clarence Thomas took exception to this expansive application of that clause. He argued that the *de minimis* use of force and the insignificant injury to the inmate do not reach the level of an Eighth Amendment violation. He phrased the issue thusly:

> [A] use of force that causes only insignificant harm to a prisoner may be immoral, it may be tortuous, it may be criminal, and it may even be remediable under other provisions of the Federal Constitution, but it is not "cruel and unusual punishment."

On another dimension of the cruel and unusual punishment question, the Rehnquist Court adopted a narrow view of its protective shield when it decided *Harmelin* v. *Michigan* (111 S. Ct. 2680) in 1991. There, the Court upheld a Michigan law that provides for a mandatory life sentence without the possibility of parole for a conviction of the possession of large quantities of drug. Brushing aside the petitioner's claim that such a mandatory sentencing policy is contrary to the Court's capital sentencing jurisprudence that requires the consideration of mitigating factors and hence abridges the cruel and unusual punishment clause, Justice Scalia held that while such "severe, mandatory penalties may be cruel, . . . they are not unusual in the constitutional sense." Emphasizing that what actually constitutes cruel and unusual punishment does not include consideration of "the particular offense," he concluded that the clause was intended to proscribe "certain methods of punishment," not "disproportionate" sentences.

In dissent, Justice White found some support for the petitioner's proportionality argument in the "excessive fines" clause of the Eighth Amendment. Consequently, it would not be unreasonable to conclude that the imposition of "punishment that is grossly disproportionate to the offense" for which one has been convicted infringes the cruel and unusual punishment clause.

Another issue before the Court was whether the First Amendment guarantees of freedom of speech and assembly apply to inmate organizational activities with respect to the formation of a prisoners' union. In *Jones* v. *North Carolina Prisoners' Labor Union, Inc.* (433 U.S. 119, 1977),[24] the Supreme Court balanced away these First Amendment guarantees in favor of a state's overriding interest in the maintenance of prison decorum and security. The Court noted that such an organization, where grievances would be aired in an adversarial relationship with prison officials, "surely would rank high on anyone's list of potential trouble spots."

The Court has also considered a number of claims that focus on the application of constitutional guarantees to parole and probation revocation. In the height of the Court's sensitivity to the rights of the accused during the 1960s, it held in *Mempa* v. *Rhay* (389 U.S. 128, 1967) that when a sentencing hearing is included in a probation revocation proceeding, a stage of the criminal process is involved and the probationer is therefore entitled to counsel. Absent a sentencing component, however, the Court ruled that neither a hearing nor counsel is required in the revocation proceeding.

Five years later, in *Morrissey* v. *Brewer* (408 U.S. 471, 1972), the Court held that while revocation of parole is not a part of a criminal prosecution, the

---

[24]See Chapter 3 for discussion of the First Amendment issues considered by the Court.

deprivation of liberty involved requires that due process be observed. Accordingly, parolees are entitled to a hearing when they are placed in custody to ascertain whether there is probable cause that they have violated their parole. Additionally, the Court held that a parolee is entitled to a "more comprehensive" hearing prior to a revocation decision. This was reaffirmed a year later in *Gagnon* v. *Scarpelli* (411 U.S. 778) when, at the same time, the Court asserted the necessity for a flexible "constitutional rule" with respect to the right to counsel in such proceedings. As Justice Powell contended, "there will [be] certain cases in which fundamental fairness . . . will require that the state provide at its expense counsel for indigent probationers or parolees."

When lower courts construed *Morrissey* and its progeny to invalidate Nebraska's discretionary parole procedure, the Court disagreed. In *Greenholtz* v. *Inmates of the Nebraska Penal and Correctional Complex* (442 U.S. 1, 1979), Chief Justice Burger maintained that there was a constitutional difference between a deprivation of the liberty one has (as in *Morrissey*, when parole revocation was at issue) and the "conditional liberty that one desires" (as in the discretionary parole release involved in this case). He concluded that the state's two-stage procedure for determining parole eligibility did not abridge due process because the inmate was not afforded a full-scale hearing at the initial interview stage, where the question of suitability for parole is determined. Provision for such a hearing at the second stage, once the inmate has been determined to be suitable, was held to be sufficient.

WILSON v. SEITER
___ U.S. ___; ___ L. Ed. 2d ___; 111 S. Ct. 2321 (1991)

JUSTICE SCALIA *delivered the opinion of the Court.*

This case presents the questions whether a prisoner claiming that conditions of confinement constitute cruel and unusual punishment must show a culpable state of mind on the part of prison officials and, if so, what state of mind is required.

Petitioner Pearly L. Wilson is a felon incarcerated at the Hocking Correctional Facility (HCF) in Nelsonville, Ohio. Alleging that a number of the conditions of his confinement constitute cruel and unusual punishment in violation of the Eighth and Fourteenth Amendments, he brought this action under 42 U.S.C. § 1983 . . . [against officials] of the Ohio Department of Rehabilitation and Correction. . . . The complaints alleged overcrowding, excessive noise, insufficient locker storage space, inadequate heating and cooling, improper ventilation, unclean and inadequate restrooms, unsanitary dining facilities and food preparation, and housing with mentally and physically ill inmates. Petitioner sought declaratory and injunctive relief, as well as $900,000 in compensatory and punitive damages.

The parties filed cross-motions for summary judgment with supporting affidavits. Petitioner's affidavits described the challenged conditions and charged that the authorities, after notification, had failed to take remedial action. Respondents' affidavits denied that some of the alleged conditions existed, and described efforts by prison officials to improve the others.

The District Court granted summary judgment for respondents. The Court of Appeals for the Sixth Circuit affirmed, and we granted certiorari.

I

The Eighth Amendment . . . prohibits the infliction of "cruel and unusual punishments" on those convicted of crimes. In *Estelle* v. *Gamble,* 429 U.S. 97 (1976), we first acknowledged that the provision could be applied to some deprivations that were not specifically part of the sentence but were suffered during imprisonment. We rejected, however, the inmate's claim in that case that prison doctors had inflicted cruel and unusual punishment by inadequately attending to his medical needs—because he had failed to establish that they possessed a sufficiently culpable state of mind. Since, we said, only the " 'unnecessary *and wanton* infliction of pain' " implicates the Eighth Amendment, . . . a prisoner advancing such a claim must, at a minimum, allege "deliberate indifference" to his "serious" medical needs. "It is *only* such indifference" that can violate the Eighth Amendment. . . .

Estelle relied in large measure on an earlier case, *Louisiana es rel. Francis* v. *Resweber,* 329 U.S. 459 (1947), which involved not a prison deprivation but an effort to subject a prisoner to a second electrocution after the first attempt failed by reason of a malfunction in the electric chair. There Justice Reed, writing for a plurality of the Court, emphasized that the Eighth Amendment prohibited "the *wanton* infliction of pain." . . . Because the first attempt had been thwarted by an "unforeseeable accident," the officials lacked the culpable state of mind necessary for the punishment to be regarded as "cruel," regardless of the actual suffering inflicted. "The situation of the unfortunate victim of this accident is just as though he had suffered the identical amount of mental anguish and physical pain in any other occurrence, such as, for example, a fire in the cell block." Justice Frankfurter, concurring solely on the basis of the Due Process Clause of the Fourteenth Amendment, emphasized that the first attempt had failed because of "an innocent misadventure." . . .

After *Estelle*, we next confronted an Eighth Amendment challenge to a prison deprivation in *Rhodes* v. *Chapman*, 452 U.S. 337 (1981). In that case, inmates at the Southern Ohio Correctional Facility contended that the lodging of two inmates in a single cell ("double celling") constituted cruel and unusual punishment. We rejected that contention, concluding that it amounts "[a]t most . . . to a theory that double celling inflicts pain" that violates the Eighth Amendment. The Constitution, we said, "does not mandate comfortable prisons," and only those deprivations denying "the minimal civilized measure of life's necessities," are sufficiently grave to form the basis of an Eighth Amendment violation.

Our holding in *Rhodes* turned on the objective component of an Eighth Amendment prison claim (was the deprivation sufficiently serious?), and we did not consider the subjective component (did the officials act with a sufficiently culpable state of mind?). That *Rhodes* had not eliminated the subjective component was made clear by our next relevant case, *Whitley* v. *Albers,* 475 U.S. 312 (1986). There an inmate shot by a guard during an attempt to quell a prison disturbance contended that he had been subjected to cruel and unusual punishment. We stated:

> After incarceration, only the unnecessary and wanton infliction of pain . . . constitutes cruel and unusual punishment forbidden by the Eighth Amendment. To be cruel and unusual punishment, conduct that does not purport to be punishment at all must involve more than ordinary lack of due care for the prisoner's interests or safety. . . . It is *obduracy and wantonness, not inadvertence or error in good faith*, that characterize the conduct prohibited by the Cruel and Unusual Punishments Clause, whether that conduct occurs in connec-

tion with establishing conditions of confinement, supplying medical needs, or restoring official control over a tumultuous cellblock.

These cases mandate inquiry into a prison official's state of mind when it is claimed that the official has inflicted cruel and unusual punishment. . . . Petitioner concedes that this is so with respect to *some* claims of cruel and unusual prison conditions. He acknowledges, for instance, that if a prison boiler malfunctions accidentally during a cold winter, an inmate would have no basis for an Eighth Amendment claim, even if he suffers objectively significant harm. . . . Petitioner, and the United States as *amicus curiae* in support of petitioner, suggests that we should draw a distinction between "short-term" or "one-time" conditions (in which a state of mind requirement would apply) and "continuing" or "systemic" conditions (where official state of mind would be irrelevant). We perceive neither a logical nor a practical basis for that distinction. The source of the intent requirement is not the predilection itself, which bans only cruel and unusual *punishment.* If the pain inflicted is not formally meted out *as punishment* by the statute or the sentencing judge, some mental element must be attributed to the inflicting officer before it can qualify. As Judge Posner has observed:

> The infliction of punishment is a deliberate act intended to chastise or deter. This is what the word means today; it is what it meant in the eighteenth century. . . . [I]f [a] guard accidentally stepped on [a] prisoner's toe and broke it, this would not be punishment in anything remotely like the accepted meaning of the word, whether we consult the usage of 1791, or 1868, or 1985. *Duckworth* v. *Franzen,* 780 F.2d 645, 652 (CA7 1985) cert. denied, 479 U.S. 816 (1986). . . .

The long duration of a cruel prison condition may make it easier to *establish* knowledge and hence some form of intent, . . . but there is no logical reason why it should cause the *requirement* of intent to evaporate. The proposed short-term/long-term distinction also defies rational implementation. Apart from the difficulty of determining the day or hour that divides the two categories (is it the same for *all* conditions?) the violations alleged in specific cases often consist of composite conditions that do not lend themselves to such pigeonholing. . . .

II

Having determined that Eighth Amendment claims based on official conduct that does not purport to be the penalty formally imposed for a crime require inquiry into state of mind, it remains for us to consider what state of mind applies in cases challenging prison conditions. As described above, our cases say that the offending conduct must be *wanton*. *Whitley* makes clear, however, that in this context wantonness does not have a fixed meaning but must be determined with "due regard for differences in the kind of conduct against which an Eighth Amendment objection is lodged." 475 U.S., at 320. Where (as in *Whitley*) officials act in response to a prison disturbance, their actions are necessarily taken "in haste, under pressure," and balanced against "competing institutional concerns for the safety of prison staff or other inmates." *Ibid.* In such an emergency situation, we found that wantonness consisted of acting " 'maliciously and sadistically for the very purpose of causing harm.' " . . . In contrast, "the State's responsibility to attend to the medical needs of prisoners does not ordinarily clash with other equally important governmental responsibilities," . . . so that in that context, as *Estelle* held "deliberate indifference would constitute wantonness." Respondents counter that "deliberate indifference" is appropriate only in "cases involving personal injury of a physical nature," and that a malice standard should be applied in cases such as this, which "do not involve . . . detriment to bodily integrity, pain, injury, or loss of life." . . .

We do not agree with respondents' suggestion that the "wantonness" of conduct depends upon its effect upon the prisoner. *Whitley* teaches that, assuming the conduct is harmful enough to satisfy the objective component of an Eighth Amendment claim, . . . whether it can be characterized as "wanton" depends upon the constraints facing the *official*. From that standpoint, we see no significant distinction between claims alleging inadequate medical care and those alleging inadequate "conditions of confinement." Indeed, the medical care a prisoner receives is just as much a "condition" of his confinement as the food he is fed, the clothes he is issued, the temperature he is subjected to in his cell, and the protection he is afforded against other inmates. There is no indication that, as a general matter, the actions of prison officials with respect to these nonmedical conditions are taken under materially different constraints than their actions with respect to medical conditions. . . .

III

We now consider whether, in light of the foregoing analysis, the Sixth Circuit erred in affirming the District Court's grant of summary judgment in respondents' favor. . . .

. . . A court cannot dismiss any challenged condition, petitioner contends, as long as other conditions remain in dispute, for each condition must be "considered as part of the overall conditions challenged." Petitioner based this contention upon our observation in *Rhodes* that conditions of confinement, "alone or in combination," may deprive prisoners of the minimal civilized measure of life's necessities. As other courts besides the Court of Appeals here have understood, . . . our statement in *Rhodes* was not meant to establish the broad proposition that petitioner asserts. *Some* conditions of confinement may establish an Eighth Amendment violation "in combination" when each would not do so alone, but only when they have a mutually enforcing effect that produces the deprivation of a single, identifiable human need such as food, warmth, or exercise—for example, a low cell temperature at night combined with a failure to issue blankets. . . . To say that some prison conditions may interact in this fashion is a far cry from saying that all prison conditions are a seamless web for Eighth Amendment purposes. Nothing so amorphous as "overall conditions" can rise to the level of cruel and unusual punishment when no specific deprivation of a single human need exists. While we express no opinion on the relative gravity of the various claims that the Sixth Circuit found to pass and fail the threshold test of serious deprivation, we reject the contention made here that no claim can be found to fail that test in isolation. . . .

. . . It appears . . . that the court believed that the criterion of liability was whether the respondents acted "maliciously and sadistically for the very purpose of causing harm." . . . To be sure, mere negligence would satisfy neither that nor the more lenient "deliberate indifference" standard, so that any error on the point may have been harmless. Conceivably, however, the court would have given further thought to its finding of "[a]t best . . . negligence" if it realized that that was not merely an argument *a fortiori*, but a determination almost essential to the judgment. Out of an abundance of caution, we vacate the judgment of the Sixth Circuit and remand the case for reconsideration under the appropriate standard.

[The concurring opinion of JUSTICE WHITE, with whom JUSTICE MARSHALL, JUSTICE BLACKMUN, and JUSTICE STEVENS join, is not reprinted here.]

JUSTICE O'CONNOR *delivered the opinion of the Court.*

This case requires us to decide whether the use of excessive physical force against a prisoner may constitute cruel and unusual punishment when the inmate does not suffer serious injury. We answer that question in the affirmative.

I

At the time of the incident that is the subject of this suit, petitioner Keith Hudson was an inmate at the state penitentiary in Angola, Louisiana. Respondents Jack McMillian, Marvin Woods, and Arthur Mezo served as corrections security officers at the Angola facility. During the early morning hours of October 30, 1983, Hudson and McMillian argued. Assisted by Woods, McMillian then placed Hudson in handcuffs and shackles, took the prisoner out of his cell, and walked him toward the penitentiary's "administrative lockdown" area. Hudson testified that, on the way there, McMillian punched Hudson in the mouth, eyes, chest, and stomach while Woods held the inmate in place and kicked and punched him from behind. He further testified that Mezo, the supervisor on duty, watched the beating but merely told the officers "not to have too much fun." As a result of this episode, Hudson suffered minor bruises and swelling of his face, mouth, and lip. The blows also loosened Hudson's teeth and cracked his partial dental plate, rendering it unusable for several months.

Hudson sued the three corrections officers in Federal District Court under 42 U.S.C. § 1983, alleging a violation of the Eighth Amendment's prohibition on cruel and unusual punishments and seeking compensatory damages. The parties consented to disposition of the case before a Magistrate, who found that McMillian and Woods used force when there was no need to do so and that Mezo expressly condoned their actions. The Magistrate awarded Hudson damages of $800.

The Court of Appeals for the Fifth Circuit reversed. It held that inmates alleging use of excessive force in violation of the Eighth Amendment must prove: (1) significant injury; (2) resulting "directly and only from the use of force that was clearly excessive to the need"; (3) the excessiveness of which was objectively unreasonable; and (4) that the action constituted an unnecessary and wanton infliction of pain. The court determined that respondents' use of force was objectively unreasonable because no force was required. Furthermore, "[t]he conduct of McMillian and Woods qualified as clearly excessive and occasioned unnecessary and wanton infliction of pain." However, Hudson could not prevail on his Eighth Amendment claim because his injuries were "minor" and required no medical attention. . . .

II

. . . [The Court has adopted as the] legal standard that should govern the Eighth Amendment claim of an inmate shot by a guard during a prison riot . . . the settled rule that " 'the unnecessary and wanton infliction of pain . . . constitutes cruel and unusual punishment forbidden by the Eighth Amendment,' " (quoting *Ingraham* v. *Wright,* 430 U.S. 651, 670, 1970).

What is necessary to establish an "unnecessary and wanton infliction of pain," we said, varies according to the nature of the alleged constitutional violation. For example, the appropriate inquiry when an inmate alleges that prison officials failed to attend to serious medical needs is whether the officials exhibited "deliberate indifference." See *Estelle* v. *Gamble,* 429 U.S. 97, 104 (1976). This standard is appropriate because the State's responsibility to provide inmates with medical care ordinarily does not conflict with competing administrative concerns.

By contrast, officials confronted with a prison disturbance must balance the threat unrest poses to inmates, prison workers, administrators, and visitors against the harm inmates may suffer if guards use force. Despite the weight of these competing concerns, corrections officials must make their decisions "in haste, under pressure, and frequently without the luxury of a second chance." We accordingly concluded in *Whitley* [v. *Albers,* 475 U.S. 312, 1986] that application of the deliberate indifference standard is inappropriate when authorities use force to put down a prison disturbance. Instead, "the question whether the measure taken inflicted unnecessary and wanton pain and suffering ultimately turns on 'whether force [was] applied in a good faith effort to maintain or restore discipline or maliciously and sadistically for the very purpose of causing harm.' "

Many of the concerns underlying our holding in *Whitley* arise whenever guards use force to keep order. Whether the prison disturbance is a riot or a lesser disruption, corrections officers must balance the need "to maintain or restore discipline" through force against the risk of injury to inmates. Both situations may require prison officials to act quickly and decisively. Likewise, both implicate the principle that " '[p]rison administrators . . . should be accorded wide-ranging deference in the adoption and execution of policies and practices that in their judgment are needed to preserve internal order and discipline and to maintain institutional security.' " In recognition of these similarities, we hold that whenever prison officials stand accused of using excessive physical force in violation of the Cruel and Unusual Punishments Clause, the core judicial inquiry is that set out in *Whitley*: whether force was applied in a good-faith effort to maintain or restore discipline, or maliciously and sadistically to cause harm. . . .

A

Under the *Whitley* approach, the extent of injury suffered by an inmate is one factor that may suggest "whether the use of force could plausibly have been thought necessary" in a particular situation, "or instead evinced such wantonness with respect to the unjustified infliction of harm as is tantamount to a knowing willingness that it occur." In determining whether the use of force was wanton and unnecessary, it may also be proper to evaluate the need for application of force, the relationship between that need and the amount of force used, the threat "reasonably perceived by the responsible officials," and "any efforts made to temper the severity of a forceful response." The absence of serious injury is therefore relevant to the Eighth Amendment inquiry, but does not end it.

Respondents nonetheless assert that a significant injury requirement of the sort imposed by the Fifth Circuit is mandated by what we have termed the "objective component" of Eighth Amendment analysis. See *Wilson* v. *Seiter*, 501 U.S. ___, 111 S. Ct. 2321, 2326 (1991). *Wilson* extended the deliberate indifference standard applied to Eighth Amendment claims involving medical care to claims about conditions of confinement. In taking this step, we suggested that the subjective aspect of an Eighth Amendment claim (with which the Court was concerned) can be distinguished from the objective facet of the same claim. Thus, courts considering a prisoner's claim must ask both if "the officials

act[ed] with a sufficiently culpable state of mind" and if the alleged wrongdoing was objectively "harmful enough" to establish a constitutional violation.

. . . What is necessary to show sufficient harm for purposes of the Cruel and Unusual Punishments Clause depends upon the claim at issue, for two reasons. First, "[t]he general requirement that an Eighth Amendment claimant allege and prove the unnecessary and wanton infliction of pain should . . . be applied with due regard for differences in the kind of conduct against which an Eighth Amendment objection is lodged." Second, the Eighth Amendment's prohibition of cruel and unusual punishments " 'draw[s] its meaning from the evolving standards of decency that mark the progress of a maturing society,' " and so admits of few absolute limitations. *Rhodes* v. *Chapman*, 452 U.S. 337, 346 (1981).

The objective component of an Eighth Amendment claim is therefore contextual and responsive to "contemporary standards of decency." For instance, extreme deprivations are required to make out a conditions-of-confinement claim. Because routine discomfort is "part of the penalty that criminal offenders pay for their offenses against society," "only those deprivations denying 'the minimal civilized measure of life's necessities' are sufficiently grave to form the basis of an Eighth Amendment violation." A similar analysis applies to medical needs. Because society does not expect that prisoners will have unqualified access to health care, deliberate indifference to medical needs amounts to an Eighth Amendment violation only if those needs are "serious."

In the excessive force context, society's expectations are different. When prison officials maliciously and sadistically use force to cause harm, contemporary standards of decency always are violated. This is true whether or not significant injury is evident. Otherwise, the Eighth Amendment would permit any physical punishment, no matter how diabolic or inhuman, inflicting less than some arbitrary quantity of injury. Such a result would have been as unacceptable to the drafters of the Eighth Amendment as it is today. . . .

That is not to say that every malevolent touch by a prison guard gives rise to a federal cause of action. See *Johnson* v. *Glick*, 481 F.2d, at 1033 ("Not every push or shove, even if it may later seem unnecessary in the peace of a judge's chambers, violates a prisoner's constitutional rights.") The Eighth Amendment's prohibition of "cruel and unusual" punishment necessarily excludes from constitutional recognition *de minimis* uses of physical force, provided that the use of force is not of a sort " 'repugnant to the conscience of mankind.' "

In this case, the Fifth Circuit found Hudson's claim untenable because his injuries were "minor." Yet the blows directed at Hudson, which caused bruises, swelling, loosened teeth, and a cracked dental plate, are not *de minimis* for Eighth Amendment purposes. The extent of Hudson's injuries thus provides no basis for dismissal of his § 1983 claim.

B

The dissent's theory that *Wilson* requires an inmate who alleges excessive use of force to show serious injury *in addition to* the unnecessary and wanton infliction of pain misapplies *Wilson* and ignores the body of our Eighth Amendment jurisprudence. . . . *Wilson* presented neither an allegation of excessive force nor any issue relating to what was dubbed the "objective component" of an Eighth Amendment claim. . . .

The dissent's argument that claims based on excessive force and claims based on conditions of confinement are no different in kind is likewise unfounded. Far from rejecting *Whitley*'s insight that the unnecessary and wanton infliction of pain standard must be applied with regard for the nature of the alleged Eighth Amendment violation, the *Wilson* Court adopted it. How could it be otherwise when the constitutional touchstone is whether punishment is cruel and unusual? To deny, as the dissent does, the difference between punching a prisoner in the face and serving him unappetizing food is to ignore the " 'concepts of dignity, civilized standards, humanity, and decency' " that animate the Eighth Amendment.

C

Respondents argue that, aside from the significant injury test applied by the Fifth Circuit, their conduct cannot constitute an Eighth Amendment violation because it was "isolated and unauthorized." The beating of Hudson, they contend, arose from "a personal dispute between correctional security officers and a prisoner," and was against prison policy. Respondents invoke the reasoning of courts that have held the use of force by prison officers under such circumstances beyond the scope of "punishment" prohibited by the Eighth Amendment. . . .

We take no position on respondent's legal argument because we find it inapposite on this record. The Court of Appeals left intact the Magistrate's determination that the violence at issue in this case was "not an isolated assault." Indeed, there was testimony that McMillian and Woods beat another prisoner shortly after they finished with Hudson. To the extent that respondents rely on the unauthorized nature of their acts, they make a claim not addressed by the Fifth Circuit, not presented by the question on which we granted certiorari, and accordingly, not before this Court. Moreover, respondents ignore the Magistrate's finding that Lieutenant Mezo, acting as a supervisor, "expressly condoned the use of force in this instance."

The judgment of the Court of Appeals is

Reversed.

[The concurring opinion of JUSTICE STEVENS is not reprinted here.]

JUSTICE BLACKMUN, *concurring in the judgment.*

The Court today appropriately puts to rest a seriously misguided view that pain inflicted by an excessive use of force is actionable under the Eighth Amendment only when coupled with "significant injury," e.g., injury that requires medical attention or leaves permanent marks. Indeed, were we to hold to the contrary, we might place various kinds of state-sponsored torture and abuse—of the kind ingeniously designed to cause pain but without a telltale "significant injury"—entirely beyond the pale of the Constitution. In other words, the constitutional prohibition of "cruel and unusual punishments" then might not constrain prison officials from lashing prisoners with leather straps, whipping them with rubber hoses, beating them with naked fists, shocking them with electric currents, asphyxiating them short of death, intentionally exposing them to undue heat or cold, or forcibly injecting them with psychosis-inducing drugs. These techniques, commonly thought to be practiced only outside this Nation's borders, are hardly unknown within this Nation's prisons. See, e.g. *Campbell* v. *Grammer*, 889 F.2d 797, 802 (CA8 1989) (use of high-powered fire hoses); *Jackson* v. *Bishop*, 404 F.2d 571, 574–575 (CA8 1968) (use of the "Tucker Telephone," a hand-cranked device that generated electric shocks to sensitive body parts, and flogging with leather strap). . . .

I

Citing rising caseloads, respondents, represented by the Attorney General of Louisiana, and joined by the States of Texas, Hawaii, Nevada, Wyoming, and Florida as *amici curiae*, suggest that a "significant injury" requirement is necessary to curb the number of court filings by prison inmates. We are informed that the "significant injury requirement has been very effective in the Fifth Circuit in helping to control its system-wide docket management problems."

This audacious approach to the Eighth Amendment assumes that the interpretation of an explicit constitutional protection is to be guided by pure policy preferences for the paring down of prisoner petitions. Perhaps judicial overload is an appropriate concern in determining whether statutory standing to sue should be conferred upon certain plaintiffs. . . . But this inherently self-interested concern has no appropriate role in interpreting the contours of a substantive constitutional right.

Since the burden on the courts is presumably worth bearing when a prisoner's suit has merit, the States' "concern" is more aptly termed a "conclusion" that such suits are simply without merit. One's experience on the federal bench teaches the contrary. Moreover, were particular classes of cases to be nominated for exclusion from the federal courthouse, we might look first to cases in which federal law is not sensitively at issue rather than to those in which fundamental constitutional rights are at stake. The right to file for legal redress in the courts is as valuable to a prisoner as to any other citizen. Indeed, for the prisoner it is more valuable. Inasmuch as one convicted of a serious crime and imprisoned usually is divested of the franchise, the right to file a court action stands . . . as his most "fundamental political right, because preservative of all rights."

Today's ruling . . . does not open the floodgates for filings by prison inmates. By statute, prisoners—alone among other § 1983 claimants—are required to exhaust administrative remedies. Moreover, prison officials are entitled to a determination before trial whether they acted in an objectively reasonable manner, thereby entitling them to a qualified immunity defense. Additionally, a federal district court is authorized to dismiss a prisoner's complaint *in forma pauperis* "if satisfied that the action is frivolous or malicious." These measures should be adequate to control any docket-management problems that might result from meritless prisoner claims.

II

I do not read anything in the Court's opinion to limit injury cognizable under the Eighth Amendment to physical injury. It is not hard to imagine inflictions of psychological harm—without corresponding physical harm—that might prove to be cruel and unusual punishment. The issue was not presented here, because Hudson did not allege that he feared that the beating incident would be repeated or that it had caused him anxiety and depression.

As the Court makes clear, the Eighth Amendment prohibits the unnecessary and wanton infliction of "pain," rather than "injury." "Pain" in its ordinary meaning surely includes a notion of psychological harm. I am unaware of any precedent of this Court to the effect that psychological pain is not cognizable for constitutional purposes. If anything, our precedent is to the contrary.

To be sure, as the Court's opinion intimates, *de minimis* or nonmeasurable pain is not actionable under the Eighth Amendment. But psychological pain can be more than *de minimis*. Psychological pain often may be clinically diagnosed and quantified through well established methods, as in the ordinary tort context where damages for pain and suffering are regularly awarded. I have no doubt that to read a "physical pain" or "physical injury" requirement into the Eighth Amendment would be no less pernicious and without foundation than the "significant injury requirement" we reject today.

JUSTICE THOMAS, *with whom* **JUSTICE SCALIA** *joins, dissenting.*

* * *

I

* * *

In my view, a use of force that causes only insignificant harm to a prisoner may be immoral, it may be tortious, it may be criminal, and it may even be remediable under other provisions of the Federal Constitution, but it is not "cruel and unusual punishment." In concluding to the contrary, the Court today goes far beyond our precedents.

A

Until recent years, the Cruel and Unusual Punishment Clause was not deemed to apply at all to deprivations that were not inflicted as part of the sentence for a crime. For generations, judges and commentators regarded the Eighth Amendment as applying only to torturous punishments meted out by statutes or sentencing judges, and not generally to any hardship that might befall a prisoner during incarceration. In *Weems* v. *United States*, 217 U.S. 349

(1910), the Court extensively chronicled the background of the amendment, discussing its English antecedents, its adoption by Congress, its construction by this Court, and the interpretation of analogous provisions by state courts. Nowhere does *Weems* even hint that the Clause might regulate not just criminal sentences but the treatment of prisoners. Scholarly commentary also viewed the Clause as governing punishments that were part of the sentence. See T. Cooley, Constitutional Limitations, 329. . . .

Surely prison was not a more congenial place in the early years of the Republic than it is today; nor were our judges and commentators so naive as to be unaware of the often harsh conditions of prison life. Rather, they simply did not conceive of the Eighth Amendment as protecting inmates from harsh treatment. Thus, historically, the lower courts routinely rejected prisoner grievances by explaining that the courts had no role in regulating prison life. . . .

B

We made clear in *Estelle* that the Eighth Amendment plays a very limited role in regulating prison administration. The case involved a claim that prison doctors had inadequately attended an inmate's medical needs. We rejected the claim because the inmate failed to allege "acts or omissions sufficiently harmful to evidence *deliberate indifference* to *serious* medical needs" (emphasis added). From the outset, thus, we specified that the Eighth Amendment does not apply to every deprivation, or even every unnecessary deprivation, suffered by a prisoner, but *only* that narrow class of deprivations involving "serious" injury inflicted by prison officials acting with a culpable state of mind. We have since described these twin elements as the "objective" and "subjective" components of an Eighth Amendment prison claim.

We have never found a violation of the Eighth Amendment in the prison context when an inmate has failed to establish either of these elements. . . .

C

Given *Estelle, Rhodes, Whitley,* and *Wilson,* one might have assumed that the Court would have little difficulty answering the question presented in this case by upholding the Fifth Circuit's "significant injury" requirement. Instead, the Court announces that "[t]he objective component of an Eighth Amendment claim is . . . contextual and responsive to contemporary standards of decency." In the context of claims alleging the excessive use of physical force, the Court then asserts, the serious deprivation requirement is satisfied by no serious deprivation at all. "When prison officials maliciously and sadistically use force to cause harm, contemporary standards of decency always are violated." *Ibid.* Ascertaining prison officials' state of mind, in other words, is the *only* relevant inquiry in deciding whether such cases involve "cruel and unusual punishment." In my view, this approach is an unwarranted and unfortunate break with our Eighth Amendment prison jurisprudence.

The Court purports to derive the answer to this case from *Whitley.* The sum and substance of an Eighth Amendment violation, the Court asserts, is " ' "the unnecessary and wanton infliction of pain." ' " (quoting *Whitley,* 475 U.S., at 319, 106 S. Ct., at 1084). This formulation has the advantage, from the Court's perspective, of eliminating the objective component. As noted above, however, the only dispute in *Whitley* concerned the subjective component; the prisoner, who had been shot, had self-evidently been subjected to an objectively serious injury. *Whitley* did not say, as the Court does today, that the *objective* component is contextual, and that an Eighth Amendment claim may succeed where a prisoner is not seriously injured. Rather, *Whitley* stands for the proposition that, assuming the existence of an objectively serious deprivation, the culpability of an official's state of mind depends on the context in which he acts. "*Whitley* teaches that, *assuming* the conduct is harmful enough to satisfy the objective component of an Eighth Amendment claim, whether it can be characterized as 'wanton' depends upon the constraints facing the official." Whether officials subject a prisoner to the "unnecessary and wanton infliction of pain" is simply one way to describe the state of mind inquiry that was at issue in *Whitley* itself. As *Wilson* made clear, that inquiry is necessary but not sufficient when a prisoner seeks to show that he has been subjected to cruel and unusual punishment.

Perhaps to compensate for its elimination of the objective component in excessive force cases, the Court simultaneously makes it harder for prisoners to establish the subjective component. As we explained in *Wilson,* "deliberate indifference" is the baseline mental state required to establish an Eighth Amendment violation. Departure from this baseline is justified where, as in *Whitley,* prison officials act in response to an emergency; in such situations their conduct cannot be characterized as "wanton" unless it is taken "maliciously and sadistically for the very purpose of causing harm." The Court today extends the heightened mental state applied in *Whitley* to *all* excessive force cases, even where no competing institutional concerns are present. . . . I do not agree. Many excessive force cases do not arise from guards' attempts to "keep order." (In this very case, the basis for petitioner's Eighth Amendment claim is that the guards hit him when there was no need for them to use any force at all.) The use of excessive physical force is by no means invariably (in fact, perhaps not even predominantly) accompanied by a "malicious and sadistic" state of mind. I see no justification for applying the extraordinary *Whitley* standard to all excessive force cases, without regard to the constraints facing prison officials. The Court's unwarranted extension of *Whitley*, I can only suppose, is driven by the implausibility of saying that minor injuries imposed upon prisoners with anything less than a "malicious and sadistic" state of mind can amount to "cruel and unusual punishment." . . .

D

* * *

If the Court is to be taken at its word that "the unnecessary and wanton infliction of pain" upon a prisoner *per se* amounts to "cruel and unusual punishment," the implications of today's opinion are sweeping. For this formulation replaces the objective component described in our prior cases with a "necessity" component. Many prison deprivations, however, are not "necessary," at least under any meaningful definition of the word. Thus, under today's analysis, *Rhodes* was wrongly decided. Surely the "double celling" of inmates was not "necessary" to fulfill the State's penal mission; in fact, the prison in that case had been designed for individual cells, but was simply overcrowded. We rejected the prisoners' claim in *Rhodes* not because we determined that double-celling [*sic*] was "necessary," but because the deprivations alleged were not sufficiently serious to state a claim of cruel and unusual punishment. After today, the "necessity" of a deprivation is apparently the only relevant inquiry beyond the wantonness of official conduct. This approach, in my view, extends the Eighth Amendment beyond all reasonable limits.

II

Today's expansion of the Cruel and Unusual Punishment Clause beyond all bounds of history and precedent is, I suspect, yet another manifestation of the pervasive view that the Federal Constitution must address all ills in our society. Abusive behavior by prison guards is deplorable conduct that properly evokes outrage and contempt. But that does not mean that it is invariably unconstitutional. The Eighth Amendment is not, and should not be turned into, a National Code of Prison Regulation. To reject the notion that the infliction of concededly "minor" injuries can be considered either "cruel" or "unusual" "punishment" (much less cruel and unusual punishment) is not to say that it amounts to acceptable conduct. Rather, it is to recognize that primary responsibility for preventing and punishing such conduct rests not with the Federal Constitution but with the laws and regulations of the various States.

Petitioner apparently could have, but did not, seek redress for his injuries under state law. Respondents concede that if available state remedies were not constitutionally adequate, petitioner would have a claim under the Due Process Clause of the Fourteenth Amendment. I agree with respondents that this is the appropriate, and appropriately limited, federal constitutional inquiry in this case. . . .

Because I conclude that, under our precedents, a prisoner seeking to establish that he has been subjected to "cruel and unusual punishment" must always show that he has suffered a serious injury, I would affirm the judgment of the Fifth Circuit.

FEATURED CASES

Hernandez v. *New York*   *Georgia* v. *McCollum*

During the "criminal law explosion" of the 1960s, the Supreme Court handed down a number of decisions on the scope of the fair trial guarantees proclaimed in the Sixth Amendment.[25] In several cases, guarantees that had previously been construed as limiting the federal government only were made binding on the states. The historic right to a trial by jury in criminal cases was made obligatory on the states in *Duncan* v. *Louisiana*, 391 U.S. 145 (1968). The *Duncan* case involved a conviction for simple battery that, under Louisiana law, carries a maximum penalty of a two-year jail term and/or a fine of not more than $300. The defendant was sentenced to only 60 days in jail and was fined $150. However, because the trial court had denied his request for a jury trial, the Supreme Court held that the statutory penalty was heavy enough to classify the offense as "serious." Hence, the Court concluded that the Fourteenth Amendment entitled the accused to the jury trial guarantee proclaimed in the Sixth Amendment. (Cf. *Baldwin* v. *New York*, 399 U.S. 66, 1970, reaffirming *Duncan*, where the Court examines extensively the difference between "serious" and "petty" offenses.)

Did *Duncan* fasten the twelve-member jury requirement on the states? In *Williams* v. *Florida* (399 U.S. 78, 1970), the Court sustained a state statutory provision for a six-person jury, holding that the essential purposes served by a jury can be accomplished by the smaller number. However, the Court felt that provision for a jury of fewer than six "threatens substantially" the trial by jury guarantee and rejected a state provision for a five-person jury for trials of misdemeanors in *Ballew* v. *Georgia* (435 U.S. 223, 1978).

A unique procedure designed to lessen the demands of the jury trial was considered and approved by the Court in *Ludwig* v. *Massachusetts* (427 U.S. 618, 1976). Specifically, a statutory procedure permitting a "two-tier" criminal trial system was at issue. Initially, if defendants plead not guilty, they

can get a nonjury trial only. If a guilty verdict results therefrom, they are then entitled to a jury trial. They can also get a jury trial by "admitting sufficient finding of fact" in the first-tier proceeding if the judge enters a judgment of conviction. If defendants make a guilty plea initially, they are entitled to a second-tier proceeding for determination of their sentence. Justice Blackmun's majority opinion emphasized that the jury trial is not impaired by this procedure because the accused is not "unduly burdened" by moving to the "second-tier" (the jury trial). Nor does the procedure, argued Blackmun, constitute double jeopardy, for this constitutional guarantee does not "prohibit a [s]tate from affording a defendant two opportunities to avoid conviction and secure an acquittal." Justices Brennan, Stewart, and Marshall joined Justice Stevens in dissent. They complained of the burdens imposed on the defendant by a second trial, such as stale witnesses and lawyers, unavailability of witnesses, and improper influences of the first trial on the second, and they condemned what they considered the real aim of the procedure—to discourage jury trials by placing a burden on those who opt for them.

In other dimensions of the jury trial guarantee, the Court has held that: (1) persons may not be systematically excluded from juries because of race (*Norris* v. *Alabama*, 294 U.S. 587, 1935); (2) the Fourteenth Amendment supports the right of a black defendant to have prospective jurors questioned on their possible racial prejudice, particularly in the context of racial issue cases (*Ham* v. *South Carolina*, 409 U.S. 524, 1973), although the nature of the questions asked is left to the discretion of the trial judge (note, however, *Ristaino* v. *Ross*, 424 U.S. 589, 1976, where the Court limited significantly the scope of *Ham* to cases where "racial issues [are] inextricably bound up with the conduct of the trial," allowing trial judges discretion on whether to pose questions directed specifically at racial prejudice; also note that *Ham* was reaffirmed in *Turner* v. *Murray*, 106 S. Ct. 1683, 1986, as the Court enunciated a rule that entitles a defendant in an interracial capital crime "to have prospective jurors informed of the race of the victim and questioned on the issue of racial bias," but

[25]Quite often the public dimension of the criminal trial guarantees collides with the interest of the accused to obtain a fair trial. Because of the crucial importance of the First Amendment issues involved and the Court's attention to them, a discussion of these issues, together with illustrative cases, may be found in Chapter 3.

a majority could not be found to determine if *Turner* should be construed as negating the *Ristaino* limitation of *Ham*); (3) states may not exempt women, as an identifiable group, from jury duty because it would negate the "fair cross-section of the community" requirement as noted in *Taylor* v. *Louisiana* (419 U.S. 522, 1975) and *Duren* v. *Missouri* (439 U.S. 357, 1979); and (4) states are "precluded from systematic exclusion" of identifiable racial groups (blacks) from grand juries that indict and petit juries that convict white persons (*Peters* v. *Kiff*, 407 U.S. 493, 1971).

The question of racial exclusion in the jury selection process noted in *Norris*, and recognized initially in *Strauder* v. *West Virginia* (100 U.S. 303, 1880) over a half-century earlier, continues to produce cases that require the Court to determine the scope and nature of the equal protection guarantee for black Americans. One of the most troublesome of these kinds of questions involves the widely used prosecutorial practice of excluding all blacks from jury venires in criminal cases (where blacks are defendants) through use of the peremptory challenge. Initially, the Court's position that was enunciated in *Swain* v. *Alabama* (380 U.S. 202, 1965) recognized the peremptory as a valid prosecutorial practice so long as it was not used purposely to exclude blacks from jury service. Noting that striking all blacks from particular jury venires does not in and of itself constitute a constitutional violation, defendants raising such a claim were required to shoulder the burden of proof. As a result, *Swain* was widely read as insulating the peremptory challenge. But some 20 years later, in *Batson* v. *Kentucky* (106 S. Ct. 1712, 1986), the Court concluded that the prosecution must shoulder the burden of justifying its use when a black defendant establishes a prima facie case of racial discrimination. While many applauded the decision in *Batson* as a realistic view of a "shameful" racist practice, some thought, as did Justice Marshall in his concurrence, that racial discrimination in this criminal context will not be eliminated until the practice is abolished completely.

In a subsequent peremptory challenge action, the Rehnquist Court refused to construe *Batson* as requiring the rejection of a New York prosecutor's use of peremptories to exclude prospective Latino jurors from the trial jury of Latino defendants. In *Hernandez* v. *New York* (111 S. Ct. 1859, 1991), Justice Anthony Kennedy, in announcing the Court's judgment, emphasized the state court's finding of the prosecutor's "race-neutral explanation" for excluding the Latino jurors. The lower courts accepted the prosecutor's explanation that he thought the potential Latino jurors "might have difficulty in accepting the translator's rendition of Spanish-language testimony" as valid and without discriminatory intent. Hence Kennedy concluded that the ethnic exclusion in that context did not abridge the *Batson* requirements.

In an interesting "twist" of the peremptory-exclusion practice, a white defendant challenged the prosecutor's action striking blacks from the venire in *Powers* v. *Ohio* (111 S. Ct. 1364, 1991). On the key issue of the white defendant's standing to raise the issue of exclusion of blacks from the trial jury, Justice Kennedy held for the seven-to-two majority that the equal protection clause supports a defendant's challenge to race-based peremptory challenges, even though the defendant and the challenged juror are of different races. Underscoring the Court's longstanding position that "racial discrimination in the jury selection process cannot be tolerated," the justice concluded that a state may not follow neutral, nonracial principles in the development of jury lists and then resort to racial exclusion practices (through peremptory challenges) in the final selection stages. (Cf. *Holland* v. *Illinois*, 493 U.S. 474, 1990, where Justice Scalia held for a five-to-four majority that while a *white* defendant could challenge on "fair cross-section of the community" grounds a prosecutor's peremptory exclusion of all blacks from the jury venire, that Sixth Amendment requirement does not prevent either side from using peremptories to exclude cognizable racial groups from the final jury selected, "as long as the venire itself is drawn from [a] fair cross-section of the community." Scalia emphasized that the Sixth Amendment's imperative is a trial by an impartial jury, not a representative one.)

The Rehnquist Court examined the peremptory challenge practice in the context of civil litigation in *Edmondson* v. *Leesville Concrete Co.* (111 S. Ct. 2077, 1991), where a black worker was injured on the job site and sued Leesville for negligence. At trial, the defendant company used two of its permitted peremptory challenges to remove black prospective jurors. The plaintiff's subsequent request that the defendant should be required to meet the race-neutral explanation requirement of *Batson* was denied by the lower courts, and in a six-to-three decision the Supreme Court reversed. The critical part of the decision was the Court's holding that a private defendant's use of the peremptory challenge jury exclusion technique was subject to equal protection analysis. Justice Kennedy reasoned that because the peremptory process had its source in state authority, the private litigant, when using it, takes on the character of a "government actor" subject to the constraints of the equal protection clause.

The Court struck down a longstanding practice employed in the trials of capital punishment cases in *Witherspoon* v. *Illinois* (391 U.S. 510, 1968), which involved an appeal challenging the practice of excusing all prospective jurors who indicate that they have conscientious scruples against capital punishment. It held that such a procedure results in the selection of a "prosecution-prone" jury that is more likely than the average jury to make a finding of guilt and to impose the death penalty. In an opinion for the six-to-three majority, Justice Potter Stewart contended that "a state may not entrust the determination of whether a man should live or die to a tribunal organized to return a verdict of death." Hence, the conclusion emphasized by the Court was that the only persons called for the venire subject to exclusion by the "death penalty qualification" were those who indicated that their views on capital punishment would impair their ability to make an impartial assessment of a defendant's culpability or that they "would automatically vote against the imposition of capital punishment."

The Court explicated further the *Witherspoon* principles in several cases during the next decade. *Boulden* v. *Holman*, 394 U.S. 478, 1969; *Maxwell* v. *Bishop*, 398 U.S. 262, 1970; and *Lockett* v. *Ohio*, 438 U.S. 586, 1978. The position reiterated in those holdings was essentially that which the Court had expressed in *Witherspoon*: exclusion of a veniremember because of expressed "general objections" to the death penalty and "conscientious and religious scruples against its infliction" can only be sustained upon a finding that the veniremember has made it "unmistakably clear" that he or she would "automatically" vote against the death penalty, irrespective of the evidence and the law. In probably its most definitive statement on the *Witherspoon* standard, the Court held in *Adams* v. *Texas* (448 U.S. 38, 1980) that state statutes may not authorize exclusion on broader grounds than permitted by *Witherspoon*. In that case, the justices found defective the statutory oath required of jurors (that the mandatory penalty of death will not affect their deliberations on any issue of fact) because it, in effect, permitted exclusion of potential jurors "only because they were unable positively to state whether or not their deliberations would in any way be 'affected.' " Justice White noted for the Court that such a test is defective because it could exclude those persons who simply indicate "that they would be 'affected' by the possibility of the death penalty" but who apparently meant to convey that because of "the potential consequences of their decision," the deliberations would require a more demanding emotional involvement. White concluded that the appropriate test that follows therefrom is that "a juror may not be challenged for cause based on his views about capital punishment unless those views would prevent or substantially impair the performance of his duties as a juror in accordance with his instructions and his oath." The test was reaffirmed in 1985 in *Wainwright* v. *Witt* (105 S. Ct. 844). The Rehnquist Court, however, indicated a more restrictive construction of *Witherspoon* one year later in *Lockhart* v. *McCree* (106 S. Ct. 1758), when it overturned a ruling of the Court of Appeals for the Eighth Circuit that had held that the removal for cause of "Witherspoon excludables" abridged the "fair cross-section of the community" requirement of the Sixth Amendment jury trial provision. Chief Justice Rehnquist, who spoke for the six-to-three majority, argued that the application of the so-called "death qualification" test in the jury selection process is no more than the assurance that an impartial jury will be composed of those "who will conscientiously apply the law and find the facts." He contended further that a proper reading of *Witherspoon* does not require the exclusion from capital jury service of all persons who oppose the death penalty; rather, exclusion is restricted to those who "conscientiously" indicate that they cannot and will not follow the law in such cases. In further clarification, he asserted that the "fair cross-section of the community" principle applied to jury panels and venires and not to petit juries, contrary to the broad application urged by *McCree*.

In further elaboration of the *Witherspoon* doctrine, the Rehnquist Court considered challenges to the selection of jurors who would automatically vote to impose the death penalty on a defendant convicted of a capital offense in *Morgan* v. *Illinois* (112 S. Ct. 222) in 1992. In a six-to-three decision, Justice Byron White, speaking for the majority, held that a defendant facing the death penalty may challenge for cause a prospective juror who would automatically vote to impose the death penalty in every case. Just as a juror who is unalterably opposed to the imposition of the death penalty must be excluded because he or she cannot conscientiously fulfill the oath to follow the law and the instructions to the jury pursuant thereto, so should one who would automatically vote to impose the death penalty be excluded for the same reason. Such a juror, he emphasized, would lack the qualities of impartiality and indifference required by due process. Furthermore,

White noted, jurors who would automatically vote to impose the death penalty would not "in good faith . . . consider evidence of aggravating and mitigating circumstances" as may be required by law and included in jury instructions.

In further expansion of our Sixth Amendment jurisprudence, the Court has approved state policies that permit less than unanimous jury verdicts in noncapital criminal prosecutions despite the vigorous contention of some that such policies negate the "proof beyond a reasonable doubt" standard to which most jurisdictions are committed. (See *Apodaca* v. *Oregon*, 406 U.S. 404, and *Johnson* v. *Louisiana*, 406 U.S. 536, 1972.) The speedy trial guarantee was also made obligatory on the states in *Klopfer* v. *North Carolina* (386 U.S. 213, 1967) at the height of the so-called criminal law revolution of the Warren Court. In assessing the efficacy of claims asserting the protection of the guarantee, the Court, in *Barker* v. *Wingo* (407 U.S. 514, 1972), adopted a flexible approach, indicating that trial courts should consider such factors as: (1) length of the delay; (2) reasons for the delay; (3) the defendant's assertion of the guarantee; and (4) prejudice to the defendant. Upon a finding of a violation of the guarantee, the Court held in *Strunk* v. *United States* (412 U.S. 434, 1973) that while dismissal of the indictment may appear to be a severe remedy, "severe remedies are not necessarily unique in the application of constitutional standards."

The Speedy Trial Act enacted by Congress in 1974 rejects the *Barker* v. *Wingo* approach in federal prosecutions by requiring courts to adhere to fixed time intervals between arrest, pretrial proceedings, and the trial. Accordingly, the entire process from arrest to the commencement of the trial must take place within 100 days.

An unusual but interesting episode of the speedy trial issue was decided by the Court when it reviewed the highly publicized "Green Beret" murder case in *United States* v. *MacDonald* (456 U.S. 1, 1982). There military authorities brought charges against one of their medical officers (Captain MacDonald) for the murder of his pregnant wife and two children in their residence at Fort Bragg, North Carolina. Subsequent military proceedings led to a dismissal of the charges, and MacDonald was granted an honorable discharge. The Department of Justice continued to investigate the murders after his discharge and five years thereafter obtained an indictment and conviction in federal district court. Thereupon, the Court of Appeals for the Fourth Circuit reversed, holding that the indictment violated MacDonald's Sixth Amendment right to a speedy trial. But the Supreme Court did not accept this application of the guarantee. Instead, Chief Justice Burger contended for the six-to-three majority that the guarantee "attaches only when a formal criminal charge is instituted and a criminal prosecution begins." Consequently, the time between the dismissal of charges by the military and the indictment on civilian criminal charges is not a relevant consideration in determining if the speedy trial guarantee has been abridged.

HERNANDEZ v. NEW YORK
___ U.S. ___; ___ L. Ed. 2d ___; 111 S. Ct. 1859 (1991)

JUSTICE KENNEDY *announced the judgment of the Court and delivered an opinion in which* CHIEF JUSTICE REHNQUIST *and* JUSTICE WHITE *and* JUSTICE SOUTER *joined.*

Petitioner Dinisio Hernandez asks us to review the New York state courts' rejection of his claim that the prosecutor in his criminal trial exercised peremptory challenges to exclude Latinos from the jury by reason of their ethnicity. If true, the prosecutor's discriminatory use of peremptory strikes would violate the Equal Protection Clause as interpreted by our decision in *Batson* v. *Kentucky*. We must determine whether the prosecutor offered a race-neutral basis for challenging Latino potential jurors and, if so, whether the state courts' decision to accept the prosecutor's explanation should be sustained. . . .

I

The case comes to us on direct review of petitioner's convictions on two counts of attempted murder and two counts of criminal possession of a weapon. On a Brooklyn street, petitioner fired several shots at Charlene Calloway and her mother, Ada Saline. Calloway suffered three gunshot wounds. Petitioner missed Saline and instead hit two men in a nearby restaurant. The victims survived the incident.

. . . We concern ourselves here only with the jury selection process and the proper application of *Batson*, which had been handed down before the trial took place. After 63 potential jurors had been questioned and 9 had been empaneled, defense counsel objected that the prosecutor had used four peremptory challenges to exclude Latino potential jurors. Two of the Latino venirepersons challenged by the prosecutor had brothers who had been convicted of crimes, and the brother of one of those potential jurors was being prosecuted by the same District Attorney's office for a probation violation. Petitioner does not press his *Batson* claim, with respect to those prospective jurors, and we concentrate on the other two excluded individuals.

After petitioner raised his *Batson* objection, the prosecutor did not wait for a ruling on whether petitioner had established a prima facie case of racial discrimination. Instead, the prosecutor volunteered his reasons for striking the jurors in question. He explained:

> Your honor, my reason for rejecting the—these two jurors—I'm not certain they're Hispanics. I didn't notice how many Hispanics had been called to the panel, but my reason for rejecting these two is I feel very uncertain that they would be able to listen and follow the interpreter.

After an interruption by defense counsel, the prosecutor continued:

> We talked to them for a long time; the Court talked to them, I talked to them. I believe that in their heart they will try to follow it, but I felt there was a great deal of uncertainty as to whether they could accept the interpreter as the final arbiter of what was said by each of the witnesses, especially where there were going to be Spanish-speaking witnesses, and I didn't feel, when I asked them whether or not they could accept the interpreter's translation of it, I didn't feel that they could. They each looked away from me and said with some hesitation that they would try, not that they could, but that they would try to follow the interpreter, and I feel that in a case where the interpreter will be for the main witnesses, they would have an undue impact on the jury.

Defense counsel moved for a mistrial "based on the conduct of the District Attorney," and the prosecutor requested a chance to call a supervisor to the courtroom before the judge's ruling.

Following a recess, defense counsel renewed his motion, which the trial court denied. Discussion of the objection continued, however, and the prosecutor explained that he would have no motive to exclude Latinos from the jury.

> [T]his case involves four complainants. Each of the complainants is Hispanic. All of my witnesses, that is, civilian witnesses, are going to be Hispanic. I have absolutely no reason—there's no reason for me to want to exclude Hispanics because all the parties involved are Hispanic, and I certainly would have no reason to do that.

After further interchange among the judge and attorneys, the trial court again rejected petitioner's claim.

On appeal, the New York Supreme Court, Appellate Division, noted that though the ethnicity of one challenged bilingual juror remained uncertain, the prosecutor had challenged the only three prospective jurors with definite Hispanic surnames. The court ruled that this fact made out a prima facie showing of discrimination. The court affirmed the trial court's rejection of petitioner's *Batson* claim, however, on the ground that the prosecutor had offered race-neutral explanations for the peremptory strikes sufficient to rebut petitioner's prima facie case.

The New York Court of Appeals also affirmed the judgment. . . . We granted certiorari and now affirm.

II

In *Batson*, we outlined a three-step process for evaluating claims that a prosecutor has used peremptory challenges in a manner violating the Equal Protection Clause. The analysis set forth in *Batson* permits prompt rulings on objections to peremptory challenges without substantial disruption of the jury selection process. First, the defendant must make a prima facie showing that the prosecutor has exercised peremptory challenges on the basis of race. Second, if the requisite showing has been made, the burden shifts to the prosecutor to articulate a race-neutral explanation for striking the jurors in question. Finally, the trial court must determine whether the defendant has carried his burden of proving purposeful discrimination. This three-step inquiry delimits our consideration of the arguments raised by petitioner.

A

The prosecutor defended his use of peremptory strikes without any prompting or inquiry from the trial court. As a result, the trial court had no occasion to rule that petitioner had or had not made a prima facie showing of intentional discrimination. This departure from the normal course of proceeding need not concern us. We explained in the context of employment discrimination litigation under Title VII of the Civil Rights Act of 1964 that "[w]here the defendant has done everything that would be required of him if the plaintiff had properly made out a prima facie case, whether the plaintiff really did so is no longer relevant." *United States Postal Service Bd. of Govs. v. Aikens*, 460 U.S. 711 (1983). The same principle applies under *Batson*. Once a prosecutor has offered a race-neutral explanation for the peremptory challenges and the trial court has ruled on the ultimate question of intentional discrimination, the preliminary issue of whether the defendant had made a prima facie showing becomes moot.

B

Petitioner contends that the reasons given by the prosecutor for challenging the two bilingual jurors were not race-neutral. In evaluating the race-neutrality of an attorney's explanation, a court must determine [whether, assuming the proffered reasons for the peremptory challenges violate the Equal Protection Clause as a matter of law.] A court addressing this issue must keep in mind the fundamental principle that "official action will not be held unconstitutional solely because it results in a racially disproportionately impact. . . . Proof of racially discriminatory intent or purpose is required to show a violation of the Equal Protection Clause." " 'Discriminatory purpose' . . . implies more than intent as volition or intent as awareness of consequences. It implies that the decisionmaker . . . selected . . . a particular course of action at least in part 'because of,' not merely 'in spite of,' its adverse effects upon an identifiable group."

A neutral explanation in the context of our analysis here means an explanation based on something other than the race of the juror. At this step of the inquiry, the issue is the racial validity of the prosecutor's explanation. Unless a discriminatory intent is inherent in the prosecutor's explanation, the reason offered will be deemed race-neutral.

Petitioner argues that Spanish-language ability bears a close relation to ethnicity, and that, as a consequence, it violates the Equal Protection Clause to exercise a peremptory challenge on the ground that a Latino potential juror speaks Spanish. He points to the high correlation between Spanish-speaking language ability and ethnicity in New York, where the case was tried. . . .

The prosecutor here offered a race-neutral basis for these peremptory strikes. As explained by the prosecutor, the challenges rested neither on the intention to exclude Latino or bilingual jurors, nor on stereotypical assumptions about Latinos or bilinguals. The prosecutor's articulated basis for these challenges divided potential jurors into two classes: those whose conduct during *voir dire* would persuade him they might have difficulty in accepting the translator's rendition of Spanish-language testimony and those potential jurors who gave no such reason for doubt. Each category would include both Latinos and non-Latinos. While the prosecutor's criterion might well result in the disproportionate removal of prospective Latino jurors, that disproportionate impact does not turn the prosecutor's actions into a *per se* violation of the Equal Protection Clause.

Petitioner contends that despite the prosecutor's focus on the individual responses of these jurors, his reason for the peremptory strikes has the effect of a pure, language-based reason because "[a]ny honest bilingual juror would have answered the prosecutor in the exact same way." Petitioner asserts that a bilingual juror would hesitate in answering questions like those asked by the judge and prosecutor due to the difficulty of ignoring the actual Spanish-language testimony. In his view, no more can be expected than a commitment by a perspective juror to try to follow the interpreter's translation.

But even if we knew that a high percentage of bilingual jurors would hesitate in answering questions like these and, as a consequence, would be excluded under the prosecutor's criterion, that fact alone would not cause the criterion to fail the race-neutrality test. As will be discussed below, disparate impact should be given appropriate weight in determining whether the prosecutor acted with a forbidden intent, but it will not be conclusive in the preliminary race-neutrality step of the *Batson* inquiry. An argument relating to the impact of a classification does not alone show its purpose. Equal protection analysis turns on the intended consequences of government classifications. Unless the government actor adopted a criterion with the intent of causing the impact asserted, that impact itself does not violate the principle of race-neutrality. Nothing in the prosecutor's explanation shows that he chose to exclude jurors who hesitated in answering questions about following the interpreter *because* he wanted to prevent bilingual Latinos from serving on the jury. . . .

C

Once the prosecutor offers a race-neutral basis for

his exercise of peremptory challenges, "[t]he trial court then [has] the duty to determine if the defendant has established purposeful discrimination." While the disproportionate impact on Latinos resulting from the prosecutor's criterion for excluding these jurors does not answer the race-neutrality inquiry, it does have relevance to the trial court's decision on this question. "[A]n invidious discriminatory purpose may often be inferred from the totality of the relevant facts, including the fact, if it is true, that the [classification] bears more heavily on one race than another." If a prosecutor articulates a basis for a peremptory challenge that results in the disproportionate exclusion of members of a certain race, the trial judge may consider that fact as evidence that the prosecutor's stated reason constitutes a pretext for racial discrimination.

In the context of this trial, the prosecutor's frank admission that his ground for excusing these jurors related to their ability to speak and understand Spanish raised a plausible, though not a necessary, inference that language might be a pretext for what in fact were race-based peremptory challenges. This was not a case where by some rare coincidence a juror happened to speak the same language as a key witness, in a community where few others spoke that tongue. If it were, the explanation that the juror could have undue influence on jury deliberations might be accepted without concern that a racial generalization had come into play. But this trial took place in a community with a substantial Latino population, and petitioner and other interested parties were members of that ethnic group. It would be common knowledge in the locality that a significant percentage of the Latino population speaks fluent Spanish, and that many consider it their preferred language, the one chosen for personal communication, the one selected for speaking with the most precision and power, the one used to define the self.

The trial judge can consider these and other factors when deciding whether a prosecutor intended to discriminate. For example, though petitioner did not suggest the alternative to the trial court here, Spanish-speaking jurors could be permitted to advise the judge in a discreet way of any concerns with the translation during the course of the trial. A prosecutor's persistence in the desire to exclude Spanish-speaking jurors despite this measure could be taken into account in determining whether to accept a race-neutral explanation for the challenge.

The trial judge in this case chose to believe the prosecutor's race-neutral explanation for striking the two jurors in question, rejecting petitioner's assertion that the reasons were pretextual. In *Batson*, we explained that the trial court's decision on the ultimate question of discriminatory intent represents a finding of fact of the sort accorded great deference on appeal. . . . *Batson*'s treatment of intent to discriminate as a pure issue of fact, subject to review under a deferential standard, accords with our treatment of that issue in other equal protection cases. . . .

Deference to trial court findings on the issue of discriminatory intent makes particular sense in this context because, as we noted in *Batson*, the finding will "largely turn on evaluation of credibility." In the typical peremptory challenge inquiry, the decisive question will be whether counsel's race-neutral explanation for a peremptory challenge should be believed. There will seldom be much evidence bearing on that issue, and the best evidence often will be the demeanor of the attorney who exercises the challenge. As with the state of mind of a juror, evaluation of the prosecutor's state of mind based on demeanor and credibility lies "peculiarly within a trial judge's province."

The precise formula used for review of fact findings, of course, depends on the context. . . . On federal habeas review of a state conviction, 28 U.S.C. § 2254(d) requires the federal courts to accord state court factual findings a presumption of correctness.

This case comes to us on direct review of the state court judgment. No statute or rule governs our review of facts found by state courts in cases with this posture. The reasons justifying a deferential standard of review in other contexts, however, apply with equal force to our review of a state trial court's findings of fact made in connection with a federal constitutional claim. Our cases have indicated that, in the absence of exceptional circumstances, we would defer to state court factual findings, even when those findings relate to a constitutional issue. . . .

Petitioner advocates "independent" appellate review of a trial court's rejection of a *Batson* claim. We have difficulty understanding the nature of the review petitioner would have us conduct. Petitioner explains that "[i]ndependent review requires the appellate court to accept the findings of historical fact and credibility of the lower court unless they are clearly erroneous. Then, based on these facts, the appellate court independently determines whether there has been discrimination." But if an appellate court accepts a trial court's finding that a prosecutor's race-neutral explanation for his peremptory challenges should be believed, we fail to see how the appellate court nevertheless could find discrimination. The credibility of the prosecutor's explanation goes to the heart of the equal protection analysis, and once that has been settled, there seems nothing left to review. . . .

In the case before us, we decline to overturn the state trial court's finding on the issue of discriminatory intent unless convinced that its determination was clearly erroneous. It "would pervert the concept of federalism" to conduct a more searching review of findings made in state trial court than we conduct with respect to federal district court findings. . . .

We discern no clear error in the state trial court's determination that the prosecutor did not discriminate on the basis of the ethnicity of Latino jurors. We have said that "[w]here there are two permissible views of the evidence, the factfinder's choice between them cannot be clearly erroneous." The trial court took a permissible view of the evidence in crediting the prosecutor's explanation. Apart from the prosecutor's demeanor, which of course we have no opportunity to review, the court could have relied on the facts that the prosecutor defended his use of peremptory challenges without being asked to do so by the judge, that he did not know which jurors were Latinos, and that the ethnicity of the victims and the prosecution witnesses tended to undercut any motive to exclude Latinos from the jury. Any of these factors could be taken as evidence of the prosecutor's sincerity. The trial court, moreover, could rely on the fact that only three challenged jurors can with confidence be identified as Latinos, and that the prosecutor had a verifiable and legitimate explanation for two of those challenges. Given these factors, that the prosecutor also excluded one or two Latinos venirepersons on the basis of a subjective criterion having a disproportionate impact on Latinos does not leave us with a "definite and firm conviction that a mistake has been committed." . . .

* * *

D

Our decision today does not imply that exclusion of bilinguals from jury service is wise, or even that it is constitutional in all cases. It is a harsh paradox that one may become proficient enough in English to participate in trial, . . . only to encounter disqualification because he knows a second language as well. As the Court observed in a somewhat related context: "Mere knowledge of [a foreign] language cannot reasonably be regarded as harmful. Heretofore it has been commonly looked upon as helpful and desirable."

. . . In holding that a race-neutral reason for a peremptory challenge means a reason other than race, we do not resolve the more difficult question of the breadth with which the concept of race should be defined for equal protection purposes. We would face a quite different case if the prosecutor had justified his peremptory challenges with the explanation that he did not want Spanish-speaking jurors. It may well be, for certain ethnic groups and in some communities, that proficiency in a particular language, like skin color, should be treated as a surrogate for race under an equal protection analysis. And, as we make clear, a policy of striking all who speak a given language, without regard to the particular circumstances of the trial or the individual responses of the jurors, may be found by the trial judge to be a pretext for racial discrimination. But that case is not before us.

III

We find no error in the application by the New York courts of the three-step *Batson* analysis. . . . The state courts came to the proper conclusion that the prosecutor offered a race-neutral basis for his exercise of peremptory challenges. The trial court did not commit clear error in choosing to believe the reasons given by the prosecutor.

Affirmed.

[The opinion of JUSTICE O'CONNOR, with whom JUSTICE SCALIA joins, concurring in the judgment, is not reprinted here.]

JUSTICE STEVENS, *with whom* JUSTICE MARSHALL *joins, dissenting.*

A violation of the Equal Protection Clause requires what our cases characterize as proof of "discriminatory purpose." By definition, however, a prima facie case is one that is established by the requisite proof of invidious intent. Unless the prosecutor comes forward with an explanation for his peremptories that is sufficient to rebut that prima facie case, no additional evidence of racial animus is required to establish an equal protection violation. In my opinion, the Court therefore errs when it concludes that a defendant's *Batson* challenge fails whenever the prosecutor advances a nonpretextual justification that is not facially discriminatory.

I

In *Batson* v. *Kentucky*, we held that "a 'pattern' of strikes against black jurors included in the particular venire might give rise to an inference of discrimination" sufficient to satisfy the defendant's burden of proving an equal protection violation. "Once the defendant makes a prima facie showing, the burden shifts to the State to come forward with a neutral explanation." If the prosecutor offers no explanation, the defendant has succeeded in establishing an equal protection violation based on the evidence of invidious intent that gave rise to the prima facie case. If the prosecutor seeks to dispel the inference of discriminatory intent, in order to succeed his explanation "need not rise to the level justifying exercise of a challenge for cause." However, the prosecutor's justification must identify " 'legitimate reasons' " that are "related to the particular case to be tried" and sufficiently persuasive to "rebu[t] a defendant's prima facie case."

An avowed justification that has a significant disproportionate impact will rarely qualify as a legitimate, race-neutral reason sufficient to rebut the prima facie case because disparate impact is itself evidence of discriminatory purpose. An explanation based on a concern that can easily be accomplished by means less drastic than excluding the challenged venireperson from the petit jury will also generally not qualify as a legitimate reason because it is not in fact "related to the particular case to be tried." And, as in any other equal protection challenge to a government classification, a justification that is frivolous or illegitimate should not suffice to rebut the prima facie case.

If any explanation, no matter how insubstantial and no matter how great its disparate impact, could rebut a prima facie inference of discrimination provided only that the explanation itself was not facially discriminatory, "the Equal Protection Clause 'would be but a vain and illusory requirement.' " The Court mistakenly believes that it is compelled to reach this result because an equal protection violation requires discriminatory purpose. The Court overlooks, however, the fact that the "discriminatory purpose" which characterizes violations of the Equal Protection Clause can sometimes be established by objective evidence that is consistent with a decisionmaker's honest belief that his motive was entirely benign. "Frequently the most probative evidence of intent will be objective evidence of what actually happened," including evidence of disparate impact. The line between discriminatory purpose and discriminatory impact is neither as bright nor as critical as the Court appears to believe.

The Court therefore errs in focusing the entire inquiry on the subjective state of mind of the prosecutor. In jury selection challenges, the requisite invidious intent is established once the defendant makes out a prima facie case. No additional evidence of this intent is necessary unless the explanation provided by the prosecutor is sufficiently powerful to rebut the prima facie proof of discriminatory purpose. By requiring that the prosecutor's explanation itself provide additional, direct evidence of discriminatory motive, the Court has imposed on the defendant the added requirement that he generate evidence of the prosecutor's actual subjective intent to discriminate. Neither *Batson* nor our other equal protection holdings demand such a heightened quantum of proof.

II

Applying the principles outlined above to the facts of this case, I would reject the prosecutor's explanation without reaching the question whether the explanation was pretextual. Neither the Court nor respondent disputes that petitioner made out a prima facie case. Even assuming the prosecutor's explanation in rebuttal was advanced in good faith, the justification proffered was insufficient to dispel the existing inference of racial animus. . . .

GEORGIA v. McCOLLUM
___ U.S. ___; ___ L. Ed. 2d. ___; 112 S. Ct. 2348 (1992)

JUSTICE BLACKMUN *delivered the opinion of the Court.*

For more than a century, this Court consistently and repeatedly has reaffirmed that racial discrimination by the State in jury selection offends the Equal Protection Clause. Last Term this Court held that racial discrimination in a civil litigant's exercise of peremptory challenges also violates the Equal Protection Clause. See *Edmundson* v. *Leesville Concrete Co.*, 500 U.S. ___, 111 S. Ct. 2077 (1991). Today, we are asked to decide whether the Constitution prohibits a *criminal defendant* from engaging in purposeful racial discrimination in the exercise of peremptory challenges.

I

On August 10, 1990, a grand jury sitting in Dougherty County, Ga., returned a six-count indictment charging respondents with aggravated assault and simple battery. The indictment alleged that respondents beat and assaulted Jerry and Myra Collins. Respondents are white; the alleged victims are African-Americans. Shortly after the events, a leaflet was widely distributed in the local African-American community reporting the assault and urging community residents not to patronize respondents' business.

Before jury selection began, the prosecution moved to prohibit respondents from exercising peremptory challenges in a racially discriminatory manner. The State explained that it expected to show that the victims' race was a factor in the alleged assault. According to the State, counsel for respondents had indicated a *clear* intention to use peremptory strikes in a racially discriminatory manner, arguing that the circumstances of their case gave them the right to exclude African-American citizens from participating as jurors in the trial. Observing that 43 percent of the county's population is African-American, the State contended that, if a statistically representative panel is assembled for jury selection, 18 of the potential 42 jurors would be African-American. With 20 peremptory challenges, respondents therefore would be able to remove all the African-American potential jurors.* Relying on *Batson* v. *Kentucky*, 476 U.S. 79 (1986), the Sixth Amendment, and the Georgia Constitution, the State sought an order providing that, if it succeeded in making out a prima facie case of racial discrimination by respondents, the latter would be required to articulate a racially neutral explanation for peremptory challenges.

The trial judge denied the State's motion, holding that "[n]either Georgia nor federal law prohibits criminal defendants from exercising peremptory strikes in a racially discriminatory manner." . . .

The Supreme Court of Georgia, by a 4–3 vote, affirmed the trial court's ruling.

We granted certiorari to resolve a question left open by our prior cases—whether the Constitution prohibits a criminal defendant from engaging in purposeful racial discrimination in the exercise of peremptory challenges.

*When the defendant is indicted for an offense carrying a penalty of four or more years, Georgia law provides that he may "peremptory challenge 20 of the jurors impaneled to try him." §15-12-165.

II

* * *

In deciding whether the Constitution prohibits criminal defendants from exercising racially discriminatory peremptory challenges, we must answer four questions. First, whether a criminal defendant's exercise of peremptory challenges in a racially discriminatory manner inflicts the harms addressed by *Batson.* Second, whether the exercise of peremptory challenges by a criminal defendant constitutes state action. Third, whether prosecutors have standing to raise this constitutional challenge. Fourth, whether the constitutional rights of a criminal defendant nonetheless preclude the extension of our precedents to this case.

III

A

The majority in *Powers* [v. *Ohio*, 111 S. Ct. 1364, 1991] recognized that "*Batson* 'was designed "to serve multiple ends," ' only one of which was to protect individual defendants from discrimination in the selection of jurors." . . . [T]he extension of *Batson* in this context is designed to remedy the harm done to the "dignity of persons" and to the "integrity of the Courts."

As long ago as *Strauder* [v. *West Virginia*, 100 U.S. 303, 1880], this Court recognized that denying a person participation in jury service on account of his race unconstitutionally discriminates against the excluded juror. While "[a]n individual juror does not have a right to sit on any particular petit jury, . . . he or she does possess the right not to be excluded from one on account of race." Regardless of who invokes the discriminatory challenge, there can be no doubt that the harm is the same—in all cases, the juror is subjected to open and public racial discrimination.

But "the harm from discriminatory jury selection extends beyond that inflicted on the defendant and the excluded juror to touch the entire community." One of the goals of our jury system is "to impress upon the criminal defendant and the community as a whole that a verdict of conviction or acquittal is given in accordance with the law by persons who are fair." Selection procedures that purposefully exclude African-Americans from juries undermine that public confidence—as well they should. "The overt wrong, often apparent to the entire jury panel, casts doubt over the obligation of the parties, the jury, and indeed the court to adhere to the law throughout the trial of the cause." *Powers* v. *Ohio*, 111 S. Ct. at 1371, 1991. . . .

The need for public confidence is especially high in cases involving race-related crimes. In such cases, emotions in the affected community will inevitably be heated and volatile. Public confidence in the integrity of the criminal justice system is essential for preserving community peace in trials involving race-related crimes. . . .

Be it at the hands of the State or the defense, if a court allows jurors to be excluded because of a group bias, it is a willing participant in a scheme that could only undermine the very foundation of our system of justice—our citizens' confidence in it. Just as public confidence in criminal justice is undermined by a conviction in a trial where racial discrimination has occurred in jury selection, so is public confidence undermined where a defendant, assisted by racially discriminatory peremptory strikes, obtains an acquittal.

B

The fact that a defendant's use of discriminatory peremptory challenges harms the jurors and the community does not end our equal protection inquiry. Racial discrimination, although repugnant in all contexts, violates the Constitution only when it is attributable to state action. Thus, the second question that must be answered is whether a criminal defendant's exercise of a peremptory challenge constitutes state action for purposes of the Equal Protection Clause.

Until *Edmonson*, the cases decided by this Court that presented the problem of racially discriminatory peremptory challenges involved assertions of discrimination by a prosecutor, a quintessential state actor. In *Edmonson*, by contrast, the contested peremptory challenges were exercised by a private defendant in a civil action. In order to determine whether state action was present in that setting, the Court in *Edmonson* used the analytical framework summarized in *Lugar* v. *Edmonson Oil Co.*, 457 U.S. 922 (1982).**

The first inquiry is "whether the claimed [constitutional] deprivation has resulted from the exercise of a right or privilege having its source in state authority." *Id.*, at 939, 102 S. Ct., at 2755. "There can be no question" that peremptory challenges

satisfy this first requirement, as they "are permitted only when the government, by statute or decisional law, deems it appropriate to allow parties to exclude a given number of persons who otherwise would satisfy the requirements for service on the petit jury." As in *Edmonson*, a Georgia defendant's right to exercise peremptory challenges and the scope of that right are established by a provision of state law.

The second inquiry is whether the private party charged with the deprivation can be described as a state actor. In resolving that issue, the Court in *Edmonson* found it useful to apply three principles: 1) "the extent to which the actor relies on governmental assistance and benefits"; 2) "whether the actor is performing a traditional governmental function"; 3) "whether the injury caused is aggravated in a unique way by the incidents of governmental authority."

As to the first principle, the *Edmonson* Court found that the peremptory challenge system, as well as the jury system as a whole, "simply could not exist" without the "overt and significant participation of the government." . . .

In light of [the state's] procedures, the defendant in a Georgia criminal case relies on "governmental assistance and benefits" that are equivalent to those found in the civil context in *Edmonson*. "By enforcing a discriminatory peremptory challenge, the Court 'has . . . elected to place its power, property and prestige behind the [alleged] discrimination.' "

In regard to the second principle, the Court in *Edmonson* found that peremptory challenges perform a traditional function of government: "Their sole purpose is to permit litigants to assist the government in the selection of an impartial trier of fact." And, as the *Edmonson* Court recognized, the jury system in turn "performs the critical governmental functions of guarding the rights of litigants and 'insur[ing] continued acceptance of the laws by all of the people.' " These same conclusions apply with even greater force in the criminal context because the selection of a jury in a criminal case fulfills a unique and constitutionally compelled governmental function. . . .

Finally, the *Edmonson* Court indicated that the courtroom setting in which the peremptory challenge is exercised intensifies the harmful effects of the private litigant's discriminatory act and contributes to its characterization as state action. These concerns are equally present in the context of a criminal trial. Regardless of who precipitated the jurors' removal, the perception and the reality in a criminal trial will be that the court has ex-

---

**The Court in *Lugar* held that a private litigant is appropriately characterized as a state actor when he "jointly participates" with state officials in securing the seizure of property in which the private party claims to have rights. 457 U.S., at 932–933, 941–942.

cused jurors based on race, an outcome that will be attributed to the State. . . .

The exercise of a peremptory challenge differs significantly from other actions taken in support of a defendant's defense. In exercising a peremptory challenge, a criminal defendant is wielding the power to choose a quintessential governmental body—indeed, the institution of government on which our judicial system depends. Thus, as we held in *Edmonson*, when "a government confers on a private body the power to choose the government's employees or officials, the private body will be bound by the constitutional mandate of race neutrality."

Lastly, the fact that a defendant exercises a peremptory challenge to further his interest in acquittal does not conflict with a finding of state action. Whenever a private actor's conduct is deemed "fairly attributable" to the government, it is likely that private motives will have animated the actor's decision. Indeed, in *Edmonson*, the Court recognized that the private party's exercise of peremptory challenges constituted state action, even though the motive underlying the exercise of the peremptory challenge may be to protect a private interest. . . .

* * *

D

The final question is whether the interests served by *Batson* must give way to the rights of a criminal defendant. As a preliminary matter, it is important to recall that peremptory challenges are not constitutionally protected fundamental rights; rather, they are but one state-created means to the constitutional end of an impartial jury and a fair trial. This Court repeatedly has stated that the right to a peremptory challenge may be withheld altogether without impairing the constitutional guarantee of an impartial jury and a fair trial. . . .

We do not believe that this decision will undermine the contribution of the peremptory challenge to the administration of justice. Nonetheless, "if race stereotypes are the price for acceptance of a jury panel as fair," we reaffirm today that such a "price is too high to meet the standard of the Constitution." Defense counsel is limited to "legitimate, lawful conduct." . . . It is an affront to justice to argue that a fair trial includes the right to discriminate against a group of citizens based upon their race.

Nor does a prohibition of the exercise of discriminatory peremptory challenges violate a defendant's Sixth Amendment right to the effective assistance of counsel. Counsel can ordinarily explain the reasons for peremptory challenges without revealing anything about trial strategy or any confidential client communications. In the rare case in which the explanation for a challenge would entail confidential communications or reveal trial strategy, an *in camera* discussion can be arranged. . . . In any event, neither the Sixth Amendment right nor the attorney-client privilege gives a criminal defendant the right to carry out through counsel an unlawful course of conduct. . . .

Lastly, a prohibition of the discriminatory exercise of peremptory challenges does not violate a defendant's Sixth Amendment right to a trial by an impartial jury. The goal of the Sixth Amendment is "jury impartiality with respect to both contestants."

We recognize, of course, that a defendant has the right to an impartial jury that can view him without racial animus, which so long has distorted our system of criminal justice. We have, accordingly, held that there should be a mechanism for removing those on the venire whom the defendant has specific reason to believe would be incapable of confronting and suppressing their racism. . . .

But there is a distinction between exercising a peremptory challenge to discriminate invidiously against jurors on account of race and exercising a peremptory challenge to remove an individual juror who harbors racial prejudice. This Court firmly has rejected the view that assumptions of partiality based on race provide a legitimate basis for disqualifying a person as an impartial juror. . . . "In our heterogenous society policy as well as constitutional considerations militate against the divisive assumption—as a *per se* rule—that justice in a court of law may turn upon the pigmentation of skin, the accident of birth, or the choice of religion." *Ristaino* v. *Ross*, 424 U.S. 589, 596, n. 8 (1976). We therefore reaffirm today that the exercise of a peremptory challenge must not be based on either the race of the juror or the racial stereotypes held by the party.

IV

We hold that the Constitution prohibits a criminal defendant from engaging in purposeful discrimination in the ground of race in the exercise of peremptory challenges. Accordingly, if the State demonstrates a prima facie case of racial discrimination by the defendants, the defendants must articulate a racially neutral explanation for peremptory challenges. The judgment of the Supreme Court of Georgia is reversed and the case is remanded for further proceedings not inconsistent with this opinion.

It is so ordered.

[The concurring opinion of CHIEF JUSTICE REHNQUIST is not reprinted here.]

JUSTICE THOMAS, *concurring in the judgment.*

* * *

I write separately to express my general dissatisfaction with our continuing attempts to use the Constitution to regulate peremptory challenges. In my view, by restricting a criminal defendant's use of such challenges, this case takes us further from the reasoning and the result of *Strauder* v. *West Virginia*, 100 U.S. 303 (1880). I doubt that this departure will produce favorable consequences. On the contrary, I am certain that black criminal defendants will rue the day that this court ventured down this road that inexorably will lead to the elimination of peremptory strikes.

In *Strauder* . . . we observed that the racial composition of a jury may affect the outcome of a criminal case. We explained: "It is well known that prejudices often exist against particular classes in the community, which sway the judgment of jurors, and which, therefore, operate in some cases to deny to persons of those classes the full enjoyment of that protection which others enjoy." We thus recognized, over a century ago, the precise point that JUSTICE O'CONNOR makes today. Simply stated, securing representation of the defendant's race on the jury may help to overcome racial bias and provide the defendant with a better chance of having a fair trial.

I do not think this basic premise of *Strauder* has become obsolete. The public, in general, continues to believe that the makeup of juries can matter in certain instances. Consider, for example, how the press reports criminal trials. Major newspapers regularly note the number of whites and blacks that sit on juries in important cases. Their editors and readers apparently recognize that conscious and unconscious prejudice persists in our society and that it may influence some juries. Common experience and common sense confirm this understanding.

In *Batson*, however, this Court began to depart from *Strauder* by holding that, without some actual showing, suppositions about the possibility that jurors may harbor prejudice have no legitimacy. We said, in particular, that a prosecutor could not justify peremptory strikes "by stating merely that he challenged jurors of the defendant's race on the

assumption—or his intutive judgment—that they would be partial to the defendant because of their shared race." As noted, however, our decision in *Strauder* rested on precisely such an "assumption" or "intuition." We reasonably surmised, without direct evidence in any particular case, that all-white juries might judge black defendants unfairly.

Our departure from *Strauder* has two negative consequences. First, it produces a serious misordering of our priorities. In *Strauder*, we put the rights of defendants foremost. Today's decision, while protecting jurors, leaves defendants with less means of protecting themselves. Unless jurors actually admit prejudice during *voir dire*, defendants generally must allow them to sit and run the risk that racial animus will affect the verdict. . . . In effect, we have exalted the right of citizens to sit on juries over the rights of the criminal defendant, even though it is the defendant, not the jurors, who faces imprisonment or even death. At a minimum, I think that this inversion of priorities should give us pause.

Second, our departure from *Strauder* has taken us down a slope of inquiry that had no clear stopping point. Today, we decide only that white defendants may not strike black veniremen on the basis of race. Eventually, we will have to decide whether black defendants may strike white veniremen. Next will come the question whether defendants may exercise peremptories on the basis of sex. The consequences for defendants of our decision and of these future cases remain to be seen. But whatever the benefits were that this Court perceived in a criminal defendant's having members of his class on the jury, they have evaporated.

JUSTICE O'CONNOR, *dissenting.*

The Court reaches the remarkable conclusion that criminal defendants being prosecuted by the State act on behalf of their adversary when they exercise peremptory challenges during jury selection. The Court purports merely to follow precedents, but our cases do not compel this perverse result. To the contrary, our decisions specifically establish that criminal defendants and the lawyers are not government actors when they perform traditional trial functions.

I

It is well and properly settled that the Constitution's equal protection guarantee forbids prosecutors from exercising peremptory challenges in a racially discriminatory fashion. The Constitution, however, affords no similar protection against private action. "Embedded in our Fourteenth Amendment jurisprudence is a dichotomy between state action, which is subject to scrutiny under the Amendmen[t] . . . , and private conduct, against which the Amendment affords no shield, no matter how unfair that conduct may be." . . . The critical but straightforward question this case presents is whether criminal defendants and their lawyers, when exercising peremptory challenges as part of a defense, are state actors.

The Court's determination in this case that the peremptory challenge is a creation of state authority breaks no new ground. But disposing of this threshold matter leaves the Court with the task of showing that criminal defendants who exercise peremptories should be deemed governmental actors. What our cases require, and what the Court neglects, is a realistic appraisal of the relationship between defendants and the government that has brought them to trial.

We discussed that relationship in *Polk County* v. *Dodson*, 454 U.S. 312 (1981), which held that a public defender does not act "under color of state law" for purposes of 42 U.S.C. § 1983 "when performing a lawyer's traditional functions as counsel to a defendant in a criminal proceeding." We began our analysis by explaining that a public defender's obligations toward her client are no different than the obligations of any other defense attorney. These obligations preclude attributing the acts of defense lawyers to the State: "[T]he duties of a defense lawyer are those of a personal counselor and advocate. It is often said that lawyers are 'officers of the court.' But the Courts of Appeals are agreed that a lawyer representing a client is not, by virtue of being an officer of the court, a state actor. . . ."

We went on to stress the inconsistency between our adversarial system of justice and theories that would make defense lawyers state actors. "In our system," we said, "a defense lawyer characteristically opposes the designated representatives of the State." This adversarial posture rests on the assumption that a defense lawyer best serves the public "not by acting on behalf of the State or in concert with it, but rather by advancing 'the undivided interests of his client.' " Moreover, we pointed out that the independence of defense attorneys from state control has a constitutional dimension. . . . [T]he defense's freedom from state authority is not just empirically true, but is a constitutionally mandated attribute of our adversarial system.

Because the Court deems the "under color of state law" requirement that was not satisfied in *Dodson* identical to the Fourteenth Amendment's state action requirement, the holding of *Dodson* simply cannot be squared with today's decision. In particular, *Dodson* cannot be explained away as a case concerned exclusively with the employment status of public defenders. The *Dodson* Court reasoned that public defenders performing traditional defense functions are not state actors because they occupy the same position as other defense attorneys in relevant respects. This reasoning followed on the heels of a critical determination: defending an accused "is essentially a private function," not state action. The Court's refusal to acknowledge *Dodson*'s initial holding, on which the entire opinion turned, will not make that holding go away. . . .

From arrest, to trial, to possible sentencing and punishment, the antagonistic relationship between government and the accused is clear for all to see. Rather than squarely facing this fact, the Court . . . rests its finding of governmental action on the points that defendants exercise peremptory challenges in a courtroom and judges alter the composition of the jury in response to defendants' choices. I found this approach wanting in the context of civil controversies between private litigants, for reasons that need not be repeated here. But even if I thought *Edmonson* was correctly decided, I could not accept today's simplistic extension of it. *Dodson* makes clear that the unique relationship between criminal defendants and the State precludes attributing defendants' actions to the State, whatever is the case in civil trials. How could it be otherwise when the underlying question is whether the accused "c[an] be described in all fairness as a state actor?" As *Dodson* accords with our state action jurisprudence and with common sense, I would honor it.

What really seems to bother the Court is the prospect that leaving criminal defendants and their attorneys free to make racially motivated challenges will undermine the ideal of nondiscriminatory jury selection we espoused in *Batson*. The concept that the government alone must honor constitutional dictates, however, is a fundamental tenet of our legal order, not an obstacle to be circumvented. . . .

Considered in purely pragmatic terms, moreover, the Court's holding may fail to advance nondiscriminatory criminal justice. It is by now clear that conscious and unconscious racism can affect the way white jurors perceive minority defendants and the facts presented at their trials, perhaps determining the verdict of guilt or innocence. . . . Using peremptory challenges to secure minority representation on the jury may help to overcome such racial bias, for there is substantial reason to believe that the distorting influence of race is minimized on a racially mixed jury. As *amicus* NAACP Legal Defense and Educational Fund explained in this case:

> The ability to use peremptory challenges to exclude majority race jurors may be crucial to empaneling a fair jury. In many cases an African American, or other minority defendant, may be faced with a jury array in which his racial group is underrepresented to some degree, but not sufficiently to permit challenge under the Fourteenth Amendment. The only possible chance the defendant may have of having any minority jurors on the jury that actually tries him will be if he uses peremptories to strike members of the majority race. . . .

In a world where the outcome of a minority defendant's trial may turn on the misconceptions or biases of white jurors, there is cause to question the implications of this Court's good intentions.

That the Constitution does not give federal judges the reach to wipe all the marks of racism from every courtroom in the land is frustrating, to be sure. But such limitations are the necessary and intended consequence of the Fourteenth Amendment's state action requirement. Because I cannot accept the Court's conclusion that government is responsible for decisions criminal defendants make while fighting state prosecution, I respectfully dissent.

Other Constitutional Guarantees in the Criminal Process: Bail and Preventive Detention

---

FEATURED CASE
United States v. *Salerno*

The Eighth Amendment underscores the cardinal principle that innocence is presumed until guilt has been proved in the language that prohibits the imposition of "excessive bail." Although not expressly guaranteed as a substantive right in the Amendment, its availability is a matter of legislative policy and/or state constitutional mandate. As this policy has been applied in specific criminal prosecutions, the Supreme Court has most frequently been called upon to determine the "excessive" dimension of bail. On that question, the most notable pronouncement was set forth in *Stack* v. *Boyle* (342 U.S. 1, 1951), in its review of the $50,000 bail fixed for a number of so-called second-string Communist leaders who were accused of violating provisions of the Smith Act. Taking judicial notice of the historical purpose of bail that the accused will be present at trial, Chief Justice Fred Vinson emphasized that when bail is fixed at an amount in excess of that which is "reasonably calculated" to achieve that purpose, it is "excessive." He concluded that "[t]o infer from the fact of indictment alone a need for bail in an unusually high amount is an arbitrary act . . . [that] would inject into our own system of government the very principles of totalitarianism which Congress was seeking to guard against in passing the [Smith Act]."

When and under what conditions bail should be denied are central questions addressed in the so-called preventive detention statutes. In 1984 the Court considered the issue in the context of a juvenile criminal action in *Schall* v. *Martin* (467 U.S. 753, 1984) and concluded that the state's interest in using preventive detention, or "P. D.," for protection of both the juvenile and society was sufficient to withstand a due process challenge. A more comprehensive inquiry of "P. D." was undertaken by the Court in an adult criminal context in *United States* v. *Salerno* (107 S. Ct. 2095) in 1987. There it considered and rejected a facial constitutional challenge to the preventive detention provision of the Bail Reform Act of 1984. Under the statute's provisions, detention is imposed on those accused of specified serious felonies when the prosecution "demonstrates with clear and convincing evidence" that release of the accused on bail would pose a threat to the community and other persons. Taking notice of the required procedural safeguards available to the accused in an adversary judicial proceeding, the Court stressed the need for judicial deference to legislative regulatory power for the remediation of increasing criminal activity of persons free on bail pending trial. Consequently, the detention policy prescribed in the Bail Reform Act is a *regulatory* measure, not *penal*, and outweighs the individual liberty interest advanced.

UNITED STATES v. SALERNO
481 U.S. 738; 95 L. Ed. 2d 697; 107 S. Ct. 2095 (1987)

CHIEF JUSTICE REHNQUIST *delivered the opinion of the Court.*

The Bail Reform Act of 1984 allows a federal court to detain an arrestee pending trial if the Government demonstrates, by clear and convincing evidence after an adversary hearing, that no release conditions "will reasonably assure . . . the safety of any other person and the community." The United States Court of Appeals for the Second Circuit struck down this provision of the Act [holding that] . . . this type of pretrial detention violates "substantive due process." We granted certiorari because of a conflict among the Courts of Appeals regarding the validity of the Act. We hold that, as against the facial attack mounted by these respondents, the Act fully comports with constitutional requirements. We therefore reverse.

I

Responding to "the alarming problem of crimes committed by persons on release," . . . Congress formulated the Bail Reform Act as the solution to a bail crisis in the federal courts. The Act represents the National Legislature's considered response to numerous perceived deficiencies in the federal bail process. By providing for sweeping changes in both the way federal courts consider bail applications and the circumstances under which bail is granted, Congress hoped to "give the courts adequate authority to make release decisions that give appropriate recognition to the danger a person may pose to others if released."

To this end . . . the Act requires a judicial officer to determine whether an arrestee shall be detained. Section 3142(e) provides that "[i]f, after a hearing pursuant to the provisions of subsection (f), the judicial officer finds that no condition or combination of conditions will reasonably assure the appearance of the person as required and the safety of any other person and the community, he shall order the detention of the person prior to trial." Section 3142(f) provides the arrestee with a number of procedural safeguards. "He may request the presence of counsel at the detention hearing, he may testify and present witnesses in his behalf, as well as proffer evidence, and he may cross-examine other witnesses appearing at the hearing. If the judicial officer finds that no condi-

tions of pretrial release can reasonably assure the safety of other persons and the community, he must state his findings of fact in writing, . . . and support his conclusion with clear and convincing evidence." . . .

The judicial officer is not given unbridled discretion in making the detention determination. Congress has specified the considerations relevant to that decision. These factors include the nature and seriousness of the charges, the substantiality of the Government's evidence against the arrestee, the arrestee's background and characteristics, and the nature and seriousness of the danger posed by the suspect's release. Should a judicial officer order detention, the detainee is entitled to expedited appellate review of the detention order.

Respondents Anthony Salerno and Vincent Cafaro were arrested on March 21, 1986, after being charged in a 29-count indictment alleging various Racketeer Influenced and Corrupt Organizations Act (RICO) violations, mail and wire fraud offenses, extortion, and various criminal gambling violations. The RICO counts alleged 35 acts of racketeering activity, including fraud, extortion, gambling, and conspiracy to commit murder. At respondents' arraignment, the Government moved to have Salerno and Cafaro detained . . . on the ground that no condition of release would assure the safety of the community or any person. The District Court held a hearing at which the Government made a detailed proffer of evidence. The Government's case showed that Salerno was the "boss" of the Genovese Crime Family of La Cosa Nostra and that Cafaro was a "captain" in the Genovese Family. According to the Government's proffer, based in large part on conversations intercepted by a court-ordered wiretap, the two respondents had participated in wide-ranging conspiracies to aid their illegitimate enterprises through violent means. The Government also offered the testimony of two of its trial witnesses, who would assert that Salerno personally participated in two murder conspiracies. Salerno opposed the motion for detention, challenging the credibility of the Government's witnesses. He offered the testimony of several character witnesses as well as a letter from his doctor stating that he was suffering from a serious medical condition. Cafaro presented no evidence at the hearing, but instead characterized the wiretap conversations as merely "tough talk."

The District Court granted the Government's detention motion, concluding that the Government had established by clear and convincing evidence that no condition or combination of conditions of release would ensure the safety of the community or any person. . . .

Respondents appealed, contending that to the extent that the Bail Reform Act permits pretrial detention on the ground that the arrestee is likely to commit future crimes, it is unconstitutional on its face. Over a dissent, the United States Court of Appeals for the Second Circuit agreed. Although the court agreed that pretrial detention could be imposed if the defendants were likely to intimidate witnesses or otherwise jeopardize the trial process, it found "[the Act's] authorization of pretrial detention [on the ground of future dangerousness] repugnant to the concept of substantive due process, which we believe prohibits the total deprivation of liberty simply as a means of preventing future crimes." The court concluded that the Government could not, consistent with due process, detain persons who had not been accused of any crime merely because they were thought to present a danger to the community. It reasoned that our criminal law system holds persons accountable for past actions, not anticipated future actions. Although a court could detain an arrestee who threatened to flee before trial, such detention would be permissible because it would serve the basic objective of the criminal system—bringing the accused to trial. . . . The Court of Appeals . . . found our decision in *Schall* v. *Martin*, upholding postarrest pretrial detention of juveniles, inapposite because juveniles have a lesser interest in liberty than do adults. The dissenting judge concluded that on its face, the Bail Reform Act adequately balanced the Federal Government's compelling interest in public safety against the detainee's liberty interests.

II

A facial challenge to a legislative Act is . . . the most difficult challenge to mount successfully, since the challenger must establish that no set of circumstances exists under which the Act would be valid. The fact that the Bail Reform Act might operate unconstitutionally under some conceivable set of circumstances is insufficient to render it wholly invalid, since we have not recognized an "overbreadth" doctrine outside the limited context of the First Amendment. We think respondents have failed to shoulder their heavy burden to demonstrate that the Act is "facially" unconstitutional.

Respondents present two grounds for invalidating the Bail Reform Act's provision permitting pretrial detention on the basis of future dangerousness. First, they rely upon the Court of Appeals' conclusion that the Act exceeds the limitations placed upon the Federal Government by the Due Process Clause of the Fifth Amendment. Second, they contend that the Act contravenes the Eighth Amendment's proscription against excessive bail. We treat these contentions in turn.

A

. . . This Court has held that the Due Process Clause protects individuals against two types of government action. So-called "substantive due process" prevents the Government from engaging in conduct that "shocks the conscience" or interferes with rights "implicit in the concept of ordered liberty." When government action depriving a person of life, liberty, or property survives substantive due process scrutiny, it must still be implemented in a fair manner. This requirement has traditionally been referred to as "procedural" due process.

Respondents first argue that the Act violates substantive due process because the pretrial detention it authorizes constitutes impermissible punishment before trial. The Government, however, has never argued that pretrial detention could be upheld if it were "punishment." The Court of Appeals assumed that pretrial detention under the Bail Reform Act is regulatory, not penal, and we agree that it is.

As an initial matter, the mere fact that a person is detained does not inexorably lead to the conclusion that the Government has imposed punishment. To determine whether a restriction on liberty constitutes impermissible punishment or permissible regulation, we first look to legislative intent. Unless Congress expressly intended to impose punitive restrictions, the punitive/regulatory distinction turns on "whether an alternative purpose to which [the restriction] may rationally be connected is assignable for it, and whether it appears excessive in relation to the alternative purpose assigned [to it]."

We conclude that the detention imposed by the Act falls on the regulatory side of the dichotomy. The legislative history of the Bail Reform Act clearly indicates that Congress did not formulate the pretrial detention provisions as punishment for dangerous individuals. Congress instead perceived pretrial detention as a potential solution to a pressing societal problem. There is no doubt that preventing danger to the community is a legitimate regulatory goal.

Nor are the incidents of pretrial detention excessive in relation to the regulatory goal Congress sought to achieve. The Bail Reform Act carefully limits the circumstances under which detention may be sought to the most serious of crimes. . . . The arrestee is entitled to a prompt detention hearing, and the maximum length of pretrial detention is limited by the stringent time limitations of the Speedy Trial Act. Moreover, as in *Schall* v. *Martin*, the conditions of confinement envisioned by the Act "appear to reflect the regulatory purposes relied upon by the" Government. . . . We conclude, therefore, that the pretrial detention contemplated by the Bail Reform Act is regulatory in nature and does not constitute punishment before trial in violation of the Due Process Clause.

. . . Respondents characterize the Due Process Clause as erecting an impenetrable "wall" in this area that "no governmental interest—rational, important, compelling or otherwise—may surmount."

We do not think the Clause lays down any such categorical imperative. We have repeatedly held that the Government's regulatory interest in community safety can, in appropriate circumstances, outweigh an individual's liberty interest. For example, in times of war or insurrection, when society's interest is at its peak, the Government may detain individuals whom the Government believes to be dangerous. . . . Even outside the exigencies of war, we have found that sufficiently compelling governmental interests can justify detention of dangerous persons. Thus, we have found no absolute constitutional barrier to detention of potentially dangerous resident aliens pending deportation proceedings. . . . We have also held that Government may detain mentally unstable individuals who present a danger to the public, and dangerous defendants who become incompetent to stand trial. We have approved of postarrest regulatory detention of juveniles when they present a continuing danger to the community. Even competent adults may face substantial liberty restrictions as a result of the operation of our criminal justice system. If the police suspect an individual of a crime, they may arrest and hold him until a neutral magistrate determines whether probable cause exists. Finally, respondents concede and the Court of Appeals noted that an arrestee may be incarcerated until trial if he presents a risk of flight, or a danger to witnesses. . . .

The Government's interest in preventing crime by arrestees is both legitimate and compelling. . . . The Bail Reform Act . . . narrowly focuses on a particularly acute problem in which the Government interests are overwhelming. The Act operates only on individuals who have been arrested for a specific category of extreme serious offenses. Congress specifically found that these individuals are far more likely to be responsible for dangerous acts in the community after arrest. Nor is the Act by any means a scattershot attempt to incapacitate those who are merely suspected of these serious crimes. The Government must first of all demonstrate probable cause to believe that the charged crime has been committed by the arrestee, but that is not enough. In a full-blown adversary hearing, the Government must convince a neutral decision maker by clear and convincing evidence that no conditions of release can reasonably assure the safety of the community or any person. While the Government's general interest in preventing crime is compelling, even this interest is heightened when the Government musters convincing proof that the arrestee, already indicted or held to answer for a serious crime, presents a demonstrable danger to the community. Under these narrow circumstances, society's interest in crime prevention is at its greatest.

On the other side of the scale, of course, is the individual's strong interest in liberty. We do not minimize the importance and fundamental nature of this right. But, as our cases hold, this right may, in circumstances where the Government's interest is sufficiently weighty, be subordinated to the greater needs of society. We think that Congress's careful delineation of the circumstances under which detention will be permitted satisfied this standard. When the Government proves by clear and convincing evidence that an arrestee presents an identified and articulable threat to an individual or the community, we believe that, consistent with the Due Process Clause, a court may disable the arrestee from executing that threat. Under these circumstances, we cannot categorically state that pretrial detention "offends some principle of justice so rooted in the traditions and conscience of our people as to be ranked as fundamental."

Finally, we may dispose briefly of respondents' facial challenge to the procedures of the Bail Reform Act. To sustain them against such a challenge, we need only find them "adequate to authorize the pretrial detention of at least some [persons] charged with crimes," whether or not they might be insufficient in some particular circumstances. We think they pass that test. . . .

We think . . . extensive safeguards suffice to repel a facial challenge. The protections are more exacting than those we found sufficient in the juvenile context, and they far exceed what we found necessary to effect limited postarrest detention. . . . Given the legitimate and compelling regulatory purpose of the Act and procedural protections it offers, we conclude that the act is not facially invalid under the Due Process Clause of the Fifth Amendment.

B

Respondents also contend that the Bail Reform Act violates the Excessive Bail Clause of the Eighth Amendment. . . . We think that the Act survives a challenge founded upon the Eighth Amendment.

The Eighth Amendment addresses pretrial release by providing merely that "[e]xcessive bail shall not be required." . . . Respondents . . . contend that this Clause grants them right to bail calculated solely upon considerations of flight. They rely on *Stack* v. *Boyle*, in which the Court stated that "[b]ail set at figure higher than an amount reasonably calculated [to ensure the defendant's presence at trial] is 'excessive' under the Eighth Amendment." In respondents' view, since the Bail Reform Act allows a court essentially to set bail at an infinite amount for reasons not related to the risk of flight, it violates the Excessive Bail Clause. Respondents concede that the right to bail they have discovered in the Eighth Amendment is not absolute. A court may, for example, refuse bail in capital cases. And, as the Court of Appeals noted and respondents admit, a court may refuse bail when the defendant presents a threat to the judicial process by intimidating witnesses. Respondents characterize these exceptions as consistent with what they claim to be the sole purpose of bail—to ensure integrity of the judicial process.

While we agree that a primary function of bail is to safeguard the courts' role in adjudicating the guilt or innocence of defendants, we reject the proposition that the Eighth Amendment categorically prohibits the Government from pursuing other admittedly compelling interests through regulation of pretrial release. . . .

III

In our society liberty is the norm, and detention prior to trial or without trial is the carefully limited exception. We hold that the provisions for pretrial detention in the Bail Reform Act of 1984 fall within that carefully limited exception. The Act authorizes the detention prior to trial of arrestees charged with serious felonies who are found after an adversary hearing to pose a threat to the safety of individuals or to the community which no condition of release can dispel. . . . We are unwilling to say that this Congressional determination, based as it is upon that primary concern of every Government—a concern for the safety and indeed the lives of its citizens—on its face violates either the Due Process Clause of the Fifth Amendment or the Excessive Bail Clause of the Eighth Amendment.

The judgment of the Court of Appeals is therefore

Reversed.

JUSTICE MARSHALL, *with whom* JUSTICE BRENNAN *joins, dissenting.*

This case brings before the Court for the first time a statute in which Congress declares that a person innocent of any crime may be jailed indefinitely, pending the trial of allegations which are legally presumed to be untrue, if the Government shows to the satisfaction of a judge that the accused is likely to commit crimes, unrelated to the pending charges, at any time in the future. Such statutes, consistent with the usages of tyranny and the excesses of what bitter experience teaches us to call the police state, have long been thought incompatible with the fundamental human rights protected by our Constitution. Today a majority of this Court holds otherwise. Its decision disregards basic principles of justice established centuries ago and enshrined beyond the reach of governmental interference in the Bill of Rights. . . .

III

The essence of this case may be found, ironically enough, in a provision of the Act to which the majority does not refer. . . . [It] provides that "[n]othing in this section shall be construed as modifying or limiting the presumption of innocence." But the very pith and purpose of this statute is an abhorrent limitation of the presumption of innocence. The majority's untenable conclusion that the present Act is constitutional arises from a specious denial of the role of the Bail Clause and the Due Process Clause in protecting the invaluable guarantee afforded by the presumption of innocence.

"The principle that there is a presumption of innocence in favor of the accused is the undoubted law, axiomatic and elementary, and its enforcement lies at the foundation of the administration of our criminal law." Our society's belief, reinforced over the centuries, that all are innocent until the State has proved them to be guilty, like the companion principle that guilt must be proved beyond a reasonable doubt, is "implicit in the concept of ordered liberty" and is established beyond legislative contravention in the Due Process Clause.

The statute now before us declares that persons who have been indicted may be detained if a judicial officer finds clear and convincing evidence that they pose a danger to individuals or to the community. The statute does not authorize the Government to imprison anyone it has evidence is dangerous; indictment is necessary. But let us suppose that a defendant is indicted and the Government shows by clear and convincing evidence that he is dangerous and should be detained pending a trial, at which trial the defendant is acquitted. May the Government continue to hold the defendant in detention based upon its showing that he is dangerous? The answer cannot be yes, for that would allow the Government to imprison someone for uncommitted crimes based upon "proof" not beyond a reasonable doubt. The result must therefore be that once the indictment has failed, detention cannot continue. But our fundamental principles of justice declare that the defendant is as innocent on the day before his trial as he is on the morning after his acquittal. Under this statute an untried indictment somehow acts to permit a detention, based on other charges, which after an acquittal would be unconstitutional. The conclusion is inescapable that the indictment has been turned into evidence, if not that the defendant is guilty of the crime charged, then that left to his own devices he will soon be guilty of something else. "If it suffices to accuse, what will become of the innocent?" *Coffin* v. *United States*, 156 U.S., at 455 (quoting Ammianus Marcellinus, *Rerum Gestarum Libri ui Supersunt*, L. XVIII, c.1, A.D. 359.). . . .

To be sure, an indictment is not without legal consequences. It establishes that there is probable cause to believe that an offense was committed, and that the defendant committed it. Upon probable cause a warrant for the defendant's arrest may issue; a period of administrative detention may occur before the evidence of probable cause is presented to a neutral magistrate. . . . The finding of probable cause conveys power to try, and the power to try imports of necessity the power to assure that the processes of justice will not be evaded or obstructed. "Pretrial detention to prevent future crimes against society at large, however, is not justified by any concern for holding a trial on the charges for which a defendant has been arrested." The detention purportedly authorized by this statute bears no relation to the Government's power to try charges supported by a finding of probable cause, and thus the interests it serves are outside the scope of interests which may be considered in weighing the excessiveness of bail under the Eighth Amendment.

It is not a novel proposition that the Bail Clause plays a vital role in protecting the presumption of innocence. Reviewing the application of bail pending appeal by members of the American Communist Party convicted under the Smith Act, Justice Jackson wrote:

> Grave public danger is said to result from what [the defendants] may be expected to do, in addition to what they have done since their conviction. If I assume that defendants are disposed to commit every opportune disloyal act helpful to Communist countries, it is still difficult to reconcile with traditional American law the jailing of persons by the courts because of anticipated but as yet uncommitted crimes. Imprisonment to protect society from predicted but unconsummated offenses is . . . unprecedented in this country and . . . fraught with danger of excesses and injustice. . . . Williamson v. United States, 95 L.Ed 1379, 1382 (1950).

As Chief Justice Vinson wrote for the Court in *Stack* v. *Boyle*, "Unless th[e] right to bail before trial is preserved, the presumption of innocence, secured only after centuries of struggle, would lose its meaning."

IV

There is a connection between the peculiar facts of this case and the evident constitutional defects in the statute which the Court upholds today. Respondent Cafaro was originally incarcerated for an indeterminate period at the request of the Government, which believed (or professed to believe) that his release imminently threatened the safety of the community. That threat apparently vanished, from the Government's point of view, when Cafaro agreed to act as a covert agent of the Government. There could be no more eloquent demonstration of the coercive power of authority to imprison upon prediction, or of the dangers which the almost inevitable abuses pose to the cherished liberties of a free society.

"It is a fair summary of history to say that the safeguards of liberty have frequently been forged in controversies involving not very nice people." *United States* v. *Rabinowitz*, 339 U.S. 56, 69 (1950) (Frankfurter, J., dissenting). Honoring the presumption of innocence is often difficult; sometimes we must pay substantial social costs as a result of our commitment to the values we espouse. But at the end of the day, the presumption of innocence protects the innocent; the shortcuts we take with those whom we believe to be guilty injure only those wrongfully accused and, ultimately, ourselves.

Throughout the world today there are men, women, and children interned indefinitely, awaiting trials which may never come or which may be a mockery of the word, because their governments believe them to be "dangerous." Our Constitution, whose construction began two centuries ago, can shelter us forever from the evils of such unchecked power. Over two hundred years it has slowly, throughout efforts, grown more durable, more expansive, and more just. But it cannot protect us if we lack the courage, and the self-restraint, to protect ourselves. Today a majority of the Court applies itself to an ominous exercise in demolition. Theirs is truly a decision which will go forth without authority, and come back without respect.

I dissent.

[The dissenting opinion of JUSTICE STEVENS is not reprinted here.]

Other Constitutional Guarantees in the Criminal Process: Confrontation and Cross-Examination

---

FEATURED CASE
Coy v. *Iowa*

The Sixth Amendment guarantees the accused the right to confront and cross-examine his or her accusers, and the Court made this right applicable to state criminal proceedings in *Pointer* v. *Texas* (380 U.S. 400, 1965). The Court cited both *Malloy* [v. *Hogan*, 378 U.S. 1, 1964] and *Gideon* [v. *Wainwright*, 372 U.S. 335, 1963] emphasizing that the confrontation guarantee is an essential fundamental of a fair trial and the principal means to test the reliability of a witness and the truthfulness of his or her testimony. Additionally, Justice Hugo Black emphasized that the standards that should govern the enforcement of the guarantee in state proceedings are the same as those applied to federal actions.

In another case decided the same day as *Pointer* (*Douglas* v. *Alabama*, 380 U.S. 415), the Court stressed the essentiality of cross-examination in the criminal process, noting that it is "a primary interest" secured by the confrontation clause. This principle was reaffirmed a decade later in *Davis* v. *Alaska* (415 U.S. 308, 1974), where the Court held that state policy protecting the anonymity of juvenile offenders could not be asserted to restrict a defendant's cross-examination of an accuser, because it would diminish the confrontation guarantee.

But the Court, in reaffirming the principle a decade later in *Delaware* v. *Van Arsdale* (106 S. Ct. 1431, 1986), appeared to open the door for its later contraction when it held that pleadings alleging that judicial restrictions on cross-examination efforts impinge on the confrontation guarantee are subject to "harmless error" analysis. And the very next term the narrowing of the guarantee became evident in *Kentucky* v. *Spicer* (107 S. Ct. 2658, 1987), when the Court held that a defendant could be excluded from an in-chambers hearing to determine if two of his child victims of sodomy were competent to testify at trial. But the Court indicated some hesitancy in moving too far in this direction (even when the aim was to protect juvenile victims from the trauma of confronting their alleged assailants) during the next term in its decision in *Coy* v. *Iowa* (108 S. Ct. 2798, 1988). There it found that the Iowa statute that allowed the placement of a screen between a defendant and his juvenile sexual assault victim created a "legislatively imposed presumption of trauma" that short-circuited the requirement of "individualized findings" of the need for "special protection" of the victim during his/her testimony. Asserting that "a more obvious or damaging" infringement of the confrontation guarantee "is difficult to imagine," Justice Scalia concluded that the state's preferred interest was insufficient to justify an exception to the confrontation guarantee.

The other dimension of this Sixth Amendment guarantee—"to have compulsory process for obtaining witnesses in his favor"—was made binding on the states two years after *Pointer* in *Washington* v. *Texas* (388 U.S. 14, 1967). At issue was a statutory procedure that prohibited persons charged or convicted as coparticipants in the same crime from testifying for one another, but that allowed the prosecution to use them to testify against one another. Chief Justice Earl Warren, who spoke for the Court, emphasized the right of the accused not only to confront and challenge the testimony of prosecution witnesses but also to present their own witnesses to establish their defense. The defendant, concluded the Chief Justice, has just as much right to present his or her version of the facts to the jury as the prosecution.

COY v. IOWA
___ U.S. ___; ___ L. Ed. 2d ___; 108 S. Ct. 2798 (1988)

JUSTICE SCALIA., *delivered the opinion of the Court.*

Appellant was convicted of two counts of lascivious acts with a child after a jury trial in which a screen placed between him and the two complaining witnesses blocked him from their sight. Appellant contends that this procedure, authorized by state statute, violated his Sixth Amendment right to confront the witnesses against him.

I

In August 1985, appellant was arrested and charged with sexually assaulting two 13-year-old girls earlier that month while they were camping out in the backyard of the house next-door to him. According to the girls, the assailant entered their tent, after they were asleep, wearing a stocking over his head, shined a flashlight in their eyes, and warned them not to look at him; neither was able to describe his face. In November 1985, at the beginning of appellant's trial, the State made a motion pursuant to a recently enacted statute . . . to allow the complaining witnesses to testify either via closed-circuit television or behind a screen. The trial court approved the use of a large screen to be placed between appellant and the witness stand during the girls' testimony. After certain lighting adjustments in the courtroom, the screen would enable appellant dimly to perceive the witnesses, but the witnesses to see him not at all.

Appellant objected strenuously to use of the screen based first of all on his Sixth Amendment confrontation rights. He argued that, although the device might succeed in its apparent aim of making the complaining witnesses feel less uneasy in giving their testimony, the Confrontation Clause directly addressed this issue by giving criminal defendants a right to face-to-face confrontation. He also argued that his right to due process was violated, since the procedure would make him appear guilty and thus erode the presumption of inno-

cence. The trial court rejected both constitutional claims, though it instructed the jury to draw no inference of guilt from the screen. The Iowa Supreme Court affirmed appellant's conviction.

II

The Sixth Amendment gives a criminal defendant the right "to be confronted with the witnesses against him." This language "comes to us on faded parchment" . . . with a lineage that traces back to the beginnings of Western legal culture. . . .

Most of this Court's encounters with the Confrontation Clause have involved either the admissibility of out-of-court statements . . . or restrictions on the scope of cross-examination. . . . The reason for that is not, as the State suggests, that there is at least some room for doubt (and hence litigation) as to the extent to which the Clause includes those elements, whereas, as Justice Harlan put it, "[s]imply as a matter of English" it confers at least "a right to meet face-to-face all those who appear and give evidence at trial. . . ."

We have never doubted . . . that the Confrontation Clause guarantees the defendant a face-to-face meeting with witnesses appearing before the trier of fact. . . .

[R]ecently, we have described the "literal right to 'confront' the witness at the time of trial" as forming "the core of the values furthered by the Confrontation Clause." Last term, the plurality opinion in *Pennsylvania* v. *Ritchie*, 480 U.S. 39, 51 (1987), stated that "[t]he Confrontation Clause provides two types of protection for a criminal defendant: the right to physically face those who testify against him, and the right to conduct cross-examination."

The Sixth Amendment's guarantee of face-to-face encounter between witness and accused serves ends related both to appearances and to reality. This opinion is embellished with references to and quotations from antiquity in part to convey that there is something deep in human nature that regards face-to-face confrontation between accused and accuser as "essential to a fair trial in a criminal prosecution." What was true of old is no less true in modern times. . . .

The perception that confrontation is essential to fairness has persisted over the centuries because there is much truth to it. A witness "may feel quite differently when he has to repeat his story looking at the man whom he will harm greatly by distorting or mistaking the facts. He can now understand what sort of human being that man is." Z. Chafee, The Blessings of Liberty 35 (1956). . . . It is always more difficult to tell a lie about a person "to his face" than "behind his back." In the former context, even if the lie is told, it will often be told less convincingly. The Confrontation Clause does not, of course, compel the witness to fix his eyes upon the defendant; he may studiously look elsewhere, but the trier of fact will draw its own conclusions. Thus the right to face-to-face confrontation serves much the same purpose as a less explicit component of the Confrontation Clause that we have had more frequent occasion to discuss—the right to cross-examine the accuser [sic]; both "ensur[e] the integrity of the fact-finding process." The State can hardly gainsay the profound effect upon a witness of standing in the presence of the person the witness accuses, since that is the very phenomenon it relies upon to establish the potential "trauma" that allegedly justified the extraordinary procedure in the present case. That face-to-face presence may, unfortunately, upset the truthful rape victim or abused child; but by the same token it may confound and undo the false accuser, or reveal the child coached by a malevolent adult. It is a truism that constitutional protections have costs.

. . . [Was] the right to confrontation . . . violated in this case[?] The screen at issue was specifically designed to enable the complaining witnesses to avoid viewing appellant as they gave their testimony, and the record indicates that it was successful in this objective. It is difficult to imagine a more obvious or damaging violation of the defendant's right to a face-to-face encounter. The State suggests that the confrontation interest at stake here was outweighed by the necessity of protecting victims of sexual abuse. It is true that we have in the past indicated that rights conferred by the Confrontation Clause are not absolute, and may give way to other important interests. The rights referred to in those cases, however, were not the rights narrowly and explicitly set forth in the Clause, but rather rights that are, or were asserted to be, reasonably implicit—namely, the right to cross-examine, see *Chambers* v. *Mississippi*, 410 U.S.

284, 295 (1973), the right to exclude out-of-court statements, see *Ohio* v. *Roberts*, 448 U.S. at 63–65, (1980), and the asserted right to face-to-face confrontation at some point in the proceedings other than the trial itself, *Kentucky* v. *Stincer*, 482 U.S. 730 (1987). To hold that our determination of what implications are reasonable must take into account other important interests is not the same as holding that we can identify exceptions, in light of other important interests, to the irreducible literal meaning of the clause: "a right to *meet face-to-face* all those who appear and give evidence *at trial.*" . . . We leave for another day, however, the question if whether any exceptions exist. Whatever they may be, they would surely be allowed only when necessary to further an important public policy. The State maintains that such necessity is established here by the statute, which creates a legislatively imposed presumption of trauma. Our cases suggest, however, that even as to exceptions from the normal implications of the Confrontation Clause, as opposed to its most literal application, something more than the type of generalized finding underlying such a statute is needed when the exception is not "firmly . . . rooted in our jurisprudence." . . . The exception created by the Iowa statute . . . in 1985 could hardly be viewed as firmly rooted. Since there have been no individualized findings that these particular witnesses needed special protection, the judgment here could not be sustained by any conceivable exception. . . .

We find it unnecessary to reach appellant's due process claim. Since his constitutional right to face-to-face confrontation was violated, we reverse the judgment of the Iowa Supreme Court and remand the case.

It is so ordered.

JUSTICE KENNEDY *took no part in the consideration or decision of this case.*

[The concurring opinion of JUSTICE O'CONNOR, with whom JUSTICE WHITE joined, is not reprinted here.]

JUSTICE BLACKMUN, *with whom* THE CHIEF JUSTICE *joins, dissenting.*

Appellant was convicted by an Iowa jury on two counts of engaging in lascivious acts with a child. Because, in my view, the procedures employed at appellant's trial did not offend either the Confrontation Clause or the Due Process Clause, I would affirm his conviction. Accordingly,

I respectfully dissent.

* * *

I

A

Two witnesses against appellant in this case were the 13-year-old girls he was accused of sexually assaulting. During their testimony, as permitted by a state statute, a one-way screening device was placed between the girls and appellant, blocking the man accused of sexually assaulting them from the girls' line of vision. This procedure did not interfere with what this Court previously has recognized as the "purposes of confrontation." Specifically, the girls' testimony was given under oath, was subject to unrestricted cross-examination, and "the jury that [was] to decide the defendant's fate, [could] observe the demeanor of the witness[es] in making [their] statement[s], thus aiding the jury in assessing [their] credibility." In addition, the screen did not prevent appellant from seeing and hearing the girls and conferring with counsel during their testimony, did not prevent the girls from seeing and being seen by the judge and counsel, as well as by the jury, and did not prevent the jury from seeing the demeanor of the defendant while the girls testified. Finally, the girls were informed that appellant could see and hear them while they were on the stand. Thus, appellant's *sole* complaint is the very narrow objection that the girls could not see him while they testified about the sexual assault they endured.

The Court describes appellant's interest in ensuring that the girls could see him while they testified as "the irreducible literal meaning of the Clause." Whatever may be the significance of this characterization, in my view it is not borne out by logic or precedent. While I agree with the concurrence that "[t]here is nothing novel" in the proposition that the Confrontation Clause "reflects a preference" for the witness to be able to see the defendant, . . . I find it necessary to discuss my disagreement with the Court as to the place of this "preference" in the constellation of rights provided by the Confrontation Clause for two reasons. First, the minimal extent of the infringement on appellant's Confrontation Clause interests is relevant in considering whether competing public policies justify the procedures employed in this case. Second, I fear that the Court's apparent fascination with the witness' ability to see the defendant will lead the States that are attempting to adopt innovations to facilitate the testimony of child-victims of sex abuse to sacrifice other, more central, confrontation interests, such as the right to cross-examination or to have the trier of fact observe the testifying witness.

The weakness of the Court's support for its characterization of appellant's claim as involving "the irreducible literal meaning of the Clause" is reflected in its reliance on literature, anecdote, and dicta from opinions that a majority of this Court did not join. The majority cites only opinion of the Court that, in my view, possibly could be understood as ascribing substantial weight to a defendant's right to ensure that witnesses against him are able to see him while they are testifying. . . .

Whether or not "there is something deep in human nature" that considers critical the ability of a witness to see the defendant while the witness is testifying, that was not a part of the common law's view of the confrontation requirement. "There never was at common law any recognized right to an indispensable thing called confrontation *as distinguished from cross-examination.*"

That [the] ability of a witness to see the defendant while the witness is testifying does not constitute an essential part of the protections afforded by the Confrontation Clause is also demonstrated by the exceptions to the rule against hearsay, which allow the admission of out-of-court statements against a defendant. . . . [The Court has] held that the admission of an out-of-court statement of a co-conspirator did not violate the Confrontation Clause. In reaching that conclusion, the Court did not consider even worthy of mention the fact that the declarant could not see the defendant at the time he made his accusatory statement. Instead, the plurality opinion concentrated on the reliability of the statement and the effect cross-examination might have had. . . .

In fact, many hearsay statements are made outside the presence of the defendant, and thus implicate the confrontation right asserted here. Yet, as the majority seems to recognize, this interest has not been the focus of this Court's decisions considering the admissibility of such statements.

Finally, the importance of this interest to the Confrontation Clause is belied by the simple observation that, had blind witnesses testified against appellant, he could raise no serious objection to their testimony, notwithstanding the identity of that restriction on confrontation and the one here presented. . . .

* * *

B

Indisputably, the state interests behind the Iowa statute are of considerable importance. Between 1976 and 1985, the number of reported incidents of child maltreatment in the United States rose from .67 million to over 1.9 million, with an estimated 11.7 percent of those cases in 1985 involving allegations of sexual abuse. . . . The prosecution of these child sex-abuse cases poses substantial difficulties because of the emotional trauma frequently suffered by child witnesses who must testify about the sexual assaults they have suffered. "[T]o a child who does not understand the reason for confrontation, the anticipation and experience of being in close proximity to the defendant can be overwhelming." . . . Although research in this area is still in its early stages, studies of children who have testified in court indicate that such testimony is "associated with increased behavioral disturbance in children." . . .

Thus, the fear and trauma associated with a child's testimony in front of the defendant has [sic] serious identifiable consequences: It may cause psychological injury to the child, and it may so overwhelm the child as to prevent the possibility of effective testimony, thereby undermining the truth-finding function of the trial itself. Because of these effects, I agree with the concurring opinion that a State properly may consider the protection of child witnesses to be an important public policy. In my view, this important public policy, embodied in the Iowa statute that authorized the use of the screening device, outweighs the narrow Confrontation Clause right at issue here—the "preference" for having the defendant within the witness' sight while the witness testifies.

Appellant argues, and the Court concludes, that even if a societal interest can justify a restriction on a child witness' ability to see the defendant while the child testifies, the State must show in each case that such a procedure is essential to protect the child's welfare. I disagree. As the many rules allowing the admission of out-of-court statements demonstrate, legislative exceptions to the Confrontation Clause of general applicability are commonplace. I would not impose a different rule here by requiring the State to make a predicate showing in each case. . . .

Commentary

Juvenile Rights

To what extent are the various constitutional safeguards guaranteed to adults accused of crime available to juveniles? The Court considered this crucial question in *In re Gault* (387 U.S. 1) in 1967. In reversing a juvenile court decision that had committed a youngster to an industrial school for the remainder of his minority (six years), the Court held that in such proceedings the due process clause of the Fourteenth Amendment requires that: (1) adequate notice of the hearings be given; (2) the child be informed of his or her right to counsel (including assigned counsel); and (3) the privileges against self-incrimination and confrontation be extended to him or her. Justice Abe Fortas's opinion for the five-man majority was careful to limit the holdings to the actual "proceedings" process. He concluded that the unique values of the juvenile system would in no way be impaired by this "constitutional domestication." See also *Breed* v. *Jones* (421 U.S. 519, 1975), where the guarantee against double jeopardy was held applicable to such proceedings, but note the Court's refusal to construe a juvenile's request to consult with his probation officer as per se invocation of *Miranda* interrogation requirements. See *Fare* v. *Michael C.*, 442 U.S. 707 (1979).

In *McKeiver* v. *Pennsylvania* and *In re Burrus* (403 U.S. 528, 1971), however, the Court did not agree that such "constitutional domestication" includes the right to trial by jury in juvenile court delinquency proceedings. Noting that "fundamental fairness" is the essential ingredient of due process in such proceedings, Justice Harry Blackmun's plurality opinion emphasized that there are other instruments of the juvenile process that can best serve its purpose and that states should not be impeded in searching for improvements by the imposition of jury trials. Such trials, he concluded, are not indispensable to a "fair and equitable" proceeding. He cautioned that injection of the jury trial in juvenile matters as a matter of right could well burden juvenile courts with many of the evils characteristic of modern criminal courts, such as lengthy delays and possibly damaging public proceedings.

Justice Douglas, in dissent, focused on the results coming from such proceedings. He contended that where the state uses the juvenile proceeding as a forum for the prosecution of a criminal act out of which is issued a confinement order for a period of time or where such a possibility is a stark reality, the procedural protections afforded adults must be available to juveniles. After all, he continued, the Court made it clear in *Gault* that the guarantees protected by the Bill of Rights and the Fourteenth Amendment are not exclusively for adults.

However, in its apparent disposition to broaden the discretion of the states in the administration of criminal procedures, the Burger Court upheld New York's juvenile preventive detention statute in *Schall* v. *Martin* (104 S. Ct. 2403, 1984). For Justice William Rehnquist, who spoke for the six-to-three majority, pretrial detention is designed to accomplish a "legitimate governmental objective" in protecting society from pretrial criminal activity. In providing for a range of postdetention guarantees (habeas corpus review appeals, etc.), Rehnquist concluded that the statute does not abridge that "fundamental fairness" that due process requires.

SELECTED REFERENCES

Bedau, Hugo A. "The Death Penalty in America: Yesterday and Today," 95 *Dickinson Law Review* 759 (Summer 1991).

Bohm, Robert M. *The Death Penalty In America* (Cincinnati: Anderson Publishing Co., 1991).

Brennan, William J. "Constitutional Adjudication and the Death Penalty: A View from the Court," 100 *Harvard Law Review* 313 (December 1986).

Chapman, Frank. "The Death Penalty, U.S.A.: Racist and Class Violence," 66 *Political Affairs* 17 (July 1987).

Clark, Homer H. "Children and the Constitution," 1992 *University of Illinois Law Review* 1 (Winter 1992).

Feeney, Floyd, and Jackson, Patrick G. "Public Defenders, Assigned Counsel, Retained Counsel: Does the Type of Criminal Defense Counsel Matter?" 22 *Rutgers Law Journal* 361 (Winter 1991).

Goldberg, Stephanie. "*Batson* and the Straight Face Test: Courts Split on Gender-Based Jury Picks, Permissible Stereotyping," 78 *ABA Journal* 82 (August 1992).

Hazel, Thomas. "Toward a Uniform Statutory Standard for Effective Assistance of Counsel after *Strickland*," 17 *Loyola University (Chicago) Law Journal* 203 (Winter 1983).

Higginbotham, Patrick E. "Juries and the Death Penalty," 41 *Case-Western Law Review* 1047 (1991).

Hinton, Melissa C. "Has *Batson* Been Stretched Too Far?" 57 *Missouri Law Review* 569 (Spring 1992).

Israel, Jerrold. "Criminal Procedure, the Burger Court, and the Legacy of the Warren Court," 75 *Michigan Law Review* 1319 (June 1979).

Kirk, Bradley R. "Milking the New Sacred Cow: The Supreme Court Limits the Peremptory Challenge on Racial Grounds . . . ," 19 *Pepperdine Law Review* 691 (January 1992).

Klien, Richard. "The Emperor Gideon Has No Clothes: The Empty Promise of the Constitutional Right to Effective Assistance of Counsel," 13 *Hastings Constitutional Law Quarterly* 625 (Summer 1986).

Mayer, Albert. "The *Weeks* Exclusionary Rule: A Bizarre and Senseless Impediment to Judicial Integrity" 62 *New York State Bar Journal* 53 (October 1990).

Mushlin, Michael B. "*Gideon* v. *Wainwright*: What Does the Right to Counsel Guarantee Today?" 10 *Pace Law Review* 327 (Spring 1990).

Nardulli, Peter. "The Societal Costs of the Exclusionary Rule Revisited," 1987 *University of Illinois Law Review* 223 (1987).

Ogletree, Charles J. "Are Confessions Really Good for the Soul? A Proposal to Mirandize *Miranda*," 100 *Harvard Law Review* 1826 (May 1987).

Radelet, M. L. "Choosing Those Who Will Die: Race and the Death Penalty," 43 *Florida Law Review* 1 (January 1991).

Roehnert, Henrick A. "Warrantless Administrative Searches of the Person without Probable Cause or Particularized Suspicion: New Contours of the Fourth Amendment," 21 *New Mexico Law Review* 389 (Spring 1991).

Smith, Diane K. "The Right of Effective Counsel: The Sixth Amendment Giveth and the Trial Court Taketh Away," 16 *Thurgood Marshall Law Review* 225 (Fall 1990).

Race, Color, and the Constitution[1]

Introductory Commentary

As the last decade of the twentieth century began, the comprehensive effort undertaken in the nation over the previous four decades to strike down racial segregation and eliminate deeply rooted and pervasive racially discriminatory practices in our national life had almost ground to a halt. To be sure, the much-heralded *Brown* v. *Board of Education* (347 U.S. 483) case of 1954 and its progeny of the decades that followed, when coupled with federal legislative and executive initiatives, produced major changes in America's race policies. Just as the policies of the "First Reconstruction," which were designed to aid blacks in the transition from slavery to equality in the American society, met with stiff resistance, so were the policies of the second era of "Reconstruction" resisted by those who opposed the change from a racially segregated order to an integrated one. But despite such resistance, significant strides were made toward the integration of blacks and other minorities into major dimensions of America's political, economic, and social order. Blacks, whites, browns, and others attend many of the same public schools throughout the country. "Black power" became a reality in some jurisdictions in the country as political participation was enhanced by congressional voting rights legislation. Accommodations open to the public—such as hotels, restaurants, and recreation facilities—became available for those who had the money to use them. Many of the barriers to the purchase of real estate tumbled. And employment opportunities in the private sector have been broadened by federal equal opportunity and affirmative action policies.

The method employed to implement some of these policies, such as busing for school desegregation and affirmative action plans utilizing goals and/or quotas provoked considerable criticism and controversy in both the public and private sectors. While school desegregation controversies have all but faded from the national policy forum, affirmative action policies continue to occupy a prominent position on the national agenda, as African American and other minority leaders now see their efforts to close the inequality gap between them and white America retrogressing. To be sure, the optimism engendered by some of the actions of the Carter administration between 1977 and 1981 faded into dismay with the insensitivity and aggressive opposition to civil rights policies that characterized the Reagan and Bush administrations between 1981 and 1993. On the one hand, through its rhetoric and actual practice, the Carter administration gave both sympathy and support to civil rights advancement. President Carter, for example, appointed a record number of African Americans and members of other minority groups to important governmental positions. Even so, however, an unease was developing that the national mood on race policy issues was slowly changing in a way that could put the brakes on the drive for full equality.

The 1980 elections confirmed this assessment.

[1]Voting rights issues are considered in Chapter 6.

Indeed, the election of Ronald Reagan as president in 1980 and again in 1984 functioned to alter significantly the role of the federal government in the equality struggle of blacks and other minorities. The Reagan administration began to implement its perception of the national mood during its first term, and the effort was accelerated at the outset of the second term. Justice Department officials scaled down civil rights enforcement efforts. Consent decrees, meeting the minimum requirements of *Brown*, supplanted full-scale litigation that had in earlier years produced a fuller compliance with the standards enunciated by the judiciary. The Reagan administration gave little or no support to congressional efforts to strengthen federal fair housing laws. State and local governments were under lessened federal pressure to adhere to the submission requirements of Section 5 of the Voting Rights Act of 1965. And early in Reagan's second term, Justice Department officials sought to get many local governments to curtail or drop affirmative action programs, despite their success in achieving their objectives. Additionally, sympathetic Carter administration officials directing key civil rights agencies were replaced by officials whose rhetoric and actions underscored the low priority that the Reagan administration accorded civil rights.

Moreover, several actions of the Supreme Court during Reagan's first term appeared to reflect the administration's negative view of some of these racial equality policies and the approaches for implementing them. Some observers, for example, believe that the Court's 1984 decision in the *Memphis Firefighters* case (467 U.S. 561) was a significant catalyst in the administration's "war" on affirmative action policies led by Attorney General Edwin Meese. Additionally, the sex discrimination decision in the *Grove City College* v. *Bell* (465 U.S. 555) case (also decided in 1984) was viewed as indicative of a decisional trend toward a more restrictive interpretation of both civil rights laws as well as constitutional provisions related to the equality principle.

The Reagan administration's policy position on several civil rights issues was reflected most significantly in several court decisions shortly after he left office in 1989. To be sure, his three appointees (O'Connor, Scalia, and Kennedy) aligned themselves with Chief Justice Rehnquist and Justice Byron White to form a solid conservative bloc in this policy area to forge a reexamination of certain issues that civil rights interests had thought were well entrenched in our jurisprudence. In *City of Richmond* v. *J. A. Croson Co.* (109 S. Ct. 706, 1989), for example, that bloc refused to accept the *Full-*

ilove v. *Klutznick* (448 U.S. 448, 1980) decision of a decade earlier as a precedent to support a similar minority contractor set-aside program initiated by local government. The justices reasoned that such local governments did not have the broad authority to forge such a policy as was available to Congress under the Fourteenth Amendment.

Several months after the *Croson* ruling was announced, the Court handed down three decisions in June, 1989 that collectively indicated that the rhetoric of the Reagan administration had found its way into our constitutional law. In rapid succession, the Court first stripped away the core of a precedent of some 20 years (*Griggs* v. *Duke Power Co.* [401 U. S. 424, 1971)], when it held in *Wards Cove Packing Co.* v. *Atonio* (109 S. Ct. 2115, 1989) that an employee charging an employer with discriminatory employment practices and policies must shoulder the heavy burden of proving that such employer policies and practices are unnecessary. The relevant civil rights statute (Title VII of the 1964 Civil Rights Act) was construed narrowly to disallow a mere showing of discriminatory effect. Next, the Court dealt a blow to the effectiveness of consent decrees as mechanisms to implement affirmative action programs when it ruled in *Martin* v. *Wilks* (109 S. Ct. 2180, 1989) that nonparties to such agreements alleging that their interests are affected adversely by its provisions may bring actions to reopen it. And, in the third case (*Lorance* v. *A.T. & T. Technologies, Inc.*, 109 S. Ct. 2261, 1989), the Court again construed Title VII narrowly, making it more difficult for those bringing discriminatory actions by requiring them to adhere to very strict time limits.

After this spate of anti–civil rights decisions, the Court seemed to draw back slightly when it decided in *Patterson* v. *McLean Credit Union* (109 S. Ct. 2363, 1989) not to overturn *Runyon* v. *McCrary*, (427 U.S. 1601), the 1976 ruling that construed the 1866 Civil Rights Act as prohibiting private acts of racial discrimination as well as those resulting from public action. But it then underscored the limited nature of its ruling by holding that the statute was not to be construed to condemn employer actions such as racial harassment. For many in the civil rights community, the Court's narrow reading of the 1866 Act as well as its pro-employer reading of Title VII in the *Wards Cove*, *Martin*, and *Lorance* cases represented serious setbacks in the march to equal employment opportunity.

Almost immediately, efforts were marshaled in the Congress to counter the impact of these decisions. Obviously, since they were statutory construction decisions (the Court's determination of the congressional policy intent), Congress was in a position to make its intent clear by enacting new legislation that had the effect of setting aside the Court's 1989 rulings.

This chapter summarizes Court actions that have been crucial in the erosion and elimination of the legal supports of racial discrimination in various areas of American life. Attention is further given to legislative and executive efforts to move beyond Court decisions in effecting racial policies. But the chapter also focuses on judicial, legislative, and administrative actions that serve to thwart or inhibit the enforcement and implementation of civil rights policies. In general, the chapter discusses those issues that will undoubtedly occupy center stage in the race policy arena for the remainder of the 1990s.

SOME JUDICIAL STANDARDS AND EQUAL PROTECTION REVIEW

The constitutional protection against state-enforced racial discrimination is lodged in the equal protection clause of the Fourteenth Amendment. Although construed over the years to proscribe other forms of discriminatory treatment, such as gender and durational residency, the clause has been the major constitutional weapon that blacks have employed in their struggle for equality since World War II.

In its early approach to cases involving discriminatory classification schemes, the Supreme Court invoked its *rationality* standard of review. In according great deference to the legislature, the Court deemed it was sufficient merely to show that the classification is itself reasonable and has a rational relationship to a legitimate state interest. This has usually been considered a lenient standard of re-

view and has been used by the Supreme Court in testing the constitutionality of classification schemes involving economic and commercial questions. See, e.g., *San Antonio Independent School District* v. *Rodriguez* (411 U.S. 1, 1973).

In its review of classification schemes based on race, the Court has resorted to a more exacting standard. This *strict scrutiny* standard of review, as it has been characterized, is triggered when a "suspect class" (such as race) is embraced in the classification or when the classification is alleged to abridge a "fundamental right," such as the right to travel or to privacy. Invalidity of a classification scheme under this standard is presumed unless it can be shown that the legislation is necessary to promote a legitimate, overriding state interest and that less intrusive alternatives are not available.

In the early 1970s, Justice Thurgood Marshall, with whom Justice William O. Douglas concurred, questioned what he considered was much too rigid an approach to equal protection review. Rejecting what he perceived was the majority's view—that the broad spectrum of equal protection cases fall neatly into one of two categories, thereby triggering mere rationality or strict scrutiny review—Marshall argued for an approach employing variable degrees of scrutiny depending on such factors as (1) "the constitutional and societal importance of the interests adversely affected"; and (2) the "invidiousness of the basis upon which the particular classification is drawn"; *San Antonio Independent School District* v. *Rodriguez* (411 U.S. 1 at 98, 1973). This type of "mid-level scrutiny," as it has been labeled, provides the Court with yet another approach in its review of an ever-increasing number of cases reaching the courts under the equal protection clause.

Establishing the Legal Basis of Racial Segregation

FEATURED CASE
Plessy v. *Ferguson*

For more than a half-century following the Civil War, the judiciary's actions were not generally supportive of efforts promoting racial justice. While the Civil War and Reconstruction brought about the enactment of the Thirteenth, Fourteenth, and Fifteenth Amendments, several early decisions of the Supreme Court, such as those in the *Civil Rights*

Cases (109 U.S. 3, 1883), effectively thwarted, or at least put into mothballs, the efforts to make their objectives more than empty guarantees. This created a climate conducive to fostering rather than eliminating racial segregation. Consequently, as the situation in the South returned to "normalcy," white southerners, again fully in control of their state legislatures, were able to design rather comprehensive systems of racial segregation in both the public and private sectors of society.

The Court gave approval and added impetus to such segregation practices when, in *Plessy* v. *Ferguson* (163 U.S. 537, 1896), it upheld as a valid exercise of state police power a Louisiana statute requiring racial segregation of passengers on trains. The Court construed the statute's racial separation provisions as nondiscriminatory. Segregation of the races was not the discrimination proscribed by the equal protection clause. However, the first Justice John Marshall Harlan, the lone dissenter, took issue with his fellow justices, maintaining that "the Constitution is color-blind" and does not permit authorities to consider race in their actions. Thereafter, the *Plessy* precedent became the legal support for racial segregation in almost all areas of American life.

Separate and Unequal: Public Education from Plessy to Brown

FEATURED CASES

Brown v. Board of Education I   Brown v. Board of Education II

The racially segregated system of dual public schools became a permanent fixture in 17 states and the District of Columbia after the *Plessy* decision. In its development, the emphasis was on the "separate," but not on the "equal," dimension of the doctrine. In fact, it was not until 1936 that any court considered fully the standard of equality and the appropriate relief to be granted when inequality is found. Furthermore, it was not a challenge to the largest arena of public education—the common elementary and secondary schools—but to a higher educational institution that was involved. And, somewhat paradoxically, it was a state court—the Maryland Court of Appeals—that initiated judicial scrutiny of the equality offered under the separate-but-equal doctrine.[2] In *Pearson* v. *Murray* (182 Atl. 590, 1936), a qualified black applicant was denied admission to the University of Maryland School of Law solely because of race. Instead, the applicant was offered an out-of-state scholarship, which covered expenses for his legal education elsewhere. While refusing to rule on the issue of segregated education, the state court did examine the standard of equality afforded and found the policy deficient. Adhering to the doctrine of the "present" nature of constitutional rights, the court held immediate equality could only be furnished by Murray's admission to the white law school.

This was essentially the position adopted by the United States Supreme Court two years later in *Missouri ex rel. Gaines* v. *Canada* (305 U.S. 337, 1938). Like Maryland, Missouri provided blacks an opportunity to obtain legal education via the out-of-state scholarship arrangement. However, the Supreme Court held that admission to the white law school was the only appropriate remedy consistent with the constitutional standard of equality. The Court also gave notice that it would no longer ignore the "equal" part of the separate-but-equal formula. Chief Justice Charles Evans Hughes, who delivered the Court's opinion, stressed equality of *treatment* in rejecting the scholarship arrangement. In short, the equal protection clause required Missouri to provide black applicants a legal education within the state. The Court reaffirmed the *Gaines* doctrine 10 years later in *Sipuel* v. *Board of Regents of the University of Oklahoma* (322 U.S. 631, 1948).

Missouri and five southern states responded to the *Gaines* ruling by establishing separate law schools for blacks.[3] This action inevitably led to litigation focusing on comparable facilities of separate schools in determining the standard of equality required by the equal protection clause, and, in the Texas law school segregation case, *Sweatt* v. *Painter* (339 U.S. 629, 1950), the Court found that the educational opportunities provided at a segregated black law school were not equal to those afforded white students at the University of Texas. Although the Court stopped short of overturning the separate-but-equal doctrine per se, as urged by

[2]The Supreme Court had considered several peripheral issues growing out of segregated schools but did not have to consider the standard of equality. See *Cumming* v. *Board of Education* (175 U.S. 528, 1899); *Berea College* v. *Kentucky* (211 U.S. 45, 1908); and *Gong Lum* v. *Rice* (275 U.S. 78, 1927).

[3]Texas, Louisiana, Florida, North Carolina, and South Carolina.

petitioner, it was apparent that the doctrine had been eroded. In fact, the language of Chief Justice Fred Vinson's opinion appeared to forecast its doom, when he noted that there were "qualities which are incapable of objective measurement" and that the law school "cannot be effective in isolation from the individuals and institutions with which the law interacts."

The Court clarified further the standard of equality as applied to higher education in its decision in *McLaurin* v. *Oklahoma State Regents* (339 U.S. 637, 1950), announced the same day as *Sweatt*. There it condemned internal segregation practices to which a black graduate student was subjected as impairing his "ability to study, to engage in discussions and exchange views with other students, and, in general, to learn his profession."

Immediately following the *Sweatt* and *McLaurin* decisions, the legal attack on segregated education shifted to the elementary and secondary school level. The first action, brought in December 1950, challenged the constitutionality of South Carolina's school segregation laws. Similar challenges were made in Kansas, Virginia, Delaware, and the District of Columbia during the following year. The constitutional issue of racially segregated educational facilities was argued in each case, but the lower courts held steadfastly to the separate-but-equal doctrine. However, Chancellor Collins J. Seitz, of a Delaware state court, did grant partial relief because of a finding of unequal facilities.

The four challenges to state systems were consolidated for Supreme Court argument and decision in *Brown* v. *Board of Education of Topeka, Kansas* (347 U.S. 483, 1954), and they raised the same issue under the equal protection clause of the Fourteenth Amendment. The District of Columbia case, *Bolling* v. *Sharpe* (347 U.S. 497, 1954), raised the same question, but was decided under the due process clause of the Fifth Amendment because the equal protection clause of the Fourteenth Amendment is not applicable to the District's policies. In *Brown*, speaking for a unanimous Court on May 17, 1954, Chief Justice Earl Warren declared the separate-but-equal doctrine unconstitutional in public education, thus overruling the *Plessy* precedent. The Court went to the core of the problem and considered not only tangible inequalities, but also the nature and consequences of segregation.

Probably anticipating the impact of the decision, the Court announced its judgment but delayed a decree. After examination of additional briefs and further arguments on the question of the appropriate remedy during the 1954 fall term, the implementation decree was announced on May 31, 1955 (*Brown II*). The "immediacy" argument of the victorious appellants was rejected, and the Court leaned more toward the "gradualism" urged by the appellees. The cases were remanded to the federal district courts with instructions to order local school districts to proceed with desegregation of public schools "with all deliberate speed."

PLESSY v. FERGUSON
163 U.S. 537; 41 L. Ed. 256; 16 S. Ct. 1138 (1896)

JUSTICE BROWN *delivered the opinion of the Court.*

This case turns upon the constitutionality of an act of the general assembly of the State of Louisiana, passed in 1890, providing for separate railway carriages for the white and colored races. . . .

The first section of the statute enacts "that all railway companies carrying passengers in their coaches in this state shall provide equal but separate accommodations for the white and colored races, by providing two or more passenger coaches for each passenger train, or by dividing the passenger coaches by a partition so as to secure separate accommodations: *Provided,* That this section shall be construed to apply to street railroads. No person or persons shall be permitted to occupy any coaches other than the ones assigned to them, on account of the race they belong to."

By the second section it was enacted "that the officers of such passenger trains shall have power and are hereby required to assign each passenger to the coach or compartment used for the race to which such passenger belongs: any passenger insisting on going into a coach or compartment to which by race he does not belong, shall be liable to a fine of $25 or in lieu thereof to imprisonment for a period of not more than twenty days in the parish prison."

* * *

The information filed in the criminal district court charged in substance that Plessy, being a passenger between two stations within the State of Louisiana, was assigned by officers of the company to the coach used for the race to which he belonged, but he insisted upon going into a coach used by the race to which he did not belong. Neither in the information nor plea was his particular race or color averred.

The petition for the writ of prohibition averred that petitioner was seven-eighths Caucasian and one-eighth African blood; that the mixture of colored blood was not discernible in him, and that he was entitled to every right, privilege, and immunity secured to citizens of the United States of the white race; and that, upon such theory, he took possession of a vacant seat in a coach where passengers of the white race were accommodated, and was ordered by the conductor to vacate said coach and take a seat in another assigned to persons of the colored race, and having refused to comply with such demand he was forcibly ejected with the aid of a police officer, and imprisoned in the parish jail to answer a charge of having violated the above act.

The constitutionality of this act is attacked upon the ground that it conflicts both with the Thirteenth Amendment of the Constitution, abolishing slavery, and the Fourteenth Amendment, which prohibits certain restrictive legislation on the part of the States.

1. That it does not conflict with the Thirteenth Amendment, which abolished slavery and involuntary servitude, except as a punishment for crime, is too clear for argument

.

* * *

A statute which implies merely a legal distinction between the white and colored races—a distinction which is founded in the color of the two races, and which must always exist so long as white men are distinguished from the other race by color—has no tendency to destroy the legal equality of the two races, or reestablish a state of involuntary servitude. Indeed, we do not understand that the Thirteenth Amendment is strenuously relied upon by the plaintiff in error in this connection.

2. By the Fourteenth Amendment, all persons born or naturalized in the United States, and subject to the jurisdiction thereof, are made citizens of the United States and of the State wherein they reside; and the States are forbidden from making or enforcing any law which shall abridge the privileges or immunities of citizens of the United States, or shall deprive any person of life, liberty, or property without due process of law, or deny to any person within their jurisdiction the equal protection of the laws.

* * *

The object of the Amendment was undoubtedly to enforce the absolute equality of the two races before the law, but in the nature of things it could not have been intended to abolish distinctions based upon color, or to enforce social, as distinguished from political, equality, or a commingling of the two races upon terms unsatisfactory to either. Laws permitting and even requiring their separation in places where they are liable to be brought into contact do not necessarily imply the inferiority of either race to the other, and have been generally, if not universally, recognized as within the competency of the state legislatures in the exercise of their police power. The most common instance of this is connected with the establishment of separate schools for white and colored children, which have been held to be a valid exercise of the legislative power even by courts of States where the political rights of the colored race have been longest and most earnestly enforced.

One of the earliest of these cases is that of *Roberts* v. *Boston*, 5 Cush. 198, in which the supreme judicial court of Massachusetts held that the general school committee of Boston had power to make provision for the instruction of colored children in separate schools established exclusively for them, and to prohibit their attendance upon the other schools. . . . It was held that the powers of the committee extended to the "establishment of separate schools for children of different ages, sexes, and colors." . . . Similar laws have been enacted by Congress under its general power of legislation over the District of Columbia . . . as well as by the legislatures of many of the States, and have been generally, if not uniformly, sustained by the courts. . . .

Laws forbidding the intermarriage of the two races may be said in a technical sense to interfere with the freedom of contract, and yet have been universally recognized as within the police power of the State, *State* v. *Gibson*, 36 Ind. 389 (10 Am. Rep. 42).

The distinction between interfering with the political equality of the negro and those requiring the separation of the two races in schools, theaters, and railway carriages, has been frequently drawn by this court. Thus in *Strauder* v. *West Virginia*, 100 U.S. 303, it was held that a law of West Virginia limiting to white male persons, twenty-one years of age and citizens of the State, the right to sit upon juries, was a discrimination which implied a legal inferiority in civil society, which lessened the security of the right of the colored race, and was a step towards reducing them to a condition of servility. . . .

Much nearer, and, indeed almost directly in point, is the case of the *Louisville, N.O. & T.R. Co.* v. *Mississippi*, 133 U.S. 587, wherein the railway company was indicted for a violation of a statute of Mississippi, enacting that all railroads carrying passengers should provide equal, but separate, accommodations for the white and colored races, by providing two or more passenger cars for each passenger train, or by dividing the passenger cars by a partition, so as to secure separate accommodations. The case was presented in a different aspect from the one under consideration, inasmuch as it was an indictment against the railway company for failing to provide the separate accommodations, but the question considered was the constitutionality of the law. In that case, the supreme court of Mississippi, 66 Miss. 662, had held that the statute applied solely to commerce within the State, and, that being the construction of the state statute by its highest court, was accepted as conclusive. "If it be a matter," said the court, "respecting commerce wholly within a state, and not interfering with commerce between the states, then, obviously, there is no violation of the commerce clause of the Federal Constitution. . . . No question arises under this section as to the power of the state to separate in different compartments interstate passengers, or to affect in any manner, the privileges and rights of such passengers. All that we can consider is, whether the state has the power to require that railroad trains within her limits shall have separate accommodations for the two races; that affecting only commerce within the states is no invasion of the powers given to Congress by the commerce clause."

* * *

[I]t is . . . suggested by the learned counsel for the plaintiff in error that the same argument that will justify the state legislature in requiring railways to provide separate accommodations for the two races will also authorize them to require separate cars to be provided for people whose hair is of a certain color, or who are aliens, or who belong to certain nationalities, or to enact laws requiring colored people to walk upon one side of the street, and white people upon the other, or requiring white men's houses to be painted white, and colored men's black, or their vehicles or business signs to be of different colors, upon the theory that one side of the street is as good as the other, or that a house or vehicle of one color is as good as one of another color. The reply to all this is that every exercise of the police power must be reasonable, and extend only to such laws as are enacted in good faith for the promotion of the public good, and not for the annoyance or oppression of a particular class. . . .

So far, then, as a conflict with the Fourteenth Amendment is concerned, the case reduces itself to the question whether the statute of Louisiana is a reasonable regulation, and with respect to this there must necessarily be a large discretion on the part of the legislature. In determining the question of reasonableness it is at liberty to act with reference to the established usages, customs, and traditions of the people, and with a view to the promotion of their comfort, and the preservation of the public peace and good order. Gauged by this standard, we cannot say that a law which authorizes or even requires the separation of the two races in public conveyances is unreasonable or more obnoxious to the Fourteenth Amendment than the acts of Congress requiring separate schools for colored children in the District of Columbia, the constitutionality of which does not seem to have been questioned, or the corresponding acts of state legislatures.

We consider the underlying fallacy of the plaintiff's argument to consist in the assumption that the enforced separation of the two races stamps the colored race with a badge of inferiority. If this be so, it is not by reason of anything found in the act, but solely because the colored race chooses to put that construction upon it. The argument necessarily assumes that if, as has been more than once the case, and is not unlikely to be so again, the colored race would become the dominant power in the state legislature, and should enact a law in precisely similar terms, it would thereby relegate the white race to an inferior position. We imagine that the white race, at least, would not acquiesce in this assumption. The argument also assumes that social prejudices may be overcome by legislation, and that equal rights cannot be secured to the negro except by an enforced commingling of the two races. We cannot accept this proposition. If the two races are to meet on terms of social equality, it must be the result of natural affinities, a mutual appreciation of each other's merits and a voluntary consent of individuals. . . . Legislation is powerless to eradicate racial instincts or to abolish distinctions based upon physical differences, and the attempt to do so can only result in accentuating the difficulties of the present situation. If the civil and political rights of both races be equal, one cannot be inferior to the other civilly or politically. If one race be inferior to the other socially, the Constitution of the United States cannot put them upon the same plane.

It is true that the question of the proportion of colored blood necessary to constitute a colored person, as distinguished from a white person, is one upon which there is a difference of opinion in the different States, some holding that any visible admixture of black stamps the person as belonging to the colored race (*State* v. *Chavers*, 5 Jones, L. 11); others that it depends upon the predominance of blood (*Gray* v. *State*, 4 Ohio 354; *Monroe* v. *Collins*, 17 Ohio St. 665); and still others that the predominance of white blood must only be in the proportion of three fourths (*People* v. *Dean*, 14 Mich. 406; *Jones* v. *Com.* 80 Va. 544). But these are questions to be determined under the laws of each State and are not properly put in issue in this case. Under the allegation of his petition it may undoubtedly become a question of importance whether, under the laws of Louisiana, the petitioner belongs to the white or colored race.

The judgment of the court below is therefore affirmed.

[JUSTICE BREWER did not hear the argument or participate in the decision of this case.]

JUSTICE HARLAN, *dissenting.*

* * *

[W]e have before us a state enactment that compels, under penalties, the separation of the two races in railroad passenger coaches, and makes it a crime for a citizen of either race to enter a coach that has been assigned to citizens of the other race.

Thus the State regulates the use of a public highway by citizens of the United States solely upon the basis of race.

However apparent the injustice of such legislation may be, we have only to consider whether it is consistent with the Constitution of the United States.

* * *

In respect of civil rights, common to all citizens, the Constitution of the United States does not, I think, permit any public authority to know the race of those entitled to be protected in the enjoyment of such rights. Every true man has pride of race, and under appropriate circumstances, when the rights of others, his equals before the law, are not to be affected, it is his privilege to express such pride and to take such action based upon it as to him seems proper. But I deny that any legislative body or judicial tribunal may have regard to the race of citizens when the civil rights of those citizens are involved. Indeed such legislation as that here in question is inconsistent, not only with that equality of rights which pertains to citizenship, national and state, but with the personal liberty enjoyed by every one within the United States. [The Thirteenth, Fourteenth and Fifteenth Amendments] removed the race line from our governmental systems. They had, as this Court has said, a common purpose, namely, to secure "to a race recently emancipated, a race that through many generations have [*sic*] been held in slavery, all the civil rights that the superior race enjoys." They declared, in legal effect, this court has further said, "that the law in the states shall be the same for the black as for the white: that all persons, whether colored or white, shall stand equal before the laws of the states, and, in regard to the colored race, for whose protection that amendment was primarily designed, that no discrimination shall be made against them by law because of their color." We also said: "The words of the Amendment, it is true, are prohibitory, but they contain a necessary implication of a positive immunity, or right, most valuable to the colored race—the right to exemption from unfriendly legislation against them distinctively as colored—exemption from legal discriminations, implying inferiority in civil society, lessening the security of their enjoyment of the rights which others enjoy, and discrimination which are steps towards reducing them to the condition of a subject race." . . .

It was said in argument that the statute of Louisiana does not discriminate against either race, but prescribes a rule applicable alike to white and colored citizens. But this argument does not meet the difficulty. Everyone knows that the statute in question had its origin in the purpose, not so much to exclude white persons from railroad cars occupied by blacks, as to exclude colored people from coaches occupied or assigned to white persons. Railroad corporations of Louisiana did not make discrimination among whites in the matter of accommodation for travelers. The thing to accomplish was, under the guise of giving equal accommodation for whites and blacks, to compel the latter to keep to themselves while traveling in railroad passenger coaches. No one would be so wanting in candor to assert the contrary. The fundamental objection, therefore, to the statute is that it interferes with the personal freedom of citizens. "Personal liberty," it has been well said, "consists in the power of locomotion, of changing situation, or removing one's person to whatsoever place one's own inclination may direct, without imprisonment or restraint, unless by due course of law." 1 Bl. Com. 134. If a white man and a black man choose to occupy the same public conveyance on a public highway, it is their right to do so, and no government, proceeding alone on grounds of race, can prevent it without infringing the personal liberty of each.

It is one thing for railroad carriers to furnish, or to be required by law to furnish, equal accommodations for all whom they are under a legal duty to carry. It is quite another thing for government to forbid citizens of the white and black races from traveling in the same pubic conveyance, and to punish officers of railroad companies for permitting persons of the two races to occupy the same passenger coach. If a State can prescribe as a rule of civil conduct, that whites and blacks shall not travel as passengers in the same railroad coach, why may it not so regulate the use of the streets of its cities and towns as to compel white citizens to keep on one side of the street and black citizens to keep on the other? Why may it not, upon like grounds, punish whites and blacks who ride together in street cars or in open vehicles on a public road or street? Why may it not require sheriffs to assign whites to one side of the courtroom and blacks to the other? And why may it not also prohibit the commingling of the two races in the galleries of legislative halls or in public assemblages convened for the political questions of the day? Further, if this statute of Louisiana is consistent with the personal liberty of citizens, why may not the State require the separation in railroad coaches of native and naturalized citizens of the United States, or of Protestants and Roman Catholics?

The answer given at the argument to these questions was that regulations of the kind they suggest would be unreasonable, and could not, therefore, stand before the law. Is it meant that the determination of questions of legislative power depends upon the inquiry whether the statute whose validity is questioned is, in the judgment of the courts, a reasonable one, taking all the circumstances into consideration? A statute may be unreasonable merely because a sound public policy forbade its enactment. But I do not understand that the courts have anything to do with the policy or expediency of legislation. A statute may be valid, and yet upon grounds of public policy may well be characterized as unreasonable. Mr. Sedgwick correctly states the rule when he says that the legislative intention being clearly ascertained, "the courts have no other duty to perform than to execute the legislative will, without any regard to their views as to the wisdom or justice of the particular enactment." Sedgw. Stat. & Const. L. 324. . . .

The white race deems itself to be the dominant race in this country. And so it is, in prestige, in achievements, in education, in wealth, and in power. So, I doubt not that it will continue to be for all time, if it remains true to its great heritage and holds fast to the principles of constitutional liberty. But in view of the Constitution, in the eye of the law, there is in this country no superior, dominant, ruling class of citizens. There is no caste here. Our Constitution is color-blind, and neither knows nor tolerates classes among citizens. In respect of civil rights, all citizens are equal before the law. The humblest is the peer of the most powerful. The law regards man as man, and takes no account of his surroundings or of his color when his civil rights as guaranteed by the supreme law of the land are involved. It is therefore to be regretted that this high tribunal, the final expositor of the fundamental law of the land, has reached the conclusion that it is competent for a state to regulate the enjoyment by citizens of their civil rights solely upon the basis of race.

In my opinion, the judgment this day rendered will, in time, prove to be quite as pernicious as the decision made by this tribunal in the *Dred Scott Case*. . . . The recent amendments of the Constitution, it was supposed, had eradicated the principles (announced in that decision) from our institutions. But it seems that we have yet, in some of the states, a dominant race, a superior class of citizens, which assumes to regulate the enjoyment of civil rights, common to all citizens, upon the basis of race. The present decision, it may well be apprehended, will not stimulate aggressions, more or less brutal and irritating, upon the admitted rights of colored citizens, but will encourage the belief that it is possible, by means of state enactments, to defeat the beneficent purposes which the people of the United States had in view when they adopted the recent amendments of the Constitution. . . . Sixty millions of whites are in no danger from the presence here of eight millions of blacks. The destinies of the two races in this country are indissolubly linked together, and the interests of both require that the common government of all shall not permit the seeds of race hate to be planted under the sanction of law. What can more certainly arouse race hate, what more certainly create and perpetuate a feeling of distrust between these races, than state enactments which in fact proceed on the ground that colored citizens are so inferior and degraded that they cannot be allowed to sit in public coaches occupied by white citizens? That, as all will admit, is the real meaning of such legislation as was enacted in Louisiana.

The sure guaranty of the peace and security of each race is the clear, distinct, unconditional recognition by our governments, national and state, of every right that inheres in civil freedom, and of the equality before the law of all citizens of the United States without regard to race. State enactments, regulating the enjoyment of civil rights, upon the basis of race, are cunningly devised to defeat legitimate results of the war, under the pretense of recognizing equality of rights, and can have no other result than to render permanent peace impossible and to keep alive a conflict of races, the continuance of which must do harm to all concerned.

* * *

The arbitrary separation of citizens, on the basis of race, while they are on a public highway, is a badge of servitude wholly inconsistent with the civil freedom and the equality before the law established by the Constitution. It cannot be justified upon any legal grounds.

If evils will result from the commingling of the two races upon public highways established for the benefit of all, they will be infinitely less than those that will surely come from state legislation regulating the enjoyment of civil rights upon the basis of race. We boast of the freedom enjoyed by our people above all other peoples. But it is difficult to reconcile that boast with a state of the law which, practically, puts the brand of servitude and degradation upon a large class of our fellow citizens, our equals before the law. The thin disguise of "equal" accommodations for passengers in railroad coaches will not mislead anyone, or atone for the wrong this day done.

* * *

I am of opinion that the statute of Louisiana is inconsistent with the personal liberty of citizens, white and black, in that State, and hostile to both the spirit and letter of the Constitution of the United States. If laws of like character should be enacted in the several States of the Union, the effect would be in the highest degree mischievous. Slavery as an institution tolerated by law would, it is true, have disappeared from our country, but there would remain a power in the States, by sinister legislation, to interfere with the full enjoyment of the blessings of freedom: to regulate civil rights, common to all citizens, upon the basis of race; and to place in a condition of legal inferiority a large body of American citizens, now constituting a part of the political community, called the people of the United States, for whom and by whom, through representatives, our government is administered. Such a system is inconsistent with the guarantee given by the Constitution to each state of a republican form of government, and may be stricken down by Congressional action, or by the courts in the discharge of their solemn duty to maintain the supreme law of the land anything in the Constitution or laws of any State to the contrary notwithstanding.

For the reasons stated, I am constrained to withhold my assent from the opinion and judgment of the majority.

BROWN v. BOARD OF EDUCATION OF TOPEKA, KANSAS I
347 U.S. 483; 98 L. Ed. 873; 74 S. Ct. 686 (1954)

CHIEF JUSTICE WARREN *delivered the opinion of the Court.*

These cases came to us from the States of Kansas, South Carolina, Virginia, and Delaware. They are premised on different facts and different local conditions, but a common legal question justified their consideration together in this consolidated opinion.

In each of the cases, minors of the Negro race, through their legal representatives, seek aid of the courts in obtaining admission to the public schools of their community on a non segregated basis. . . . In each of the cases other than the Delaware case, a three-judge federal district court denied relief to the plaintiffs on the so-called "separate but equal" doctrine, announced by the Court in *Plessy* v. *Ferguson*. . . . In the Delaware case, the Supreme

Court of Delaware adhered to that doctrine, but ordered that the plaintiffs be admitted to the white schools because of their superiority to the Negro schools.

The plaintiffs contend that segregated public schools are not "equal" and cannot be made "equal," and that hence they are deprived of the equal protection of the laws. Because of the obvious importance of the question presented, the Court took jurisdiction. Argument was heard in the 1952 Term, and reargument was heard this Term on certain questions propounded by the Court.

Reargument was largely devoted to the circumstances surrounding the adoption of the Fourteenth Amendment in 1868. It covered exhaustively consideration of the Amendment in Congress, ratification by the States, then existing practices in racial segregation, and the views of proponents and opponents of the Amendment. This discussion and our own investigation convince us that, although these sources cast some light, it is not enough to resolve the problem with which we are faced. At best, they are inconclusive. The most avid proponents of the post-War Amendments undoubtedly intended them to remove all legal distinctions among "all persons born or naturalized in the United States." Their opponents just as certainly were antagonistic to both the letter and spirit of the Amendments and wished them to have the most limited effect. What others in Congress and the state legislatures had in mind cannot be determined with any degree of certainty.

An additional reason for the inconclusive nature of the Amendment's history, with respect to segregated schools, is the status of public education at that time. In the South, the movement toward free common schools, supported by general taxation, had not yet taken hold. Education for white children was largely in the hands of private groups. Education for Negroes was almost nonexistent, and practically all of the race was illiterate. In fact, any education of Negroes was forbidden by law in some States. Today, in contrast, many Negroes have achieved outstanding success in the arts and sciences as well as in the business and professional world. It is true that public education had already advanced further in the North, but the effect of the Amendment on Northern States was generally ignored in the Congressional debates. Even in the North, the conditions of public education did not approximate those existing today. The curriculum was usually rudimentary; ungraded schools were common in rural areas; the school term was but three months a year in many States; and compulsory school attendance was virtually unknown. As a consequence, it is not surprising that there should be so little in the history of the Fourteenth Amendment relating to its intended effect on public education.

In the first cases in this Court construing the Fourteenth Amendment, decided shortly after its adoption, the Court interpreted it as proscribing all state-imposed discriminations against the Negro race. The doctrine of "separate but equal" did not make its appearance in the Court until 1896 in the case of *Plessy* v. *Ferguson*, . . . involving not education but transportation. American courts have since labored with the doctrine for over half a century. In this Court, there have been six cases involving the "separate but equal" doctrine in the field of public education. In *Cumming* v. *Board of Education of Richmond County* and *Gong Lum* v. *Rice,* the validity of the doctrine itself was not challenged. In more recent cases, all on the graduate school level, inequality was found in that specific benefits enjoyed by white students were denied to Negro students of the same educational qualifications (*State of Missouri ex. rel. Gaines* v. *Canada, Sipuel* v. *Board of Regents of University of Oklahoma, Sweatt* v. *Painter,* and *McLaurin* v. *Oklahoma State Regents*). In none of these cases was it necessary to reexamine the doctrine to grant relief to the Negro plaintiff. And in *Sweatt* v. *Painter,* . . . the Court expressly reserved decision on the question whether *Plessy* v. *Ferguson* should be held inapplicable to public education.

* * *

In approaching this problem, we cannot turn the clock back to 1868 when the Amendment was adopted, or even to 1896 when *Plessy* v. *Ferguson* was written. We must consider public education in the light of its full development and its present place in American life throughout the Nation. Only in this way can it be determined if segregation in public schools deprives these plaintiffs of the equal protection of the laws.

Today, education is perhaps the most important function of state and local governments. Compulsory school attendance laws and the great expenditures for education both demonstrate our recognition of the importance of education to our democratic society. It is required in the performance of our most basic public responsibilities, even service in the armed forces. It is the very foundation of good citizenship. Today it is a principal instrument in awakening the child to cultural values, in preparing him for later professional training, and in helping him to adjust normally to his environment. In these days, it is doubtful that any child may reasonably be expected to succeed in life if he is denied the opportunity of an education. Such an opportunity, where the State has undertaken to provide it, is a right which must be made available to all on equal terms.

We come then to the question presented: Does segregation of children in public schools solely on the basis of race, even though the physical facilities and other "tangible" factors may be equal, deprive the children of the minority group of equal educational opportunities? We believe that it does.

In *Sweatt* v. *Painter* . . . in finding that a segregated law school for Negroes could not provide them equal educational opportunities, this Court relied in large part on "those qualities which are incapable of objective measurement but which make for greatness in a law school." In *McLaurin* v. *Oklahoma State Regents* . . . the Court, in requiring that a Negro admitted to a white graduate school be treated like all other students, again resorted to intangible considerations:" . . . his ability to study, to engage in discussion and exchange views with other students, and, in general, to learn his profession." Such considerations apply with added force to children in grade and high schools. To separate them from others of similar age and qualifications solely because of their race generates a feeling of inferiority as to their status in the community that may affect their hearts and minds in a way unlikely ever to be undone. The effect of this separation on their educational opportunities was well stated by a finding in the Kansas case by a court which nevertheless felt compelled to rule against the Negro plaintiffs:

> Segregation of white and colored children in public schools has a detrimental effect upon the colored children. The impact is greater when it has the sanction of the law; for the policy of separating the races is usually interpreted as denoting the inferiority of the negro group. A sense of inferiority affects the motivation of a child to learn. Segregation with the sanction of law, therefore, has a tendency to retard the educational and mental development of negro children and to deprive them of the benefits they would receive in a racial[ly] integrated school system.

Whatever may have been the extent of psychological knowledge at the time of *Plessy* v. *Ferguson*, this finding is amply supported by modern authority. Any language in *Plessy* v. *Ferguson* contrary to this finding is rejected.

We conclude that in the field of public education the doctrine of "separate but equal" has no place. Separate educational facilities are inherently unequal. Therefore, we hold that the plaintiffs and others similarly situated for whom the actions have been brought are, by the reason of the segregation complained of, deprived of the equal protection of the laws guaranteed by the Fourteenth Amendment. This disposition make unnecessary any discussion whether such segregation also violates the Due Process Clause of the Fourteenth Amendment.

Because these are class actions because of the wide applicability of the decision, and because of the great variety of local conditions, the formulation of decrees in these cases presents problems of considerable complexity. . . . In order that we may have the full assistance of the parties in formulating decrees, the cases will be restored to the docket, and the parties are requested to present further argument on [the appropriate decree]. The Attorney General of the United States is again invited to participate. The Attorneys General of the States requiring or permitting segregation in public education will also be permitted to appear as *amici curiae* upon request to do so by September 15, 1954, and submission of briefs by October 1, 1954.

Cases ordered restored to docket for further argument on question of appropriate decrees.

It is so ordered.

BROWN v. BOARD OF EDUCATION OF TOPEKA, KANSAS II
349 U.S. 294; 99 L. Ed. 1083; 75 S. Ct. 753 (1955)

CHIEF JUSTICE WARREN *delivered the opinion of the Court.*

These cases were decided on May 17, 1954. The opinions of that date, declaring the fundamental principle that racial discrimination in public education is unconstitutional, are incorporated herein by reference. All provisions of federal, state, or local law requiring or permitting such discrimination must yield to this principle. There remains for consideration the manner in which relief is to be accorded.

Because these cases arose under different local conditions and their disposition will involve a variety of local problems, we requested further argument on the question of relief. In view of the nationwide importance of the decision, we invited the Attorney General of the United States and the Attorneys General of all States requiring or permitting racial discrimination in public education to present their views on that question. The parties, the United States, and the States of Florida, North Carolina, Arkansas, Oklahoma, Maryland, and Texas filed briefs and participated in the oral argument.

These presentations were informative and helpful to the Court in its consideration of the complexities arising from the transition to a system of public education freed of racial discrimination. The presentations also demonstrated that substantial steps to eliminate racial discrimination in public schools have already been taken, not only in some of the communities in which these cases arose, but in some of the States appearing as *amici curiae,* and in other States as well. Substantial progress has been made in the District of Columbia and in the communities in Kansas and Delaware involved in this litigation. The defendants in the cases coming to us from South Carolina and Virginia are awaiting the decision of this Court concerning relief.

Full implementation of these constitutional principles may require solution of varied local school problems. School authorities have the primary responsibility for elucidating, assessing, and solving these problems; courts will have to consider whether the action of school authorities constitutes good faith implementation of the governing constitutional principles. Because of their proximity to local conditions and the possible need for further hearings, the courts which originally heard these cases can best perform this judicial appraisal. Accordingly, we believe it appropriate to remand the cases to those courts.

In fashioning and effectuating the decrees, the courts will be guided by equitable principles. Traditionally, equity has been characterized by a practical flexibility in shaping its remedies and by a facility for adjusting and reconciling public and private needs. These cases call for the exercise of these traditional attributes of equity power. At stake is the personal interest of the plaintiffs in admission to public schools as soon as practicable on a nondiscriminatory basis. To effectuate this interest may call for elimination of a variety of obstacles in making the transition to school systems operated in accordance with the constitutional principles set forth in our May 17, 1954, decision. Courts of equity may properly take into account the public interest in the elimination of such obstacles in a systematic and effective manner. But it would go without saying that the validity of these constitutional principles cannot be allowed to yield simply because of disagreement with them.

While giving weight to these public and private considerations, the courts will require that the defendants make a prompt and reasonable start toward full compliance with our May 17, 1954, ruling. Once such a start has been made, the courts may find that additional time is necessary to carry out the ruling in an effective manner. The burden rests upon the defendants to establish that such time is necessary in the public interest and is consistent with good faith compliance at the earliest practicable date. To that end, the courts may consider problems related to administration, arising from the physical condition of the school plant, the school transportation system, personnel, revision of school districts and attendance areas into compact units to achieve a system of determining admission to the public schools on a nonracial basis, and a revision of local laws and regulations which may be necessary in solving the foregoing problems. They will also consider the adequacy of any plans the defendants may propose to meet these problems and to effectuate a transition to a racially nondiscriminatory school system. During this period of transition, the courts will retain jurisdiction of these cases.

The judgments below, except that in the Delaware case, are accordingly reversed and remanded to the District Courts to take such proceedings and enter such orders and decrees consistent with this opinion as are necessary and proper to admit to public schools on a racially nondiscriminatory basis with all deliberate speed the parties to these cases. The judgment in the Delaware case—ordering the immediate admission of the plaintiffs to schools previously attended only by white children—is affirmed on the basis of the principle stated in our May 17, 1954, opinion, but the case is remanded to the Supreme Court of Delaware for such further proceedings as that court may deem necessary in light of this opinion.

Implementing Brown: *Generations of Plans and Litigation*

FEATURED CASES

Milliken v. *Bradley*   *Board of Education of Oklahoma City Public Schools* v. *Dowell*
Freeman v. *Pitts*   *Missouri* v. *Jenkins*

The Court's decree mandating the implementation of Brown placed primary responsibility for moving from racially segregated public school systems to desegregated unitary ones on local school governing authorities under the supervision of federal district courts in their respective jurisdictions. Even the unitiated's casual examination of the sociopolitical context in which these public officials perform their functions would have little hesitation in concluding that the goals of Brown would not be achieved without profound unsettling effects over an extended period of time.

In practice, district courts showed considerable leniency in passing on local desegregation plans. They tolerated procedural maneuvers and often granted delays that were hardly consistent with the intent of the Court's "deliberate speed" formula, for many school boards were also under heavy local pressures to resist, evade, or at least delay final desegregation orders. In addition, there were threats of violence. But in *Cooper* v. *Aaron* (358 U.S. 1, 1958) the Supreme Court made it clear that it would not tolerate postponement of court orders (and hence enjoyment of constitutional rights) in the face of threatened or actual violence.

While the Court used strong language in *Cooper* to condemn obstruction to desegregation efforts, it showed considerable leniency and deference to lower courts when presented with plans designed to keep the number of blacks attending schools with whites at a minimum. It approved pupil-placement plans and grade-a-year plans, and allowed to stand a variety of freedom-of-choice and free transfer plans, all of which contributed to the disappointingly slow pace of desegregation during the decade immediately following *Brown*.[4]

But other more blatant evasion efforts were blunted. In *Griffin* v. *Prince Edward County School Board* (377 U.S. 218, 1964), for example, the Court refused to allow authorities to abandon public education when faced with a final order to effect desegregation. In rejecting this method of defiance, the Court took the unusual step of empowering the federal district court to order the taxing authority to exercise its power in providing funds "to reopen, operate, and maintain" the public school system on a nondiscriminatory basis. In the same action, the mushrooming "private white academies" (an alternative to desegregated schools) were blunted in their attempts to gain sustenance from the public trough in the form of various tuition-grant arrangements and tax exemptions for their financial backers.

While there were occasional expressions of discontent with the slow pace of school desegregation, such as in Justice Goldberg's opinion in *Watson* v. *Memphis* (373 U.S. 526, 1963) and the Court's decision in *Rogers* v. *Paul* (382 U.S. 198, 1965), very little was done until Congress provided some support with the enactment of the Civil Rights Act of 1964. It contained a title on public school desegregation that denies federal financial assistance to any program administered in a racially discriminatory manner. Pursuant to this provision, the U.S. Office of Education, late in 1964, made eligibility for federal aid contingent on compliance with a court-ordered desegregation plan or, in the absence thereof, compliance with guidelines for school desegregation issued by the Department of Health, Education and Welfare, popularly known as the *HEW Guidelines*.

The new policy had an immediate impact, since the withholding of federal financial aid would have serious fiscal consequences for many school districts where no effort at all or at most a token effort had been made to desegregate schools. Faced with the possibility of a loss of substantial funds, especially in view of the passage of the Elementary and Secondary Education Act of 1965, most districts grudgingly moved to comply with the *Guidelines*.[5]

Indeed, the most authoritative statement on the

---

[4]See *Kelly* v. *Board of Education* (270 F.2d 209, 6th Cir., 1959); *Shuttlesworth* v. *Birmingham Board of Education* (358 U.S. 101, 1958); and *Green* v. *County School Board of New Kent County* (391 U.S. 430, 1968).

[5]These first *Guidelines*, issued in April 1965, set the fall of 1967 as the target date for the desegregation of all public school systems. A revision of the *Guidelines* in March 1968 moved the target date to the opening of the 1968–69 school year, or, at the latest, the opening of the 1969–70 year. Without abandoning the 1969–70 target, the Nixon administration adopted a flexible policy under which delays in implementing desegregation plans would be granted if warranted by "bona fide educational and administrative problems."

constitutionality of the *HEW Guidelines* was given by Circuit Judge John Minor Wisdom of the Court of Appeals for the Fifth Circuit in *United States* v. *Jefferson County Board of Education* (372 F.2d 836, 1966). In reversing district court holdings involving seven school districts in Alabama and Louisiana, Judge Wisdom held that the standards for desegregation prescribed by the *Guidelines* are within the rationale of the *Brown* ruling and the congressional objectives of the Civil Rights Act of 1964. In what must be considered the most far-reaching statement on the obligation of school boards, Judge Wisdom asserted that "the law imposes an absolute duty to integrate, in the sense that a disproportionate concentration of Negroes in certain schools cannot be ignored [for] racial mixing of students is a high priority goal."

A significant statement on the obligations that *Brown* imposed on local school boards to dismantle segregated schools systems was made by the Supreme Court while striking down the "freedom-of-choice" plan in *Green* v. *County School Board of New Kent County* (391 U.S. 430, 1968). Justice Brennan's opinion for the Court emphasized that the burden of a school board was to come forth with realistically workable plans for a speedier and more effective conversion to a unitary, nonracial school system. Brennan's emphasis on speed was underscored further one year later when a unanimous Court blunted the Nixon administration's effort to delay the court-ordered desegregation of 33 Mississippi school districts in *Alexander* v. *Holmes County Board of Education* (396 U.S. 19, 1969). The Court maintained that the standard of "all deliberate speed [was no longer] constitutionally permissible" and that the operation of segregated schools must be terminated "at once." Although the Court reaffirmed its intolerance for delay in several cases decided immediately thereafter, several justices (including Chief Justice Burger) indicated in dissent a preference for greater lower court discretion in applying the "at once" standard. See, e.g., *Carter* v. *West Feliciana Parish School Board* (396 U.S. 290, 1970). In the end, notwithstanding scattered instances of violent resistance, desegregation proceeded rather swiftly throughout the Fourth and Fifth Circuits, which contained the bulk of districts where de jure segregation had been firmly embedded for almost a century. The immediate result was that there was a larger percentage of blacks and whites attending the same schools in the South than in other parts of the country.[6]

[6]For an interesting discussion of this phenomenon, see J. Harvie Wilkinson, *From* Brown *to* Bakke: *The Supreme Court and School Integration: 1954–1978* (New York: Oxford University Press, 1979), pp. 118–125.

"IT'S NOT THE BUS, IT'S US": DESEGREGATION MOVES NORTH

Some defenders of racially segregated public schools in the South frequently called attention to the racially segregated schools in other sections of the country, complaining that *Brown* was not being fairly enforced. While concern was initially focused on the areas where state policy mandated racially separate schools, the 1970s saw judicial and administrative efforts directed at de facto segregation as practiced in the public schools of the North and West. To be sure, some scattered lower court action on the problem during the 1960s illuminated several dimensions of the problem. In the Gary, Indiana, case of *Bell* v. *School City of Gary, Ind.* (324 F.2d 209, 1963) for example, residential segregation was pinpointed as a crucial variable, and when coupled with a "neighborhood school" policy, the resulting segregated schools were predictable. But Circuit Judge F. Ryan Duffy, speaking for a unanimous panel of the Seventh Circuit, would not accept the plaintiffs' argument of school official responsibility for population shifts that affected the racial character of school attendance districts. There was no constitutional duty "to change innocently arrived-at school attendance districts." When the Supreme Court denied certiorari, *Bell* became the legal support for northern-type de facto school segregation, although other circuits were not bound thereby. (See also *Downs* v. *Kansas City*, 336 F.2d 988, 10th Cir., 1964; and *Deal* v. *Cincinnati Board of Education*, 369 F.2d 55, 6th Cir., 1966. But compare *Hobson* v. *Hansen*, 269 F. Supp. 407, 1967, where Circuit Judge J. Skelly Wright of the District of Columbia Circuit, sitting in the D.C. district court pursuant to 23 U.S.C. § 291 (c), made an expansive interpretation of *Brown* in an effort to dismantle de facto segregation in the District's school system.)

The de jure–de facto distinction was finally before the Supreme Court in *Keyes* v. *School District No. 1, Denver, Colorado* (413 U.S. 921) in 1973. Advancing the "segregative intent" test as the "differentiating factor between de jure and de facto segregation," the Court asserted that a finding of intentional and purposeful segregation in a "meaningful portion of the school system" supported a finding that de jure segregation characterized the entire system. Since the board could not prove that its policies and practices with respect to such matters as site location, attendance zones, assignment and transfer options for students, and assignment of faculty and staff, considered together with the neighborhood school policy, were not designed to create or maintain racially segregated inner-city schools, Justice Brennan concluded for the Court that de jure segregation existed and that there was no need to consider the de facto "neighborhood school policy."

In a concurring opinion, Justice Lewis Powell, echoing the charges of many apologists of southern school systems, noted that many northern school systems were as fully segregated as those of the South before the implementation of *Brown*. He charged that this northern system was being condoned under the "de facto–de jure distinction" and urged that it should be discarded and replaced with constitutional principles of national rather than merely regional application.

Crucial to the effectiveness of the desegregation effort in most large metropolitan areas is the movement of large numbers of children from their neighborhood schools to other areas of the district by bus. But the possibility of such a remedy being forced on school districts produced emotional rhetoric against what came to be popularized as "forced busing."[7] Also contributing to the exacerbation of the issue was the anti-busing rhetoric of the 1968 presidential campaign. But despite such campaign rhetoric and the subsequent condemnation of "forced busing" by President Nixon, the president's newly appointed Chief Justice led the Court in approving busing as an acceptable remedy to dismantle de jure segregation within a specific district.

In *Swann* v. *Charlotte-Mecklenburg Board of Education* (402 U.S. 1, 1971), Chief Justice Burger, speaking for a unanimous Court, made it clear that where there was a long history of school segregation and where school authorities had defaulted in their constitutional duty to produce an acceptable desegregation plan, lower federal courts possessed considerable discretion in fashioning equitable remedial relief. Consequently, the district court's plan that included the limited use of mathematical ratios of black and white pupils, the pairing and grouping of noncontiguous school zones, and a system of bus transportation to implement the racial ratio scheme was a constitutionally acceptable means of dismantling the dual system. In approving the busing component of the district court's order, the Chief Justice noted that the district had employed a bus transportation system for years and that the distances traveled and the amount of time required in the instant plan compared favorably with Charlotte's previous transportation plan.

But Burger's language did provide some comfort to opponents of busing when he maintained that the continued existence of a few one-race or largely one-race schools within a district does not in and of itself constitute a violation of *Brown*. Presumably, extensive busing would be required if a change in racial composition were to be effected. He further recognized that a valid objection to busing can be made when distance and time of travel are so great as to constitute a health risk or when they "impinge significantly on the educational process."

In another busing decision (*North Carolina State Board of Education* v. *Swann*, 402 U.S. 43, 1971), the Court affirmed a lower court decision that had ruled unconstitutional a North Carolina antibusing law. The key part of the statute prohibited the assignment of pupils to schools on the basis of race, the "involuntary busing of students," and the expenditure of public funds for such busing. Chief Justice Burger, speaking for a unanimous Court, made it clear that the statute could not stand because it limits a school authority's discretion that could impede the dismantling of a dual segregated system. Such a policy, he concluded, "must give way when it operates to hinder vindication of federal constitutional guarantees."[8]

For some whites opposed to busing for any number of reasons, *Swann* and its progeny hastened their flight to the suburbs.[9] But their apprehension over the possibility of their children being bused back to the inner cities from which they had fled was eased somewhat by the Burger Court's stance on *interdistrict* busing. On this issue, the Nixon administration's antibusing position was clearly evident in the votes of his appointees. Having split four-to-four on the first interdistrict busing case presented it in 1973, involving three districts in the Richmond, Virginia, metropolitan

---

[7]For a comprehensive examination of the issue see Gary Orfield, *Must We Bus? Segregated Schools and National Policy* (Washington, D.C.: The Brookings Institution, 1978).

[8]One year after its first busing decision, the Court's line of unanimous school desegregation decisions was broken in *Wright* v. *Emporia* (407 U.S. 451, 1972). Nevertheless, the five-to-four majority struck down an attempt of a city to detach itself from a county school unit under a desegregation order and establish a separate district coterminus with the white residential area. See also *United States* v. *Scotland Neck City Board of Education* (407 U.S. 493, 1972).

[9]Many critics of school desegregation found support in Professor James Coleman's controversial 1975 study in which he concluded that busing for desegregation contributed significantly to the exodus of whites from big city school systems. ("Liberty and Equality in School Desegregation," 6 *Social Policy* 9, January-February, 1976.)

area,[10] the Court enunciated a policy one year later with all nine justices participating in the decision of *Milliken* v. *Bradley* (418 U.S. 717). There, a federal district court utilized the interdistrict busing remedy to dismantle racially segregated schools in the three-county Detroit metropolitan area embracing 53 districts. The lower court reasoned that because of the residential patterns, the only effective remedy for the elimination of segregated schools was a two-way busing arrangement between the central city and the suburbs. In short, the court concluded that a plan limited to Detroit would only produce an all-black city system surrounded by a number of all-white suburban systems. The Court of Appeals for the Sixth Circuit agreed with this conclusion and noted that the proposed interdistrict remedy could be fashioned because of the power that the state exercises in the control of local school districts. But, by a five-to-four vote (with Justice Potter Stewart joining the four Nixon appointees), the Supreme Court rejected such an expansive application of busing to effect remedial relief, emphasizing that there was no constitutional violation by the suburban districts. The Chief Justice held, however, that interdistrict busing was a permissible remedy where discriminatory acts in one district produced discrimination in the other or where there was collusive action in the gerrymandering of the districts involved.

Justice Thurgood Marshall, who was chief counsel for the petitioners in *Brown*, expressed his outrage at the majority position in a sharp dissent. Characterizing the ruling as an "emasculation of our constitutional guarantee of equal protection of the laws," Marshall complained that the decision had the effect of saying to black children in inner city schools of large metropolitan areas that they have no remedy to enforce their constitutional rights as declared in *Brown*.

Notwithstanding *Milliken*, busing was still a remedy that could be employed where a violation of *Brown* was found, even involving central city–suburban arrangements. This was underscored, for example, when, in *Newberry Area Council* v. *Board of Education of Jefferson County, Kentucky* (510 F.2d 1358, cert. denied, 421 U.S. 931, 1975), the Supreme Court refused to overturn a metropolitan desegregation plan ordered by lower federal courts that embraced the city of Louisville, Kentucky, and its surrounding suburban area. But this and a number of other post-*Swann* intradistrict busing orders only heightened opposition to desegregation efforts in which the reassignment of pupils (and their transportation by bus) was an essential ingredient of the plan. From Pontiac, Michigan, to Boston, Massachusetts, and Dayton and Columbus, Ohio, to Los Angeles, California, the cry was the same—"no forced busing" of children from their neighborhoods. Some of the opposition came from black parents, whose children had shouldered a disproportionate share of the burden in the movement of students from one locale to another.

But the Supreme Court refused to deny lower courts the busing remedy in fashioning relief where school systems were adjudged to be in violation of *Brown*. In both the Columbus and Dayton, Ohio, cases of 1979 (*Columbus Board of Education* v. *Penick*, 443 U.S. 449; *Dayton Board of Education* v. *Brickman II*, 443 U.S. 526),[11] the Supreme Court affirmed rulings of the Court of Appeals for the Sixth Circuit ordering systemwide desegregation upon finding that the respective boards had intentionally operated racially segregated schools on a systemwide basis prior to and after *Brown*. Subsequent actions to dismantle these segregated systems involved the busing of significant numbers of students.

When desegregation efforts were undertaken in northern urban areas, many members of Congress (some of whom had helped to enact the stringent "funds cutoff" desegregation enforcement provision in the 1964 Civil Rights Act) were not so insistent on the implementation of that provision as it hit close to home. When, for example, HEW deferred payment of some $32 million of federal funds to the Chicago school system in 1965 pending an investigation of charges that the system was not operating in compliance with *Brown*, a number of prominent Illinois members of Congress, who had given crucial support in passing the 1964 legislation to enforce *Brown*, reassessed their positions. Thereafter, attempts to restrict HEW's enforcement authority increased in the Congress. Amendments to federal aid-to-education proposals de-

---

[10]In *Bradley* v. *School Board of the City of Richmond* (388 F. Supp. 67, 1972), Federal District Judge Robert Mehrige, upon finding that the undesirable racial imbalance of the Richmond and two adjoining suburban districts stemmed partly from invidious state action, ordered the consolidation of the three districts and extensive two-way busing between the city and the suburban counties.

[11]In an earlier ruling in the Dayton controversy (*Dayton Board of Education* v. *Brickman I*, 433 U.S. 406, 1977), the Court had set aside a systemwide plan because the lower court's general finding of "cumulative violations" was not sufficient to support the scope of the remedy. On remand, a more particularized finding of particular segregative acts was required.

signed to weaken or curtail the federal effort to enforce compliance with *Brown* appeared regularly.[12]

After President Nixon's election in 1968 and the *Swann* decision in 1971, congressional efforts to curb busing as a remedy for school desegregation intensified. Much of this effort was directed toward legislating restrictions on the use of busing in designing desegregation remedies. But most of such proposals were of dubious constitutionality and, although popular among many members, none emerged from the Congress until July 1974 (Title II of the 1974 of the Elementary And Secondary Education Act Amendments). But the antibusing provisions incorporated in that massive aid-to-education act of 1974 were so watered down from the intense debate in Congress that President Ford (who found the act awaiting his action when he suddenly became president upon the resignation of President Nixon), in signing the measure, expressed dissatisfaction with the weak antibusing provisions.[13]

Efforts to curb busing as a desegregation remedy continued during the Carter administration. The antibusing forces in Congress were finally successful in attaching an antibusing provision as a *rider* to the 1981 appropriations measure for the Commerce, Justice, and State departments in the final days of the 96th Congress. The essential thrust of the measure was directed at the Justice Department and prohibited it from bringing desegregation actions against local school districts where busing would be included as a remedy. Just five weeks before he left office, however, President Carter vetoed the measure because he believed it would set a dangerous precedent for congressional incursions into the domain of executive law enforcement responsibilities.

Congressional antibusing efforts continued during the Reagan administration, and on occasions, each house passed separate measures designed to curb the use of the busing remedy. Some of them would have denied the use of federal money to support any busing dimension of a desegregation plan. Others would have prohibited the Department of Justice from participating in cases where the busing remedy would be used to effect relief. The last major effort to get Congress to ban busing for school desegregation purposes was undertaken by Senator Jesse Helms (R., N.C.) during President Reagan's second term. After his antibusing bill was killed in committee in 1986 (S. 37), Helms attempted to accomplish his objective with an amendment to the Higher Education Act of 1986. Like many earlier efforts, it too was a court-curbing measure. Its key provision would have prohibited federal courts from mandating busing plans that would require travel in excess of 10 miles round-trip. But, as in the earlier efforts, the Senate rejected the amendment.[14]

Antibusing rhetoric and efforts also intensified in the executive branch during the Reagan administration, as the president moved to accomplish a major objective of many of his supporters. Working through the assistant attorney general charged with the enforcement of civil rights laws (H. Bradford Reynolds), a "new leniency" was emphasized in the enforcement of *Brown*. Compliance litigation was shunted aside for voluntary measures adopted in negotiated consent decrees. Stressing the use of magnet-school concept to attain an acceptable racial mix, these decrees almost always relegated mandatory busing to a remedy of last resort. (See *United States* v. *Chicago Board of Education*, 88 F.R.D. 679, 1981).

The Reagan administration's antibusing effort was also directed at the modification and/or withdrawal of existing busing mandates. In 1982, for example, the Department of Justice, for the first time since busing was approved as a desegregation remedy in *Swann*, petitioned lower federal courts to stop the busing plan then in effect in East Baton Rouge Parish, Louisiana, and Nashville, Tennessee. In neither instance did the courts grant the request, and the Supreme Court refused to review the Nashville case when the Justice Department sought to use the appeal for a reexamination of *Swann*. See *Metropolitan County Board of Education of Nashville* v. *Kelley* (103 S. Ct. 834, 1983).

Another strategy of antibusing forces was to use the popular initiative and referendum to impose

[12]For an excellent summary of those efforts, see Gary Orfield, "Congress, the President, and Antibusing Legislation," vol. 7 *Journal of Law and Education* 81, at 88–136 (January 1975).

[13]The act prohibits the busing of a student beyond the school "next closest" to his residence or busing that poses a health risk or impinges significantly "on the educational process" of students. Also, the act includes a provision that specifies that nothing in the measure is intended "to modify or diminish the authority of the courts . . . to enforce fully the Fifth and Fourteenth Amendments. . . . " This was considered by some as giving courts a green light to order extensive busing simply on a finding that there is no other remedy to protect the constitutional rights involved. See U.S.C., 1975 Supp., Title 20, secs. 1701 (6b) and 1714.

[14]Senator Lowell Weicker (R., Conn.) led a successful filibuster against another 1986 antibusing effort in the Senate, where an attempt was made to attach an amendment to the Health and Human Services funding bill for fiscal year 1987 that would have denied use of federal funds for the involuntary busing of pupils and/or teachers to implement a desegregation plan.

busing restrictions. But such efforts had mixed results. In *Washington* v. *Seattle School District No. 1* (458 U.S. 457, 1982), for example, a popularly adopted statute prohibiting the assignment of pupils to schools outside their neighborhood was struck down as a violation of the equal protection clause of the Fourteenth Amendment. The statute allowed exceptions for assignment outside the neighborhood for any number of purposes, but singled out racial desegregation as a "prohibited" purpose. This, contended Justice Harry Blackmun speaking for the five-to-four majority, was at odds with *Hunter* v. *Erickson, infra,* because it structured a "decision-making process" where subsequent "state action placed special burdens on racial minorities."

On the same day, however, the Court did not find a California busing policy so flawed in *Crawford* v. *Board of Education of City of Los Angeles* (458 U.S. 527, 1982). The constitutional provision, adopted through the popular initiative process, limited the remedial power of state courts in mandating busing for the implementation of desegregation to only the kinds of situations where federal courts would be required to use the busing remedy to correct a Fourteenth Amendment violation. The Court noted that in this case (unlike the Seattle case) all the people had done in their initiative was to decide that, in effecting school desegregation, it was more appropriate for state courts to apply the standards demanded by the Fourteenth Amendment than the exacting standards of the state constitution. Justice Lewis Powell, who spoke for the eight-to-one majority, agreed with the lower court finding that there was no "discriminatory intent." Rather, the provision was adopted to advance "legitimate nondiscriminatory objectives."

After two decades of federal court supervision of the process of dismantling the racially based dual public school systems, some districts sought to terminate that scrutiny on the ground that they were now operating unitary systems in full compliance with *Brown*. Many prodesegregation forces were wary of such termination efforts, fearing that without court supervision some districts would pursue policies that could lead to the resegregation of the schools. But in *Pasadena City Board of Education* v. *Spangler* (427 U.S. 424, 1976), the Court took a step in the direction of terminating such judicial supervision when Justice Rehnquist asserted for the six-to-two majority that "once the affirmative duty to desegregate has been accomplished and racial discrimination through official action is eliminated from the system," school governing boards are not required to make annual adjustments in the racial composition of student bodies caused by demographic fluctuation. Noting that in this case school authorities had implemented the district court's order to obtain racial neutrality with respect to attendance, the Court ruled that the district court was not entitled to require school authorities to make a year-by-year adjustment of its attendance zones. Three years later the district court relinquished complete authority over the school board.

Efforts to terminate federal court supervision met with mixed results in other jurisdictions around the country. Following the views enunciated in *Pasadena*, the Court of Appeals for the Fourth Circuit made it clear in *Riddick by Riddick* v. *School Board of City of Norfolk* (784 F.2d 521, 1986) that once a desegregation plan achieves its objective of dismantling a segregated system and attaining a unitary one, the district court's role ends. The Court stressed, however, that such a finding does not bar any future court intervention where there is evidence of intentional actions by school authorities that lead to resegregation.

The Rehnquist Court has continued to countenance the move away from the judicial supervision of school district desegregation efforts once they have attained a unitary status, even when such districts continue to maintain a number of one-race schools because of a variety of demographic factors. In *Board of Education of Oklahoma City Public Schools* v. *Dowell* (111 S. Ct. 630, 1991), for example, Chief Justice Rehnquist emphasized the value of local participation in school governance in schools that were no longer vestiges of state-imposed segregation policies. Asserting that "school desegregation decrees are not intended to operate in perpetuity," the Chief Justice supported the dissolution of a desegregation decree once a district had "operated in compliance with it for a reasonable period of time." For him, the "reasonable period of time" was that period required to remedy the effects of the past state-imposed segregation policies. In the end, the Chief Justice provided some guidance to lower courts in future termination actions:

> In considering whether the vestiges of *de jure* segregation had been eliminated as far as practicable, the District Court should look not only at student assignments, but to every facet of school operations—faculty, staff, transportation, extra-curricular activities and facilities. . . .

In a sharp dissent, Justice Thurgood Marshall,

joined by Justices Blackmun and Stevens, complained that the majority had departed form the central aim of the Court's desegregation jurisprudence—the elimination of racially segregated schools and the prevention of their recurrence. Arguing that desegregation decrees should not be lifted "so long as conditions likely to inflict the stigmatic injury condemned in *Brown I* persist," Marshall objected to the majority's acceptance of some one-race schools and underscored the availability of "feasible steps" that could be used "to avoid one-race schools." He, as the leading architect of the attack on school segregation while chief counsel for the Legal Defense and Education Fund of the NAACP, underscored his dismay of the Court's action when he asserted:

> The practical question now before us is whether, 13 years after [the Oklahoma City School Board was directed to eliminate its dual segregated system], the same . . . Board should have been allowed to return many of its elementary schools to their former one-race status. The majority today suggests that 13 years of desegregation was enough.

In the end, Marshall was concerned that the majority did not provide the guidance that district courts should have in dealing with the vestiges of past de jure segregation.

That the termination of the judicial superintendence of school board desegregation efforts is becoming the school issue of the 1990s is evidenced by the Court's return to it in the term following its *Dowell* ruling in the context of *Freeman* v. *Pitts* (112 S. Ct. 1430, 1992). In that case, eight of the justices (Justice Thomas did not participate because he had not been confirmed when oral arguments were heard) agreed that lower courts could terminate their supervision of school desegregation efforts, but there was considerable disagreement on "timing," that is, whether court supervision could be terminated in one category (student assignments) yet continued in another (faculty assignments). Additionally, the justices were not of one mind on whether full superintendence should be maintained until every facet of school operations has been desegregated. Justice Kennedy, whose opinion was supported by Chief Justice Rehnquist and Justices White, Scalia, and Souter, took the position that the lower courts may disengage from supervision in some areas of school operations while continuing surveillance in others. But Justice Scalia would accelerate the withdrawal of court superintendence when there is no longer intentional discrimination in the operation of a school system. This standard could certainly launch a massive return to the old "neighborhood school" model that reflects the segregated housing patterns in much of the county. But Justices Blackmun, Stevens, and O'Connor cautioned that the district courts should be required to undertake a searching examination of a school board's full array of actions to determine if they have in anyway contributed to continued segregation. Certainly, the kinds of reservations raised in these concurrences will almost certainly spawn another "generation of litigation" before the objective of *Brown* is fully realized.

While the Court was grappling with the "termination of judicial superintendence" of desegregation efforts, it was confronted with the troublesome issue of financing their implementation in *Missouri* v. *Jenkins* (110 S. Ct. 1651, 1990). Growing weary of the desegregation question, some school boards refused to commit their declining revenues to meet the costs associated with desegregation initiatives. But a bare five-to-four majority of the Court would not permit school boards to escape from their obligations under *Brown* by arguing insufficient fiscal capacity to implement desegregation programs. Here the Court upheld the power of a federal district judge to direct Kansas City, Missouri, school authorities to increase the property tax levy to pay for its magnet school desegregation effort. In taking this extraordinary remedial action, the Court was careful to stress that judges *do not* possess the power to *impose taxation*. But the Court did make it clear that restrictive state policies on the taxing powers that may inhibit school authorities in their efforts to comply with federal constitutional requirements in the school desegregation process may be modified or set aside to the extent required to meet the constitutional obligation.

CHIEF JUSTICE BURGER *delivered the opinion of the Court.*

We granted certiorari in these consolidated cases to determine whether a federal court may impose a multidistrict, areawide remedy to a single district *de jure* segregation problem absent any finding that the other included school districts have failed to operate unitary school systems within their districts, absent any claim or finding that the boundary lines of any affected school district were established with the purpose of fostering racial segregation in public schools, absent any finding that the included districts committed acts which effected segregation within the other districts, and absent a meaningful opportunity for the included neighboring school districts to present evidence or be heard on the propriety of a multidistrict remedy or on the question of constitutional violations by those neighboring districts.

The action was commenced in August of 1970 by the respondents, the Detroit Branch of the National Association for the Advancement of Colored People and individual parents and students, on behalf of a class . . . to include "all school children of the City of Detroit and all Detroit resident parents who have children of school age." The named defendants in the District Court included the Governor of Michigan, the Attorney General, the State Board of Education, the State Superintendent of Public Instruction, and the Board of Education of the City of Detroit. . . . In their complaint respondents attacked the constitutionality of a statute of the State of Michigan known as Act 48 of the 1970 Legislature on the ground that it put the State of Michigan in the position of unconstitutionally interfering with the execution and operation of a voluntary plan of partial high school desegregation. . . . The complaint also alleged that the Detroit Public School System was and is segregated on the basis of race as a result of the official policies and actions. . . .

Initially the matter was tried on respondents' motion for preliminary injunction to restrain the enforcement of Act 48 so as to permit the April 7 Plan to be implemented. On that issue, the District Court ruled that respondents were not entitled to a preliminary injunction since at that stage there was no proof that Detroit had a dual segregated school system. On appeal, the Court of Appeals found that the "implementation of the April 7 Plan was [unconstitutionally] thwarted by state action in the form of the Act of the Legislature of Michigan." . . . The case was remanded to the District Court for an expedited trial on the merits.

. . . On September 27, 1971, the District Court issued its findings and conclusions on the issue of segregation finding that "Government actions and inaction at all levels, federal, state and local, have combined, with those of private organizations, such as loaning institutions and real estate associations and brokerage firms, to establish and to maintain the pattern of residential segregation throughout the Detroit metropolitan area." . . .

The District Court found that the Detroit Board of Education created and maintained optional attendance zones within Detroit neighborhoods undergoing racial transition and between high school attendance areas of opposite predominant racial compositions. These zones, the court found, had the "natural probable, foreseeable and actual effect" of allowing White pupils to escape identifiably Negro schools. . . . [T]he District Court concluded, the natural and actual effect of these acts was the creation and perpetuation of school segregation within Detroit.

The District Court found that in the operation of its school transportation program, which was designed to relieve overcrowding, the Detroit Board had admittedly bused Negro Detroit pupils in predominantly Negro schools which were beyond or away from closer White schools with available space. . . .

With respect to the Detroit Board of Education's practices in school construction, the District found that Detroit school construction generally tended to have segregative effect with the great majority of schools being built in either overwhelmingly all Negro or all White neighborhoods so that the new schools opened as predominantly one-race schools. . . .

The District Court also found that the State of Michigan had committed several constitutional violations with respect to the exercise of its general responsibility for, and supervision of, public education. The State, for example, was found to have failed, until the 1971 Session of the Michigan Legislature, to provide authorization or funds for the transportation of pupils within Detroit regardless of their poverty or distance from the school to which they were assigned: during this same period the State provided many neighboring, mostly White, suburban districts the full range of state supported transportation.

The District Court found that the State, through Act 48, acted to "impede, delay and minimize racial integration in Detroit schools.". . .

Accordingly, the District Court proceeded to order the Detroit Board of Education to submit desegregation plans limited to the segregation problems found to be existing within the city of Detroit. At the same time, however, the state defendants were directed to submit desegregation plans encompassing the three-county metropolitan area despite the fact that the school districts of these three counties were not parties to the action and despite the fact that there had been no claim that these outlying counties, encompassing some 85 separate school districts, had committed constitutional violations. An effort to appeal these orders to the Court of Appeals was dismissed on the ground that the orders were not appealable. . . .

Upon granting the motion to intervene, on March 15, 1972, the District Court advised the petitioning intervenors that the court had previously set March 22, 1972, as the date for the filing of briefs on the legal propriety of a "metropolitan" plan of desegregation and, accordingly, that the intervening school districts would have one week to muster their legal arguments on the issue. . . .

On March 28, 1972, the District Court issued its findings and conclusions on the three "Detroit-only" plans submitted by the city Board and the respondents. It found that the best of the three plans "would make the Detroit system more identifiably Black, . . . thereby increasing the flights of Whites from the city and the system." From this the court concluded that the plan "would not accomplish desegregation within the corporate geographical limits of the city." Accordingly, the District Court held that "it must look beyond the limits of the Detroit school district for a solution to the problem." . . .

During the period from March 28, 1972, to April 14, 1972, the District Court conducted hearings on a metropolitan plan. . . . [I]t designated 53 of the 85 suburban school districts plus Detroit as the "desegregation area" and appointed a panel to prepare and submit "an effective desegregation plan" for the Detroit schools that would encompass the entire desegregation area. The plan was to be based on 15 clusters, each containing part of the Detroit system and two or more suburban districts, and was to "achieve the greatest degree of actual desegregation to the end that, upon imple-

mentation, no school, grade or classroom [would be] substantially disproportionate to the overall pupil racial composition."

On July 11, 1972, and in accordance with a recommendation by the court-appointed desegregation panel, the District Court ordered the Detroit Board of Education to purchase or lease "at least" 295 school buses for the purposes of providing transportation under an interim plan to be developed for the 1972–1973 school year. The costs of this acquisition were to be borne by the state defendants.

On June 12, 1973, a divided Court of Appeals, sitting *en banc*, affirmed in part, vacated in part and remanded for further proceedings. The Court of Appeals held, first, that the record supported the District Court's findings and conclusions on the constitutional violations. . . .

The Court of Appeals also agreed with the District Court that "any less comprehensive a solution than a metropolitan area plan would result in an all black school system immediately surrounded by practically all white suburban school systems, with an overwhelming white majority population in the total metropolitan area." The court went on to state that it could "not see how such segregation can be any less harmful to the minority students than if the same result were accomplished within one school district."

Accordingly, the Court of Appeals concluded that "the only feasible desegregation plan involves the crossing of the boundary lines between the Detroit School District and adjacent or nearby school districts for the limited purpose of providing an effective desegregation plan." It reasoned that such a plan would be appropriate because of the State's violations, and could be implemented because of the State's authority to control local school districts. Without further elaboration, and without any discussion of the claims that no constitutional violation by the outlying districts had been shown and that no evidence on that point had been allowed, the Court of Appeals held:

> [T]he State has committed *de jure* acts of segregation and . . . the State controls the instrumentalities whose action is necessary to remedy the harmful effects of the State acts.

An interdistrict remedy was thus held to be "within the equity powers of the District Court." . . .

Viewing the record as a whole, it seems clear that the District Court and the Court of Appeals shifted the primary focus from a Detroit remedy to the metropolitan area only because of their conclusion that total desegregation of Detroit would not produce the racial balance which they perceived as desirable. Both courts proceeded on an assumption that the Detroit schools could not be truly desegregated—in their view of what constituted desegregation—unless the racial composition of the student body of each school substantially reflected the racial composition of the population of the metropolitan area as a whole. . . .

In *Swann*, which arose in the context of a single independent school district, the Court held:

> If we were to read the holding of the District Court to require as a matter of substantive constitutional right, any particular degree of racial balance or mixing, that approach would be disapproved and we would be obliged to reverse. 402 U.S., at 24, 1971.

The clear import of this language from *Swann* is that desegregation, in the sense of dismantling a dual school system, does not require any particular racial balance in each "school, grade or classroom." . . .

The Michigan educational structure involved in this case, in common with most States, provides for a large measure of local control and a review of the scope and character of these local powers indicates the extent to which the interdistrict remedy approved by the two courts could disrupt and alter the structure of public education in Michigan. The metropolitan remedy would require, in effect, consolidation of 54 independent school districts historically administered as separate units into a vast new super school district. Entirely apart from the logistical and other serious problems attending large-scale transportation of students, the consolidation would give rise to an array of other problems in financing and operating this new school system. Some of the more obvious questions would be: What would be the status and authority of the present popularly elected school boards? Would the children of Detroit be within the jurisdiction and operating control of a school board elected by the parents and residents of other districts? What board or boards would levy taxes for school operations in these 54 districts constituting the consolidated metropolitan area? What provisions could be made for assuring substantial equality in tax levies among the 54 districts, if this were deemed requisite? What provisions would be made for financing? Would the validity of long-term bonds be jeopardized unless approved by all of the component districts as well as the State? What body would determine that portion of the curricula now left to the discretion of local school boards? Who would

establish attendance zones, purchase school equipment, locate and construct new schools, and indeed attend to all the myriad day-to-day decisions that are necessary to school operations affecting potentially more than three quarters of a million pupils?

It may be suggested that all of these vital operational problems are yet to be resolved by the District Court, and that this is the purpose of the Court of Appeals' proposed remand. But it is obvious from the scope of the interdistrict remedy itself that absent a complete restructuring of the laws of Michigan relating to school districts the District Court will become first a *de facto* "legislative authority" to resolve these complex questions, and then the "school superintendent" for the entire area. This is a task which few, if any, judges are qualified to perform and one which would deprive the people of control of schools through their elected representatives.

Of course, no state law is above the Constitution. School district lines and the present laws with respect to local control are not sacrosanct, and if they conflict with the Fourteenth Amendment federal courts have a duty to prescribe appropriate remedies. . . . But our prior holdings have been confined to violations and remedies within a single school district. We therefore turn to address, for the first time, the validity of a remedy mandating cross-district or interdistrict consolidation to remedy a condition of segregation found to exist in only one district.

The controlling principle consistently expounded in our holdings is that the scope of the remedy is determined by the nature and extent of the constitutional violation. Before the boundaries of separate and autonomous school districts may be set aside by consolidating the separate units for remedial purposes or by imposing a cross-district remedy, it must first be shown that there has been a constitutional violation within one district that produces a significant segregative effect in another district. Specifically it must be shown that racially discriminatory acts of the state or local school district, or of a single school district have been a substantial cause of interdistrict segregation. Thus an interdistrict remedy might be in order where the racially discriminatory acts of one or more school districts caused racial segregation in an adjacent district, or where district lines have been deliberately drawn on the basis of race. In such circumstances an interdistrict remedy would be appropriate to eliminate the interdistrict segregation directly caused by the constitutional violation. Conversely, without an interdistrict violation and interdistrict effect, there is no constitutional wrong calling for an interdistrict remedy.

The record before us, voluminous as it is, contains evidence of *de jure* segregated conditions only in the Detroit schools. . . . With no showing of significant violation by the 53 outlying school districts and no evidence of any interdistrict violation or effect, the court went beyond the original theory of the case as framed by the pleadings and mandated a metropolitan area remedy. To approve the remedy ordered by the court would impose on the outlying districts, not shown to have committed any constitutional violation, a wholly impermissible remedy based on a standard not hinted at in *Brown I* and *II* or any holding of this Court. . . .

The constitutional right of the Negro respondents residing in Detroit is to attend a unitary school system in that district. Unless petitioners drew the district lines in a discriminatory fashion, or arranged for White students residing in the Detroit district to attend schools in Oakland and Macomb Counties, they were under no constitutional duty to make provisions for Negro students to do so. . . .

We conclude that the relief ordered by the District Court and affirmed by the Court of Appeals was based upon an erroneous standard and was unsupported by record evidence that acts of the outlying districts affected the discrimination found to exist in the schools of Detroit. Accordingly, the judgment of the Court of Appeals is vacated and the case is remanded for further proceedings consistent with this opinion leading to prompt formulation of a decree directed to eliminating the segregation found to exist in Detroit city schools, a remedy which has been delayed since 1970.

Reversed and remanded.

JUSTICE MARSHALL, *with whom* JUSTICE DOUGLAS, JUSTICE BRENNAN, *and* JUSTICE WHITE *join, dissenting.*

In *Brown* v. *Board of Education I*, 347 U.S. 483 (1954), this Court held that segregation of children in public schools on the basis of race deprives minority group children of equal educational opportunities and therefore denies them the equal protection of the laws under the Fourteenth Amendment. This Court recognized then that remedying decades of segregation in public education would not be an easy task. . . .

After 20 years of small, often difficult steps toward that great end, the Court today takes a giant step backwards. Notwithstanding a record showing widespread and pervasive racial segregation in the educational system provided by the State of Michigan for children in Detroit, this Court holds that the District Court was powerless to require the State to remedy its constitutional violation in any meaningful fashion. Ironically purporting to base its result on the principle that the scope of the remedy in a desegregation case should be determined by the nature and the extent of the constitutional violation, the Court's answer is to provide no remedy at all for the violation proved in this case, thereby guaranteeing that Negro children in Detroit will receive the same separate and inherently unequal education in the future as they have been unconstitutionally afforded in the past.

I cannot subscribe to this emasculation of our constitutional guarantee of equal protection of the laws and must respectfully dissent. Our precedents, in my view, firmly establish that where, as here, state-imposed segregation has been demonstrated, it becomes the duty of the State to eliminate root and branch all vestiges of racial discrimination and to achieve the greatest possible degree of actual desegregation. I agree with both the District Court and the Court of Appeals that, under the facts of this case, this duty cannot be fulfilled unless the State of Michigan involves outlying metropolitan area school districts in its desegregation remedy. Furthermore, I perceive no basis either in law or in the practicalities of the situation justifying the State's interposition of school district boundaries as absolute barriers to the implementation of an effective desegregation remedy. Under established and frequently used Michigan procedures, school district lines are both flexible and permeable for a wide variety of purposes, and there is no reason why they must now stand in the way of meaningful desegregation relief. . . .

Nowhere in the Court's opinion does the majority confront, let alone respond to, the District Court's conclusion that a remedy limited to the city of Detroit would not effectively desegregate the Detroit city schools. I, for one, find the District Court's conclusion well supported by the record and its analysis compelled by our prior cases. . . .

[T]he District Court's decision to expand its desegregation decree beyond the geographical limits of the city of Detroit rested in large part on its conclusions (A) that the State of Michigan was ultimately responsible for curing the condition of segregation within the Detroit city schools, and (B) that the Detroit-only remedy would not accomplish this task. In my view, both of these conclusions are well supported by the facts of this case and by this Court's precedents.

To begin with, the record amply supports the District Court's findings that the State of Michigan, through state officers and state agencies, has engaged in purposeful acts which created or aggravated segregation in the Detroit schools. The State Board of Education, for example, prior to 1962, exercised its authority to supervise local school site selection in a manner which contributed to segregation. Furthermore, the State's continuing authority, after 1962, to approve school building construction plans had intertwined the State with site selection decisions of the Detroit Board of Education which had the purpose and effect of maintaining segregation.

The State had also stood in the way of past efforts to desegregate the Detroit city schools. In 1970, for example, the Detroit School Board had begun implementation of its own desegregation plan for its high schools, despite considerable public and official resistance. The State Legislature intervened by enacting Act 48 of the Public Acts of 1970, specifically prohibiting implementation of the desegregation plan and thereby continuing the growing segregation of the Detroit school system. Adequate desegregation of the Detroit system was also hampered by discriminatory restrictions placed by the State on the use of transportation within Detroit. While state aid for transportation was provided by statute for suburban districts, many of which were highly urbanized, aid for intracity transportation was excepted. One of the effects of this restriction was to encourage the construction of small walk-in neighborhood schools in Detroit, thereby lending aid to the intentional policy of creating a school system which reflected, to the greatest extent feasible, extensive residential segregation. Indeed, that one of the purposes of the transportation restriction was to impede desegregation was evidenced when the Michigan Legislature amended the State Transportation Aid Act to cover intracity transportation but expressly prohibited the allocation of funds for cross busing of students within a school district to achieve racial balance.

Under Michigan law "a school district is an agency of the State government." It is "a legal division of territory, created by the State for educational purposes, to which the State has granted such powers as are deemed necessary to permit the district to function as a State agency." Racial discrimination by the school district, an agency of the State, is therefore racial discrimination by the State itself, forbidden by the Fourteenth Amendment.

Most significantly for present purposes, the State has wide-ranging powers to consolidate and merge school districts, even without the consent of the districts themselves or the local citizenry. . . . Indeed, recent years have witnessed an accelerated program of school district consolidations, mergers, and annexations, many of which were state imposed. . . . Furthermore, the State has broad powers to transfer property from one district to another, again without the consent of the local school districts affected by the transfer. . . .

Whatever may be the history of public education in other parts of our Nation, it simply flies in the face of reality to say, as does the majority, that in Michigan, "No single tradition in public education is more deeply rooted than local control over the operation of schools." . . . As the State's supreme court has said: "We have repeatedly emphasized that education in this State is not a local concern, but belongs to the State at large." . . .

The continued racial identifiability of the Detroit schools under a Detroit-only remedy is not simply a reflection of their high percentage of Negro students. What is or is not a racially identifiable vestige of *de jure* segregation must necessarily depend on several factors. Foremost among these should be the relationship between the schools in question and the neighboring community. For these purposes the city of Detroit and its surrounding suburbs must be viewed as a single community. Detroit is closely connected to its suburbs in many ways, and the metropolitan area is viewed as a single cohesive unit by its residents. . . .

It is a hollow remedy indeed where "after supposed 'desegregation' the schools are segregated in fact." *Hobson* v. *Hansen*, 269 F. Supp. 401, 495 (D.D.C. 1967). We must do better than "substitute . . . one segregated school system for another segregated school system." *Wright*, 407 U.S., at 456. To suggest, as does the majority, that a Detroit-only plan somehow remedies the effects of *de jure* segregation of the races is, in my view, to make a solemn mockery of *Brown I*'s holding that separate educational facilities are inherently unequal and of *Swann*'s unequivocal mandate that the answer to *de jure* segregation is the greatest possible degree of actual desegregation.

One final set of problems remains to be considered. We recognized in *Brown II*, and have reemphasized ever since, that in fashioning relief in desegregation cases, "the courts will be guided by equitable principles. Traditionally equity has been characterized by a practical flexibility in shaping its remedies and by a facility for adjusting and reconciling public and private needs."

Though not resting its holding on this point,

the majority suggests that various equitable considerations militate against interdistrict relief. The Court refers to, for example, financing and administrative problems, the logistical problems attending large-scale transportation of students, and the prospect of the District Court's becoming a "*de facto* 'legislative authority' and 'school superintendent' for the entire area." The entangling web of problems woven by the Court, however, appears on further consideration to be constructed of the flimsiest of threads. . . .

Some disruption, of course, is the inevitable product of any desegregation decree, whether it operates within one district or on an interdistrict basis. As we said in *Swann*, however,

> Absent a constitutional violation there would be no basis for judicially ordering assignment of students on a racial basis. All things being equal, with no history of discrimination, it might well be desirable to assign pupils to schools nearest their homes. But all things are not equal in a system that has been deliberately constructed and maintained to enforce racial segregation. The remedy for such segregation may be admin-

istratively awkward, inconvenient, and even bizarre in some situations and may impose burdens on some; but all awkwardness and inconvenience cannot be avoided. . . . 402 U.S., at 28.

Desegregation is not and was never expected to be an easy task. Racial attitudes ingrained in our Nation's childhood and adolescence are not quickly thrown aside in its middle years. But just as the inconvenience of some cannot be allowed to stand in the way of the rights of others, so public opposition, no matter how strident, cannot be permitted to divert this Court from the enforcement of the constitutional principles at issue in this case. Today's holding, I fear, is more a reflection of a perceived public mood that we have gone far enough in enforcing the Constitution's guarantee of equal justice than it is the product of neutral principles of law. In the short run, it may seem to be the easier course to allow our great metropolitan areas to be divided up each into two cities— one white, the other black—but it is a course, I predict, our people will ultimately regret.

I dissent.

BOARD OF EDUCATION OF OKLAHOMA CITY PUBLIC SCHOOLS, INDEPENDENT SCHOOL DISTRICT v. ROBERT DOWELL
498 U. S. 237; 112 L. Ed. 2d 715; 111 S. Ct. 630 (1991)

CHIEF JUSTICE REHNQUIST *delivered the opinion of the Court.*

Petitioner Board of Education of Oklahoma City sought dissolution of a decree entered by the District Court imposing a school desegregation plan. The District Court granted relief over the objection of respondents. The Court of Appeals reversed, holding that the Board would be entitled to such relief only upon " '[n]othing less than a clear showing of grievous wrong evoked by new and unforeseen conditions. . . . ' " We hold that the Court of Appeals' test is more stringent than is required either by our cases dealing with injunctions or by the Equal Protection Clause of the Fourteenth Amendment. . . .

I

In 1961 . . . black students and their parents sued . . . the Board of Education of Oklahoma City (Board), to end *de jure* segregation in the public

schools. In 1963, the District Court found that Oklahoma City had intentionally segregated both schools and housing in the past, and that Oklahoma City was operating a "dual" school system—one that was intentionally segregated by race. In 1965, the District Court found that the School Board's attempt to desegregate by using neighborhood zoning failed to remedy past segregation because residential segregation resulted in one-race schools. Residential segregation had once been state imposed, and it lingered due to discrimination by some realtors and financial institutions. The District Court found that school segregation had caused some housing segregation. In 1972, finding that previous efforts had not been successful at eliminating state-imposed segregation, the District Court ordered the Board to adopt . . . [a desegregation plan] under which kindergartners would be assigned to neighborhood schools unless their parents opted otherwise; children in grades 1–4 would attend formerly all white schools, and thus black children would be bused to those schools; children in grade five would attend formerly black schools, and thus white children would be bused to those schools; students in the upper grades would be bused to various areas in order to maintain integrated schools; and in integrated neighborhoods there would be stand-alone schools for all grades.

In 1977, after complying with the desegregation decree for five years, . . . [t]he District Court [granted the Board's motion terminating its jurisdiction, noting]:

> The Court has concluded that [the desegregation plan] worked and that substantial compliance with the constitutional requirements has been achieved. The Court does not foresee that the termination of its jurisdiction will result in the dismantlement of the Plan or any affirmative action by the defendant to undermine the unitary system so slowly and painfully accomplished over the 16 years during which the cause has been pending before this court. . . .

. . . The School Board, as now constituted, has manifested the desire and intent to follow the law. The court believes that the present members and their successors on the Board will now and in the future continue to follow the constitutional desegregation requirements. "Now . . . , the Board is entitled to pursue in good faith its legitimate policies without the continuing constitutional supervision of this Court." . . .

In 1984, the School Board faced demographic changes that led to greater burdens on young black children. As more and more neighborhoods became integrated, more stand-alone schools were established, and young black students had to be bused further from their inner-city houses to outlying white areas. In an effort to alleviate this burden and to increase parental involvement, the Board adopted the Student Reassignment Plan (SRP). Any student could transfer from a school where he or she was in the majority to a school where he or she would be in the minority. Faculty and staff integration was retained, and an "equity officer" was appointed.

In 1985, respondents filed a "Motion to Reopen the Case," contending that the School District had not achieved "unitary" status and that the SRP was a return to segregation. Under the SRP, 11 of 64 elementary schools would be greater than 90% black, 22 would be greater than 90% white plus other minorities, and 31 would be racially mixed. The District Court refused to reopen the case, holding that its 1977 finding of unitariness was res judicata as to those who were then parties to the action, and that the district remained unitary. The

District Court found that the School Board, administration, faculty, support staff, and student body were integrated, and transportation, extracurricular activities, and facilities within the district were equal and nondiscriminatory. Because unitariness had been achieved, the District Court concluded that court-ordered desegregation must end.

The Court of Appeals for the Tenth Circuit reversed. It held that, while the 1977 order finding the district unitary was binding on the parties, nothing in that order indicated that the 1972 injunction itself was terminated. The court reasoned that the finding that the system was unitary merely ended the District Court's active supervision of the case, and because the school district was still subject to the desegregation decree, respondents could challenge the SRP. The case was remanded to determine whether the decree should be lifted or modified.

On remand, the District Court found that demographic changes made the . . . Plan unworkable, that the Board had done nothing for 25 years to promote residential segregation, and that the school district had bused students for more than a decade in good-faith compliance with the court's orders. The District Court found that present residential segregation was the result of private decisionmaking and economics, and that it was too attenuated to be a vestige of former school segregation. It also found that the district had maintained its unitary status, and that the neighborhood assignment plan was not designed with discriminatory intent. The court concluded that the previous injunctive decree should be vacated and the school district returned to local control.

The Court of Appeals again reversed, holding that " 'an injunction takes on a life of its own and becomes an edict quite independent of the law it is meant to effectuate.' " That court approached the case "not so much as one dealing with desegregation, but as one dealing with the proper application of the federal law on injunctive remedies." Relying on *United States* v. *Swift & Co.*, 296 U.S. 106 (1932), it held that a desegregation decree remains in effect until a school district can show "grievous wrong evoked by new and unforeseen conditions," and "dramatic changes in conditions unforeseen at the time of the decree that . . . impose extreme and unexpectedly oppressive hardships on the obligor." Given that a number of schools would return to being primarily one-race schools under the SRP, circumstances in Oklahoma City had not changed enough to justify modification of the decree. The Court of Appeals held that, despite the unitary finding, the Board had the " 'affirmative duty . . . not to take any action that would impede the process of disestablishing the dual system and its effects.' "

We granted the Board's petition for certiorari, to resolve a conflict between the standard laid down by the Court of Appeals in this case and that laid down in *Spangler* v. *Pasadena City Board of Education*, and *Riddick* v. *School Bd. of City of Norfolk*. We now reverse the Court of Appeals.

II

We must first consider whether respondents may contest the District Court's 1987 order dissolving the injunction which had imposed the desegregation decree. Respondents did not appeal from the District Court's 1977 order finding that the school system had achieved unitary status, and petitioners contend that the 1977 order bars respondents from contesting the 1987 order. We disagree, for the 1977 order did not dissolve the desegregation decree, and the District Court's unitariness finding was too ambiguous to bar respondents from challenging later action by the Board.

The lower courts have been inconsistent in their use of the term "unitary." . . . We think it is a mistake to treat words such as "dual" and "unitary" as if they were actually found in the Constitution. The constitutional command of the Fourteenth Amendment is that "[n]o State shall . . . deny to any person . . . the equal protection of the laws." Courts have used the terms "dual" to denote a school system which has engaged in intentional segregation of students by race, and "unitary" to describe a school system which has been brought into compliance with the command of the Constitution. We are not sure how useful it is to define these terms more precisely, or to create subclasses within them. But there is no doubt that the differences in usage described above do exist. The District Court's 1977 order is unclear with respect to what it meant by unitary and the necessary result of that finding. We therefore decline to overturn the conclusion of the Court of Appeals that while the 1977 order of the District Court did bind the parties as to the unitary character of the district, it did not finally terminate the Oklahoma City school litigation. In *Pasadena City Bd. of Education* v. *Spangler*, 427 U.S. 424 (1976), we held that a school board is entitled to a rather precise statement of its obligations under a desegregation decree. If such a decree is to be terminated or dissolved, respondents as well as the school board are entitled to a like statement from the court.

* * *

III

* * *

. . . In the present case, a finding by the District Court that the Oklahoma City School District was being operated in compliance with the commands of the Equal Protection Clause of the Fourteenth Amendment, and that it was unlikely that the school board would return to its former ways, would be a finding that the purposes of the desegregation litigation had been fully achieved. No additional showing of "grievous wrong evoked by new and unforeseen conditions" is required of the school board. . . .

. . . From the very first, federal supervision of local school systems was intended as a temporary measure to remedy past discrimination. *Brown* considered the "complexities arising from the transition to a system of public education freed of racial discrimination" holding that the implementation of desegregation was to proceed "with all deliberate speed." . . .

. . . [School desegregation decrees] are not intended to operate in perpetuity. Local control over the education of children allows citizens to participate in decisionmaking, and allows innovation so that school programs can fit local needs. The legal justification for displacement of local authority by an injunctive decree in a school desegregation case is a violation of the Constitution by the local authorities. Dissolving a desegregation decree after the local authorities have operated in compliance with it for a reasonable period of time properly recognizes that "necessary concern for the important values of local control of public school systems dictates that a federal court's regulatory control of such systems not extend beyond the time required to remedy the effects of past intentional discrimination. . . . "

. . . [I]n deciding whether to modify or dissolve a desegregation decree, a school board's compliance with previous court orders is obviously relevant. . . .

. . . [T]he [Oklahoma City School] Board complied with the decree in good faith until 1985. Not only do the personnel of school boards change over time, but the same passage of time enables the District Court to observe the good faith of the school board in complying with the decree. The test espoused by the Court of Appeals would condemn a school district, once governed by a board which intentionally discriminated, to judicial tutelage for the indefinite future. Neither the principles governing the entry and dissolution of injunctive decrees, nor the commands of the Equal Protection Clause of the Fourteenth Amendment, require any such Draconian result.

. . . [W]e think that the preferable course is to remand the case to that court so that it may decide, in accordance with this opinion, whether the Board made a sufficient showing of constitutional compliance as of 1985, when the SRP was adopted, to allow the injunction to be dissolved. The District Court should address itself to whether the Board had complied in good faith with the desegregation decree since it was entered, and whether the vestiges of past discrimination had been eliminated to the extent practicable. . . .

In considering whether the vestiges of *de jure* segregation had been eliminated as far as practicable, the District Court should look not only at student assignments, but "to every facet of school operations—faculty, staff, transportation, extracurricular activities and facilities." . . .

After the District Court decides whether the Board was entitled to have the decree terminated, it should proceed to decide respondent's challenge to the SRP. A school district which has been released from a injunction imposing a desegregation plan no longer requires court authorization for the promulgation of policies and rules regulating matters such as assignment of students and the like, but it of course remains subject to the mandate of the Equal Protection Clause of the Fourteenth Amendment. If the Board was entitled to have the decree terminated as of 1985, the District Court would then evaluate the Board's decision to implement the SRP under appropriate equal protection principles.

The judgment of the Court of Appeals is reversed, and the case is remanded to the District Court for further proceedings consistent with this opinion.

It is so ordered.

[JUSTICE SOUTER took no part in the consideration or decision of this case.]

JUSTICE MARSHALL, *with whom* JUSTICE BLACKMUN *and* JUSTICE STEVENS *join, dissenting.*

. . . The practical question now before us is whether, 13 years after [a desegregation] injunction was imposed, the same School Board should have been allowed to return many of its elementary schools to their former one-race status. The majority today suggests that 13 years of desegregation was enough. The Court remands the case for further evaluation of whether the purposes of the

injunctive decree were achieved sufficient to justify the decree's dissolution. However, the inquiry it commends to the District Court fails to recognize explicitly the threatened reemergence of one-race schools as a relevant "vestige" of *de jure* segregation.

In my view, the standard for dissolution of a school desegregation decree must reflect the central aim of our school desegregation precedents. In *Brown* v. *Board of Education,* a unanimous Court declared that racially "[s]eparate educational facilities are inherently unequal." . . .

Remedying this evil and preventing its recurrence were the motivations animating our requirement that formerly *de jure* segregated school districts take all feasible steps at racially identifiable schools.

I believe a desegregation decree cannot be lifted so long as conditions likely to inflict the stigmatic injury condemned in *Brown I* persist and there remain feasible methods of eliminating such conditions. Because the record here shows, and the Court of Appeals found, that feasible steps could be taken to avoid one-race schools, it is clear that the purposes of the decree have not yet been achieved and the Court of Appeals' reinstatement of the decree should be affirmed.

I therefore dissent.

* * *

II

I agree with the majority that the proper standard for determining whether a school desegregation decree should be dissolved is whether the purposes of the desegregation litigation, as incorporated in the decree, have been fully achieved. . . . I strongly disagree with the majority, however, on what must be shown to demonstrate that a decree's purposes have been fully realized. In my view, a standard for dissolution of a desegregation decree must take into account the unique harm associated with a system of racially identifiable schools and must expressly demand the elimination of such schools.

Our pointed focus in *Brown I* upon the stigmatic injury caused by segregated schools explains our unflagging insistence that formerly *de jure* segregated school districts extinguish all vestiges of school segregation. The concept of stigma also gives us guidance as to what conditions must be eliminated before a decree can be deemed to have served its purpose. . . .

Remedying and avoiding the recurrence of this stigmatizing injury have been the guiding objectives of this Court's desegregation jurisprudence.

... These concerns inform the standard by which the Court determines the effectiveness of a proposed desegregation remedy. . . .

Concern with stigmatic injury also explains the Court's requirement that a formerly *de jure* segregated school district provide its victims with "make whole" relief. . . . In order to achieve such "make whole" relief, school systems must redress any effects traceable to former *de jure* segregation. . . .

Similarly, avoiding reemergence of the harm condemned in *Brown I* accounts for the Court's insistence on remedies that insure lasting integration of formerly segregated systems. Such school districts are required to "make every effort to achieve the greatest possible degree of actual desegregation and [to] be concerned with the elimination of one-race schools." . . . This focus on "achieving and preserving an integrated school system" stems from the recognition that the reemergence of racial separation in such schools may revive the message of racial inferiority implicit in the former policy of state-enforced segregation.

Just as it is central to the standard for evaluating the formation of a desegregation decree, so should the stigmatic injury associated with segregated schools be central to the standard for dissolving a decree. The Court has indicated that "the ultimate end to be brought about" by a desegregation remedy is "a unitary, nonracial system of public education." We have suggested that this aim is realized once school officials have "eliminate[d] from the public schools all vestiges of state-imposed segregation," whether they inhere in the school's "faculty, staff, transportation, extracurricular activities and facilities," or even in "the community and administration['s] attitudes toward [a] school." Although the Court has never explicitly defined what constitutes a "vestige" of state-enforced segregation, the function that this concept has performed in our jurisprudence suggests that it extends to any condition that is likely to convey the message of inferiority implicit in a policy of segregation. So long as such conditions persist, the purposes of the decree cannot be deemed to have been achieved. . . .

III

Applying the standard I have outlined, I would affirm the Court of Appeals' decision ordering the District Court to restore the desegregation decree. For it is clear on this record that removal of the decree will result in a significant number of racially identifiable schools that could be eliminated. . . .

It is undisputed that replacing the Finger Plan [the original plan] with a system of neighborhood school assignments for grades K–4 resulted in a system of racially identifiable schools. Under the SRP, over one-half of Oklahoma City's elementary schools now have student bodies that are either 9% Afro-American or 9% non-Afro-American. Because the principal vestige of *de jure* segregation persists, lifting the decree would clearly be premature at this point. . . .

The majority equivocates on the effect to be given to the reemergence of racially identifiable schools. . . . And, by rendering "*res nova*" the issue whether residential segregation in Oklahoma City is a vestige of former school segregation, the majority accepts at least as a theoretical possibility that vestiges may exist beyond those identified in *Green*. Nonetheless, the majority hints that the District Court could ignore the effect of residential segregation in perpetuating racially identifiable schools if the Court finds residential segregation to be "the result of private decisionmaking and economics." Finally, the majority warns against the application of a standard that would subject formerly segregated school districts to the "Draconian" fate of "judicial tutelage for the indefinite future."

This equivocation is completely unsatisfying. First, it is well established that school segregation "may have a profound reciprocal effect on the racial composition of residential neighborhoods." The record in this case amply demonstrates this form of complicity in residential segregation on the part of the Board. . . .

Second, there is no basis for the majority's apparent suggestion that the result should be different if residential segregation is now perpetuated by "private decisionmaking." . . . Even more important, it fails to account for the unique role of the School Board in creating "all-Negro" schools clouded by the stigma of segregation. . . . That such negative "personal preferences" exist should not absolve a school district that played a role in creating such "preferences" from its obligation to desegregate the schools to the maximum extent possible.

I also reject the majority's suggestion that the length of federal judicial supervision is a valid factor in assessing a dissolution. The majority is correct that the Court has never contemplated perpetual judicial oversight of former *de jure* segregated school districts. Our jurisprudence requires, however, that the job of school desegregation be fully completed and maintained so that the stigmatic harm identified in *Brown I* will not recur upon lifting the decree. Any doubt on the issue whether the School Board has fulfilled its remedial obligations should be resolved in favor of the Afro-American children affected by this litigation.

In its concern to spare local school boards the "Draconian" fate of "indefinite" "judicial tutelage," the majority risks subordination of the constitutional rights of Afro-American children to the interest of school board autonomy. The courts must consider the value of local control, but that factor primarily relates to the feasibility of a remedial measure, not whether the constitutional violation has been remedied. *Swann* establishes that if fur-ther desegregation is "reasonable, feasible, and workable," then it must be undertaken. . . .

We should keep in mind that the court's active supervision of the desegregation plan process ceased in 1977. Retaining the decree does not require a return to active supervision. It may be that a modification of the decree which will improve its effectiveness and give the school district more flexibility in minimizing busing is appropriate in this case. But retaining the decree seems a slight burden on the school district compared with the risk of not delivering a full remedy to the Afro-American children in the school system. . . .

FREEMAN v. PITTS
___ U.S. ___; ___ L. Ed. 2d ___; 112 S. Ct. 1430 (1992)

JUSTICE KENNEDY *delivered the opinion of the Court.*

Dekalb County, Georgia, is a major suburban area of Atlanta. This case involves a court-ordered desegregation decree for the DeKalb County School System (DCSS). DCSS now serves some 73,000 students in kindergarten through high school and is the 32nd largest elementary and secondary school system in the Nation.

DCSS has been subject to the supervision and jurisdiction of the United States District Court for the Northern District of Georgia since 1969, when it was ordered to dismantle its dual school system. In 1986, petitioners filed a motion for final dismissal. The District Court ruled that DCSS had not achieved unitary status in all respects but had done so in student attendance and three other categories. In its order the District Court relinquished remedial control as to those aspects of the system in which unitary status had been achieved, and retained supervisory authority only for those aspects of the school system in which the district was not in full compliance. The Court of Appeals for the Eleventh Circuit reversed, holding that a district court should retain full remedial authority over a school system until it achieves unitary status in six categories at the same time for several years. We now reverse the judgment of the Court of Appeals and remand, holding that a district court is permitted to withdraw judicial supervision with respect to discrete categories in which the school district has achieved compliance with a court-ordered desegregation plan. A district court need not retain active control over every aspect of school administration until a school district has demonstrated unitary status in all facets of its system.

I

A

For decades before our decision in *Brown* v. *Board of Education* . . . DCSS was segregated by law. DCSS's initial response to the mandate of *Brown II* was an all too familiar one. Interpreting "all deliberate speed" as giving latitude to delay steps to desegregate, DCSS took no positive action toward desegregation until the 1966–1967 school year, when it did nothing more than adopt a freedom of choice transfer plan. Some black students chose to attend former *de jure* white schools, but the plan had no significant effect on the former *de jure* black schools.

In 1968 we decided *Green* v. *New Kent County School Bd.* . . . [and] held that adoption of a freedom of choice plan does not, by itself, satisfy a school district's mandatory responsibility to eliminate all vestiges of a dual system. *Green* was a turning point in our law . . . [as] we stated that " '[t]he time for mere "deliberate speed" has run out.' " . . . We said that the obligation of school districts once segregated by law was to come forward with a plan that "promises realistically to work, and promises realistically to work *now*." . . . The case before us requires an understanding and assessment of how DCSS responded to the directives set forth in *Green*.

Within two months of our ruling in *Green*, respondents, who are black school children and their parents, instituted this class action in the United States District Court for the Northern District of Georgia. After the suit was filed, DCSS voluntarily began working with the Department of Health, Education and Welfare to devise a comprehensive and final plan of desegregation. The District Court in June 1969 entered a consent order approving the proposed plan, which was to be implemented in the 1969–1970 school year. The order abolished the freedom of choice plan and adopted a neighborhood school attendance plan that had been proposed by the DCSS and accepted by the Department of Health, Education and Welfare subject to a minor modification. Under the plan all of the former *de jure* black schools were closed and their students were reassigned among the remaining neighborhood schools. The District Court retained jurisdiction.

Between 1969 and 1986 respondents sought only infrequent and limited judicial intervention into the affairs of DCSS. They did not request significant changes in student attendance zones or student assignment policies. In 1976 DCSS was ordered: to expand its Minority-to-Majority (M-to-M) student transfer program, allowing students in a school where they are in the majority race to transfer to a school where they are in the minority; to establish a bi-racial committee to oversee the transfer program and future boundary line changes; and to reassign teachers so that the ratio of black to white teachers in each school would be, in substance, similar to the racial balance in the school population systemwide. From 1977 to 1979 the District Court approved a boundary line change for one elementary school attendance zone and rejected DCSS proposals to restrict the M-to-M transfer program. In 1983 DCSS was ordered to make further adjustments to the M-to-M transfer program.

In 1986 petitioners filed a motion for final dismissal of the litigation. They sought a declaration that DCSS had satisfied its duty to eliminate the dual education system, that is to say a declaration that the school system had achieved unitary status. The District Court approached the question whether DCSS had achieved unitary status by asking whether DCSS was unitary with respect to each of the factors identified in *Green*. The court considered an additional factor that is not named in *Green*: the quality of education being offered to the white and black student populations.

The District Court found DCSS to be "an innovative school system that has travelled the often

long road to unitary status almost to its end," noting that "the court has continually been impressed by the successes of the DCSS and its dedication to providing a quality education for all students within that system." It found that DCSS is a unitary system with regard to student assignments, transportation, physical facilities, and extracurricular activities [the *Green* factors], and ruled that it would order no further relief in those areas. The District Court stopped short of dismissing the case, however, because it found that DCSS was not unitary in every respect. The court said that vestiges of the dual system remain in the areas of teacher and principal assignments, resource allocation, and quality of education. DCSS was ordered to take measures to address the remaining problem.

B

. . . Here, as in most cases where the issue is the degree of compliance with a school desegregation decree, a critical beginning point is the degree of racial imbalance in the school district, that is to say a comparison of the proportion of majority to minority students in individual schools with the proportions of the races in the district as a whole. This inquiry is fundamental, for under the former *de jure* regimes racial exclusion was both the means and the end of a policy motivated by disparagement of or hostility towards the disfavored race. In accord with this principle, the District Court began its analysis with an assessment of the current racial mix in the schools throughout DCSS and the explanation for the racial imbalance it found. The respondents did not contend on appeal that the findings of fact were clearly erroneous and the Court of Appeals did not find them to be erroneous. The Court of Appeals did disagree with the conclusion reached by the District Court respecting the need for further supervision of racial balance in student assignments.

In the extensive record that comprises this case, one fact predominates: remarkable changes in the racial composition of the county presented DCSS and the District Court with a student population in 1986 far different from the one they set out to integrate in 1969. Between 1950 and 1985, DeKalb County grew from 70,000 to 450,000 in total population, but most of the gross increase in student enrollment had occurred by 1969. . . . Although the public school population experienced only modest changes between 1969 and 1986 (remaining in the low 70,000s), a striking change occurred in the racial proportions of the student population. The school system that the District Court ordered desegregated in 1969 had 5.6% black students; by 1986 the percentage of black students was 47%.

To compound the difficulty of working with these radical demographic changes, the northern and southern parts of the county experienced much different growth patterns. The District Court found that "[a]s the result of these demographic shifts, the population of the northern half of DeKalb County is now predominantly white and the southern half of DeKalb County is predominantly black." In 1970, there were 7,615 nonwhites living in the northern part of DeKalb County and 11,508 nonwhites in the southern part of the county. By 1980, there were 15,365 nonwhites living in the northern part of the county, and 87,583 nonwhites in the southern part. Most of the growth in the nonwhite population in the southern portion of the county was due to the migration of black persons from the city of Atlanta. Between 1975 and 1980 alone, approximately 64,000 black citizens moved into southern DeKalb County, most of them coming from Atlanta. During the same period, approximately 37,000 white citizens moved out of southern DeKalb County to the surrounding counties.

The District Court made findings with respect to the number of nonwhite citizens in the northern and southern parts of the county for the years 1970 and 1980 without making parallel findings with respect to white citizens. Yet a clear picture does emerge. During the relevant period, the black population in the southern portion of the county experienced tremendous growth while the white population did not, and the white population in the northern part of the county experienced tremendous growth while the black population did not.

The demographic changes that occurred during the course of the desegregation order are an essential foundation for the District Court's analysis of the current racial mix of DCSS. As the District Court observed, the demographic shifts have had "an immense effect on the racial compositions of the DeKalb County schools." From 1976 to 1986, enrollment in elementary schools declined overall by 15%, while black enrollment in elementary schools increased by 86%. During the same period, overall high school enrollment declined by 16%, while black enrollment in high school increased by 119%. These effects were even more pronounced in the southern portion of DeKalb County.

Concerned with racial imbalance in the various schools of the district, respondents presented evidence that during the 1986–1987 school year DCSS had the following features: (1) 47% of the students attending DCSS were black; (2) 50% of the black students attended schools that were over 90% black; (3) 62% of all black students attended schools that had more than 20% more blacks than the systemwide average; (4) 27% of white students attended schools that were more than 90% white; (5) 59% of the white students attended schools that had more than 20% more whites than the systemwide average; (6) of the 22 DCSS high schools, five had student populations that were more than 90% black, while five other schools had student populations that were more than 80% white; and (7) of the 74 elementary schools in DCSS, 18 are over 90% black, while 10 are over 90% white. (The respondents' evidence on these points treated all nonblack students as white. The District Court noted that there was no evidence that nonblack minority students comprised even one percent of DCSS student population.)

Respondents argued in the District Court that this racial imbalance in student assignment was a vestige of the dual system, rather than a product of independent demographic forces. In addition to the statistical evidence that the ratio of black students to white students in individual schools varied to a significant degree from the systemwide average, respondents contend that DCSS had not used all available desegregative tools in order to achieve racial balancing. Respondents pointed to the following alleged shortcomings in DCSS desegregative efforts: (1) DCSS did not break the county into subdistricts and racially balance each subdistrict; (2) DCSS failed to expend sufficient funds for minority learning opportunities; (3) DCSS did not establish community advisory organizations; (4) DCSS did not make full use of the freedom of choice plan; (5) DCSS did not cluster schools, that is, it did not create schools for separate grade levels which could be used to establish a feeder pattern; (6) DCSS did not institute its magnet school program as early as it might have; and (7) DCSS did not use busing to facilitate urban to suburban exchanges.

According to the District Court, respondents conceded that the 1969 order assigning all students to their neighborhood schools "effectively desegregated DCSS for a period of time" with respect to student assignment. The District Court noted, however, that despite this concession the respondents contended there was an improper imbalance in two schools even in 1969. Respondents made much of the fact that despite the small percentage of blacks in the county in 1969, there were then two schools that contained a majority of black students: Terry Mill Elementary School was 76% black, and Stoneview Elementary School was 51% black.

The District Court found the racial imbalance in these schools was not a vestige of the prior *de jure* system. It observed that both the Terry Mill and Stoneview schools were *de jure* white schools before the freedom of choice plan was put in place. It cited expert witness testimony that Terry Mill had become a majority black school as a result of demographic shifts unrelated to the actions of petitioners or their predecessors. In 1966, the overwhelming majority of students at Terry Mill were white. By 1967, due to migration of black citizens from Atlanta into DeKalb County—and into the neighborhood surrounding the Terry Mill school in particular—23% of the students at Terry Mill were black. By 1968, black students comprised 50% of the school population at Terry Mill. By 1969, when the plan was put in effect, the percentage had grown to 76%. In accordance with the evidence of demographic shifts, and in the absence of any evidence to suggest that the former dual system contributed in any way to the rapid racial transformation of the Terry Mill student population, the District Court found that the pre-1969 unconstitutional acts of petitioners were not responsible for the high percentage of black students at the Terry Mill school in 1969. Its findings in this respect are illustrative of the problems DCSS and the District Court faced in integrating the whole district.

Although the District Court found that DCSS was desegregated for at least a short period under the court-ordered plan of 1969, it did not base its finding that DCSS had achieved unitary status with respect to student assignment on that circumstance alone. Recognizing that "[t]he achievement of unitary status in the area of student assignment cannot be hedged on the attainment of such status for a brief moment," the District Court examined the interaction between DCSS policy and demographic shifts in DeKalb County.

The District Court noted that DCSS had taken specific steps to combat the effects of demographics on the racial mix of the schools. Under the 1969 order, a biracial committee had reviewed all proposed changes in the boundary lines of school attendance zones. Since the original desegregation order, there had been about 170 such changes. It was found that only three had a partial segregative effect. An expert testified, and the District Court found, that even those changes had no significant effect on the racial mix of the school population. . . .

The District Court also noted that DCSS, on its own initiative, started an M-to-M program in the 1972 school year. The program was a marked success. Participation increased with each passing year, so that in the 1986–1987 school year, 4,500 of the 72,000 students enrolled in DCSS participated. An expert testified that the impact of an M-to-M program goes beyond the number of students transferred because students at the receiving school also obtain integrated learning experiences. The District Court found that about 19% of the students attending DCSS had an integrated learning experience as a result of the M-to-M program.

In addition, in the 1980's, DCSS instituted a magnet school program in schools located in the middle of the county. The magnet school programs included a performing arts program, two science programs, and a foreign language program. There was testimony in the District Court that DCSS also had plans to operate additional magnet programs in occupational education and gifted and talented education, as well as a preschool program and an open campus. By locating these programs in the middle of the county, DCSS sought to attract black students from the southern part of the county and white students from the northern part.

Further, the District Court found that DCSS operates a number of experience programs integrated by race, including a writing center for fifth and seventh graders, a driving range, summer school programs, and a dialectical speech program. DCSS employs measures to control the racial mix in each of these special areas.

In determining whether DCSS has achieved unitary status with respect to student assignment, the District Court saw its task as one of deciding if petitioners "have accomplished maximum practical desegregation of the DCSS or if the DCSS must still do more to fulfill their affirmative constitutional duty." Petitioners and respondents presented conflicting expert testimony about the potential effects that desegregative techniques not deployed might have had upon the racial mix of the schools. The District Court found that petitioners' experts were more reliable, citing their greater familiarity with DCSS, their experience and their standing within the expert community. The District Court made these findings:

[The actions of DCSS] achieved maximum practical desegregation from 1969 to 1986. The rapid population shifts in DeKalb County were not caused by any action on the part of the DCSS. These demographic shifts were inevitable as the result of suburbanization, that is, work opportunities arising in DeKalb County as well as the City of Atlanta, which attracted blacks to DeKalb; the decline in the number of children born to white families during this period while the number of children born to black families did not decrease; blockbusting of formerly white neighborhoods leading to selling and buying real estate in the DeKalb area on a highly dynamic basis; and the completion of Interstate 20, which made access from DeKalb County into the City of Atlanta much easier. . . . There is no evidence that the school system's previous unconstitutional conduct may have contributed to this segregation. This court is convinced that any further actions taken by defendants, while the actions might have made marginal adjustments in the population trends, would not have offset the factors that were described above and the same racial segregation would have occurred at approximately the same speed.

The District Court added:

[A]bsent massive bussing, which is not considered as a viable option by either the parties or this court, the magnet school program and the M-to-M program, which the defendents voluntarily implemented and to which the defendants obviously are dedicated, are the most effective ways to deal with the effects on student attendance of the residential segregation existing in DeKalb County at this time.

Having found no constitutional violation with respect to student assignment, the District Court next considered the other *Green* factors, beginning with faculty and staff assignments. The District Court first found that DCSS had fulfilled its constitutional obligation with respect to hiring and retaining minority teachers and administrators. . . . The District Court also noted that DCSS has an "equally exemplary record" in retention of black teachers and administrators. Nevertheless, the District Court found that DCSS had not achieved or maintained a ratio of black to white teachers and administrators in each school to approximate the ratio of black to white teachers and administrators throughout the system. See *Singleton* v. *Jackson Municipal Separate School Dist.*, 419 F.2d 1211 (CA5 1969), cert. denied, 396 U.S. 1032 (1970). In other words, a racial imbalance existed in the assignment of minority teachers and administrators. The District Court found that in the 1984–1985 school year, seven schools deviated by more than 10% from the systemwide average of 26.4% minority teachers in elementary schools and 24.9% minority teachers in high schools. The District Court also found that black principals and administrators were overrepresented in schools with high per-

centages of black students and underrepresented in schools with low percentages of black students.

The District Court found that the crux of the problem to be that DCSS has relied on the replacement process to attain a racial balance in teachers and other staff and has avoided using mandatory reassignment. DCSS gave as its reason for not using mandatory reassignment that the competition among local school districts is stiff, and that it is difficult to attract and keep qualified teachers if they are required to work far from their homes. In fact, because teachers prefer to work close to their homes, DCSS has a voluntary transfer program in which teachers who have taught at the same school for a period of three years may ask for a transfer. Because most teachers request to be transferred to schools near their homes, this program makes compliance with the objective of racial balance in faculty and staff more difficult.

The District Court stated that it was not "unsympathetic to the difficulties that DCSS faces in this regard," but held that the law of the circuit requires DCSS to comply with *Singleton*. The court ordered DCSS to devise a plan to achieve compliance with *Singleton*, noting that "[i]t would appear that such compliance will necessitate reassignment of both teachers and principals." With respect to faculty, the District Court noted that meeting *Singleton* would not be difficult, citing petitioners' own estimate that most schools' faculty could conform by moving, at most, two or three teachers.

Addressing the more ineffable category of quality of education, the District Court rejected most of respondents' contentions that there was racial disparity in the provision of certain educational resources (e.g., teachers with advanced degrees, teachers with more experience, library books), contentions made to show that black students were not being given equal educational opportunity. The District Court went further, however, and examined the evidence concerning achievement of black students in DCSS. It cited expert testimony praising the overall educational program in the district, as well as objective evidence of black achievement: black students at DCSS made greater gains on the Iowa Tests of Basic Skills (ITBS) than white students, and black students at DCSS are more successful than black students nationwide on the Scholastic Aptitude Test (SAT). It made the following finding:

While there will always be something more that the DCSS can do to improve the chances for black students to achieve academic success, the court cannot find, as plaintiffs urge, that the DCSS has been negligent in its duties to implement programs to assist black students. The DCSS is a very innovative school system. It has implemented a number of programs to enrich the lives and enhance the academic potential of all students, both blacks and whites. Many remedial programs are targeted in the majority black schools. Programs have been implemented to involve the parents and off-set negative socio-economic factors. If the DCSS has failed in any way in this regard, it is not because the school system has been negligent in its duties. . . .

Despite its finding that there was no intentional violation, the District Court found that DCSS had not achieved unitary status with respect to quality of education because teachers in schools with disproportionately high percentages of white students tended to be better educated and have more experience than their counterparts in schools with disproportionately high percentages of black students, and because per pupil expenditures in majority white schools exceeded per pupil expenditures in majority black schools. From these findings, the District Court ordered DCSS to equalize spending and remedy the other problems.

The final *Green* factors considered by the District Court were: (1) physical facilities, (2) transportation, and (3) extracurricular activities. The District Court noted that although respondents expressed some concerns about the use of portable classrooms in schools in the southern portion of the county, they in effect conceded that DCSS has achieved unitary status with respect to physical facilities.

In accordance with its factfinding, the District Court held that it would order no further relief in the areas of student assignment, transportation, physical facilities and extracurricular activities. The District Court, however, did order DCSS to establish a system to balance teacher and principal assignments and to equalize per pupil expenditures throughout DCSS. Having found that blacks were represented on the school board and throughout DCSS administration, the District Court abolished the biracial committee as no longer necessary.

Both parties appealed to the United States Court of Appeals for the Eleventh Circuit. The Court of Appeals affirmed the District Court's ultimate conclusion that DCSS has not yet achieved unitary status, but reversed the District Court's ruling that DCSS has no further duties in the area of student assignment. The Court of Appeals held that the District Court erred by considering the six *Green* factors as separate categories. The Court of

Appeals rejected the District Court's incremental approach, an approach that has also been adopted by the Court of Appeals for the First Circuit, *Morgan* v. *Nucci*, 831 F.2d 313, 318–319 (1987), and held that a school system achieves unitary status only after it has satisfied all six factors at the same time for several years. Because, under this test, DCSS had not achieved unitary status at any time, the Court of Appeals held that DCSS could "not shirk its constitutional duties by pointing to demographic shifts occurring prior to unitary status." The Court of Appeals held that petitioners bore the responsibility for the racial imbalance, and in order to correct that imbalance would have to take actions that "may be administratively awkward, inconvenient, and even bizarre in some situations," *Swann* v. *Charlotte-Mecklenburg Bd. of Education*, 402 U.S. 1 (1971), such as pairing and clustering of schools, drastic gerrymandering of school zones, grade reorganization, and busing. . . .

II

Two principal questions are presented. The first is whether a district court may relinquish its supervision and control over those aspects of a school system in which there has been compliance with a desegregation decree if other aspects of the system remain in noncompliance. As we answer this question in the affirmative, the second question is whether the Court of Appeals erred in reversing the District Court's order providing for incremental withdrawal of supervision in all the circumstances of this case.

A

The duty and responsibility of a school district once segregated by law is to take all steps necessary to eliminate the vestiges of the unconstitutional *de jure* system. This is required in order to insure that the principal wrong of the *de jure* system, the injuries and stigma inflicted upon the race disfavored by the violation, is no longer present. This was the rationale and the objective of *Brown I* and *Brown II*. . . .

The concept of unitariness has been a helpful one in defining the scope of the district court's authority, for it conveys the central idea that a school district that was once a dual system must be examined in all of its facets, both when a remedy is ordered and in the later phases of desegregation when the question is whether the district court's remedial control ought to be modified, lessened, or withdrawn. But, as we explained last term in

Board of Education of Oklahoma City v. *Dowell,* 498 U.S. 237; 111 S. Ct. 630, 636 (1991), the term "unitary" is not a precise concept:

> [I]t is a mistake to treat words such as "dual" and "unitary" as if they were actually found in the Constitution. . . . Courts have used the terms "dual" to denote a school system which has engaged in intentional segregation of students by race, and "unitary" to describe a school system which has been brought into compliance with the command of the Constitution. We are not sure how useful it is to define these terms more precisely, or to create subclasses within them.

It follows that we must be cautious not to attribute to the term a utility it does not have. The term "unitary" does not confine the discretion and authority of the District Court in a way that departs from traditional equitable principles.

That the term "unitary" does not have fixed meaning or content is not inconsistent with the principles that control the exercise of power. The essence of a court's equity power lies in its inherent capacity to adjust remedies in a feasible and practical way to eliminate the conditions or redress the injuries caused by unlawful action. Equitable remedies must be flexible if these underlying principles are to be enforced with fairness and precision. The requirement of a unitary school system must be implemented according to this prescription.

Our application of these guiding principles in *Pasadena City Bd. of Education* v. *Spangler* is instructive. There we held that a District Court exceeded its remedial authority in requiring annual readjustment of school attendance zones in the Pasadena school district when changes in the racial makeup of the schools were caused by demographic shifts "not attributed to any segregative acts on the part of the [school district]." In so holding we said:

> It may well be that petitioners have not yet totally achieved the unitary system contemplated by . . . *Swann.* . . . But that does not undercut the force of the principle underlying the quoted language from *Swann.* In this case the District Court approved a plan designed to obtain racial neutrality in the attendance of students at Pasadena's public schools. No one disputes that the initial implementation of this plan accomplished *that* objective. That being the case, the District Court was not entitled to require the [Pasadena Unified School District] to rearrange its attendance zones each year so as to ensure that the racial mix desired by the court was maintained in perpetuity. For having once implemented a racially neutral attendance pattern in order to remedy the perceived constitutional violations on the part of the defen-

dants, the District Court had fully performed its function of providing the appropriate remedy for previous racially discriminatory attendance patterns. . . .

Today, we make explicit the rationale that was central in *Spangler.* A federal court in a school desegregation case has the discretion to order an incremental or partial withdrawal of its supervision and control. This discretion derives both from the constitutional authority which justified its intervention in the first instance and its ultimate objectives in formulating the decree. The authority of the court is invoked at the outset to remedy particular constitutional violations. In construing the remedial authority of the district courts, we have been guided by the principles that "judicial powers may be exercised only on the basis of a constitutional violation," and that "the nature of the violation determines the scope of the remedy." A remedy is justifiable only insofar as it advances the ultimate objective of alleviating the initial constitutional violation.

We have said that the court's end purpose must be to remedy the violation and in addition to restore state and local authorities to the control of a school system that is operating in compliance with the Constitution. Partial relinquishment of control, where justified by the facts of the case, can be an important and significant step in fulfilling the district court's duty to return the operations and control of schools to local authorities. In *Dowell,* we emphasized that federal judicial supervision of local school systems was intended as a "temporary measure." Although this temporary measure has lasted decades, the ultimate objective has not changed—to return school districts to the control of local authorities. Just as a court has the obligation at the outset of a desegregation decree to structure a plan so that all available resources of the court are directed to comprehensive supervision of its decree, so too must a court provide an orderly means for withdrawing from control when it is shown that the school district has attained the requisite degree of compliance. A transition phase in which control is relinquished in a gradual way is an appropriate means to this end.

As we have long observed, "local autonomy of school districts is a vital national tradition." Returning schools to the control of local authorities at the earliest practicable date is essential to restore their true accountability in our governmental system. When the school district and all state entities participating with it in operating the schools make decisions in the absence of judicial supervision, they can be held accountable to the citizenry, to the political process, and to the courts in the ordinary course. . . . [O]ne of the prerequisites to relinquishment of control in whole or in part is that a school district has demonstrated its commitment to a course of action that gives full respect to the equal protection guarantees of the Constitution. Yet it must be acknowledged that the potential for discrimination and racial hostility is still present in our country, and its manifestations may emerge in new and subtle forms after the effects of *de jure* desegregation have been eliminated. It is the duty of the State and its subdivisions to ensure that such forces do not shape or control the policies of its school systems. Where control lies, so too does responsibility.

We hold that, in the course of supervising desegregation plans, federal courts have the authority to relinquish supervision and control of school districts in incremental stages, before full compliance has been achieved in every area of school operations. While retaining jurisdiction over the case, the court may determine that it will not order further remedies in areas where the school district is in compliance with the decree. That is to say, upon a finding that a school system subject to a court-supervised desegregation plan is in compliance in some but not all areas, the court in appropriate cases may return control to the school system in those areas where compliance has been achieved, limiting further judicial supervision to operations that are not yet in full compliance with the court decree. In particular, the district court may determine that it will not order further remedies in the area of student assignments where racial imbalance is not traceable, in a proximate way, to constitutional violations.

A court's discretion to order the incremental withdrawal of its supervision in a school desegregation case must be exercised in a manner consistent with the purposes and objectives of its equitable power. Among the factors which must inform the sound discretion of the court in ordering partial withdrawal are the following: whether there has been full and satisfactory compliance with the decree in those aspects of the system where supervision is to be withdrawn; whether retention of judicial control is necessary or practicable to achieve compliance with the decree in other facets of the school system; and whether the school district has demonstrated, to the public and to the parents and students of the once disfavored race, its good faith commitment to the whole of the court's decree and to those provisions of the law and the Constitution that were the predicate for judicial intervention in the first instance.

In considering these factors a court should give particular attention to the school system's record of compliance. A school system is better positioned to demonstrate its good-faith commitment to a constitutional course of action when its policies form a consistent pattern of lawful conduct directed to eliminating earlier violations. And with the passage of time the degree to which racial imbalances continue to represent vestiges of a constitutional violation may diminish, and the practicability and efficacy of various remedies can be evaluated with more precision. . . .

B

We reach now the question whether the Court of Appeals erred in prohibiting the District Court from returning to DCSS partial control over some of its affairs. We decide that the Court of Appeals did err in holding that, as a matter of law, the District Court had no discretion to permit DCSS to regain control over student assignment, transportation, physical facilities, and extracurricular activities, while retaining court supervision over the areas of faculty and administrative assignments and the quality of education, where full compliance had not been demonstrated.

It was an appropriate exercise of its discretion for the District Court to address the elements of a unitary system discussed in *Green*, to inquire whether other elements ought to be identified, and to determine whether minority students were being disadvantaged in ways that required the formulation of new and further remedies to insure full compliance with the court's decree. Both parties agreed that quality of education was a legitimate inquiry in determining DCSS compliance with the desegregation decree, and the trial court found it workable to consider the point in connection with its findings on resource allocation. Its order retaining supervision over this aspect of the case has not been challenged by the parties and we need not examine it except as it underscores the school district's record of compliance in some areas but not others. The District Court's approach illustrates that the *Green* factors need not be a rigid framework. It illustrates also the uses of equitable discretion. By withdrawing control over areas where judicial supervision is no longer needed, a district court can concentrate both its own resources and those of the school district on the areas where the effects of *de jure* discrimination have not been eliminated and further action is necessary in order to provide real and tangible relief to minority students. . . .

That there was racial imbalance in student attendance zones was not tantamount to a showing that the school district was in noncompliance with the decree or with its duties under the law. Racial balance is not to be achieved for its own sake. It is to be pursued when racial imbalance has been caused by a constitutional violation. Once the racial imbalance due to the *de jure* violation has been remedied, the school district is under no duty to remedy imbalance that is caused by demographic factors. . . . If the unlawful *de jure* policy of a school system has been the cause of the racial imbalance in student attendance, that condition must be remedied. The school district bears the burden of showing that any current imbalance is not traceable, in a proximate way, to the prior violation.

The findings of the District Court that the population changes which occurred in DeKalb County were not caused by the policies of the school district, but rather by independent factors, are consistent with the mobility that is a distinct characteristic of our society. In one year (from 1987 to 1988) over 40 million Americans, or 17.6 percent of the total population, moved households. . . . In such a society it is inevitable that the demographic makeup of school districts, based as they are on political subdivisions such as counties and municipalities, may undergo rapid change. . . .

Where resegregation is a product not of state action but of private choices, it does not have constitutional implications. It is beyond the authority and beyond the practical ability of the federal courts to try to counteract these kinds of continuous and massive demographic shifts. To attempt such results would require ongoing and never-ending supervision by the courts of school districts simply because they were once *de jure* segregated. Residential housing choices, and their attendant effects on the racial composition of schools, present an ever-changing pattern, one difficult to address through judicial remedies.

In one sense of the term, vestiges of past segregation by state decree do remain in our society and in our schools. Past wrongs to the black race, wrongs committed by the State and in its name, are a stubborn fact of history. And stubborn facts of history linger and persist. But though we cannot escape our history, neither must we overstate its consequences in fixing legal responsibilities. The vestiges of segregation that are the concern of the law in a school case may be subtle and intangible but nonetheless they must be so real that they have a casual link to the *de jure* violation being remedied. It is simply not always the case that demographic forces causing population change bear any

real and substantial relation to a *de jure* violation. And the law need not proceed on that premise.

As the *de jure* violation becomes more remote in time and these demographic changes intervene, it becomes less likely that a current racial imbalance in a school district is a vestige of the prior *de jure* system. The causal link between current conditions and the prior violation is even more attenuated if the school district has demonstrated its good faith. In light of its finding that the demographic changes in DeKalb County are unrelated to the prior violation, the District Court was correct to entertain the suggestion that DCSS had no duty to achieve systemwide racial balance in the student population. . . .

We next consider whether retention of judicial control over student attendance is necessary or practicable to achieve compliance in other facets of the school system. Racial balancing in elementary and secondary school student assignments may be a legitimate remedial device to correct other fundamental inequities that were themselves caused by the constitutional violation. We have long recognized that the *Green* factors may be related or interdependant. Two or more *Green* factors may be intertwined or synergistic in their relation, so that a constitutional violation in one area cannot be eliminated unless the judicial remedy addresses other matters as well. We have observed, for example, that student segregation and faculty segregation are often related problems. . . . As a consequence, a continuing violation in one area may need to be addressed by remedies in another. . . .

There was no showing that racial balancing was an appropriate mechanism to cure other deficiencies in this case. It is true that the school district was not in compliance with respect to faculty assignments, but the record does not show that student reassignments would be a feasible or practical way to remedy this defect. . . .

The requirement that the school district show its good faith commitment to the entirety of a desegregation plan so that parents, students and the public have assurance against further injuries or stigma also should be a subject for more specific findings. We stated in *Dowell* that the good faith compliance of the district with the court order over a reasonable period of time is a factor to be considered in deciding whether or not jurisdiction could be relinquished. . . . A history of good-faith compliance is evidence that any current racial imbalance is not the product of a new *de jure* violation, and enables the district court to accept the school board's representation that it has accepted the principle of racial equality and will not suffer intentional discrimination in the future. . . .

When a school district has not demonstrated good faith under a comprehensive plan to remedy ongoing violations, we have without hesitation approved comprehensive and continued district court supervision. . . .

. . . [T]he District Court in this case stated that throughout the period of judicial supervision it has been impressed by the successes DCSS has achieved and its dedication to providing a quality education for all students, and that DCSS "has travelled the often long road to unitary status almost to its end." With respect to those areas where compliance had not been achieved, the District Court did not find that DCSS had acted in bad faith or engaged in further acts of discrimination since the desegregation plan went into effect. This, though, may not be the equivalent of a finding that the school district has an affirmative commitment to comply in good faith with the entirety of a desegregation plan, and further proceedings are appropriate for this purpose as well.

The judgment is reversed and the case is remanded to the Court of Appeals. It should determine what issues are open for its further consideration in light of the previous briefs and arguments of the parties and in light of the principles set forth in this opinion. Thereupon it should order further proceedings as necessary or order an appropriate remand to the District Court.

Each party is to bear its own costs.

It is so ordered.

[JUSTICE THOMAS took no part in the consideration or decision of this case.]

JUSTICE SCALIA, *concurring.*

* * *

Our decision will be of great assistance to the citizens of DeKalb County, who for the first time since 1969 will be able to run their own public schools, at least so far as student assignments are concerned. It will have little effect, however, upon the many other school districts throughout the country that are still being supervised by federal judges, since it turns upon the extraordinarily rare circumstance of a *finding* that no portion of the current racial imbalance is a remnant of prior *de jure* discrimination. While it is perfectly appropriate for the Court to decide this case on that narrow basis, we must resolve—if not today, then soon—what is to be done in the vast majority of other districts, where, though our cases continue to profess that judicial

oversight of school operations is a temporary expedient, democratic processes remain suspended, with no prospect of restoration, 38 years after *Brown* v. *Board of Education.* . . .

Identifying and undoing the effects of some violations of the law is easy. . . . That is not so with respect to the effects of unconstitutionally operating a legally segregated school system; they are uncommonly difficult to identify and to separate from the effects of other causes. But one would not know that from our instructions to the lower courts on this subject, which tend to be at a level of generality that assumes facile reduction to specifics. "[Desegregation] decrees," we have said, "exceed appropriate limits if they are aimed at eliminating a condition that does not violate the Constitution or does not flow from such a violation." . . . We have never sought to describe how one identifies a condition as the effluent of a violation, or how a "vestige" or a "remnant" of past discrimination is to be recognized. Indeed, we have not even betrayed an awareness that these tasks are considerably more difficult than calculating the amount of taxes unconstitutionally paid. It is time for us to abandon our studied disregard of that obvious truth, and to adjust our jurisprudence to its reality.

Since parents and school boards typically want children to attend schools in their own neighborhood, "[t]he principal cause of racial and ethnic imbalance in . . . public schools across the country—North and South—is the imbalance in residential patterns." That imbalance in residential patterns, in turn, "doubtless result[s] from a mélange of past happenings prompted by economic considerations, private discrimination, discriminatory school assignments, or a desire to reside near people of one's own race or ethnic background." Consequently, residential segregation "is a national, not a southern phenomenon" which exists " 'regardless of the character of local laws and policies, and regardless of the extent of other forms of segregation or discrimination.' " . . .

Racially imbalanced schools are hence the product of a blend of public and private actions, and any assessment that they would not be segregated, or would not be *as* segregated, in the absence of a particular one of those factors is guesswork. It is similarly guesswork, of course, to say that they *would* be segregated, or would be *as* segregated, in the absence of one of those factors. Only in rare cases such as this one and *Spangler*, where the racial imbalance had been temporarily corrected after the abandonment of *de jure* segregation, can it be asserted with any degree of confidence that the past discrimination is no longer playing a proximate role. Thus, allocation of the burden of proof foreordains the result in almost all of the "vestige of past discrimination" cases. If, as is normally the case under our Equal Protection jurisprudence (and in the law generally), we require the plaintiffs to establish the asserted facts entitling them to relief—that the racial imbalance they wish corrected is at least in part the vestige of an old *de jure* system—the plaintiffs will almost always lose. Conversely, if we alter our normal approach and require the school authorities to establish the negative—that the imbalance is *not* attributable to their past discrimination—the plaintiffs will almost always win.

Since neither of these alternatives is entirely palatable, an observer unfamiliar with the history surrounding this issue might suggest that we avoid the problem by requiring only that the school authorities establish a regime in which parents are free to disregard neighborhood-school assignment, and to send their children (with transportation paid) to whichever school they choose. So long as there is free choice, he would say, there is no reason to require that the schools be made identical. The constitutional right is equal racial access to schools, not access to racially equal schools; whatever racial imbalances such a free-choice system might produce would be the product of private forces. We apparently envisioned no more than this in our initial post-*Brown* cases. . . .

. . . "From the very first, federal supervision of local school systems was intended as a *temporary* measure to remedy past discrimination." *Dowell,* 498 U.S., at, 111 S. Ct., at 637 (emphasis added). We envisioned it as temporary partly because "[n]o single tradition in public education is more deeply rooted than local control over the operation of schools," *Milliken* v. *Bradley,* 418 U.S. 717, 741, (1974) (*Milliken I*), and because no one's interest is furthered by subjecting the nation's educational system to "judicial tutelage for the indefinite future." . . . But we also envisioned it as temporary, I think, because the rational basis for the extraordinary presumption of causation simply must dissipate as the *de jure* system and the school boards who produced it recede further into the past. Since a multitude of private factors has shaped school systems in the years after abandonment of *de jure* segregation—normal migration, population growth (as in this case), "white flight" from the inner cities, increases in the costs of new facilities—the percentage of the current makeup of school systems attributable to the prior, government-enforced discrimination has diminished with

each passing year, to the point where it cannot realistically be assumed to be a significant factor.

At some time, we must acknowledge that it has become absurd to assume, without any further proof, that violations of the Constitution dating from the days when Lyndon Johnson was President, or earlier, continue to have an appreciable effect upon current operation of schools. We are close to that time. While we must continue to prohibit, without qualification, all racial discrimination in the operation of public schools, and to afford remedies that eliminate not only the discrimination but its identified consequences, we should consider laying aside the extraordinary, and increasingly counterfactual, presumption of *Green.* We must soon revert to the ordinary principles of our law, of our democratic heritage, and of our educational tradition: that plaintiffs alleging Equal Protection violations must prove intent and causation and not merely the existence of racial disparity; that public schooling, even in the South, should be controlled by locally elected authorities acting in conjunction with parents, and that it is "desirable" to permit pupils to attend "schools nearest their homes." . . .

JUSTICE BLACKMUN, *with whom* JUSTICE STEVENS *and* JUSTICE O'CONNOR *join, concurring in the judgment.*

* * *

I write separately for two purposes. First, I wish to be precise about my understanding of what it means for the District Court in this case to retain jurisdiction while relinquishing "supervision and control" over a subpart of a school system under desegregation decree. Second, I write to elaborate on factors the District Court should consider in determining whether racial imbalance is traceable to board actions and to indicate where, in my view, it failed to apply these standards.

I

Beginning with *Brown,* and continuing through the Court's most recent school-desegregation decision in *Board of Education of Oklahoma City* v. *Dowell,* 498 U.S. 237, 111 S. Ct. 630 (1991), this Court has recognized that when the local government has been running *de jure* segregated schools, it is the operation of a racially segregated school *system* that must be remedied, not discriminatory policy in some discrete subpart of that system. Consequently, the

Court in the past has required and decides again today that even if the school system ceases to discriminate with respect to one of the *Green*-type factors, "the [district] court should retain jurisdiction until it is clear that state-imposed segregation has been *completely removed*." ...

That the District Court's jurisdiction should continue until the school board demonstrates full compliance with the Constitution follows from the reasonable skepticism that underlies judicial supervision in the first instance. This Court noted in *Dowell*: "A district court need not accept at face value the profession of a school board which has intentionally discriminated that it will cease to do so in the future." 498 U.S., at ___, 111 S. Ct., at 637. It makes little sense, it seems to me, for the court to disarm itself by renouncing jurisdiction in one aspect of a school system, while violations of the Equal Protection Clause persist in other aspects of the same system. ... It would seem especially misguided to place unqualified reliance on the school board's promises in this case, because the two areas of the school system the District Court found still in violation of the Constitution—expenditures and teacher assignments—are two of the *Green* factors over which DCSS exercises the greatest control.

The obligations of a district court and a school district under its jurisdiction have been clearly articulated in the Court's many desegregation cases. Until the desegregation decree is dissolved under the standards set forth in *Dowell*, the school board continues to have "the affirmative duty to take whatever steps might be necessary to convert a unitary system in which racial discrimination would be eliminated root and branch." The duty remains enforceable by the district court without any new proof of a constitutional violation, and the school district has the burden of proving that its actions are eradicating the effects of the former *de jure* regime.

Contrary to the Court of Appeals' conclusion, however, retaining jurisdiction does not obligate the district court in all circumstances to maintain active supervision and control, continually ordering reassignment of students. The "duty" of the district court is to guarantee that the school district "eliminate[s] the discriminatory effects of the past as well as to bar like discrimination in the future." This obligation requires the court to review school board actions to ensure that each one "will further rather than delay conversion to a unitary, nonracial nondiscriminatory school system." But this obligation does not always require the district

court to order new, affirmative action simply because of racial imbalance in student assignment.

Whether a district court must maintain active supervision over student assignment, and order new remedial actions depends on two factors. As the Court discusses, the district court must order changes in student assignment if it "is necessary or practicable to achieve compliance in other facets of the school system." The district court also must order affirmative action in school attendance if the school district's conduct was a "contributing cause" of the racially identifiable school. ... It is the application of this latter causation requirement that I now examine in more detail.

II

A

DCSS claims that it need not remedy the segregation in DeKalb County schools because it was caused by demographic changes for which DCSS has no responsibility. It is not enough, however, for DCSS to establish that demographics exacerbated the problem; it must prove that its own policies did not contribute. Such contribution can occur in at least two ways: DCSS may have contributed to the demographic changes themselves, or it may have contributed directly to the racial imbalance in the schools.

To determine DCSS' possible role in encouraging the residential segregation, the court must examine the situation with special care. "[A] connection between past segregative acts and present segregation may be present even when not apparent and ... close examination is required before concluding that the connection does not exist." Close examination is necessary because what might seem to be purely private preferences in housing may in fact have been created, in part, by actions of the school district.

> People gravitate toward school facilities, just as schools are located in response to the needs of the people. The location of schools may thus influence the patterns of residential development of a metropolitan area and have important impact on composition of inner-city neighborhoods. Swann, 402 U.S., at 20–21.

This interactive effects between schools and housing choices may occur because many families are concerned about the racial composition of a prospective school and will make residential decisions accordingly. Thus, schools that are demonstrably black or white provide a signal to these families, perpetuating and intensifying the residential movement.

School systems can identify a school as "black" or "white" in a variety of ways; choosing to enroll a racially identifiable student population is only the most obvious. The Court has noted: "[T]he use of mobile classrooms, the drafting of student transfer policies, the transportation of students, and the assignment of faculty and staff, on racially identifiable bases, have the clear effect of earmarking schools according to their racial composition." Because of the various methods for identifying schools by race, even if a school district manages to desegregate student assignments at one point, its failure to remedy the constitutional violation in its entirety may result in resegregation, as neighborhoods respond to the racially identifiable schools. Regardless of the particular way in which the school district has encouraged residential segregation, this Court's decisions require that the school district remedy the effect that such segregation has had on the school system.

In addition to exploring the school district's influence on residential segregation, the District Court here should examine whether school board actions might have contributed to school segregation. Actions taken by a school district can aggravate or eliminate school segregation independent of residential segregation. School board policies concerning placement of new schools and closure of old schools and programs such as magnet classrooms and majority-to-minority (M-to-M) transfer policies affect the racial composition of the schools. A school district's failure to adopt policies that effectively desegregate its schools continues the violation of the Fourteenth Amendment. The Court many times has noted that a school district is not responsible for all of society's ills, but it bears full responsibility for schools that have never been desegregated.

B

The District Court's opinion suggests that it did not examine DCSS' actions in light of the foregoing principles. The court did note that the migration farther into the suburbs was accelerated by "white flight" from black schools and the "blockbusting" of former white neighborhoods. It did not examine, however, whether DCSS might have encouraged that flight by assigning faculty and principals so as to identify some schools as intended respectively for black students or white students. Nor did the court consider how the placement of schools, the attendance zone boundaries, or the use of mobile classrooms might have affected residential movement. The court, in my view, failed to consider the many ways DCSS may have contributed to the demographic shifts.

Nor did the District Court correctly analyze whether DCSS' past actions had contributed to the school segregation independent of residential segregation. The court did not require DCSS to bear the "heavy burden" of showing that student assignment policies—policies that continued the effects of the dual system—served important and legitimate ends. Indeed, the District Court said flatly that it would "not dwell on what might have been," but would inquire only as to "what else should be done now." But this Court's decisions *require* the District Court to "dwell on what might have been." In particular, they require the court to examine the past to determine whether racial imbalance in the schools is attributable in part to the former *de jure* segregated regime or any later actions by school officials.

As the Court describes, the District Court placed great emphasis on its conclusion that DCSS, in response to the court order, had desegregated student assignment in 1969. DCSS' very first action taken in response to the court decree, however, was to shape attendance zones to result in two schools that were more than 50% black, despite a districtwide black student population of less than 6%. Within a year, another school became majority black, followed by 4 others within the next 2 years. Despite the existence of these schools, the District Court found that DCSS effectively had desegregated for a short period of time with respect to student assignment. The District Court justified this finding by linking the school segregation exclusively to residential segregation existing prior to the court order.

But residential segregation that existed *prior* to the desegregation decree cannot provide an excuse. It is not enough that DCSS adopt race-neutral policies in response to a court desegregation decree. Instead, DCSS is obligated to "counteract the continuing effects of past school segregation." Accordingly, the school district did not meet its affirmative duty simply by adopting a neighborhood-school plan, when already existing residential segregation inevitably perpetuated the dual system.

Virtually all the demographic changes that DCSS claims caused the school segregation occurred after 1975. Of particular relevance to the causation inquiry, then, are DCSS' actions prior to 1975; failures during that period to implement the

1969 decree render the school district's contentions that its noncompliance is due simply to demographic changes less plausible.

A review of the record suggests that from 1969 until 1975, DCSS failed to desegregate its schools. During that period, the number of students attending racially identifiable schools actually increased, and increased more quickly than the increase in black students. By 1975, 73% of black elementary students and 56% of black high school students were attending majority black schools, although the percentages of black students in the district population were just 20% and 13%, respectively.

Of the 13 new elementary schools DCSS opened between 1969 and 1975, six had a total of four black students in 1975. One of the two high schools DCSS opened had no black students at all. The only other measure taken by DCSS during the 1969–1975 period was to adopt the M-to-M transfer program in 1972. Due, however, to limitations imposed by the school district administrators—including a failure to provide transportation, "unnecessary red tape," and limits on available transfer schools—only one-tenth of 1% of the students were participating in the transfer program as of the 1975–1976 school year.

In 1976, when the District Court reviewed DCSS' actions in the M-to-M program, it concluded that DCSS' limitations on the program "perpetuate the vestiges of a dual system." Noting that the Department of Health, Education and Welfare had found that DCSS had ignored its responsibility affirmatively to eradicate segregation and perpetuate desegregation, the District Court found that attendance zone changes had perpetuated the dual system in the county.

Thus, in 1976, before most of the demographic changes, the District Court found that DCSS had not complied with the 1969 order to eliminate the vestiges of its former *de jure* school system. Indeed, the 1976 order found that DCSS had contributed to the growing racial imbalance of its schools. Given these determinations in 1976, the District Court, at a minimum, should have required DCSS to prove that, but for the demographic changes be-

tween 1976 and 1985, its actions would have been sufficient to "convert promptly to a system without a 'white' school and a 'Negro' school, but just schools." The available evidence suggests that this would be a difficult burden for DCSS to meet.

DCSS has undertaken only limited remedial actions since the 1976 court order. The number of students participating in the M-to-M program has expanded somewhat, comprising about 6% of the current student population. The district also has adopted magnet programs, but they involve fewer than 1% of the system's students. Doubtless DCSS could have started and expanded its magnet and M-to-M programs more promptly; it could have built and closed more schools with a view toward promoting integration of both schools and neighborhoods; redrawn attendance zones; integrated its faculty and administrators; and spent its funds equally. But it did not. DCSS must prove that the measures it actually implemented satisfy its obligation to eliminate the vestiges of *de jure* segregation originally discovered in 1969, and still found to exist in 1976.

III

The District Court apparently has concluded that DCSS should be relieved of the responsibility to desegregate because such responsibility would be burdensome. To be sure, changes in demographic patterns aggravated the vestiges of segregation and made it more difficult for DCSS to desegregate. But an integrated school system is no less desirable because it is difficult to achieve, and it is no less a constitutional imperative because that imperative has gone unmet for 38 years.

Although respondents challenged the District Court's causation conclusions in the Court of Appeals, that court did not reach the issue. Accordingly, in addition to the issues the Court suggests be considered in further proceedings, I would remand for the Court of Appeals to review, under the foregoing principles, the District Court's finding that DCSS has met its burden of proving the racially identifiable schools are in no way the result of past segregative action.

JUSTICE WHITE *delivered the opinion of the Court.*

The United States District Court for the Western District of Missouri imposed an increase in the property taxes levied by the Kansas City, Missouri, School District (KCMSD) to ensure funding for the desegregation of KCMSD's public schools. We granted certiorari to consider the State of Missouri's argument that the District Court lacked the power to raise local property taxes. For the reasons given below, we hold that the District Court abused its discretion in imposing the tax increase. We also hold, however, that the modifications of the District Court's order made by the Court of Appeals do satisfy equitable and constitutional principles governing the District Court's power.

I

In 1977, KCMSD and a group of KCMSD students filed a complaint alleging that the State of Missouri and surrounding school districts had operated a segregated public school system in the Kansas City metropolitan area. The District Court realigned KCMSD as a party defendant, *School Dist. of Kansas City* v. *Missouri*, 460 F. Supp. 421 (WD Mo. 1978), and KCMSD filed a cross-claim against the State, seeking indemnification for any liability that might be imposed on KCMSD for intradistrict segregation. After a lengthy trial, the District Court found that KCMSD and the State had operated a segregated school system within the KCMSD.

The District Court thereafter issued an order detailing the remedies necessary to eliminate the vestiges of segregation and the financing necessary to implement those remedies. The District Court originally estimated the total cost of the desegregation remedy to be almost $88,000,000 over three years, of which it expected the State to pay $67,592,072 and KCMSD to pay $20,140,472. The court concluded, however, that several provisions of Missouri law would prevent KCMSD from being able to pay its share of the obligation. The Missouri Constitution limits local property taxes to $1.25 per $100 of assessed valuation unless a majority of the voters in the district approve a higher levy, up to $3.25 per $100; the levy may be raised above $3.25 per $100 only if two-thirds of the vot-

ers agree. The "Hancock Amendment" requires property tax rates to be rolled back when property is assessed at a higher valuation to ensure that taxes will not be increased solely as a result of re-assessments. The Hancock Amendment thus prevents KCMSD from obtaining any revenue increase as a result of increases in the assessed valuation of real property. "Proposition C" allocates one cent of every dollar raised by the state sales tax to a schools trust fund and requires school districts to reduce property taxes by an amount equal to 50% of the previous year's sales tax receipts in the district. However, the trust fund is allocated according to a formula that does not compensate KCMSD for the amount lost in property tax revenues, and the effect of Proposition C is to divert nearly half of the sales tax collected in KCMSD to other parts of the State.

The District Court believed that it had the power to order a tax increase to ensure adequate funding of the desegregation plan, but it hesitated to take this step. It chose instead to enjoin the effect of the Proposition C rollback to allow KCMSD to raise an additional $4,000,000 for the coming fiscal year. The court ordered KCMSD to submit to the voters a proposal for an increase in taxes sufficient to pay for its share of the desegregation remedy in following years.

The Court of Appeals for the Eighth Circuit affirmed the District Court's findings of liability and remedial order in most respects. The Court of Appeals agreed with the State, however, that the District Court had failed to explain adequately why it had imposed most of the cost of the desegregation plan on the State. The Eighth Circuit ordered the District Court to divide the cost equally between the State and KCMSD.

Proceedings before the District Court continued during the appeal. In its original remedial order, the District Court had directed KCMSD to prepare a study addressing the usefulness of "magnet schools" to promote desegregation. A year later, the District Court approved KCMSD's proposal to operate six magnet schools during the 1986–1987 school year. The court again faced the problem of funding, for KCMSD's efforts to persuade the voters to approve a tax increase had failed, as had its efforts to seek funds from the Kansas City Council and the state legislature. Again hesitating to impose a tax increase itself, the court continued its injunction against the Proposition C rollback to enable KCMSD to raise an additional $6,500,000.

In November 1986, the District Court endorsed a marked expansion of the magnet school program. It adopted in substance a KCMSD proposal that every high school, every middle school, and half of the elementary schools in KCMSD become magnet schools by the 1991–1992 school year. It also approved the $142,736,025 budget proposed by KCMSD for implementation of the magnet school plan, as well as the expenditure of $52,858,301 for additional capital improvements.

The District Court next considered, as the Court of Appeals had directed, how to shift the cost of desegregation to KCMSD. The District Court concluded that it would be "clearly inequitable" to require the population of KCMSD to pay half of the desegregation cost, and that "even with Court help it would be very difficult for the KCMSD to fund more than 25% of the costs of the entire remedial plan." The court reasoned that the State should pay for most of the desegregation cost under the principle that " 'the person who starts the fire has more responsibility for the damages caused than the person who fails to put it out,' " and that apportionment of damages between the State and KCMSD according to fault was supported by the doctrine of comparative fault in tort, which had been adopted by the Missouri Supreme Court in 1983. The District Court then held that the State and KCMSD were 75% and 25% at fault, respectively, and ordered them to share the cost of the desegregation remedy in that proportion. To ensure complete funding of the remedy, the court also held the two tortfeasors jointly and severally liable for the cost of the plan.

Three months later, the District Court adopted a plan requiring $187,450,334 in further capital improvements. By then it was clear that KCMSD would lack the resources to pay for its 25% share of the desegregation cost. KCMSD requested that the District Court order the State to pay for any amount that KCMSD could not meet. The District Court declined to impose a greater share of the cost on the State, but it accepted that KCMSD had "exhausted all available means of raising additional revenue." Finding itself with "no choice but to exercise its broad equitable powers and enter a judgment that will enable the KCMSD to raise its share of the cost of the plan," and believing that the "United States Supreme Court has stated that a tax may be increased 'if necessary to raise funds adequate to . . . operate and maintain without racial discrimination a public school system,' "

(quoting *Griffin* v. *Prince Edward County School Bd.*, 377 U.S. 218, 233, [1964]), the court ordered the KCMSD property tax levy raised from $2.05 to $4.00 per $100 of assessed valuation through the 1991–1992 school year. KCMSD was also directed to issue $150,000,000 in capital improvement bonds.

The State appealed, challenging the scope of the desegregation remedy, the allocation of the cost between the State and KCMSD, and the tax increase. . . . A panel of the Eighth Circuit affirmed in part and reversed in part. 855 F. 2d 1295 (1988). With respect to the would-be intervenors, the Court of Appeals upheld the denial of intervention. The scope of the desegregation order was also upheld against all the State's objections, as was the allocation of costs.

Turning to the property tax increase, the Court of Appeals rejected the State's argument that a federal court lacks the judicial power to order a tax increase. The Court of Appeals agreed with the District Court that *Griffin* v. *Prince Edward County School Bd.* had established the District Court's authority to order county officials to levy taxes. Accepting also the District Court's conclusion that state law prevented KCMSD from raising funds sufficient to implement the desegregation remedy, the Court of Appeals held that such state-law limitations must fall to the command of the Constitution.

Although the Court of Appeals thus "affirm[ed] the actions that the [District] [C]ourt has taken to this point," it agreed with the State that principles of federal/state comity required the District Court to use "minimally obtrusive methods to remedy constitutional violations." The Court of Appeals thus required that in the future, the District Court should not set the property tax rate itself but should authorize KCMSD to submit a levy to the state tax collection authorities and should enjoin the operation of state laws hindering KCMSD from adequately funding the remedy. The Court of Appeals reasoned that permitting the school board to set the levy itself would minimize disruption of state laws and processes and would ensure maximum consideration of the views of state and local officials. . . .

[Subsequently petition for a rehearing was denied in an order of October 14, 1988.]

On December 31, 1988, 78 days after the issuance of the order denying rehearing and 134 days after the entry of the Court of Appeals' judgment, Jackson County [in which KCMSD is located] presented to this Court an application for extension of time in which to file a petition for certiorari. The Clerk of this Court returned the application to Jackson County as untimely. App. 503. According to the Clerk, the 90-day period in which Jackson County could petition for certiorari began to run on August 19, 1988, and expired on November 17, 1988. The Clerk informed Jackson County that although the timely filing of a "petition for rehearing" with the Court of Appeals tolls the running of the 90-day period, the filing of a "petition for rehearing en banc" does not toll the time.

On January 10, 1989, the Clerk of the Eighth Circuit issued an order amending the order of October 14, 1988. The amended order stated: This Court's mandate which was issued on October 14, 1988, is hereby recalled.

> There are three (3) petitions for rehearing with suggestions for rehearing en banc pending before the Court. It is hereby ordered that the petitions for rehearing and the petitions for rehearing with suggestions for rehearing en banc are denied.

> This order is entered nunc pro tunc effective October 14, 1988. The Court's mandate shall now issue forthwith. *Id.*, at 513 (emphasis added).

The State, Jackson County, and Clark Group (a group of local taxpayers) filed petitions for certiorari within 90 days of the October 14, 1988, order. The State's petition argued that the remedies imposed by the District Court were excessive in scope and that the property tax increase violated Article III, the Tenth Amendment, and principles of federal/state comity. We denied the petitions of Jackson. We granted the State's petition, limited to the question of the property tax increase. . . .

III

We turn to the tax increase imposed by the District Court. The State urges us to hold that the tax increase violated Article III, the Tenth Amendment, and principles of federal/state comity. We find it unnecessary to reach the difficult constitutional issues, for we agree with the State that the tax increase contravened the principles of comity that must govern the exercise of the District Court's equitable discretion in this area.

It is accepted by all the parties, as it was by the courts below, that the imposition of a tax increase by a federal court was an extraordinary event. In assuming for itself the fundamental and delicate power of taxation the District Court not only intruded on local authority but circumvented it altogether. Before taking such a drastic step the District Court was obliged to assure itself that no permissible alternative would have accomplished the required task. We have emphasized that although the "remedial powers of an equity court must be adequate to the task, . . . they are not unlimited," and one of the most important considerations governing the exercise of equitable power is a proper respect for the integrity and function of local government institutions. Especially is this true where, as here, those institutions are ready, willing, and—but for the operation of state law curtailing their powers—able to remedy the deprivation of constitutional rights themselves.

The District Court believed that it had no alternative to imposing a tax increase. But there was an alternative, the very one outlined by the Court of Appeals: it could have authorized or required KCMSD to levy property taxes at a rate adequate to fund the desegregation remedy and could have enjoined the operation of state laws that would have prevented KCMSD from exercising this power. The difference between the two approaches is far more than a matter of form. Authorizing and directing local government institutions to devise and implement remedies not only protects the function of those institutions but, to the extent possible, also places the responsibility for solutions to the problems of segregation upon those who have themselves created the problems.

As *Brown* v. *Board of Education* observed, local authorities have the "primary responsibility for elucidating, assessing, and solving" the problems of desegregation. This is true as well of the problems of financing desegregation, for no matter has been more consistently placed upon the shoulders of local government than that of financing public schools. As was said in another context, "[t]he very complexity of the problems of financing and managing a . . . public school system suggests that 'there will be more than one constitutionally permissible method of solving them,' and that . . . 'the legislature's efforts to tackle the problems' should be entitled to respect." *San Antonio Independent School District* v. *Rodriguez*, 411 U.S. 1 (1973). By no means should a district court grant local government *carte blanche*, but local officials should at least have the opportunity to devise their own solutions to these problems.

The District Court therefore abused its discretion in imposing the tax itself. The Court of Appeals should not have allowed the tax increase to stand and should have reversed the District Court in this respect.

IV

We stand on different ground when we review the modifications to the District Court's order made by the Court of Appeals. As explained . . . the Court of Appeals held that the District Court in the future should authorize KCMSD to submit a levy to the state tax collection authorities adequate to fund its budget and should enjoin the operation of state laws that would limit or reduce the levy below that amount.

The State argues that the funding ordered by the District Court violates principles of equity and comity because the remedial order itself was excessive. As the State puts it, "[t]he only reason that the court below needed to consider an unprecedented tax increase was the equally unprecedented cost of its remedial programs." We think this argument aims at the scope of the remedy rather than the manner in which the remedy is to be funded and thus falls outside our limited grant of certiorari in this case. As we denied certiorari on the first question presented by the State's petition, which did challenge the scope of the remedial order, we must resist the State's efforts to argue that point now. We accept, without approving or disapproving, the Court of Appeals' conclusion that the District Court's remedy was proper.

The State has argued here that the District Court, having found the State and KCMSD jointly and severally liable, should have allowed any monetary obligations that KCMSD could not meet to fall on the State rather than interfere with state law to permit KCMSD to meet them. Under the circumstances of this case, we cannot say it was an abuse of discretion for the District Court to rule that KCMSD should be responsible for funding its share of the remedy. The State strenuously opposed efforts by respondents to make it responsible for the cost of implementing the order and had secured a reversal of the District Court's earlier decision placing on it all of the cost of substantial portions of the order. The District Court declined to require the State to pay for KCMSD's obligations because it believed that the Court of Appeals had ordered it to allocate the costs between the two governmental entities. Furthermore, if the District Court had chosen the route now suggested by the State, implementation of the remedial order might have been delayed if the State resisted efforts by KCMSD to obtain contribution.

It is true that in *Milliken* v. *Bradley*, we stated that the enforcement of a money judgment against the State did not violate principles of federalism because "[t]he District Court . . . neither attempted to restructure local governmental entities nor . . . mandat[ed] a particular method or structure of state or local financing." But we did not there state that a District Court could never set aside state laws preventing local governments from raising funds sufficient to satisfy their constitutional obligations just because those funds could also be obtained from the States. To the contrary, 42 U.S.C. § 1983 (1982 ed.), on which respondents' complaint is based, is authority enough to require each tortfeasor to pay its share of the cost of the remedy if it can, and apportionment of the cost is part of the equitable power of the District Court.

We turn to the constitutional issues. The modifications ordered by the Court of Appeals cannot be assailed as invalid under the Tenth Amendment. "The Tenth Amendment's reservation of non-delegated powers to the States is not implicated by a federal-court judgment enforcing the express prohibitions of unlawful state conduct enacted by the Fourteenth Amendment." *Milliken* v. *Bradley*, 433 U.S. at 291, 1974 "The Fourteenth Amendment . . . was avowedly directed against the power of the States," *Pennsylvania* v. *Union Gas Co.*, 109 S. Ct. 2273 at 2302, 1989 . . . and so permits a federal court to disestablish local government institutions that interfere with its commands.

Finally, the State argues that an order to increase taxes cannot be sustained under the judicial power of Article III. Whatever the merits of this argument when applied to the District Court's own order increasing taxes, a point we have not reached, a court order directing a local government body to levy its own taxes is plainly a judicial act within the power of a federal court. We held as much in *Griffin* v. *Prince Edward County School Bd.* where we stated that a District Court, faced with a county's attempt to avoid desegregation of the public schools by refusing to operate those schools, could "require the [County] Supervisors to exercise the power that is theirs to levy taxes to raise funds adequate to reopen, operate, and maintain without racial discrimination a public school system. . . . "

The State maintains, however, that . . . the federal judicial power can go no further than to require local governments to levy taxes *as authorized under state law*. In other words, the State argues that federal courts cannot set aside state-imposed limitations on local taxing authority because to do so is to do more than to require the local government "to exercise the power *that is theirs*." We disagree. . . .

It is therefore clear that a local government with taxing authority may be ordered to levy taxes in excess of the limit set by state statute where there is reason based in the Constitution for not observing the statutory limitation. Here the KCMSD may be ordered to levy taxes despite the statutory limitations on its authority in order to compel the discharge of an obligation imposed on KCMSD by the Fourteenth Amendment. To hold otherwise would fail to take account of the obligations of local governments, under the Supremacy Clause, to fulfill the requirements that the Constitution imposes on them.

However wide the discretion of local authorities in fashioning desegregation remedies may be, "if a state-imposed limitation on a school authority's discretion operates to inhibit or obstruct the operation of a unitary school system or impede the disestablishing of a dual school system, it must fall; state policy must give way when it operates to hinder vindication of federal constitutional guarantees." *North Carolina State Board of Education* v. *Swann*, 402 U.S. 43 at 45, 1971. Even though a particular remedy may not be required in every case to vindicate constitutional guarantees, where (as here) it has been found that a particular remedy is required, the State cannot hinder the process by preventing a local government from implementing that remedy.

Accordingly, the judgment of the Court of Appeals is affirmed insofar as it required the District Court to modify its funding order and reversed insofar as it allowed the tax increase imposed by the District Court to stand. The case is remanded for further proceedings consistent with this opinion.

It is so ordered.

JUSTICE KENNEDY, *with whom* THE CHIEF JUSTICE, JUSTICE O'CONNOR, *and* JUSTICE SCALIA *join, concurring in part and concurring in the judgment.*

In agreement with the Court that we have jurisdiction to decide this case, I join Part II of the opinion. I agree also that the District Court exceeded its authority by attempting to impose a tax. The Court is unanimous in its holding, that the Court of Appeals' judgment affirming "the actions that the [district] court has taken to this point," must be reversed. This is consistent with our precedents and the basic principles defining judicial power.

In my view, however, the Court transgresses these same principles when it goes further, much further, to embrace by broad dictum an expansion of power in the federal judiciary beyond all precedent. Today's casual embrace of taxation imposed by the unelected, life-tenured federal judiciary disregards fundamental precepts for the democratic control of public institutions. I cannot acquiesce in the majority's statements on this point, and should there arise an actual dispute over the collection of taxes as here contemplated in a case that is not, like this one, premature, we would not confirm the outcome of premises adopted with so little constitutional justification. The Court's statements, in my view, cannot be seen as necessary for its judgment, or as precedent for the future, and I cannot join Parts III and IV of the Court's opinion.

* * *

II

. . . The description of the judicial power nowhere includes the word "tax" or anything that resembles it. This reflects the Framers' understanding that taxation was not a proper area for judicial involvement. "The judiciary . . . has no influence over either the sword or the purse, no direction either of the strength or of the wealth of the society, and can take no active resolution whatever." The Federalist, No. 78. . . .

Our cases throughout the years leave no doubt that taxation is not a judicial function. . . .

A judicial taxation order is but an attempt to exercise a power that always has been thought legislative in nature. The location of the federal taxing power sheds light on today's attempt to approve judicial taxation at the local level. Article I, § 8, cl. 1, begins with the statement that "[t]he Congress shall have Power To lay and collect Taxes. . . . " As we have said, "[t]axation is a legislative function, and Congress . . . is the sole organ for levying taxes." . . . *National Cable Television Assn., Inc.* v. *United States*, 415 U.S. 336 (1974).

The confinement of taxation to the legislative branches, both in our Federal and State Governments, was not random. It reflected our ideal that the power of taxation must be under the control of those who are taxed. This truth animated all our colonial and revolutionary history. . . .

The power of taxation is one that the federal judiciary does not possess. In our system "the legislative department alone has access to the pockets of people," The Federalist, No. 48, . . .for it is the legislature that is accountable to them and represents their will. The authority that would levy the tax at issue here shares none of these qualities. . . . The operation of tax systems is among the most difficult aspects of public administration.

The Court relies on dicta from *Griffin* v. *School*

Bd. of Prince Edward County to support its statements on judicial taxation. In *Griffin,* the Court faced an unrepentant and recalcitrant school board that attempted to provide financial support for white schools while refusing to operate schools for black schoolchildren. We stated that the district court could "require the Supervisors to exercise the power that is theirs to levy taxes to raise funds adequate to reopen, operate, and maintain without racial discrimination a public school system." There is no occasion in this case to discuss the full implications of *Griffin*'s observation, for it has no application here. *Griffin* endorsed the power of a federal court to order the local authority to exercise existing authority to tax.

This case does not involve an order to a local government with plenary taxing power to impose a tax, or an order directed at one whose taxing power has been limited by a state law enacted in order to thwart a federal court order. An order of this type would find support in the *Griffin* dicta, and present a closer question than the one before us. Yet that order might implicate as well the "perversion of the normal legislative process" that we have found troubling in other contexts. A legislative vote taken under judicial compulsion blurs lines of accountability by making it appear that a decision was reached by elected representatives when the reality is otherwise. For this reason, it is difficult to see the difference between an order to tax and direct judicial imposition of a tax. . . .

IV

This case is a stark illustration of the ever-present question whether ends justify means. Few ends are more important than enforcing the guarantee of equal educational opportunity for our Nation's children. But rules of taxation that override state political strictures not themselves subject to any constitutional infirmity raise serious questions of federal authority, questions compounded by the odd posture of a case in which the Court assumes the validity of a novel conception of desegregation remedies we never before have approved. The historical record of voluntary compliance with the decree of *Brown* v. *Board of Education* is not a proud chapter in our constitutional history, and the judges of the District Courts and Courts of Appeals have been courageous and skillful in implementing its mandate. But courage and skill must be exercised with due regard for the proper and historic role of the courts.

I do not acknowledge the troubling departures in today's majority opinion as either necessary or appropriate to ensure full compliance with the Equal Protection Clause and its mandate to eliminate the cause and effects of racial discrimination in the schools. Indeed, while this case happens to arise in the compelling context of school desegregation, the principles involved are not limited to that context. There is no obvious limit to today's discussion that would prevent judicial taxation in cases involving prisons, hospitals, or other public institutions, or indeed to pay a large damages award levied against a municipality under 42 U.S.C. § 1983. This assertion of judicial power in one of the most sensitive of policy areas, that involving taxation, begins a process that over time could threaten fundamental alteration of the form of government our Constitution embodies.

James Madison observed: "Justice is the end of government. It is the end of civil society. It ever has been, and ever will be pursued, until it be obtained, or until liberty be lost in the pursuit." The Federalist, No. 51. In pursuing the demand of justice for racial equality, I fear that the Court today loses sight of other basic political liberties guaranteed by our constitutional system, liberties that can coexist with a proper exercise of judicial remedial powers adequate to correct constitutional violations.

Brown *in the Academy: Racial Segregation and Discrimination in Higher Education*

FEATURED CASES

United States v. *Fordice*   *Regents of the University of California* v. *Bakke*

Just as state segregation policies separated elementary and secondary school pupils on the basis of race, so did those states provide for racial segregation in their institutions of higher learning. In addition to the establishment of "Negro" colleges and universities by the several states of the "Old Confederacy," a number of private colleges were developed and maintained by churches and other private philanthropy to make higher education accessible for "Negro" students. By the time of *Brown*, public authorities were operating some 32 of these institutions, and private sources maintained more than 40 of them. Together these "historic black colleges and universities" (HBCUs) nurtured and developed most of the nation's African-American professional class and leaders. To be sure, leaders like Supreme Court Justice Thurgood Marshall, Dr. Martin Luther King, Jr., President Clinton's Transition Team Chair Vernon Jordan, former United Nations Ambassador Andrew Young and former Congressperson Barbara Jordan completed their undergraduate education at those institutions. Because so many African American students found the culture of the HBCUs more conducive to their total development, considerable efforts have been undertaken during the post-*Brown* era to maintain the publicly supported ones as identifiable African-American institutions despite the mandate of *Brown I* and *Brown II*. Hence, very little was done to alter their character. A token few "other" race students enrolled at the traditional "white" institutions and the HBCUs under nondiscriminatory admissions policies. Even occasional pressure from the Justice and Education Departments failed to alter significantly the racial character of these institutions.

Maintaining essentially a dual system of comprehensive colleges and universities is an expensive undertaking, and the fiscal resources problem is compounded in the states where most of the HBCUs are located because of their very weak revenue capacities. Hence, in the allocation of resources, the HBCUs almost always did not receive their fair share.

While many attempts were made to ameliorate this condition (e.g., increased federal support for the historic black colleges and universities [HBCUs] under Title III of the Higher Education Act of 1965) African Americans in Mississippi in the mid-1970s instituted a challenge to the funding disparity between the traditionally "white" colleges and universities and the HBCUs in that state. The federal government later joined in that challenge, resulting in the Supreme Court's decision in *United States* v. *Fordice* (112 S. Ct. 2727) in 1992.

While the plaintiffs' position alleging the discriminatory allocation of resources was sustained, that victory was tempered with unforeseen negative possibilities. Some African-American defenders of the HBCUs remain wary of the future of many of the publicly supported schools in a context of white-dominated legislatures and governing boards where the fiscal capacity to sustain higher education continues to deteriorate. These supporters fear that state authorities may move to comply with the *Fordice* ruling by terminating their HBCUs as identifiable, freestanding institutions. The immediate consequence would be that African-American students would have to turn to the traditionally white universities and colleges to seek higher education in the state, but their numbers would then probably decline as they would be confronted with more restrictive admissions policies.

In his concurring opinion, Justice Thomas recognized this possibility, but cautioned that the standard advanced by the Court in this higher education context is less stringent than that forged in the 1968 *Green* case to achieve compliance with *Brown* at the elementary and secondary school levels. Here, he noted, the essence of the Court's holding was that states are *required to reform policies still in force from the old de jure segregation era that have discriminatory effects, "to the extent practiced and consistent with sound educational policies"* (emphasis added). Thomas concluded that this standard "does not compel the elimination of all observed racial imbalance" and hence does not portend "the destruction of [HBCUs] nor the severing of those institutions from their distinctive histories and traditions." But the policy options that *Fordice* appears to leave to states that continue to operate essentially "white" and "black" colleges and universities will undoubtedly spawn litigation for the remainder of this century.

THE PREFERENTIAL ADMISSIONS CONTROVERSY

During the 1960s and the early 1970s, a number of traditionally white institutions of higher learning adopted admissions policies designed to increase the number of minority students in their general student population. Such policies were generically referred to as "affirmative action" programs and came under sharp attack in the early 1970s with the ever-increasing scarcity of resources to support education, particularly higher education. As white applicants found space limitations thwarting their admission to professional schools, some of them alleged that the affirmative action programs had also placed them at a disadvantage in their quest for admission.

When this controversial issue was presented in *DeFunis* v. *Odegaard* (416 U.S. 312, 1974), the Court was able to avoid making a decision on it. In that case, the white petitioner charged the University of Washington Law School with a violation of the equal protection clause of the Fourteenth Amendment in denying him admission while admitting "minority" applicants with lower qualifications. The university acknowledged that the petitioner's grades and Law School Aptitude Test scores were higher than those of some 36 black, Latino, and other minority students who were admitted, but justified its policy by indicating its use of a broad range of other factors, in addition to raw grades and test scores, to arrive at its admissions decisions. It further defended its administrative discretion to expand opportunities for legal education to minorities whose past access to the legal profession had been negligible. But a state trial court disagreed and ordered DeFunis's admission in 1971. When the state supreme court reversed that ruling, DeFunis took the issue to the U.S. Supreme Court. Pending disposition of the appeal, however, he was allowed to remain in school.

Hence, when the Court considered the case in 1974, DeFunis was nearing completion of his studies (having enrolled for his last semester), and the majority ducked the issue by holding that the case was moot. The Court did concede, however, that the issue would most likely be before it in the near future. Three years later, it did come back, when, in February 1977, the case of *Regents of the University of California* v. *Bakke* (438 U. S. 265, 1978) was accepted for review, and raised legal issues somewhat similar to those in the *DeFunis* case. The minority admissions program at the Medical School of the University of California at Davis provided for separate reviews of minority and white applicants. Sixteen places in the entering class of 100 were, for all practical purposes, set aside for minority students. When Bakke was denied admission to one of the remaining 84 slots, he charged that the special minority program allowed the admission of students whose overall qualifications were inferior to his and operated to exclude him solely on the basis of race. To Bakke, this was *reverse discrimination*, which not only violated the equal protection clause of the Fourteenth Amendment, but a central provision (Title VI) of the 1964 Civil Rights Act as well.

A California trial court agreed, holding that the special minority admissions program really operated as a racial quota system in violation of the cited constitutional and statutory provisions. Additionally, that court proscribed the use of race as a criterion in admissions decisions. However, Bakke's admission was not ordered because of insufficient proof of his admissibility "but for the special admissions program." The California Supreme Court modified this ruling, finding the *strict scrutiny* standard of review applicable, and held that the program violated the equal protection clause of the Fourteenth Amendment. Contrary to the trial court, it further held that the burden of proof under *strict scrutiny* shifted to the university, and since this burden was not satisfied, Bakke should be admitted. Thereupon, the university, despite the urging of some major civil rights groups not to do so, sought review by the Supreme Court.

Responding to the difficult and complex questions the case presented, the justices divided in such a manner as to allow both sides in this widely publicized case to gain something. There was no Court opinion, but Justice Lewis Powell announced the Court's judgment and was supported by the Chief Justice and Justices Stewart, Rehnquist, and Stevens in holding that the special minority admissions program at Davis operated to exclude persons because of race, thereby abridging the equal protection clause of the Fourteenth Amendment.

But the other four justices, Brennan, White, Marshall, and Blackmun, who disagreed with Powell's characterization of the admissions programs, joined him in holding that university officials may consider race as one of a number of factors in their admissions determinations.

In waffling on this, the Court preserved its options for the consideration of affirmative action programs that had been fashioned to accomplish equal employment opportunities, that are considered in the next section.

JUSTICE WHITE *delivered the opinion of the Court.*

In 1954, this Court held that the concept of " 'separate but equal' " has no place in the field of public education. The following year, the Court ordered an end to segregated public education "with all deliberate speed." Since these decisions, the Court has had many occasions to evaluate whether a public school district has met its affirmative obligation to dismantle its prior *de jure* segregated system in elementary and secondary schools. In this case we decide what standards to apply in determining whether the State of Mississippi has met this obligation in the university context.

I

Mississippi launched its public university system in 1848 by establishing the University of Mississippi, an institution dedicated to the higher education exclusively of white persons. In succeeding decades, the State erected additional post-secondary schools, single-race educational facilities. Alcorn State University opened its doors in 1871 as "an agricultural college for the education of Mississippi's black youth." Creation of four more exclusively white institutions followed: Mississippi State University (1880), Mississippi University for Women (1885), University of Southern Mississippi (1912), and Delta State University (1925). The State added two more solely black institutions in 1940 and 1950: in the former year, Jackson State University, which was charged with training "black teachers for the black public schools," and in the latter year, Mississippi Valley State University, whose functions were to educate teachers primarily for rural and elementary schools and to provide vocational instruction to black students.

Despite this Court's decisions in *Brown I* and *Brown II*, Mississippi's policy of *de jure* segregation continued. The first black student was not admitted to the University of Mississippi until 1962, and then only by court order. For the next 12 years the segregated public university system in the State remained largely intact. Mississippi State University, Mississippi University for Women, University of Southern Mississippi, and Delta State University each admitted at least one black student during these years, but the student composition of these

institutions was still almost completely white. During this period, Jackson State and Mississippi Valley State were exclusively black; Alcorn State had admitted five white students by 1968.

In 1969, the United States Department of Health, Education and Welfare (HEW) initiated efforts to enforce Title VI of the Civil Rights Act of 1964, 42 U.S.C. § 2000d.* HEW requested that the State devise a plan to disestablish the formerly *de jure* segregated university system. In June 1973, the Board of Trustees of State Institutions of Higher Learning submitted a Plan of Compliance, which expressed the aims of improving educational opportunities for all Mississippi citizens by setting numerical goals on the enrollment of other-race students at State universities, hiring other-race faculty members, and instituting remedial programs and special recruitment efforts to achieve these goals. HEW rejected this Plan as failing to comply with Title VI because it did not go far enough in the areas of student recruitment and enrollment, faculty hiring, elimination of unnecessary program duplication, and institutional funding practices to ensure that "a student's choice of institution or campus, henceforth, will be based on other than racial criteria." The Board reluctantly offered amendments, prefacing its reform pledge to HEW with this statement: "With deference, it is the position of the Board of Trustees . . . that the Mississippi system of higher education is in compliance with Title VI of the Civil Rights Act of 1964." At this time, the racial composition of the State's universities had changed only marginally from the levels of 1968, which were almost exclusively single-race.** Though HEW refused to accept the modified Plan, the Board adopted it anyway. But even the limited effects of this Plan in disestablishing the prior *de jure* segregated system were substantially con-

---

*This provision states: "No person in the United States shall, on the ground of race, color, or national origin, be excluded from participation in, be denied the benefits of, or be subjected to discrimination, under any program or activity receiving Federal financial assistance."

**For the 1974–1975 school year, black students comprised 4.1 percent of the full-time undergraduate enrollments at University of Mississippi; at Mississippi State University, 7.5 percent; at University of Southern Mississippi, 8.0 percent; at Delta State University, 12.6 percent; at Mississippi University for Women, 13.0 percent. At Jackson State, Alcorn State, and Mississippi Valley State, the percentages of black students were 96.6 percent, 99.9 percent, and 100 percent, respectively. Brief for United States 7.

stricted by the state legislature, which refused to fund it until Fiscal Year 1978, and even then at well under half the amount sought by the Board.

Private petitioners initiated this lawsuit in 1975. They complained that Mississippi had maintained the racially segregative effects of its prior dual system of post-secondary education in violation of the Fifth, Ninth, Thirteenth, and Fourteenth Amendments, 42 U.S.C. §§ 1981 and 1983, and Title VI of the Civil Rights Act of 1964, 42 U.S.C. § 2000d. Shortly thereafter, the United States filed its complaint in intervention, charging that State officials had failed to satisfy their obligation under the Equal Protection Clause of the Fourteenth Amendment and Title VI to dismantle Mississippi's dual system of higher education.

After this lawsuit was filed, the parties attempted for 12 years to achieve a consensual resolution of their differences through voluntary dismantlement by the State of its prior separated system. The Board of Trustees implemented reviews of existing curricula and program "mission" at each institution. In 1981, the Board issued "Mission Statements" that identified the extant purpose of each public university. These "missions" were clustered into three categories: comprehensive, urban, and regional.

"Comprehensive" universities were classified as those with the greatest existing resources and program offerings. All three such institutions (University of Mississippi, Mississippi State, and Southern Mississippi) were exclusively white under the prior *de jure* segregated system. The Board authorized each to continue offering doctoral degrees and to assert leadership in certain disciplines. Jackson State, the sole urban university, was assigned a more limited research and degree mission, with both functions geared toward its urban setting. It was exclusively black at its inception. The "regional" designation was something of a misnomer, as the Board envisioned those institutions primarily in an undergraduate role, rather than a "regional" one in the geographical sense of serving just the localities in which they were based. Only the universities classified as "regional" included institutions that, prior to desegregation, had been either exclusively white—Delta State and Mississippi University for Women—or exclusively black—Alcorn State and Mississippi Valley.

By the mid-1980s, 30 years after *Brown*, more than 99 percent of Mississippi's white students were enrolled at University of Mississippi, Mississippi State, Southern Mississippi, Delta State, and Mississippi University for Women. The student bodies at these universities remained predomi-nantly white, averaging between 80 and 90 percent white students. Seventy-one percent of the State's black students attended Jackson State, Alcorn State, and Mississippi Valley, where the racial composition ranged from 92 to 99 percent black.

II

By 1987, the parties concluded that they could not agree on whether the State had taken steps to dismantle its prior *de jure* segregated system. They proceeded to trial. Both sides presented voluminous evidence on a full range of educational issues spanning admissions standards, faculty and administrative staff recruitment, program duplication, on-campus discrimination, institutional funding disparities, and satellite campuses. Petitioners argued that in various ways the State continued to reinforce historic, race-based distinctions among the universities. Respondents argued generally that the State had fulfilled its duty to disestablish its state-imposed segregative system by implementing and maintaining good-faith, nondiscriminatory race-neutral policies and practices in student admission, faculty hiring, and operations. Moreover, they suggested, the State had attracted significant numbers of qualified black students to those universities composed mostly of white persons. Respondents averred that the mere continued existence of racially identifiable universities was not unlawful given the freedom of students to choose which institution to attend and the varying objectives and features of the State's universities.

At trial's end, based on the testimony of 71 witnesses and 56,700 pages of exhibits, the District Court entered extensive findings of fact, . . . including a description at the time of the trial, in those areas of the higher education system under attack by plaintiffs: admission requirements and recruitment; institutional classification and assignment of missions; duplication of programs; facilities and finance; the land grant institutions; faculty and staff; and governance.

The court's conclusions of law followed. As an overview, the court outlined the common ground in the case: "Where a state has previously maintained a racially dual system of public education established by law, it assumes an 'affirmative duty' to reform those policies and practices which required or contributed to the separation of the races." Noting that courts unanimously hold that the affirmative duty to dismantle a racially dual structure in elementary and secondary schools also governs in the higher education context, the court observed that there was disagreement whether

Green v. *New Kent County School Bd.*, 391 U.S. 430 (1968), applied in all of its aspects to formerly dual systems of higher education, i.e., whether "some level of racial mixture at previously segregated institutions of higher learning is not only desirable but necessary to 'effectively' desegregate the system." Relying on a Fifth Circuit three-judge court decision, *Alabama State Teachers Assn. (ASTA)* v. *Alabama Public School and College Authority*, 289 F. Supp. 784 (MD Ala. 1968), our *per curiam* affirmance of that case, 393 U.S. 4000 (1969), and its understanding of our later decision in *Bazemore* v. *Friday*, 478 U.S. 385 (1986), the court concluded that in the higher education context, "the affirmative duty to desegregate does not contemplate either restricting choice or the achievement of any degree of racial balance." Thus, the court stated: "While student enrollment and faculty and staff hiring patterns are to be examined, greater emphasis should instead be placed on current state higher education policies and practices in order to insure that such policies and practices are racially neutral, developed and implemented in good faith, and do not substantially contribute to the continued racial identifiability of individual institutions."

When it addressed the same aspects of the university system covered by the factfindings in light of the foregoing standard, the court found no violation of federal law in any of them. "In summary, the court finds that current actions on the part of the defendants demonstrate conclusively that the defendants are fulfilling their affirmative duty to disestablish the former *de jure* segregated system of higher education."

The Court of Appeals reheard the case en banc and affirmed the decision of the District Court. *Ayers* v. *Allain*, 914 F.2d 676 (CA 5 1990). With a single exception, it did not disturb the District Court's findings of fact or conclusions of law. The en banc majority agreed that "Mississippi was . . . constitutionally required to eliminate invidious racial distinctions and dismantle its dual system." That duty, the court held, had been discharged since "the record makes clear that Mississippi has adopted and implemented race–neutral policies for operating its colleges and universities and that all students have real freedom of choice to attend the college or university they wish. . . . "

III

* * *

. . . [T]he primary issue in this case is whether the State has met its affirmative duty to dismantle its prior dual university system.

Our decisions establish that a State does not discharge its constitutional obligations until it eradicates policies and practices traceable to its prior *de jure* dual system that continue to foster segregation. Thus we have consistently asked whether existing racial identifiability is attributable to the State . . . and examined a wide range of factors to determine whether the State has perpetuated its formerly *de jure* segregation in any facet of its institutional system. . . .

The Court of Appeals concluded that the State had fulfilled its affirmative obligation to disestablish its prior *de jure* segregated system by adopting and implementing race-neutral policies governing its college and university system. Because students seeking higher education had "real freedom" to choose the institution of their choice, the State need do no more. Even though neutral policies and free choice were not enough to dismantle a dual system of primary or secondary schools, the Court of Appeals thought that universities "differ in character fundamentally" from lower levels of schools, sufficiently so that our decision in *Bazemore* v. *Friday* justified the conclusion that the conclusion that the State had dismantled its former dual system.

Like the United States, we do not disagree with the Court of Appeals' observation that a state university system is quite different in very relevant respects from primary and secondary schools. Unlike attendance at the lower level schools, a student's decision to seek higher education has been a matter of choice. . . . Students who qualify for admission enjoy a range of choices of which institution to attend. Thus, as the Court of Appeals stated, "[i]t hardly needs mention that remedies common to public school desegregation, such as pupil assignments, busing, attendance quotas, and zoning, are unavailable when persons may freely choose whether to pursue an advanced education and, when the choice is made, which of several universities to attend."

We do not agree with the Court of Appeals or the District Court, however, that the adoption and implementation of race-neutral policies alone suffice to demonstrate that the State has completely abandoned its prior dual system. That college attendance is by choice and not by assignment does not mean that a race-neutral admissions policy cures the constitutional violation of a dual system. In a system based on choice, student attendance is determined not simply by admissions policies, but also by many other factors. Although some of these factors clearly cannot be attributed to State policies, many can be. Thus, even after a State dismantles its segregative *admissions* policy, there may still be state action that is traceable to the State's prior *de jure* segregation and that continues to foster segregation. The Equal Protection Clause is offended by "sophisticated as well as simple-minded modes of discrimination." *Lane* v. *Wilson*, 307 U.S. 268, 275 (1939). If policies traceable to the *de jure* system are still in force and have discriminatory effects, those policies too must be reformed to the extent practicable and consistent with sound educational practices. . . .

. . . If the State perpetuates policies and practices traceable to its prior system that continue to have segregative effects—whether by influencing student enrollment decisions or by fostering segregation in other facets of the university system— and such policies are without sound educational justification and can be practically eliminated, the State has not satisfied its burden of proving that it has dismantled its prior system. Such policies run afoul of the Equal Protection Clause, even though the State has abolished the legal requirement that whites and blacks be educated separately and has established racially neutral policies not animated by a discriminatory purpose. Because the standard applied by the District Court did not make these inquiries, we hold that the Court of Appeals erred in affirming the District Court's ruling that the State had brought itself into compliance with the Equal Protection Clause in the operation of its higher education system.

IV

Had the Court of Appeals applied the correct legal standard, it would have been apparent from the undisturbed factual findings of the District Court that there are several surviving aspects of Mississippi's prior dual system which are constitutionally suspect; for even though such policies may be race neutral on their face, they substantially restrict a person's choice of which institution to enter and they contribute to the racial identifiability of the eight public universities. Mississippi must justify these policies or eliminate them.

. . . In highlighting certain remnants of the prior system that are readily apparent from the findings of fact made by the District Court and affirmed by the Court of Appeals, we by no means suggest that the Court of Appeals need not examine, in light of the proper standard, each of the other policies now governing the State's university system that have been challenged or that are challenged on remand in light of the standard that we articulate today. With this caveat in mind, we address four policies of the present system: admission standards, program duplication, institutional mis-

sion assignments, and continued operation of all eight public universities.

We deal first with the current admissions policies of Mississippi's public universities. As the District Court found, the three flagship historically white universities in the system—University of Mississippi, Mississippi State University, and University of Southern Mississippi—enacted policies in 1963 requiring all entrants to achieve a minimum composite score of 15 on the American College Testing Program (ACT). The court described the "discriminatory taint" of this policy, an obvious reference to the fact that, at the time, the average ACT score for white students was 18 and the average score for blacks was 7. The District Court concluded, and the en banc Court of Appeals agreed, that present admissions standards derived from policies enacted in the 1970's to redress the problem of student unpreparedness. Obviously, this mid-passage justification for perpetuating a policy enacted originally to discriminate against black students does not make the present admissions standards any less constitutionally suspect.

The present admission standards are not only traceable to the *de jure* system and were originally adopted for a discriminatory purpose, but they also have present discriminatory effects. Every Mississippi resident under 21 seeking admission to the university system must take the ACT. Any applicant who scores at least 15 qualifies for automatic admission to any of the five historically white institutions except Mississippi University for Women, which requires a score of 18 for automatic admission unless the student has a 3.0 high school grade average. Those scoring less than 15 but at least 13 automatically qualify to enter Jackson State University, Alcorn State University, and Mississippi Valley State University. Without doubt, these requirements restrict the range of choices of entering students as to which institution they may attend in a way that perpetuates segregation. Those scoring 13 or 14, with some exceptions, are excluded from the five historically white universities and if they want a higher education must go to one of the historically black institutions or attend a junior college with the hope of transferring to a historically white institution.†

† The District Court's finding that "(v)ery few black students, if any, are actually denied admission to a Mississippi university as a first time freshman for failure to achieve the minimal ACT score," *Ayers* v. *Allain*, 674 F. Supp. 1523 (ND Miss. 1987), ignores the inherent self-selection that accompanies public announcement of "automatic" admissions standards. It is logical to think that some percentage of black students who fail to score 15 do *not* seek admission to one of the historically white universities because of this automatic admission standard.

Proportionately more blacks than whites face this choice: in 1985, 72 percent of Mississippi's white high school seniors achieved an ACT composite score of 15 or better, while less than 30 percent of black high school seniors earned that score. It is not surprising then that Mississippi's universities remain predominantly identifiable by race.

The segregative effect of this automatic entrance standard is especially striking in light of the differences in minimum automatic entrance scores among the regional universities in Mississippi's system. The minimum score for automatic admission to Mississippi University for Women (MUW) is 18; it is 13 for the historically black universities. Yet MUW is assigned the same institutional mission as two other regional universities, Alcorn State and Mississippi Valley—that of providing quality undergraduate education. The effects of the policy fall disproportionately on black students who might wish to attend MUW; and though the disparate impact is not as great, the same is true of the minimum standard ACT score of 15 at Delta State University—the other "regional" university—as compared to the historically black "regional" universities where a score of 13 suffices for automatic admission. The courts below made little if any effort to justify in educational terms those particular disparities in entrance requirements or to inquire whether it was practicable to eliminate them.

We also find inadequately justified by the courts below or by the record before us the differential admissions requirements between universities with dissimilar programmatic missions. We do not suggest that absent a discriminatory purpose different programmatic missions accompanied by different admission standards would be constitutionally suspect simply because one or more schools are racially identifiable. But here the differential admission standards are remnants of the dual system with a continuing discriminatory effect, and the mission assignments "to some degree follow the historical racial assignments." Moreover, the District Court did not justify the differing admission standards based on the different mission assignments. It observed only that in the 1970s, the Board of Trustees justified a minimum ACT score of 15 because too many students with lower scores were not prepared for the historically white institutions and that imposing the 15 score requirement on admissions to the historically black institutions would decimate attendance at those universities. The District Court also stated that the mission of the regional universities had the more modest function of providing quality undergraduate education. Certainly the comprehensive universities are also, among other things,

educating undergraduates. But we think the 15 ACT test score for automatic admission to the comprehensive universities, as compared with a score of 13 for the regionals, requires further justification in terms of sound educational policy.

Another constitutionally problematic aspect of the State's use of the ACT test scores is its policy of denying automatic admission if an applicant fails to earn the minimum ACT score specified for the particular institution, without also resorting to the applicant's high school grades as an additional factor in predicting college performance. The United States produced evidence that the American College Testing Program (ACTP), the administering organization of the ACT, discourages use of ACT scores as the sole admissions criterion on the ground that it gives an incomplete "picture" of the student applicant's ability to perform adequately in college. One ACTP report presented into evidence suggests that "it would be foolish" to substitute a 3- or 4-hour test in place of a student's high school grades as a means of predicting college performance. The record also indicated that the disparity between black and white students' high school grade averages was much narrower than the gap between their average ACT scores, thereby suggesting that an admissions formula which included grades would increase the number of black students eligible for automatic admission to all of Mississippi's public universities.‡

The United States insists that the State's refusal to consider information which would better predict college performance than ACT scores alone is irrational in light of most States' use of high school grades and other indicators along with standardized test scores. The District Court observed that the Board of Trustees was concerned with grade inflation and the lack of comparability in grading practices and course offerings among the State's diverse high schools. Both the District Court and the Court of Appeals found the concern ample justification for the failure to consider high school grade performance along with ACT scores. In our view, such justification is inadequate because the ACT requirement was originally adopted for discriminatory purposes, the current requirement is traceable to that decision and seemingly continues to have segregative effects, and the State

‡In 1985, 72 percent of white students in Mississippi scored 15 or better on the ACT, whereas only 30 percent of black students achieved that mark, a difference of nearly 2¹/₂ times. By contrast, the disparity among grade averages was not nearly so wide. 43.8 percent of white high school students and 30.5 percent of black students averaged at least a 3.0, and 62.2 percent of whites and 49.2 percent of blacks earned at least a 2.5 grade point average. . . .

has so far failed to show the "ACT-only" admission standard is not susceptible to elimination without eroding sound educational policy.

A second aspect of the present system that necessitates further inquiry is the widespread duplication of programs. "Unnecessary" duplication refers, under the District Court's definition, "to those instances where two or more institutions offer the same nonessential or noncore program. Under this definition, all duplication at the bachelor's level of nonbasic liberal arts and sciences course work and all duplication at the master's level and above are considered to be unnecessary." The District Court found that 34.6 percent of the 29 undergraduate programs are "unnecessarily duplicated" by the historically white universities, and that 90 percent of the graduate programs at the historically black institutions are unnecessarily duplicated at the historically white institutions. In its conclusions of law on this point, the District Court nevertheless determined that "there is no proof" that such duplication "is directly associated with the racial identifiability of institutions," and that "there is no proof that the elimination of unnecessary program duplication would be justifiable from an educational standpoint or that its elimination would have a substantial effect on student choice."

The District Court's treatment of this issue is problematic from several different perspectives. First, the court appeared to impose the burden of proof on the plaintiffs to meet a legal standard the court itself acknowledged was not yet formulated. It can hardly be denied that such duplication was part and parcel of the prior dual system of higher education—the whole notion of "separate but equal" required duplicative programs in two sets of schools—and that the present unnecessary duplication is a continuation of that practice. *Brown* and its progeny, however, established that the burden of proof falls on the *State*, and not the aggrieved plaintiffs, to establish that it has dismantled its prior *de jure* segregated system. The court's holding that petitioners could not establish the constitutional defect of unnecessary duplication, therefore, improperly shifted the burden away from the State. Second, implicit in the District Court's finding of "unnecessary" duplication is the absence of any educational justification and the fact that some if not all duplication may be practically eliminated. Indeed, the District Court observed that such duplication "cannot be justified economically or in terms of providing quality education." Yet by stating that "there is no proof" that elimination of unnecessary duplication would decrease institutional racial identifiability, affect student choice, and pro-

mote educationally sound policies, the court did not make clear whether it had directed the parties to develop evidence on these points, and if so, on what that evidence revealed. Finally, by treating this issue in isolation, the court failed to consider the combined effects of unnecessary program duplication with other policies, such as differential admissions standards, in evaluating whether the State had met its duty to dismantle its prior *de jure* segregated system.

We next address Mississippi's scheme of institutional mission classification, and whether it perpetuates the State's formerly *de jure* dual system. The District Court found that, throughout the period of *de jure* segregation, University of Mississippi, Mississippi State University, and University of Southern Mississippi were the flagship institutions in the state system. They received the most funds, initiated the most advanced and specialized programs, and developed the widest range of curricular functions. At their inception, each was restricted for the education solely of white persons. The missions of Mississippi University for Women and Delta State University (DSU), by contrast, were more limited than their other all-white counterparts during the period of legalized segregation. MUW and DSU were each established to provide undergraduate education solely for white students in the liberal arts and such other fields as music, art education, and home economics. When they were founded, the three exclusively black universities were more limited in their assigned academic missions than the five all-white institutions. Alcorn State, for example, was designated to serve as "an agricultural college for the education of Mississippi's black youth." Jackson State and Mississippi Valley State were established to train black teachers. Though the District Court's findings do not make this point explicit, it is reasonable to infer that state funding and curriculum decisions throughout the period of *de jure* segregation were based on the purposes for which these institutions were established.

In 1981, the State assigned certain missions to Mississippi's public universities as they then existed. It classified University of Mississippi, Mississippi State, and Southern Mississippi as "comprehensive" universities having the most varied programs and offering graduate degrees. Two of the historically white institutions, Delta State University and Mississippi University for Women, along with two of the historically black institutions, Alcorn State University and Mississippi Valley State University, were designated as "regional" universities with more limited programs and devoted primarily to undergraduate education. Jackson State University was classified as an "urban" university whose mission was defined by its urban location. . . .

The institutional mission designations adopted in 1981 have as their antecedents the policies enacted to perpetuate racial separation during the *de jure* segregated regime. . . . That different missions are assigned to the universities surely limits to some extent an entering student's choice as to which university to seek admittance. While the courts below both agreed that the classification and mission assignments were made without discriminatory purpose, the Court of Appeals found that the record "supports the plaintiffs' argument that the mission designations had the effect of maintaining the more limited program scope at the historically black universities." We do not suggest that absent discriminatory purpose the assignment of different missions to various institutions in a State's higher education system would raise an equal protection issue where one or more of the institutions become or remain predominantly black or white. But here the issue is whether the State has sufficiently dismantled its prior dual system; and when combined with the differential admission practices and unnecessary program duplication, it is likely that the mission designations interfere with student choice and tend to perpetuate the segregated system. On remand, the court should inquire whether it would be practicable and consistent with sound educational practices to eliminate any such discriminatory effects of the State's present policy of mission assignments.

Fourth, the State attempted to bring itself into compliance with the Constitution by continuing to maintain and operate all eight higher educational institutions. The existence of eight instead of some lesser number was undoubtably occasioned by State laws forbidding the mingling of the races. And as the District Court recognized, continuing to maintain all eight universities in Mississippi is wasteful and irrational. The District Court pointed especially to the facts that Delta State and Mississippi Valley are only 35 miles apart and that only 20 miles separate Mississippi State and Mississippi University for Women. It was evident to the District Court that "the defendants undertake to fund more institutions of higher learning than are justified by the amount of financial resources available to the state," but the court concluded that such fiscal irresponsibility was a policy choice of the legislature rather than a feature of a system subject to constitutional scrutiny.

Unquestionably, a larger rather than a smaller number of institutions from which to choose in it-

self makes for different choices, particularly when examined in the light of other factors present in the operation of the system, such as admissions, program duplication, and institutional mission designations. Though certainly closure of one or more institutions would decrease the discriminatory effects of the present system, based on the present record we are unable to say whether such action is constitutionally required. Elimination of program duplication and revision of admissions criteria may make institutional closure unnecessary. However, on remand this issue should be carefully explored by inquiring and determining whether retention of all eight institutions itself affects student choice and perpetuates the segregated higher education system, whether maintenance of each of the universities is educationally justifiable, and whether one or more of them can be practicably closed or merged with other existing institutions.

Because the former *de jure* segregated system of public universities in Mississippi impeded the free choice of prospective students, the State in dismantling that system must take the necessary steps to ensure that this choice now is truly free. The full range of policies and practices must be examined with this duty in mind. That an institution is predominantly white or black does not in itself make out a constitutional violation. But surely the State may not leave in place policies rooted in its prior officially segregated system that serve to maintain the racial identifiability of its universities if those policies can practicably be eliminated without eroding sound educational policies.

If we understand private petitioners to press us to order the upgrading of Jackson State, Alcorn State, and Mississippi Valley *solely* so that they may be publicly financed, exclusively black enclaves by private choice, we reject that request. The State provides these facilities for *all* its citizens and it has not met its burden under *Brown* to take affirmative steps to dismantle its prior *de jure* system when it perpetuates a separate, but "more equal" one. Whether such an increase in funding is necessary to achieve a full dismantlement under the standards we have outlined, however, is a different question, and one that must be addressed on remand.

Because the District Court and the Court of Appeals failed to consider the State's duties in their proper light, the cases must be remanded. To the extent that the State has not met its affirmative obligation to dismantle its prior dual system, it shall be adjudged in violation of the Constitution and Title VI and remedial proceedings shall be conducted. The decision of the Court of Appeals is vacated, and the cases are remanded for further proceedings consistent with this opinion.

It is so ordered.

[The concurring opinion of JUSTICE O'CONNOR is not reprinted here.]

JUSTICE THOMAS, *concurring.*

"We must rally to the defense of our schools. We must repudiate this unbearable assumption of the right to kill institutions unless they conform to one narrow standard." W.E.B. Du Bois, Schools, 13 *The Crisis* 111, 112 (1917). . . .

A challenged policy does not survive under the standard we announce today if it began during the prior *de jure* era, produces adverse impacts, and persists without sound educational justification. When each of these elements has been met, I believe, we are justified in not requiring proof of a present specific intent to discriminate. It is safe to assume that a policy adopted during the *de jure* era, if it produces segregative effects, reflects a discriminatory intent. As long as that intent remains, of course, such a policy cannot continue. And given an initially tainted policy, it is eminently reasonable to make the State bear the risk of nonpersuasion with respect to intent at some future time, both because the State has created the dispute through its own prior unlawful conduct, and because discriminatory intent does tend to persist through time . . . . Although we do not formulate our standard in terms of a burden shift with respect to intent, the factors we do consider—the historical background of the policy, the degree of its adverse impact, and the plausibility of any justification asserted in its defense—are precisely those factors that go into determining intent under *Washington* v. *Davis*, 426 U.S. 229, (1976). Thus, if a policy remains in force, without adequate justification and despite tainted roots and segregative effect, it appears clear—clear enough to presume conclusively—that the State has failed to disprove discriminatory intent.

. . . I find most encouraging the Court's emphasis on "sound *educational* practices" (emphasis added). . . . From the beginning, we have recognized that desgregation remedies cannot be designed to ensure the elimination of any remnant at any price, but rather must display "a practical flexibility" and "a facility for adjusting and reconciling public and private needs." Quite obviously, one compelling need to be considered is the *educa-*

tional need of the present and future *students* in the Mississippi university system, for whose benefit the remedies will be crafted.

In particular, we do not foreclose the possibility that there exists "sound educational justification" for maintaining historically black colleges *as such.* Despite the shameful history of state-enforced segregation, these institutions have survived and flourished. Indeed, they have expanded as opportunities for blacks to enter historically white institutions have expanded. Between 1954 and 1980, for example, enrollment at historically black colleges increased from 70,000 to 200,000 students, while degrees awarded increased from 13,000 to 32,000. See S. Hill, National Center for Education Statistics, The Traditionally Black Institutions of Higher Education 1860 to 1982, pp. xiv–xv (1985). These accomplishments have not gone unnoticed:

> The colleges founded for Negroes are both a source of pride to blacks who have attended them and a source of hope to black families who want the benefits of higher learning for their children. They have exercised leadership in developing educational opportunities for young blacks at all levels of instruction, and especially in the South, they are still regarded as key institutions for enhancing the general quality of the lives of black Americans. Carnegie Commission on Higher Education, From Isolation to Mainstream: Problems of the Colleges Founded for Negroes 11 (1971).

I think it undisputable that these institutions have succeeded in part because of their distinctive histories and traditions; for many, historically black colleges have become "a symbol of the highest attainments of black culture." J. Preer, Lawyers v. Educators: Black Colleges and Desegregation in Public Higher Education 2 (1982). Obviously, a State cannot maintain such traditions by closing particular institutions, historically white or historically black, to particular racial groups. Nonetheless, it hardly follows that a State cannot operate a diverse assortment of institutions—including historically black institutions—open to all on a race-neutral basis, but with established traditions and programs that might disproportionately appeal to one race or another. No one, I imagine, would argue that such institutional *diversity* is without "sound educational justification," or that it is even remotely akin to program *duplication*, which is designed to separate the races for the sake of separating the races. The Court at least hints at the importance of this value when it distinguishes *Green* in part on the ground that colleges and universities "are not fungible." Although I agree that a State is not constitutionally *required* to maintain its historically black institutions as such, I do not understand our opinion to hold that a State is *forbidden* from doing so. It would be ironic, to say the least, if the institutions that sustained blacks during segregation were themselves destroyed in an effort to combat its vestiges.

JUSTICE SCALIA, *concurring in the judgment in part and dissenting in part.*

* * *

III

I must add a few words about the unanticipated consequences of today's decision. Among petitioners' contentions is the claim that the Constitution requires Mississippi to correct funding disparities between its HBIs and HWIs. The Court rejects that—as I think it should, since it is students and not colleges that are guaranteed equal protection of the law. But to say that the Constitution does not *require* equal funding is not to say that the Constitution *prohibits* it (emphasis in original). The citizens of a State may conclude that if certain of their public educational institutions are used predominantly by blacks, it is desirable to fund those institutions more or less equally.

Ironically enough, however, today's decision seems to prevent adoption of such a conscious policy. What the Court says about duplicate programs is as true of equal funding: the requirement "was part and parcel of the prior dual system." Moreover, equal funding, like program duplication, facilitates continued segregation—enabling students to attend schools where their own race predominates without paying a penalty in the quality of education. Nor could such an equal funding policy be saved on the basis that it serves what the Court calls a "sound educational justification." The only conceivable *educational* value it furthers is that of fostering schools in which blacks receive their education in a "majority" setting; but to acknowledge that as a "value" would contradict the compulsory-integration philosophy that underlies *Green.* Just as vulnerable, of course, would be all other programs that have the effect of facilitating the continued existence of predominantly black institutions: elevating an HBI to comprehensive status (where the Court inexplicably suggests that this action may be required); offering a so-called Afrocentric curriculum, as has been done recently on an experimental basis in some secondary and primary schools, see Jarvis, *Brown* and the Afrocentric Curriculum, 101 Yale L.J. 1285, 1287, and n. 12 (1992); preserving eight separate universities, which is perhaps Mississippi's single policy most segregative in effect; or providing funding for HBIs as HBIs, see Pub. L. 99-498, Title III, § 301(a), 100 Stat. 1294, 20 U.S.C. §§ 1060–1063c, which does just that.

But this predictable impairment of HBIs should come as no surprise; for incidentally facilitating—indeed, even tolerating—the continued existence of HBIs is not what the Court's test is about, and has never been what *Green* is about.... What the Court's test is designed to achieve is the elimination of predominantly black institutions. While that may be good social policy, the present petitioners, I suspect, would not agree; and there is much to be said for the Court of Appeals' perception in *Ayers*, 914 F.2d, at 687, that "if no [state] authority exists to deny [the student] the right to attend the institution of his choice, he is done a severe disservice by remedies which, in seeking to maximize integration, minimize diversity and vitiate his choices." But whether or not the Court's antagonism to unintegrated schooling is good policy, it is assuredly not good constitutional law. There is nothing unconstitutional about a "black" school in the sense, not of a school that blacks *must* attend and that whites *cannot* but of a school that, as a consequence of private choice in residence or in school selection, contains, and has long contained, a large black majority.... (emphasis in original). In a perverse way, in fact, the insistence, whether explicit or implicit, that such institutions not be permitted to endure perpetuates the very stigma of black inferiority that *Brown I* sought to destroy. Not only Mississippi but Congress itself seems out of step with the drum that the Court beats today, judging by its passage of an Act entitled "Strengthening Historically Black Colleges and Universities," which authorizes the Education Department to provide money grants to historically black colleges. The implementing regulations designate Alcorn State University, Jackson State University, and Mississippi Valley State University as eligible recipients.

* * *

The Court was asked to decide today whether, in the provision of university education, a State satisfies its duty under *Brown I* by removing discriminatory barriers to admissions. That question required us to choose between the standards established in *Green* and *Bazemore*, both of which cases involved (as, for the most part, this does) free-choice plans that failed to end *de facto* segregation. Once the confusion engendered by the Court's something-for-all, guidance-to-none opinion has been dissipated, it will become apparent that, essentially, the Court has adopted *Green*.

I would not predict, however, that today's opinion will succeed in producing the same result as *Green*—*viz.*, compelling the States to compel racial "balance" in their schools—because of several practical imperfections: because the Court deprives district judges of the most efficient (and perhaps the only effective) *Green* remedy, mandatory student assignment; because some contradictory elements of the opinion (its suggestion, for example, that Mississippi's mission designations foster, rather than deter, segregation) will prevent clarity of application; and because the virtually standardless discretion conferred upon district judges will permit them to do pretty much what they please. What I do predict is a number of years of litigation-driven confusion and destabilization in the university systems of all the formerly *de jure* States, that will benefit neither blacks nor whites, neither predominantly black institutions nor predominantly white ones. Nothing good will come of this judicially ordained turmoil, except the public recognition that any Court that would knowingly impose it must hate segregation. We must find some other way of making that point.

REGENTS OF THE UNIVERSITY OF CALIFORNIA v. BAKKE
438 U.S. 265; 57 L. Ed. 2d 750; 98 S. Ct. 2733 (1978)

JUSTICE POWELL *announced the judgment of the Court.*

This case presents a challenge to the special admissions program of the petitioner, the Medical School of the University of California at Davis, which is designed to assure the admission of a specified number of students from certain minority groups. The Superior Court of California sustained respondent's challenge, holding that petitioner's program violated the California Constitution, Title VI of the Civil Rights Act of 1964 . . . and the Equal Protection Clause of the Fourteenth Amendment. The court enjoined petitioner from considering respondent's race or the race of any other applicant in making admissions decisions. It refused, however, to order respondent's admission to the Medical School, holding that he had not carried his burden of proving that he would have been admitted but for the constitutional and statutory violations. The Supreme Court of California affirmed those portions of the trial court's judgment . . . . It modified that portion of the judgment denying respondent's requested injunction and directed the trial court to order his admission.

For the reasons stated in the following opinion, I believe that so much of the judgment of the California court as holds petitioner's special admissions program unlawful and directs that respondent be admitted to the Medical School must be affirmed. For the reasons expressed in a separate opinion, my Brothers THE CHIEF JUSTICE, JUSTICE STEWART, JUSTICE REHNQUIST, and JUSTICE STEVENS concur in this judgment.

I also conclude for the reasons stated in the following opinion that the portion of the court's judgment enjoining petitioner from according any consideration to race in its admissions process must be reversed. For reasons expressed in separate opinions, my Brothers JUSTICE BRENNAN, JUSTICE WHITE, JUSTICE MARSHALL, and JUSTICE BLACKMUN concur in this judgment.

Affirmed in part and reversed in part.

I

The Medical School of the University of California at Davis opened in 1968 with an entering class of 50 students. In 1971, the size of the entering class was increased to 100 students, a level at which it remains. No admissions program for disadvantaged or minority students existed when the school opened, and the first class contained three Asians but no blacks, no Mexican-Americans, and no American Indians. Over the next two years, the faculty devised a special admissions program to increase the representation of "disadvantaged" students in each medical school class. The special program consisted of a separate admissions system operating in coordination with the regular admissions process.

Under the regular admissions procedure, a candidate could submit his application to the Medical

School beginning in July of the year preceding the academic year for which admission was sought. Because of the large number of applications, the admissions committee screened each one to select candidates for further consideration. Candidates whose overall undergraduate grade point averages fell below 2.5 on a scale of 4.0 were summarily rejected. About one out of six applicants was invited for a personal interview. Following the interviews, each candidate was rated on a scale of 1 to 100 by his interviewers and four other members of the admissions committee. The rating embraced the interviewers' summaries, the candidate's overall grade point average, grade point average in science courses, scores on the Medical College Admissions Test (MCAT), letters of recommendation, extracurricular activities, and other biographical data. The ratings were added together to arrive at each candidate's "benchmark" score. . . . The full committee then reviewed the file and scores of each applicant and made offers of admission. . . .

The special admissions program operated with a separate committee, a majority of whom were members of minority groups. On the 1973 application form, candidates were asked to indicate whether they wished to be considered as "economically and/or educationally disadvantaged" applicants; on the 1974 form the question was whether they wished to be considered as members of a "minority group," which the Medical School apparently viewed as "Blacks," "Chicanos," "Asians," and "American Indians." If these questions were answered affirmatively, the application was forwarded to the special admissions committee. No formal definition of "disadvantaged" was ever produced, but the chairman of the special committee screened each application to see whether it reflected economic or educational deprivation. Having passed this initial hurdle, the applications then were rated by the special committee in a fashion similar to that used by the general admissions committee, except that special candidates did not have to meet the 2.5 grade point average cutoff applied to regular applicants. About one-fifth of the total number of special applicants were invited for interviews in 1973 and 1974. Following each interview, the special committee assigned each special applicant a benchmark score. The special committee then presented its top choices to the general admissions committee. The latter did not rate or compare the special candidates against the general applicants, but could reject recommended special candidates for failure to meet course requirements or other specific deficiencies. The special committee continued to recommend special applicants until a number prescribed by faculty vote were admitted. While the overall class size was still 50, the prescribed number was 8; in 1973 and 1974, when the class size had doubled to 100, the prescribed number of special admissions also doubled, to 16.

From the year of the increase in class size—1971—through 1974, the special program resulted in the admission of 21 black students, 30 Mexican-Americans, and 12 Asians, for a total of 63 minority students. Over the same period, the regular admissions program produced 1 black, 6 Mexican-Americans, and 37 Asians, for a total of 44 minority students. Although disadvantaged whites applied to the special program in large numbers, none received an offer of admission through that process. . . .

Allan Bakke is a white male who applied to the Davis Medical School in both 1973 and 1974. In both years Bakke's application was considered under the general admissions program, and he received an interview. . . . Despite a strong benchmark score of 468 out of 500 (in 1973), Bakke was rejected. His application had come late in the year, and no applicants in the general admissions process with scores below 470 were accepted after Bakke's application was completed. There were four special admissions slots unfilled at that time, however, for which Bakke was not considered. . . .

Bakke's 1974 application was completed early in the year. . . . Again, Bakke's application was rejected. In neither year did the chairman of the admissions committee . . . exercise his discretion to place Bakke on the waiting list. In both years, applicants were admitted under the special program with grade point averages, MCAT scores, and benchmark scored significantly lower than Bakke's.

After the second rejection, Bakke filed the instant suit in the Supreme Court of California.

II

* * *

In this Court the parties neither briefed nor argued the applicability of Title VI of the Civil Rights Act of 1964. Rather, as had the California court, they focused exclusively upon the validity of the special admissions program under the Equal Protection Clause. Because it was possible, however, that a decision on Title VI might obviate resort to constitutional interpretation, see *Ashwander* v. *TVA*, . . . we requested supplementary briefing on the statutory issue. . . .

B

The language of § 601, 78 Stat. 252, [Title VI] like that of the Equal Protection Clause, is majestic in its sweep:

> No person in the United States shall, on the ground of race, color, or national origin, be excluded from participation in, be denied the benefits of, or be subjected to discrimination under any program or activity receiving Federal financial assistance.

The concept of "discrimination," like the phrase "equal protection of the laws," is susceptible of varying interpretations. . . . We must, therefore, seek whatever aid is available in determining the precise meaning of the statute before us. . . . Examination of the voluminous legislative history of Title VI reveals a congressional intent to halt federal funding of entities that violate a prohibition of racial discrimination similar to that of the Constitution. Although isolated statements of various legislators, taken out of context, can be marshaled in support of the proposition that § 601 enacted a purely colorblind scheme, without regard to the reach of the Equal Protection Clause, these comments must be read against the background of both the problem that Congress was addressing and the broader view of the statute that emerges from a full examination of the legislative debates.

The problem confronting Congress was discrimination against Negro citizens at the hands of recipients of federal moneys. . . . Over and over again, proponents of the bill detailed the plight of Negroes seeking equal treatment in such programs. There simply was no reason for Congress to consider the validity of hypothetical preferences that might be accorded minority citizens; the legislators were dealing with the real and pressing problem of how to guarantee those citizens equal treatment.

In addressing that problem, supporters of Title VI repeatedly declared that the bill enacted constitutional principles. . . .

In the Senate, Senator Humphrey declared that the purpose of Title VI was "to insure that Federal funds are spent in accordance with the Constitution and the moral sense of the Nation." . . . Senator Ribicoff agreed that Title VI embraced the constitutional standard: "Basically, there is a constitutional restriction against discrimination in the use of federal funds; and Title VI simply spells out the procedure to be used in enforcing that restriction." . . . Other Senators expressed similar views.

Further evidence of the incorporation of a constitutional standard into Title VI appears in the repeated refusals of the legislation's supporters precisely to define the term "discrimination." Opponents sharply criticized this failure, but proponents of the bill merely replied that the meaning of "discrimination" would be made clear by reference to the Constitution or other existing law. . . .

In view of the clear legislative intent, Title VI must be held to proscribe only those racial classifications that would violate the Equal Protection Clause of the Fifth Amendment.

III

A

Petitioner does not deny that decisions based on race or ethnic origin by faculties and administrations of state universities are reviewable under the Fourteenth Amendment. . . . For his part, respondent does not argue that all racial or ethnic classifications are *per se* invalid. . . . The parties do disagree as to the level of judicial scrutiny to be applied to the special admissions program. Petitioner argues that the court below erred in applying strict scrutiny, as this inexact term has been applied in our cases. That level of review, petitioner asserts, should be reserved for classifications that disadvantage "discrete and insular minorities." See *United States* v. *Carolene Products Co.* . . . Respondent, on the other hand, contends that the California court correctly rejected the notion that the degree of scrutiny accorded a particular racial or ethnic classification hinges upon membership in a discrete and insular minority and duly recognized that the "rights established (by the Fourteenth Amendment) are personal rights." *Shelley* v. *Kraemer.* . . .

En route to this crucial battle over the scope of judicial review, the parties fight a sharp preliminary action over the proper characterization of the special admissions program. Petitioner prefers to view it as establishing a "goal" of minority representation in the Medical School. Respondent, echoing the courts below, labels it a racial quota.

This semantic distinction is beside the point: The special admissions program is undeniably a classification based on race and ethnic background. To the extent that there existed a pool of at least minimally qualified minority applicants to fill the 16 special admissions seats, white applicants could compete only for 84 seats in the entering class, rather than the 100 open to minority applicants. Whether this limitation is described as a quota or a goal, it is a line drawn on the basis of race and ethnic status. . . .

It is settled beyond question that the "rights created by the first section of the Fourteenth Amendment are, by its terms, guaranteed to the individual. The rights established are personal rights." *Shelley* v. *Kraemer*. . . . The guarantee of equal protection cannot mean one thing when applied to one individual and something else when applied to a person of another color. If both are not accorded the same protection, then it is not equal.

Nevertheless, petitioner argues that the court below erred in applying strict scrutiny to the special admissions program because white males, such as respondent, are not a "discrete and insular minority" requiring extraordinary protection from the majoritarian political process. . . . This rationale, however, has never been invoked in our decisions as prerequisite to subjecting racial or ethnic distinctions to strict scrutiny. Nor has this Court held that discreteness and insularity constitute necessary preconditions to a holding that a particular classification is invidious. . . . These characteristics may be relevant in deciding whether or not to add new types of classifications to the list of "suspect" categories or whether a particular classification survives close examination. . . . Racial and ethnic classifications, however, are subject to stringent examination without regard to these additional characteristics. We declared as much in the first cases explicitly to recognize racial distinctions as suspect:

> Distinctions between citizens solely because of their ancestry are by their very nature odious to a free people whose institutions are founded upon the doctrine of equality. *Hirabayashi*, 320 U.S., at 100.

> [A]ll legal restrictions which curtail the civil rights of a single group are immediately suspect. That is not to say that all such restrictions are unconstitutional. It is to say that courts must subject them to the most rigid scrutiny. *Korematsu*, 323 U.S., at 216.

The Court has never questioned the validity of those pronouncements. Racial and ethnic distinctions of any sort are inherently suspect and thus call for the most exacting judicial examination.

B

This perception of racial and ethnic distinctions is rooted in our Nation's constitutional and demographic history. The Court's initial view of the Fourteenth Amendment was that its "one pervading purpose" was "the freedom of the slave race, the security and firm establishment of that freedom, and the protection of the newly-made free-man and citizen from the oppressions of those who had formerly exercised dominion over him." Slaughter-House Cases. . . . The Equal Protection Clause, however, was "[v]irtually strangled in infancy by post-civil-war judicial reactionism." It was relegated to decades of relative desuetude while the Due Process Clause of the Fourteenth Amendment, after a short germinal period, flourished as a cornerstone in the Court's defense of property and liberty of contract. . . . In that cause, the Fourteenth Amendment's "one pervading purpose" was displaced. . . . It was only as the era of substantive due process came to a close . . . that the Equal Protection Clause began to attain a genuine measure of vitality. . . .

By that time it was no longer possible to peg the guarantees of the Fourteenth Amendment to the struggle for equality of one racial minority. During the dormancy of the Equal Protection Clause, the United States had become a Nation of minorities. Each had to struggle—and to some extent struggles still—to overcome the prejudices not of a monolithic majority, but of a "majority" composed of various minority groups of whom it was said—perhaps unfairly in many cases—that a shared characteristic was a willingness to disadvantage other groups. As the Nation filled with the stock of many lands, the reach of the Clause was gradually extended to all ethnic groups seeking protection from official discrimination. See *Strauder* v. *West Virginia*, 100 U.S. 303, 308 (1880) (Celtic Irishmen) (dictum): *Yick Wo* v. *Hopkins*, 118 U.S. 356 (1886) (Chinese); *Traux* v. *Raich*, 239 U.S. 33, 41 (1915) (Austrian resident aliens); *Korematsu, supra* (Japanese); *Hernandez* v. *Texas*, 347 U.S. 475 (1954) (Mexican-Americans). . . .

Although many of the Framers of the Fourteenth Amendment conceived of its primary function as bridging the vast distance between members of the Negro race and the white "majority," . . . the Amendment itself was framed in universal terms, without reference to color, ethnic origin, or condition of prior servitude. As this Court recently remarked in interpreting the 1866 Civil Rights Act to extend to claims of racial discrimination against white persons, "the 39th Congress was intent upon establishing in the federal law a broader principle than would have been necessary simply to meet the particular and immediate plight of the newly freed Negro slaves." *McDonald* v. *Sante Fe Trail Transportation Co.* . . . And that legislation was specifically broadened in 1870 to ensure that "all persons," not merely "citizens" would enjoy equal rights under the law. See *Runyon* v. *McCrary* . . . Indeed, it is not unlikely that among the Framers were many who would have applauded a reading of the Equal Protection Clause that states a principle of universal application and is responsive to the racial, ethnic, and cultural diversity of the Nation. . . .

Over the past 30 years, this Court has embarked upon the crucial mission of interpreting the Equal Protection Clause with the view of assuring to all persons "the protection of equal laws" . . . in a Nation confronting a legacy of slavery and racial discrimination. . . . Because the landmark decisions in this area arose in response to the continued exclusion of Negroes from the mainstream of American society, they could be characterized as involving discrimination by the "majority" white race against the Negro minority. But they need not be read as depending upon that characterization for their results. It suffices to say that "[o]ver the years, this Court has consistently repudiated '[d]istinctions between citizens solely because of their ancestry' as being 'odious to a free people whose institutions are founded upon the doctrine of equality.'" *Loving* v. *Virginia*, 388 U.S. 1, 11 (1967), quoting *Hirabayashi* . . . .

Petitioner urges us to adopt for the first time a more restrictive view of the Equal Protection Clause and hold that discrimination against members of the white "majority" cannot be suspect if its purpose can be characterized as "benign." The clock of our liberties, however, cannot be turned back to 1868. . . . It is far too late to argue that the guarantee of equal protection to all persons permits the recognition of special wards entitled to a degree of protection greater than that accorded others. "The Fourteenth Amendment is not directed solely against discrimination due to a 'two-class theory'—that is, based upon differences between 'white' and Negro." *Hernandez*, 347 U.S., at 478.

Once the artificial line of a "two-class theory" of the Fourteenth Amendment is put aside, the difficulties entailed in varying the level of judicial review according to a perceived "preferred" status of a particular racial or ethnic minority are intractable. The concepts of "majority" and "minority" necessarily reflect temporary arrangements and political judgments. . . . [T]he white "majority" itself is composed of various minority groups, most of which can lay claim to a history of prior discrimination at the hands of the State and private individuals. Not all of these groups can receive preferential treatment and corresponding judicial tolerance of distinctions drawn in terms of race and nationality, for then the only "majority" left would be a new minority of white Anglo-Saxon

Protestants. There is no principled basis for deciding which groups would merit "heightened judicial solicitude" and which would not. Courts would be asked to evaluate the extent of the prejudice and consequent harm suffered by various minority groups. Those whose societal injury is thought to exceed some arbitrary level of tolerability then would be entitled to preferential classifications at the expense of individuals belonging to other groups. Those classifications would be free from exacting judicial scrutiny. As these preferences began to have their desired effect, and the consequences of past discrimination were undone, new judicial rankings would be necessary. The kind of variable sociological and political analysis necessary to produce such rankings simply does not lie within the judicial competence—even if they otherwise were politically feasible and socially desirable.

Moreover, there are serious problems of justice connected with the idea of preference itself. First, it may not always be clear that a so-called preference is in fact benign. Courts may be asked to validate burdens imposed upon individual members of a particular group in order to advance the group's general interest. See *United Jewish Organizations* v. *Carey*. . . . Nothing in the Constitution supports the notion that individuals may be asked to suffer otherwise impermissible burdens in order to enhance the societal standing of their ethnic groups. Second, preferential programs may only reinforce common stereotypes holding that certain groups are unable to achieve success without special protection based on a factor having no relationship to individual worth. See *DeFunis* v. *Odegaard* . . . . Third, there is a measure of inequity in forcing innocent persons in respondent's position to bear the burdens of redressing grievances not of their making.

By hitching the meaning of the Equal Protection Clause to these transitory considerations, we would be holding, as a constitutional principle, that judicial scrutiny of classifications touching on racial and ethnic background may vary with the ebb and flow of political forces. Disparate constitutional tolerance of such classifications well may serve to exacerbate racial and ethnic antagonisms rather than alleviate them. . . . *United Jewish Organizations, supra*, at 173–174 (BRENNAN, J., concurring in part). Also, the mutability of a constitutional principle, based upon shifting political and social judgments, undermines the changes for consistent application of the Constitution from one generation to the next, a critical feature of its coherent interpretation. . . .

If it is the individual who is entitled to judicial protection against classifications based upon his racial or ethnic background because such distinctions impinge upon personal rights, rather than the individual only because of his membership in a particular group, then constitutional standards may be applied consistently. Political judgments regarding the necessity for the particular classification may be weighed in the constitutional balance . . . but the standard of justification will remain constant. This is as it should be, since those political judgments are the product of rough compromise struck by contending groups within the democratic process. When they touch upon an individual's race or ethnic background, he is entitled to a judicial determination that the burden he is asked to bear on that basis is precisely tailored to serve a compelling governmental interest. The Constitution guarantees that right to every person regardless of his background . . . .

C

Petitioner contends that on several occasions this Court has approved preferential classifications without applying the most exacting scrutiny. Most of the cases upon which petitioner relies are drawn from three areas: school desegregation, employment discrimination, and sex discrimination. Each of the cases cited presented a situation materially different from the facts of this case.

The school desegregation cases are inapposite. Each involved remedies for clearly determined constitutional violations. . . . Racial classifications thus were designed as remedies for the vindication of constitutional entitlement. Moreover, the scope of the remedies was not permitted to exceed the extent of the violations. . . . Here, there was no judicial determination of constitutional violation as a predicate for the formulation of a remedial classification.

The employment discrimination cases also do not advance petitioner's cause. For example, in *Franks* v. *Bowman Transportation Co.*, 424 U.S. 747 (1976), we approved a retroactive award of seniority to a class of Negro truckdrivers who had been the victims of discrimination—not just by society at large, but by the respondent in that case. While this relief imposed some burdens on other employees, it was held necessary " 'to make [the victims] whole for injuries suffered on account of unlawful employment discrimination.' " . . . The Courts of Appeals have fashioned various types of racial preferences as remedies for constitutional or statutory violations resulting in identified, race-based injuries to individuals held entitled to the preference. . . . Such preferences also have been upheld where a legislative or administrative body charged with the responsibility made determinations of past discrimination by the industries affected, and fashioned remedies deemed appropriate to rectify the discrimination. . . . But we have never approved preferential classifications in the absence of proved constitutional or statutory violations.

Nor is petitioner's view as to the applicable standard supported by the fact that gender-based classifications are not subjected to this level of scrutiny . . . Gender-based distinctions are less likely to create the analytical and practical problems present in preferential programs premised on racial or ethnic criteria. With respect to gender there are only two possible classifications. The incidence of the burdens imposed by preferential classifications is clear. There are no rival groups which can claim that they, too, are entitled to preferential treatment. . . . In sum, the Court has never viewed such classification as inherently suspect or as comparable to racial or ethnic classifications for the purpose of equal protection analysis. . . .

[P]etitioner contends that our recent decision in *United Jewish Organizations* v. *Carey* . . . indicates a willingness to approve racial classifications designed to benefit certain minorities, without denominating the classifications as "suspect." The State of New York had redrawn its reapportionment plan to meet objections of the Department of Justice under § 5 of the Voting Rights Act of 1965. . . . Specifically, voting districts were redrawn to enhance the electoral power of certain "nonwhite" voters found to have been the victims of unlawful "dilution" under the original reapportionment plan. *United Jewish Organizations* . . . properly is viewed as a case in which the remedy for an administrative finding of discrimination encompassed measures to improve the previously disadvantaged group's ability to participate, without excluding individuals belonging to any other group from enjoyment of the relevant opportunity—meaningful participation in the electoral process.

In this case, unlike . . . *United Jewish Organizations*, there has been no determination by the legislature or a responsible administrative agency that the University engaged in a discriminatory practice requiring remedial efforts. Moreover, the operation of petitioner's special admissions program is quite different from the remedial measures approved in those cases. It prefers the designated minority groups at the expense of other individuals who are totally foreclosed from competition for the 16 special admissions seats in every

Medical School class. Because of that foreclosure, some individuals are excluded from enjoyment of a state-provided benefit—admission to the Medical School—they otherwise would receive. When a classification denies an individual opportunities or benefits enjoyed by others solely because of his race or ethnic background, it must be regarded as suspect. . . .

IV

We have held that in "order to justify the use of a suspect classification, a State must show that its purpose or interest is both constitutionally permissible and substantial, and that its use of the classification is 'necessary . . . to the accomplishment' of its purpose of the safeguarding of its interest." . . . The special admissions program purports to serve the purposes of: (i) "reducing the historic deficit of traditionally disfavored minorities in medical schools and in the medical profession". . . ; (ii) countering the effects of societal discrimination; (iii) increasing the number of physicians who will practice in communities currently underserved; and (iv) obtaining the educational benefits that flow from an ethnically diverse student body. It is necessary to decide which, if any, of these purposes is substantial enough to support the use of a suspect classification.

A

If petitioner's purpose is to assure within its student body some specified percentage of a particular group merely because of its race or ethnic origin, such a preferential purpose must be rejected not as insubstantial but as facially invalid. Preferring members of any one group for no reason other than race or ethnic origin is discrimination for its own sake. . . .

B

The State certainly has a legitimate and substantial interest in ameliorating, or eliminating where feasible, the disabling effects of identified discrimination. The line of school desegregation cases, commencing with *Brown*, attests to the importance of this state goal and the commitment of the judiciary to affirm all lawful means toward its attainment. . . . That goal was far more focused than the remedying of the effects of "societal discrimination," an amorphous concept of injury that may be ageless in its reach into the past.

We have never approved a classification that aids persons perceived as members of relatively victimized groups at the expense of other innocent individuals in the absence of judicial, legislative, or administrative findings of constitutional or statutory violations. . . . After such findings have been made, the governmental interest in preferring members of the injured groups at the expense of others is substantial, since the legal rights of the victims must be vindicated. In such a case, the extent of the injury and the consequent remedy will have been judicially, legislatively, or administratively defined. Also, the remedial action usually remains subject to continuing oversight to assure that it will work the least harm possible to other innocent persons competing for the benefit. Without such findings of constitutional or statutory violations, it cannot be said that the Government has any greater interest in helping one individual than in refraining from harming another. Thus, the Government has no compelling justification for inflicting such harm.

Petitioner does not purpose to have made, and is in no position to make, such findings. Its broad mission is education, not the formulation of any legislative policy or the adjudication of particular claims of illegality. . . . [I]solated segments of our vast governmental structures are not competent to make those decisions, at least in the absence of legislative mandates and legislatively determined criteria. . . . Before relying upon these sorts of findings in establishing a racial classification, a governmental body must have the authority and capability to establish, in the record, that the classification is responsive to identified discrimination. . . . Lacking this capability, petitioner has not carried its burden of justification on this issue.

Hence, the purpose of helping certain groups whom the faculty of the Davis Medical School perceived as victims of "societal discrimination" does not justify a classification that imposes disadvantages upon persons like respondent, who bear no responsibility for whatever harm the beneficiaries of the special admissions program are thought to have suffered. To hold otherwise would be to convert a remedy heretofore reserved for violations of legal rights into a privilege that all institutions throughout the Nation could grant at their pleasure to whatever groups are perceived as victims of societal discrimination. That is a step we have never approved. . . .

C

Petitioner identifies, as another purpose of its program, improving the delivery of health-care services to communities currently underserved. It may be assumed that in some situations a State's interest in facilitating the health care of its citizens is sufficiently compelling to support the use of a suspect classification. But there is virtually no evidence in the record indicating that petitioner's special admissions program is either needed or geared to promote that goal. . . .

D

The fourth goal asserted by petitioner is the attainment of a diverse student body. This clearly is a constitutionally permissible goal for an institution of higher education. Academic freedom, though not a specifically enumerated constitutional right, long has been viewed as a special concern of the First Amendment. The freedom of a university to make its own judgments as to education includes the selection of its student body. . . . The atmosphere of "speculation, experiment and creation"—so essential to the quality of higher education—is widely believed to be promoted by a diverse student body. . . .

Thus, in arguing that its universities must be accorded the right to select those students who will contribute the most to the "robust exchange of ideas," petitioner invokes a countervailing constitutional interest, that of the First Amendment. In this light, petitioner must be viewed as seeking to achieve a goal that is of paramount importance in the fulfillment of its mission.

It may be argued that there is greater force to these views at the undergraduate level than in a medical school where the training is centered primarily on professional competency. But even at the graduate level, our tradition and experience lend support to the view that the contribution of diversity is substantial. In *Sweatt* v. *Painter*, 339 U.S. 629, at 634 (1950) the Court made a similar point with specific reference to legal education:

> The law school, the proving ground for legal learning and practice, cannot be effective in isolation from the individuals and institutions with which the law interacts. Few students and no one who has practiced law would choose to study in an academic vacuum, removed from the interplay of ideas and the exchange of views with which the law is concerned.

Physicians serve a heterogeneous population. An otherwise qualified medical student with a particular background—whether it be ethnic, geographic, culturally advantaged or disadvantaged—may bring to a professional school of medicine experiences, outlooks, and ideas that enrich the training of its student body and better equip its graduates to render with understanding their vital service to humanity.

Ethnic diversity, however, is only one element in a range of factors a university properly may consider in attaining the goal of a heterogeneous student body. Although a university must have wide discretion in making the sensitive judgments as to who should be admitted, constitutional limitations protecting individual rights may not be disregarded. . . . As the interest of diversity is compelling in the context of a university's admissions program, the question remains whether the program's racial classification is necessary to promote this interest. . . .

V

A

It may be assumed that the reservation of a specified number of seats in each class for individuals from the preferred ethnic groups would contribute to the attainment of considerable ethnic diversity in the student body. But petitioner's argument that this is the only effective means of serving the interest of diversity is seriously flawed. In a most fundamental sense the argument misconceives the nature of the state interest that would justify consideration of race or ethnic background. It is not an interest in simple ethnic diversity, in which a specified percentage of the student body is in effect guaranteed to be members of selected ethnic groups, with the remaining percentage an undifferentiated aggregation of students. The diversity that furthers a compelling state interest encompasses a far broader array of qualifications and characteristics of which racial or ethnic origin is but a single though important element. Petitioner's special admissions program, focused solely on ethnic diversity, would hinder rather than further attainment of genuine diversity. . . .

The experience of other university admissions programs, which take race into account in achieving the educational diversity valued by the First Amendment, demonstrates that the assignment of a fixed number of places to a minority group is not a necessary means toward that end. An illuminating example is found in the Harvard College program:

> In recent years Harvard College has expanded the concept of diversity to include students from disadvantaged economic, racial and ethnic groups. Harvard College now recruits not only Californians or Louisianians but also blacks and Chicanos and other minority students. . . .
>
> In practice, this new definition of diversity has meant

that race has been a factor in some admission decisions. When the Committee on Admissions reviews the large middle group of applicants who are "admissible" and deemed capable of doing good work in their courses, the race of an applicant may tip the balance in his favor just as geographic origin or a life spent on a farm may tip the balance in other candidates' cases. A farm boy from Idaho can bring something to Harvard College that a Bostonian cannot offer. Similarly, a black student can usually bring something that a white person cannot offer. . . .

In Harvard College admissions the Committee has not set target-quotas for the number of blacks, or of musicians, football players, physicists or Californians to be admitted in a given year. . . . But that awareness (of the necessity of including more than a token number of black students) does not mean that the Committee sets a minimum number of blacks or of people from west of the Mississippi who are to be admitted. It means only that in choosing among thousands of applicants who are not only "admissible" academically but have other strong qualities, the Committee, with a number of criteria in mind, pays some attention to distribution among many types and categories of students. . . .

In such an admissions program, race or ethnic background may be deemed a "plus" in a particular applicant's file, yet it does not insulate the individual from comparison with all other candidates for the available seats. The file of a particular black applicant may be examined for his potential contribution to diversity without the factor of race being decisive when compared, for example, with that of an applicant identified as an Italian-American if the latter is thought to exhibit qualities more likely to promote beneficial educational pluralism. Such qualities could include exceptional personal talents, unique work or service experience, leadership potential, maturity, demonstrated compassion, a history of overcoming disadvantage, ability to communicate with the poor, or other qualifications deemed important. In short, an admissions program operated in this way is flexible enough to consider all pertinent elements of diversity in light of the particular qualifications of each applicant, and to place them on the same footing for consideration, although not necessarily according them the same weight. . . .

This kind of program treats each applicant as an individual in the admission process. The applicant who loses out on the last available seat to another candidate receiving a "plus" on the basis of ethnic background will not have been foreclosed from all consideration for that seat simply because he was not the right color or had the wrong sur-

name. It would mean only that his combined qualifications, which may have included similar nonobjective factors, did not outweigh those of the other applicant. His qualifications would have been weighed fairly and competitively, and he would have no basis to complain of unequal treatment under the Fourteenth Amendment.

It has been suggested that an admissions program which considers race only as one factor is simply a subtle and more sophisticated—but no less effective—means of according racial preference than the Davis program. A facial intent to discriminate, however, is evident in petitioner's preference program and not denied in this case. No such facial informity exists in an admissions program where race or ethnic background is simply one element—to be weighed fairly against other elements—in the selection process. . . .

B

In summary, it is evident that the Davis special admissions program involves the use of an explicit racial classification never before countenanced by this Court. It tells applicants who are not Negro, Asian, or Chicano that they are totally excluded from a specific percentage of the seats in an entering class. No matter how strong their qualifications, quantitative and extracurricular, including their own potential for contribution to educational diversity, they are never afforded the chance to compete with applicants from the preferred groups for the special admission seats. At the same time, the preferred applicants have the opportunity to compete for every seat in the class.

The fatal flaw in petitioner's preferential program is its disregard of individual rights as guaranteed by the Fourteenth Amendment. *Shelley* v. *Kraemer*, 334 U.S., at 22. Such rights are not absolute. But when a State's distribution of benefits or imposition of burdens hinges on ancestry or the color of a person's skin, that individual is entitled to a demonstration that the challenged classification is necessary to promote a substantial state interest. Petitioner has failed to carry this burden. For this reason, that portion of the California court's judgment holding petitioner's special admissions program invalid under the Fourteenth Amendment must be affirmed.

C

In enjoining petitioner from ever considering the race of any applicant, however, the courts below failed to recognize that the State has a substantial interest that legitimately may be served by a properly devised admissions program involving the competitive consideration of race and ethnic origin. For this reason, so much of the California court's judgment as enjoins petitioner from any consideration of the race of any applicant must be reversed.

VI

With respect to respondent's entitlement to an injunction directing his admission to the Medical School, petitioner has conceded that it could not carry its burden of proving that, but for the existence of its unlawful special admissions program, respondent still would not have been admitted. Hence, respondent is entitled to the injunction, and that portion of the judgment must be affirmed. . . .

JUSTICE BRENNAN, JUSTICE WHITE, JUSTICE MARSHALL, *and* JUSTICE BLACKMUN, *concurring in the judgment in part and dissenting in part.*

The court today, in reversing in part the judgment of the Supreme Court of California, affirms the constitutional power of Federal and State Governments to act affirmatively to achieve equal opportunity for all. The difficulty of the issue presented—whether Government may use race-conscious programs to redress the continuing effects of past discrimination—and the mature consideration which each of our Brethren has brought to it have resulted in many opinions, no single one speaking for the Court. But this should not and must not mask the central meaning of today's opinions: Government may take race into account when it acts not to demean or insult any racial group, but to remedy disadvantages cast on minorities by past racial prejudice, at least when appropriate findings have been made by judicial, legislative, or administrative bodies with competence to act in this area.

THE CHIEF JUSTICE, and our Brothers STEWART, REHNQUIST and STEVENS, have concluded that Title VI of the Civil Rights Act of 1964 . . . prohibits programs such as that at the Davis Medical School. On this statutory theory alone, they would hold that respondent Allan Bakke's rights have been violated and that he must, therefore, be admitted to the Medical School. Our Brother POWELL, preaching the Constitution, concludes that, although race may be taken into account in university admissions, the particular special admissions program used by petitioner, which resulted in the exclusion of respondent

Bakke, was not shown to be necessary to achieve petitioner's stated goals. Accordingly, these Members of the Court form a majority of five affirming the judgment of the Supreme Court of California insofar as it holds that respondent Bakke "is entitled to an order that he be admitted to the University." . . .

We agree with JUSTICE POWELL that, as applied to the case before us, Title VI goes no further in prohibiting the use of race than the Equal Protection Clause of the Fourteenth Amendment itself. We also agree that the effect of the California Supreme Court's affirmance of the judgment of the Superior Court of California would be to prohibit the University from establishing in the future affirmative action programs that take race into account. . . . Since we conclude that the affirmative admissions program at the Davis Medical School is constitutional, we would reverse the judgment below in all respects. JUSTICE POWELL agrees that some uses of race in university admissions are permissible and, therefore, he joins with us to make five votes reversing the judgment below insofar as it prohibits the University from establishing race-conscious programs in the future. . . .

* * *

Davis's articulated purpose of remedying the effects of past societal discrimination is, under our cases, sufficiently important to justify the use of race-conscious admissions programs where there is a sound basis for concluding that minority underrepresentation is substantial and chronic, and that the handicap of past discrimination is impeding access of minorities to the Medical School.

[The separate opinion of JUSTICE WHITE is not reprinted here.]

JUSTICE MARSHALL.

I agree with the judgment of the Court only insofar as it permits a university to consider the race of an applicant in making admissions decisions. I do not agree that petitioner's admissions program violates the Constitution. For it must be remembered that, during most of the past 200 years, the Constitution as interpreted by this Court did not prohibit the most ingenious and pervasive forms of discrimination against the Negro. Now, when a State acts to remedy the effects of the legacy of discrimination, I cannot believe that this same Constitution stands as a barrier . . . .

[Here JUSTICE MARSHALL gives a lengthy review of the 350 years of the Negro in the United States.]

* * *

The position of the Negro today in America is the tragic but inevitable consequence of centuries of unequal treatment. Measured by any benchmark of comfort or achievement, meaningful equality remains a distant dream for the Negro. . . .

A Negro child today has a life expectancy which is shorter by more than five years than that of a white child. The Negro child's mother is over three times more likely to die of complications in childbirth, and the infant mortality rate for Negroes is nearly twice that for whites. The median income of the Negro family is only 60% that of the median of a white family, and the percentage of Negroes who live in families with incomes below the poverty line is nearly four times greater than that of whites.

When the Negro child reaches working age, he finds that America offers him significantly less than it offers his white counterpart. For Negro adults, the unemployment rate is twice that of whites, and the unemployment rate for Negro teenagers is nearly three times that of white teenagers. . . . Although Negroes represent 11.5% of the population, they are only 1.2% of the lawyers and judges, 2% of the physicians, 2.3% of the dentists, 1.1% of the engineers, and 2.6% of the college and university professors.

The relationship between those figures and the history of unequal treatment afforded to the Negro cannot be denied. At every point from birth to death the impact of the past is reflected in the still disfavored position of the Negro.

In light of the sorry history of discrimination and its devastating impact on the lives of Negroes, bringing the Negro into the mainstream of American life should be a state interest of the highest order. To fail to do so is to ensure that America will forever remain a divided society.

I do not believe that the Fourteenth Amendment requires us to accept that fate. Neither its history nor our past cases lend any support to the conclusion that a university may not remedy the cumulative effects of society's discrimination by giving consideration to race in an effort to increase the number and percentage of Negro doctors.

This Court long ago remarked that

in any fair and just construction of any section or phrase of these [Civil War] amendments, it is necessary to look to the purpose which we have said was the pervading spirit of them all, the evil which they were designed to remedy. . . . Slaughter-House Cases, 16 Wall., at 72.

It is plain that the Fourteenth Amendment was not intended to prohibit measures designed to remedy the effects of the Nation's past treatment of Negroes. . . .

While I applaud the judgment of the Court that a university may consider race in its admissions process, it is more than a little ironic that, after several hundred years of class-based discrimination against Negroes, the Court is unwilling to hold that a class-based remedy for that discrimination is permissible. In declining to so hold, today's judgment ignores the fact that for several hundred years Negroes have been discriminated against, not as individuals, but rather solely because of the color of their skins. It is unnecessary in 20th century America to have individual Negroes demonstrate that they have been victims of racial discrimination; the racism of our society has been so pervasive that none, regardless of wealth or position, has managed to escape its impact. The experience of Negroes in America has been different in kind, not just in degree, from that of other ethnic groups. It is not merely the history of slavery alone but also that a whole people were marked as inferior by the law. And that mark has endured. The dream of America as the great melting pot has not been realized for the Negro; because of his skin color he never even made it into the pot.

These differences in the experience of the Negro make it difficult for me to accept that Negroes cannot be afforded greater protection under the Fourteenth Amendment where it is necessary to remedy the effects of past discrimination. In the Civil Rights Cases, . . . the Court wrote that the Negro emerging from slavery must cease "to be the special favorite of the laws." 109 U.S., at 25. . . . We cannot in light of the history of the last century yield to that view. Had the Court in that decision and others been willing to "do for human liberty and the fundamental rights of American citizenship, what it did . . . for the protection of slavery and the rights of the masters of fugitive slaves", *id.*, at 52 (Harlan, J., dissenting), we would not need now to permit the recognition of any "special wards."

Most importantly, had the Court been willing in 1896, in *Plessy* v. *Ferguson*, to hold that the Equal Protection Clause forbids differences in treatment based on race, we would not be faced with this dilemma in 1978. We must remember however, that the principle that the "Constitution is color-blind" appeared only in the opinion of the lone dissenter . . . . The majority of the Court rejected the principle of color blindness, and for the next 60 years, from *Plessy* to *Brown* v. *Board of Education,* ours was a Nation where, by law, an individual could be given "special" treatment based on the color of his skin.

It is because of a legacy of unequal treatment that we now must permit the institutions of this society to give consideration to race in making decisions about who will hold the positions of influence, affluence, and prestige in America. For far too long, the doors to those positions have been shut to Negroes. If we are ever to become a fully integrated society, one in which the color of a person's skin will not determine the opportunities available to him or her, we must be willing to take steps to open those doors. I do not believe that anyone can truly look into America's past and still find that a remedy for the effects of that past is impermissible.

It has been said that this involves only the individual, Bakke, and this University. I doubt, however, that there is a computer capable of determining the number of persons and institutions that may be affected by the decision in this case. For example, we are told by the Attorney General of the United States that at least 27 federal agencies have adopted regulations requiring recipients of federal funds to take "*affirmative action* to overcome the effects of conditions which resulted in limiting participation . . . by persons of a particular race, color, or national origin . . . " (emphasis added). I cannot even guess the number of state and local governments that have set up affirmative action programs, which may be affected by today's decision.

I fear that we have come full circle. After the Civil War our Government started several "affirmative action" programs. This Court in the Civil Rights Cases and *Plessy* v. *Ferguson* destroyed the movement toward complete equality. For almost a century no action was taken, and this nonaction was with the tacit approval of the courts. Then we had *Brown* v. *Board of Education* and the Civil Rights Acts of Congress, followed by numerous affirmative action programs. Now, we have this Court again stepping in, this time to stop affirmative action programs of the type used by the University of California.

[The separate opinion of JUSTICE BLACK-MUN is not reprinted here.]

JUSTICE STEVENS, *with whom* THE CHIEF JUSTICE, JUSTICE STEWART, *and* JUSTICE REHNQUIST *join, concurring in the judgment in part and dissenting in part.*

* * *

Our settled practice . . . is to avoid the decision of a constitutional issue if a case can be fairly decided on a statutory ground. "If there is one doctrine more deeply rooted than any other in the process of constitutional adjudication it is that we ought not to pass on questions of constitutionality . . . unless such adjudication is unavoidable." *Spector Motor Co.* v. *McLaughlin.* . . . The more important the issue, the more force there is to this doctrine. In this case, we are presented with a constitutional question of undoubted and unusual importance. Since, however, a dispositive statutory claim was raised at the very inception of this case, and squarely decided in the portion of the trial court judgment affirmed by the California Supreme Court, it is our plain duty to confront it. Only if petitioner should prevail on the statutory issue would it be necessary to decide whether the University's admissions program violated the Equal Protection Clause of the Fourteenth Amendment. . . .

Title VI is an integral part of the far-reaching Civil Rights Act of 1964. No doubt, when this legislation was being debated, Congress was not directly concerned with the legality of "reverse discrimination" or "affirmative action" programs. Its attention was focused on the problem at hand, the "glaring . . . discrimination against Negroes which exists throughout our Nation." . . . Title VI stands for "the general principle that no person . . . be excluded from participation . . . on the ground of race, color, or national origin under any program or activity receiving Federal financial assistance." . . . This same broad view of Title VI and § 601 was echoed throughout the congressional debate and was stressed by every one of the major spokesmen for the Act.

Petitioner contends, however, that exclusion of applicants on the basis of race does not violate Title VI if the exclusion carries with it no racial stigma. No such qualification or limitation of § 601's categorical prohibition of "exclusion" is justified by the statute or its history. . . .

. . . The statutory prohibition against discrimination in federally funded projects contained in § 601 is more than a simple paraphrasing of what the Fifth or Fourteenth Amendment would require. The Act's proponents plainly considered Title VI consistent with their view of the Constitution, and they sought to provide an effective weapon to implement that view. As a distillation of what the supporters of the Act believed the Constitution demanded of State and Federal Governments, § 601 has independent force, with language and emphasis in addition to that found in the Constitution.

As with other provisions of the Civil Rights Act,

Congress's expression of its policy to end racial discrimination may independently proscribe conduct that the Constitution does not. However, we need not decide the congruence—or lack of congruence—of the controlling statute and the Constitution since the meaning of the Title VI ban on exclusion is clear: Race cannot be the basis of excluding anyone from participation in a federally funded program. . . .

Eliminating Job Bias and the Affirmative Action Controversy

FEATURED CASES

Griggs v. *Duke Power Company*   *City of Richmond, Virginia* v. *J. A. Croson Company*
Washington v. *Davis*   *Wards Cove Packing Company* v. *Atonio*   *Brenda Patterson* v. *McClean Credit Union*

The civil rights revolution of the 1960s produced the first major federal legislative action directed at racial discrimination in the job market. To be sure, several token steps had been taken by the executive during World War II and in the period thereafter. But since these initiatives were confined to federal employment and, to a lesser extent, to employers performing services for the federal government under contract, the impact was very slight. Additionally, several northern states adopted fair employment practices legislation during the 1950s with uneven results.

But a major breakthrough came with the enactment of Title VII of the 1964 Civil Rights Act, which forbade discrimination based on race, color, sex, religion, or national origin by both employers and labor unions. Initially covering those establishments with 100 or more employees, the coverage number has been reduced in successive stages to 25 or more.

This legislation withstood its first major challenge in *Griggs* v. *Duke Power Company* (401 U.S. 424, 1971), when the Supreme Court unanimously held that the act bars the use of employment practices that operate to exclude blacks if the practices are unrelated to job performance. In that case, black employees of the Duke Power Company contested requirements that conditioned employment in, or transfer to, jobs within the company upon having completed high school or passing a standardized intelligence test. The practical effect of

these requirements was to preclude blacks from employment in or promotion to jobs in the highest paying departments of the company. Chief Justice Burger, speaking for the Court, said that the act "proscribes not only overt discrimination but also practices that are fair in form, but discriminatory in operation." "The touchstone," noted Burger, "is business necessity [and] if an employment practice which operates to exclude Negroes cannot be shown to be related to job performance, the practice is prohibited." To Duke Power's contention that the requirements were made without the intention of discrimination against blacks, Burger said that "good intent or absence of discriminatory intent does not redeem employment procedures or testing mechanisms that operate as 'built-in headwinds' for minority groups and are unrelated to measuring job capability."

Subsequently, in *McDonnell Douglas Corp.* v. *Green* (411 U.S. 792, 1973), the Court set forth some of the factors that a complainant could use in establishing a prima facie case of racial discrimination. These include a showing that the complainant: (1) belongs to a racial minority; (2) applied and was qualified for a job for which the employer was seeking applicants; and (3) was rejected despite his or her qualifications; and that the employer continued to accept applications for the position from persons with similar qualifications.

In 1976 the title was construed to prohibit discrimination against whites. In *McDonald* v. *Sante Fe Trail Transportation Co.* (424 U.S. 905, 1976), Justice Thurgood Marshall, speaking for the Court, underscored the even-handed prohibition against racial discrimination as the intent of the Congress in enacting the measure, as had been held in *Duke Power Company*. Furthermore, Marshall contended that the challenged discrimination was additionally prohibited by the 1870 Civil Rights Act as codified in 42 U.S.C.A. Section 1981.

Finally, in *Washington* v. *Davis* (426 U.S. 229), decided late in the 1975 term, the Court considered the nature of recruiting procedures, scrutinizing in particular the personnel test administered to police applicants in Washington, D.C. In what some have characterized as a crippling blow to the aspirations of black would-be employees, the Court reversed the court of appeals and held that the more stringent statutory standards of Title VII were inapplicable in resolving the Fifth Amendment issue of invidious discrimination raised. Despite the radically disproportionate impact of the testing and selection procedures involved, the Court held that where a constitutional claim is raised, aggrieved blacks must show that administrators had a *discriminatory intent*; mere showing of a disproportionate racial impact of the selection mechanisms is not enough.

Just one year later, in *Teamsters* v. *United States* (431 U.S. 324, 1977), the Court rejected the positions of the Justice Department and the Equal Employment Opportunity Commission when it ruled that Title VII does not forbid the use of seniority systems that perpetuate the effects of pre-act racially discriminatory employment practices. In a bitter disappointment to civil rights groups, the seven-to-two majority held that it was not the intention of Congress when enacting Title VII to displace preexisting seniority systems, even where they resulted in seniority advantages for white over black employees. The majority contended that the white employee's seniority should not be adversely affected because of the discriminatory policies and practices of his or her employer. As long as there is no proof of a "discriminatory intent" of the employer by continuing to use the pre-act seniority system, Title VII is not breached.

Applying a rationale similar to that supporting race-conscious admissions policies in higher education, the Court approved the use of such remedies by employers operating in the private sector in its ruling in *United States Steelworkers of America* v. *Weber* (443 U.S. 193) in 1979. In a cooperative effort to achieve a more proportionate racial balance in the local work force, union and manage-

ment agreed to implement a training program aimed at increasing the ranks of blacks in skilled positions in the company from which they (blacks) were excluded in the past. Central to this voluntary effort was a preferential admissions component to achieve the goals of training larger numbers of blacks than whites. In sustaining the arrangement against a charge of "reverse discrimination" by a white applicant who was not admitted to the training program, the Court made it clear that the program was consistent with the intent of the framers of Title VII of the 1964 Civil Rights Act. The Court emphasized that the statute should be viewed as a "catalyst" for employers and unions in their efforts to remedy the past effects of racial discrimination in employment practices and not as a barrier. In short, the plan was well within the discretionary area left to private employers by Title VII.

That the principle of affirmative action is incompatible with longstanding seniority principles traditionally embedded in labor contracts has presented some thorny questions for courts enforcing the nondiscriminatory provisions of Title VII. In their efforts to achieve a better racial balance of employees in key service areas like firefighting and police departments, a number of cities agreed to institute (not without the objection of many white employees) affirmative action hiring programs during the 1970s. But when economic hard times plunged many municipal governments into fiscal difficulty, employee layoffs resulted, putting the affirmative action and seniority principles on a collision course. Should the traditional seniority practice (requiring "the last hired to be the first fired") be followed and bring to a halt the objective of a better racial balance of employees, or should there be a modification of or moratorium on the seniority principle to protect the gains of minority employees? The question had profound implications for the struggle for racial equality, since racially discriminatory hiring policies prior to Title VII had provided a significant seniority advantage to white employees.

Several lower federal courts, including those in Boston, Detroit, and Memphis, decided to sustain the affirmative action principle. The Supreme Court sidestepped the conflict in 1983 when it held in *Boston Firefighters Union, Local 718* v. *Boston Chapter, NAACP*, and *Boston Police Patrolmen's Association* v. *Castro* (103 S. Ct. 2076), that an appeal of a district court ruling (affirmed by the court of appeals) that had set aside the seniority principle in order to preserve affirmative action hiring programs in the Boston fire and police departments was moot. The state legislature had responded to the district court ruling by appropriating additional revenue enabling the departments to reinstate the aggrieved white employees. But one year later, however, in *Firefighters Union No. 1784* v. *Stotts* (104 S. Ct. 2576, 1984), the Court was presented a "live" conflict involving the affirmative action program in the Memphis Fire Department and upheld the seniority principle. Speaking for the majority, Justice Byron White argued that the district court's action modifying the consent decree (in which the affirmative action hiring plan was couched), contrary to the wishes of the city, was limited by Title VII of the 1964 Civil Rights Act. Furthermore, he rejected the notion advanced by the court of appeals, that judges possess inherent power to order actions that are required to accomplish the objectives sought by such consent decrees. Instead, he maintained, Title VII limits their actions in awarding relief (such as seniority in the context of this case) only to those individual employees who prove that they have been "actual victims of discriminatory employment practices." Thus, White appeared to provide precedential support for the Reagan administration's effort to eliminate group-based remedies from affirmative action law. But in two subsequent rulings in 1986, the Court did not read *Stotts* as forging such a restrictive construction of Title VII. First, in *Firefighters* v. *City of Cleveland* (106 S. Ct. 3063), Justice Brennan made it clear for a six-to-three majority that Title VII is not to be construed so narrowly as to preclude a consent decree remedy for discrimination against minority firefighters in promotions that may benefit some minority persons who may not have been the actual victims of discriminatory treatment. Pointing to the statutory provision (Section 706g) that the white firefighters association invoked in opposing the consent decree remedy, Brennan noted that the provision is intended to restrict the latitude of a court from imposing certain kinds of race-conscious relief after trial and does not apply to consent decree–fashioned relief arrangements. Brennan went a step further in the other case—*Sheet Metal Workers* v. *Equal Employment Opportunity Commission* (106 S. Ct. 3019)—when he argued that section 706g is not to be construed as precluding the authority of district courts to fashion remedies that may prescribe race-conscious arrangements that may "incidentally benefit individuals who were not actual victims of discrimination."

In a third ruling handed down in 1986, the Court continued to indicate its displeasure with affirmative action plans that made possible the abrogation of seniority rights of white employees as a means of preserving targeted minority representation in the work force. At issue in *Wygant* v. *Jackson, Michigan Board of Education* (476 U.S. 267, 1986), was a layoff policy that the teachers' union had been persuaded to accept in a collective bargaining agreement that extended preferential treatment to minority teachers. When circumstances necessitated implementation of the policy, the result was that white teachers with greater seniority were laid off, while the positions of minority teachers with less seniority were preserved. A plurality of the justices (Powell, Burger, Rehnquist, and O'Connor) agreed with the complaining white teachers that such a policy constituted an abridgment of equal protection of the laws. They were joined in the judgment by Justice Byron White.

Justice Powell, who wrote the plurality opinion, rejected generalized societal discrimination and minority role model justifications as insufficient to justify the application of the race-conscious remedy. Rather, he contended that the board's burden was to present convincing evidence of past discrimination and then "narrowly tailor the remedy" that was to be used in accomplishing its objective. He concluded that there were "less intrusive measures" that could be used to attain the objectives of the school board than the use of racial preference in the layoff of teachers.

In a concurring opinion, Justice White would limit the remedy to the "actual victims" of discrimination. He could not accept a policy that required the layoff of white teachers "to make room for black [teachers]" absent proof of actual victimization. In dissent, Justice Thurgood Marshall, who was joined by Justices Brennan and Blackmun, argued that the race-preferential remedy here was adopted to achieve "important governmental interests" and was "substantially related" thereto. Justice Stevens, the fourth dissenter, contended that the important public interest that the layoff policy was designed to achieve justified the adverse consequences for some of the board's white teachers.

In the following term, the Rehnquist Court had its first opportunity to examine the affirmative action question in both the race and gender contexts. In the first case, the Alabama state police employment practices were at issue in *United States* v. *Paradise* (480 U.S. 149, 1987). The crucial dimension of the relief ordered by the district court was a "one-black-for-one-white" promotion arrangement to be used as an interim measure until the Department was found to be "implementing valid promotion procedures." The equal protection objection to this relief measure was made by the Reagan Justice Department and several white troopers who alleged that they would be adversely affected by it. But the Supreme Court, in a narrow five-to-four decision, rejected that contention, with Justice Brennan once again asserting that such a race-conscious remedy was justified in pursuit of a "compelling governmental interest" to eradicate longstanding egregious discrimination in that area of public employment. Furthermore, he contended, the relief was "narrowly tailored" to deal with the specific discriminatory practices involved.

The Rehnquist Court considered a gender-based affirmative action plan in *Johnson* v. *Transportation Agency, Santa Clara County, CA* (480 U.S. 616, 1987). There it rejected a Title VII challenge to a public agency's affirmative action plan that allowed the consideration of the sex of an applicant in making promotions to positions in which women had been traditionally underrepresented. Speaking for the six-to-three majority, Justice Brennan recognized the existence of a "manifest imbalance" in the job category to which the female applicant was promoted (it should be noted that the female applicant's rating on the promotional examination was slightly lower than that of the male applicant who brought the challenge) and concluded that the agency's consideration of the applicant's sex is constitutionally justified in correcting such imbalances. Furthermore, it should be noted that there was no question that the applicant was qualified to hold the position of dispatcher about which the controversy centered.

Another congressional action designed to enhance the economic position of minority contractors met with litigatory resistance in *Fullilove* v. *Klutznick* (448 U.S. 448, 1980). Minority contractors (often operating with meager resources) were usually at a disadvantage in competing for contracts and usually did not receive them. This situation was ameliorated somewhat when Congress included in the Public Works Employment Act of 1977 a "minority business enterprise" provision. MBE, as the provision was popularly known, required the secretary of commerce to exact from the state and local governments applying for grants under the act assurances that at least 10 percent of each grant would be expended in contracts with minority business enterprises.

Immediately, the "10 percent set-aside," as it was labeled, was denounced as a "quota" regulatory measure that deprived some contractors of access to a portion of governmental contracting opportunities. Congress, it was argued, is constitutionally required to act in a "color-blind" manner.

In rejecting such status quo arguments, the Court stressed the broad remedial powers of Congress to remedy the effects of past racial discrimination. The "limited use of racial and ethnic criteria" to effect remedies in this area of government operation was certainly within its authority, said Chief Justice Warren Burger, and meets the strict scrutiny standard required in such governmental efforts.

In the years that followed the *Fullilove* ruling, a number of state and local governments adopted little "set-aside" programs to assure that minority contractors constantly would be able to get their share of the construction dollars awarded by various agencies of government in those governmental units. To be sure, a number of minority contractors prospered in varying degrees as a result of these inclusive policies. But just as in *Fullilove*, some white contractors resisted these initiatives, charging that the implementation of such policies resulted in unconstitutional "reverse" discrimination.

White contractors were joined in their attack on the "set-aside" plans by the Reagan administration, which had mounted a heavy attack on race-based affirmative action policies generally. The issue was before the Court in a local governmental context when it considered the case of *City of Richmond, Virginia* v. *J. A. Croson Co.* (109 S. Ct. 706) during the 1988 term. In a six-to-three decision affirming the court of appeals' rejection of Richmond's 30 percent set-aside program, the Court held that government policies that utilize race-conscious numerical remedies are "suspect" and are subject to "strict scrutiny" review. Speaking for the Court, Justice Sandra Day O'Connor argued that the kind of race-conscious numerical remedy at issue in Richmond can only pass constitutional muster by a showing of a "compelling state interest" in the redress of specific "identified discrimination." Rejecting the contention of affirmative action proponents that numerical disparity (the absence of blacks or a token presence) is proof of discrimination, O'Connor, embraced the meritocracy theory as the appropriate standard to govern agency selection and/or award decisions. Emphasizing this point, she contended, "[W]here special qualifications are necessary, the relevant statistical pool for purposes of demonstrating discriminatory exclusion must be the number of minorities qualified to undertake the particular task" at issue.

In a concurring opinion, Justice Antonin Scalia argued that "compensatory justice" types of affirmative action plans (those adopted to remedy generalized past societal discrimination) should not be accorded constitutional sanction. Furthermore, he asserted, "[T]here is only one circumstance in which the states may act by race to 'undo the effects of past discrimination': where that is necessary to eliminate their own maintenance of a system of unlawful racial classification."

In the major dissent, Justice Thurgood Marshall indicated his displeasure with the majority for taking "a deliberate and giant step backward in [the] Court's affirmative action jurisprudence." On the merits, he argued that the Constitution does not prohibit Richmond from allocating a portion of its resources to allow minority contractors an opportunity to participate in the delivery of city services. Consequently, he stated, neither ordinary scrutiny (rational basis) nor strict scrutiny was the appropriate constitutional standard to apply to cases like this one. Hence, for Marshall, this kind of affirmative action case called for an equal protection inquiry that seeks to determine if the plan "serves important governmental objectives" and is "substantially related to the achievement of those objectives." Underscoring the appropriateness of this kind of mid-level scrutiny for the race-conscious remedial policies, Marshall took very sharp exception to the majority's adoption of strict scrutiny as the appropriate standard for the equal protection review of race remediation policies as an "unwelcomed development."

The furor over the *Croson* ruling had hardly subsided when the Court dealt another blow to affirmative action interests in *Wards Cove Packing Company* v. *Atonio* (109 S. Ct. 2115, 1989). In rejecting the challenges of employees of two Alaskan salmon canning companies alleging discriminatory employment practices in violation of Title VII, a conservative five-to-four majority of the Court construed the burden of proof requirements to make it more difficult for a plaintiff in a disparate impact case to prevail. Here the plaintiffs had marshaled considerable evidence of discrimination in job assignments (minorities were in disproportionately large numbers in the lower positions and very few were assigned to the higher-paying positions) sufficient to convince the court of appeals of a prima facie case of the disparate impact of the employer's employment practices. Such a finding shifts the burden of proof to the employer to justify the "business necessity" of the employment practices.

But Justice White, speaking for the majority (Rehnquist, O'Connor, Scalia, and Kennedy) rejected the lower court's ruling as a misreading of the Court's relevant precedents and a misunderstanding of the purpose of Title VII. Making it more difficult for plaintiffs to prove a violation of Title VII based on data showing racial imbalance in particular positions in an employer's work force, White asserted that such race-based statistical comparisons are insufficient to sustain a disparate impact claim. What is required, he argued, is a showing of disproportionality that focuses on "the pool of qualified job applicants" or the "qualified population in the labor force."

Probably the most disheartening part of White's opinion for the affirmative action interests was the way he treated the burden-of-proof issue. Noting that the dispositive issue in a disparate impact case is whether "legitimate employment goals of the employer" are served by the "challenged practice," he maintained that although the employer is required to produce evidence to support "a business justification for the challenged practice," the burden of proof remains with the plaintiff—"the ultimate burden of proving that discrimination against a protected group has been caused by a specific employment practice remains with the plaintiff *at all times.*"

Additionally, the Court fastened heavier demands on plaintiffs in their effort to establish a prima facie case of disparate impact of an employment practice or policy. Under this holding, plaintiffs are now required to "isolate and identify specific employee practices that are allegedly responsible for any observed statistical disparities."

In a major dissent, Justice John Paul Stevens accused the majority of judicial activism by "turning a blind eye to the meaning and purpose of Title VII." He noted that since *Duke Power* in 1971, the Court and federal enforcement agencies had all interpreted Title VII to prohibit employment practices that had discriminatory effects as well as those that were intended to discriminate. He concluded that such a construction of the statute had helped to accomplish the equal employment opportunity objectives, and he decried the majority's retreat from that effort.

Justice Harry Blackmun wrote a brief dissent in which he called attention to the racial climate out of which affirmative action policies were developed and chastised his colleagues for disregarding it. Apparently echoing the concerns of many civil rights interests that the majority was acting as if it were writing on a "clean slate" in this policy area, the justice noted bluntly that "one wonders whether the majority still believes that race discrimination . . . against nonwhites is a problem in our society or even remembers that it ever was."

While affirmative action interests were still reeling from the *Wards Cove* ruling, the Court delivered another setback for affirmative action interests just one week later in *Martin* v. *Wilks* (109 S.

Ct. 2180, 1989). Here the consent decree as a mechanism for the implementation of affirmative action goals was the target of the Court's conservative majority, as it upheld a ruling of the Court of Appeals for the Eleventh Circuit that had overturned a federal district court consent decree settlement of a racial discrimination suit against the Birmingham Fire Department. The core stipulation in the decree provided for the hiring and promotion of equal numbers of blacks and whites until such time as the black contingent in the several firefighter positions approximates the proportion of blacks in the local civilian labor force. The appeals court agreed with the white firefighter plaintiffs that implementation of the numerical-based remedy in the consent decree would constitute "reverse discrimination" and that they (the white firefighters) should be allowed to reopen the consent decree and make their case.

In its affirmance of that position, the majority, speaking through Chief Justice Rehnquist, asserted that a consent decree, while settling matters among parties to a lawsuit, "does not conclude the rights of strangers (the white firefighters here) to those proceedings." The Chief Justice then swung the courthouse door wide open to a potentially large number of lawsuits by groups challenging affirmative action programs in a variety of employment contexts that have been couched in consent decrees over the past two decades when he concluded that the decree is only to be considered binding on parties who were part of the original lawsuit.

Justice John Paul Stevens underscored that possibility in his sharp dissent. Characterizing the result reached by the majority as "unfathomable" and "counterproductive," he warned that the decision would "subject large employers who seek to comply with the law by remedying past discrimination to a never ending stream of litigation and potential liability."

On the same decision day, the Court, with a slightly different line-up of justices (Justice O'Connor did not participate and Justice Stevens supplied the fifth vote), handed down a ruling that makes it significantly more difficult for a plaintiff to bring an action challenging an allegedly discriminatory seniority system. In *Lorance* v. *American Telephone and Telegraph Co.* (109 S. Ct. 2261, 1989), Justice Antonin Scalia's opinion for the Court held that the female and the black employees, who had discovered in a personnel action some time after the employer had modified seniority rules that the changes had an adverse impact on them, were too late to bring a discrimination action under Title VII. He noted that, in complaints alleging discrimination in violation of the title, actions must be brought within 300 days of the alleged violation.

For many civil rights leaders and their supporters, the Court's narrow interpretation of the applicable antidiscrimination laws in these affirmative action rulings represented a major step toward acceptance of the disgruntled white employees' complaints of reverse discrimination. To be sure, the Court's conservative majority did not overturn any of the antidiscrimination laws in the several rulings, but the construction of those laws made it significantly more difficult for the "protected" classes (minorities and women) to prevail in their complaints of discriminatory treatment in the several dimensions of employment.

In the congressional session following the Court's 1989 anti-affirmative action rulings, civil rights forces got Congress to enact amendatory legislation to overturn the Court's narrow interpretation of the relevant law in the several cases. But many opponents of affirmative action convinced President Bush that the net effect of the amendatory legislation would be to "force" employers to adopt hiring quotas to protect themselves from employment discrimination actions. The expected veto sent the measure back to the Congress, where a bipartisan group led by Senator John Danforth (R., Mo.) was able to fashion a measure that the president could sign in 1991. Not unnoticed in the president's altered position on this legislation was the impact of ex–Ku Klux Klansman David Duke's significant appeal (as a Republican candidate) in the Louisiana gubernatorial election and the troublesome sexual harassment allegations brought against the president's African American nominee (Appeals Court Judge Clarence Thomas) to fill a Supreme Court vacancy. The image of a president insensitive to the efforts of diverse forces (including respected members of his own party) to rid the American work place of employment discrimination was not the kind of baggage he needed to carry in his 1992 reelection effort.

While the measure essentially restored the *Griggs* v. *Duke Power Company* interpretation of Title VII, which had been shunted aside in the *Wards Cove* decision, it also allows limited monetary damage awards for victims of employment discrimination based on sex, religion, and disability. Other key provisions of the new legislation negate and/or lessen the impact of the decisions in *Wilks, McLean Credit Union*, and *Lorance*. Many expect that the climate that spawned the retrogressive actions on employment discrimination during the 1980s will be replaced with the more vigorous enforcement of existing law under the Clinton administration.

The Court, however, did not give any indication that it was backing away from its narrow construction of employment discrimination law in the 1989 decisions when it handed down the decision in *St. Mary's Honor Center* v. *Hicks* (113 S. Ct. 2742, 1993) during the final days of its 1992 term. There, in a 5-to-4 decision, the burden of proof required of employees, who sue their employers for engaging in discriminatory practices against them, was made more demanding. Justice Antonin Scalia argued for the majority that proof that an employer's proffered explanation for the adverse action against an employee was not credible is simply not enough. Additionally, Scalia maintained, the employee must present *evidence of intentional discrimination* as the reason for the adverse action against him or her. (emphasis added). Certainly such a requirement makes it extremely difficult for an employee-plaintiff to prevail. Evidence of intentional discrimination will be almost impossible to uncover unless an employer is incredibly inept and careless. In the end, it could well be that civil rights leaders will mount an effort in Congress for remedial legislation as was done after the 1989 decision in this area of the law.

GRIGGS v. DUKE POWER COMPANY
401 U.S. 424; 28 L. Ed. 2d 158; 91 S. Ct. 849 (1971)

CHIEF JUSTICE BURGER *delivered the opinion of the Court.*

We granted the writ in this case to resolve the question whether an employer is prohibited by the Civil Rights Act of 1964, Title VII, from requiring a high school education or passing of a standardized general intelligence test as a condition of employment in or transfer to jobs when (a) neither standard is shown to be significantly related to successful job performance, (b) both requirements operate to disqualify Negroes at a substantially higher rate than white applicants, and (c) the jobs in question formerly had been filled only by white employees as part of a longstanding practice of giving preference to whites.

Congress provided, in Title VII of the Civil Rights Act of 1964, for class actions for enforcement of provisions of the Act and this proceeding was brought by a group of incumbent Negro employees against Duke Power Company. . . . At the time this action was instituted, the Company had 95 employees at the Dan River Station, 14 of whom were Negroes; 13 of these are petitioners here.

The District Court found that prior to July 2, 1965, the effective date of the Civil Rights Act of 1964, the Company openly discriminated on the basis of race in the hiring and assigning of employees at its Dan River plant. The plant was organized into five operating departments: (1) Labor, (2) Coal Handling, (3) Operations, (4) Maintenance, and (5) Laboratory and Test. Negroes were employed only in the Labor Department where the highest paying jobs paid less than the lowest paying jobs in the other four "operating" departments in which only whites were employed. Promotions were normally made within each department on the basis of job seniority. Transferees into a department usually began in the lowest position.

In 1955 the Company instituted a policy of requiring a high school education for initial assignment to any department except Labor, and for transfer from the Coal Handling to any "inside" department (Operations, Maintenance, or Laboratory). When the Company abandoned its policy of restricting Negroes to the Labor Department in 1965, completion of high school also was made a prerequisite to transfer from Labor to any other department. From the time the high school requirement was instituted to the time of trial, however, white employees hired before the time of the high school education requirement continued to perform satisfactorily and achieve promotions in the "operating" departments. Findings on this score are not challenged.

The Company added a further requirement for new employees on July 2, 1965, the date on which Title VII became effective. To qualify for placement in any but the Labor Department it became necessary to register satisfactory scores on two professionally prepared aptitude tests, as well as to have a high school education. Completion of high school alone continued to render employees eligible for transfer to the four desirable departments from which Negroes had been excluded if the incumbent had been employed prior to the time of the new requirement. In September 1965 the Company began to permit incumbent employees who lacked a high school education to qualify for transfer from Labor or Coal Handling to an "inside" job by passing two tests—the Wonderlic Personnel Test, which purports to measure general intelligence, and the Bennett Mechanical Aptitude Test. Neither was directed or intended to measure the ability to learn to perform a particular job or category of jobs. The requisite scores used for both initial hiring and transfer approximated the national median for high school graduates.

The District Court had found that while the Company previously followed a policy of overt racial discrimination in a period prior to the Act, such conduct had ceased. The District Court also concluded that Title VII was intended to be prospective only and, consequently, the impact of prior inequities was beyond the reach of corrective action authorized by the Act.

The Court of Appeals was confronted with a question of first impression, as are we, concerning the meaning of Title VII. After careful analysis a majority of that court concluded that a subjective test of the employer's intent should govern, particularly in a close case, and that in this case there was no showing of a discriminatory purpose in the adoption of the diploma and test requirements. On this basis, the Court of Appeals concluded there was no violation of the Act.

The Court of Appeals reversed the District Court in part, rejecting the holding that residual discrimination arising from prior employment practices was insulated from remedial action. The Court of Appeals noted, however, that the District Court was correct in its conclusion that there was no finding of a racial purpose of invidious intent in the adoption of the high school diploma requirement or general intelligence test and that these standards had been applied fairly to whites and Negroes alike. It held that, in the absence of a discriminatory purpose, use of such requirements was permitted by the Act. In so doing, the Court of Appeals rejected the claim that because these two requirements operated to render ineligible a markedly disproportionate number of Negroes, they were unlawful under Title VII unless shown to be job-related. . . .

The objective of Congress in the enactment of Title VII is plain from the language of the statute. It was to achieve equality of employment opportunities and remove barriers that have operated in the past to favor an identifiable group of white employees over other employees. Under the Act, practices, procedures, or tests neutral on their face, and even neutral in terms of intent, cannot be maintained if they operate to "freeze" the status quo of prior discriminatory employment practices.

The Court of Appeals' opinion, and the partial dissent, agreed that, on the record in the present case, "whites fare far better on the Company's alternative requirements" than Negroes. This consequence would appear to be directly traceable to race. Basic intelligence must have the means of articulation to manifest itself fairly in a testing process. Because they are Negroes, petitioners have long received inferior education in segregated schools and this Court expressly recognized these differences in *Gaston County* v. *United States*, 395 U.S. 285 (1969). There, because of the inferior education received by Negroes in North Carolina, this Court barred the institution of a literacy test for voter registration on the ground that the test would abridge the right to vote indirectly on account of race. Congress did not intend by Title VII, however, to guarantee a job to every person regardless of qualifications. In short, the Act does not command that any person be hired simply because he was formerly the subject of discrimination, or because he is a member of a minority group. Discriminatory preference for any group, minority or majority, is precisely and only what Congress has proscribed. What is required by Congress is the removal of artificial, arbitrary, and unnecessary barriers to employment when the barriers operate invidiously to discriminate on the basis of racial or other impermissible classification.

Congress has now provided that tests or criteria for employment or promotion may not provide equality of opportunity only in the sense of the fabled offer of milk to the stork and the fox. On the contrary, Congress has now required that the posture and condition of the job seeker be taken into account. It has—to resort again to the fable—provided that the vessel in which the milk is proffered be one all seekers can use. The Act proscribes not only overt discrimination but also practices that are fair in form, but discriminatory in operation. The touchstone is business necessity. If an employment practice which operates to exclude Negroes cannot be shown to be related to job performance, the practice is prohibited.

On the record before us, neither the high school completion requirement nor the general intelligence test is shown to bear a demonstrable relationship to successful performance of the jobs for which it was used. Both were adopted, as the Court of Appeals noted, without meaningful study of their relationship to job-performance ability. Rather, a vice president of the Company testified, the requirements were instituted on the Company's judgment that they generally would improve the overall quality of the work force.

The evidence, however, shows that employees

who have not completed high school or taken the tests have continued to perform satisfactorily and make progress in departments for which the high school and test criteria are now used. The promotion record of present employees who would not be able to meet the new criteria thus suggests the possibility that the requirements may not be needed even for the limited purpose of preserving the avowed policy of advancement within the Company....

The Court of Appeals held that the Company had adopted the diploma and test requirements without any "intention to discriminate against Negro employees." We do not suggest that either the District Court or the Court of Appeals erred in examining the employer's intent; but good intent or absence of discriminatory intent does not redeem employment procedures or testing mechanisms that operate as "built-in headwinds" for minority groups and are unrelated to measuring job capability....

The facts of this case demonstrate the inadequacy of broad and general testing devices as well as the infirmity of using diplomas or degrees as fixed measures of capability. History is filled with examples of men and women who rendered highly effective performance without the conventional badges of accomplishment in terms of certificates, diplomas, or degrees. Diplomas and tests are useful servants, but Congress had mandated the common-sense proposition that they are not to become masters of reality.

The Company contends that its general intelligence tests are specifically permitted by section 703(h) of the Act. That section authorizes the use of "any professionally developed ability test" that is not "designed, intended, or used to discriminate because of race...."

The Equal Employment Opportunity Commission, having enforcement responsibility, has issued guidelines interpreting section 703(h) to permit only the use of job-related tests. The administrative interpretation of the Act by the enforcing agency is entitled to great deference.... Since the Act and its legislative history support the Commission's construction, this affords good reason to treat the Guidelines as expressing the will of Congress....

Nothing in the Act precludes the use of testing or measuring procedures; obviously they are useful. What Congress has forbidden is giving these devices and mechanisms controlling force unless they are demonstrably a reasonable measure of job performance. Congress has not commanded that the less qualified be preferred over the better qualified simply because of minority origins. Far from disparaging job qualifications as such, Congress has made such qualifications the controlling factor, so that race, religion, nationality, and sex become irrelevant. What Congress has commanded is that any tests used must measure the person for the job and not the person in the abstract.

The judgment of the Court of Appeals is, as to that portion of the judgment appealed from, reversed.

[JUSTICE BRENNAN took no part in the consideration or decision of this case.]

CITY OF RICHMOND, VIRGINIA v. J. A. CROSON COMPANY
488 U.S. 469; 102 L. Ed. 2d 854; 109 S. Ct. 706 (1989)

JUSTICE O'CONNOR *announced the judgment of the Court and delivered the opinion of the Court with respect to Parts I, III-B, and IV, an opinion with respect to Part II, in which* THE CHIEF JUSTICE *and* JUSTICE WHITE *join, and an opinion with respect to Parts III-A and V, in which* THE CHIEF JUSTICE, JUSTICE WHITE, *and* JUSTICE KENNEDY *join.*

In this case, we confront once again the tension between the Fourteenth Amendment's guarantee of equal treatment to all citizens, and the use of race-based measures to ameliorate the effects of past discrimination on the opportunities enjoyed by members of minority groups in our society. In *Fullilove* v. *Klutznick*, 448 U.S. 448 (1980), we held that a congressional program requiring that 10% of certain federal construction grants be awarded to minority contractors did not violate the equal protection principles embodied in the Due Process Clause of the Fifth Amendment. Relying largely on our decision in *Fullilove*, some lower federal courts have applied a similar standard of review in assessing the constitutionality of state and local minority set-aside provisions under the Equal Protection

Clause of the Fourteenth Amendment. . . . Since our decision two Terms ago in *Wygant* v. *Jackson Board of Education*, 476 U.S. 267 (1986), the lower federal courts have attempted to apply its standards in evaluating the constitutionality of state and local programs which allocate a portion of public contracting opportunities exclusively to minority-owned businesses. . . . We noted probable jurisdiction in this case to consider the applicability of . . . *Wygant* to a minority set-aside program adopted by the city of Richmond, Virginia.

I

On April 11, 1983, the Richmond City Council adopted the Minority Business Utilization Plan (the Plan). The Plan required prime contractors to whom the city awarded construction contracts to subcontract at least 30% of the dollar amount of the contract to one or more Minority Business Enterprises (MBEs). . . . The 30% set-aside did not apply to city contracts awarded to minority-owned prime contractors.

The Plan defined an MBE as "[a] business at least fifty-one (51) percent of which is owned and controlled . . . by minority group members." "Minority group members" were defined as "[c]itizens of the United States who are Blacks, Spanish-speaking, Orientals, Indians, Eskimos, or Aleuts." . . . The Plan declared that it was "remedial" in nature, and enacted "for the purpose of promoting wider participation by minority business enterprises in the construction of public projects." The Plan expired on June 30, 1988, and was in effect for approximately five years. . . .

The Plan was adopted by the Richmond City Council after a public hearing. Seven members of the public spoke to the merits of the ordinance: five were in opposition, two in favor. Proponents of the set-aside provision relied on a study which indicated that, while the general population of Richmond was 50% black, only .67% of the city's prime construction contracts had been awarded to minority businesses in the 5-year period from 1978 to 1983. It was also established that a variety of contractors' associations, whose representatives appeared in opposition to the ordinance, had virtually no minority businesses within their membership. . . . The city's legal counsel indicated his view that the ordinance was constitutional under this Court's decision in *Fullilove* v. *Klutznick* . . . .

There was no direct evidence of race discrimination on the part of the city in letting contracts, or any evidence that the city's prime contractors had discriminated against minority-owned subcontractors. . . .

Opponents of the ordinance questioned both its wisdom and its legality. They argued that a disparity between minorities in the population of Richmond and the number of prime contracts awarded to MBEs had little probative value in establishing discrimination in the construction industry. . . .

[The J. A. Croson Co.] brought this action under 42 U.S.C. § 1983 in the Federal District Court for the Eastern District of Virginia, arguing that the Richmond ordinance was unconstitutional on its face and as applied in this case.

The District Court upheld the Plan in all respects. . . . In its original opinion, a divided panel of the Fourth Circuit Court of Appeals affirmed. . . . Both courts applied a test derived from "the common concerns articulated by the various Supreme Court opinions" in *Fullilove* v. *Klutznick* . . . and *University of California Regents* v. *Bakke* . . . .

The majority found that national findings of discrimination in the construction industry, when considered in conjunction with the statistical study concerning the awarding of prime contracts in Richmond, rendered the city council's conclusion that low minority participation in city contracts was due to past discrimination "reasonable." . . . The panel opinion then turned to the second part of its "synthesized *Fullilove*" test, examining whether the racial quota was "narrowly tailored to the legislative goals of the Plan." . . .

The panel held that to remedy the effects of past discrimination, "a set-aside program for a period of five years obviously must require more than a 0.67% set-aside to encourage minorities to enter the contracting industry and to allow existing minority contractors to grow." *Ibid*. Thus, in the court's view the 30% figure was "reasonable in light of the undisputed fact that minorities constitute 50% of the population of Richmond." . . .

We . . . vacated that opinion . . . and remanded the case for further consideration in light of our intervening decision in *Wygant* v. *Jackson Board of Education*. . . .

On remand, a divided panel of the Court of Appeals struck down the Richmond set-aside program as violating both prongs of strict scrutiny under the Equal Protection Clause of the Fourteenth Amendment. . . .

I

* * *

The principal opinion in *Fullilove*, written by Chief Justice Burger, did not employ "strict scrutiny" or any other traditional standard of equal protection review. The Chief Justice noted at the outset that although racial classifications call for close examination, the Court was at the same time "bound to approach [its] task with appropriate deference to the Congress, a coequal branch charged by the Constitution with the power to 'provide for the . . . general Welfare of the United States' and 'to enforce by appropriate legislation' the equal protection guarantees of the Fourteenth Amendment." The principal opinion asked two questions: First, were the objectives of the legislation within the power of Congress? Second, was the limited use of racial and ethnic criteria a permissible means for Congress to carry out its objectives within the constraints of the Due Process Clause?

On the issue of Congressional power, the Chief Justice found that Congress's commerce power was sufficiently broad to allow it to reach the practices of prime contractors on federally funded local construction projects. . . . Congress could mandate state and local government compliance with the set-aside program under its § 5 power to enforce the Fourteenth Amendment. . . .

The Chief Justice next turned to the constraints on Congress's power to employ race-conscious remedial relief. His opinion stressed two factors in upholding the MBE set-aside. First was the unique remedial powers of Congress under § 5 of the Fourteenth Amendment:

> Here we deal . . . not with the limited remedial powers of a federal court, for example, but with the broad remedial powers of Congress. It is fundamental that *in no organ of government, state or federal, does there repose a more comprehensive remedial power than in the Congress,* expressly charged by the Constitution with competence and authority to enforce equal protection guarantees. . . . (emphasis added).

Because of these unique powers, the Chief Justice concluded that "Congress not only may induce voluntary action to assure compliance with existing federal statutory or constitutional antidiscrimination provisions, but also, where Congress has authority to *declare certain conduct unlawful,* it may, as here, authorize and induce state action to avoid such conduct." *Id.,* at 483–484 (emphasis added).

In reviewing the legislative history behind the Act, the principal opinion focused on the evidence before Congress that a nationwide history of past discrimination has reduced minority participation in federal construction grants. The Chief Justice also noted that Congress drew on its experience under § 8(a) of the Small Business Act of 1953, which had extended aid to minority businesses . . . [and he] concluded that "Congress had abundant historical basis from which it could conclude that traditional procurement practices, when applied to minority businesses, could perpetuate the effects of prior discrimination."

The second factor emphasized by the principal opinion in *Fullilove* was the flexible nature of the 10% set-aside. Two "congressional assumptions" underlay the MBE program: first, that the effects of past discrimination had impaired the competitive position of minority businesses, and second, that "adjustment for the effects of past discrimination" would assure that at least 10% of the funds from the federal grant program would flow to minority businesses. The Chief Justice noted that both of these "assumptions" could be "rebutted" by a grantee seeking a waiver of the 10% requirement. Thus a waiver could be sought where minority businesses were not available to fill the 10% requirement or, more importantly, where an MBE attempted "to exploit the remedial aspects of the program by charging an unreasonable price, *i.e.,* a price not attributable to the present effects of prior discrimination." The Chief Justice indicated that without this fine-tuning to remedial purpose, the statute would not have "pass[ed] muster." . . .

Appellant and its supporting *amici* rely heavily on *Fullilove* for the proposition that a city council, like Congress, need not make specific findings of discrimination to engage in race-conscious relief. Thus, appellant argues "[i]t would be a perversion of federalism to hold that the federal government has a compelling interest in remedying the effects of racial discrimination in its own public works program, but a city government does not." . . .

What appellant ignores is that Congress, unlike any State or political subdivision, has a specific constitutional mandate to enforce the dictates of the Fourteenth Amendment. The power to "enforce" may at times also include the power to define situations which *Congress* determines threaten principles of equality and to adopt prophylactic rules to deal with those situations. . . .

That Congress may identify and redress the effects of society-wide discrimination does not mean that, *a fortiori,* the States and their political subdivisions are free to decide that such remedies are appropriate. Section 1 of the Fourteenth Amendment is an explicit *constraint* on state power, and the States must undertake any remedial efforts in accordance with that provision. To hold otherwise would be to cede control over the content of the Equal Protection Clause to the 50 state legislatures and their myriad political subdivisions. The mere recitation of a benign or compensatory purpose for the use of a racial classification would essentially entitle the States to exercise the full power of Congress under § 5 of the Fourteenth Amendment and insulate any racial classification from judicial scrutiny under § 1. We believe that such a result would be contrary to the intentions of the Framers of the Fourteenth Amendment, who desired to place clear limits on the States' use of race as a criterion for legislative action, and to have the federal courts enforce those limitations. . . .

We do not, as JUSTICE MARSHALL's dissent suggests, . . . find in § 5 of the Fourteenth Amendment some form of federal preemption in matters of race. We simply note what should be apparent to all—§ 1 of the Fourteenth Amendment stemmed from a distrust of state legislative enactments based on race: § 5 is . . . " 'a *positive* grant of legislative power' " to Congress. . . . Thus, our treatment of an exercise of Congressional power in *Fullilove* cannot be dispositive here . . . .

It would seem equally clear, however, that a state or local subdivision (if delegated the authority from the State) has the authority to eradicate the effects of private discrimination within its own legislative jurisdiction. This authority must, of course, be exercised within the constraints of § 1 of the Fourteenth Amendment. Our decision in *Wygant* is not to the contrary. *Wygant* addressed the constitutionality of the use of racial quotas by local school authorities pursuant to an agreement reached with the local teachers' union. It was in the context of addressing the school board's power to adopt a race-based layoff program affecting its own work force that the *Wygant* plurality indicated that the Equal Protection Clause required "some showing of prior discrimination by the governmental unit involved." As a matter of state law, the city of Richmond has legislative authority over its procurement policies and can use its spending powers to remedy private discrimination, if it identifies that discrimination with the particularity required by the Fourteenth Amendment. To this extent, on the question of the city's competence, the Court of Appeals erred in following *Wygant* by rote in a case involving a state entity which has state-law authority to address discriminatory practices within local commerce under its jurisdiction.

Thus, if the city could show that it had essentially become a "passive participant" in a system of racial exclusion practiced by elements of the local construction industry, we think it clear that the city could take affirmative steps to dismantle such a system. It is beyond dispute that any public entity, state or federal, has a compelling interest in assuring that public dollars, drawn from the tax contributions of all citizens, do not serve to finance the evil of private prejudice. . . .

III

A

The Richmond Plan denies certain citizens the opportunity to compete for a fixed percentage of public contracts based solely upon their race. To whatever racial group these citizens belong, their "personal rights" to be treated with equal dignity and respect are implicated by a rigid rule erecting race as the sole criterion in an aspect of public decision making.

Absent searching judicial inquiry into the justification for such race-based measures, there is simply no way of determining what classifications are "benign" or "remedial" and what classifications are in fact motivated by illegitimate notions of racial inferiority or simple racial politics. Indeed, the purpose of strict scrutiny is to "smoke out" illegitimate uses of race by assuring that the legislative body is pursuing a goal important enough to warrant use of a highly suspect tool. The test also ensures that the means chosen "fit" this compelling goal so closely that there is little or no possibility that the motive for the classification was illegitimate racial prejudice or stereotype.

Classifications based on race carry a danger of stigmatic harm. Unless they are strictly reserved for remedial settings, they may in fact promote notions of racial inferiority and lead to a politics of racial hostility. . . . We thus reaffirm the view expressed by the plurality in *Wygant* that the standard of review under the Equal Protection Clause is not dependent on the race of those burdened or benefited by a particular classification. . . .

Our continued adherence to the standard of review employed in *Wygant* does not, as JUSTICE MARSHALL's dissent suggests, indicate that we view "racial discrimination as largely a phenomenon of the past" or that "government bodies need no longer preoccupy themselves with rectifying racial injustice." . . . States and their local subdivisions have many legislative weapons at their disposal both to punish and prevent present discrimination and to remove arbitrary barriers to minority advancement. Rather, our interpretation of § 1 stems from our agreement with the view expressed by Justice Powell in *Bakke*, that "[t]he guarantee of equal protection cannot mean one thing when applied to one individual and something else when applied to a person of another color." . . .

Under the standard proposed by JUSTICE MARSHALL's dissent, "[r]ace-conscious classifications designed to further remedial goals" are forthwith subject to a relaxed standard of review. How the dissent arrives at the legal conclusion that a racial classification is "designed to further remedial goals," without first engaging in an examination of the factual basis for its enactment and the nexus between its scope and that factual basis, we are not told. However, once the "remedial" conclusion is reached, the dissent's standard is singularly deferential and bears little resemblance to the close examination of legislative purpose we have engaged in when reviewing classifications based either on race or gender. . . . The dissent's watered-down version of equal protection review effectively assures that race will always be relevant in American life, and that the "ultimate goal" of "eliminat[ing] entirely from governmental decisionmaking such irrelevant factors as a human being's race" . . . will never be achieved. . . .

In this case, blacks comprise approximately 50% of the population of the city of Richmond. Five of the nine seats on the City Council are held by blacks. The concern that a political majority will more easily act to the disadvantage of a minority based on unwarranted assumptions or incomplete facts would seem to militate for, not against, the application of heightened judicial scrutiny in this case. . . .

In *Bakke*, the Court confronted a racial quota employed by the University of California at Davis Medical School. Under the plan, 16 out of 100 seats in each entering class at the school were reserved exclusively for certain minority groups. Among the justifications offered in support of the plan were the desire to "reduc[e] the historic deficit of traditionally disfavored minorities in medical school and the medical profession" and the need to "counte[r] the effects of societal discrimination." Five Members of the Court determined that none of these interests could justify a plan that completely eliminated nonminorities from consideration for a specified percentage of opportunities. . . .

JUSTICE POWELL's opinion applied heightened scrutiny under the Equal Protection Clause to the racial classification at issue . . . . He indicated that for the governmental interest in remedying past discrimination to be triggered, "judicial, legislative, or administrative findings of constitutional or statutory violations" must be made. Only

then does the Government have a compelling interest in favoring one race over another.

In *Wygant*, four Members of the Court applied heightened scrutiny to a race-based system of employee layoffs. JUSTICE POWELL, writing for the plurality, again drew the distinction between "societal discrimination," which is an inadequate basis for race-conscious classifications, and the type of identified discrimination that can support and define the scope of race-based relief. The challenged classification in that case tied the layoff of minority teachers to the percentage of minority students enrolled in the school district. The lower courts had upheld the scheme, based on the theory that minority students were in need of "role models" to alleviate the effects of prior discrimination in society. This Court reversed, with a plurality of four justices reiterating the view expressed by Justice Powell in *Bakke* that "[s]ocietal discrimination, without more, is too amorphous a basis for imposing a racially classified remedy." . . .

B

* * *

Appellant argues that it is attempting to remedy various forms of past discrimination that are alleged to be responsible for the small number of minority businesses in the local contracting industry. Among these the city cites the exclusion of blacks from skilled construction trade unions and training programs. This past discrimination has prevented them "from following the traditional path from laborer to entrepreneur." The city also lists a host of nonracial factors which would seem to face a member of any racial group attempting to establish a new business enterprise, such as deficiencies in working capital, inability to meet bonding requirements, unfamiliarity with bidding procedures, and disability caused by an inadequate track record.

While there is no doubt that the sorry history of both private and public discrimination in this country had contributed to a lack of opportunities for black entrepreneurs, this observation, standing alone, cannot justify a rigid racial quota in the awarding of public contracts in Richmond, Virginia. . . . [A]n amorphous claim that there has been past discrimination in a particular industry cannot justify the use of an unyielding racial quota.

It is sheer speculation how many minority firms there would be in Richmond absent past societal discrimination. . . . Defining these sorts of injuries as "identified discrimination" would give local governments license to create a patchwork of racial preference based on statistical generalizations about any particular field of endeavor.

These defects are readily apparent in this case. The 30% quota cannot in any realistic sense be tied to any injury suffered by anyone. The District Court relied upon five predicate "facts" in reaching its conclusion that there was an adequate basis for the 30% quota: (1) the ordinance declares itself to be remedial; (2) several proponents of the measure stated their views that there had been past discrimination in the construction industry; (3) minority businesses received .67% of prime contracts from the city while minorities constituted 50% of the city's population; (4) there were very few minority contractors in local and state contractors' associations; and (5) in 1977 Congress made a determination that the effects of past discrimination had stifled minority participation in the construction industry nationally.

None of these "findings," singly or together, provide the city of Richmond with a "strong basis in evidence for its conclusion that remedial action was necessary." . . . There is nothing approaching a prima facie case of a constitutional or statutory violation by *anyone* in the Richmond construction industry. . . .

Racial classifications are suspect, and that means that simple legislative assurances of good intention cannot suffice.

The District Court . . . relied on the highly conclusionary statement of a proponent of the Plan that there was racial discrimination in the construction industry "in this area, and the State, and around the nation." It is also noted that the city manager had related his view that racial discrimination still plagued the construction industry in his home city of Pittsburgh. These statements are of little probative value in establishing identified discrimination in the Richmond construction industry. The fact-finding process of legislative bodies is generally entitled to a presumption of regularity and deferential review by the judiciary. . . . But when a legislative body chooses to employ a suspect classification, it cannot rest upon a generalized assertion as to the classification's relevance to its goals. . . . A governmental actor cannot render race a legitimate proxy for a particular condition merely by declaring that the condition exists. The history of racial classifications in this country suggests that blind judicial deference to legislative or executive pronouncements of necessity has no place in equal protection analysis. . . .

Reliance on the disparity between the number of prime contracts awarded to minority firms and the minority population of the city of Richmond is similarly misplaced. There is no doubt that "[w]here gross statistical disparities can be shown, they alone in a proper case may constitute prima facie proof of a pattern or practice of discrimination" under Title VII. . . . But it is equally clear that "[w]hen special qualifications are required to fill particular jobs, comparisons to the general population (rather than to the smaller group of individuals who possess the necessary qualifications) may have little probative value." . . .

In the employment context, we have recognized that for certain entry-level positions or positions requiring minimal training, statistical comparisons of the racial composition of an employer's work force to the racial composition of the relevant population may be probative of a pattern of discrimination. . . . But where special qualifications are necessary, the relevant statistical poll for purposes of demonstrating discriminatory exclusion must be the number of minorities qualified to undertake the particular task. . . .

. . . [N]one of the evidence presented by the city points to any identified discrimination in the Richmond construction industry. We, therefore, hold that the city has failed to demonstrate a compelling interest in apportioning public contracting opportunities on the basis of race. To accept Richmond's claim that past societal discrimination alone can serve as the basis for rigid racial preferences would be to open the door to competing claims for "remedial relief" for every disadvantaged group. The dream of a Nation of equal citizens in a society where race is irrelevant to personal opportunity and achievement would be lost in a mosaic of shifting preferences based on inherently unmeasurable claims of past wrongs. "Courts would be asked to evaluate the extent of the prejudice and consequent harm suffered by various minority groups. Those whose societal injury is thought to exceed some arbitrary level of tolerability then would be entitled to preferential classifications. . . . " We think such a result would be contrary to both the letter and spirit of a constitutional provision whose central command is equality. . . .

The foregoing analysis applies only to the inclusion of blacks within the Richmond set-aside program. There is *absolutely no evidence* of past discrimination against Spanish-speaking, Oriental, Indian, Eskimo, or Aleut persons in any aspect of the Richmond construction industry. The District Court took judicial notice of the fact that the vast majority of "minority" persons in Richmond were black. Sup. App. 207. It may well be that Richmond has never had an Aleut or Eskimo citizen. The random inclusion of racial groups that, as a practical matter, may never have suffered from discrimination in the construction industry in Richmond suggests that perhaps the city's purpose was not in fact to remedy past discrimination.

If a 30% set-aside was "narrowly tailored" to compensate black contractors for past discrimination, one may legitimately ask why they are forced to share this "remedial relief" with an Aleut citizen who moves to Richmond tomorrow? The gross overinclusiveness of Richmond's racial preference strongly impugns the city's claim of remedial motivation. . . .

IV

. . . [I]t is almost impossible to assess whether the Richmond Plan is narrowly tailored to remedy prior discrimination since it is not linked to identified discrimination in any way. We limit ourselves to two observations in this regard.

First, there does not appear to have been any consideration of the use of race-neutral means to increase minority business participation in city contracting. . . .

Second, the 30% quota cannot be said to be narrowly tailored to any goal, except perhaps outright racial balancing. It rests upon the "completely unrealistic" assumption that minorities will choose a particular trade in lockstep proportion to their representation in the local population. . . .

Given the existence of an individualized procedure, the city's only interest in maintaining a quota system rather than investigating the need for remedial action in particular cases would seem to be simple administrative convenience. But the interest in avoiding the bureaucratic effort necessary to tailor remedial relief to those who truly have suffered the effects of prior discrimination cannot justify a rigid line drawn on the basis of a suspect classification. . . . Under Richmond's scheme, a successful black, Hispanic, or Oriental entrepreneur from anywhere in the country enjoys an absolute preference over other citizens based solely on their race. We think it obvious that such a program is not narrowly tailored to remedy the effects of prior discrimination.

V

Nothing we say today precludes a state or local entity from taking action to rectify the effects of identified discrimination within its jurisdiction. If the city of Richmond had evidence before it that nonmi-

nority contractors were systematically excluding minority businesses from subcontracting opportunities, it could take action to end the discriminatory exclusion. Where there is a significant statistical disparity between the number of qualified minority contractors willing and able to perform a particular service and the number of such contractors actually engaged by the locality or the locality's prime contractors, an inference of discriminatory exclusion could arise. . . . Under such circumstances, the city could act to dismantle the closed business system by taking appropriate measures against those who discriminate on the basis of race or other illegitimate criteria. . . . In the extreme case, some form of narrowly tailored racial preference might be necessary to break down patterns of deliberate exclusion.

Nor is local government powerless to deal with individual instances of racially motivated refusals to employ minority contractors. Where such discrimination occurs, a city would be justified in penalizing the discriminator and providing appropriate relief to the victim of such discrimination. . . . Moreover, evidence of a pattern of individual discriminatory acts can, if supported by appropriate statistical proof, lend support to a local government's determination that broader remedial relief is justified.

Even in the absence of evidence of discrimination, the city has at its disposal a whole array of race-neutral devices to increase the accessibility of city contracting opportunities to small entrepreneurs of all races. Simplification of bidding procedures, relaxation of bonding requirements, and training and financial aid for disadvantaged entrepreneurs of all races would open the public contracting market to all those who have suffered the effects of past societal discrimination or neglect. Many of the formal barriers to new entrants may be the product of bureaucratic inertia more than actual necessity, and may have a disproportionate effect on the opportunities open to new minority firms. Their elimination or modification would have little detrimental effect on the city's interests and would serve to increase the opportunities available to minority business without classifying individuals on the basis of race. The city may also act to prohibit discrimination in the provision of credit or bonding by local suppliers and banks. Business as usual should not mean business pursuant to the unthinking exclusion of certain members of our society from its rewards.

. . . The city points to no evidence that qualified minority contractors have been passed over for city contracts or subcontracts, either as a group or in any individual case. Under such circumstances, it is simply impossible to say that the city has demonstrated "a strong basis in evidence for its conclusion that remedial action was necessary."

Proper findings in this regard are necessary to define both the scope of the injury and the extent of the remedy necessary to cure its effects. Such findings also serve to assure all citizens that the deviation from the norm of equal treatment of all racial and ethnic groups is a temporary matter, a measure taken in the service of the goal of equality itself. Absent such findings, there is a danger that a racial classification is merely the product of unthinking stereotypes or a form of racial politics. "[I]f there is no duty to attempt either to measure the recovery by the wrong or to distribute that recovery within the injured class in an even-handed way, our history will adequately support a legislative preference for almost any ethnic, religious, or racial group with the political strength to negotiate 'a piece of the action' for its members." *Fullilove*, 448 U.S., at 539 (STEVENS, J., dissenting). Because the city of Richmond has failed to identify the need for remedial action in the awarding of its public construction contracts, its treatment of its citizens on a racial basis violates the dictates of the Equal Protection Clause. Accordingly, the judgment of the Court of Appeals for the Fourth Circuit is

Affirmed.

JUSTICE SCALIA, *concurring in the judgment.*

I agree with much of the Court's opinion and, in particular, with its conclusion that strict scrutiny must be applied to all governmental classification by race, whether or not its asserted purpose is "remedial" or "benign." I do not agree, however, with the Court's dicta suggesting that, despite the Fourteenth Amendment, state and local governments may in some circumstances discriminate on the basis of race in order (in a broad sense) "to ameliorate the effects of past discrimination." The benign purpose of compensating for social disadvantages, whether they have been acquired by reason of prior discrimination or otherwise, can no more be pursued by the illegitimate means of racial discrimination than can other assertedly benign purposes we have repeatedly rejected. . . . The difficulty of overcoming the effects of past discrimination is as nothing compared with the difficulty of eradicating from our society the source of those effects, which is the tendency—fatal to a nation such as ours—to classify and judge men and women on the basis of their country of origin or the color of their skin. A solution to the first problem that aggravates the second is no solution at all. . . . At least where state or local action is at issue, only a social emergency rising to the level of imminent danger to life and limb—for example, a prison race riot, requiring temporary segregation of inmates . . . can justify an exception to the principle embodied in the Fourteenth Amendment that "[o]ur Constitution is color-blind, and neither knows nor tolerates classes among citizens." . . .

We have in some contexts approved the use of racial classifications by the Federal Government to remedy the effects of past discrimination. I do not believe that we must or should extend those holdings to the States. . . . And we have permitted federal courts to prescribe quite severe race-conscious remedies when confronted with egregious and persistent unlawful discrimination, see *e.g., United States* v. *Paradise*, 480 U.S. 149 (1987); *Sheet Metal Workers* v. *EEOC*, 478 U.S. 421 (1986). . . . [H]owever, . . . it is one thing to permit racially based conduct by the Federal Government—whose legislative powers concerning matters of race were explicitly enhanced by the Fourteenth Amendment . . . —and quite another to permit it by the precise entities against whose conduct in matters of race that Amendment was specifically directed. . . .

A sound distinction between federal and state (or local) action based on race rests not only upon the substance of the Civil War Amendments, but upon social reality and governmental theory. It is a simple fact that what Justice Stewart described in *Fullilove* as "the dispassionate objectivity [and] the flexibility that are needed to mold a race-conscious remedy around the single objective of eliminating the effects of past or present discrimination"—political qualities already to be doubted in a national legislature . . . —are substantially less likely to exist at the state or local level. The struggle for racial justice has historically been a struggle by the national society against oppression in the individual States. . . .

In my view there is only one circumstance in which the States may act *by race* to "undo the effects of past discrimination": where that is necessary to eliminate their own maintenance of a system of unlawful racial classification. . . .

In his final book, Professor Bickel wrote:

[A] racial quota derogates the human dignity and individuality of all to whom it is applied; it is invidious in principle as well as in practice. Moreover, it can easily be turned against those it purports to help. The history of the racial quota is a history of subjugation, not beneficence. Its evil lies not in its name, but in its effects: a quota is a divider of society, a creator of castes, and it is all the worse for its racial base, especially in a society desperately striving for an equality that will make race irrelevant. (Bickel, *The Morality of Consent*, at 133.)

Those statements are true and increasingly prophetic. Apart from their societal effects, however, which are "in the aggregate disastrous," *id.*, at 134, it is important not to lose sight of the fact that even "benign" racial quotas have individual victims, whose very real injustice we ignore whenever we deny them enforcement of their right not to be disadvantaged on the basis of race. . . . As Justice Douglas observed: "A DeFunis who is white is entitled to no advantage by virtue of that fact; nor is he subject to any disability, no matter what his race or color. Whatever his race, he had a constitutional right to have his application considered on its individual merits in a racially neutral manner." *DeFunis* v. *Odegaard*, 416 U.S. 312, 337 (1974) (DOUGLAS, J., dissenting). When we depart from this American principle we play with fire, and much more than an occasional *DeFunis, Johnson,* or *Croson* burns.

It is plainly true in our society that blacks have suffered discrimination immeasurably greater than any directed at other racial groups. But those who believe that racial preferences can help to "even the score" display, and reinforce, a manner of thinking by race that was the source of the injustice and that will, if it endures within our society, be the source of more injustice still. The relevant proposition is not that it was blacks, or Jews, or Irish who were discriminated against, but that it was individual men and women, "created equal," who were discriminated against. And the relevant resolve is that that should never happen again. Racial preferences appear to "even the score" (in some small degree) only if one embraces the proposition that our society is appropriately viewed as divided into races, making it right that injustice rendered in the past to a black man should be compensated for by discriminating against a white. Nothing is worth that embrace. Since blacks have been disproportionately disadvantaged by racial discrimination, any race-neutral remedial program aimed at the disadvantaged *as such* will have a disproportionately beneficial impact on blacks. Only such a program, and not one that operates on the basis of race, is in accord with the letter and the spirit of our Constitution.

Since I believe that the appellee here had a constitutional right to have its bid succeed or fail under a decision-making process uninfected with racial bias, I concur in the judgment of the Court.

JUSTICE MARSHALL, *with whom* JUSTICE BRENNAN *and* JUSTICE BLACKMUN *join, dissenting.*

It is a welcome symbol of racial progress when the former capital of the Confederacy acts forthrightly to confront the effects of racial discrimination in its midst. In my view, nothing in the Constitution can be construed to prevent Richmond, Virginia, from allocating a portion of its contracting dollars for businesses owned or controlled by members of minority groups. Indeed, Richmond's set-aside program is indistinguishable in all meaningful respects from—and in fact was patterned upon—the federal set-aside plan which this court upheld in *Fullilove* v. *Klutznick.* . . .

A majority of this Court holds today, however, that the Equal Protection Clause of the Fourteenth Amendment blocks Richmond's initiative. . . . I find deep irony in second-guessing Richmond's judgment on this point. As much as any municipality in the United States. Richmond knows what racial discrimination is; a century of decisions by this and other federal courts has richly documented the city's disgraceful history of public and private racial discrimination. In any event, the Richmond City Council *has* supported its determination that minorities have been wrongly excluded from local construction contracting. Its proof includes statistics showing that minority-owned businesses have received virtually no city contracting dollars and rarely if ever belonged to area trade associations; testimony by municipal officials that discrimination has been widespread in the local construction industry; and the same exhaustive and widely publicized federal studies relied on in *Fullilove*, studies which showed that pervasive discrimination in the Nation's tight-knit construction industry had operated to exclude minorities from public contracting. These are precisely the types of statistical and testimonial evidence which, until today, this Court had credited in cases approving of race-conscious measures designed to remedy past discrimination.

More fundamentally, today's decision marks a deliberate and giant step backward in this Court's affirmative action jurisprudence. Cynical of one municipality's attempt to redress the effects of past racial discrimination in a particular industry, the majority launches a grapeshot attack on race-conscious remedies in general. The majority's unnecessary pronouncements will inevitably discourage or prevent governmental entities, particularly states and localities, from acting to rectify the scourge of past discrimination. This is the harsh reality of the majority's decision, but it is not the Constitution's command. . . .

II

"Agreement upon a means of applying the Equal Protection Clause to an affirmative-action program has eluded this Court every time the issue has come before us." *Wygant* v. *Jackson Board of Education*, 476 U.S. 267, 301 (1986) (MARSHALL, J., dissenting). My view has long been that race-conscious classifications designed to further remedial goals "must serve important governmental objectives and must be substantially related to achievement of those objectives" in order to withstand constitutional scrutiny. . . . Analyzed in terms of this two-prong standard, Richmond's set-aside, like the federal program on which it was modeled, is "plainly constitutional." . . .

A

1

Turning first to the governmental interest inquiry, Richmond has two powerful interests in setting aside a portion of public contracting funds for minority-owned enterprises. The first is the city's interest in eradicating the effects of past racial discrimination. It is far too late in the day to doubt that remedying such discrimination is a compelling, let alone an important, interest. . . .

Richmond has a second compelling interest in setting aside . . . a portion of its contracting dollars. That interest is the prospective one of preventing the city's own spending decisions from reinforcing and perpetuating the exclusionary effects of past discrimination. . . .

The majority pays only lip service to this additional governmental interest. But our decisions have often emphasized the danger of the Government tacitly adopting, encouraging, or furthering racial discrimination even by its own routine operations. . . .

The majority is wrong to trivialize the continuing impact of government acceptance or use of private institutions or structures once wrought by discrimination. When government channels all its contracting funds to a white-dominated community of established contractors whose racial homogeneity is the product of private discrimination, it does more than place its imprimatur on the practices which forged and which continue to define that community. It also provides a measurable boost to those economic entities that have thrived

within it, while denying important economic benefits to those entities which, but for prior discrimination, might well be better qualified to receive valuable government contracts. In my view, the interest in ensuring that the Government does not reflect and reinforce prior private discrimination in dispensing public contracts is every bit as strong as the interest in eliminating private discrimination—an interest which this Court has repeatedly deemed compelling. . . . The more government bestows its rewards on those persons or businesses that were positioned to thrive during a period of private racial discrimination, the tighter the dead-hand grip of prior discrimination becomes on the present and future. Cities like Richmond may not be constitutionally required to adopt set-aside plans. But there can be no doubt that when Richmond acted affirmatively to stem the perpetuation of patterns of discrimination through its own decision making, it served an interest of the highest order.

2

The remaining question with respect to the "governmental interest" prong of equal protection analysis is whether Richmond has proffered satisfactory proof of past racial discrimination to support its twin interests in remediation and in governmental nonperpetuation. . . . [W]e have required that government adduce evidence that, taken as a whole, is sufficient to support its claimed interest and to dispel the natural concern that it acted out of mere "paternalistic stereotyping, not on a careful consideration of modern social conditions." . . .

The varied body of evidence on which Richmond relied provides a "strong," "firm," and "unquestionably legitimate" basis upon which the City Council could determine that the effects of past racial discrimination warranted a remedial and prophylactic governmental response. . . . [T]o suggest that the facts on which Richmond has relied do not provide a sound basis for its finding of past racial discrimination simply blinks credibility.

The majority's perfunctory dismissal of the testimony of Richmond's appointed and elected leaders is also deeply disturbing. These officials—including council members, a former mayor, and the present city manager—asserted that race discrimination in area contracting had been widespread, and that the set-aside ordinance was a sincere and necessary attempt to eradicate the effects of this discrimination. The majority, however, states that where racial classifications are concerned, "simple legislative assurances of good intention cannot suffice." It similarly discounts as minimally probative the City Council's designation of its set-aside plan as remedial. "[B]lind judicial deference to legislative or executive pronouncements," the majority explains, "has no place in equal protection analysis."

No one, of course, advocates "blind judicial deference" to the findings of the City Council or the testimony of city leaders. The majority's suggestion that wholesale deference is what Richmond seeks is a classic straw-man argument. But the majority's trivialization of the testimony of Richmond's leaders is dismaying in a far more serious respect. By disregarding the testimony of local leaders and the judgment of local government, the majority does violence to the very principles of comity within our federal system which this Court has long championed. Local officials, by virtue of their proximity to, and their expertise with, local affairs, are exceptionally well qualified to make determinations of public good "within their respective spheres of authority." The majority, however, leaves any traces of comity behind in its headlong rush to strike down Richmond's race-conscious measure. . . .

When the legislatures and leaders of cities with histories of pervasive discrimination testify that past discrimination has infected one of their industries, armchair cynicism like that exercised by the majority has no place. It may well be that "the autonomy of a state is an essential component of federalism" . . . and that "each State is sovereign within its own domain, governing its citizens and providing for their general welfare," . . . but apparently this is not the case when federal judges, with nothing but their impressions to go on, choose to disbelieve the explanations of these local governments and officials. Disbelief is particularly inappropriate here in light of the fact that appellee Croson, which had the burden of proving unconstitutionality at trial, has at *no point* come forward with *any* direct evidence that the City Council's motives were anything other than sincere. . . .

B

In my judgment, Richmond's set-aside plan also comports with the second prong of the equal protection inquiry, for it is substantially related to the interests it seeks to serve in remedying past discrimination and in ensuring that municipal contract procurement does not perpetuate that discrimination. The most striking aspect of the city's ordinance is the similarity it bears to the "appropriately limited" federal set-aside provision upheld in *Fullilove*. Like the federal provision, Richmond's is limited to five years in duration and was not re-

newed when it came up for reconsideration in 1988. Like the federal provision, Richmond's contains a waiver provision freeing from its subcontracting requirements those nonminority firms that demonstrate that they cannot comply with its provisions. Like the federal provision, Richmond's has a minimal impact on innocent third parties. While the measure affects 30% of *public* contracting dollars, that translates to only 3% of overall Richmond area contracting.

Finally, like the federal provision, Richmond's does not interfere with any vested right of a contractor to a particular contract; instead it operates entirely prospectively. *Ibid.* Richmond's initiative affects only future economic arrangements and imposes only a diffuse burden on nonminority competitors—here, businesses owned or controlled by nonminorities which seek subcontracting work on public construction projects. The plurality in *Wygant* emphasized the importance of this not disrupting the settled and legitimate expectations of innocent parties. . . .

These factors, far from "justify[ing] a preference of any size or duration," are precisely the factors to which this Court looked in *Fullilove*. . . .

III

I would ordinarily end by analysis at this point and conclude that Richmond's ordinance satisfies both the governmental interest and substantial relationship prongs of our Equal Protection Clause analysis. However, I am compelled to add more, for the majority has gone beyond the facts of this case to announce a set of principles which unnecessarily restrict the power of governmental entities to take race-conscious measures to redress the effects of prior discrimination.

A

Today, for the first time, a majority of this Court has adopted strict scrutiny as its standard of Equal Protection Clause review of race-conscious remedial measures. This is an unwelcome development. A profound difference separates governmental actions that seek to remedy the effects of prior racism or to prevent neutral governmental activity from perpetuating the effects of such racism. . . .

Racial classifications "drawn on the presumption that one race is inferior to another or because they put the weight of government behind racial hatred and separatism" warrant the strictest judicial scrutiny because of the very irrelevance of these rationales. By contrast, racial classifications drawn for the purpose of remedying the effects of discrimination that itself was race-based have a highly pertinent basis: the tragic and indelible fact that discrimination against blacks and other racial minorities in this Nation has pervaded our Nation's history and continues to scar our society. As I stated in *Fullilove*: "Because the consideration of race is relevant to remedying the continuing effects of past racial discrimination, and because governmental programs employing racial classifications for remedial purposes can be crafted to avoid stigmatization, . . . such programs should not be subjected to conventional 'strict scrutiny'—scrutiny that is strict in theory, but fatal in fact."

In concluding that remedial classifications warrant no different standard of review under the Constitution than the most brute and repugnant forms of state-sponsored racism, a majority of this Court signals that it regards racial discrimination as largely a phenomenon of the past, and that government bodies need no longer preoccupy themselves with rectifying racial injustice. I, however, do not believe this Nation is anywhere close to eradicating racial discrimination or its vestiges. In constitutionalizing its wishful thinking, the majority today does a grave disservice not only to those victims of past and present racial discrimination in this Nation whom government has sought to assist, but also to this Court's long tradition of approaching issues of race with the utmost sensitivity.

B

I am also troubled by the majority's assertion that, even if it did not believe generally in strict scrutiny of race-based remedial measures, "the circumstances of this case" require this Court to look upon the Richmond City Council's measure with the strictest scrutiny. The sole such circumstance which the majority cites, however, is the fact that blacks in Richmond are a "dominant racial grou[p]" in the city. In support of this characterization of dominance, the majority observed that "blacks comprise approximately 50% of the population of the city of Richmond" and that "[f]ive of the nine seats on the City Council are held by blacks."

While I agree that the numerical and political supremacy of a given racial group is a factor bearing upon the level of scrutiny to be applied, this Court has never held that numerical inferiority, standing alone, makes a racial group "suspect" and thus entitled to strict scrutiny review. Rather, we have identified *other* "traditional indicia of suspectness": whether a group has been "saddled with such disabilities, or subjected to such a history of

purposeful unequal treatment, or relegated to such a position of political powerlessness as to command extraordinary protection from the majoritarian political process."

It cannot seriously be suggested that nonminorities in Richmond have any "history of purposeful unequal treatment." Nor is there any indication that they have any disabilities that have characteristically afflicted those groups this Court has deemed suspect. Indeed, the numerical and political dominance of nonminorities within the State of Virginia and the Nation as a whole provide an enormous political check against the "simple racial politics" at the municipal level which the majority fears. If the majority really believes that groups like Richmond's nonminorities, which comprise approximately half the population but which are outnumbered even marginally in political fora, are deserving of suspect class status for these reasons alone, this Court's decisions denying suspect status to women, see *Craig* v. *Boren*, 429 U.S. 190, 197 (1976), and to persons with below-average incomes, see *San Antonio Independent School Dist.*, [411 U.S. 1] at 28, stand on extremely shaky ground. . . .

In my view, the "circumstances of this case" underscore the importance of *not* subjecting to a strict scrutiny straitjacket the increasing number of cities which have recently come under minority leadership and are eager to rectify, or at least prevent the perpetuation of, past racial discrimination. In many cases, these cities will be the ones with the most in the way of prior discrimination to rectify. Richmond's leaders had just witnessed decades of publicly sanctioned racial discrimination in virtually all walks of life—discrimination amply documented in the decisions of the federal judiciary. This history of "purposefully unequal treatment" forced upon minorities, not imposed by them, should raise an inference that minorities in Richmond had much to remedy—and that the 1983 set-aside was undertaken with sincere remedial goals in mind, not "simple racial politics." . . .

C

Today's decision, finally, is particularly noteworthy for the daunting standard it imposes upon States and localities contemplating the use of race-conscious measures to eradicate the present effects of prior discrimination and prevent its perpetuation. The majority restricts the use of such measures to situations in which a State or locality can put forth "a prima facie case of a constitutional or statutory violation." In so doing, the majority calls into question the validity of the business set-asides which dozens of municipalities across this Nation have adopted on the authority of *Fullilove*.. . . .

IV

The majority today sounds a full-scale retreat from the Court's long-standing solicitude to race-conscious remedial efforts "directed toward deliverance of the century-old promise of equality of economic opportunity." The new and restrictive tests it applies scuttle one city's effort to surmount its discriminatory past, and imperil those of dozens more localities. I, however, profoundly disagree with the cramped vision of the Equal Protection Clause which the majority offers today and with its application of that vision to Richmond Virginia's laudable set-aside plan. The battle against pernicious racial discrimination or its effects is nowhere near won.

I must dissent.

WASHINGTON v. DAVIS
426 U.S. 229; 48 L. Ed. 2d 597; 96 S. Ct. 2040 (1976)

JUSTICE WHITE *delivered the opinion of the Court.*

This case involves the validity of a qualifying test administered to applicants for positions as police officers in the District of Columbia Metropolitan Police Department. The test was sustained by the District Court but invalidated by the Court of Appeals. We are in agreement with the District Court and hence reverse the judgment of the Court of Appeals.

I

This action began on April 10, 1970, when two Negro police officers filed suit against the then Commissioner of the District of Columbia, the Chief of the District's Metropolitan Police Department and the Commissioners of the United States Civil Service Commission. An amended complaint . . . alleged that the promotion policies of the Department were racially discriminatory and sought a declaratory judgment and an injunction. The respondents Harley and Sellers were permitted to intervene, their amended complaint asserting that their applications to become officers in the Department had been rejected, and that the Department's recruiting procedures discriminated on the basis of race against black applicants by a series of practices including, but not limited to, a written personnel test which excluded a disproportionately high number of Negro applicants. These practices were asserted to violate respondents' rights "under the due process clause of the Fifth Amendment to the United States Constitution, under 42 U.S.C. § 1981 and under D.C. Code § 1-320." Defendants answered, and discovery and various other proceedings followed. Respondents then filed a motion for partial summary judgment with respect to the recruiting phase of the case, seeking a declaration that the test administered to those applying to become police officers is "unlawfully discriminatory and therefore in violation of the Due Process Clause of the Fifth Amendment." . . . The District of Columbia defendants, petitioners here, and the federal parties also filed motions for summary judgment with respect to the recruiting aspects of the case asserting that respondents were entitled to relief on neither constitutional nor statutory grounds. The District Court granted petitioner's and denied respondents' motions. . . .

According to the findings and conclusions of the District Court, to be accepted by the Department and to enter an intensive 17-week training program, the police recruit was required to satisfy certain physical and character standards, to be a high school graduate or its equivalent and to receive a grade of at least 40 on "Test 21," which is "an examination that is used generally throughout the federal service," which "was developed by the Civil Service Commission not the Police Department" and which was "designed to test verbal ability, vocabulary, reading and comprehension." . . .

The validity of Test 21 was the sole issue before the court on the motions for summary judgment. The District Court noted that there was no claim of "an intentional discrimination or purposeful discriminatory actions" but only a claim that Test 21 bore no relationship to job performance and "has a highly discriminatory impact in screening out black candidates." 348 F. Supp., at 16. Petitioners' evidence, the District Court said, warranted three conclusions: "(a) The number of black police officers, while substantial, is not proportionate to the population mix of the city. (b) A higher percentage of blacks fail the Test than whites. (c) The Test has not been validated to establish its reliability for measuring subsequent job performance." *Ibid.* This showing was deemed sufficient to shift the burden of proof to the defendants in the action, petitioners here; but the court nevertheless concluded that on the undisputed facts respondents were not entitled to relief. The District Court relied on several factors. Since August 1969, 44% of the new police force recruits had been black; that figure also represented the proportion of blacks on the total force and was roughly equivalent to 20–29-year-old blacks in the 50-mile radius in which the recruiting efforts of the Police Department had been concentrated. It was undisputed that the Department had systematically and affirmatively sought to enroll black officers many of whom passed the test but failed to report for duty. The District Court rejected the assertion that Test 21 was culturally slanted to favor whites and was "satisfied that the undisputable facts prove the test to be reasonably and directly related to the requirements of the police recruit training program and that it is neither so designed nor operates to discriminate against otherwise qualified blacks." 348 F. Supp., at 17. It was thus not necessary to show that Test 21 was not only a useful indicator of training school performance but had also been validated in terms of job performance—"the lack of job performance validation does not defeat the Test, given its direct relationship to recruiting and the valid part it plays in this process." The District Court ultimately concluded that "the proof is wholly lacking that a police officer qualifies on the color of his skin rather than ability" and that the Department "should not be required on this showing to lower standards or to abandon efforts to achieve excellence." 348 F. Supp., at 18.

. . . [R]espondents brought the case to the Court of Appeals claiming that their summary judgment motion, which rested on purely constitutional grounds, should have been granted. The tendered constitutional issue was whether the use of Test 21 invidiously discriminated against Negroes. . . . The Court of Appeals, addressing that issue, announced that it would be guided by *Griggs* v. *Duke Power Co.*, 401 U.S. 424 (1971), a case involving the interpretation and application of Title VII of the Civil Rights Act of 1964, and held that the statutory standards elucidated in that case were to govern the due process question tendered in this one. . . . The court went on to declare that lack of discriminatory intent in designing and administering Test 21 was irrelevant; the critical fact was rather that a far greater proportion of blacks— four times as many—failed the test than did whites. This disproportionate impact, standing alone and without regard to whether it indicated a discriminatory purpose, was held sufficient to establish a constitutional violation, absent proof by petitioners that the test was an adequate measure of job performance in addition to being an indicator of probable success in the training program, a burden which the court ruled petitioners had failed to discharge. That the Department had made substantial efforts to recruit blacks was held beside the point and the fact that the racial distribution of recent hirings and of the Department itself might be roughly equivalent to the racial makeup of the surrounding community, broadly conceived, was put aside as a "comparison [not] material to this appeal." . . . The Court of Appeals, over a dissent, accordingly reversed the judgment of the District Court and directed that respondents' motion for partial summary judgment be granted. . . .

II

Because the Court of Appeals erroneously applied the legal standards applicable to Title VII cases in resolving the constitutional issue before it, we reverse its judgment in respondents' favor. . . .

As the Court of Appeals understood Title VII, employees or applicants proceeding under it need not concern themselves with the employer's possible discriminatory purpose but instead may focus solely on the racially differential impact of the challenged hiring or promotion practices. This is not the constitutional rule. We have never held that the constitutional standard for adjudicating claims of invidious racial discrimination is identical to the standards applicable under Title VII, and we decline to do so today.

The central purpose of the Equal Protection Clause of the Fourteenth Amendment is the prevention of official conduct discriminating on the basis of race. It is also true that the Due Process Clause of the Fifth Amendment contains an equal protection component, prohibiting the United States from invidiously discriminating between individuals or groups. . . . But our cases have not embraced the proposition that a law or other official act, without regard to whether it reflects a racially discriminatory purpose, is unconstitutional *solely* because it has a racially disproportionate impact. . . .

This is not to say that the necessary discriminatory racial purpose must be expressed or appear on the face of the statute, or that a law's disproportionate impact is irrelevant in cases involving Constitution-based claims of racial discrimination. . . . With a prima facie case made out, "the burden of proof shifts to the State to rebut the presumption of unconstitutional act by showing that permissible racially neutral selection criteria and procedures have produced the monochromatic result." *Alexander* v. *Louisiana*, 405 U.S. 625, at 632 (1972). . . .

Necessarily, an invidious discriminatory purpose may often be inferred from the totality of the relevant facts, including the fact, if it is true, that the law bears more heavily on one race than another. It is also not infrequently true that the discriminatory impact . . . may for all practical purposes demonstrate unconstitutionality because in various circumstances the discrimination is very difficult to explain on nonracial grounds. Nevertheless, we have not held that a law, neutral on its face and serving ends otherwise within the power of government to pursue, is invalid under the Equal Protection Clause simply because it may affect a greater proportion of one race than of another. Disproportionate impact is not irrelevant, but it is not the sole touchstone of an invidious racial discrimination forbidden by the Constitution. Standing alone, it does not trigger the rule . . . that racial classifications are to be subjected to the strictest scrutiny and are justifiable only by the weightiest of considerations. . . .

As an initial matter, we have difficulty understanding how a law establishing a racially neutral qualification for employment is nevertheless racially discriminatory and denies "any person equal protection of the laws" simply because a greater proportion of Negroes fail to qualify than members of other racial or ethnic groups. Had respondents, along with all others who had failed Test 21, whether white or black, brought an action claiming that the test denied each of them equal protection of the laws as compared with those who had passed with high enough scores to qualify them as police recruits, it is most unlikely that their challenge would have been sustained. Test 21, which is administered generally to prospective government employees, concededly seeks to ascertain whether those who take it have acquired a particular level of verbal skill; and it is untenable that the Constitution prevents the government from seeking modestly to upgrade the communicative abilities of its employees rather than to be satisfied with some lower level of competence, particularly where the job requires special ability to communicate orally and in writing. Respondents, as Negroes, could no more successfully claim that the test denied them equal protection than could white applicants who also failed. The conclusion would not be different in the face of proof that more Negroes than whites had been disqualified by Test 21. That other Negroes also failed to score well would, alone, not demonstrate that respondents individually were being denied equal protection of the laws by the application of an otherwise valid qualifying test being administered to prospective police recruits.

Nor on the facts of the case before us would the disproportionate impact of Test 21 warrant the conclusion that it is a purposeful device to discriminate against Negroes and hence an infringement of the constitutional rights of respondents as well as other black applicants. Even agreeing with the District Court that the differential racial effect of Test 21 called for further inquiry, we think the District Court correctly held that the affirmative efforts of the Metropolitan Police Department to recruit black officers, the changing racial composition of the recruit classes and of the force in general, and the relationship of the test to the training program negated any inference that the Department discriminated on the basis of race or that "a police officer qualifies on the color of his skin rather than ability." 348 F. Supp., at 18.

Under Title VII, Congress provided that when hiring and promotion practices disqualifying substantially disproportionate numbers of blacks are challenged, discriminatory purpose need not be proved, and that it is an insufficient response to demonstrate some rational basis for the challenged practices. It is necessary, in addition, that they be "validated" in terms of job performance in any one of several ways, perhaps by ascertaining the minimum skill, ability or potential necessary for the position at issue and determining whether the qualifying tests are appropriate for the selection of qualified applicants for the job in question. However this process proceeds, it involves a more probing judicial review of, and less deference to, the seemingly reasonable acts of administrators and executives than is appropriate under the Constitution where special racial impact, without discriminatory purpose, is claimed. We are not disposed to adopt this more rigorous standard for the purposes of applying the Fifth and the Fourteenth Amendments in cases such as this.

A rule that a statute designed to serve neutral ends is nevertheless invalid, absent compelling justification, if in practice it benefits or burdens one race more than another would be far reaching and would raise serious questions about, and perhaps invalidate, a whole range of tax, welfare, public service, regulatory, and licensing statutes that may be more burdensome to the poor and to the average black than to the more affluent white.

Given that rule, such consequences would perhaps be likely to follow. However, in our view, extension of the rule beyond those areas where it is already applicable by reason of statute, such as in the field of public employment, should await legislative prescription. . . .

III

We also hold that the Court of Appeals should have affirmed the judgment of the District Court granting the motions for summary judgment filed by petitioners and the federal parties. Respondents were entitled to relief on neither constitutional nor statutory grounds.

The submission of the defendants in the District Court was that Test 21 complied with all applicable statutory as well as constitutional requirements; and they appear not to have disputed that under the statutes and regulations governing their conduct standards similar to those obtaining under Title VII had to be satisfied. The District Court also assumed (that Title VII standards were to control the case identified) the determinative issue as whether Test 21 was sufficiently job related and proceeded to uphold use of the test because it was "directly related to a determination of whether the applicant possesses sufficient skills requisite to the demands of the curriculum a recruit must master at the police academy." 348 F. Supp., at 17. The Court of Appeals reversed because the relationship between Test 21 and training school success, if demonstrated at all, did not satisfy what it deemed to be the crucial requirement of a direct relationship between performance on Test 21 and performance on the policeman's job.

We agree with petitioners and the federal respondents that this was error. The advisability of the police recruit training course informing the recruit about his upcoming-job, acquainting him with its demands and attempting to impart a modicum of required skills seems conceded. It is also apparent to us, as it was to the District Judge, that some minimum verbal and communicative skill would be very useful, if not essential, to satisfactory progress in the training regimen. . . .

The District Court's accompanying conclusion that Test 21 was in fact directly related to the requirements of the police training program was supported by a validation study, as well as by other evidence of record: [The record includes a validation study of Test 21's relationship to performance in the recruit training program made by D. L. Futransky of the Standards Division, Bureau of Policies and Standards, United States Civil Service Commission] and we are not convinced that this conclusion was erroneous. . . .

JUSTICE BRENNAN, *with whom* JUSTICE MARSHALL *joins, dissenting.*

The Court holds that the job qualification examination (Test 21) . . . does not unlawfully discriminate on the basis of race under either constitutional or statutory standards.

Initially, it seems to me that the Court should not pass on the statutory questions, because they are not presented by this case. . . . As I understand the opinion, the Court . . . holds that Test 21 is job-related under § 3304, but not necessarily under Title VII. But that provision, by the Court's own analysis, is no more in the case than Title VII; respondents' "complaint asserted no claim under § 3304." . . . If it was "plain error" for the Court of Appeals to apply a statutory standard to this case, as the Court asserts . . . then it is unfortunate that the Court does not recognize that it is also plain error to address the statutory issues in Part III of its opinion.

Nevertheless, although it appears unnecessary to reach the statutory questions, I will accept the Court's conclusion that respondents were entitled to summary judgment if they were correct in their statutory arguments, and I would affirm the Court of Appeals because petitioners have failed to prove that Test 21 satisfies the applicable statutory standards. All parties' arguments and both lower court decisions were based on Title VII standards. In this context, I think it wrong to focus on § 3304 to the exclusion of the Title VII standards, particularly because the Civil Service Commission views the job-relatedness standards of Title VII and § 3304 as identical. . . .

But the CSC [Civil Service Commission] instructions cited by the Court do not support the District Court's conclusion. More importantly, the brief filed in this Court by the CSC takes the position that petitioners did not satisfy the burden of proof imposed by the CSC guidelines. It also appears that longstanding regulations of the Equal Employment Opportunity Commission (EEOC)—previously endorsed by this Court—require a result contrary to that reached by the Court. Furthermore, the Court's conclusion is inconsistent with my understanding of the interpretation of Title VII in *Griggs* and *Albermarle.* I do not find this conclusion 'much more sensible' and with all respect I suggest that today's decision has the potential of significantly weakening statutory safeguards against discrimination in employment. . . .

* * *

. . . The CSC maintains that a positive correlation between scores on entrance examinations and the criterion of success in training may establish the job-relatedness of an entrance test—thus relieving an employer from the burden of providing a relationship to job performance after training—but only subject to certain limitations. . . . . Applying its standards the CSC concludes that none of the evidence presented in the District Court established "the appropriateness of using Recruit School Final Averages as the measure of training performance or the relationship of the Recruit School program to the job of a police officer." *Id.*, at 30.

The CSC's standards thus recognize that Test 21 can be validated by a correlation between Test 21 scores and recruits' averages on training examinations only if (1) the training averages predict job performance or (2) the averages are proven to measure performance in job-related training. There is no proof that the recruits' average is correlated with job performance after completion of training. . . . And although a positive relationship to the recruits' average might be sufficient to validate Test 21 if the average were proven to reflect mastery of material on the training curriculum that was in turn demonstrated to be relevant to job performance, the record is devoid of proof in this regard. First, there is no demonstration by petitioners that the training course examinations measure comprehension of the training curriculum: indeed, these examinations do not even appear in the record. Furthermore, the Futransky study simply designated an average of 85 on the examination as a "good" performance and assumed that a recruit with such an average learned the material taught in the training course. Without any further proof of the significance of a score of 85, and there is none in the record, I cannot agree that Test 21 is predictive of "success in training."

II

Today's decision is also at odds with EEOC regulations issued pursuant to explicit authorization in Title VII. 42 U.S.C. § 2000e–12(a). Although the dispute in this case is not within the EEOC's jurisdiction . . . the proper construction of Title VII nevertheless is relevant. Moreover, the 1972 extension of Title VII to public employees gave the same substantive protection to those employees as had previously been accorded in the private sector . . . .

The EEOC regulations require that the validity of a job qualification test be proven by "empirical data demonstrating that the test is predictive of or significantly correlated with important elements of work behavior which comprise or are relevant to the job or jobs for which candidates are being evaluated." . . . This construction of Title VII was approved in *Albemarle*, where we quoted this provision and remarked that "[t]he message of these Guidelines is the same as that of the *Griggs* case." 422 U.S., at 431. . . .

III

The Court also says that its conclusion is not foreclosed by *Griggs* and *Albemarle*, but today's result plainly conflicts with those cases. *Griggs* held that "[i]f an employment practice which operates to exclude Negroes cannot be shown to be *related to job performance,* the practice is prohibited." 401 U.S., at 431. Once a discriminatory impact is shown, the employer carries the burden of proving that the challenged practice "bear[s] a *demonstrable relationship to successful performance of the jobs* for which it was used." . . .

Albemarle read *Griggs* to require that a discriminatory test be validated through proof "by professionally acceptable methods" that it is " 'predictive of or significantly correlated with *important* elements of work behavior *which comprise or are relevant to the job or jobs* for which candidates are being evaluated.' " 422 U.S., at 431. Further, we rejected the employer's attempt to validate a written test by proving that it was related to supervisors' job performance ratings, because there was no demonstration that the ratings accurately reflected job performance. We were unable "to determine whether the criteria *actually* considered were sufficiently related to the [employer's] legitimate interest in job-specific ability to justify a testing system with a racially discriminatory impact." . . . To me, therefore, these cases read Title VII as requiring proof of a significant relationship to job performance to establish the validity of a discriminatory test. . . . Petitioners do not maintain that there is a demonstrated correlation between Test 21 scores and job performance. Moreover, their validity study was unable to discern a significant positive relationship between training averages and job performance. Thus, there is no proof of a correlation—either direct or indirect—between Test 21 and performance of the job of being a police officer. . . .

Today's reduced emphasis on a relationship to job performance is also inconsistent with clearly expressed congressional intent. The Conference Report on the 1972 amendments to Title VII states as follows:

> In any area where the new law does not address itself, or in any areas where a specific contrary intention is not indicated, it was assumed that the present case law as developed by the courts would continue to govern the applicability and construction of Title VII. 118 Cong. Rec. 7166.

The pre-1972 judicial decisions dealing with standardized tests used as job qualification requirements uniformly follow the EEOC regulations discussed above and insist upon proof of a relationship to job performance to prove that a test is job-related. Furthermore, the Court ignores Congress' explicit hostility towards the use of written tests as job-qualification requirements: Congress disapproved the CSC's "use of general ability tests which are not aimed at any direct relationship to specific jobs." . . .

Finally, it should be observed that every federal court, except the District Court in this case, presented with proof identical to that offered to validate Test 21 has reached a conclusion directly opposite to that of the Court today. Sound policy considerations support the view that, at a minimum, petitioners should have been required to prove that the police training examinations either measure job-related skills or predict job performance. Where employers try to validate written qualification tests by proving a correlation with written examinations in a training course, there is a substantial danger that people who have good verbal skills will achieve high scores on both tests due to verbal ability, rather than "job-specific ability." As a result, employers could validate any entrance examination that measures only verbal ability by giving another written test that measures verbal ability at the end of a training course. Any contention that the resulting correlation between examination scores would be evidence that the initial test is "job-related" is plainly erroneous. It seems to me, however, that the Court's holding in this case can be read as endorsing this dubious proposition. Today's result will prove particularly unfortunate if it is extended to govern Title VII cases. . . .

WARDS COVE PACKING CO., INC., ET AL. v. FRANK ATONIO, ET AL.
___ U.S. ___; ___ L. Ed. 2d ___; 109 S. Ct. 2115 (1989)

JUSTICE WHITE *delivered the opinion of the Court.*

Title VII of the Civil Rights Act of 1964 makes it an unfair employment practice for an employer to discriminate against any individual with respect to hiring or the terms and conditions of employment because of such individual's race, color, religion, sex, or national origin; or to limit, segregate, or classify his employees in ways that would adversely affect any employee because of the employee's race, color, religion, sex, or national origin. *Griggs* v. *Duke Power Co.*, 401 U.S. 424, 431 (1971), construed Title VII to proscribe "not only overt discrimination but also practices that are fair in form but discriminatory in practice." Under this basis for liability, which is known as the "disparate impact" theory and which is involved in this case, a facially neutral employment practice may be deemed violative of Title VII without evidence of the employer's subjective intent to discriminate that is required in a "disparate treatment" case.

I

The claims before us are disparate-impact claims, involving the employment practices of petitioners, two companies that operate salmon canneries in . . . Alaska. The canneries operate only during the salmon runs in the summer months. They are inoperative and vacant for the rest of the year. In May or June of each year, a few weeks before the salmon runs begin, workers arrive and prepare the equipment and facilities for the canning operation. Most of these workers possess a variety of skills. When salmon runs are about to begin, the workers who will operate the cannery lines arrive, remain as long as there are fish to can, and then depart. The canneries are then closed down, winterized, and left vacant until the next spring. During the off season, the companies employ only a small number of individuals at their headquarters in Seattle and Astoria, Oregon, plus some employees at the winter shipyard in Seattle. . . .

Jobs at the canneries are of two general types: "cannery jobs" on the cannery line, which are unskilled positions; and "noncannery jobs," which fall into a variety of classifications. Most noncannery jobs are classified as skilled positions. Cannery jobs are filled predominantly by nonwhites, Filipinos, and Alaska Natives. The Filipinos are hired through and dispatched by Local 37 of the International Longshoremen Workers Union pursuant to a hiring hall agreement with the Local. The Alaska Natives primarily reside in villages near the remote cannery locations. Noncannery jobs are filled with predominantly white workers, who are hired during the winter months from the companies' offices in Washington and Oregon. Virtually all of the noncannery jobs pay more than cannery positions. The predominantly white noncannery workers and the predominantly nonwhite cannery employees live in separate dormitories and eat in separate mess halls.

In 1974, respondents, a class of nonwhite cannery workers who were (or had been) employed at the canneries, brought this Title VII action against petitioners. Respondents alleged that a variety of petitioners' hiring/promotion practices—*e.g.*, nepotism, a rehire preference, a lack of objective hiring criteria, separate hiring channels, a practice of not promoting from within—were responsible for the racial stratification of the work force, and had denied them and other nonwhites employment as noncannery workers on the basis of race. Respondents also complained of petitioners' racially segregated housing and dining facilities. All of respondents' claims were advanced under both the disparate-treatment and disparate-impact theories of Title VII liability.

The District Court held a bench trial, after which it entered 172 findings of fact . . . [and] then rejected all of respondents' disparate-treatment claims. It also rejected the disparate-impact challenges involving the subjective employment criteria used by petitioners to fill these noncannery positions, on the ground that those criteria were not subject to attack under a disparate-impact theory. *Id.*, at I-102. Petitioner's "objective" employment practices (*e.g.*, an English language requirement, alleged nepotism in hiring, failure to post noncannery openings, the rehire preference, etc.) were found to be subject to challenge under the disparate-impact theory, but these claims were rejected for failure of proof. Judgment was entered for petitioners.

On appeal, a panel of the Ninth Circuit affirmed, but that decision was vacated when the Court of Appeals agreed to hear the case en banc.

The en banc hearing was ordered to settle an intracircuit conflict over the question whether subjective hiring practices could be analyzed under a disparate-impact model; the Court of Appeals held—as this Court subsequently ruled . . . —that disparate-impact analysis could be applied to subjective hiring practices. The Ninth Circuit also concluded that in such a case, "[o]nce the plaintiff class has shown disparate-impact caused by specific, identifiable employment practices or criteria, the burden shifts to the employer," to "prov[e the] business necessity" of the challenged practice. Because the en banc holding on subjective employment practices reversed the District Court's contrary ruling, the en banc Court of Appeals remanded the case to a panel for further proceedings.

On remand, the panel applied the en banc ruling to the facts of this case. It held that respondents had made out a prima facie case of disparate impact in hiring for both skilled and unskilled noncannery positions. The panel remanded the case for further proceedings, instructing the District Court that it was the employer's burden to prove that any disparate impact caused by its hiring and employment practices was justified by business necessity. Neither the en banc court nor the panel disturbed the District Court's rejection of the disparate-treatment claims.

Petitioners [then] sought review of the Court of Appeals' decision in this Court. . . .

II

In holding that respondents had made out a prima facie case of disparate impact, the Court of Appeals relied solely on respondents' statistics showing a high percentage of nonwhite workers in the cannery jobs and a low percentage of such workers in the noncannery positions. Although statistical proof can alone make out a prima facie case, . . . the Court of Appeals' ruling here misapprehends our precedents and the purposes of Title VII, and we therefore reverse.

"There can be no doubt," . . . "that the . . . comparison . . . misconceived the role of statistics in employment discrimination cases." The "proper comparison [is] between the racial composition of [the at-issue jobs] and the racial composition of the qualified . . . population in the relevant labor market." It is such a comparison—between the racial composition of the qualified persons in the labor market and the persons holding at-issue jobs—that generally forms the proper basis for the initial inquiry in a disparate impact case. Alternatively, in cases where such labor market statistics will be difficult if not impossible to ascertain, we have recognized that certain other statistics–such as measures indicating the racial composition of "otherwise-qualified applicants" for at-issue jobs—are equally probative for this purpose. . . .

It is clear to us that the Court of Appeals' acceptance of the comparison between the racial composition of the cannery work force and that of the noncannery work force, as probative of a prima facie case of disparate impact in the selection of the latter group of workers, was flawed for several reasons. Most obviously, with respect to the skilled noncannery jobs at issue here, the cannery work force in no way reflected "the pool of *qualified* job applicants" or the "*qualified* population in the labor force." Measuring alleged discrimination in the selection of accountants, managers, boat captains, electricians, doctors, and engineers—and the long list of other "skilled" noncannery positions found to exist by the District Court . . . by comparing the number of nonwhites occupying these jobs to the number of nonwhites filling cannery worker positions is nonsensical. If the absence of minorities holding such skilled positions is due to a dearth of qualified nonwhite applicants (for reasons that are not petitioners' fault), petitioners' selection methods or employment practices cannot be said to have had a "disparate impact" on nonwhites . . . .

The Court of Appeals also erred with respect to the unskilled noncannery positions. Racial imbalance in one segment of an employer's work force does not, without more, establish a prima facie case of disparate impact with respect to the selection of workers for the employer's other positions, even where workers for the different positions may have somewhat fungible skills (as is arguably the case for cannery and unskilled noncannery workers). As long as there are no barriers or practices deterring qualified nonwhites from applying for noncannery positions, if the percentage of selected applicants who are nonwhite is not significantly less than the percentage of qualified applicants who are nonwhite, the employer's selection mechanism probably does not operate with a disparate impact on minorities. . . .

III

Since the statistical disparity relied on by the Court of Appeals did not suffice to make out a prima facie case, any inquiry by us into whether the specific challenged employment practices of petition-

ers caused that disparity is pretermitted, as is any inquiry into whether the disparate impact that any employment practice may have had was justified by business considerations. Because we remand for further proceedings, however, on whether a prima facie case of disparate impact has been made in defensible fashion in this case, we address two other challenges petitioners have made to the decision of the Court of Appeals.

A

* * *

Our disparate-impact cases have always focused on the impact of *particular* hiring practices on employment opportunities for minorities. Just as an employer cannot escape liability under Title VII by demonstrating that, "at the bottom line," his work force is racially balanced (where particular hiring practices may operate to deprive minorities of employment opportunities . . .), a Title VII plaintiff does not make out a case of disparate impact simply by showing that, "at the bottom line," there is racial *imbalance* in the work force. As a general matter, a plaintiff must demonstrate that it is the application of a specific or particular employment practice that has created the disparate impact under attack. Such a showing is an integral part of the plaintiff's prima facie case in a disparate-impact suit under Title VII.

Here, respondents have alleged that several "objective" employment practices (*e.g.*, nepotism, separate hiring channels, rehire preferences), as well as the use of "subjective decision making" to select noncannery workers, have had a disparate impact on nonwhites. Respondents base this claim on statistics that allegedly show a disproportionately low percentage of nonwhites in the at-issue positions. However, even if on remand respondents can show that nonwhites are underrepresented in the at-issue jobs in a manner that is acceptable under the standards set forth in Part II, *supra*, this alone will *not* suffice to make out a prima facie case of disparate impact. Respondents will also have to demonstrate that the disparity they complain of is the result of one or more of the employment practices that they are attacking here, specifically showing that each challenged practice has a significantly disparate impact on employment opportunities for whites and nonwhites. To hold otherwise would result in employers being potentially liable for "the myriad of innocent causes that may lead to statistical imbalances in the composition of their work forces." . . .

Some will complain that this specific causation requirement is unduly burdensome on Title VII plaintiffs. But liberal civil discovery rules give plaintiffs broad access to employers' records in an effort to document their claims. Also, employers falling within the scope of the Uniform Guidelines on Employee Selection Procedures . . . are required to "maintain . . . records or other information which will disclose the impact which its tests and other selection procedures have upon employment opportunities of persons by identifiable race, sex, or ethnic group[s.]" . . . Plaintiffs as a general matter will have the benefit of these tools to meet their burden of showing a causal link between challenged employment practices and racial imbalances in the work force; respondents presumably took full advantage of these opportunities to build their case before the trial in the District Court was held.

Consequently, on remand, the courts below are instructed to require, as part of respondents' prima facie case, a demonstration that specific elements of the petitioners' hiring process have a significantly disparate impact on nonwhites.

B

If, on remand, respondents meet the proof burdens outlined above, and establish a prima facie case of disparate impact with respect to any of petitioners' employment practices, the case will shift to any business justification petitioners offer for their use of these practices. . . .

(1)

Though we have phrased the query differently in different cases, it is generally well-established that at the justification stage of such a disparate impact case, the dispositive issue is whether a challenged practice serves, in a significant way, the legitimate employment goals of the employer. . . . . The touchstone of this inquiry is a reasoned review of the employer's justification for his use of the challenged practice. A mere insubstantial justification in this regard will not suffice, because such a low standard of review would permit discrimination to be practiced through the use of spurious, seemingly neutral employment practices. At the same time, though, there is no requirement that the challenged practice be "essential" or "indispensable" to the employer's business for it to pass muster: this degree of scrutiny would be almost impossible for most employers to meet, and would result in a host of evils we have identified above.

In this phase, the employer carries the burden of producing evidence of a business justification for his employment practice. The burden of persuasion, however, remains with the disparate-impact plaintiff. To the extent that the Ninth Circuit held otherwise in its en banc decision in this case, . . . or in the panel's decision on remand, suggesting that the persuasion burden should shift to the petitioners once the respondents established a prima facie case of disparate impact—its decisions were erroneous. "[T]he ultimate burden of proving that discrimination against a protected group has been caused by a specific employment practice remains with the plaintiff *at all times*" . . . (emphasis added). This rule conforms with the usual method for allocating persuasion and production burdens in the federal courts . . . and more specifically, it conforms to the rule in disparate-treatment cases that the plaintiff bears the burden of disproving an employer's assertion that the adverse employment action or practice was based solely on a legitimate neutral consideration. . . . We acknowledge that some of our earlier decisions can be read as suggesting otherwise . . . . But to the extent that those cases speak of an employers' "burden of proof" with respect to a legitimate business justification defense, . . . they should have been understood to mean an employer's production—but not persuasion—burden. . . . . The persuasion burden here must remain with the plaintiff, for it is he who must prove that it was "because of such individual's race, color," etc., that he was denied a desired employment opportunity. . . .

IV

For the reasons given above, the judgment of the Court of Appeals is reversed, and the case is remanded for further proceedings consistent with this opinion.

It is so ordered.

JUSTICE STEVENS, *with whom* JUSTICE BRENNAN, JUSTICE MARSHALL, *and* JUSTICE BLACKMUN *join, dissenting.*

Fully 18 years ago, this Court unanimously held that Title VII of the Civil Rights Act of 1964 prohibits employment practices that have discriminatory effects as well as those that are intended to discriminate. *Griggs* v. *Duke Power Co.,* 401 U.S. 424 (1971). Federal courts and agencies consistently have enforced that interpretation, thus promoting our national goal of eliminating barriers that define economic opportunity not by aptitude and ability but by race, color, national origin, and other traits that are easily identified but utterly irrelevant to one's qualification for a particular job. Regrettably, the Court retreats from these efforts in its review of an interlocutory judgment respecting the "peculiar facts" of this lawsuit. Turning a blind eye to the meaning and purpose of Title VII, the majority's opinion perfunctorily rejects a long-standing rule of law and underestimates the probative value of evidence of a racially stratified work force. I cannot join this latest sojourn into judicial activism.

I

I would have thought it superfluous to recount at this late date the development of our Title VII jurisprudence, but the majority's facile treatment of settled law necessitates such a primer. This Court initially considered the meaning of Title VII in *Griggs* v. *Duke Power Co.*, 401 U.S. 424 (1971), in which a class of utility company employees challenged the conditioning of entry into higher paying jobs upon a high school education or passage of two written tests. Despite evidence that "these two requirements operated to render ineligible a markedly disproportionate number of Negroes," the Court of Appeals had held that because there was no showing of an intent to discriminate on account of race, there was no Title VII violation. Chief Justice Burger's landmark opinion established that an employer may violate the statute even when acting in complete good faith without any invidious intent. Focusing on § 703(a)(2), he explained:

> The objective of Congress in the enactment of Title VII is plain from the language of the statute. It was to achieve equality of employment opportunities and remove barriers that have operated in the past to favor an identifiable group of white employees over other employees. Under the Act, practices, procedures, or tests neutral on their face, and even neutral in terms of intent, cannot be maintained if they operate to "freeze" the status quo of prior discriminatory employment practices. *Griggs*, 401 U.S., at 429–430.

The opinion in *Griggs* made it clear that a neutral practice that operates to exclude minorities is nevertheless lawful if it serves a valid business purpose. "The touchstone is business necessity," the Court stressed. Because "Congress directed the thrust of the Act to the *consequences* of employment practices, not simply the motivation[,] . . . Congress has placed on the employer the burden of showing that any given requirement must have a manifest relationship to the employment in question" (emphasis in original). Congress has de-

clined to act—as the Court now sees fit—to limit the reach of this "disparate impact" theory, . . . indeed it has extended its application. This approval lends added force to the *Griggs* holding. . . . .

Decisions of this Court and other federal courts repeatedly have recognized that while the employer's burden in a disparate treatment case is simply one of coming forward with evidence of legitimate business purpose, its burden in a disparate impact case is proof of an affirmative defense of business necessity. Although the majority's opinion blurs that distinction, thoughtful reflection on common-law pleading principles clarifies the fundamental differences between the two types of "burdens of proof." In the ordinary civil trial, the plaintiff bears the burden of persuading the trier of fact that the defendant has harmed her. . . . . The defendant may undercut plaintiff's efforts both by confronting plaintiff's evidence during her case in chief and by submitting countervailing evidence during its own case. But if the plaintiff proves the existence of the harmful act, the defendant can escape liability only by persuading the factfinder that the act was justified or excusable. . . . The plaintiff in turn may try to refute this affirmative defense. Although the burdens of producing evidence regarding the existence of harm or excuse thus shift between the plaintiff and the defendant, the burden of proving either proposition remains throughout on the party asserting it.

In a disparate treatment case there is no "discrimination" within the meaning of Title VII unless the employer intentionally treated the employee unfairly because of race. Therefore, the employee retains the burden of proving the existence of intent at all times. If there is direct evidence of intent, the employee may have little difficulty persuading the factfinder that discrimination has occurred. But in the likelier event that intent has to be established by inference, the employee may resort to the *McDonnell/Burdine* [*McDonnell Douglas Corp.* v. *Green*, 411 U.S. 792, (1973) and *Texas Dept. of Community Affairs* v. *Burdine*, 450 U.S. 248 (1981)] inquiry. In either instance, the employer may undermine the employee's evidence but has no independent burden of persuasion.

In contrast, intent plays no role in the disparate impact inquiry. The question, rather, is whether an employment practice has a significant, adverse effect on an identifiable class of workers—regardless of the cause or motive for the practice. The employer may attempt to contradict the factual basis for this effect; that is, to prevent the employee from establishing a prima facie case. But when an employer is faced with sufficient proof of disparate impact, its only recourse is to justify the practice by explaining why it is necessary to the operation of business. Such a justification is a classic example of an affirmative defense.

Failing to explore the interplay between these distinct orders of proof, the Court announces that our frequent statements that the employer shoulders the burden of proof respecting business necessity "should have been understood to mean an employer's production—but not persuasion—burden." Our opinion always have emphasized that in a disparate impact case the employer's burden is weighty. "The touchstone," the Court said in *Griggs*, "is business necessity." . . . I am thus astonished to read that the "touchstone of this inquiry is a reasoned review of the employer's justification for his use of the challenged practice. . . . [T]here is no requirement that the challenged practice be . . . 'essential.' " This casual—almost summary—rejection of the statutory construction that developed in the wake of *Griggs* is most disturbing. I have always believed that the *Griggs* opinion correctly reflected the intent of the Congress that enacted Title VII. . . .

Also troubling is the Court's apparent redefinition of the employees' burden of proof in a disparate impact case. No prima facie case will be made, it declares, unless the employees " 'isolat[e] and identif[y] the specific employment practices that are allegedly responsible for any observed statistical disparities.' " . . . This additional proof requirement is unwarranted. It is elementary that a plaintiff cannot recover upon proof of injury alone; rather, the plaintiff must connect the injury to an act of the defendant in order to establish prima facie that the defendant is liable. . . . Thus in a disparate impact case, proof of numerous questionable employment practices ought to fortify an employee's assertion that the practices caused racial disparities. Ordinary principles of fairness require that Title VII actions be tried like "any lawsuit." . . . The changes the majority makes today, tipping the scales in favor of employers, are not faithful to those principles. . . .

III

The majority's opinion begins with recognition of the settled rule that "a facially neutral employment practice may be deemed violative of Title VII without evidence of the employer's subjective intent to discriminate that is required in a 'disparate treatment' case." It then departs from the body of law engendered by this disparate impact theory, reformulating the order of proof and the weight of the parties' burdens. Why the Court undertakes these unwise changes in elementary and eminently fair rules is a mystery to me.

I respectfully dissent.

JUSTICE BLACKMUN, *with whom* JUSTICE BRENNAN *and* JUSTICE MARSHALL *join, dissenting.*

. . . Today a bare majority of the Court takes three major strides backwards in the battle against race discrimination. It reaches out to make last Term's plurality opinion in *Watson* v. *Fort Worth Bank and Trust*, 487 U.S. ___ (1988), the law, thereby upsetting the long-standing distribution of burdens of proof in Title VII disparate-impact cases. It bars the use of internal workforce comparisons in the making of a prima facie case of discrimination, even where the structure of the industry in question renders any other statistical comparison meaningless. And it requires practice-by-practice statistical proof of causation, even where, as here, such proof would be impossible . . . .

. . . The salmon industry as described by this record takes us back to the kind of overt and institutionalized discrimination we have not dealt with in years: a total residential and work environment organized on principles of racial stratification and segregation, which . . . resembles a plantation economy. . . . This industry long has been characterized by a taste for discrimination of the old-fashioned sort: a preference for hiring nonwhites to fill its lowest-level positions, on the condition that they stay there. The majority's legal rulings essentially immunize these practices from attack under a Title VII disparate-impact analysis.

Sadly, this comes as no surprise. One wonders whether the majority still believes that race discrimination—or, more accurately, race discrimination against nonwhites—is a problem in our society, or even remembers that it ever was. . . .

JUSTICE KENNEDY *delivered the opinion of the Court.*

In this case we consider important issues respecting the meaning and coverage of one of our oldest civil rights statutes, 42 U.S.C. § 1981.

I

Petitioner Brenda Patterson, a black woman, was employed by respondent McLean Credit Union as a teller and a file coordinator, commencing in May 1972. In July 1982, she was laid off. After the termination, petitioner commenced this action in District Court. She alleged that respondent, in violation of 42 U.S.C. § 1981, had harassed her, failed to promote her to an intermediate accounting clerk position, and then discharged her, all because of her race. Petitioner also claimed this conduct amounted to an intentional infliction of emotional distress, actionable under North Carolina tort law.

The District Court determined that a claim for racial harassment is not actionable under § 1981 and declined to submit that part of the case to the jury. The jury did receive and deliberate upon petitioner's § 1981 claims based on alleged discrimination in her discharge and the failure to promote her, and it found for respondent on both claims. As for petitioner's state law claim, the District Court directed a verdict for respondent on the ground that the employer's conduct did not rise to the level of outrageousness required to state a claim for intentional infliction of emotional distress under applicable standards of North Carolina law.

In the Court of Appeals, petitioner raised two matters which are relevant here. First, she challenged the District Court's refusal to submit to the jury her § 1981 claim based on racial harassment. Second, she argued that the District Court erred in instructing the jury that in order to prevail on her § 1981 claim of discriminatory failure to promote, she must show that she was better qualified than the white employee who she alleges was promoted in her stead. The Court of Appeals affirmed.

. . . After oral argument on these issues, we requested the parties to brief and argue an additional question:

"Whether or not the interpretation of 42 U.S.C. § 1981 adopted by this Court in *Runyon* v. *McCrary*, 427 U.S. 160 (1976), should be reconsidered."

We now decline to overrule our decision in *Runyon* v. *McCrary.* We hold further that racial harassment relating to the conditions of employment is not actionable under § 1981 because that provision does not apply to conduct which occurs after the formation of a contract and which does not interfere with the right to enforce established contract obligations. Finally, we hold that the District Court erred in instructing the jury regarding petitioner's burden in proving her discriminatory promotion claim.

II

In *Runyon,* the Court considered whether § 1981 prohibits private schools from excluding children who are qualified for admission, solely on the basis of race. We held that § 1981 did prohibit such conduct, noting that it was already well established in prior decisions that § 1981 "prohibits racial discrimination in the making and enforcement of private contracts." . . . Some Members of this Court believe that *Runyon* was decided incorrectly, and others consider it correct on its own footing, but the question before us is whether it ought now to be overturned. We conclude after reargument that *Runyon* should not be overruled, and we now reaffirm that § 1981 prohibits racial discrimination in the making and enforcement of private contracts.

The Court has said often and with great emphasis that "the doctrine of *stare decisis* is of fundamental importance to the rule of law." . . . Although we have cautioned that "*stare decisis* is a principle of policy and not a mechanical formula of adherence to the latest decision," it is indisputable that *stare decisis* is a basic self-governing principle within the Judicial Branch, which is entrusted with the sensitive and difficult task of fashioning and preserving a jurisprudential system that is not based upon "an arbitrary discretion." The Federalist, No. 78. . . .

Our precedents are not sacrosanct, for we have overruled prior decisions where the necessity and propriety of doing so has been established. Nonetheless, we have held that "any departure from the doctrine of *stare decisis* demands special justification." We have said also that the burden borne by the party advocating the abandonment of an established precedent is greater where the Court is asked to overrule a point of statutory construction. Considerations of *stare decisis* have special force in the area of statutory interpretation, for here, unlike in the context of constitutional interpretation, the legislative power is implicated, and Congress remains free to alter what we have done. . . .

We conclude, upon direct consideration of the issue, that no special justification has been shown for overruling *Runyon*. In cases where statutory precedents have been overruled, the primary reason for the court's shift in position has been the intervening development of the law, through either the growth of judicial doctrine or further action taken by Congress. Where such changes have removed or weakened the conceptual underpinnings from the prior decision, . . . or where the later law has rendered the decision irreconcilable with competing legal doctrines or policies, . . . the Court has not hesitated to overrule an earlier decision. Our decision in *Runyon* has not been undermined by subsequent changes or development in the law. . . .

. . . [I]t has sometimes been said that a precedent becomes more vulnerable as it becomes outdated and after being " 'tested by experience, has been found to be inconsistent with the sense of justice or with social welfare.' " Whatever the effect of this consideration may be in statutory cases, it offers no support for overruling *Runyon*. In recent decades, state and federal legislation has been enacted to prohibit private racial discrimination in many aspects of our society. Whether *Runyon*'s interpretation of § 1981 as prohibiting racial discrimination in the making and enforcement of private contracts is right or wrong as an original matter, it is certain that it is not inconsistent with the prevailing sense of justice in this country. To the contrary, *Runyon* is entirely consistent with our society's deep commitment to the eradication of discrimination based on a person's race or the color of his or her skin. . . .

We decline to overrule *Runyon* and acknowledge that its holding remains the governing law in this area.

III

Our conclusion that we should adhere to our decision in *Runyon* that § 1981 applies to private conduct is not enough to decide this case. We must decide also whether the conduct of which petitioner complains falls within one of the enumerated rights protected by § 1981.

A

Section 1981 reads as follows:

> All persons within the jurisdiction of the United States shall have the same right in every State and Territory to make and enforce contracts, to sue, be parties, give evidence, and to the full and equal benefit of all laws and proceedings for the security of persons and property as is enjoyed by white citizens, and shall be subject to like punishment, pains, penalties, taxes, licenses, and exactions of every kind, and to no other.

The most obvious feature of the provision is the restriction of its scope to forbidding discrimination in the "mak[ing] and enforce[ment]" of contracts alone. Where an alleged act of discrimination does not involve the impairment of one of these specific rights, § 1981 provides no relief. Section 1981 cannot be construed as a general proscription of racial discrimination in all aspects of contract relations, for it expressly prohibits discrimination only in the making and enforcement of contracts. . . .

By its plain terms, the relevant provision in § 1981 protects two rights: "the same right . . . to make . . . contracts" and "the same right . . . to . . . enforce contracts." The first of these protections extends only to the formation of a contract, but not to problems that may arise later from the conditions of continuing employment. The statute prohibits, when based on race, the refusal to enter into a contract with someone, as well as the offer to make a contract only on discriminatory terms. But the right to make contracts does not extend, as a matter of either logic of semantics, to conduct by the employer after the contract relation has been established, including breach of the terms of the contract or imposition of discriminatory working conditions. Such postformation conduct does not involve the right to make a contract, but rather implicates the performance of established contract obligations and the conditions of continuing employment, matters more naturally governed by state contract law and Title VII. . . .

The second of these guarantees, "the same right . . . to . . . enforce contracts . . . as is enjoyed by white citizens," embraces protection of a legal process, and of a right of access to legal process, that will address and resolve contract-law claims without regard to race. In this respect, it prohibits discrimination that infects the legal process in ways that prevent one from enforcing contract rights, by reason of his or her race, and this is so whether this discrimination is attributed to a statute or simply to existing practices. . . .

B

Applying these principles to the case before us, we agree with the Court of Appeals that petitioner's racial harassment claim is not actionable under § 1981. Petitioner has alleged that during her employment with respondent, she was subjected to various forms of racial harassment from her supervisor. As summarized by the Court of Appeals, petitioner testified that

> [her supervisor] periodically stared at her for several minutes at a time; that he gave her too many tasks, causing her to complain that she was under too much pressure: that among the tasks given her were sweeping and dusting, jobs not given to white employees. On one occasion, she testified, [her supervisor] told [her] that blacks are known to work slower than whites. According to [petitioner, her supervisor] also criticized her in staff meetings while not similarly criticizing white employees.

Petitioner also alleges that she was passed over for promotion, not offered training for higher-level jobs, and denied wage increases, all because of her race.

With the exception perhaps of her claim that respondent refused to promote her to a position as an accountant, none of the conduct which petitioner alleges as part of the racial harassment against her involves either a refusal to make a contract with her or the impairment of her ability to enforce her established contract rights. Rather, the conduct which petitioner labels as actionable racial harassment is postformation conduct by the employer relating to the terms and conditions of continuing employment. . . . [I]t is plain to us that what petitioner is attacking are the conditions of her employment.

This type of conduct, reprehensible though it be if true, is not actionable under § 1981, which covers only conduct at the initial formation of the contract and conduct which impairs the right to enforce contract obligations through legal process. Rather, such conduct is actionable under the more expansive reach of Title VII of the Civil Rights Act of 1964. . . .

Interpreting § 1981 to cover postformation conduct unrelated to an employee's right to enforce her contract, such as incidents relating to the conditions of employment, is not only inconsistent with that statute's limitation to the making and enforcement of contracts, but would also undermine the detailed and well-crafted procedures for conciliation and resolution of Title VII claims. In Title VII, Congress set up an elaborate administrative procedure, implemented through the EEOC [Equal Employment Opportunity Commission], that is designed to assist in the investigation of claims of racial discrimination in the workplace and to work towards the resolution of these claims through conciliation rather than litigation. . . . Only after these procedures have been exhausted, and the plaintiff has obtained a "right to sue" letter from the EEOC, may she bring a Title VII action in court. Section 1981, by contrast, provides no administrative review or opportunity for conciliation.

Where conduct is covered by both § 1981 and Title VII, the detailed procedures of Title VII are rendered a dead letter, as the plaintiff is free to pursue a claim by bringing suit under § 1981 without resort to those statutory prerequisites. We agree that, after *Runyon*, there is some necessary overlap between Title VII and § 1981, and that where the statutes do in fact overlap we are not at liberty "to infer any positive preference for one over the other." We should be reluctant, however, to read an earlier statute broadly where the result is to circumvent the detailed remedial scheme constructed in a later statute. That egregious racial harassment of employees is forbidden by a clearly applicable law (Title VII), moreover, should lessen the temptation for this Court to twist the interpretation of another statute (§ 1981) to cover the same conduct. In the particular case before us, we do not know for certain why petitioner chose to pursue only remedies under § 1981, and not under Title VII. But in any event, the availability of the latter statute should deter us from a tortuous construction of the former statute to cover this type of claim.

By reading § 1981 not as a general proscription of racial discrimination in all aspects of contract relations, but as limited to the enumerated rights within its express protection, specifically the right to make and enforce contracts, we may preserve the integrity of Title VII's procedures without sacrificing any significant coverage of the civil rights laws. . . .

V

The law now reflects society's consensus that discrimination based on the color of one's skin is a profound wrong of tragic dimension. Neither our words nor our decisions should be interpreted as signaling one inch of retreat from Congress' policy to forbid discrimination in the private, as well as the public, sphere. Nevertheless, in the area of private discrimination, to which the ordinance of the

Constitution does not extend, our role is limited to interpreting what Congress may do and has done. The statute before us, which is only one part of Congress' extensive civil rights legislation, does not cover the acts of harassment alleged here.

In sum, we affirm the Court of Appeals' dismissal of petitioner's racial harassment claim as not actionable under § 1981. The Court of Appeals erred, however, in holding that petitioner could succeed in her discriminatory promotion claim under § 1981 only by proving that she was better qualified for the position of intermediate accounting clerk than the white employee who in fact was promoted. The judgment of the Court of Appeals is therefore vacated insofar as it relates to petitioner's discriminatory promotion claim, and the case is remanded for further proceedings consistent with this opinion.

It is so ordered.

JUSTICE BRENNAN, *with whom* JUSTICE MARSHALL *and* JUSTICE BLACKMUN *join, and with whom* JUSTICE STEVENS *joins as to Parts II-B, II-C, and III, concurring in the judgment in part and dissenting in part.*

What the Court declines to snatch away with one hand, it takes with the other. Though the Court today reaffirms § 1981's applicability to private conduct, it simultaneously gives this landmark civil rights statute a needlessly cramped interpretation. The Court has to strain hard to justify this choice to confine § 1981 within the narrowest possible scope, selecting the most pinched reading of the phrase "same right to make a contract," ignoring powerful historical evidence about the Reconstruction Congress' concerns, and bolstering its parsimonious rendering by reference to a statute enacted nearly a century after § 1981, and plainly not intended to affect its reach. When it comes to deciding whether a civil rights statute should be construed to further our Nation's commitment to the eradication of racial discrimination, the Court adopts a formalistic method of interpretation antithetical to Congress' vision of a society in which contractual opportunities are equal. I dissent from the Court's holding that § 1981 does not encompass Patterson's racial harassment claim.

. . . Since deciding *Runyon*, we have upon a number of occasions treated as settled law its interpretation of § 1981 as extending to private discrimination. . . . We have also reiterated our holding in *Jones* [v. *Alfred H. Mayer Co.*, 392 U.S. 409 (1968)] that § 1982 similarly applies to private discrimina-tion in the sale or rental of real or personal property—a holding arrived at through an analysis of legislative history common to both § 1981 and § 1982.

The Court's reaffirmation of this long and consistent line of precedents establishing that § 1981 encompasses private discrimination is based upon its belated decision to adhere to the principle of *stare decisis*—a decision that could readily and would better have been made before the Court decided to put *Runyon* and its progeny into question by ordering reargument in this case. While there is an exception to *stare decisis* for precedents that have proved "outdated, . . . unworkable, or otherwise legitimately vulnerable to serious reconsideration," . . . it has never been arguable that *Runyon* falls within it. Rather, *Runyon* is entirely consonant with our society's deep commitment to the eradication of discrimination based on a person's race or the color of her skin . . . . In the past, this Court has overruled decisions antagonistic to our Nation's commitment to the ideal of a society in which a person's opportunities do not depend on her race, . . . and I find it disturbing that the Court has in this case chosen to reconsider, without any request from the parties, a statutory construction so in harmony with that ideal.

Having decided, however, to reconsider *Runyon*, and now to reaffirm it by appeal to *stare decisis*, the Court glosses over what are in my view two very obvious reasons for refusing to overrule this interpretation of § 1981: that *Runyon* was correctly decided, and that in any event Congress has ratified our construction of the statute. . . .

[Here follows an extensive review of the Court's decisions involving the interpretation of Section 1981.]

Even were there doubts as to the correctness of *Runyon*, Congress has in effect ratified our interpretation of § 1981, a fact to which the Court pays no attention. We have justified our practice of according special weight to statutory precedents . . . by reference to Congress' ability to correct our interpretations when we have erred. To be sure, the absence of legislative correction is by no means in all cases determinative, for where our prior interpretation of a statute was plainly a mistake, we are reluctant to " 'place on the shoulders of Congress the burden of the Court's own error.' " . . . Where our prior interpretation of congressional intent was plausible, however—which is the very least that can be said for our construction of § 1981 in *Runyon*—we have often taken Congress' subsequent inaction as probative to varying degrees, depending upon circumstances, of its acquiescence.

... Given the frequency with which Congress has in recent years acted to overturn this Court's mistaken interpretations of civil rights statutes, its failure to enact legislation to overturn *Runyon* appears at least to some extent indicative of a congressional belief that *Runyon* was correctly decided. It might likewise be considered significant that no other legislative developments have occurred that cast doubt on our interpretation of § 1981. . . .

There is no cause, though, to consider the precise weight to attach to the fact that Congress has not overturned or otherwise undermined *Runyon*. For in this case we have more positive signs of Congress' views. Congress has considered and rejected an amendment that would have rendered § 1981 unavailable in most cases as a remedy for private employment discrimination, which is evidence of congressional acquiescence that is "something other than mere congressional silence and passivity." . . . In addition, Congress has built upon our interpretation of § 1981 in enacting a statute that provides for the recovery of attorney's fees in § 1981 actions.

After the Court's decision in *Jones* v. *Alfred H. Mayer Co.*, Congress enacted the Equal Employment Opportunity Act of 1972, . . . amending Title VII of the Civil Rights Act of 1964. . . . During Congress' consideration of this legislation—by which time there had been ample indication that § 1981 was being interpreted to apply to private acts of employment discrimination—it was suggested that Title VII rendered redundant the availability of a remedy for employment discrimination under provisions derived from the Civil Rights Act of 1866. Some concluded that Title VII should be made, with limited exceptions, the exclusive remedy for such discrimination. . . .

[But] Congress in 1972 assumed that § 1981 reached private discrimination, and declined to alter its availability as an alternative to those remedies provided by Title VII. The Court in *Runyon* properly relied upon Congress' refusal to adopt an amendment that would have made § 1981 inapplicable to racially discriminatory actions by private employers, and concluded, as I do, that "[t]here could hardly be a clearer indication of congressional agreement with the view that § 1981 *does* reach private acts of racial discrimination."

Events since our decision in *Runyon* confirm Congress' approval of our interpretation of § 1981. . . .

The Court holds that § 1981, insofar as it gives an equal right to make a contract, "covers only conduct at the initial formation of the contract." . . . This narrow interpretation is not, as the Court would have us believe, the inevitable result of the statutory grant of an equal right "to make contracts." On the contrary, the language of § 1981 is quite naturally read as extending to cover postformation conduct that demonstrates that the contract was not really made on equal terms at all. It is indeed clear that the statutory language of § 1981 imposes some limit upon the type of harassment claims that are cognizable under § 1981, for the statute's prohibition is against discrimination in the making and enforcement of contracts; but the Court mistakes the nature of that limit. In my view, harassment is properly actionable under the language of §1981 mandating that all persons "shall have the same right . . . to make . . . contracts . . . as is enjoyed by white citizens" if it demonstrates that the employer has in fact imposed discriminatory terms and hence has not allowed blacks to make a contract on an equal basis.

The question in a case in which an employee makes a § 1981 claim alleging racial harassment should be whether the acts constituting harassment were sufficiently severe or pervasive as effectively to belie any claim that the contract was entered into in a racially neutral manner. Where a black employee demonstrates that she has worked in conditions substantially different from those enjoyed by similarly situated white employees, and can show the necessary racial animus, a jury may infer that the black employee has not been afforded the same right to make an employment contract as white employees. Obviously, as respondent conceded at oral argument. . . . if an employer offers a black and a white applicant for employment the same written contract, but then tells the black employee that her working conditions will be much worse than those of the white hired for the same job because "there's a lot of harassment going on in this work place and you have to agree to that," it would have to be concluded that the white and black had not enjoyed an equal right to make a contract. . . .

. . . I believe the evidence in this case brings petitioner's harassment claim firmly within the scope of § 1981. Petitioner testified at trial that during her 10 years at McLean she was subjected to racial slurs; given more work than white employees and assigned the most demeaning tasks: passed over for promotion, not informed of promotion opportunities, and not offered training.

I agree that the District Court erred when it instructed the jury as to petitioner's burden in proving her claim that McLean violated § 1981 by failing to promote her, because she is black, to an intermediate accounting clerk position. The District Court instructed the jury that Patterson had to prove not only that she was denied a promotion because of her race, but also that she was better qualified than the white employee who had allegedly received the promotion. That instruction is inconsistent with the scheme of proof we have carefully designed, in analogous cases, "to bring the litigants and the court expeditiously and fairly to [the] ultimate question" of whether the defendant intentionally discriminated against the plaintiff. . . .

I . . . agree that petitioner's promotion discrimination claim must be remanded because of the District Court's erroneous instruction as to petitioner's burden. It seems to me, however, that the Court of Appeals was correct when it said that promotion-discrimination claims are cognizable under § 1981 because they "go to the very existence and nature of the employment contract." The Court's disagreement with this common-sense view, and its statement that "the question whether a promotion claim is actionable under § 1981 depends upon whether the nature of the change in position was such that it involved the opportunity to enter into a new contract with the employer," display nicely how it seeks to eliminate with technicalities the protection § 1981 was intended to afford—to limit protection to the form of the con-

tract entered into, and not to extend it, as Congress intended, to the substance of the contract as it is worked out in practice. Under the Court's view, the employer may deny any number of promotions solely on the basis of race, safe from a § 1981 suit, provided it is careful that promotions do not involve new contracts. It is admittedly difficult to see how a "promotion"—which would seem to imply different duties and employment terms—could be achieved without a new contract, and it may well be as a result that promotion claims will always be cognizable under § 1981. Nevertheless, the same criticisms I have made of the Court's decision regarding harassment claims apply here: proof that an employee was not promoted because she is black—while all around white peers are advanced—shows that the black employee has in substance been denied the opportunity to contract on the equal terms that § 1981 guarantees.

In summary, I would hold that the Court of Appeals erred in deciding that petitioner's racial harassment claim is not cognizable under § 1981. It likewise erred in holding that petitioner could succeed in her promotion-discrimination claim only by proving that she was better qualified for the position of intermediate accounting clerk than the white employee who was in fact promoted.

"But Not Next Door": The Controversy over Racially Segregated Housing

---

FEATURED CASE
Jones v. *Mayer*

For the most part, where people live is determined by those forces controlling the private housing market. But public housing authorities have not been without significant influence. Exacerbating the problem has been the acceptance by many whites of a number of myths regarding the residential behavior of minority groups, particularly blacks. Commonly shared views that property values drop and neighborhoods deteriorate when blacks move in have generally been accepted as truisms by frightened whites. Hence, when the phenomenon of "blockbusting" occurs and one black family moves in, almost immediately most of the homes on that block and in that neighborhood are put on the market by fleeing whites.

Early attempts to seal off a neighborhood by

legislation were rejected by the Supreme Court in *Buchanan* v. *Warley* (245 U.S. 60, 1917), because the Louisville, Kentucky, ordinance was a direct violation of the equal protection clause. The Court also struck a blow at the perpetrators of racially segregated housing areas when it held in *Shelley* v. *Kraemer* (334 U.S. 1, 1948) and *Hurd* v. *Hodge* (334 U.S. 24, 1948) that privately executed "restrictive covenants" were unenforceable in the courts. The judicial action involved would be *state* action to enforce racial discrimination and hence violative of the equal protection clause. See also *Barrows* v. *Jackson* (346 U.S. 249, 1953).

Such judicial holdings had little or no impact on opening up the housing market. Blacks were still restricted to certain residential areas either by the practices of real estate brokers or by mortgage institutions, with varying degrees of pressure from neighborhood associations. In addition, the *Buchanan* decision was often skirted by the public housing "location" decisions of local governments, as major housing projects were usually constructed with an eye to the maintenance of racially segregated neighborhoods. Consequently, federal money has, at times, supported segregated housing policies of communities across the nation.

Major attention was directed at equal access to housing during the civil rights movement of the 1960s. Efforts there and other pressures produced a number of state and local "open occupancy" laws designed to bring under regulation certain real estate practices that had undergirded the segregated housing market. Typically banned were such practices as racially separate listings and mortgage company policies restricting loans to black buyers to specified areas. The courts have upheld such fair housing laws as a valid exercise of state power to achieve a nondiscriminatory housing market.

Attempts by some groups to constitutionally seal off this policy area from legislative action have been rebuffed. In California, for example, a state constitutional amendment, overwhelmingly approved through the popular initiative and referendum in 1964, that repealed the state's fair housing laws and prohibited the legislature from the future enactment of such legislation was struck down in *Reitman* v. *Mulkey* (387 U.S. 369, 1967). Noting the amendment's "immediate objective," the California Supreme Court found its adoption to be an unconstitutional state involvement in promoting racial discrimination contrary to the equal protection clause. In affirming on the same equal protection grounds, the U.S. Supreme Court made it clear that the enjoyment of constitutional rights may not be submitted to a popular referendum. The Court reemphasized this proposition two years later in *Hunter* v. *Erickson* (393 U.S. 385, 1969), in striking down an Akron, Ohio, charter amendment requiring the city council to submit any fair housing ordinance to a popular referendum.

On the national front, the Johnson administration's efforts to get Congress to enact a national fair housing law proved successful shortly after the assassination of the Reverend Martin Luther King, Jr., in 1968. Undoubtedly, this tragedy and the widespread urban violence that followed in its wake helped to spur congressional approval of the measure known as the 1968 Fair Housing Law.

The law bans discrimination in the sale and rental of 80 percent of the nation's housing.

Excluded from its provisions are owner-occupied dwellings of four units or less and privately owned single family homes where sale and rental transactions do not involve the services of a real estate broker. The nondiscriminatory provisions were also extended to financing and brokerage services. The Department of Housing and Urban Development (HUD) is charged with seeking voluntary compliance, but enforcement is possible through civil actions by individuals and by the attorney general, who is authorized to file suits against the offender(s) where a pattern or general practice of discrimination is found.

After a decade of experience under the act, supporters of fair housing concluded that discrimination in the nation's housing market could not be eliminated through the conciliatory means to which HUD was limited. Consequently, a major effort, with strong support from the Carter administration, was made in the 96th Congress to strengthen the enforcement authority of HUD. A bill authorizing HUD to initiate administrative actions before administrative law judges, who had the power to assess civil penalties up to $10,000, passed the House of Representatives, only to be killed by a Senate filibuster in the waning days of the second session. The bill also included provisions to deal with the problem of "red-lining" (a practice of denying mortgage money to neighborhoods undergoing racial change) and to expand coverage to home appraisers and insurers.

Apparently the presidential election campaign of 1988 provided a needed catalyst to bring the efforts to strengthen the Fair Housing Act to a successful conclusion. Major amendments to the act were incorporated in the Fair Housing Amendments Act of 1988 and had the backing of both President Reagan and Republican presidential candidate George Bush. Passing both houses with overwhelming votes, key provisions directed at racial discrimination strengthened HUD's enforcement authority. While retaining the power to attempt conciliation of housing discrimination complaints, the Department can resort to more stringent measures if the conciliation effort is unsuccessful. Upon determination that conciliation will not resolve the controversy, HUD can then issue a "charge of housing discrimination," which allows the plaintiff or the defendant to seek resolution of the dispute through a newly created administrative law judge procedure or through a regular federal court trial. As an indication of Congress's intent to get tough on violators, the administrative law judges are given authority to impose fines that can range from $10,000 for an initial violation up to $50,000 for persistent violators. Of course, such actions are reviewable by federal courts.

Just two months after the passage of the 1968 Fair Housing Act, another law that could be employed in the battle against housing discrimination came to light when the Supreme Court resurrected an amorphous federal statute that had been passed in 1866 to enforce the Thirteenth Amendment and construed it in the case of *Jones* v. *Mayer* (392 U.S. 409, 1968) to apply to private discrimination in the housing market. This provision of the Civil Rights Act of 1866, the Court held, which guarantees to black citizens the same right "enjoyed by white[s] . . . to inherit, purchase, lease, sell, hold, and convey real and personal property," also prohibits racial discrimination in the sale of housing by a private developer. Justice Potter Stewart, who wrote the Court's opinion, said that the statute's language was "plain and unambiguous" in its declaration of property rights available to *all* citizens. Furthermore, Justice Stewart had no doubt about the authority of Congress to act. He noted that the act was grounded in the Thirteenth Amendment, and that its enabling section empowered Congress to enact "all laws necessary and proper to abolish all badges and incidents of slavery." Stewart emphasized that the Court's action in no way "diminished the significance" of the 1968 Fair Housing Law since there were vast differences between the two measures. He noted, for example, that the 1866 act was "a general statute applicable only to racial discrimination in the rental and sale of property" with remedial relief available only through private action, while, on the other hand, the 1968 statute was a comprehensive housing measure applicable to a number of discriminatory practices and exempting specific types of units, and "enforceable by a complete arsenal of federal authority."

As noted, some public agencies have been essential supports of racial segregation in public housing. This was well illustrated in *Hills* v. *Gautreaux* (425 U.S. 234, 1976), where location of public housing in the Chicago metropolitan area was at issue. There, lower federal courts found that the Chicago Housing Authority, with financial sup-

port from HUD, had violated the Fourteenth Amendment and federal statutes in deliberately selecting sites for public housing on a racially discriminatory basis. In its affirmance, the Supreme Court agreed with the court of appeals that it was constitutionally permissible to consider the entire metropolitan area in fashioning relief, since that was the "relevant housing market."

Despite this ruling, the dispersal of public and other types of low-income housing in Chicago and its suburban area is highly improbable for the foreseeable future. Chief among the barriers are the powers retained by local governments (recognized in the Court's opinion in *Gautreaux*) over zoning and land use in general. And the Supreme Court made it clear that the invocation of such powers to block the construction of low-income housing does not offend the Constitution. In *Village of Arlington Heights, Illinois* v. *Metropolitan Housing Development Corp.* (429 U.S. 254, 1977), the Court fastened on would-be developers and proponents of low-income and public housing the very strict burden of proving a "discriminatory intent." As Justice Lewis Powell argued for the Court, showing that the "ultimate effect" of the Arlington Heights zoning decision was racially discriminatory was insufficient; there must be a showing that the "motivating factor in the rezoning decision" was purposefully and intentionally to discriminate on the basis of race.

As a result of the *Gautreaux* decision and the very meager federal financial support for housing development in the late 1970s and early 1980s, practically no new low-income housing was constructed in the nation's larger metropolitan centers. Instead, public housing authorities have focused their efforts on arrangements that involve housing units in the private housing market. Among the most widely used of these arrangements are rent subsidies (grants to assist the would-be public housing resident meet the higher rent charged in privately operated housing) and the scattered-site housing program (in which public housing authorities acquire private housing units throughout the metropolitan area and make it available for those who qualify for public housing).

JUSTICE STEWART *delivered the opinion of the Court.*

In this case we are called upon to determine the scope and the constitutionality of an Act of Congress, 42 U.S.C. Sec. 1982, which provides that:

> All citizens of the United States shall have the same rights, in every State and Territory, as is enjoyed by white citizens thereof to inherit, purchase, lease, sell, hold, and convey real and personal property.

On September 2, 1965, the petitioners filed a complaint in the District Court for the Eastern District of Missouri, alleging that the respondents had refused to sell them a home in the Paddock Woods community of St. Louis County for the sole reason that petitioner . . . is a Negro. Relying in part upon Sec. 1982, the petitioners sought injunctive and other relief. The District Court sustained the respondents' motion to dismiss the complaint, and the Court of Appeals for the Eighth Circuit affirmed, concluding that Sec. 1982 applies only to state action and does not reach private refusals to sell. . . . [W]e reverse the judgment of the Court of Appeals [and] hold that Sec. 1982 bars *all* racial discrimination, private as well as public, in the sale or rental of property, and that the statute, thus construed, is a valid exercise of the power of Congress to enforce the Thirteenth Amendment.

At the outset, it is important to make clear precisely what this case does *not* involve. Whatever else it may be, 42 U.S.C. Sec. 1982 is not a comprehensive open housing law. In sharp contrast to the Fair Housing Title (Title VIII) of the Civil Rights Act of 1968, . . . the statute in this case deals only with racial discrimination and does not address itself to discrimination on grounds of religion or national origin. It does not deal specifically with discrimination in the provision of services or facilities in connection with the sale or rental of a dwelling. It does not prohibit advertising or other representations that indicate discriminatory preferences. It does not refer explicitly to discrimination in financing arrangements or in the provision of brokerage services. It does not empower a federal administrative agency to assist aggrieved parties. It makes no provision for intervention by the Attorney General. And, although it can be enforced by injunction, it contains no provision expressly authorizing a federal court to order the payment of damages.

Thus, although Sec. 1982 contains none of the exemptions that Congress included in the Civil Rights Act of 1968, it would be a serious mistake to suppose that Sec. 1982 in any way diminishes the significance of the law recently enacted by Congress . . . .

. . . [T]he Civil Rights Act of 1968 . . . underscored the vast differences between, on the one hand, a general statute applicable only to racial discrimination in the rental and sale of property and enforceable only by private parties acting on their own initiative, and, on the other hand, a detailed housing law, applicable to a broad range of discriminatory practices and enforceable by a complete arsenal of federal authority. Having noted these differences, we turn to a consideration of Sec. 1982 itself.

This Court has had occasion to consider the scope of 42 U.S.C. Sec. 1982 in 1948, in *Hurd* v. *Hodge*, 334 U.S. 24. That case arose when property owners in the District of Columbia sought to enforce racially restrictive covenants against the Negro purchasers of several homes in their block. A federal district court enforced the restrictive agreements by declaring void the deeds of the Negro purchasers. It enjoined further attempts to sell or lease them the properties in question and directed them to "remove themselves and all of their personal belongings" from the premises within 60 days. The Court of Appeals for the District of Columbia affirmed, and this Court granted certiorari to decide whether Sec. 1982 . . . barred enforcement of the racially restrictive agreements in that case.

The agreements in *Hurd* covered only two-thirds of the lots of a single city block, and preventing Negroes from buying or renting homes in that specific area would not have rendered them ineligible to do so elsewhere in the city. Thus, if Sec. 1982 had been thought to do no more than grant Negro citizens the legal capacity to buy and rent property free of prohibitions that wholly disabled them because of their race, judicial enforcement of the restrictive covenants at issue would not have violated Sec. 1982. But this Court took a broader view of the statute. Although the covenants could have been enforced without denying the general right of Negroes to purchase or lease real estate, the enforcement of those covenants would nonetheless have denied the Negro purchasers "the same right (as is enjoyed by white citizens . . . to inherit, purchase, lease, sell, hold, and convey real and personal property)" 334 U.S., at 34. That result, this Court concluded, was prohibited by Sec. 1982. To suggest otherwise, the Court said, "is to reject the plain meaning of language" *Ibid.*

Hurd v. *Hodge* . . . squarely held, therefore, that a Negro citizen who is denied the opportunity to purchase the home he wants "[s]olely because of [his] race and color," 334 U.S., at 34, has suffered the kind of injury that Sec. 1982 was designed to prevent . . . . The basic source of the injury in *Hurd* was, of course, the action of private individuals—white citizens who had agreed to exclude Negroes from a residential area. But an arm of the Government—in that case, a federal court—had assisted in the enforcement of that agreement. Thus *Hurd* v. *Hodge* . . . did not present the question whether *purely* private discrimination, unaided by any action on the part of government, would violate Sec. 1982 if its effects were to deny a citizen the right to rent or buy property solely because of his race or color.

The only federal court (other than the Court of Appeals in this case) that has ever squarely confronted that question held that a wholly private conspiracy among white citizens to prevent a Negro from leasing a farm violated Sec. 1982. *United States* v. *Morris*, 125 F. 322. It is true that a dictum in *Hurd* said that Sec. 1982 was directed only toward "governmental action," 334 U.S., at 31, but neither *Hurd* nor any other case before or since has presented that precise too much issue for adjudication in this Court. Today we face that issue for the first time.

We begin with the language of the statute itself. In plain and unambiguous terms, Sec. 1982 grants to all citizens, without regard to race or color, "the same right" to purchase and lease property "as is enjoyed by white citizens." As the Court of Appeals in this case evidently recognized, that right can be impaired as effectively by "those who place property on the market" as by the State itself. For, even if the State and its agents lend no support to those who wish to exclude persons from their communities on racial grounds, the fact remains that, whenever property "is placed on the market for whites only, whites have a right denied to Negroes." So long as a Negro citizen who wants to buy or rent a home can be turned away simply because he is not white, he cannot be said to enjoy "the *same* right . . . as is enjoyed by white citizens . . . to . . . purchase [and] lease . . . real and personal property." 42 U.S.C. Sec. 1982 (emphasis added).

On its face, therefore, Sec. 1982 appears to prohibit *all* discrimination against Negroes in the sale or rental of property—discrimination by private owners as well as discrimination by public authorities. Indeed, even the respondents seem to concede that, if Sec. 1982 "means what it says"—to use the words of the respondents' brief—then it must encompass every racially motivated refusal to sell or rent and cannot be confined to officially sanctioned segregation in housing. Stressing what they consider to be the revolutionary implications of so literal a reading of Sec. 1982, the respondents argue that Congress cannot possibly have intended any such result. Our examination of the relevant history, however, persuades us that Congress meant exactly what it said. [Here follows a review of the legislative history of the statute.]

* * *

As we said in a somewhat different setting two Terms ago, "We think that history leaves no doubt that, if we are to give [the law] the scope that its origins dictate, we must accord it a sweep as broad as its language," *United States* v. *Price*, 383 U.S. 787, 801. "We are not at liberty to seek ingenious analytical instruments," *ibid.*, to carve from Sec. 1982 an exception for private conduct—even though its application to such conduct in the present context is without established precedent. And, as the Attorney General of the United States said at the oral argument of this case. "The fact that the statute lay partially dormant for many years cannot be held to diminish its force today."

The remaining question is whether Congress has power under the Constitution to do what Sec. 1982 purports to do: to prohibit all racial discrimination, private and public, in the sale and rental of property. Our starting point is the Thirteenth Amendment, for it was pursuant to that constitutional provision that Congress originally enacted what is now Sec. 1982. The Amendment consists of two parts. Section 1 states:

> Neither slavery nor involuntary servitude, except as a punishment for a crime whereof the party shall have been duly convicted, shall exist within the United States, or any place subject to their jurisdiction.

Section 2 provides:

> Congress shall have power to enforce this article by appropriate legislation.

As its text reveals, the Thirteenth Amendment "is not a mere prohibition of State laws establishing or upholding slavery, but an absolute declaration that slavery or involuntary servitude shall not exist in any part of the United States." *Civil Rights Cases*, 109 U.S. 3, 20, 1883. It has never been doubted, therefore, "that the power vested in Congress to enforce the article by appropriate legislation," *ibid.*, includes the power to enact laws "direct and primary, operating upon the acts of individuals, whether sanctioned by State legislation or not." *Id.*, at 23.

Thus, the fact that Sec. 1982 operates upon the unofficial acts of private individuals, whether or not sanctioned by state law, presents no constitutional problems. If Congress has power under the Thirteenth Amendment to eradicate conditions that prevent Negroes from buying and renting property because of their race or color, then no federal statute calculated to achieve that objective can be thought to exceed the constitutional power of Congress simply because it reaches beyond state action to regulate the conduct to private individuals. The constitutional question in this case, therefore, comes to this: Does the authority of Congress to enforce the Thirteenth Amendment "by appropriate legislation" include the power to eliminate all racial barriers to the acquisition of real and personal property? We think the answer to that question is plainly yes.

"By its own unaided force and effect," the Thirteenth Amendment "abolished slavery, and established universal freedom." *Civil Rights Cases*, 109 U.S. 3, 20. Whether or not the Amendment *itself* did any more than that—a question not involved in this case—it is at least clear that the Enabling Clause of that Amendment empowered Congress to do much more. For that clause clothed "Congress with power to pass *all laws necessary and proper for abolishing all badges and incidents of slavery in the United States.*" *Ibid.* (Emphasis added by JUSTICE STEWART.)

* * *

. . . Surely Congress has the power under the Thirteenth Amendment rationally to determine what are the badges and the incidents of slavery, and the authority to translate that determination into effective legislation. Nor can we say that the determination Congress has made is an irrational one. For this Court recognized long ago that, whatever else they may have encompassed, the badges and incidents of slavery—its "burdens and disabilities"—included restraints upon "those fundamental rights which are the essence of civil freedom, namely, the same right . . . to inherit, purchase, lease, sell and convey property, as is enjoyed by white citizens."

Civil Rights Cases, 109 U. S. 3, 22. Just as the Black Codes, enacted after the Civil War to restrict the free exercise of those rights, were substitutes for the slave system, so the exclusion of Negroes from white communities became a substitute for the Black Codes. And when racial discrimination herds men into ghettos and makes their ability to buy property turn on the color of their skin, then it too is a relic of slavery.

Negro citizens North and South, who saw in the Thirteenth Amendment a promise of freedom— freedom to "go and come at pleasure" and to "buy and sell when they please"—would be left with "a mere paper guarantee" if Congress were powerless to assure that a dollar in the hands of a Negro will purchase the same thing as a dollar in the hands of a white man. At the very least, the freedom that Congress is empowered to secure under the Thirteenth Amendment includes the freedom to buy whatever a white man can buy, the right to live wherever a white man can live. If Congress cannot say that being a free man means at least this much, then the Thirteenth Amendment made a promise the Nation cannot keep.

The judgment is reversed.

JUSTICE DOUGLAS, *concurring.*

Enabling a Negro to buy and sell real and personal property is a removal of one of many badges of slavery. . . .

The true curse of slavery is not what it did to the black man, but what it has done to the white man. For the existence of the institution produced the notion that the white man was of a superior character, intelligence, and morality. The blacks were little more than livestock—to be fed and fattened for the economic benefits they could bestow through their labors, and to be subjected to authority, often with cruelty, to make clear who was master and who slave.

Some badges of slavery remain today. While the institution has been outlawed, it has remained in the minds and hearts of many white men. Cases which have come to this Court depict a spectacle of slavery unwilling to die. We have seen contrivances by States designed to thwart Negro voting, *e.g., Lane* v. *Wilson*, 307 U.S. 268. Negroes have been excluded over and again from juries solely on account of their race, *e.g., Strauder* v. *West Virginia*, 100 U.S. 303, or have been forced to sit in segregated seats in court rooms, *Johnson* v. *Virginia*, 373 U.S. 61. They have been made to attend segregated and inferior schools, *e.g., Brown* v. *Board of Education*, 347 U.S. 483, or been denied entrance to colleges or graduate schools because of their color, *e.g., Pennsylvania* v. *Board of Trusts,* 353 U.S. 230; *Sweatt* v. *Painter,* 339 U.S. 629. Negroes have been prosecuted for marrying whites, *e.g., Loving* v. *Virginia,* 388 U.S. 1. They have been forced to live in segregated residential districts, *Buchanan* v. *Warley,* 245 U.S. 60, and residents of white neighborhoods have denied them entrance, *e.g., Shelley* v. *Kraemer,* 334 U.S. 1. Negroes have been forced to use segregated facilities in going about their daily lives, being excluded from railway coaches, *Plessy* v. *Ferguson,* 163 U.S. 537; public parks, *New Orleans* v. *Detiege,* 358 U.S. 54; restaurants, *Lombard* v. *Louisiana,* 373 U.S. 267; public beaches, *Mayor of Baltimore* v. *Dawson,* 350 U.S. 877; municipal golf courses, *Holmes* v. *City of Atlanta,* 350 U.S 879; amusement parks, *Griffin* v. *Maryland,* 378 U.S. 130; busses, *Gayle* v. *Browder,* 352 U.S. 903; public libraries, *Brown* v. *Louisiana,* 383 U.S. 131. A state court judge in Alabama convicted a Negro woman of contempt of court because she refused to answer him when he addressed her as "Mary," although she had made the simple request to be called "Miss Hamilton." *Hamilton* v. *Alabama,* 376 U.S. 650.

That brief sampling of discriminatory practices, many of which continue today, stands almost as an annotation to what Frederick Douglass (1817–1895) wrote a century earlier:

> Of all the races and varieties of men which have suffered from this feeling, the colored people of this country have endured most. They can resort to no disguises which will enable them to escape its deadly aim. They carry in front the evidence which marks them for persecution. They stand at the extreme point of difference from the Caucasian race, and their African origin can be instantly recognized, though they may be several removes from the typical African race. They may remonstrate like Shylock— "Hath not a Jew eyes? hath not a Jew hands, organs, dimensions, senses, affections, passions? fed with the same food, hurt with the same weapons, subject to the same diseases, healed by the same means, warmed and cooled by the same summer and winter, as a Christian is?"—but such eloquence is unavailing. They are Negroes—and that is enough, in the eye of this unreasoning prejudice, to justify indignity and violence. In nearly every department of American life they are confronted by this insidious influence. It fills the air. It meets them at the workshop and factory, when they apply for work. It meets them at the church, at the hotel, at the ballot-box, and worst of all, it meets them in the jury-box. Without crime or offense against law or gospel, the colored man is the Jean Valjean of American society. He has escaped from the galleys, and hence all presumptions are against him. The workshop denies him work, and the inn denies him shelter; the ballot-box a fair vote, and the jury-box a fair trial. He has ceased to be the slave of an individual, but has in some sense become the slave of society. He may not now be bought and sold like a beast in the market, but he is the trammeled victim of a prejudice, well calculated to repress his manly ambition, paralyze his energies, and make him a dejected and spiritless man, if not a sullen enemy to society, fit to prey upon life and property and to make trouble generally.*

Today the black is protected by a host of civil rights laws. But the forces of discrimination are still strong.

A member of his race, duly elected by the people to a state legislature, is barred from that assembly because of his views on the Vietnam war. *Bond* v. *Floyd,* 385 U.S. 116.

Real estate agents use artifice to avoid selling "white property" to the blacks. The blacks who travel the country, though entitled by law to the facilities for sleeping and dining that are offered all tourists, *Heart of Atlanta Motel* v. *United States,* 379 U.S. 241, may well learn that the "vacancy" sign does not mean what it says, especially if the motel has a swimming pool.

On entering a half-empty restaurant they may find "reserved" signs on all unoccupied tables.

The black is often barred from a labor union because of his race.

He learns that the order directing admission of his children into white schools has not been obeyed "with all deliberate speed," *Brown* v. *Board of Education,* 349 U.S. 294, 301, "but has been delayed by numerous strategies and devices." State laws, at times, have even encouraged discrimination in housing. *Reitman* v. *Mulkey,* 387 U.S. 369.

This recital is enough to show how prejudices, once part and parcel of slavery, still persist. The men who sat in Congress in 1866 were trying to remove some of the badges or "customs" of slavery when they enacted Sec. 1982. And, as my Brother STEWART shows, the Congress that passed the so-called Open Housing Act of 1968 did not undercut any of the grounds on which Sec. 1982 rests.

JUSTICE HARLAN, *whom* JUSTICE WHITE *joins, dissenting.*

The decision in this case appears to me to be the most ill-considered and ill-advised.

*Excerpt from Frederick Douglass, The Color Line, The North American Review, June 1881, IV The Life and Writings of Frederick Douglass, 343–344 (1955).

* * *

. . . I believe that the Court's construction of Sec. 1982 as applying to purely private action is almost surely wrong, and at the least is open to serious doubt. The issue of constitutionality of Sec. 1982, as construed by the Court, and of liability under the Fourteenth Amendment alone, also present formidable difficulties. Moreover, the political processes of our own era have, since the date of oral argument in this case, given birth to a civil rights statute embodying "fair housing" provisions which would at the end of this year make available to others, though apparently not to the petitioners themselves, the type of relief which the petitioners now seek. It seems to me that this latter factor so diminishes the public importance of this case that by far the wisest course would be for this Court to refrain from decision and to dismiss the writ as improvidently granted.

I shall deal first with the Court's construction of Sec. 1982, which lies at the heart of its opinion. . . .

The Court's opinion focuses upon the statute's legislative history, but it is worthy of note that the precedents in this Court are distinctly opposed to the Court's view of the statute.

In the *Civil Rights Cases,* 109 U.S. 3, decided less than two decades after the enactment of the Civil Rights Act of 1866, from which Sec. 1982 is derived, the Court said in dictum of the 1866 Act:

This law is clearly corrective in its character, intended to counteract and furnish redress against State laws and proceedings, and customs having the force of law, which sanction the wrongful acts specified . . . . The Civil Rights Bill here referred to is analogous in its character to what a law would have been under the original Constitution, declaring that the validity of contracts should not be impaired, and that if any person bound by a contract should refuse to comply with it, under color or pretence that it had been rendered void or invalid by a State law, he should be liable in an action upon it in the courts of the United States, with the addition of a penalty for setting up such an unjust and unconstitutional defence. *Id.,* at 16–17.

In *Corrigan* v. *Buckley,* 271 U.S. 323, the question was whether the courts of the District of Columbia might enjoin prospective breaches of racially restrictive covenants. The Court held that it was without jurisdiction to consider the petitioners' argument that the covenant was void because it contravened the Fifth, Thirteenth, and Fourteenth Amendments and their implementing statutes. . . .
In *Hurd* v. *Hodge,* 334 U.S. 24, the issue was again whether the courts of the District might enforce racially restrictive covenants. At the outset of the process of reasoning by which it held that judicial enforcement of such a covenant would violate the predecessor to Sec. 1982, the Court said:

We may start with the proposition that the statute does not invalidate private restrictive agreements so long as the purpose of those agreements are achieved by the parties through voluntary adherence to the terms. The action toward which the provisions of the statute under consideration is [*sic*] directed is governmental action. . . .

Like the Court, I begin analysis of Sec. 1982 by examining its language. In its present form, the section provides:

All citizens of the United States shall have the same right, in every State and Territory, as is enjoyed by white citizens thereof to inherit, purchase, lease, sell, hold and convey real and personal property.

The Court finds it "plain and unambiguous" . . . that this language forbids purely private as well as state-authorized discrimination. With all respect, I do not find it so. For me, there is an inherent ambiguity in the term "right," as used in Sec. 1982. The "right" referred to may either be a right to equal status under law, in which case the statute operates only against state-sanctioned discrimination, or it may be an "absolute" right enforceable against private individuals. To me, the words of the statute, taken alone, suggest the former interpretation, not the latter.

Further, since intervening revisions have not been meant to alter substance, the intended meaning of Sec. 1982 must be drawn from the words in which it was originally enacted. Section 1982 originally was a part of Section 1 of the Civil Rights Act of 1866. . . . Sections 1 and 2 of that Act provided in relevant part:

That all persons born in the United States and not subject to any foreign power . . . are hereby declared to be citizens of the United States; and such citizens, of every race and color. . . . shall have the same right, in every State and Territory in the United States, . . . to inherit, purchase, lease, sell, hold and convey real and personal property . . . as is enjoyed by white citizens, and shall be subject to like punishments, pains, and penalties, and to none other, any law, statute, ordinance, regulation, or custom, to the contrary notwithstanding.

Sec. 2. . . . That any person who, under color of any law, statute, ordinance, regulation, or custom, shall subject, or cause to be subjected, any inhabitant of any State or Territory to the deprivation of any right secured or protected by this act . . . shall be deemed guilty of a misdemeanor. . . .

It seems to me that this original wording indicates even more strongly than the present language that Sec. 1 of the Act (as well as Sec. 2, which is explicitly so limited) was intended to apply only to action taken pursuant to state or community authority, in the form of a "law, statute, ordinance, regulation, or custom." . . .

[Here follows an examination of the legislative history of the statute to show that the debates do not overwhelmingly support the majority's interpretation.]

* * *

The . . . analysis of the language, structure, and legislative history of the 1866 Civil Rights Act shows, I believe, that the Court's thesis that the Act was meant to extend to purely private action is open to the most serious doubt, if indeed it does not render that thesis wholly untenable. Another, albeit less tangible, consideration points in the same direction. Many of the legislators who took part in the congressional debates inevitably must have shared the individualistic ethic of their time, which emphasized personal freedom and embodies a distaste for governmental interference which was soon to culminate in the era of laissez-faire. It seems to me that most of these men would have regarded it as a great intrusion on individual liberty for the Government to take from a man the power to refuse for personal reasons to enter into purely private transaction involving the disposition of property, albeit those personal reasons might reflect racial bias. It should be remembered that racial prejudice was not uncommon in 1866, even outside the South. Although Massachusetts had recently enacted the Nation's first law prohibiting racial discrimination in public accommodations, Negroes could not ride within Philadelphia streetcars or attend public schools with white children in New York City. Only five States accorded equal voting rights to Negroes, and it appears that Negroes were allowed to serve on juries only in Massachusetts. Residential segregation was the prevailing pattern almost everywhere in the North. There were no state "fair housing" laws in 1866, and it appears that none has ever been proposed. In this historical context, I cannot conceive that a bill thought to prohibit purely private discrimination not only in the sale or rental of housing but in *all* property transactions would not have received a great deal

of criticism explicitly directed to this feature. The fact that the 1866 Act received *no* criticism of this kind is for me strong additional evidence that it was not regarded as extending so far.

In sum, the most which can be said with assurance about the intended impact of the 1866 Civil Rights Act upon purely private discrimination is that the Act probably was envisioned by most members of Congress as prohibiting official, community-sanctioned discrimination in the South, engaged in pursuant to local "customs" which in the recent time of slavery probably were embodied in laws or regulations . . . . Adoption of a "state action" construction of the Civil Rights Act would therefore have the additional merit of bringing its interpretation into line with that of the Fourteenth Amendment, which this Court has consistently held to reach only "state action." This seems especially desirable in light of the Fourteenth Amendment, at least in the minds of its congressional proponents, was to assure that the rights conferred by the then recently enacted Civil Rights Act could not be taken away by a subsequent Congress.

The foregoing, I think, amply demonstrates that the Court has chosen to resolve this case by according to a loosely worded statute a meaning which is open to the strongest challenge in light of the statute's legislative history.

* * *

The fact that a case is "hard" does not, of course, relieve a judge of his duty to decide it. Since, the Court did vote to hear this case, I normally would consider myself obligated to decide whether the petitioners are entitled to relief on either of the grounds on which they rely. After mature reflection, however, I have concluded that this is one of those rare instances in which an event which occurs after the hearing of argument so diminishes a case's public significance, when viewed in light of the difficulty of the questions presented as to justify this Court in dismissing the writ as improvidently granted.

The occurrence to which I refer is the recent enactment of the Civil Rights Act of 1968. . . . Title VIII of that Act contains comprehensive "fair housing" provisions, which by the terms of Sec. 803 will become applicable on January 1, 1969, to persons who, like the petitioners, attempt to buy houses from developers. Under those provisions, such persons will be entitled to injunctive relief and damages from developers who refuse to sell to them on account of race or color, unless the parties are able to resolve their dispute by other means. Thus, the type of relief which the petitioners seek will be available within seven months time under the terms of a presumptively constitutional Act of Congress. In these circumstances, it seems obvious that the case has lost most of its public importance, and I believe that it would be much the wiser course for this Court to refrain from deciding it. I think it particularly unfortunate for the Court to persist in deciding this case on the basis of a highly questionable interpretation of a sweeping, century-old statute which, as the Court acknowledges . . . contains none of the exemptions which the Congress of our own time found it necessary to include in a statute regulating relationships so personal in nature. In effect, this Court, by its construction of Sec. 1982, has extended the coverage of federal "fair housing" laws far beyond that which Congress in its wisdom chose to provide in the Civil Rights Act of 1968. The political process now having taken hold again in this very field, I am at a loss to understand why the Court should have deemed it appropriate or, in the circumstances of this case, necessary to proceed with such precipitous and insecure strides.

I am not dissuaded from my view by the circumstance that the 1968 Act was enacted after oral argument in this case, at a time when the parties and *amici curiae* had invested time and money in anticipation of a decision on the merits, or by the fact that the 1968 Act apparently will not entitle these petitioners to the relief which they seek. For the certiorari jurisdiction was not conferred upon this Court "merely to give the defeated party in the . . . Court of Appeals another hearing," *Magnum Co.* v. *Coty*, 262 U.S. 159, 164, or "for the benefit of the particular litigants." *Rice* v. *Sioux City Cemetery*, 349 U.S. 70, 74, but to decide issues, "the settlement of which is important to the public as distinguished from . . . the parties," *Layne & Bowler Corp.* v. *Western Well Works, Inc.*, 261 U.S. 387, 393. I deem it far more important that this Court should avoid, if possible, the decision of constitutional and unusually difficult statutory questions than that we fulfill the expectations of every litigant who appears before us.

Commentary

From the Courts to the Streets to the Congress: Attaining Equal Access to Public Accommodations

When the Supreme Court declared the public accommodations provisions of the 1875 Civil Rights Act unconstitutional in the *Civil Rights Cases* (109 U.S. 3) in 1883, private entrepreneurs were left free (except where state law decreed otherwise) to make racial distinctions in providing a variety of "public accommodations" services to the public. As a result, a rigid racial segregation practice developed in the South and in some areas outside the South in which blacks could obtain restaurant service only (if at all) in small dining areas in or near the kitchen or could view motion pictures only from the balcony or separately designated "colored" sections of local theaters. Motel and hotel accommodations were generally nonexistent except for second- and third-rate facilities in the "colored" section of town. The "white only" sign of warning of the racial exclusion policy generally was enough to keep the "unknowing" black from seeking service at the establishment.

In the early 1960s, the entrenched segregation policies and practices in this area became a target of the civil rights movement. The vigorous campaigns launched against segregated lunch counters, restaurants, motels, and theaters were largely undertaken by aroused black college and high school students. The tactics employed were markedly different from those used in the school segregation controversy—sit-ins and massive demonstrations were substituted for court challenges. Of course, these tactics themselves became the subject of much litigation. The objective was to prod the conscience of the various communities and the nation generally into a reexamination of racial segregation as a moral proposition. Beginning in 1960, demonstrations spread throughout the South, and thousands of demonstrators were arrested and jailed. Although numerous appeals were taken to the Supreme Court, the Court was able to dispose of the cases without tackling the tough constitutional issue of segregated accommodations. (See *Garner* v. *Louisiana* 368 U.S. 157, 1961). Apparently, most of the justices were not yet ready to reexamine the *Civil Rights Cases* (109 U.S. 3, 1883), where the Court limited the command of the equal protection clause to state action only, excluding the discriminatory actions of private individuals who provide various accommodations for the public.

In a few scattered instances, segregation practices were abandoned as a result of demonstrations, but in the end it took the public accommodations title (Title II) of the 1964 Civil Rights Act to ban this form of private discrimination. This legislation was challenged immediately after President Johnson signed it. But a federal district court in Georgia sustained the constitutionality of the act and denied attempts to enjoin its enforcement as applied to a restaurant and a motel. In Alabama, however, a federal district court held the public accommodations title unconstitutional as applied to a local eating establishment. Upon appeal of both rulings, the Supreme Court held the legislation to be a valid exercise of the commerce power (*Heart of Atlanta Motel* v. *United States*, 379 U.S. 241, and *Katzenback* v. *McClung*, 379 U.S. 294, 1974).

Initial expansive interpretations of Title II blunted the efforts of some to circumvent it by employing the subterfuge of the "private club." In *Daniel* v. *Paul* (395 U.S. 298, 1969), for example, the Lake Nixon Club (a recreational facility near Little Rock, Arkansas) attempted to continue its "white only" policy by selling memberships in the "private club" only to whites. In brushing aside this simple subterfuge, Justice William J. Brennan found that the operations of the club generally, and its snack bar in particular, were so affected by interstate commerce that the entire facility was a place of public accommodation within the meaning of the 1964 act. Cf. *United States* v. *Northwest Louisiana Restaurant Club* (256 F. Supp. 151, W.D. La. 1966).

By 1970, much of the vigorous resistance to compliance had subsided. In the years that have followed, use of the major public accommodations (hotels, motels, restaurants) by blacks has become commonplace, particularly in the large urban areas. So to what extent blacks now benefit from the wide range of private sector public accommodations is essentially determined by economic factors.

SELECTED REFERENCES

Armstrong, Margalynne. "Desegregation Through Private Litigants Using Equitable Remedies to Achieve the Purposes of the Fair Housing Act," 64 *Temple Law Review* 909 (Winter 1991).

Bell, Derrick, Jr. *And We Are Not Saved: The Elusive Quest for Racial Justice* (New York: Basic Books, 1987).

———. "Racial Realism," 24 *Connecticut Law Review* 363 (Winter 1992).

Bunch, Kenyon D. "Patrick E. Higginbothan's Third Road to Desegregating Higher Education: Something Old or Something New?" 18 *Ohio Northern University Law Review* 11 (1991).

Frye, Joycelyn, et. al. "The Rise and Fall of the United States Commission on Civil Rights," 22 *Harvard Civil Rights–Civil Liberties Law Review* 450 (Spring 1987).

Graglia, Lino A. "Race Preferences, Quotas, and the Civil Rights Act of 1991," 41 *DePaul Law Review* 1117 (Summer 1992).

Guinier, Lani. "Keeping the Faith: Black Voters in the Post-Reagan Era," 24 *Harvard Civil Rights–Civil Liberties Law Review* 393 (Spring 1989).

Hanell, Joy. "The Future of Desegregation after *Dowell*: Returning to Pre-*Brown* Days," 56 *Missouri Law Review* 1141 (Fall 1991).

Kujovich, Gilo. "Equal Opportunity in Higher Education and the Black College: The Era of Separate, but Equal," 72 *Minnesota Law Review* 29 (October 1987).

Landsberg, Brian K. "Race and the Rehnquist Court," 66 *Tulane Law Review* 1267 (May 1992).

Miller, Binny. "Who Shall Rule and Govern? Local Legislative Delegations, Rural Politics, and the Voting Rights Act," 102 *Yale Law Journal* 105 (October 1992).

Moore, G. A., and Braswell, M. K. "Quotas and the Codification of the Disparate Impact Theory: What Did *Griggs* Really Say and Did Not Say?" 55 *Albany Law Review* 459 (1991).

Nieman, Donald. *Promises to Keep: African-Americans and the Constitutional Order, 1776 to the Present* (New York: Oxford University Press, 1990).

Ray-Holmes, Sunanda. "The Changing Disparate Impact Theory of Employment Discrimination," 34 *Howard Law Journal* 331 (1991).

Rutherglen, George. "After Affirmative Action: Conditions and Consequences of Ending Preferences in Employment," 1992 *University of Illinois Law Review* 339 (1992).

Saks, Richard, "Redemption or Exemption: Racial Discrimination in Judicial Elections under the Voting Rights Act," 66 *Chicago-Kent Law Review* 245 (1990).

Starr, Paul. "Building Minority Institutions: Alternatives to Affirmative Action," 49 *Current* 34 (February 1992).

Chapter 6

Political Participation

Gomillion v. Lightfoot   South Carolina v. Katzenbach   City of Mobile, Alabama v. Bolden
Thornburg v. Gingles   Chisom v. Roemer   Presley v. Etowah County Commission
Baker v. Carr   Davis v. Bandemer   Shaw v. Reno

Introductory Commentary

Protection of the right to vote and expansion of the electorate were twin concerns of the civil rights movement during the 1960s. Civil rights leaders and advocates of "black power" focused considerable attention on the potential of black voters at all levels of government. For almost a century, this potential had been blunted by the imposition of a variety of strategies, both official and unofficial, to bar the ballot box to black citizens. While many officially prescribed and implemented barriers were eventually negated by the courts, blacks did not make a significant impact on elections in many sections of the country until Congress passed the Voting Rights Act in 1965. The immediate results in many local areas, particularly in the South, with its heavy concentration of black population, were startling. The U.S. Commission on Civil Rights reported in 1975[1] that between 1964 and 1972 more than 1.1 million new black voters were registered in the seven southern states[2] covered in the Act. This represented an increase of the percentage of eligible blacks registered from 29 percent to more than 56 percent. Blacks continued to respond to politi-

cal education efforts throughout the 1970s and into the 1980s, and the percentage increase in the registration of the voting age population surpassed that of other racial groups in the U.S. electorate. Certainly, this enlarged black electorate across the country, and more particularly in the South, led directly to the election of blacks to a wide variety of local offices and to both houses of state legislatures in the South for the first time since Reconstruction. In addition, a congressional district in four of those states elected an African American to Congress. While these electoral gains slowed toward the end of the 1970s, the Joint Center for Political and Economic Studies reported that after the 1992 election cycle, there were some 8,000 African American elected officials at the national, state, and local levels.

One of the most visible of these successful politicians, of course, was Douglas Wilder, who was elected governor of Virginia in 1990 and thus became the first African American to be elected as a state governor in the nation's history.[3] Also highly prominent are U. S. Senator Carol Mosely-Braun, who was elected in Illinois in the tumultuous 1992 elections,[4] and the 39 African Americans who were

---

[1]U. S. Commission on Civil Rights, *The Voting Rights Act: Ten Years After* (Washington, D.C.; Civil Rights Commission, 1975).

[2]Alabama, Georgia, Louisiana, Mississippi, North Carolina (40 counties), South Carolina, and Virginia. When the four other southern states not covered by the act (Arkansas, Florida, Tennessee, and Texas) are included, the increases are even more pronounced. In 1964, there were approximately 2.2 million blacks registered in those 11 states, and the number had increased to almost 5.45 million by the 1986 elections. See Unites States Department of Commerce, Bureau of the Census Statistical Abstract of the United States, 1987, p. 250.

[3]Another African American, P.B.S. Pinchback, as lieutenant governor of Louisiana during Reconstruction, served briefly as governor in 1872.

[4]Braun is only the second African American elected to the U.S. Senate in this century. Edward Brooke (R., Mass.) was elected in 1966 and served one term. Hiram Revels (D., Miss.) was appointed to serve out a term, and Blanche K. Bruce (D., Miss.) was elected to a full term during Reconstruction.

elected to the House of Representatives that year. In the last three decades, African American mayors were also elected in some of the nations's largest cities, including New York City, Los Angeles, Chicago, Detroit, Denver, Atlanta, New Orleans, Kansas City, Cleveland, Washington, D.C., Philadelphia, and Birmingham.

Also contributing significantly to the energizing of African American political participation during the 1980s were the two unprecedented campaigns of the Reverend Jesse Jackson for the Democratic presidential nomination in 1984 and 1988. Both efforts greatly increased the overall political consciousness of blacks and other "locked-out" groups, such as women, Hispanics, and the poor. Some idea of the impact of Jackson's 1984 campaign on black Americans, for example, can be obtained from Table 6.1.

The accelerated drive of African Americans to share fully in the political process since the passage of the Voting Rights Act did not go unchallenged by entrenched white political elites. The possibility that African Americans might assume control of the governmental machinery in some heavily black areas was met by white legislative majorities employing sophisticated techniques of re-

sistance. The at-large election, for example, replaced single-member district elections. Diluting black voting strength by reapportionment gerrymandering (dispersing black voters in several electoral districts) stymied black encroachment on the political status quo, and the annexation of all-white suburban territory to urban voting districts (adding more white voters) was the answer to heavy black concentrations in central cities. The Democratic "runoff," or "second primary," used mostly in the South seems to pose additional barriers to black political influence. Such actions and structures have fostered considerable litigation in the past, and we may see greater attention being given to the application of political pressure on policy-making machinery in concert with the litigation strategy used in the past as we move to the twenty-first century.

We now review major developments in the long struggle of African Americans to gain access to effective participation in the political system. Also examined in this chapter is the reapportionment revolution of the 1960s and beyond, where litigation was the critical strategy used to gain equality of representation, making certain that one person's vote would count the same as any other person's.

Table 6.1
Southern Voter Registration, 1980–86 (Selected States)

State	White Registration			Black Registration		
	1980	1984	1986	1980	1984	1986
Alabama	1,700,000	1,664,000	1,807,000	350,000	482,000	508,000
Arkansas	1,056,000	964,000	1,030,000	130,000	155,000	157,000
Florida	4,331,000	4,337,000	4,677,000	489,000	517,000	576,000
Georgia	1,800,000	1,787,000	1,990,000	450,000	512,000	576,000
Louisiana	1,550,000	1,609,000	1,580,000	465,000	535,000	551,000
Mississippi	1,152,000	1,144,000	1,193,000	330,000	406,000	450,000
N. Carolina	2,314,000	2,369,000	2,468,000	440,000	565,000	585,000
S. Carolina	916,000	848,000	932,000	320,000	331,000	371,000
Tennessee	2,200,000	2,082,000	2,186,000	300,000	348,000	358,000
Texas	6,020,000	6,042,000	7,068,000	620,000	720,000	875,000
Virginia	1,942,000	1,908,000	2,097,000	360,000	378,000	442,000
TOTAL	24,981,000	24,754,000	27,028,000	4,254,000	4,949,000	5,450,000

Source: *Statistical Abstract of the United States*, 1987, p. 250.

Negating Black Political Participation: State Defiance of the Fifteenth Amendment

FEATURED CASE

Gomillion v. *Lightfoot*

Despite the voting rights guarantee of the Fifteenth Amendment, systematic exclusion of black Americans from the electoral process was commonplace for almost a century after the amendment's adoption. This condition was in large measure a consequence of our federal system. States not only exercise power to determine who can vote in state and local contests, but, in practice, one's participation in federal elections is essentially in the hands of state officials as well.

Putting aside earlier practices of threats and physical intimidation, states devised several legal schemes to circumvent the Fifteenth Amendment and thwart its objective. Several states had plans that included a property-holding requirement for voting and a poll tax. In addition, a "grandfather" clause was included that allowed the use of lineage to gain exemption from the voting rights requirements, but it did not pass Supreme Court scrutiny in *Guinn* v. *United States* (238 U.S. 347, 1915).

However, a decision of the Supreme Court in 1921, in *Newberry* v. *United States* (256 U.S. 232), holding that a primary was "in no real sense" a part of the federal election process, facilitated the perfection and spread of the "white primary" as one of the most effective schemes fencing blacks out of the political process. Initially stymied by the "state action" barrier of the Fourteenth Amendment because the exclusion of blacks from the Democratic Party primaries was directly traceable to official actions, the Texas Democratic Convention skirted this constitutional barrier when it acted as a "private voluntary group" to exclude blacks. In *Grovey* v. *Townsend* (295 U.S. 45, 1935), the Supreme Court agreed that the subsequent exclusion of blacks from the party's primary election was not constitutionally defective because of the private character of the action.

By 1941, a change in judicial attitude about the status of primary elections was indicated in *United States* v. *Classic* (313 U.S. 299). Involved was the federal prosecution of a Louisiana election official for ballot fraud in a congressional primary election. The district court had rejected federal regulation of such contests largely on the authority of the *Newberry* decision. But in reversing this holding, the Supreme Court held that the right to vote in such primary elections is secured by the federal Constitution and that Congress has the authority to regulate primaries "when they are a step in the exercise by the people of their choice of representatives in Congress."

The *Classic* decision clearly forecasted the downfall of the white primary by rejecting the "private status" theory of primary elections. In fact that downfall came only three years later in *Smith* v. *Allwright* (321 U.S. 649, 1944), when the Court had before it another challenge to the Texas white primary system. The Court thus eliminated this impediment to black suffrage by directly reversing *Grovey* v. *Townsend*. It ruled that political parties and party primaries were so regulated by massive state legislation that such action was for all practical purposes "state action." Hence, party action, which discriminated against blacks, was really state action contrary to the command of the Fifteenth Amendment.

Several schemes designed to resurrect the white primary proved to be little more than delaying nuisances. The South Carolina effort to make the party a truly private club by repealing some 150 statutory provisions governing primary elections was rejected by the lower federal courts, and the Supreme Court denied certiorari (*Rice* v. *Elmore*, 333 U.S. 875, 1948). A Texas county's evasive scheme took the form of a preprimary election from which black voters were excluded. The winner then filed in the regular Democratic primary and was usually elected without opposition. In *Terry* v. *Adams* (345 U.S. 461, 1953), the Supreme Court rejected the "private status" claim of the "Jaybird" group and held that its primary was an integral part of the election process that must conform with the Fifteenth Amendment.

Despite the death of the white primary, blacks attempting to vote in many southern areas continued to meet stiff resistance from both official and nonofficial sources. Cumbersome registration procedures and "understanding" tests administered by hostile registration officials in an atmosphere of fear as well as threatened economic intimidation succeeded in keeping all but a few blacks off voter registration rolls. The larger the potential black vote, the more determined was the white resistance. For example, when the large black registration in Tuskegee, Alabama (seat of Macon County), presaged a possible takeover of city government by black officials, the state legislature enacted a statute gerrymandering nearly all resident blacks out of the city. In declaring the act unconstitutional in *Gomillion* v. *Lightfoot* (364 U.S. 339,

1960), the Supreme Court rejected Alabama's "political-question" argument. It held that while in form the act was merely a redefinition of municipal boundaries, "the inescapable human effect of [that] essay in geometry and geography" was to deprive blacks of their voting rights secured by the Fifteenth Amendment.

GOMILLION v. LIGHTFOOT
364 U.S. 339; 5 L. Ed. 2d 110; 81 S. Ct. 125 (1960)

JUSTICE FRANKFURTER *delivered the opinion of the Court.*

This litigation challenges the validity, under the United States Constitution, of Local Act No. 140, passed by the Legislature of Alabama in 1957, redefining the boundaries of the City of Tuskegee. Petitioners, Negro citizens of Alabama who were, at the time of this redistricting measure, residents of the City of Tuskegee, brought an action in the United States District Court for the Middle District of Alabama for a declaratory judgment that Act 140 is unconstitutional, and for an injunction to restrain the Mayor and officers of Tuskegee and the officials of Macon County, Alabama, from enforcing the Act against them and other Negroes similarly situated. Petitioners' claim is that enforcement of the statute . . . will constitute a discrimination against them in violation of the Due Process and Equal Protection Clauses of the Fourteenth Amendment to the Constitution and will deny them the right to vote in defiance of the Fifteenth Amendment.

The respondents moved for dismissal of the action for failure to state a claim upon which relief could be granted and for lack of jurisdiction of the District Court. The court granted the motion, stating, "This Court has no control over, no supervision over, and no power to change any boundaries of municipal corporations fixed by a duly convened and elected legislative body, acting for the people of the State of Alabama." . . . On appeal, the Court of Appeals for the Fifth Circuit, affirmed the judgment, one judge dissenting. . . . We brought the case here since serious questions were raised concerning the power of a State over its municipalities in relation to the Fourteenth and Fifteenth Amendments. . . .

. . . The sole question is whether the allegations entitle . . . [petitioners] to make good on their claim that they are being denied rights under the United States Constitution. The complaint . . . allege[s] the following facts: Prior to Act 140 the

City of Tuskegee was square in shape; the Act transformed it into a strangely irregular twenty-eight-sided figure. . . . The essential inevitable effect of this redefinition of Tuskegee's boundaries is to remove from the city all save only four or five of its 400 Negro voters while not removing a single white voter or resident. The result of the Act is to deprive the Negro petitioners discriminatorily of the benefits of residence in Tuskegee, including, inter alia, the right to vote in municipal elections.

These allegations, if proven, would abundantly establish that Act 140 was not an ordinary geographic redistricting measure even within familiar abuses of gerrymandering. If these allegations upon a trial remained uncontradicted or unqualified, the conclusion would be irresistible, tantamount for all practical purposes to a mathematical demonstration, that the legislation is solely concerned with segregating white and colored voters by fencing Negro citizens out of town so as to deprive them of their preexisting municipal vote.

It is difficult to appreciate what stands in the way of adjudging a statute having this inevitable effect invalid in light of the principles by which this Court must judge, and uniformly has judged, statutes that, however speciously defined, obviously discriminate against colored citizens. "The [Fifteenth] Amendment nullifies sophisticated as well as simple minded modes of discrimination." *Lane* v. *Wilson*, 307 U.S. 268, 275 (1939) . . .

The complaint amply alleges a claim of racial discrimination. Against this claim the respondents have never suggested, either in their brief or in oral argument, any countervailing municipal function which Act 140 is designed to serve. The respondents invoke generalities expressing the State's unrestricted power—unlimited, that is, by the United States Constitution—to establish, destroy, or reorganize by contraction or expansion its political subdivisions, to wit, cities, counties, and other local units. We freely recognize the breadth and importance of this aspect of the State's political power. To exalt this power into an absolute is to misconceive the reach and rule of this Court's decisions. . . .

* * *

. . . [T]he cases that have come before this Court regarding legislation by States dealing with their political subdivisions fall into two classes: (1) those in which it is claimed that the State, by virtue of the prohibition against impairment of the obligation of contract (Art 1, Sec. 10) and of the Due Process Clause of the Fourteenth Amendment, is without power to extinguish, or alter the boundaries of, an existing municipality; and (2) in which it is claimed that the State has no power to change the identity of a municipality whereby citizens of a pre-existing municipality suffer serious economic disadvantages.

Neither of these claims is supported by such a specific limitation upon State power as confines the States under the Fifteenth Amendment. As to the first category, it is obvious that the creation of municipalities—clearly a political act—does not come within the conception of a contract under the Dartmouth College Case. . . . As to the second, if one principle clearly emerges from the numerous decisions of this Court dealing with taxation it is that the Due Process Clause affords no immunity against mere inequalities in tax burdens, nor does it afford protection against their increase as an indirect consequence of a State's exercise of its political powers.

Particularly in dealing with claims under broad provisions of the Constitution, which derive content by an interpretive process of inclusion and exclusion, it is imperative that generalizations, based on and qualified by the concrete situations that gave rise to them, must not be applied out of context in disregard of variant controlling facts. Thus, a correct reading of . . . kindred cases is not that the State has plenary power to manipulate in every conceivable way, for every conceivable purpose, the affairs of its municipal corporations, but rather that the State's authority is unrestrained by the particular prohibitions of the Constitution considered in those cases.

* * *

. . . [T]he Court has never acknowledged that the States have power to do as they will with municipal corporations regardless of consequences. Legislative control of municipalities, no less than other state power, lies within the scope of relevant limitations imposed by the United States Constitution.

* * *

The respondents find another barrier to the trial of this case in *Colegrove* v. *Green*, 328 U.S. 549 (1946). . . . In that case the Court passed on an Illinois law governing the arrangement of congressional districts within that State. The complaint rested upon the disparity of population between the different districts which rendered the effectiveness of each individual's vote in some districts far less than in others. This disparity came to pass solely through shifts in population between 1901, when Illinois organized its congressional districts, and 1946, when the complaint was lodged. During this entire period elections were held under the districting scheme devised in 1901. The Court affirmed the dismissal of the complaint on the ground that it presented a subject not meet for adjudication. The decisive facts in this case . . . are wholly different from the considerations found controlling in *Colegrove*.

. . . The petitioners here complain that affirmative legislative action deprives them of their votes and the consequent advantages that the ballot affords. When a legislature thus singles out a readily isolated segment of a racial minority for special discriminatory treatment, it violates the Fifteenth Amendment. In no case involving unequal weight in voting distribution that has come before the Court did the decision sanction a differentiation on racial lines whereby approval was given to unequivocal withdrawal of the vote solely from colored citizens. Apart from all else, these considerations lift this controversy out of the so-called "political" arena and into the conventional sphere of constitutional litigation.

. . . A statute which is alleged to have worked unconstitutional deprivations of petitioners' rights is not immune to attack simply because the mechanism employed by the legislature is a redefinition of municipal boundaries. According to the allegations here made, the Alabama Legislature has not merely redrawn the Tuskegee city limits with incidental inconvenience to the petitioners; it is more accurate to say that it has deprived the petitioners of the municipal franchise and consequent rights and to that end it has incidentally changed the city's boundaries. While in form this is merely an act redefining metes and bounds, if the allegations are established, the inescapable human effect of this essay is to despoil colored citizens, and only colored citizens, of their theretofore enjoyed voting rights. That was not *Colegrove* v. *Green*.

When a State exercises power wholly within the domain of state interest, it is insulated from federal judicial view. But such insulation is not carried over when the state power is used as an instrument for circumventing a federally protected right. . . .

For these reasons, the principal conclusions of the District Court and the Court of Appeals are clearly erroneous and the decision below must be reversed.

JUSTICE WHITTAKER, *concurring.*

I concur in the Court's judgment, but not in the whole of its opinion. It seems to me that the decision should be rested not on the Fifteenth Amendment, but rather on the Equal Protection Clause of the Fourteenth Amendment to the Constitution. I am doubtful that the averments of the complaint, taken for present purposes to be true, show a purpose by Act No. 140 to abridge petitioners' "right . . . to vote," in the Fifteenth Amendment sense. It seems to me that the "right . . . to vote" that is guaranteed by the Fifteenth Amendment is but the same right to vote as is enjoyed by all others within the same election precinct, ward or other political division. And, inasmuch as no one has the right to vote in a political division, or in a local election concerning only an area in which he does not reside, it would seem to follow that one's right to vote in Division A is not abridged by a redistricting that places his residence in Division B *if* he there enjoys the same voting privileges as all others in that Division, even though the redistricting was done by the State for the purpose of placing a racial group of citizens in Division B rather than A.

But it does seem clear to me that accomplishment of a State's purpose—to use the Court's phrase—of "fencing Negro citizens out of" Division A and into Division B is an unlawful segregation of races of citizens, in violation of the Equal Protection Clause of the Fourteenth Amendment . . . and, . . . I would think the decision should be rested on that ground. . . .

From the Streets to the Congress: Renewing the Fifteenth Amendment's Commitment

---

FEATURED CASES

South Carolina v. Katzenbach   City of Mobile, Alabama v. Bolden   Thornburg v. Gingles
Chisom v. Roemer   Presley v. Etowah County Commission

African American leaders and civil rights activists correctly recognized that judicial declarations alone would not secure the ballot for African Americans. Hence, they marshaled forces for a concerted effort to break the remaining resistance to black suffrage by concentrating on presidential and congressional action to implement the Fifteenth Amendment. Their efforts resulted in the Civil Rights Acts of 1957 and 1960, and the Voting Rights Act of 1965.

Although the acts of 1957 and 1960 were generally viewed by African Americans and civil rights groups as rather mild palliatives for a serious defect in our democratic political system, the fact that Congress had finally taken some action to enforce the Fifteenth Amendment was considered a significant step in southern African Americans' equality.[5] The chief defect of these acts was their continued reliance on the courts. Litigation could be dragged on for a long period in the courtrooms of local federal judges, some of whom might reasonably be expected to be sympathetic to maintenance of the status quo.

The 1964 Civil Rights Act, while primarily directed at discrimination in public accommodations and other areas, dealt a crippling blow to the literacy and "understanding" tests that had been effective in thwarting African American voter registration. In *Lassiter* v. *Northampton County Board of Elections* (360 U.S. 45, 1959), the Supreme Court had warned that although literacy tests were constitutional, they could not be employed as instruments of racial discrimination. But evidence gathered by the Civil Rights Commission indicated that this warning had been largely ignored by southern registrars. Consequently, the act provided that reg-

---

[5]The 1957 act created a Civil Rights Commission and charged it with, among other duties, gathering evidence of denials of the right to vote. More significantly, blacks were relieved of the burden of filing their own lawsuits, as the attorney general was empowered to seek injunctions against those conspiring to deny the right to vote. The 1960 act continued to place reliance on the courts. Upon application of the attorney general and after a finding of a persistent pattern of discrimination, federal district judges were empowered to appoint referees to register qualified persons to vote in both federal and state elections.

istration officials had to apply their standards equally and administer their tests in writing, keeping the test papers for possible review.

After the 1964 elections, there was considerable evidence that the black person's right to vote had still not been secured in many areas of the South. The registration machinery was still in the hands of state and local officials, most of whom were opposed to black voting rights. At President Johnson's urging and following massive demonstrations in the South, Congress passed a comprehensive voting rights act in 1965. Its major improvement over the earlier laws was the provision for federal machinery for voter registration. In addition, the act suspended the use of literacy, "understanding," and other tests in states and voting districts where less than 50 percent of the voting-age residents were registered in 1964 or had actually voted in the 1964 presidential election. Initially, the "coverage" formula made the act applicable to the states of Alabama, Georgia, Louisiana, Mississippi, South Carolina, Virginia, 26 counties in North Carolina, Alaska, and a few counties in several other states. Criminal sanctions could be applied also to anyone attempting to harm, threaten, or prevent persons from voting or civil rights workers from assisting potential voters. Also the act directed the Justice Department to institute injunctive action against the enforcement of the poll tax requirement in the five states retaining it.

One of the discrimination devices suspended by the act—the "understanding" test—had been struck down in the case of *Louisiana* v. *United States* (380 U.S. 145, 1965) by the time the president signed the measure. In that case, the Supreme Court upheld a district court ruling invalidating the Louisiana constitutional and statutory provisions that required every applicant for voting to "be able to understand" and "give a reasonable interpretation" of any provision of the state or federal constitution. Justice Hugo Black's opinion for the Court emphasized the discriminatory manner in which the test had been applied:

> The applicant facing a registrar in Louisiana . . . [is] compelled to leave his voting fate to that official's uncontrolled power to determine whether the applicant's understanding of the Federal or State Constitution is satisfactory. As the evidence showed, colored people, even some with the most advanced education and scholarship, were declared by voting registrars with less education to have an unsatisfactory understanding of . . . [those constitutions]. This is not a test but a trap, sufficient to stop even the most brilliant man on his way to the voting booth.

Not unexpectedly, officials in Louisiana, Alabama, and Mississippi immediately challenged the act's constitutionality. The challenges came in the form of state court injunctions forbidding local election officials to enter on voting rolls the names of persons registered by federal examiners. Instead of instituting actions under Section 12(d) of the act to dissolve these injunctions, the attorney general filed a motion to bring action in the original jurisdiction of the Supreme Court against the three states. In the meantime, South Carolina brought an injunction action in the original jurisdiction of the Court against enforcement of the act by the attorney general. After a consideration of the complex jurisdictional questions posed by these simultaneous actions, the Supreme Court agreed to hear the South Carolina suit—*South Carolina* v. *Katzenbach* (383 U.S. 301, 1966)—and upheld the act primarily on the authority of Congress to enact legislation to enforce the Fifteenth Amendment.

Soon after the *South Carolina* decision, the Court struck down the poll tax as violative of the equal protection clause in *Harper* v. *Virginia Board of Elections* (383 U.S. 663, 1966). Justice William O. Douglas, speaking for the Court, maintained that "voter qualifications have no relation to wealth nor to paying or not paying" a tax, and concluded that "wealth, like race, creed, or color, is not germane to one's ability to participate intelligently in the electoral process."

The 1965 Voting Rights Act also contains a provision designed to aid Spanish-speaking voters. It provides that no person who has obtained at least a sixth-grade education from an accredited school in the United States or its territories, in which the predominant classroom language was other than English, shall be denied the right to vote because of his or her inability to read or write English. The provision had particular relevance for New York City with its large Puerto Rican population, where literacy in English was required as a condition for voting. In *Katzenbach* v. *Morgan* (384 U.S. 641, 1966), the Supreme Court reversed a ruling of the District Court for the District of Columbia and upheld the provision's constitutionality as a valid exercise of congressional power to enforce the equal protection clause of the Fourteenth Amendment.

Probably the most controversial provision of the Act is Section 5. It requires that "covered" jurisdictions must get from the District Court for the District of Columbia a declaratory judgment that an electoral change "does not have the purpose and will not have the effect of denying or abridging the right to vote on account of race or color." But the act makes possible speedier implementation of electoral changes by allowing states to submit them and get approval from the attorney general. Should the attorney general approve the changes, private parties may still institute court challenges thereto. (See *Allen* v. *State Board of Election*, 393 U.S. 544, 1969; *Perkins* v. *Matthews*, 400 U.S. 379, 1971; and *Georgia* v. *United States*, 411 U.S. 622, 1973.)

The electoral law and procedural changes that have been reviewed under Section 5 undoubtedly reflect the concern of white policymakers about the monumental increases of black registered voters in a number of governmental units. The most widely used changes to resist possible black electoral successes in such areas include the switch from single-member to multimember districts with at-large election schemes and central city annexation of white suburban areas. In addition, white officials did not lose sight of the possibilities that reapportionment offered in their actions to limit black electoral strength.

An early example of the switch to an at-large scheme challenged under Section 5 was in *Fairley* v. *Patterson* (consolidated with *Allen* v. *State Board of Elections* and two other cases challenging voting procedure changes, 393 U.S. 544, 1969), where the court struck down a Mississippi statute that permitted a switch from single-member election districts to countywide at-large elections for county supervisors. Chief Justice Warren rejected the argument advanced by the state officials that Section 5 was not intended to apply to a change from district to at-large voting, arguing that the legislative history of the section underscores clearly the intention of Congress to have such change subject to its scrutiny. The type of changes at issue, Warren concluded, could dilute black voting strength and nullify their ability to elect candidates of their choice.

Two years after this ruling, the Court considered the multimember district scheme in the context of the Fourteenth Amendment in *Whitcomb* v. *Chavis* (403 U.S. 124, 1971). At issue was an Indiana legislative districting plan that provided for a mixture of single- and multimember districts. In rejecting the claim of black voters in the Indianapolis "ghetto" that multimember districting (joining them with larger groups of white voters) unconstitutionally diluted their voting strength, the Court held that such districts are not inherently unconstitutional simply because the proportion of black voters is insufficient to elect a black legislator. Justice Byron White, who spoke for the majority on the issue, noted that since there had been no finding that blacks "had less opportunity than did [white] residents [of the multi-

member district] to participate in the political process and to elect legislators of their choice," the invidious discrimination required to sustain a Fourteenth Amendment violation had not been proved. He concluded that the underrepresentation alleged by black voters was more the result of losing elections than the result of any "built-in bias." To White, the "cancelling out" of black voting strength found by the court below was but "a mere euphemism for political defeat at the polls."

Justice Douglas was joined in dissent by Justices Brennan and Marshall. They contended that "the [essential] test for multimember districts is whether there are invidious effects." They had little doubt that these effects were present since, to them, the effect of the plan was to "purposively wash blacks out of the system."

Two years later the Court applied its *Whitcomb* standards in *White* v. *Regester* (412 U.S. 755, 1973) in the election of state legislators from the multimember districts in two Texas counties. Examining the history of black and Mexican-American political participation in the two counties (the long history of official segregation; the small number of blacks [only two since Reconstruction] elected from the area; white-dominated slate-making; and technical rules of the electoral process) within the context of the multimember scheme, the Court concluded that the Texas legislative apportionment plan was invidiously discriminatory in violation of the equal protection clause.[6]

The Court continued to apply the demanding standard requiring proof of purposeful discrimination in challenges to multimember, at-large election schemes in *City of Mobile, Alabama* v. *Bolden* (446 U.S. 55, 1980) and *Rogers* v. *Herman Lodge* (458 U.S. 613, 1982). In the *Mobile* case, blacks constituted 40 percent of the city's population but had never been elected to its three-member city commission, allegedly because of its at-large election scheme. Relief was granted by the district court upon a finding that the at-large election system discriminated against blacks. The Supreme Court's reversal that followed reiterated the need to prove purposeful discrimination to sustain a Fourteenth or Fifteenth Amendment violation, as well as a violation of the Voting Rights Act, and the record below contained no such proof. In the *Rogers* case,

[6]The Court of Appeals for the Fifth Circuit formulated and set forth specific guidelines for measuring vote dilution in *Zimmer* v. *McKiethen* (485 F. 2d 1297, 1973). These included such factors as (1) lack of access to the slate-making process; (2) a history of locking blacks out of the electoral process; and (3) a state policy underlying the preference for multimember districts and at-large voting schemes.

however, the Court held that the district court's findings about the Burke County, Georgia, scheme were sufficient to support the existence of intentional and purposeful discrimination.

The more exacting standard of proof preferred by the Court in the *Mobile* case was overcome by Congress in its 1982 Voting Rights Act extension legislation, which amended Section 2 to allow the establishment of proof of a violation by showing that the electoral processes in question have a discriminatory effect or result. Whether this legislative shift will influence the Court to adopt the less demanding standard in cases where only constitutional challenges are raised must await further litigation. Thus far into the early 1990s the Court had not done so. Hence, for those challenging electoral processes and procedures as discriminatory the most viable option will undoubtedly be to bring those actions under Section 2, which allows courts to review the "totality of circumstances" in applying the "results" test.

The Court advanced a "non-retrogression" standard in a reapportionment challenge brought under Section 5 in *Beer* v. *United States* (425 U.S. 130, 1976). There, black voters alleged that the New Orleans city council reapportionment action following the 1970 census was invidiously discriminatory because the five single-member election districts were drawn in such a fashion as to preclude the election of black candidates in all except one, although blacks constituted 45 percent of the city's population. Furthermore, they asserted that the discrimination was compounded by the requirement that two of the seven members were to be elected at-large.

Considering the historical position of blacks in New Orleans politics, the Court concluded that black voting strength had been enhanced by the reapportionment, since there would be a 100 percent increase of black representation in the city council—from none to one member. To be sure, the Court accepted a plan with an obvious discriminatory effect, because it did not result in "retrogression" in the position of blacks in city council elections.[7]

Black voters have continued to raise the complaint that some at-large electoral mechanisms have adversely diluted their voting strength, thereby blocking their chances of winning office in such

jurisdiction. In its most definitive statement on the issue, the Court held in *Thornburg* v. *Gingles* (478 U.S. 30, 1986) that vote dilution charges flowing from the implementation of a multimember district election mechanism adopted by North Carolina for the election of some state legislators after the 1980 census were actionable under Section 2 of the Voting Rights Act. To be successful in such an action, however, the plaintiffs "must demonstrate that, under the totality of such circumstances," the employment of the multimember scheme produces "unequal access to the electoral process." "The essence of such a claim," said Justice Brennan, is that the multimember mechanism "interacts with social and historical conditions to cause an inequality in the opportunities enjoyed by black and white voters to elect their preferred representatives." He asserted that critical in demonstrating such a claim are such factors as (1) lingering effects of past discrimination; (2) the extent of racially polarized voting in the electoral jurisdiction; (3) the appeal to racial bias in the election campaigns; and (4) a pattern of racial bloc voting over an extended period. He concluded that when the district court, considering "the totality of circumstances," found that these factors "acted in concert with the multimember districting scheme to impair the ability of geographically insular and politically cohesive groups of black voters to participate equally in the political process and to elect candidates of their choice," its finding of illegal vote dilution in violation of Section 2 of the Voting Rights Act was appropriate.

While the multimember, at-large election schemes were used in some jurisdictions to minimize black electoral advances, political strategists in other areas turned to territorial annexation to achieve the same objective. In 1969, the city of Richmond, Virginia, annexed approximately 23 miles of surrounding Chesterfield County. Before the annexation, 52 percent of the city's population was black, but the annexation brought in an additional 45,705 whites and only 1,557 blacks, thereby decreasing the proportion of blacks in the city to 42 percent. Under Section 5 of the 1965 Voting Rights Act, the city's request for the approval of the annexation action was initially denied by the attorney general because of the dilution of black voting strength that would result. However, at the attorney general's suggestion, Richmond eliminated an existing at-large election structure and replaced it with single-member districts to overcome the adverse racial impact of the annexation. Upon submission to the District Court of the District of Columbia, however, both the annexation and the

---

[7]Cf. *City of Lockhart* v. *United States* (460 U.S. 125, 1983), where the Court held that although the city's revised election plan did not allow improvement of the voting strength of Mexican-Americans, the revision did not violate Section 2 of the Voting Rights Act because it did not result in any retrogression of their position.

system of nine wards established for elections thereunder were found defective under Section 5 because of the "invidious purpose underlying the annexation" and the failure of the ward election plan to "compensate for the [resulting] dilution of black voting power."

But in a five-to-three decision in *City of Richmond, Va.* v. *United States* (422 U.S. 387, 1975) (Justice Powell did not participate), the Supreme Court set aside this ruling. Justice White reasoned that the annexation, which had reduced black political strength, was not defective under Section 5 of the Voting Rights Act since the subsequent electoral structure "fairly recognizes [black] political strength." The majority made it clear that it could not accept the argument that the right to vote was abridged because blacks had fewer seats on a city council after annexation. To them, the crucial issue was whether the election system adopted for the selection of the council afforded blacks "representation reasonably equivalent to their political strength in the enlarged community." In the end, the Court remanded the case to the district court to consider the issue of purposeful discrimination, the record being incomplete on it. (But compare the Court's holding in *City of Rome, Ga.* v. *United States*, 446 U.S. 156, 1980).

When finally made operational by the district court in August 1967, the nine wards were fashioned so that four contained black majorities, four contained white majorities, and one was structured as a "swing" district containing approximately equal numbers of whites and blacks. In the first election under the newly structured wards, held on March 1, 1977, blacks were elected to five of the nine seats.

The Supreme Court appeared to give Section 5 of the Voting Rights Act a more expansive interpretation in upholding New York's 1974 state legislative reapportionment scheme, which was designed to enhance black representation. In a seven-to-one decision (Justice Marshall did not participate) in *United Jewish Organizations of Williamsburgh, Inc.* v. *Carey* (U.S. 144, 1977), the Court rejected the challenge of a Hasidic Jewish community, which argued that the structuring of districts to produce black majorities diminished their voting strength by dispersing them into two districts. In upholding the legislature's authority to consider race in its redistricting efforts, the justices were in disagreement about the supporting rationale; hence, no opinion commanded majority support. In announcing the judgment, Justice White's opinion, fully supported by Justice Stevens and only partly by Justices Brennan, Blackmun, and Rehnquist, contended that the Constitution was not abridged by New York in its effort to comply with Section 5 of the Voting Rights Act of 1965 by establishing specific minority racial majorities in legislative districts. The creation of nonwhite majorities in the districts involved, he argued, "was reasonably related to the constitutionally valid statutory mandate of maintaining nonwhite voting strength." Justices Brennan and Blackmun left White, however, when he argued that even if there were no statutory support for the reapportionment, New York's use of racial quotas to establish nonwhite majority districts did not offend the Fourteenth and Fifteenth Amendments. In making this argument he emphasized that the redistricting "did not minimize or unfairly cancel out white voting strength."

In dissent, Chief Justice Burger was troubled by the aura of the "racial gerrymander" that he felt was the result of setting racial quotas of voters. He contended that New York should undo the racial injustices of the past by reapportioning along racially neutral lines. In a philosophical vein, the Chief Justice was disturbed at what fragmented representation by race does to the "American melting-pot ideal."

While African American representation in the legislative and executive arenas was enhanced significantly by the Court's expansive application of the Voting Rights Act, their successes in states judicial elections were scant indeed. Using such electoral arrangements as the runoff election, majority vote approval, and multimember districts, African American judicial candidates were rarely successful. Entrenched political elites had resisted the application of the provisions of the Voting Rights Act to elective judicial positions by arguing that the act applied to legislative representation only. But challenges to that construction were mounted in Georgia, Louisiana, and Texas in the late 1980s, leading to the Supreme Court's decisions in *Georgia State Board of Elections* v. *Brooks* (111 S. Ct. 288, 1990), *Chisom* v. *Roemer* (111 S. Ct. 2354, 1991), and *Houston Lawyers Association* v. *Texas Attorney General* (111 S. Ct. 2376, 1991), in which the Court held that judicial elections are covered by Section 2 of the Voting Rights Act. Speaking for the six-to-three majority in *Roemer*, Justice John Paul Stevens focused on legislative intent and concluded that Congress had employed terms such as "representatives of their choice" and "standard, practice, or procedure" as "inclusive" terms that without doubt embrace judicial elections. Hence, the Voting Rights Act opened up another electoral arena for greater African American representation.

Immediately following the judgeship decisions, the Court refused to extend Section 5 of the act to certain local governmental structural changes in financial management by its decisions in *Presley* v. *Etowah County Commission* (112 S. Ct. 820, 1992) and *Mack* v. *Russell County Commission* (112 S. Ct. 820, 1992). There, when African Americans were elected to the office of county commissioner, the revenue allocation authority that had traditionally been assigned the commissioner for use in his or her district was transferred to the full commission, where allocation decisions for each district would be made by the white majority. Rejecting the plea of the African American commissioners that the restructuring of the revenue allocation system should be considered as the kind of change contemplated in Section 5 of the Voting Rights Act (and thus subject to the approval of the attorney general before implementation), Justice Kennedy asserted for the six-to-three majority that such internal procedural changes in a government's financial management could not be construed as "voting changes." For him, redistributing power among officials of a governmental body had no direct relationship to voting for office.

In a dissenting opinion joined by Justices Blackmun and White, Justice Stevens took notice of the timing of the action to transfer the financial allocating authority from individual commissioners to the commission itself. The critical factor producing that change was the election of an African American for the first time. In the end, Justice Stevens thought the Court should have deferred to the statutory interpretation, urged by the Bush administration, that would have subjected the change at issue to preclearance under Section 5.

There is little doubt that the continued federal scrutiny of state and local election law changes (including legislative reapportionment) has blunted attempts to evade the Voting Rights Act. Table 6.2 indicates the scope of that scrutiny from 1976 through 1985. Certainly, blacks and other minorities consider the maintenance of such a review mechanism essential if their full potential as participants in the political processes is to be realized.

Consequently, the act, originally intended to be effective for a five-year period, has been extended by Congress three times at the vigorous insistence of civil rights groups and their supporters who feared that removal of federal scrutiny of the electoral policies and practices of the "covered states" would lead to a restoration of the racially discriminatory requirements that were in general use prior to the act. Thus, in 1970, Congress brushed aside proposals of the Nixon administration that would

Table 6.2
Section 5 Preclearance Activity of the Attorney General, 1976–85

	Number of Submissions	Number of Proposed Changes	Number of Objections to the Changes Filed
1976	2,685	6,902	63
1977	1,817	3,122	43
1978	1,946	4,653	38
1979	1,914	3,420	23
1980	2,422	7,312	32
1981	2,001	6,072	21
1982	2,800	13,330	41
1983	3,000	10,000	80
1984	3,400	16,700	n.a.*
1985	2,800	12,000	102

*Not included in the attorney general's report.
Source: *Annual Reports of the Attorney General of the United States.*

have significantly weakened the act by altering the Section 5 preclearance provision, and extended the act for another five years. This ritual was repeated just before the expiration date in 1975, when the act was renewed for seven years.[8] Significant changes produced by these renewals include a nationwide ban on the use of literacy tests; an updating of the time to be used in the "triggering" mechanism of Section 4 of the act that sets forth the procedure for determining which states and jurisdictions therein are to be "covered"; and the provision for the use of bilingual election materials in "covered" jurisdictions that contain large numbers of non–English-reading voters.

The most controversial extension struggle came in 1982 under the Reagan administration. Sections 2 and 5 were the focus of much of the debate. The 1980 Supreme Court decision in *Mobile* triggered the debate on the standard to be used to prove discriminatory actions prohibited in Section 2. In *Mobile*, the Court held that proof of a "discriminatory intent" was required to prove a voting discrimination violation under the Fifteenth Amendment. But the act's supporters were successful in getting Congress to reject this more exacting standard of proof to sustain violations of the VRA and included in Section 2 the less exacting "discriminatory effect" standard for proving a discriminatory violation.

The Section 5 preclearance provision was extended for 25 years, thus continuing Justice Department scrutiny of election law changes in the "covered" states and jurisdictions. A controversial

[8]For an insightful analysis of the politics of the Voting Rights Act renewal actions, see Charles S. Bullock and Charles M. Lamb, *Implementation of Civil Rights Policy* (Monterey, Calif.: Brooks/Cole Publishing Co., 1984), ch. 2.

"bail-out" provision, which became effective in 1984, makes it possible for "covered" states to be relieved of Section 5 scrutiny upon proving to a three-judge panel in the District of Columbia that they have a clean record in voting rights actions for the previous 10-year period.

SOUTH CAROLINA v. KATZENBACH
383 U.S. 301; 15 L. Ed. 769; 86 S. Ct. 803 (1966)

CHIEF JUSTICE WARREN *delivered the opinion of the Court.*

By leave of the Court . . . South Carolina has filed a bill of complaint, seeking a declaration that selected provisions of the Voting Rights Act of 1965 violate the Federal Constitution, and asking for an injunction against enforcement of these provisions by the Attorney General. . . .

Recognizing that the questions presented were of urgent concern to the entire country, we invited all of the States to participate in this proceeding as friends of the Court. A majority responded by submitting or joining in briefs on the merits, some supporting South Carolina and others the Attorney General.* Seven of these States also requested and received permission to argue the case orally at our hearing. Without exception, despite the emotional overtones of the proceeding, the briefs and oral arguments were temperate, lawyer-like and constructive. . . .

The Voting Rights Act was designed by Congress to banish the blight of racial discrimination in voting, which has infected the electoral process in parts of our country for nearly a century. The Act creates stringent new remedies for voting discrimination where it persists on a pervasive scale, and in addition the statute strengthens existing remedies for pockets of voting discrimination elsewhere in the country. Congress assumed the power to prescribe these remedies from section 2 of the Fifteenth Amendment, which authorizes the National Legislature to effectuate by "appropriate" measures the constitutional prohibition against racial discrimination in voting. We hold that the sections of the Act which are properly before us are an appropriate means for carrying out Congress' constitutional responsibilities and are consonant with all other provisions of the Constitution. We therefore deny South Carolina's request that enforcement of these sections of the Act be enjoined.

The constitutional propriety of the Voting Rights Act of 1965 must be judged with reference to the historical experience which it reflects. Before enacting the measure, Congress explored with great care the problem of racial discrimination in voting. . . . At the close of . . . deliberations, the verdict of both chambers was overwhelming. The House approved the bill by a vote of 328–74, and the measure passed the Senate by a margin of 79–18.

Two points emerge vividly from the voluminous legislative history of the Act contained in the committee hearings and the floor debates. First: Congress felt itself confronted by an insidious and pervasive evil which had been perpetuated in certain parts of our country through unremitting and ingenious defiance of the Constitution. Second: Congress concluded that the unsuccessful remedies which it had prescribed in the past would have to be replaced by sterner and more elaborate measures in order to satisfy the clear commands of the Fifteenth Amendment. . . .

[Here followed a review of Congressional remedies from 1870 to 1964.]

* * *

Despite the earnest efforts of the Justice Department and of many federal judges, these new laws [enacted in 1956, 1960, and 1964] have done little to cure the problem of voting discrimination. According to estimates by the Attorney General during hearings on the Act, registration of voting-age Negroes in Alabama rose only from 14.2% to 19.4% between 1958 and 1964; in Louisiana it barely inched ahead from 31.7% to 31.8% between 1956 and 1965; and in Mississippi it increased only from 4.4% to 6.4% between 1954 and 1964. In each instance, registration of voting-age whites ran roughly 50 percentage points or more ahead of Negro registration.

The previous legislation has proved ineffective

---

*States supporting South Carolina: Alabama, Georgia, Louisiana, Mississippi, and Virginia. States supporting the Attorney General: California, Illinois, and Massachusetts, joined by Hawaii, Indiana, Iowa, Kansas, Maine, Maryland, Michigan, Montana, New Hampshire, New Jersey, New York, Oklahoma, Oregon, Pennsylvania, Rhode Island, Vermont, West Virginia, and Wisconsin.

for a number of reasons. Voting suits are unusually onerous to prepare, sometimes requiring as many as 6,000 man-hours spent combing through registration records in preparation for trial. Litigation has been exceedingly slow, in part because of the ample opportunities for delay afforded voting officials and others involved in the proceedings. Even when favorable decisions have finally been obtained, some of the States affected have merely switched to discriminatory devices not covered by the federal decrees or have enacted difficult new tests designed to prolong the existing disparity between white and Negro registration. Alternatively, certain local officials have defied and evaded court orders or have simply closed their registration offices to freeze the voting rolls. The provision of the 1960 law authorizing registration by federal officers has had little impact on local maladministration because of its procedural complexities.

* * *

The Voting Rights Act of 1965 reflects Congress' firm intention to rid the country of racial discrimination in voting. The heart of the Act is a complex scheme of stringent remedies aimed at areas where voting discrimination has been most flagrant. Section 4(a)–(d) lays down a formula defining the States and political subdivision to which these new remedies apply. The first of the remedies, contained in section 4(a), is the suspension of literacy tests and similar voting qualifications for a period of five years from the last occurrence of substantial voting discrimination. Section 5 prescribes a second remedy, the suspension of all new voting regulations pending review by federal authorities to determine whether their use would perpetuate voting discrimination. The third remedy, covered in sections 6(b), 7, 9, and 13(a), is the assignment of federal examiners on certification by the Attorney General to list qualified applicants who are thereafter entitled to vote in all elections.

Other provisions of the Act prescribe subsidiary cures for persistent voting discrimination. Section 8 authorizes the appointment of federal pollwatchers in places to which federal examiners have already been assigned. Section 10(d) excuses those made eligible to vote in sections of the country covered by section 4(b) of the Act from paying accumulated past poll taxes for state and local elections. Section 12(e) provides for balloting by persons denied access to the polls in areas where federal examiners have been appointed.

The remaining remedial portions of the Act are aimed at voting discrimination in any area of the country where it may occur. Section 2 broadly prohibits the use of voting rules to abridge exercise of the franchise on racial grounds. Sections 3, 6(a), and 13(b) strengthen existing procedures for attacking voting discrimination by means of litigation. Section 4(e) excuses citizens educated in American schools conducted in a foreign language from passing English-language literacy tests. Section 10(a)–(c) facilitates constitutional litigation challenging the imposition of all poll taxes for state and local elections. Sections 11 and 12(a)–(d) authorize civil and criminal sanctions against interference with the exercise of rights guaranteed by the Act.

. . . The only sections of the Act to be reviewed at this time are sections 4(a)–(d), 5, 6(b), 7, 9, 13(a), and certain procedural portions of section 14, all of which are presently in actual operation in South Carolina. We turn now to a . . . description of these provisions and their present status.

Coverage Formula

The remedial sections of the Act assailed by South Carolina automatically apply to any State, or to any separate political subdivision such as a county or parish, for which two findings have been made: (1) the Attorney General has determined that on November 1, 1964, it maintained a "test or device," and (2) the Director of the Census has determined that less than 50% of its voting-age residents were registered on November 1, 1964, or voted in the presidential election of 1964. These findings are not reviewable in any court and are final upon publication in the Federal Register.

* * *

South Carolina was brought within the coverage formula of the Act on August 7, 1965, pursuant to appropriate administrative determinations which have not been challenged in this proceeding. On the same day, coverage was also extended to Alabama, Alaska, Georgia, Louisiana, Mississippi, Virginia, 26 counties in North Carolina, and one county in Arizona. Two more counties in Arizona, one county in Hawaii, and one county in Idaho were added to the list on November 19, 1965. Thus far Alaska, the three Arizona counties, and the single county in Idaho have asked the District Court for the District of Columbia to grant a declaratory judgment terminating statutory coverage.

Suspension of Tests

In a State or political subdivision covered by section 4(b) of the Act, no person may be denied the right to vote in any election because of his failure to comply with a "test or device." Section 4(a).

On account of this provision, South Carolina is temporarily barred from enforcing the portion of its voting laws which requires every applicant for registration to show that he:

> Can both read and write any section of [the State] Constitution submitted to [him] by the registration officer or can show that he owns, and has paid all taxes collectible during the previous year on, property in this State assessed at three hundred dollars or more. SC Code Ann. section 23–62(4) (1965 Supp.).

The Attorney General has determined that the property qualification is inseparable from the literacy test, and South Carolina makes no objection to this finding. Similar tests and devices have been temporarily suspended in the other sections of the country listed above.

Review of New Rules

In a State or political subdivision covered by section 4(b) of the Act, no person may be denied the right to vote in any election because of his failure to comply with a voting qualification or procedure different from those in force on November 1, 1964. This suspension of new rules is terminated, however, under either of the following circumstances: (1) if the area has submitted the rules to the Attorney General, and he had not interposed an objection within 60 days, or (2) if the area has obtained a declaratory judgment from the District Court for the District of Columbia, determining that the rules will not abridge the franchise on racial grounds. . . .

South Carolina altered its voting laws in 1965 to extend the closing hour at polling places from 6 P.M. to 7 P.M. . . . the Attorney General . . . does not challenge the amendment. There are indications in the record that other sections of the country listed above have also altered their voting laws since November 1, 1964.

Federal Examiners

In any political subdivision covered by section 4(b) of the Act, the Civil Service Commission shall appoint voting examiners whenever the Attorney General certifies either of the following facts: (1) that he has received meritorious written complaints from at least 20 residents alleging that they have been disenfranchised under color of law because of their race, or (2) that the appointment of examiners is otherwise necessary to effectuate the guarantees of the Fifteenth Amendment. In making the latter determination, the Attorney General must consider, among other factors, whether the registration ratio of non-whites to whites seems reasonably attributable to racial discrimination, or whether there is substantial evidence of good-faith efforts to comply with the Fifteenth Amendment. . . .

. . . Any person who meets the voting requirements of state law, insofar as these have not been suspended by the Act, must promptly be placed on a list of eligible voters. . . . Any person listed by an examiner is entitled to vote in all elections held more than 45 days after his name has been transmitted. . . .

On October 30, 1965, the Attorney General certified the need for federal examiners in two South Carolina counties, and examiners appointed by the Civil Service Commission have been serving there since November 8, 1965. Examiners have also been assigned to 11 counties in Alabama, five parishes in Louisiana, and 19 counties in Mississippi. . . .

These provisions of the Voting Rights Act of 1965 are challenged on the fundamental ground that they exceed the powers of Congress and encroach on an area reserved to the States by the Constitution. South Carolina and certain of the amici curiae also attack specific sections of the Act for more particular reasons. They argue that the coverage formula prescribed in section 4(a)–(d) violates the principle of the equality of States, denies due process by employing an invalid presumption and by barring judicial review of administrative findings, constitutes a forbidden bill of attainder, and impairs the separation of powers by adjudicating guilt through legislation. They claim that the review of new voting rules required in section 5 infringes Article III by directing the District Court to issue advisory opinions. They contend that the assignment of federal examiners authorized in section 6(b) abridges due process by precluding judicial review of administrative findings and impairs the separation of powers by giving the Attorney General judicial functions; also that the challenge procedure prescribed in section 9 denies due process on account of its speed. Finally, South Carolina and certain of the amici curiae maintain that sections 4(a) and 5, buttressed by section 14(b) of the Act, abridge due process by limiting litigation to a distant forum.

. . . The objections to the Act which are raised under these provisions may . . . be considered only as additional aspects of the basic question presented by the case: Has Congress exercised its powers under the Fifteenth Amendment in an appropriate manner with relation to the States?

The ground rules for resolving this question are clear. The language and purpose of the Fifteenth Amendment, the prior decisions construing its several provisions, and the general doctrines of constitutional interpretation, all point to one fundamental principle. As against the reserved powers of the States, Congress may use any rational means to effectuate the constitutional prohibition of racial discrimination in voting. . . .

Section 1 of the Fifteenth Amendment declares that "[t]he right of citizens of the United States to vote shall not be denied or abridged by the United States or by any State on account of race, color, or previous condition of servitude." This declaration has always been treated as self-executing and has repeatedly been construed, without further legislative specification, to invalidate state voting qualifications or procedures which are discriminatory on their face or in practice. . . . [S]tates "have broad powers to determine the conditions under which the right of suffrage may be exercised." [However, t]he gist of the matter is that the Fifteenth Amendment supersedes contrary exertions of state power. "When a State exercised power wholly within the domain of state interest, it is insulated from federal judicial review. But such insulation is not carried over when state power is used as an instrument for circumventing a federally protected right." *Gomillion* v. *Lightfoot*, 364 U.S., at 347, 1960. . . .

South Carolina contends that the [previous] cases are precedents only for the authority of the judiciary to strike down state statutes and procedures—that to allow an exercise of this authority by Congress would be to rob the courts of their rightful constitutional role. On the contrary, section 2 of the Fifteenth Amendment expressly declares that "Congress shall have power to enforce this article by appropriate legislation." By adding this authorization, the Framers indicated that Congress was to be chiefly responsible for implementing the rights created in section 1. "It is the power of Congress which has been enlarged. Congress is authorized to *enforce* the prohibitions by appropriate legislation. Some legislation is contemplated to make the [Civil War] amendments fully effective." *Ex parte Virginia*, 100 U.S. 339, 345, 1880. . . . Accordingly, in addition to the courts, Congress has full remedial powers to effectuate the constitutional prohibition against racial discrimination in voting.

Congress has repeatedly exercised these powers in the past, and its enactments have repeatedly been upheld. . . .

The basic test to be applied in a case involving section 2 of the Fifteenth Amendment is the same as in all cases concerning the express powers of Congress with relation to the reserved powers of the States. Chief Justice Marshall laid down the classic formulation, 50 years before the Fifteenth Amendment was ratified:

Let the end be legitimate, let it be within the scope of the constitution, and all means which are appropriate, which are plainly adapted to that end, which are not prohibited, but consist with the letter and spirit of the constitution, are constitutional. *McCulloch* v. *Maryland*, 4 Wheat 316, 421, 1819. . . .

The Court has subsequently echoed his language in describing each of the Civil War Amendments:

> Whatever legislation is appropriate, that is, adapted to carry out the objects the amendments have in view, whatever tends to enforce submission to the prohibitions they contain, and to secure to all persons the enjoyment of perfect equality of civil rights and the equal protection of the laws against State denial or invasion, if not prohibited, is brought within the domain of congressional power. *Ex parte Virginia*, 100 U.S., at 345.

* * *

Congress exercised its authority under the Fifteenth Amendment in an inventive manner when it enacted the Voting Rights Act of 1965. First: The measure prescribes remedies for voting discrimination which go into effect without any need for prior adjudication. This was clearly a legitimate response to the problem, for which there is ample precedent under other constitutional provisions. . . . Congress had found that case-by-case litigation was inadequate to combat widespread and persistent discrimination in voting, because of the inordinate amount of time and energy required to overcome the obstructionist tactics invariably encountered in these lawsuits. After enduring nearly a century of systematic resistance to the Fifteenth Amendment, Congress might well decide to shift the advantage of time and inertia from the perpetrators of the evil to its victims. . . .

Second: The Act intentionally confines these remedies to a small number of States and political subdivisions which in most instances were familiar to Congress by name. This, too, was a permissible method of dealing with the problem. Congress had learned that substantial voting discrimination presently occurs in certain sections of the country, and it knew no way of accurately forecasting whether the evil might spread elsewhere in the future. In acceptable legislative fashion, Congress chose to limit its attention to the geographic areas where immediate action seemed necessary.

* * *

After enduring nearly a century of widespread resistance to the Fifteenth Amendment, Congress has marshalled an array of potent weapons against the evil, with authority in the Attorney General to employ them effectively. Many of the areas directly affected by this development have indicated their willingness to abide by any restraints legitimately imposed upon them. We here hold that the portions of the Voting Rights Act properly before us are a valid means for carrying out the commands of the Fifteenth Amendment. Hopefully, millions of non-white Americans will now be able to participate for the first time on an equal basis in the government under which they live. We may finally look forward to the day when truly "[t]he right of citizens of the United States to vote shall not be denied or abridged by the United States or by any State on account of race, color, or previous condition of servitude."

The bill of complaint is

Dismissed.

JUSTICE BLACK, *concurring and dissenting.*

Though . . . I agree with most of the Court's conclusions, I dissent from its holding that every part of section 5 of the Act is constitutional. Section 4(a), to which section 5 is linked, suspends for five years all literacy tests and similar devices in those States coming within the formula of section 4(b). Section 5 goes on to provide that a State covered by section 4(b) can in no way amend its constitution or laws relating to voting without first trying to persuade the Attorney General of the United States or the Federal District Court for the District of Columbia that the new proposed laws do not have the purpose and will not have the effect of denying the right to vote to citizens on account of their race or color. I think this section is unconstitutional on at least two grounds.

The Constitution gives federal courts jurisdiction over cases and controversies only. If it can be said that any case or controversy arises under this section which gives the District Court for the District of Columbia jurisdiction to approve or reject state laws or constitutional amendments, then the case or controversy must be between a State and the United States Government. But it is hard for me to believe that a justiciable controversy can arise in the constitutional sense from a desire by the United States Government or some of its officials to determine in advance what legislative provisions a State may enact or what constitutional amendments it may adopt. If this dispute between the Federal Government and the States amounts to a case or controversy it is a far cry from the traditional constitutional notion of a case or controversy as a dispute over the meaning of enforceable laws or the manner in which they are applied. And if by this section Congress has created a case or controversy, and I do not believe it has, then it seems to me that the most appropriate judicial forum for settling these important questions is this Court acting under its original Art. III, section 2, jurisdiction to try cases in which a State is a party. At least a trial in this Court would treat the States with dignity to which they should be entitled as constituent members of our Federal Union.

The form of words and the manipulation of presumptions used in section 5 to create the illusion of a case or controversy should not be allowed to cloud the effect of that section. By requiring a State to ask a federal court to approve the validity of a proposed law which has in no way become operative, Congress had asked the State to secure precisely the type of advisory opinion our Constitution forbids. . . .

My second and more basic objection to section 5 is that Congress has here exercised its power under section 2 of the Fifteenth Amendment through the adoption of means that conflict with the most basic principles of the Constitution. As the Court says the limitations of the power granted under section 2 are the same as the limitations imposed on the exercise of any of the powers expressly granted Congress by the Constitution. . . . Section 5, by providing that some of the States cannot pass state laws or adopt state constitutional amendments without first being compelled to beg federal authorities to approve their policies, so distorts our constitutional structure of government as to render any distinction drawn in the Constitution between state and federal power almost meaningless. One of the most basic premises upon which our structure of government was founded was that the Federal Government was to have certain specific and limited powers and no others, and all other power was to be reserved either "to the States respectively, or to the people." Certainly if all the provisions of our Constitution which limit the power of the Federal Government and reserve other power to the States are to mean anything, they mean at least that the States have power to pass laws and amend their constitutions without first sending their officials hundreds of miles away to beg federal authorities to approve them. Moreover, it seems to me that section 5 which gives federal officials power to veto state laws they do not like is in direct conflict with the clear command of our Constitution that "The United States shall guarantee to every State in this Union a Republican Form of Government." I cannot help but believe that the inevitable effect of any such law which forces any one of the States to entreat federal authorities in faraway places for approval of local laws before they can become effective is to create the impression that the State or States treated in this way are little more than conquered provinces. And if one law concerning voting can make the States plead for this approval by a distant federal court or the United States Attorney General, other laws on different subjects can force the States to seek the advance approval not only of the Attorney General but of the President himself or any other chosen members of his staff. It is inconceivable to me that such a radical degradation of state power was intended in any of the provisions of our Constitution or its Amendments. Of course I do not mean to cast any doubt whatever upon the indisputable power of the Federal Government to invalidate a state law once enacted and operative on the ground that it intrudes into the area of supreme federal power. But the Federal Government has heretofore always been content to exercise this power to protect federal supremacy by authorizing its agents to bring lawsuits against state officials once an operative state law has created an actual case and controversy. A federal law which assumes the power to compel the States to submit in advance any proposed legislation they have for approval by federal agents approaches dangerously near to wiping the States out as useful and effective units in the government of our country. I cannot agree to any constitutional interpretation that leads inevitably to such a result.

* * *

In this and other prior Acts Congress has quite properly vested the Attorney General with extremely broad power to protect voting rights of citizens against discrimination on account of race or color. Section 5 viewed in this context is of very minor importance and in my judgment is likely to serve more as an irritant to the States than as an aid to the enforcement of the Act. I would hold section 5 invalid for the reasons stated above with full confidence that the Attorney General has ample power to give vigorous, expeditious and effective protection to the voting rights of all citizens.

CITY OF MOBILE, ALABAMA v. BOLDEN
446 U.S. 55; 64 L. Ed. 2d 47; 100 S. Ct. 1490 (1980)

JUSTICE STEWART *announced the judgment of the Court and delivered an opinion in which* THE CHIEF JUSTICE, JUSTICE POWELL, *and* JUSTICE REHNQUIST *join.*

The City of Mobile, Ala., has since 1911 been governed by a City Commission consisting of three members elected by the voters of the city at-large. The question in this case is whether this at-large system of municipal elections violates the rights of Mobile's Negro voters in contravention of federal statutory or constitutional law.

The appellees brought this suit in the Federal District Court for the Southern District of Alabama as a class action on behalf of all Negro citizens of Mobile. . . . The complaint alleged that the practice of electing the City Commissioners at-large unfairly diluted the voting strength of Negroes in violation of § 2 of the Voting Rights Act of 1965, of the Fourteenth Amendment and of the Fifteenth Amendment. Following a bench trial, the District Court found that the constitutional rights of the appellees had been violated, entered a judgment in their favor, and ordered that the City Commission be disestablished and replaced by a municipal government consisting of a Mayor and a City Council with members elected from single-member districts. . . . The Court of Appeals affirmed the judgment in its entirety . . . agreeing that Mobile's at-large elections operated to discriminate against Negroes in violation of the Fourteenth and Fifteenth Amendments . . . and finding that the remedy formulated by the District Court was appropriate. . . . The case was originally argued in the 1978 Term, and was reargued in the present Term.

I

In Alabama, the form of municipal government a city may adopt is governed by state law. . . . In [1911] the Alabama Legislature authorized every large municipality to adopt a commission form of government. Mobile established its City Commission in the same year, and has maintained that basic system of municipal government ever since.

The three Commissioners jointly exercise all legislative, executive and administrative power in the municipality. They are required after election to designate one of their number as Mayor, a largely ceremonial office, but no formal provision is made for allocating specific executive or administrative duties among the three. As required by the state law enacted in 1911, each candidate for the Mobile City Commission runs for election in the city at-large for a term of four years in one of three numbered posts, and may be elected only by a majority of the total vote. This is the same basic electoral system that is followed by literally thousands of municipalities and other local governmental units throughout the Nation. . . .

The Court's early decisions under the Fifteenth Amendment established that it imposes but one limitation on the powers of the States. It forbids them to discriminate against Negroes in matters having to do with voting. See *Ex parte Yarbrough*, 110 U.S. 651, 665. . . . *United States* v. *Reese*, 92 U.S. 214, 1876. . . . The Amendment's command and effect are wholly negative. "The Fifteenth Amendment does not confer the right of suffrage upon anyone," but has "invested the citizens of the United States with a new constitutional right which is within the protecting power of Congress. That right is exemption from discrimination in the exercise of the elective franchise on account of race, color, or previous condition of servitude." *Id.*, at 217–218.

Our decisions, moreover, have made clear that action by a State that is racially neutral on its face violates the Fifteenth Amendment only if motivated by a discriminatory purpose. In *Guinn* v. *United States*, 238 U.S. 347, 1915 . . . this Court struck down a "grandfather" clause in a state constitution exempting from the requirement that voters be literate any person or the descendants of any person who had been entitled to vote before January 1, 1866. . . .

[T]he Court did not hesitate to hold the grandfather clause unconstitutional because it was not "possible to discover any basis in reason for the standard thus fixed than the purpose" to circumvent the Fifteenth Amendment, *Id.*, at 365.

The Court's more recent decisions confirm the principle that racially discriminatory motivation is a necessary ingredient of a Fifteenth Amendment violation. . . .

[Here Justice Stewart discusses *Gomillion* v. *Lightfoot*, 364 U.S. 339 (1960), *Wright* v. *Rockefeller*, 376 U.S. 52 (1964), and the Texas white primary cases.]

. . . Having found that Negroes in Mobile "register and vote without hindrance," the District Court and Court of Appeals were in error in believing that the appellants invaded the protection of that Amendment in the present case.

The Court of Appeals also agreed with the District Court that Mobile's at-large electoral system violates the Equal Protection Clause of the Fourteenth Amendment. . . .

The claim that at-large electoral schemes unconstitutionally deny to some persons the Equal Protection of the Laws has been advanced in numerous cases before this Court. That contention has been raised most often with regard to multimember constituencies within a state legislative apportionment system. The constitutional objection to multimember districts is not and cannot be that, as such, they depart from apportionment on a population basis in violation of *Reynolds* v. *Sims*, 377 U.S. 533, 1964 . . . and its progeny. Rather the focus in such cases has been on the lack of representation multimember districts afford various elements of the voting population in a system of representative legislative democracy. "Criticism [of multimember districts] is rooted in their winner-take-all aspects,their tendency to submerge minorities . . . , a general preference for legislatures reflecting community interests as closely as possible and disenchantment with political parties and elections as devices to settle policy differences between contending interests." *Whitcomb* v. *Chavis*, 403 U.S. 124, 158–159, 1971. . . .

Despite repeated constitutional attacks upon multimember legislative districts, the Court has consistently held that they are not unconstitutional *per se*, e.g., *White* v. *Regester*, 412 U.S. 755, 1973; *Whitcomb* v. *Chavis*, . . . We have recognized, however, that such legislative apportionments could violate the Fourteenth Amendment if their purpose were invidiously to minimize or cancel out the voting potential of racial or ethnic minorities. . . . To prove such a purpose it is not enough to show that the group allegedly discriminated against has not elected representatives in proportion to its numbers. . . . A plaintiff must prove that the disputed plan was "conceived or operated as [a] purposeful device to further racial discrimination." . . .

This burden of proof is simply one aspect of the basic principle that only if there is purposeful discrimination can there be a violation of the Equal Protection Clause of the Fourteenth Amendment. See *Washington* v. *Davis*, 426 U.S. 229, 1976; *Village of Arlington Heights* v. *Metropolitan Housing Development Corp.*, 429 U.S. 252, 1977; *Personnel Adm'r of Massachusetts* v. *Feeney*, 442 U.S. 256, 1979. . . .

In only one case has the Court sustained a claim that multimember legislative districts unconstitutionally diluted the voting strength of a discrete group. That case was *White* v. *Regester, supra*. There the Court upheld a constitutional challenge by Negroes and Mexican-Americans to parts of a legislative reapportionment adopted by the State of Texas. The plaintiffs alleged that the multimember districts for the two counties in which they resided minimized the effect of their votes in violation of the Fourteenth Amendment, and the Court held that the plaintiffs had been able to "produce evidence to support the finding that the political processes leading to nomination and election were not equally open to participation by the group[s] in question." 412 U.S., at 766. . . . In so holding, the Court relied upon evidence in the record that included a long history of official discrimination against minorities as well as indifference to their needs and interests on the part of white elected officials. The Court also found in each county additional factors that restricted the access of minority groups to the political process. In one county, Negroes effectively were excluded from the process of slating candidates for the Democratic Party, while the plaintiffs in the other county were Mexican-Americans who "suffer[ed] a cultural and language barrier" that made "participation in community processes extremely difficult, particularly . . . with respect to the political life" of the county. *Id.*, at 768.

White v. *Regester* is thus consistent with "the basic equal protection principle that the invidious equality of a law claimed to be racially discriminatory must ultimately be traced to a racially discriminatory purpose," *Washington* v. *Davis*, 426 U.S., at 240. The Court stated the constitutional question in *White* to be whether the "multimember districts [were] being used invidiously to minimize or cancel out the voting strength of racial groups," . . . strongly indicating that only a purposeful dilution of the plaintiff's vote would offend the Equal Protection Clause. . . . But where the character of a law is readily explainable on grounds apart from race, as would nearly always be true where, as here, an entire system of local governance is brought to

question, disproportionate impact alone cannot be decisive, and courts must look to other evidence to support a finding of discriminatory purpose. . . .

We may assume, for present purposes, that an at-large election of city officials with all the legislative, executive and administrative power of the municipal government is constitutionally indistinguishable from the election of a few members of a state legislative body in multimember districts—although this may be a rash assumption. But even making this assumption, it is clear that the evidence in the present case fell far short of showing that the appellants "conceived or operated [a] purposeful device to further racial discrimination." *Whitcomb* v. *Chavis*, 403 U.S., at 149. . . .

We turn finally to the arguments advanced in Part I of JUSTICE MARSHALL's dissenting opinion. The theory of this dissenting opinion—a theory much more extreme than that espoused by the District Court or the Court of Appeals—appears to be that every "political group," or at least every such group that is in the minority, has a federal constitutional right to elect candidates in proportion to its numbers. Moreover, a political group's "right" to have its candidates elected is said to be a "fundamental interest," the infringement of which may be established without proof that a State has acted with the purpose of impairing anybody's access to the political process. This dissenting opinion finds the "right" infringed in the present case because no Negro has been elected to the Mobile City Commission.

Whatever appeal the dissenting opinion's view may have as a matter of political theory, it is not the law. The Equal Protection Clause of the Fourteenth Amendment does not require proportional representation as an imperative of political organization. The entitlement that the dissenting opinion assumes to exist simply is not to be found in the Constitution of the United States. . . .

Almost a hundred years ago the Court unanimously held that "the Constitution of the United States does not confer the right of suffrage upon any one. . . . " *Minor* v. *Happersett*, 21 Wall. 162, 178. . . . It is for the States "to determine the conditions under which the right of suffrage may be exercised . . . , absent of course the discrimination which the Constitution condemns," *ibid.* It is true, as the dissenting opinion states, that the Equal Protection Clause confers a substantive right to participate in elections on an equal basis with other qualified voters. . . . But this right to equal participation in the electoral process does not protect any "political group," however defined, from electoral defeat.

The dissenting opinion erroneously discovers

the asserted entitlement to group representation within the "one person-one vote" principle of *Reynolds* v. *Sims* . . . and its progeny. Those cases established that the Equal Protection Clause guarantees the right of each voter to "have his vote weighted equally with those of all other citizens." . . . There can be, of course, no claim that the "one person–one vote" principle has been violated in this case, because the city of Mobile is a unitary electoral district and the Commission elections are conducted at-large. It is therefore obvious that nobody's vote has been "diluted" in the sense in which that word was used in the *Reynolds* case.

The dissenting opinion-places an extraordinary interpretation on these decisions, an interpretation not justified by *Reynolds* v. *Sims* itself or by any other decision of this Court. It is, of course, true that the right of a person to vote on an equal basis with other voters draws much of its significance from the political associations that its exercise reflects, but it is an altogether different matter to conclude that political groups themselves have an independent constitutional claim to representation. And that Court's decisions hold squarely that they do not. . . .

The fact is that the Court has sternly set its face against the claim, however phrased, that the Constitution somehow guarantees proportional representation. . . .

The judgment is reversed, and the case is remanded to the Court of Appeals for further proceedings.

It is so ordered.

[The concurring opinions of JUSTICE BLACKMUN and JUSTICE STEVENS and the dissenting opinions of JUSTICE BRENNAN and JUSTICE WHITE are not reprinted here.]

JUSTICE MARSHALL, *dissenting.*

. . . The plurality would require plaintiffs in vote-dilution cases to meet the stringent burden of establishing discriminatory intent with the meaning of *Washington* v. *Davis*, 426 U.S. 229 (1976); *Arlington Heights* v. *Metropolitan Housing Corp.*, 429 U.S. 252 (1977); and *Personnel Administrator of Mass.* v. *Feeney*, 442 U.S. 256 (1979). In my view, our vote-dilution decisions require only a showing of discriminatory impact to justify the invalidation of a multimember districting scheme, and, because they are premised on the fundamental interest in voting protected by the Fourteenth Amendment, the discriminatory-impact standard adopted by them is unaffected by *Washington* v. *Davis, supra,* and its progeny. Furthermore, an intent require-

ment is inconsistent with the protection against denial or abridgement of the vote on account of race embodied in the Fifteenth Amendment and in § 2 of the Voting Rights Act of 1965, 42 U.S.C. § 1973. Even if, however, proof of discriminatory intent were necessary to support a vote-dilution claim, I would impose upon the plaintiffs a standard of proof less rigid than that provided by *Personnel Administrator of Mass.* v. *Feeney, supra.*

The Court does not dispute the proposition that multimember districting can have the effect of submerging electoral minorities and overrepresenting electoral majorities. It is for this reason that we developed a strong preference for single-member districting in court-ordered reapportionment plans. . . . Furthermore, and more important for present purposes, we decided a series of vote-dilution cases under the Fourteenth Amendment that were designed to protect electoral minorities from precisely the combination of electoral laws and historical and social factors found in the present cases. In my view, the plurality's treatment of these cases is fanciful. Although we have held that multimember districts are not unconstitutional *per se*, . . . there is simply no basis for the plurality's conclusion that under our prior cases proof of discriminatory intent is a necessary condition for the invalidation of multimember districting. . . .

[I]n *White* v. *Regester*, 412 U.S. 756 (1973), we invalidated the challenged multimember districting plans because their characteristics, when combined with historical and social factors, had the discriminatory effect of denying the plaintiff Negroes and Mexican-Americans equal access to the political process. . . . We stated that

> [i]t is not enough that the racial group allegedly discriminated against has not had legislative seats in proportion to its voting potential. The plaintiff's burden is to produce evidence to support findings that the political processes leading to nomination and election were not equally open to participation by the group in question—that its members had less opportunity than did other residents in the district to participate in the political processes and to elect legislators of their choice. *Id.,* at 765–766.

It is apparent that a showing of discriminatory intent in the creation or maintenance of multimember districts is as unnecessary after *White* as it was under our earlier vote-dilution decisions. Under this line of cases, an electoral districting plan is invalid if it has the effect of affording an electoral minority "less opportunity than . . . other residents in the district to participate in the political processes and to elect legislators of their choice," *id.*, at 766. It is also apparent that the Court in *White* considered equal access to the political process as meaning more than merely allowing the minority the opportunity to vote. *White* stands for the proposition that an electoral system may not relegate an electoral minority to political impotence by diminishing the importance of its vote. The plurality's approach requiring proof of discriminatory purpose in the present cases is, then, squarely contrary to *White* and its predecessors.

The plurality fails to apply the discriminatory effect standard of *White* v. *Regester* because that approach conflicts with what the plurality takes to be an elementary principle of law. "[O]nly if there is purposeful discrimination," announced the plurality, "can there be a violation of the Equal Protection Clause of the Fourteenth Amendment." . . . That proposition is plainly overbroad. It fails to distinguish between two distinct lines of equal protection decisions: those involving suspect classifications and those involving fundamental rights.

We have long recognized that under the Equal Protection Clause classifications based on race are "constitutionally suspect" . . . and are subject to the "most rigid scrutiny," regardless of whether they infringe on an independently protected constitutional right. . . . Under *Washington* v. *Davis* . . . , a showing of discriminatory purpose is necessary to impose strict scrutiny on facially neutral classifications having a racially discriminatory impact. Perhaps because the plaintiffs in the present cases are Negro, the plurality assumes that their vote-dilution claims are premised on the suspect-classification branch of our equal protection cases, and that under *Washington* v. *Davis* . . . they are required to prove discriminatory intent. That assumption fails to recognize that our vote-dilution decisions are rooted in a different strand of equal protection jurisprudence.

Under the Equal Protection Clause, if a classification "impinges upon a fundamental right explicitly or implicitly protected by the Constitution, . . . strict judicial scrutiny" is required . . . regardless of whether the infringement was intentional. . . . [O]ur cases recognize a fundamental right to equal electoral participation that encompasses protection against vote dilution. Proof of discriminatory purpose is, therefore, not required to support a claim of vote dilution. The plurality's erroneous conclusion to the contrary is the result of a failure to recognize the central distinction between *White* v. *Regester* . . . and *Washington* v. *Davis* . . . : the former involved an infringement of a constitutionally protected right, while the latter dealt with a claim of racially discriminatory distribution

of an interest to which no citizen has a constitutional entitlement. . . .

Nearly a century ago, the Court recognized the elementary proposition upon which our structure of civil rights is based: "[T]he political franchise of voting is . . . a fundamental political right, because preservative of all rights." *Yick Wo* v. *Hopkins*, 118 U.S. 356, 370 (1886). We reiterated that theme in our landmark decision in *Reynolds* v. *Sims*, 377 U.S. 533, 561–562 (1964), and stated that, because "the right of suffrage is a fundamental matter in a free and democratic society[,] . . . any alleged infringement of the right of citizens to vote must be carefully and meticulously scrutinized." *Ibid.* . . .

Reynolds v. *Sims* and its progeny focused solely on the discriminatory effects of malapportionment. They recognize that, when population figures for the representational districts of a legislature are not similar, the votes of citizens in larger districts do not carry as much weight in the legislature as do votes cast by citizens in smaller districts. The equal protection problem attacked by the "one person–one vote" principle is, then, one of vote dilution: under *Reynolds*, each citizen must have an "equally effective voice" in the election of representatives. . . . In the present cases, the alleged vote dilution, though caused by the combined effects of the electoral structure and social and historical factors rather than by unequal population distribution, is analytically the same concept; the unjustified abridgement of a fundamental right. It follows, then, that a showing of discriminatory intent is just as unnecessary under the vote-dilution approach adopted in *Fortson* v. *Dorsey*, 379 U.S. 433, 1965 . . . as it is under our reapportionment cases.

Indeed, our vote-dilution cases have explicitly acknowledged that they are premised on the infringement of a fundamental right, not on the Equal Protection Clause's prohibition of racial discrimination. . . .

Until today, this Court had never deviated from this principle. . . . [See *Burns* v. *Richardson*, 384 U.S. 73 (1966); *Whitcomb* v. *Chavis, supra; Gaffney* v. *Cummings*, 412 U.S. 735 (1973); *Dallas County* v. *Reese*, 421 U.S. 477 (1975); and *United Jewish Organizations* v. *Carey*, 430 U.S. 144 (1977).]

. . . The plurality's response is that my approach amounts to nothing less than a constitutional requirement of proportional representation for groups. . . . That assertion amounts to nothing more than a red herring: I explicitly reject the notion that the Constitution contains any such requirement. . . . The constitutional protection against vote dilution found in our prior cases does not extend to those situations in which a group has merely failed to elect representatives in proportion to its share of the population. To prove unconstitutional vote dilution, the group is also required to carry the far more onerous burden of demonstrating that it has been effectively fenced out of the political process. . . . Typical of the plurality's mischaracterization of my position is its assertion that would provide protection against vote dilution for "every 'political group,' or at least every such group that is in the minority." . . . The vote-dilution doctrine can logically apply only to groups whose electoral discreteness and insularity allow dominant political factions to ignore them. . . . In short, the distinction between a requirement of proportional representation and the discriminatory effect test I espouse is by no means a difficult one, and it is hard for me to understand why the plurality insists on ignoring it. . . .

The plaintiffs convinced the District Court that Mobile Negroes were unable to use alternative avenues of political influence. They showed that Mobile Negroes still suffered pervasive present effects of massive historical, official and private discrimination, and that the city commission had been quite unresponsive to the needs of the minority community. The City of Mobile has been guilty of such pervasive racial discrimination in hiring employees that extensive intervention by the Federal District Court has been required. . . . Negroes are grossly underrepresented on city boards and committees. . . . The city's distribution of public services is racially discriminatory. . . . City officials and police were largely unmoved by Negro complaints about police brutality and a "mock lynching." . . . The District Court concluded that "[t]his sluggish and timid response is another manifestation of the low priority given to the needs of the black citizens and of the [commissioners'] political fear of a white backlash vote when black citizens' needs are at stake." . . .

Today the plurality gives short shrift to the argument that proof of discriminatory intent is not a necessary condition to relief under [the Fifteenth Amendment]. . . . I have examined this issue in another context and reached the contrary result. *Beer* v. *United States*, 425 U.S. 130, 146–149, and nn. 3–5 (1976) (dissenting opinion). I continue to believe that "a showing of purpose or of effect is alone sufficient to demonstrate unconstitutionality." *Id.*, at 149, n. 5. . . .

The Fifteenth Amendment . . . assuredly strikes down the diminution as well as the outright denial of the exercise of the franchise. An interpretation holding that the Amendment reaches only complete abrogation of the vote would render the Amendment essentially useless, since it is not a difficult task to imagine schemes in which the Negro's marking of the ballot is a meaningless exercise.

The Court has long understood that the right to vote encompasses protection against vote dilution. "[T]he right to have one's vote counted" is of the same importance as "the right to put a ballot in a box." *United States* v. *Mosley*, 238 U.S. 383, 386 (1915). . . . The right to vote is protected against the diluting effect of ballot-box stuffing. *United States* v. *Saylor*, 322 U.S. 385 (1944); *Ex parte Siebold*, 100 U.S. 371 (1880). Indeed, this Court has explicitly recognized that the Fifteenth Amendment protects against vote dilution. In *Terry* v. *Adams*, 345 U.S. 461 (1953), and *Smith* v. *Allwright*, 321 U.S. 649 (1944), the Negro plaintiffs did not question their access to the ballot for general elections. Instead they argued, and the Court recognized, that the value of their votes had been diluted by their exclusion from participation in primary elections and in the slating of candidates by political parties. The Court's struggles with the concept of "state action" in those decisions were necessarily premised on the understanding that vote dilution was a claim cognizable under the Fifteenth Amendment.

Wright v. *Rockefeller*, 376 U.S. 52 (1964), recognized that an allegation of vote dilution resulting from the drawing of district lines stated a claim under the Fifteenth Amendment. The plaintiffs in that case argued that congressional districting in New York violated the Fifteenth Amendment because district lines had been drawn in a racially discriminatory fashion. . . . More recently, in *United Jewish Organizations* v. *Carey*, 430 U.S. 144 (1977), we again treated an allegation of vote dilution arising from a redistricting scheme as stating a claim under the Fifteenth Amendment. . . .

It is plain, then, that the Fifteenth Amendment shares the concept of vote dilution developed in such Fourteenth Amendment decisions as *Reynolds* v. *Sims* and *Fortson* v. *Dorsey*. . . . In fact, under the Court's unified view of the protections of the right to vote accorded in disparate portions of the Constitution, the concept of vote dilution is a core principle of the Seventeenth and Nineteenth Amendments as well as the Fourteenth and Fifteenth. . . .

An interpretation of the Fifteenth Amendment limiting its prohibitions to the outright denial of the ballot would convert the words of the Amendment into language illusory in symbol and hollow in substance. Surely today's decision should not be read as endorsing that interpretation. . . .

. . . In holding that racial discrimination claims under the Equal Protection Clause must be supported by proof of discriminatory intent, the court in *Washington* v. *Davis* . . . signaled some movement away from the doctrine that such proof is irrelevant to constitutional adjudication. Although the Court . . . attempted mightily to distinguish *Palmer* v. *Thompson*, 403 U.S. 217 (1971), . . . its decision was in fact based upon a judgment that, in light of modern circumstances, the Equal Protection Clause's ban on racial discrimination in the distribution of constitutional gratuities should be interpreted as prohibiting only intentional official discrimination.

These vacillations in our approach to the relevance of discriminatory purpose belie the plurality's determination that our prior decisions require such proof to support Fifteenth Amendment claims. To the contrary, the Court today is in the same unsettled position with regard to the Fifteenth Amendment as it was four years ago in *Washington* v. *Davis* regarding the Fourteenth Amendment's prohibition on racial discrimination. The absence of old answers mandates a new inquiry.

The Court in *Washington* v. *Davis* required a showing of discriminatory purpose to support racial discrimination claims largely because it feared that a standard based solely on disproportionate impact would unduly interfere with the far-ranging governmental distribution of constitutional gratuities. Underlying the Court's decision was a determination that, since the Constitution does not entitle any person to such governmental benefits, courts should accord discretion to those officials who decide how the Government shall allocate its scarce resources. If the plaintiff proved only that governmental distribution of constitutional gratuities had a disproportionate effect on a racial minority, the Court was willing to presume that the officials who approved the allocation scheme either had made an honest error or had foreseen that the decision would have a discriminatory impact and had found persuasive, legitimate reasons for imposing it nonetheless. These assumptions about the good faith of officials allowed the Court to conclude that, standing alone, a showing that a governmental policy had a racially discriminatory impact did not indicate that the affected minority had suffered the stigma, frustration, and unjust treatment prohibited under the suspect classification branch of our equal protection jurisprudence.

Such judicial deference to official decisionmaking has no place under the Fifteenth Amendment.

Section 1 of that Amendment differs from the Fourteenth Amendment's prohibition on racial discrimination in two crucial respects: it explicitly recognizes the right to vote free of hindrances related to race, and it sweeps no further. In my view, these distinctions justify the conclusion that proof of racially discriminatory impact should be sufficient to support a claim under the Fifteenth Amendment. The right to vote is of such fundamental importance in the constitutional scheme that the Fifteenth Amendment's command that it shall not be "abridged" on account of race must be interpreted as providing that the votes of citizens of all races shall be of substantially equal weight. Furthermore, a disproportionate-impact test under the Fifteenth Amendment would not lead to constant judicial intrusion into the process of official decisionmaking. Rather, the standard would reach only those decisions having a discriminatory effect upon the minority's vote. The Fifteenth Amendment cannot tolerate that kind of decision, even if made in good faith, because the Amendment grants racial minorities the full enjoyment of the right to vote, not simply protection against the unfairness of intentional vote dilution along racial lines.

In addition, it is beyond dispute that a standard based solely upon the motives of official decision makers creates significant problems of proof for plaintiffs and forces the inquiring court to undertake an unguided, torturous look into the minds of officials in the hope of guessing why certain policies were adopted and others rejected. . . . An approach based on motivation creates the risk that officials will be able to adopt policies that are the products of discriminatory intent so long as they sufficiently mask their motives through the use of subtlety and illusion. *Washington* v. *Davis* is premised on the notion that this risk is insufficient to overcome the deference the judiciary must accord to governmental decisions about the distribution of constitutional gratuities. That risk becomes intolerable, however, when the precious right to vote protected by the Fifteenth Amendment is concerned.

I continue to believe, then, that under the Fifteenth Amendment an "[e]valuation of the purpose of a legislative enactment is just too ambiguous a task to be the sole tool of constitutional analysis. . . . [A] demonstration of effect ordinarily should suffice. If, of course, purpose may conclusively be shown, it too should be sufficient to demonstrate a statute's unconstitutionality." *Beer* v. *United States*, 425 U.S. 130, 149, n. 5 (1976) (MARSHALL, J., dissenting). The plurality's refusal in this case even to consider this approach bespeaks an indifference to the plight of minorities who, through no fault of their own, have suffered diminution of the right preservative of all other rights.

If it is assumed that proof of discriminatory intent is necessary to support the vote-dilution claims in these cases, the question becomes what evidence will satisfy this requirement.

The plurality assumes, without any analysis, that these cases are appropriate for the application of the rigid test developed in *Personnel Administrator of Mass.* v. *Feeney* . . . requiring that "the decision maker . . . selected or reaffirmed a particular course of action at least in part 'because of,' not merely 'in spite of,' its adverse effects upon an identifiable group." In my view, the *Feeney* standard creates a burden of proof far too extreme to apply in vote-dilution cases.

The Court has acknowledged that the evidentiary inquiry involving discriminatory intent must necessarily vary depending upon the factual context. . . . One useful evidentiary tool, long recognized by the common law, is the presumption that "[e]very man must be taken to contemplate the probable consequences of the act he does." *Townsend* v. *Wather*, 103 Eng. Rep. 579, 580–581 (K.B. 1808). The Court in *Feeney, supra*, at 279 and n. 25, acknowledged that proof of foreseeability of discriminatory consequences could raise a "strong inference that the adverse effects were desired," but refused to treat this presumption as conclusive in cases alleging discriminatory distribution of constitutional gratuities.

I would apply the common-law foreseeability presumption to the present cases. The plaintiffs surely proved that maintenance of the challenged multimember districting would have the foreseeable effect of perpetuating the submerged electoral influence of Negroes, and that this discriminatory effect could be corrected by implementation of a single-member districting plan. Because the foreseeable disproportionate impact was so severe, the burden of proof should have shifted to the defendants, and they should have been required to show that they refused to modify the districting schemes in spite of, not because of, their severe discriminatory effect. . . . Reallocation of the burden of proof is especially appropriate in these cases, where the challenged state action infringes the exercise of a fundamental right. The defendants would carry their burden of proof only if they showed that they considered submergence of the Negro vote a detriment, not a benefit, of the multimember systems, that they accorded minority citizens the same respect given to whites, and that they nevertheless decided to maintain the systems for legitimate reasons. . . .

Furthermore, if proof of discriminatory purpose is to be required in these cases, this standard would comport with my view that the degree to which the Government must justify a decision depends upon the importance of the interests infringed by it. . . .

The plurality also fails to recognize that the maintenance of multimember districts in the face of foreseeable discriminatory consequences strongly suggests that officials are blinded by "racially selective sympathy and indifference." Like outright racial hostility, selective racial indifference reflects a belief that the concerns of the minority are not worthy of the same degree of attention paid to problems perceived by whites. When an interest as fundamental as voting is diminished along racial lines, a requirement that discriminatory purpose must be proved should be satisfied by a showing that official action was produced by this type of pervasive bias. In the present case, the plaintiffs presented strong evidence of such bias; they showed that Mobile officials historically discriminated against Negroes, that there are pervasive present effects of this past discrimination, and that officials have not been responsive to the needs of the minority community. It takes only the smallest of inferential leaps to conclude that the decisions to maintain multimember districting having obvious discriminatory effects represent, at the very least, selective racial sympathy and indifference resulting in the frustration of minority desires, the stigmatization of the minority as second-class citizens, and the perpetuation of inhumanity.

The American approach to government is premised on the theory that, when citizens have the unfettered right to vote, public officials will make decisions by the democratic accommodation of competing beliefs, not by deference to the mandates of the powerful. The American approach to civil rights is premised on the complementary theory that the unfettered right to vote is preservative of all other rights. The theoretical foundations for these approaches are shattered where, as in the present cases, the right to vote is granted in form, but denied in substance.

It is time to realize that manipulating doctrines and drawing improper distinctions under the Fourteenth and Fifteenth Amendments, as well as under Congress's remedial legislation enforcing those Amendments, make this Court an accessory to the perpetuation of racial discrimination. The plurality's requirement of proof of *intentional dis-*

crimination, so inappropriate in today's cases, may represent an attempt to bury the legitimate concerns of the minority beneath the soil of a doctrine almost as impermeable as it is specious. If so, the superficial tranquility created by such measures can be but shortlived. If this Court refuses to honor our long-recognized principle that the Constitution "nullifies sophisticated as well as simpleminded modes of discrimination," *Lane* v. *Wilson,* 307 U.S. 268, 275 (1939), it cannot expect the victims of discrimination to respect political channels of seeking redress.

I dissent.

THORNBURG v. GINGLES
478 U.S. 30; 92 L. Ed. 2d 25; 106 S. Ct. 2752 (1986)

JUSTICE BRENNAN *announced the judgment of the Court and delivered the opinion of the Court with respect to Parts I, II, III-A, III-B, IV-A, and V, an opinion with respect to Part III-C, in which* JUSTICE MARSHALL, JUSTICE BLACKMUN, *and* JUSTICE STEVENS *join, and an opinion with respect to Part IV-B, in which* JUSTICE WHITE *joins.*

This case requires that we construe for the first time § 2 of the Voting Rights Act of 1965, as amended June 29, 1982. 42 U.S.C. § 1973. The specific question to be decided is whether the three-judge District Court, convened in the Eastern District of North Carolina . . . correctly held that the use in a legislative redistricting plan of multimember districts in five North Carolina legislative districts violated § 2 by impairing the opportunity of black voters "to participate in the political process and to elect representatives of thei choice."

I

Background

In April 1982, the North Carolina General Assembly enacted a legislative redistricting plan for the State's Senate and House of Representatives. Appellees, black citizens of North Carolina who are registered to vote, challenged seven districts, one single-member and six multimember districts, alleging that the redistricting scheme impaired black citizens' ability to elect representatives of their choice in violation of the Fourteenth and Fifteenth Amendments to the United States Constitution and of § 2 of the Voting Rights Act.

After appellees brought suit, but before trial, Congress amended § 2. The amendment was largely a response to this Court's plurality opinion in *Mobile* v. *Bolden,* 446 U.S. 55 (1980), which had declared that, in order to establish a violation of either § 2 or of the Fourteenth or Fifteenth Amendments, minority voters must prove that a contested electoral mechanism was intentionally adopted or maintained by state officials for a discriminatory purpose. Congress substantially revised § 2 to make clear that a violation could be proven by showing discriminatory effect alone and to establish as the relevant legal standard the "results test." . . .

Section 2, as amended, 96 Stat. 134, reads as follows:

(a) No voting qualification or prerequisite to voting or standard, practice, or procedure shall be imposed or applied by any State or political subdivision in a manner which results in a denial or abridgement of the right of any citizen of the United States to vote on account of race or color, or in contravention of the guarantees set forth in section 4(f)(2), as provided in subsection (b).

(b) A violation of subsection (a) is established if, based on the totality of the circumstances, it is shown that the political processes leading to nomination or election in the State or political subdivision are not equally open to participation by members of a class of citizens protected by subsection (a) in that its members have less opportunity than other members of the electorate to participate in the political process and to elect representatives of their choice. The extent to which members of a protected class have been elected to office in the State or political subdivision is one circumstance which may be considered: *Provided,* That nothing in this section establishes a right to have members of a protected class elected in numbers equal to their proportion in the population. Codified at 42 U.S.C. § 1973 . . .

The District Court applied the "totality of the

circumstances" test . . . [and] held that the redistricting scheme violated § 2 because it resulted in the dilution of black citizens' votes in all seven disputed districts. In light of this conclusion, the court did not reach appellees' constitutional claims. . . .

Preliminarily, the court found that black citizens constituted a distinct population and registered-voter minority in each challenged district. The court noted that at the time the multimember districts were created, there were concentrations of black citizens within the boundaries of each that were sufficiently large and contiguous to constitute effective voting majorities in single-member districts lying wholly within the boundaries of the multimember districts. With respect to the challenged single-member district, Senate District No. 2, the court also found that there existed a concentration of black citizens within its boundaries and within those of adjoining Senate District No. 6 that was sufficient in numbers and in contiguity to constitute an effective voting majority in a single-member district. The District Court then proceeded to find that the following circumstances combined with the multimember districting scheme to result in the dilution of black citizens' votes.

First, the court found that North Carolina had officially discriminated against its black citizens with respect to their exercise of the voting franchise from approximately 1900 to 1970 by employing at different times a poll tax, a literacy test, a prohibition against bullet (single-shot) voting and designated seat plans for multimember districts. The court observed that even after the removal of direct barriers to black voter registration, such as the poll tax and literacy test, black voter registration remained relatively depressed; in 1982 only 52.7% of age-qualified blacks statewide were registered to vote, whereas 66.7% of whites were registered. The District Court found these statewide depressed levels of black voter registration to be present in all of the disputed districts and to be traceable, at least in part, to the historical pattern of statewide official discrimination.

Second, the court found that historic discrimination in education, housing, employment, and health services had resulted in a lower socioeconomic status for North Carolina blacks as a group than for whites. The court concluded that this lower status both gives rise to special group interests and hinders blacks' ability to participate effectively in the political process and to elect representatives of their choice.

Third, the court considered other voting procedures that may operate to lessen the opportunity of black voters to elect candidates of their choice. It noted that North Carolina has a majority vote requirement for primary elections and, while acknowledging that no black candidate for election to the State General Assembly had failed to win solely because of this requirement, the court concluded that it nonetheless presents a continuing practical impediment to the opportunity of black voting minorities to elect candidates of their choice. The court also remarked on the fact that North Carolina does not have a subdistrict residency requirement for members of the General Assembly elected from multimember districts, a requirement which the court found could offset to some extent the disadvantages minority voters often experience in multimember districts.

Fourth, the court found that white candidates in North Carolina have encouraged voting along color lines by appealing to racial prejudice. It noted that the record is replete with specific examples of racial appeals, ranging in style from overt and blatant to subtle and furtive, and in date from the 1890s to the 1984 campaign for a seat in the United States Senate. The court determined that the use of racial appeals in political campaigns in North Carolina persists to the present day and that its current effect is to lessen to some degree the opportunity of black citizens to participate effectively in the political processes and to elect candidates of their choice.

Fifth, the court examined the extent to which blacks have been elected to office in North Carolina, both statewide and in the challenged districts. It found, among other things, that prior to World War II, only one black had been elected to public office in this century. While recognizing that "it has now become possible for black citizens to be elected to office at all levels of state government in North Carolina" . . . the court found that, in comparison to white candidates running for the same office, black candidates are at a disadvantage in terms of relative probability of success. It also found that the overall rate of black electoral success has been minimal in relation to the percentage of blacks in the total state population. For example, the court noted, from 1971 and 1982 there were at any given time only two to four blacks in the 120-member House of Representatives—that is, only 1.6% to 3.3% of House members were black. From 1975 to 1983 there were at any one time only one or two blacks in the 50-member State Senate—that is, only 2% to 4% of State Senators were black. By contrast, at the time of the District Court's opinion, blacks constituted about 22.4% of the total state population.

With respect to the success in this century of black candidates in the contested districts . . . , the court found that only one black had been elected to House District 36—after this lawsuit began. Similarly, only one black had served in the Senate from District 22, from 1975–1980. Before the 1982 election, a black was elected only twice to the House from District 39 (part of Forsyth County); in the 1982 contest two blacks were elected. Since 1973 a black citizen had been elected each 2-year term to the House from District 23 (Durham County), but no black had been elected to the Senate from Durham County. In House District 21 (Wake County), a black had been elected twice to the House, and another black served two terms in the State Senate. No black had ever been elected to the House or Senate from the area covered by House District No. 8, and no black person had ever been elected to the Senate from the area covered by Senate District No. 2.

The court did acknowledge the improved success of black candidates in the 1982 elections, in which 11 blacks were elected to the State House of Representatives, including 5 blacks from the multimember districts at issue here. However, the court pointed out that the 1982 election was conducted after the commencement of this litigation. The court found the circumstances of the 1982 election sufficiently aberrational and the success by black candidates too minimal and too recent in relation to the long history of complete denial of elective opportunities to support the conclusion that black voters' opportunities to elect representatives of their choice were not impaired.

Finally, the court considered the extent to which voting in the challenged districts was racially polarized. Based on statistical evidence presented by expert witnesses, supplemented to some degree by the testimony of lay witnesses, the court found that all of the challenged districts exhibit severe and persistent racially polarized voting.

Based on these findings, the court declared the contested portions of the 1982 redistricting plan violative of § 2 and enjoined appellants from conducting elections pursuant to those portions of the plan. Appellants, the Attorney General of North Carolina and others, took a direct appeal to this Court . . . with respect to five of the multimember districts—[and we] . . . affirm with respect to all of the districts except House District 23. With regard to District 23, the judgment of the District Court is reversed and remanded for further proceedings.

II

Section 2 and Vote Dilution Through Use of Multimember Districts

An understanding both of § 2 and of the way in which multimember districts can operate to impair blacks' ability to elect representatives of their choice is prerequisite to an evaluation of appellants' contentions. . . .

A

Section 2 and Its Legislative History

Subsection 2(a) prohibits all States and political subdivisions from imposing *any* voting qualifications or prerequisites to voting, or any standards, practices, or procedures which result in the denial or abridgement of the right to vote of any citizen who is a member of a protected class of racial and language minorities. Subsection 2(b) establishes that § 2 has been violated where the "totality of the circumstances" reveal that "the political processes leading to nomination or election . . . are not equally open to participation by members of a [protected class] . . . in that its members have less opportunity than other members of the electorate to participate in the political process and to elect representatives of their choice." While explaining that "[t]he extent to which members of a protected class have been elected to office in the State or political subdivision is one circumstance which may be considered" in evaluating an alleged violation, § 2(b) cautions that "nothing in [§ 2] establishes a right to have members of a protected class elected in numbers equal to their proportion in the population."

The Senate Report which accompanied the 1982 amendments elaborates on the nature of § 2 violations and on the proof required to establish these violations. First and foremost, the Report dispositively rejects the position of the plurality in *Mobile* v. *Bolden,* 446 U.S. 55 (1980), which required proof that the contested electoral practice or mechanism was adopted or maintained with the intent to discriminate against minority voters. The intent test was repudiated for three principal reasons—it is "unnecessarily divisive because it involves charges of racism on the part of individual officials or entire communities," it places an "inordinately difficult" burden of proof on plaintiffs, and it "asks the wrong question." . . . The "right" question, as the Report emphasizes repeatedly, is whether "as a result of the challenged practice or structure plaintiffs do not have an equal opportunity to participate in the political processes and to elect candidates of their choice." . . .

In order to answer this question, a court must assess the impact of the contested structure or practice on minority electoral opportunities "on the basis of objective factors." . . . The Senate Report specifies factors which typically may be relevant to a § 2 claim: the history of voting-related discrimination in the State or political subdivision; the extent to which voting in the elections of the State or political subdivision is racially polarized; the extent to which the State or political subdivision has used voting practices or procedures that tend to enhance the opportunity for discrimination against the minority group, such as unusually large election districts, majority vote requirements, and prohibitions against bullet voting; the exclusion of members of the minority group from candidate-slating processes; the extent to which minority group members bear the effects of past discrimination in areas such as education, employment, and health, which hinder their ability to participate effectively in the political process; the use of overt or subtle racial appeals in political campaigns; and the extent to which members of the minority group have been elected to public office in the jurisdiction. The Report notes also that evidence demonstrating that elected officials are unresponsive to the particularized needs of the members of the minority group and that the policy underlying the State's or the political subdivision's use of the contested practice or structure is tenuous may have probative value. . . . While the enumerated factors will often be pertinent to certain types of § 2 violations, particularly to vote dilution claims, other factors may also be relevant and may be considered. . . . Furthermore, the Senate Committee observed that "there is no requirement that any particular number of factors be proved, or that a majority of them point one way or the other." . . . Rather, the Committee determined that "the question whether the political processes are 'equally open' depends upon a searching practical evaluation of the 'past and present reality' " . . . and on a "functional" view of the political process. . . .

B

Vote Dilution Through the Use of Multimember Districts

* * *

. . . This Court has long recognized that multimember districts and at-large voting schemes may " 'operate to minimize or cancel out the voting strength of racial [minorities in] the voting population.' " . . . The theoretical basis for this type of impairment is that where minority and majority voters consistently prefer different candidates, the majority, by virtue of its numerical superiority, will regularly defeat the choices of minority voters. . . . Multimember districts and at-large election schemes, however, are not *per se* violative of minority voters' rights. . . . Minority voters who contend that the multimember form of districting violates § 2 must prove that the use of a multimember electoral structure operates to minimize or cancel out their ability to elect their preferred candidates . . . S. Rep. 16.

While many or all of the factors listed in the Senate Report may be relevant to a claim of vote dilution through submergence in multimember districts, unless there is a conjunction of the following circumstances, the use of multimember districts generally will not impede the ability of minority voters to elect representatives of their choice. Stated succinctly, a bloc voting majority must *usually* be able to defeat candidates supported by a politically cohesive, geographically insular minority group. . . . These circumstances are necessary preconditions for multimember districts to operate to impair minority voters' ability to elect representatives of their choice for the following reasons. First, the minority group must be able to demonstrate that it is sufficiently large and geographically compact to constitute a majority in a single-member district. If it is not, as would be the case in a substantially integrated district, the *multimember form* of the district cannot be responsible for minority voters' inability to elect its candidates. . . . Second, the minority group must be able to show that it is politically cohesive. If the minority group is not politically cohesive, it cannot be said that the selection of a multimember electoral structure thwarts distinctive minority group interests. . . . Third, the minority must be able to demonstrate that the white majority votes sufficiently as a bloc to enable it—in the absence of special circumstances, such as the minority candidate running unopposed—usually to defeat the minority's preferred candidate. . . . In establishing this last circumstance, the minority group demonstrates that submergence in a white multimember district impedes its ability to elect its chosen representatives.

Finally, we observe that the usual predictability of the majority's success distinguishes structural dilution from the mere loss of an occasional election. . . .

Racially Polarized Voting

Having stated the general legal principles relevant to claims that § 2 has been violated through the use of multimember districts, we turn to the arguments of appellants and of the United States as *amici curiae* addressing racially polarized voting. . . .

A

The District Court's Treatment of Racially Polarized Voting

The investigation conducted by the District Court into the question of racial bloc voting credited some testimony of lay witnesses, but relied principally on statistical evidence presented by appellees' expert witnesses . . . [that examined] data concerning the voting patterns of the two races, including estimates of the percentages of members of each race who voted for black candidates.

The court's initial consideration of these data took the form of a three-part inquiry: Did the data reveal any correlation between the race of the voter and the selection of certain candidates? Was revealed correlation statistically significant? and, Was the difference in black and white voting patterns "substantively significant"? The District Court found that blacks and whites generally preferred different candidates and, on that basis, found voting in the districts to be racially correlated. . . . Finally, . . . the court found that in all but two of the 53 elections the degree of racial bloc voting was "so marked as to be substantively significant, in the sense that the results of the individual election would have been different depending upon whether it had been held among only the white voters or only the black voters."

The court also reported its findings . . . that a high percentage of black voters regularly supported black candidates and that most white voters were extremely reluctant to vote for black candidates. The court then considered the relevance to the existence of legally significant white bloc voting of the fact that black candidates have won some elections. It determined that in most instances, special circumstances, such as incumbency and lack of opposition, rather than a diminution in usually severe white bloc voting, accounted for these candidates' success. The court also suggested that black voters' reliance on bullet voting was a significant factor in their successful efforts to elect candidates of their choice. Based on all of the evidence before it, the trial court concluded that each of the districts experiences

racially polarized voting "in a persistent and severe degree." . . .

B

The Degree of Bloc Voting that is Legally Significant Under Sec. 2

1

* * *

2

The Standard for Legally Significant Racial Bloc Voting

* * *

[T]he extent of bloc voting necessary to demonstrate that a minority's ability to elect its preferred representatives is impaired varies according to several factual circumstances[;] the degree of bloc voting which constitutes the threshold of legal significance will vary from district to district. Nonetheless, it is possible to state some general principles, and we proceed to do so. . . .

[T]he question whether a given district experiences legally significant racially polarized voting requires discrete inquiries into minority and white voting practices. A showing that a significant number of minority group members usually vote for the same candidates is one way of proving the political cohesiveness necessary to a vote dilution claim. . . . And, in general, a white bloc vote that normally will defeat the combined strength of minority support plus white "crossover" votes rises to the level of legally significant white bloc voting. The amount of white bloc voting that can generally "minimize or cancel" . . . black voters' ability to elect representatives of their choice, however, will vary from district to district according to a number of factors, including the nature of the allegedly dilutive electoral mechanism; the presence or absence of other potentially dilutive electoral devices, such as majority vote requirements, designated posts, and prohibitions against bullet voting; the percentage of registered voters in the district; and, in multimember districts, the number of candidates in the field. . . .

Because loss of political power through vote dilution is distinct from the mere inability to win a particular election, a pattern of racial bloc voting that extends over a period of time is more probative of a claim that a district experiences legally significant polarization than are the results of a single election. . . . [I]n a district where elections are shown usually to be polarized, the fact that racially polarized voting is not present in one or a few individual elections does not necessarily negate the conclusion that the district experiences legally significant bloc voting. Furthermore, the success of a minority candidate in a particular election does not necessarily prove that the district did not experience polarized voting in that election; special circumstances, such as the absence of an opponent, incumbency, or the utilization of bullet voting may explain minority electoral success in a polarized contest.

As must be apparent, the degree of racial bloc voting that is cognizable as an element of a § 2 vote dilution claim will vary according to a variety of factual circumstances. Consequently, there is no simple doctrinal test for the existence of legally significant racial bloc voting. However, the foregoing general principles should provide courts with substantial guidance in determining whether evidence that black and white voters generally prefer different candidates rises to the level of legal significance under § 2.

3

Standard Utilized by the District Court

* * *

The District Court's findings concerning black support for black candidates in the five multi-member districts at issue here clearly establish the political cohesiveness of black voters. As is apparent from the District Court's tabulated findings . . . black voters' support for black candidates was overwhelming in almost every election. In all but 5 of 16 primary elections, black support for black candidates ranged between 71% and 92%; and in the general elections, black support for black Democrat candidates ranged between 87% and 96%.

In sharp contrast to its findings of strong black support for black candidates, the District Court found that a substantial majority of white voters would rarely, if ever, vote for a black candidate. In the primary elections, white support for black candidates ranged between 8% and 50%, and in the general elections it ranged between 28% and 49%.

The court also determined that, on average, 81.7% of white voters did not vote for any black candidate in the primary elections. In the general elections, white voters almost always ranked black candidates either last or next to last in the multi-candidate field, except in heavily Democratic areas where white voters consistently ranked black candidates last among the Democrats, if not last or next

to last among all candidates. The court further observed that approximately two-thirds of white voters did not vote for black candidates in general elections, even after the candidate had won the Democratic primary and the choice was to vote for a Republican or for no one. . . .

We conclude that the District Court's approach, which tested data derived from three election years in each district, and which revealed that blacks strongly supported black candidates, while, to the black candidates' usual detriment, whites rarely did, satisfactorily addresses each facet of the proper legal standard. . . .

C
Evidence of Racially Polarized Voting

* * *

4

Race of Candidate as Primary Determinant of Voter Behavior

North Carolina's and the United States' suggestion that racially polarized voting means that voters select or reject candidates *principally* on the basis of the *candidate's race* is . . . misplaced.

[B]oth the language of § 2 and a functional understanding of the phenomenon of vote dilution mandate the conclusion that the race of the candidate *per se* is irrelevant to racial bloc voting analysis. Section 2(b) states that a violation is established if it can be shown that members of a protected minority group "have less opportunity than other members of the electorate to . . . elect representatives *of their choice*" (emphasis added). Because both minority and majority voters often select members of their own race as their preferred representatives, it will frequently be the case that a black candidate is the choice of blacks, while a white candidate is the choice of whites. Cf. "Letter to the Editor from Chandler Davidson," 17 *New Perspectives* 38 (Fall 1985). Indeed, the facts of this case illustrate that tendency—blacks preferred black candidates, whites preferred white candidates. Thus, as a matter of convenience, we and the District Court may refer to the preferred representative of black voters as the "black candidate" and to the preferred representative of white voters as the "white candidate." Nonetheless, the fact that race of voter and race of candidate is often correlated is not directly pertinent to a § 2 inquiry. Under § 2, it is the *status* of the candidate as the *chosen representative of a particular racial group*, not the race of the candidate, that is important. . . .

5

Racial Animosity as Primary Determinant of Voter Behavior

* * *

In amending § 2, Congress rejected the requirement announced by this Court in *Bolden, supra,* that § 2 plaintiffs must prove the discriminatory intent of state or local governments in adopting or maintaining the challenged electoral mechanism. Appellants' suggestion that the discriminatory intent of individual white voters must be proven in order to make out a § 2 claim must fail for the very reasons Congress rejected the intent test with respect to governmental bodies. . . .

The grave threat to racial progress and harmony which Congress perceived from requiring proof that racism caused the adoption or maintenance of a challenged electoral mechanism is present to a much greater degree in the proposed requirement that plaintiffs demonstrate that racial animosity determined white voting patterns. Under the old intent test, plaintiffs might succeed by proving only that a limited number of elected officials were racist; under the new intent test plaintiffs would be required to prove that most of the white community is racist in order to obtain judicial relief. It is difficult to imagine a more racially divisive requirement.

A second reason Congress rejected the old intent test was that in most cases it placed an "inordinately difficult burden" on § 2 plaintiffs. . . . The new intent test would be equally, if not more, burdensome. In order to prove that a *specific factor*—racial hostility—*determined* white voters' ballots, it would be necessary to demonstrate that other potentially relevant *causal factors*, such as socioeconomic characteristics and candidate expenditures, do not correlate better than racial animosity with white voting behavior. . . .

Focusing on the discriminatory intent of voters, rather than the behavior of the voters, also asks the wrong question. All that matters under § 2 and under a functional theory of vote dilution is voter behavior, not its explanations. Moreover, . . . requiring proof that racial considerations actually *caused* voter behavior will result—contrary to Congressional intent—in situations where a black minority that functionally has been totally excluded from the political process will be unable to establish a § 2 violation. . . .

6

Summary

In sum, we would hold that the legal concept of racially polarized voting, as it relates to claims of vote dilution, refers only to the existence of a correlation between the race of voters and the selection of certain candidates. Plaintiffs need not prove causation or intent in order to prove a prima facie case of racial bloc voting, and defendants may not rebut that case with evidence of causation or intent. . . .

V

Ultimate Determination of Vote Dilution

* * *

A

* * *

We reaffirm our view that the clearly erroneous test of Rule 52(a) is the appropriate standard for appellate review of a finding of vote dilution. As both amended § 2 and its legislative history make clear, in evaluating a statutory claim of vote dilution through districting, the trial court is to consider the "totality of the circumstances" and to determine, based "upon a searching practical evaluation of the 'past and present reality' " . . . whether the political process is equally open to minority voters. " 'This determination is peculiarly dependent upon the facts of each case,' " . . . and requires "an intensely local appraisal of the design and impact" of the contested electoral mechanisms. . . . The fact that amended § 2 and its legislative history provide legal standards which a court must apply to the facts in order to determine whether § 2 has been violated does not alter the standard of review. . . .

The District Court in this case carefully considered the totality of the circumstances and found that in each district racially polarized voting; the legacy of official discrimination in voting matters, educational, housing, employment, and health services; and the persistence of campaign appeals to racial prejudice acted in concert with the multimember districting scheme to impair the ability of geographically insular and politically cohesive groups of black voters to participate equally in the political process and to elect candidates of their choice. It found that the success a few black candidates have enjoyed in these districts is too recent, too limited, and, with regard to the 1982 elections, perhaps too aberrational, to disprove its conclusion. Excepting House District 23, with respect to which the District Court committed legal error, . . . we affirm the District Court's judgment. We cannot say that the District Court, composed of local judges who are well-acquainted with the political realities of the State, clearly erred in concluding that use of a multimember electoral structure has caused black voters in the districts other than House District 23 to have less opportunity than white voters to elect representatives of their choice.

The judgment of the District Court is

Affirmed in part, reversed in part.

CHISOM v. ROEMER
___ U.S. ___; 112 L. Ed. 2d 838; 111 S. Ct. 2354 (1991)

JUSTICE STEVENS *delivered the opinion of the Court.*

* * *

In 1982, Congress amended sec. 2 of the Voting Rights Act to make clear that certain practices and procedures that result in the denial or abridgment of the right to vote are forbidden even though the absence of proof of discriminatory intent protects them from constitutional challenge.* The question presented by this case is whether this "results test" protects the right to vote in state judicial elections. We hold that the coverage provided by the 1982 amendment is coextensive with the coverage provided by the Act prior to 1982 and that judicial elections are embraced within that coverage.

I

Petitioners represent a class of approximately 135,000 black registered voters in Orleans Parish, Louisiana. They brought this action against the Governor and other state officials (respondents) to challenge the method of electing justices of the Louisiana Supreme Court from the New Orleans area. The United States intervened to support the claims advanced by the plaintiff class.

The Louisiana Supreme Court consists of seven justices, five of whom are elected from five single-member Supreme Court Districts, and two of whom are elected from one multi-member Supreme Court District. . . . The one multimember [*sic*] district, the First Supreme Court District, consists of the parishes of Orleans, St. Bernard, Plaquemines, and Jefferson. Orleans Parish contains about half of the population of the First Supreme Court District and about half of the registered voters in that district. More than one-half of the registered voters of Orleans Parish are black, whereas more than three-fourths of the registered voters in the other three parishes are white.

Petitioners allege that "the present method of electing two Justices to the Louisiana Supreme Court at-large from the New Orleans area impermissibly dilutes minority voting strengths" in violation of sec. 2 of the Voting Rights Act. Furthermore, petitioners claimed in the courts below that the current electoral system within the First Supreme Court District violates the Fourteenth and Fifteenth Amendments of the Federal Constitution because the purpose and effect of this election practice "is to dilute, minimize, and cancel the voting strength" of black voters in Orleans Parish.

Petitioners seek a remedy that would divide the First District into two districts, one for Orleans Parish and the second for the other three parishes. If this remedy were adopted, the seven members of the Louisiana Supreme Court would each represent a separate single-member judicial district, and each of the two new districts would have approximately the same population. According to petitioners, the new Orleans Parish district would also

---

*[Section 2 of the Voting Rights Act as amended reads] "Section 2. (a) No voting qualification or prerequisite to voting or standard, practice or procedure shall be imposed or applied by any State or subdivision in a manner which results in a denial or abridgment of the right of any citizen of the United States to vote on account of race or color. . . .

"(b) A violation of subsection (a) is established if, based on the totality of circumstances, it is shown that the political processes leading to nomination or election in the State or political subdivision are not equally open to participation by members of a class of citizens protected by subsection (a) in that its members have less opportunity than other members of the electorate to participate in the political process and to elect representatives of their choice. The extent to which members of a protected class have been elected to office in the State or political subdivision is one circumstance which may be considered: Provided, That nothing in this section establishes a right to have members of a protected class elected in numbers equal to their proportion in the population."

have a majority black population and majority black voter registration.

The District Court granted respondents' motion to dismiss the complaint. It held that the constitutional claims were insufficient because the complaint did not adequately allege a specific intent to discriminate. With respect to the statutory claim, the court held that sec. 2 is not violated unless there is an abridgment of minority voters' opportunity "to elect representatives of their choice." The court concluded that because judges are not "representatives," judicial elections are not covered by sec. 2.

The Court of Appeals for the Fifth Circuit reversed. . . . After agreeing with the recently announced opinion in *Mallory* v. *Eyrich,* 839 F.2d 275 (CA6 1988), it noted that the broad definition of the terms "voting" and "vote" in sec. 14(c)(1) of the original Act expressly included judicial elections within the coverage of sec. 2. It also recognized Congress' explicit intent to expand the coverage under the Act. The court rejected the State's contention that the term "representatives" in the 1982 amendment was used as a word of limitation. Instead, the court concluded that representative " 'denotes anyone selected or chosen by popular election from among a field of candidates to fill an office, including judges.' " It also gleaned support for its construction of sec. 2 from the fact that the Attorney General had "consistently supported an expansive, not restrictive, construction of the Act." Finally, the court held that the constitutional allegations were sufficient to warrant a trial, and reinstated all claims.

After the case was remanded to the District Court, the United States filed a complaint in intervention in which it alleged that the use of a multi-member district to elect two members of the Louisiana Supreme Court is a "standard, practice or procedure" that "results in a denial or abridgment of the right to vote on account of race or color in violation of Section 2 of the Voting Rights Act." After a nonjury trial, however, the District Court concluded that the evidence did not establish a violation of sec. 2 under the standards set forth in *Thornburg* v. *Gingles,* 478 U.S. 3 (1986). The District Court also dismissed the constitutional claims. Petitioners and the United States appealed. While their appeal was pending, the Fifth Circuit, sitting en banc in another case, held that judicial elections were not covered under sec. 2 of the Act as amended. *League of United Latin American Citizens Council No. 4434* v. *Clements,* 914 F.2d 62 (1990) (hereinafter *LULAC*).

The majority in *LULAC* concluded that Congress' use of the word "representatives" in the phrase "to elect representatives of their choice" in sec. 2(b) of the Act indicated that Congress did not intend to authorize vote dilution claims in judicial elections. . . .

In the majority's view, it was "factually false" to characterize judges as representatives because public opinion is "irrelevant to the judge's role." "The judiciary serves no representative function whatever: the judge represents no one." The majority concluded that judicial offices "are not 'representative' ones, and their occupants are not representatives." . . .

Following the en banc decision in *LULAC,* the Court of Appeals remanded this case to the District Court with directions to dismiss the complaint. . . .

II

[T]his case presents us solely with a question of statutory construction. That question involves only the scope of the coverage of sec. 2 of the Voting Rights Act, as amended in 1982. . . .

It is . . . undisputed that sec. 2 applied to judicial elections prior to the 1982 amendment, and that sec. 5 of the amended statute continues to apply to judicial elections. . . . The only matter in dispute is whether the test for determining the legality of such a practice, which was added to the statute in 1982, applies in judicial elections as well as in other elections. . . .

III

* * *

[Under] the 1982 amendment to sec. 2, . . . proof of intent is no longer required to prove a sec. 2 violation. Now plaintiffs can prevail . . . by demonstrating that a challenged election practice has resulted in the denial or abridgment of the right to vote based on color or race. Congress not only incorporated the results test in the paragraph that formerly constituted the entire sec. 2, but also designated that paragraph as subsection (a) and added a new subsection (b) to make clear that an application of the results test requires an inquiry into "the totality of the circumstances." . . .

Respondents contend, and the *LULAC* majority agreed, that the Congress' choice of the word "representatives" in the phrase "have less opportunity than other members of the electorate to participate in the political process and to elect representatives of their choice" in section 2(b) is evidence of congressional intent to exclude vote dilution claims involving judicial elections from the coverage of sec. 2. We reject that construction because we are convinced that if Congress had such an intent, Congress would have made it explicit in the statute, or at least some of the Members would have identified or mentioned it at some point in the unusually extensive legislative history of the 1982 amendment. . . .

IV

* * *

Any abridgment of the opportunity of members of a protected class to participate in the political process inevitably impairs their ability to influence the outcome of an election. As the statute is written, however, the inability to elect representatives of their choice is not sufficient to establish a violation unless, under the totality of circumstances, it can also be said that the members of the protected class have less opportunity to participate in the political process. The statute does not create two separate and distinct rights. Subsection (a) covers every application of a qualification, standard, practice, or procedure that results in a denial or abridgement of "*the right*" to vote. The singular form is also used in subsection (b) when referring to an injury to members of the protected class who have less "opportunity" than others "to participate in the political process and to elect representatives of their choice." It would distort the plain meaning of the sentence to substitute the word "or" for the word "and." Such radical surgery would be required to separate the opportunity to participate from the opportunity to elect. . . .

The results mandated by the 1982 amendment is applicable to all claims arising under sec. 2. If the word "representatives" did place a limit on the coverage of the Act for judicial elections, it would exclude all claims involving such elections from the protection of sec. 2. For all such claims must allege an abridgment of the opportunity to participate in the political process and to elect representatives of one's choice. Even if the wisdom of Solomon would support the *LULAC* majority's proposal to preserve claims based on an interference with the right to vote in judicial elections while eschewing claims based on the opportunity to elect judges, we have no authority to divide a unitary claim created by Congress.

V

Both respondents and the *LULAC* majority place their principal reliance on Congress' use of the word "representatives" instead of "legislators" in the phrase "to participate in the political process and to elect representatives of their choice." When Congress borrowed the phase from *White* v. *Regester*, it replaced "legislators" with "representatives." This substitution indicates, at the very least, that Congress intended the amendment to cover more than legislative elections. Respondents argue, and the majority agreed, that the term "representatives" was used to extend sec. 2 coverage to executive officials, but not to judges. We think, however, that the better reading of the word "representatives" describes the winners of representative, popular elections. If executive officers such as prosecutors, sheriffs, state attorneys general, and state treasurers can be considered "representatives" simply because they are chosen by popular election, then the same reasoning should apply to elected judges . . . and that ideally public opinion should be irrelevant to the judge's role because the judge is often called upon to disregard, or even to defy, popular sentiment. The Framers of the Constitution had a similar understanding of the judicial role, and as a consequence, they established that Article III judges would be appointed, rather than elected, and would be sheltered from public opinion by receiving life tenure and salary protection. Indeed these views were generally shared by the States during the early years of the Republic. Louisiana, however, has chosen a different course. It has decided to elect its judges and to compel judicial candidates to vie for popular support just as other political candidates do.

The fundamental tension between the ideal character of the judicial office and the real world of electoral politics cannot be resolved by crediting judges with total indifference to the popular will while simultaneously requiring them to run for elected office. When each of several members of a court must be a resident of a separate district, and must be elected by the voters of that district, it seems both reasonable and realistic to characterize the winners as representatives of that district. Indeed, at one time the Louisiana Bar Association characterized the members of the Louisiana Supreme Court as representatives for that reason: "Each justice and judge now in office shall be considered as a representative of the judicial district within which is situated the parish of his residence at the time of his election." Louisiana could, of course, exclude its judiciary from the coverage of the Voting Rights Act by changing to a system in which judges are appointed, and in that way, it could enable its judges to be indifferent to popular opinion. The reasons why Louisiana has chosen otherwise are precisely the reasons why it is appropriate for sec. 2, as well as sec. 5, of the Voting Rights Act to continue to apply to its judicial elections.

The close connection between sec. 2 and sec. 5 further undermines respondents' view that judicial elections should not be covered under sec. 2. Section 5 requires certain States to submit changes in their voting procedures to the District Court of the District of Columbia or to the Attorney General for preclearance. Section 5 uses language similar to that of sec. 2 in defining prohibited practices: "any voting qualification or prerequisite to voting, or standard, practice, or procedure with respect to voting." This Court has already held that sec. 5 applies to judicial elections. If sec. 2 did not apply to judicial elections, a State covered by sec. 5 would be precluded from implementing a new voting procedure having discriminatory effects with respect to judicial elections, whereas a similarly discriminatory system already in place could not be challenged under sec. 2. It is unlikely that Congress intended such an anomalous result. . . .

VII

* * *

Congress enacted the Voting Rights Act of 1965 for the broad remedial purpose of "rid[ding] the country of racial discrimination in voting." In *Allen* v. *State Board of Elections*, 393 U.S. 544 (1969), we said that the Act should be interpreted in a manner that provides "the broadest possible scope" in combatting racial discrimination. Congress amended the Act in 1982 in order to relieve plaintiffs of the burden of proving discriminatory intent, after a plurality of this Court had concluded that the original Act, like the Fifteenth Amendment, contained such a requirement. See *Mobile* v. *Bolden*, 446 U.S. 55 (1980). Thus, Congress made clear that a violation of sec. 2 could be established by proof of discriminatory results alone. It is difficult to believe that Congress, in an express effort to broaden the protection afforded by the Voting Rights Act, withdrew, without comment, an important category or elections from the protection. Today we reject such an anomalous view and hold that state judicial elections are included within the ambit of sec. 2 as amended.

The judgment of the Court of Appeals is reversed and the case is remanded for further proceedings consistent with this opinion.

It is so ordered.

JUSTICE SCALIA, *with whom* THE CHIEF JUSTICE *and* JUSTICE KENNEDY *join, dissenting.*

Section 2 of the Voting Rights Act is not some all-purpose weapon for well-intentioned judges to wield as they please in the battle against discrimination. It is a statute. I thought we had adopted a regular method for interpreting the meaning of the language in a statute: first, find the ordinary meaning of the language in its textual context, and second, using established canons of construction, ask whether there is any clear indication that some permissible meaning other than the ordinary one applies. If not—and especially if a good reason for the ordinary meaning appears plain—we apply that ordinary meaning. . . .

Today, however, the Court adopts a method quite out of accord with that usual practice. It begins not with what the statute says, but with an expectation about what the statute must mean absent particular phenomena ("*we are convinced* that if Congress had . . . an intent [to exclude judges] Congress would have made it explicit in the statute, or at least some of the Members would have identified or mentioned it at some point in the unusually extensive legislative history" . . . [emphasis added]; and the Court then interprets the words of the statute to fulfill its expectation. Finding nothing in the legislative history affirming that judges were excluded from the coverage of sec. 2, the Court gives the phrase "to elect representatives" the quite extraordinary meaning that covers the elections of judges).

As method, this is just backwards, and however much we may be attracted by the result it produces in particular case, we should in every case resist it. Our job begins with a text that Congress has passed and the President has signed. We are to read the words of that text as any ordinary Member of Congress would have read them and apply the meaning so determined. In my view, that reading reveals that sec. 2 extends to vote dilution claims for the elections of representatives only, and judges are not representatives. . . .

I

* * *

The 1982 amendments . . . radically transformed the Act. As currently written, that statute proscribes intentional discrimination only if it has a discriminatory effect, but proscribes practices with discriminatory effect whether or not intentional. This new "results" criterion provides a powerful, albeit sometimes blunt, weapon with which to attack even the most subtle forms of discrimination. The question we confront here is how broadly the new remedy applies. The foundation of the Court's analysis, the itinerary for its journey in the wrong direction, is the following statement: "It is difficult to believe that Congress, in an express effort to broaden the protection afforded by the Voting Rights Act, withdrew, without comment, an important category of elections from that protection." There are two things wrong with this. First is the notion that Congress cannot be credited with having achieved anything of major importance by simply saying it, in ordinary language in the text of the statute, "without comment" in the legislative history. As the Court colorfully puts it, if the dog of legislative history has not barked, nothing of great significance can have transpired. Apart from the questionable wisdom of assuming that dogs will bark when something important is happening, we have forcefully and explicitly rejected the Conan Doyle approach to statutory construction in the past. . . . We are here to apply the statute, not legislative history, and certainly not the absence of legislative history. Statutes are the law though sleeping dogs lie.

The more important error in the Court's starting-point, however, is the assumption that the effect of excluding judges from the revised sec. 2 would be to "withdr[aw] . . . an important category of elections from [the] protection [of the Voting Rights Act]." There is absolutely no question here of *withdrawing* protection. Since the pre-1982 content of sec. 2 was coextensive with the Fifteenth Amendment, the entirety of that protection subsisted in the Constitution, and could be enforced through the other provisions of the Voting Rights Act. Nothing was lost from the prior coverage; *all* of the new "results" protection was an add-on. The issue is not, therefore, as the Court would have it, whether Congress has cut back on the coverage of the Voting Rights Act; the issue is how far it has extended it. Thus, even if a court's expectations were a proper basis for interpreting the text of the statute, while there would be reason to expect that Congress was not "withdrawing" protection, there is no particular reason to expect that the supplemental protection it provided was any more extensive than the text of the statute said. . . .

The court, petitioners, and petitioners' *amici* have labored mightily to establish that there is a meaning of "representatives" that would include judges . . . and no doubt there is. But our job is not to scavenge the world of English usage to discover whether there is any possible meaning of "representatives" which suits our preconception that the statute includes judges; our job is to determine whether the *ordinary* meaning includes them, and if it does not, to ask whether there is any solid indication in the text or structure of the statute that something other than ordinary meaning was intended.

There is little doubt that the ordinary meaning of "representatives" does not include judges, see *Webster's Second New International Dictionary* (1950). The court's feeble argument to the contrary is that "representatives" means those who "are chosen by popular election." On that hypothesis, the fan-elected members of the baseball All-Star teams are "representatives"—hardly a common, if even a permissible, usage. Surely the word "representative" connotes one who is not only *elected by* the people, but who also, at a minimum, *acts on behalf of* the people. Judges do that in a sense—but not in the ordinary sense. . . .

Finally, the Court suggests that there is something "anomalous" about extending coverage under sec. 5 of the Voting Rights Act to the election of judges, while not extending coverage under sec. 2 to the same elections. This simply misconceives the different roles of sec. 2 and sec. 5. The latter requires certain jurisdictions to preclear changes in election methods before those changes are implemented; it is a means of assuring in advance the absence of all electoral illegality, not only that which violates the Voting Rights Act but that which violates the Constitution as well. In my view, judges are within the scope of sec. 2 for nondilution claims, and thus for those claims, sec. 5 preclearance would enforce the Voting Rights Act with respect to judges. Moreover, intentional discrimination in the election of judges, whatever its form, is constitutionally prohibited, and the preclearance provision of sec. 5 gives the government a method by which to prevent that. The scheme makes entire sense without the need to bring judges within the "to elect" provision.

All this is enough to convince me that there is sense to the ordinary meaning of "representative" in sec. 2(b)—that there is reason to Congress's choice—and since there is, then, under our normal presumption, that ordinary meaning prevails. I would read sec. 2 as extending vote dilution claims to elections for "representatives," but not to elections for judges. For other claims under sec. 2, however—those resting on the "to participate in the political process" provision rather than the "to elect" provision—no similar restriction would apply. Since the claims here are exclusively claims of dilution. I would affirm the judgment of the Fifth Circuit. . . .

. . . The Court transforms the meaning of sec. 2,

not because the ordinary meaning is irrational, or inconsistent with other parts of the statute, . . . but because it does not fit the Court's conception of what Congress must have had in mind. When we adopt a method that psychoanalyzes Congress rather than reads its laws, when we employ a tinkerer's toolbox, we do great harm. Not only do we reach the wrong results with respect to the statute at hand, but we poison the well of future legislation, depriving legislators of the assurance that ordinary terms, used in an ordinary context, will be given a predictable meaning. Our highest responsibility in the field of statutory construction is to read the laws in a consistent way, giving Congress a sure means by which it may work the people's will. We have ignored that responsibility today.

I respectfully dissent.

PRESLEY v. ETOWAH COUNTY COMMISSION
____ U.S. ____; ____ L. Ed. 2d ____; 112 S. Ct. 820 (1992)

JUSTICE KENNEDY *delivered the opinion of the Court.*

In various Alabama counties voters elect members of county commissions whose principal function is to supervise and control the maintenance, repair, and construction of the county roads. The consolidated appeals now before us concern certain changes in the decision-making authority of the elected members on two different county commissions, and the question to be decided is whether these were changes "with respect to voting" within the meaning of § 5 of the Voting Rights Act of 1965, as amended. The case has significance well beyond the two county commissions; for the appellants, and the United States as *amicus curiae*, ask us to adopt a rule embracing the routine actions of state and local governments at all levels. We must interpret the provisions of § 5, which require a jurisdiction covered by the Act to obtain either judicial or administrative preclearance before enforcing any new "voting qualification or prerequisite to voting, or standard, practice, or procedure with respect to voting."

I

* * *

A

We consider first the Etowah County Commission. On November 1, 1964, commission members were elected at large under a "residency district" system. The entire electorate of Etowah County voted on candidates for each of the five seats. Four of the seats corresponded to the four residency districts of the county. Candidates were required to reside in the appropriate district. The fifth member, the chairman, was not subject to a district residency requirement, though residency in the county itself was a requirement.

Each of the four residency districts functioned as a road district. The commissioner residing in the district exercised control over a road shop, equipment, and road crew for that district. It was the practice of the commission to vote as a collective body on the division of funds among the road districts, but once funds were divided each commissioner exercised individual control over spending priorities within his district. The chairman was responsible for overseeing the solid waste authority, preparing the budget, and managing the courthouse building and grounds.

Under a consent decree issued in 1986 . . . the commission is being restructured, so that after a transition period there will be a six-member commission, with each of the members elected by the voters of a different district. The changes required by the consent decree were precleared by the Attorney General. For present purposes, it suffices to say that when this litigation began the commission consisted of four holdover members who had been on the commission before the entry of the consent decree and two new members elected from new districts. Commissioner Williams, who is white, was elected from new district 6, and Commissioner Presley, who is black, was elected from new district 5. Presley is the principal appellant in the Etowah County case. His complaint relates not to the elections but to actions taken by the four holdover members when he and Williams first took office.

On August 25, 1987, the commission passed the "Road Supervision Resolution." It provided that each holdover commissioner would continue to control the workers and operations assigned to his respective road shop, which, it must be remembered, accounted for all the road shops the county had. It also gave the four holdovers joint responsibility for overseeing the repair, maintenance, and improvement of all the roads of Etowah County in order to pick up the roads in the districts where the new commissioners resided. The new commissioners, now foreclosed from exercising any authority over roads, were given other functions under the resolution. Presley was to oversee maintenance of the county courthouse and Williams the operation of the engineering department. The Road Supervision Resolution was passed by a 4–2 margin, with the two new commissioners dissenting.

The same day the Road Supervision Resolution was passed, the commission passed a second, the so-called "Common Fund Resolution." It provides in part that

> all monies earmarked and budgeted for repair, maintenance and improvement of the streets, roads and public ways of Etowah County [shall] be placed and maintained in common accounts, [shall] not be allocated, budgeted or designated for use in districts, and [shall] be used county-wide in accordance with need, for the repair, maintenance and improvement of all streets, roads and public ways in Etowah County which are under the jurisdiction of the Etowah County Commission.

This had the effect of altering the prior practice of allowing each commissioner full authority to determine how to spend the funds allocated to his own district. The Etowah County Commission did not seek judicial or administrative preclearance of either the Road Supervision Resolution or the Common Fund Resolution. The District Court held that the Road Supervision Resolution was subject to preclearance but that the Common Fund Resolution was not. No appeal was taken from the first ruling, so only the Common Fund Resolution is before us in the Etowah County case.

B

We turn next to the background of the Russell County Commission. On November 1, 1964, it had three commissioners. Like the members of the Etowah County Commission before the consent decree change, Russell County Commissioners were elected at large by the entire electorate, subject to a requirement that a candidate for commissioner reside in the district corresponding to the seat he or she sought. A 1972 federal court order . . . required that the commission be expanded to include five members. The two new members were both elected at large from one newly-created residency district for Phoenix City, the largest city in

Russell County. Following the implementation of the court order, each of the three rural commissioners had individual authority over his own road shop, road crew, and equipment. The three rural commissioners also had individual authority for road and bridge repair and construction within their separate residency districts. Although funding for new construction and major repair projects was subject to a vote by the entire commission, individual commissioners could authorize expenditures for routine repair and maintenance work as well as routine purchase orders without seeking approval from the entire commission.

Following the indictment of one commissioner on charges of corruption in Russell County road operations, in May 1979 the commission passed a resolution delegating control over road construction, maintenance, personnel, and inventory to the county engineer, an official appointed by the entire commission and responsible to it. The engineer's previous duties had been limited to engineering and surveying services for the separate road shops, and running a small crew devoted to pothole repair. Although the May 1979 resolution may have sufficed for the necessary delegation of authority to the county engineer[,] . . . the commission also requested the state legislature to pass implementing legislation. The Alabama Legislature did so on July 30, 1979. . . . The parties refer to abolition of the individual road districts and transfer of responsibility for all road operations to the county engineer as the adoption of a "Unit System." Neither the resolution nor the statute which authorized the Unit System was submitted for preclearance under § 5.

Litigation involving the Russell County Commission led to a 1985 consent decree . . . that enlarged the commission to seven members and replaced the at-large election system with elections on a district-by-district basis. Without any mention of the Unit System changes, the consent decree was precleared by the Department of Justice under § 5. Following its implementation, appellants Mack and Gosha were elected in 1986. They are Russell County's first black county commissioners in modern times.

C

In May 1989, the appellants in both cases now before us filed a single complaint in the District Court for the Middle District of Alabama, alleging racial discrimination in the operation of the Etowah and Russell County Commissions in violation of prior court orders, the Constitution, Title VI of the Civil Rights Act of 1964, 42 U.S.C. §

2000d, and § 2 of the Voting Rights Act. . . . In a series of amended complaints, the appellants added claims under § 5. The § 5 claims alleged that Etowah County had violated the Act by failing to obtain preclearance of the 1987 Road Supervision and Common Fund Resolutions, and that Russell County had failed to preclear the 1979 change to the Unit System. . . . [A] three-judge District Court was convened to hear the appellants' § 5 claims. . . . The other claims still pend in the District Court.

With respect to the issues now before us, a majority of the District Court held that neither the Common Fund Resolution of the Etowah County Commission nor the adoption of the Unit System in Russell County was subject to § 5 preclearance. The court held that changes in the responsibilities of elected officials are subject to preclearance when they "effect a significant relative change in the powers exercised by, or responsible to, substantially different constituencies of voters." Applying its test, the court found that the Common Fund Resolution in Etowah County did not effect a significant change, and adoption of the Unit System in Russell County did not transfer authority among officials responsible to different constituencies. . . . We affirm the District Court but adopt a different interpretation of § 5 as the rationale for our decision.

II

We first considered the Voting Rights Act in *South Carolina* v. *Katzenbach*, 383 U.S. 301 (1966). Although we acknowledged that suspension of new voting regulations pending preclearance was an extraordinary departure from the traditional course of relations between the States and the Federal Government, we held it constitutional as a permitted congressional response to the unremitting attempts by some state and local officials to frustrate their citizens' equal enjoyment of the right to vote.

After *South Carolina* v. *Katzenbach* upheld the Voting Rights Act against a constitutional challenge, it was not until we heard *Allen* v. *State Board of Elections*, 393 U.S. 544 (1969), that we were called upon to decide whether particular changes were covered by § 5. There we rejected a narrow construction, one which would have limited § 5 to state rules prescribing who may register to vote. We held that the section applies also to state rules relating to the qualifications of candidates and to state decisions as to which offices shall be elective. We observed that "[t]he Voting Rights Act was aimed at the subtle, as well as the obvious, state regulations which have the effect of denying citizens their right to vote because of their race." *Id.*, at 565, 89 S. Ct., at 831. Our decision, and its rationale, have proven sound, and we adhere to both.

In giving a broad construction to § 5 in *Allen*, we noted that "Congress intended to reach any state enactment which altered the election law of a covered State in even a minor way." Relying on this language and its application in later cases, appellants and the United States now argue that because there is no *de minimis* exception to § 5, the changes at issue here must be subject to preclearance. This argument, however, assumes the answer to the principle question in the case: whether the changes at issue are changes in voting, or as we phrased it in *Allen*, "election law."

We agree that all changes in voting must be precleared and with *Allen*'s holding that the scope of § 5 is expansive within its sphere of operation. That sphere comprehends all changes to rules governing voting, changes effected through any of the mechanisms described in the statute. Those mechanisms are any "qualification or prerequisite" or any "standard, practice or procedure with respect to voting."

The principle that § 5 covers voting changes over a wide range is well illustrated by the separate cases we considered in the single opinion for the Court in *Allen*. *Allen* involved four cases. The eponymous *Allen* v. *State Board of Elections*, 393 U.S. 544, at 570, 1969, concerned a change in the procedures for the casting of write-in ballots. In *Whitley* v. *Williams*, there were changes in the requirements for independent candidates running in general elections. The challenged procedure in *Fairley* v. *Patterson* resulted in a change from single-district voting to at-large voting. The remaining case, *Bunton* v. *Patterson*, involved a statute which provided that officials who in previous years had been elected would be appointed. We held that the changes in each of the four cases were covered by § 5.

Our cases since *Allen* reveal a consistent requirement that changes subject to § 5 pertain only to voting. Without implying that the four typologies exhaust the statute's coverage, we can say [that] later cases fall within one of the four factual contexts presented in the *Allen* cases. . . .

. . . [W]hether the changes are of procedure or substance, each has a direct relation to voting and the election process.

III

A comparison of the changes at issue here with those in our prior decisions demonstrates that the present cases do not involve changes covered by the Act.

A

The Etowah County Commission's Common Fund Resolution is not a change within any of the categories recognized in *Allen* or our later cases. It has no connection to voting procedures: It does not affect the manner of holding elections, it alters or imposes no candidacy qualifications or requirements, and it leaves undisturbed the composition of the electorate. It also has no bearing on the substance of voting power, for it does not increase or diminish the number of officials for whom the electorate may vote. Rather, the Common Fund Resolution concerns the internal operations of an elected body.

The appellants argue that the Common Fund Resolution is a covered change because after its enactment each commissioner has less individual power than before the resolution. A citizen casting a ballot for a commissioner today votes for an individual with less authority than before the resolution, and so, it is said, the value of the vote has been diminished.

Were we to accept the appellants' proffered reading of § 5, we would work an unconstrained expansion of its coverage. Innumerable state and local enactments having nothing to do with voting affect the power of elected officials. When a state or local body adopts a new governmental program or modifies an existing one it will often be the case that it changes the powers of elected officials. So too, when a state or local body alters its internal operating procedures, for example by modifying its subcommittee assignment system, it "implicate[s] an elected official's decision-making authority." . . .

Appellants and the United States fail to provide a workable standard for distinguishing between changes in rules governing voting and changes in the routine organization and functioning of government. Some standard is necessary, for in a real sense every decision taken by government implicates voting. This is but the felicitous consequence of democracy, in which power derives from the people. Yet no one would contend that when Congress enacted the Voting Rights Act it meant to subject all or even most decisions of government in covered jurisdictions to federal supervision. Rather, the Act by its terms covers any "voting qualification or prerequisite to voting, or standard, practice, or procedure with respect to voting." A faithful effort to implement the design of the statute must begin by drawing lines between those

governmental decisions that involve voting and those that do not. . . .

Under the view advanced by appellants and the United States, every time a state legislature acts to diminish or increase the power of local officials, preclearance would be required. Governmental action decreasing the power of local officials could carry with it a potential for discrimination against those who represent racial minorities at the local level. At the same time, increasing the power of local officials will entail a relative decrease in the power of state officials, and that too could carry with it a potential for discrimination against state officials who represent racial minorities at the state level. The all but limitless minor changes in the allocation of power among officials and the constant adjustments required for the efficient governance of every covered State illustrate the necessity for us to formulate workable rules to confine the coverage of § 5 to its legitimate sphere: voting.

Changes which affect only the distribution of power among officials are not subject to § 5 because such changes have no direct relation to, or impact on, voting. The Etowah County Commission's Common Fund Resolution was not subject to the preclearance requirement.

B

We next consider Russell County's adoption of the Unit System and its concomitant transfer of operations to the county engineer. Of the four categories of changes in rules governing voting we have recognized to date, there is not even an arguable basis for saying that adoption of the Unit System fits within any of the first three. As to the fourth category, it might be argued that the delegation of authority to an appointed official is similar to the replacement of an elected official with an appointed one, the change we held subject to § 5 in *Bunton* v. *Patterson*. This approach, however, would ignore the rationale for our holding: "after the change, [the citizen] is prohibited from electing an officer formerly subject to the approval of the voters." In short, the change in *Bunton* v. *Patterson* involved a rule governing voting not because it affected a change in the relative authority of various officials, but because it changed an elective office to an appointive one.

The change in *Russell County* does not prohibit voters "from electing an officer formerly subject to the[ir] approval." Both before and after the change the citizens of Russell County were able to vote for the members of the Russell County Commission. To be sure, after the 1979 resolution each commissioner exercised less direct authority over road operations, that authority having been delegated to an official answerable to the commission. But as we concluded with respect to Etowah County, the fact that an enactment alters an elected official's powers does not in itself render the enactment a rule governing voting.

It is a routine part of governmental administration for appointive positions to be created or eliminated, and for their powers to be altered. Each time this occurs the relative balance of authority is altered in some way. The making or unmaking of an appointive post often will result in the erosion or accretion of the powers of some official responsible to the electorate, but it does not follow that those changes are covered by § 5. By requiring preclearance of changes with respect to voting, Congress did not mean to subject such routine matters of governance to federal supervision. Were the rule otherwise, neither state nor local governments could exercise power in a responsible manner within a federal system. . . .

IV

The United States urges that despite our understanding of the language of § 5, we should defer to its administrative construction of the provision. We have recognized that "the construction placed upon the [Voting Rights] Act by the Attorney General . . . is entitled to considerable deference." But the principle has its limits. Deference does not mean acquiescence. As in other contexts in which we defer to an administrative interpretation of a statute, we do so only if Congress has not expressed its intent with respect to the question, and then only if the administrative interpretation is reasonable. Because the first of these conditions is not satisfied in the cases before us we do not defer to the Attorney General's interpretation of the Act. . . .

. . . [Section] 5 is unambiguous with respect to the question whether it covers changes other than changes in rules governing voting: It does not. The administrative position in the present case is not entitled to deference, for it suggests the contrary. The United States argues that the changes are covered by § 5 because they implicate the decision-making authority of elected officials, even though they are not changes in rule governing voting. This argument does not meet the express requirement of the statute.

V

Nothing we say implies that the conduct at issue in these cases is not actionable under a different re-

medial scheme. The Voting Rights Act is not an all-purpose antidiscrimination statute. The fact that the intrusive mechanisms of the Act do not apply to other forms of pernicious discrimination does not undermine its utility in combating the specific evils it was designed to address. . . .

If federalism is to operate as a practical system of governance and not a mere poetic ideal, the States must be allowed both predictability and efficiency in structuring their governments. Constant minor adjustments in the allocation of power among state and local officials serve this elemental purpose.

Covered changes must bear a direct relation to voting itself. That direct relation is absent in both cases now before us. The changes in Etowah and Russell Counties affected only the allocation of power among governmental officials. They had no impact on the substantive question whether a particular office would be elective or the procedural question how an election would be conducted. Neither change involves a new "voting qualification or prerequisite to voting, or standard, practice, or procedure with respect to voting."

The judgment of the District Court is affirmed.

It is so ordered.

JUSTICE STEVENS, *with whom* JUSTICE WHITE *and* JUSTICE BLACKMUN *join, dissenting.*

In 1986, an important event occurred in each of two Alabama counties with long histories of white-dominated political processes. In Etowah County, a black commissioner was elected to the county commission for the first time in recent history, and in Russell County, two black commissioners were elected to the county commission for the first time in "modern times." Because of the three resolutions at issue in this case—two adopted in Etowah County after Commissioner Presley's election and one adopted in Russell County before the election of Commissioners Mack and Gosha—none of the three newly-elected black commissioners was able to exercise the decisionmaking authority that had been traditionally associated with his office.

As I shall explain, this is a case in which a few pages of history are far more illuminating than volumes of logic and hours of speculation about hypothetical line-drawing problems. Initially, however, it is important to note that a different decision in these cases would not impose any novel or significant burden on those jurisdictions that remain covered under § 5 of the Voting Rights Act of 1965.

Prior to these cases, federal courts had uniformly agreed with the Attorney General's interpretation that § 5 covered transfers of decision-making power that had a potential for discrimination against minority voters.* On at least eight occasions since 1975, the Department of Justice has refused to preclear changes in the power of elected officials that had a potentially discriminatory impact on black voters. The Department has routinely precleared numerous other transfers of authority after determining that they had no discriminatory purpose or effect. There is no evidence that the prevailing practice imposed any special burden on covered jurisdictions. For example, in this fiscal year the Attorney General has processed over 17,000 preclearance requests, and has approved over 99 percent of them without any undue delay. It is, therefore, simply hyperbole for the Court to suggest that if we adopted the Attorney General's position in this case "neither state nor local governments could exercise power in a responsible manner within a federal system."

In all of our prior cases interpreting § 5 of the Voting Rights Act, the Court has agreed with the Attorney General's construction of this important statute. I share the Court's view that the "considerable deference" to which the Attorney General's construction is entitled does not mean automatic "acquiescence", however, I strongly disagree with the Court that our task in these cases is "to formulate workable rules to confine the coverage of § 5 to its legitimate sphere: voting." For reasons that I shall explain, even if the Attorney General, participating in these cases as *amicus curiae*, has asked the Court to adopt a broader rationale than is necessary or appropriate, a narrower basis for a decision is obviously available in the *Etowah County* case and, in my judgment, in the *Russell County* case as well.

* See *Horry County* v. *United States*, 449 F. Supp. 990 (D.C. 1978) (statute providing for election of public officials who were formerly appointed by Governor required preclearance under § 5); *Hardy* v. *Wallace*, 603 F. Supp. 174 (N.D. Ala. 1985) (statute changing appointive power over local racing commission from local legislative delegation to Governor required preclearance under § 5); *County Council of Sumter County* v. *United States*, 555 F. Supp. 694 (D.C. 1983) (law that eliminated legal power of Governor and General Assembly over local affairs and vested it in county council elected at large by county voters required preclearance under § 5); *Robinson* v. *Alabama State Department of Education*, 652 F. Supp. 484 (MD Ala. 1987) (transfer of authority from Board of Education whose members were elected county-wide to one whose members were appointed by the city council required § 5 pre clearance).

I

* * *

During the first few years after the enactment of § 5, the federal courts gave its text a narrow literal construction that confined its coverage to the political subdivisions that registered voters and to the practices that directly concerned the registration and voting process. . . .

In *Allen* and [its progeny, noting] . . . the broad remedial purposes of the Act, the Court held that a change from district to at-large voting for county supervisors, a change that made an important county office appointive rather than elective, and a change that altered the requirements for independent candidates, were all covered voting practices. . . .

The Court's construction of the Act in *Allen*, as requiring preclearance of changes in covered jurisdictions that were responsive to the increase in the number of black registered voters, was consistent with the concern that justified the extraordinary remedy set forth in § 5 itself, particularly the concern that recalcitrant white majorities could be expected to devise new stratagems to maintain their political power if not closely scrutinized. . . .

Thus, § 5 was understood to be "a 'vital element' of the Act," and was designed to be flexible enough to ensure that " 'new subterfuges will be promptly discovered and enjoined.' " Section 5, as construed by the Court, was not limited to a "simple inventory of voting procedures," but rather, was understood to address "the reality of changed practices as they affect Negro voters." *Georgia* v. *United States*, 411 U.S. 526, 531, (1973).

In subsequent cases, this Court has reaffirmed the broad scope of § 5 coverage, as first articulated in *Allen*.

The reenactment of § 5 in 1970, in 1975, and in 1982 reflected congressional approval of *Allen*'s broad interpretation of the Act. Indeed, congressional comments quoted in our opinion in *Perkins* v. *Matthews*, 400 U.S. 379, 1971, expressly endorsed an interpretation of § 5 that takes into account white resistance to progress in black registration.

One Congressman who had supported the 1965 Act observed, "When I voted for the Voting Rights Act of 1965, I hoped that 5 years would be ample time. But resistance to progress has been more subtle and more effective than I thought possible. A whole arsenal of racist weapons has been perfected. Boundary lines have been gerrymandered, elections have been switched to an at-large basis, counties have been consolidated, elective offices have been abolished where blacks had a chance of winning, the appointment process has been substituted for the elective process, election officials have withheld the necessary information for voting or running for office, and both physical and economic intimidation have been employed.

Section 5 was intended to prevent the use of most of these devices."

Since the decision in *Allen,* the debate on reenactment of § 5 in 1970, and the issuance of regulations by the Department of Justice, it has been recognized that the replacement of an elective office that might be won by a black candidate with an appointive office is one of the methods of maintaining a white majority's political power that § 5 was designed to forestall. As a practical matter, such a change has the same effect as a change that makes an elected official a mere figurehead by transferring his decisionmaking authority to an appointed official, or to a group of elected officials controlled by the majority. Although this type of response to burgeoning black registration may not have been prevalent during the early history of the Act, it has been an active concern of the Attorney General since 1976. In my judgment, such a change in the reallocation of decisionmaking authority in an elective office, at least in its most blatant form, is indistinguishable from, and just as unacceptable as, gerrymandering boundary lines or switching elections from a district to an at-large basis.

II

The two resolutions adopted by the Etowah County Commission on August 25, 1987, less than 9 months after the county's first black commissioner took office, were an obvious response to the redistricting of the county that produced a majority black district from which a black commissioner was elected. In my view, it was wrong for the District Court to divorce the two parts of this consolidated response and to analyze the two resolutions separately. The characterization of the Road Supervision Resolution as a change with a "potential for discrimination" that was "blatant and obvious," and that should be enjoined unless subjected to § 5 preclearance, applies equally to the Common Fund Resolution. Both resolutions diminished the decisionmaking authority of the newly-elected black commissioner, and both were passed on the same day and in response to the districting changes effected by the same consent decree.

At the very least, I would hold that the reallocation of decisionmaking authority of an elective office that is taken (1) after the victory of a black candidate, and (2) after the entry of a consent decree designed to give black voters an opportunity to have representation on an elective body, is covered by § 5. . . .

III

The record indicates that the resolution challenged in the *Russell County* case may well have had a nondiscriminatory, anticorruption purpose. It would not be covered by the narrow standard that I have proposed as a "workable rule" for deciding the *Etowah County* case. I would, however, adopt a broader standard that would require preclearance in this case as well. The proper test, I believe, is suggested by the examples of resistance to the increase in black registration that were noted in our opinion in *Perkins* v. *Matthews, supra.*

Changes from district voting to at-large voting, the gerrymandering of district boundary lines, and the replacement of an elected official with an appointed official, all share the characteristic of enhancing the power of the majority over a segment of the political community that might otherwise be adequately represented. A resolution that reallocates decisionmaking power by transferring authority from an elected district representative to an official, or a group, controlled by the majority, has the same potential for discrimination against the constituents in the disadvantaged districts. The Russell County Resolution satisfies that test, and therefore, like both Etowah County Resolutions, should have been precleared. To hold otherwise, as the Court does today, leaves covered States free to evade the requirements of § 5, and to undermine the purpose of the Act, simply by transferring the authority of an elected official, who happens to be black, to another official or group controlled by the majority.

The Court today rejects the Attorney General's position that transfers of authority are covered under § 5 when "they implicate the decisionmaking authority of elected officials." It does so because it fears that such a rule creates line-drawing problems and moves too far afield from "voting." Whether or not the rationale advocated by the Attorney General in this case is appropriate, his judgment concerning the proper disposition of these two cases is unquestionably correct.

I would therefore reverse in both cases.

FEATURED CASES

Baker v. Carr   Davis v. Bandemer   Shaw v. Reno

Simultaneous with the voting rights revolution was the drive to reapportion state legislatures. Here was a controversy involving the failure of rural-oriented state legislatures to honor reapportionment provisions of their state constitutions. This situation had caused those areas that had increased in population—cities and suburbs—to become increasingly underrepresented in state legislatures, while those areas that had stood still or had in fact lost population became increasingly overrepresented. For some time, the Supreme Court had refused to enter the controversy, relying mainly on the "political question" doctrine (*Colegrove* v. *Green*, 328 U.S. 549, 1946). And although *Gomillion* v. *Lightfoot*, discussed above, raised the political question issue anew, the Court was able to circumvent it by saying that unlike *Colegrove, supra,* where the state (Illinois) had failed to act, in *Gomillion* the state (Alabama) had taken "affirmative action" to deprive blacks of their right to vote.

But in 1962, just two years after *Gomillion*, the Court found in *Baker* v. *Carr* (396 U.S. 186, 1962), that the "political question" doctrine was not a barrier to considering reapportionment since that doctrine, upon close reexamination, had not even commanded a majority in *Colegrove*. In any event, the Court held in *Baker* that reapportionment was a justiciable question subject to judicial remedies. And the judicial remedy was not long forthcoming. On June 15, 1964, in *Reynolds* v. *Sims* (377 U.S. 533), the Court stated that the "one man, one vote" formula was the constitutional rule to be followed in the reapportionment of both houses of state legislatures. Subsequent Court decisions have generally applied this rule to other elective bodies. (See, for example, *Avery* v. *Midland County*, 390 U.S. 474, 1968; but compare and contrast *Sailors* v. *Board of Education of Kent County*, 387 U.S. 203; and *Abate* v. *Mundt*, 403 U.S. 182, 1971.)

The Court, in effect, fashioned its *Reynolds* decision, *supra,* largely on the basis of two earlier cases, *Gray* v. *Sanders* (372 U.S. 368, 1963) and *Wesberry* v. *Sanders* (376 U.S. 1, 1964). In *Wesberry,* for example, the Court said that "while it may not be possible to draw congressional districts with mathematical precision . . . [the Constitution requires] as

nearly as is practicable [that] one man's vote in a congressional election is to be worth as much as another's." The Court had occasion in *Kirkpatrick* v. *Preisler* (394 U.S. 526, 1969) to elucidate on *Wesberry*'s "as nearly as practicable" standard. Here the Court rejected "Missouri's argument that there is a fixed numerical or percentage population variance small enough to be considered *de minimis* and to satisfy without question the 'as nearly as practicable' standard." That standard, said the Court, "requires that the state make a good-faith effort to achieve precise mathematical equality." Cf. *Wells* v. *Rockefeller* (394 U.S. 542), decided the same day.

But four years later, in *Mahan* v. *Howell* (410 U.S. 315, 1973), the Court took notice of the variety of factors that come into play in the apportionment of state and local legislative districts and refused to extend the more demanding *Kirkpatrick* equality standard to them. Consequently, the Court set aside a district court ruling that had struck down Virginia's 1971 state legislative redistricting where the population variance between the largest and smallest districts was 16.4 percent. Justice William Rehnquist, speaking for the majority, condemned what he characterized as the "absolute equality" test of *Kirkpatrick* and *Wells* because its application would have the effect of "impair[ing] the normal function of state and local governments." Noting that more flexibility is permissible in state than in congressional redistricting, Rehnquist concluded that the population variations resulted from Virginia's effort to preserve "the integrity of political subdivision lines" and was "within tolerable constitutional limits." See also *Gaffney* v. *Cummings* (412 U.S. 735, 1970) and *White* v. *Regester* (412 U.S. 755, 1973), as well as *Chapman* v. *Meier* (420 U.S. 1, 1975), where more exacting standards are applied to judicially imposed reapportionment than to plans emanating from legislative bodies.

When New Jersey's congressional reapportionment action that followed the 1980 census was before the Court a decade later in *Karcher* v. *Daggett* (462 U.S. 725, 1983), the five-to-four majority made it clear that the less exacting equality standard permitted in *Mahan* was not to be construed as a retreat from *Kirkpatrick* when states redraw their congressional districts. Justice William J. Brennan's opinion for the majority underscored the "precise mathematical equality" standard that flows from Article 1, section 2 of the Constitution and held that such a standard "permits only the limited population variances between congressional districts which are unavoidable despite a good-faith effort to achieve absolute equality." He concluded that New Jersey's action, where the population deviation between the largest and smallest districts was less than one percent (0.6984), did not meet the burden of demonstrating a "good-faith effort" to attain the precise equality standard.

While the Court had considered the issue of racial gerrymandering in a number of reapportionment actions since the decision in *Gomillion* v. *Lightfoot* in 1960, it was not until its ruling in *Davis* v. *Bandemer* (106 S. Ct. 2787) in 1986 that it made a comprehensive ruling on partisan political gerrymandering. There, in the context of a challenge to the 1981 Indiana legislative apportionment action, the Court made it clear that such challenges present justiciable causes under the equal protection clause of the Fourteenth Amendment. But having opened the courthouse door for such challenges, Justice White made it clear that the burden of proof of such a violation would be a heavy one. "The mere lack of proportional representation" or "intentional drawing of district boundaries for partisan ends and for no other reason" was not considered sufficient to establish proof of a constitutional violation. As the justice pointed out, the "mere fact that a particular apportionment scheme makes it more difficult for a particular group in a particular district to elect the representatives of its choice does not render that scheme constitutionally infirm." He concluded that a violation is indicated "only when [an] electoral system is arranged in a manner that will consistently degrade a voter's or a group of voters' influence on the political process as a whole." Consequently, the majority was not convinced that the Indiana scheme produced such a result.

Actions in other areas point to an "opening up" of the electoral process. In 1972, for example, the Court struck down lengthy residency requirements for voting in state elections as violative of the equal protection clause (*Dunn* v. *Blumstein*, 405 U.S. 330). Here the Court declared invalid Tennessee requirements that made one year of residency in the state and three months of residency in the county prerequisites for voting.

Similarly, the Voting Rights Act Amendments of 1970 included a provision prohibiting "durational" residence requirements for voting in presidential elections. Specifically, states were precluded from closing voter registration more than 30 days prior to such elections. In adopting this policy, Congress specifically found that lengthy residency requirements do "not bear a reasonable relationship to any compelling state interest in the conduct of presidential elections." In addition, the 1970 amendments barred the use of literacy tests in all elections for a five-year period and lowered the voting age to 18 for national, state, and local elections. The Supreme Court, in *Oregon* v. *Mitchell* (400 U.S. 112, 1970), upheld the constitutionality of each of these amendments except the lowered voting age as applied to state and local elections. The Court reasoned that Congress did not possess the power to fasten such a requirement on the states and their local units. But the Twenty-Sixth Amendment to the Constitution, ratified in 1971, accomplished this objective of lowering the voting age to 18 for all elections.

BAKER v. CARR
369 U.S. 186; 7 L. Ed. 2d 663; 82 S. Ct. 691 (1962)

JUSTICE BRENNAN *delivered the opinion of the Court.*

This civil action was brought under 42 U.S.C. §§1983 and 1988 to redress the alleged deprivation of federal constitutional rights. The complaint, alleging that by means of a 1901 statute of Tennessee apportioning the members of the General Assembly among the State's 95 counties, "these plaintiffs and others similarly situated, are denied the equal protection of the laws accorded them by the Fourteenth Amendment to the Constitution of the

United States by virtue of the debasement of their votes," was dismissed by a three-judge court convened under 28 U.S.C. §2281 in the Middle District of Tennessee. The court held that it lacked jurisdiction of the subject matter and also that no claim was stated upon which relief could be granted. . . . We noted probable jurisdiction of the appeal. . . . We hold that the dismissal was error, and remand the case to the District Court for trial and further proceedings consistent with this opinion.

The General Assembly of Tennessee consists of the Senate with 33 members and the House of Representatives with 99 members.

Tennessee's standard for allocating legislative representation among her counties is the total number of qualified voters resident in the respective counties, subject only to minor qualifications. Decennial reapportionment in compliance with the constitutional scheme was effected by the General Assembly each decade from 1871 to 1901. The 1871 apportionment was preceded by an 1870 statute requiring an enumeration. The 1881 apportionment involved three statutes, the first authorizing an enumeration, the second enlarging the Senate from 25 to 33 members and the House from 75 to 99 members, and the third apportioning the membership of both Houses. In 1891 there were both an enumeration and an apportionment. In 1901 the General Assembly abandoned separate enumeration in favor of reliance upon the Federal Census and passed the Apportionment Act here in controversy. In the more than 60 years since that action, all proposals in both Houses of the General Assembly for reapportionment have failed to pass.

Between 1901 and 1961, Tennessee has experienced substantial growth and redistribution of her population. In 1901 the population was 2,020,616, of whom 487,380 were eligible to vote. The 1960 Federal Census reports the State's population at 3,567,089, of whom 2,092,891 are eligible to vote. The relative standings of the counties in terms of qualified voters have changed significantly. It is primarily the continued application of the 1901 Apportionment Act to this shifted and enlarged voting population which gives rise to the present controversy.

The District Court was uncertain whether our cases withholding federal judicial relief rested upon a lack of federal jurisdiction or upon the inappropriateness of the subject matter for judicial consideration—what we have designated "nonjusticiability." The distinction between the two grounds is significant. In the instance of nonjusticiability, consideration of the cause is not wholly and immediately foreclosed; rather, the Court's inquiry necessarily proceeds to the point of deciding whether the duty asserted can be judicially molded. In the instance of lack of jurisdiction the cause either does not "arise under" the Federal Constitution, laws or treaties (or fall within one of the other enumerated categories of Art. III, §2), or is not a "case or controversy" within the meaning of that section; or the case is not one described by any jurisdictional statute. Our conclusion, . . . *infra*, that this case presents no nonjusticiable "political question" settles the only possible doubt that it is a case or controversy. Under the present heading of "Jurisdiction of the Subject Matter" we hold only that the matter set forth in the complaint does arise under the Constitution.

Article III, §2, of the Federal Constitution provides that "The judicial Power shall extend to all Cases, in Law and Equity, arising under this Constitution, the Laws of the United States, and Treaties made, or which shall be made, under their Authority. . . . " It is clear that the cause of action is one which "arises under" the Federal Constitution. The complaint alleges that the 1901 statute effects an apportionment that deprives the appellants of the equal protection of the laws in violation of the Fourteenth Amendment. Dismissal of the complaint upon the ground of lack of jurisdiction of the subject matter would, therefore, be justified only if that claim were "so attenuated and unsubstantial as to be absolutely devoid of merit," . . . or "frivolous." . . . That the claim is unsubstantial must be "very plain." . . . Since the District Court obviously and correctly did not deem the asserted federal constitutional claim unsubstantial and frivolous, it should not have dismissed the complaint for want of jurisdiction of the subject matter.

The appellees refer to *Colegrove* v. *Green*, 328 U.S. 549 (1946), as authority that the District Court lacked jurisdiction of the subject matter. Appellees misconceive the holding of that case. The holding was precisely contrary to their reading of it. Seven members of the Court participated in the decision. Unlike many other cases in this field which have assumed without discussion that there was jurisdiction, all three opinions filed in *Colegrove* discussed the question. Two of the opinions expressing the views of four of the Justices, a majority, flatly held that there was jurisdiction of the subject matter. JUSTICE BLACK joined by JUSTICE DOUGLAS and JUSTICE MURPHY stated: "It is my judgment that the District Court had jurisdiction. . . . " . . .JUSTICE RUTLEDGE, writing separately, expressed agreement with this conclusion. . . . Indeed, it is even questionable that the opinion of JUSTICE FRANKFURTER, joined by JUSTICE REED and JUSTICE BURTON, doubted jurisdiction of the subject matter. . . .

We hold that the District Court has jurisdiction of the subject matter of the federal constitutional claim asserted in the complaint.

We hold that the appellants do have standing to maintain this suit. Our decisions plainly support this conclusion. Many of the cases have assumed rather than articulated the premise in deciding the merits of similar claims. And *Colegrove* v. *Green* . . . squarely held that voters who allege facts showing disadvantage to themselves as individuals have standing to sue.

In holding that the subject matter of this suit was not justiciable, the District Court relied on *Colegrove* v. *Green, supra*, and subsequent per curiam cases. The court stated: "From a review of these decisions there can be no doubt that the federal rule . . . is that the federal courts . . . will not intervene in cases of this type to compel legislative reapportionment." . . . We understand the District Court to have read the cited cases as compelling the conclusion that since the appellants sought to have a legislative apportionment held unconstitutional, their suit presented a "political question" and was therefore nonjusticiable. We hold that this challenge to an apportionment presents no nonjusticiable "political question." The cited cases do not hold the contrary.

Of course, the mere fact that the suit seeks protection of a political right does not mean it presents a political question. . . . Rather, it is argued that apportionment cases, whatever the actual working of the complaint, can involve no federal constitutional right except one resting on the guaranty of a republican form of government, and that complaints based on that clause have been held to present political questions which are nonjusticiable.

We hold that the claim pleaded here neither rests upon nor implicates the Guaranty Clause and that its justiciability is therefore not foreclosed by our decisions of cases involving that clause. The District Court misinterpreted *Colegrove* v. *Green* and other decisions of this Court on which it relied. Appellants' claim that they are being denied equal protection is justiciable, and if "discrimination is sufficiently shown, the right to relief under the equal protection clause is not diminished by the fact that the discrimination relates to political rights." . . . To show why we reject the argument based on the Guaranty Clause, we must examine the authorities under it. But because there appears to be some uncertainty as to why those cases did present political questions, and specifically as to whether this apportionment case is like those cases, we deem it necessary first to consider the contours of the "political question" doctrine.

That review reveals that in the Guaranty Clause cases and in the other "political question" cases, it is the relationship between the judiciary and the coordinate branches of the Federal Government, and not the federal judiciary's relationship to the States, which gives rise to the "political question."

We have said that "[i]n determining whether a question falls within [the political question] category, the appropriateness under our system of government of attributing finality to the action of the political departments and also the lack of satisfactory criteria for a judicial determination are dominant considerations." . . . The nonjusticiability of a political question is primarily a function of the separation of powers. Much confusion results from the capacity of the "political question" label to obscure the need for case-by-case inquiry. Deciding whether a matter has in any measure been committed by the Constitution to another branch of government, or whether the action of that branch exceeds whatever authority has been committed, is itself a delicate exercise in constitutional interpretation, and is a responsibility of this Court as ultimate interpreter of the Constitution.

It is apparent that several formulations which vary slightly according to the settings in which the questions arise may describe a political question, although each has one or more elements which identify it as essentially a function of the separation of powers. Prominent on the surface of any case held to involve a political question is found a textually demonstrable constitutional commitment of the issue to a coordinate political department; or a lack of judicially discoverable and manageable standards for resolving it; or the impossibility of deciding without an initial policy determination of a kind clearly for nonjudicial discretion; or the impossibility of a court's undertaking independent resolution without expressing lack of the respect due coordinate branches of government; or an unusual need for unquestioning adherence to a political decision already made; or the potentiality of embarrassment from multifarious pronouncements by various departments on one question.

Unless one of these formulations is inextricable from the case at bar, there should be no dismissal for nonjusticiability on the ground of a political question's presence. The doctrine of which we treat is one of "political questions," not one of "political cases." The courts cannot reject as "no law suit" a bona fide controversy as to whether some action denominated "political" exceeds constitutional authority. The cases we have reviewed show the necessity for discriminating inquiry into the precise facts and posture of the particular case, and the impossibility of resolution by any semantic cataloguing.

Clearly, several factors were thought by the Court in *Luther* v. *Borden* (48 U.S. 1, 1849), to make the question there "political"; the commitment to the other branches of the decision as to which is the lawful state government; the unambiguous action by the President, in recognizing the charter government as the lawful authority; the need for finality in the executive's decision; and the lack of criteria by which a court could determine which form of government was republican.

But the only significance that *Luther* could have for our immediate purposes is in its holding that the Guaranty Clause is not a repository of judicially manageable standards which a court could utilize independently in order to identify a State's lawful government. The Court has since refused to resort to the Guaranty Clause—which alone had been invoked for the purpose—as the source of a constitutional standard for invalidating state action.

We come, finally, to the ultimate inquiry whether our precedents as to what constitutes a nonjusticiable "political question" bring the case before us under the umbrella of that doctrine. A natural beginning is to note whether any of the common characteristics which we have been able to identify and label descriptively are present. We find none: The question here is the consistency of state action with the Federal Constitution. We have no question decided, or to be decided by a political branch of government coequal with this Court. Nor do we risk embarrassment of our government abroad, or grave disturbance at home if we take issue with Tennessee as to the constitutionality of her action here challenged. Nor need the appellants, in order to succeed in this action, ask the Court to enter upon policy determinations for which judicially manageable standards are lacking. Judicial standards under the Equal Protection Clause are well developed and familiar, and it has been open to courts since the enactment of the Fourteenth Amendment to determine, if on the particular facts they must, that a discrimination reflects no policy, but simply arbitrary and capricious action.

This case does, in one sense, involve the allocation of political power within a State, and the appellants might conceivably have added a claim under the Guaranty Clause. Of course, as we have seen, any reliance on that clause would be futile.

But because any reliance on the Guaranty Clause could not have succeeded, it does not follow that appellants may not be heard on the equal protection claim which in fact they tender. True, it must be clear that the Fourteenth Amendment claim is not so enmeshed with those political question elements which render Guaranty Clause claims nonjusticiable as actually to present a political question itself. But we have found that not to be the case here.

We conclude then that the nonjusticiability of claims resting on the Guaranty Clause, which arises from their embodiment of questions that were thought "political," can have no bearing upon the justiciability of the equal protection claim presented in this case. Finally, we emphasize that it is the involvement in Guaranty Clause claims of the elements thought to define "political questions," and no other feature, which could render them nonjusticiable. Specifically, we have said that such claims are not held nonjusticiable because they touch matters of state governmental organization. Brief examination of a few cases demonstrates this.

When challenges to state action respecting matters of "the administration of the affairs of the State and the officers through whom they are conducted" have rested on claims of constitutional deprivation which are amenable to judicial correction, this Court has acted upon its view of the merits of the claim. . . . Only last Term, in *Gomillion* v. *Lightfoot*, . . . we applied the Fifteenth Amendment to strike down a redrafting of municipal boundaries which effected a discriminatory impairment of voting rights, in the face of what a majority of the Court of Appeals thought to be a sweeping commitment to state legislatures of the power to draw and redraw such boundaries.

Gomillion was brought by a Negro who had been a resident of the City of Tuskegee, Alabama, until the municipal boundaries were so recast by the State Legislature as to exclude practically all Negroes. The plaintiff claimed deprivation of the right to vote in municipal elections. The District Court's dismissal for want of jurisdiction and failure to state a claim upon which relief could be granted was affirmed by the Court of Appeals. This Court unanimously reversed. This Court's answer to the argument that States enjoyed unrestricted control over municipal boundaries was:

Legislative control of municipalities, no less than other state power, lies within the scope of relevant limitations imposed by the United States Constitution. . . . The opposite conclusion, urged upon us by respondents, would sanction the achievement by a State of any impairment of voting rights whatever so long as it was cloaked in the garb of the realignment of political subdivisions. "It is inconceivable that guarantees embedded in the Constitution of the United States may thus be manipulated out of existence." . . .

To a second argument, that *Colegrove* v. *Green, supra,* was a barrier to hearing the merits of the case, the Court responded that *Gomillion* was lifted "out of the so-called 'political' arena and into the conventional sphere of constitutional litigation" because here was discriminatory treatment of a racial minority violating the Fifteenth Amendment.

Article I, §§2, 4, and 5, and Amendment XIV, §2, relate only to congressional elections and obviously do not govern apportionment of state legislatures. However, our decisions in favor of justiciability even in light of those provisions plainly afford no support for the District Court's conclusion that the subject matter of this controversy presents a political question. Indeed, the refusal to award relief in *Colegrove* resulted only from the controlling view of a want of equity.

We conclude that the complaint's allegations of a denial of equal protection present a justiciable constitutional cause of action upon which appellants are entitled to a trial and a decision. The right asserted is within the reach of judicial protection under the Fourteenth Amendment.

The judgment of the District Court is reversed and the cause is remanded for further proceedings consistent with this opinion.

[JUSTICE WHITTAKER did not participate in the decision of this case.]

[The concurring opinions of JUSTICES DOUGLAS and STEWART are omitted.]

JUSTICE CLARK, *concurring.*

One emerging from the rash of opinions with their accompanying clashing of views may well find himself suffering a mental blindness. The Court holds that the appellants have alleged a cause of action. However, it refuses to award relief here— although the facts are undisputed—and fails to give the District Court any guidance whatever. One dissenting opinion, bursting with words that go through so much and conclude with so little, condemns the majority action as "a massive repudiation of the experience of our whole past." Another describes the complaint as merely asserting conclu-

sory allegations that Tennessee's apportionment is "incorrect," "arbitrary," "obsolete," and "unconstitutional." I believe it can be shown that this case is distinguishable from earlier cases dealing with the distribution of political power by a State, that a patent violation of the Equal Protection Clause of the United States Constitution has been shown, and that an appropriate remedy may be formulated.

Although I find the Tennessee apportionment statute offends the Equal Protection Clause, I would not consider intervention by this Court into so delicate a field if there were any other relief available to the people of Tennessee. But the majority of the people of Tennessee have no "practical opportunities for exerting their political weight at the polls" to correct the existing "invidious discrimination." Tennessee has no initiative and referendum. I have searched diligently for other "practical opportunities" present under the law. I find none other than through the federal courts. The majority of the voters have been caught up in a legislative straitjacket. Tennessee has an "informed, civically militant electorate" and "an aroused popular conscience," but it does not sear "the conscience of the people's representatives." This is because the legislative policy has riveted the present seats in the Assembly to their respective constituencies, and by the votes of their incumbents a reapportionment of any kind is prevented. The people have been rebuffed at the hands of the Assembly; they have tried the constitutional convention route, but since the call must originate in the Assembly it, too, has been fruitless. They have tried Tennessee courts with the same result, and Governors have fought the tide only to flounder. It is said that there is recourse in Congress and perhaps that may be, but from a practical standpoint this is without substance. To date Congress has never undertaken such a task in any State. We therefore must conclude that the people of Tennessee are stymied and without judicial intervention will be saddled with the present discrimination in the affairs of their state government.

Finally, we must consider if there are any appropriate modes of effective judicial relief. The federal courts are of course not forums for political debate, nor should they resolve themselves into state constitutional conventions or legislative assemblies. Nor should their jurisdiction be exercised in the hope that such a declaration as is made today may have the direct effect of bringing on legislative action and relieving the courts of the problem of fashioning relief. To my mind this would be nothing less than blackjacking the

Assembly into reapportioning the State. If judicial competence were lacking to fashion an effective decree, I would dismiss this appeal.

As John Rutledge (later Chief Justice) said 175 years ago in the course of the Constitutional Convention, a chief function of the Court is to secure the national rights. Its decision today supports the proposition for which our forebears fought and many died, namely, that to be fully conformable to the principle of right, the form of government must be representative. That is the keystone upon which our government was founded and lacking which no republic can survive. It is well for this Court to practice self-restraint and discipline in constitutional adjudication, but never in its history have those principles received sanction where the national rights of so many have been so clearly infringed for so long a time. National respect for the courts is more enhanced through the forthright enforcement of those rights rather than by rendering them nugatory through the interposition of subterfuges. In my view the ultimate decision today is in the greatest tradition of this Court.

JUSTICE FRANKFURTER, *whom* JUSTICE HARLAN *joins, dissenting.*

The Court today reverses a uniform course of decision established by a dozen cases, including one by which the very claim now sustained was unanimously rejected only five years ago. The impressive body of rulings thus cast aside reflected the equally uniform course of our political history regarding the relationship between population and legislative representation—a wholly different matter from denial of the franchise to individuals because of race, color, religion or sex. Such a massive repudiation of the experience of our whole past in asserting destructively novel judicial power demands a detailed analysis of the role of this Court in our constitutional scheme. Disregard of inherent limits in the effective exercise of the Court's "judicial power" not only presages the futility of judicial intervention in the essentially political conflict of forces by which the relation between population and representation has time out of mind been and now is determined. It may well impair the Court's position as the ultimate organ of the "supreme Law of the Land" in that vast range of legal problems, often strongly entangled in popular feeling, on which this Court must pronounce. The Court's authority—possessed of neither the purse nor the sword—ultimately rests on sustained public confidence in its moral sanction. Such feeling must be nourished by the Court's complete de-

tachment, in fact and in appearance, from injecting itself into the clash of political forces in political settlements.

A hypothetical claim resting on abstract assumptions is now for the first time made the basis for affording illusory relief for a particular evil, even though it foreshadows deeper and more pervasive difficulties in consequence. The claim is hypothetical and the assumptions are abstract because the Court does not vouchsafe the lower courts—state and federal—guidelines for formulating specific, definite, wholly unprecedented remedies for the inevitable litigations that today's umbrageous disposition is bound to stimulate in connection with politically motivated reapportionments in so many States. In such a setting, to promulgate jurisdiction in the abstract is meaningless. It is as devoid of reality as "a brooding omnipresence in the sky," for it conveys no intimation what relief, if any, a District Court is capable of affording that would not invite legislatures to play ducks and drakes with the judiciary. For this Court to direct the District Court to enforce a claim to which the Court has over the years consistently found itself required to deny legal enforcement and at the same time to find it necessary to withhold any guidance to the lower court how to enforce this turnabout, new legal claim, manifests an odd—indeed an esoteric—conception of judicial propriety. One of the Court's supporting opinions, as elucidated by commentary, unwittingly affords a disheartening preview of the mathematical quagmire (apart from divers judicially inappropriate and elusive determinants) into which this Court today catapults the lower courts of the country without so much as adumbrating the basis for a legal calculus as a means of extrication. Even assuming the indispensible intellectual disinterestedness on the part of judges in such matters, they do not have accepted legal standards or criteria or even reliable analogies to draw upon for making judicial judgments. To charge courts with the task of accommodating the incommensurable factors of policy that underlie these mathematical puzzles is to attribute, however flatteringly, omnicompetence to judges. The Framers of the Constitution persistently rejected a proposal that embodied this assumption, and Thomas Jefferson never entertained it.

Recent legislation, creating a district appropriately described as "an atrocity of ingenuity," is not unique. Considering the gross inequality among legislative electoral units within almost every State, the Court naturally shrinks from asserting that in districting at least substantial equality is a constitutional requirement enforceable by courts. Room continues to be allowed for weighting. This of course implies that geography, economics, urban-rural conflict, and all the other nonlegal factors which have throughout our history entered into political districting are to some extent not to be ruled out in the undefined vista now opened up by review in the federal courts of state reapportionments. To some extent—aye, there's the rub. In effect, today's decision empowers the courts of the country to devise what should constitute the proper composition of the legislatures of the fifty States. If state courts should for one reason or another find themselves unable to discharge this task, the duty of doing so is put on the federal courts or on this Court, if State views do not satisfy this court's notion of what is proper districting.

We were soothingly told at the bar of this Court that we need not worry about the kind of remedy a court could effectively fashion once the abstract constitutional right to have courts pass on a statewide system of electoral districting is recognized as a matter of judicial rhetoric, because legislatures would heed the Court's admonition. This is not only a euphoric hope. It implies a sorry confession of judicial impotence in place of a frank acknowledgment that there is not under our Constitution a judicial remedy for every political mischief, for every undesirable exercise of legislative power. The Framers carefully and with deliberate forethought refused so to enthrone the judiciary. In this situation, as in others of like nature, appeal for relief does not belong here. Appeal must be to an informed, civically militant electorate. In a democratic society like ours, relief must come through an aroused popular conscience that sears the conscience of the people's representatives. In any event there is nothing judicially more unseemly nor more self-defeating than for this Court to make *in terrorem* pronouncements, to indulge in merely empty rhetoric, sounding a word of promise to the ear, sure to be disappointing to the hope. . . .

What, then, is this question of legislative apportionment? Appellants invoke the right to vote and to have their votes counted. But they are permitted to vote and their votes are counted. They go to the polls, they cast their ballots, they send their representatives to the state councils. Their complaint is simply that the representatives are not sufficiently numerous or powerful—in short, that Tennessee has adopted a basis of representation with which they are dissatisfied. Talk of "debasement" or "dilution" is circular talk. One cannot speak of "debasement" or "dilution" of the value of a vote until there is first defined a standard of reference as to what a vote should be worth. What is actually asked of the Court in this case is to choose among competing bases of representation—ultimately, really, among competing theories of political philosophy—in order to establish an appropriate frame of government for the State of Tennessee and thereby for all the States of the Union.

In such a matter, abstract analogies which ignore the facts of history deal in unrealities; they betray reason. This is not a case in which a State has, through a device however oblique and sophisticated, denied Negroes or Jews or redheaded persons a vote, or given them only a third or a sixth of a vote. That was *Gomillion* v. *Lightfoot*. . . . What Tennessee illustrates is an old and still widespread method of representation—representation by local geographical division, only in part respective of population—in preference to others, others, forsooth, more appealing. Appellants contest this choice and seek to make this Court the arbiter of the disagreement. They would make the Equal Protection Clause the charter of adjudication, asserting that the equality which it guarantees comports, if not the assurance of equal weight to every voter's vote, at least the basic conception that representation ought to be proportionate to population, a standard by reference to which the reasonableness of apportionment plans may be judged.

To find such a political conception legally enforceable in the broad and unspecific guarantee of equal protection is to rewrite the Constitution. . . . Certainly, "equal protection" is no more secure a foundation for judicial judgment of the permissibility of varying forms of representative government than is "Republican Form." Indeed since "equal protection of the laws" can only mean an equality of persons standing in the same relation to whatever governmental action is challenged, the determination whether treatment is equal presupposes a determination concerning the nature of the relationship. This, with respect to apportionment, means an inquiry into the theoretic base of representation in an acceptably republican state. For a court could not determine the equal-protection issue without in fact first determining the Republican-Form issue, simply because what is reasonable for equal protection purposes will depend upon what frame of government basically is allowed. To divorce "equal protection" from "Republican Form" is to talk about half a question.

Manifestly, the Equal Protection Clause supplies no clearer guide for judicial examination of apportionment methods than would the Guaranty Clause itself. Apportionment, by its character, is a subject of extraordinary complexity, involving—even after the fundamental theoretical issues concerning what is to be represented in a representative legislature have been fought out or compromised—considerations of geography, demography, electoral convenience, economic and social cohesions or divergencies among particular local groups, communications, the practical effects of political institutions like the lobby and the city machine, ancient traditions and ties of settled usage, respect for proven incumbents of long experience and senior status, mathematical mechanics, censuses compiling relevant data, and a host of others. Legislative responses throughout the country to the reapportionment demands of the 1960 Census have glaringly confirmed that these are not factors that lend themselves to evaluations of a nature that are the staple of judicial determinations or for which judges are equipped to adjudicate by legal training or experience or native wit. And this is the more so true because in every strand of this complicated, intricate web of values meet the contending forces of partisan politics. The practical significance of apportionment is that the next election results may differ because of it. Apportionment battles are overwhelmingly party or intra-party contests. It will add a virulent source of friction and tension in federal-state relations to embroil the federal judiciary in them.

Dissenting opinion of JUSTICE HARLAN, *whom* JUSTICE FRANKFURTER *joins.*

I can find nothing in the Equal Protection Clause or elsewhere in the Federal Constitution which expressly or impliedly supports the view that state legislatures must be so structured as to reflect with approximate equality the voice of every voter. Not only is that proposition refuted by history, as shown by my Brother FRANKFURTER, but it strikes deep into the heart of our federal system. Its acceptance would require us to turn our backs on the regard which this Court has always shown for the judgment of state legislatures and courts on matters of basically local concern.

In the last analysis, what lies at the core of this controversy is a difference of opinion as to the function of representative government. It is surely beyond argument that those who have the responsibility for devising a system of representation may permissibly consider that factors other than bare numbers should be taken into account. The existence of the United States Senate is proof enough of that. To consider that we may ignore the Tennessee Legislature's judgment in this instance because that body was the product of an asymmetrical electoral apportionment would in effect be to assume the very conclusion here disputed. Hence we must accept the present form of the Tennessee Legislature as the embodiment of the State's choice, or, more realistically, its compromise, between competing political philosophies. The federal courts have not been empowered by the Equal Protection Clause to judge whether this resolution of the State's internal political conflict is desirable or undesirable, wise or unwise.

From a reading of the majority and concurring opinions one will not find it difficult to catch the premises that underlie this decision. The fact that the appellants have been unable to obtain political redress of their asserted grievances appears to be regarded as a matter which would lead the Court to stretch to find some basis for judicial intervention. While the Equal Protection Clause is invoked, the opinion for the Court notably eschews explaining how, consonant with past decisions, the undisputed facts in this case can be considered to show a violation of that constitutional provision. The majority seems to have accepted the argument, pressed at the bar, that if this Court merely asserts authority in this field, Tennessee and other "malapportioning" States will quickly respond with appropriate political action, so that this Court need not be greatly concerned about the federal courts becoming further involved in these matters. At the same time the majority has wholly failed to reckon with what the future may hold in store if this optimistic prediction is not fulfilled. Thus, what the Court is doing reflects more an adventure in judicial experimentation than a solid piece of constitutional adjudication. Whether dismissal of this case should have been for want of jurisdiction or . . . for failure of the complaint to state a claim upon which relief could be granted, the judgment of the District Court was correct.

In conclusion, it is appropriate to say that one need not agree, as a citizen, with what Tennessee had done or failed to do, in order to deprecate, as a judge, what the majority is doing today. Those observers of the Court who see it primarily as the last refuge for the correction of all inequality or injustice, no matter what its nature or source, will no doubt applaud this decision and its break with the past. Those who consider that continuing national respect for the Court's authority depends in large measure upon its wise exercise of self-restraint and discipline in constitutional adjudication, will view the decision with deep concern.

I would affirm.

JUSTICE WHITE *announced the judgment of the Court and delivered the opinion of the Court as to Part II and an opinion in which* JUSTICE BRENNAN, JUSTICE MARSHALL, *and* JUSTICE BLACKMUN *joined as to Parts I, III, and IV.*

In this case, we review a judgment from a three-judge District Court, which sustained an equal protection challenge to Indiana's 1981 state apportionment on the basis that the law unconstitutionally diluted the votes of Indiana Democrats. Although we find such political gerrymandering to be justiciable, we conclude that the District Court applied an insufficiently demanding standard in finding unconstitutional vote dilution. Consequently, we reverse.

I

The Indiana Legislature . . . consists of a House of Representatives and a Senate. There are 100 members of the House of Representatives and 50 members of the Senate. The members of the House serve two-year terms, with elections held for all seats every two years. The members of the Senate serve four-year terms, and Senate elections are staggered so that half of the seats are up for election every two years. The members of both Houses are elected from legislative districts; but, while all Senate members are elected from single-member districts, House members are elected from a mixture of single-member and multimember districts. The division of the State into districts is accomplished by legislative enactment, which is signed by the Governor into law. . . .

In early 1981, the General Assembly initiated the process of reapportioning the State's legislative districts pursuant to the 1980 census. At this time, there were Republican majorities in both the House and the Senate, and the Governor was Republican. . . . Bills were introduced in both Houses. [A] reapportionment plan was duly passed and approved by the Governor. This plan provided 50 single-member districts for the Senate; for the House, it provided 7 triple-member, 9 double-member, and 61 single-member districts. In the Senate plan, the population deviation between districts was 1.15%; in the House plan, the deviation was 1.05%. The multimember districts generally included the more metropolitan areas of the

State, although not every metropolitan area was in a multimember district. Marion County, which included Indianapolis, was combined with portions of its neighboring counties to form five triple-member districts. Fort Wayne was divided into parts, and each part was combined with portions of the surrounding county or counties to make double-member districts. On the other hand, South Bend was divided and put partly into a double-member district and partly into a single-member district (each part combined with part of the surrounding county or counties). Although county and city lines were not consistently followed, township lines generally were. . . .

In early 1982, this suit was filed by several Indiana Democrats (here the appellees) . . . alleging that the 1981 reapportionment plans constituted a political gerrymander intended to disadvantage Democrats. Specifically, they contended that the particular district lines that were drawn and the mix of single and multimember districts were intended to and did violate their right, as Democrats, to equal protection under the Fourteenth Amendment. A three-judge District Court was convened to hear these claims.

In November 1982, before the case went to trial, elections were held under the new districting plan. All of the House seats and half of the Senate seats were up for election. Over all the House races statewide, Democratic candidates received 51.9% of the vote. Only 43 Democrats, however, were elected to the House. Over all the Senate races statewide, Democratic candidates received 53.1% of the vote. Thirteen (of 25) Democrats were elected. In Marion and Allen Counties, both divided into multimember House districts, Democratic candidates drew 46.6% of the vote, but only 3 of the 21 House seats were filled by Democrats.

On December 13, 1984, a divided District Court issued a decision declaring the reapportionment to be unconstitutional, enjoining the appellants from holding elections pursuant to the 1981 redistricting, ordering the General Assembly to prepare a new plan, and retaining jurisdiction over the case.

To the District Court majority, the results of the 1982 elections seemed "to support an argument that there is a built-in bias favoring the majority party, the Republicans, which instituted the reapportionment plan." . . . Although the court thought that these figures were unreliable predictors of future elections, it concluded that they warranted further examination of the circumstances surrounding the passage of the reapportionment statute. . . . In the course of this further examination, the court noted the irregular shape of some district lines, the peculiar mix of single- and multi-member districts, and the failure of the district lines to adhere consistently to political subdivision boundaries to define communities of interest. The court also found inadequate the other explanations given for the configuration of the districts, such as adherence to the one-person, one-vote imperative and the Voting Rights Act's no retrogression requirement. These factors, concluded the court, evidenced an intentional effort to favor Republican incumbents and candidates and to disadvantage Democratic voters. This was achieved by "stacking" Democrats into districts with large Democratic majorities and "splitting" them in other districts so as to give Republicans safe but not excessive majorities in those districts. Because the 1982 elections indicated that the plan also had a discriminatory effect in that the proportionate voting influence of Democratic voters had been adversely affected, and because any scheme "which purposely inhibit[s] or prevent[s] proportional representation cannot be tolerated," . . . the District Court invalidated the statute.

The defendants appealed, seeking review of the District Court's rulings that the case was justiciable and that, if justiciable, an equal protection violation had occurred.* . . .

II

We address first the question whether this case presents a justiciable controversy or a nonjusticiable political question. Although the District Court

*Consolidated with this suit in the proceedings below was another lawsuit, filed by the Indiana NAACP. The NAACP suit challenged the plans as unconstitutional dilutions of the black vote in Indiana in violation of the Fourteenth and Fifteenth Amendments and the Voting Rights Act of 1965, 42 U.S.C. §1973 (as amended).

In rejecting the NAACP claims, the District Court majority found that "the voting efficacy of the NAACP plaintiffs was impinged upon because of their politics and not because of their race. It is not in dispute that blacks in this state vote overwhelmingly Democratic." 603 R. Supp., at 1489–1490. Consequently, the majority found no Fifteenth Amendment or Voting Rights Act violation. The dissent concurred with this result but gave different reasons for reaching this conclusion.

The NAACP did not appeal these dispositions. Consequently, the only claims now before us are the political gerrymandering claims.

never explicitly stated that the case was justiciable, its holding clearly rests on such a finding. The appellees urge that this Court has in the past acknowledged and acted upon the justiciability of pure political gerrymandering claims. The appellants contend that we have affirmed on the merits decisions of lower courts finding such claims to be nonjusticiable.

A

Since *Baker* v. *Carr*, 369 U.S. 186 (1962), we have consistently adjudicated equal protection claims in the legislative districting context regarding inequalities in population between districts. In the course of these cases, we have developed and enforced the "one person, one vote" principle. . . .

Our past decisions also make clear that even where there is no population deviation among the districts, racial gerrymandering presents a justiciable equal protection claim. In the multimember district context, we have reviewed, and on occasion rejected, districting plans that unconstitutionally diminished the effectiveness of the votes of racial minorities. . . . We have also adjudicated claims that the configuration of single-member districts violated equal protection with respect to racial and ethnic minorities, although we have never struck down an apportionment plan because of such a claim. . . .

In the multimember district cases, we have also repeatedly stated that districting that would "operate to minimize or cancel out the voting strength of racial or political elements of the voting population" would raise a constitutional question. . . . Finally, in *Gaffney* v. *Cummings*, [412 U.S. 735, 1973], we upheld against an equal protection political gerrymandering challenge a state legislative single-member redistricting scheme that was formulated in a bipartisan effort to try to provide political representation on a level approximately proportional to the strength of political parties in the State. In that case, we adjudicated the type of purely political equal protection claim that is brought here, although we did not, as a threshold matter, expressly hold such a claim to be justiciable. Regardless of this lack of a specific holding, our consideration of the merits of the claim in *Gaffney* in the face of a discussion of justiciability in appellant's brief, combined with our repeated reference in other opinions to the constitutional deficiencies of plans that dilute the vote of political groups, at the least supports an inference that these cases are justiciable.

In the years since *Baker* v. *Carr*, both before and after *Gaffney*, however, we have also affirmed a number of decisions in which the lower courts rejected the justiciability of purely political gerrymandering claims. . . . Although these summary affirmances arguably support an inference that these claims are not justiciable, there are other cases in which federal or state courts adjudicated political gerrymandering claims and we summarily affirmed or dismissed for want of a substantial federal question. . . .

These sets of cases may look in different directions, but to the extent that our summary affirmances indicate the nonjusticiability of political gerrymander cases, we are not bound by those decisions. As we have observed before, "[i]t is not at all unusual for the Court to find it appropriate to give full consideration to a question that has been the subject of previous summary action." *Washington* v. *Yakima Indian Nation*, 439 U.S. 463, 477, N. 20 (1979). . . . The issue that the appellants would have us find to be precluded by these summary dispositions is an important one, and it deserves further consideration.

B

The issue here . . . does not concern districts of unequal size. Not only does everyone have the right to vote and to have his vote counted, but each elector may vote for and be represented by the same number of lawmakers. Rather, the claim is that each political group in a State should have the same chance to elect representatives of its choice as any other political group. Nevertheless, the issue is one of representation, and we decline to hold that such claims are never justiciable.

Our racial gerrymander cases such as *White* v. *Regester, supra,* and *Whitcomb* v. *Chavis, supra,* indicate as much. In those cases, there was no population variation among the districts, and no one was precluded from voting. The claim instead was that an identifiable racial or ethnic group had an insufficient chance to elect a representative of its choice and that district lines should be redrawn to remedy this alleged defect. In both cases, we adjudicated the merits of such claims, rejecting the claim in *Whitcomb* and sustaining it in *Regester*. Just as clearly, in *Gaffney* v. *Cummings* . . . , the claim was that the legislature had manipulated district lines to afford political groups in various districts an enhanced opportunity to elect legislators of their choice. Although advising caution, we said that "we must . . . respond to [the] claims . . . that even if acceptable populationwise, the . . . plan was invidiously discriminatory because a 'political fairness principle' was followed. . . ." 412 U.S., at

751–752. We went on to hold that the statute at issue did not violate the Equal Protection Clause.

These decisions support a conclusion that this case is justiciable. As *Gaffney* demonstrates, that the claim is submitted by a political group, rather than a racial group, does not distinguish it in terms of justiciability. . . .

III

Having determined that the political gerrymandering claim in this case is justiciable, we turn to the question whether the District Court erred in holding that appellees had alleged and proved a violation of the Equal Protection Clause.

A

Preliminarily, we agree with the District Court that the claim made by the appellees in this case is a claim that the 1981 apportionment discriminates against Democrats on a statewide basis. Both the appellees and the District Court have cited instances of individual districting within the State which they believe exemplify this discrimination, but the appellees' claim as we understand it is that Democratic voters over the State as a whole, not Democratic voters in particular districts, have been subjected to unconstitutional discrimination. . . . Although the statewide discrimination asserted here was allegedly accomplished through the manipulation of individual district lines, the focus of the equal protection inquiry is necessarily somewhat different from that involved in the review of individual districts.

We also agree with the District Court that in order to succeed the Bandemer plaintiffs were required to prove both intentional discrimination against an identifiable political group and an actual discriminatory effect on that group. . . . Further, we are confident that if the law challenged here had discriminatory effects on Democrats, this record would support a finding that the discrimination was intentional. Thus, we decline to overturn the District Court's finding of discriminatory intent as clearly erroneous.

Indeed, quite aside from the anecdotal evidence, the shape of the House and Senate Districts, and the alleged disregard for political boundaries, we think it most likely that whenever a legislature redistricts, those responsible for the legislation will know the likely political composition of the new districts and will have a prediction as to whether a particular district is a safe one for a Democratic or Republican candidate or is a competitive district that either candidate might win. . . .

As long as redistricting is done by a legislature, it should not be very difficult to prove that the likely political consequences of the reapportionment were intended.

B

We do not accept, however, the District Court's legal and factual bases for concluding that the 1981 Act visited a sufficiently adverse effect on the appellees' constitutionally protected rights to make out a violation of the Equal Protection Clause. The District Court held that because any apportionment scheme that purposely prevents proportional representation is unconstitutional, Democratic voters need only show that their proportionate voting influence has been adversely affected. Our cases, however, clearly foreclose any claim that the Constitution requires proportional representation or that legislatures in reapportioning must draw district lines to come near as possible to allocating seats to the contending parties in proportion to what their anticipated statewide vote will be. . . .

The typical election for legislative seats in the United States is conducted in described geographical districts, with the candidate receiving the most votes in each district winning the seat allocated to that district. If all or most of the districts are competitive—defined by the District Court in this case as districts in which the anticipated split in the party vote is within the range of 45% to 55%—even a narrow statewide preference for either party would produce an overwhelming majority for the winning party in the state legislature. This consequence, however, is inherent in winner-take-all, district-based elections, and we cannot hold that such a reapportionment law would violate the Equal Protection Clause because the voters in the losing party do not have representation in the legislature in proportion to the statewide vote received by their party candidates. As we have said: "[W]e are unprepared to hold that district-based elections decided by plurality vote are unconstitutional in either single- or multimember districts simply because the supporters of losing candidates have no legislative seats assigned to them." . . . It is also true of a statewide claim as well as an individual district claim. . . .

In cases involving individual multimember districts, we have required a substantially greater showing of adverse effects than a mere lack of proportional representation to support a finding of unconstitutional vote dilution. Only where there is

evidence that excluded groups have "less opportunity to participate in the political processes and to elect candidates of their choice" have we refused to approve the use of multimember districts. . . .

These holdings rest on a conviction that the mere fact that a particular apportionment scheme makes it more difficult for a particular group in a particular district to elect the representatives of its choice does not render that scheme constitutionally infirm. This conviction, in turn, stems from a perception that the power to influence the political process is not limited to winning elections. An individual or a group of individuals who votes for a losing candidate is usually deemed to be adequately represented by the winning candidate and to have as much opportunity to influence that candidate as other voters in the district. We cannot presume that such a situation, without actual proof to the contrary, that the candidate elected will entirely ignore the interests of those voters. This is true even in a safe district where the losing group loses election after election. Thus, a group's electoral power is not unconstitutionally diminished by the simple fact of an apportionment scheme that makes winning elections more difficult, and a failure of proportional representation alone does not constitute impermissible discrimination under the Equal Protection Clause. . . .

As with individual districts, where unconstitutional vote dilution is alleged in the form of statewide political gerrymandering, the mere lack of proportional representation will not be sufficient to prove unconstitutional discrimination. Again, without specific supporting evidence, a court cannot presume in such a case that those who are elected will disregard the disproportionately underrepresented group. Rather, unconstitutional discrimination occurs only when the electoral system is arranged in a manner that will consistently degrade a voter's or a group of voters' influence on the political process as a whole. . . .

. . . In a challenge to an individual district [the] inquiry focuses on the opportunity of members of the group to participate in party deliberations in the slating and nominations of candidates, their opportunity to register and vote, and hence their chance to directly influence the election returns and to secure the attention of the winning candidate. Statewide, however, the inquiry centers on the voters' direct or indirect influence on the elections of the state legislature as a whole. And, as in individual district cases, an equal protection violation may be found only where the electoral system substantially disadvantages certain voters in their opportunity to influence the political process effectively. In this context, such a finding of unconstitutionality must be supported by evidence of continued frustration of the will of a majority of the voters or effective denial to a minority of voters of a fair chance to influence the political process.

Based on these views, we would reject the District Court's apparent holding that any interference with an opportunity to elect a representative of one's choice would be sufficient to allege or make out an equal protection violation, unless justified by some acceptable state interest that the State would be required to demonstrate. In addition to being contrary to the above described conception of an unconstitutional political gerrymander, such a low threshold for legal action would invite attack on all or almost all reapportionment statutes. District-based elections hardly ever produce a perfect fit between votes and representation. The one-person, one-vote imperative often mandates departure from this result as does the noretrogression rule required by §5 of the Voting Rights Act. Inviting attack on minor departures from some supposed norm would too much embroil the judiciary in second-guessing what has consistently been referred to as a political task for the legislature, a task that should not be monitored too closely unless the express or tacit goal is to effect its removal from legislative halls. We decline to take a major step toward that end, which would be so much at odds with our history and experience. . . .

* * *

D

In response to our approach, JUSTICE POWELL suggests an alternative method for evaluating equal protection claims of political gerrymandering. In his view, courts should look at a number of factors in considering these claims: the nature of the legislative procedures by which the challenged redistricting was accomplished and the intent behind the redistricting; the shapes of the districts and their conformity with political subdivision boundaries; and "evidence concerning population disparities and statistics tending to show vote dilution" (POWELL, J., concurring in part and dissenting in part). The District Court in this case reviewed these factors in reaching its ultimate conclusion that unconstitutional vote dilution had occurred, and JUSTICE POWELL concludes that its finding on these factors—and on the ultimate question of vote discrimination—should be upheld. According to JUS-

TICE POWELL, those findings adequately support a conclusion that "the boundaries of the voting districts have been distorted deliberately and arbitrarily to achieve illegitimate ends."

[T]he crux of JUSTICE POWELL's analysis seems to be that—at least in some cases—the intentional drawing of district boundaries for partisan ends and for no other reason violates the Equal Protection Clause in and of itself. We disagree, however, with this conception of a constitutional violation. Specifically, even if a state legislature redistricts with specific intention of disadvantaging one political party's election prospects, we do not believe that there has been an unconstitutional discrimination against members of that party unless the redistricting does in fact disadvantage it at the polls.

Moreover, . . . a mere lack of proportionate results in one election cannot suffice in this regard. . . . In the statewide political gerrymandering context, . . . prior cases lead to the . . . conclusion that equal protection violations may be found only where a history (actual or projected) of disproportionate results appears in conjunction with similar indicia. The mere lack of control of the General Assembly after a single election does not rise to the requisite level.

This requirement of more than a showing of possibly transitory results is where we appear to depart from JUSTICE POWELL. Stripped of its "factors" verbiage, JUSTICE POWELL's analysis turns on a determination that a lack of proportionate election results can support a finding of an equal protection violation, at least in some circumstances. Here, the only concrete effect on the Democrats in Indiana in terms of election results that the District Court had before it was one election in which the percentage of Democrats elected was lower than the percentage of total Democratic votes cast. In JUSTICE POWELL's view, this disproportionality, when combined with clearly discriminatory intent on the part of the 1981 General Assembly and the manipulation of district lines in the apportionment process, is sufficient to conclude that fair representation has been denied.

The factors other than disproportionate election results, however, do not contribute to a finding that Democratic voters have been disadvantaged in fact. They support a finding that an intention to discriminate was present and that districts were drawn in accordance with that intention, but they do not show any actual disadvantage beyond that shown by the election results. It surely cannot be an actual disadvantage in terms of fair representation on a group level just to be placed in a district with a supermajority of the Democratic voters or a district that departs from preexisting political boundaries. Only when such placement affects election results and political power statewide has an actual disadvantage occurred. . . .

In sum, we decline to adopt the approach enunciated by JUSTICE POWELL. In our view, that approach departs from our past cases and invites judicial interference in legislative districting whenever a political party suffers at the polls. We recognize that our own view may be difficult of application. Determining when an electoral system has been "arranged in a manner that will consistently degrade a voter's or a group of voters' influence on the political process as a whole," is of necessity a difficult inquiry. Nevertheless, we believe that it recognizes the delicacy of intruding on this most political of legislative functions and is at the same time consistent with our prior cases regarding individual multimember districts, which have formulated a parallel standard.

IV

In sum, we hold that political gerrymandering cases are properly justiciable under the Equal Protection Clause. We also conclude, however, that a threshold showing of discriminatory vote dilution is required for a prima facie case of an equal protection violation. In this case, the findings made by the District Court of an adverse effect on the appellees do not surmount the threshold requirement. Consequently, the judgment of the District Court is

Reversed.

JUSTICE O'CONNOR, *with whom* THE CHIEF JUSTICE *and* JUSTICE REHNQUIST *join, concurring in the judgment.*

Today the Court holds that claims of political gerrymandering lodged by members of one of the political parties that make up our two-party system are justiciable under the Equal Protection Clause of the Fourteenth Amendment. Nothing in our precedents compels us to take this step, and there is every reason not to do so. I would hold that the partisan gerrymandering claims of major political parties raise a nonjusticiable political question that the judiciary should leave to the legislative branch as the Framers of the Constitution unquestionably intended. Accordingly, I would reverse the District Court's judgment on the grounds that appellees' claim is nonjusticiable.

There can be little doubt that the emergence of a strong and stable two-party system in this country has contributed enormously to sound and effective government. The preservation and health of our political institutions, state and federal, depends [*sic*] to no small extent on the continued vitality of our two-party system, which permits both stability and measured change. The opportunity to control the drawing of electoral boundaries through the legislative process of appointment is a critical and traditional part of politics in the United States, and one that plays no small role in fostering active participation in the political parties at every level. Thus, the legislative business of apportionment is fundamentally a political affair, and challenges to the manner in which an apportionment has been carried out—by the very parties that are responsible for this process—present a political question in the truest sense of the term.

To turn these matters over to the federal judiciary is to inject the courts into the most heated partisan issues. It is predictable that the courts will respond by moving away from the nebulous standard a plurality of the court fashions today and toward some form of rough proportional representation for all political groups. The consequences of this shift will be as immense as they are unfortunate. I do not believe, and the Court offers not a shred of evidence to suggest, that the Framers of the Constitution intended the judicial power to encompass the making of such fundamental choices about how this Nation is to be governed. Nor do I believe that the proportional representation towards which the Courts expansion of equal protection doctrine will lead as consistent with our history, our traditions, or our political institutions. . . .

The step taken today is a momentous one, which if followed in the future can only lead to political instability and judicial malaise. If members of the major political parties are protected by the Equal Protection Clause from dilution of their voting strength, then members of every identifiable group that possesses distinctive interests and tends to vote on the basis of those interests should be able to bring similar claims. Federal courts will have no alternative but to attempt to recreate the complex process of legislative apportionment in the context of adversary litigation in order to reconcile the competing claims of political, religious, ethnic, racial, occupational, and socioeconomic groups. . . . Even if there were some way of limiting such claims to organized political parties, the fact remains that the losing party or the losing group of legislators in every reapportionment will now be invited to fight the battle anew in federal court. Apportionment is so important to legislators and political parties that the burden of proof the plurality places on political gerrymandering plaintiffs is unlikely to deter the routine lodging of such complaints. Notwithstanding the plurality's threshold requirement of discriminatory effects, the Court's holding that political gerrymandering claims are justifiable has opened the door to pervasive and unwarranted judicial superintendence of the legislative task of apportionment. There is simply no clear stopping point to prevent the gradual evolution of a requirement of roughly proportional representation for every cohesive political group....

In my view, where a radical minority group is characterized by "the traditional indicia of suspectness" and is vulnerable to exclusion from the political process, . . . individual voters who belong to that group enjoy some measure of protection against intentional dilution of their group voting strength by means of racial gerrymandering. As a matter of past history and present reality, there is a direct and immediate relationship between the racial minority's group voting strength in particular community and the individual rights of its members to vote and to participate in the political process. In these circumstances, the stronger nexus between individual rights and group interests, and the greater warrant the Equal Protection Clause gives the federal courts to intervene for protection against racial discrimination, suffices to render racial gerrymandering claims justiciable.

Even so, the individual's right is infringed only if the racial minority group can prove that it has "essentially been shut out of the political process." . . .

I would avoid the difficulties generated by the plurality's efforts to continue the effects of a generalized group right to equal representation by not recognizing such a right in the first instance. To allow district courts to strike down apportionment plans on the basis of their prognostications as to the outcome of future elections or future apportionments invites "findings" on matters as to which neither judges nor anyone else have any confidence. Once it is conceded that "a group's electoral power is not unconstitutionally diminished by the simple fact of an apportionment scheme that makes winning elections more difficult," the virtual impossibility of reliably predicting how difficult it will be to win an election in 2, or 4, or 10 years should, in my view, weigh in favor of holding such challenges nonjusticiable. Racial gerrymandering should remain justiciable, for the harms it engenders run counter to the central thrust of the Fourteenth Amendment. But no such justification can be given for judicial intervention on behalf of mainstream political parties, and the risks such intervention poses to our political institutions are unacceptable. "Political affiliation is the keystone of the political trade. Race, ideally, is not." *United Jewish Organizations of Williamsburgh, Inc.* v. *Carey*, 430 U.S. 144, 171 n. 1 (1977) (BRENNAN, J., concurring).

RUTH O. SHAW, ET AL. v. JANET RENO, ATTORNEY GENERAL, ET AL.
___ U.S. ___; ___ L. Ed. 2d ___; 113 S. Ct. 2816 (1993)

JUSTICE O'CONNOR *delivered the opinion of the Court.*

This case involves two of the most complex and sensitive issues this Court has faced in recent years: the meaning of the constitutional "right" to vote, and the propriety of race-based state legislation designed to benefit members of historically disadvantaged racial minority groups. As a result of the 1990 census, North Carolina became entitled to a twelfth seat in the United States House of Representatives. The General Assembly enacted a reapportionment plan that included one majority-black congressional district. After the Attorney General of the United States objected to the plan pursuant to sec. 5 of the Voting Rights Act of 1965, . . . the

General Assembly passed new legislation creating a second majority-black district. Appellants allege that the revised plan, which contains district boundary lines of dramatically irregular shape, constitutes an unconstitutional racial gerrymander. The question before us is whether appellants have stated a cognizable claim.

I

The voting age population of North Carolina is approximately 78% white, 20% black, and 1% Native American; the remaining 1% is predominantly Asian. . . . The black population is relatively dispersed; blacks constitute a majority of the general population in only 5 of the State's 100 counties. . . .

The largest concentrations of black citizens live in the Coastal Plain, primarily in the northern part. . . . The General Assembly's first redistricting plan contained one majority-black district centered in that area of the State. . . .

Under sec. 5, the State remained free to seek a declaratory judgment from the District Court for the District of Columbia notwithstanding the Attorney General's objection. It did not do so. Instead, the General Assembly enacted a revised redistricting plan . . . that included a second majority-black district. . . .

The first of the two majority-black districts contained in the revised plan, District 1, is somewhat hook shaped. Centered in the northeast portion of the State, it moves southward until it tapers to a narrow band; then, with fingerlike extensions, it reaches far into the southernmost part of the State near the South Carolina border. District 1 has been compared to a "Rorschach ink-blot test," *Shaw* v. *Barr*, 808 F. Supp. 461, 476 (EDNC 1992) (Voorhees, C.J., concurring in part and dissenting in part), and a "bug splattered on a windshield," *Wall Street Journal*, Feb. 4, 1992, p. A14.

The second majority-black district, District 12, is even more unusually shaped. It is approximately 160 miles long and, for much of its length, no wider than the I-85 corridor. It winds in snake-like fashion through tobacco country, financial centers, and manufacturing areas "until it gobbles in enough enclaves of black neighborhoods." . . . Northbound and southbound drivers on I-85 sometimes find themselves in separate districts in one county, only to "trade" districts when they enter the next county. Of the 10 counties through which District 12 passes, five are cut into three different districts; even towns are divided. At one point the district remains contiguous only because it intersects at a single point with two other districts before crossing over them. . . .

The Attorney General did not object to the General Assembly's revised plan. But numerous North Carolinians did. The North Carolina Republican Party and individual voters brought suit in Federal District Court alleging that the plan constituted an unconstitutional political gerrymander under *Davis* v. *Bandemer*, 478 U.S. 109 (1986). That claim was dismissed, see *Pope* v. *Blue*, 809 F. Supp. 392 (WDNC 1992), and this Court summarily affirmed, 506 U.S. (1992).

Shortly after the complaint in *Pope* v. *Blue* was filed, appellants instituted the present action in the United States District Court for the Eastern District of North Carolina. Appellants alleged not that the revised plan constituted a political gerry-

mander, nor that it violated the "one person, one vote" principle, . . . but that the State had created an unconstitutional racial gerrymander. . . .

. . . Appellants sought declaratory and injunctive relief against the state appellees. They sought similar relief against the federal appellees, arguing, alternatively, that the federal appellees had misconstrued the Voting Rights Act or that the Act itself was unconstitutional.

The three-judge District court granted the federal appellees' motion to dismiss. . . .

The majority first took judicial notice of a fact omitted from appellants' complaint: that appellants are white. It rejected the argument that race-conscious redistricting to benefit minority voters is per se unconstitutional. The majority also rejected appellants' claim that North Carolina's reapportionment plan was impermissible. . . . The purposes of favoring minority voters and complying with the Voting Rights Act are not discriminatory in the constitutional sense, the court reasoned, and majority-minority districts have an impermissibly discriminatory effect only when they unfairly dilute or cancel out white voting strength. Because the State's purpose here was to comply with the Voting Rights Act and because the General Assembly's plan did not lead to proportional underrepresentation of white voters statewide, the majority concluded that appellants had failed to state an equal protection claim. . . .

II

A

* * *

B

. . . Our focus is on appellant's claim that the State engaged in unconstitutional racial gerrymandering. That argument strikes a powerful historical chord: It is unsettling how closely the North Carolina plan resembles the most egregious racial gerrymanders of the past.

An understanding of the nature of appellants' claim is critical to our resolution of the case. In their complaint, appellants did not claim that the General Assembly's reapportionment plan unconstitutionally "diluted" white voting strength. They did not even claim to be white. Rather, appellants' complaint alleged that the deliberate segregation of voters into separate districts on the basis of race violated their constitutional right to participate in a "color-blind electoral process. . . . "

Despite their invocation of the ideal of a "color-blind" Constitution, . . . appellants appear to concede that race-conscious redistricting is not always unconstitutional. . . . That concession is wise: This Court never has held that race-conscious state decision-making is impermissible in all circumstances. What appellants object to is redistricting legislation that is so extremely irregular on its face that it rationally can be viewed only as an effort to segregate the races for purposes of voting, without regard for traditional districting principles and without sufficiently compelling justification. For the reasons that follow, we conclude that appellants have stated a claim upon which relief can be granted under the Equal Protection Clause. . . .

III

A

The Equal Protection Clause provides that "[n]o State shall . . . deny to any person within its jurisdiction the equal protection of the laws." . . . Its central purpose is to prevent the States from purposefully discriminating between individuals on the basis of race. . . . Laws that explicitly distinguish between individuals on racial grounds fall within the core of that prohibition.

No inquiry into legislative purpose is necessary when the racial classification appears on the face of the statute. See *Personnel Administrator of Massachusetts* v. *Feeney*, 442 U.S. 256, 272 (1979). . . . Express racial classifications are immediately suspect because, "[a]bsent searching judicial inquiry . . . , there is simply no way of determining what classifications are 'benign' or 'remedial' and what classifications are in fact motivated by illegitimate notions of racial inferiority or simple racial politics." *Richmond* v. *J.A. Croson Co.*, 488 U.S. 469, 493 (1989). . . .

Classifications of citizens solely on the basis of race "are by their very nature odious to a free people whose institutions are founded upon the doctrine of equality." *Hirabayashi* v. *United States*, 320 U.S. 81, 100 (1943). . . . They threaten to stigmatize individuals by reason of their membership in a racial group and to incite racial hostility. . . . Accordingly, we have held that the Fourteenth Amendment requires state legislation that expressly distinguishes among citizens because of their race to be narrowly tailored to further a compelling governmental interest. . . .

These principles apply not only to legislation that contains explicit racial distinctions, but also to those "rare" statutes that, although race-neutral, are, on their face, "unexplainable on ground other than race." *Arlington Heights* v. *Metropolitan Housing*

Development Corp., 429 U.S. 252, 266 (1977). As we explained in *Feeney*: "A racial classification, regardless of purported motivation, is presumptively invalid and can be upheld only upon an extraordinary justification. . . . This rule applies as well to a classification that is ostensibly neutral but is an obvious pretext for racial discrimination. *Yick Wo* v. *Hopkins*, 118 U.S. 356; *Guinn* v. *United States*, 238 U.S. 347; cf. *Lane* v. *Wilson*, 307 U.S. 268; *Gomillion* v. *Lightfoot*, 364 U.S. 339." . . .

B

Appellants contend that redistricting legislation that is so bizarre on its face that it is "unexplainable on ground other than race," *Arlington Heights*, *supra*, at 266, demands the same close scrutiny that we give other state laws that classify citizens by race. Our voting rights precedents support that conclusion. . . .

Wright [v. *Rockefeller*, 376 U.S. 52, 1964] illustrates the difficulty of determining from the face of a single-member districting plan that it purposefully distinguishes between voters on the basis of race. A reapportionment statute typically does not classify persons at all; it classifies tracts of land, or addresses. Moreover, redistricting differs from other kinds of state decision-making in that the legislature always is aware of race when it draws district lines, just as it is aware of age, economic status, religious and political persuasion, and a variety of other demographic factors. That sort of race consciousness does not lead inevitably to impermissible race discrimination. As *Wright* demonstrates, when members of a racial group live together in one community, a reapportionment plan that concentrates members of the group in one district and excludes them from others may reflect wholly legitimate purposes. The district lines may be drawn, for example, to provide for compact districts of contiguous territory, or to maintain the integrity of political subdivisions. . . .

The difficulty of proof, of course, does not mean that a racial gerrymander, once established, should receive less scrutiny under the Equal Protection Clause than other state legislation classifying citizens by race. Moreover, it seems clear to us that proof sometimes will not be difficult at all. In some exceptional cases, a reapportionment plan may be so highly irregular that, on its face, it rationally cannot be understood as anything other than an effort to "segregat[e] . . . voters" on the basis of race. *Gomillion*, *supra*, at 341. *Gomillion*, in which a tortured municipal boundary line was drawn to exclude black voters, was such a case. So, too, would be a case in which a State concentrated a dispersed minority population in a single district by disregarding traditional districting principles such as compactness, contiguity, and respect for political subdivisions. We emphasize that these criteria are important not because they are constitutionally required—they are not, . . . but because they are objective factors that may serve to defeat a claim that a district has been gerrymandered on racial lines. . . .

Put differently, we believe that reapportionment is one area in which appearances do matter. A reapportionment plan that includes in one district individuals who belong to the same race, but who are otherwise widely separated by geographical and political boundaries, and who may have little in common with one another but the color of their skin, bears an uncomfortable resemblance to political apartheid. It reinforces the perception that members of the same racial group—regardless of their age, education, economic status, or the community in which they live—think alike, share the same political interests, and will prefer the same candidates at the polls. We have rejected such perceptions elsewhere as impermissible racial stereotypes. See, e.g., *Holland* v. *Illinois*, 493 U.S. 474, 484, n. 2 (1990). . . .

The message that such districting sends to elected representatives is equally pernicious. When a district obviously is created solely to effectuate the perceived common interests of one racial group, elected officials are more likely to believe that their primary obligation is to represent only the members of that group, rather than their constituency as a whole. This is altogether antithetical to our system of representative democracy. As Justice Douglas explained in his dissent in *Wright* v. *Rockefeller* nearly 30 years ago: "Here the individual is important, not his race, his creed, or his color. The principle of equality is at war with the notion that District A must be represented by a Negro, as it is with the notion that District B must be represented by a Caucasian, District C by a Jew, District D by a Catholic, and so on. . . . That system, by whatever name it is called, is a divisive force in a community, emphasizing differences between candidates and voters that are irrelevant in the constitutional sense. . . .

. . . "When racial or religious lines are drawn by the State, the multiracial, multireligious communities that our Constitution seeks to weld together as one become separatist; antagonisms that relate to race or to religion rather than to political issues are generated; communities seek not the best representative but the best racial or religious partisan. Since that system is at war with the democratic ideal, it should find no footing here. 376 U.S., at 66–67 (dissenting opinion).

For these reasons, we conclude that a plaintiff challenging a reapportionment statute under the Equal Protection Clause may state a claim by alleging that the legislation, though race-neutral on its face, rationally cannot be understood as anything other than an effort to separate voters into different districts on the basis of race, and that the separation lacks sufficient justification. It is unnecessary for us to decide whether or how a reapportionment plan that, on its face, can be explained in nonracial terms successfully could be challenged. Thus, we express no view as to whether "the intentional creation of majority-minority districts, without more" always gives rise to an equal protection claim. . . . We hold only that, on the facts of this case, plaintiffs have stated a claim sufficient to defeat the state appellees' motion to dismiss.

C

* * *

IV

* * *

V

Racial classifications of any sort pose the risk of lasting harm to our society. They reinforce the belief, held by too many for too much of our history, that individuals should be judged by the color of their skin. Racial classifications with respect to voting carry particular dangers. Racial gerrymandering, even for remedial purposes, may balkanize us into competing racial factions; it threatens to carry us further from the goal of a political system in which race no longer matters—a goal that the Fourteenth and Fifteenth Amendments embody, and to which the Nation continues to aspire. It is for these reasons that race-based districting by our state legislatures demands close judicial scrutiny.

In this case, the Attorney General suggested that North Carolina could have created a reasonably compact second majority-minority district in the south-central to southeastern part of the State. We express no view as to whether appellants successfully could have challenged such a district under the Fourteenth Amendment. We also do not decide whether appellants' complaint stated a claim under constitutional provisions other than the Fourteenth Amendment. Today we hold only that appellants have stated a claim under the

Equal Protection Clause by alleging that the North Carolina General Assembly adopted a reapportionment scheme so irrational on its face that it can be understood only as an effort to segregate voters into separate voting districts because of their race, and that the separation lacks sufficient justification. If the allegation of racial gerrymandering remains uncontradicted, the District Court further must determine whether the North Carolina plan is narrowly tailored to further a compelling governmental interest. Accordingly, we reverse the judgment of the District Court and remand the case for further proceedings consistent with this opinion

It is so ordered.

JUSTICE WHITE, *with whom* JUSTICE BLACKMUN *and* JUSTICE STEVENS *join, dissenting.*

The facts of this case mirror those presented in *United Jewish Organizations of Williamsburgh, Inc.* v. *Carey*, 430 U.S. 144 (1977) (*UJO*), where the Court rejected a claim that creation of a majority-minority district violated the Constitution, either as a per se matter or in light of the circumstances leading to the creation of such a district. Of particular relevance, five of the Justices reasoned that members of the white majority could not plausibly argue that their influence over the political process had been unfairly canceled, see *id.,* at 165–168 (opinion of WHITE, J., joined by REHNQUIST CJ. and STEVENS, JJ.). . . . Accordingly, they held that plaintiffs were not entitled to relief under the Constitution's Equal Protection Clause. On the same reasoning, I would affirm the District Court's dismissal of appellants' claim in this instance.

The Court today chooses not to overrule, but rather to sidestep, *UJO.* It does so by glossing over the striking similarities, focusing on surface differences, most notably the (admittedly unusual) shape of the newly created district, and imagining an entirely new cause of action. Because the holding is limited to such anomalous circumstances, it perhaps will not substantially hamper a State's legitimate efforts to redistrict in favor of racial minorities. Nonetheless, the notion that North Carolina's plan, under which whites remain a voting majority in a disproportionate number of congressional districts, and pursuant to which the State has sent its first black representatives since Reconstruction to the United States Congress, might have violated appellants' constitutional rights is both a fiction and a departure from settled equal protection principles. Seeing no good reason to engage in either,

I dissent.

I

A

The grounds for my disagreement with the majority are simply stated: Appellants have not presented a cognizable claim, because they have not alleged a cognizable injury. To date, we have held that only two types of state voting practices could give rise to a constitutional claim. The first involves direct and outright deprivation of the right to vote, for example by means of a poll tax or literacy test. See, e.g., *Guinn* v. *United States*, 238 U.S. 347 (1915). . . . The second type of unconstitutional practice is that which "affects the political strength of various groups," *Mobile* v. *Bolden* 446 U.S. 55, 83 (1980) . . . in violation of the Equal Protection Clause. As for this latter category, we have insisted that members of the political or racial group demonstrate that the challenged action have the intent and effect of unduly diminishing their influence on the political process.

Although this severe burden has limited the number of successful suits, it was adopted for sound reasons. . . .

. . . . [A] number of North Carolina's political subdivisions have interfered with black citizens' meaningful exercise of the franchise, and are therefore subject to secs. 4 and 5 of the Voting Rights Act. In other words, North Carolina was found by Congress to have " 'resorted to the extraordinary stratagem of contriving new rules of various kinds for the sole purpose of perpetuating voting discrimination in the face of adverse federal court decrees' " and therefore "would be likely to engage in 'similar maneuvers in the future in order to evade the remedies for voting discrimination contained in the Act itself.' " *McCain* v. *Lybrand*, 465 U.S. 236, 245 (1984). . . . Like New York, North Carolina failed to prove to the Attorney General's satisfaction that its proposed redistricting had neither the purpose nor the effect of abridging the right to vote on account of race or color. . . .

In light of this background, it strains credulity to suggest that North Carolina's purpose in creating a second majority-minority district was to discriminate against members of the majority group by "impair[ing] or burden [ing their] opportunity . . . to participate in the political process." The State has made no mystery of its intent, which was to respond to the Attorney General's objections, by improving the minority group's prospects of electing a candidate of its choice. I doubt that this constitutes a discriminatory purpose as defined in the Court's equal protection cases—i.e., an intent to aggravate "the unequal distribution of electoral power." . . . But even assuming that it does, there is no question that appellants have not alleged the requisite discriminatory effects. Whites constitute roughly 76 percent of the total population and 79 percent of the voting age population in North Carolina. Yet, under the State's plan, they still constitute a voting majority in 10 (or 83 percent) of the 12 congressional districts. Though they might be dissatisfied at the prospect of casting a vote for a losing candidate—a lot shared by many, including a disproportionate number of minority voters—surely they cannot complain of discriminatory treatment.

II

* * *

III

Although I disagree with the holding that appellants' claim is cognizable, the Court's discussion of the level of scrutiny it requires warrants a few comments. I have no doubt that a State's compliance with the Voting Rights Act clearly constitutes a compelling interest. . . . Here, the Attorney General objected to the State's plan on the ground that it failed to draw a second majority-minority district for what appeared to be pretextual reasons. Rather than challenge this conclusion, North Carolina chose to draw the second district. As *UJO* held, a State is entitled to take such action. . . .

The Court, while seemingly agreeing with this position, warns that the State's redistricting effort must be "narrowly tailored" to further its interest in complying with the law. It is evident to me, however, that what North Carolina did was precisely tailored to meet the objection of the Attorney General to its prior plan. Hence, I see no need for

a remand at all, even accepting the majority's basic approach to this case.

Furthermore, how it intends to manage this standard, I do not know. Is it more "narrowly tailored" to create an irregular majority-minority district as opposed to one that is compact but harms other State interests such as incumbency protection or the representation of rural interest? Of the following two options—creation of two minority influence districts or of a single majority-minority district—is one "narrowly tailored" and the other not? Once the Attorney General has found that a proposed redistricting change violates sec. 5's non-retrogression principle in that it will abridge a racial minority's right to vote, does "narrow tailoring" mean that the most the State can do is preserve the status quo? Or can it maintain that change, while attempting to enhance minority voting power in some other manner? This small sample only begins to scratch the surface of the problems raised by the majority's test. But it suffices to illustrate the unworkability of a standard that is divorced from any measure of constitutional harm. In that, State efforts to remedy minority vote dilution are wholly unlike what typically has been labeled "affirmative action." To the extent that no other racial group is injured, remedying a Voting Rights Act violation does not involve preferential treatment. . . . It involves, instead, an attempt to equalize treatment, and to provide minority voters with an effective voice in the political process. The Equal Protection Clause of the Constitution, surely, does not stand in the way.

IV

Since I do not agree that petitioners alleged an Equal Protection violation and because the Court of Appeals faithfully followed the Court's prior cases,

I dissent and would affirm the judgment below.

SELECTED REFERENCES

Alfange, Dean, Jr. "Gerrymandering and the Constitution: Into the Thorns of the Thicket at Last," 1986 *Supreme Court Review* 175 (1986).

Anderson, John M. "Politics and Purpose: Hide and Seek in the Gerrymandering Thicket after *Davis* v. *Bandemer*," 136 *University of Pennsylvania Law Review* 183 (November 1987).

Ballard, Gregory G. "Application of Section 2 of the Voting Rights Act to Runoff Election Laws," 91 *Columbia Law Review* 1127 (June 1991).

Barber, Steve, et al. "The Purging of Empowerment: Voter Purge Laws and the Voting Rights Act," 23 *Harvard Civil Rights–Civil Liberties Law Review* 483 (Summer 1988).

Cipollone, Pasquale A. "Section 2 of the Voting Rights Act and Judicial Elections: Application and Remedy," 58 *University of Chicago Law Review* 733 (Spring 1991).

Guinier, Lani. "The Triumph of Tokenism: The Voting Rights Act and the Theory of Black Electoral Success," 89 *Michigan Law Review* 1077 (March 1991).

Hamilton, Charles V. *The Bench and the Ballot: Southern Federal Judges and Black Voters* (New York: Oxford University Press, 1973).

Haydel, Judith. "Section 2 of the Voting Rights Act of 1965: A Challenge to State Judicial Election Systems," 73 *Judicature* 68 (August–September 1989).

Martin, Philip L. "Supreme Court and State Legislative Reapportionment: The Retreat from Absolutism," 9 *Valparaiso University Law Review* 31 (Fall 1974).

McKenzie, Roy, and Krauss, Ronald. "Section 2 of the Voting Rights Act: An Analysis of the 1982 Amendment," 19 *Harvard Civil Rights–Civil Liberties Law Review* 155 (Winter 1984).

Montague, Bill. "The Voting Rights Act Today," 74 *ABA Journal* 52 (August 1988).

Note. "Fair and Effective Voting Strength under Section 2 of the Voting Rights Act: The Impact of *Thornburg* v. *Gingles* in Minority Vote Dilution Litigation," 34 *Wayne Law Review* 303 (Fall 1987).

Schuck, Peter H. "The Thickest Thicket: Partisan Gerrymandering and Judicial Regulation of Politics," 87 *Columbia Law Review* 1325 (November 1987).

Simpson, William. "The Primary Runoff: Racism's Reprieve?" 65 *North Carolina Law Review* 359 (January 1987).

Chapter 7

Sex, Privacy, and Poverty

Frontiero v. *Richardson*   *Craig et al.* v. *Boren*   *Mississippi University for Women et al.* v. *Hogan*
Grove City College v. *Bell*   *Griswold et al.* v. *Connecticut*   *Roe* v. *Wade*
Webster v. *Reproductive Health Services*   *Planned Parenthood* v. *Casey*   *Bowers* v. *Hardwick*
Cruzan v. *Missouri*   *Wyman* v. *James*   *San Antonio Independent School District* v. *Rodriguez*
Kadrmas v. *Dickinson Public Schools*

Introductory Commentary

One of the effects of the civil rights movement has been the awakening of other minorities as well as white Americans to the racism, sexism, and injustices that continue to exist in the United States. As the last two chapters demonstrate, African Americans have long been treated unfairly because of race and color. But so have others. Chicanos and Latinos, for example, have also endured deprivations with respect to education, employment, and political participation. And the difficulties suffered by people of color have been compounded by the fact that many of them also belong to another group that has long been ignored—the poor. Although it is true that in raw numbers the white poor is the largest group, on a proportionate basis American people of color continue to shoulder a much heavier burden of the pains and problems of being poor. Indeed, despite changing definitions of poverty, almost one out of every three blacks in this country lives in poverty.

Women as a group have also long suffered from "minority" deprivations, for they too encounter inequities in education, employment, and legal status. Although finally securing the right to vote in 1920 by virtue of the Nineteenth Amendment, women are still clamoring for equal rights by way of constitutional interpretation and legislative enactment. But men are also complaining, charging that they too are being discriminated against because of sex. As a result, the legal battle over women's rights is now being fought within the more general context of "gender-based discrimination," which, as we shall see, holds important implications for the law and politics of gender-based classifications under the Constitution.

Similarly, the right of privacy, which came to the fore in the mid-1960s, is also clearly on the center stage of law and politics. While deeply ingrained in our constitutional and legal history, much of the development of this right, particularly in recent years, has taken place in the context of issues relating to women's rights and sexual freedoms. These "personal autonomy" issues, however, have triggered conflicts with other rights and concerns, such as those involving fetuses and surrogate mothers. For example, in *International Union, UAW* v. *Johnson Controls* (1991) there was such a direct conflict of rights. In *Johnson Controls*, the employer had a "fetal protection" policy that barred all fertile women from jobs involving actual or potential lead exposure exceeding Occupational Safety and Health Administration standards. The Supreme Court ruled that such a pregnancy policy was facially discriminatory on the basis of sex and thus violated Title VII of the Civil Rights Act of 1964 in that it was not a bona fide occupational qualification that would have been an exception to Title VII restrictions on discrimination. In *Johnson Controls*, the Court chose to protect the "autonomy" of women to choose their employment over the rights of employers to make discriminations that would minimize potential liability from suits stemming from "injured pregnant women."

As we shall see, the Court is increasingly being asked to choose among different interests that are represented in the range of possible legal institutional circumstances and that are now being adjusted to take into account the presence of women, gays and lesbians, and the poor. Employment and job security, military service, fair and equal access to education, housing, and health care are among the many contexts in which the Court has had (and is likely to continue to have) to make difficult choices.

In this chapter, we shall study these and similar conflicts of interests reflective of a changing society by focusing on three major themes: (1) equal rights for women in the context of gender-based discrimination; (2) the definition and development of the right of privacy; and (3) an emerging body of law that attempts to deal with the rights of the poor.

Equal Rights for Women and Gender-Based Discrimination

FEATURED CASES

Frontiero v. Richardson   Craig et al. v. Boren   Mississippi University for Women et al. v. Hogan
Grove City College v. Bell

THE EVOLUTION OF JUDICIAL POLICIES

Early decisions of the Supreme Court indicated that there were reasonable justifications to conclude that women could be treated differently from men, especially in such matters as job opportunities and conditions of employment. (See, for example, *Bradwell* v. *Illinois*, 83 U.S. 130, 1872, especially the concurring opinion of Justice Bradley at 141–142; and *Muller* v. *Oregon*, 208 U.S. 412, 1908.) And, of most importance, the Court held that such differential treatment did not abridge the federal Constitution. Moreover, the theories advanced in these earlier decisions were reflected in a Supreme Court decision as late as 1948. In *Goesaert* v. *Cleary* (335 U.S. 464, 1948), for example, the Court rejected an equal protection challenge and upheld a Michigan law that denied issuance of a bartender's license to any woman except one who was "the wife or daughter of the male owner" of a licensed liquor establishment. Speaking for the majority, Justice Frankfurter maintained that the statutory classification scheme was "not without a basis in reason." The legislature, he contended, had a reasonable basis for believing serious moral and social problems could result from women tending bars. Consequently, legislatures are not without power to "devise preventive measures." Justifying the "wife-daughter" exemption, Frankfurter concluded that "the legislature need not go to the full length of the prohibition if it believes that as to a defined group of females other factors are operating which either eliminate or reduce the moral and social problems otherwise calling for prohibition." But Justice Rutledge, joined by Justices Douglas and Murphy, dissented. While noting that the equal protection clause does not require a legislature to devise classification schemes with mathematical precision, Rutledge argued, however, that it "does require lawmakers to refrain from invidious distinctions of the sort drawn by the statute challenged in this case." Indeed, he continued, the "inevitable result of the classification (some, not *all*, women are prevented from becoming bartenders) belies the assumption that the statute was motivated by a legislative solicitude for the moral and physical well-being of women, who, but for the law, would be employed as barmaids."

Spurred by the egalitarian mood of the 1960s, litigation involving women's rights is on the increase, and it would be difficult for any court today to maintain theories underlying *Goesaert* and earlier cases such as *Muller* v. *Oregon, supra.* As the California Supreme Court put it in 1971, *Goesaert* was decided "well before the recent and major growth of public concern about and opposition to sex discrimination," *Sail'er Inn, Inc.* v. *Kirby* (485 P. 2d 529, fn. 15). In the *Sail'er Inn* case, the California Supreme Court struck down a statute, similar to the one involved in the 1948 *Goesaert* case, as violative of the California constitution, the 1964 Civil Rights Act, and the Fourteenth Amendment. The statute forbade women to work as bartenders. If such statutes applied to racial or ethnic minorities, said the court, they would "readily be recognized as invidious and impermissible." Consequently, the California Supreme Court concluded that sexual classifications should be "properly treated as suspect, particularly when . . . made with respect to employment."

Beginning in 1971, the U.S. Supreme Court also started to scrutinize gender-based discrimination more carefully. Women's rights advocates now began to win victories in the Supreme Court. Clearly a watershed victory came in *Reed* v. *Reed* (404 U.S. 71, 1972), in which the Court declared for the first time that sex discrimination was violative of the equal protection clause of the Fourteenth Amendment. In *Reed*, the Court held as violative of the equal protection clause a provision of the Idaho Probate Code that in determining the administrator of estates from among persons in the same class, "males must be preferred to females." Speaking for the majority in *Reed*, Chief Justice Burger said that "to give a mandatory preference to members of either sex over members of the other, merely to accomplish the elimination of hearings on the merits, is to make the very kind of arbitrary legislative choice forbidden by the Equal Protection Clause." In another case, *Stanton* v. *Stanton* (421 U.S. 7, 1975), involving a Utah statute in which child support payments for male children were extended until age 21 but for females only until age 18, the Supreme Court in an eight-to-one decision ruled that the gender-based classification had no rational relationship to the objective of the statute. Consequently, it was a denial of equal protection under the Fourteenth Amendment. The Court primarily relied upon *Reed* in deciding *Stanton*. Similarly, in *Craig et al.* v. *Boren* (429 U.S. 190, 1976), it held unconstitutional an Oklahoma statute that prohibited the sale of 3.2 percent beer to males under 21 years and to females under 18 years of age. *Reed* again was controlling, since the Oklahoma beer statute in this instance invidiously discriminated against 18-to-21-year-old males.

In a 1973 decision, the Court indicated that military service regulations cannot treat dependents of female members of the armed forces differently from the way they treat dependents of male members (*Frontiero* v. *Richardson*, 411 U.S. 671, 1973). An important aspect of the case is that a plurality of the justices in *Frontiero* concluded that sex was a "suspect" classification and should be treated accordingly. The *Frontiero* decision was cited by the Court in *Weinberger* v. *Weisenfeld* (420 U.S. 636, 1975) as justification to declare unconstitutional Section 402 (g) of the Social Security Act. This section provided survivors' benefits, based on earnings, to the widow and minor children of a deceased husband, but not to the widower of a deceased wife and mother. Writing for a unanimous Court, Justice Brennan concluded that the gender-based distinction was "entirely irrational" and therefore a denial of equal protection. Similarly, in a 1977 ruling, *Califano* v. *Goldfarb* (430 U.S. 199), the Court by a five-to-four majority held unconstitutional a requirement of the Social Security system that widowers, but not widows, had to prove their financial dependence on their deceased spouses to be eligible for survivors' benefits. (But in *Califano* v. *Webster*, 430 U.S. 313, 1977, the Court upheld a provision of the Social Security Act that could provide women with higher old-age benefits than men. In a per curiam opinion, the Court found "that the statutory scheme here bears a closer analogy to *Kahn* and *Ballard, infra,* than to the schemes found invalid in *Weisenfeld* and *Goldfarb, supra.*" Rather than "archaic and overbroad generalizations" or "role-typing" based on stereotypes, the Court found that "the only discernable purpose" of the provision involved in *Webster* was to redress "society's longstanding disparate treatment of women." It was not, said the Court, the "accidental byproduct of a traditional way of thinking about females.")

In early 1974, the Supreme Court sought to resolve the confused state of the law on maternity leaves for women. In *Lafleur* (*Lafleur* v. *Cleveland Board of Education*, 414 U.S. 632), a Court of Appeals (465 F. 2d 1184, 1972) had held that a school board rule requiring pregnant teachers to take unpaid leaves of absence beginning three months before the child's birth was "arbitrary and unreasonable." The appeals court said that "pregnant women teachers have been singled out for unconstitutionally unequal restrictions upon their employment" because of their sex. On the other hand, however, a federal district court in Connecticut had upheld a teaching contract clause requiring pregnant teachers to apply for and take leaves of absence to begin not less than four months prior to the expected date of birth of the child. (*Green* v. *Waterford Bd. of Education*, 349 F. Supp. 687, D. Conn., 1972). In *Green* the district court indicated that the traditional standard of equal protection review "whether the classification at issue is without any reasonable basis"—was to be applied in the case and concluded that the maternity leave section of the contract was "not so lacking in rational basis as to constitute a denial of equal protection."

However, the U.S. Supreme Court majority agreed with the Court of Appeals ruling in the

Lafleur case. Justice Potter Stewart, who delivered the opinion for the Court, held that the arbitrary cutoff dates embraced in maternity leave regulations are violative of due process "since they create a conclusive presumption that every teacher who is four or five months pregnant is physically incapable of continuing her duties." "Such a rule," Stewart continued, contains the "irrebuttable presumption of physical incompetency" and ignores the differences among individuals in their capacities to perform their duties during pregnancy. Stewart concluded that "neither the necessity for continuity of instruction nor the state interest in keeping physically unfit teachers out of the classroom can justify the sweeping mandatory leave regulations involved."

Chief Justice Burger and Justice William Rehnquist dissented because they felt that the board's regulation was well within permissible limits of legislative classification statutes. Justice Rehnquist, with whom Burger joined in dissent, stated that "if legislative bodies are to be permitted to draw a general line anywhere short of the delivery room," they could "find no judicial standard of measurement" that would invalidate those involved in this case. Furthermore, he concluded that the Court's "disenchantment with irrebuttable presumptions and its preference for individualized determination is in the last analysis nothing less than an attack upon the very notion of lawmaking itself." (In light of *Lafleur* and *Green, Johnson Controls* may be reconsidered as an indication of the current evolution of the law in addressing and balancing the complex issues surrounding pregnancy and employment interests.)

The Court continued to support women's rights in *Taylor* v. *Louisiana* (419 U.S. 522, 1975). Here the appellant, a male convicted in 1972 for aggravated kidnapping, challenged the Louisiana jury selection procedure under which he had been tried and convicted, in which women were excluded from service in a jury trial unless they had previously filed for it.[1] The question before the Court was whether the presence of a fair cross-section of the community is essential to fulfillment of the Sixth Amendment's guarantee of an impartial jury trial in criminal prosecutions. Writing for an eight-to-one majority, Justice White declared that "restricting jury service to only special groups or excluding identifiable segments playing major roles in the community cannot be squared with the constitutional concept of jury trial. . . . [I]t is

no longer tenable to hold that women as a class may be excluded or given automatic exemptions based solely on sex if the consequence is that criminal jury venires are almost totally male." (Cf. *Duren* v. *Missouri*, 439 U.S. 357, 1979, holding inconsistent with the Sixth Amendment fair cross-section requirement a state scheme affording "any woman" exemption from jury duty.)

Several other 1979 decisions also found the Court striking down gender-based discrimination. In *Califano* v. *Westcott* (443 U.S. 76, 1979), the Court held unconstitutional under the due process clause of the Fifth Amendment a provision of the Social Security Act that "provides benefits to families whose dependent children have been deprived of parental support because of the unemployment of the father, but does not provide such benefits when the mother becomes unemployed." The Court found the provision was not substantially related to the attainment of any important and valid statutory goals, but "it is, rather, part of the 'baggage of sexual stereotypes' . . . that presumes the father has 'primary responsibility to provide a home and its essentials' " . . . while the mother is the "center of home and family life."

In *Caban* v. *Mohammed* (441 U.S. 380, 1979), the Court held unconstitutional a New York statutory scheme that permits an unwed mother, but not an unwed father, to prevent the adoption of their child simply by withholding her consent. Justice Powell, who spoke for the Court, stated that the "undifferentiated distinction between unwed mothers and unwed fathers applicable in all circumstances where adoption of a child of theirs is at issue, does not bear a substantial relationship" to any important state interest. Accordingly, the Court found the New York law violative of the equal protection clause of the Fourteenth Amendment. And in *Orr* v. *Orr* (440 U.S. 268, 1979), the Court found violative of equal protection an Alabama law imposing alimony obligations on husbands *but* not on wives. Similarly, in a 1982 decision, the Court held that refusal of a state's nursing school to admit a qualified male applicant violated the equal protection clause of the Fourteenth Amendment (*Mississippi University for Women* v. *Hogan*, 458 U.S. 718).

Overall, the decisions in *Reed, Frontiero, Stanton, Boren, Weisenfeld, Taylor, Goldfarb, Duren, Westcott, Caban, Orr,* and *Hogan* represent the interests of those wishing to overturn gender-based classifications. (And although the Court upheld such a classification in *Califano* v. *Webster*, that case can be read as an attempt "to compensate women for past economic discrimination.")

[1]On December 31, 1974, the Louisiana constitution eliminated the special provision for female jury service.

To be sure, however, the Court has also represented the interests of those who believe that they have important and sufficient reasons to maintain gender-based classifications. For example, in *Geduldig* v. *Aiello* (417 U.S. 484, 1974), the Supreme Court reversed a federal district court's judgment that California's disability insurance program, which excluded disabilities resulting from normal pregnancy and childbirth, violated the equal protection clause of the Fourteenth Amendment. The Court said it could "not agree that the exclusion of this disability from coverage amounts to invidious discrimination under the Equal Protection Clause." Writing for the majority, Justice Stewart observed that the state "does not discriminate with respect to persons or groups who are eligible for disability insurance protection." He noted that the "classification challenged in this case relates to the asserted under-inclusiveness of the set of risks that the State has selected to insure." But, said Stewart, "there is nothing in the Constitution . . . that requires the State to subordinate or compromise its legitimate interests solely to create a more comprehensive social insurance program than it already has." Concluded Stewart:

> There is no evidence in the record that the selection of the risks insured by the program worked to discriminate against any definable group or class from the program. There is no risk from which men are protected and women are not. Likewise, there is no risk from which women are protected and men are not.

Justice Brennan, joined by Justices Douglas and Marshall, dissented. "[T]he economic effects caused by pregnancy-related disabilities," said Brennan, "are functionally indistinguishable from the effects caused by any other disability. . . . " "[B]y singling out for less favorable treatment a gender-linked disability peculiar to women," continued Brennan, "the State has created a double standard for disability compensation: a limitation is imposed upon the disabilities for which women workers may recover, while men receive full compensation for all disabilities suffered, including those that affect only or primarily their sex, such as prostatectomies, circumcision, hemophilia, and gout." Brennan chided the majority for not applying a more strict standard of judicial scrutiny to such gender-based classification programs. "Yet," continued Brennan, "by its decision today, the Court appears willing to abandon that higher standard of review without satisfactorily explaining what differentiates the gender-based classification employed in this case from those found unconsti-

tutional in *Reed* and *Frontiero*." He thought that "the Court's decision threatens to return men and women to a time when 'traditional' equal protection analysis sustained legislation classification that treated differently members of a particular sex solely because of their sex." "I cannot," he said, "join the Court's apparent retreat." Citing his position in *Frontiero* v. *Richardson*, Brennan concluded that he continued to hold the "view that classifications based upon sex, like classification based upon race, alienage, or national origin, are inherently suspect."

In another decision, the Court upheld a Florida statute that granted widows a $500 property tax exemption and no analogous benefit for widowers (*Kahn* v. *Shevin*, 416 U.S. 361, 1974). In an opinion by Justice Douglas, the Court stated that the Florida state tax law was "reasonably designed to further the state policy of cushioning the financial impact of spousal loss upon the sex for whom that loss imposes a disproportionately heavy burden." The Court has "long held," said Douglas, that ". . . where taxation is concerned and no specific federal right, apart from equal protection, is imperiled, the states have large leeway in making classifications and drawing lines which in their judgment produce reasonable systems of taxation." But Justices Brennan, Marshall, and White dissented. Brennan, joined in his opinion by Marshall, stated that "gender-based classifications cannot be sustained merely because they promote legitimate governmental interests. . . . " And Justice White, in a separate dissent, said he found the "discrimination invidious and violative of the Equal Protection Clause."

In *Schlesinger* v. *Ballard* (419 U.S. 498, 1975), the Supreme Court ruled that the U.S. Navy's mandatory discharge procedures requiring separation of male line officers twice passed over for promotion, but allowing female line officers to serve 13 years regardless of promotions, did not constitute unlawful discrimination on the basis of sex in violation of the due process clause of the Fifth Amendment. Writing for the majority, Justice Stewart said that "the different treatment of men and women . . . reflects, not archaic and overbroad generalizations, but, instead, the demonstrable fact that male and female line officers in the Navy are not similarly situated with respect to opportunities for professional service." "In both *Reed* and *Frontiero*," he continued, "the reason asserted to justify the challenged gender-based classifications was administrative convenience, and that alone." "Here, on the contrary," concluded Stewart, "the operation of statutes in question results in a flow of promotions commensurate with the Navy's current needs and serves to motivate qualified commissioned officers to so conduct themselves that they may realistically look forward to higher levels of command."

Justice Brennan, with whom Justices Douglas and Marshall joined, dissented. Brennan held to the belief " . . . that a legislative classification that is premised solely upon gender must be subjected to close judicial scrutiny." Further, he said that the Court had gone "far to conjure up a legislative purpose which may have underlain the gender-based distinction here attached." "I find nothing in the statutory scheme or the legislative history," reasoned Brennan, "to support the supposition that Congress intended, by assuring women but not men line lieutenants in the Navy in a 13-year tenure, to compensate women for other forms of disadvantage visited upon them by the Navy."

Several other decisions indicate that the Court is reluctant to invalidate all gender-based classification. In *General Electric* v. *Gilbert* (429 U.S. 125, 1976), the Court held that a disability insurance plan that failed to cover pregnancy-related disabilities was not sex discrimination under Title VII of the Civil Rights Act of 1964. But the Court's interpretation of Title VII was overturned by Congress.

In 1978, Congress amended Title VII by passing the Pregnancy Discrimination Act, indicating that discrimination on account of "pregnancy, childbirth, and related conditions" was impermissible sex discrimination, and that in terms of employment, pregnancy "shall be treated the same" as other temporary disabilities. Subsequently, in a 1983 case (*Newport News Shipbuilding* v. *EEOC*, 462 U.S. 669), the Court stated that the 1978 act "makes clear that it is discriminatory to treat pregnancy-related conditions less favorably than other medical conditions."

But in 1987 the Court was faced with the question of whether Title VII preempts statutes that give preferential treatment to pregnancy. Here, however, despite claims that Title VII did preempt such laws, the Court upheld a California law requiring employers to provide pregnancy leaves for employees (*California Federal Savings and Loan Association* v. *Guerra*, 107 S. Ct. 683, 1987).

In *Personnel Administrator of Massachusetts* v. *Feeney* (442 U.S. 256, 1979) the Court upheld a Massachusetts law that gave a lifetime preference to all veterans over nonveterans who qualify for state civil service positions, despite the fact that such preference had a disproportionate impact on women. Justice Stewart, speaking for the majority, viewed the statute as "a preference for veterans of either sex over nonveterans of either sex, not for men over women." In addition, the Court upheld a California statutory rape law against the charge that the statute unlawfully discriminated on the basis of gender, since men alone were held criminally liable thereunder. (*Michael M.* v. *Superior Court of Sonoma County*, 450 U.S. 464, 1981. Cf. *Kirchberg* v. *Feinstra*, 450 U.S. 455, which decided the same as *Michael M.*) Justice Rehnquist announced the judgment of the Court and delivered an opinion in which he said that gender-based classifications are not "inherently suspect" and "thus we do not apply so-called 'strict scrutiny' to those classifications." Such classifications, he continued, will be upheld if they bear a "substantial relationship" to "important governmental objectives."[2]

Justice Rehnquist used similar reasoning in speaking for a 6-to-3 Court majority in *Rostker* v. *Goldberg*, which upheld the constitutionality of the "male-only" military draft registration. No one, said Rehnquist, could deny that "the government's interest in raising and supporting armies is an 'important governmental interest.' " In addition, Rehnquist found that under "established policy" and congressional statutes, "women as a group, . . . unlike men, are not eligible for combat." "The existence of the combat restrictions," said Rehnquist, "clearly indicates the basis for Congress to exempt women from registration." "The purpose of registration," he said, "was to prepare for a draft of combat troops," and "since women are excluded from combat, Congress concluded that they would not be needed in event of a draft, and therefore decided not to register them." Then Justice Rehnquist drove the point home:

> The reason women are exempt from registration is not because military needs can be met by drafting men. This is not a case of Congress arbitrarily choosing to burden one of two similarly situated groups, such as would be the case with an all-black or all-white, or an all-Catholic or all-Lutheran, or an all-Republican or an all-Democratic registration. Men and women, because of the combat restrictions on women, are simply not similarly situated for purposes of a draft or registration for a draft (453 U.S., at p. 80).

[2] Consider also the implications for women's rights in *McCarty* v. *McCarty* (453 U.S. 210, 1981), where the Court held that the military retirement system confers no entitlement to retired pay upon the retired member's spouse, and does not embody even a limited "community property concept." Since military personnel are overwhelmingly male, the ruling's negative effects fall "almost entirely on women." See Linda Greenhouse, "Court's Sex Rulings: A Subtle Step Backward," *The New York Times*, July 1, 1981, p. 1, col. 2, and p. 9, col. 1.

Consequently, Rehnquist held that the decision of Congress to authorize the registration of men only did not violate the equal protection of the laws as guaranteed by the due process clause of the Fifth Amendment.

Overall, then, *Geduldig, Kahn, Schlesinger, General Electric, Guerra, Feeney, Michael M.,* and *Rostker* reflect that the Court majority is far from ready to treat sex as a "suspect class" and to subject it to "strict scrutiny" analysis. Rather, the cases represent the continuing conflict in the Court over attempts to apply "something-in-between" (perhaps an "intermediate" standard) as opposed to the "strict scrutiny" and "rational-basis" standards to adjudge gender-based statutes that are alleged to run afoul of the equal protection clause of the Fourteenth Amendment or the due process clause of the Fifth Amendment.

It also seems likely that in the future, statutory rather than constitutionally based rights could prove very crucial to the future of the women's movement. This certainly was reflected in a 1981 decision (*County of Washington, Oregon et al.* v. *Gunther,* 452 U.S. 161). Here the Court, by a narrow five-to-four vote, held that the Civil Rights Act of 1964, which forbids discrimination in employment on the basis of sex as well as race, is not limited to the "equal pay for equal work" standard approved by Congress in the Equal Pay Act of 1963. Justice Brennan, who spoke for the Court, declared explicitly that the Court was not deciding whether the Civil Rights Act countenanced litigation based on the "comparative worth" theory, which holds that work of comparable difficulty and value to an organization should warrant comparable pay. Nonetheless, some women's groups did view the Court ruling as holding important potential for women, in that, as a result of the decision "the door is now open to challenge employers who keep women in the kinds of jobs that are low paid solely because they are traditionally held by women."[3]

In *Johnson* v. *Transportation Agency of Santa Clara County, California* (1987) (see Chapter 5), the Court upheld an affirmative action plan that permitted qualified women, even though scoring slightly lower on certain tests than white males, to be promoted to jobs that in the past had been closed to them.

Other decisions illuminate the possible importance of statutory rights for the future of the women's movement. In *Hishon* v. *King & Spalding* (104 S. Ct. 2229, 1984) the Court held that Title VII of the Civil Rights Act of 1964 was applicable to allegations brought by a woman associate charging that her employer law firm had denied her partnership status because of sex discrimination. Chief Justice Burger, who spoke for a unanimous Court, said that "once a contractual relationship of employment is established, the provisions of Title VII attach," and forbid unlawful discrimination as to the " 'terms, conditions, or privileges of employment' which clearly include benefits that are part of an employment contract." (see Chapter 3.) However, the interests of women's rights did not fare as well in the 1984 case *Grove City College* v. *Bell,* 104 S. Ct. 1211. Here the Court narrowly construed a 1972 federal statute so as to limit the scope and effect of its antisex discrimination provisions. But in subsequent legislation, Congress was able to overcome the *Grove City* ruling (see Chapter 1).

CONSTITUTIONAL POLITICS: THE SAGA OF THE ERA

But those interested in women's rights have not been content to leave their cause to statutes alone. Feminist advocates and their supporters have persisted in their drive to secure women's rights on a more fundamental basis by pushing for a constitutional amendment. Popularly called the Equal Rights Amendment (ERA), the amendment simply states that "equality of rights under the law shall not be denied or abridged by the United States or by any other state on account of sex." Under its terms, Congress is authorized to pass appropriate legislation to enforce its provisions. ERA supporters have prevailed in the Congress, which passed a proposal for such an amendment in 1972, but they have been unable to negotiate the tough terrain of ratification politics. Even though Congress approved an extended period for ratification of the amendment (June 30, 1982), the ERA still fell 3 states short of the 38 states needed for ratification.

Nonetheless, the equal rights battle remains alive. Proponents continue to hold that neither existing constitutional and statutory protections nor incremental expansions of these protections are adequate. On the other hand, ERA opponents contend that the amendment is unnecessary in view of existing and developing federal and state law, and the possibility that the amendment could be used against the best interests of women (for example, that it could subject women to compul-

[3] "High Court Widens Grounds for Women to Seek Equal Pay," *The New York Times,* June 9, 1981, p. 1, col. 1, and p. 10, col. 3. Statement of Judith Lichtman, Executive Director of Women's Legal Defense Fund.

sory selective service, and could more generally disrupt family and home life). Regardless of the ERA's fate, however, the battle over equal rights for women, and gender-based classifications more generally, seems likely to continue for some time to come.

FRONTIERO v. RICHARDSON
411 U.S. 671; 36 L. Ed. 2d 583; 93 S. Ct. 1764 (1973)

JUSTICE BRENNAN *announced the judgment of the Court and an opinion in which* JUSTICE DOUGLAS, JUSTICE WHITE, *and* JUSTICE MARSHALL *join.*

The question before us concerns the right of a female member of the uniformed services to claim her spouse as a "dependent" for the purposes of obtaining increased quarters allowances and medical and dental benefits under 36 U.S.C. sections 401, 403, and 10 U.S.C. sections 1072, 1076, on an equal footing with male members. Under these statutes, a serviceman may claim his wife as a "dependent" without regard to whether she is in fact dependent upon him for any part of her support. A servicewoman, on the other hand, may not claim her husband as a "dependent" under these programs unless he is in fact dependent upon her for over one-half of his support. Thus, the question for decision is whether this difference in treatment constitutes an unconstitutional discrimination against servicewomen in violation of the Due Process Clause of the Fifth Amendment. A three-judge District Court for the Middle District of Alabama, one judge dissenting, rejected this contention and sustained the constitutionality of the provisions of the statutes making this distinction. . . .

In an effort to attract career personnel through re-enlistment, Congress established . . . a scheme for the provision of fringe benefits to members of the uniformed services on a competitive basis with business and industry. Thus, . . . a member of the uniformed services with dependents is entitled to an increased "basic allowance for quarters" and . . . a member's dependents are provided comprehensive medical and dental care.

Appellant Sharron Frontiero, a lieutenant in the United States Air Force, sought increased quarters allowances, and housing and medical benefits for her husband, appellant Joseph Frontiero, on the ground that he was her "dependent." Although such benefits would automatically have been granted with respect to the wife of a male member of the uniformed services, appellant's application was denied because she failed to demonstrate that her husband was dependent on her for more than one-half of his support. Appellants then commenced this suit, contending that, by making this distinction, the statutes unreasonably discriminate on the basis of sex in violation of the Due Process Clause of the Fifth Amendment. In essence, appellants asserted that the discriminatory impact of the statutes is two-fold: first, as a procedural matter, a female member is required to demonstrate her spouse's dependency, while no such burden is imposed upon male members; and second, as a substantive matter, a male member who does not provide more than one-half of his wife's support receives benefits, while a similarly situated female member is denied such benefits. Appellants therefore sought a permanent injunction against the continued enforcement of these statutes and an order directing the appellees to provide Lieutenant Frontiero with the same housing and medical benefits that a similarly situated male member would receive.

Although the legislative history of these statutes sheds virtually no light on the purposes underlying the differential treatment accorded male and female members, a majority of the three-judge District Court surmised that Congress might reasonably have concluded that, since the husband in our society is generally the "breadwinner" in the family and the wife typically the "dependent" partner—"it would be more economical to require married female members claiming husbands to prove actual dependency than to extend the presumption of dependency to such members." Indeed, given the fact that approximately 99% of all members of the uniformed services are male, the District Court speculated that such differential treatment might conceivably lead to a "considerable saving of administrative expense and manpower." *Ibid.*

II

At the outset, appellants contend that classifications based upon sex, like classifications based upon race, alienage, and national origin, are inherently suspect and must therefore be subjected to close judicial scrutiny. We agree and, indeed, find at least implicit support for such an approach in our unanimous decision only last Term in *Reed* v. *Reed*, 404 U.S. 71 (1971).

In *Reed*, the Court considered the constitutionality of an Idaho statute providing that, when two individuals are otherwise equally entitled to appointment as administrator of an estate, the male applicant must be preferred to the female. Appellant, the mother of the deceased, and appellee, the father, filed competing petitions for appointment as administrator of their son's estate. Since the parties, as parents of the deceased, were members of the same entitlement class, the statutory preference was invoked and the father's petition was therefore granted. Appellant claimed that this statute, by giving a mandatory preference to males over females without regard to their individual qualifications, violated the Equal Protection Clause of the Fourteenth Amendment.

The Court noted that the Idaho statute "provides that different treatment be accorded to the applicants on the basis of their sex; it thus establishes a classification subject to scrutiny under the Equal Protection Clause." Under "traditional" equal protection analysis, a legislative classification must be sustained unless it is "patently arbitrary" and bears no rational relationship to a legitimate governmental interest. . . .

In an effort to meet this standard, appellee contended that the statutory scheme was a reasonable measure designed to reduce the workload on probate courts by eliminating one class of contests. Moreover, appellee argued that the mandatory preference for male applicants was in itself reasonable since "men [are] as a rule more conversant with business affairs than . . . women." Indeed, appellee maintained that "it is a matter of common knowledge, that women still are not engaged in politics, the professions, business or industry to the extent that men are." And the Idaho Supreme Court, in upholding the constitutionality of this statute, suggested that the Idaho Legislature might reasonably have concluded that in general men are better qualified to act as administrators than are women.

Despite these contentions, however, the Court held the statutory preference for male applicants unconstitutional. . . . The Court . . . held that, even though the State's interest in achieving administrative efficiency "is not without some legitimacy," "[t]o give a mandatory preference to members of either sex over members of the other, merely to accomplish the elimination of hearings on the mer-

its, is to make the very kind of arbitrary legislative choice forbidden by the [Constitution]. . . . " This departure from "traditional" rational basis analysis with respect to sex-based classifications is clearly justified.

There can be no doubt that our Nation has had a long and unfortunate history of sex discrimination. Traditionally, such discrimination was rationalized by an attitude of "romantic paternalism" which, in practical effect, put women not on a pedestal, but in a cage. Indeed, this paternalistic attitude became so firmly rooted in our national consciousness that, exactly 100 years ago, a distinguished member of this Court was able to proclaim:

> Man is, or should be, a woman's protector and defender. The natural and proper timidity and delicacy which belongs to the female sex evidently unfits it for many of the occupations of civil life. The constitution of the family organization, which is founded in the divine ordinance, as well as in the nature of things, indicates the domestic sphere as that which properly belongs to the domain and functions of womanhood. The harmony, not to say identity, of interests, and views which belong, or should belong, to the family institution is repugnant to the ideas of a woman adopting a distinct and independent career from that of her husband. . . .
>
> . . . The paramount destiny and mission of woman are to fulfill the noble and benign offices of wife and mother. This is the law of the Creator. *Bradwell* v. *Illinois*, 83 US [16 Wall] 130 (Bradley, J., concurring).

As a result of notions such as these, our statute books gradually became laden with gross, stereotypical distinctions between the sexes and, indeed, throughout much of the 19th century the position of women in our society was, in many respects, comparable to that of blacks under the pre–Civil War slave codes. Neither slaves nor women could hold office, serve on juries, or bring suit in their own names, and married women traditionally were denied the legal capacity to hold or convey property or to serve as legal guardians of their own children. . . . It is true, of course, that the position of women in America has improved markedly in recent decades. Nevertheless, it can hardly be doubted that, in part because of the high visibility of the sex characteristic, women still face pervasive, although at times more subtle, discrimination in our educational institutions, on the job market and, perhaps most conspicuously, in the political arena. . . .

Moreover, since sex, like race and national origin, is an immutable characteristic determined solely by the accident of birth, the imposition of special disabilities upon the members of a particular sex because of their sex would seem to violate "the basic concept of our system that legal burdens should bear some relationship to individual responsibility. . . . " And what differentiates sex from such nonsuspect statutes as intelligence or physical disability, and aligns it with the recognized suspect criteria, is that the sex characteristic frequently bears no relation to ability to perform or contribute to society. As a result, statutory distinctions between the sexes often have the effect of invidiously relegating the entire class of females to inferior legal status without regard to the actual capabilities of its individual members.

We might also note that, over the past decade, Congress has itself manifested an increasing sensitivity to sex-based classifications. In Title VII of the Civil Rights Act of 1964, for example, Congress expressly declared that no employer, labor union, or other organization subject to the provisions of the Act shall discriminate against any individual on the basis of "race, color, religion, *sex*, or national origin." Similarly, the Equal Pay Act of 1963 provides that no employer covered by the Act "shall discriminate . . . between employees on the basis of *sex*." And section 1 of the Equal Rights Amendment, passed by Congress on March 22, 1972, and submitted to the legislatures of the States for ratification, declares that "[e]quality of rights under the law shall not be denied or abridged by the United States or by any State on account of sex." Thus, Congress has itself concluded that classifications based upon sex are inherently invidious, and this conclusion of a coequal branch of government is not without significance to the question presently under consideration. . . .

With these considerations in mind, we can only conclude that classifications based on sex, like classifications based upon race, alienage, or national origin, are inherently suspect and must therefore be subjected to strict judicial scrutiny. Applying the analysis mandated by that stricter standard of review, it is clear that the statutory scheme now before us is constitutionally invalid. . . .

III

. . . [T]he Government concedes that the differential treatment accorded men and women under these statutes serves no purpose other than mere "administrative convenience." In essence, the Government maintains that, as an empirical matter,

wives in our society frequently are dependent upon their husbands, while husbands rarely are dependent upon their wives. Thus, the Government argues that Congress might reasonably have concluded that it would be both cheaper and easier simply conclusively to presume that wives of male members are financially dependent upon their husbands, while burdening female members with the task of establishing dependency in fact.

The Government offers no concrete evidence, however, tending to support its view that such differential treatment in fact saves the Government any money. In order to satisfy the demands of strict judicial scrutiny, the Government must demonstrate, for example, that it is actually cheaper to grant increased benefits with respect to *all* male members, than it is to determine which male members are in fact entitled to such benefits and to grant increased benefits only to those members whose wives actually meet the dependency requirement. Here, however, there is substantial evidence that, if put to the test, many of the wives of male members would fail to qualify for benefits. And in light of the fact that the dependency determination with respect to the husbands of female members is presently made solely on the basis of affidavits, rather than through the more costly hearing process, the Government's explanation of the statutory scheme is, to say the least, questionable.

In any case, our prior decisions make clear that, although efficacious administration of governmental programs is not without some importance, "the Constitution recognizes higher values than speed and efficiency." . . . And when we enter into the realm of "strict judicial scrutiny," there can be no doubt that "administrative convenience" is not a shibboleth, the mere recitation of which dictates constitutionality. . . . On the contrary, any statutory scheme which draws a sharp line between the sexes, *solely* for the purpose of achieving administrative convenience, necessarily commands "dissimilar treatment for men and women who are . . . similarly situated," and therefore involves the "very kind of arbitrary legislative choice forbidden by the [Constitution]. . . . " We therefore conclude that, by according differential treatment to male and female members of the uniformed services for the sole purpose of achieving administrative convenience, the challenged statutes violate the Due Process Clause of the Fifth Amendment insofar as they require a female member to prove the dependency of her husband.

Reversed.

JUSTICE STEWART *concurs in the judgment, agreeing that the statutes before us work an invidious discrimination in violation of the Constitution.* Reed *v.* Reed, *404, (1971), U.S. 71.*

JUSTICE REHNQUIST *dissents for the reasons stated by Judge Rives in his opinion for the District Court.* Frontiero *v.* Laird, *341 F. Supp. 201 (1972).*

[The opinion of JUSTICE POWELL, with whom THE CHIEF JUSTICE and JUSTICE BLACKMUN join, concurring in the judgment, is not reprinted here.]

CRAIG ET AL. v. BOREN, GOVERNOR OF OKLAHOMA ET AL.
429 U.S. 190; 50 L. Ed. 2d 397; 97 S. Ct. 451 (1976)

JUSTICE BRENNAN *delivered the opinion of the Court.*

The interaction of two sections of an Oklahoma statute prohibits the sale of "nonintoxicating" 3.2% beer to males under the age of 21 and to females under the age of 18. The question to be decided is whether such a gender-based differential constitutes a denial to males 18–20 years of age of the equal protection of the laws in violation of the Fourteenth Amendment.

Analysis may appropriately begin with the reminder that *Reed* emphasized that statutory classifications that distinguish between males and females are "subject to scrutiny under the Equal Protection Clause." . . . To withstand constitutional challenge, previous cases establish that classifications by gender must serve important governmental objectives and must be substantially related to achievement of those objectives. Thus, in *Reed,* the objectives of "reducing the workload on probate courts" . . . and "avoiding intrafamily controversy" . . . were deemed of insufficient importance to sustain use of an overt gender criterion in the appointment of administrators of intestate decedents' estates. Decisions following *Reed* similarly have rejected administrative ease and convenience as sufficiently important objectives to justify gender-based classifications. . . . And only two Terms ago *Stanton* v. *Stanton* . . . (1975), expressly stating that *Reed* v. *Reed* was "controlling," . . . held that *Reed* required invalidation of a Utah differential age-of-majority statute, notwithstanding the statute's coincidence with and furtherance of the State's purpose of fostering "old notions" of role typing and preparing boys for their expected performance in the economic and political worlds. . . .

Reed v. *Reed* has also provided the underpinning for decisions that have invalidated statutes employing gender as an inaccurate proxy for other, more germane bases of classification. Hence, "archaic and overbroad" generalizations, *Schlesinger* v. *Ballard,* . . . concerning the financial position of servicewomen, *Frontiero* v. *Richardson,* . . . and working women, *Weinberger* v. *Wiesenfeld* . . . (1975), could not justify use of a gender line in determining eligibility for certain governmental entitlements. Similarly, increasingly outdated misconceptions concerning the role of females in the home rather than in the "marketplace and world of ideas" were rejected as loose-fitting characterizations incapable of supporting state statutory schemes that were premised upon their accuracy. *Stanton* v. *Stanton, supra,* Taylor v. *Louisiana* . . . (1975). In light of the weak congruence between gender and the characteristic or trait that gender purported to represent, it was necessary that the legislatures choose either to realign their substantive laws in a gender-neutral fashion, or to adopt procedures for identifying those instances where the sex-centered generalization actually comported with fact. . . .

In this case, too, "*Reed,* we feel, is controlling . . . ," *Stanton* v. *Stanton.* . . . We turn then to the question whether, under *Reed,* the difference between males and females with respect to the purchase of 3.2% beer warrants the differential in age drawn by the Oklahoma statute. We conclude that it does not.

The District Court recognized that *Reed* v. *Reed* was controlling. In applying the teachings of that case, the court found the requisite important governmental objective in the traffic-safety goal proffered by the Oklahoma Attorney General. It then concluded that the statistics introduced by the appellees established that the gender-based distinction was substantially related to achievement of that goal.

We accept for purposes of discussion the District Court's identification of the objective underlying the Oklahoma law as the enhancement of traffic safety. Clearly, the protection of public health and safety represents an important function of state and local governments. However, appellees' statistics in our view cannot support the conclusion that the gender-based distinction closely serves to achieve that objective and therefore the distinction cannot under *Reed* withstand equal protection challenge.

Moreover, the statistics exhibit a variety of other shortcomings that seriously impugn their value to equal protection analysis. Setting aside the obvious methodological problems, the surveys do not adequately justify the salient features of Oklahoma's gender-based traffic-safety law. None purports to measure the use and dangerousness of 3.2% beer as opposed to alcohol generally, a detail that is of particular importance since, in light of its low alcohol level, Oklahoma apparently considers the 3.2% beverage to be "nonintoxicating." . . . Moreover, many of the studies, while graphically documenting the unfortunate increase in driving while under the influence of alcohol, make no effort to relate their findings to age-sex differentials as involved here. Indeed, the only survey that explicitly centered its attention upon young drivers and their use of beer—albeit apparently not of the diluted 3.2% variety—reached results that hardly can be viewed as impressive in justifying either a gender or age classification.

There is no reason to belabor this line of analysis. It is unrealistic to expect either members of the judiciary or state officials to be well versed in the rigors of experimental or statistical technique. But this merely illustrates that proving broad sociological propositions by statistics is a dubious business, and one that inevitably is in tension with the normative philosophy that underlies the Equal Protection Clause. Suffice to say that the showing offered by the appellees does not satisfy us that sex represents a legitimate, accurate proxy for the regulation of drinking and driving. In fact, when it is further recognized that Oklahoma's statute prohibits only the selling of 3.2% beer to young males and not their drinking the beverage once acquired (even after purchase by their 18–20-year-old female companions), the relationship between gender and traffic safety becomes far too tenuous to satisfy *Reed*'s requirement that the gender-based difference be substantially related to achievement of the statutory objective.

We hold, therefore, that under *Reed*, Oklahoma's 3.2% beer statute invidiously discriminates against males 18–20 years of age.

[The concurring opinions of JUSTICES POW-ELL, STEVENS, BLACKMUN, and STEWART are omitted.]

CHIEF JUSTICE BURGER, *dissenting.*

I am in general agreement with Justice Rehnquist's dissent, but even at the risk of compounding the obvious confusion created by those voting to reverse the District Court, I will add a few words.

Of the merits, we have only recently recognized that our duty is not "to create substantive constitutional rights in the name of guaranteeing equal protection of the laws." *San Antonio School Dist.* v. *Rodriguez* . . . (1973). Thus, even interests of such importance in our society as public education and housing do not qualify as "fundamental rights" for equal protection purposes because they have no textually independent constitutional status. . . . Though today's decision does not go so far as to make gender-based classifications "suspect," it makes gender a disfavored classification. Without an independent constitutional basis supporting the right asserted or disfavoring the classification adopted, I can justify no substantive constitutional protection other than the normal . . . protection afforded by the Equal Protection Clause.

The means employed by the Oklahoma Legislature to achieve the objectives sought may not be agreeable to some judges, but since eight Members of the Court think the means not irrational, I see no basis for striking down the statute as violative of the Constitution simply because we find it unwise, unneeded, or possibly even a bit foolish.

JUSTICE REHNQUIST, *dissenting.*

The Court's disposition of this case is objectionable on two grounds. First is its conclusion that *men* challenging a gender-based statute which treats them less favorably than women may invoke a more stringent standard of judicial review than pertains to most other types of classifications. Second is the Court's enunciation of this standard, without citation to any source, as being that "classifications by gender must serve *important* governmental objectives and must be *substantially* related to achievement of those objectives." *Ante*, at 197 (emphasis added). The only redeeming feature of the Court's opinion, to my mind, is that it apparently signals a retreat by those who joined the plurality opinion in *Frontiero* v. *Richardson* . . . (1973) from their view that sex is a "suspect" classification for purposes of equal protection analysis. I think the Oklahoma statute challenged here need pass only the "rational basis" equal protection analysis expounded in cases such as *McGowan* v. *Maryland* . . . (1961), and I believe that it is constitutional under that analysis.

In *Frontiero* v. *Richardson, supra,* the opinion for the plurality sets forth the reasons of four justices for concluding that sex should be regarded as a suspect classification for purposes of equal protection analysis. These reasons center on our Nation's "long and unfortunate history of sex discrimination," . . . which has been reflected in a whole range of restrictions on the legal rights of women, not the least of which have concerned the ownership of property and participation in the electoral process. Noting that the pervasive and persistent nature of the discrimination experienced by women is in part the result of their ready identifiability, the plurality rested its invocation of strict scrutiny largely upon the fact that "statutory distinctions between the sexes often have the effect of invidiously relegating the entire class of females to inferior legal status without regard to the actual capabilities of its individual members." . . .

Subsequent to *Frontiero*, the Court has declined to hold that sex is a suspect class, *Stanton* v. *Stanton*, . . . and no such holding is imported by the Court's resolution of this case. However, the Court's application here of an elevated or "intermediate" level scrutiny, like that invoked in cases dealing with discrimination against females, raises the question of why the statute here should be treated any differently from countless legislative classifications unrelated to sex which have been upheld under a minimum rationality standard. . . .

Most obviously unavailable to support any kind of special scrutiny in this case, is a history or pattern of past discrimination, such as was relied on by the plurality in *Frontiero* to support its invocation of strict scrutiny. There is no suggestion in the Court's opinion that males in this age group are in any way peculiarly disadvantaged, subject to systematic discriminatory treatment, or otherwise in need of special solicitude from the courts.

It is true that a number of our opinions contain broadly phrased dicta implying that the same test should be applied to all classifications based on sex, whether affecting females or males. E.g., *Frontiero* v. *Richardson* . . . ; *Reed* v. *Reed* . . . (1971). However, before today, no decision of this Court has applied an elevated level of scrutiny to invalidate a statutory discrimination harmful to males, except where the statute impaired an important personal interest protected by the Constitution. There being no such interest here, and there being no plausible argument that this is a discrimination against females, the Court's reliance on our previous sex-discrimination cases is ill-founded. It treats gender classification as a talisman which—without regard to the rights involved or the persons affected—calls into effect a heavier burden of judicial review.

The Court's conclusion that a law which treats males less favorably than females "must serve important governmental objectives and must be substantially related to achievement of those objectives" apparently comes out of thin air. The Equal Protection Clause contains no such language, and none of our previous cases adopt that standard. I would think we have had enough difficulty with the two standards of review which our cases have recognized—the norm of "rational basis," and the "compelling state interest" required where a "suspect classification" is involved—so as to counsel weightily against the insertion of still another "standard" between those two. How is this court to divine what objectives are important? How is it to determine whether a particular law is "substantially" related to the achievement of such objective, rather than related in some other way to its achievement? Both of the phrases used are so diaphanous and elastic as to invite subjective judicial preferences or prejudices relating to particular types of legislation, masquerading as judgments whether such legislation is directed at "important" objectives or, whether the relationship to those objectives is "substantial" enough.

I would have thought that if this Court were to leave anything to decision by the popularly elected branches of the Government, where no constitutional claim other than that of equal protection in invoked, it would be the decision as to what governmental objectives to be achieved by law are "important," and which are not. As for the second part of the Court's new test, the Judicial Branch is probably in no worse position than the Legislative or Executive Branches to determine if there is any rational relationship between a classification and the purpose which it might be thought to serve. But the introduction of the adverb "substantially" requires courts to make subjective judgments as to operational effects, for which neither their expertise nor their access to data fits them. And even if we manage to avoid both confusion and the mirroring of our own preferences in the development of this new doctrine, the thousands of judges in other courts who must interpret the Equal Protection Clause may not be so fortunate.

The applicable rational-basis test is one which

permits the States a wide scope of discretion in enacting laws which affect some groups of citizens differently than others. The constitutional safeguard is offended only if the classification rests on grounds wholly irrelevant to the achievement of the State's objective. State legislatures are presumed to have acted within their constitutional power despite the fact that, in practice, their laws result in some inequality. A statutory discrimination will not be set aside if any state of facts reasonably may be conceived to justify it. *McGowan* v. *Maryland.* . . .

Our decisions indicate that application of the Equal Protection Clause in a context not justifying an elevated level of scrutiny does not demand "mathematical nicety" or the elimination of all inequality. Those cases recognize that the practical problems of government may require rough accommodations of interests, and hold that such accommodations should be respected unless no reasonable basis can be found to support them. . . .

The Court appears to hold that evidence, on its face, fails to support the distinction drawn in the statute. The Court notes that only 2% of males (as against 0.18% of females) in the age group were arrested for drunk driving, and that this very low figure establishes "an unduly tenuous 'fit'" between maleness and drunk driving in the 18–20-year-old group. On this point the Court misconceives the nature of the equal protection inquiry.

The rationality of a statutory classification for equal protection purposes does not depend upon the statistical "fit" between the class and the trait sought to be singled out. It turns on whether there may be a sufficiently higher incidence of the trait within the included class than in the excluded class to justify different treatment. Therefore the present equal protection challenge to this gender-based discrimination poses only the question whether the incidence of drunk driving among young men is sufficiently greater than among young women to justify differential treatment. Notwithstanding the Court's critique of the statistical evidence, that evidence suggests clear differences between the drinking and driving habits of young men and women. Those differences are grounds enough for the State reasonably to conclude that young males pose by far the greater drunk-driving hazard, both in terms of sheer numbers and in terms of hazard on a per-driver basis. The gender-based difference in treatment in this case is therefore not irrational.

The Oklahoma Legislature could have believed that 18–20-year-old males drive substantially more and tend more often to be intoxicated than their female counterparts; that they prefer beer and admit to drinking and driving at a higher rate than females; and that they suffer traffic injuries out of proportion to the part they make up of the population. Under the appropriate rational-basis test for equal protection, it is neither irrational nor arbitrary to bar them from making a purchase of 3.2% beer, which purchase might in many cases be made by a young man who immediately returns to his vehicle with the beverage in his possession. The record does not give any good indication of the true proportion of males in the age group who drink and drive (except that it is no doubt greater than the 2% who are arrested), but whatever it may be, I cannot see that the mere purchase right involved could conceivably raise a due process question. There being no violation of either equal protection or due process, the statute should accordingly be upheld.

MISSISSIPPI UNIVERSITY FOR WOMEN ET AL. v. HOGAN
458 U.S. 718; 73 L. Ed. 2d 1090; 102 S. Ct. 3331 (1982)

JUSTICE O'CONNOR *delivered the opinion of the Court.*

This case presents the narrow issue of whether a state statute that excludes males from enrolling in a state-supported professional nursing school violates the Equal Protection Clause of the Fourteenth Amendment.

I

The facts are not in dispute. In 1884, the Mississippi Legislature created the Mississippi Industrial Institute and College for the Education of White Girls of the State of Mississippi, now the oldest state-supported all-female college in the United States. . . . The school, known today as Mississippi University for Women (MUW), has from its inception limited its enrollment to women.

In 1971, MUW established a School of Nursing, initially offering a 2-year associate degree. Three years later, the school instituted a 4-year baccalaureate program in nursing and today also offers a graduate program. The School of Nursing has its own faculty and administrative officers and establishes its own criteria for admission.

Respondent, Joe Hogan, is a registered nurse but does not hold a baccalaureate degree in nursing. Since 1974, he has worked as a nursing supervisor in a medical center in Columbus, the city in which MUW is located. In 1979, Hogan applied for admission to the MUW School of Nursing's baccalaureate program. Although he was otherwise qualified, he was denied admission to the School of Nursing solely because of his sex. School officials informed him that he could audit the courses in which he was interested, but could not enroll for credit. . . .

Hogan filed an action in the United States District Court of the Northern District of Mississippi, claiming the single-sex admissions policy of MUW's School of Nursing violated the Equal Protection Clause of the Fourteenth Amendment. Hogan sought injunctive and declaratory relief, as well as compensatory damages.

Following a hearing, the District Court denied preliminary injunctive relief. . . . The court concluded that maintenance of MUW as a single-sex school bears a rational relationship to the State's legitimate interest "in providing the greatest practical range of educational opportunities for its female student population." . . . Furthermore, the court stated, the admissions policy is not arbitrary because providing single-sex education affords unique benefits to students. . . . Stating that the case presented no issue of fact, the court informed Hogan that it would enter summary judgment dismissing his claim unless he tendered a factual issue. When Hogan offered no further evidence, the District Court entered summary judgment in favor of the State. . . .

The Court of Appeals for the Fifth Circuit reversed, holding that, because the admissions policy discriminates on the basis of gender, the District Court improperly used a "rational relationship" test to judge the constitutionality of the policy. . . . Instead, the Court of Appeals stated, the proper test is whether the State has carried the heavier burden of showing that the gender-based classification is substantially related to an important governmental objective. . . . Recognizing that the State has a significant interest in providing educational opportunities for all its citizens, the court then found that the State had failed to show that providing a unique educational opportunity for females, but not for males, bears a substantial relationship to that interest. . . .

We begin our analysis aided by several firmly established principles. Because the challenged policy expressly discriminates among applicants on the basis of gender, it is subject to scrutiny under the Equal Protection Clause of the Fourteenth Amendment. . . . That this statutory policy discriminates against males rather than against females does not exempt it from scrutiny or reduce the standard of review. . . . Our decisions also establish that the party seeking to uphold a statute that classifies individuals on the basis of their gender must carry the burden of showing an "exceedingly persuasive justification" for the classification. . . . The burden is met only by showing at least that the classification serves "important governmental objectives and that the discriminatory means employed" are "substantially related to the achievement of those objectives." . . .

Although the test for determining the validity of a gender-based classification is straightforward, it must be applied free of fixed notions concerning the roles and abilities of males and females. Care must be taken in ascertaining whether the statutory objective itself reflects archaic and stereotypic notions. Thus, if the statutory objective is to exclude or "protect" members of one gender because they are presumed to suffer from an inherent handicap or to be innately inferior, the objective itself is illegitimate. . . .

If the State's objective is legitimate and important, we next determine whether the requisite direct, substantial relationship between objective and means is present. The purpose of requiring that close relationship is to assure that the validity of a classification is determined through reasoned analysis rather than through the mechanical application of traditional, often inaccurate, assumptions about the proper roles of men and women. The need for the requirement is amply revealed by reference to the broad range of statutes already invalidated by this Court, statutes that relied upon the simplistic, outdated assumption that gender could be used as a "proxy for other, more germane bases of classification," *Craig* v. *Boren* . . . (1976), to establish a link between objective and classification.

Applying this framework, we now analyze the arguments advanced by the State to justify its refusal to allow males to enroll for credit in MUW's School of Nursing. . . .

The State's primary justification for maintaining the single-sex admissions policy of MUW's School of Nursing is that it compensates for discrimination against women and, therefore, constitutes educational affirmative action. . . . As applied to the School of Nursing, we find the State's argument unpersuasive.

In limited circumstances, a gender-based classification favoring one sex can be justified if it intentionally and directly assists members of the sex that is disproportionately burdened. . . . However, we consistently have emphasized that "the mere recitation of a benign, compensatory purpose is not an automatic shield which protects against any inquiry into the actual purposes underlying, a statutory scheme." *Weinberger* v. *Weisenfeld* . . . (1975). The same searching analysis must be made, regardless of whether the State's objective is to eliminate family controversy, *Reed* v. *Reed* . . . (1971), to achieve administrative efficiency, *Frontiero* v. *Richardson* . . . (1973), or to balance the burdens borne by males and females.

It is readily apparent that a State can evoke a compensatory purpose, to justify an otherwise discriminatory classification only if members of the gender benefited by the classification actually suffer a disadvantage related to the classification. We considered such a situation in *Califano* v. *Webster* . . . (1977), which involved a challenge to a statutory classification that allowed women to eliminate more low-earning years than men for purposes of computing Social Security retirement benefits. Although the effect of the classification was to allow women higher monthly benefits than were available to men with the same earning history, we upheld the statutory scheme, noting that it took into account that women "as such have been unfairly hindered from earning as much as men" and "work[ed] directly to remedy" the resulting economic disparity. . . .

A similar pattern of discrimination against women influenced our decision in *Schlesinger* v. *Ballard* (1975). . . . There, we considered a federal statute that granted female Naval officers a 13-year tenure of commissioned service before mandatory discharge, but accorded male officers only a 9-year tenure. We recognized that, because women were barred from combat duty, they had had fewer opportunities for promotion than had their male counterparts. By allowing women an additional four years to reach a particular rank before subjecting them to mandatory discharge, the statute directly compensated for other statutory barriers to advancement.

In sharp contrast, Mississippi has made no showing that women lacked opportunities to obtain training in the field of nursing or to attain positions of leadership in that field when the MUW School of Nursing opened its door or that women currently are deprived of such opportunities. In fact, in 1970, the year before the School of Nursing's first class enrolled, women earned 94 percent of the nursing baccalaureate degrees conferred in Mississippi and 98.6 percent of the degrees earned nationwide. . . . That year was not an aberration; one decade earlier, women had earned all the nursing degrees conferred in Mississippi and 98.9 percent of the degrees conferred nationwide. . . . As one would expect, the labor force reflects the same predominance of women in nursing. When MUW's School of Nursing began operation, nearly 98 percent of all employed registered nurses were female. . . .

Rather than compensate for discriminatory barriers faced by women, MUW's policy of excluding males from admission to the School of Nursing tends to perpetuate the stereotyped view of nursing as an exclusively women's job. By assuring that Mississippi allots more openings in its state-supported nursing schools to women than it does to men, MUW's admissions policy lends credibility to the old view that women, not men, should become nurses, and makes the assumption that nursing is a field for women a self-fulfilling prophecy. . . . Thus, we conclude that, although the State recited a "benign, compensatory purpose," it failed to establish that the alleged objective is the actual purpose underlying the discriminatory classification.

The policy is invalid also because it fails the second part of the equal protection test, for the State has made no showing that the gender-based classification is substantially and directly related to its proposed compensatory objective. To the contrary, MUW's policy of permitting men to attend classes as auditors fatally undermines its claim that women, at least those in the School of Nursing, are adversely affected by the presence of men.

MUW permits men who audit to participate fully in classes. Additionally, both men and women take part in continuing education courses offered by the School of Nursing, in which regular nursing students also can enroll. . . . The uncontroverted record reveals that admitting men to nursing classes does not affect teaching style, . . . that the presence of men in the classroom would not affect the performance of the female nursing students, . . . and that men in coeducational nursing schools do not dominate the classroom. In sum, the record in this case is flatly inconsistent with the claim that excluding men from the School of Nursing is necessary to reach any of MUW's educational goals.

Thus, considering both the asserted interest and relationship between the interest and the methods used by the State, we conclude that the State has fallen far short of establishing the "exceedingly persuasive justification" needed to sustain the gender-based classification. Accordingly, we hold that MUW's policy of denying males the right to enroll for credit in its School of Nursing violates the Equal Protection Clause of the Fourteenth Amendment. . . .

JUSTICE POWELL, *with whom* JUSTICE REHNQUIST *joins, dissenting.*

The Court's opinion bows deeply to conformity. Left without honor—indeed, held unconstitutional—is an element of diversity that has characterized much of American education and enriched much of American life. The Court in effect holds today that no State now may provide even a single institution of higher learning open only to women students. It gives no heed to the efforts of the State of Mississippi to provide abundant opportunities for young men and young women to attend coeducational institutions, and none to the preferences of the more than 40,000 young women who over the years have evidenced their approval of an all-women's college by choosing Mississippi University for Women (MUW) over seven coeducational universities within the State. The Court decides today that the Equal Protection Clause makes it unlawful for the State to provide women with a traditionally popular and respected choice of educational environment. It does so in a case instituted by one man, who represents no class, and whose primary concern is personal convenience.

It is undisputed that women enjoy complete equality of opportunity in Mississippi's public system of higher education. Of the State's 8 universities and 16 junior colleges, all except MUW are coeducational. At least two other Mississippi universities would have provided respondent with the nursing curriculum that he wishes to pursue. No other male has joined in his complaint. The only groups with any personal acquaintance with MUW to file *amicus* briefs are female students and alumnae of MUW. And they have emphatically rejected respondent's arguments, urging that the State of Mississippi be allowed to continue offering the choice from which they have benefited.

Nor is respondent significantly disadvantaged by MUW's all-female tradition. His constitutional complaint is based upon a single asserted harm: that he must *travel* to attend the state-supported nursing schools that concededly are available to him. The Court characterizes this injury as one of "inconvenience." . . . This description is fair and accurate, though somewhat embarrassed by the fact that there is, of course, no constitutional right to attend a state-supported university in one's home town. Thus the Court, to redress respondent's injury of inconvenience, must rest its invalidation of MUW's single-sex program on a mode of "sexual stereotype" reasoning that has no application whatever to the respondent or to the "wrong" of which he complains. At best this is anomalous. And ultimately the anomaly reveals legal error—

that of applying a heightened equal protection standard, developed in cases of genuine sexual stereotyping, to a narrowly utilized state classification that provides an *additional* choice for women. Moreover, I believe that Mississippi's educational system should be upheld in this case even if this inappropriate method of analysis is applied. . . .

Coeducation, historically, is a novel educational theory. From grade school through high school, college, and graduate and professional training, much of the Nation's population during much of our history has been educated in sexually segregated classrooms. At the college level, for instance, until recently some of the most prestigious colleges and universities—including most of the Ivy League—had long histories of single-sex education. As Harvard, Yale, and Princeton remained all-male colleges well into the second half of this century, the "Seven Sister" institutions established a parallel standard of excellence for women's colleges. . . .

The sexual segregation of students has been a reflection of, rather than an imposition upon, the preference of those subject to the policy. It cannot be disputed, for example, that the highly qualified women attending the leading women's colleges could have earned admission to virtually any college of their choice. Women attending such colleges have chosen to be there, usually expressing a preference for the special benefits of single-sex institutions. Similar decisions were made by the colleges that elected to remain open to women only.

The arguable benefits of single-sex colleges also continue to be recognized by students of higher education. The Carnegie Commission on Higher Education has reported that it "favor[s] the continuation of colleges for women. They provide an element of diversity . . . and [an environment in which women] generally . . . speak up more in their classes, . . . hold more positions of leadership on campus, . . . and . . . have more role models and mentors among women teachers and administrators." . . . A 10-year empirical study by the Cooperative Institutional Research Program of the American Council of Education and the University of California, Los Angeles, also has affirmed the distinctive benefits of single-sex colleges and universities. As summarized in A. Astin, *Four Critical Years*, 232 (1977), the data established that

[b]oth [male and female] single-sex colleges facilitate student involvement in several areas: academic, interaction with faculty, and verbal aggressiveness. . . . Men's and women's colleges also have a positive effect on intellectual self-esteem. Students at single-sex colleges are more satisfied than students at coeducation-

al colleges with virtually all aspects of college life. . . . The only area where students are less satisfied is social life. . . .

The issue in this case is whether a State transgresses the Constitution when—within the context of a public system that offers a diverse range of campuses, curricula, and educational alternatives—it seeks to accommodate the legitimate personal preferences of those desiring the advantages of an all-women's college. In my view, the Court errs seriously by assuming—without argument or discussion—that the equal protection standard generally applicable to sex discrimination is appropriate here. That standard was designed to free women from "archaic and overbroad generalizations. . . ." *Schlesinger* v. *Ballard* . . . (1976). In no previous case have we applied it to invalidate state efforts to *expand* women's choices. Nor are there prior sex discrimination decisions by this Court in which a male plaintiff, as in this case, had the choice of an equal benefit.

The cases cited by the Court therefore do not control the issue now before us. In most of them women were given no opportunity for the same benefit as men. Cases involving male plaintiffs are equally inapplicable. In *Craig* v. *Boren* . . . (1976), a male under 21 was not permitted to buy beer anywhere in the State, and women were afforded no choice as to whether they would accept the "statistically measured but loose-fitting generalities concerning the drinking tendencies of aggregate groups." . . . A similar situation prevailed in *Orr* v. *Orr* . . . (1979), where men had no opportunity to seek alimony from their divorced wives, and women had no escape from the statute's stereotypical announcement of "the State's preference for an allocation of family responsibilities under which the wife plays a dependent role. . . ."

By applying a heightened equal protection analysis to this case, the Court frustrates the liberating spirit of the Equal Protection Clause. It prohibits the States from providing women with an opportunity to choose the type of university they prefer. And yet it is these women whom the Court regards as the *victims* of an illegal, stereotyped perception of the role of women in our society. The Court reasons this way in a case in which no woman has complained, and the only complainant is a man who advances no claims on behalf of anyone else. His claim, it should be recalled, is not that he is being denied a substantive educational opportunity, or even the right to attend an all-male or a coeducational college. . . . It is *only* that the colleges open to him are located at inconvenient distances. . . .

The Court views this case as presenting a serious equal protection claim of sex discrimination. I do not, and I would sustain Mississippi's right to continue MUW on a rational-basis analysis. But I need not apply this "lowest tier" of scrutiny. I can accept for present purposes the standard applied by the Court: that there is a gender-based distinction that must serve an important governmental objective by means that are substantially related to its achievement. . . . The record in this case reflects that MUW has a historic position in the State's educational system dating back to 1884. More than 2,000 women presently evidence their preference for MUW by having enrolled there. The choice is one that discriminates invidiously against no one. And the State's purpose in preserving that choice is legitimate and substantial. Generations of our finest minds, both among educators and students, have believed that single-sex, college-level institutions afford distinctive benefits. There are many persons, of course, who have different views. But simply because there are these differences is no reason—certainly none of constitutional dimension—to conclude that no substantial state interest is served when such a choice is made available.

In arguing to the contrary, the Court suggests that the MUW is so operated as to "perpetuate the stereotyped view of nursing as an exclusively women's job." . . . But as the Court itself acknowledges, . . . MUW's School of Nursing was not created until 1971—about 90 years after the single-sex campus itself was founded. This hardly supports a link between nursing as a woman's profession and MUW's single-sex admission policy. Indeed, MUW's School of Nursing was established at the coeducational University of Mississippi at Jackson. . . . The School of Nursing makes up only one part—a relatively small part—of MUW's diverse modern university campus and curriculum. The other departments on the MUW campus offer a typical range of degrees and a typical range of subjects. There is no indication that women suffer fewer opportunities at other Mississippi state campuses because of MUW's admission policy.

In sum, the practice of voluntarily chosen single-sex education is an honored tradition in our country, even if it now rarely exists in state colleges and universities. Mississippi's accommodation of such student choices is legitimate because it is completely consensual and is important because it permits students to decide for themselves the type of college education they think will benefit them most. Finally, Mississippi's policy is substantially related to its long-respected objective. . . .

A distinctive feature of America's tradition has been respect for diversity. This has been characteristic of the peoples from numerous lands who have built our country. It is the essence of our democratic system. At stake in this case as I see it is the preservation of a small aspect of this diversity. But that aspect is by no means insignificant, given our heritage of available choice between single-sex and coeducational institutions of higher learning. The Court answers that there is discrimination—not just that which may be tolerable, as for example between those candidates for admission able to contribute most to an educational institution and those able to contribute less—but discrimination of constitutional dimension. But, having found "discrimination," the Court finds it difficult to identify the victims. It hardly can claim that women are discriminated against. A constitutional case is held to exist solely because one man found it inconvenient to travel to any of the other institutions made available to him by the State of Mississippi. In essence he insists that he has a right to attend a college in his home community. This simply is not a sex discrimination case. The Equal Protection Clause was never intended to be applied to this kind of case.

GROVE CITY COLLEGE v. BELL
465 U.S. 555; 77 L. Ed. 2d 1450; 104 S. Ct. 1211 (1984)

JUSTICE WHITE *delivered the opinion of the Court.*

Section 901(a) of Title IX of the Education Amendments of 1972 . . . prohibits sex discrimination in "any education program or activity receiving Federal financial assistance," and . . . directs agencies awarding most types of assistance to promulgate regulations to ensure that recipients adhere to that prohibition. Compliance with departmental regulations may be secured by termination of assistance "to the particular program, or part thereof, in which . . . noncompliance has been . . . found" or by "any other means authorized by law." . . .

This case presents several questions concerning the scope and operation of these provisions and the regulations established by the Department of Education. We must decide, first, whether Title IX applies at all to Grove City College, which accepts no direct assistance but enrolls students who receive federal grants that must be used for educational purposes. If so, we must identify the "education program or activity" at Grove City that is "receiving Federal financial assistance" and determine whether federal assistance to that program may be terminated solely because the College violates the Department's regulations by refusing to execute an Assurance of Compliance with Title IX. Finally, we must consider whether the application of Title IX to Grove City infringes the First Amendment rights of the College or its students.

Petitioner Grove City College is a private, coeducational, liberal arts college that has sought to preserve its institutional autonomy by consistently refusing state and federal financial assistance. Grove City's desire to avoid federal oversight has led it to decline to participate, not only in direct institutional aid programs, but also in federal student assistance programs under which the College would be required to assess students' eligibility and to determine the amounts of loans, work-study funds, or grants they should receive. Grove City has, however, enrolled a large number of students who receive Basic Educational Opportunity Grants (BEOGs) . . . under the Department of Education's Alternate Disbursement System (ADS).

The Department concluded that Grove City was a "recipient" of "Federal financial assistance" as those terms are defined in the regulations implementing Title IX, . . . and, in July 1977, it requested that the College execute the Assurance of Compliance required. . . . If Grove City had signed the Assurance, it would have agreed to

[c]omply, to the extent applicable to it, with Title IX . . . and all applicable requirements imposed by or pursuant to the Department's regulation . . . to the end that . . . no person shall, on the basis of sex, be . . . subjected to discrimination under any education program or activity for which [it] receives or benefits from Federal financial assistance from the Department. . . .

When Grove City persisted in refusing to execute an Assurance, the Department initiated proceedings to declare the College and its students ineligible to receive BEOGs. The Administrative Law

Judge held that the federal financial assistance received by Grove City obligated it to execute an Assurance of Compliance and entered an order terminating assistance until Grove City "corrects its noncompliance with Title IX and satisfies the Department that it is in compliance" with the applicable regulations . . .

Grove City and four of its students then commenced this action in the District Court for the Western District of Pennsylvania, which concluded that the students' BEOGs constituted "Federal financial assistance" to Grove City but held, on several grounds, that the Department could not terminate the students' aid because of the College's refusal to execute an Assurance of Compliance. . . . The Court of Appeals reversed. . . . It first examined the language and legislative history of Title IX and held that indirect, as well as direct, aid triggered coverage . . . and that institutions whose students financed their educations with BEOGs were recipients of federal financial assistance within the meaning of Title IX. Although it recognized that Title IX's provisions are program-specific, the court likened the assistance flowing to Grove City through its students to non-earmarked aid, and, with one judge dissenting, declared that "[w]here the federal government furnishes indirect or non-earmarked aid to an institution, it is apparent to us that the institution itself must be the 'program'." . . . Finally, the Court of Appeals concluded that the Department could condition financial aid upon the execution of an Assurance of Compliance and that the Department had acted properly in terminating federal financial assistance to the students and Grove City despite the lack of evidence of actual determination.

We granted certiorari, . . . and we now affirm the Court of Appeals' judgment that the Department could terminate BEOGs received by Grove City's students to force the College to execute an Assurance of Compliance.

In defending its refusal to execute the Assurance of Compliance required by the Department's regulations, Grove City first contends that neither it nor any "education program or activity" of the college receives any federal financial assistance within the meaning of Title IX by virtue of the fact that some of its students receive BEOGs and use them to pay for their education. We disagree.

Grove City provides a well-rounded liberal arts education and a variety of educational programs and student services. The question is whether any of those programs or activities "receiv[es] Federal financial assistance" within the meaning of Title IX when students finance their education with BEOGs. The structure of the Education Amendments of 1972, in which Congress both created the BEOG program and imposed Title IX's nondiscrimination requirement, strongly suggests an affirmative conclusion. BEOGs were aptly characterized as a "centerpiece of the bill," . . . and Title IX "relate[d] directly to [its] central purpose." . . . In view of this connection and Congress's express recognition of discrimination in the administration of student financial aid programs, it would indeed by anomalous to discover that one of the primary components of Congress's comprehensive "package of federal aid," . . . was not intended to trigger coverage under Title IX.

It is not surprising to find, therefore, that the language of §901(a) contains no hint that Congress perceived a substantive difference between direct institutional assistance and aid received by a school through its students. The linchpin of Grove City's argument that none of its programs receives any federal assistance is a perceived distinction between direct and indirect aid, a distinction that finds no support in the text of §901(a). Nothing in §901(a) suggests that Congress elevated form over substance by making the application of the nondiscrimination principle dependent on the manner in which a program or activity receives federal assistance. There is no basis in the statute for the view that only institutions that themselves apply for federal aid or receive checks directly from the federal government are subject to regulation. . . . As the Court of Appeals observed "by its all-inclusive terminology [§901(a)] appears to encompass *all* forms of federal aid to education, direct or indirect." . . . We have recognized the need to " 'accord [Title IX] a sweep as broad as its language,' " . . . and we are reluctant to read into §901(a) a limitation not apparent on its face.

Our reluctance grows when we pause to consider the available evidence of Congress's intent. The economic effect of direct and indirect assistance often is indistinguishable, . . . and the BEOG program was structured to ensure that it effectively supplements the College's own financial aid program. Congress undoubtedly comprehended this reality in enacting the Education Amendments of 1972. The legislative history of the amendments is replete with statements evincing Congress's awareness that the student assistance programs established by the amendments would significantly aid colleges and universities. In fact, one of the stated purposes of the student aid provisions was to "provid[e] assistance to institutions of higher education." . . .

Congress's awareness of the purpose and effect of its student aid programs also is reflected in the sparse legislative history of Title IX itself. Title IX was patterned after Title VI of the Civil Rights Act of 1964. . . . The drafters of Title VI envisioned that the receipt of student aid funds would trigger coverage, and, since they approved identical language, we discern no reason to believe that the Congressmen who voted for Title IX intended a different result. . . .

With the benefit of clear statutory language, powerful evidence of Congress's intent, and a long-standing and coherent administrative construction of the phrase "receiving Federal financial assistance," we have little trouble concluding that Title IX coverage is not foreclosed because federal funds are granted to Grove City's students rather than directly to one of the College's educational programs. There remains the question, however, of identifying the "education program or activity" of the College that can properly be characterized as "receiving" federal assistance through grants to some of the students attending the College.

An analysis of Title IX's language and legislative history led us to conclude in *North Haven Board of Education* v. *Bell* . . . that "an agency's authority under Title IX both to promulgate regulations and to terminate funds is subject to the program-specific limitations of §§901 and 902." Although the legislative history contains isolated suggestions that entire institutions are subject to the nondiscrimination provision whenever one of their programs received federal assistance, . . . we cannot accept the Court of Appeals' conclusion that in the circumstances present here Grove City itself is a "program or activity" that may be regulated in its entirety. Nevertheless, we find no merit in Grove City's contention that a decision treating BEOGs as "Federal financial assistance" cannot be reconciled with Title IX's program-specific language since BEOGs are not tied to any specific "education program or activity."

If Grove City participated in the BEOG program through the RDS [Regular Disbursement System] we would have no doubt that the "education program or activity receiving Federal financial assistance" would not be the entire College; rather, it would be its student financial aid program. RDS institutions receive federal funds directly, but can use them only to subsidize or expand their financial aid programs and to recruit students who might otherwise be unable to enroll. In short, the assistance is earmarked for the recipient's financial aid program. Only by ignoring Title IX's program-specific language could we conclude that funds received under the RDS, awarded to eligible students and paid back to the school when tuition comes due, represent federal aid to the entire institution.

We see no reason to reach a different conclusion merely because Grove City has elected to participate in the ADS [Alternate Disbursement System]. Although Grove City does not itself disburse students' awards, BEOGs clearly augment the resources that the College itself devotes to financial aid. As is true of the RDS, however, the fact that federal funds eventually reach the College's general operating budget cannot subject Grove City to institution-wide coverage. Grove City's choice of administrative mechanisms, we hold, neither expands nor contracts the breadth of the "program or activity"—the financial aid program—that receives federal assistance and that may be regulated under Title IX.

To the extent that the Court of Appeals' holding that BEOGs received by Grove City's students constitute aid to the entire institution rests on the possibility that federal funds received by one program or activity free up the College's own resources for use elsewhere, the Court of Appeals' reasoning is doubly flawed. First, there is no evidence that the federal aid received by Grove City's students results in the diversion of funds from the College's own financial aid program to other areas within the institution. Second, and more important, the Court of Appeals' assumption that Title IX applies to programs receiving a larger share of a school's own limited resources as a result of federal assistance earmarked for use elsewhere within the institution is inconsistent with the program-specific nature of the statute. Most federal educational assistance has economic ripple effects throughout the aided institution, and it would be difficult, if not impossible, to determine which programs or activities derive such indirect benefits. Under the Court of Appeals' theory, an entire school would be subject to Title IX merely because one of its students received a small BEOG or because one of its departments received an earmarked federal grant. This result cannot be squared with Congress's intent.

The Court of Appeals' analogy between student financial aid received by an educational institution and non-earmarked direct grants provides a more plausible justification for its holding, but it too is faulty. Student financial aid programs, we believe, are *sui generis*. In neither purpose nor effect can BEOGs be fairly characterized as unrestricted grants that institutions may use for whatever purpose they desire. The BEOG program was designed, not merely to increase the total resources available to educational institutions, but to enable them to offer their services to students who had previously been unable to afford higher education. It is true, of course, that substantial portions of the BEOGs received by Grove City's students ultimately find their way into the College's general operating budget and are used to provide a variety of services to the students through whom the funds pass. However, we have found no persuasive evidence suggesting that Congress intended that the Department's regulatory authority follow federally aided students from classroom to classroom, building to building, or activity to activity. In addition, as Congress recognized in considering the Education Amendments of 1972, the economic effect of student aid is far different from the effect of non-earmarked grants to institutions themselves since the former, unlike the latter, increases both an institution's resources and its obligations. . . . In that sense, student financial aid more closely resembles many earmarked grants.

We conclude that the receipt of BEOGs by some of Grove City's students does not trigger institution-wide coverage under Title IX. In purpose and effect, BEOGs represent federal financial assistance to the College's own financial aid program, and it is that program that may properly be regulated under Title IX.

Since Grove City operates an "education program or activity receiving Federal financial assistance," the Department may properly demand that the College execute an Assurance of Compliance with Title IX. . . . Grove City contends, however, that the Assurance it was requested to sign was invalid, both on its face and as interpreted by the Department, in that it failed to comport with Title IX's program-specific character. Whatever merit that objection might have had at the time, it is not now a valid basis for refusing to execute an Assurance of Compliance.

The Assurance of Compliance regulation itself does not, on its face, impose institution-wide obligations. Recipients must provide assurance only that "each education program or activity operated by . . . [them] *and to which this part applies* will be operated in compliance with this part." . . . The regulations apply, by their terms, "to every recipient and to *each education program or activity* operated by such recipient *which receives or benefits from Federal financial assistance*." . . . [C]onsistent with the program-specific requirements of Title IX, the covered education program is the College's financial aid program.

A refusal to execute a proper program-specific Assurance of Compliance warrants termination of

federal assistance to the student financial aid program. . . . We conclude therefore, that the Department may properly condition federal financial assistance on the recipient's assurance that it will conduct the aided program or activity in accordance with Title IX and the applicable regulations.

Grove City's final challenge to the Court of Appeals' decision—that conditioning federal assistance on compliance with Title IX infringes First Amendment rights of the College and its students—warrants only brief consideration. Congress is free to attach reasonable and unambiguous conditions to federal financial assistance that educational institutions are not obligated to accept. . . . Grove City may terminate its participation in the BEOG program and thus avoid the requirements of §901(a). Students affected by the Department's action may either take their BEOGs elsewhere or attend Grove City without federal financial assistance. Requiring Grove City to comply with Title IX's prohibition of discrimination as a condition for its continued eligibility to participate in the BEOG program infringes no First Amendment rights of the College or its students.

[The concurring opinions of JUSTICE POWELL and JUSTICE STEVENS are omitted.]

* * *

JUSTICE BRENNAN, *with whom* JUSTICE MARSHALL *joins, concurring in part and dissenting in part.* . . .

I cannot join Part III of the Court's opinion, in which the Court interprets the language in Title IX that limits application of the statute to "any education program or activity" receiving federal monies. By conveniently ignoring these controlling indicia of Congressional intent, the Court also ignores the primary purposes for which Congress enacted Title IX. The result—allowing Title IX coverage for the College's financial aid program, but rejecting institution-wide coverage even though federal monies benefit the entire College—may be superficially pleasing to those who are uncomfortable with federal intrusion into private educational institutions, but it has no relationship to the statutory scheme enacted by Congress.

The Court has twice before had occasion to ascertain the precise scope of Title IX. See *North Haven Board of Education* v. *Bell* . . . (1982); *Cannon* v. *University of Chicago* . . . (1979). In both cases, the Court emphasized the broad Congressional purposes underlying enactment of the statute. In *Cannon*, while holding that Title IX confers a private cause of action on individual plaintiffs, we noted that the primary Congressional purpose behind the statute was "to avoid the use of federal resources to support discriminatory practices," and that this purpose "is generally served by the statutory procedure for the termination of federal financial support for institutions engaged in discriminatory practices." . . . In *North Haven*, while holding that employment discrimination is within the reach of Title IX, we expressed "no doubt that 'if we are to give [Title IX] the scope that its origins dictate, we must accord it a sweep as broad as its language.' " . . . And although we acknowledged that an agency's authority "both to promulgate regulations and to terminate funds is subject to the program-specific limitation of §§901 and 902," . . . we explicitly refused to define "program" at that time. . . .

When reaching that question today, the Court completely disregards the broad remedial purposes of Title IX that consistently have controlled our prior interpretations of this civil rights statute. Moreover, a careful examination of the statute's legislative history, the accepted meaning of similar statutory language in Title VI, and the postenactment history of Title IX will demonstrate that the Court's narrow definition of "program or activity" is directly contrary to Congressional intent. . . .

A proper application of Title IX to the circumstances of this case demonstrates beyond peradventure that the Court has unjustifiably limited the statute's reach. Grove City College enrolls approximately 140 students who utilize Basic Educational Opportunity Grants (BEOGs) to pay for their education at the College. Although the grant monies are paid directly to the students, the Court properly concludes that the use of these federal monies at the College means that the College "receives Federal financial assistance" within the meaning of Title IX. The Court also correctly notes that a principal purpose underlying Congressional enactment of the BEOG program is to provide funds that will benefit colleges and universities as a whole. It necessarily follows, in my view, the entire undergraduate institution operated by Grove City College is subject to the antidiscrimination provisions included in Title IX.

In determining the scope of Title IX coverage, the primary focus should be on the purposes meant to be served by the particular federal funds received by the institution. In this case, Congress has clearly indicated that BEOG monies are intended to benefit any college or university that enrolls students receiving such grants. As the Court repeatedly recognizes, "[t]he legislative history of the [Education Amendments of 1972] is replete with statements evincing Congress's awareness that the student assistance programs established by the amendments would significantly aid colleges and universities. In fact, one of the stated purposes of the student aid provisions was to provid[e] assistance to institutions of higher education." . . . ("The history of [the reenactments of the statutory authorization for BEOGs] makes clear that Congress regards BEOGs and other forms of student aid as a critical source of support for educational institutions.")

In many respects, therefore, Congress views financial aid to students, and in particular BEOGs, as the functional equivalent of general aid to institutions. Given this undeniable and clearly stated Congressional purpose, it would seem to be self-evident that Congress intended colleges or universities enrolling students who receive BEOGs to be covered, in their entirety, by the antidiscrimination provisions of Title IX. That statute's primary purpose, after all, is to ensure that federal monies are not used to support discriminatory practices. . . .

Under the Court's holding, in contrast, Grove City College is prohibited from discriminating on the basis of sex in its own "financial aid program," but is free to discriminate in other "programs or activities" operated by the institution. Underlying this result is the unstated and unsupportable assumption that monies received through BEOGs are meant only to be utilized by the College's financial aid program. But it is undisputed that BEOG monies, paid to the institution as tuition and fees and used in the general operating budget, are utilized to support most, and perhaps all, of the facilities and services that together comprise Grove City College.

The absurdity of the Court's decision is further demonstrated by examining its practical effect. According to the Court, the "financial aid program" at Grove City College may not discriminate on the basis of sex because it is covered by Title IX, but the College is not prohibited from discriminating in its admissions, its athletic programs, or even its various academic departments. The Court thus sanctions practices that Congress clearly could not have intended: for example, after today's decision, Grove City College would be free to segregate male and female students in classes run by its mathematics department. This would be so even though the affected students are attending the College with the financial assistance provided by federal funds. If anything about Title IX were ever certain, it is that discriminatory practices like the one just described were meant to be prohibited by the statute.

The Court, moreover, does not offer any defensible justification for its holding. First, the Court states that it has "no doubt" that BEOGs administered through the Regular Disbursement System (RDS) are received, not by the entire College, but by its financial aid program. Thus, the Court reasons, BEOGs administered through the Alternate Disbursement System (ADS) must also be received only by the financial aid program. The premise of this syllogism, however, simply begs the question presented; until today's decision, there was considerable doubt concerning the reach of Title IX in a college or university administering BEOGs through the RDS. Indeed, the extent to which Title IX covers an educational institution receiving Title IX is the same regardless of the procedural mechanism chosen by the College to disburse the student aid. With this argument, therefore, the Court is simply restating the question presented by the case.

Second, the Court rejects the notion that the federal funds disbursed under the BEOG program are received by the entire institution because they effectively "free up" the College's own resources for use by all programs or activities that are operated by Grove City College. But coverage of an entire institution that receives BEOGs through its students is not dependent upon such a theory. Instead Title IX coverage for the whole undergraduate institution at Grove City College is premised on the Congressional intent that BEOG monies would provide aid for the college or university as a whole. Therefore, whatever merit the Court's argument may have for federal monies that are intended solely to benefit a particular aspect of an educational institution, such as a research grant designed to assist a specific laboratory or professor, . . . the freeing-up theory is simply irrelevant when the federal financial assistance is meant to benefit the entire institution.

Third, the Court contradicts its earlier recognition that BEOGs are no different from general aid to a college or university by claiming that "student financial aid programs . . . are *sui generis.*" . . . Although this assertion serves to limit severely the effect of the Court's holding, it is wholly unexplained, especially in light of the forceful evidence of Congressional intent to the contrary. Indeed, it would be more accurate to say that financial aid for students is the prototypical method for funneling federal aid to institutions of higher education.

Finally, although not explicitly offered as a rationale, the Court's holding might be explained by its willingness to defer to the Government's position as it has been represented to this Court. But until the Government filed its briefs in this case, it had consistently argued that Title IX coverage for the entire undergraduate institution operated by Grove City College was authorized by the statute. . . . The latest position adopted by the Government, irrespective of the motivations that might underlie this recent change, is therefore entitled to little, if any, deference. . . . The interpretation of statutes as important as Title IX should not be subjected so easily to shifts in policy by the executive branch.

In sum the program-specific language in Title IX was designed to ensure that the reach of the statute is dependent upon the scope of federal financial assistance provided to an institution. When that financial assistance is clearly intended to serve as federal aid for the entire institution, the institution as a whole should be covered by the statute's prohibition on sex discrimination. Any other interpretation clearly disregards the intent of Congress and severely weakens the antidiscrimination provisions included in Title IX. I therefore cannot join in Part III of the Court's opinion.

The Right of Privacy

FEATURED CASES

Griswold et al. v. *Connecticut*	*Roe* v. *Wade*	*Webster* v. *Reproductive Health Services*
Planned Parenthood v. *Casey*	*Bowers* v. *Hardwick*	*Cruzan* v. *Missouri*

The constitutional right of privacy is deeply rooted in American history. Indeed, the issue of privacy, as Alan Westin documents in his *Privacy and Freedom* (New York: Atherton, 1967), has been with us for some time. The adoption of the Fourth Amendment in 1791, with its prohibition against unreasonable searches and seizures, was an implicit recognition of the right of privacy. However, technological advances and other pressures on privacy have led to a more explicit recognition in our public law of the importance of safeguarding the right of privacy as against competing interests such as public morality and law enforcement. In their 1890 seminal article on the right of privacy, for example, Samuel Warren and Louis Brandeis called attention to new and increasing threats to privacy.[4] And after his appointment to the Supreme Court in 1916, Brandeis continued to champion the cause of privacy. Then and now "wiretapping" and other search and seizure cases have provided lively contexts in which to debate the right to privacy. (See, e.g., *Katz* v. *United States*, 389 U.S. 347, 1967; and *California* v. *Ciraolo*, 476 U.S. 207, 1986). A fundamental question that comes to the fore in such situations is whether governmental intrusion for the purposes of crime control is a necessary evil consistent with the needs of a changing society, or an unacceptable infringement on the privacy and freedom that individuals have a constitutional right to expect.

Over the last 25 years, the issue of privacy versus governmental intrusion has illuminated additional dimensions of the rights and freedoms of individuals in their social behavior and relations. As such, it has involved relations and behavior patterns with respect to such hotly contested subjects as contraception, reproduction, and sexual orientation. On one side of the debate, for example, is the view that activities involving individual autonomy and relations among consenting adults are (or at least should be) outside the scope of government regulation. On the other side is the opinion that government must (and should) play a role in regulating sexual behavior either under the rationale of promoting social morality, or under the rationale of regulating conduct to protect third parties ranging from fetuses to the terminally ill.

In this section, we shall examine the discussion on the range of possible governmental involvement in such matters. Although the most hotly contested controversies have been over abortion and gay and lesbian rights, the conceptual (and actual) stress on the rights of privacy has increased as technological changes are forcing society (and government) to deal with such issues as surrogate motherhood, the use of fetal tissue to treat diseases, and the public health dimensions regarding the transmission of AIDS (e.g., compulsory testing).

BEYOND THE FOURTH AMENDMENT: PRIVACY AS A CONSTITUTIONAL RIGHT

In 1965 the Supreme Court took a major step toward recognizing a constitutional right of privacy. By a seven-to-two vote, the Court held in *Griswold* v. *Connecticut* (381 U.S. 479) that a Connecticut law that forbade the dissemination of birth control information was violative of the right of marital privacy. Justice Douglas, who spoke for the majority, said the Connecticut law interfered with "a right of privacy older than the Bill of Rights." Douglas spoke of "zones of privacy" and admitted that privacy as a specific right is not protected by the Constitution. However, he thought it was within a "penumbra" of certain fundamental guarantees such as those enunciated in the First, Third, Fourth, and Fifth Amendments. In this formulation, Douglas also cited the Ninth Amendment, which declares that the delineation of certain rights in the Bill of Rights does not mean that there are not other rights "retained by the people."

Justice Black issued a sharp dissent. He attacked the majority for creating a constitutional right of privacy when there was nothing in the Constitution to warrant such a development. Moreover, Black differed with the manner by which the Court had developed its own notion of

[4]The Right to Privacy, 4 *Harvard Law Review* 193 (1890).

the right of privacy and incorporated it into the meaning of the due process clause of the Fourteenth Amendment. Black had long warned the Court that the due process clause was meant to include *only* the provisions of the first eight amendments as limitations on the states and *no more*. To do otherwise, Black said, allowed the Court to write its own notions of due process rather than those intended by the framers of the Fourteenth Amendment. (*Griswold* was also cited with approval in *Eisenstadt* v. *Baird*, 405 U.S. 438, 1972.)

The 1973 celebrated "Abortion Cases" gave the Court a most visible opportunity to review the issue of whether there is a constitutional right of privacy. And the Court used this opportunity to reaffirm its *Griswold* position, namely that there is a constitutional right of privacy that limits the states in their actions. Justice Blackmun, who spoke for the Court in a seven-to-two decision in *Roe* v. *Wade* (410 U.S. 113, 1973), admitted that "the Constitution does not explicitly mention any right of privacy." However, he indicated that "in a line of decisions . . . going back perhaps as far as . . . 1891, the Court has recognized that a right of personal privacy, or a guarantee of certain areas or zones of privacy does exist under the Constitution." Justices White and Rehnquist dissented. Their dissents, as well as how Justice Blackmun balanced this constitutional right of privacy against competing state interests, are reprinted in this chapter.

Several 1977 Supreme Court decisions bear directly on the abortion issue. In one case, *Maher* v. *Roe* (432 U.S. 464), a six-to-three Court majority ruled that neither the Constitution nor current federal law requires states to spend Medicaid funds for elective (i.e., nontherapeutic) abortions in the first trimester. (Also see *Beal* v. *Doe*, 432 U.S. 438.) By the same majority, the Court also ruled in a St. Louis case, *Poelker* v. *Doe* (432 U.S. 519), that city public hospitals were under no constitutional obligation to provide or permit elective abortions. And in *Harris* v. *McRae* (448 U.S. 297, 1980), the Court held that under the Social Security Act, which provided federal financial assistance to cover certain medical costs of needy people, participating states are not obligated to pay for medically necessary abortions for which Congress has withheld federal funds. Thus the Court in *Harris* was able to uphold the well-publicized Hyde amendment, which permits Medicaid funds to be used only for abortions performed to save the life of the mother and under certain other special circumstances. Justices Stevens, Brennan, and Marshall

gave strong dissents. Brennan said that "both by design and in effect [the Hyde amendment] serves to coerce indigent pregnant women to bear children they would otherwise not elect to have." Overall, the impact of *Maher*, *Poelker*, and *Harris* does appear, to quote from Marshall's dissent in *Harris*, "to deny to the poor the constitutional right recognized in *Roe* v. *Wade* (1973). . . . "

This trend that Marshall saw in *Harris* has not abated. State and city regulations continue to mandate procedures and conditions under which abortions may take place. To be sure, some of these regulations have been declared invalid, but others have been upheld. (Cf. *Planned Parenthood Assn. of Kansas City* v. *Ashcroft*, 1983; and *City of Akron* v. *Akron Center for Reproductive Health*, 1983.)

In *Thornburgh* v. *American College of Obstetricians and Gynecologists* (1986), the Court dealt once again with state regulations that sought to narrow or restrict a woman's right to an abortion. Here the Court held that six provisions of a Pennsylvania statute impermissibly deterred a woman's right to an abortion. Although *Thornburgh* strongly reaffirms *Roe* v. *Wade*, its narrow five-to-four majority indicates vividly the eroding support in the Court for the principles of that earlier 1973 decision in *Roe* v. *Wade*.

By its 1989 decision in *Webster* v. *Reproductive Health Services*, however, a new and vibrant Rehnquist Court majority signaled that the Court was prepared to uphold state restrictions on abortion that it had held unconstitutional in the past. Here, by a narrow five-to-four vote, the Court held that Missouri could ban the use of public funds, employees, or facilities in assisting or performing a nontherapeutic abortion. Although the Court's decision placed additional pressure on the *Roe* v. *Wade* edifice, it did not topple *Roe*, as Justice O'Connor blocked the Scalia–Rehnquist push to reconsider *Roe*.

Recently, in *Planned Parenthood* v. *Casey* (112 S. Ct. 2791, 1992), the Supreme Court surprised legal and political analysts by upholding the basic guarantees of *Roe*. The Supreme Court, though, upheld most of Pennsylvania's statutory restrictions, including a 24-hour waiting period. Importantly, a plurality of Justices O'Connor, Kennedy, and Souter announced a new test—a state statute would be deemed violative of *Roe* and thus unconstitutional if it placed an "undue burden" on a woman's abortion rights.

Casey was surprising in that after several appointments by Presidents Reagan and Bush, and an especially confrontational confirmation of Justice Thomas, *Roe* still remained standing. The debate among legal scholars currently is whether the new standard of the existence of an "undue burden" is a workable conceptual structure. Also, as Justice Scalia noted in *Casey*, thus echoing a concern that he voiced in *Webster*, the evaluation of the "undue burden" standard keeps the Court in the business of evaluating abortion rights, something that he sees as a role best left to the political branches.

As manifest in recent cases, the Supreme Court seems to have reached a "compromise" position based on a distinction between private and public activity. States may regulate, albeit minimally, the private provision of abortions through the use, for example, of a waiting period. Regulation would be justified on the basis that restrictions would only be used to allow the woman to make an "informed" decision, as occurs in typical doctor-patient relations. However, the basic right to obtain an abortion outside the purview of government would remain intact. In contrast to the regulation of a private service, especially as seen by *Webster*, states may try to get out of the business of providing abortions.

Although this evolution in Supreme Court jurisprudence may seem to fit better with the societal notions of privacy, it does raise some fundamental questions. For example, how tightly may the public and private spheres be drawn? Recently, in *Rust* v. *Sullivan* (111 S. Ct. 1759, 1991), the Court upheld the Department of Health and Human Services' interpretation of Title X of the Public Health Service Act of 1970. The affirmed interpretation, issued in 1988, required that health care recipients of governmental funds under Title X could not counsel clients on matters regarding abortion. In fact, all abortion activities had to be kept "physically and financially separate" from other family counseling activities available in Title X projects. The petitioners argued that such restrictions violated the free speech rights of health care providers to inform the patient of all relevant options. The Court rejected this position, arguing that any restrictions arose as a consequence of accepting public money for the Title X program. The majority made it clear that the regulations did not restrict individuals who chose to act privately. By contrast, Justice Blackmun dissented, arguing that the Court was upholding the viewpoint-based suppression of speech solely because it was imposed on those dependent on the government for economic support.

To reiterate, the heart of the problem is the parameters of the public/private distinction when giving content to a constitutional right premised on the concept of privacy. After all, once the Supreme Court a fundamental right has declared, there might arise an equal protection problem with respect to whether all citizens can afford to make the right a reality. At bottom one might ask whether some citizens (e.g., the poor) may receive, because of economics, less than the full measure of their constitutional rights.

PRIVACY IN VARIED CONTEXTS

The notion of privacy has also been present in other contexts. Take, for example, the issues in *Public Utilities Commission* v. *Pollak* (343 U.S. 451, 1952). Here the Capital Transit Company, with the approval of the Public Utilities Commission of the District of Columbia, arranged with an FM station for special programs to be piped in over a streetcar radio. The special programs consisted of about 90 percent music, 5 percent news announcements, and 5 percent commercial advertisements. Two passengers thought that this practice infringed upon their constitutional right of privacy under the Fifth Amendment. But Justice Burton, speaking for the Court majority, said:

> This position wrongly assumes that the Fifth Amendment secures to each passenger on a public vehicle regulated by the Federal Government a right of privacy substantially equal to the privacy to which he is entitled in his own home. However complete his right of privacy may be at home, it is substantially limited by the rights of others when its possessor travels on a public thoroughfare or rides in a public conveyance.

Justice Douglas dissented, and Justice Black dissented in part. Justice Frankfurter did not participate in the case since "[his] feelings [were] so strongly engaged as a victim of the practice in controversy. . . ." Justice Douglas's dissent emphasized "the right to be let alone," which he argued "is . . . the beginning of all freedom." Said Douglas:

> The present case involves a form of coercion to make people listen. The listeners are of course in a public place; they are on streetcars, traveling to and from home. In one sense it can be said that those who ride streetcars do so voluntarily. Yet in a practical sense they are forced to ride, since this mode of transportation is today essential for many thousands. Compulsion which comes from circumstances can be as real as compulsion which comes from a command. . . . When we force people to listen to another's ideas, we give the propagandist a powerful weapon. . . . Once a man is forced to submit to one type of radio

program, he can be forced to submit to another. It may be but a short step from a cultural program to a political program.

Twenty-two years later Justice Douglas saw his *Pollak* dissent largely vindicated by the Court in *Lehman* v. *City of Shaker Heights* (418 U.S. 298, 1974). Here the Court upheld the constitutionality of a transit system's advertising policy that provided space for commercial ads and public service messages but not for political advertising. In his plurality opinion, Justice Blackmun said that the decision to forbid political advertising was a "managerial decision . . . little different from deciding to impose a 10-, 25-, or 35-cent fare or from changing schedules or the location of bus stops." The selling of advertisement space was incidental to the company's primary function, and the ban served to avoid administrative problems such as space allocations to different political candidates, the public impression of favoritism toward a particular candidate, and the invasion of privacy of the transit company's passengers. Addressing the equal protection question, Justice Blackmun found the objectives of the political advertisement prohibition to be "reasonable legislative objectives"; hence discrimination between nonpolitical and political advertising was justified. Justice Douglas gave the judgment a five-man majority, but would have reached the conclusion based entirely on "captive audience" and "right to privacy" arguments reminiscent of his dissent in *Pollak*. Dissenting, Justice Brennan argued that principles of free speech and equal protection prohibited discrimination based solely on content.

How much privacy can one have in his or her own home? The door-to-door canvasser has long been a constant irritant to the late sleeper, the night-shift worker, or the person who just wants to be let alone. At first, some door-to-door canvassing seems to have been protected by the First Amendment, but some not. Noncommercial canvassing, for example, came within the First Amendment guarantees in *Martin* v. *Struthers* (319 U.S. 141, 1943). Here the Court was faced with an ordinance that made it unlawful "for any person distributing handbills, circulars, or other advertisements to ring the doorbell, sound the doorknocker, or otherwise summon the inmate or inmates to the door for the purpose of receiving such handbills, circulars, or other advertisements they or any person with them may be distributing." When a Jehovah's Witness was convicted under this ordinance for distributing advertisements for a religious meeting, the Supreme Court declared the ordinance invalid as a denial of free speech and press. Justice Black delivered the opinion for the five-to-four majority. Justices Reed, Roberts, and Jackson dissented.

On the other side of the ledger, some Court decisions suggested that commercial canvassing is clearly subject to local regulation. (*Green River* v. *Bunger*, 58 P.2d 456, *Bunger* v. *Green River*, 300 U.S. 638, 1937; and *Breard* v. *Alexandria*, 341 U.S. 622, 1951.) The Court held to this view in *Breard* despite the free speech and free press problem raised by an Alexandria, Louisiana, city ordinance against door-to-door commercial canvassing as applied in this instance to magazine solicitors. Justice Reed, who had dissented in *Struthers*, now spoke for the Court majority in *Breard*. To Reed, the constitutionality of the ordinance turned on "a balancing of the conveniences between some householders' desires for privacy and the publisher's right to distribute publications in the precise way that those soliciting for him think brings the best results." But Justice Black, in an opinion joined by Justice Douglas, dissented, stating that "[t]he constitutional sanctuary for the press must necessarily include liberty to publish and circulate." "In view of our economic system," reasoned Black, "it must also include freedom to solicit paying subscribers." In recent years, the Black-Douglas position seems to represent the prevailing view of the Court. Indeed, the noncommercial/commercial distinction suggested in *Struthers* and *Breard* appears now to be all but obliterated. (See *Bigelow* v. *Virginia*, 1975; and *Virginia State Board of Pharmacy* v. *Virginia Citizens Consumer Council*, 1976.)

The Court has also considered privacy in the context of other First Amendment issues, including the matter of obscenity. The Court decision in *Stanley* v. *Georgia* (394 U.S. 557, 1969) seems to have turned primarily on the right of privacy. Here the Court upheld the right of the private possession of obscene materials for private use in one's home. (See the general discussion on obscenity.) Another interesting case involving obscenity and the right of privacy came to the Supreme Court in *Rowan* v. *United States Post Office Department* (397 U.S. 728, 1970), where the right to be let alone versus the right to communicate (under the First Amendment) was before the Court. At issue was a provision of the Postal Revenue and Salary Act of 1967 under which householders could insulate themselves from advertisements that offer for sale "matter which the addressee in his sole discretion believes to be erotically arousing or sexually provocative." The postmaster general, once an addressee gives notice that he or she has received ads that he or she believes to be within this statutory category and does not wish to receive them, is obliged to order the sender "to refrain from other mailings" to that addressee. The postmaster general must also: (1) order the sender to delete the addressee's name from all mailing lists owned or controlled by the sender; and (2) prohibit the sender from selling or renting any mailing lists that include the addressee's name.

A federal district court upheld the act, construing it to prohibit future mailings similar to those originally sent to the addressee. Chief Justice Burger, speaking for the Court, gave the act a more restrictive scope, but upheld its constitutionality. He found that the act's purpose was "to allow the addressee complete and unfettered discretion in electing whether or not he desired to receive further material from a particular sender." By focusing on the prohibition of any further mailings rather than of similar mailings, Burger relieved the addressee of the "further burdens of scrutinizing the [sender's] mail for objectionable material" and avoided a situation that "would interpose the Postmaster General between the sender and the addressee and, at the least, create the appearance if not the substance of governmental censorship." Thus, Burger held that the statute did not violate the sender's constitutional right to communicate. "Without doubt," he concluded, "the public postal system is an indispensable adjunct of every civilized society and communication is imperative to a healthy social order. But the right of every person 'to be let alone' must be placed on the scales with the right of others to communicate."

The notion of the right of privacy was also involved in the *New York Times* v. *Sullivan* sequence of cases concerning damage to one's reputation and defamation of character. (See Chapter 3.) Particular attention should be called to *Time, Inc.* v. *Hill* (385 U.S. 374, 1967), where the Court in effect held that the right of privacy under a New York privacy statute was insufficient to overcome the free press and speech guarantees of the First Amendment.

The right of privacy has also been discussed in the context of family life and family living arrangements. For example, in *Moore* v. *East Cleveland* (431 U.S. 494, 1977), the Court held invalid a housing ordinance that restricted occupancy to single families and defined "family" in such a way as to prevent two grandsons of the appellant from living with her. (Cf. *Village of Belle Terre* v. *Boraas*, 416 U.S. 1, 1974, which upheld an ordinance on the types of groups—unrelated individuals—that could occupy a single dwelling unit.) Justice Powell announced the judgment of the Court and wrote an opinion that was joined by Justices Brennan, Marshall, and Blackmun. Powell said that the ordinance on its face "selects certain categories of relatives who may live together and declares that others may not," in this instance "making it a crime for a grandmother to live with a grandson." Powell noted the "intrusive" nature of the ordinance and said that the Court "had long recognized that freedom of personal choice in matters of marriage and family life is one of the liberties protected by the . . . Fourteenth Amendment." Under such circumstances, Powell said, the Court "must examine carefully the importance of the governmental interests advanced and the extent to which they are served by the regulation." After doing so, Powell found the ordinance unconstitutional and indicated that it serves "marginally, at best," the objectives cited by the city—preventing overcrowding, minimizing traffic and parking congestion, and avoiding an undue financial burden on East Cleveland's school system.

Does a uniformed police officer have a right of privacy to his personal appearance when viewed in the context of a police regulation that prescribes the "style and length" of a male police officer's hair? In *Kelly* v. *Johnson* (425 U.S. 238, 1976), the Court held that such a police regulation did not infringe any "liberty" interest protected by the Fourteenth Amendment. Justice Rehnquist, who spoke for the Court, distinguished *Kelly* from *Roe, Eisenstadt*, and *Griswold*. "Each of those cases," said Rehnquist, "involved a substantial claim of infringement on the individual's freedom of choice with respect to certain basic matters of procreation, marriage, and family life." Moreover, continued Rehnquist, the respondent seeks "the protection of the Fourteenth Amendment, not as a member of the citizenry at large, but on the contrary as an employee of the police department. . . . " Given the importance of the law enforcement function, and the relation of organization, dress, and equipment to that function, Rehnquist concluded that "the regulation . . . did not violate any right guaranteed by the Fourteenth Amendment. . . . " Justice Marshall, joined by Justice Brennan, issued a sharp dissent. "To say," observed Marshall, "that the liberty guarantee of the Fourteenth Amendment does not encompass matters of personal appearance would be fundamentally inconsistent with the values of privacy, self-identity, autonomy, and personal integrity that I have always assumed the Constitution was designed to protect. . . . "

In general, the recent clamor to "return" the

country to "law and order" has also increased pressures on those who champion the right of privacy. Official actions designed to stop "coddling" criminals and "protect society" (such as "stop and frisk" searches, the use of undercover agents, bugging, wiretapping, and other measures) certainly portend to collide sooner or later with the right of privacy. Issues related to the right of privacy are raised especially by those who see a relation between law and order and the need to maintain certain moral standards. Much of this controversy concerns "morals" legislation that involves "crimes without victims" (such as prostitution, homosexual relations among consenting adults, adultery, and abortion). There is anything but consensus on whether such activities should be "crimes" and thus subject to criminal penalties, or should be primarily left to matters of individual choice.

Obviously, it is with respect to these "crimes without victims" that the "right of privacy" is more forcefully raised. Indeed, unlike a few years ago, some "victims" of such "victimless" crimes (e.g., homosexuals) are no longer willing to accept the verdict imposed by restrictive "morals" legislation, and they now openly organize to protect their rights. But in 1986, gay rights were dealt a setback as the Supreme Court, in *Bowers* v. *Hardwick* (478 U.S. 186, 1986), decided that the constitutional right of privacy did not include homosexual sodomy. The Court in fact limited the constitutional right of privacy to cover activities that manifested a connection to "family, marriage or procreation," and it accepted the right of a state to pass legislation reflecting a set of moral beliefs. In doing so, the Court explicitly distinguished among "victimless" activities, and grouped homosexual behavior with such restricted activities as the possession and use of illegal drugs, adultery, and incest. Moreover, the Court acknowledged that about 25 states had statutes restricting sodomy, thus undercutting the argument that sodomy was historically accepted in the United States. Nonetheless, continuing developments indicate clearly that the battle over homosexual rights is far from over.

In another context, the regulation of so-called victimless activity entered a new area in 1990. In *Cruzan* v. *Missouri* (110 S. Ct. 2841, 1990), the Supreme Court had to decide whether a comatose individual had a constitutional right to be free of governmental interference that maintained her on life-support technology. In denying the patient's "right to die" by being removed from life support, the Court upheld Missouri's interest in requiring "clear and convincing" evidence of the patient's wishes, something that was not furnished by her family. Justice Brennan, in dissent, argued that the individual's right to be free from governmental interference was impermissibly burdened by the procedural obstacles of evidence that the state had put in place. In reaction, Justice Scalia's concurrence made it clear that this, like abortion, was yet another field the Supreme Court should not enter.

PRIVACY AND CONGRESSIONAL LEGISLATION

Although our focus here has been mainly on the judiciary, mention should be made of pertinent actions in other governmental arenas. For example, in an apparent response to revelations made during the Watergate hearings, Congress attempted to protect citizens from invasions of their privacy by passing the Privacy Act of 1974. As enacted, the law provides individuals with access to personal information on themselves that may be contained in agency files. It authorizes people to challenge such information and to seek injunctive relief if necessary to correct or amend what is contained in the files. Except as authorized by statute or approval by the individual, or as pursuant to an official law enforcement activity, the Privacy Act also prohibits government agencies from keeping records that describe an individual's exercise of his or her rights under the First Amendment. Moreover, it forbids agencies that maintain files for one purpose to make such files available to other agencies for a second purpose without the consent of the individual involved. In addition, the act requires federal agencies to keep records only as may be lawful and necessary as well as current and accurate. Agencies must also disclose the existence of all their data banks and files that contain information on individuals.

Also in 1974, Congress overrode a presidential veto and passed the Freedom of Information Act Amendments. In effect, the amendments are designed to overcome certain deficiencies in the Freedom of Information Act of 1966 by increasing public access to government information. For example, while classified materials remain exempt, the amendments tighten the reins on government agencies that improperly classify or otherwise restrict public access to information. Under the 1974 provisions, federal judges may review, *in camera*, contested agency decisions to determine whether the classification of certain documents is appropriate within the terms of the legislation. The 1974 amendments also set definite time limits within which agencies must respond to requests for information. In addition, Congress passed the Family Educational Rights and Privacy Act of 1974. Essentially, the law was designed to protect the confidentiality and privacy of student records in educational institutions. It required educational institutions to allow parents or students, if over 18, to see student files. Further, such institutions were required to obtain the consent of parents or students before releasing information in student files to third parties. Certain clarifying amendments to the law were subsequently made to sharpen and further delineate provisions on the disclosure of student records.

The 1978 Supreme Court decision in *Zurcher* v. *Stanford Daily* (436 U.S. 547) spurred Congress to pass additional privacy legislation in 1980. Referred to as the Privacy Protection Act of 1980, the law was designed to overcome the *Zurcher* ruling, which held that the Constitution posed no barrier to police officials' use of warrants to make unannounced searches of newspaper offices for evidence. The third-party search had been made pursuant to a warrant in a situation where state authorities had "probable cause" to believe that relevant evidence was located in the *Stanford Daily's* office, although neither the newspaper nor its reporters were suspected of criminal activity. The Court decision sparked sharp protests and broad concern not only from newspapers and news organizations, but from other professional groups (lawyers, physicians, and psychiatrists) who thought their confidential records and relationships with clients could be jeopardized by the decision.[5] Although the search was found to be constitutional, the Court in *Zurcher* nonetheless contemplated that future legislation might be passed to prohibit such searches. In its opinion, the Court said:

> Of course, the Fourth Amendment does not prevent or advise against legislative or executive efforts to establish non-constitutional protections against possible abuses of the search warrant procedure, but we decline to reinterpret the Amendment to impose a general constitutional barrier against warrants to search newspaper premises, to require resort to subpoenas as a general rule, or to demand prior notice and hearing in connection with the issuance of search warrants.

Thus, the Privacy Protection Act of 1980 may be

viewed as an attempt to establish these "non-constitutional protections." Essentially, the act bars federal, state, and local law enforcement officers from searching and seizing documentary materials from news organizations and others engaged in First Amendment activities. Moreover, the law prohibits such officials from using warrants to search newsrooms and offices of other organizations working in the First Amendment area. Rather than using warrants, which are generally executed without prior warning, law enforcement officials under the new law must now go to court and obtain subpoenas requiring that certain materials be produced by those holding them. Subpoenas are generally viewed as less intrusive and may be challenged in court *before* being enforced. To be sure, the law provides several exceptions to the new subpoena rule, for example, if there is reason to believe that giving notice of a subpoena would result in the destruction, alteration, or concealment of the materials in question. The law also mandates the attorney general to issue guidelines and procedures for federal officials to use in searches for evidence held by people who are not suspected of crime nor working in First Amendment areas. This provision and the resulting guidelines may serve to quiet the concerns of medical groups and others about protecting confidential and privileged relationships.

THE ISSUE OF PRIVACY: A CONCEPTUAL FRAMEWORK

Privacy, as this brief overview demonstrates, is a somewhat amorphous, elusive issue. It is hard to harness and understand. However, in *The Right to Privacy* (St. Paul: West Publishing Co., 1976), P. Allan Dionisopoulos and Craig Ducat have provided "three conceptual cores about which the doctrine might usefully be spun."[6] The first of these "conceptual cores" or contexts, is "place-oriented conceptions of privacy," or "privacy that inheres in the place or property." This, of course, defines the right of privacy in spatial terms, as, for example, in the metaphor that one's home is one's castle. In this regard, the Fourth Amendment was used to carve out certain "constitutionally protected areas," such as those exemplified by the Court in the *Olmstead* line of cases. (*Olmstead* v. *U.S.*, 277 U.S. 438, 1928.) Other examples of "privacy inhering in the place" are illustrated by court decisions such as *Stanley* v. *Georgia, Public Utilities*

---

[5]For example, see the views of the American Medical Association, the American Psychiatric Association, and the City Bar of New York in *Hearings on the Privacy Protection Act*, Comm. on the Judiciary, 96th Cong., 2d Sess., on S. 115., S. 1790, and S. 1816, March 28, 1980.

[6]Materials in this section are based largely on their book.

Commission v. *Pollak*, and *Erznoznik* v. *City of Jacksonville* (422 U.S. 205, 1975).

The second conceptual core or context in which privacy may be viewed is referred to by Dionisopoulos and Ducat as "person-oriented conceptions of privacy," or "privacy inhering in the person." Here the attempt is to "define the right of privacy in terms of the person." In short, the emphasis is shifted from place or property to the person involved. Supreme Court decisions that exemplify this "person-oriented" conception of privacy include the Abortion Cases, *Time, Inc.* v. *Hill, Kelly* v. *Johnson*, and *Schmerber* v. *California* (384 U.S. 757, 1966).

Just as in the other conceptual cores, a number of lower court decisions exemplify this person-oriented conception of privacy. One of the most complicated and touching cases in this regard touched on whether a person in a persistent moribund state of life, such as Karen Quinlan, had a "right to die." (See *Matter of Quinlan*, 355 A.2d 647, 1976.) Another interesting and well-publicized situation was that of free-lance photographer Ronald Galella, whose tactics in attempting to practice his trade by photographing Jacqueline Onassis (formerly Mrs. John F. Kennedy) and her minor children led to litigation that imposed certain restrictions on Galella's activities. Mrs. Onassis had charged, among other things, that Galella's activities constituted harassment and an invasion of privacy. (*Galella* v. *Onassis*, 353 F. Supp. 196, 1972; 487 F. 2d 986, 1973.) Finally, a New Jersey court held that "surrogate mother" contracts were void against the public policy of the state. (*In the Matter of Baby M*, 537 A.2d 1227, 1988.) In that case, William Stern and Mary Beth Whitehead had entered into a contract in which Stern's sperm was artificially inseminated in Whitehead in an effort to produce a child for the Sterns. The conflict arose out of Whitehead's refusal to give up the child that was born as the contract required. Although the contract was void, the court awarded custody of the child to the father with visitation rights for Whitehead. To be sure, the legal and social issues of this case are complex. However, with advances in medical technology, reproductive rights issues will create a host of problems that will present the Supreme Court with profound questions about person-oriented rights of privacy in future years.

The third conceptual context suggested by Dionisopoulos and Ducat for analyzing privacy has to do with how the right "inheres in certain relationships." Some of these relationships enjoy special constitutional-legal protections, such as the

marital relationship in *Griswold* v. *Connecticut* (381 U.S. 479, 1965). But certain others may not enjoy such protection, such as same-sex marriages (*Singer* v. *Hara*, 522 P.2d 1187, 1974) and homosexuality (*Doe* v. *Commonwealth's Attorney for City of Richmond*, 403 F. Supp. 1199, 425 U.S. 901, 1976. Also see *Bd. of Ed. of Okla. City* v. *Nat'l Gay Rights Task Force*, 729 F.2d 1270; 105 S. Ct. 1858, 1985.)[7] In *Bowers* v. *Hardwick* (1986), the Court explicitly upheld for the first time state criminal laws outlawing consensual sexual conduct between homosexuals. The Court held that such conduct is not protected by the constitutional right of privacy.

In general, these three conceptual cores, or contexts, suggested by Dionisopoulos and Ducat provide a more tangible framework by which to analyze the right of privacy. But it remains to be seen whether this or any other framework can lead us, or, of more importance, the Court, better to assess the increasing problems of privacy in a constitutional context.

In this regard, Jed Rubenfeld has suggested an interesting and undoubtedly provocative framework by which to understand the right of privacy.[8] Rather than using the concept of "privacy" to justify the restraints on government conduct, as is done in the constitutional prohibition on laws banning abortion, he suggests that we consider the right to privacy in terms of what the law brings about "affirmatively." Laws implicate privacy because of their consequences for shaping the course of a person's life. Moreover, because the conflicts over the scope of the right of privacy usually cluster around sexual expression with such matters as contraception, abortion, and sexual orientation, they touch the very essence of defining one's personhood. Thus laws that force people along certain paths such as bearing children are deemed totalitarian in nature and against our shared conception of government.

This "path-shaping" view of the law that privacy seeks to limit may have profound implications for our reading of various of the Supreme Court holdings discussed here. Under this conception, the self-determination of one's life path would argue that women should have complete control over their reproductive destiny, whether in terms of abortion or surrogate motherhood, that homosexuals should have complete control over their sex-

[7]For a perceptive analysis of the constitutional basis on which more protection should be offered certain groups, see Jose Gomez, "The Public Expression of Lesbian/Gay Personhood as Protected Speech," 1 *Law and Inequality* 121 (1983).

[8]See Rubenfeld, "The Right of Privacy," 102 *Harvard Law Review* 737 (1989).

ual expression, and that terminally ill patients should have complete control over their right to refuse treatment. One might argue that the state, in this scheme, is obligated not to interfere until requested.

Although this underpinning idea of self-deter-mination has intuitive appeal, we have seen in a variety of chapters in this book that one's behavior, no matter how self-fulfilling, influences and affects the destinies of others. In this context, it is useful to consider the limits of individualism and the rule of law.

GRISWOLD ET AL. v. CONNECTICUT
381 U.S. 479; 14 L. Ed. 510; 85 S. Ct. 1678 (1965)

JUSTICE DOUGLAS *delivered the opinion of the Court.*

Appellant Griswold is Executive Director of the Planned Parenthood League of Connecticut. Appellant Buxton is a licensed physician and a professor at the Yale Medical School, who served as Medical Director for the League at its Center in New Haven—a center open and operating from November 1 to November 10, 1961, when appellants were arrested.

They gave information, instructions, and medical advice to *married persons* as to the means of preventing conception. They examined the wife and prescribed the best contraceptive device or material for her use. Fees were usually charged, although some couples were serviced free.

The statutes whose constitutionality is involved in this appeal are §§53–32 and 54–196 of the General Statutes of Connecticut (1958 rev.). The former provides:

Any person who uses any drug, medicinal article or instrument for the purpose of preventing conception shall be fined not less than fifty dollars or imprisoned not less than sixty days nor more than one year or be both fined and imprisoned.

Section 54–196 provides:

Any person who assists, abets, counsels, causes, hires, or commands another to commit any offense may be prosecuted and punished as if he were the principal offender.

The appellants were found guilty as accessories and fined $100 each, against the claim that the accessory statute as so applied violated the Fourteenth Amendment. . . .

We think that appellants have standing to raise the constitutional rights of the married people with whom they had a professional relationship. . . . Certainly the accessory should have standing to assert that the offense which he is charged with assisting is not, or cannot constitutionally be, a crime.

* * *

Coming to the merits, we are met with a wide range of questions that implicate the Due Process Clause of the Fourteenth Amendment. Overtones of some arguments suggest that *Lochner* v. *New York*, 198 U.S. 45, 1905, should be our guide. But we decline that invitation as we did in *West Coast Hotel Co.* v. *Parrish*, 300 U.S. 379, 1937. We do not sit as a superlegislature to determine the wisdom, need, and propriety of laws that touch economic problems, business affairs, or social conditions. This law, however, operates directly on an intimate relation of husband and wife and their physician's role in one aspect of that relation.

The association of people is not mentioned in the Constitution nor in the Bill of Rights. The right to educate a child in a school of the parents' choice—whether public or private or parochial—is also not mentioned. Nor is the right to study any particular subject or any foreign language. Yet the First Amendment has been construed to include certain of those rights.

By *Pierce* v. *Society of Sisters, supra,* the right to educate one's children as one chooses is made applicable to the States by the force of the First and Fourteenth Amendments. By *Meyer* v. *Nebraska* . . . the same dignity is given the right to study the German language in a private school. In other words, the State may not, consistently with the spirit of the First Amendment, contract the spectrum of available knowledge. The right of freedom of speech and press includes not only the right to utter or to print, but the right to distribute, the right to receive, the right to read . . . and freedom of inquiry, freedom of thought, and freedom to teach . . . —indeed the freedom of the entire university community. . . . Without those peripheral rights the specific rights would be less secure. And so we reaffirm the principle of the *Pierce* and the *Meyer* cases.

In *NAACP* v. *Alabama* . . . we protected the "freedom to associate and privacy in one's associations," noting that freedom of association was a peripheral First Amendment right. Disclosure of membership lists of a constitutionally valid association, we held, was invalid "as entailing the likelihood of a substantial restraint upon the exercise by petitioner's members of their right to freedom of association." In other words, the First Amendment has a penumbra where privacy is protected from governmental intrusion. In like context, we have protected forms of "association" that are not political in the customary sense but pertain to the social, legal, and economic benefit of the members. *NAACP* v. *Button*. . . . In *Schware* v. *Board of Bar Examiners* . . . we held it not permissible to bar a lawyer from practice because he had once been a member of the Communist Party. The man's "association with that Party" was not shown to be "anything more than a political faith in a political party" . . . and was not action of a kind proving bad moral character. . . .

Those cases involved more than the "right of assembly"—a right that extends to all irrespective of their race or ideology. *De Jonge* v. *Oregon*. . . . The right of "association," like the right of belief (*Board of Education* v. *Barnette*), is more than the right to attend a meeting; it includes the right to express one's attitudes or philosophies by membership in a group or by affiliation with it or by other lawful means. Association in that context is a form of expression of opinion; and while it is not expressly included in the First Amendment its existence is necessary in making the express guarantees fully meaningful.

The foregoing cases suggest that specific guarantees in the Bill of Rights have penumbras, formed by emanations from those guarantees that help give them life and substance. . . . Various guarantees create zones of privacy. The right of association contained in the penumbra of the First Amendment is one, as we have seen. The Third Amendment in its prohibition against the quartering of soldiers "in any house" in time of peace without the consent of the owner is another facet of that privacy. The Fourth Amendment explicitly affirms the "right of the people to be secure in their persons, houses, papers, and effects, against unreasonable searches and seizures." The Fifth Amendment in its Self-Incrimination Clause en-

ables the citizen to create a zone of privacy which government may not force him to surrender to his detriment. The Ninth Amendment provides: "The enumeration in the Constitution, of certain rights, shall not be construed to deny or disparage others retained by the people."

The Fourth and Fifth Amendments were described in *Boyd* v. *United States* . . . as protection against all governmental invasions "of the sanctity of a man's home and the privacies of life." We recently referred in *Mapp* v. *Ohio* . . . to the Fourth Amendment as creating a "right to privacy, no less important than any other right carefully and particularly reserved to the people." . . .

We have had many controversies over these penumbral rights of "privacy and repose." See, e.g., *Breard* v. *Alexandria* . . . ; *Public Utilities Comm'n* v. *Pollak*. . . . These cases bear witness that the right of privacy which presses for recognition here is a legitimate one.

The present case, then, concerns a relationship lying within the zone of privacy created by several fundamental constitutional guarantees. And it concerns a law which, in forbidding the *use* of contraceptives rather than regulating their manufacture or sale, seeks to achieve its goals by means having a maximum destructive impact upon that relationship. Such a law cannot stand in light of the familiar principle, so often applied by this Court, that a "governmental purpose to control or prevent activities constitutionally subject to state regulation may not be achieved by means which sweep unnecessarily broadly and thereby invade the area of protected freedoms." *NAACP* v. *Alabama*. . . . Would we allow the police to search the sacred precincts of marital bedrooms for telltale signs of the use of contraceptives? The very idea is repulsive to the notions of privacy surrounding the marriage relationship.

We deal with a right of privacy older than the Bill of Rights—older than our political parties, older than our school system. Marriage is a coming together for better or for worse, hopefully enduring, and intimate to the degree of being sacred. It is an association that promotes a way of life, not causes; a harmony in living, not political faiths; a bilateral loyalty, not commercial or social projects. Yet it is an association for as noble a purpose as any involved in our prior decisions.

Reversed.

JUSTICE GOLDBERG, *whom* THE CHIEF JUSTICE *and* JUSTICE BRENNAN *join, concurring.*

I agree with the Court that Connecticut's birth-control law unconstitutionally intrudes upon the right of marital privacy, and I join in its opinion and judgment. Although I have not accepted the view that "due process" as used in the Fourteenth Amendment incorporates all of the first eight amendments, . . . I do agree that the concept of liberty protects those personal rights that are fundamental, and is not confined to the specific terms of the Bill of Rights. My conclusion that the concept of liberty is not so restricted and that it embraces the right of marital privacy though that right is not mentioned explicitly in the Constitution is supported both by numerous decisions of this Court, referred to in the Court's opinion, and by the language and history of the Ninth Amendment. In reaching the conclusion that the right of marital privacy is protected, as being within the protected penumbra of specific guarantees of the Bill of Rights, the Court refers to the Ninth Amendment. I add these words to emphasize the relevance of that Amendment to the Court's holding.

* * *

The Court, in a series of decisions, has held that the Fourteenth Amendment absorbs and applies to the States those specifics of the first eight amendments which express fundamental personal rights. The language and history of the Ninth Amendment reveal that the Framers of the Constitution believed that there are additional fundamental rights, protected from governmental infringement, which exist alongside those fundamental rights specifically mentioned in the first eight constitutional amendments.

The Ninth Amendment reads, "The enumeration in the Constitution, of certain rights, shall not be construed to deny or disparage others retained by the people." . . .

* * *

While this Court has had little occasion to interpret the Ninth Amendment, "[i]t cannot be presumed that any clause in the Constitution is intended to be without effect." *Marbury* v. *Madison.* In interpreting the Constitution, "real effect should be given to all the words it uses." *Myers* v. *United States,* 272 U.S. 52. The Ninth Amendment to the Constitution may be regarded by some as a recent discovery and may be forgotten by others, but since 1791 it has been a basic part of the Constitution which we are sworn to uphold. To hold that a right so basic and fundamental and so deep-rooted in our society as the right of privacy in marriage may be infringed because that right is not guaranteed in so many words by the first eight amendments to the Constitution is to ignore the Ninth Amendment and to give it no effect whatsoever. Moreover, a judicial construction that this fundamental right is not protected by the Constitution because it is not mentioned in explicit terms by one of the first eight amendments or elsewhere in the Constitution would violate the Ninth Amendment, which specifically states that "[t]he enumeration in the Constitution, of certain rights, shall not be *construed* to deny or disparage others retained by the people." (Emphasis added.)

. . . I do not take the position of my Brother Black . . . that the entire Bill of Rights is incorporated in the Fourteenth Amendment, and I do not mean to imply that the Ninth Amendment is applied against the States by the Fourteenth. Nor do I mean to state that the Ninth Amendment constitutes an independent source of rights protected from infringement by either the States or the Federal Government. Rather, the Ninth Amendment shows a belief of the Constitution's authors that fundamental rights exist that are not expressly enumerated in the first eight amendments and an intent that the list of rights included there not be deemed exhaustive. . . . The Ninth Amendment simply shows the intent of the Constitution's authors that other fundamental personal rights should not be denied such protection or disparaged in any other way simply because they are not specifically listed in the first eight constitutional amendments. I do not see how this broadens the authority of the Court; rather it serves to support what this Court has been doing in protecting fundamental rights.

Nor am I turning somersaults with history in arguing that the Ninth Amendment is relevant in a case dealing with a *State*'s infringement of a fundamental right. While the Ninth Amendment—and indeed the entire Bill of Rights—originally concerned restrictions upon *federal* power, the subsequently enacted Fourteenth Amendment prohibits the States as well from abridging fundamental personal liberties. And, the Ninth Amendment, in indicating that not all such liberties are specifically mentioned in the first eight amendments, is surely relevant in showing the existence of other fundamental personal rights, now protected from state, as well as federal, infringement. In sum, the Ninth Amendment simply lends strong support to the view that the "liberty" protected by the Fifth and Fourteenth Amendments from infringement by the Federal Government or the States is not restricted to rights specifically mentioned in the first eight amendments. . . .

* * *

Although the Constitution does not speak in so many words of the right of privacy in marriage, I cannot believe that it offers these fundamental rights no protection. The fact that no particular provision of the Constitution explicitly forbids the State from disrupting the traditional relation of the family—a relation as old and as fundamental as our entire civilization—surely does not show that the Government was meant to have the power to do so. Rather, as the Ninth Amendment expressly recognizes, there are fundamental personal rights such as this one, which are protected from abridgment by the Government though not specifically mentioned in the Constitution.

* * *

[The concurring opinions of JUSTICE HARLAN and JUSTICE WHITE are **omitted**.]

JUSTICE BLACK, *with whom* JUSTICE STEWART *joins, dissenting.*

The Court talks about a constitutional "right of privacy" as though there is some constitutional provision or provisions forbidding any law ever to be passed which might abridge the "privacy" of individuals. But there is not. There are, of course, guarantees in certain specific constitutional provisions which are designed in part to protect privacy at certain times and places with respect to certain activities. Such, for example, is the Fourth Amendment's guarantee against "unreasonable searches and seizures." But I think it belittles that Amendment to talk about it as though it protects nothing but "privacy." To treat it that way is to give it a niggardly interpretation, not the kind of liberal reading I think any Bill of Rights provision should be given. The average man would very likely not have his feelings soothed any more by having his property seized openly than by having it seized privately and by stealth. He simply wants his property left alone. And a person can be just as much, if not more, irritated, annoyed and injured by an unceremonious public arrest by a policeman as he is by a seizure in the privacy of his office or home.

One of the most effective ways of diluting or expanding a constitutionally guaranteed right is to substitute for the crucial word or words of a constitutional guarantee another word or words, more or less flexible and more or less restrictive in meaning. This fact is well illustrated by the use of the term "right of privacy" as a comprehensive substitute for the Fourth Amendment's guarantee against "unreasonable searches and seizures." "Privacy" is a broad, abstract and ambiguous concept which can easily be shrunken in meaning but which can also, on the other hand, easily be interpreted as a constitutional ban against many things other than searches and seizures. I have expressed the view many times that First Amendment freedoms, for example, have suffered from a failure of the courts to stick to the simple language of the First Amendment in construing it, instead of invoking multitudes of words substituted for those the Framers used. . . . For these reasons I get nowhere in this case by talk about a constitutional "right of privacy" as an emanation from one or more constitutional provisions. I like my privacy as well as the next one, but I am nevertheless compelled to admit that government has a right to invade it unless prohibited by some specific constitutional provision. For these reasons I cannot agree with the Court's judgment and the reasons it gives for holding this Connecticut law unconstitutional.

* * *

My Brother Goldberg has adopted the recent discovery that the Ninth Amendment as well as the Due Process Clause can be used by this Court as authority to strike down all state legislation which this Court thinks violates "fundamental principles of liberty and justice," or is contrary to the "traditions and [collective] conscience of our people." He also states, without proof satisfactory to me, that in making decisions on this basis judges will not consider "their personal and private notions." One may ask how they can avoid considering them. Our Court certainly has no machinery with which to take a Gallup Poll. And the scientific miracles of this age have not yet produced a gadget which the Court can use to determine what traditions are rooted in the "[collective] conscience of our people." Moreover, one would certainly have to look far beyond the language of the Ninth Amendment to find that the Framers vested in this Court any such awesome veto powers over lawmaking, either by the States or by the Congress. Nor does anything in the history of the Amendment offer any support for such a shocking doctrine. The whole history of the adoption of the Constitution and Bill of Rights points the other way, and the very material quoted by my Brother Goldberg shows that the Ninth Amendment was intended to protect against the idea that "by enumerating particular exceptions to the grant of power" to the Federal Government, "those rights which were not singled out, were intended to be assigned into the hands of the General Government [the United States], and were consequently insecure." That Amendment was passed, not to broaden the powers of this Court or any other department of "the General Government," but, as every student of history knows, to assure the people that the Constitution in all its provisions was intended to limit the Federal Government to the powers granted expressly or by necessary implication. If any broad, unlimited power to hold laws unconstitutional because they offend what this Court conceives to be the "[collective] conscience of our people" is vested in this Court by the Ninth Amendment, the Fourteenth Amendment, or any other provision of the Constitution, it was not given by the Framers, but rather has been bestowed on the Court by the Court. This fact is perhaps responsible for the peculiar phenomenon that for a period of a century and a half no serious suggestion was ever made that the Ninth Amendment, enacted to protect state powers against federal invasion, could be used as a weapon of federal power to prevent state legislatures from passing laws they consider appropriate to govern local affairs. Use of any such broad, unbounded judicial authority would make of this Court's members a day-to-day constitutional convention.

I repeat so as not to be misunderstood that this Court does have power, which it should exercise, to hold laws unconstitutional where they are forbidden by the Federal Constitution. My point is that there is no provision of the Constitution which either expressly or impliedly vests power in this Court to sit as a supervisory agency over acts of duly constituted legislative bodies and set aside their laws because of the Court's belief that the legislative policies adopted are unreasonable, unwise, arbitrary, capricious or irrational. The adoption of such a loose, flexible, uncontrolled standard for holding laws unconstitutional, if ever it is finally achieved, will amount to a great unconstitutional shift of power to the courts which I believe and am constrained to say will be bad for the courts and worse for the country. Subjecting federal and state laws to such an unrestrained and unrestrainable judicial control as to the wisdom of legislative enactments would, I fear, jeopardize the separation of governmental powers that the Framers set up and at the same time threaten to take away much of the power of States to govern themselves which the Constitution plainly intended them to have.

I realize that many good and able men have eloquently spoken and written, sometimes in rhapsodical strains, about the duty of this Court to keep the Constitution in tune with the times. The idea is that the Constitution must be changed from time to time and that this Court is charged with a duty to make those changes. For myself, I must with all deference reject that philosophy. The Constitution makers knew the need for change and provided for it. Amendments suggested by the people's elected representatives can be submitted to the people or their elected agents for ratification. That method of change was good for our Fathers, and being somewhat old-fashioned I must add it is good enough for me. And so, I cannot rely on the Due Process Clause or the Ninth Amendment or any mysterious and uncertain natural law concept as a reason for striking down this state law. The Due Process Clause with an "arbitrary and capricious" or "shocking to the conscience" formula was liberally used by this Court to strike down economic legislation in the early decades of this century, threatening, many people thought, the tranquility and stability of the Nation. See, e.g., *Lochner v. New York*. . . . That formula, based on subjective considerations of "natural justice," is no less dangerous when used to enforce this Court's views about personal rights than those about economic rights. I had thought that we had laid that formula, as a means for striking down state legislation, to rest once and for all in cases like *West Coast Hotel Co.* v. *Parrish*. . . .

* * *

The late Judge Learned Hand, after emphasizing his view that judges should not use the due process formula suggested in the concurring opinions today or any other formula like it to invalidate legislation offensive to their "personal preferences," made the statement, with which I fully agree, that:

> For myself it would be most irksome to be ruled by a bevy of Platonic Guardians, even if I knew how to choose them, which I assuredly do not.

So far as I am concerned, Connecticut's law as applied here is not forbidden by any provision of the Federal Constitution as that Constitution was written, and I would therefore affirm.

[The dissenting opinion of JUSTICE STEWART is omitted.]

JUSTICE BLACKMUN *delivered the opinion of the Court.*

This Texas federal appeal and its Georgia companion, *Doe* v. *Bolton*, present constitutional challenges to state criminal abortion legislation. The Texas statutes under attack here are typical of those that have been in effect in many States for approximately a century. The Georgia statutes, in contrast, have a modern cast and are a legislative product that, to an extent at least, obviously reflects the influences of recent attitudinal change, of advancing medical knowledge and techniques, and of new thinking about an old issue. . . .

The Texas statutes that concern us . . . make it a crime to "procure an abortion," as therein defined, or to attempt one, except with respect to "an abortion procured or attempted by medical advice for the purpose of saving the life of the mother." Similar statutes are in existence in a majority of the States. . . .

[Appellant] Roe alleged that she was unmarried and pregnant; that she wished to terminate her pregnancy by an abortion "performed by a competent, licensed physician, under safe, clinical conditions"; that she was unable to get a "legal" abortion in Texas because her life did not appear to be threatened by the continuation of her pregnancy; and that she could not afford to travel to another jurisdiction in order to secure a legal abortion under safe conditions. She claimed that the Texas statutes were unconstitutionally vague and that they abridged her right of personal privacy, protected by the First, Fourth, Fifth, Ninth, and Fourteenth Amendments. . . .

. . . On the merits, the District Court held that the "fundamental right of single women and married persons to choose whether to have children is protected by the Ninth Amendment, through the Fourteenth Amendment," and that the Texas criminal abortion statutes were void on their face because they were both unconstitutionally vague and constituted an overbroad infringement of the plaintiffs' Ninth Amendment rights. The court then held that abstention was warranted with respect to the requests for an injunction. It therefore dismissed the Doe complaint, declared the abortion statutes void, and dismissed the application for injunctive relief.

The plaintiffs . . . have appealed to this Court from that part of the District Court's judgment denying the injunction. . . .

The principal thrust of appellant's attack on the Texas statutes is that they improperly invade a right, said to be possessed by the pregnant woman, to choose to terminate her pregnancy. Appellant would discover this right in the concept of personal "liberty" embodied in the Fourteenth Amendment's Due Process Clause; or in personal, marital, familial, and sexual privacy said to be protected by the Bill of Rights or its penumbras, see *Griswold* v. *Connecticut*, . . . or among those rights reserved to the people by the Ninth Amendment. . . . Before addressing this claim, we feel it desirable briefly to survey, in several aspects, the history of abortion, for such insight as that history may afford us, and then to examine the state purposes and interests behind the criminal abortion laws.

[The Court here reviews the history of abortion in terms of Ancient Attitudes, The Hippocratic Oath, The Common Law, The English Statutory Law, and The American Law. The Court also summarizes the positions of the American Medical Association, the American Public Health Association, and the American Bar Association.]

It is thus apparent that at common law, at the time of adoption of our Constitution, and throughout the major portion of the 19th century, abortion was viewed with less disfavor than under most American statutes currently in effect. Phrasing it another way, a woman enjoyed a substantially broader right to terminate a pregnancy than she does in most States today. At least with respect to the early stage of pregnancy, and very possibly without such a limitation, the opportunity to make this choice was present in this country well into the 19th century. Even later, the law continued for some time to treat less punitively an abortion procured in early pregnancy. . . .

Three reasons have been advanced to explain historically the enactment of criminal abortion laws in the 19th century and to justify their continued existence.

It has been argued occasionally that these laws were the product of a Victorian social concern to discourage illicit sexual conduct. Texas, however, does not advance this justification in the present case, and it appears that no court or commentator has taken the argument seriously. The appellants and *amici* contend, moreover, that this is not a proper state purpose at all and suggest that, if it were, the Texas statutes are overbroad in protecting it since the law fails to distinguish between married and unwed mothers.

A second reason is concerned with abortion as a medical procedure. When most criminal abortion laws were first enacted, the procedure was a hazardous one for the woman. . . . Thus it has been argued that a State's real concern in enacting a criminal abortion law was to protect the pregnant woman, that is, to restrain her from submitting to a procedure that placed her life in serious jeopardy.

Modern medical techniques have altered this situation. Appellants and various *amici* refer to medical data, indicating that abortion in early pregnancy, that is, prior to the end of first trimester, although not without its risk, is now relatively safe. Mortality rates for women undergoing early abortions, where the procedure is legal, appear to be as low as or lower than the rates for normal childbirth. Consequently, any interest of the State in protecting the woman from an inherently hazardous procedure, except when it would be equally dangerous for her to forgo it, has largely disappeared. Of course, important state interests in the area of health and medical standards do remain. The State has a legitimate interest in seeing to it that abortion, like any other medical procedure, is performed under circumstances that insure maximum safety for the patient. . . . The prevalence of high mortality rates at illegal "abortion mills" strengthens, rather than weakens, the State's interest in regulating the conditions under which abortions are performed. Moreover, the risk to the woman increases as her pregnancy continues. . . .

The third reason is the State's interest—some phrase it in terms of duty—in protecting prenatal life. Some of the argument for this justification rests on the theory that a new human life is present from the moment of conception. The State's interest and general obligation to protect life then extends, it is argued, to prenatal life. Only when the life of the pregnant mother herself is at stake, balanced against the life she carries within her, should the interest of the embryo or fetus not prevail. Logically, of course, a legitimate state interest in this area need not stand or fall on acceptance of the belief that life begins at conception or at some point prior to live birth. In assessing the State's interest, recognition may be given to the less rigid claim that as long as at least *potential* life is involved, the State may assert interests beyond the protection of the pregnant woman alone. . . .

It is with these interests and the weight to be attached to them, that this case is concerned.

The Constitution does not explicitly mention any rights of privacy. In a line of decisions, however, . . . the Court has recognized that a right of personal privacy, or a guarantee of certain areas or zones of privacy, does exist under the Constitution. In varying contexts the Court or individual justices have indeed found at least the roots of that right in the First Amendment, *Stanley* v. *Georgia* (1969); in the Fourth and Fifth Amendments, *Terry* v. *Ohio* (1968), *Katz* v. *United States* (1967); . . . in the penumbras of the Bill of Rights, *Griswold* v. *Connecticut* (1965); in the Ninth Amendment, or in the concept of liberty guaranteed by the first section of the Fourteenth Amendment, see *Meyer* v. *Nebraska* (1923). These decisions make it clear that only personal rights that can be deemed "fundamental" or "implicit in the concept of ordered liberty," *Palko* v. *Connecticut* (1937), are included in this guarantee of personal privacy. They also make it clear that the right has some extension to activities relating to marriage, *Loving* v. *Virginia*, procreation, *Skinner* v. *Oklahoma*, contraception, *Eisenstadt* v. *Baird*, family relationships, *Prince* v. *Massachusetts*, and child rearing and education, *Pierce* v. *Society of Sisters*, *Meyer* v. *Nebraska*.

This right of privacy, whether it be founded in the Fourteenth Amendment's concept of personal liberty and restrictions upon state action, as we feel it is, or, as the District Court determined, in the Ninth Amendment's reservation of rights to the people, is broad enough to encompass a woman's decision whether or not to terminate her pregnancy. The detriment that the State would impose upon the pregnant woman by denying this choice altogether is apparent. Specific and direct harm medically diagnosable even in early pregnancy may be involved. Maternity, or additional offspring, may force upon the woman a distressful life and future. Psychological harm may be imminent. Mental and physical health may be taxed by child care. There is also the distress, for all concerned, associated with the unwanted child, and there is the problem of bringing a child into a family already unable, psychologically and otherwise, to care for it. In other cases, as in this one, the additional difficulties and continuing stigma of unwed motherhood may be involved. All these are factors the woman and her responsible physician necessarily will consider in consultation.

On the basis of elements such as these, appellants and some *amici* argue that the woman's right is absolute and that she is entitled to terminate her pregnancy at whatever time, in whatever way, and for whatever reason she alone chooses. With this we do not agree. Appellants' arguments that Texas either has no valid interest at all in regulating the abortion decision, or no interest strong enough to support any limitation upon the woman's sole determination, is unpersuasive. The Court's decisions recognizing a right of privacy also acknowledge that some state regulation in areas protected by that right is appropriate. As noted above, a state may properly assert important interests in safeguarding health, in maintaining medical standards, and in protecting potential life. At some point in pregnancy, these respective interests become sufficiently compelling to sustain regulation of the factors that govern the abortion decision. The privacy right involved, therefore, cannot be said to be absolute. In fact, it is not clear to us that the claim asserted by some *amici* that one has an unlimited right to do with one's body as one pleases bears a close relationship to the right of privacy previously articulated in the Court's decisions. The Court has refused to recognize an unlimited right of this kind in the past. *Jacobson* v. *Massachusetts* (1905) (vaccination); *Buck* v. *Bell* (1927) (sterilization).

We therefore conclude that the right of personal privacy includes the abortion decision, but that this right is not unqualified and must be considered against important state interests in regulation. . . .

Where certain "fundamental rights" are involved, the Court has held that regulation limiting these rights may be justified only by a "compelling state interest," . . . and that legislative enactments must be narrowly drawn to express only the legitimate state interests at stake. . . .

The District Court held that the appellee failed to meet his burden of demonstrating that the Texas statute's infringement upon Roe's rights was necessary to support a compelling state interest, and that, although the defendant presented "several compelling justifications for state presence in the area of abortions," the statutes outstripped these justifications and swept "far beyond any areas of compelling state interest." Appellant and appellee both contest that holding. Appellant, as has been indicated, claims an absolute right that bars any state imposition of criminal penalties in the area. Appellee argues that the State's determination to recognize and protect prenatal life from and after conception constitutes a compelling state interest. As noted above, we do not agree fully with either formulation.

The appellee and certain *amici* argue that the fetus is a "person" within the language and meaning of the Fourteenth Amendment. In support of this they outline at length and in detail the well-known facts of fetal development. If this suggestion of personhood is established, the appellant's case, of course, collapses, for the fetus's right to life is then guaranteed specifically by the Amendment. The appellant conceded as much on reargument. On the other hand, the appellee conceded on reargument that no case could be cited that holds that a fetus is a person within the meaning of the Fourteenth Amendment.

The Constitution does not define "person" in so many words. Section 1 of the Fourteenth Amendment contains three references to "person." The first, in defining "citizens," speaks of "persons born or naturalized in the United States." The word also appears both in the Due Process Clause and in the Equal Protection Clause. "Person" is used in other places in the Constitution. . . . But in nearly all these instances, the use of the word is such that it has application only postnatally. None indicates, with any assurance, that it has any possible prenatal application.

All this, together with our observation, *supra*, that throughout the major portion of the 19th century prevailing legal abortion practices were far freer than they are today, persuades us that the word "person," as used in the Fourteenth Amendment, does not include the unborn. . . .

This conclusion, however, does not of itself fully answer the contentions raised by Texas, and we pass on to other considerations.

The pregnant woman cannot be isolated in her privacy. She carries an embryo and, later, a fetus, if one accepts the medical definitions of the developing young in the human uterus. . . . The situation therefore is inherently different from marital intimacy, or bedroom possession of obscene material, or marriage, or procreation, or education, with which *Eisenstadt, Griswold, Stanley, Loving, Skinner, Pierce*, and *Meyer* were respectively concerned. As we have intimated above, it is reasonable and appropriate for a State to decide that at some point in time another interest, that of health of the mother or that of potential human life, becomes significantly involved. The woman's privacy is no longer sole, and any right of privacy she possesses must be measured accordingly.

Texas urges that, apart from the Fourteenth Amendment, life begins at conception and is present throughout pregnancy, and that therefore the State has a compelling interest in protecting that life from and after conception. We need not resolve the difficult question of when life begins.

When those trained in the respective disciplines of medicine, philosophy, and theology are unable to arrive at any consensus, the judiciary, at this point in the development of man's knowledge, is not in a position to speculate as to the answer. . . .

In areas other than criminal abortion the law has been reluctant to endorse any theory that life, as we recognize it, begins before live birth or to accord legal rights to the unborn except in narrowly defined situations and except when the rights are contingent upon live birth. . . . [T]he unborn have never been recognized in the law as persons in the whole sense.

In view of all this, we do not agree that, by adopting one theory of life, Texas may override the rights of the pregnant woman that are at stake. We repeat, however, that the State does have an important and legitimate interest in preserving and protecting the health of the pregnant woman, whether she be a resident of the State or a nonresident who seeks medical consultation and treatment there, and that it has still *another* important and legitimate interest in protecting the potentiality of human life. These interests are separate and distinct. Each grows in substantiality as the woman approaches term and, at a point during pregnancy, each becomes "compelling."

With respect to the State's important and legitimate interest in the health of the mother, the "compelling" point, in the light of present medical knowledge, is at approximately the end of the first trimester. This is so because of the now established medical fact . . . that until the end of the first trimester mortality in abortion is less than mortality in normal childbirth. It follows that, from and after this point, a State may regulate the abortion procedure to the extent that the regulation reasonably relates to the preservation and protection of maternal health. Examples of permissible state regulation in this area are requirements as to the qualifications of the person who is to perform the abortion; as to the licensure of that person; as to the facility in which the procedure is to be performed, that is, whether it must be a hospital or may be a clinic or some other place of less-than-hospital status; as to the licensing of the facility; and the like.

This means, on the other hand, that, for the period of pregnancy prior to this "compelling" point, the attending physician, in consultation with his patient, is free to determine, without regulation by the State, that in his medical judgment the patient's pregnancy should be terminated. If that decision is reached, the judgment may be effectuated by an abortion free of interference by the State.

With respect to the State's important and legitimate interest in potential life, the "compelling" point is at viability. This is so because the fetus then presumably has the capability of meaningful life outside the mother's womb. State regulation protective of fetal life after viability thus has both logical and biological justifications. If the State is interested in protecting fetal life after viability, it may go so far as to proscribe abortion during that period except when it is necessary to preserve the life or health of the mother.

Measured against these standards, the Texas Penal Code, in restricting legal abortions to those "procured or attempted by medical advice for the purpose of saving the life of the mother," sweeps too broadly. The statute makes no distinction between abortions performed later, and it limits to a single reason, "saving" the mother's life, the legal justification for the procedure. The statute, therefore, cannot survive the constitutional attack made upon it here. . . .

*Affirmed in part
and reversed in part.*

[The concurring opinion of JUSTICE STEWART is omitted here.]

JUSTICE REHNQUIST, *dissenting.*

The Court's opinion brings to the decision of this troubling question both extensive historical fact and a wealth of legal scholarship. While its opinion thus commands my respect, I find myself nonetheless in fundamental disagreement with those parts of it which invalidate the Texas statute in question, and therefore dissent. . . .

I have difficulty in concluding, as the Court does, that the right of "privacy" is involved in this case. Texas by the statute here challenged bars the performance of a medical abortion by a licensed physician on a plaintiff such as Roe. A transaction resulting in an operation such as this is not "private" in the ordinary usage of that word. Nor is the "privacy" which the Court finds here even a distant relative of the freedom from searches and seizures protected by the Fourth Amendment to the Constitution which the Court has referred to as embodying a right of privacy.

If the Court means by the term "privacy" no more than that the claim of a person to be free from unwanted state regulation of consensual transactions may be a form of "liberty" protected by the Fourteenth Amendment, there is no doubt that similar claims have been upheld in our earlier decisions on the basis of that liberty. I agree with the statement of Justice Stewart in his concurring opinion that the "liberty," against deprivation of which without due process the Fourteenth Amendment protects, embraces more than the rights found in the Bill of Rights. But that liberty is not guaranteed absolutely against deprivation, but only against deprivation without due process of law. The test traditionally applied in the area of social and economic legislation is whether or not a law such as that challenged has a rational relation to a valid state objective. The Due Process Clause of the Fourteenth Amendment undoubtedly does place a limit on legislative power to enact laws such as this, albeit a broad one. If the Texas statute were to prohibit an abortion even where the mother's life is in jeopardy, I have little doubt that such a statute would lack a rational relation to a valid state objective under the test stated *supra*. But the Court's sweeping invalidation of any restrictions on abortion during the first trimester is impossible to justify under that standard, and the conscious weighing of competing factors which the Court's opinion apparently substitutes for the established test is far more appropriate to a legislative judgment than to a judicial one.

The Court eschews the history of the Fourteenth Amendment in its reliance on the "compelling state interest" test. But the Court adds a new wrinkle to this test by transposing it from the legal considerations associated with the Equal Protection Clause of the Fourteenth Amendment to this case arising under the Due Process Clause of the Fourteenth Amendment. Unless I misapprehend the consequences of this transplanting of the "compelling state interest test," the Court's opinion will accomplish the seemingly impossible feat of leaving this area of the law more confused than it found it.

While the Court's opinion quotes from the dissent of Justice Holmes in *Lockner* v. *New York* (1905), the result it reaches is more closely attuned to the majority opinion of Justice Peckham in that case. As in *Lockner* and similar cases applying substantive due process standards to economic and social welfare legislation, the adoption of the compelling state interest standard will inevitably require this Court to examine the legislative policies and pass on the wisdom of these policies in the very process of deciding whether a particular state interest put forward may or may not be "compelling." The decision here to break the term of pregnancy into three distinct terms and to outline the permissible restrictions the State may impose in each one, for example, partakes more of judicial legislation than it does of a determination of the intent of the drafters of the Fourteenth Amendment.

The fact that a majority of the States, reflecting after all the majority sentiment in those States, have had restrictions on abortions for at least a century seems to me as strong an indication there is that the asserted right to an abortion is not "so rooted in the traditions and conscience of our people as to be ranked as fundamental." Even today, when society's views on abortion are changing, the very existence of the debate is evidence that the "right" to an abortion is not so universally accepted as the appellants would have us believe. . . .

WEBSTER v. REPRODUCTIVE HEALTH SERVICES ET AL.
492 U.S. 490; 106 L. Ed. 2d 410; 109 S. Ct. 3040 (1989)

CHIEF JUSTICE REHNQUIST *announced the judgment of the Court and delivered the opinion of the Court with respect to Parts I, II-A, II-B, and II-C, and an opinion with respect to Parts II-D and III, in which* JUSTICE WHITE *and* JUSTICE KENNEDY *join.*

This appeal concerns the constitutionality of a Missouri statute regulating the performance of abortions. The United States Court of Appeals for the Eighth Circuit struck down several provisions of the statute on the ground that they violated this Court's decision in *Roe* v. *Wade*, 410 U.S. 113 (1973), and cases following it. We noted probable jurisdiction, 488 U.S. ___ (1989), and now reverse.

I

In June 1986, the Governor of Missouri signed into law Missouri Senate Committee Substitute for House Bill No. 1596 (hereinafter Act or statute), which amended existing state law concerning unborn children and abortions.

The Act consisted of 20 provisions, 5 of which are now before the Court. The first provision, or preamble, contains "findings" by the state legislature that "[t]he life of each human being begins at conception," and that "unborn children have protectable interests in life, health, and well-being." The Act further requires that all Missouri laws be interpreted to provide unborn children with the same rights enjoyed by other persons, subject to the Federal Constitution and this Court's precedents. Among its other provisions, the Act requires that, prior to performing an abortion on any woman whom a physician has reason to believe is 20 or more weeks pregnant, the physician ascertain whether the fetus is viable by performing "such medical examinations and tests as are necessary to make a finding of the gestational age, weight, and lung maturity of the unborn child." The Act also prohibits the use of public employees and facilities to perform or assist abortions not necessary to save the mother's life, and it prohibits the use of public funds, employees, or facilities for the purpose of "encouraging or counseling" a woman to have an abortion not necessary to save her life.

In July 1986, five health professionals employed by the State and two nonprofit corporations brought this class action in the United States District Court for the Western District of Missouri to challenge the constitutionality of the Missouri statute. Plaintiffs, appellees in this Court, sought declaratory and injunctive relief on the ground that certain statutory provisions violated the First, Fourth, Ninth, and Fourteenth Amendments to the Federal Constitution. They asserted violations of various rights, including the "privacy rights of pregnant women seeking abortions"; the "woman's right to an abortion"; the "righ[t] to practice medicine"; the pregnant woman's "right to life due to inherent risks involved in childbirth"; and the woman's right to "receive . . . adequate medical advice and treatment" concerning abortions. . . .

Several weeks after the complaint was filed, the District Court temporarily restrained enforcement of several provisions of the Act. Following a 3-day trial in December 1986, the District Court declared seven provisions of the Act unconstitutional and enjoined their enforcement. . . . These provisions included the preamble, . . . the "informed consent" provision, which required physicians to inform the pregnant woman of certain facts before performing an abortion; . . . the requirement that post-16-week abortions be performed only in hospitals; . . . the mandated tests to determine viability; and the prohibition on the use of public funds, employees, and facilities to perform or assist non-therapeutic abortions and the restrictions on the use of public funds, employees, and facilities to encourage or counsel women to have such abortions.

The Court of Appeals for the Eighth Circuit affirmed, with one exception not relevant to this appeal. The Court of Appeals determined that Missouri's declaration that life begins at conception was "simply an impermissible state adoption of a theory of when life begins to justify its abortion regulations." [I]t further held that the requirement that physicians perform viability tests was an unconstitutional legislative intrusion on a matter of medical skill and judgment. The Court of Appeals invalidated Missouri's prohibition on the use of public facilities and employees to perform or assist abortions not necessary to save the mother's life. It distinguished our decisions in *Harris* v. *McRae* (1980), and *Maher* v. *Roe* (1977), on the ground that "[t]here is a fundamental difference between providing direct funding to effect the abortion decision and allowing staff physicians to perform abortions at an existing publicly owned hospital." The Court of Appeals struck down the provision prohibiting the use of public funds for "encouraging or counseling" women to have non-therapeutic abortions, for the reason that this provision was both overly vague and inconsistent with the right to an abortion enunciated in *Roe* v. *Wade.* The court also invalidated the hospitalization requirement for 16-week abortions, and the prohibition on the use of public employees and facilities for abortion counseling, but the State has not appealed those parts of the judgment below.

II

Decision of this case requires us to address four sections of the Missouri Act: (a) the preamble; (b) the prohibition on the use of public facilities or employees to perform abortions; (c) the prohibition on public funding of abortion counseling; and (d) the requirement that physicians conduct viability tests prior to performing abortions. We address these *seriatim.*

A

The Act's preamble, as noted, sets forth "findings" by the Missouri legislature that "[t]he life of each human being begins at conception," and that "[u]nborn children have protectable interests in life, health, and well-being." The Act then mandates that state laws be interpreted to provide unborn children with "all the rights, privileges, and immunities available to other persons, citizens, and residents of this state," subject to the Constitution and this Court's precedents. In invalidating the preamble, the Court of Appeals relied on this Court's dictum that "a State may not adopt one theory of when life begins to justify its regulation of abortions." It rejected Missouri's claim that the preamble was "abortion-neutral," and "merely determine[d] when life begins in a non-abortion context, a traditional state prerogative." The court thought that "[t]he only plausible inference" from the fact that "every remaining section of the bill save one regulates the performance of abortions" was that "the state intended its abortion regulations to be understood against the backdrop of its theory of life."

The State contends that the preamble itself is prefatory and imposes no substantive restrictions on abortions, and that appellees therefore do not have standing to challenge it. Appellees, on the other hand, insist that the preamble is an operative part of the Act intended to guide the interpretation of other provisions of the Act. They maintain, for example, that the preamble's definition of life may prevent physicians in public hospitals from dispensing certain forms of contraceptives, such as the intrauterine device.

In our view, the Court of Appeals misconceived the meaning of the *Akron* dictum, which was only that a State could not "justify" an abortion regulation otherwise invalid under *Roe* v. *Wade* on the ground that it embodied the State's view about when life begins. Certainly the preamble does not by its terms regulate abortion or any other aspect of appellees' medical practice. The Court has emphasized that *Roe* v. *Wade* "implies no limitation on the authority of a State to make a value judgment favoring childbirth over abortion." The preamble can be read simply to express that sort of value judgment.

We think the extent to which the preamble's language might be used to interpret other state statutes or regulations is something that only the courts of Missouri can definitively decide. . . . It will be time enough for federal courts to address the meaning of the preamble should it be applied to restrict the activities of appellees in some concrete way. Until then, this Court "is not empowered to decide . . . abstract propositions, or to declare, for the government of future cases, principles or rules of law which cannot affect the result as to the thing in issue in the case before it." . . . We therefore need not pass on the constitutionality of the Act's preamble.

B

Section 188.210 provides that "[i]t shall be unlawful for any public employee within the scope of his employment to perform or assist an abortion, not necessary to save the life of the mother," while Sec. 188.215 makes it "unlawful for any public facility to be used for the purpose of performing or assisting an abortion not necessary to save the life of the mother." The Court of Appeals held that these provisions contravened this Court's abortion decisions. We take the contrary view.

As we said earlier this Term in *DaShaney* v. *Winnebago County, Dept. of Social Services*, 489 U.S. 189, 196 (1989), "our cases have recognized that the Due Process Clauses generally confer no affirmative right to governmental aid, even where such aid may be necessary to secure life, liberty, or property interests of which the government itself may not deprive the individual." In *Maher* v. *Roe*, the Court upheld a Connecticut welfare regulation under which Medicaid recipients received payments for medical services related to childbirth, but not for non-therapeutic abortions. The Court rejected the claim that this unequal subsidization of childbirth and abortion was impermissible under *Roe* v. *Wade*. As the Court put it:

> The Connecticut regulation before us is different in kind from the laws invalidated in our previous abortion decisions. The Connecticut regulation places no obstacles—absolute or otherwise—in the pregnant woman's path to an abortion. An indigent woman who desires an abortion suffers no disadvantage as a consequence of Connecticut's decision to fund childbirth; she continues as before to be dependent on private sources for the service she desires. The State may have made childbirth a more attractive alternative, thereby influencing the woman's decision, but it has imposed no restriction on access to abortions that was not already there. The indigence that may make it difficult—and in some cases, perhaps, impossible—for some women to have abortions is neither created nor in any way affected by the Connecticut regulation.

Relying on *Maher*, the Court in *Poelker* v. *Doe* (1977) held that the city of St. Louis committed "no constitutional violation . . . in electing, as a policy choice, to provide publicly financed hospital services for childbirth without providing corresponding services for non-therapeutic abortions."

More recently, in *Harris* v. *McRae* (1980) the Court upheld "the most restrictive version of the Hyde Amendment."

. . . The Court of Appeals distinguished these cases on the ground that "[t]o prevent access to a public facility does more than demonstrate a political choice in favor of childbirth; it clearly narrows and in some cases forecloses the availability of abortion to women." The court reasoned that the ban on the use of public facilities "could prevent a woman's chosen doctor from performing an abortion because of his unprivileged status at other hospitals or because a private hospital adopted a similar anti-abortion stance." It also thought that "[s]uch a rule could increase the cost of obtaining an abortion and delay the timing of it as well."

We think that this analysis is much like that which we rejected in *Maher, Poelker*, and *McRae*. As in those cases, the State's decision here to use public facilities and staff to encourage childbirth over abortion "places no governmental obstacle in the path of a woman who chooses to terminate her pregnancy." Just as Congress' refusal to fund abortions in *McRae* left "an indigent woman with at least the same range of choice in deciding whether to obtain a medically necessary abortion as she would have had if Congress had chosen to subsidize no health care costs at all," Missouri's refusal to allow public employees to perform abortions in public hospitals leaves a pregnant woman with the same choices as if the State had chosen not to operate any public hospitals at all. The challenged provisions only restrict a woman's ability to obtain an abortion to the extent that she chooses to use a physician affiliated with a public hospital. This circumstance is more easily remedied, and thus considerably less burdensome, than indigence, which "may make it difficult—and in some cases, perhaps, impossible—for some women to have abortions" without public funding. Having held that the State's refusal to fund abortions does not violate *Roe* v. *Wade*, it strains logic to reach a contrary result for the use of public facilities and employees. If the State may "make a value judgment favoring childbirth over abortion and . . . implement that judgment by the allocation of public funds," surely it may do so through the allocation of other public resources, such as hospitals and medical staff.

The Court of Appeals sought to distinguish our cases on the additional ground that "[t]he evidence here showed that all of the public facility's costs in providing abortion services are recouped when the patient pays." Absent any expenditure of public funds, the court thought that Missouri was "expressing" more than "its preference for childbirth over abortions," but rather was creating an "obstacle to exercise of the right to choose an abortion [that could not] stand absent a compelling state interest." We disagree.

"Constitutional concerns are greatest . . . when the State attempts to impose its will by the force of law; the State's power to encourage actions deemed to be in the public interest is necessarily far broader." Nothing in the Constitution requires States to enter or remain in the business of performing abortions. Nor . . . do private physicians and their patients have some kind of constitutional right of access to public facilities for the performance of abortions. . . . Indeed, if the State does recoup all of its costs in performing abortions, and no state subsidy, direct or indirect, is available, it is difficult to see how any procreational choice is burdened by the State's ban on the use of its facilities or employees for performing abortions.

Maher, Poelker, and *McRae* all support the view that the State need not commit any resources to facilitating abortions, even if it can turn a profit by doing so. In *Poelker*, the suit was filed by an indigent who could not afford to pay for an abortion, but the ban on the performance of non-therapeutic abortions in city-owned hospitals applied whether or not the pregnant woman could pay. (BRENNAN, J., dissenting). The Court emphasized that the Mayor's decision to prohibit abortions in city hospitals was "subject to public debate and approval or disapproval at the polls," and that "the Constitution does not forbid a State or city, pursuant to democratic processes, from expressing a preference for normal childbirth as St. Louis has done." Thus we uphold the Act's restrictions on the use of public employees and facilities for the performance or assistance of non-therapeutic abortions.

C

The Missouri Act contains three provisions relating to "encouraging or counseling a woman to have an abortion not necessary to save her life." Section 188.205 states that no public funds can be used for this purpose; Sec. 188.210 states that public employees cannot, within the scope of their employment, engage in such speech; and Sec. 188.215 forbids such speech in public facilities. The Court of Appeals did not consider Sec. 188.205 separately from Sec. 188.210 and Sec. 188.215. It held that all three of these provisions were unconstitutionally vague, and that "the ban on using public funds, employees, and facilities to encourage or counsel a women to have an abortion is an unacceptable infringement of the woman's Fourteenth Amendment right to choose an abortion after receiving the medical information necessary to exercise the right knowingly and intelligently."

Missouri has chosen only to appeal the Court of Appeals' invalidation of the public funding provision, 188.205. See Juris. Statement I–II. A threshold question is whether this provision reaches primary conduct, or whether it is simply an instruction to the State's fiscal officers not to allocate funds for abortion counseling. We accept, for purposes of decision, the State's claim that 188.205 "is not directed at the conduct of any physician or health care provider, private or public," but "is directed solely at those persons responsible for expending public funds."

Appellees contend that they are not "adversely" affected under the State's interpretation of Sec. 188.205, and therefore that there is no longer a case or controversy before us on this question. Plaintiffs are masters of their complaints and remain so at the appellate stage of a litigation. A majority of the Court agrees with appellees that the controversy over Sec. 188.205 is now moot, because appellees' argument amounts to a decision to no longer seek a declaratory judgment that Sec. 188.205 is unconstitutional and accompanying declarative relief. . . .

D

[*This section joined only by* JUSTICES WHITE *and* KENNEDY *and thus is a plurality, not majority opinion.*]

Section 188.029 of the Missouri Act provides:

Before a physician performs an abortion on a woman he has reason to believe is carrying an unborn child of twenty or more weeks gestational age, the physician shall first determine if the unborn child is viable by using and exercising that degree of care, skill, and proficiency commonly exercised by the ordinarily skillful, careful, and prudent physician engaged in similar practice under the same or similar conditions. In making this determination of viability, the physician shall perform or cause to be performed such medical examinations and tests as are necessary to make a finding of the gestational age, weight, and lung maturity of the unborn child and shall enter such findings and determination of viability in the medical record of the mother.

As with the preamble, the parties disagree over the meaning of this statutory provision. The State emphasizes the language of the first sentence, which speaks in terms of the physician's determination of viability being made by the standards of ordinary skill in the medical profession. Appellees stress the language of the second sentence, which prescribes such "tests as are necessary" to make a finding of gestational age, fetal weight, and lung maturity.

The Court of Appeals reads Sec. 188.029 as requiring that after 20 weeks "doctors *must* perform tests to find gestational age, fetal weight, and lung maturity." The court indicated that the tests needed to determine fetal weight at 20 weeks are "unreliable and inaccurate" and would add $125 to $250 to the cost of an abortion. It also stated that "amniocentesis, the only method available to de-termine lung maturity, is contrary to accepted medical practice until 28–30 weeks of gestation, expensive, and imposes significant health risks for both the pregnant woman and the fetus."

We must first determine the meaning of Sec. 188.029 under Missouri law. Our usual practice is to defer to the lower court's construction of a state statute, but we believe the Court of Appeals has "fallen into plain error" in this case. . . .

We think the viability-testing provision makes sense only if the second sentence is read to require only those tests that are useful to making subsidiary findings as to viability. . . .

The viability-testing provision of the Missouri Act is concerned with promoting the State's interest in potential human life rather than in maternal health. Section 188.029 creates what is essentially a presumption of viability at 20 weeks, which the physician must rebut with tests indicating that the fetus is not viable prior to performing an abortion. It also directs the physician's determination as to viability by specifying consideration, if feasible, of gestational age, fetal weight, and lung capacity. The District Court found that "the medical evidence is uncontradicted that a 20-week fetus is *not* viable," and that "23-1/2 to 24 weeks gestation is the earliest point in pregnancy where a reasonable possibility of viability exists." But it also found that there may be a 4-week error in estimating gestational age, which supports testing at 20 weeks.

In *Roe* v. *Wade*, the Court recognized that the State has "important and legitimate" interests in protecting maternal health and in the potentiality of human life. During the second trimester, the State "may, if it chooses, regulate the abortion procedure in ways that are reasonably related to maternal health." After viability, when the State's interest in potential human life was held to become compelling, the State "may, if it chooses, regulate, and even proscribe, abortion except where it is necessary in appropriate medical judgment for the preservation of the life or health of the mother."

In *Colautti* v. *Franklin* (1979), upon which appellees rely, the Court held that a Pennsylvania statute regulating the standard of care to be used by a physician performing an abortion of a possible viable fetus was void for vagueness. But in the course of reaching that conclusion, the Court reaffirmed its earlier statement in *Planned Parenthood of Central Missouri* v. *Danforth* (1976) that " 'the determination of whether a particular fetus *is* viable is, and must be, a matter for the judgment of the responsible attending physician.' " . . .

We think that the doubt cast upon the Missouri statute by these cases is not so much a flaw in the statute as it is a reflection of the fact that the rigid trimester analysis of the course of a pregnancy enunciated in *Roe* has resulted in subsequent cases like *Colautti* and *Akron* making constitutional law in this area a virtual Procrustean bed. . . .

Stare decisis is a cornerstone of our legal system, but it has less power in constitutional cases, where, save for constitutional amendments, this Court is the only body able to make needed changes. We have not refrained from reconsideration of a prior construction of the Constitution that has proved "unsound in principle and unworkable in practice." . . . We think the *Roe* trimester framework falls into that category.

In the first place, the rigid *Roe* framework is hardly consistent with the notion of a Constitution cast in general terms, as ours is, and usually speaking in general principles, as ours does. The key elements of the *Roe* framework—trimesters and viability—are not found in the text of the Constitution or in any place else one would expect to find a constitutional principle. Since the bounds of the inquiry are essentially indeterminate, the result has been a web of legal rules that have become increasingly intricate, resembling a code of regulations rather than a body of constitutional doctrine. As JUSTICE WHITE has put it, the trimester framework has left this Court to serve as the country's "*ex officio* medical board with powers to approve or disapprove medical and operative practices and standards throughout the United States." . . .

In the second place, we do not see why the State's interest in protecting potential human life should come into existence only at the point of viability, and that there should therefore be a rigid line allowing state regulation after viability but prohibiting it before viability. . . .

The tests that Sec. 188.029 requires the physician to perform are designed to determine viability. The State here has chosen viability as the point at which its interest in potential human life must be safeguarded. . . . It is true that the tests in question increase the expense of abortion, and regulate the discretion of the physician in determining the viability of the fetus. Since the tests will undoubtedly show in many cases that the fetus is not viable, the tests will have been performed for what were in fact second-trimester abortions. But we are satisfied that the requirement of these tests permissibly furthers the State's interest in protecting potential human life, and we therefore believe Sec. 188.029 to be constitutional.

The dissent takes us to task for our failure to join in a "great issues" debate as to whether the Constitution includes an "unenumerated" general right to privacy as recognized in cases such as *Griswold* v. *Connecticut* (1965) and *Roe*. But *Griswold* v. *Connecticut*, unlike *Roe*, did not purport to adopt a whole framework, complete with detailed rules and distinctions, to govern the cases in which the asserted liberty interest would apply. As such, it was far different from the opinion, if not the holding, of *Roe* v. *Wade*, which sought to establish a constitutional framework for judging state regulation of abortion during the entire term of pregnancy. . . .

The dissent also accuses us . . . of cowardice and illegitimacy in dealing with "the most politically divisive domestic legal issue of our time." There is no doubt that our holding today will allow some governmental regulation of abortion that would have been prohibited under the language of cases such as *Colautti* v. *Franklin* (1979) and *Akron* v. *Akron Center for Reproductive Health, Inc.* (1983). But the goal of constitutional adjudication is surely not to remove inexorably "politically divisive" issues from the ambit of the legislative process, whereby the people through their elected representatives deal with matters of concern to them. The goal of constitutional adjudication is to hold true the balance between that which the Constitution puts beyond the reach of the democratic process and that which it does not. We think we have done that today. The dissent's suggestion, that legislative bodies, in a Nation where more than half of our population is women, will treat our decision today as an invitation to enact abortion regulation reminiscent of the dark ages not only misreads our views but does scant justice to those who serve in such bodies and the people who elect them.

III

Both appellants and the United States as *amicus curiae* have urged that we overrule our decision in *Roe* v. *Wade*. . . . The facts of the present case, however, differ from those at issue in *Roe*. Here, Missouri has determined that viability is the point at which its interest in potential human life must be safeguarded. In *Roe*, on the other hand, the Texas statute criminalized the performance of *all* abortions, except when the mother's life was at stake. This case therefore affords us no occasion to revisit the holding of *Roe*, which was that the Texas statute unconstitutionally infringed the right to an abortion derived from the Due Process Clause, and we leave it undisturbed. To the extent indicated in our opinion, we would modify and narrow *Roe* and succeeding cases.

Because none of the challenged provisions of the Missouri Act properly before us conflict with the Constitution, the judgment of the Court of Appeals is

Reversed.

JUSTICE O'CONNOR, *concurring in part and concurring in the judgment.*

I concur in Parts I, II-A, II-B, and II-C of the Court's opinion.

II

D

In its interpretation of Missouri's "determination of viability" provision, Mo. Rev. Stat. Sec. 188.029 (1986), see *ante,* at 15–23, the plurality has proceeded in a manner unnecessary to deciding the question at hand. I agree with the plurality that it was plain error for the Court of Appeals to interpret the second sentence of Mo. Rev. Stat. Sec. 188.029 as meaning that "doctors *must* perform tests to find gestational age, fetal weight, and lung maturity." 851 F.2d, at 1075, n. 5 (emphasis in original). When read together with the first sentence of Sec. 188.029—which requires a physician to "determine if the unborn child is viable by using and exercising that degree of care, skill, and proficiency commonly exercised by the ordinary skillful, careful, and prudent physician engaged in similar practice under the same or similar conditions"—it would be contradictory nonsense to read the second sentence as requiring a physician to perform viability examinations and tests in situations where it would be careless and imprudent to do so. The plurality is quite correct: "the viability-testing provision makes sense only if the second sentence is read to require only those tests that are useful to making subsidiary findings as to viability," *ante,* at 16, and, I would add, only those examinations and tests that it would not be imprudent or careless to perform in the particular medical situation before the physician.

Unlike the plurality, I do not understand these viability testing requirements to conflict with any of the Court's past decisions concerning state regulation of abortion. Therefore, there is no necessity to accept the State's invitation to reexamine the constitutional validity of *Roe* v. *Wade.* Where there is no need to decide a constitutional question, it is a venerable principle of this Court's adjudicatory processes not to do so for "[t]he Court will not 'anticipate a question of constitutional law in advance of the necessity of deciding it.' " Neither will it generally "formulate a rule of consti-

tutional law broader than is required by the precise facts to which it is to be applied." Quite simply, "[i]t is not the habit of the Court to decide questions of a constitutional nature unless absolutely necessary to a decision of the case." The Court today has accepted the State's every interpretation of its abortion statute and has upheld, under our existing precedents, every provision of that statute which is properly before us. Precisely for this reason reconsideration of *Roe* falls not into any "good-cause exception" to this "fundamental rule of judicial restraint. . . . " When the constitutional invalidity of a State's abortion statute actually turns on the constitutional validity of *Roe* v. *Wade,* there will be time enough to reexamine *Roe.* And to do so carefully.

* * *

I do not think the second sentence of Sec. 188.029, as interpreted by the Court, imposes a degree of state regulation on the medical determination of viability that in any way conflicts with prior decisions of this Court. As the plurality recognizes, the requirement that, where not imprudent, physicians perform examinations and tests useful to making subsidiary findings to determine viability "promot[es] the State's interest in potential human life rather than in maternal health." No decision of this Court has held that the State may not directly promote its interest in potential life when viability is possible. Quite the contrary. In *Thornburgh* v. *American College of Obstetricians and Gynecologists* (1986), the Court considered a constitutional challenge to a Pennsylvania statute requiring that a second physician be present during an abortion performed "when viability is possible." For guidance, the Court looked to the earlier decision in *Planned Parenthood Assn. of Kansas City, Missouri, Inc.* v. *Ashcroft* (1988), upholding a Missouri statute requiring the presence of a second physician during an abortion performed after viability. The *Thornburgh* majority struck down the Pennsylvania statute merely because the statute had no exception for emergency situations and not because it found a constitutional difference between the State's promotion of its interest in potential life when viability is possible and when viability is certain.

I dissented from the Court's opinion in *Akron* because it was my view that, even apart from *Roe*'s trimester framework, which I continue to consider problematic, the *Akron* majority had distorted and misapplied its own standard for evaluating state regulation of abortion which the Court had applied with fair consistency in the past: that, previability, "a regulation imposed on a lawful abortion is not unconstitutional unless it unduly burdens the right to seek an abortion."

It is clear to me that requiring the performance of examinations and tests useful to determining whether a fetus is viable, when viability is possible, and when it would not be medically imprudent to do so, does not impose an undue burden on a woman's abortion decision. On this ground alone I would reject the suggestion that Sec. 188.029 as interpreted is unconstitutional. . . .

In sum, I concur in Parts I, II-A, II-B, and II-C of the Court's opinion and concur in the judgment of Part II-D.

JUSTICE SCALIA, *concurring in part and concurring in the judgment.*

I join Parts I, II-A, II-B, and II-C of the opinion of THE CHIEF JUSTICE. As to Part II-D, I share JUSTICE BLACKMUN's view . . . that it effectively would overrule *Roe* v. *Wade* (1973). I think that should be done, but would do it more explicitly. Since today we contrive to avoid doing it, and indeed to avoid almost any decision of national import, I need not set forth my reasons, some of which have been well recited in dissents of my colleagues in other cases.

The outcome of today's case will doubtless be heralded as a triumph of judicial statesmanship. It is not that, unless it is statesmanlike, needlessly to prolong this Court's self-awarded sovereignty over a field where it has little proper business since the answers to most of the cruel questions posed are political and not juridical—a sovereignty which therefore quite properly, but to the great damage of the Court, makes it the object of the sort of organized public pressure that political institutions in a democracy ought to receive.

JUSTICE O'CONNOR's assertion, that a " 'fundamental rule of judicial restraint' " requires us to avoid reconsidering *Roe*, cannot be taken seriously. By finessing *Roe* we do not, as she suggests, adhere to the strict and venerable rule that we should avoid " 'decid[ing] questions of a constitutional nature.' " We have not disposed of this case on some statutory or procedural ground, but have decided, and could not avoid deciding, whether the Missouri statute meets the requirements of the United States Constitution. The only choice available is whether, in deciding that constitutional question, we should use *Roe* v. *Wade* as the benchmark, or something else. What is involved, therefore, is not the rule of avoiding constitutional issues where possible, but the quite separate principle that we will not " 'formulate a rule of constitutional law broader than is required by the precise facts to which it is to be applied.' " The latter is a sound general principle, but one often departed from when good reason exists. Just this Term, for example, in an opinion authored by JUSTICE O'CONNOR, despite the fact that we had already held a racially based set-aside unconstitutional because unsupported by evidence of identified discrimination, which was all that was needed to decide the case, we went on to outline the criteria for properly tailoring race-based remedies in cases where such evidence is present. *Richmond* v. *J. A. Croson.* . . .

The real question, then, is whether there are valid reasons to go beyond the most stingy possible holding today. It seems to me there are not only valid but compelling ones. Ordinarily, speaking no more broadly than is absolutely required avoids throwing settled law into confusion; doing so today preserves a chaos that is evident to anyone who can read and count. Alone sufficient to justify a broad holding is the fact that our retaining control, through *Roe*, of what I believe to be, and many of our citizens recognize to be, a political issue, continuously distorts the public perception of the role of this Court. We can now look forward to at least another Term with carts full of mail from the public, and streets full of demonstrators, urging us—their unelected and life-tenured judges who have been awarded those extraordinary, undemocratic characteristics precisely in order that we might follow the law despite the popular will—to follow the popular will. Indeed, I expect we can look forward to even more of that than before, given our indecisive decision today. And if these reasons for taking the unexceptional course of reaching a broader holding are not enough, then consider the nature of the constitutional question we avoid: in most cases, we do no harm by not speaking more broadly than the decision requires. Anyone affected by the conduct that the avoided holding would have prohibited will be able to challenge it himself, and have his day in court to make the argument. Not so with respect to the harm that many States believed, pre-*Roe*, and many may continue to believe, is caused by largely unrestricted abortion. That will continue to occur if the States have the constitutional power to prohibit it, and would do so, but we skillfully avoid telling them so. Perhaps those abortions cannot constitutionally be proscribed. That is surely an arguable question, the question that reconsideration of *Roe* v. *Wade* entails. But what is not at all arguable, it seems to me, is that we should decide now and not insist that we be run into a corner before we grudgingly yield up our judgment. The only sound reason for the latter course is to prevent a change in the law—but to think that desirable begs the question to be decided.

It was an arguable question today whether Sec. 188.029 of the Missouri law contravened this Court's understanding of *Roe* v. *Wade,* and I would have examined *Roe* rather than examining the contravention. Given the Court's newly contracted abstemiousness, what will it take, one must wonder, to permit us to reach that fundamental question? The result of our vote today is that we will not reconsider that prior opinion, even if most of the Justices think it is wrong, unless we have before us a statute that in fact contradicts it—and even then (under our newly discovered "no-broader-than-necessary" requirement) only minor problematical aspects of *Roe* will be reconsidered, unless one expects State legislatures to adopt provisions whose compliance with *Roe* cannot even be argued with a straight face. It thus appears that the mansion of constitutionalized abortion-law, constructed overnight in *Roe* v. *Wade,* must be disassembled door-jamb by door-jamb, and never entirely brought down, no matter how wrong it may be.

Of the four courses we might have chosen today—to reaffirm *Roe,* to overrule it explicitly, to overrule it *sub silentio,* or to avoid the question—the last is the least responsible. On the question of the constitutionality of Sec. 188.029, I concur in the judgment of the Court and strongly dissent from the manner in which it has been reached.

JUSTICE BLACKMUN, *with whom* JUSTICE BRENNAN *and* JUSTICE MARSHALL *join, concurring in part and dissenting in part.*

Today, *Roe* v. *Wade,* 410 U.S. 113 (1973), and the fundamental constitutional right of women to decide whether to terminate a pregnancy, *survive but are not secure.* Although the Court extricates itself from this case without making a single, even incremental, change in the law of abortion, the plurality and JUSTICE SCALIA would overrule *Roe* (the first silently, the other explicitly) and would return to the States virtually unfettered authority to control the quintessentially intimate, personal, and life-directing decision whether to carry a fetus to term. Although today, no less than yesterday, the Constitution and the decisions of this Court prohibit a State from enacting laws that inhibit women from the meaningful exercise of that right, a plurality of this Court implicitly invites every state legislature to enact more and more restrictive abortion regulations in order to provoke more and more test cases, in the hope that sometime down the line the Court will return the law of procreative freedom to the severe limitations that generally prevailed in this country before January 22, 1973. Never in my memory has a plurality announced a judgment of this Court that so foments disregard for the law and for our standing decisions. Nor in my memory has a plurality gone about its business in such a deceptive fashion. At every level of its review, from its effort to read the real meaning out of the Missouri statute, to its intended evisceration of precedents and its deafening silence about the constitutional protections that it would jettison, the plurality obscures the portent of its analysis. With feigned restraint, the plurality announces that its analysis leaves *Roe* "undisturbed," albeit "modif[ied] and narrow[ed]." But this disclaimer is totally meaningless. The plurality opinion is filled with winks, and nods, and knowing glances to those who would do away with *Roe* explicitly, but turns a stone face to anyone in search of what the plurality conceives as the scope of a woman's right under the Due Process Clause to terminate a pregnancy free from the coercive and brooding influence of the State. The simple truth is that *Roe* would not survive the plurality's analysis, and that the plurality provides no substitute for *Roe*'s protective umbrella.

* * *

I fear for the future. I fear for the liberty and equality of the millions of women who have lived and come of age in the 16 years since *Roe* was decided. I fear for the integrity of, and public esteem for, this Court. I dissent. . . .

* * *

In the plurality's view, the viability-testing provision imposes a burden on second-trimester abortions as a way of furthering the State's interest in protecting the potential life of the fetus. Since under the *Roe* framework, the State may not fully regulate abortion in the interest of potential life (as opposed to maternal health) until the third trimester, the plurality finds it necessary, in order to save the Missouri testing provision, to throw out *Roe*'s trimester framework. In flat contradiction to *Roe,* the plurality concludes that the State's interest in potential life is compelling before viability, and upholds the testing provision because it "permissibly furthers" that state interest.

At the outset, I note that in its haste to limit

abortion rights, the plurality compounds the errors of its analysis by needlessly reaching out to address constitutional questions that are not actually presented. The conflict between Sec. 188.029 and *Roe*'s trimester framework, which purportedly drives the plurality to reconsider our past decisions, is a contrived conflict: the product of an aggressive misreading of the viability-testing requirement and a needlessly wooden application of the *Roe* framework.

The plurality's reading of Sec. 188.029 (also joined by JUSTICE O'CONNOR) is irreconcilable with the plain language of the statute and is in derogation of this Court's settled view that " 'district courts and courts of appeals are better schooled in and more able to interpret the laws of their respective States.' "

* * *

The statute's plain language requires the physician to undertake whatever tests are necessary to determine gestational age, weight, and lung maturity, regardless of whether these tests are necessary to a finding of viability, and regardless of whether the tests subject the pregnant woman or the fetus to additional health risks or add substantially to the cost of an abortion.

Had the plurality read the statute as written, it would have had no cause to reconsider the *Roe* framework. As properly construed, the viability-testing provision does not pass constitutional muster under even a rational-basis standard, the least restrictive level of review applied by this Court. By mandating tests to determine fetal weight and lung maturity for every fetus thought to be more than 20 weeks gestational age, the statute requires physicians to undertake procedures, such as amniocentesis, that, in the situation presented, have no medical justification, impose significant additional health risks on both the pregnant woman and the fetus, and bear no rational relation to the State's interest in protecting fetal life. As written, Sec. 188.029 is an arbitrary imposition of discomfort, risk, and expense, furthering no discernible interest except to make the procurement of an abortion as arduous and difficult as possible. Thus, were it not for the plurality's tortured effort to avoid the plain import of Sec. 188.029, it could have struck down the testing provision as patently irrational irrespective of the *Roe* framework.

The plurality eschews this straightforward resolution, in the hope of precipitating a constitutional crisis. Far from avoiding constitutional difficulty, the plurality attempts to *engineer a dramatic retrenchment* in our jurisprudence by exaggerating the conflict between its untenable construction of Sec. 188.029 and the *Roe* trimester framework.

No one contests that under the *Roe* framework the State, in order to promote its interest in potential human life, may regulate and even proscribe non-therapeutic abortions once the fetus becomes viable. If, as the plurality appears to hold, the testing provision simply requires a physician to use appropriate and medically sound tests to determine whether the fetus is actually viable when the estimated gestational age is greater than 20 weeks (and therefore within what the District Court found to be the margin of error for viability), then I see little or no conflict with *Roe*. Nothing in *Roe*, or any of its progeny, holds that a State may not effectuate its compelling interests in the potential life of a viable fetus by seeking to ensure that no viable fetus is mistakenly aborted because of the inherent lack of precision in estimates of gestational age. A requirement that a physician make a finding of viability, one way or the other, for every fetus that falls within the range of possible viability does no more than preserve the State's recognized authority. Although, as the plurality correctly points out, such a testing requirement would have the effect of imposing additional costs on second-trimester abortions where the tests indicated that the fetus was not viable, these costs would be merely incidental to, and a necessary accommodation of, the State's unquestioned right to prohibit non-therapeutic abortions after the point of viability. In short, the testing provision, as construed by the plurality, is consistent with the *Roe* framework and could be upheld effortlessly under current doctrine.

How ironic it is, then, and disingenuous, that the plurality scolds the Court of Appeals for adopting a construction of the statute that fails to avoid constitutional difficulties. By distorting the statute, the plurality manages to avoid invalidating the testing provision on what should have been noncontroversial constitutional grounds; having done so, however, the plurality rushes headlong into a much deeper constitutional thicket, brushing past an obvious basis for upholding Sec. 188.029 in search of a pretext for scuttling the trimester framework. Evidently, from the plurality's perspective, the real problem with the Court of Appeals' construction of Sec. 188.029 is not that it raised a constitutional difficulty, but that it raised the wrong constitutional difficulty—one not implicating *Roe*. The plurality has remedied that, traditional canons of construction and judicial forbearance notwithstanding.

Having set up the conflict between Sec. 188.029 and the *Roe* trimester framework, the plurality summarily discards *Roe*'s analytic core as " 'unsound in principle and unworkable in practice.' " This is so, the plurality claims, because the key elements of the framework do not appear in the text of the Constitution, because the framework more closely resembles a regulatory code than a body of constitutional doctrine, and because under the framework the State's interest in potential human life is considered compelling only after viability, when, in fact, that interest is equally compelling throughout pregnancy. The plurality does not bother to explain these alleged flaws in *Roe*. Bald assertion masquerades as reasoning. The object, quite clearly, is not to persuade, but to prevail.

The plurality opinion is far more remarkable for the arguments that it does not advance than for those that it does. The plurality does not even mention, much less join, the true jurisprudential debate underlying this case: whether the Constitution includes an "unenumerated" general right to privacy as recognized in many of our decisions, most notably *Griswold* v. *Connecticut* (1965) and *Roe*, more specifically, whether and to what extent such a right to privacy extends to matters of childbearing and family life, including abortion. These are questions of unsurpassed significance in this Court's interpretation of the Constitution, and mark the battleground upon which this case was fought, by the parties, by the Solicitor General as *amicus* on behalf of petitioners, and by an unprecedented number of *amici*. On these grounds, abandoned by the plurality, the Court should decide this case.

But rather than arguing that the text of the Constitution makes no mention of the right to privacy, the plurality complains that the critical elements of the *Roe* framework—trimesters and viability—do not appear in the Constitution and are, therefore, somehow inconsistent with a Constitution cast in general terms. Were this a true concern, we would have to abandon most of our constitutional jurisprudence. As the plurality well knows, or should know, the "critical elements" of countless constitutional doctrines nowhere appear on the Constitution's text. The Constitution makes no mention, for example, of the First Amendment's "actual malice" standard for proving certain libels, see *New York Times* v. *Sullivan* (1964), or of the standard for determining when speech is obscene. See *Miller* v. *California* (1973). Similarly, the Constitution makes no mention of the ratio-

nal-basis test, or the specific verbal formulations of intermediate and strict scrutiny by which this Court evaluates claims under the Equal Protection Clause. The reason is simple. Like the *Roe* framework, these tests or standards are not, and do not purport to be, rights protected by the Constitution. Rather, they are judge-made methods for evaluating and measuring the strength and scope of constitutional rights or for balancing the constitutional rights of individuals against the competing interests of government.

With respect to the *Roe* framework, the general constitutional principle, indeed the fundamental constitutional right, for which it was developed, is the right to privacy, see, e.g., *Griswold* v. *Connecticut* (1965), a species of "liberty" protected by the Due Process Clause, which under our past decisions safeguards the right of women to exercise some control over their own role in procreation. As we recently reaffirmed in *Thornburgh* v. *American College of Obstetricians and Gynecologists* (1986), few decisions are "more basic to individual dignity and autonomy" or more appropriate to that "certain private sphere of individual liberty" that the Constitution reserves from the intrusive reach of government than the right to make the uniquely personal, intimate, and self-defining decision whether to end a pregnancy. It is this general principle, the " 'moral fact that a person belongs to himself and not others nor to society as a whole,' " that is found in the Constitution. The trimester framework simply defines and limits that right to privacy in the abortion context to accommodate, not destroy, a State's legitimate interest in protecting the health of pregnant women and in preserving potential human life. Fashioning such accommodations between individual rights and the legitimate interests of government, establishing bench-marks and standards with which to evaluate the competing claims of individuals and government, lies at the very heart of constitutional adjudication. To the extent that the trimester framework is useful in this enterprise, it is not only consistent with constitutional interpretation, but necessary to the wise and just exercise of this Court's paramount authority to define the scope of constitutional rights.

The plurality next alleges that the result of the trimester framework has "been a web of legal rules that have become increasingly intricate, resembling a code of regulations rather than a body of constitutional doctrine." Again, if this were a true and genuine concern, we would have to abandon vast areas of our constitutional jurisprudence. The plurality complains that under the trimester framework the Court has distinguished between a city ordinance requiring that second-trimester abortions be performed in clinics and a state law requiring that these abortions be performed in hospitals, or between laws requiring that certain information be furnished to a woman by a physician or his assistant and those requiring that such information be furnished by the physician exclusively. Are these distinctions any finer, or more "regulatory," than the distinctions we have often drawn in our First Amendment jurisprudence, where, for example, we have held that a "released-time" program permitting public school students to leave school grounds during school hours to receive religious instruction does not violate the Establishment Clause, even though a released-time program permitting religious instruction on school grounds does violate the Clause?

* * *

That numerous constitutional doctrines result in narrow differentiations between similar circumstances does not mean that this Court has abandoned adjudication in favor of regulation. Rather, these careful distinctions reflect the process of constitutional adjudication itself, which is often highly fact-specific, requiring such determinations as whether state laws are "unduly burdensome" or "reasonable" or bear a "rational" or "necessary" relation to asserted state interests.

* * *

Finally, the plurality asserts that the trimester framework cannot stand because the State's interest in potential life is compelling throughout pregnancy, not merely after viability. The opinion contains not one word of rationale for its view of the State's interest. This "it-is-so-because-we-say-so" jurisprudence constitutes nothing other than an attempted exercise of brute force; reason, much less persuasion, has no place.

* * *

For my own part, I remain convinced, as six other Members of the Court 16 years ago were convinced, that the *Roe* framework, and the viability standard in particular, fairly, sensibly, and effectively functions to safeguard the constitutional liberties of pregnant women while recognizing and accommodating the State's interest in potential human life. The viability line reflects the biological facts and truths of fetal development; it marks that threshold moment prior to which a fetus cannot survive separate from the woman and cannot reasonably and objectively be regarded as a subject of rights or interests distinct from, or paramount to, those of the pregnant woman. At the same time, the viability standard takes account of the undeniable fact that as the fetus evolves into its postnatal form, and as it loses its dependence on the uterine environment, the State's interest in the fetus's potential human life, and in fostering a regard for human life in general, becomes compelling. . . .

Having contrived an opportunity to reconsider the *Roe* framework, and then having discarded that framework, the plurality finds the testing provision unobjectionable because it "permissibly furthers the State's interest in protecting potential human life." This newly minted standard is circular and totally meaningless. Whether a challenged abortion regulation "permissibly furthers" a legitimate state interest is the *question* that courts must answer in abortion cases, not the standard for courts to apply. In keeping with the rest of its opinion, the plurality makes no attempt to explain or to justify its new standard, either in the abstract or as applied in this case. Nor could it. The "permissibly furthers" standard has no independent meaning, and consists of nothing other than what a majority of this Court may believe at any given moment in any given case. The plurality's novel test appears to be nothing more than a dressed-up version of rational-basis review, this Court's most lenient level of scrutiny. One thing is clear, however: were the plurality's "permissibly furthers" standard adopted by the Court, for all practical purposes, *Roe* would be overruled.

* * *

The plurality pretends that *Roe* survives, explaining that the facts of this case differ from those in *Roe*: here, Missouri has chosen to assert its interest in potential life only at the point of viability, whereas, in *Roe*, Texas had asserted that interest from the point of conception, criminalizing all abortions, except where the life of the mother was at stake. This, of course, is a distinction without a difference. The plurality repudiates every principle for which *Roe* stands; in good conscience, it cannot possibly believe that *Roe* lies "undisturbed" merely because this case does not call upon the court to reconsider the Texas statute, or one like it. If the Constitution permits a State to enact any statute that reasonably furthers its interest in potential life, and if that interest arises as of conception, why would the Texas statute fail to pass muster? One suspects that the plurality agrees. It is impossible to read the plurality opinion and especially its final paragraph, without recognizing its implicit invitation to every State to enact more and more restrictive abortion laws, and to assert their interest in potential life as of the moment of conception. All these laws will satisfy the plurality's non-scrutiny, until sometime, a new regime of old dissenters and new appointees will declare what the plurality intends: that *Roe* is no longer good law.

Thus, "not with a bang, but a whimper," the plurality discards a landmark case of the last generation, and casts into darkness the hopes and visions of every woman in this country who had come to believe that the Constitution guaranteed her the right to exercise some control over her unique ability to bear children. The plurality does so either oblivious or insensitive to the fact that millions of women, and their families, have ordered their lives around the right to reproductive choice, and that this right has become vital to the full participation of women in the economic and political walks of American life. The plurality would clear the way once again for government to force upon women the physical labor and specific and direct medical and psychological harms that may accompany carrying a fetus to term. The plurality would clear the way again for the State to conscript a woman's body and to force upon her a "distressful life and future."

The result, as we know from experience, would be that every year hundreds of thousands of women, in desperation, would defy the law, and place their health and safety in the unclean and unsympathetic hands of back-alley abortionists, or they would attempt to perform abortions upon themselves, with disastrous results. Every year, many women, especially poor and minority women, would die or suffer debilitating physical trauma, all in the name of enforced morality or religious dictates or lack of compassion, as it may be.

Of the aspirations and settled understandings of American women, of the inevitable and brutal consequences of what it is doing, the tough-approach plurality utters not a word. This silence is callous. It is also profoundly destructive of this Court as an institution. To overturn a constitutional decision is a rare and grave undertaking. To overturn a constitutional decision that secured a fundamental personal liberty to millions of persons would be unprecedented in our 200 years of constitutional history. Although the doctrine of *stare decisis* applies with somewhat diminished force in constitutional cases generally, even in ordinary constitutional cases "any departure from *stare decisis* demands special justification." . . . This require-ment of justification applies with unique force where, as here, the Court's abrogation of precedent would destroy people's firm beilef, based on past decisions of this Court, that they possess an unabridgeable right to undertake certain conduct.

As discussed at perhaps too great length above, the plurality makes no serious attempt to carry "the heavy burden of persuading . . . that changes in society or in the law dictate" the abandonment of *Roe* and its numerous progeny, much less the greater burden of explaining the abrogation of a fundamental personal freedom. Instead, the plurality pretends that it leaves *Roe* standing, and refuses even to discuss the real issue underlying this case: whether the Constitution includes an unenumerated right to privacy that encompasses a woman's right to decide whether to terminate a pregnancy. . . .

This comes at a cost. The doctrine of *stare decisis* "permits society to presume that bedrock principles are founded in the law rather than in the proclivities of individuals, and thereby contributes to the integrity of our constitutional system of government, both in appearance and in fact." Today's decision involves *the most politically divisive domestic legal issue of our time.* By refusing to explain or to justify its proposed revolutionary revision in the law of abortion, and by refusing to abide not only by our precedents, but also by our canons for reconsidering those precedents, the plurality invites charges of cowardice and illegitimacy to our door. I cannot say that these would be undeserved.

For today, at least, the law of abortion stands undisturbed. For today, the women of this Nation still retain the liberty to control their destinies. But the signs are evident and very ominous, and a chill wind blows.

I dissent.

JUSTICE STEVENS, *concurring in part and dissenting in part.*

The Missouri statute defines "conception" as "the fertilization of the ovum of a female by a sperm of a male," even though standard medical texts equate "conception" with implantation in the uterus, occurring about six days after fertilization. Missouri's declaration therefore implies regulation not only of previability abortions, but also of common forms of contraception such as the IUD and the morning-after pill.

One might argue that *Griswold* does not protect a woman's choice to use an IUD or take a morning-after pill. There is unquestionably a theological basis for such an argument, just as there was unquestionably a theological basis for the Connecticut statute that the Court invalidated in *Griswold*. Our jurisprudence, however, has consistently required a secular basis for valid legislation. Because I am not aware of any secular basis for differentiating between contraceptive procedures that are effective immediately before and those that are effective immediately after fertilization, I believe it inescapably follows that the preamble to the Missouri statute is invalid under *Griswold* and its progeny.

Indeed, I am persuaded that the absence of any secular purpose for the legislative declarations that life begins at conception and that conception occurs at fertilization makes the relevant portion of the preamble invalid under the Establishment Clause of the First Amendment to the Federal Constitution. This conclusion does not, and could not, rest on the fact that the statement happens to coincide with the tenets of certain religions, or on the fact that the legislators who voted to enact it may have been motivated by religious considerations. . . .

Rather, it rests on the fact that the preamble, an unequivocal endorsement of a religious tenet of some but by no means all Christian faiths, serves no identifiable secular purpose. That fact alone compels a conclusion that the statute violates the Establishment Clause. *Wallace* v. *Jaffree* (1985).

My concern can best be explained by reference to the position on this issue that was endorsed by St. Thomas Aquinas and widely accepted by the leaders of the Roman Catholic Church for many years. The position is summarized in a report, entitled "Catholic Teaching on Abortion," prepared by the Congressional Research Service of the Library of Congress. It states in part:

> The disagreement over the status of the unformed as against the formed fetus was crucial for Christian teaching on the soul. It was widely held that the soul was not present until the formation of the fetus 40 or 80 days after conception, for males and females respectively. Thus, abortion of the "unformed" or "inanimate" fetus(from anima, soul) was something less than true homicide, rather a form of anticipatory or quasi-homicide. This view received its definitive treatment in St. Thomas Aquinas and became for a time the dominant interpretation in the Latin Church.

* * *

If the views of St. Thomas were held as widely today as they were in the Middle Ages, and if a state legislature were to enact a statute prefaced with a "finding" that female life begins 80 days after conception and male life begins 40 days after conception,

I have no doubt that this Court would promptly conclude that such an endorsement of a particular religious tenet is violative of the Establishment Clause.

In my opinion the difference between that hypothetical statute and Missouri's preamble reflects nothing more than a difference in theological doctrine. The preamble to the Missouri statute endorses the theological position that there is the same secular interest in preserving the life of a fetus during the first 40 or 80 days of pregnancy as there is after viability—indeed, after the time when the fetus has become a "person" with legal rights protected by the Constitution. To sustain that position as a matter of law, I believe Missouri has the burden of identifying the secular interests that differentiate the first 40 days of pregnancy from the period immediately before or after fertilization when, as *Griswold* and related cases establish, the Constitution allows the use of contraceptive procedures to prevent potential life from developing into full personhood. Focusing our attention on the first several weeks of pregnancy is especially appropriate because that is the period when the vast majority of abortions are actually performed.

As a secular matter, there is an obvious difference between the state interest in protecting the freshly fertilized egg and the state interest in protecting a 9-month-gestated, fully sentient fetus on the eve of birth. There can be no interest in protecting the newly fertilized egg from physical pain or mental anguish, because the capacity for such suffering does not yet exist; respecting a developed fetus, however, that interest is valid. In fact, if one prescinds the theological concept of ensoulment—or one accepts St. Thomas Aquinas's view that ensoulment does not occur for at least 40 days, a State has no greater secular interest in protecting the potential life of an embryo that is still "seed" than in protecting the potential life of a sperm or an unfertilized ovum.

* * *

Bolstering my conclusion that the preamble violated the First Amendment is the fact that the intensely divisive character of much of the national debate over the abortion issue reflects the deeply held religious convictions of many participants in the debate. The Missouri Legislature may not inject its endorsement of a particular religious tradition into this debate, for "[t]he Establishment Clause does not allow public bodies to foment such disagreement."

JUSTICE O'CONNOR, JUSTICE KENNEDY, *and* JUSTICE SOUTER *announced the judgment of the Court and delivered the opinion of the Court with respect to Parts I, II, III, V-A, V-C, and VI, an opinion with respect to Part V-E, in which* JUSTICE STEVENS *joins, and an opinion with respect to Parts IV, V-B, and V-D.*

I

Liberty finds no refuge in a jurisprudence of doubt. Yet 19 years after our holding that the Constitution protects a woman's right to terminate her pregnancy in its early stages, *Roe* v. *Wade* (1973), that definition of liberty is still questioned. Joining the respondents as *amicus curiae*, the United States, as it has done in five other cases in the last decade, again asks us to overrule *Roe.*

At issue in these cases are five provisions of the Pennsylvania Abortion Control Act of 1982 as amended in 1988 and 1989. The Act requires that a woman seeking an abortion give her informed consent prior to the abortion procedure, and specifies that she be provided with certain information at least 24 hours before the abortion is performed. For a minor to obtain an abortion, the Act requires the informed consent of one of her parents, but provides for a judicial bypass option if the minor does not wish to or cannot obtain a parent's consent. Another provision of the Act requires that, unless certain exceptions apply, a married woman seeking an abortion must sign a statement indicating that she has notified her husband of her intended abortion. The Act exempts compliance with these three requirements in the event of a "medical emergency," which is defined in the Act. In addition to the above provisions regulating the performance of abortions, the Act imposes certain reporting requirements on facilities that provide abortion services.

Before any of these provisions took effect, the petitioners, who are five abortion clinics and one physician representing himself as well as a class of physicians who provide abortion services, brought this suit seeking declaratory and injunctive relief. Each provision was challenged as unconstitutional on its face. The District Court entered a preliminary injunction against the enforcement of the regulations, and, after a 3-day bench trial, held all the provisions at issue here unconstitutional, en-

tering a permanent injunction against Pennsylvania's enforcement of them. The Court of Appeals for the Third Circuit affirmed in part and reversed in part, upholding all of the regulations except for the husband notification requirement. We granted certiorari.

The Court of Appeals found it necessary to follow an elaborate course of reasoning even to identify the first premise to use to determine whether the statute enacted by Pennsylvania meets constitutional standards. And at oral argument in this Court, the attorney for the parties challenging the statute took the position that none of the enactments can be upheld without overruling *Roe* v. *Wade.* We disagree with that analysis; but we acknowledge that our decisions after *Roe* cast doubt upon the meaning and reach of its holding. Further, THE CHIEF JUSTICE admits that he would overrule the central holding of *Roe* and adopt the rational relationship test as the sole criterion of constitutionality. State and federal courts as well as legislatures throughout the Union must have guidance as they seek to address this subject in conformance with the Constitution. Given these premises, we find it imperative to review once more the principles that define the rights of the woman and the legitimate authority of the State respecting the termination of pregnancies by abortion procedures.

After considering the fundamental constitutional questions resolved by *Roe*, principles of institutional integrity, and the rule of *stare decisis*, we are led to conclude this: the essential holding of *Roe* v. *Wade* should be retained and once again reaffirmed.

It must be stated at the outset and with clarity that *Roe's* essential holding, the holding we reaffirm, has three parts. First is a recognition of the right of the woman to choose to have an abortion before viability and to obtain it without undue interference from the State. Before viability, the State's interests are not strong enough to support a prohibition of abortion or the imposition of a substantial obstacle to the woman's effective right to elect the procedure. Second is a confirmation of the State's power to restrict abortions after fetal viability, if the law contains exceptions for pregnancies which endanger a woman's life or health. And third is the principle that the State has legitimate interests from the outset of the pregnancy in protecting the health of the woman and the life of the fetus that may become a child. These principles do not contradict one another; and we adhere to each.

II

Constitutional protection of the woman's decision to terminate her pregnancy derives from the Due Process Clause of the Fourteenth Amendment. It declares that no State shall "deprive any person of life, liberty, or property, without due process of law." The controlling word in the case before us is "liberty." Although a literal reading of the Clause might suggest that it governs only the procedures by which a State may deprive persons of liberty, for at least 105 years, at least since *Mugler* v. *Kansas* (1887), the Clause has been understood to contain a substantive component as well, one "barring certain government actions regardless of the fairness of the procedures used to implement them." *Daniels* v. *Williams* (1986). As JUSTICE BRANDEIS (joined by JUSTICE HOLMES) observed, "[d]espite arguments to the contrary which had seemed to me persuasive, it is settled that the due process clause of the Fourteenth Amendment applies to matters of procedure. Thus all fundamental rights comprised within the term liberty are protected by the Federal Constitution from invasion by the States." *Whitney* v. *California* (1927) (BRANDEIS, J., concurring). "[T]he guaranties of due process, though having their roots in Magna Carta's '*per legem terrae*' and considered as procedural safeguards 'against executive usurpation and tyranny,' have in this country 'become bulwarks also against arbitrary legislation.' " *Poe* v. *Ullman* (1961) (HARLAN, J., dissenting from dismissal on jurisdictional grounds) (quoting *Hurtado* v. *California* [1884]).

The most familiar of the substantive liberties protected by the Fourteenth Amendment are those recognized by the Bill of Rights. We have held that the Due Process Clause of the Fourteenth Amendment incorporates most of the Bill of Rights against the States. See, e.g., *Duncan* v. *Louisiana* (1968). It is tempting, as a means of curbing the discretion of federal judges, to suppose that liberty encompasses no more than those rights already guaranteed to the individual against federal interference by the express provisions of the first eight amendments to the Constitution. See *Adamson* v. *California* (1947) (BLACK, J., dissenting). But of course this Court has never accepted that view.

It is also tempting, for the same reason, to suppose that the Due Process Clause protects only those practices, defined at the most specific level, that were protected against government interference by other rules of law when the Fourteenth Amendment was ratified. But such a view would be inconsistent with our law. It is a promise of the Constitution that there is a realm of personal liberty which the government may not enter. We have vindicated this principle before. Marriage is mentioned nowhere in the Bill of Rights and interracial marriage was illegal in most States in the 19th century, but the Court was no doubt correct in finding it to be an aspect of liberty protected against state interference by the substantive component of the Due Process Clause in *Loving* v. *Virginia.* Similar examples may be found in other cases.

Neither the Bill of Rights nor the specific practices of States at the time of the adoption of the Fourteenth Amendment mark the outer limits of the substantive sphere of liberty which the Fourteenth Amendment protects. In *Griswold,* we held that the Constitution does not permit a State to forbid a married couple to use contraceptives. That same freedom was later guaranteed, under the Equal Protection Clause, for unmarried couples. *Eisenstadt* v. *Baird* (1972). Constitutional protection was extended to the sale and distribution of contraceptives in *Carey* v. *Population Services International.* It is settled now, as it was when the Court heard arguments in *Roe* v. *Wade,* that the Constitution places limits on a State's right to interfere with a person's most basic decisions about family and parenthood. . . .

The inescapable fact is that adjudication of substantive due process claims may call upon the Court in interpreting the Constitution to exercise that same capacity which by tradition courts always have exercised: reasoned judgment. Its boundaries are not susceptible of expression as a simple rule. That does not mean we are free to invalidate state policy choices with which we disagree; yet neither does it permit us to shrink from the duties of our office.

Men and women of good conscience can disagree, and we suppose some always shall disagree, about the profound moral and spiritual implications of terminating a pregnancy, even in it earliest stage. Some of us as individuals find abortion offensive to our most basic principles of morality, but that cannot control our decision. Our obligation is to define the liberty of all, not to mandate our own moral code. The underlying constitutional issue is whether the State can resolve these philosophic questions in such a definitive way that a woman lacks all choice in the matter except perhaps in those rare circumstances in which the pregnancy is itself a danger to her own life or health, or is the result of rape or incest.

It is conventional constitutional doctrine that where reasonable people disagree the government can adopt one position or the other. That theorem, however, assumes a state of affairs in which the choice does not intrude upon a protected liberty. Thus, while some people might disagree about whether or not the flag should be saluted, or disagree about the the proposition that it may not be defiled, we have ruled that a State may not compel or enforce one view or the other. See *West Virginia State Bd. of Education* v. *Barnette* (1943); *Texas* v. *Johnson* (1989).

Our law affords constitutional protection to personal decisions relating to marriage, procreation, contraception, family relationships, child rearing, and education. . . . These matters, involving the most intimate and personal choices a person may make in a lifetime, choices central to personal dignity and autonomy, are central to the liberty protected by the Fourteenth Amendment. At the heart of liberty is the right to define one's own concept of existence, of meaning, of the universe, and of the mystery of human life. Beliefs about these matters could not define the attributes of personhood were they formed under compulsion of the State.

These considerations begin our analysis of the woman's interest in terminating her pregnancy but cannot end it, for this reason: though the abortion decision may originate within the zone of conscience and belief, it is more than a philosophic exercise. Abortion is a unique act. It is an act fraught with consequences for others: for the woman who must live with the implications of her decision; for the persons who perform and assist in the procedure; for the spouse, family, and society which must confront the knowledge that these procedures exist, procedures some deem nothing short of an act of violence against innocent human life; and, depending on one's beliefs, for the life or potential life that is aborted. Though abortion is conduct, it does not follow that the State is entitled to proscribe it in all instances. That is because the liberty of the woman is at stake in a sense unique to the human condition and so unique to the law. The mother who carries a child to full term is subject to anxieties, to physical constraints, to pain that only she must bear. That these sacrifices have from the beginning of the human race been endured by the woman with a pride that ennobles her in the eyes of others and gives to the infant a bond of love cannot alone be grounds for the State to insist she make the sacrifice. Her suf-

fering is too intimate and personal for the State to insist, without more, upon its own vision of the woman's role, however dominant that vision has been in the course of our history and our culture. The destiny of the woman must be shaped to a large extent on her own conception of her spiritual imperatives and her place in society.

It should be recognized, moreover, that in some critical respects the abortion decision is of the same character as the decision to use contraception, to which *Griswold* v. *Connecticut, Eisenstadt* v. *Baird*, and *Carey* v. *Population Services International,* afford constitutional protection. We have no doubt as to the correctness of those decisions. They support the reasoning in *Roe* relating to the woman's liberty because they involve personal decisions concerning not only the meaning of procreation but also human responsibility and respect for it. As with abortion, reasonable people will have differences of opinion about these matters. One view is based on such reverence for the wonder of creation that any pregnancy ought to be welcomed and carried to full term no matter how difficult it will be to provide for the child and ensure its well-being. Another is that the inability to provide for the nurture of the infant is a cruelty to the child and an anguish to the parent. These are intimate views with infinite variations, and their deep, personal character underlay our decisions in *Griswold, Eisenstadt*, and *Carey.* The same concerns are present when the woman confronts the reality that, perhaps despite her attempts to avoid it, she has become pregnant.

It was this dimension of personal liberty that *Roe* sought to protect, and its holding invoked the reasoning and the tradition of the precedents we have discussed, granting protection to substantive liberties of the person. *Roe* was, of course, an extension of those cases and, as the decision itself indicated, the separate States could act in some degree to further their own legitimate interests in protecting pre-natal life. The extent to which the legislatures of the State might act to outweigh the interests of the woman in choosing to terminate her pregnancy was a subject of debate in both *Roe* itself and in decisions following it.

While we appreciate the weight of the arguments on behalf of the State in the case before us, arguments which in their ultimate formulation conclude that *Roe* should be overruled, the reservations any of us may have in reaffirming the central holding of *Roe* are outweighed by the explication of individual liberty we have given combined with the force of *stare decisis.* We turn now to that doctrine.

III

A

The obligation to follow precedent begins with necessity, and a contrary necessity marks its outer limits. With Cardozo, we recognize that no judicial system could do society's work if it eyed each issue afresh in every case that raised it. See B. Cardozo, The Nature of the Judicial Process, 149 (1921). Indeed, the very concept of the rule of law underlying our own Constitution requires such continuity over time that a respect for precedent is, by definition, indispensable. At the other extreme, a different necessity would make itself felt if a prior judicial ruling should come to be seen so clearly as error that its enforcement was for that very reason doomed.

Even when the decision to overrule a prior case is not, as in the rare, latter instance, virtually foreordained, it is common wisdom that the rule of *stare decisis* is not an "inexorable command" and certainly it is not such in every constitutional case. . . . Rather, when this Court reexamines a prior holding, its judgment is customarily informed by a series of prudential and pragmatic considerations designed to test the consistency of overruling a prior decision with the ideal of the rule of law, and to gauge the respective costs of reaffirming and overruling a prior case. Thus, for example, we may ask whether the rule has proved to be intolerable simply in defying practical workability; whether the rule is subject to a kind of reliance that would lend a special hardship to the consequences of overruling and add inequity to the cost of repudiation; whether related principles of law have so far developed as to have left the old rule no more than a remnant of abandoned doctrine or whether facts have so changed or come to be seen so differently, as to have robbed the old rule for significant application or justification.

So in this case we may inquire whether *Roe*'s central rule has been found unworkable; whether the rule's limitation on state power could be removed without serious inequity to those who have relied upon it or significant damage to the stability of the society governed by the rule in question; whether the law's growth in the intervening years has left *Roe*'s central rule a doctrinal anachronism discounted by society; and whether *Roe*'s premises of fact have so far changed in the ensuing two decades as to render its central holding somehow irrelevant or unjustifiable in dealing with the issue it addressed.

Although *Roe* has engendered opposition, it has in no sense proven "unworkable," representing as it does a simple limitation beyond which a state law is unenforceable. While *Roe* has, of course, required judicial assessment of state laws affecting the exercise of the choice guaranteed against government infringement, and although the need for such review will remain as a consequence of today's decision, the required determinations fall within judicial competence.

The inquiry into reliance counts the cost of a rule's repudiation as it would fall on those who have relied reasonably on the rule's continued application. Since the classic case for weighing reliance heavily in favor of following the earlier rule occurs in the commercial context, where advance planning of great precision is most obviously a necessity, it is no cause for surprise that some would find no reliance worthy of consideration in support of *Roe*.

While neither respondents nor their *amici* in so many words deny that the abortion right invites some reliance prior to its actual exercise, one can readily imagine an argument stressing the dissimilarity of this case to one involving property or contract. Abortion is customarily chosen as an unplanned response to the consequence of unplanned activity or to the failure of conventional birth control, and except on the assumption that no intercourse would have occurred but for *Roe*'s holding, such behavior may appear to justify no reliance claim. Even if reliance could be claimed on that unrealistic assumption, the argument might run, any realistic interest would be *de minimis*. This argument would be premised on the hypothesis that reproductive planning could take virtually immediate account of any sudden restoration of state authority to ban abortions.

To eliminate the issue of reliance that easily, however, one would need to limit cognizable reliance to specific instances of sexual activity. But to do this would be simply to refuse to face the fact that for two decades of economic and social developments, people have organized intimate relationships and made choices that define their views of themselves and their places in society, in reliance on the availability of abortion in the event that contraception should fail. The ability of women to participate equally in the economic and social life of the Nation has been facilitated by their ability to control their reproductive lives. The Constitution serves human values, and while the effect of reliance on *Roe* cannot be exactly measured, neither can the certain cost of overruling *Roe* for people who have ordered their thinking and living around that case be dismissed.

No evolution of legal principle has left *Roe*'s doctrinal footings weaker than they were in 1973. No development of constitutional law since the case was decided has implicitly or explicitly left *Roe* behind as a mere survivor of obsolete constitutional thinking.

It will be recognized, of course, that *Roe* stands at an intersection of two lines of decisions, but in whichever doctrinal category one reads the case, the result for present purposes will be the same. The *Roe* Court itself placed its holdings in the succession of cases most prominently exemplified by *Griswold* v. *Connecticut*. When it is so seen, *Roe* is clearly in no jeopardy, since subsequent constitutional developments have neither disturbed, nor do they threaten to diminish, the scope of recognized protection accorded to the liberty relating to intimate relationships, the family, and decisions about whether or not to beget or bear a child.

Roe, however, may be seen not only as an exemplar of *Griswold* liberty but as a rule (whether or not mistaken) of personal autonomy and bodily integrity, with doctrinal affinity to cases recognizing limits on governmental power to mandate medical treatment or to bar its rejection. If so, our cases since *Roe* accord with *Roe*'s view that a State's interest in the protection of life falls short of justifying any plenary override of individual liberty claims.

Finally, one could classify *Roe* as *sui generis*. If the case is so viewed, there clearly has been no erosion of its central determination. The original holding resting on the concurrence of seven Members of the Court in 1973 was expressly affirmed by a majority of six in 1983, see *Akron* v. *Akron Center for Reproductive Health, Inc.*, and by a majority of five in 1986, see *Thornburgh* v. *American College of Obstetricians and Gynecologists*, expressing adherence to the constitutional ruling despite legislative efforts in some States to test its limits. More recently, in *Webster* v. *Reproductive Health Services*, although two of the present authors questioned the trimester framework in a way consistent with our judgment today, a majority of the Court either decided to reaffirm or declined to address the constitutional validity of the central holding of *Roe*.

Nor will courts building upon *Roe* be likely to hand down erroneous decisions as a consequence. Even on the assumption that the central holding of *Roe* was in error, that error would go only to the strength of the state interest in fetal protection, not to the recognition afforded by the Constitution to the woman's liberty. The latter aspect of the decision fits comfortably within the framework of the Court's prior decisions including *Loving* v. *Virginia* and *Eisenstadt* v. *Baird*, the holdings of which are "not a series of isolated points," but mark a "rational continuum." As we described in *Carey* v. *Population Services International*, the liberty which encompasses those decisions

> includes "the interest in independence in making certain kinds of important decisions." While the outer limits of this aspect of [protected liberty] have not been marked by the Court, it is clear that among the decisions that an individual may make without unjustified government interference are personal decisions "relating to marriage, procreation, contraception, family relationships, and child rearing and education."

The soundness of this prong of the *Roe* analysis is apparent from a consideration of the alternative. If indeed the woman's interest in deciding whether to bear and beget a child had not been recognized as in *Roe*, the State might as readily restrict a woman's right to choose to carry a pregnancy to term as to terminate it, to further asserted state interests in population control, or eugenics, for example. Yet *Roe* has been sensibly relied upon to encounter any such suggestions, e.g., *Arnold* v. *Board of Education of Escambia County, Alabama* (CA11 1989) (relying upon *Roe* and concluding that government officials violate the Constitution by coercing a minor to have an abortion); *Avery* v. *County of Burke* (CA4 1981) (county agency inducing teenage girl to undergo unwanted sterilization on the basis of misrepresentation that she had sickle cell trait); see also *In re Quinlan* (1976) (relying on *Roe* in finding a right to terminate medical treatment). In any event, because *Roe*'s scope is confined by the fact of its concern with postconception potential life, a concern otherwise likely to be implicated only by some forms of contraception protected independently under *Griswold* and later cases, any error in *Roe* is unlikely to have serious ramifications in future cases.

We have seen how time has overtaken some of *Roe*'s factual assumptions: advances in maternal health care allow for abortions safe to the mother later in pregnancy than was true in 1973, see *Akron I*, and advances in neonatal care have advanced viability to a point somewhat earlier. But these facts go only to the scheme of time limits on the realization of competing interests, and the divergences from the factual premises of 1973 have no bearing on the validity of *Roe*'s central holding, that viability marks the earliest point at which the State's interest in fetal life is constitutionally adequate to justify a legislative ban on nontherapeutic abortions. The soundness or unsoundness of that constitutional judgment in no sense turns on whether viability occurs at approximately 28 weeks, as was usual at the time of *Roe*, at 23 to 24 weeks, as it sometimes does today, or at some moment even slightly earlier in pregnancy, as it may if fetal respiratory capacity can somehow be enhanced in the future. Whenever it may occur, the attainment of viability may continue to serve as the critical fact, just as it has done since *Roe* was decided; which is to say that no change in *Roe*'s factual underpinning has left its central holding obsolete, and none supports an argument for overruling it.

The sum of the precedential inquiry to this point shows *Roe*'s underpinnings unweakened in any way affecting its central holding. While it has engendered disapproval, it has not been unworkable. An entire generation has come of age free to assume *Roe*'s concept of liberty in defining the capacity of women to act in society, and to make reproductive decisions; no erosion of principle going to liberty or personal autonomy has left *Roe*'s central holding a doctrinal remnant; *Roe* portends no developments at odds with other precedent for the analysis of personal liberty; and no changes of fact have rendered viability more or less appropriate as the point at which the balance of interest tips. Within the bounds of normal *stare decisis* analysis, then, and subject to the considerations on which it customarily turns, the stronger argument is for affirming *Roe*'s central holding, with whatever degree of personal reluctance any of us may have, not for overruling it.

In a less significant case, *stare decisis* analysis could, and would, stop at the point we have reached. But the sustained and widespread debate *Roe* has provoked calls for some comparison between that case and others of comparable dimension that have responded to national controversies and taken on the impress of the controversies addressed. Only two such decisional lines from the past century present themselves for examination, and in each instance the result reached by the Court accorded with the principles we apply today.

The first example is that line of cases identified with *Lochner* v. *New York*, which imposed substantive limitations on legislation limiting economic autonomy in favor of health and welfare regulation, adopting, in JUSTICE HOLMES' view, the theory of *laissez-faire*. The *Lochner* decisions were exemplified by *Adkins* v. *Children's Hospital of D.C.*, (1923), in which this Court held it to be an infringement of constitutionally protected liberty of contract to require the employers of adult women to satisfy minimum wage standards. Fourteen years later, *West Coast Hotel Co.* v. *Parrish*, (1937), signalled the demise of *Lochner* by overruling *Adkins*.

In the meantime, the Depression had come and, with it, the lesson that seemed unmistakable to most people by 1937, that the interpretation of contractual freedom protected in *Adkins* rested on fundamentally false factual assumptions about the capacity of a relatively unregulated market to satisfy minimal levels of human welfare. As JUSTICE JACKSON wrote of the constitutional crisis of 1937 shortly before he came on the bench, "The older world of *laissez-faire* was recognized everywhere outside the Court to be dead." The facts upon which the earlier case had premised a constitutional resolution of social controversy had proved to be untrue, and history's demonstration of their untruth not only justified but required the new choice of constitutional principle that *West Coast Hotel* announced. Of course, it was true that the Court lost something by its misperception, or its lack of prescience, and the Court-packing crisis only magnified the loss; but the clear demonstration that the facts of economic life were different from those previously assumed warranted the repudiation of the old law.

The second comparison that the 20th century history invites is with the cases employing the separate-but-equal rule for applying the Fourteenth Amendment's equal protection guarantee. They began with *Plessy* v. *Ferguson*, (1896), holding that legislatively mandated racial segregation in public transportation works no denial of equal protection, rejecting the argument that racial separation enforced by the legal machinery of American society treats the black race as inferior. The *Plessy* Court considered "the underlying fallacy of the plaintiff's argument to consist in the assumption that the enforced separation of the two races stamps the colored race with a badge of inferiority. If this be so, it is not by reason of anything found in the act, but solely because the colored race chooses to put that construction upon it." Whether, as a matter of historical fact, the Justices in the *Plessy* majority believed this or not, this understanding of the implication of segregation was the stated justification for the Court's opinion. But this understanding of the facts and the rule it was stated to justify were repudiated in *Brown* v. *Board of Education* (1954). As one commentator observed, the question before the Court in *Brown* was "whether discrimination inheres in that segregation which is imposed by law in the twentieth century in certain specific states in the American Union. And that question has meaning and can find an answer only on the ground of history and of common knowledge about the facts of life in the times and places aforesaid." Black, The Lawfulness of the Segregation Decisions, 69 Yale Law Journal 421, 427 (1960).

The Court in *Brown* addressed these facts of life by observing that whatever may have been the understanding in *Plessy*'s time of the power of segregation to stigmatize those who were segregated with a "badge of inferiority," it was clear by 1954 that legally sanctioned segregation had just such an effect, to the point that racially separate public educational facilities were deemed inherently unequal. Society's understanding of the facts upon which a constitutional ruling was sought in 1954 was thus fundamentally different from the basis claimed for the decision in 1896. While we think *Plessy* was wrong the day it was decided we must also recognize that the *Plessy* Court's explanation for its decision was so clearly at odds with the facts apparent to the Court in 1954 that the decision to reexamine *Plessy* was on this ground alone not only justified but required.

West Coast Hotel and *Brown* each rested on facts, or an understanding of facts, changed from those which furnished the claimed justifications for the earlier constitutional resolutions. Each case was comprehensible as the Court's response to facts that the country could understand, or had come to understand already, but which the Court of an earlier day, as its own declarations disclosed, had not been able to perceive. As the decisions were thus comprehensible they were also defensible, not merely as the victories of one doctrinal school over another by dint of numbers (victories though they were), but as applications of constitutional principle to facts as they had not been seen by the Court before. In constitutional adjudication as elsewhere in life, changed circumstances may impose new obligations, and the thoughtful part of the Nation could accept each decision to overrule a prior case as a response to the Court's constitutional duty.

Because the case before us presents no such occasion it could be seen as no such response. Because neither the factual underpinnings of *Roe*'s central holding nor our understanding of it has changed (and because no other indication of weakened precedent has been shown) the Court could not pretend to be reexamining the prior law with any justification beyond a present doctrinal disposition to come out differently from the Court of 1973. To overrule prior law for no other reason than that would run counter to the view repeated in our cases, that a decision to overrule should rest on some special reason over and above the belief that a prior case was wrongly decided. ("A basic change in the law upon a ground no firmer than a change in our membership invites the popular misconception that this institution is little different from the two political branches of the Government. No misconception could do more lasting injury to this Court and to the system of law which it is our abiding mission to serve"); *Mapp* v. *Ohio*, (1961) (HARLAN, J., dissenting).

C

The examination of the conditions justifying the repudiation of *Adkins* by *West Coast Hotel* and *Plessy* by *Brown* is enough to suggest the terrible price that would have been paid if the Court had not overruled as it did. In the present case, however, as our analysis to this point makes clear, the terrible price would be paid for overruling. Our analysis would not be complete, however, without explaining why overruling *Roe*'s central holding would not only reach an unjustifiable result under principles of *stare decisis*, but would seriously weaken the Court's capacity to exercise the judicial power and to function as the Supreme Court of a Nation dedicated to the rule of law. To understand why this would be so it is necessary to understand the source of this Court's authority, the conditions necessary for its preservation, and its relationship to the country's understanding of itself as a constitutional Republic.

The root of American governmental power is revealed most clearly in the instance of the power conferred by the Constitution upon the Judiciary of the United States and specifically upon this Court. As Americans of each succeeding generation are rightly told, the Court cannot buy support for its decisions by spending money and, except to a minor degree, it cannot independently coerce obedience to its decrees. The Court's power lies, rather, in its legitimacy, a product of substance and perception that shows itself in the people's acceptance of the Judiciary as fit to determine what the Nation's law means and to declare what it demands.

The underlying substance of this legitimacy is of course the warrant for the Court's decisions in the Constitution and the lesser sources of legal principle on which the Court draws. That substance is expressed in the Court's opinions, and our contemporary understanding is such that a decision without principled justification would be no judicial act at all. But even when justification is furnished by apposite legal principle, something more is required. Because not every conscientious claim of principled justification will be accepted as such, the justification claimed must be beyond dispute. The Court must take care to speak and act in ways that allow people to accept its decisions on the terms the Court claims for them, as grounded truly in principle, not as compromises with social and political pressures having, as such, no bearing on the principled choices that the Court is obliged to make. Thus, the Court's legitimacy depends on making legally principled decisions under circumstances in which their principled character is sufficiently plausible to be accepted by the Nation.

The need for principled action to be perceived as such is implicated to some degree whenever this, or any other appellate court, overrules a prior case. This is not to say, of course, that this Court cannot give a perfectly satisfactory explanation in most cases. People understand that some of the Constitution's language is hard to fathom and that the Court's Justices are sometimes able to perceive significant facts or to understand principles of law that eluded their predecessors and that justify departures from existing decisions. However upsetting it may be to those most directly affected when one judicially derived rule replaces another, the country can accept some correction of effort without necessarily questioning the legitimacy of the Court.

In two circumstances, however, the Court would almost certainly fail to receive the benefit of the doubt in overruling prior cases. There is, first, a point beyond which frequent overruling would overtax the country's belief in the Court's good faith. Despite the variety of reasons that may inform and justify a decision to overrule, we cannot forget that such a decision is usually perceived (and perceived correctly) as, at the least, a statement that a prior decision was wrong. There is a limit to the amount of error that can plausibly be imputed to prior courts. If that limit should be exceeded, disturbance of prior rulings would be taken as evidence that justifiable reexamination of principle had given way to drives for particular results in the short term. The legitimacy of the Court would fade with the frequency of its vacillation.

That first circumstance can be described as hypothetical; the second is to the point here and now. Where, in the performance of its judicial duties, the Court decides a case in such a way as to resolve the sort of intensely divisive controversy reflected in *Roe* and those rare, comparable cases, its decision has a dimension that the resolution of the normal case does not carry. It is the dimension present whenever the Court's interpretation of the Constitution calls the contending sides of a national controversy to end their national division by accepting a common mandate rooted in the Constitution.

The Court is not asked to do this very often, having thus addressed the Nation only twice in our lifetime, in the decisions of *Brown* and *Roe*. But when the Court does act in this way, its decision requires an equally rare precedential force to counter the inevitable efforts to overturn it and to thwart its implementation. Some of those efforts may be mere unprincipled emotional reactions; others may proceed from principles worthy of profound respect. But whatever the premises of opposition may be, only the most convincing justification under accepted standards of precedent could suffice to demonstrate that a later decision overruling the first was anything but a surrender to political pressure, and an unjustified repudiation of the principle on which the Court staked its authority in the first instance. So to overrule under fire in the absence of the most compelling reason to reexamine a watershed decision would subvert the Court's legitimacy beyond any serious question. Cf. *Brown* v. *Board of Education*, (1955) (*Brown II*) ("[I]t should go without saying that the vitality of th[e] constitutional principles [announced in *Brown* v. *Board of Education*, (1954)] cannot be allowed to yield simply because of disagreement with them").

The country's loss of confidence in the judiciary would be underscored by an equally certain and equally reasonable condemnation for another failing in the overruling unnecessarily and under pressure. Some cost will be paid by anyone who approves or implements a constitutional decision where it is unpopular, or who refuses to work to undermine the decision or to force its reversal. The price my be criticism or ostracism, or it may be violence. An extra price will be paid by those who themselves disapprove of the decision's results when viewed outside of constitutional terms, but who nevertheless struggle to accept it, because they respect the rule of the law. To all those who will be so tested by the following, the Court implicitly undertakes to remain steadfast, lest in the end a price be paid for nothing. The promise of consistency, once given, binds its maker for as long as the power to stand by the decision survives and the understanding of the issue has not changed so fundamentally as to render the commitment obsolete. From the obligation of this promise the Court cannot and should not assume any exemption when duty requires it to decide a case in conformance with the Constitution. A willing breach of it would be nothing less that a breach of faith, and no Court that broke its faith with the people could sensibly expect credit for the principle in the decision by which it did that.

It is true that diminished legitimacy may be restored, but only slowly. Unlike the political branches, a Court thus weakened could not seek to regain its position with a new mandate from the voters, and even if the Court could somehow go to the polls, the loss of its principled character could not be retrieved by the casting of so many votes. Like the character of an individual, the legitimacy of the Court must be earned over time. So, indeed, must be the character of a Nation of people who aspire to live according to the rule of law. Their belief in themselves as such a people is not readily separable from their understanding of the Court invested with the authority to decide their constitutional cases and speak before all others for their constitutional ideals. If the Court's legitimacy should be undermined, then so would the country be in its very ability to see itself through its constitutional ideals. The Court's concern with legitimacy is not for the sake of the Court but for the sake of the Nation to which it is responsible.

The Court's duty in the present case is clear. In 1973, it confronted the already-divisive issue of governmental power to limit personal choice to undergo abortion, for which it provided a new resolution based on the due process guaranteed by the Fourteenth Amendment. Whether or not a new social consensus is developing on that issue, its divisiveness is no less today than in 1973, and pressure to retain it has grown only more intense. A decision to overrule *Roe*'s essential holding under the existing circumstances would address error, if error there was, at the cost of both profound and unnecessary damage to the Court's legitimacy, and to the Nation's commitment to the rule of law. It is therefore imperative to adhere to the essence of *Roe*'s original decision, and we do so today.

IV

From what we have said so far it follows that it is a constitutional liberty of the woman to have some freedom to terminate her pregnancy. We conclude that the basic decision in *Roe* was based on a constitutional analysis which we cannot now repudiate. The woman's liberty is not so unlimited, however, that from the outset the State cannot show its concern for the life of the unborn, and at a later point in fetal development the State's interest in life has sufficient force so that the right of the woman to terminate pregnancy can be restricted.

That brings us, of course, to the point where much criticism has been directed at *Roe*, a criticism that always inheres when the Court draws a specific rule from what in the Constitution is but a general

standard. We conclude, however, that the urgent claims of the woman to retain the ultimate control over her destiny and her body, claims implicit in the meaning of liberty, require us to perform that function. Liberty must not be extinguished for want of a line that is clear. And it falls to us to give some real substance to the woman's liberty to determine whether to carry her pregnancy to full term.

We conclude the line should be drawn at viability, so that before that time the woman has a right to choose to terminate her pregnancy. We adhere to the principle for two reasons. First, as we have said, is the doctrine of *stare decisis*. Any judicial act of line-drawing may seem somewhat arbitrary, but *Roe* was a reasoned statement, elaborated with great care. We have twice reaffirmed it in the face of great opposition. Although we must overrule those parts of *Thornburgh* and *Akron I* which, in our view, are inconsistent with *Roe*'s statement that the State has a legitimate interest in promoting the life or potential life of the unborn, the central premise of those cases represents an unbroken commitment by this Court to the essential holding of *Roe*. It is that premise which we reaffirm today.

The second reason is that the concept of viability, as we noted in *Roe*, is the time at which there is a realistic possibility of maintaining and nourishing a life outside the womb, so that the independent existence of the second life can in reason and all fairness be the object of state protection that now overrides the rights of the woman. Consistent with other constitutional norms, legislatures may draw lines which appear arbitrary without the necessity of offering a justification. But courts may not. We must justify the line we draw. And there is no line other than viability which is more workable. To be sure, as we have said, there may be some medical developments that affect the precise point of viability, but this is an imprecision within tolerable limits given that the medical community and all those who must apply its discoveries will continue to explore the matter. The viability line also has, as a practical matter, an element of fairness. In some broad sense it might be said that a woman who fails to act before viability has consented to the State's intervention of behalf of the developing child.

The woman's right to terminate her pregnancy before viability is the most central principle of *Roe* v. *Wade*. It is a rule of law and a component of liberty we cannot renounce.

On the other side of the equation is the interest of the State in the protection of potential life. The

Roe Court recognized the State's "important and legitimate interest in protecting the potentiality of human life." The weight to be given this state interest, not the strength of the woman's interest, was the difficult question faced in *Roe.* We do not need to say whether each of us, had we been Members of the Court when the valuation of the state interest came before it as an original matter, would have concluded, as the *Roe* Court did, that its weight is insufficient to justify a ban on abortions prior to viability even when it is subject to certain exceptions. That matter is not before us in the first instance, and coming as it does after nearly 20 years of litigation in *Roe*'s wake we are satisfied that the immediate question is not the soundness of *Roe*'s resolution of the issue, but the precedential force that must be accorded to its holding. And we have concluded that the essential holding of *Roe* should be reaffirmed.

Yet it must be remembered that *Roe* v. *Wade* speaks with clarity in establishing not only the woman's liberty but also the State's "important and legitimate interest in potential life." That portion of the decision in *Roe* has been given too little acknowledgement and implementation by the Court in its subsequent cases. Those cases decided that any regulation touching upon the abortion decision must survive strict scrutiny, to be sustained only if drawn in narrow terms to further a compelling state interest. Not all of the cases decided under that formulation can be reconciled with the holding in *Roe* itself that the State has legitimate interests in the health of the woman and in protecting the potential life within her. In resolving this tension, we choose to rely upon *Roe*, as against the later cases.

Roe established a trimester framework to govern abortion regulations. Under this elaborate but rigid construct, almost no regulation at all is permitted during the first trimester of pregnancy; regulations designed to protect the woman's health, but not to further the State's interest in potential life, are permitted during the second trimester; and during the third trimester, when the fetus is viable, prohibitions are permitted provided the life or health of the mother is not at stake. Most of our cases since *Roe* have involved the application of rules derived from the trimester framework.

The trimester framework no doubt was erected to ensure that the woman's right to choose not become so subordinate to the State's interest in promoting fetal life that her choice exists in theory but not in fact. We do not agree, however, that the trimester approach is necessary to accomplish this objective. A framework of this rigidity was unnecessary and in its later interpretation sometimes contradicted the State's permissible exercise of its powers.

Though the woman has a right to choose to terminate or continue her pregnancy before viability, it does not at all follow that the State is prohibited from taking steps to ensure that this choice is thoughtful and informed. Even in the earliest stages of pregnancy, the State may enact rules and regulations designed to encourage her to know that there are philosophic and social arguments of great weight that can be brought to bear in favor of continuing the pregnancy to full term and that there are procedures and institutions to allow adoption of unwanted children as well as a certain degree of state assistance if the mother chooses to raise the child herself. "[T]he Constitution does not forbid a State or city, pursuant to democratic processes, from expressing a preference for normal childbirth." *Webster* v. *Reproductive Health Services.* It follows that States are free to enact laws to provide a reasonable framework for a woman to make a decision that has such profound and lasting meaning. This, too, we find consistent with *Roe*'s central premises, and indeed the inevitable consequence of our holding that the State has an interest in protecting the life of the unborn.

We reject the trimester framework, which we do not consider to be part of the essential holding of *Roe.* Measures aimed at ensuring that a woman's choice contemplates the consequences for the fetus do not necessarily interfere with the right recognized in *Roe*, although those measures have been found to be inconsistent with the rigid trimester framework announced in that case. A logical reading of the central holding in *Roe* itself, and a necessary reconciliation of the liberty of the woman and the interest of the State in promoting prenatal life, require, in our view, that we abandon the trimester framework as a rigid prohibition on all previability regulation aimed at the protection of fetal life. The trimester framework suffers from these basic flaws: in its formulation it misconceives the nature of the pregnant woman's interest; and in practice it undervalues the State's interest in potential life, as recognized in *Roe.*

As our jurisprudence relating to all liberties save perhaps abortion has recognized, not every law which makes a right more difficult to exercise is, *ipso facto*, an infringement of that right. An example clarifies the point. We have held that not every ballot access limitation amounts to an infringement of the right to vote. Rather, the States are granted substantial flexibility in establishing the framework within which voters choose the candidates for whom they wish to vote (*Anderson* v. *Celebrezze*, 1992).

The abortion right is similar. Numerous forms of state regulation might have the incidental effect of increasing the cost or decreasing the availability of medical care, whether for abortion or any other medical procedure. The fact that a law which serves a valid purpose, one not designed to strike at the right itself, has the incidental effect of making it more difficult or more expensive to procure an abortion cannot be enough to invalidate it. Only where state regulation imposes an undue burden on a woman's ability to make this decision does the power of the State reach into the heart of the liberty protected by the Due Process Clause.

For the most part, the Court's early abortion cases adhered to this view. In *Maher* v. *Roe*, (1977), the Court explained: "*Roe* did not declare an unqualified 'constitutional right to an abortion,' as the District Court seemed to think. Rather, the right protects the woman from unduly burdensome interference with her freedom to decide whether or not to terminate her pregnancy." . . .

These considerations of the nature of the abortion right illustrate that it is an overstatement to describe it as a right to decide whether to have an abortion "without interference from the State" (*Planned Parenthood of Central Mo.* v. *Danforth*, (1976)). All abortion regulations interfere to some degree with a woman's ability to decide whether to terminate her pregnancy. It is, as a consequence, not surprising that despite the protestations contained in the original *Roe* opinion to the effect that the Court was not recognizing an absolute right, the Court's experience applying the trimester framework has led to the striking down of some abortion regulations which in no real sense deprived women of the ultimate decision. Those decisions went too far because the right recognized by *Roe* is a right "to be free from unwarranted governmental intrusion into matters so fundamentally affecting a person as the decision whether to bear or beget a child."

Not all governmental intrusion is of necessity unwarranted; and that brings us to the other basic flaw in the trimester framework: even in *Roe*'s terms, in practice it undervalues the State's interest in the potential life within the woman. *Roe* v. *Wade* was express in its recognition of the State's "important and legitimate interest[s] in preserving and protecting the health of the pregnant woman [and] in protecting the potentiality of human life." The trimester framework, however, does not fulfill *Roe*'s own promise that the State has an interest in protecting fetal life or potential life. *Roe* began the contradiction by using the trimester framework to forbid any regulation of abortion designed to advance that interest before viability. Before viability, *Roe* and subsequent cases treat all governmental attempts to influence a woman's decision on behalf of the potential life within her as unwarranted. This treatment is, in our judgment, incompatible with the recognition that there is a substantial state interest in potential life throughout pregnancy.

The very notion that the State has a substantial interest in potential life leads to the conclusion that not all regulations must be deemed unwarranted. Not all burdens on the right to decide whether to terminate a pregnancy will be undue. In our view, the undue burden standard is the appropriate means of reconciling the State's interest with the woman's constitutionally protected liberty.

. . . Because we set forth a standard of general application to which we intend to adhere, it is important to clarify what is meant by an undue burden.

A finding of an undue burden is a shorthand for the conclusion that a state regulation has the purpose or effect of placing a substantial obstacle in the path of a woman seeking an abortion of a nonviable fetus . . . [Thus,] we answer the question left open in previous opinions discussing the undue burden formulation, whether a law designed to further the State's interest in fetal life which imposes an undue burden on the woman's decision before fetal viability could be constitutional.

Some guiding principles should emerge. What is at stake is the woman's right to make the ultimate decision, not a right to be insulated from all others in doing so. Regulations which do no more that create a structural mechanism by which the State, or the parent or guardian of a minor, may express profound respect for the life of the unborn are permitted, if they are not a substantial obstacle to the woman's exercise of the right to choose. Unless it has that effect on her right of choice, a state measure designed to persuade her to choose childbirth over abortion will be upheld if reasonable related to that goal. Regulations designed to foster the health of a woman seeking an abortion are valid if they do not constitute an undue burden.

Even when jurists reason from shared premises, some disagreement is inevitable. . . . That is to be expected in the application of any legal standard which must accommodate life's complexity. We do not expect it to be otherwise with respect to the undue burden standard. We give this summary:

(a) To protect the central right recognized by *Roe* v. *Wade* while at the same time accommodating the State's profound interest in potential life, we will employ the undue burden analysis as explained in this opinion. An undue burden exists, and therefore a provision of law is invalid, if its purpose or effect is to place a substantial obstacle in the path of a woman seeking an abortion before the fetus attains viability.

(b) We reject the rigid trimester framework of *Roe* v. *Wade*. To promote the State's profound interest in potential life, throughout pregnancy the State may take measures to ensure that the woman's choice is informed, and measures designed to advance this interest will not be invalidated as long as their purpose is to persuade the woman to choose childbirth over abortion. These measures must not be an undue burden on the right.

(c) As with any medical procedure, the State may enact regulations to further the health or safety of a woman seeking an abortion. Unnecessary health regulations that have the purpose or effect of presenting a substantial obstacle to a woman seeking an abortion impose an undue burden on the right.

(d) Our adoption of the undue burden analysis does not disturb the central holding of *Roe* v. *Wade*, and we reaffirm that holding. Regardless of whether exceptions are made for particular circumstances, a State may not prohibit any woman from making the ultimate decision to terminate her pregnancy before viability.

(e) We also reaffirm *Roe*'s holding that "subsequent to viability, the State in promoting its interest in the potentiality of human life, may, if it chooses, regulate, and even proscribe, abortion except where it is necessary, in appropriate medical judgment, for the preservation of the life or health of the mother." *Roe* v. *Wade*, 410 U.S., at 164–165, 93 S. Ct., at 732.

These principles control our assessment of the Pennsylvania statute, and we now turn to the issue of the validity of its challenged provisions.

V

The Court of Appeals applied what it believed to be the undue burden standard and upheld each of the provisions except for the husband notification requirement. We agree generally with this conclusion, but refine the undue burden analysis in accordance with the principles articulated above. We now consider the separate statutory sections at issue.

A

Because it is central to the operation of various other requirements, we begin with the statute's definition of medical emergency. Under the statute, a medical emergency is

[t]hat condition which, on the basis of the physician's good faith clinical judgment, so complicates the medical condition of a pregnant woman as to necessitate the immediate abortion of her pregnancy to avert her death or for which a delay will create serious risk of substantial and irreversible impairment of a major bodily function.

Petitioners argue that the definition is too narrow, contending that it forecloses the possibility of an immediate abortion despite some significant health risks. If the contention were correct, we would be required to invalidate the restrictive operation of the provision, for the essential holding of *Roe* forbids a State from interfering with a woman's choice to undergo an abortion procedure if continuing her pregnancy would constitute a threat to her health.

The District Court found that there were three serious conditions which would not be covered by the statute. . . . Yet, as the Court of Appeals observed, it is undisputed that under some circumstances each of these conditions could lead to an illness with substantial and irreversible consequences. While the definition could be interpreted in an unconstitutional manner, the Court of Appeals construed the phrase "serious risk" to include those circumstances. It stated: "we read the medical emergency exception as intended by the Pennsylvania legislature to assure that compliance with its abortion regulations would not in any way pose a significant threat to the life or health of a woman." As we said in *Brockette* v. *Arcades, Inc.*, (1985), "Normally, . . . we defer to the construction of a state statute given it by the lower federal courts." Indeed, we have said that we will defer to lower court interpretations of state law unless they amount to "plain" error. *Palmer* v. *Hoffman*, (1948). This " 'reflect[s] our belief that district courts and courts of appeals are better schooled in and more able to interpret the laws of their respective States.' " *Frisby* v. *Schultz* (1988). We adhere to that course today, and conclude that, as construed by the Court of Appeals, the medical emergency definition imposes no undue burden on a woman's abortion right.

B

We next consider the informed consent requirement. Except in a medical emergency, the statute requires that at least 24 hours before performing an abortion a physician inform the woman of the nature of the procedure, the health risks of the abortion and of childbirth, and the "probable gestational age of the unborn child." . . .

Our prior decisions establish that as with any medical procedure, the State may require a woman to give her written informed consent to an abortion. In this respect, the statute is unexceptional. Petitioners challenge the statute's definition of informed consent because it includes the provision of specific information by the doctor and the mandatory 24-hour waiting period. The conclusions reached by a majority of the Justices in the separate opinions filed today and the undue burden standard adopted in the opinion require us to overrule in part some of the Court's past decisions driven by the trimester framework's prohibition of all previability regulations designed to further the State's interest in fetal life. . . .

To the extent *Akron* and *Thornburgh* find a constitutional violation when the government requires, as it does here, the giving of truthful, nonmisleading information about the nature of the procedure, the attendant health risks of the procedure, the attendant health risks and those of childbirth, and the "probable gestational age" of the fetus, those cases go too far, are inconsistent with *Roe*'s acknowledgement of an important interest in potential life, and are overruled. . . . In short, requiring that the information relating to fetal development and the assistance available should she decide to carry the pregnancy to full term is a reasonable measure to insure an informed choice, one which might cause the woman to choose childbirth over abortion. This requirement cannot be considered a substantial obstacle to obtaining an abortion, and, it follows, there is not undue burden.

Our prior cases also suggest that the "straitjacket" of particular information which must be given in each case interferes with a constitutional right of privacy between a pregnant woman and her physician. As a preliminary matter, it is worth noting that the statute now before us does not require a physician to comply with the informed consent provisions "if he or she can demonstrate by a preponderance of evidence that he or she reasonably believed that furnishing the information would have resulted in a severely adverse effect on the physical or mental health of the patient." In this respect, the statute does not prevent the physician from exercising his or her medical judgment.

Whatever constitutional status the doctor-patient relation may have as a general matter, in the present context it is derivative of the woman's position. The doctor-patient relation does not underlie or override the two more general rights under which the abortion right is justified: the right to make family decisions and the right to physical autonomy. On its own the doctor-patient relation here is entitled to the same solicitude it receives in other contexts. Thus, a requirement that a doctor give a woman certain information as part of obtaining her consent to an abortion is, for constitutional purposes, no different from a requirement that a doctor give certain specific information about any medical procedure. . . .

Since there is no evidence on this record that requiring a doctor to give the information as provided by the statute would amount in practical terms to a substantial obstacle to a woman seeking an abortion, we conclude that it is not an undue burden . . . Thus, we uphold the provision as a reasonable means to insure that the woman's consent is informed.

Our analysis of Pennsylvania's 24-hour waiting period between the provision of the information deemed necessary to informed consent and the performance of an abortion under the undue burden standard requires us to reconsider the premise behind the decision invalidating a parallel requirement. In *Akron I* we said: "Nor are we convinced that the State's legitimate concern that the woman's decision be informed is reasonably served by requiring a 24-hour delay as a matter of course." We consider that conclusion to be wrong. The idea that important decisions will be more informed and deliberate if they follow some period of reflection does not strike us as unreasonable, particularly where the statute directs that important information become part of the background of the decision. . . .

C

Section 3209 of Pennsylvania's abortion law provides, except in cases of medical emergency, that no physician shall perform an abortion on a married woman without receiving a signed statement from the woman that she had notified her spouse that she is about to undergo an abortion. The woman has the option of providing an alternative signed statement certifying that her husband could not be located; that the pregnancy is the result of spousal sexual assault which she has reported; or that the woman believes that notifying her husband will cause him or someone else to inflict bodily injury upon her. A physician who performs an abortion on a married woman without receiving the appropriate signed statement will have his or her license revoked, and is liable to the husband for damages.

The District Court heard the testimony of numerous expert witnesses, and made detailed findings of fact regarding the effect of this statute. . . . This information and the District Court's findings reinforce what common sense would suggest. In well-functioning marriages, spouses discuss important intimate decisions such as whether to bear a child. But there are millions of women in this country who are victims of regular and psychological abuse at the hands of their husbands. Should these women become pregnant, they may have very good reasons for not wishing to inform their husbands of their decision to obtain an abortion. Many may have justifiable fears of physical abuse, but may be no less fearful of the consequences of reporting prior abuse to the Commonwealth of Pennsylvania. Many may have a reasonable fear that notifying their husbands will provoke further instances of child abuse; these women are not exempt from [Section] 3209's notification requirement. Many may fear devastating forms of psychological abuse from their husbands, including verbal harassment, threats of future violence, the destruction of possessions, physical confinement to the home, the withdrawal of financial support, or the disclosure of the abortion to family and friends. These methods of psychological abuse may act as even more of a deterrent to notification than the possibility of physical violence, but women who are victims of the abuse are not exempt from [Section] 3209's notification requirement. And many women who are pregnant as a result of sexual assaults by their husbands will be unable to avail themselves of the exception for spousal sexual assault, because the exception requires that the woman have notified law enforcement authorities within 90 days of the assault, and her husband will be notified of her report once an investigation begins. If anything in this field is certain, it is that victims of spousal sexual assault are extremely reluctant to report the abuse to the government; hence, a great many spousal rape victims will not be exempt from the notification requirement imposed by [Section] 3209.

The spousal notification requirement is thus likely to prevent a significant number of women from obtaining an abortion. It does not merely make abortions a little more difficult or expensive to obtain; for many women it will impose a substantial obstacle. We must not blind ourselves to the fact that the significant number of women who fear for their safety and the safety of their children are likely to be deterred from procuring an abor-

tion as surely as if the Commonwealth had outlawed abortion in all cases. . . .

The unfortunate yet persisting conditions we document above will mean that in a large fraction of the cases in which [Section] 3209 is relevant, it will operate as a substantial obstacle to a woman's choice to undergo an abortion. It is an undue burden, and therefore invalid.

The husband's interest in the life of the child his wife is carrying does not permit the State to empower him with this troubling degree of authority over his wife. The contrary view leads to consequences reminiscent of the common law. A husband has no enforceable right to require a wife to advise him before she exercises her personal choices. . . . A State may not give to a man the kind of dominion over his wife that parents exercise over their children.

Section 3209 embodies a view of marriage consonant with the common-law status of married women but repugnant to our present understanding of marriage and of the nature of the rights secured by the Constitution. Women do not lose their constitutionally protected liberty when they marry. The Constitution protects all individuals, male or female, married or unmarried, from the abuse of governmental power, even where that power is employed for the supposed benefit of a member of the individual's family. These considerations confirm that [Section] 3209 is invalid.

D

We next consider the parental consent provision. Except in a medical emergency, an unemancipated young woman under 18 may not obtain an abortion unless she and one of her parents (or guardian) provides informed consent as defined above. If neither a parent nor a guardian provides consent, a court may authorize the performance of an abortion upon a determination that the young woman is mature and capable of giving informed consent and has in fact given her informed consent, or that an abortion would be in her best interests.

We have been over most of this ground before. Our cases establish, and we reaffirm today, that a State may require a minor seeking an abortion to obtain the consent of a parent or guardian, provided that there is an adequate judicial bypass procedure. Under these precedents, in our view, the one-parent consent requirement and judicial bypass procedure are constitutional.

The only argument made by petitioners respecting this provision and to which our prior decisions do not speak is the contention that the parental consent requirement is invalid because it requires informed parental consent. For the most part, petitioners' argument is a reprise of their argument with respect to the informed consent requirement in general, and we reject it for the reasons given above. Indeed, some of the provisions regarding informed consent have particular force with respect to minors: the waiting period, for example, may provide the parent or parents of a pregnant young woman the opportunity to consult with her in private, and to discuss the consequences of her decision in the context of the values and moral or religious principles of their family.

E

Under the recordkeeping and reporting requirements of the statute, every facility which performs abortions is required to file a report stating its name and address as well as the name and address of any related entity, such as a controlling or subsidiary organization. In the case of state-funded institutions, the information becomes public. . . . Every abortion facility must also file quarterly reports showing the number of abortions performed broken down by trimester. In all events, the identity of each woman who has had an abortion remains confidential.

In *Danforth*, (1976), we held that recordkeeping and reporting provisions "that are reasonably directed to the preservation of maternal health and that properly respect a patient's confidentiality and privacy are permissible." We think that under this standard, all the provisions at issue here except that relating to spousal notice are constitutional. Although they do not relate to the State's interest in informing the woman's choice, they do relate to health. The collection of information with respect to actual patients is a vital element of medical research, and so it cannot be said that the requirements serve no purpose other than to make abortions more difficult. Nor do we find that the requirements impose a substantial obstacle to a woman's choice. At most they might increase the cost of some abortions by a slight amount. While at some point increased cost could become a substantial obstacle, there is not such showing on the record before us.

Subsection (12) of the reporting provision requires the reporting of, among other things, a married woman's "reason for failure to provide notice" to her husband. This provision in effect requires women as a condition of obtaining an abortion, to provide the Commonwealth with the precise information we have already recognized that many women have pressing reasons not to re-

veal. Like the spousal notice requirement itself, this provision places an undue burden on a woman's choice, and must be invalidated for that reason.

VI

Our Constitution is a covenant running from the first generation of Americans to us and then to future generations. It is a coherent succession. Each generation must learn anew that the Constitution's written terms embody ideas and aspirations that must survive more ages than one. We accept our responsibility not to retreat from interpreting the full meaning of the covenant in light of all our precedents. We invoke it once again to define the freedom guaranteed by the Constitution's own promise, the promise of liberty. . . .

JUSTICE STEVENS's [opinion], *concurring in part and dissenting in part* [is omitted].

JUSTICE BLACKMUN, *concurring in part, concurring in the judgment in part, and dissenting in part.*

I join Parts I, II, III, V-A, V-C, and VI of the joint opinion of JUSTICES O'CONNOR, KENNEDY, and SOUTER.

Three years ago, in *Webster* v. *Reproductive Health Serv.*, (1989), four Members of this Court appeared poised to "cas[t] into darkness the hopes and visions of every woman in this country" who had come to believe that the Constitution guaranteed her the right to reproductive choice. All that remained between the promise of *Roe* and the darkness of the plurality was a single, flickering flame. Decisions since *Webster* gave little reason to hope that this flame would cast much light. See, e.g., *Ohio* v. *Akron Center for Reproductive Health*, (1990). But now, just when so many expected the darkness to fall, the flame has grown bright.

I do not underestimate the significance of today's joint opinion. Yet I remain steadfast in my belief that the right to reproductive choice is entitled to the full protection afforded by this Court before *Webster*. And I fear for the darkness as four Justices anxiously await the single vote necessary to extinguish the light.

I

Make no mistake, the joint opinion of JUSTICES O'CONNOR, KENNEDY, and SOUTER is an act of personal courage and constitutional principle. In contrast to previous decisions in which JUSTICES O'CONNOR and KENNEDY postponed reconsideration of *Roe* v. *Wade* (1973), the authors of the joint opinion today join JUSTICE STEVENS and me in concluding that "the essential holding of *Roe* should be retained and once again reaffirmed." In brief, five Members of this Court today recognize that "the Constitution protects a woman's right to terminate her pregnancy in its early stages."

A fervent view of individual liberty and the force of *stare decisis* have led the Court to this conclusion. Today a majority reaffirms that the Due Process Clause of the Fourteenth Amendment establishes "a realm of personal liberty which the government may not enter," a realm whose outer limits cannot be determined by interpretations of the Constitution that focus only on the specific practices of States at the time the Fourteenth Amendment was adopted. Included within this realm of liberty is " 'the right of the *individual,* married or single, to be free from unwarranted governmental intrusion into matters so fundamentally affecting a person as the decision whether to bear or beget a child.' " "These matters, involving the most intimate and personal choices central to personal dignity and autonomy, are *central* to the liberty protected by the Fourteenth Amendment." Finally, the Court today recognizes that in the case of abortion, "the liberty of the woman is at stake in a sense unique to the human condition and so unique to the law. The mother who carries a child to full term is subject to anxieties, to physical constraints, to pain that only she must bear."

The Court's reaffirmation of *Roe*'s central holding is also based on the force of *stare decisis*. "[N]o erosion of principle going to liberty or personal autonomy has left *Roe*'s central holding a doctrinal remnant; *Roe* portends no developments at odds with other precedent for the analysis of personal liberty; and no changes of fact have rendered viability more or less appropriate as the point at which the balance of interests tips." Indeed, the Court acknowledges that *Roe*'s limitation on state power could not be removed "without serious inequity to those who have relied upon it or significant damage to the stability of the society governed by the rule in question." In the 19 years since *Roe* was decided, that case has shaped more than reproductive planning—"an entire generation has come of age free to assume *Roe*'s concept of liberty in defining the capacity of women to act in society and to make reproductive decisions." The Court understands that; having "call[ed] the contending sides . . . to end their national division by accepting a common mandate rooted in the

Constitution," a decision to overrule *Roe* "would seriously weaken the Court's capacity to exercise the judicial power and to function as the Supreme Court of a Nation dedicated to the rule of law." What has happened today should serve as a model for future Justices and a warning to all who have tried to turn this Court into yet another political branch.

In striking down the Pennsylvania statute's spousal notification requirement, the Court has established a framework for evaluating abortion regulations that responds to the social context of women facing issues of reproductive choice.

. . . [W]hile I believe that the joint opinion errs in failing to invalidate the other regulations, I am pleased that the joint opinion has not ruled out the possibility that these regulations may be shown to impose an unconstitutional burden. The joint opinion makes clear that its specific holdings are based on the insufficiency of the record before it. I am confident that in the future evidence will be produced to show that "in a large fraction of the cases in which [these regulations are] relevant, [they] will operate as a substantial obstacle to a woman's choice to undergo an abortion."

Today, no less than yesterday, the Constitution and decisions of this Court require that a State's abortion restrictions be subjected to the strictest of judicial scrutiny. Our precedents and the joint opinion's principles require us to subject all non–*de minimis* abortion regulations to strict scrutiny. Under this standard, the Pennsylvania statute's provisions requiring content-based counseling, a 24-hour delay, informed parental consent, and reporting of abortion-related information must be invalidated.

. . . If there is much reason to applaud the advances made by the joint opinion today, there is far more to fear from THE CHIEF JUSTICE's opinion.

THE CHIEF JUSTICE's criticism of *Roe* follows from his stunted conception of individual liberty. While recognizing that the Due Process Clause protects more than simple physical liberty, he then goes on to construe this Court's personal-liberty cases as establishing only a laundry list of particular rights, rather than a principled account of how these particular rights are grounded in a more general right of privacy. This constricted view is reinforced by THE CHIEF JUSTICE's exclusive reliance on tradition as a source of fundamental rights. He argues that the record in favor of a right to abortion is not stronger than the record in *Michael H.* v. *Gerald D.*, (1986), where the Court found no fundamental right to engage in homosexual sodomy, or in a case involving the "firing of a gun . . . into another person's body." In THE CHIEF JUSTICE's world, a woman considering whether to terminate a pregnancy is entitled to no more protection than adulterers, murderers, and so-called "sexual deviates." Given THE CHIEF JUSTICE's exclusive reliance on tradition, people using contraceptives seem the next likely candidate for his list of outcasts.

Even more shocking than THE CHIEF JUSTICE's cramped notion of individual liberty is his complete omission of any discussion of the effects that compelled childbirth and motherhood have on women's lives. The only expression of concern with women's health is purely instrumental—for THE CHIEF JUSTICE, only when women's *psychological* health is a concern, and only to the extent that he assumes that every woman who decides to have an abortion does so without serious consideration of the moral implications of their decision. In short, THE CHIEF JUSTICE's view of the State's compelling interest in maternal health has less to do with health than it does with compelling women to be maternal.

Nor does THE CHIEF JUSTICE give any serious consideration to the doctrine of *stare decisis*. For THE CHIEF JUSTICE the facts that gave rise to *Roe* are surprisingly simple: "women become pregnant, there is a point somewhere, depending on medical technology, where a fetus becomes viable, and women give birth to children." This characterization of the issue thus allows THE CHIEF JUSTICE quickly to discard the joint opinion's reliance argument by asserting that "reproductive planning could take . . . virtually immediate account of a decision overruling *Roe*."

THE CHIEF JUSTICE's narrow conception of individual liberty and *stare decisis* leads him to propose the same standard of review proposed by the plurality in *Webster*.

States may regulate abortion procedures in ways rationally related to a legitimate state interest.

. . . Even if it is somehow "irrational" for a State to require a woman to risk her life for her child, what protection is offered for women who become pregnant through rape or incest? Is there anything arbitrary or capricious about a State's prohibiting the sins of the father from being visited upon his offspring?

But, we are reassured, there is always the protection of the democratic process. While there is much to be praised about our democracy, our country since its founding has recognized that there are certain fundamental liberties that are not to be left to the whims of an election. A woman's right to reproductive choice is one of those fundamental liberties. Accordingly, that liberty need not seek refuge at the ballot box.

In one sense, the Court's approach is a world apart from that of THE CHIEF JUSTICE and JUSTICE SCALIA. And yet in another sense, the distance between the two approaches is short—the distance is but a single vote.

I am 83 years old. I cannot remain on this Court forever, and when I do step down, the confirmation process for my successor well may focus on the issue before us today. That, I regret, may be exactly where the choice between the two worlds will be made.

CHIEF JUSTICE REHNQUIST, *with whom* JUSTICE WHITE, JUSTICE SCALIA, *and* JUSTICE THOMAS *join, concurring in the judgment in part and dissenting in part.*

The joint opinion, following its newly minted variation on *stare decisis*, retains the outer shell of *Roe* v. *Wade*, but beats a wholesale retreat from the substance of that case. We believe that *Roe* was wrongly decided, and that it can and should be overruled consistently with our traditional approach to *stare decisis* in constitutional cases. We should adopt the approach of the plurality in *Webster* v. *Reproductive Health Services*, and uphold the challenged provisions of the Pennsylvania statute in their entirety.

. . . We think, therefore, both in view of this history and of our decided cases dealing with substantive liberty under the Due Process Clause, that the Court was mistaken in *Roe* when it classified a woman's decision to terminate her pregnancy as a "fundamental right" that could be abridged only in a manner which withstood "strict scrutiny." In so concluding, we repeat the observation made in *Bowers* v. *Hardwick*, (1986):

Nor are we inclined to take a more expansive view of our authority to discover new fundamental rights imbedded in the Due Process Clause. The Court is most vulnerable and comes nearest to illegitimacy when it delays with judge-made constitutional law having little or no cognizable roots in the language or design of the Constitution.

We believe that the sort of constitutionally imposed abortion code of the type illustrated by our decisions following *Roe* is inconsistent "with the notion of a Constitution cast in general terms, as ours is, and usually speaking in general principles, as ours does." The Court in *Roe* reached too far when it analogized the right to abort a fetus to the rights involved in *Pierce*, *Meyer*, *Loving*, and *Griswold*, and thereby deemed the right to abortion fundamental.

The joint opinion of JUSTICES O'CONNOR, KENNEDY, and SOUTER cannot bring itself to say that *Roe* was correct as an original matter, but the authors are of the view that "the immediate question is not the soundness of *Roe*'s resolution of the issue, but the precedental force that must be accorded to its holding." Instead of claiming that *Roe* was correct as a matter of original constitutional interpretation, the opinion therefore contains an elaborate discussion of *stare decisis*. This discussion of the principle of *stare decisis* appears to be almost entirely dicta, because the joint opinion does not apply that principle in dealing with *Roe*. *Roe* decided that a woman had a fundamental right to an abortion. The joint opinion rejects that view. *Roe* decided that abortion regulations were to be subjected to "strict scrutiny" and could be justified only in the light of "compelling state interests." The joint opinion rejects that view. *Roe* analyzed abortion regulation under a rigid trimester framework, a framework which has guided this Court's decisionmaking for 19 years. The joint opinion rejects that framework.

Stare decisis is defined in Black's Law Dictionary as meaning "to abide by, or adhere to, decided cases." Black's Law Dictionary 1406 (6th ed. 1990). Whatever the "central holding" of *Roe* that is left after the joint opinion finishes dissecting it is surely not the result of that principle. While purporting to adhere to precedent, the joint opinion instead revises it. *Roe* continues to exist, but only in the way a storefront on a western movie set exists: a mere facade to give the illusion of reality. Decisions following *Roe*, such as *Akron* v. *Akron Center for Reproductive Health, Inc.,* (1983), and *Thornburgh* v. *American College of Obstetricians and Gynecologists,* (1986), are frankly overruled in part under the "undue burden" standard expounded in the joint opinion.

In our view, authentic principles of *stare decisis* do not require that any portion of the reasoning in *Roe* be kept intact.

. . . The joint opinion discusses several *stare decisis* factors which, it asserts, point toward retaining a portion of *Roe*. Two of these factors are that the main "factual underpinning" of *Roe* has remained the same, and that its doctrinal foundation is no

weaker now than it was in 1973. Of course, what might be called the basic facts which gave rise to *Roe* have remained the same—women become pregnant, there is a point somewhere, depending on medical technology, where a fetus becomes viable, and women give birth to children. But this is only to say that the same facts which gave rise to *Roe* will continue to give rise to similar cases. It is not a reason, in and of itself, why those cases must be decided in the same incorrect manner as was the first case to deal with the question. And surely there is no requirement, in considering whether to depart from *stare decisis* in a constitutional case, that a decision be more wrong now than it was at the time it was rendered. If that were true, the most outlandish constitutional decision could survive forever, based simply on the fact that it was no more outlandish later than it was when originally rendered.

Nor does the joint opinion faithfully follow this alleged requirement. The opinion frankly concludes that *Roe* and its progeny were wrong in failing to recognize that the State's interests in maternal health and in the protection of unborn human life exist throughout pregnancy. But there is no indication that these components of *Roe* are any more incorrect at this juncture than they were at its inception.

The joint opinion also points to the reliance interests involved in this context in its effort to explain why precedent must be followed for precedent's sake. . . . But, as the joint opinion apparently agrees, any traditional notion of reliance is not applicable here. The Court today cuts back on the protection afforded by *Roe*, and no one claims that this action defeats any reliance interest in the disavowed trimester framework. Similarly, reliance interests would not be diminished were the Court to go further and acknowledge the full error of *Roe*, as "reproductive planning could take virtually immediate account of" this action.

The joint opinion thus turns to what can only be described as an unconventional—and unconvincing—notion of reliance, a view based on the surmise that the availability of abortion since *Roe* has led to "two decades of economic and social developments" that would be undercut if the error of *Roe* were recognized. The joint opinion's assertion of this fact is underdeveloped and totally conclusory. In fact, one can not be sure to what economic and social developments the opinion is referring. Surely it is dubious to suggest that women have reached their "places in society" in reliance upon

Roe, rather than as a result of their determination to obtain higher education and compete with men and in the job market, and of society's increasing recognition of their ability to fill positions that were previously thought to be reserved only for men.

In the end, having failed to put forth any evidence to prove any true reliance, the joint opinion's argument is based solely on generalized assertions about the national psyche, on a belief that the people of this country have grown accustomed to the *Roe* decision over the last 19 years and have "ordered their thinking and living around" it. As an initial matter, one might inquire how the joint opinion can view the "central holding" of *Roe* as so deeply rooted in our constitutional culture, when it so casually uproots and disposes of that same decision's trimester framework. Furthermore, at various points in the past, the same could have been said about this Court's erroneous decisions that the Constitution allowed "separate but equal" treatment of minorities, see *Plessy* v. *Ferguson*, (1896), or that "liberty" under the Due Process Clause protected "freedom of contract." See *Adkins* v. *Children's Hospital of D.C.*, (1905). The "separate but equal" doctrine lasted 58 years after *Plessy*, and *Lochner*'s protection of contractual freedom lasted 32 years. However, the simple fact that a generation or more had grown used to these major decisions did not prevent the Court from correcting its errors in those cases, nor should it prevent us from correctly interpreting the Constitution here.

Apparently realizing that conventional *stare decisis* principles do not support its position, the joint opinion advances a belief that retaining a portion of *Roe* is necessary to protect the "legitimacy" of this Court. Because the Court must take care to render decisions "grounded truly in principle," and not simply as political and social compromises, the joint opinion properly declares it to be this Court's duty to ignore the public criticism and protest that may arise as a result of a decision. Few would quarrel with this statement, although it may be doubted that Members of this Court, holding their tenure as they do during constitutional "good behavior," are at all likely to be intimidated by such public protests.

But the joint opinion goes on to state that when the Court "resolve[s] the sort of intensely divisive controversy reflected in *Roe* and those rare, comparable cases," its decision is exempt from reconsideration under established principles of *stare decisis* in constitutional cases. This is so, the joint opinion contends, because in those "intensely divisive" cases the Court has "call[ed] the contending sides of a national controversy to end their national division by accepting a common mandate rooted in the Constitution," and must therefore take special care not to be perceived as "surrender[ing] to political pressure" and continued opposition. This is a truly novel principle, one which is contrary to both the Court's historical practice and to the Court's traditional willingness to tolerate criticism of its opinions. Under this principle, when the Court has ruled on a divisive issue, it is apparently prevented from overruling that decision from the sole reason that it was incorrect, *unless opposition to the original decision has died away*.

The first difficulty with this principle lies in its assumption that cases which are "intensely divisive" can be readily distinguished from those that are not. The question of whether a particular issue is "intensely divisive" enough to qualify for special protection is entirely subjective and dependent on the individual assumptions of the members of this Court. In addition, because the Court's duty is to ignore public opinion and criticism on issues that come before it, its members are in perhaps the worst position to judge whether a decision divides the Nation deeply enough to justify such uncommon protection. Although many of the Court's decisions divide the populace to a large degree, we have not previously on that account shied away from applying normal rules of *stare decisis* when urged to reconsider earlier decisions. Over the past 21 years, for example, the Court has overruled in whole or in part 34 of its previous constitutional decisions. See *Payne* v. *Tennessee* (listing cases).

The joint opinion picks out and discusses two prior Court rulings that it believes are of the "intensely divisive" variety, and concludes that they are of comparable dimension to *Roe*. (*Lochner* v. *New York*, and *Plessy* v. *Ferguson*) It appears to us very odd indeed that the joint opinion chooses as benchmarks two cases in which the Court chose *not* to adhere to erroneous constitutional precedent, but instead enhanced its stature by acknowledging and correcting its error, apparently in violation of the joint opinion's "legitimacy" principle. One might also wonder how it is that the joint opinion puts these, and not others, in the "intensely divisive" category, and how it assumes that these are the only two lines of cases of comparable dimension to *Roe*. There is no reason to think that either *Plessy* or *Lochner* produced the sort of public protest when they were decided that *Roe* did. There were undoubtedly large segments of the bench and bar who agreed with the dissenting views in those cases, but surely that cannot be what the Court means when it uses the term "intensely divisive," or many other cases would have to be added to the list. In terms of public protest, however, *Roe*, so far as we know, was unique. But just as the Court should not respond to that sort of protest by retreating from the decision simply to allay the concerns of the protesters, it should likewise not respond by determining to adhere to the decision at all costs lest it *seem* to be retreating under fire. Public protests should not alter the normal application of *stare decisis*, lest perfectly lawful protest activity be penalized by the Court itself.

Taking the joint opinion on its own terms, we doubt that its distinction between *Roe*, on the one hand, and *Plessy* and *Lochner*, on the other, withstands the analysis. The joint opinion acknowledges that the Court improved its stature by overruling *Plessy* in *Brown* on a deeply divisive issue. And our decision in *West Coast Hotel*, which overruled *Adkins* v. *Children's Hospital* and *Lochner*, was rendered at a time when Congress was considering President Franklin Roosevelt's proposal to "reorganize" this Court and enable him to name six additional Justices in the event that any member of the Court over the age of 70 did not elect to retire. It is difficult to imagine a situation in which the Court would face more intense opposition to a prior ruling than it did at that time, and, under the general principle proclaimed in the joint opinion, the Court seemingly should have responded to this opposition by stubbornly refusing to reexamine the *Lochner* rationale, lest it lose legitimacy by appearing to "overrule under fire."

The joint opinion agrees that the Court's stature would have been seriously damaged if in *Brown* and *West Coast Hotel* it had dug in its heels and refused to apply the normal principles of *stare decisis* to the earlier decisions. But the opinion contends that the Court was entitled to overrule *Plessy* and *Lochner* in those cases, despite the existence of the opposition to the original decisions, only because both the Nation and the Court had learned new lessons in the interim. This is at best a feebly supported *post hoc* rationalization for those decisions.

. . . The joint opinion also agrees that the Court acted properly in rejecting the doctrine of "separate but equal" in *Brown*. In fact, the opinion lauds *Brown* in comparing it to *Roe*. This is strange, in that under the opinion's "legitimacy" principle the Court would seemingly have been forced to adhere to its erroneous decision in *Plessy* because of its "intensely divisive" character. To us, adherence to *Roe* today under the guise of "legitimacy" would seem to resemble more closely adherence to *Plessy* on the same ground. Fortunately, the Court did not choose that option in *Brown*, and instead frankly repudiated *Plessy*. The joint opinion concludes that such repudiation was justified only because segregation had the effect of treating one race as inferior to another. But it can hardly be argued that this was not urged upon those who decided *Plessy*, as JUSTICE HARLAN observed in his dissent that the law at issue "puts the brand of servitude and degradation upon a large class of our fellow-citizens, our equals before the law." It is clear that the same arguments made before the Court in *Brown* simply recognized, as JUSTICE HARLAN had recognized beforehand, that the Fourteenth Amendment does not permit racial segregation; it is a judgment that the Equal Protection Clause does not permit racial segregation, no matter whether the public might come to believe that it is beneficial. On that ground it stands, and on that ground alone the Court was justified in properly concluding that the *Plessy* Court had erred.

There is also a suggestion in the joint opinion that the propriety of overruling a "divisive" decision depends in part on whether "most people" would now agree that it should be overruled. Either the demise of opposition or its progression to substantial popular agreement apparently is required to allow the Court to reconsider a divisive decision. How such agreement would be ascertained, short of public opinion poll, the joint opinion does not say. But surely even the suggestion is totally at war with the idea of "legitimacy" in whose name it is invoked. The Judicial Branch derives its legitimacy, not from following public opinion, but from deciding by its best lights whether legislative enactments of the popular branches of Government comport with the Constitution. The doctrine of *stare decisis* is an adjunct of this duty, and should be no more subject to the vagaries of public opinion than is the basic judicial task.

There are other reasons why the joint opinion's discussion of legitimacy is nonconvincing as well. In assuming that the Court is perceived as "surrender[ing] to political pressure" when it overrules a controversial decision, the joint opinion forgets that there are two sides to any controversy. The joint opinion asserts that, in order to protect its legitimacy, the Court must refrain from overruling a controversial decision lest it be viewed as favoring those who oppose the decision. But a decision to *adhere* to prior precedent is subject to the same criticism, for in such a case one can easily argue that the Court is responding to those who have demonstrated in favor of the original decision. The decision in *Roe* has engendered large demonstrations, including repeated marches on this

Court and on Congress, both in opposition and in support of that opinion. A decision either way on *Roe* can therefore be perceived as favoring one group or the other. But this perceived dilemma arises only if one assumes, as the joint opinion does, that the Court should make its decisions with a view toward speculative perceptions. If one assumes instead, as the Court surely did in both *Brown* and *West Coast Hotel,* that the Court's legitimacy is enhanced by faithful interpretation of the Constitution irrespective of public opposition, such self-engendered difficulties may be put to one side. Strong and often misguided criticism of a decision should not render the decision immune from reconsideration, lest a fetish for legitimacy penalize freedom of expression.

The end result of the joint opinion's paeans of praise for legitimacy is the enunciation of a brand new standard for evaluating state regulation of a woman's right to abortion—the "undue burden" standard. As indicated above, *Roe* v. *Wade* adopted a "fundamental right" standard under which state regulations could survive only if they met the requirement of "strict scrutiny." While we disagree with that standard, it at least had a recognized basis in constitutional law at the time *Roe* was decided. The same cannot be said for the "undue burden" standard, which is created largely out of whole cloth by the authors of the joint opinion. It is a standard which even today does not command the support of a majority of this Court. And it will not, we believe, result in the sort of "simple limitation," easily applied, which the joint opinion anticipates. In sum it is a standard which is not built to last. . . .

Despite the efforts of the joint opinion, the undue burden standard presents nothing more workable than the trimester framework which it discards today. Under the guise of the Constitution, this Court will still impart its own preferences on the States in the form of a complex abortion code.

The sum of the joint opinion's labors in the name of *stare decisis* and "legitimacy" is this: *Roe* v. *Wade* stands as sort of a judicial Potemkin Village, which may be pointed out to passers-by as a monument to the importance of adhering to the precedent. But behind the facade, an entirely new method of analysis, without any roots in the constitutional law, is imported to decide the constitutionality of state laws regulating abortion. Neither *stare decisis* nor "legitimacy" are [*sic*] truly served by such an effort.

We have stated above our belief that the Constitution does not subject state abortion regulations to heightened scrutiny. Accordingly, we think that the correct analysis is that set forth by the plu-

rality opinion in *Webster*. A woman's interest in having an abortion is a form of liberty protected by the Due Process Clause, but States may regulate abortion procedures in ways rationally related to a legitimate state interest.

. . . For the reasons stated, we therefore would hold that each of the challenged provisions of the Pennsylvania statute is consistent with the Constitution. It bears emphasis that our conclusion in this regard does not carry with it any necessary approval of these regulations. Our task is as always, to decide only whether the challenged provisions of a law comport with the United States Constitution. If, as we believe, these do, their wisdom as a matter of public policy is for the people of Pennsylvania to decide.

JUSTICE SCALIA, *with whom* THE CHIEF JUSTICE, JUSTICE WHITE, *and* JUSTICE THOMAS *join, concurring in the judgment in part and dissenting in part.*

My views on this matter are unchanged from those I set forth in my separate opinion in *Webster* v. *Reproductive Health Services* (1989), and *Ohio* v. *Akron Center for Reproductive Health* (1990). The States may, if they wish, permit abortion-on-demand, but the Constitution does not *require* them to do so. The permissibility of abortion, and the limitations upon it are to be resolved like most important questions in our democracy: by citizens trying to persuade one another and then voting. As the Court acknowledges, "where reasonable people disagree the government can adopt one position or the other." The Court is correct in adding the qualification that this "assumes a state of affairs in which the choice does not intrude upon a protected liberty,"—but the crucial part of that qualification is the penultimate word. A State's choice between two positions on which reasonable people can disagree is constitutional even when (as is often the case) it intrudes upon a "liberty" in the absolute sense. Laws against bigamy, for example, which entire societies of reasonable people disagree with—intrude upon men and women's liberty to marry and live with one another. But bigamy happens not to be a liberty specially "protected" by the Constitution.

That is, quite simply, the issue in this case: not whether the power of a woman to abort her unborn child is a "liberty" in the absolute sense; or even whether it is a liberty of great importance to many women. Of course it is both. The issue is whether it is a liberty protected by the Constitution of the United States. I am sure it is not. I reach that conclusion not because of anything so exalted as my views concerning the "concept of existence, of meaning, of the universe, and of the mystery of human life." Rather, I reach the conclusion that bigamy is not constitutionally protected because of two simple facts: (1) the Constitution says absolutely nothing about it, and (2) the longstanding traditions of American society have permitted it to be legally proscribed.

. . . I will not swell the United States Reports with repetition of what I have said before; and applying the rational basis test. I would uphold the Pennsylvania statute in its entirety. I must, however, respond to a few of the more outrageous arguments in today's opinion, which it is beyond human nature to leave unanswered. I shall discuss each of them under a quotation from the Court's opinion to which they pertain:

> *The inescapable fact is that adjudication of substantive due process claims may call upon the Court in interpreting the Constitution to exercise that same capacity which by tradition courts always have exercised: reasoned judgment.*

Assuming that the question before us is to be resolved at such a level of philosophical abstraction, in such isolation from the traditions of American society, as by simply applying "reasoned judgment," I do not see how that could possibly have produced the answer the Court arrived at in *Roe* v. *Wade*, (1973). Today's opinion describes the methodology of *Roe*, quite accurately, as weighing against the woman's interest the State's important and legitimate interest in protecting the potentiality of human life. But "reasoned judgment" does not begin by begging the question, as *Roe* and subsequent cases unquestionably did by assuming that what the State is protecting is the mere "potentiality of human life." The whole argument of abortion opponents is that what the Court calls the fetus and what others call the unborn child *is a human life*. Thus, whatever answer *Roe* came up with after conducting its "balancing" is bound to be wrong, unless it is correct that the human fetus is in some critical sense merely potentially human. There is of course no way to determine that as a legal matter; it is in fact a value judgment. Some societies have considered newborn children not yet human, or the incompetent elderly no longer so.

The authors of the joint opinion, of course, do not squarely contend that *Roe* v. *Wade* was a *correct* application of "reasoned judgment"; merely that it must be followed because of *stare decisis*. But in their exhaustive discussion of all the factors that go into the determination of when *stare decisis* should

be observed and when disregarded, they never mention "how wrong was the decision on its face?" Surely, if "[t]he Court's power lies . . . in its legitimacy, a product of substance and perception," the "substance" part of the equation demands that plain error be acknowledged and eliminated. *Roe* was plainly wrong—even on the Court's methodology of "reasoned judgment," and even more so (of course) if the proper criteria of text and tradition are applied.

The emptiness of the "reasoned judgment" that produced *Roe* is displayed in plain view by the fact that, after more than 19 years of effort by some of the brightest (and most determined) legal minds in the country, after more than 10 cases upholding abortion rights in this Court, and after dozens upon dozens of *amicus* briefs submitted in this and other cases, the best the Court can do to explain how it is that the word "liberty" *must* be thought to include the right to destroy human fetuses is to rattle off a collection of adjectives that simply decorate a value judgment and conceal a political choice.

. . . The joint opinion frankly concedes that the amorphous concept of "undue burden" has been inconsistently applied by the Members of this Court in the few brief years since that "test" was first explicitly propounded by JUSTICE O'CONNOR in her dissent from *Akron I*. Because the three Justices now wish to "set forth a standard of general application," the joint opinion announces that "it is important to clarify what is meant by an undue burden." I certainly agree with that, but I do not agree that the joint opinion succeeds in the announced endeavor. To the contrary, its effort at clarification makes clear only that the standard is inherently manipulable and will prove hopelessly unworkable in practice.

The joint opinion explains that a state regulation imposes an "undue burden" if it "has the purpose or effect of placing a substantial obstacle in the path of a woman seeking an abortion of a nonviable fetus." An obstacle is "substantial," we are told, if it is "calculated[,] [not] to inform the woman's free choice, [but to] hinder it." This latter statement cannot possibly mean what it says. *Any* regulation of abortion that is intended to advance what the joint opinion concedes is the State's "substantial" interest in protecting unborn life will be "calculated [to] hinder" a decision to have an abortion. It thus seems more accurate to say that the joint opinion would uphold abortion regulations only if they do not *unduly* hinder the woman's decisions. That, of course, brings us right back to square one: Defining an "undue burden" as an "undue hindrance" (or a "substantial obstacle") hardly "clarifies" the test. Consciously or not, the joint opinion's verbal shell game will conceal raw judicial policy choices concerning what is "appropriate" abortion legislation.

The ultimately standardless nature of the "undue burden" inquiry is a reflection of the underlying fact that the concept has no principled or coherent legal basis. As THE CHIEF JUSTICE points out, *Roe*'s strict-scrutiny standard "at least had a recognized basis in constitutional law at the time *Roe* was decided," while "[t]he same cannot be said for the 'undue burden' standard, which is created largely out of whole cloth by the authors of the joint opinion."

. . . The Court's reliance upon *stare decisis* can best be described as contrived. It insists upon the necessity of adhering not to all of *Roe*, but only to what it calls the "central holding." It seems to me that *stare decisis* ought to be applied even to the doctrine of *stare decisis*, and I confess never to have heard of this new, keep-what-you-want-and-throw-away-the-rest version. I wonder whether, as applied to *Marbury* v. *Madison*, (1803), for example, the new version of *stare decisis* would be satisfied if we allowed courts to review the constitutionality of only those statutes that (like the one in *Marbury*) pertain to the jurisdiction of the courts.

I am certainly not in a good position to dispute that the Court *has saved* the "central holding" of *Roe*, since to do that effectively I would have to know what the court has saved, which in turn would require me to understand (as I do not) what the "undue burden" test means. I must confess, however, that I have always thought, and I think a lot of other people have always thought, that the arbitrary trimester framework, which the Court today discards, was quite as central to *Roe* as the arbitrary viability test, which the Court today retains. It seems particularly ungrateful to carve the trimester framework out of the core of *Roe*, since its very rigidity (in sharp contrast to the utter indeterminability of the "undue burden" test) is probably the only reason the Court is able to say, in urging *stare decisis*, that *Roe* "has in no sense proven 'unworkable.' " I suppose the Court is entitled to call a "central holding" whatever it wants to call a "central holding"—which is, come to think of it, perhaps one of the difficulties with this modified version of *stare decisis*. I thought I might note, however, that the following portions of *Roe* have not been saved:

- Under *Roe*, requiring that a woman seeking an abortion be provided truthful information about abortion before giving informed consent is unconstitutional, if the information is designed to influence her choice, *Thornburgh, Akron I*. Under the joint opinion's "undue burden" regime (as applied today, at least) such a requirement is constitutional.

- Under *Roe*, requiring that information be provided by a doctor, rather than by nonphysician counselors, is unconstitutional, *Akron I*. Under the "undue burden" regime (as applied today, at least) it is not.

- Under *Roe*, requiring detailed reports that include demographic data about each woman who seeks an abortion is unconstitutional, *Thornburgh*. Under the "undue burden" regime (as applied today, at least) it generally is not.

The Court's description of the place of *Roe* in the social history of the United States is unrecognizable. Not only did *Roe* not, as the Court suggests, *resolve* the deeply divisive issue of abortion; it did more than anything else to nourish it, by elevating it to the national level where it is infinitely more difficult to resolve. National politics were not plagued by abortion protests, national abortion lobbying, or abortion marches on Congress, before *Roe* v. *Wade* was decided. Profound disagreement existed among our citizens over the issue—as it does over other issues, such as the death penalty—but that disagreement was being worked out at the state level. As with many other issues, the division of sentiment within each State was not as closely balanced as it was among the population of the nation as a whole, meaning not only that more people would be satisfied with the results of state-by-state resolution, but also that those results would be more stable. Pre-*Roe*, moreover, political compromise was possible.

. . . The Imperial Judiciary lives.

. . . There is a poignant aspect to today's opinion. Its length, and what might be called its epic tone, suggest that its authors believe they are bringing to an end a troublesome era in the history of our Nation and of our court. "It is the dimension" of authority, they say, to "cal[l] the contending sides of national controversy to end their national division by accepting a common mandate rooted in the Constitution."

There comes vividly to mind a portrait by Emanuel Leutze that hangs in the Harvard Law School: Roger Brooke Taney, painted in 1859, the 82d year of his life, the 24th of his Chief Justiceship, the second after his opinion in *Dred Scott*. He is all in black, sitting in a shadowed red armchair, left hand resting upon a pad of paper in his lap, right hand hanging limply, almost lifelessly, beside the inner arm of the chair. He sits facing the viewer, and staring straight out. There seems to be on his face, and in his deep-set eyes, an expression of profound sadness and disillusionment. Perhaps he always looked that way, even when dwelling upon the happiest of thoughts. But those of us who know how the lustre of his great Chief Justiceship came to be eclipsed by *Dred Scott* cannot help believing that he had that case—its already apparent consequences for the Nation—burning on his mind. I expect that two years earlier he, too, had thought himself "call[ing] the contending sides of national controversy to end their national division by accepting a common mandate rooted in the Constitution."

It is no more realistic for us in this case, than it was from him in that, to think that an issue of the sort they both involved—an issue involving life and death, freedom and subjugation—can be "speedily and finally settled" by the Supreme Court, as President James Buchanan in his inaugural address said the issue of slavery in the territories would be. Quite to the contrary, by foreclosing all democratic outlet for the deep passions this issue arouses, by banishing the issue from the political forum that gives all participants, even the losers, the satisfaction of a fair hearing and an honest fight, by continuing the imposition of a rigid national rule instead of allowing for regional differences, the Court merely prolongs and intensifies the anguish.

We should get out of this area, where we have no right to be, and where we do neither ourselves nor the country any good by remaining.

BOWERS v. HARDWICK
478 U.S. 186; ___ L. Ed. 2d ___; 108 S. Ct. 2562 (1986)

JUSTICE WHITE *delivered the opinion of the Court.*

In August 1982, respondent was charged with violating the Georgia statute criminalizing sodomy* by committing that act with another adult male in the bedroom of respondent's home. After a preliminary hearing, the District Attorney decided not to present the matter to the grand jury unless further evidence developed.

Respondent then brought suit in the Federal District Court, challenging the constitutionality of the statute insofar as it criminalized consensual sodomy.** He asserted that the Georgia sodomy statute, as administered by the defendants, placed him in imminent danger of arrest, and that the statute for several reasons violates the Federal Constitution. The District Court granted the defendants' motion to dismiss for failure to state a claim, relying on *Doe* v. *Commonwealth's Attorney for the City of Richmond*, 403 F. Supp. 1199 (ED Va. 1975), which this Court summarily affirmed, 425

*Ga. Code Ann. § 16-6-2 (1964) provides, in pertinent part, as follows:

"(a) A person commits the offense of sodomy when he performs or submits to any sexual act involving the sex organs of one person and the mouth or anus of another. . . .

"(b) A person convicted of the offense of sodomy shall be punished by imprisonment for not less than one nor more than 20 years. . . . "

**John and Mary Doe were also plaintiffs in the action. They alleged that they wished to engage in sexual activity proscribed by § 16-6-2 in the privacy of their home, App.3, and that they had

U.S. 901 (1976).

A divided panel of the Court of Appeals for the Eleventh Circuit reversed. The court first held that, because *Doe* was distinguished by later decisions, our summary affirmance in that case did not require affirmance of the District Court. Relying on our decisions in *Griswold* v. *Connecticut* (1965), *Eisenstadt* v. *Baird* (1972), *Stanley* v. *Georgia* (1969), and *Roe* v. *Wade* (1973), the court went on to hold that the Georgia statute violated respondent's fundamental rights because his homosexual activity is a private and intimate association that is beyond the reach of state regulation by reason of the Ninth Amendment and the Due Process Clause of the Fourteenth Amendment. The case was remanded for trial, at which, to prevail, the State would have to prove that the statute is supported

been "chilled and deterred" from engaging in such activity by both the existence of the statute and Hardwick's arrest. *Id.*, at 5. The District Court held, however, that because they had neither sustained, nor were in immediate danger of sustaining, any direct injury from the enforcement of the statute, they did not have proper standing to maintain the action. *Id.*, at 18. The Court of Appeals affirmed the District Court's judgment dismissing the Does' claim for lack of standing, 760 F.2d 1202, 1206–1207 (1985), and the Does do not challenge that holding in this Court.

The only claim properly before the Court, therefore, is Hardwick's challenge to the Georgia statute as applied to consensual homosexual sodomy. We express no opinion on the constitutionality of the Georgia statute as applied to other acts of sodomy.

by a compelling interest and is the most narrowly drawn means of achieving that end.

Because other Courts of Appeals have arrived at judgments contrary to that of the Eleventh Circuit in this case, we granted the State's petition for certiorari questioning the holding that its sodomy statute violates the fundamental rights of homosexuals. We agree with the State that the Court of Appeals erred, and hence reverse its judgment.

This case does not require a judgment on whether laws against sodomy between consenting adults in general, or between homosexuals in particular, are wise or desirable. It raises no question about the right or propriety of state legislative decisions to repeal their laws that criminalize homosexual sodomy, or of state court decisions invalidating those laws on state constitutional grounds. The issue presented is whether the Federal Constitution confers a fundamental right upon homosexuals to engage in sodomy and hence invalidates the laws of the many States that still make such conduct illegal and have done so for a very long time. The case also calls for some judgment about the limits of the Court's role in carrying out its constitutional mandate.

We first register our disagreement with the Court of Appeals and with respondent that the Court's prior cases have construed the Constitution to confer a right of privacy that extends to homosexual sodomy and for all intents and purposes have decided this case. The reach of this line of cases was sketched in *Carey* v. *Population Services International* (1977). *Pierce* v. *Society of Sisters* (1925) and *Meyer* v. *Nebraska* (1923) were described as dealing with child rearing and education; *Prince* v. *Massachusetts* (1942), with procreation; *Loving* v. *Virginia* (1967), with marriage; *Griswold* v. *Connecticut* and *Eisenstadt* v. *Baird*, with contraception; and *Roe* v. *Wade* (1973), with abortion. The latter three cases were interpreted as construing the Due Process Clause of the Fourteenth Amendment to confer a fundamental individual right to decide whether or not to beget or bear a child. *Carey* v. *Population Services International*.

Accepting the decisions in these cases and the above description of them, we think it evident that none of the rights announced in those cases bears any resemblance to the claimed constitutional right of homosexuals to engage in acts of sodomy that is asserted in this case. No connection between family, marriage, or procreation on the one hand and homosexual activity on the other has been demonstrated, either by the Court of Appeals or by respondent. Moreover, any claim that these cases nevertheless stand for the proposition that any kind of private sexual conduct between consenting adults is constitutionally insulated from state proscription is unsupportable. Indeed, the Court's opinion in *Carey* twice asserted that the privacy right, which the *Griswold* line of cases found to be one of the protections provided by the Due Process Clause, did not reach so far.

Precedent aside, however, respondent would have us announce, as the Court of Appeals did, a fundamental right to engage in homosexual sodomy. This we are quite unwilling to do. It is true that despite the language of the Due Process Clauses of the Fifth and Fourteenth Amendments, which appears to focus only on the processes by which life, liberty, or property is taken, the cases are legion in which those Clauses have been interpreted to have substantive content, subsuming rights that to a great extent are immune from federal or state regulation or proscription. Among such cases are those recognizing rights that have little or no textual support in the constitutional language. *Meyer, Prince,* and *Pierce* fall in this category, as do the privacy cases from *Griswold* to *Carey*.

Striving to assure itself and the public that announcing rights not readily identifiable in the Constitution's text involves much more than the imposition of the justices' own choice of values on the States and the Federal Government, the Court has sought to identify the nature of the rights qualifying for heightened judicial protection. In *Palko* v. *Connecticut* (1937), it was said that this category includes those fundamental liberties that are "implicit in the concept of ordered liberty," such that "neither liberty nor justice would exist if [they] were sacrificed." A different description of fundamental liberties appeared in *Moore* v. *East Cleveland* (1977) (opinion of POWELL, J.), where they are characterized as those liberties that are "deeply rooted in this Nation's history and tradition."

It is obvious to us that neither of these formulations would extend a fundamental right to homosexuals to engage in acts of consensual sodomy. Proscriptions against that conduct have ancient roots. See generally, "Survey on the Constitutional Right to Privacy in the Context of Homosexual Activity," 40 *U. Miami L. Rev.* 521, 525 (1986). Sodomy was a criminal offense at common law and was forbidden by the laws of the original thirteen States when they ratified the Bill of Rights. In 1868, when the Fourteenth Amendment was ratified, all but 5 of the 37 States in the Union had criminal sodomy laws. In fact, until 1961, all 50 States outlawed sodomy, and today, 24 States and the District of Columbia continue to provide criminal penalties for sodomy performed in private and between consenting adults. Against this background, to claim that a right to engage in such conduct is "deeply rooted in this Nation's history and tradition" or "implicit in the concept of ordered liberty" is, at best, facetious.

Nor are we inclined to take a more expansive view of our authority to discover new fundamental rights imbedded in the Due Process Clause. The Court is most vulnerable and comes nearest to illegitimacy when it deals with judge-made constitutional law having little or no cognizable roots in the language or design of the Constitution. That this is so was painfully demonstrated by the face-off between the Executive and the Court in the 1930s, which resulted in the repudiation of much of the substantive gloss that the Court had placed on the Due Process Clause of the Fifth and Fourteenth Amendments. There should be, therefore, great resistance to expand the substantive reach of those Clauses, particularly if it requires redefining the category of rights deemed to be fundamental. Otherwise, the Judiciary necessarily takes to itself further authority to govern the country without express constitutional authority. The claimed right pressed on us today falls far short of overcoming this resistance.

Respondent, however, asserts that the result should be different where the homosexual conduct occurs in the privacy of the home. He relies on *Stanley* v. *Georgia* (1969), where the Court held that the First Amendment prevents conviction for possessing and reading obscene material in the privacy of the home: "If the First Amendment means anything, it means that a State has no business telling a man, sitting alone in his house, what books he may read or what films he may watch."

Stanley did protect conduct that would not have been protected outside the home, and it partially prevented the enforcement of state obscenity laws; but the decision was firmly grounded in the First Amendment. The right pressed upon us here has no similar support in the text of the Constitution, and it does not qualify for recognition under the prevailing principles for construing the Fourteenth Amendment. Its limits are also difficult to discern. Plainly enough, otherwise, illegal conduct is not always immunized whenever it occurs in the home. Victimless crimes, such as the possession and use of illegal drugs, do not escape the law where they are committed at home. *Stanley* itself recognized that its holding offered no protection for the possession in the home of drugs, firearms,

or stolen goods. And if respondent's submission is limited to the voluntary sexual conduct between consenting adults, it would be difficult, except by fiat, to limit the claimed right to homosexual conduct while leaving exposed to prosecution adultery, incest, and other sexual crimes even though they are committed in the home. We are unwilling to start down that road.

Even if the conduct at issue here is not a fundamental right, respondent asserts that there must be a rational basis for the law and that there is none in this case other than the presumed belief of a majority of the electorate in Georgia that homosexual sodomy is immoral and unacceptable. This is said to be an inadequate rationale to support the law. The law, however, is constantly based on notions of morality, and if all laws representing essential moral choices are to be invalidated under the Due Process Clause, the courts will be very busy indeed. Even respondent makes no such claim, but insists that majority sentiments about the morality of homosexuality should be declared inadequate. We do not agree, and are unpersuaded that the sodomy laws of some 25 States should be invalidated on this basis.

Accordingly, the judgment of the Court of Appeals is

Reversed.

[The concurring opinion of CHIEF JUSTICE BURGER is omitted.]

JUSTICE POWELL, *concurring.*

I join the opinion of the Court. I agree with the Court that there is no fundamental right—i.e., no substantive right under the Due Process Clause—as that claimed by respondent and found to exist by the Court of Appeals. This is not to suggest, however, that respondent may not be protected by the Eighth Amendment of the Constitution. The Georgia statute at issue in this case, Ga. Code Ann. § 16-6-2, authorizes a court to imprison a person for up to 20 years for a single private, consensual act of sodomy. In my view, a prison sentence for such conduct—certainly a sentence of long duration—would create a serious Eighth Amendment issue. Under the Georgia statute a single act of sodomy, even in the private setting of a home, is a felony comparable in terms of the possible sentence imposed to serious felonies such as aggravated battery, first degree arson, and robbery.

In this case, however, respondent has not been tried, much less convicted and sentenced.[†] Moreover, respondent has not raised the Eighth Amendment issue below. For these reasons this constitutional argument is not before us.

JUSTICE BLACKMUN, *with whom* JUSTICE BRENNAN, JUSTICE MARSHALL, *and* JUSTICE STEVENS *join, dissenting.*

This case is no more about "a fundamental right to engage in homosexual sodomy," as the Court purports to declare, than *Stanley* v. *Georgia* was about a fundamental right to watch obscene movies. . . . Rather, this case is about "the most comprehensive of rights and the right most valued by civilized men," namely, "the right to be left alone." *Olmstead* v. *United States* (1928) (BRANDEIS, J., dissenting).

The statute at issue denies individuals the right to decide for themselves whether to engage in particular forms of private, consensual sexual activity. The Court concludes that § 16-6-2 is valid essentially because "the laws of . . . many States . . . still make such conduct illegal and have done so for a very long time." But the fact that the moral judgments expressed by statutes like § 16-6-2 may be "natural and familiar . . . ought not to conclude our judgment upon the question whether statutes embodying them conflict with the Constitution of the United States." . . . Like JUSTICE HOLMES, I believe that "[i]t is revolting to have no better reason for a rule of law than that so it was laid down in the time of Henry IV. It is still more revolting if the grounds upon which it was laid down have vanished long since, and the rule simply persists from blind imitation of the past." HOLMES, "The Path of the Law," 10 *Harv. L. Rev.* 457, 469 (1897). I believe we must analyze respondent's claim in the light of the values that underlie the constitutional right to privacy. If that right means anything, it means that, before Georgia can prosecute its citizens for making choices about the most intimate aspects of their lives, it must do more than assert that the choice they have made is an "abominable crime not fit to be named among Christians."

In its haste to reverse the Court of Appeals and hold that the Constitution does "confe[r] a fundamental right upon homosexuals to engage in sodomy," the Court relegates the actual statute being challenged to a footnote and ignores the procedural posture of the case before it. A fair reading of the statute and of the complaint clearly reveals that the majority has distorted the question this case presents.

First, the Court's almost obsessive focus on homosexual activity is particularly hard to justify in light of the broad language Georgia has used. Unlike the Court, the Georgia Legislature has not proceeded on the assumption that homosexuals are so different from other citizens that their lives may be controlled in a way that would not be tolerated if it limited the choices of those other citizens. Rather, Georgia has provided that "[a] person commits the offense of sodomy when he performs or submits to any sexual act involving the sex organs of one person and the mouth or anus of another." The sex or status of the persons who engage in the act is irrelevant as a matter of state law. In fact, to the extent I can discern a legislative purpose for Georgia's 1968 enactment of § 16-6-2, that purpose seems to have been to broaden the coverage of the law to reach heterosexual as well as homosexual activity.[‡] I therefore see no basis for the Court's decision to treat this case as an "as applied" challenge to § 16-6-2, or for Georgia's attempt, both in its brief and at oral argument, to defend § 16-6-2 solely on the grounds that it prohibits homosexual activity. Michael Hardwick's standing may rest in significant part on Georgia's apparent willingness to enforce against homosexuals a law it seems not to have any desire to enforce against heterosexuals. But his claim that § 16-6-2 involves an unconstitutional intrusion into his privacy and his right of intimate association does not depend in any way on his sexual orientation.

[†]It was conceded at oral argument that, prior to the complaint against respondent Hardwick, there had been no reported decision involving prosecution for private homosexual sodomy under this statute for several decades. See *Thompson* v. *Aldredge*, 187 Ga. 467, 200 S.E. 799 (1939). Moreover, the State has declined to present the criminal charge against Hardwick to a grand jury, and this is a suit for declaratory judgment brought by respondents challenging the validity of the statute. The history of nonenforcement suggests the moribund character today of laws criminalizing this type of private consensual conduct. Some 26 states have repealed similar statutes. But the constitutional validity of the Georgia statute was put in issue by respondents, and, for the reasons stated by the Court, I cannot say that conduct condemned for hundreds of years has now become a fundamental right.

[‡]Until 1968, Georgia defined sodomy as "the carnal knowledge and connection against the order of nature, by man with man, or in the same unnatural manner with woman." In *Thompson* v. *Aldredge* (1939), the Georgia Supreme Court held that §26-5901 did not prohibit lesbian activity. And in *Riley* v. *Garrett* (1963), the Georgia Supreme Court held that § 26-5901 did not prohibit heterosexual cunnilingus. Georgia passed the act-specific statute currently in force "perhaps in response to the restrictive court decisions such as *Riley*." Note, "The Crimes Against Nature," 16 *J. Pub. L.* 159, 167, n. 47 (1967).

Second, I disagree with the Court's refusal to consider whether § 16-6-2 runs afoul of the Eighth or Ninth Amendments or the Equal Protection Clause of the Fourteenth Amendment. . . . Respondent's complaint expressly invoked the Ninth Amendment . . . and he relied heavily before this Court on *Griswold* v. *Connecticut* (1965), which identifies that Amendment as one of the specific constitutional provisions giving "life and substance" to our understanding of privacy. Of more importance, the procedural posture of the case requires that we affirm the Court of Appeals' judgment if there is any ground on which respondent may be entitled to relief. This case is before us on petitioner's motion to dismiss for failure to state a claim. It is a well-settled principle of law that "a complaint should not be dismissed merely because a plaintiff's allegations do not support the particular legal theory he advances, for the court is under a duty to examine the complaint to determine if the allegations provide for relief on any possible theory." . . . Thus, even if respondent did not advance claims based on the Eighth or Ninth Amendments, or on the Equal Protection Clause, his complaint should not be dismissed if any of those provisions could entitle him to relief. I need not reach either the Eighth Amendment or the Equal Protection Clause issues because I believe that Hardwick has stated a cognizable claim that § 16-6-2 interferes with constitutionally protected interests in privacy and freedom of intimate association. But neither the Eighth Amendment nor the Equal Protection Clause is so clearly irrelevant that a claim resting on either provision should be peremptorily dismissed. The Court's cramped reading of the issue before it makes for a short opinion, but it does little to make for a persuasive one.

"Our cases long have recognized that the Constitution embodies a promise that a certain private sphere of individual liberty will be kept largely beyond the reach of government." *Thornburgh* v. *American College of Obstetricians & Gynecologists* (1986). In constructing the right to privacy, the Court has proceeded along two somewhat distinct, albeit complementary, lines. First, it has recognized a privacy interest with reference to certain decisions that are properly for the individual to make. E.g., *Roe* v. *Wade* (1973); *Pierce* v. *Society of Sisters* (1925). Second, it has recognized a privacy interest with reference to certain places without regard for the particular activities in which the individuals who occupy them are engaged. E.g., *United States* v. *Karo* (1984); *Payton* v. *New York* (1980); *Rios* v. *United States* (1960). The case before us implicates both the decision and the spatial aspects of the right to privacy.

The Court concludes today that none of our prior cases dealing with various decisions that individuals are entitled to make free of governmental interference "bears any resemblance to the claimed constitutional right of homosexuals to engage in acts of sodomy that is asserted in this case." While it is true that these cases may be characterized by their connection to protection of the family, see *Roberts* v. *United States Jaycees* (1984), the Court's conclusion that they extend no further than this boundary ignores the warning in *Moore* v. *East Cleveland* (1977) (plurality opinion), against "clos[ing] our eyes to the basic reasons why certain rights associated with the family have been accorded shelter under the Fourteenth Amendment's Due Process Clause." We protect those rights not because they contribute, in some direct and material way, to the general public welfare, but because they form so central a part of an individual's life. "[T]he concept of privacy embodies the 'moral fact that a person belongs to himself and not others nor to society as a whole.'" *Thornburgh* v. *American Coll. of Obst. & Gyn.* (STEVENS, J., concurring), quoting Fried, "Correspondence," 6 *Phil. & Pub. Affairs* 288–289 (1977). And so we protect the decision whether to marry precisely because marriage "is an association that promotes a way of life, not causes; a harmony in living, not political faiths; a bilateral loyalty, not commercial or social projects." *Griswold* v. *Connecticut*. We protect the decision whether to have a child because parenthood alters so dramatically an individual's self-definition, not because of demographic considerations or the Bible's command to be fruitful and multiply. And we protect the family because it contributes so powerfully to the happiness of individuals, not because of a preference for stereotypical households. The Court recognized in *Roberts*, 468 U.S., at 619, that the "ability independently to define one's identity that is central to any concept of liberty" cannot truly be exercised in a vacuum; we all depend on the "emotional enrichment of close ties with others." *Ibid.*

Only the most willful blindness could obscure the fact that sexual intimacy is "a sensitive, key relationship of human existence, central to family life, community welfare, and the development of human personality." *Paris Adult Theatre* v. *Slaton* (1973). The fact that individuals define themselves in a significant way through their intimate sexual relationships with others suggests, in a Nation as diverse as ours, that there may be many "right" ways of conducting those relationships, and that much of the richness of a relationship will come from the freedom an individual has to *choose* the form and nature of these intensely personal bonds.

See Karst, "The Freedom of Intimate Association," 89 *Yale L. J.* 624, 637 (1980).

In a variety of circumstances we have recognized that a necessary corollary of giving individuals freedom to choose how to conduct their lives is acceptance of the fact that different individuals will make different choices. For example, in holding that the clearly important state interest in public education should give way to a competing claim by the Amish to the effect that extended formal schooling threatened their way of life, the Court declared: "There can be no assumption that today's majority is 'right' and the Amish and others like them are 'wrong.' A way of life that is odd or even erratic but interferes with no rights or interests of others is not to be condemned because it is different." *Wisconsin* v. *Yoder* (1972). The Court claims that its decision today merely refuses to recognize a fundamental right to engage in homosexual sodomy; what the Court really has refused to recognize is the fundamental interest all individuals have in controlling the nature of their intimate associations with others.

The behavior for which Hardwick faces prosecution occurred in his own home, a place to which the Fourth Amendment attaches special significance. The Court's treatment of this aspect of the case is symptomatic of its overall refusal to consider the broad principles that have informed our treatment of privacy in specific cases. Just as the right to privacy is more than the mere aggregation of a number of entitlements to engage in specific behavior, so too, protecting the physical integrity of the home is more than merely a means of protecting specific activities that often take place there. Even when our understanding of the contours of the right to privacy depends on "reference to a 'place,' " *Katz* v. *United States*, 389 U.S., at 361 (HARLAN, J., concurring), "the essence of a Fourth Amendment violation is 'not the breaking of [a person's] doors, and the rummaging of his drawers,' but rather is 'the invasion of his indefeasible right of personal security, personal liberty and private property.' " . . .

The Court's interpretation of the pivotal case of *Stanley* v. *Georgia* (1969) is entirely unconvincing. *Stanley* held that Georgia's undoubted power to punish the public distribution of constitutionally unprotected, obscene material did not permit the State to punish the private possession of such material. According to the majority here, *Stanley* relied entirely on the First Amendment and thus, it is claimed, sheds no light on cases not involving printed materials. But that is not what *Stanley* said. Rather, the *Stanley* Court anchored its holding in the Fourth Amendment's special protection for the individual in his home:

> The makers of our Constitution undertook to secure conditions favorable to the pursuit of happiness. They recognized the significance of man's spiritual nature, of his feelings and of his intellect. They knew that only a part of the pain, pleasure and satisfactions of life are to be found in material things. They sought to protect Americans in their beliefs, their thoughts, their emotions and their sensations. . . . These are the rights that appellant is asserting in the case before us. He is asserting the right to read or observe what he pleases—the right to satisfy his intellectual and emotional needs in the privacy of his own home. (Quoting *Olmstead* v. *United States*; BRANDEIS, J., dissenting.)

The central place that *Stanley* gives Justice Brandeis's dissent in *Olmstead*, a case raising *no* First Amendment claim, shows that *Stanley* rested as much on the Court's understanding of the Fourth Amendment as it did on the First. . . . Indeed, the right of an individual to conduct intimate relationships in the intimacy of his or her own home seems to me to be the heart of the Constitution's protection of privacy.

The Court's failure to comprehend the magnitude of the liberty interests at stake in this case leads it to slight the question whether petitioner, on behalf of the State, has justified Georgia's infringement on these interests. I believe that neither of the two general justifications for § 16-6-2 that petitioner has advanced warrants dismissing respondent's challenge for failure to state a claim.

First, petitioner asserts that the acts made criminal by the statute may have serious adverse consequences for "the general public health and welfare," such as spreading communicable diseases or fostering other criminal activity. Inasmuch as this case was dismissed by the District Court on the pleadings, it is not surprising that the record before us is barren of any evidence to support petitioner's claim. In light of the state of the record, I see no justification for the Court's attempt to equate the private, consensual sexual activity at issue here with the "possession in the home of drugs, firearms, or stolen goods," to which *Stanley* refused to extend its protection. None of the behavior so mentioned in *Stanley* can properly be viewed as "[v]ictimless"; drugs and weapons are inherently dangerous, and for property to be "stolen," someone must have been wrongfully deprived of it. Nothing in the record before the Court provides any justification for finding the activity forbidden by § 16-6-2 to be physically dangerous, either to the persons engaged in it or to others.

The core of petitioner's defense of § 16-6-2, however, is that respondent and others who engage in the conduct prohibited by § 16-6-2 interfere with Georgia's exercise of the "right of the Nation and of the States to maintain a decent society." Essentially, petitioner argues, and the Court agrees, that the fact that the acts described in § 16-6-2 "for hundreds of years, if not thousands, have been uniformly condemned as immoral" is a sufficient reason to permit a State to ban them today.

I cannot agree that either the length of time a majority has held its convictions or the passions with which it defends them can withdraw legislation from this Court's scrutiny. . . . As JUSTICE JACKSON wrote so eloquently for the Court in *West Virginia Board of Education* v. *Barnette* (1943), "we apply the limitations of the Constitution with no fear that freedom to be intellectually and spiritually diverse or even contrary will disintegrate the social organization. . . . [F]reedom to differ is not limited to things that do not matter much. That would be a mere shadow of freedom. The test of its substance is the right to differ as to things that touch the heart of the existing order." It is precisely because the issue raised by this case touches the heart of what makes individuals what they are that we should be especially sensitive to the rights of those whose choices upset the majority.

The assertion that "traditional Judeo-Christian values proscribe" the conduct involved cannot provide an adequate justification for § 16-6-2. That certain, but by no means all, religious groups condemn the behavior at issue gives the State no license to impose their judgments on the entire citizenry. The legitimacy of secular legislation depends instead on whether the State can advance some justification for its law beyond its conformity to religious doctrine. . . . A State can no more punish private behavior because of religious intolerance than it can punish such behavior because of racial animus. "The Constitution cannot control such prejudices, but neither can it tolerate them. Private biases may be outside the reach of the law, but the law cannot, directly or indirectly give them effect." No matter how uncomfortable a certain group may make the majority of this Court, we have held that "[m]ere public intolerance or animosity cannot constitutionally justify the deprivation of a person's physical liberty." . . .

. . . This case involves no real interference with the rights of others, for the mere knowledge that other individuals do not adhere to one's value system cannot be a legally cognizable interest, let alone an interest that can justify invading the houses, hearts, and minds of citizens who choose to live their lives differently.

It took but three years for the Court to see the error in its analysis in *Minersville School District* v. *Gobitis* (1940), and to recognize that the threat to national cohesion posed by a refusal to salute the flag was vastly outweighed by the threat to those same values posed by compelling such a salute. See *West Virginia Board of Education* v. *Barnette* (1943). I can only hope that here, too, the Court soon will reconsider its analysis and conclude that depriving individuals of the right to choose for themselves how to conduct their intimate relationships poses a far greater threat to the values most deeply rooted in our Nation's history than tolerance of nonconformity could ever do. Because I think the Court today betrays those values, I dissent.

JUSTICE STEVENS, *with whom* JUSTICE BRENNAN *and* JUSTICE MARSHALL *join, dissenting.*

Like the statute that is challenged in this case, the rationale of the Court's opinion applies equally to the prohibited conduct regardless of whether the parties who engage in it are married or unmarried, or are of the same or different sexes. Sodomy was condemned as an odious and sinful type of behavior during the formative period of the common law. That condemnation was equally damning for heterosexual and homosexual sodomy. Moreover, it provided no special exemption for married couples. The license to cohabit and to produce legitimate offspring simply did not include any permission to engage in sexual conduct that was considered a "crime against nature."

The history of the Georgia statute before us clearly reveals this traditional prohibition of heterosexual, as well as homosexual, sodomy. Indeed, at one point in the twentieth century, Georgia's law was construed to permit certain sexual conduct between homosexual women even though such conduct was prohibited between heterosexuals. The history of the statutes cited by majority as proof for the proposition that sodomy is not constitutionally protected similarly reveals a prohibition on heterosexual, as well as homosexual, sodomy.

Because the Georgia statute expresses the traditional view that sodomy is an immoral kind of conduct regardless of the identity of the persons who engage in it, I believe that a proper analysis of its constitutionality requires consideration of two questions: First, may a State totally prohibit the described conduct by means of a neutral law applying without exception to all persons subject to its jurisdiction? If not, may the State save the statute by announcing that it will only enforce the law against homosexuals? The two questions merit separate discussion.

Our prior cases make two propositions abundantly clear. First, the fact that the governing majority in a State has traditionally viewed a particular practice as immoral is not a sufficient reason for upholding a law prohibiting the practice; neither history nor tradition could save a law prohibiting miscegenation from constitutional attack. Second, individual decisions by married persons, concerning the intimacies of their physical relationship, even when not intended to produce offspring, are a form of "liberty" protected by the Due Process Clause of the Fourteenth Amendment. Moreover, this protection extends to intimate choices by unmarried as well as married persons. . . .

. . . Society has every right to encourage its individual members to follow particular traditions in expressing affection for one another and in gratifying their personal desires. It, of course, may prohibit an individual from imposing his will on another to satisfy his own selfish interests. It also may prevent an individual from interfering with, or violating, a legally sanctioned and protected relationship, as marriage. And it may explain the relative advantages and disadvantages of different forms of intimate expression. But when individual married couples are isolated from observation by others, the way in which they voluntarily choose to conduct their intimate relations is a matter for them—not the State—to decide.# The essential "liberty" that animated the development of the law in cases like *Griswold, Eisenstadt,* and *Carey* surely embraces the right to engage in nonreproductive, sexual conduct that others may consider offensive or immoral.

Paradoxical as it may seem, our prior cases thus establish that a State may not prohibit sodomy within "the sacred precincts of marital bedrooms," or, indeed, between unmarried heterosexual adults. In all events, it is perfectly clear that the State of Georgia may not totally prohibit the conduct proscribed by § 16-6-2 of the Georgia Criminal Code.

#Indeed, the Georgia Attorney General concedes that Georgia's statute would be unconstitutional if applied to a married couple. See Tr. of Oral Arg. 8 (stating that application of the statute to a married couple "would be unconstitutional" because of the "right of marital privacy as identified by the Court in *Griswold*"). Significantly, Georgia passed the current statute three years after the Court's decision in *Griswold*.

If the Georgia statute cannot be enforced as it is written—if the conduct it seeks to prohibit is a protected form of liberty for the vast majority of Georgia's citizens—the State must assume the burden of justifying a selective application of its law. Either the persons to whom Georgia seeks to apply its statute do not have the same interest in "liberty" that others have, or there must be a reason why the State may be permitted to apply a generally applicable law to certain persons that it does not apply to others.

The first possibility is plainly unacceptable. Although the meaning of the principle that "all men are created equal" is not always clear, it surely must mean that every free citizen has the same interest in "liberty" that the members of the majority share. From the standpoint of the individual, the homosexual and the heterosexual have the same interest in deciding how he will live his own life, and, more narrowly, how he will conduct himself in his personal and voluntary associations with his companions. State intrusion into the private conduct of either is equally burdensome.

The second possibility is similarly unacceptable. A policy of selective application must be supported by a neutral and legitimate interest—something more substantial than a habitual dislike for, or ignorance about, the disfavored group. Neither the State nor the Court has identified any such interest in this case. The Court has posited as a justification for the Georgia statute "the presumed belief of a majority of the electorate in Georgia that homosexual sodomy is immoral and unacceptable." But the Georgia electorate has expressed no such belief; instead, its representatives enacted a law that presumably reflects the belief that *all sodomy* is immoral and unacceptable. Unless the Court is prepared to conclude that such a law is constitutional, it may not rely on the work product of the Georgia Legislature to support its holding. For the Georgia statute does not single out homosexuals as a separate class meriting special disfavored treatment.

Nor, indeed, does the Georgia prosecutor even believe that all homosexuals who violate this statute should be punished. This conclusion is evident from the fact that the respondent in this very case has formally acknowledged in his complaint and in court that he has engaged, and intends to continue to engage, in the prohibited conduct, yet the State has elected not to process criminal charges against him. As JUSTICE POWELL points out, moreover, Georgia's prohibition on private, consensual sodomy has not been enforced for decades. The record of nonenforcement, in this case and in the last several decades, belies the

Attorney General's representations about the importance of the State's selective application of its generally applicable law.

Both the Georgia statute and the Georgia prosecutor thus completely fail to provide the Court with any support for the conclusion that homosexual sodomy, *simpliciter*, is considered unacceptable conduct in that State, and that the burden of justifying a selective application of the generally applicable law has been met. . . .

CRUZAN v. MISSOURI
497 U.S. 261; 111 L. Ed. 2d 224; 110 S.Ct. 2841 (1990)

CHIEF JUSTICE REHNQUIST *delivered the opinion of the Court.*

Petitioner Nancy Beth Cruzan was rendered incompetent as a result of severe injuries sustained during an automobile accident. Co-petitioners Lester and Joyce Cruzan, Nancy's parents and co-guardians, sought a court order directing the withdrawal of their daughter's artificial feeding and hydration equipment after it became apparent that she had virtually no chance of recovering her cognitive faculties. The Supreme Court of Missouri held that because there was no clear and convincing evidence of Nancy's desire to have life-sustaining treatment withdrawn under such circumstances, her parents lacked authority to effectuate such a request. We granted certiorari, and now affirm.

On the night of January 11, 1983, Nancy Cruzan lost control of her car as she traveled down Elm Road in Jasper County, Missouri. The vehicle overturned, and Cruzan was discovered lying face down in a ditch without detectable respiratory or cardiac function. Paramedics were able to restore her breathing and heartbeat at the accident site, and she was transported to a hospital in an unconscious state. An attending neurosurgeon diagnosed her as having sustained probable cerebral contusions compounded by significant anoxia (lack of oxygen). The Missouri trial court in this case found that permanent brain damage generally results after 6 minutes in an anoxic state; it was estimated that Cruzan was deprived of oxygen from 12 to 14 minutes. She remained in a coma for approximately three weeks and then progressed to an unconscious state in which she was able to orally ingest some nutrition. In order to ease feeding and further the recovery, surgeons implanted a gastrostomy feeding and hydration tube in Cruzan with the consent of her then husband. Subsequent rehabilitative effort proved unavailing. She now lies in a Missouri state hospital in what is commonly referred to as a persistent vegetative state: generally, a condition in which a person exhibits motor reflexes but evinces no indications of significant cognitive function.* The State of Missouri is bearing the cost of her care.

*The State Supreme Court, adopting much of the trial court's findings, described Nancy Cruzan's medical condition as follows:

". . . (1) [H]er respiration and circulation are not artificially maintained and are within the normal limits of a thirty-year-old female; (2) she is oblivious to her environment except for reflexive responses to sound and perhaps painful stimuli; (3) she suffered anoxia of the brain resulting in a massive enlargement of the ventricles filling with cerebrospinal fluid in the area where the brain has degenerated and [her] cerebral cortical atrophy is irreversible, permanent, progressive and ongoing; (4) her highest cognitive brain function is exhibited by her grimacing, perhaps in recognition of ordinarily painful stimuli, indicating the experience of pain and apparent response to sound; (5) she is a spastic quadriplegic; (6) her four extremities are contracted with irreversible muscular and tendon damage to all extremities; (7) she has no cognitive or reflexive ability to swallow food or water to maintain her daily essential needs and. . . . she will never recover her ability to swallow sufficient [sic] to satisfy her needs. In sum, Nancy is diagnosed as in a persistent vegetative state. She is not dead. She is not terminally ill. Medical experts testified that she could live another thirty years." *Cruzan* v. *Harmon*, 760 S.W.2d 408, 411 (Mo. 1989) (en banc) (quotations omitted; footnote omitted).

In observing that Cruzan was not dead, the court referred to the following Missouri statute:

"For all legal purposes, the occurrence of human death shall be determined in accordance with the usual and customary standards of medical practice, provided that death shall not be determined to have occurred unless the following minimal conditions have been met:
"(1) When respiration and circulation are not artificially maintained, there is an irreversible cessation of spontaneous respiration and circulation; or
"(2) When respiration and circulation are artificially maintained, and there is total and irreversible cessation of all brain function, including the brain stem, and that such determination is made by a licensed physician." Mo. Rev. Stat. Sec. 194.005 (1986).

Since Cruzan's respiration and circulation were not being artifi-

After it had become apparent that Nancy Cruzan had virtually no chance of regaining her mental faculties her parents asked hospital employees to terminate the artificial nutrition and hydration procedures. All agree that such a removal would cause her death. The employees refused to honor the request without court approval. The parents then sought and received authorization from the state trial court for termination. The court found that a person in Nancy's condition had a fundamental right under the State and Federal Constitutions to refuse or direct the withdrawal of "death prolonging procedures." The court also found that Nancy's "expressed thoughts at age twenty-five in somewhat serious conversation with a housemate friend that if sick or injured she would not wish to continue her life unless she could live at least halfway normally suggests that given her present condition she would not wish to continue on with her nutrition and hydration."

The Supreme Court of Missouri reversed by a divided vote. The court recognized a right to refuse treatment embodied in the common law doctrine of informed consent, but expressed skepticism about the application of that doctrine in the circumstances of this case. The court also declined to read a broad right of privacy into the State Constitution which would "support the right of a person to refuse medical treatment in every circumstance," and expressed doubt as to whether such a right existed under the United States Constitution. It then decided that the Missouri Living Will statute embodied a state policy strongly favoring the preservation of life. The court found that Cruzan's statements to her roommate regarding her desire to live or die under certain conditions were "unreliable for the purpose of determining her intent," . . . "and thus insufficient to

cially maintained, she obviously fit within the first proviso of the statute.

Dr. Fred Plum, the creator of the term "persistent vegetative state" and a renowned expert on the subject, has described the "vegetative state" in the following terms:

" 'Vegetative state describes a body which is functioning entirely in terms of its internal controls. It maintains temperature. It maintains heart beat and pulmonary ventilation. It maintains digestive activity. It maintains reflex activity of muscles and nerves for low level conditioned responses. But there is no behavioral evidence of either self-awareness or awareness of the surroundings in a learned manner.' "

See also Brief for American Medical Association et al., as *Amici Curiae,* 6 ("The persistent vegetative state can best be understood as one of the conditions in which patients have suffered a loss of consciousness").

support the co-guardians' claim to exercise substituted judgment on Nancy's behalf." It rejected the argument that Cruzan's parents were entitled to order the termination of her medical treatment, concluding that "no person can assume that choice for an incompetent in the absence of the formalities required under Missouri's Living Will statutes or the clear and convincing, inherently reliable evidence absent here." The court also expressed its view that "[b]road policy questions bearing on life and death are more properly addressed by representative assemblies" than judicial bodies.

We granted certiorari to consider the question of whether Cruzan has a right under the United States Constitution which would require the hospital to withdraw life-sustaining treatment from her under these circumstances.

At common law, even the touching of one person by another without consent and without legal justification was a battery. Before the turn of the century, this Court observed that "[n]o right is held more sacred, or is more carefully guarded, by the common law, than the right of every individual to the possession and control of his own person, free from all restraint or interference of others, unless by clear and unquestionable authority of law." This notion of bodily integrity has been embodied in the requirement that informed consent is generally required for medical treatment. Justice Cardozo, while on the Court of Appeals of New York, aptly described this doctrine: "Every human being of adult years and sound mind has a right to determine what shall be done with his own body; and a surgeon who performs an operation without his patient's consent commits an assault, for which he is liable in damages." The informed consent doctrine has become firmly entrenched in American tort law.

The logical corollary of the doctrine of informed consent is that the patient generally possesses the right not to consent, that is, to refuse treatment. Until about 15 years ago and the seminal decision in *In re Quinlan,* the number of right-to-refuse-treatment decisions were relatively few. Most of the earlier cases involved patients who refused medical treatment forbidden by their religious beliefs, thus implicating First Amendment rights as well as common law rights of self-determination. More recently, however, with the advance of medical technology capable of sustaining life well past the point where natural forces would have brought certain death in earlier times, cases involving the right to refuse life-sustaining treatment have burgeoned.

In the *Quinlan* case, young Karen Quinlan suffered severe brain damage as the result of anoxia, and entered a persistent vegetative state. Karen's father sought judicial approval to disconnect his daughter's respirator. The New Jersey Supreme Court granted the relief, holding that Karen had a right of privacy grounded in the Federal Constitution to terminate treatment. Recognizing that this right was not absolute, however, the court balanced it against asserted state interests. Noting that the State's interest "weakens and the individual's right to privacy grows as the degree of bodily invasion increases and the prognosis dims," the court concluded that the state interests had to give way in that case. The court also concluded that the "only practical way" to prevent the loss of Karen's privacy right due to her incompetence was to allow her guardian and family to decide "whether she would exercise it in these circumstances."

After *Quinlan*, however, most courts have based a right to refuse treatment either solely on the common law right to informed consent or on both the common law right and a constitutional privacy right.

* * *

As these cases demonstrate, the common law doctrine of informed consent is viewed as generally encompassing the right of a competent individual to refuse medical treatment. Beyond that, these decisions demonstrate both similarity and diversity in their approaches to decision of what all agree is a perplexing question with unusually strong moral and ethical overtones. State courts have available to them for decision a number of sources—state constitutions, statutes, and common law—which are not available to us. In this Court, the question is simply and starkly whether the United States Constitution prohibits Missouri from choosing the rule of decision which it did. This is the first case in which we have been squarely presented with the issue of whether the United States Constitution grants what is in common parlance referred to as a "right to die." We follow the judicious counsel of our decision in *Twin City Bank* v. *Nebeker*, (1897), where we said that in deciding "a question of such magnitude and importance . . . it is the [better] part of wisdom not to attempt, by any general statement, to cover every possible phase of the subject."

The Fourteenth Amendment provides that no State shall "deprive any person of life, liberty, or property, without due process of law." The principle that a competent person has a constitutionally protected liberty interest in refusing unwanted medical treatment may be inferred from our prior decisions.

* * *

But determining that a person has a "liberty interest" under the Due Process Clause does not end the inquiry; "whether respondent's constitutional rights have been violated must be determined by balancing his liberty interests against the relevant state interests." *Youngberg* v. *Romeo*, 457 U.S. 307, 321 (1982). See also *Mills* v. *Rogers*, 457 U.S. 291, 299 (1982).

Petitioners insist that under the general holdings of our cases, the forced administration of life-sustaining medical treatment, and even of artificially-delivered food and water essential to life, would implicate a competent person's liberty interest. Although we think the logic of the cases . . . would embrace such a liberty interest, the dramatic consequences involved in refusal of such treatment would inform the inquiry as to whether the deprivation of that interest is constitutionally permissible. But for purposes of this case, we assume that the United States Constitution would grant a competent person a constitutionally protected right to refuse life-saving hydration and nutrition.

Petitioners go on to assert that an incompetent person should possess the same right in this respect as is possessed by a competent person.

* * *

The difficulty with petitioners' claim is that in a sense it begs the question: an incompetent person is not able to make an informed and voluntary choice to exercise a hypothetical right to refuse treatment or any other right. Such a "right" must be exercised for her, if at all, by some sort of surrogate. Here, Missouri has in effect recognized that under certain circumstances a surrogate may act for the patient in electing to have hydration and nutrition withdrawn in such a way as to cause death, but it has established a procedural safeguard to assure that the action of the surrogate conforms as best it may to the wishes expressed by the patient while competent. Missouri requires that evidence of the incompetent's wishes as to the withdrawal of treatment be proved by clear and convincing evidence. The question, then, is whether the United States Constitution forbids the establishment of this procedural requirement by the State. We hold that it does not.

Whether or not Missouri's clear and convincing

evidence requirement comports with the United States Constitution depends in part on what interests the State may properly seek to protect in this situation. Missouri relies on its interest in the protection and preservation of human life, and there can be no gainsaying this interest. As a general matter, the States—indeed, all civilized nations—demonstrate their commitment to life by treating homicide as serious crime. Moreover, the majority of States in this country have laws imposing criminal penalties on one who assists another to commit suicide. We do not think a State is required to remain neutral in the face of an informed and voluntary decision by a physically-able adult to starve to death.

But in the context presented here, a State has more particular interests at stake. The choice between life and death is a deeply personal decision of obvious and overwhelming finality. We believe Missouri may legitimately seek to safeguard the personal element of this choice through the imposition of heightened evidentiary requirement. It cannot be disputed that the Due Process Clause protects an interest in life as well as an interest in refusing life-sustaining medical treatment. Not all incompetent patients will have loved ones available to serve as surrogate decisionmakers. And even where family members are present, "[t]here will, of course, be some unfortunate situations in which family members will not act to protect a patient." . . . A State is entitled to guard against potential abuses in such situations. Similarly, a State is entitled to consider that a judicial proceeding to make a determination regarding an incompetent's wishes may very well not be an adversarial one, with the added guarantee of accurate factfinding that the adversary process brings with it. See *Ohio v. Akron Center for Reproductive Health,* 497 U.S. 502, 515-516 (1990). Finally, we think a State may properly decline to make judgments about the "quality" of life that a particular individual may enjoy, and simply assert an unqualified interest in the preservation of human life to be weighed against the constitutionally protected interests of the individual.

In our view, Missouri has permissibly sought to advance these interests through the adoption of a "clear and convincing" standard of proof to govern such proceedings. "The function of a standard of proof, as that concept is embodied in the Due Process Clause and in the realm of factfinding, is to 'instruct the factfinder concerning the degree of confidence our society thinks he should have in the correctness of factual conclusions for a particular type of adjudication.' " . . . "This Court has

mandated an intermediate standard of proof—'clear and convincing evidence'—when the individual interests at stake in a state proceeding are both 'particularly important' and 'more substantial than mere loss of money.' " Thus, such a standard has been required in deportation proceedings, in denaturalization proceedings, in civil commitment proceedings, and in proceedings for the termination of parental rights. Further, this level of proof, "or an even higher one, has traditionally been imposed in cases involving allegations of civil fraud, and in a variety of other kinds of civil cases involving such issues as . . . lost wills, oral contracts to make bequests, and the like."

We think it self-evident that the interests at stake in the instant proceedings are more substantial, both on an individual and societal level, than those involved in a run-of-the-mi[ll] civil dispute. But not only does the standard of proof reflect the importance of a particular adjudication, it also serves as "a societal judgment about how the risk of error should be distributed between the litigants." The more stringent the burden of proof a party must bear, the more that party bears the risk of an erroneous decision. We believe that Missouri may permissibly place an increased risk of an erroneous decision on those seeking to terminate an incompetent individual's life-sustaining treatment. An erroneous decision not to terminate results in a maintenance of the status quo; the possibility of subsequent developments such as advancements in medical science, the discovery of new evidence regarding the patient's intent, changes in the law, or simply the unexpected death of the patient despite the administration of life-sustaining treatment, at least create the potential that a wrong decision will eventually be corrected or its impact mitigated. An erroneous decision to withdraw life-sustaining treatment, however, is not susceptible of correction. . . . [O]ne of the factors which led the Court to require proof by clear and convincing evidence in a proceeding to terminate parental rights was that a decision in such a case was final and irrevocable. The same must surely be said of the decision to discontinue hydration and nutrition of a patient such as Nancy Cruzan, which all agree will result in her death.

It is also worth noting that most, if not all, States simply forbid oral testimony entirely in determining the wishes of parties in transactions which, while important, simply do not have the consequences that a decision to terminate a person's life does. At common law and by statute in most States, the parole evidence rule prevents the variations of the terms of a written contract by oral testimony.

The statute of frauds makes unenforceable oral contracts to leave property by will, and statutes regulating the making of wills universally require that those instruments be in writing. There is no doubt that statutes requiring wills to be in writing, and statutes of frauds which require that a contract to make a will be in writing, on occasion frustrate the effectuation of the intent of a particular decedent, just as Missouri's requirement of proof in this case may have frustrated the effectuation of the not-fully-expressed desires of Nancy Cruzan. But the Constitution does not require general rules to work faultlessly; no general rule can.

In sum, we conclude that a State may apply a clear and convincing evidence standard in proceedings where a guardian seeks to discontinue nutrition and hydration for a person diagnosed to be in a persistent vegetative state. We note that many courts which have adopted some sort of substituted judgment procedure in situations like this, whether they limit consideration of evidence to the prior expressed wishes of the incompetent individual, or whether they allow more general proof of what the individual's decision would have been, require a clear and convincing standard of proof for such evidence.

* * *

The Supreme Court of Missouri held that in this case the testimony adduced at trial did not amount to clear and convincing proof of the patient's desire to have hydration and nutrition withdrawn. In so doing, it reversed a decision of the Missouri trial court which had found that the evidence "suggest[ed]" Nancy Cruzan would not have desired to continue such measures, but which had not adopted the standard of "clear and convincing evidence" enunciated by the Supreme Court. The testimony adduced at trial consisted primarily of Nancy Cruzan's statement made to a housemate about a year before her accident that she would not want to live should she face life as a "vegetable," and other observations to the same effect. The observations did not deal in terms with withdrawal of medical treatment or of hydration and nutrition. We cannot say that the Supreme Court of Missouri committed constitutional error in reaching the conclusion that it did.

Petitioners alternatively contend that Missouri must accept the "substituted judgment" of close family members even in the absence of substantial proof that their views reflect the views of the patient. They rely primarily upon our decisions in *Michael H.* v. *Gerald D.*, 491 U.S. ___ (1989), and

Parham v. *J.R.*, 442 U.S. 584 (1979). But we do not think these cases support their claim. In *Michael H.*, we *upheld* the constitutionality of California's favored treatment of traditional family relationships; such a holding may not be turned around into a constitutional requirement that a State *must* recognize the primacy of those relationships in a situation like this. And in *Parham*, where the patient was a minor, we also *upheld* the constitutionality of a state scheme in which parents made certain decisions for mentally ill minors. Here again petitioners would seek to turn a decision which allowed a State to rely on family decisionmaking into a constitutional requirement that the State recognize such decisionmaking. But constitutional law does not work that way.

No doubt is engendered by anything in this record but that Nancy Cruzan's mother and father are loving and caring parents. If the State were required by the United States Constitution to repose a right of "substituted judgment" with anyone, the Cruzans would surely qualify. But we do not think the Due Process Clause requires the State to repose judgment on these matters with anyone but the patient herself. Close family members may have a strong feeling—a feeling not at all ignoble or unworthy, but not entirely disinterested, either—that they do not wish to witness the continuation of the life of a loved one which they regard as hopeless, meaningless, and even degrading. But there is no automatic assurance that the view of close family members will necessarily be the same as the patient's would have been had she been confronted with the prospect of her situation while competent. All of the reasons previously discussed for allowing Missouri to require clear and convincing evidence of the patient's wishes lead us to conclude that the State may choose to defer only to those wishes, rather than confide the decision to close family members.

The judgment of the Supreme Court of Missouri is

Affirmed.

[JUSTICE O'CONNOR's concurring opinion is omitted.]

JUSTICE SCALIA, *concurring.*

The various opinions in this case portray quite clearly the difficult, indeed agonizing, questions that are presented by the constantly increasing power of science to keep the human body alive for longer than any reasonable person would want to inhabit it. The States have begun to grapple with these problems through legislation. I am concerned, from the tenor of today's opinions, that we are poised to confuse that enterprise as successfully as we have confused the enterprise of legislating concerning abortion—requiring it to be conducted against a background of federal constitutional imperatives that are unknown because they are being newly crafted from Term to Term. That would be a great misfortune.

While I agree with the Court's analysis today, and therefore join in its opinion, I would have preferred that we announce, clearly and promptly, that the federal courts have no business in this field; that American law has always accorded the State the power to prevent, by force if necessary, suicide—including suicide by refusing to take appropriate measures necessary to preserve one's life; that the point at which life becomes "worthless," and the point at which the means necessary to preserve it become "extraordinary" or "inappropriate," are neither set forth in the Constitution nor known to the nine Justices of this Court any better than they are known to nine people picked at random from the Kansas City telephone directory; and hence, that even when it *is* demonstrated by clear and convincing evidence that a patient no longer wishes certain measures to be taken to preserve her life, it is up to the citizens of Missouri to decide, through their elected representatives, whether that wish will be honored. It is quite impossible (because the Constitution says nothing about the matter) that those citizens will decide upon a line less lawful than the one we would choose; and it is unlikely (because we know no more about "life-and-death" than they do) that they will decide upon a line less reasonable.

* * *

Petitioners rely on three distinctions to separate Nancy Cruzan's case from ordinary suicide: (1) that she is permanently incapacitated and in pain; (2) that she would bring on her death not by any affirmative act but merely declining treatment that provides nourishment; and (3) that preventing her from effectuating her presumed wish to die requires violation of her bodily integrity. None of these suffices. Suicide was not excused even when committed "to avoid those ills which [persons] had not the fortitude to endure." . . . "The life of those to whom life has become a burden—of those who are hopelessly diseased or fatally wounded—nay, even the lives of criminals condemned to death, are under the protection of the law, equally as the lives of those who are in the full tide of life's enjoyment, and anxious to continue to live." *Blackburn* v. *State*, (1873). Thus, a man who prepared a poison, and placed it within reach of his wife, "to put an end to her suffering" from a terminal illness was convicted of murder, *People* v. *Roberts*, (1920); the "incurable suffering of the suicide, as a legal question, could hardly affect the degree of criminality. . . . " Note, 30 Yale L.J. 408, 412 (1921) (discussing *Roberts*). Nor would the imminence of the patient's death have affected liability. "The lives of all are equally under the protection of the law, and under that protection to their last moment. . . . [Assisted suicide] is declared by the law to be murder, irrespective of the wishes or the condition of the party to whom the poison is administered. . . . "

The second asserted distinction—suggested by the recent cases canvassed by the Court concerning the right to refuse treatment, relies on the dichotomy between action and inaction. Suicide, it is said, consists of an affirmative act to end one's life; refusing treatment is not an affirmative act "causing" death, but merely a passive acceptance of the natural process of dying. I readily acknowledge that the distinction between action and inaction has some bearing upon the legislative judgment of what ought to be prevented as suicide—though even there it would seem to me unreasonable to draw the line precisely between action and inaction, rather than between various forms of inaction. It would not make much sense to say that one may not kill oneself by walking into the sea, but may sit on the beach until submerged by the incoming tide; or that one may not intentionally lock oneself into a cold storage locker, but may refrain from coming indoors when the temperature drops below freezing. Even as a legislative matter, in other words, the intelligent line does not fall between action and inaction but between those forms of inaction that consist of abstaining from "ordinary" care and those that consist of abstaining from "excessive" or "heroic" measures. Unlike action *vs.* inaction, that is not a line to be discerned by logic or legal analysis, and we should not pretend that it is.

But to return to the principal point for present purposes: the irrelevance of the action-inaction distinction. Starving oneself to death is no different from putting a gun to one's temple as far as the common law definition of suicide is concerned; the cause of death in both cases is the suicide's conscious decision to "pu[t] an end to his own existence." . . . Of course the common law rejected the action-inaction distinction in other contexts involving the taking of human life as well.

It is not surprising, therefore, that the early cases considering the claimed right to refuse medical treatment dismissed as specious the nice distinction between "passively submitting to death and actively seeking it. The distinction may be merely verbal, as it would be if an adult sought death by starvation instead of a drug. If the State may interrupt one mode of self-destruction, it may with equal authority interfere with the other."

The third asserted basis of distinction—that frustrating Nancy Cruzan's wish to die in the present case requires interference with her bodily integrity—is likewise inadequate, because such interference is impermissible only if one begs the question whether her refusal to undergo the treatment on her own is suicide. It has always been lawful not only for the State, but even for private citizens, to interfere with bodily integrity to prevent a felony. . . . That general rule has of course been applied to suicide. At common law, even a private person's use of force to prevent suicide was privileged.

. . . It is not even reasonable, much less required by the Constitution, to maintain that although the State has the right to prevent a person from slashing his wrists it does not have the power to apply physical force to prevent him from doing so, nor the power, should he succeed, to apply, coercively if necessary, medical measures to stop the flow of blood. The state-run hospital, I am certain, is not liable under 42 U.S.C. Sec. 1983 for violation of constitutional rights, nor the private hospital liable under general tort law, if, in a State where suicide is unlawful, it pumps out the stomach of a person who has intentionally taken an overdose of barbiturates, despite that person's wishes to the contrary.

The dissents of JUSTICES BRENNAN and STEVENS make a plausible case for our intervention here only by embracing—the latter explicitly and the former by implication—a political principle that the States are free to adopt, but that is demonstrably not imposed by the Constitution. "The State," says JUSTICE BRENNAN, "has no legitimate general interest in someone's life, completely abstracted from the interest of the person living that life, that could outweigh the person's choice *to avoid medical treatment.*" (emphasis added). The italicized phrase sounds moderate enough, and is all that is needed to cover the pre-

sent case—but the proposition cannot *logically* be so limited. One who accepts it must also accept, I think, that the State has no such legitimate interest that could outweigh "the person's choice *to put an end to her life.*" Similarly, if one agrees with JUSTICE BRENNAN that "the State's general interest in life must accede to Nancy Cruzan's particularized and intense interest in self-determination *in her choice of medical treatment,*" (emphasis added), he must also believe that the State must accede to her "particularized and intense interest in self-determination *in her choice whether to continue living or to die.*" For insofar as balancing the relative interests of the State and the individual is concerned, there is nothing distinctive about accepting death through the refusal of "medical treatment," as opposed to accepting it through the refusal of food, or through the failure to shut off the engine and get out of the car after parking in one's garage after work. Suppose that Nancy Cruzan were in precisely the condition she is in today, except that she could be fed and digest food and water *without* artificial assistance. How is the State's "interest" in keeping her alive thereby increased, or her interest in deciding whether she wants to continue living reduced? It seems to me, in other words, that JUSTICE BRENNAN's position ultimately rests upon the proposition that it is none of the State's business if a person wants to commit suicide. JUSTICE STEVENS is explicit on the point: "Choices about death touch the core of liberty. . . . [N]ot much may be said with confidence about death unless it is said from faith, and that alone is reason enough to protect the freedom to conform choices about death to individual conscience." This is a view that some societies have held, and that our States are free to adopt if they wish. But it is not a view imposed by our constitutional traditions, in which the power of the State to prohibit suicide is unquestionable.

What I have said above is not meant to suggest that I would think it desirable, if we were sure that Nancy Cruzan wanted to die, to keep her alive by the means at issue here. I assert only that the Constitution has nothing to say about the subject. To raise up a constitutional right here we would have to create out of nothing (for it exists neither in text nor tradition) some constitutional principle whereby, although the State may insist that an individual come in out of the cold and eat food, it may not insist that he take medicine; and although it may pump his stomach empty of poison he has ingested, it may not fill his stomach with food he has failed to ingest. Are there, then, no reasonable and humane limits that ought not to be exceeded in requiring an individual to preserve his own life? There obviously are, but they are not set forth in the Due Process Clause. What assures us that those limits will not be exceeded is the same constitutional guarantee that is the source of most of our protection—what protects us, for example, from being assessed a tax of 100% of our income above the subsistence level, from being forbidden to drive cars, or from being required to send our children to school for 10 hours a day, none of which horribles is categorically prohibited by the Constitution. Our salvation is the Equal Protection Clause, which requires the democratic majority to accept for themselves and their loved ones what they impose on you and me. This Court need not, and has no authority to, inject itself into every field of human activity where irrationality and oppression may theoretically occur, and if it tries to do so it will destroy itself.

* * *

JUSTICE BRENNAN, *with whom* JUSTICE MARSHALL *and* JUSTICE BLACKMUN *join, dissenting.*

Medical technology has effectively created a twilight zone of suspended animation where death commences while life, in some form, continues. Some patients, however, want no part of life sustained only by medical technology. Instead, they prefer a plan of medical treatment that allows nature to take its course and permits them to die with dignity.

Nancy Cruzan has dwelt in that twilight zone for six years. She is oblivious to her surroundings and will remain so. Her body twitches only reflexively, without consciousness. The areas of her brain that once thought, felt, and experienced sensations have degenerated badly and are continuing to do so. The cavities remaining are filling with cerebrospinal fluid. The " 'cerebral cortical atrophy is irreversible, permanent, progressive and ongoing.' " . . . "Nancy will never interact meaningfully with her environment again. She will remain in a persistent vegetative state until her death." Because she cannot swallow, her nutrition and hydration are delivered through a tube surgically implanted in her stomach.

A grown woman at the time of the accident, Nancy had previously expressed her wish to forgo continuing medical care under circumstances such as these. Her family and her friends are convinced that this is what she would want. A guardian ad litem appointed by the trial court is also convinced that this is what Nancy would want. Yet the Missouri Supreme Court, alone among state courts deciding such a question, has determined that an irreversibly vegetative patient will remain a passive prisoner of medical technology—for Nancy, perhaps for the next 30 years.

Today the Court, while tentatively accepting that there is some degree of constitutionally protected liberty interest in avoiding unwanted medical treatment, including life-sustaining medical treatment such as artificial nutrition and hydration, affirms the decision of the Missouri Supreme Court. The majority opinion, as I read it, would affirm that decision on the ground that a State may require "clear and convincing" evidence of Nancy Cruzan's prior decision to forgo life-sustaining treatment under circumstances such as hers in order to ensure that her actual wishes are honored. Because I believe that Nancy Cruzan has a fundamental right to be free of unwanted artificial nutrition and hydration, which right is not outweighed by any interests of the State, and because I find that the improperly biased procedural obstacles imposed by the Missouri Supreme Court impermissibly burden that right, I respectfully dissent. Nancy Cruzan is entitled to choose to die with dignity.

I

A

"[T]he timing of death—once a matter of fate—is now a matter of human choice." Office of Technology Assessment Task Force, Life Sustaining Technologies and the Elderly 41 (1988). Of the approximately two million people who die each year, 80% die in hospitals and long-term care institutions, and perhaps 70% of those after a decision to forgo life-sustaining treatment has been made. Nearly every death involves a decision whether to undertake some medical procedure that could prolong the process of dying. Such decisions are difficult and personal. They must be made on the basis of individual values, informed by medical realities, yet within a framework governed by law. The role of the courts is confined to defining that framework, delineating the ways in which government may and may not participate in such decisions.

The question before this Court is a relatively narrow one: whether the Due Process Clause allows Missouri to require a now incompetent patient in an irreversible persistent vegetative state to remain on life-support absent rigorously clear and convincing evidence that avoiding the treatment represents the patient's prior, express choice. If a fundamental right is at issue, Missouri's rule of decision must be scrutinized under the standards this Court has always applied in such circumstances. As we said in *Zablocki* v. *Redhail*, (1978), if a requirement imposed by a State "significantly interferes with the exercise of a fundamental right, it cannot be upheld unless it is supported by sufficiently important state interests and is closely tailored to effectuate only those interests." The Constitution imposes on this Court the obligation to "examine carefully . . . the extent to which [the legitimate government interests advanced] are served by the challenged regulation." . . . An evidentiary rule, just as a substantive prohibition, must meet these standards if it significantly burdens a fundamental liberty interest. Fundamental rights "are protected not only against heavy-handed frontal attack, but also from being stifled by more subtle governmental interference." *Bates* v. *Little Rock*, (1960).

B

The starting point for our legal analysis must be whether a competent person has a constitutional right to avoid unwanted medical care. Earlier this Term, this Court held that the Due Process Clause of the Fourteenth Amendment confers a significant liberty interest in avoiding unwanted medical treatment. *Washington* v. *Harper*, (1990). Today, the Court concedes that our prior decisions "support the recognition of a general liberty interest in refusing medical treatment." The Court, however, avoids discussing either the measure of that liberty interest or its application by assuming, for purposes of this case only, that a competent person has a constitutionally protected liberty interest in being free of unwanted artificial nutrition and hydration.

* * *

But if a competent person has a liberty interest to be free of unwanted medical treatment . . . it must be fundamental. "We are dealing here with [a decision] which involves one of the basic civil rights of man."

* * *

The right to be free from medical attention without consent, to determine what shall be done with one's own body, *is* deeply rooted in this Nation's traditions, as the majority acknowledges. This right has long been "firmly entrenched in American tort law" and is securely grounded in the earliest common law. . . . Thus, freedom from unwanted medical attention is unquestionably among those principles "so rooted in the traditions and conscience of our people as to be ranked as fundamental."

That there may be serious consequences involved in refusal of the medical treatment at issue here does not vitiate the right under our common law tradition of medical self-determination. It is "a well-established rule of general law . . . that it is the patient, not the physician, who ultimately decides if treatment—any treatment—is to be given at all. . . . The rule has never been qualified in its application by either the nature or purpose of the treatment, or the gravity of the consequences of acceding to or forgoing it."

* * *

II

A

The right to be free from unwanted medical attention is a right to evaluate the potential benefit of treatment and its possible consequences according to one's own values and to make a personal decision whether to subject oneself to the intrusion. For a patient like Nancy Cruzan, the sole benefit of medical treatment is being kept metabolically alive. Neither artificial nutrition nor any other form of medical treatment available today can cure or in any way ameliorate her condition. Irreversibly vegetative patients are devoid of thought, emotion, and sensation; they are permanently and completely unconscious.

* * *

There are also affirmative reasons why someone like Nancy might choose to forgo artificial nutrition and hydration under these circumstances. Dying is personal. And it is profound. For many, the thought of an ignoble end, steeped in decay, is abhorrent. A quiet, proud death, bodily integrity intact, is a matter of extreme consequence.

* * *

B

Although the right to be free of unwanted medical intervention, like other constitutionally protected interests, may not be absolute, no state interest could outweigh the rights of an individual in Nancy Cruzan's position. Whatever a State's possible interests in mandating life-support treatment under other circumstances, there is no good to be obtained here by Missouri's insistence that Nancy

Cruzan remain on life-support systems if it is indeed her wish not to do so. Missouri does not claim, nor could it, that society as a whole will be benefited by Nancy's receiving medical treatment. No third party's situation will be improved and no harm to others will be averted.

The only state interest asserted here is a general interest in the preservation of life. But the State has no legitimate general interest in someone's life, completely abstracted from the interest of the person living that life, that could outweigh the person's choice to avoid medical treatment.... Thus, the State's general interest in life must accede to Nancy Cruzan's particularized and intense interest in self-determination in her choice of medical treatment. There is simply nothing legitimately within the State's purview to be gained by superseding her decision.

Moreover, there may be considerable danger that Missouri's rule of decision would impair rather than serve any interest the State does have in sustaining life. Current medical practice recommends use of heroic measures if there is a scintilla of a chance that the patient will recover, on the assumption that the measures will be discontinued should the patient improve. When the President's Commission in 1982 approved the withdrawal of life support equipment from irreversibly vegetative patients, it explained that "[a]n even more troubling wrong occurs when a treatment that might save life or improve health is not started because the health care personnel are afraid that they will find it very difficult to stop the treatment if, as is fairly likely, it proves to be of little benefit and greatly burdens the patient."

* * *

III

This is not to say that the State has no legitimate interests to assert here. As the majority recognizes, Missouri has a *parens patriae* interest in providing Nancy Cruzan, now incompetent, with as accurate as possible a determination of how she would exercise her rights under these circumstances. Second, if and when it is determined that Nancy Cruzan would want to continue treatment, the State may legitimately assert an interest in providing that treatment. But *until* Nancy's wishes have been determined, the only state interest that may be asserted is an interest in safeguarding the accuracy of that determination.

Accuracy, therefore, must be our touchstone. Missouri may constitutionally impose only those procedural requirements that serve to enhance the accuracy of a determination of Nancy Cruzan's wishes or are at least consistent with an accurate determination. The Missouri "safeguard" that the Court upholds today does not meet that standard. The determination needed in this context is whether the incompetent person would choose to live in a persistent vegetative state on life-support or to avoid this medical treatment. Missouri's rule of decision imposes a markedly asymmetrical evidentiary burden. Only evidence of specific statements of treatment choice made by the patient when competent is admissible to support a finding that the patient, now in a persistent vegetative state, would wish to avoid further medical treatment. Moreover, this evidence must be clear and convincing. No proof is required to support a finding that the incompetent person would wish to continue treatment.

* * *

B

Even more than its heightened evidentiary standard, the Missouri court's categorical exclusion of relevant evidence dispenses with any semblance of accurate factfinding. The court adverted to no evidence supporting its decision, but held that no clear and convincing, inherently reliable evidence had been presented to show that Nancy would want to avoid further treatment. In doing so, the court failed to consider statements that Nancy had made to family members and a close friend. The court also failed to consider testimony from Nancy's mother and sister that they were certain that Nancy would want to discontinue artificial nutrition and hydration, even after the court found that Nancy's family was loving and without malignant motive. The court also failed to consider the conclusions of the guardian ad litem, appointed by the trial court, that there was clear and convincing evidence that Nancy would want to discontinue medical treatment and that this was in her best interests. The court did not specifically define what kind of evidence it would consider clear and convincing, but its general discussion suggests that only a living will or equivalently formal directive from the patient when competent would meet this standard.

Too few people execute living wills or equivalently formal directives for such an evidentiary rule to ensure adequately that the wishes of incompetent persons will be honored. While it might be a wise social policy to encourage people to furnish such instructions, no general conclusion about a patient's choice can be drawn from the absence of formalities. The probability of becoming irreversibly vegetative is so low that many people may not feel an urgency to marshal formal evidence of their preferences. Some may not wish to dwell on their own physical deterioration and mortality. Even someone with a resolute determination to avoid life-support under circumstances such as Nancy's would still need to know that such things as living wills exist and how to execute one. Often legal help would be necessary, especially given the majority's apparent willingness to permit States to insist that a person's wishes are not truly known unless the particular medical treatment is specified.

* * *

. . . When Missouri enacted a living will statute, it specifically provided that the absence of a living will does not warrant a presumption that a patient wishes continued medical treatment. Thus, apparently not even Missouri's own legislature believes that a person who does not execute a living will fails to do so because he wishes continuous medical treatment under all circumstances.

The testimony of close friends and family members, on the other hand, may often be the best evidence available of what the patient's choice would be. It is they with whom the patient most likely will have discussed such questions and they who know the patient best.

* * *

The Missouri court's disdain for Nancy's statements in serious conversations not long before her accident, for the opinions of Nancy's family and friends as to her values, beliefs, and certain choice, and even for the opinion of an outside objective factfinder appointed by the State evinces a disdain for Nancy Cruzan's own right to choose. The rules by which an incompetent person's wishes are determined must represent every effort to determine those wishes. The rule that the Missouri court adopted and that this Court upholds, however, skews the result away from a determination that as accurately as possible reflects the individual's own preferences and beliefs.

* * *

C

I do not suggest that States must sit by helplessly if the choices of incompetent patients are in danger

of being ignored. Even if the Court had ruled that Missouri's rule of decision is unconstitutional, as I believe it should have, States would nevertheless remain free to fashion procedural protections to safeguard the interests of incompetents under these circumstances. The Constitution provides merely a framework here: protections must be genuinely aimed at ensuring decisions commensurate with the will of the patient, and must be reliable as instruments to that end. Of the many States which have instituted such protections, Missouri is virtually the only one to have fashioned a rule that lessens the likelihood of accurate determinations. In contrast, nothing in the Constitution prevents States from reviewing the advisability of a family decision, by requiring a court proceeding or by appointing an impartial guardian ad litem.

There are various approaches to determining an incompetent patient's treatment choice in use by the several States today and there may be advantages and disadvantages to each and other approaches not yet envisioned. The choice, in largest part, is and should be left to the States, so long as each State is seeking, in a reliable manner, to discover what the patient would want. But with such momentous interests in the balance, States must avoid procedures that will prejudice the decision.

* * *

D

Finally, I cannot agree with the majority that where it is not possible to determine what choice an incompetent patient would make, a State's role as *parens patriae* permits the State automatically to make that choice itself. . . . Under fair rules of evidence, it is improbable that a court could not determine what the patient's choice would be. Under the rule of decision adopted by Missouri and upheld today by this Court, such occasions might be numerous. But in neither case does it follow that it is constitutionally acceptable for the State invariably to assume the role of deciding for the patient. A State's legitimate interest in safeguarding a patient's choice cannot be furthered by simply appropriating it.

The majority justifies its position by arguing that, while close family members may have a strong feeling about the question, "there is no automatic assurance that the view of close family members will necessarily be the same as the patient's would have been had she been confronted with the prospect of her situation while competent." I cannot quarrel with this observation. But it leads only to another question: Is there any reason to suppose that a State is *more* likely to make the choice that the patient would have made than someone who knew the patient intimately? To ask this is to answer it. As the New Jersey Supreme Court observed: "Family members are best qualified to make substituted judgments for incompetent patients not only because of their peculiar grasp of the patient's approach to life, but also because of their special bonds with him or her. . . . It is . . . they who treat the patient as a person, rather than a symbol of a cause." *In re Jobes* (1987). The State, in contrast, is a stranger to the patient.

A State's inability to discern an incompetent patient's choice still need not mean that a State is rendered powerless to protect that choice. But I would find that the Due Process Clause prohibits a State from doing more than that. A State may ensure that the person who makes the decision on the patient's behalf is the one whom the patient himself would have selected to make that choice for him. And a State may exclude from consideration anyone having improper motives. But a State generally must either repose the choice with the person whom the patient himself would most likely have chosen as proxy or leave the decision to the patient's family.

IV

As many as 10,000 patients are being maintained in persistent vegetative states in the United States, and the number is expected to increase significantly in the near future. Medical technology, developed over the past 20 or so years, is often capable of resuscitating people after they have stopped breathing or their hearts have stopped beating. Some of those people are brought fully back to life. Two decades ago, those who were not and could not swallow and digest food, died. Intravenous solutions could not provide sufficient calories to maintain people for more than a short time. Today, various forms of artificial feeding have been developed that are able to keep people metabolically alive for years, even decades. . . . The new medical technology can reclaim those who would have been irretrievably lost a few decades ago and restore them to active lives. For Nancy Cruzan, it failed, and for others with wasting incurable disease it may be doomed to failure. In these unfortunate situations, the bodies and preferences and memories of the victims do not escheat to the State; nor does our Constitution permit the State or any other government to commandeer them. No singularity of feeling exists upon which such a government might confidently rely as *parens patriae.* . . . Yet Missouri and this Court have displaced Nancy's own assessment of the processes associated with dying. They have discarded evidence of her will, ignored her values, and deprived her of the right to a decision as closely approximating her own choice as humanly possible. They have done so disingenuously in her name, and openly in Missouri's own. That Missouri and this Court may truly be motivated only by concern for incompetent patients makes no matter. As one of our most prominent jurists warned us decades ago: "Experience should teach us to be most on our guard to protect liberty when the government's purposes are beneficent. . . . The greatest dangers to liberty lurk in insidious encroachment by men of zeal, well meaning but without understanding." *Olmstead* v. *United States*, (1928) (BRANDEIS, J., dissenting).

I respectfully dissent.

[JUSTICE STEVENS's *dissenting opinion is omitted.*]

The Poor in Court: Expanding and Contracting Rights

FEATURED CASES:

Wyman v. *James*   *San Antonio Independent School District* v. *Rodriguez*
Kadrmas v. *Dickinson Public Schools*

Poverty remains one of the most pervasive and vexing problems in American society. Poor people in America experience deprivation and discrimination solely because of their low socioeconomic status. In the most affluent nation on earth, the poor barely subsist. Their everyday life is burdened by inadequate food and clothing, dilapidated housing, high unemployment, grossly inferior schools, and high crime rates. It is as if they live in another country, another world—and most of them do!

In actual numbers, whites form the majority of poor people in this country. Nonetheless, because blacks, Latinos, and other persons of color constitute a disproportionate number of those in poverty, the drive to eliminate poverty and live a decent life may be viewed as part of the overall civil rights struggle. This perception, of course, can engender support as well as arouse opposition. Consequently, not unlike other interests, the nation's poor have also resorted to the judiciary in attempts to achieve their objectives. Much of this activity has been centered on safeguarding the rights of the poor in the criminal justice system, an area where their plight and problems have been well documented. In the main, these matters are discussed in Chapter 4, dealing with rights of the accused. Our major concern here is with the stance of the Supreme Court on problems of poverty in noncriminal areas.

In reviewing cases in this chapter, it is important not only to understand the path that the law has taken, but also to imagine the alternative paths *not* chosen. One might argue that each path represents the public commitments made by the American people as to the type of society in which they want to live. In this context, issues surrounding the poor and other marginalized groups are difficult to understand using traditional methods of constitutional interpretation because, as we have seen in other chapters, such methods usually focus on the restraints on governmental power and not on the possible affirmative obligations of the government toward achieving a more just society.

It is thought that one reason for the current failure to go down the jurisprudential path of actively promoting a more just society through law is the difficulty that governmental bodies, especially courts, have in choosing the proper goals and in getting prevailing interests to give concrete support for such goals. As our case law exemplifies, the transfer of resources from those who "have" to those who "have not" presents vexing problems in translating public commitment into reality. An important question raised here is which, if any, of our governmental institutions—the executive, Congress, or especially the Supreme Court—has the appropriate institutional competence and ability to provide the leadership to overcome such problems.

In this regard, and before examining the various lines of cases, it may be useful to consider the incisive and provocative views of Yale Law School Professor Charles L. Black, Jr.[9] Black argues that the public commitments to safeguard "life, liberty and the pursuit of happiness" made by the American people in the Declaration of Independence are hypocritical given the reality of poverty in America. He states simply and directly that "the possession of a decent material basis for life is an indispensable condition, to almost all people and at almost all times, to this " 'pursuit.' " Moreover, Black argues that the Preamble and Article I, sec. 8, of the Constitution "carry forward the very themes of the pursuit of happiness" by empowering and creating in Congress an affirmative obligation to tax and spend for the general welfare. Although he acknowledges the problem of articulating the "level of general welfare" to be satisfied, he points out that the circumstances in which "half of our black children under six lived in poverty in 1984" is clearly not a level from which happiness may be pursued.

Black sets forth a variety of bases for the proposition that Congress is bound by affirmative obligations to give content to a constitutional right to a decent livelihood. He is, however, less certain of the institutional competence of courts to effectu-

[9]Charles L. Black, Jr., "Further Reflections on the Constitutional Justice of Livelihood," 86 *Columbia Law Review*, 1103 (1986).

ate these affirmative obligations. Yet Black, although less certain, still offers hope: "I believe that there has been no Supreme Court Justice in this century who has not voted to support some right that could on no commonsense basis be said to be named in the Constitution; the great majority have cast such votes in some numbers over a wide range." Yet, to go from this possibility to the affirmative use of judicial power to overcome poverty and to change the socioeconomic circumstances of such marginalized persons remains a distant hope that would seem especially difficult to realize. Indeed, in the cases of *Spallone v. United States* (110 S. Ct. 625, 1990) and *Missouri v. Jenkins* (110 S. Ct. 1651, 1990), the Court defined some rather sharp limits on the use of judicial power to promote a more just society.

Nonetheless, Black does challenge us to imagine that in the three or four lifetimes since the founding of our country, the public commitments of the nation, especially with respect to race relations, have shown some, albeit slow, progress away from the hypocrisy between, on one hand the noble words and commitments embodied in the Declaration of Independence and the Constitution, and on the other the stark reality and practice in the everyday lives of many Americans who seem to be trapped in poverty. The question remains as to which institution will lead the way.

Articles such as Black's challenge us to reconceive of contemporary problems in ways that permit a more just balancing of rights and obligations. Remember, if you will, earlier chapters in which Tribe and Rubenfeld tried to reexamine the constitutional rights of free speech and privacy in terms of the affirmative promotion of individual rights rather than only their protection *from* the influence of government (See Chapter 3, and Chapter 7). As we go through the following cases, consider whether the Supreme Court could (or should) have functioned so as to foster a more affirmative obligation of government to fulfill our national commitments for a more just society.

WELFARE BENEFITS

In a series of earlier cases, the Court was faced with questions concerning the requirements and conditions under which welfare benefits are administered to the poor. In *King* v. *Smith* (392 U.S. 309, 1968), for example, the Court held invalid an Alabama regulation that denied federally provided benefits (Aid to Families with Dependent Children, AFDC) "to the children of a mother who 'cohabits' in or outside her home with any single or married able-bodied man." Chief Justice Earl Warren's majority opinion striking down the regulation first cited the AFDC program's definition of a "dependent child": "an age-qualified [under 18 or under 21 and a student] needy child . . . who has been deprived of parental support or care by reason of the death, continued absence from the home, or physical or mental incapability of a parent, and who is living with any one of several listed relatives." In this case, Mrs. Smith's children lost benefits in 1966 because "a Mr. Williams came to her home on weekends and had sexual relations with her." By viewing a "substitute father" as "a nonabsent parent within the federal statute," said Warren, Alabama "denies aid to an otherwise eligible needy child on the basis that his substitute parent is not absent from the home." Warren examined two justifications Alabama gave for its interpretation of the "nonabsent" wording. Alabama first said that its regulation "discourages illicit sexual relationships and illegitimate births." Further, the state contended that the regulation "puts families in which there is an informal 'marital' relationship on a par with those in which there is an ordinary marital relationship, because families of the latter sort are not eligible for AFDC assistance."

As to the first argument, Warren said that "Congress has determined that immorality and illegitimacy should be dealt with through rehabilitative measures rather than measures that punish dependent children, and that protection of such children is the paramount goal of AFDC." "It is simply inconceivable," continued Warren, "that Alabama is free to discourage immorality and illegitimacy by the device of absolute disqualification of needy children." Warren said Alabama's second argument "fails to take account of the circumstance that children of fathers living in the home are in a very different position from children of mothers who cohabit with men not their fathers: The child's father has a legal duty to support him, while the unrelated substitute father, at least in Alabama, does not." Warren concluded that "Congress intended the term 'parent' in [the AFDC statute] to include only those persons with a legal duty of support."

A different type of state regulation was at issue in *Shapiro* v. *Thompson* (394 U.S. 618, 1969). Several states and the District of Columbia required welfare recipients to reside within their jurisdiction for one year before receiving benefits. These rules, which allegedly tended to discourage the poor from moving to such jurisdictions, were held in *Shapiro* to create classifications that constituted invidious discrimination violative of the equal protection clause of the Fourteenth Amendment. In his majority opinion, Justice William J. Brennan noted that the "waiting period device is well suited to discourage the influx of poor families in need of assistance." "An indigent who desires to migrate, resettle, find a new job, start a new life," said Brennan, "will doubtless hesitate if he knows that he must risk making the move without the possibility of falling back on state welfare assistance during his first year of residence, when his need may be most acute." For Brennan, such purposeful action to inhibit migration by the poor is "irrational and unconstitutional" under traditional equal protection tests.

One of the most oft-cited justifications supporting the residency classification policy is that it is essential to protect the state's welfare resources from claims of indigents who move to a state only to get larger benefits. But to Brennan, "a State may no more try to fence out those indigents who seek higher benefits than it may try to fence out indigents generally." He further noted that "the fundamental right of interstate movement" was affected by the classification and that therefore "its constitutionality must be judged by the stricter standard of whether it promotes a *compelling* state interest." "Under this standard," he concluded, "the waiting period requirement clearly violates the Equal Protection Clause."

Justice John M. Harlan, in dissent, was extremely critical of the majority's use of the "compelling interest" equal protection doctrine. He was especially upset because the majority could make a statutory classification subject to the compelling interest test "if the result of the classification may be to affect a fundamental right, regardless of the basis of the classification." Harlan felt that such a doctrine was "unfortunate because it creates an exception which threatens to swallow the standard equal protection rule," and it was "unnecessary" because "the right affected is one assured by the Federal Constitution" and "any infringement can be dealt with under the Due Process Clause."

Overall, the *Shapiro* holding, especially when examined in light of *Dunn* v. *Blumstein* (405 U.S. 336, 1972, prohibiting lengthy residency requirements for voting in state and local elections), has considerable importance for the poor. At least two of the onerous burdens encountered when the poor move from one state to another—lack of welfare benefits when they are most acutely needed and exclusion from voting—are eliminated by these decisions.[10] (Cf. *Memorial Hospital* v. *Maricopa County*, 415 U.S. 250, 1974, where the Court held violative of the equal protection clause an Arizona law that required a one-year residence in a county as a condition for an indigent to receive nonemergency hospitalization or medical care at the county's expense.)

In *Goldberg* v. *Kelly* (397 U.S. 254, 1970), the Court held that procedural due process requires a state to afford a welfare recipient an opportunity for an evidentiary hearing *prior* to the termination of public assistance payments. Speaking for the majority, Justice Brennan noted that while some governmental benefits may be terminated administratively without affording the recipient a pretermination evidentiary hearing, welfare benefits were outside this category. Indeed, said Brennan:

> For qualified recipients, welfare provides the means to obtain essential food, clothing, housing and medical care. Thus, the crucial factor in this context—a factor not present in the case of the blacklisted governmental contractor, the discharged government employee, the taxpayer denied a tax exemption, or virtually anyone else whose government entitlements are ended—is that the termination of aid pending resolution of a controversy over eligibility may deprive an *eligible* recipient of the very means by which to live while he waits. Since he lacks independent resources, his situation becomes immediately desperate.

To meet the requisites of due process in this context, concluded Brennan, a recipient must "have timely and adequate notice detailing the reasons for a proposed termination and an effective opportunity to defend by confronting any adverse witnesses and by presenting his own arguments and evidence orally."

Chief Justice Warren Burger and Justices Hugo Black and Potter Stewart dissented. Their position was best articulated by Justice Black, who suggested that the new procedure would "lead to constitutionally imposed, time-consuming delays of a full adversary process of administrative and judicial review." Black was also concerned about persons receiving aid without being eligible. He said that officials probably erroneously added names to the welfare lists "in order to alleviate immediate suffering, and undoubtedly some people are drawing relief who are not entitled under the law to do so."

[10]In this connection, consider *Bullock* v. *Carter* (405 U.S. 134, 1972) and *Lubin* v. *Panish* (415 U.S. 709, 1974) with respect to rights of the poor in the political process. (Cf. *Simon* v. *Eastern Kentucky Welfare Rights Organization*, 426 U.S. 26, 1976.)

"In other words," he continued, "although some recipients might be on the lists for payment wholly because of deliberate fraud on their part, the Court holds that the government is helpless and must continue, until after an evidentiary hearing, to pay money that it does not owe, never has owed, and never could owe." Overall, however, the views of the dissenters did not go completely unheeded, for in *Mathews* v. *Eldridge* (424 U.S. 319, 1976) the Court somewhat tempered the potential impact of *Goldberg* by holding that evidentiary hearings were not required before social security benefits could be terminated.

Other regulations imposed by states in the administration of welfare programs indicate still additional problems faced by the poor. For example, in *Dandridge* v. *Williams* (397 U.S. 471, 1970), decided only two weeks after *Goldberg*, the Court upheld a Maryland regulation under which most families received AFDC benefits in accordance with their standard of need (determined by family size), but which imposed a ceiling of $250 per month on the grant "regardless of the size of the family and its actual need." In his majority opinion, Justice Potter Stewart said that the Court "need not explore all the reasons that the State advances in justification of the regulation." "It is enough," he asserted, "that a solid foundation for the regulation can be found in the State's legitimate interest in encouraging employment and in avoiding discrimination between welfare families and the families of the working poor." Stewart noted that "the Equal Protection Clause does not require a State to choose between attacking every aspect of a problem or not attacking the problem at all." The Maryland rule, continued Stewart, is "rationally based and free from invidious discrimination."

Justices Douglas, Brennan, and Marshall dissented. They believed that the Maryland regulation was inconsistent with the Social Security Act that created the AFDC program. Justice Marshall was particularly concerned about "the Court's emasculation of the Equal Protection Clause as a constitutional principle applicable to the area of social welfare administration." He argued that the appellees here were "needy dependent children and families who are discriminated against by the State." "The basis of that discrimination—the classification of individuals into large and small families," continued Marshall, "is too arbitrary and too unconnected to the asserted rationale, the impact on those discriminated against—the denial of even a subsistence existence—too great, and the supposed interests served too contrived and attenu-

ated to meet the requirements of the Constitution."

A year later, in *Wyman* v. *James* (400 U.S. 309, 1971), the Court upheld a New York regulation that required—as a condition to continuance of public assistance—periodic caseworker visitations to homes of AFDC recipients. Here Mrs. James, who began receiving AFDC assistance shortly after her son's birth in 1967, refused such a visit by a caseworker in her home, and, as a consequence, lost AFDC benefits. Justice Harold Blackmun, speaking for the Court, concluded that "the home visitation as structured by the New York statutes and regulations is a reasonable administrative tool [which] serves a valid and proper administrative purpose for the dispensation of the AFDC program." Hence, he asserted, "it is not an unwarranted invasion of personal privacy and violates no right guaranteed by the Fourth Amendment," because such visits do "not descend to the level of unreasonableness." Blackmun distinguished several other cases that turned on Fourth Amendment issues, including one case (*See* v. *City of Seattle*, 387 U.S. 541, 1967) in which a commercial warehouse owner refused to let a fire department representative enter his warehouse as a part of a "routine, periodic city-wide" inspection. The Court in *See* held that such administrative entry can be prevented unless it is carried out pursuant to a warrant.

This distinction did not impress Justice Thurgood Marshall who, joined by Justices Douglas and Brennan, issued a sharp dissent. He did not understand "why a commercial warehouse deserves more protection than this poor woman's home." He also attacked the two explanations set forth to justify the home visit rule. The first, "to protect dependent children from 'abuse' and 'exploitation,'" is concededly to prevent "heinous crimes," said Marshall, "but [such interests] are not confined to indigent households." Marshall wondered whether "the majority [would] sanction, in the absence of probable cause, compulsory visits to all American homes for the purpose of discovering child abuse." The second justification was based on the contention that home visits were necessary to determine whether the family was eligible for AFDC benefits. Marshall noted that "federal [AFDC] regulations do not require the home visit." Concluding, Marshall declared that he found "no little irony in the fact that the burden of today's departure from principled adjudication is placed upon the lowly poor."

In *Jefferson* v. *Hackney* (406 U.S. 535, 1972), the Court upheld a Texas scheme (necessitated by a state constitutional ceiling on welfare assistance grants) under which AFDC benefits were reduced by greater proportions than other welfare assistance programs. The Texas system provided for 100 percent implementation of the old-age assistance benefit, 95 percent of aid to the blind and to the disabled, but only 75 percent to AFDC recipients. The appellants claimed a violation of equal protection "because the proportion of AFDC recipients who are black or Mexican-American is higher than the proportion of the aged, blind or disabled welfare recipients who fall within these minority groups." (While less than 40 percent of those on old-age assistance were blacks or Mexican-Americans, 87 percent of those on AFDC were in these minority groups.) Justice William Rehnquist's majority opinion rejected the equal protection argument, stating that the Court "cannot say that Texas's decision to provide somewhat lower welfare benefits for AFDC recipients is invidious or irrational." Rehnquist described the allegations of racial discrimination as "unproven" and cited the district court's finding that "payment by Texas of a lesser percentage of unmet needs to the recipients of AFDC than to other recipients of other welfare programs is not the result of racial or ethnic prejudice."

In computing benefits, Texas employs a percentage reduction procedure that results in lower benefits that would tend to penalize those who earn outside income. Some other states use alternative computation procedures that, using the same factual base, result in higher benefits to the recipient. Acknowledging that "the two systems of accounting for outside income yield somewhat different results," and demonstrating that the Texas method results in lower actual benefits paid out, Rehnquist nevertheless contended that "if Texas were to switch to the alternative system of recognizing outside income, it would be forced to lower its percentage reduction factor, in order to keep down its welfare budget." "Lowering the percentage," he said, "would result in less money for those who need the welfare benefits the most—those with no outside income—and the State has been unwilling to do this."

Justices Douglas, Brennan, and Marshall dissented, indicating that in their view the Texas AFDC computation scheme was violative of the Social Security Act. Douglas, for example, said the majority "ignores the explicit congressional policy in favor of work incentives and upholds a system which provides penalties and disincentives for those who seek employment." Marshall not only presented strong statutory arguments against the majority's position on reduction computations but

also indicated that "the disparity [in the percentage reductions] between the various social welfare programs is not permissible under the federal statutory framework."

Assessing the record of the Burger Court in welfare law litigation, Professor Gayle Binion has suggested that although recipients have achieved some successes, especially in early years of the Burger Court, in later terms (1976–80) there has been a "precipitous decline" in the level of support for welfare claims.[11] Binion offers two explanations for this declining support. "First and most apparent," says Binion, "is that the Court has simply become ideologically less disposed to support the interests of those dependent on welfare, whether out of change in personal convictions or a perception that public support for these interests has declined." Second, Binion attributes the decline to the increasing deference of the Burger Court during the same period to the political branches of the federal government, that is, "to both the Congress and the Secretary of HEW (HHS)."

POVERTY, PUBLIC SCHOOLS, AND THE PROPERTY TAX

In *San Antonio Independent School District* v. *Rodriguez* (411 U.S. 1), a 1973 decision, the Supreme Court rejected challenges to the Texas system of financing public school education. Here, Rodriguez contended that the Texas system of supplementing state aid to school districts by means of an *ad valorem* tax on property within the jurisdiction of the individual school district violated the equal protection clause. Rodriguez, whose children attended schools in a district with lower per pupil expenditures but higher property tax rates than in other area districts, argued that substantial differences in per pupil expenditures among the districts resulted from the differences in the value of the property taxed within each district. Justice Lewis Powell, speaking for a five-to-four majority of the Court, said that the financing system, although not perfect, "abundantly satisfies" the constitutional standard for equal protection since the system "rationally furthers a legitimate state purpose or interest." Powell said that the traditional equal protection standard applied, since "the Texas system does not operate to the peculiar disadvantage of any suspect class" and since education, although an important state service, is not a "fundamental"

[11]Gayle Binion, "The Disadvantaged before the Burger Court," *Law and Policy Quarterly* 37 (January 1982).

right because it is not "explicitly or implicitly guaranteed by the Constitution." Justices Brennan, White, Douglas, and Marshall dissented.

One effect of *Rodriguez* is that relief from such inequities has been sought in state courts and legislatures. And some relief has come about. A number of states, through court rulings and legislative enactments, have made sweeping reforms in this regard. But the fact that other states have refused to overturn existing methods of financing public education must temper any notion of circumventing *Rodriguez* on a massive scale. (Cf. *Serrano* v. *Priest*, 487 P.2d 1241, 1977, cert. denied in *Clowes* v. *Serrano*, 432 U.S. 907, 1977.)

Nonetheless, the legal (and political) battle over spending disparities between rich schools and poor schools continues unabated as evidenced clearly by the fact that as of 1992 some twenty three states were embroiled in lawsuits over such matters. (See William Celis 3d, "23 States Face Suits on School Funds," *The New York Times*, September 2, 1992, p. B5)

THE POOR AND HOUSING

Several decisions of the Supreme Court held considerable importance for the poor with respect to housing. In *James* v. *Valtierra* (402 U.S. 137, 1971), for example, the Court upheld a California statute that "provided that no low-rent [federally financed] housing project should be developed, constructed or acquired in any manner by a state public body until the project was approved by a majority of those voting at a community election." A federal district court agreed with the plaintiffs, who contended the statute denied them equal protection of the laws and enjoined its enforcement. But on appeal the Supreme Court reversed. In his opinion for the majority, Justice Black rejected the plaintiff's argument "that the mandatory nature of the . . . referendum constitutes unconstitutional discrimination because it hampers persons desiring public housing from achieving their objective when no such roadblock faces other groups seeking to influence other public decisions to their advantage." To him, it was clear that the referendum procedure "ensures that all the people of a community will have a voice in a decision which may lead to large expenditures of local governmental funds for increased public services and to lower tax revenues." The California referendum statute, he concluded, is a "procedure for democratic decision-making" that does not violate the equal protection clause.

Justice Marshall, joined by Justices Brennan and Blackmun, dissented. Marshall said that the California statute "on its face constitutes invidious discrimination which the Equal Protection Clause of the Fourteenth Amendment plainly prohibits." He contended further that "singling out the poor to bear a burden not placed on any other class of citizens tramples the values the Fourteenth Amendment was designed to protect."

At issue in *Warth* v. *Seldin* (422 U.S. 490, 1975) was the allegedly discriminatory zoning laws of Penfield, New York, a Rochester suburb, which effectively prevented low- and middle-income blacks and Puerto Ricans from moving in. The suit was brought by several groups. These included several area residents with low or middle incomes who were members of racial minorities; several Rochester taxpayers who claimed that the discriminatory practices of Penfield resulted in higher taxes; and a nonprofit organization whose purpose was to alleviate the housing shortage of the Rochester area for lower-income people. In a five-to-four decision, the Court ruled that the above groups did not have the standing requisite to bring such action. Justice Powell, who wrote the majority opinion, held that none of the petitioners had met the "threshold requirement" of "clearly . . . demonstrating that he is a proper party to invoke judicial resolution of the dispute and the exercise of the court's remedial powers."

The decision in *Warth*, especially considered in light of *San Antonio*, illustrates the plight of the poor in trying to achieve parity with their wealthier "neighbors." On the one hand, the poor are denied relief with respect to financial inequities that exist between school districts or communities. On the other hand, it is possible for the wealthy to exclude the poor through certain zoning regulations. Thus, the options for poor people to achieve some sense of parity on the local level have been greatly narrowed by these Court actions. (But cf. *Hills* v. *Gautreaux*, 1976, and *Arlington Heights* v. *Metropolitan Housing Authority*, 1977, Chapter 5.

A long-standing concern of the poor—the rights of indigent renters—came before the Supreme Court in the 1970s. In *Lindsey* v. *Normet* (405 U.S. 56, 1972), Lindsey and other tenants refused to pay their monthly rent unless certain substandard conditions were remedied, and Normet threatened to evict them. The appellants filed a class action suit seeking a declaratory judgment that three provisions of the Oregon Forcible Entry and Wrongful Detainer (FED) statute were unconstitutional. The appellants attacked primarily, (1) the requirement of a trial no later than six days after service of the complaint unless security for the accruing rent is provided; (2) the limitation of triable issues to the tenant's default (the landlord's breach of duty to maintain the premises was excluded); and (3) the requirement of posting bond on appeal that amounted to twice the rent expected to accrue pending the appellate decision. The entire bond was forfeited if the lower court decision was affirmed.

Justice White delivered the opinion of the Court. He took note that the appellants contended "that the 'need for decent shelter' and the 'right to retain peaceful possession of one's home' are fundamental interests which are particularly important to the poor and which may be trenched upon only after the State demonstrates a superior interest. . . . " Accordingly, the appellants felt that the Court should apply the "strict scrutiny" standard of equal protection. But Justice White disagreed, and in doing so reflected a more general reluctance of the Court to declare a "constitutional war" on poverty. Said White:

> We do not denigrate the importance of decent, safe, and sanitary housing. But the Constitution does not provide judicial remedies for every social and economic ill. We are unable to perceive in that document any constitutional guarantee of access to dwellings of a particular quality or any recognition of the right of a tenant to occupy the real property of his landlord beyond the terms of his lease, without payment of rent or otherwise contrary to the terms of the relevant agreement. Absent constitutional mandate, the assurance of adequate housing and the definition of landlord-tenant relationships is a legislative and not a judicial function. Nor should we forget that the Constitution expressly protects against confiscation of private property or the income therefrom.

Consequently, White used the "rationality standard" and found that the first two issues raised by the appellants did not violate either the equal protection clause or the due process clause. However, White found that the double bond prerequisite for appealing an FED action violated the equal protection clause because it arbitrarily discriminated against tenants wishing to appeal adverse FED decisions without effectuating the state's purpose of preserving the property issue. "The discrimination against the poor who could pay their rent pending an appeal but cannot post the double bond," said White, "is particularly obvious." "For them, as a practical matter," observed White, "appeal is foreclosed, no matter how meritorious their case may be." White noted that the "nonindigent FED appellant also is confronted by a substantial barrier to

appeal faced by no other civil litigant in Oregon." Consequently, White concluded that "the discrimination against the class of FED appellants is arbitrary and irrational, and the double-bond requirement . . . violates the Equal Protection Clause."

Also at issue was the refusal of a judge to allow a jury trial to a renter who was being sued by his landlord for repossession of property (*Pernell* v. *Southhall Realty*, 416 U.S. 363, 1974). The appellant refused payments to "set-off" costs he had incurred in performing certain repair work and for the landlord's failure to maintain the premises in compliance with District of Columbia housing regulations. In the majority opinion, Justice Marshall stated that either party has the right to a jury trial by the Seventh Amendment. In general, *Pernell* and to an extent *Lindsey* recognize that renters, too, have certain rights and are entitled to seek redress on constitutional grounds.

ACCESS TO THE COURTS

In *Boddie* v. *Connecticut* (401 U.S. 371, 1971), the Court held that states cannot deny access to their courts to people seeking divorces solely because of inability to pay court costs. The case involved indigent welfare recipients who desired divorces but who were unable to pay the necessary filing and other court fees (about $60 in all) in order to obtain a hearing. They claimed that the due process and equal protection clauses required Connecticut to grant them access to courts. In accepting Boddie's due process contention, Justice John Harlan's opinion for the Court emphasized the state's authority over the marriage status. "Given the basic position of the marriage relationship in this society's hierarchy of values and the concomitant state monopolization of the means for legally dissolving [it]," he asserted, "due process does prohibit the State from denying, solely because of inability to pay access to its courts to individuals who seek judicial dissolution of their marriages." Harlan's opinion in *Boddie*, however, is self-limiting, since two important factors must be present in cases attempting to use the result as a binding precedent: (1) the presence of a fundamental or basic interest; and (2) "state monopolization" over resolution of the dispute.

Several of the other opinions in *Boddie*, however, were not so limited. Justice Douglas, for example, concurred, saying that the decision should have rested on the broader base of equal protection. "An invidious discrimination based on property," said Douglas, "is adequate for this case."

Justice Brennan, in another concurring opinion, said that "[t]he right to be heard in some way at some time extends to all proceedings entertained by courts." "The possible distinctions suggested by the Court today," cautioned Brennan, "will not withstand analysis." Brennan was concerned over the "state monopolization" language used by Harlan in the majority opinion.

But the Burger Court moved away from this "access" trend in civil matters with two five-to-four decisions in 1973. First, in *United States* v. *Kras* (409 U.S. 434, 1973), the inability of an unemployed indigent to pay the $50 filing fee in a bankruptcy petition was at issue. A federal district court had agreed with the petitioner's argument that denying him the opportunity to file for bankruptcy because of his inability to pay the filing fee violated the due process and equal protection guarantees of the Fifth Amendment. Relying on the *Boddie* decision, the district court concluded that "a discharge in bankruptcy was a 'fundamental interest' that could be denied only when a 'compelling government interest' was demonstrated." But a five-member majority of the Supreme Court rejected this reliance on *Boddie* as misplaced. Speaking for them, Justice Harold Blackmun maintained that bankruptcy should not be regarded as a fundamental right that demands the showing of a "compelling governmental interest" to justify significant regulation. Furthermore, he contended, this subject does not touch upon "the suspect criteria of race, nationality or alienage." Hence, he argued, "rational justification" was the appropriate standard and Congress had met it. For example, while the court action sought in *Boddie* was the only way to dissolve the marriage, the statute involved in *Kras* permits "negotiated agreements" and very low installment payments. In short, the indigent bankrupt is offered effective alternatives. In the end, he held, any extension of the *Boddie* principle to bankruptcy proceedings should start with the Congress.

The dissenting justices (Douglas, Stewart, Brennan, and Marshall) were sharply critical of the majority for in effect holding, as Justice Stewart remarked, "that some of the poor are too poor even to go bankrupt." Because they believed that access to the courts to determine the claim of a legal right is fundamental, any denial of that access because of inability to pay filing fees constituted for them the kind of invidious discrimination between rich and poor contrary to equal protection.

The second case, *Ortwein* v. *Schwab* (410 U.S. 656, 1973), involved an action by welfare recipients, without payment of the required $25 filing fee, to have a court review of an Oregon administrative action reducing their benefits. The Supreme Court affirmed the Oregon court's denial of relief. In its per curiam opinion, the Court cited *Kras* rather than *Boddie* as the governing precedent, noting that the interest alleged by the welfare recipients (to have administrative action reducing their benefits judicially reviewed), was far less significant than that asserted by the indigent divorce seekers in *Boddie*.

The same four dissenters restated their argument advanced in *Kras*. As Justice William O. Douglas noted, the majority's action simply "broadens and fortifies the 'private preserve' for the affluent . . . [by upholding] a scheme of judicial review whereby justice remains a luxury for the wealthy." Furthermore, Douglas noted, *Kras* should not be considered applicable to this case because relief through "nonjudicial accommodation" was not available. Even more crucial was the fact that the majority's ruling permits a state to deny "initial access to the courts for review of an adverse administrative determination."

The Supreme Court did not exhibit this kind of deference to state procedures permitting prejudgment garnishment of wages (in Wisconsin and about 20 other states) and prejudgment seizure of goods under writs of replevin (in Pennsylvania and Florida) without any prior hearing. In 1969, in *Sniadach* v. *Family Finance Corporation* (395 U.S. 337), the Court indicated that wages were "a specialized type of property" and that the consequences of wage garnishment (hardship on wage earners with families to support) were quite severe. Justice Douglas's brief majority opinion stated that "[w]here the taking of one's property is so obvious, it needs no extended argument to conclude that absent notice and a prior hearing this prejudgment garnishment procedure violates the fundamental principles of due process."

Three years later, in *Fuentes* v. *Shevin* (407 U.S. 67, 1972), the Court in a four-to-three decision ruled that due process requires that an opportunity for a hearing be provided before the state can authorize its agents to seize property in the possession of a debtor upon the application of his or her creditor. Justice Stewart's majority opinion noted that the "essential reason for the hearing requirement is to prevent unfair and mistaken deprivations of property." "Due process," said Stewart, "is afforded only by the kinds of 'notice' and 'hearing' that are aimed at establishing the validity, or at least the probable validity, of the underlying claim against the alleged debtor *before* he can be deprived of his property." Chief Justice Burger and

Justices White and Blackmun did not believe that the Constitution guarantees such a right to a defaulting buyer-debtor. In Justice White's dissenting opinion, supported by Burger and Blackmun, the creditor's property interest is considered just "as deserving as that of the debtor." White argued that under the Court's historic view of what procedures due process requires "under any given set of circumstances," the creditors had the right under state laws to take possession of the property *pending final hearing*. White told the majority that it should best leave such legislative matters to the experts employed by legislative bodies. Certainly he did not think the procedures struck down were "some barbaric hangover from bygone days."

By 1974, Justice White's dissent in *Fuentes* was, in great measure, accepted by the Court majority in *Mitchell* v. *W.T. Grant Co.* (416 U.S. 600, 1974). Here the Court upheld a Louisiana sequestration statute permitting creditors to secure a court order for their immediate repossession of goods without prior notice to the defaulting debtor. However, the statute gives the debtor the opportunity for a full hearing subsequent to the repossession. Speaking for a five-to-four Court majority, Justice White rejected the "petitioner's broad assertion that the Due Process Clause of the United States Constitution guaranteed to him the use and possession of the goods until all issues in the case were judicially resolved after full adversary proceedings had been completed." "The very nature of due process," said White, "negates any concept of inflexible procedures universally applicable to every imaginable situation." Applying this principle to the instant case, White observed:

> The question is not whether a debtor's property may be seized by his creditors, *pendente lite*, where they hold no present interest in the property sought to be seized. The reality is that both seller and buyer had rights as a matter of state law. Resolution of the due process question must take account not only of the interests of the buyer of the property but those of the seller as well.

Prior cases upon which the petitioner relied, reasoned White, "merely stand for the proposition that a hearing must be had before one is *finally* deprived of his property" (emphasis added). "Considering the Louisiana procedure as a whole," said White, "we are convinced that the State has reached a constitutional accommodation of the respective interests of buyer and seller."

Justice Stewart, in a dissent joined by Justices Douglas and Marshall, strongly attacked the majority for not following *Fuentes*. Said Stewart: "The only perceivable change that has occurred since *Fuentes* is in the makeup of this Court." Stewart pinpointed this membership change by indicating in a footnote . . . that although Justices Powell and Rehnquist had seen on the Court when *Fuentes* was announced, they were not on the Court when the case was argued and hence did not participate in its consideration or decision. "A basic change in the law upon a ground no firmer than a change in our membership," warned Stewart, "invites the popular misconception that this institution is little different from the two political branches of the Government." "No misconception," concluded Stewart, "could do more lasting injury to this Court and to the system of law which it is our abiding mission to serve."

Overall, and after her well developed empirically based study of "The Disadvantaged before the Burger Court," Binion suggests "that the Court's jurisprudence is to be faulted as much for its inappropriate application of principle as for its application of inappropriate principle."[12] She then outlines and describes a "newest equal protection" standard so as to overcome pitfalls of earlier standards. Binion believes that this "newest" standard "which questions the contextual reasonableness of the classifications rather than only their effectiveness, [would] restore judicial protection to equal protection." However, while not minimizing the role of tests or standards in judicial decision-making, it is perhaps well for us to remain constantly alert to the observation made by Jack Peltason some time ago, to the effect that in the final analysis it is judges, not "tests" or "standards" or "doctrines," that determine judicial outcomes.[13]

LAWYERS, LEGAL SERVICES, AND RIGHTS OF THE POOR

In general, the availability of legal services is a major key as to whether poor persons can really use the law and courts to attain their objectives. Lawyers are needed to negotiate the legal terrain: draft legislation, phrase issues, develop arguments, and suggest strategies and rationales to achieve their goals. But legal services cost money, a resource that is alien to those in poverty. Consequently, going to court to vindicate their rights is a

[12]Ibid, pp. 59–60.
[13]See generally Jack W. Peltason, *Federal Courts in the Political Process* (Garden City, NY: Doubleday, 1955).

luxury poor people cannot afford on their own.[14] Early on, the primary burden of providing legal services for the poor fell on privately funded and operated legal aid societies. However, the services these groups could provide, including some offered by local bar associations, were not sufficient to meet the need. This situation did (and does) pose some serious problems and dilemmas. For example, in a country that prides itself on having a "government of laws" where all persons are subject to the rule of law, could (and can) we afford to have those in poverty effectively denied access and participation in our legal justice system solely because they are too poor to use it? Could (and can) we afford to ignore the linkages between race and poverty, which show that a very large and disproportionate number of blacks (about one out of every three) as compared to whites (about one out of every ten) live in poverty? To do so, of course, would mean that access to courts and to the legal justice system is effectively determined along wealth and poverty lines that are very much tainted by a lingering racism. In any event, the egalitarian sentiments of the 1960s led President Lyndon B. Johnson and the Congress to declare a "War on Poverty" in which the full range of the nation's resources, including law and courts, would be used. As a result, a new federally funded Legal Services Program (LSP) was established in 1965 and represented the most important development in providing legal services for the poor.

Free legal services that provide representation for indigent defendants in the criminal justice area have generally met with widespread approval and support. To be sure, decisions of the Supreme Court, such as *Gideon* v. *Wainwright* (372 U.S. 335, 1963), have spurred and kindled this support. However, many recognized that the poor need legal services to protect and promote their interests in noncriminal areas as well. Thus, with federally funded legal services, more of these needs could be met. For one thing, poor persons could now begin actively to use the legal justice system to achieve their rights and policy objectives, for example, food, decent housing, good educational opportunities, and jobs. And rather than rely exclusively on "band-aid" approaches (i.e., attending the needs of individual clients with the present structure of the law), more aggressive LSP lawyers began to use more general approaches, such as class action suits and other law reform activities, that would "revise the structure of the world in which the poor live"[15] However, this law reform posture of the federal LSP, not unexpectantly, met with trouble. In vindicating and promoting the rights and interests of poor people. LSP lawyers were almost inevitably led to attack the "system," and did indeed become embroiled in issues (e.g., school desegregation, landlord-tenant rights) that stood to affect the futures and fortunes of not only the poor, but those (e.g., the wealthy) who had long used the courts and legal system to protect their interests and to preserve the status quo. As a result, the federally funded Legal Services Program has increasingly come under attack leading to various restrictions and limitations on LSP functions and attorneys. This anti-LSP trend had accelerated during the Nixon administration and by the time of the Reagan years reached such proportions that the matter of federally funded Legal Services was no longer a problem of reorganization, limitations, or budget cuts, but rather one of whether to maintain or fund a legal services program at all.[16] In fact, President Reagan did recommend eliminating funds for the Legal Services Corporation (LSC) entirely, which would have effectively killed the program. This recommendation created sharp divisions and fierce debate. For example, Republican Senator Orrin Hatch (Utah), chairman of the Labor and Human Resources Committee within whose jurisdiction LSC falls, supported the president and favored abolishing the corporation. "Though I have supported legal services in the vain hope they will concentrate on really helping the poor," said Hatch, "personally I have come to the conclusion that they will never do that."[17] The senator stated that legal aid lawyers had spent "millions of dollars in what we call lawyer activism for liberal social programs instead of working for the common needs of the poor."

[14]The relative importance of legal representation for protecting the rights of indigents is pointed up quite starkly by the majority and dissenting opinions in the 1981 case of *Lassiter* v. *Department of Social Services of Durham County, North Carolina* (452 U.S. 18). By a narrow five-to-four vote, the Court held that the Constitution does not require the appointment of counsel for indigent parents in every parental status termination proceedings and indicated that the constitutional right of indigent litigants to the appointment of counsel exists "only where, if he loses, he [the litigant] may be deprived of his physical liberty."

[15]Statement of Earl Johnson, second director of the federal LSP, 1976, as quoted in Philip Hannon. "From Politics to Reality: An Historical Perspective of the Legal Services Corporation," 25 *Emory Law Journal* 639, 1976, at p. 642.
[16]The Legal Services Program, formerly a part of the Office of Economic Opportunity, was reorganized and set up as a separate independent corporation in 1974, and was formally designated the Legal Services Corporation. For an overview of these developments, see *ibid.*
[17]Quotations in section are from *The Congressional Quarterly*, March 21, 1981, p. 529.

However, Attorney F. William McCalpin, chairman of the LSC board of directors and speaking in support of the program, placed the matter in broad political perspective. In testimony before a congressional committee, he warned that President Reagan's overall budget cuts affecting the poor "will raise feelings of alienation and frustration to a level we have not seen in fifteen years." "In those circumstances," said McCalpin, "we need equal access to justice to keep the controversies in balance, within the system." "That's what legal services is all about," concluded McCalpin, and "I urge you not to retreat from the principle of equal justice under law."

But President Reagan did not give up on his fight to curtail the LSP sharply or even to kill it outright. As Senator Thomas Eagleton (D., Mo.) aptly put it:

> There are three ways to kill a program, and the president with respect to legal services has tried all three. One way is to kill it outright. That didn't succeed. Another is to fund it at such a low level as to make it inoperative. From Reagan's point of view he made a little progress on that, he got the budget cut. And the third way is to put the management and oversight of the program in unfriendly hands.[18]

Civil rights advocates and others would suggest that Eagleton's comments were not applicable only to the LSP, but were equally descriptive of the overall record and attitude of the Reagan administration with respect to programs affecting civil rights and the poor in general.

In any case, the nature and sharpness of the LSC debate, especially when coupled with the disposition of many establishment types (e.g., the American Bar Association) to save the program, attest to the relation of the goals of the LSC to the general values to which we are attached as a nation. They also attest to how lawyers can use law and courts as avenues to achieve particular objectives, even for poor people. However, although successful in some important respects, such as *Shapiro* v. *Thompson*, Legal Services lawyers can also attest to the difficulties involved in attempts to "constitutionalize" and win more rights for poor people.[19] Let us now take a closer look at the stance of the Court on these matters during the Reagan-Bush years of 1980–92.

[18]Stuart Taylor, Jr., "Legal Aid for the Poor: Reagan's Longest Brawl," *The New York Times,* June 8, 1984, p. 16.

[19]Krislov, "OEO Lawyers Fail to Constitutionalize a Right to Welfare: A Study in Uses and Limits of the Judicial Process," 58 *Minnesota Law Review* 211 (1973).

THE REAGAN AND BUSH YEARS: LIMITATIONS ON ACHIEVING ECONOMIC JUSTICE THROUGH COURTS AND THE LAW

As a result of budgetary cutbacks and key appointments of justices and administration officials, it is clear that the Reagan and Bush administrations did not focus on how to overcome the problems of the poor and marginalized. As realized in the jurisprudence of the decade, the 1980s were marked by an increasing concern with self-interest and the perspective that social justice was not a value that could be promoted through the rule of law. This tone, grudging in its views of public commitments toward the collective "pursuit of happiness," stood in contrast to the attitude in the 1970s, when the legal debate, as we have seen, focused on the scope of the distribution of benefits. A significant trend in some of the cases of the 1980s was an emphasis on the limitations on the use of judicial authority to fill the gap brought on by an increasing reluctance by the political branches to give content to the demands of the poor and marginalized. A few recent cases illustrate the results of the sea change that marked the 1980s.

Earlier we looked at the path that society took in regulating welfare benefits during the 1970s. In *Goldberg* and *Dandridge*, respectively, we saw that the receipt of welfare benefits was to be accompanied by due process safeguards. However, receipt could also be restricted by conditions reinforcing a state interest in promoting employment and nondiscrimination between welfare recipients and the working poor. However, during the 1980s, when fewer resources were available, greater pressures were put upon legislatures to cut back on public assistance or, at the very minimum, to increase restrictions on its receipt. But, by and large, Congress and the courts tried to ensure that although conditions were placed on the receipt of public benefits, such conditions did not require the sacrifice of fundamental constitutional rights. It could be argued, though, that the Supreme Court has recently shifted its position and placed the receipt of public benefits in conflict with the possession of fundamental constitutional rights.

In *Lyng* v. *International Union, UAW* (108 S. Ct. 1184, 1988), the Court, by a five-to-three vote, held that 1981 amendments to the Food Stamp Act of 1977 did not interfere with the recipient's First Amendment right to association. In 1981, Congress amended the Food Stamp Act to restrict the level of eligibility for benefits for certain households if such eligibility arose after a drop in income due to participation in a labor strike. The plaintiffs argued that the statute's restrictions were unconstitutionally coercive in limiting union participation. In writing for the Court, Justice White reinforced the traditional notion that welfare benefits were a privilege, not a right, by holding that the First Amendment did not require the federal government to provide food stamps to lessen the "economic hardship" that would accompany a labor dispute (108 S. Ct., at 1191). In dissent, Justice Marshall rejected the Court's rational basis analysis of the statute and argued that the amendments were too broad to meet the government's interest in limiting the receipt of food stamps to those who wanted to work. He argued that the amendments were not neutral in that employers received governmental benefits during strikes and felt that the amendments reflected a "public animus" toward a particular group—strikers (108 S. Ct., at 1198)— that thus violated the equal protection clause of the Fourteenth Amendment.

The Supreme Court also used a rational basis test to uphold a North Dakota statute that allowed school districts to charge students for transportation to a school. In *Kadrmas* v. *Dickinson Public Schools* (108 S. Ct. 2481, 1988), a family near the poverty level sued to enjoin the school system from enforcing the fee because it would violate the equal protection clause of the Fourteenth Amendment. In a five-to-four decision, the United States Supreme Court affirmed the Supreme Court of North Dakota's rejection of the family's claims. Justice O'Connor argued that the Court had dismissed prior attempts to classify wealth, or more appropriately, the lack of it, as a category that required "strict scrutiny" by courts. She asserted that the statute was rationally related to the goals of the state in fulfilling the expectations of the families that had supported school reorganization plans. In dissent, Justice Marshall found that even though the statute did not prevent the Kadrmas child from attending school, the transportation fee denied the poor access to basic education, which he considered to be a fundamental right.

In both *Lyng* and *Kadrmas*, the Court indirectly displayed benign neglect, if not some hostility, to the working and nonworking poor by permitting an increase in the costs of obtaining welfare benefits. In *Lyng*, the poor would have to make choices that those who were better off did not as to the exercise of other constitutional rights. In *Kadrmas*, the exercise of the disputed right itself, in this case public education, was made more difficult by the imposition of a transportation fee. In both cases, the Court displayed a cramped view of the affirma-

tive obligation of government to enable people to achieve self-determination. It is quite straightforward that the poor can do very little about their lot if their chosen activities, such as association or public education, require them to sacrifice subsistence. In addition, the symbol of the Court accommodating such restrictions by the state only added an air of legitimacy to the sea change of Reagan administration politics.

The limitations on using law to promote social justice have also affected the legal system—both lawyers and judges. The most striking example of the emphasis in the 1980s on self-interest and the economics of using law to promote social justice could be seen in *Mallard* v. *United States District Court* (109 S. Ct. 1814, 1991). *Mallard* required the Supreme Court to interpret Congress's intent in 28 U.S.C. § 1915, which authorized federal courts to use their judicial authority to enable the poor to sue without incurring costs and fees. At the heart of the conflict was a provision of the statute that was ambiguous as to whether attorney compliance in representing the poor client at the request of the judge was to be mandatory or voluntary. At stake was the public commitment toward representing the poor, which would go beyond the simple economics of such representation. It is obvious that the market for an effective attorney's services would always result in much more money to be made in selling services to a private client than to a court in order to assist the poor.

In *Mallard*, an attorney was requested by a court to represent two prison inmates and one former inmate in a civil rights matter. The attorney made an unsuccessful motion to withdraw, offering the excuse of lack of expertise. The lower courts had interpreted Section 1915(d) to allow for compulsory appointment. In a five-to-four decision, Justice Brennan held that the statute did not authorize a federal court to require an attorney to represent an indigent. Justice Anthony Kennedy concurred, emphasizing that the role of the Supreme Court was to separate out the requirements of the statute from the general obligations of the profession and of society. By contrast, Justice John Paul Stevens, in dissent, argued that the duty of attorneys was instead defined by a tradition of providing legal assistance to the poor and the marginalized.

The economics of indigent representation was also apparent in *FTC* v. *Superior Court Trial Lawyers Association* (110 S. Ct. 768, 1990). In that case, criminal defense lawyers in Washington, D.C., who represented indigents organized a boycott of their legal services in an effort to force the local government to increase their hourly rates. Over time, inadequate compensation had led to a diminishing supply of lawyers to assist indigents. Moreover, the ones that remained were overburdened with huge caseloads, little administrative support, and, as a result, little time to research any case effectively. By increasing their fees, the boycotters hoped to obtain better and more effective representation for the poor.

In litigating this case, it is ironic that the focus on the poor dropped out. The case was framed in terms of the First Amendment rights of the boycotters to be heard as against the antitrust laws that tried to preserve competition for services. In a six-to-three decision, the Supreme Court concluded that the boycott was a per se violation of the Sherman Antitrust Act in that it constituted a "naked restraint" on trade. The Supreme Court rejected the boycotters' claim that their action deserved protection in that it constituted political speech that sought to vindicate the rights of indigent defendants. The thrust of the Court's argument was that groups could not be permitted to avoid the antitrust laws by substituting their own conception about the public welfare (110 S. Ct., at 777). In making such an argument, the Court reinforced the prevailing economic ideology of competition and self-interest at the expense of trying to find alternative ways to commit the public to the representation of indigents.

Mallard and *Superior Court Trial Lawyers Association* both focused on the role of lawyers in the administration of justice for the poor and the marginalized. By contrast, in the cases of *Spallone* v. *United States* (110 S. Ct. 625, 1990) and *Missouri* v. *Jenkins* (110 S.Ct. 1651, 1990), the Supreme Court focused on the role of federal judges in encouraging the legal system to fulfill its public commitments to socioeconomic justice. In *Spallone*, a federal district judge used his contempt powers to impose sanctions on the city of Yonkers, New York, and on individual council members in order to coerce them to remedy his earlier finding that the city had intentionally created and maintained racial segregation in housing. Because of severe public opposition to court-mandated remedies, the City Council had refused to build public housing. The Supreme Court, in a five-to four decision, overturned the personal contempt citations of the council members and limited federal courts' powers to apply coercive remedies. Chief Justice Rehnquist argued that courts were obliged to tailor their remedies narrowly to use the "least possible power adequate to the end proposed" (110 S.

Ct., at 632). In dissent, Justice Brennan feared that this decision would only give a signal to recalcitrant local officials to resist the remedial powers of federal courts.

In *Jenkins*, a federal district court found that Kansas City had created and maintained a segregated school system. The federal judge ordered an ambitious remedial program consisting of magnet schools, capital improvements, and new educational programs. Because the local district lacked the funds to pay for its share of the remedies, the district court judge both levied an increase in the property tax rate that was prohibited by the state constitution and imposed a surcharge on the income of those living and working in the district. The Court of Appeals for the Eighth Circuit reversed only as to the surcharge on income. The Supreme Court, on the other hand, went further, holding unanimously that the district court's direct imposition of a property tax was an abuse of discretion. In concurring, Justice Kennedy wanted the Court to assert clearly that "taxation is not a judicial function" and that the role of judges was limited to deciding controversies between parties before the court and not to remedy social ills (110 S. Ct., at 1669–70).

CONCLUSION

Over the last five years, the Supreme Court has begun to give realization to the Reagan administration's political legacy of contracting the role of government in the lives of Americans. Moreover, such contraction of public authority has occurred in a focused way. In the main, the emphasis has been on retracting the role of government from the group of citizens who probably need it and want it the most. As we have seen, the Supreme Court's analysis of equal protection is currently exclusive, denying any special judicial scrutiny to issues that implicate wealth classifications.

In addition, the scope not only of governmental authority but also of legal authority has shrunk vis-á-vis the poor. The legal profession has now become much more cost-conscious about the value of *pro bono* time and its obligations to make such contributions. Further, led by the Supreme Court, the self-conception of judicial authority to induce the political system to remedy racial and economic injustice has changed to reflect a more cramped role. In contrast to the conception of judges in the 1960s and 1970s as active participants and managers in the political process, courts and judges played a more limited role in the national political process in the 1980s.[20]

As a result of this limited role of governmental and legal authority in the promotion of economic and social justice, a transformed conception of the role of courts and law seemed to have emerged by the end of the 1980s. It may be argued that the path that the country has taken is to fashion law sensitive to the needs and concerns of prevailing interests (e.g., law for the middle and upper classes instead of for all Americans). The profound implication of this transformation is that law has effectively been reduced as a force to redress the inequities and concerns of emerging and aspiring interests. This is especially salient, for example, in light of cases that force the poor to choose between the vindication of their political rights and their subsistence, making it much more difficult for such marginalized individuals to achieve their full potential.

Despite this present bleak assessment, it is useful to consider comments made by Charles Black in 1986 relative to the dynamics involved as the path of law winds through time:

> The country is now infatuated with an idol called the "economy," which most high priests seem to agree is doing real well, though millions of children are not getting enough to eat, and millions of adults who want work cannot find it. But winds change; they always have, and doubtless they always will. A period of no power is a period for the reformation of thought, to the end that when power returns it may be more skillfully, more fittingly, used. The way I want to see thought reformed is by our ceasing to view the elimination of poverty as a sentimental matter, as a matter of compassion, and our starting to look on it as a matter of justice, constitutional right.[21]

We must wait to see whether the new Democratic Clinton administration, like Professor Black, will look upon poverty "as a matter of justice, [and] constitutional right." Indeed, it remains to be seen if certain early actions and inclinations of President Clinton, in contrast to those of Reagan and Bush, will lead to an overall political-legal environment in which courts and elective political institutions will deal more actively with poverty and related matters.

---

[20]Compare Abram Chayes, "The Role of the Judge in Public Law Litigation," 89 *Harvard Law Review* 1281 (1976), and Owen M. Fiss, "The Supreme Court, 1978 Term—Forward: The Forms of Justice," 93 *Harvard Law Review* 1 (1979) (a broader, more managerial role for judges) with R. Bork, *The Tempting of America* (New York: Free Press, 1990) (a narrower, more umpirelike role for judges).

[21]Black, "Further Reflections," p. 1115.

WYMAN v. JAMES
400 U.S. 309; 27 L. Ed. 2d 408; 91 S. Ct. 381 (1971)

JUSTICE BLACKMUN *delivered the opinion of the Court.*

This appeal presents the issue whether a beneficiary of the program for Aid to Families with Dependent Children (AFDC) may refuse a home visit by the caseworker without risking the termination of benefits.

The New York State and City social services commissioners appeal from a judgment and decree of a divided three-judge District Court holding invalid and unconstitutional in application section 134 of the New York Social Services Law, section 175 of the New York Policies Governing the Administration of Public Assistance, and sections 351.10 and 351.21 of Title 18 of the New York Code of Rules and Regulations, and granting injunctive relief. . . .

The District Court majority held that a mother receiving AFDC relief may refuse, without forfeiting her right to that relief, the periodic visit which the cited New York statutes and regulations prescribe as a condition for the continuance of assistance under the program. The beneficiary's thesis, and that of the District Court majority, is that home visitation is a search and, when not consented to or when not supported by a warrant based on probable cause, violates the beneficiary's Fourth and Fourteenth Amendment rights.

Judge McLean, in dissent, thought it unrealistic to regard the home visit as a search; felt that the requirement of a search warrant to issue only upon a showing of probable cause would make the AFDC program "in effect another criminal statute" and would "introduce a hostile arm's length element into the relationship" between worker and mother, "a relationship which can be effective only when it is based upon mutual confidence and trust"; and concluded that the majority's holding struck "a damaging blow" to an important social welfare program. 303 F. Supp., at 946.

. . . The pertinent facts . . . are not in dispute.

Plaintiff Barbara James is the mother of a son, Maurice, who was born in May 1967. They reside in New York City. Mrs. James first applied for AFDC assistance shortly before Maurice's birth. A caseworker made a visit to her apartment at that time without objection. The assistance was authorized.

Two years later, on May 8, 1969, a caseworker wrote Mrs. James that she would visit her home on May 14. Upon receipt of this advice, Mrs. James telephoned the worker that, although she was willing to supply information "reasonable and relevant" to her need for public assistance, any discussion was not to take place at her home. The worker told Mrs. James that she was required by law to visit in her home and that refusal to permit the visit would result in the termination of assistance. Permission was still denied.

On May 13 the City Department of Social Services sent Mrs. James a notice of intent to discontinue assistance because of the visitation refusal. The notice advised the beneficiary of her right to a hearing before a review officer. The hearing was requested and was held on May 27. Mrs. James appeared with an attorney at that hearing. They continued to refuse permission for a worker to visit the James home, but again expressed willingness to cooperate and to permit visits elsewhere. The review officer ruled that the refusal was a proper ground for the termination of assistance. . . . A notice of termination was issued on June 2.

Thereupon, without seeking a hearing at the state level, Mrs. James, individually and on behalf of Maurice, and purporting to act on behalf of all other persons similarly situated, instituted the present civil rights suit under 42 U.S.C. section 1983. She alleged the denial of rights guaranteed to her under the First, Third, Fourth, Fifth, Sixth, Ninth, Tenth, and Fourteenth Amendments, and under Subchapters IV and XVI of the Social Security Act and regulations thereunder. She further alleged that she and her son have no income, resources, or support other than the benefits received under the AFDC program. She asked for declaratory and injunctive relief. A temporary restraining order was issued on June 13, *James* v. *Goldberg*, 302 F. Supp. 478 (SDNY 1969), and the three-judge District Court was convened.

The federal aspects of the AFDC program deserve mention. They are provided for in Subchapter IV, Part A, of the Social Security Act of 1935, 49 Stat. 627, as amended, 42 U.S.C. sections 601–610 (1964 ed. and Supp. V). Section 401 of the Act, 42 U.S.C. section 601 (1964 ed., Supp. V), specified its purpose, namely, "encouraging the care of dependent children in their own homes or in the homes of relatives by enabling each State to furnish financial assistance and rehabilitation and other services . . . to needy dependent children and the parents or relatives with whom they are living to help maintain and strengthen family life. . . . " The same section authorizes the federal appropriation for payments to States that qualify. Section 402, 42 U.S.C. section 602 (1964 ed., Supp. V), provides that a state plan, among other things, must "provide for granting an opportunity for a fair hearing before the State agency to any individual whose claim for aid to families with dependent children is denied or is not acted upon with reasonable promptness"; . . . and must "provide that where the State agency has reason to believe that the home in which a relative and child receiving aid reside is unsuitable for the child because of the neglect, abuse, or exploitation of such child it shall bring such condition to the attention of the appropriate court or law enforcement agencies in the State. . . . "

When a case involves a home and some type of official intrusion into that home, as this case appears to do, an immediate and natural reaction is one of concern about Fourth Amendment rights and the protection which that Amendment is intended to afford. Its emphasis indeed is upon one of the most precious aspects of personal security in the home: "The right of the people to be secure in their persons, houses, papers, and effects. . . . " This Court has characterized that right as "basic to a free society." . . .

This natural and quite proper protective attitude, however, is not a factor in this case, for the seemingly obvious and simple reason that we are not concerned here with any search by the New York social service agency in the Fourth Amendment meaning of that term. It is true that the governing statute and regulations appear to make mandatory the initial home visit and the subsequent periodic "contacts" (which may include home visits) for the inception and continuance of aid. It is also true that the caseworker's posture in the home visit is perhaps, in a sense, both rehabilitative and investigative. But this latter aspect, we think is given too broad a character and far more emphasis than it deserves if it is equated with a search in the traditional criminal law context. We note, too, that the visitation in itself is not forced or compelled, and that the beneficiary's denial of permission is not a criminal act. If consent to the visitation is withheld, no visitation takes place. The aid then never begins or merely ceases, as the case may be. There is no entry of the home and there is no search.

If, however, we were to assume that a caseworker's home visit, before or subsequent to the beneficiary's initial qualification for benefits, somehow (perhaps because the average beneficiary might feel she is in no position to refuse consent to the visit), and despite its interview nature, does possess some of the characteristics of a search in the traditional sense, we nevertheless conclude that the visit does not fall within the Fourth Amendment's proscription. This is because it does not descend to the level of unreasonableness. It is unreasonableness which is the Fourth Amendment's standard. . . .

There are a number of factors that compel us to conclude that the home visit proposed for Mrs. James is not unreasonable:

1. The public's interest in this particular segment of the area of assistance to the unfortunate is protection and aid for the dependent child whose family requires such aid for that child. . . . The dependent child's needs are paramount, and only with hesitancy would we relegate those needs, in the scale of comparative values, to a position secondary to what the mother claims as her rights.
2. The agency, with tax funds provided from federal as well as from state sources, is fulfilling a public trust. The State, working through its qualified welfare agency, has appropriate and paramount interest and concern in seeing and assuring that the intended and proper objects of that tax-produced assistance are the ones who benefit from the aid it dispenses. Surely it is not unreasonable, in the Fourth Amendment sense or in any other sense of that term, that the State have at its command a gentle means, of limited extent and of practical and considerate application, of achieving that assurance.
3. One who dispenses purely private charity naturally has an interest in and expects to know how his charitable funds are utilized and put to work. The public, when it is the provider, rightly expects the same. . . .
4. The emphasis of the New York statutes and regulations is upon the home, upon "close contact" with the beneficiary, upon restoring the aid recipient "to a condition of self-support," and upon the relief of his distress. The federal emphasis is no different. . . .

5. The home visit, it is true, is not required by federal statute or regulation. But it has been noted that the visit is "the heart of welfare administration"; that it affords "a personal rehabilitative orientation, unlike that of most federal programs"; and that the "more pronounced service orientation" effected by Congress with the 1956 amendments to the Social Security Act "gave redoubled importance to the practice of home visiting." . . . The home visit is an established routine in States besides New York.
6. The means employed by the New York agency are significant. Mrs. James received written notice several days in advance of the intended home visit. The date was specified. . . . Privacy is emphasized. The applicant-recipient is made the primary source of information as to eligibility. Outside informational sources, other than public records, are to be consulted only with the beneficiary's consent. Forcible entry or entry under false pretenses or visitation outside working hours or snooping in the home are forbidden. . . . All this minimizes any "burden" upon the homeowner's right against unreasonable intrusion.
7. Mrs. James, in fact, on this record presents no specific complaint of any unreasonable intrusion of her home and nothing that supports an inference that the desired home visit had as its purpose the obtaining of information as to criminal activity. She complains of no proposed visitation at an awkward or retirement hour. She suggests no forcible entry. She refers to no snooping. She describes no impolite or reprehensible conduct of any kind. She alleges only, in general and nonspecific terms, that on previous visits and, on information and belief, on visitation at the home of other aid recipients, "questions concerning personal relationships, beliefs and behavior are raised and pressed which are unnecessary for a determination of continuing eligibility." Paradoxically, this same complaint could be made of a conference held elsewhere than in the home, and yet this is what is sought by Mrs. James. The same complaint could be made of the census taker's questions. . . . What Mrs. James appears to want from the agency that provides her and her infant son with the necessities of life is the right to receive those necessities upon her own informational terms, to utilize the Fourth Amendment as a wedge for imposing those terms, and to avoid questions of any kind.
8. We are not persuaded, as Mrs. James would have us be, that all information pertinent to the issue of eligibility can be obtained by the agency through an interview at a place other than the home, or, as the District Court majority suggested, by examining a lease or a birth certificate, or by periodic medical examinations, or by interviews with school personnel. Although these

secondary sources might be helpful, they would not always assure verification of actual residence or of actual physical presence in the home. . . .

9. The visit is not one by police or uniformed authority. It is made by a caseworker of some training whose primary objective is, or should be, the welfare, not the prosecution, of the aid recipient for whom the worker has profound responsibility. . . . The caseworker is not a sleuth but rather, we trust, is a friend to one in need.

10. The home visit is not a criminal investigation, does not equate with a criminal investigation, and despite the announced fears of Mrs. James and those who would join her, is not in aid of any criminal proceeding. . . .

Mrs. James is not being prosecuted for her refusal to permit the home visit and is not about to be so prosecuted. Her wishes in that respect are fully honored. We have not been told, and have not found, that her refusal is made a criminal act by any applicable New York or federal statute. The only consequence of her refusal is that the payment of benefits ceases. Important and serious as this is, the situation is no different than if she had exercised a similar negative choice initially and refrained from applying for AFDC benefits. . . .

Our holding today does not mean, of course, that a termination of benefits upon refusal of a home visit is to be upheld against constitutional challenge under all conceivable circumstances. . . .

We therefore conclude that the home visitation as structured by the New York statutes and regulations is a reasonable administrative tool; that it serves a valid and proper administrative purpose for the dispensation of the AFDC program; that it is not an unwarranted invasion of personal privacy; and that it violates no right guaranteed by the Fourth Amendment.

Reversed and remanded with directions to enter a judgment of dismissal. It is so ordered.

JUSTICE WHITE *concurs in the judgment and joins the opinion of the Court with the exception of Part IV thereof.*

JUSTICE DOUGLAS, *dissenting.*

We are living in a society where one of the most important forms of property is government largesse which some call the "new property." . . .

The question in this case is whether receipt of largesse from the Government makes the *home* of the beneficiary subject to access by an inspector of the agency of oversight, even though the Fourth Amendment's procedure for access to one's *house* or *home* is not followed. The penalty here is not, of course, invasion of the privacy of Barbara James, only her loss of federal or state largesse. That, however, is merely rephrasing the problem. Whatever the semantics, the central question is whether the Government by force of its largesse has the power to "buy up" rights guaranteed by the Constitution. But for the assertion of her constitutional right, Barbara James in this case would have received the welfare benefit. . . .

These cases are in the tradition of *United States* v. *Chicago, M., St. P. & P. R. Co.*, 281 U.S. 311, 328–329, where JUSTICE SUTHERLAND, writing for the Court, said:

[T]he rule is that the right to continue the exercise of a privilege granted by the state cannot be made to depend upon the grantee's submission to a condition prescribed by the state which is hostile to the provisions of the federal Constitution.

What we said in those cases is as applicable to Fourth Amendment rights as to those of the First. . . .

Is a search of her home without a warrant made "reasonable" merely because she is dependent on government largesse?

Judge Skelly Wright has stated the problem succinctly:

Welfare has long been considered the equivalent of charity and its recipients have been subjected to all kinds of dehumanizing experiences in the government's effort to police its welfare payments. In fact, over half a billion dollars are expended annually for administration and policing in connection with the Aid to Families with Dependent Children program. Why such large sums are necessary for administration and policing has never been adequately explained. No such sums are spent policing the government subsidies granted to farmers, airlines, steamship companies, and junk mail dealers, to name but a few. The truth is that in this subsidy area society has simply adopted a double standard, one for aid to business and the farmer and a different one for welfare. "Poverty, Minorities, and Respect for Law," 1970 *Duke L. J.* 425, 437–438.

If the welfare recipient was not Barbara James but a prominent, affluent cotton or wheat farmer receiving benefit payments for not growing crops, would not the approach be different? Welfare in aid of dependent children, like social security and unemployment benefits, has an aura of suspicion. There doubtless are frauds in every sector of public welfare, whether the recipient be a Barbara James or someone who is prominent or influential. But constitutional rights—here the privacy of the *home*—are obviously not dependent on the poverty or on the affluence of the beneficiary . . .

I would place the same restrictions on inspectors entering the *homes* of welfare beneficiaries as are on inspectors entering the *homes* of those on the payroll of the government, or the *homes* of those who work for those having government contracts. . . .

The bureaucracy of modern government is not only slow, lumbering, and oppressive; it is omnipresent. It touches everyone's life at numerous points. It pries more and more into private affairs, breaking down the barriers that individuals erect to give them some insulation from the intrigues and harassments of modern life. Isolation is not a constitutional guarantee; but the sanctity of the sanctuary of the home is such—as marked and defined by the Fourth Amendment. . . . What we do today is to depreciate it.

I would sustain the judgment of the three-judge court in the present case.

The Court's assertion that this case concerns no search "in the Fourth Amendment meaning of that term" is neither "obvious" nor "simple." I should have thought that the Fourth Amendment governs all intrusions by agents of the public upon personal security. . . .

Even if the Fourth Amendment does not apply to each and every governmental entry into the home, the welfare visit is not some sort of purely benevolent inspection. No one questions the motives of the dedicated welfare caseworker. Of course, caseworkers seek to be friends, but the point is that they are also required to be sleuths. . . .

Actually, the home visit is precisely the type of inspection proscribed by *Camara* and its companion case, *See* v. *City of Seattle*, 387 U.S. 541 (1967), except that the welfare visit is a more severe intrusion upon privacy and family dignity. Both the home visit and the searches in those cases may convey benefits to the householder. Fire inspectors give frequent advice concerning fire prevention, wiring capacity, and other matters, and obvious self-interest causes many to welcome the fire or safety inspection. Similarly, the welfare caseworker may provide welcome advice on home manage-

ment and child care. Nonetheless, both searches may result in the imposition of civil penalties—loss or reduction of welfare benefits or an order to upgrade a housing defect. The fact that one purpose of the visit is to provide evidence that may lead to an elimination of benefits is sufficient to grant appellee protection, since *Camara* stated that the Fourth Amendment applies to inspections which can result in only civil violations, 387 U.S., at 531. But here the case is stronger since the home visit, like many housing inspections, may lead to criminal convictions. . . . Appellants offer scant explanation for their refusal even to attempt to utilize public records, expenditure receipts, documents such as leases, nonhome interviews, personal financial records, sworn declaration, etc.—all sources that government agencies regularly accept as adequate to establish eligibility for other public benefits. In this setting, it ill behooves appellants to refuse to utilize informational sources less drastic than an invasion of the privacy of the home. . . .

Although the Court does not agree with my conclusion that the home visit is an unreasonable search, its opinion suggests that even if the visit were unreasonable, appellee has somehow waived her right to object. Surely the majority cannot believe that valid Fourth Amendment consent can be given under the threat of the loss of one's sole means of support. Nor has Mrs. James waived her rights. Had the Court squarely faced the question of whether the State can condition welfare payments on the waiver of clear constitutional rights, the answer would be plain. The decisions of this Court do not support the notion that a State can use welfare benefits as a wedge to coerce "waiver" of Fourth Amendment rights. . . .

In deciding that the homes of AFDC recipients are not entitled to protection from warrantless searches by welfare caseworkers, the Court declines to follow prior case law and employs a rationale that, if applied to the claims of all citizens, would threaten the vitality of the Fourth Amendment. This Court has occasionally pushed beyond established constitutional contours to protect the vulnerable and to further basic human values. I find no little irony in the fact that the burden of today's departure from principled adjudication is placed upon the lowly poor. . . . I am not convinced; and, therefore, I must respectfully dissent.

JUSTICE POWELL *delivered the opinion of the Court.*

This suit attacking the Texas system of financing public education was initiated by Mexican-American parents whose children attend the elementary and secondary schools in the Edgewood Independent School District, an urban school district in San Antonio, Texas. They brought a class action on behalf of school children throughout the State who are members of minority groups or who are poor and reside in school districts having a low property tax base. . . . In December 1971 [a three-judge federal district court held] the Texas school finance system unconstitutional under the Equal Protection Clause of the Fourteenth Amendment. The State appealed, and . . . [f]or the reasons stated in this opinion we reverse the decision of the District Court.

I

Until recent times Texas was a predominantly rural State and its population and property wealth were spread relatively evenly across the State. Sizable differences in the value of assessable property between local school districts became increasingly evident as the State became more industrialized and as rural-to-urban population shifts became more pronounced. The location of commercial and industrial property began to play a significant role in determining the amount of tax resources available to each school district. These growing disparities in population and taxable property between districts were responsible in part for increasingly notable differences in levels of local expenditure for education.

In due time it became apparent to those concerned with financing public education that contributions from the Available School fund were not sufficient to ameliorate these disparities. . . .

Recognizing the need for increased state funding to help offset disparities in local spending and to meet Texas's changing educational requirements, the state legislature in the late 1940s undertook a thorough evaluation of public education with an eye toward major reform. In 1947 an 18-member committee, composed of educators and legislators, was appointed to explore alternative systems in other States and to propose a funding scheme that would guarantee a minimum of basic educational offering to each child and that would help overcome inter-district disparities in taxable resources. The Committee's efforts led to the passage of . . . bills . . . establishing the Texas Minimum Foundation School Program. Today this Program accounts for approximately half of the total educational expenditures in Texas. . . .

The design of this complex system was twofold. First, it was an attempt to assure that the Foundation Program would have an equalizing influence on expenditure levels between school districts by placing the heaviest burden on the school districts most capable of paying. Second, the Program's architects sought to establish a Local Fund Assignment that would force every school district to contribute to the education of its children but that would not by itself exhaust any district's resources. Today every school district does impose a property tax from which it derives locally expendable funds in excess of the amount necessary to satisfy its Local Fund Assignment under the Foundation Program. . . .

The school district in which appellees reside, the Edgewood Independent School District, has been compared throughout this litigation with the Alamo Heights Independent School District. This comparison between the least and most affluent districts in the San Antonio area serves to illustrate the manner in which the dual system of finance operates and to indicate the extent to which substantial disparities exist despite the State's impressive progress in recent years. Edgewood is one of seven public school districts in the metropolitan area. Approximately 22,000 students are enrolled in its 25 elementary and secondary schools. The district is situated in the core-city sector of San Antonio in a residential neighborhood that has little commercial or industrial property. The residents are predominantly of Mexican-American descent: approximately 90 percent of the student population is Mexican-American and over 6 percent is Negro. The average assessed property value per pupil is $5,960—the lowest in the metropolitan area—and the median family income ($4,686) is also the lowest. At an equalized rate of $1.05 per $100 of assessed property—the highest in the metropolitan area—the district contributed $26 to the education of each child for the 1967–1968 school year above its Local Fund Assignment for the

Minimum Foundation Program. The Foundation Program contributed $222 per pupil for a state-local total of $248. Federal funds added another $108 for a total of $356 per pupil.

Alamo Heights is the most affluent school district in San Antonio. Its six schools, housing approximately 5,000 students, are situated in a residential community quite unlike the Edgewood District. The school population is predominantly Anglo, having only 18 percent Mexican-Americans and less than 1 percent Negroes. The assessed property value per pupil exceeds $49,000, and the median family income is $8,001. In 1967–1968 the local tax rate of $.85 per $100 of valuation yielded $333 per pupil over and above its contribution to the Foundation Program. Coupled with the $225 provided from that Program, the district was able to supply $558 per student. Supplemented by a $36 per pupil grant from federal sources, Alamo Heights spent $594 per pupil.

Although the 1967–1968 school year figures provide the only complete statistical breakdown for each category of aid, more recent partial statistics indicate that the previously noted trend of increasing state aid has been significant. For the 1970–1971 school year, the Foundation School Program allotment for Edgewood was $356 per pupil, a 62 percent increase over the 1967–1968 school year. Indeed, state aid alone in 1970–1971 equaled Edgewood's entire 1967–1968 school budget from local, state, and federal sources. Alamo Heights enjoyed a similar increase under the Foundation Program, netting $491 per pupil in 1970–1971.* These recent figures also reveal the extent to which these two districts' allotments were funded from their own required contributions to

*Although the Foundation Program has made significantly greater contributions to both school districts over the last several years, it is apparent that Alamo Heights has enjoyed a larger gain. The sizable difference between the Alamo Heights and Edgewood grants is due to the emphasis in the State's allocation formula on the guaranteed minimum salaries for teachers. Higher salaries are guaranteed to teachers having more years of experience and possessing more advanced degrees. Therefore, Alamo Heights, which has a greater percentage of experienced personnel with advanced degrees, receives more State support. . . . Because more dollars have been given to districts that already spend more per pupil, such Foundation formulas have been described as "anti-equalizing." The formula, however, is anti-equalizing only if viewed in absolute terms. The percentage disparity between the two Texas districts is diminished substantially by State aid. Alamo Heights derived in 1967–1968 almost 13 times as much money from local taxes as Edgewood did. The State aid grants to each district in 1970–1971 lowered the ratio to approximately two to one., i.e., Alamo Heights had a little more than twice as much money to spend per pupil from its combined State and local resources.

the Local Fund Assignment. Alamo Heights, because of its relative wealth, was required to contribute out of its local property tax collections approximately $100 per pupil, or about 20 percent of its Foundation grant. Edgewood, on the other hand, paid only $8.46 per pupil, which is about 2.4 percent of its grant. It does appear then that, at least as to these two districts, the Local Fund Assignment does reflect a rough approximation of the relative taxpaying potential of each.

Despite these recent increases, substantial interdistrict disparities in school expenditures found by the District Court to prevail in San Antonio and in varying degrees throughout the State still exist. And it was these disparities, largely attributable to differences in the amounts of money collected through local property taxation, that led the District Court to conclude that Texas's dual system of public school finance violated the Equal Protection Clause. The District Court held that the Texas system discriminates on the basis of wealth in the manner in which education is provided for its people. Finding that wealth is a "suspect" classification and that education is a "fundamental" interest, the District Court held that the Texas system could be sustained only if the State could show that it was premised upon some compelling state interest. On this issue the court concluded that "not only are defendants unable to demonstrate compelling state interests . . . they fail even to establish a reasonable basis for these classifications."

Texas virtually concedes that its historically rooted dual system of financing education could not withstand the strict judicial scrutiny that this Court has found appropriate in reviewing legislative judgments that interfere with fundamental constitutional rights or that involve suspect classifications. If, as previous decisions have indicated, strict scrutiny means that the State's system is not entitled to the usual presumption of validity, that the State rather than the complainants must carry a "heavy burden of justification," that the State must demonstrate that its educational system has been structured with "precision" and is "tailored" narrowly to serve legitimate objectives, and that it has selected the "least drastic means" for effectuating its objectives, the Texas financing system and its counterparts in virtually every other State will not pass muster. The State candidly admits that "no one familiar with the Texas system would contend that it has yet achieved perfection." Apart from its conclusion that educational finance in Texas has "defects" and "imperfections," the State defends the system's rationality with vigor and disputes the District Court's finding that it lacks a "reasonable basis."

This, then, establishes the framework for our analysis. We must decide, first, whether the Texas system for financing public education operates to the disadvantage of some suspect class or impinges upon a fundamental right explicitly or implicitly protected by the Constitution, thereby requiring strict judicial scrutiny. If so, the judgment of the District Court should be affirmed. If not, the Texas scheme must still be examined to determine whether it rationally furthers some legitimate, articulated state purpose and therefore does not constitute an invidious discrimination in violation of the Fourteenth Amendment.

II

The District Court's opinion does not reflect the novelty and complexity of the constitutional questions posed by appellees' challenge to Texas's system of school finance. In concluding that strict judicial scrutiny was required, that court relied on decisions dealing with the rights of indigents to equal treatment in the criminal trial and appellate processes, and on cases disapproving wealth restrictions on the right to vote. Those cases, the District Court concluded, established wealth as a suspect classification. Finding that the local property tax system discriminated on the basis of wealth, it regarded those precedents as controlling. It then reasoned, based on decisions of this Court affirming the undeniable importance of education, that there is a fundamental right to education and that, absent some compelling state justification, the Texas system could not stand.

We are unable to agree that this case, which in significant aspects is *sui generis*, may be so neatly fitted into the conventional mosaic of constitutional analysis under the Equal Protection Clause. Indeed, for the several reasons that follow, we find neither the suspect classification nor the fundamental interest analysis persuasive.

A

The wealth discrimination discovered by the District Court in this case, and by several other courts that have recently struck down school financing laws in other States, is quite unlike any of the forms of wealth discrimination heretofore reviewed by this Court. Rather than focusing on the unique features of the alleged discrimination, the courts in these cases have virtually assumed their findings of a suspect classification through a simplistic process

of analysis: since, under the traditional systems of financing public schools, some poorer people receive less expensive educations than other more affluent people, these systems discriminate on the basis of wealth. This approach largely ignores the hard threshold questions, including whether it makes a difference for purposes of consideration under the Constitution that the class of disadvantaged "poor" cannot be identified or defined in customary equal protection terms, and whether the relative—rather than absolute—nature of the asserted deprivation is of significant consequence. Before a State's laws and the justifications for the classifications they create are subjected to strict judicial scrutiny, we think these threshold considerations must be analyzed more closely than they were in the court below.

The case comes to us with no definitive description of the classifying facts or delineation of the disfavored class. Examination of the District Court's opinion and of appellees' complaint, briefs, and contentions at oral argument suggests, however, at least three ways in which the discrimination claimed here might be described. The Texas system of school finance might be regarded as discriminating (1) against "poor" persons whose incomes fall below some identifiable level of poverty or who might be characterized as functionally "indigent," or (2) against those who are relatively poorer than others, or (3) against all those who, irrespective of their personal incomes, happen to reside in relatively poorer school districts. Our task must be to ascertain whether, in fact, the Texas system has been shown to discriminate on any of these possible bases. . . .

[Here follows an examination of the Court's precedents that consider discrimination against indigents.]

Only appellees' first possible basis for describing the class disadvantaged by the Texas school finance system discrimination against a class of definably "poor" persons might arguably meet the criteria established in [our] prior cases. Even a cursory examination, however, demonstrates that neither of the two distinguishing characteristics of wealth classifications can be found here. First, in support of their charge that the system discriminates against the "poor," appellees have made no effort to demonstrate that it operates to the peculiar disadvantage of any class fairly definable as indigent, or as composed of persons whose incomes are beneath any designated poverty level. Indeed, there is reason to believe that the poorest families are not necessarily clustered in the poorest property districts. A recent and exhaustive study of school districts in Connecticut concluded that "[i]t is clearly incorrect . . . to contend that the 'poor' live in 'poor' districts." . . . [T]he Connecticut study found, not surprisingly, that the poor were clustered around commercial and industrial areas—those same areas that provide the most attractive sources of property tax income for school districts. Whether a similar pattern would be discovered in Texas is not known, but there is no basis on the record in this case for assuming that the poorest people—defined by reference to any level of absolute impecunity—are concentrated in the poorest districts.

Second, neither appellees nor the District Court addressed the fact that . . . lack of personal resources has not occasioned an absolute deprivation of the desired benefit. The argument here is not that the children in districts having relatively low assessable property values are receiving no public education; rather, it is that they are receiving a poorer quality education than that available to children in districts having more assessable wealth. Apart from the unsettled and disputed question whether the quality of education may be determined by the amount of money expended for it, a sufficient answer to appellees' argument is that at least where wealth is involved the Equal Protection Clause does not require absolute equality of precisely equal advantages. Nor indeed, in view of the infinite variables affecting the educational process, can any system assure equal quality of education except in the most relative sense. Texas asserts that the Minimum Foundation Program provides an "adequate" education for all children in the State. By providing 12 years of free public school education, and by assuring teachers, books, transportation and operating funds, the Texas Legislature has endeavored to "guarantee, for the welfare of the state as a whole, that all people shall have at least an adequate program of education. This is what is meant by 'A Minimum Foundation Program of Education.' " The State repeatedly asserted in its briefs in this Court that it has fulfilled this desire and that it now assures "every child in every school district an adequate education." No proof was offered at trial persuasively discrediting or refuting the State's assertion.

For these two reasons—the absence of any evidence that the financing system discriminates against any definable category of "poor" people or that it results in the absolute deprivation of education—the disadvantaged class is not susceptible to identification in traditional terms.

[A]ppellees and the District Court may have embraced a second or third approach, the second of which might be characterized as a theory of relative or comparative discrimination based on family income. Appellees sought to prove that a direct correlation exists between the wealth of families within each district and the expenditures therein for education. That is, along a continuum, the poorer the family the lower the dollar amount of education received by the family's children.

The principal evidence adduced in support of this comparative discrimination claim is an affidavit submitted by Professor Joele S. Berke of Syracuse University's Educational Finance Policy Institute. The District Court, relying in major part upon this affidavit and apparently accepting the substance of appellees' theory, noted, first, a positive correlation between the wealth of school districts, measured in terms of assessable property per pupil, and their levels of per-pupil expenditures. Second, the court found a similar correlation between district wealth and the personal wealth of its residents, measured in terms of median family income.

If, in fact, these correlations could be sustained, then it might be argued that expenditures on education—equated by appellees to the quality of education—are dependent on personal wealth. Appellees' comparative discrimination theory would still face serious unanswered questions, including whether a bare positive correlation or some higher degree of correlation is necessary to provide a basis for concluding that the financing system is designated to operate to the peculiar disadvantage of the comparatively poor, and whether a class of this size and diversity could ever claim the special protection accorded "suspect" classes. These questions need not be addressed in this case, however, since appellees' proof fails to support their allegations or the District Court's conclusions. . . .

This brings us, then, to the third way in which the classification scheme might be defined—*district* wealth discrimination. Since the only correlation indicated by the evidence is between district property wealth and expenditures, it may be argued that discrimination might be found without regard to the individual income characteristics of district residents. Assuming a perfect correlation between district property wealth and expenditures from top to bottom, the disadvantaged class might be viewed as encompassing every child in every district except the district that has the most assessable wealth and spends the most on education. Alternatively, as suggested in JUSTICE MARSHALL's dissenting opinion, the class might be defined more restrictively to include children in districts with assessable property which falls below the statewide average, or median, or below some other artificially defined level.

However described, it is clear that appellees' suit asks this Court to extend its most exacting scrutiny to review a system that allegedly discriminates against a large, diverse, and amorphous class, unified only by the common factor of residence in districts that happen to have less taxable wealth than other districts. The system of alleged discrimination and the class it defines have none of the traditional indicia of suspectness: the class is not saddled with such disabilities, or subjected to such a history of purposeful unequal treatment, or relegated to such a position of political powerlessness as to command extraordinary protection from the majoritarian political process.

We thus conclude that the Texas system does not operate to the peculiar disadvantage of any suspect class. But in recognition of the fact that this Court has never heretofore held that wealth discrimination alone provides an adequate basis for invoking strict scrutiny, appellees have not relied solely on this contention. They also assert that the State's system impermissibly interferes with the exercise of a "fundamental" right and that accordingly the prior decisions of this Court require the application of the strict standard of judicial review. It is this question—whether education is a fundamental right, in the sense that it is among the rights and liberties protected by the Constitution—which has so consumed the attention of courts and commentators in recent years.

B

. . . The lesson of [our] cases in addressing the question now before the Court is plain. It is not the province of this Court to create substantive constitutional rights in the name of guaranteeing equal protection of the laws. Thus the key to discovering whether education is "fundamental" is not to be found in comparisons of the relative societal significance of education as opposed to subsistence in housing. Nor is it to be found by weighing whether education is as important as the right to travel. Rather, the answer lies in assessing whether there is a right to education explicitly or implicitly guaranteed by the Constitution. . . .

Education, of course, is not among the rights afforded explicit protection under our Federal Constitution. Nor do we find any basis for saying it is implicitly so protected. As we have said, the undisputed importance of education will not alone

cause this Court to depart from the usual standard for reviewing a State's social and economic legislation. It is appellees' contention, however, that education is distinguishable from other services and benefits provided by the State because it bears a peculiarly close relationship to other rights and liberties accorded protection under the Constitution. Specifically, they insist that education is itself a fundamental personal right because it is essential to the effective exercise of First Amendment freedoms and to intelligent utilization of the right to vote. In asserting a nexus between speech and education, appellees urge that the right to speak is meaningless unless the speaker is capable of articulating his thoughts intelligently and persuasively. The "marketplace of ideas" is an empty forum for those lacking basic communicative tools. Likewise, they argue that the corollary right to receive information becomes little more than a hollow privilege when the recipient has not been taught to read, assimilate, and utilize available knowledge.

A similar line of reasoning is pursued with respect to the right to vote. . . .

We need not dispute any of these propositions. The Court has long afforded zealous protection against unjustifiable governmental interference with the individual's rights to speak and to vote. Yet we have never presumed to possess either the ability or the authority to guarantee to the citizenry the most *effective* speech or the most *informed* electoral choice. That these may be desirable goals of a system of freedom of expression and a representative form of government is not to be doubted. These are indeed goals to be pursued by a people whose thoughts and beliefs are freed from governmental interference. But they are not values to be implemented by judicial intrusion into otherwise legitimate state activities. . . .

We have carefully considered each of the arguments supportive of the District Court's, finding that education is a fundamental right or liberty and have found those arguments unpersuasive. . . .

C

We need not rest our decision, however, solely on the inappropriateness of the strict scrutiny test. A century of Supreme Court adjudication under the Equal Protection Clause affirmatively supports the application of the traditional standard of review, which requires only that the State's system be shown to bear some rational relationship to legitimate state purposes. This case represents far more than a challenge to the manner in which Texas provides for the education of its children. We have here nothing less than a direct attack on the way in which Texas has chosen to raise and disburse state and local tax revenues. We are asked to condemn the State's judgment in conferring on political subdivisions the power to tax local property to supply revenues for local interests. In so doing, appellees would have the Court intrude in an area in which it has traditionally deferred to state legislatures. This Court has often admonished against such interferences with the State's fiscal policies under the Equal Protection Clause. . . .

Thus we stand on familiar grounds when we continue to acknowledge that the justices of this Court lack both the experience and the familiarity with local problems so necessary to the making of wise decisions with respect to the raising and disposition of public revenues. . . . No scheme of taxation, whether the tax is imposed on property, income, or purchases of goods and services, has yet been devised which is free of all discriminatory impact. In such a complex arena in which no perfect alternatives exist, the Court does well not to impose too rigorous a standard of scrutiny lest all local fiscal schemes become subjects of criticism under the Equal Protection Clause.

In addition to matters of fiscal policy, this case also involves the most persistent and difficult questions of educational policy, another area in which this Court's lack of specialized knowledge and experience counsels against premature interference with the informed judgments made at the state and local levels. Education, perhaps even more than welfare assistance, presents a myriad of "intractable economic, social, and even philosophical problems." The very complexity of the problems of financing and managing a statewide public school system suggest that "there will be more than one constitutionally permissible method of solving them," and that, within the limits of rationality, "the legislature's efforts to tackle the problems" should be entitled to respect. . . . In such circumstances the judiciary is well advised to refrain from interposing on the States' inflexible constitutional restraints that could circumscribe or handicap the continued research and experimentation so vital to finding even partial solutions to educational problems and to keeping abreast of ever-changing conditions. . . .

III

Appellees further urge that the Texas system is unconstitutionally arbitrary because it allows the availability of local taxable resources to turn on "happenstance." They see no justification for a system that allows as they contend, the quality of education to fluctuate on the basis of the fortuitous positioning of the boundary lines of political subdivisions and the location of valuable commercial and industrial property. But any scheme of local taxation—indeed the very existence of identifiable local governmental units—requires the establishment of jurisdictional boundaries that are inevitably arbitrary. It is equally inevitable that some localities are going to be blessed with more taxable assets than others. Nor is local wealth a static quantity. Changes in the level of taxable wealth within any district may result from any number of events, some of which local residents can and do influence. For instance, commercial and industrial enterprises may be encouraged to locate within a district by various actions—public and private.

Moreover, if local taxation for local expenditure is an unconstitutional method of providing for education, then it may be an equally impermissible means of providing other necessary services customarily financed largely from local property taxes, including local police and fire protection, public health and hospitals, and public utility facilities of various kinds. We perceive no justification for such a severe denigration of local property taxation and control as would follow from appellees' contentions. It has simply never been within the constitutional prerogative of this Court to nullify statewide measures for financing public services merely because the burdens or benefits thereof fall unevenly depending upon the relative wealth of the political subdivisions in which citizens live.

In sum, to the extent that the Texas system of school finance results in unequal expenditures between children who happen to reside in different districts, we cannot say that such disparities are the product of a system that is so irrational as to be invidiously discriminatory. . . . We are unwilling to assume for ourselves a level of wisdom superior to that of legislators, scholars, and educational authorities in 49 States, especially where the alternatives proposed are only recently conceived and nowhere yet tested. The constitutional standard under the Equal Protection Clause is whether the challenged state action rationally furthers a legitimate state purpose or interest. We hold that the Texas plan abundantly satisfies this standard. . . .

Reversed.

[The concurring opinion of JUSTICE POTTER STEWART and the dissenting opinions of JUSTICES WILLIAM J. BRENNAN and BYRON WHITE are not reprinted here.]

JUSTICE MARSHALL, *with whom* JUSTICE DOUGLAS *concurs, dissenting.*

The Court today decides, in effect, that a State may constitutionally vary the quality of education which it offers its children in accordance with the amount of taxable wealth located in the school districts within which they reside. The majority's decision represents an abrupt departure from the mainstream of recent state and federal court decisions concerning the unconstitutionality of state educational financing schemes dependent upon taxable local wealth. More unfortunately, though, the majority's holding can only be seen as a retreat from our historic commitment to equality of educational opportunity and as unsupportable acquiescence in a system which deprives children in their earliest years of the chance to reach their full potential as citizens. The Court does this despite the absence of any substantial justification for a scheme which arbitrarily channels educational resources in accordance with the fortuity of the amount of taxable wealth within each district.

In my judgment, the right of every American to an equal start in life, so far as the provision of a state service as important as education is concerned, is far too vital to permit state discrimination on grounds as tenuous as those presented by this record. Nor can I accept the notion that it is sufficient to remit these appellees to the vagaries of the political process which, contrary to the majority's suggestion, has proven singularly unsuited to the task of providing a remedy for this discrimination. I, for one, am unsatisfied with the hope of an ultimate "political" solution sometime in the indefinite future while, in the meantime, countless children unjustifiably receive inferior educations that "may affect their hearts and minds in a way unlikely ever to be undone." I must therefore respectfully dissent.

I

The Court acknowledges that "substantial interdistrict disparities in school expenditures" exist in Texas. . . . But instead of closely examining the seriousness of these disparities and the invidiousness of the Texas financing scheme, the Court undertakes an elaborate exploration of the efforts Texas has purportedly made to close the gaps between its districts in terms of levels of district wealth and resulting educational funding. Yet, however, praiseworthy Texas's equalizing efforts, the issue in this case is not whether Texas is doing its best to ameliorate the worst features of a discriminatory scheme, but rather whether the scheme itself is in fact unconstitutionally discriminatory in the face of the Fourteenth Amendment's guarantee of equal protection of the laws. When the Texas financing scheme is taken as a whole I do not think it can be doubted that it produces a discriminatory impact on substantial numbers of the school-age children of the State of Texas. . . .

A

It is clear . . . that the disparity of per pupil revenues cannot be dismissed as the result of lack of local effort—that is, lower tax rates by property-poor districts. To the contrary, . . . data . . . indicate that the poorest districts tend to have the highest tax rates and the richest districts tend to have the lowest tax rates. Yet despite the apparent *extra* effort being made by the poorest districts, they are unable even to begin to match the richest districts in terms of the production of local revenues. . . . Without more, this state-imposed system of educational funding presents a serious picture of widely varying treatment of Texas school districts, and thereby of Texas school children, in terms of the amount of funds available for public education. . . .

The majority continually emphasizes how much state aid has, in recent years, been given to property-poor Texas school districts. What the Court fails to emphasize is the cruel irony of how much more state aid is being given to property-rich Texas school districts on top of their already substantial local property tax revenues. Under any view, then, it is apparent that the state aid provided by the Foundation School Program fails to compensate for the large funding variations attributable to the local property tax element of the Texas financing scheme. And it is these stark differences in the treatment of Texas school districts and school children inherent in the Texas financing scheme, not the absolute amount of state aid provided to any particular school district, that are the crux of this case. There can, moreover, be no escaping the conclusion that the local property tax which is dependent upon taxable district property wealth is an essential feature of the Texas scheme for financing public education. . . .

B

. . . At the very least, in view of the substantial interdistrict disparities in funding and in resulting educational inputs shown by appellees to exist under the Texas financing scheme, the burden of proving that these disparities do not in fact affect the quality of children's education must fall on the appellants. . . .

[T]he appellants and the majority may believe that the Equal Protection Clause cannot be offended by substantial unequal state treatment of persons who are similarly situated so long as the State provides everyone with some unspecified amount of education which evidently is "enough." The basis for such a novel view is far from clear. It is, of course, true that the Constitution does not require precise equality in the treatment of all persons. . . . But this Court has never suggested that because some "adequate" level of benefits is provided to all, discrimination in the provision of services is therefore constitutionally excusable. The Equal Protection Clause is not addressed to the minimal sufficiency but rather to the unjustifiable inequalities of state action. It mandates nothing less than that "all persons similarly circumstanced shall be treated alike." . . .

In my view, then, it is inequality—not some notion of gross adequacy—of educational opportunity that raises a question of denial of equal protection of the laws. I find any other approach to the issue unintelligible and without directing principle. Here appellees have made a substantial showing of wide variations in educational funding and the resulting educational opportunity afforded to the school children of Texas. This discrimination is, in large measure, attributable to significant disparities in the taxable wealth of local Texas school districts. This is a sufficient showing to raise a substantial question of discriminatory state action in violation of the Equal Protection Clause. . . .

C

. . . I believe it is sufficient that the overarching form of discrimination in this case is between the school children of Texas on the basis of the taxable property wealth of the districts in which they happen to live. To understand both the precise nature of this discrimination and the parameters of the disadvantaged class it is sufficient to consider the constitutional principle which appellees contend is controlling in the context of educational financing. In their complaint appellees asserted that the Constitution does not permit local district wealth to be determinative of educational opportunity. This is simply another way of saying, as the District Court concluded, that consistent with the guarantee of equal protection of the laws, "the quality of public education may not be a function of wealth, other than the wealth of the state as a whole." Under such a principle, the children of a district are excessively advantaged if that district has more taxable property per pupil than the average amount of taxable property per pupil considering the State as a whole. By contrast, the children of a district are disadvantaged if that district has less taxable property per pupil than the same average. The majority attempts to disparage such a definition of the disadvantaged class as the product of an "artificially defined level" of district wealth. But such is clearly not the case, for this is the definition unmistakably dictated by the constitutional principal for which appellees have argued throughout the course of this litigation. And I do not believe that a clearer definition of either the disadvantaged class of Texas school children or the allegedly unconstitutional discrimination suffered by the members of that class under the present Texas financing scheme could be asked for, much less needed. Whether this discrimination, against the school children of property-poor districts, inherent in the Texas financing scheme is violative of the Equal Protection Clause is the question to which we must now turn.

II

A

To begin, I must once more voice my disagreement with the Court's rigidified approach to equal protection analysis. The Court apparently seeks to establish today that equal protection cases fall into one of two neat categories which dictate the appropriate standard of review—strict scrutiny or mere rationality. But this Court's decisions in the field of equal protection defy such easy categorization. A principled reading of what this Court has done reveals that it has applied a spectrum of standards in reviewing discrimination allegedly violative of the Equal Protection Clause. This spectrum clearly comprehends variations in the degree of care with which the Court will scrutinize particular classifications, depending, I believe, on the constitutional and societal importance of the interest adversely affected and the recognized invidiousness of the basis on which the particular classification is drawn. I find in fact that many of the Court's recent decisions embody the very sort of reasoned approach to equal protection analysis for which I previously argued—that is, an approach in which "concentration [is] placed upon the character of the classification in question, the relative importance to the individuals in the class discriminated against of the governmental benefits that they do not receive, and the asserted state interests in support of the classification."

I therefore cannot accept the majority's labored efforts to demonstrate that fundamental interests, which call for strict scrutiny of the challenged classification, encompass only established rights which we are somehow bound to recognize from the text of the Constitution itself. To be sure, some interests which the Court has deemed to be fundamental for purposes of equal protection analysis are themselves constitutionally protected rights. . . . But it will not do to suggest that the "answer" to whether an interest is fundamental for purposes of equal protection analysis is *always* determined by whether that interest "is a right . . . explicitly or implicitly guaranteed by the Constitution." . . .

C

. . . We are told that in every prior case involving a wealth classification, the members of the disadvantaged class have "shared two distinguishing characteristics: because of their impecunity they were completely unable to pay for some desired benefit, and as a consequence, they sustained an absolute deprivation of a meaningful opportunity to enjoy that benefit." I cannot agree. . . .

This is not to say that the form of wealth classification in this case does not differ significantly from those recognized in the previous decisions of this Court. Our prior cases have dealt essentially with discrimination on the basis of personal wealth. Here, by contrast, the children of the disadvantaged Texas school districts are being discriminated against not necessarily because of their personal wealth or the wealth of their families, but because of the taxable property wealth of the residents of the districts in which they happen to live. The appropriate question, then, is whether the same degree of judicial solicitude and scrutiny that has previously been afforded wealth classifications is warranted here.

As the Court points out, no previous decision has deemed the presence of just a wealth classification to be sufficient basis to call forth "rigorous judicial scrutiny" of allegedly discriminatory state action. That wealth classifications alone have not necessarily been considered to bear the same high degree of suspectness as have classifications based on, for instance, race or alienage may be explainable on a number of grounds. The "poor" may not be seen as politically powerless as certain discrete and insular minority groups. Personal poverty may entail much the same social stigma as historically attached to certain racial or ethnic groups. But personal poverty is not a permanent disability; its shackles may be escaped. Perhaps, most importantly, though, personal wealth may not necessarily share the general irrelevance as a basis for legislative action that race or nationality is recognized to have. While the "poor" have frequently been a legally disadvantaged group, it cannot be ignored that social legislation must frequently take cognizance of the economic status of our citizens. Thus, we have generally gauged the invidiousness of wealth classifications with an awareness of the importance of the interests being affected and the relevance of personal wealth to those interests.

When evaluated with these considerations in mind, it seems to me that discrimination on the basis of group wealth in this case likewise calls for careful judicial scrutiny. First, it must be recognized that while local district wealth may serve other interests, it bears no relationship whatsoever to the interest of Texas school children in the educational opportunity afforded them by the State of Texas. Given the importance of that interest, we must be particularly sensitive to the invidious characteristics of any form of discrimination that is not clearly intended to serve it, as opposed to some other distinct state interest. Discrimination on the basis of group wealth may not, to be sure, reflect the social stigma frequently attached to personal poverty. Nevertheless, insofar as group wealth discrimination involves wealth over which the disadvantaged individual has no significant control, it represents in fact a more serious basis of discrimination than does personal wealth. For such discrimination is no reflection of the individual's characteristics or his abilities. And thus particularly in the context of a disadvantaged class composed of children—we have previously treated discrimination on a basis which the individual cannot control as constitutionally disfavored.

In the final analysis, then, the invidious characteristics of the group wealth classification present in this case merely serve to emphasize the need for careful judicial scrutiny of the State's justifications for the resulting interdistrict discrimination in the educational opportunity afforded to the school children of Texas. . . .

O'CONNOR, J., *delivered the opinion of the Court, in which* REHNQUIST, C. J., *and* WHITE, SCALIA, *and* KENNEDY, JJ. *joined.* MARSHALL, J., *filed a dissenting opinion, in which* BRENNAN, J., *joined.* STEVENS, J., *filed a dissenting opinion in which* BLACKMUN, J., joined.

JUSTICE O'CONNOR *delivered the opinion of the Court.*

Appellants urge us to hold that the Equal Protection Clause forbids a State to allow some local school boards, but not others, to assess a fee for transporting pupils between their homes and the public schools. Applying well-established equal protection principles, we reject this claim and affirm the constitutionality of the challenged statute.

I

North Dakota is a sparsely populated State, with many people living on isolated farms and ranches. One result has been that some children, as late as the mid-20th century, were educated in "the one-room schools where, in many cases, there were twenty or more pupils with one teacher attempting in crowded conditions and under other disadvantages to give instructions in all primary grades." *Herman* v. *Medicine Lodge School Dist. No. 8*, (ND 1955). The State has experimented with various ameliorative devices at different times in its history. Beginning in 1907, for example, it has adopted a series of policies that "in certain circumstances required and in other circumstances merely authorized [local public] school districts to participate in transporting or providing compensation for transporting students to school." 402 NW2d 897, 900 (ND 1987).

Since 1947, the legislature has authorized and encouraged thinly populated school districts to consolidate or "reorganize" themselves into larger districts so that education can be provided more efficiently. Reorganization proposals, which obviously must contemplate an increase in the distance that some children travel to school, are required by law to include provisions for transporting students back and forth from their homes. The details of these provisions may vary from district to district, but once a reorganization plan is adopted the transportation provisions can be changed only with approval of the voters.

Appellee Dickinson Public Schools, which serves a relatively populous area, has chosen not to participate in such a reorganization. Until 1973, this school system provided free bus service to students' homes. After a plebiscite of the bus users, Dickinson's School Board instituted door-to-door bus service and began charging a fee. During the period relevant to this case, about 13% of the students rode the bus; their parents were charged $97 per year for one child or $150 per year for two children. Such fees covered approximately 11% of the cost of providing the bus service, and the remainder was provided from state and local tax revenues.

In 1979, the State enacted the legislation at issue in this case. This statute expressly indicates that nonreorganized school districts, like Dickinson, may charge a fee for transporting students to school; such fees, however, may not exceed the estimated cost to the school district of providing the service. The current version of this provision, which for convenience will be referred to as the "1979 statute," states in full:

> Charge for bus transportation optional. The school board of any school district which has not been reorganized may charge a fee for schoolbus service provided to anyone riding on buses provided by the school district. For schoolbus service which was started prior to July 1, 1981, the total fees collected may not exceed an amount equal to the difference between the state transportation payment and the local school district's cost for transportation during the preceding school year. Any districts that have not previously provided transportation for pupils may establish charges based on costs estimated by the school board during the year that transportation is provided.

Appellants are a Dickinson schoolchild, Sarita Kadrmas, and her mother, Paula. The Kadrmas family, which also includes Mrs. Kadrmas' husband and two preschool children, lives about 16 miles from Sarita's school. Mr. Kadrmas works sporadically in the North Dakota oil fields, and the family's annual income at the time of trial was at or near the officially defined poverty level. Until 1985, the Kadrmas family had agreed each year to pay the fee for busing Sarita to school. Having fallen behind on these and other bills, however, the family refused to sign a contract obligating them to pay $97 for the 1985 school year. Accordingly, the school bus no longer stopped for Sarita, and the family arranged to transport her to school privately. The costs they incurred that year for Sarita's transportation exceeded $1,000, or about 10 times the fee charged by the school district for bus service. This arrangement continued until the spring of 1987, when Paula Kadrmas signed a bus service contract for the remainder of the 1986 school year and paid part of the fee. Mrs. Kadrmas later signed another contract for the 1987 school year, and paid about half of the fee for that period.

In September 1986, appellants, along with others who have since withdrawn from the case, filed an action in state court seeking to enjoin appellees—the Dickinson Public Schools and various school district officials—from collecting any fee for the bus service. The action was dismissed on the merits, and an appeal was taken to the Supreme Court of North Dakota. After rejecting a state-law challenge, which is not at issue here, the court considered appellants' claim that the busing fee violates the Equal Protection Clause of the Fourteenth Amendment. The court characterized the 1979 statute as "purely economic legislation," which "must be upheld unless it is patently arbitrary and fails to bear a rational relationship to any legitimate government purpose." The court then concluded "that the charges authorized [by the statute] are rationally related to the legitimate governmental objective of allocating limited resources and that the statute does not discriminate on the basis of wealth so as to violate federal or state equal protection rights." The court also rejected the contention that the distinction drawn by the statute between reorganized and nonreorganized school districts violates the Equal Protection Clause. The distinction, the court found, serves the legitimate objective of promoting reorganization "by alleviating parental concerns regarding the cost of student transportation." Three justices dissented on state-law grounds. We noted probable jurisdiction, and now affirm.

* * *

Unless a statute provokes "strict judicial scrutiny" because it interferes with a "fundamental right" or discriminates against a "suspect class," it will ordinarily survive an equal protection attack so long as the challenged classification is rationally related to a legitimate governmental purpose. See *Rodriguez,*

supra. Appellants contend that Dickinson's user fee for bus service unconstitutionally deprives those who cannot afford to pay it of "minimum access to education." Sarita Kadrmas, however, continued to attend school during the time that she was denied access to the school bus. Appellants must therefore mean to argue that the busing fee unconstitutionally places a greater obstacle to education in the path of the poor than it does in the path of wealthier families. Alternately, appellants may mean to suggest that the Equal Protection Clause affirmatively requires government to provide free transportation to school, at least for some class of students that would include Sarita Kadrmas. Under either interpretation of appellants' position, we are evidently being urged to apply a form of strict or "heightened" scrutiny to the North Dakota statute. Doing so would require us to extend the requirements of the Equal Protection Clause beyond the limits recognized in our cases, a step we decline to take.

We have previously rejected the suggestion that statutes having different effects on the wealthy and the poor should on that account alone be subjected to strict equal protection scrutiny. Nor have we accepted the proposition that education is a "fundamental right," like equality of the franchise, which should trigger strict scrutiny when government interferes with an individual's access to it.

Relying primarily on *Plyler* v. *Doe,* however, appellants suggest that North Dakota's 1979 statute should be subjected to "heightened" scrutiny. This standard of review, which is less demanding than "strict scrutiny" but more demanding than the standard rational relation test, has generally been applied only in cases that involved discriminatory classifications based on sex or illegitimacy. See, e.g., *Mississippi University for Women* v. *Hogan* (1982). In *Plyler,* which did not fit this pattern, the State of Texas had denied to the children of illegal aliens the free public education that it made available to other residents. Applying a heightened level of equal protection scrutiny, the Court concluded that the State had failed to show that its classification advanced a substantial state interest. We have not extended this holding beyond the "unique circumstances" that provoked its "unique confluence of theories and rationales." *Plyler, supra.* Nor do we think that the case before us today is governed by the holding in *Plyler.* Unlike the children in that case, Sarita Kadrmas has not been penalized by the government for illegal conduct by her parents. On the contrary, Sarita was denied access to the school bus only because her parents would not agree to pay the same user fee charged to all other families that took advantage of the service. Nor do we see any reason to suppose that this user fee will "promot[e] the creation and perpetuation of a subclass of illiterates within our boundaries, surely adding to the problems and costs of unemployment, welfare, and crime." ("A schoolboard may waive any fee if any pupil or his parent or guardian shall be unable to pay such fees. No pupil's rights or privileges, including the receipt of grades or diplomas, may be denied or abridged for nonpayment of fees.") *Plyler, supra.* The case before us does not resemble *Plyler,* and we decline to extend the rationale of that decision to cover this case.

Appellants contend, finally, that whatever label is placed on the standard of review, this case is analogous to decisions in which we have held that government may not withhold certain especially important services from those who are unable to pay for them.

Leaving aside other distinctions that might be found between these cases and the one before us today, each involved a rule that barred indigent litigants from using the judicial process in circumstances where they had no alternative to that process. Decisions invalidating such rules are inapposite here. In contrast to the "utter exclusiveness of court access and court access and court remedy," *United States* v. *Kras* (1973), North Dakota does not maintain a legal or a practical monopoly on the means of transporting children to school. Thus, unlike the complaining parties in all the cases cited by appellants, the Kadrmas family could and did find a private alternative to the public school bus service for which Dickinson charged a fee. That alternative was more expensive, to be sure, and we have no reason to doubt that genuine hardships were endured by the Kadrmas family when Sarita was denied access to the bus. Such facts, however, do not imply that the Equal Protection Clause has been violated. In upholding a filing fee for voluntary bankruptcy actions, for example, we observed: "[B]ankruptcy is not the only method available to a debtor for the adjustment of his legal relationship with his creditors. . . . However unrealistic the remedy may be in a particular situation, a debtor, in theory, and often in actuality, may adjust his debts by negotiated agreement with his creditors." *Kras* at 445. Similarly, we upheld a statute that required indigents to pay a filing fee for appellate review of adverse welfare benefits decisions. *Ortwein* v. *Schwab,* (1973). Noting that the case did not involve a "suspect classification," we held that the "applicable standard is that of rational justification." It is plain that the busing fee in this case more closely resembles the fees that were upheld in *Kras* and *Ortwein* than it resembles the fees that were invalidated in the cases on which appellants rely. Those cases therefore do not support the suggestion that North Dakota's 1979 statute violates the Equal Protection Clause.

Applying the appropriate test—under which a statute is upheld if it bears a rational relation to a legitimate government objective—we think it is quite clear that a State's decision to allow local school boards the option of charging patrons a user fee for bus service is constitutionally permissible. The Constitution does not require that such service be provided at all, and it is difficult to imagine why choosing to offer the service should entail a constitutional obligation to offer it for free. No one denies that encouraging local school districts to provide school bus service is a legitimate state purpose or that such encouragement would be undermined by a rule requiring that general revenues be used to subsidize an optional service that will benefit a minority of the district's families. It is manifestly rational for the State to refrain from undermining its legitimate objective with such a rule.

Appellants contend that, even without the application of strict or heightened scrutiny, the 1979 statute violates equal protection because it permits user fees for bus service only in nonreorganized school districts. This distinction, they say, can be given no rational justification whatsoever. The principles governing our review of this claim are well established. "The Fourteenth Amendment does not prohibit legislation merely because it is special, or limited in its application to a particular geographical or political subdivision of the state."

Rather, the Equal Protection Clause is offended only if the statute's classification "rests on grounds wholly irrelevant to the achievement of the State's objective." Social and economic legislation, like the statute at issue in this case, moreover, "carries with it a presumption of a rationality that can only be overcome by a clear showing of arbitrariness and irrationality." "[W]e will not overturn such a statute unless the varying treatment of different groups or persons is so unrelated to the achievement of any combination of legitimate purposes that we can only conclude that the legislature's actions were irrational." In performing this analysis, we are not bound only by explanations of the statute's rationality that may be offered by litigants or other courts. Rather, those challenging the legislative judgment must convince us "that the legislative facts on which the classification is apparently based could not reasonably be conceived to be true by the governmental decisionmaker."

Applying these principles to the present case, we conclude that appellants have failed to carry the "heavy burden" of demonstrating that the challenged statute is both arbitrary and irrational.

* * *

In sum, the statute challenged in this case discriminates against no suspect class and interferes with no fundamental right. Appellants have failed to carry the heavy burden of demonstrating that the statute is arbitrary and irrational. The Supreme Court of North Dakota correctly concluded that the statute does not violate the Equal Protection Clause of the Fourteenth Amendment, and

its judgment is affirmed.

JUSTICE MARSHALL, *with whom* JUSTICE BRENNAN *joins, dissenting.*

In *San Antonio Independent School Dist.* v. *Rodriguez*, (1973), I wrote that the Court's holding was a "retreat from our historic commitment to equality of educational opportunity and [an] insupportable acquiescence in a system which deprives children in their earliest years of the chance to reach their full potential." Today, the Court continues the retreat from the promise of equal educational opportunity by holding that a school district's refusal to allow an indigent child who lives 16 miles from the nearest school to use a school-bus service without paying a fee does not violate the Fourteenth Amendment's Equal Protection Clause. Because I do not believe that this Court should sanction discrimination against the poor with respect to "perhaps the most important function of state and local governments," *Brown* v. *Board of Education*, (1954), I dissent.

The Court's opinion suggests that this case does not concern state action that discriminates against the poor with regard to the provision of a basic education. The Court notes that the particular governmental action challenged in this case involves the provision of transportation, rather than the provision of educational services. Moreover, the Court stresses that the denial of transportation to Sarita Kadrmas did not in fact prevent her from receiving an education; notwithstanding the denial of bus service, Sarita's family ensured that she attended school each day. To the Court, then, this case presents no troublesome questions; indeed, the Court's facile analysis suggests some perplexity as to why this case ever reached this Court.

I believe the Court's approach forgets that the Constitution is concerned with "sophisticated as well as simple-minded modes of discrimination." *Lane* v. *Wilson*, (1939). This case involves state action that places a special burden on poor families in their pursuit of education. Children living far from school can receive a public education only if they have access to transportation; as the state court noted in this case, "a child must reach the schoolhouse door as a prerequisite to receiving the educational opportunity offered therein." Indeed, for children in Sarita's position, imposing a fee for transportation is no different in practical effect from imposing a fee directly for education. Moreover, the fee involved in this case discriminated against Sarita's family because it necessarily fell more heavily upon the poor than upon wealthier members of the community. This case therefore presents the question whether a State may discriminate against the poor in providing access to education. I regard this question as one of great urgency.

As I have stated on prior occasions, proper analysis of equal protection claims depends less on choosing the "formal label" under which the claim should be reviewed than upon identifying and carefully analyzing the real interests at stake. In particular, the Court should focus on "the character of the classification in question, the relative importance to individuals in the class discriminated against of the governmental benefits that they do not receive, and the asserted state interests in support of the classification." *Dandridge* v. *Williams*, (1970). (MARSHALL, J., dissenting); see *San Antonio Independent School Dist.* v. *Rodriguez*, (MARSHALL, J., dissenting). Viewed from this perspective, the discrimination inherent in the North Dakota statute fails to satisfy the dictates of the Equal Protection Clause.

The North Dakota statute discriminates on the basis of economic status. This Court has determined that classifications based on wealth are not automatically suspect. Such classifications, however, have a measure of special constitutional significance. See e.g., *McDonald* v. *Board of Election Comm'rs of Chicago* (1969) ("[A] careful examination on our part is especially warranted where lines are drawn on the basis of wealth . . ."); *Harper* v. *Virginia Bd. of Elections* (1966) ("Lines drawn on the basis of wealth or property . . . are traditionally disfavored"). This Court repeatedly has invalidated statutes, on their face or as applied, that discriminated against the poor. See, e.g., *Bullock* v. *Carter* (1972); *Griffin* v. *Illinois* (1956). The Court has proved most likely to take such action when the laws in question interfered with the access of the poor to the political and judicial processes. One source of these decisions, in my view, is a deep distrust of policies that specially burden the access of disadvantaged persons to the governmental institutions and processes that offer members of our society an opportunity to improve their status and better their lives. The intent of the Fourteenth Amendment was to abolish caste legislation. See *Plyler* v. *Doe*, (1982). When state action has the predictable tendency to entrap the poor and create a permanent underclass, that intent is frustrated. Thus, to the extent that a law places discriminatory barriers between the indigent and the basic tools and opportunities that might enable them to rise, exacting scrutiny should be applied.

The statute at issue here burdens a poor person's interest in an education. The extraordinary nature of this interest cannot be denied. This Court's most famous statement on the subject is contained in *Brown* v. *Board of Education*:

> [E]ducation is perhaps the most important function of state and local governments. Compulsory school attendance laws and the great expenditures for education both demonstrate our recognition of the importance of education to our democratic society. It is required in the performance of our most basic public responsibilities, even service in the armed forces. It is the very foundation of good citizenship. Today it is a principal instrument in awakening the child to cultural values, in preparing him for later professional training, and in helping him to adjust normally to his environment. In these days, it is doubtful that any child may reasonably be expected to succeed in life if he is denied the opportunity of an education.

Since *Brown*, we frequently have called attention to the vital role of education in our society. We have noted that "education is necessary to prepare citizens to participate effectively and intelligently in our open political system . . . " *Wisconsin* v. *Yoder* (1972). We have also recognized that education prepares individuals to become self-reliant participants in our economy. A statute that erects special obstacles to education in the path of the poor naturally tends to consign such persons to their current disadvantaged status. By denying equal opportunity to exactly those who need it most, the law not only militates against the ability of each poor child to advance herself or himself, but also increases the likelihood of the creation of a discrete and permanent underclass. Such a statute is difficult to reconcile with the framework of equality embodied in the Equal Protection Clause.

This Court's decision in *Plyler* v. *Doe* supports these propositions. The Court in *Plyler* upheld the right of the children of illegal aliens to receive the free public education that the State of Texas made available to other residents. The Court in that case engaged in some discussions of alienage, a classification not relevant here. The decision, however, did not rest upon this basis. Rather, the Court made clear that the infirmity of the Texas law stemmed from its differential treatment of a discrete and disadvantaged group of children with respect to the provision of education. The Court stated that education is not "merely some governmental 'benefit' indistinguishable from other forms of social welfare legislation." The Court further commented that the state law "poses an affront to one of the goals of the Equal Protection Clause: the abolition of governmental barriers presenting unreasonable obstacles to advancement on the basis of merit." Finally, the Court called attention to the tendency of the Texas law to create a distinct underclass of impoverished illiterates who would be unable to participate in and contribute to society. The *Plyler* Court's reasoning is fully applicable here. As in *Plyler*, the State in this case has acted to burden the educational opportunities of a disadvantaged group of children, who need an education to become full participants in society.

The State's rationale for this policy is based entirely on fiscal considerations. The State has allowed Dickinson and certain other school districts to charge a non-waiveable flat fee for bus service so that these districts may recoup part of the costs of the service. The money that Dickinson collects from applying the busing fee to indigent families, however, represents a minuscule proportion of the costs of the bus service. As the Court notes, all of the fees collected by Dickinson amount to only 10% of the cost of providing the bus service, and the fees collected from poor families represent a small fraction of the total fees. Exempting indigent families from the busing fee therefore would not require Dickinson to make any significant adjustments in either the operation or the funding of the bus service. Indeed, as the Court states, most school districts in the State provide full bus service without charging any fees at all. The state interest involved in this case is therefore insubstantial; it does not begin to justify the discrimination challenged here.

The Court's decision to the contrary "demonstrates once again a callous indifference to the realities of life for the poor." These realities may not always be obvious from the Court's vantage point, but the Court fails in its constitutional duties when it refuses, as it does today, to make even the effort to see. For the poor, education is often the only route by which to become full participants in our society. In allowing a State to burden the access of poor persons to an education, the Court denies equal opportunity and discourages hope. I do not believe the Equal Protection Clause countenances such a result. I therefore dissent.

SELECTED REFERENCES

Baer, Judith A. "Sexual Equality and the Burger Court," 31 *Western Political Quarterly* 470 (1978).

Black, Charles L., Jr. "Further Reflections on the Constitutional Justice of Livelihood," 86 *Columbia Law Review* 1103 (1986).

Binion, Gayle. "The Disadvantaged before the Burger Court," 4 *Law and Policy Quarterly* 37 (January 1982).

Brigham, John. *Civil Liberties and American Democracy* (Washington, D.C.: Congressional Quarterly, Inc., 1984), ch. 4.

Burns, Michael M. "The Exclusion of Women from Influential Men's Clubs: The Inner Sanctum and the Myth of Full Equality," 18 *Harvard Civil Rights–Civil Liberties Law Review* 321 (Summer 1983).

Celis, William, 3rd. "23 States Face Suits on School Funds," *The New York Times*, September 2, 1992, p. B-5.

Crowley, Donald. "Implementing Serrano: A Study in Judicial Impact," 4 *Law and Policy Quarterly* 299 (July 1982).

Dionisopoulos, P. Allan, and Ducat, Craig. *The Right to Privacy: Essays and Cases* (St. Paul, Minn.: West Publishing Co., 1976).

Edelman, P. B. "The Next Century of Our Constitution: Rethinking Our Duty to the Poor," 39 *Hastings Law Journal* (November 1987).

"Equal Rights for Women: A Symposium on the Proposed Constitutional Amendment," 6 *Harvard Civil Rights–Civil Liberties Law Review* 2 (1971).

Franklin, Charles H., and Kosaki, Liane C. "The Republican Schoolmaster: The Supreme Court, Public Opinion, and Abortion," 83 *American Political Science Review* 751 (1989).

Gomèz, José. "The Public Expression of Lesbian/Gay Personhood as Protected Speech," 1 *Law and Inequality* 121 (1963).

"Government Drug Testing and Individual Privacy Rights: Crying Wolf in the Workplace," 5 *Yale Law and Policy Review* 235 (Fall/Winter 1986).

Hansen, Susan B. "State Implementation of Supreme Court Decisions: Abortion Since *Roe* v. *Wade*," 42 *Journal of Politics* 372 (May 1980).

Lawrence, Susan E. *The Poor in Court: The Legal Services Program and Supreme Court Decision Making* (Princeton: Princeton University Press, 1990).

Mansbridge, Jane J. *Why We Lost the ERA* (Chicago: University of Chicago Press, 1986).

McCloskey, Herbert, and Brill, Alida. *Dimensions of Tolerance: What Americans Believe about Civil Liberties* (New York: Russell Sage Foundation, 1963), ch. 5.

O'Connor, Karen. *Women's Organizations Use of Courts* (Lexington, Mass.: Lexington Books, 1980).

Paul, Eve W., and Schaap, Paula. "Abortion and the Law in 1980," 25 *New York Law School Review* 497 (1980).

Posner, R. A. "Uncertain Protection of Privacy by the Supreme Court." 1979 *Supreme Court Review* 173 (1979).

Rubenfeld, Jed. "The Right of Privacy," 102 *Harvard Law Review* 737 (1989).

Shuldiner, Paul. "Visual Rape: A Look at the Dubious Legality of Strip Searches," 13 *John Marshall Law Review* 273 (1980).

Subcommittee of the Committee on Government Operations House of Representatives. *Privacy and 1984: Public Opinions on Privacy Issues* (Hearings, 98th Cong., 1st Sess., April 4, 1984).

"The Supreme Court as Superlegislature Emasculates the Right to Privacy: *Bowers* v. *Hardwick*," 21 *Suffolk University Law Review* 853 (Fall 1987).

The Constitution of the United States of America

We, the People of the United States, in order to form a more perfect Union, establish Justice, insure domestic Tranquility, provide for the common defence, promote the general Welfare, and secure the Blessings of Liberty to ourselves and our Posterity, do ordain and establish this Constitution for the United States of America.

ARTICLE I

Section 1. All legislative Powers herein granted shall be vested in a Congress of the United States, which shall consist of a Senate and House of Representatives.

Section 2. The House of Representatives shall be composed of Members chosen every second Year by the People of the several States, and the Electors in each State shall have the Qualifications requisite for Electors of the most numerous Branch of the State Legislature.

No Person shall be a Representative who shall not have attained to the Age of twenty-five Years, and been seven Years a Citizen of the United States, and who shall not, when elected, be an Inhabitant of that State in which he shall be chosen.

Representatives and direct Taxes shall be apportioned among the several States which may be included within this Union, according to their respective Numbers, which shall be determined by adding to the whole Number of free Persons, including those bound to Service for a Term of Years, and excluding Indians not taxed, three-fifths of all other persons. The actual Enumeration shall be made within three Years after the first Meeting of the Congress of the United States, and within every subsequent Term of ten Years, in such Manner as they shall by Law direct. The Number of Representatives shall not exceed one for every thirty Thousand, but each State shall have at Least one Representative; and until such enumeration shall be made, the State of New-Hampshire shall be entitled to chuse three, Massachusetts eight, Rhode-Island and Providence Plantations one, Connecticut five, New York six, New-Jersey four, Pennsylvania eight, Delaware one, Maryland six, Virginia ten, North-Carolina five, South-Carolina five, and Georgia three.

When vacancies happen in the Representation from any State, the Executive Authority thereof shall issue Writs of Election to fill such Vacancies.

The House of Representatives shall chuse their Speaker and other Officers; and shall have the sole Power of Impeachment.

Section 3. The Senate of the United States shall be composed of two Senators from each State, chosen by the Legislature thereof, for six Years; and each Senator shall have one Vote.

Immediately after they shall be assembled in

Consequence of the first election, they shall be divided as equally as may be into three Classes. The Seats of the Senators of the first Class shall be vacated at the Expiration of the Second Year, of the Second Class at the Expiration of the fourth Year, and of the third Class at the Expiration of the sixth Year, so that one-third may be chosen every second Year; and if Vacancies happen by Resignation, or otherwise, during the Recess of the Legislature of any State, the Executive therefore may make temporary Appointments until the next Meeting of the Legislature, which shall then fill such Vacancies.

No person shall be a Senator who shall not have attained to the Age of thirty Years, and been nine Years a Citizen of the United States, and who shall not, when elected, be an Inhabitant of that State for which he shall be chosen.

The Vice-President of the United States shall be President of the Senate, but shall have no Vote, unless they be equally divided.

The Senate shall chuse their other Officers, and also a President pro tempore, in the Absence of the Vice-President, or when he shall exercise the Office of President of the United States.

The Senate shall have the sole Power to try all impeachments. When sitting for that Purpose, they shall be on Oath or affirmation. When the President of the United States is tried, the Chief Justice shall preside: And no Person shall be convicted without the Concurrence of two-thirds of the Members present.

Judgment in Cases of Impeachment shall not extend further than to removal from Office, and disqualification to hold and enjoy any Office of honor, Trust or Profit under the United States; but the Party convicted shall nevertheless be liable and subject to Indictment, Trial, Judgment and Punishment, according to Law.

Section 4. The Times, Places and Manner of holding Elections for Senators and Representatives, shall be prescribed in each State by the Legislature thereof; but the Congress may at any time by Law make or alter such Regulations, except as to the Places of chusing Senators.

The Congress shall assemble at least once in every Year, and such Meeting shall be on the first Monday in December, unless they shall by Law appoint a different Day.

Section 5. Each House shall be the judge of the Elections, Returns and Qualifications of its own Members, and a Majority of each shall constitute a Quorum to do Business; but a smaller Number may adjourn from day to day, and may be authorized to compel the Attendance of absent Members, in such Manner, and under such Penalties as each House may provide.

Each House may determine the Rules of its Proceedings, punish its Members for disorderly Behaviour, and, with the Concurrence of two-thirds, expel a member.

Each House shall keep a Journal of its Proceedings, and from time to time publish the same excepting such Parts as may in their Judgment require Secrecy, and the Yeas and Nays of the Members of either House on any question shall at the Desire of one fifth of those Present, be entered on the journal.

Neither House, during the Session of Congress, shall, without the Consent of the other, adjourn for more than three days, not to any other Place than that in which the two Houses shall be sitting.

Section 6. The Senators and Representatives shall receive a Compensation for their Services, to be ascertained by Law, and paid out of the Treasury of the United States. They shall in all Cases, except Treason, Felony and Breach of the peace, be privileged from Arrest during their Attendance at the Session of their respective Houses, and in going to and returning from the same; and for any Speech or Debate in either House, they shall not be questioned in any other Place.

No Senator or Representative shall, during the Time for which he was elected, be appointed to any civil Office under the Authority of the United States, which shall have been created, or the Emoluments whereof shall have been encreased during such time; and no Person holding any Office under the United States, shall be a Member of either House during his Continuance in Office.

Section 7. All Bills for raising Revenue shall originate in the House of Representatives; but the Senate may propose or concur with Amendments as on other Bills.

Every Bill which shall have passed the House of Representatives and the Senate, shall, before it become a Law, be presented to the President of the United States; If he approve he shall sign it, but if not he shall return it, with his Objections to that House in which it shall have originated, who shall enter the Objections at large on their Journal, and proceed to reconsider it. If after such Reconsideration two-thirds of that House shall agree to pass the Bill, it shall be sent, together with the Objections, to the other House, by which it shall likewise be reconsidered, and if approved by two-thirds of that House, it shall become a Law. But in all such Cases the Votes of both Houses shall be determined by Yeas and Nays, and the Names of the Persons voting for and against the Bill shall be entered on the Journal of each House respectively. If any Bill shall not be returned by the President within ten Days (Sundays excepted) after it shall have been presented to him, the Same shall be a Law, in like Manner as if he had signed it, unless the Congress by their Adjournment prevent its Return, in which Case it shall not be a Law.

Every Order, Resolution, or Vote to which the Concurrence of the Senate and House of Representatives may be necessary (except on a question of Adjournment) shall be presented to the President of the United States; and before the Same shall take Effect, shall be approved by him, or, being disapproved by him, shall be repassed by two-thirds of the Senate and House of Representatives, according to the Rules and Limitations prescribed in the Case of a Bill.

Section 8. The Congress shall have Power

To lay and collect Taxes, Duties, Imposts and Excises, to pay the Debts and provide for the common Defence and general Welfare of the United States; but all Duties, Imposts and Excises shall be uniform throughout the United States;

To borrow money on the credit of the United States;

To regulate Commerce with foreign Nations, and among the several States, and with the Indian Tribes;

To establish a uniform Rule of Naturalization, and uniform Laws on the subject of Bankruptcies throughout the United States;

To coin Money, regulate the Value thereof, and of foreign Coin, and fix the Standard of Weights and Measures;

To provide for the Punishment of counterfeiting the Securities and current Coin of the United States;

To Establish Post Offices and Post Roads;

To promote the Progress of Science and useful Arts, by securing for limited Times to Authors and Inventors the exclusive Right to their respective Writings and Discoveries;

To constitute Tribunals inferior to the supreme Court;

To define and punish Piracies and Felonies committed on the high Seas, and Offences against the Law of Nations;

To declare War, grant Letters of Marque and Reprisal, and make Rules concerning Captures on Land and Water;

To raise and support Armies, but no Appropriation of Money to that Use shall be for a longer Term than two Years;

To provide and maintain a Navy;

To make Rules for the Government and Regulation of the land and naval Forces;

To provide for calling forth the Militia to execute the Laws of the Union, suppress Insurrections and repel Invasions;

To provide for organizing, arming, and disciplining, the Militia, and for governing such Part of them as may be employed in the Service of the United States, reserving to the States respectively, the Appointment of Officers, and the Authority of training the Militia according to the discipline prescribed by Congress;

To exercise exclusive Legislation in all Cases whatsoever, over such District (not exceeding ten Miles square) as may, by Cession of particular States, and the Acceptance of Congress, become the Seat of the Government of the United States, and to exercise like Authority over all Places purchased by the Consent of the Legislature of the State in which the Same shall be, for the Erection of Forts, Magazines, Arsenals, dock-Yards, and other needful Buildings;—And

To make all Laws which shall be necessary and proper for carrying into Execution the foregoing Powers, and all other Powers vested by this Constitution in the Government of the United States, or in any Department or Officer thereof.

Section 9. The Migration or Importation of Such Persons as any of the States now existing shall think proper to admit, shall not be prohibited by the Congress prior to the Year one thousand eight hundred and eight, but a Tax or duty may be imposed on such Importation, not exceeding ten dollars for each Person.

The privilege of the Writ of Habeas Corpus shall not be suspended, unless when in Cases of Rebellion or Invasion the public Safety may require it.

No Bill or Attainder or ex post facto Law shall be passed.

No Capitation, or other direct, Tax shall be laid, unless in Proportion to the Census or Enumeration herein before directed to be taken.

No Tax or Duty shall be laid on Articles exported from any State. No Preference shall be given by any Regulation of Commerce or Revenue to the Ports of one State over those of another; nor shall Vessels bound to, or from, one State, be obliged to enter, clear, or pay Duties in another.

No money shall be drawn from the Treasury,

but in Consequence of Appropriations made by Law, and a regular Statement and Account of the Receipts and Expenditures of all public Money shall be published from time to time.

No Title of Nobility shall be granted by the United States:—And no Person holding any Office of Profit or Trust under them, shall, without the Consent of the Congress, accept of any present, Emolument, Office, or Title, of any kind whatever from any King, Prince, or foreign State.

Section 10. No State shall enter into any Treaty, Alliance, or Confederation; grant Letters of Marque and Reprisal; coin Money; emit Bills of Credit; make any Thing but gold and silver Coin a Tender in Payment of Debts; pass any Bill of Attainder, ex post facto Law, or Law impairing the Obligation of Contracts, or grant any Title of Nobility.

No State shall, without Consent of Congress, lay any Imposts or Duties on Imports or Exports, except what may be absolutely necessary for executing its inspection Laws; and the net Produce of all Duties and Imposts, laid by any State on Imports or Exports, shall be for the Use of the Treasury of the United States; and all such Laws shall be subject to the Revision and Control of the Congress.

No State shall, without the Consent of Congress, lay any Duty of Tonnage, keep Troops, or Ships of War in time of Peace, enter into any Agreement or Compact with another State, or with a foreign Power, or engage in War, unless actually invaded, or in such imminent Danger as will not admit of delay.

ARTICLE II

Section 1. The executive Power shall be vested in a President of the United States of America. He shall hold his Office during the Term of four Years, and, together with the Vice-President, chosen for the same Term, be elected as follows:

Each State shall appoint, in such Manner as the Legislature thereof may direct, a Number of Electors, equal to the whole Number of Senators and Representatives to which the State may be entitled in the Congress; but no Senator or Representative, or Person holding an Office of Trust or Profit under the United States, shall be appointed an Elector.

The Electors shall meet in their respective States, and vote by Ballot for two Persons, of whom one at least shall not be an Inhabitant of the same State with themselves. And they shall make a List of all the Persons voted for, and of the Number of Votes for each; which List they shall sign and cer-

tify, and transmit sealed to the Seat of the Government of the United States, directed to the President of the Senate. The President of the Senate shall, in the Presence of the Senate and House of Representatives, open all the Certificates, and the Votes shall then be counted. The Person having the greatest Number of Votes shall be the President, if such Number be a Majority of the whole Number of Electors appointed; and if there be more than one who have such Majority, and have an equal Number of Votes, then the House of Representatives shall immediately chuse by Ballot one of them for President; and if no Person have a Majority, then from the five highest on the List the said House shall in like Manner chuse the President. But in chusing the President, the Votes shall be taken by States, the Representation from each State having one Vote; A quorum for this Purpose shall consist of a Member or Members from two-thirds of the States and a Majority of all the States shall be necessary to a Choice. In every Case, after the Choice of the President the Person having the greatest Number of Votes of the Electors shall be the Vice-President. But if there should remain two or more who have equal Votes, the Senate shall chuse from them by Ballot the Vice President.

The Congress may determine the Time of chusing the Electors, and the Day on which they shall give their Votes; which Day shall be the same throughout the United States.

No person except a natural born Citizen, or a Citizen of the United States, at the time of the Adoption of this Constitution, shall be eligible to the Office of President; neither shall any Person be eligible to that Office who shall not have attained to the Age of thirty-five Years, and been fourteen years a Resident within the United States.

In case of the removal of the President from Office, or of his Death, Resignation, or Inability to discharge the Powers and Duties of the said Office, the Same shall devolve on the Vice-President, and the Congress may by Law provide for the Case of Removal, Death, Resignation or Inability, both of the President and Vice-President, declaring what Officer shall then act as President, and such Officer shall act accordingly, until the Disability be removed, or a President shall be elected.

The President shall, at stated Times, receive for his Services, a Compensation, which shall neither be encreased nor diminished during the Period for which he shall have been elected, and he shall not receive within that Period any other Emolument from the United States, or any of them.

Before he enter on the Execution of his Office, he shall take the following Oath or Affirmation: "I do solemnly swear (or affirm) that I will faithfully execute the Office of President of the United States, and will to the best of my Ability, preserve, protect and defend the Constitution of the United States."

Section 2. The President shall be Commander in Chief of the Army and Navy of the United States, and of the militia of the several States, when called into the actual Service of the United States; he may require the Opinion, in writing, of the principal Officer in each of the Executive Departments, upon any Subject relating to the Duties of their respective Offices, and he shall have Power to grant Reprieves and Pardons for Offences against the United States, except in Cases of Impeachment.

He shall have Power, by and with the Advice and Consent of the Senate, to make Treaties, provided two-thirds of the Senators present concur; and he shall nominate, and by and with the Advice and Consent of the Senate, shall appoint Ambassadors, other public Ministers and Consuls, Judges of the supreme Court, and other Officers of the United States, whose Appointments are not herein otherwise provided for, and which shall be established by law. But the Congress may by Law vest the Appointment of such inferior Officers, as they think proper, in the President alone, in the Courts of Law, or in the Heads of Departments.

The President shall have Power to fill up all Vacancies that may happen during the Recess of the Senate, by granting Commissions which shall expire at the End of their next Session.

Section 3. He shall from time to time give to the Congress Information of the State of the Union, and recommend to their Consideration such Measures as he shall judge necessary and expedient; he may, on extraordinary Occasions, convene both Houses, or either of them, and in Case of Disagreement between them, with Respect to the Time of Adjournment, he may adjourn them to such Time as he shall think proper; he shall receive Ambassadors and other public Ministers; he shall take Care that the Laws be faithfully executed, and shall Commission all the Officers of the United States.

Section 4. The President, Vice-President and all civil Officers of the United States, shall be removed from Office on Impeachment for, and Conviction of, Treason, Bribery, or other high Crimes and Misdemeanors.

ARTICLE III

Section 1. The judicial Power of the United States, shall be vested in one supreme Court and in such inferior Courts as the Congress may from time to time ordain and establish. The Judges, both of the supreme and inferior Courts, shall hold their Offices during good Behaviour, and shall, at stated Times, receive for their Services, a Compensation, which shall not be diminished during their Continuance in Office.

Section 2. The Judicial Power shall extend to all Cases, in Law and Equity, arising under this Constitution, the Laws of the United States, and Treaties made, or which shall be made, under their Authority; to all Cases affecting Ambassadors, other public Ministers and Consuls; to all Cases of admiralty and maritime Jurisdiction; to Controversies to which the United States shall be a Party; to Controversies between two or more States, [between a State and Citizens of another State,] between Citizens of different States, between Citizens of the same State claiming Lands under Grants of different States, and between a State, or the Citizens thereof, and foreign States, Citizens or Subjects.

In all Cases affecting Ambassadors, other public Ministers and Consuls, and those in which a State shall be a Party, the supreme Court shall have original Jurisdiction. In all the other Cases before mentioned, the supreme Court shall have appellate Jurisdiction, both as to Law and Fact, with such Exceptions, and under such Regulations as the Congress shall make.

The trial of all crimes, except in Cases of Impeachment, shall be by Jury; and such Trial shall be held in the State where the said Crimes shall have been committed; but when not committed within any State, the Trial shall be at such Place or Places as the Congress may by Law have directed.

Section 3. Treason against the United States, shall consist only in levying War against them, or in adhering to their Enemies, giving them Aid and Comfort. No Person shall be convicted of Treason unless on the Testimony of two Witnesses to the same overt Act, or on Confession in open Court.

The Congress shall have Power to declare the Punishment of Treason, but no Attainder of Treason shall work Corruption of Blood, or Forfeiture except during the Life of the Person attainted.

ARTICLE IV

Section 1. Full Faith and Credits shall be given in each State to the public Acts, Records, and judicial Proceedings of every other State. And the Congress may by general Laws prescribe the Manner in which such Acts, Records and Proceedings shall be proved, and the Effect thereof.

Section 2. The Citizens of each State shall be entitled to all Privileges and immunities of Citizens in the several States.

A Person charged in any State with Treason, Felony, or other Crime, who shall flee from Justice and be found in another State, shall, on demand of the executive Authority of the State from which he fled, be delivered up, to be removed to the State having Jurisdiction of the Crime.

No Person held to Service or Labour in one State, under the Laws thereof, escaping into another, shall, in Consequence of any Law or Regulation therein, be discharged from such Service or Labour, but shall be delivered up on Claim of the Party to whom such Service or Labour may be due.

Section 3. New States may be admitted by Congress into this Union; but no new State shall be formed or erected within the Jurisdiction of any other State; nor any State be formed by the Junction of two or more States, or Parts of States, without the Consent of the Legislatures of the States concerned as well as of the Congress.

The Congress shall have Power to dispose of and make all needful Rules and Regulations respecting the Territory or other Property belonging to the United States; and nothing in this Constitution shall be so construed as to Prejudice any Claims of the United States, or of any particular State.

Section 4. The United States shall guarantee to every State in this Union a Republican Form of Government, and shall protect each of them against Invasion; and on Application of the Legislature, or of the Executive (when the Legislature cannot be convened) against domestic Violence.

ARTICLE V

The Congress, whenever two-thirds of both Houses shall deem it necessary, shall propose Amendments to this Constitution, or, on the Application of the Legislatures of two-thirds of the several States, shall call a Convention for proposing Amendments, which, in either Case, shall be valid to all Intents and Purposes, as part of this Constitution, when ratified by the Legislatures of three-fourths of the several States, or by Conventions in three-fourths thereof, as the one or the other Mode of Ratification may be proposed by the Congress; Provided, that no Amendment which may be made prior to the Year One thousand eight hundred and eight shall in any Manner affect the first and fourth Clauses in the Ninth Section of the first Article; and that no State, without its Consent, shall be deprived of its equal Suffrage in the Senate.

ARTICLE VI

All Debts contracted and Engagements entered into, before the Adoption of this Constitution, shall be as valid against the United States under this Constitution, as under the Confederation.

This Constitution, and the Laws of the United States which shall be made in Pursuance thereof; and all treaties made, or which shall be made, under the Authority of the United States, shall be the supreme Law of the Land; and the Judges in every State shall be bound thereby, any Thing in the Constitution or Laws of any State to the Contrary notwithstanding.

The Senators and Representatives beforementioned, and the Members of the several State Legislatures, and all executive and judicial Officers, both of the United States and of the several States, shall be bound by Oath or Affirmation, to support this Constitution; but no religious Test shall be required as a Qualification to any Office or public Trust under the United States.

ARTICLE VII

The Ratification of the Conventions of nine States, shall be sufficient for the Establishment of this Constitution between the States so ratifying the Same.

ARTICLES IN ADDITION TO, AND AMENDMENT OF THE CONSTITUTION OF THE UNITED STATES OF AMERICA, PROPOSED BY CONGRESS, AND RATIFIED BY THE LEGISLATURES OF THE SEVERAL STATES, PURSUANT TO THE FIFTH ARTICLE OF THE ORIGINAL CONSTITUTION.

AMENDMENT I [1791]

Congress shall make no law respecting an establishment of religion, or prohibiting the free exercise thereof; or abridging the freedom of speech, or of the press; or the right of the people peaceably to assemble, and to petition the Government for a redress of grievances.

AMENDMENT II [1791]

A well regulated Militia, being necessary to the security of a free State, the right of the people to keep and bear Arms, shall not be infringed.

AMENDMENT III [1791]

No Soldier shall, in time of peace be quartered in any house, without the consent of the Owner, nor in time of war, but in a manner to be prescribed by law.

AMENDMENT IV [1791]

The right of the people to be secure in their persons, houses, papers, and effects, against unreasonable searches and seizures, shall not be violated, and no Warrants shall issue, but upon probable cause, supported by Oath or affirmation, and particularly describing the place to be searched, and the persons or things to be seized.

AMENDMENT V [1791]

No person shall be held to answer for a capital, or otherwise infamous crime, unless on a presentment or indictment of a Grand Jury, except in cases arising in the land or naval forces, or in the Militia, when in actual service in time of War or public danger; nor shall any person be subject for the same offence to be twice put in jeopardy of life or limb; nor shall be compelled in any criminal case to be a witness against himself, nor be deprived of life, liberty, or property, without due process of law; nor shall private property be taken for public use, without just compensation.

AMENDMENT VI [1791]

In all criminal prosecutions, the accused shall enjoy the right to a speedy and public trial, by an impartial jury of the State and district wherein the crime shall have been committed, which district shall have been previously ascertained by law, and to be informed of the nature and cause of the accusation; to be confronted with the witnesses against him; to have compulsory process for obtaining witnesses in his favor, and to have the Assistance of Counsel for his defence.

AMENDMENT VII [1791]

In Suits at common law, where the value in controversy shall exceed twenty dollars, the right of trial by jury shall be preserved, and no fact tried by jury, shall be otherwise re-examined in any Court of the United States, than according to the rules of the common law.

AMENDMENT VIII [1791]

Excessive bail shall not be required, nor excessive fines imposed, nor cruel and unusual punishments inflicted.

AMENDMENT IX [1791]

The enumeration in the Constitution, of certain rights, shall not be construed to deny or disparge others retained by the people.

AMENDMENT X [1791]

The powers not delegated to the United States by the Constitution, nor prohibited by it to the States, are reserved to the States respectively, or to the people.

AMENDMENT XI [1798]

The judicial power of the United States shall not be construed to extend to any suit in law or equity, commenced or prosecuted against one of the United States by Citizens of another State or by Citizens or Subjects of any Foreign State.

AMENDMENT XII [1804]

The Electors shall meet in their respective states, and vote by ballot for President and Vice-President, one of whom, at least, shall not be an inhabitant of the same state with themselves; they shall name in their ballots the person voted for as President, and in distinct ballots the person voted for as Vice-President, and they shall make distinct lists of all persons voted for as President, and of all persons voted for as Vice President, and of the number of votes for each, which lists they shall sign and certify, and transmit sealed to the seat of the government of the United States, directed to the President of the Senate;—The President of the Senate shall, in the presence of the Senate and House of Representatives, open all the certificates and the votes shall then be counted;—The person having the greatest number of votes for President, shall be the President, if such number be a majority of the whole number of Electors appointed; and if no person have such majority, then from the persons having the highest numbers not exceeding three on the list of those voted for as President, the House of Representatives shall choose immediately, by ballot, the President. But in choosing the President the votes shall be taken by states, the representation from each state having one vote; a quorum for this purpose shall consist of a member or members from two-thirds of the states, and a majority of all the states shall be necessary to a choice. And if the House of Representatives shall not choose a President whenever the right of choice shall devolve upon them, before the fourth day of March next following, then the Vice-President shall act as President, as in the face of the death or other constitutional disability of the President.—The person having the greatest number of votes as Vice-President, shall be the Vice-President, if such number be a majority, then from the two highest numbers on the list, the Senate shall choose the Vice-President; a quorum for the purpose shall consist of two-thirds of the whole number of Senators, and a majority of the whole number shall be necessary to a choice. But no person constitutionally ineligible to the office of President shall be eligible to that of Vice-President of the United States.

AMENDMENT XIII [1865]

Section 1. Neither slavery nor involuntary servitude, except as a punishment for crime whereof the party shall have been duly convicted, shall exist within the United States, or any place subject to their jurisdiction.

Section 2. Congress shall have power to enforce this article by appropriate legislation.

AMENDMENT XIV [1868]

Section 1. All persons born or naturalized in the United States, and subject to the jurisdiction thereof, are citizens of the United States and of the State wherein they reside. No State shall make or enforce any law which shall abridge the privileges or immunities of citizens of the United States; nor shall any State deprive any person of life, liberty, or property, without due process of law; nor deny to any person within its jurisdiction the equal protection of the laws.

Section 2. Representatives shall be apportioned among the several States according to their respective numbers, counting the whole number of persons in each State, excluding Indians not taxed. But when the right to vote at any election for the choice of electors for President and Vice President of the United States, Representatives in Congress, the Executive and Judicial officers of a State, or the members of the Legislature thereof, is denied to any of the male inhabitants of such State, being twenty-one years of age, and citizens of the United States, or in any way abridged, except for participation in rebellion, or other crime, the basis of representation therein shall be reduced in the proportion which the number of such male citizens shall bear to the whole number of male citizens twenty-one years of age in such State.

Section 3. No person shall be a Senator or Representative in Congress, or elector of President and Vice President, or hold any office, civil or military, under the United States, or under any State, who, having previously taken an oath, as a member of Congress, or as an officer of the United States, or as a member of any State legislature, or as an executive or judicial officer of any State, to support the Constitution of the United States, shall have engaged in insurrection or rebellion against the same, or given aid or comfort to the enemies thereof. But Congress may by a vote of two-thirds of each House, remove such disability.

Section 4. The validity of the public debt of the United States, authorized by law, including debts incurred for payment of pensions and bounties for services in suppressing insurrection or rebellion, shall not be questioned. But neither the United States nor any State shall assume or pay any debt or obligation incurred in aid of insurrection or rebellion against the United States, or any claim for the loss or emancipation of any slave; but all such debts, obligations and claims shall be held illegal and void.

Section 5. The Congress shall have power to enforce, by appropriate legislation, the provisions of this article.

AMENDMENT XV [1870]

Section 1. The right of citizens of the United States to vote shall not be denied or abridged by the United States or by any State on account of race, color, or previous condition of servitude.

Section 2. The Congress shall have power to enforce this article by appropriate legislation.

AMENDMENT XVI [1913]

The Congress shall have power to lay and collect taxes on incomes, from whatever source derived, without apportionment among the several States, and without regard to any census or enumeration.

AMENDMENT XVII [1913]

The Senate of the United States shall be composed of two Senators from each State, elected by the people thereof, for six years; and each Senator shall have one vote. The electors in each State shall have qualifications requisite for electors of the most numerous branch of the State legislatures.

When vacancies happen in the representation of any State in the Senate, the executive authority of such State shall issue writs of election to fill such vacancies: *Provided,* That the legislature of any State may empower the executive thereof to make temporary appointments until the people fill the vacancies by election as the legislature may direct.

This amendment shall not be so construed as to affect the election or term of any Senator chosen before it becomes valid as part of the Constitution.

AMENDMENT XVIII [1919]

Section 1. After one year from the ratification of this article the manufacture, sale, or transportation of intoxicating liquors within, the importation thereof into, or the exportation thereof from the United States and all territory subject to the jurisdiction thereof for beverage purposes is hereby prohibited.

Section 2. The Congress and the several States shall have concurrent power to enforce this article by appropriate legislation.

Section 3. This article shall be inoperative unless it shall have been ratified as an amendment to the Constitution by the legislatures of the several States, as provided in the Constitution, within seven years from the date of the submission hereof to the States by the Congress.

AMENDMENT XIX [1920]

The right of citizens of the United States to vote shall not be denied or abridged by the United States or by any State on account of sex.

Congress shall have power to enforce this article by appropriate legislation.

AMENDMENT XX [1933]

Section 1. The terms of the President and Vice President shall end at noon on the 20th day of January, and the terms of Senators and Representatives at noon on the 3d day of January, of the years in which such terms would have ended if this article had not been ratified; and the terms of their successors shall then begin.

Section 2. The Congress shall assemble at least once in every year, and such meeting shall begin at noon on the 3rd day of January, unless they shall by law appoint a different day.

Section 3. If, at the time fixed for the beginning of the term of the President, the President elect shall have died, the Vice President elect shall become President. If a President shall not have been chosen before the time fixed for the beginning of his term, or if the President elect shall have failed to qualify, then the Vice President elect shall act as President until a President shall have qualified; and the Congress may by law provide for the case wherein neither a President elect nor a Vice President elect shall have qualified, declaring who shall then act as President, or the manner in which one who is to act shall be selected, and such person shall act accordingly until a President or Vice President shall have qualified.

Section 4. The Congress may by law provide for the case of the death of any of the persons from whom the House of Representatives may choose a President whenever the right of choice shall have devolved upon them, and for the case of the death of any of the persons from whom the Senate may choose a Vice President whenever the right of choice shall have devolved upon them.

Section 5. Sections 1 and 2 shall take effect on the 15th day of October following the ratification of this article.

Section 6. This article shall be inoperative unless it shall have been ratified as an amendment to the Constitution by the legislatures of three-fourths of the several States within seven years from the date of its submission.

AMENDMENT XXI [1933]

Section 1. The eighteenth article of amendment to the Constitution of the United States is hereby repealed.

Section 2. The transportation or importation into any State, Territory, or possession of the United States for delivery or use therein of intoxicating liquors, in violation of the laws thereof, is hereby prohibited.

Section 3. This article shall be inoperative unless it shall have been ratified as an amendment to the Constitution by conventions in the several States, as provided in the Constitution, within seven years from the date of the submission hereof to the States by the Congress.

AMENDMENT XXII [1951]

Section 1. No person shall be elected to the office of the President more than twice, and no person who has held the office of President, or acted as President, for more than two years of a term to which some other person was elected President shall be elected to the office of President more than once. But this Article shall not apply to any person holding the office of President when this Article was proposed by the Congress, and shall not prevent any person who may be holding the office of President, or acting as President, during the term within which this Article becomes operative from holding the office of President or acting as President during the remainder of such term.

Section 2. This article shall be inoperative unless it shall have been ratified as an amendment to the Constitution by the legislatures of three-fourths of the several States within seven years from the date of its submission to the States by the Congress.

AMENDMENT XXIII [1961]

Section 1. The District constituting the seat of Government of the United States shall appoint in such manner as the Congress may direct:

A number of electors of President and Vice President equal to the whole number of Senators and Representatives in Congress to which the District would be entitled if it were a State, but in no event more than the least populous State; they shall be in addition to those appointed by the States, but they shall be considered, for the purposes of the election of President and Vice President, to be electors appointed by a State; and they shall meet in the District and perform such duties as provided by the twelfth article of amendment.

Section 2. The Congress shall have power to enforce this article by appropriate legislation.

AMENDMENT XXIV [1964]

Section 1. The right of citizens of the United States to vote in any primary or other election for President or Vice President, for electors for President or Vice President, or for Senator or Representative in Congress, shall not be denied or abridged by the United States or any State by reason of failure to pay any poll tax or other tax.

Section 2. The Congress shall have power to enforce this article by appropriate legislation.

AMENDMENT XXV [1967]

Section 1. In case of the removal of the President from office or his death or resignation, the Vice President shall become President.

Section 2. Whenever there is a vacancy in the office of the Vice President, the President shall nominate a Vice President who shall take the office upon confirmation by a majority vote of both houses of Congress.

Section 3. Whenever the President transmits to the President pro tempore of the Senate and the Speaker of the House of Representatives his written declaration that he is unable to discharge the powers and duties of his office, and until he transmits to them a written declaration to the contrary, such powers and duties shall be discharged by the Vice President as Acting President.

Section 4. Whenever the Vice President and a majority of either the principal officers of the executive departments or of such other body as Congress may by law provide, transmit to the President pro tempore of the Senate and the Speaker of the House of Representatives their written declaration that the President is unable to discharge the powers and duties of his office, the Vice President shall immediately assume the powers and duties of the office as Acting President.

Thereafter, when the President transmits to the President pro tempore of the Senate and the Speaker of the House of Representatives his written declaration that no inability exists, he shall resume the powers and duties of his office unless the Vice President and a majority of either the principal officers of the executive department or of such other body as Congress may by law provide, trans-mit within four days to the President pro tempore of the Senate and the Speaker of the House of Representatives their written declaration that the President is unable to discharge the powers and duties of his office. Thereupon Congress shall decide the issue, assembling within forty-eight hours for that purpose if not in session. If the Congress, within twenty-one days after receipt of the latter written declaration, or, if Congress is not in session, within twenty-one days after Congress is required to assemble, determines by two-thirds vote of both houses that the President is unable to discharge the powers and duties of his office, the Vice President shall continue to discharge the same as Acting President; otherwise, the President shall resume the powers and duties of his office.

AMENDMENT XXVI [1971]

Section 1. The right of citizens of the United States, who are eighteen years of age or older, to vote shall not be denied or abridged by the United States or by any State on account of age.

Section 2. The Congress shall have power to enforce this article by appropriate legislation.

Table of Cases

NOTE: Page numbers followed by n denote cases cited in footnotes. Entries in bold are featured cases.

In the Matter of Baby M, 647
Irwin v. Dowd, 242

Jackson v. Bishop, 401
Jackson v. Georgia, 359n
Jacobellis v. Ohio, 275–276, 281
Jacobson v. Massachusetts, 655
James v. Goldberg, 728
James v. Headley, 348
Jamison v. Texas, 168
Jefferson v. Hackney, 717
Jenkins v. Georgia, 277
Jimmy Swaggart Ministries v. Board of Equalization of California, 105–106, 110–114
Johnson v. Avery, 392
Johnson v. Glick, 400
Johnson v. Louisiana, 408
Johnson v. New Jersey, 329
Johnson v. Robinson, 133
Johnson v. Transportation Agency, Santa Clara County, California, 507, 622
Johnson v. United States, 322
Johnson v. United States Postal Service, 116n
Johnson v. Virginia, 545
Johnson v. Zerbst, 347, 351–352
Jones v. Barnes, 349
Jones v. Com., 438
Jones v. Mayer, 538–540, 542–550
Jones v. North Carolina Prisoners' Labor Union, Inc., 395
Jones v. Opelika, 134
Jones v. United States, 299, 303
Joseph Burstyn, Inc. v. Wilson, 185
Jurek v. Texas, 360n

Kadrmas v. Dickinson Public Schools, 714, 725, 741–746
Kahn v. Shevin, 618, 620, 622
Karcher v. Daggett, 594
Karcher v. May, 51
Katzenbach v. Morgan, 557
Katzenback v. McClung, 550
Katz v. United States, 321, 640, 654, 699
Kelly v. Board of Education, 444n
Kelly v. Johnson, 644, 647
Kentucky v. Spicer, 425
Kentucky v. Stincer, 427
Ker v. California, 297
Keyes v. School District No. 1, Denver, Colorado, 445
Keyishian v. Board of Regents, 150, 152
King v. Smith, 715
Kingsley Books v. Brown, 277
Kingsley International Pictures v. Regents of State University of New York, 278
Kirby v. Illinois, 348
Kirchberg v. Feinstra, 621
Kirkpatrick v. Preisler, 594–595
Klopfer v. North Carolina, 17, 408
Knight v. State, 355
Kolender v. Lawson, 315
Korematsu, 495
Kovacs v. Cooper, 164, 180
Kunz v. New York, 157

Lafleur v. Cleveland Board of Education, 618–619

Lamb's Chapel v. Steigerwald, 162
Landmark Communication, Inc. v. Virginia, 138
Lane v. Wilson, 486, 545, 554, 575, 611, 744
Lanzetta v. New Jersey, 140
Largent v. Texas, 172
Larkin v. Grendel's Den, Inc., 94
Lassiter v. Department of Social Services of Durham County, North Carolina, 723n
Lassiter v. Northampton County Board of Elections, 556
Layne & Bowler Corp. v. Western Well Works, Inc., 549
League of United Latin American Citizens Council No. 4434 v. Clements, 583–584
Lechmere, Inc. v. NLRB, 163, 196
Lee v. Weisman, 48, 51, 78–88
Lehman v. City of Shaker Heights, 643
Lehman v. Shaker Heights, 186
Lemon v. Kurtzman, 30, 32–38, 41, 43–47, 51–53, 59, 61–62, 66–71, 73–75, 77–78, 80, 88–89, 93, 96–97, 102–103, 106, 113–114
Lepiscope v. United States, 392n
Levitt v. Committee for Public Education, 31, 31n, 43
Lindsey v. Normet, 719–720
Linmark Associates v. Township of Willingboro, 165
Lipp v. Norris, 134
Lloyd Corporation v. Tanner, 5, 195–197, 199–200, 241
Lochner v. New York, 648, 652, 676, 689–690
Lockett v. Ohio, 360, 407
Lockhart v. McCree, 407
Lombard v. Louisiana, 546
Long v. District Court, 392
Lorance v. A.T.&T. Technologies, Inc., 432, 509
Los Angeles v. Taxpayers for Vincent, 165, 274
Louisiana v. United States, 557
Louisiana es rel. Francis v. Resweber, 396
Louisville, N.O. & T.R. Co. v. Mississippi, 437
Lovell v. City of Griffin, 140, 156, 168
Loving v. Virginia, 496, 546, 654–655, 672, 675, 688, 695
Ludwig v. Massachusetts, 405
Lugar v. Edmonson Oil Co., 415n, 415–416, 418
Luther v. Borden, 598
Lynch v. Donnelly, 67, 89–104
Lyng v. International Union, UAW, 724–725
Lyng v. Northwest Indian Cemetery Protective Association, 117

Mack v. Russell County Commission, 561, 590, 592–593
Magnum Co. v. Coty, 549
Mahan v. Howell, 594
Maher v. Roe, 641, 658–660, 681
Maine v. Moulton, 345
Mallard v. United States District Court, 725–726
Mallory v. Eyrich, 583
Mallory v. United States, 328–329, 338
Malloy v. Hogan, 17, 328, 425
Manual Enterprises v. Day, 275
Mapp v. Ohio, 17, 297–298, 298n, 301–305, 310–311, 328–329, 649, 677
Marbury v. Madison, 2, 650, 693
Marcus v. Search Warrant, 277
Marshall v. Barlow, 318n
Marsh v. Alabama, 195
Marsh v. Chambers, 67, 80, 91, 93, 103
Martin v. Struthers, 164, 169, 171–172, 643
Martin v. Wilks, 432, 508–509
Maryland v. Munson, 157
Massachusetts v. Sheppard, 300